T0183168

Lecture Notes in Artificial Intelligence 9121

Subseries of Lecture Notes in Computer Science

More information about this series at http://www.springer.com/series/1244

Enrique Onieva · Igor Santos
Eneko Osaba · Héctor Quintián
Emilio Corchado (Eds.)

Hybrid Artificial Intelligent Systems

10th International Conference, HAIS 2015
Bilbao, Spain, June 22–24, 2015
Proceedings

 Springer

Editors
Enrique Onieva
University of Deusto
Bilbao
Spain

Igor Santos
University of Deusto
Bilbao
Spain

Eneko Osaba
University of Deusto
Bilbao
Spain

Héctor Quintián
Universidad de Salamanca
Salamanca
Spain

Emilio Corchado
Universidad de Salamanca
Salamanca
Spain

ISSN 0302-9743   ISSN 1611-3349 (electronic)
Lecture Notes in Artificial Intelligence
ISBN 978-3-319-19643-5   ISBN 978-3-319-19644-2 (eBook)
DOI 10.1007/978-3-319-19644-2

Library of Congress Control Number: 2015939923

LNCS Sublibrary: SL7 – Artificial Intelligence

Springer International Publishing AG Switzerland is part of Springer Science+Business Media
(www.springer.com)

Preface

This volume of *Lecture Notes on Artificial Intelligence* (LNAI) includes papers presented at HAIS 2015 held in the beautiful seaside city of Bilbao, Spain, June 2015.

The International Conference on Hybrid Artificial Intelligence Systems (HAIS), has become a unique, established, and broad interdisciplinary forum for researchers an practitioners who are involved in developing and applying symbolic and sub-symbolic techniques aimed at the construction of highly robust and reliable problem-solving techniques and bringing the most relevant achievements in this field.

Hybridization of intelligent techniques, coming from different computational intelligence areas, has become popular because of the growing awareness that such combinations frequently perform better than the individual techniques such as neurocomputing, fuzzy systems, rough sets, evolutionary algorithms, agents and multiagent systems, etc.

Practical experience has indicated that hybrid intelligence techniques might be helpful for solving some of the challenging real-world problems. In a hybrid intelligence system, a synergistic combination of multiple techniques is used to build an efficient solution to deal with a particular problem. This is, thus, the setting of the HAIS conference series, and its increasing success is proof of the vitality of this exciting field.

HAIS 2015 received 190 technical submissions. After a rigorous peer-review process, the international Program Committee selected 60 papers, which are published in this conference proceedings.

The selection of papers was extremely rigorous in order to maintain the high quality of the conference and we would like to thank the Program Committee for their hard work in the reviewing process. This process is very important to the creation of a conference of high standard and the HAIS conference would not exist without their help.

The large number of submissions is certainly not only testimony to the vitality and attractiveness of the field but an indicator of the interest in the HAIS conferences themselves.

HAIS 2015 enjoyed outstanding keynote speeches by distinguished guest speakers: Prof. Enrique Zuazua – Research Professor at Ikerbasque (Basque Country, Spain), Prof. Miguel Angel Sotelo – University of Alcalá (Spain), and Prof. Michal Wozniak – Wroclaw University of Technology (Poland).

HAIS 2015 teamed up with *Neurocomputing* (Elsevier) and the *Logic Journal of the IGPL* Oxford Journals for a suite of special issues including selected papers from HAIS 2015.

Particular thanks go to the conference main sponsors, IEEE-Spanish Section, IEEE Systems, Man and Cybernetics – Spanish Chapter, University of Salamanca, University of Deusto, DeustoTech, and The International Federation for Computational Logic, who jointly contributed in an active and constructive manner to the success of this initiative.

We would like to thank Alfred Hofmann and Anna Kramer from Springer for their help and collaboration during this demanding publication project.

June 2015

Enrique Onieva
Igor Santos
Eneko Osaba
Héctor Quintián
Emilio Corchado

Organization

General Chair

Emilio Corchado   University of Salamanca, Spain

International Advisory Committee

Ajith Abraham   Machine Intelligence Research Labs, Europe
Antonio Bahamonde   President of the Spanish Association
     for Artificial Intelligence, AEPIA
Andre de Carvalho   University of São Paulo, Brazil
Sung-Bae Cho   Yonsei University, Korea
Juan M. Corchado   University of Salamanca, Spain
José R. Dorronsoro   Autonomous University of Madrid, Spain
Michael Gabbay   Kings College London, UK
Ali A. Ghorbani   UNB, Canada
Mark A. Girolami   University of Glasgow, UK
Manuel Graña   University of País Vasco, Spain
Petro Gopych   Universal Power Systems USA-Ukraine LLC, Ukraine
Jon G. Hall   The Open University, UK
Francisco Herrera   University of Granada, Spain
César Hervás-Martínez   University of Córdoba, Spain
Tom Heskes   Radboud University Nijmegen, The Netherlands
Dusan Husek   Academy of Sciences of the Czech Republic,
     Czech Republic
Lakhmi Jain   University of South Australia, Australia
Samuel Kaski   Helsinki University of Technology, Finland
Daniel A. Keim   University Konstanz, Germany
Isidro Laso   D.G. Information Society and Media, European
     Commission
Marios Polycarpou   University of Cyprus, Cyprus
Witold Pedrycz   University of Alberta, Canada
Václav Snášel   VSB-Technical University of Ostrava, Czech Republic
Xin Yao   University of Birmingham, UK
Hujun Yin   University of Manchester, UK
Michał Woźniak   Wroclaw University of Technology, Poland
Aditya Ghose   University of Wollongong, Australia
Ashraf Saad   Armstrong Atlantic State University, USA
Fanny Klett   German Workforce Advanced Distributed Learning
     Partnership Laboratory, Germany

Paulo Novais	Universidade do Minho, Portugal
Rajkumar Roy	The EPSRC Centre for Innovative Manufacturing in Through-life Engineering Services, UK
Amy Neustein	Linguistic Technology Systems, USA
Jaydip Sen	Innovation Lab, Tata Consultancy Services Ltd., India

Program Committee

Emilio Corchado	University of Salamanca, Spain (Chair)
Abdel-Badeeh M. Salem	Ain Shams University, Egypt
Aboul Ella Hassanien	Cairo University, Egypt
Adolfo Rodríguez	University of León, Spain
Ajith Abraham	Machine Intelligence Research Labs, Europe
Alberto Fernández	Universidad Rey Juan Carlos, Spain
Alberto Ochoa	Juarez City University, Mexico
Aldo Franco Dragoni	Università Politecnicadelle Marche, Italy
Alfredo Cuzzocrea	ICAR-CNR and University of Calabria, Italy
Alicia Troncoso	Pablo de Olavide University, Spain
Álvaro Herrero	University of Burgos, Spain
Amelia Zafra	University of Córdoba, Spain
Ana M. Bernardos	Universidad Politécnica de Madrid, Spain
Ana María Madureira	Polytechnic University of Porto, Portugal
Anca Andreica	University of Babes-Bolyai, Romania
André C.P.L.F. de Carvalho	University of São Paulo, Brazil
Andreea Vescan	University of Babes-Bolyai, Romania
Andrés Ortiz	University of Málaga, Spain
Ángel Arroyo	University of Burgos, Spain
Angelos Amanatiadis	Democritus University of Thrace, Greece
Anna Burduk	Wroclaw University of Technology, Poland
António Dourado	University of Coimbra, Portugal
Antonio Masegosa	University of Deusto, Spain
Arkadiusz Kowalski	Wroclaw University of Technology, Poland
Arturo de la Escalera	University Carlos III de Madrid, Spain
Arturo Hernández-Aguirre	CIMAT, Mexico
Asier Perallos	University of Deusto, Spain
Barna Iantovics	Petru Maior University of Tg. Mures, Romania
Belén Vaquerizo	University of Burgos, Spain
Bernardete Ribeiro	University of Coimbra, Portugal
Bingyang Zhao	Tsinghua University, China
Blanca Cases Gutierrez	University of País Vasco/EHU, Spain
Bogdan Trawinski	Wroclaw University of Technology, Poland
Borja Fernandez-Gauna	University of País Vasco/EHU, Spain
Bozena Skolud	Silesian University of Technology, Poland
Bruno Baruque	University of Burgos, Spain
Camelia Chira	University of Babes-Bolyai, Romania
Camelia Pintea	North University of Baia-Mare, Romania

José Luis Verdegay	University of Granada, Spain
José M. Armingol	University Carlos III de Madrid, Spain
José M. Molina	University of Seville, Spain
José Manuel López	University of País Vasco/EHU, Spain
José R. Villar	University of Oviedo, Spain
José Ramón Cano	University of Jaén, Spain
Jose Ranilla	University of Oviedo, Spain
José Riquelme	University of Seville, Spain
Jovita Nenortaite	Kaunas Technology University, Baltic States
Juan Álvaro Muñoz	University of Almería, Spain
Juan F. De Paz Santana	University of Salamanca, Spain
Juan Humberto Sossa	CIC-IPN, Mexico
Juan José Flores	University of Michoacana, Mexico
Juan Manuel Gorriz	University of Granada, Spain
Juan Pavón	Universidad Complutense de Madrid, Spain
Julián Luengo	University of Granada, Spain
Julio César Ponce	Universidad Autónoma de Aguascalientes, Mexico
Krzysztof Kalinowski	Silesian University of Technology, Poland
Lauro Snidaro	University of Udine, Italy
Lenka Lhotska	Czech Technical University in Prague, Czech Republic
Leocadio G. Casado	University of Almeria, Spain
Lourdes Sáiz	University of Burgos, Spain
Manuel Grana	University of Basque Country, Spain
Marcilio De Souto	LIFO/University of Orleans, France
María Guijarro	Universidad Complutense de Madrid, Spain
María Jose Del Jesus	Universidad de Jaén, Spain
María Martínez Ballesteros	University of Seville, Spain
María R Sierra	Universidad de Oviedo, Spain
Mario Köeppen	Kyushu Institute of Technology, Japan
Marios Policarpou	University of Cyprus, Cyprus, Cyprus
Martí Navarro	Universidad Politécnica de Valencia, Spain
Martin Macas	Czech Technical University in Prague, Czech Republic
Matjaz Gams	Jozef Stefan Institute, Slovenia
Miguel Ángel Patricio	Universidad Carlos III de Madrid, Spain
Miguel Ángel Veganzones	GIPSA-lab, Grenoble-INP, France
Miroslav Bursa	Czech Technical University in Prague, Czech Republic
Michal Wozniak	Wroclaw University of Technology, Poland
Mohammed Chadli	University of Picardie Jules Verne, France
Nicola Di Mauro	Università di Bari, Italy
Nima Hatami	University of California, USA
Noelia Sanchez-Maroño	University of A Coruña, Spain
Oscar Fontenla-Romero	University of A Coruña, Spain
Ozgur Koray Sahingoz	Turkish Air Force Academy, Turkey
Paula M. Castro Castro	University of A Coruña, Spain
Paulo Novais	University of Minho, Portugal
Pavel Brandstetter	VSB-Technical University of Ostrava, Czech Republic

Pedro López   University of Deusto, Spain
Peter Rockett   University of Sheffield, UK
Petrica Claudiu Pop   North University of Baia Mare, Romania
Rafael Alcala   University of Granada, Spain
Ramón Moreno   Universidad del País Vasco, Spain
Ramon Rizo   Universidad de Alicante, Spain
Ricardo Del Olmo   Universidad de Burgos, Spain
Robert Burduk   Wroclaw University of Technology, Poland
Rodolfo Zunino   University of Genoa, Italy
Roman Senkerik   Tomas Bata University in Zlin, Czech Republic
Ronald Yager   Iona College, USA
Rubén Fuentes-Fernández   Universidad Complutense de Madrid, Spain
Sean Holden   University of Cambridge, UK
Sebastián Ventura   University of Cordoba, Spain
Stella Heras   Universidad Politécnica de Valencia, Spain
Sung-Bae Cho   Yonsei University, Korea
Theodore Pachidis   Kavala Institute of Technology, Greece
Tomasz Kajdanowicz   Wroclaw University of Technology, Poland
Urko Zurutuza   Mondragon University, Spain
Urszula Stanczyk   Silesian University of Technology, Poland
Václav Snášel   VSB-Technical University of Ostrava, Czech Republic
Vasile Palade   Oxford University, UK
Waldemar Małopolski   Cracow University of Technology, Poland
Wei-Chiang Hong   Oriental Institute of Technology, Taiwan
Wiesław Chmielnicki   Jagiellonian University, Poland
Yannis Marinakis   Technical University of Crete, Greece
Ying Tan   Peking University, China
Yusuke Nojima   Osaka Prefecture University, Japan
Zuzana Oplatkova   Tomas Bata University in Zlin, Czech Republic

Organizing Committee

Emilio Corchado   University of Salamanca, Spain
Héctor Quintián   University of Salamanca, Spain
Eneko Osaba   University of Deusto, Spain
Enrique Onieva   University of Deusto, Spain
Borja Sanz   University of Deusto, Spain
Igor Santos   University of Deusto, Spain
Iker Pastor-López   University of Deusto, Spain
Sendoa Rojas   University of Deusto, Spain
Itziar Salaberria   University of Deusto, Spain
Pedro López   University of Deusto, Spain
Antonio Masegosa   University of Deusto, Spain
Jose Galviria de-la-Puerta   University of Deusto, Spain

Contents

Bio-inspired Models and Evolutionary Computation

Learning Algorithms

Hybrid Intelligent Systems for Data Mining and Applications

Classification and Cluster Analysis

Data Mining and Knowledge Discovery

Frequent Sets Discovery in Privacy Preserving Quantitative Association Rules Mining

Piotr Andruszkiewicz$^{(\boxtimes)}$

Institute of Computer Science, Warsaw University of Technology, Warsaw, Poland
P.Andruszkiewicz@ii.pw.edu.pl

Abstract. This paper deals with discovering frequent sets for quantitative association rules mining with preserved privacy. It focuses on privacy preserving on an individual level, when true individual values, e.g., values of attributes describing customers, are not revealed. Only distorted values and parameters of the distortion procedure are public. However, a miner can discover hidden knowledge, e.g., association rules, from the distorted data. In order to find frequent sets for quantitative association rules mining with preserved privacy, not only does a miner need to discretise continuous attributes, transform them into binary attributes, but also, after both discretisation and binarisation, the calculation of the distortion parameters for new attributes is necessary. Then a miner can apply either MASK (Mining Associations with Secrecy Konstraints) or MMASK (Modified MASK) to find candidates for frequent sets and estimate their supports. In this paper the methodology for calculating distortion parameters of newly created attributes after both discretisation and binarisation of attributes for quantitative association rules mining has been proposed. The new application of MMASK for finding frequent sets in discovering quantitative association rules with preserved privacy has been also presented. The application of MMASK scheme for frequent sets mining in quantitative association rules discovery on real data sets has been experimentally verified. The results of the experiments show that both MASK and MMASK can be applied in frequent sets mining for quantitative association rules with preserved privacy, however, MMASK gives better results in this task.

Keywords: Privacy preserving data mining · Quantitative association rules · Frequent sets · Discretisation · MMASK

1 Introduction

Since privacy concerns related to a possible misuse of knowledge discovered by means of data mining techniques have been raised [1], many attempts have been made to provide privacy preserving techniques [2]. Thus, a new domain, privacy preserving data mining, emerged.

In the case of preserving privacy on an individual level, that the paper focuses on, individual values of user's (object's) characteristics (values of attributes)

© Springer International Publishing Switzerland 2015
E. Onieva et al. (Eds.): HAIS 2015, LNAI 9121, pp. 3–15, 2015.
DOI: 10.1007/978-3-319-19644-2_1

are preserved. A miner is able to discover hidden knowledge, e.g., to build a model, find association rules, however, exact object's characteristics (e.g., true vales of an attribute *Salary*) are not provided. This can be obtained through the reconstruction-based approach. Privacy incorporation in the reconstruction-based approach is done by changing the original individual values (for instance, user's answers) in a random way by means of a randomisation-based method and revealing only modified values. The distorted data as well as parameters of a randomisation-based method used to distort the data can be published or passed to a third party. Knowing distorted individual values and parameters of a randomisation-based method, one is able to perform data mining tasks. To this end, firstly original distributions of values of attributes are reconstructed (estimated) based on the distorted values and the parameters, secondly a data mining model is built based on the reconstructed distributions and the distorted data. The model is created without the need to access the original data. In this paper, the centralised scenario, where the distorted records are stored in a centralised database, was assumed.

Privacy Preserving Association Rules Mining deals with discovering associations with preserved privacy. In order to perform such a task, a miner can find frequent sets and then calculate association rules.

For the first step the MASK (Mining Associations with Secrecy Konstraints[1]) [3] scheme can be employed. This scheme estimates an original support of candidate itemsets based on a counted support of itemsets or itemsubsets in a distorted database and parameters of a distortion procedure and, in the consequence, enables a miner to discover frequent sets. Having frequent sets and their supports estimated association rules can be discovered easily. More details on MASK scheme can be found in Sect. 3. The optimisation for MASK that eliminates exponential complexity in estimating a support of an itemset with respect to its cardinality and improves the accuracy of the results is called MMASK (Modified MASK) [4] (for details please refer to Sect. 3.3).

In this paper, the extension of the applicability of MMASK to quantitative association rules mining with preserved privacy by discretisation and binarisation of attributes has been proposed. Moreover, the method for calculating distortion parameters for new attributes in order to apply MMASK has been presented.

The remainder of this paper is organized as follows: Sect. 2 presents related work. Section 3 reviews the MASK scheme and the idea of the MMASK optimisation. In Sect. 4, the idea of applying MASK and MMASK in frequent sets mining for quantitative association rules is discussed. The experimental results are highlighted in Sect. 5. Finally, Sect. 6, summarises the conclusions of the study and outline future avenues to explore.

2   Related Work

Since the notion of Privacy Preserving Data Mining was introduced, association rules mining and classification with incorporated privacy have been widely discussed [5–7]. Only solutions closely related to the proposal were mentioned.

---

[1] The authors use Konstraints instead of Constraints to achieve abbreviation: MASK.

A framework for mining association rules from a centralised distorted database was proposed in [3]. A scheme called MASK (detailed description of MASK can be found in Sect. 3) attempts to simultaneously provide a high degree of privacy to a user and retain a high degree of accuracy in the mining results. To address efficiency, several optimisations for MASK were originally proposed in the same paper. The main optimisation, which reduces time complexity, requires randomisation factors to be constant for all items. This is the most important disadvantage of this optimisation, because it does not allow using different randomisation factors for different items, and in consequence, privacy levels. Non-uniform randomisation factors help to achieve higher accuracy [5] because people have different privacy concerns about different attributes. Another optimisation, called EMASK (Efficient MASK), was proposed in [6]. In general, EMASK does not break the exponential complexity of reconstructing an original support with respect to the length of an intemset and does not allow different randomisation factors when an item is present in an original database and when it is not.

In [5] a general framework for privacy preserving association rules mining was proposed. It allows attributes to be randomised using different randomisation factors, based on their privacy levels. An efficient algorithm RE, Recursive Estimation, for mining frequent itemsets under this framework was also developed in [5]. The RE algorithm uses different randomisation factors, but it does not break an exponential complexity in estimating a support of an itemset.

In [4] the MMASK optimisation for MASK was proposed. It breaks exponential complexity in estimating a support of an itemset with respect to its cardinality. Not only does this optimisation allow attributes to be randomised using different randomisation factors, based on their privacy levels, but also allows attributes to have different randomisation factors for each value; that is, when an item is present in an original database and when it is not. In [8] the *reduction relaxation* which, when combined with the relaxation, enables a miner to decrease and control the false negative coefficient for different lengths of frequent itemsets discovered during the process of association rules mining was introduced.

The discussion on privacy preserving quantitative association rules mining was started in [9]. However, the idea was only sketched and no empirical verification was done. In [10] and [11] the problem of hiding quantitative association rules with preserved privacy was discussed.

In this paper, the new application of MMASK [4] for finding frequent sets in quantitative association rules mining with preserved privacy has been proposed. The new usage of MMASK has been experimentally tested and the results are presented herein.

3   Mining Associations with Secrecy Konstraints (MASK) Scheme and Idea of MMASK Optimisation

In this section, basics of the MASK scheme [3] for Privacy Preserving Data Mining over centralised data are described. The MASK scheme is used to estimate an original support of an itemset; that is, support of an itemset in a database with original values of attributes, based on distorted transactions as the original values of attributes are not accessible in the real scenario. The idea of MMASK optimisation, which eliminates exponential complexity in estimating a support of an itemset with respect to its cardinality, is also presented.

3.1   Distortion Procedure in MASK Scheme

In order to distort a transactional data set in the original MASK scheme, the following basic randomisation method for binary attributes was used.

Given a binary attribute with possible values of 0 and 1, each (original) value is kept with the probability p or flipped with the probability $1 - p$ [3,6]. All attributes are distorted in the same manner, however, each attribute may have a different value of the probability p. Moreover, each original value of an attribute may have a different probability of keeping an original value or flipping it. Let p denote the probability that the value 1 is kept and q that the value 0 is kept. Distorted values of binary attributes create a new database and are supplied to a miner. The only information a miner gets is a distorted database and values of probability p and q for each attribute.

3.2   Estimating n-itemset Support in MASK

Let $\mathcal{T}$ be a true data set[2] represented by matrix $\mathbf{T}$. Let denote a distorted data set, obtained accordingly to the distortion procedure for binary attributes presented in the previous section, as $\mathcal{D}$ and its matrix representation as $\mathbf{D}$.

Now the matrices $\mathbf{C^D}$ and $\mathbf{C^T}$ will be defined:

$$
\mathbf{C^D} = \begin{bmatrix} C^D_{2^n-1} \\ \cdot \\ \cdot \\ \cdot \\ C^D_1 \\ C^D_0 \end{bmatrix}, \quad
\mathbf{C^T} = \begin{bmatrix} C^T_{2^n-1} \\ \cdot \\ \cdot \\ \cdot \\ C^T_1 \\ C^T_0 \end{bmatrix}. \tag{1}
$$

C^T_k and C^D_k are the numbers of tuples in $\mathbf{T}$ and $\mathbf{D}$, respectively, that have a binary form of k (in n bits) for a given itemset. For a 2-itemset C^T_0 refers to the number of 00's and C^T_2 to the number of 10's in $\mathbf{T}$.

The matrix $\mathbf{M}$ is defined as follows:

$$
\mathbf{M} = \begin{bmatrix}
m_{0,0} & m_{0,1} & m_{0,2} & \cdots & m_{0,2^n-1} \\
m_{1,0} & m_{1,1} & m_{1,2} & \cdots & m_{1,2^n-1} \\
\vdots & & & \ddots & \vdots \\
m_{2^n-1,0} & m_{2^n-1,1} & m_{2^n-1,2} & \cdots & m_{2^n-1,2^n-1}
\end{bmatrix}, \tag{2}
$$

---

[2] In real applications a true data set is not stored. Only distorted tuples are collected.

where $m_{i,j}$ is a probability that a tuple of the form C_j^T in matrix $\mathbf{T}$ is changed to a tuple of the form C_i^D in $\mathbf{D}$.

For instance, $m_{1,2}$ for a 2-itemset is the probability that a tuple 10 is distorted to a tuple 01 during the distortion process and $m_{1,2} = (1-p)(1-p)$, if p is the same for considered items. The value of $m_{1,2}$ results from the changes made for both items $(1-p$ probability was used) and the independent distortion for both items (multiplication of the probabilities was used).

A support of an n-itemset in the true matrix $\mathbf{T}$ can be estimated using the following equation:

$$\mathbf{C}^T = \mathbf{M}^{-1}\mathbf{C}^D. \tag{3}$$

3.3 Reducing the Number of Items in Estimating n-itemsets Support in MMASK Optimisation

The reduction of a number of items in estimating the original support of an n-itemset X can be obtained by choosing for an itemset X a subset of distorted transactions for estimation of the true support.

Let *reduction threshold* denote the maximal length of an itemset used in estimating the support of an n-itemset X, reduction threshold $< n$.

The true support of X can be estimated as the support of a reduced itemset $R \subset X$ in transactions which support $X \backslash R$ in a true database, where $|R| <$ reduction threshold.

As there is no access to a true database $\mathcal{T}$, the subset of the chosen distorted transactions $\mathcal{D_R}$ from the distorted database $\mathcal{D}$, $\mathcal{D_R} \subset \mathcal{D}$, should support $X \backslash R$ in the true database $\mathcal{T}$ with a high probability. The CTS algorithm for choosing distorted transactions which support a given itemset $X \backslash R$ in the true database $\mathcal{T}$ with a high probability was proposed in [4]. A probability that a distorted transaction supports a given itemset in the true database is estimated based on the distorted set of transactions.

For more details on MMASK, please refer to [4] and [8].

4 Frequent Sets Discovery for Quantitative Rules in Privacy Preserving

In order to find frequent sets for quantitative rules mining without preserved privacy, a miner can discretise continuous attributes, then transform them into binary attributes and use, e.g., Apriori algorithm.

With preserved privacy, after discretisation and binarisation the calculation of the distortion parameters for new attributes is needed. And then either MASK or MMASK can be applied. In this paper, the methodology for calculating the distortion parameters of newly created attributes after both discretisation and binarisation of attributes for quantitative association rules mining and the new application of MMASK for finding frequent sets in discovering quantitative association rules with preserved privacy have been proposed. In order to achieve the final goal, the presented solution hybridises different areas, namely association rules mining, statistical reconstruction of random variable's distributions, and heuristics in MMASK transaction choosing algorithm.

Frequent sets discovery for quantitative rules with preserved privacy is performed as follows:

1. Discretise continuous attributes and calculate new distortion parameters,
2. Binarise discretised and nominal attributes, for each unique value of an attribute create a binary attribute, and calculate new distortion parameters,
3. Apply MMASK algorithm to find frequent sets based on binary attributes and new distortion parameters.

It is important to store rules of discretising and binarising attributes and take into account that the frequent sets came from continuous or nominal attributes while calculating quantitative association rules based on frequent sets.

In the following subsections, discretisation and binarisation for quantitative rules, especially the solution for calculating the probabilities of changing/retaining the original value for transformed attributes[3], will be described. As binary attributes[4] will be obtained after transformation, MMASK can be applied to find frequent sets.

4.1 Discretisation

The solution for continuous attributes is to discretise an attribute and calculate the probabilities of changing/retaining the original value. This solution applies to both techniques of distorting continuous attributes, namely the additive perturbation technique [13] and the retention replacement perturbation [14]. The chosen perturbation technique does not have the influence on discretisation process but it influences the way that the distortion procedure parameters are calculated.

The method for calculating elements of matrix $\mathbf{P}'$[5] is the same for both perturbation techniques [15]. A miner is looking for the probability that the value of nominal attribute A will be equal to v_i given that the vale of continuous attribute X is equal to x.

$$P(A = v_i | X = x) = P(X' \in I_i | X = x); \; i = 1...k, \tag{4}$$

where X' is the continuous attribute after distortion and I_i is the i-th interval, which corresponds to v_i value.

The computation of these probabilities for the retention replacement perturbation will be shown. Let there be k intervals after discretisation, i.e., k values of the nominal attribute, where p is the probability that the original value of the continuous attribute is kept, p does not depend on x (the given value of X

---

[3] For details about the probabilities of changing/retaining the original value and the matrix of retaining/changing values of nominal attribute please refer to [12].

[4] In this paper, the term item and binary attribute is used interchangeably.

[5] $\mathbf{P}'$ is a matrix of retaining/changing values of discretised (nominal) attribute.

attribute) neither on the probability $P(X' \in I_i|R')$, where R' means that the original value x is changed and R means that the original value x is retained.

$$P(X' \in I_i|X = x)$$

$$= pP(X' \in I_i|R) + (1 - p)P(X' \in I_i|R') \tag{5}$$

$$= \begin{cases} p + (1 - p)P(X' \in I_i|R'); & x \in I_i \\ (1 - p)P(X' \in I_i|R'); & x \notin I_i \end{cases}$$

For the uniform perturbation and intervals with the same length $P(X' \in I_i|R') = \frac{1}{k}$ and

$$P(X' \in I_i|X = x) = \begin{cases} p + (1 - p)\frac{1}{k}; & x \in I_i \\ (1 - p)\frac{1}{k}; & x \notin I_i. \end{cases} \tag{6}$$

Using the above probabilities, the discretised nominal attribute is binarised to k binary attributes.

4.2   Binarisation

A nominal attribute A with k possible values is binarised to k binary attributes - A_1 to A_k. An attribute A_i has the value of 1 when the attribute A is equal to the i-th value or 0 otherwise. This transformation is applied to both nominal attributes and discretised attributes.

There are two possible scenarios of distorting nominal attributes [15]. The first is to transform a nominal attribute to k binary attributes and then distort all k attributes. The second is to distort a nominal attribute and after that transform it to k binary attributes.

The first scenario may result in wrong values of k attributes, e.g., two 1's simultaneously.

In both scenarios parameters of distorting procedure should be chosen. For binary attributes distorted after the transformation, the probability of retaining the original value of 1 (p_i) and corresponding probability for 0 (q_i) for each attribute ($i = 1, ..., k$) are chosen. Usually $p_i = p$, $i = 1, ..., k$ and $q_i = q$, $i = 1, ..., k$. In the special case q_i is equal to p_i. Distorting and estimating the support the independence of the attributes $A_1, ..., A_k$ is assumed.

In the second scenario the distortion parameters for the nominal attribute before the transformation are chosen. Then the attribute is distorted. After that the calculation of p_i and q_i for all binary attributes is performed, $i = 1, ..., k$. The calculation of the probabilities for this case will be shown.

Let the attribute A has k values $v_1, v_2, v_3, ..., v_k$. Let assume that the probability of retaining the original value for each possible value of the attribute is equal to p. The probability of changing the value is the same for each value of the attribute and is equal to $\frac{1-p}{k-1}$. Thus the matrix of retaining/changing values of nominal attribute ($\mathbf{P}$) looks as follows:

$$\mathbf{P} = \begin{pmatrix} p & \frac{1-p}{k-1} & \frac{1-p}{k-1} & \cdots & \frac{1-p}{k-1} \\ \frac{1-p}{k-1} & p & \frac{1-p}{k-1} & \cdots & \frac{1-p}{k-1} \\ \vdots & \vdots & \vdots & \ddots & \vdots \\ \frac{1-p}{k-1} & \frac{1-p}{k-1} & \frac{1-p}{k-1} & \cdots & p \end{pmatrix}. \tag{7}$$

Let p'_i and q'_i be the probabilities of retaining the value of 1 and 0 for i-th binary attribute, respectively. In our case $p'_i = p'$ and $q'_i = q'$ for $i = 1...k$, because the probabilities for all values of the nominal attributes are symmetrical, according to our assumptions.

At the first glance, $p' = p$. To calculate q', let look at the matrix $\mathbf{P}$ once again. For the sake of simplicity, q'_1, i.e., the probability that 0 of the binary attribute which comes from v_1 will be kept, is considered.

$$\begin{aligned} q'_i = q'_1 &= P_A(\{v_2, v_3, ..., v_k\} | \{v_2, v_3, ..., v_k\}) \\ &= P_A(v_2)[P_A(v_2 \to v_2) + P_A(v_2 \to v_3) + ... + \\ P_A(v_2 &\to v_k)] + P_A(v_3)[P_A(v_3 \to v_2) + P_A(v_3 \to v_3) \\ &+ ... + P_A(v_3 \to v_k)] + ... + P_A(v_k)[P_A(v_k \to v_2) \\ &+ P_A(v_k \to v_3) + ... + P_A(v_k \to v_k)], \end{aligned} \tag{8}$$

where $Pr(v_p \to v_r)$ is the probability that value v_p will be changed to value v_r.

Let assume that $P_A(v_i) = \frac{1}{k}$, i.e., there is the same number of samples in the training data set for each value of the attribute.

If there is a particular training set, one can estimate the original number of samples for each value of the attribute and alter the calculations of $\mathbf{P'}$.

Let assume that $P_A(v_i) = \frac{1}{k}$, then

$$q'_i = q'_1 = \frac{1}{k-1}(k-1)[(k-2)\frac{1-p}{k-1} + p] = \frac{k-2p}{k-1}. \tag{9}$$

Finally, matrix $\mathbf{P'}$ has the following elements:

$$\mathbf{P'} = \begin{bmatrix} p & 1 - \frac{k-2p}{k-1} \\ 1-p & \frac{k-2p}{k-1} \end{bmatrix}. \tag{10}$$

During the estimation of the support in the second scenario the independence of attributes $A_1...A_k$ was assumed.

The presented solution is easily extensible to any specific $\mathbf{P}$ matrix.

5   Experimental Evaluation

In this section, the results of the experiments conducted to assess the usefullness of MMASK in finding frequent sets for quantitative rules are presented.

5.1   Error Measures

In the experiments three kinds of measures have been used, namely Support Error, Identity Error [3], and Accuracy of Identity [4]:

- Support Error (ρ): This measure reflects the average relative error in the reconstructed support values for those itemsets that are correctly identified to be frequent. Denoting the reconstructed support by *recSupport* and the actual support by *actSupport*, the support error is computed over all frequent itemsets F as follows:

$$\rho = \frac{1}{|F|} \Sigma_{x \in F} \frac{|recSupport_x - actSupport_x|}{actSupport_x} * 100 \ [\%]. \tag{11}$$

This measure is computed separately for each length of itemsets; that is, for 1-itemsets, 2-item- sets, etc.

- Identity Error (σ): This measure reflects the percentage error in identifying frequent itemsets and has two components: σ^+ indicating the percentage of false positives, and σ^- indicating the percentage of false negatives. Denoting the reconstructed set of frequent itemsets with R and the correct set of frequent itemsets with F, these measures are computed as follows:

$$\sigma^+ = \frac{|R \setminus F|}{|F|} * 100 \ [\%], \quad \sigma^- = \frac{|F \setminus R|}{|F|} * 100 \ [\%]. \tag{12}$$

- Accuracy of Identity (f): This measure reflects the accuracy of identifying frequent itemsets (shows how many sets are correctly identified to be frequent).

$$f = |F \cap R| \tag{13}$$

5.2   Experimental Results

13 UCI [16] datasets have been examined and below the representative results for *Breast*, *Australian*, and *Diabetes* datasets are presented (the remaining results were skipped due to limited space).

In the experiments MASK and MMASK without the relaxation for frequent sets discovery in Privacy Preserving Quantitative Association Rules Mining were compared. The discretisation (as presented in Sect. 4.1) that divided values of an attribute into 4 value intervals with equal number of samples in each interval was used. Then nominal and transformed attributes were binarised as described in Sect. 4.2. After that the attributes were distorted.

The first set of experiments was conducted on the real dataset *Breast* with 200 % privacy (Table 1). Table 2 presents the results of frequent sets mining on *Australian* dataset with 150 % privacy. The results from the experiments on *Diabetes* dataset with 200 % privacy level can be found in Table 3. The *Level*, which corresponds to the consecutive iterations in Apriori-like algorithms, indicates the length of frequent itemsets, $|F_0|$ indicates the number of frequent itemsets at a

Table 1. The results of mining the frequent sets in dataset *Breast* with 200 % privacy and parameters: reduction threshold = 3, minimum support = 0.02

Level	$|Fo|$	$|Fr|$	ρ_r	$\sigma-_r$	$\sigma+_r$	f_r	$|Frm|$	ρ_{rm}	$\sigma-_{rm}$	$\sigma+_{rm}$	f_{rm}
1	29	31	15.9	0.0	6.9	29	31	15.9	0.0	6.9	29
2	320	328	70.0	20.3	22.8	255	328	70.0	20.3	22.8	255
3	1192	1163	108.9	49.4	47.0	603	1163	108.9	49.4	47.0	603
4	1863	1091	98.6	76.9	35.5	430	1183	73.6	73.4	36.9	496
5	1648	255	69.8	91.3	6.7	144	453	57.9	85.0	12.4	248
6	988	17	64.3	98.6	0.3	14	86	54.0	92.7	1.4	72
7	407	0	-	100.0	0.0	0	10	62.0	97.5	0.0	10
8	87	0	-	100.0	0.0	0	0	-	100	0.0	0
9	8	0	-	100.0	0.0	0	0	-	100	0.0	0

Table 2. The results of mining the frequent sets in dataset *Australian* with 150 % privacy and parameters: reduction threshold = 3, minimum support = 0.02

Level	$|Fo|$	$|Fr|$	ρ_r	$\sigma-_r$	$\sigma+_r$	f_r	$|Frm|$	ρ_{rm}	$\sigma-_{rm}$	$\sigma+_{rm}$	f_{rm}
1	48	48	21.0	4.2	4.2	46	48	21.0	4.2	4.2	46
2	772	656	196.3	36.8	21.8	488	656	196.3	36.8	21.8	488
3	4056	3016	252.5	71.3	45.6	1166	3016	252.5	71.3	45.6	1166
4	8911	4161	266.2	93.3	40.0	595	3916	220.2	92.3	36.3	683
5	9786	1417	189.1	99.6	14.1	41	1565	124.9	98.8	14.8	118
6	5878	79	-	100.0	1.3	0	148	141.8	99.9	2.4	4
7	2060	0	-	100.0	0.0	0	0	-	100.0	0.0	0
8	398	0	-	100.0	0.0	0	0	-	100.0	0.0	0
9	30	0	-	100.0	0.0	0	0	-	100.0	0.0	0

given level, $|F_r|$ ($|F_{rm}|$) shows the number of mined frequent itemsets from the distorted database using MASK (MMASK). The other columns are the measures defined in Sect. 5.1.

As shown in Tables 1, 2, 3, MMASK in most cases discovers the same or more true frequent sets ($|F_{rm}| \geq |F_r|$) than MASK. For the first three levels, the number of correctly identified frequent sets is the same for MASK and MMASK because reduction threshold = 3 was used (MMASK is equivalent to MASK for levels less or equal to the reduction threshold). The advantage of MMASK is especially clear for higher levels, where MASK cannot find the frequent sets which MMASK does. For instance, in Table 1 MASK did not find any frequent set for level 7 and MMASK found 10 sets that all are correctly identified as frequent sets (the false positive coefficient ($\sigma+$) is equal to 0). MMASK also achieves better support error (ρ) for levels greater than reduction threshold; that is, it estimates better the support of correctly identified frequent sets. Moreover,

Table 3. The results of mining the frequent sets in dataset *Diabetes* with 200 % privacy and parameters: reduction threshold = 3, minimum support = 0.01

Level	$|Fo|$	$|Fr|$	ρ_r	$\sigma-_r$	$\sigma+_r$	f_r	$|Frm|$	ρ_{rm}	$\sigma-_{rm}$	$\sigma+_{rm}$	f_{rm}
1	33	32	13.6	3.0	0.0	32	32	13.6	3.0	0.0	32
2	448	367	71.4	23.0	4.9	345	367	71.4	23.0	4.9	345
3	3010	1323	295.2	66.5	10.5	1008	1323	295.2	66.5	10.5	1008
4	3922	854	451.7	92.0	13.8	313	1069	241.3	89.9	17.1	398
5	1330	47	423.4	99.7	3.2	4	132	182.3	99.0	8.9	13
6	194	0	-	100.0	0.0	0	3	-	100.0	1.5	0
7	9	0	-	100.0	0.0	0	0	-	100.0	0.0	0

MMASK achieves better false negative coefficient (smaller values of $\sigma-$) for levels greater than the reduction threshold because of the higher number of identified (correctly and incorrectly) frequent sets; that is, more indentified frequent sets give less chance to miss some true frequent sets. On the other hand, MMASK has worse false positive coefficient (higher values of $\sigma-$) because more identified (correctly and incorrectly) frequent sets produce more sets incorrectly indicated as frequent.

The results of the experiments show that frequent sets mining for privacy preserving quantitative association rules discovery is feasible and suggest superiority of MMASK over MASK in this task.

6   Conclusions and Future Work

The use of MMASK scheme for frequent sets mining in quantitative association rules discovery on real data sets has been investigated. The results of the experiments suggest that MMASK gives better results than MASK when applied in frequent sets mining for quantitative association rules with preserved privacy.

In future work, the investigation of the possibility of extending the MMASK scheme with the relaxations usage to quantitative association rules is planned. Using relaxation, a miner can control the number of discovered frequent itemsets of particular length and, in consequence, reduce the false negative coefficient. The higher relaxation (applied at the begining of the discovery process) results in more discovered frequent itemsets for all lengths of itemsets. The reduction relaxation applied on a particular level makes the number of discovered frequent itemsets higher for this and higher levels.

The MMASK scheme in generalised association rules [17] can be also used. Furthermore, the investigation of the possibility of privacy preserving incorporation in other algorithms for associations mining, e.g., Eclat, MaxClique [18], can be performed.

References

1. Clifton, C., Marks, D.: Security and privacy implications of data mining. In: ACM SIGMOD Workshop on Research Issues on Data Mining and Knowledge Discovery, Montreal, Canada, University of British Columbia Department of Computer Science, pp. 15–19 (1996)
2. Verykios, V.S., Bertino, E., Fovino, I.N., Provenza, L.P., Saygin, Y., Theodoridis, Y.: State-of-the-art in privacy preserving data mining. SIGMOD Rec. **33**(1), 50–57 (2004)
3. Rizvi, S.J., Haritsa, J.R.: Maintaining data privacy in association rule mining. In: VLDB 2002: Proceedings of the 28th International Conference on Very Large Data Bases, VLDB Endowment, pp. 682–693 (2002)
4. Andruszkiewicz, P.: Optimization for MASK scheme in privacy preserving data mining for association rules. In: Kryszkiewicz, M., Peters, J.F., Rybiński, H., Skowron, A. (eds.) RSEISP 2007. LNCS (LNAI), vol. 4585, pp. 465–474. Springer, Heidelberg (2007)
5. Xia, Y., Yang, Y., Chi, Y.: Mining association rules with non-uniform privacy concerns. In: Das, G., Liu, B., Yu, P.S. (eds.) DMKD, pp. 27–34. ACM (2004)
6. Agrawal, S., Krishnan, V., Haritsa, J.R.: On addressing efficiency concerns in privacy preserving data mining. CoRR cs.DB/0310038 (2003)
7. Andruszkiewicz, P.: Hierarchical combining of classifiers in privacy preserving data mining. In: Polycarpou, M., de Carvalho, A.C.P.L.F., Pan, J.-S., Woźniak, M., Quintian, H., Corchado, E. (eds.) HAIS 2014. LNCS, vol. 8480, pp. 573–584. Springer, Heidelberg (2014)
8. Andruszkiewicz, P.: Reduction relaxation in privacy preserving association rules mining. In: Morzy, T., Härder, T., Wrembel, R. (eds.) ADBIS 2012. AISC, vol. 186, pp. 1–8. Springer, Heidelberg (2013)
9. Chen, Z.Y., hua Liu, G.: Quantitative association rules mining methods with privacy-preserving. In: PDCAT, pp. 910–912. IEEE Computer Society (2005)
10. SathiyaPriya, K., Sadasivam, G.S., Celin, N.: A new method for preserving privacy in quantitative association rules using dsr approach with automated generation of membership function. In: 2011 World Congress on Information and Communication Technologies (WICT), pp. 148–153 (2011)
11. SathiyaPriya, K., Sadasivam, G.S., Aarthi, V.C., Divya, K., Suganya, C.J.P.: Privacy preserving quantitative association rule mining. In: Trends in Innovative Computing 2012 - Intelligent Systems Design, pp. 155–160 (2012)
12. Andruszkiewicz, P.: Probability distribution reconstruction for nominal attributes in privacy preserving classification. In: ICHIT 2008: Proceedings of the 2008 International Conference on Convergence and Hybrid Information Technology, pp. 494–500. IEEE Computer Society, Washington, DC (2008)
13. Agrawal, R., Srikant, R.: Privacy-preserving data mining. In: Chen, W., Naughton, J.F., Bernstein, P.A. (eds.) SIGMOD Conference, pp. 439–450. ACM (2000)
14. Agrawal, R., Srikant, R., Thomas, D.: Privacy preserving olap. In: SIGMOD 2005: Proceedings of the 2005 ACM SIGMOD International Conference on Management of Data, pp. 251–262. ACM, New York (2005)
15. Andruszkiewicz, P.: Privacy preserving classification with emerging patterns. In Saygin, Y., Yu, J.X., Kargupta, H., Wang, W., Ranka, S., Yu, P.S., Wu, X., (eds.) ICDM Workshops, pp. 100–105. IEEE Computer Society (2009)
16. Asuncion, A., Newman, D.J.: UCI machine learning repository (2007)

17. Srikant, R., Agrawal, R.: Mining generalized association rules. In: Dayal, U., Gray, P.M.D., Nishio, S. (eds.) VLDB, pp. 407–419. Morgan Kaufmann (1995)
18. Zaki, M.J.: Scalable algorithms for association mining. IEEE Trans. Knowl. Data Eng. **12**(3), 372–390 (2000)

An Instance of Social Intelligence in the Internet of Things: Bread Making Recipe Recommendation by ELM Regression

Manuel Graña and J. David Nuñez-Gonzalez[✉]

Computational Intelligence Group, UPV/EHU, Leioa, Spain
manuel.grana@ehu.eus,jdnunez001@gmail.com

Abstract. The Social and Smart project proposes a new framework for the interaction between users and their household appliances, where social interaction becomes an intelligent social network of users and appliances which is able to provide intelligent responses to the needs of the users. In this paper we focus on one incrasingly common appliance in the european homes: the bread-maker. There are a number of satisfaction parameters which can be specified by the user: crustiness, fragance, baking finish, and softness. A bread making recipe is composed mainly of the temperatures and times for each of the baking stages: first leavening, second leavening, precooking, cooking and browning. Although a thoroughful real life experimentation and data collection is being carried out by project partners, there are no data available for training/testing yet. Thus, in order to test out ideas we must resort to synthetic data generated using a very abstract model of the satisfaction parameters resulting from a given recipe. The recommendation in this context is carried by a couple of Extreme Learning Machine (ELM) regression models trained to predict the satisfaction parameters from the recipe input, and the other the inverse mapping from the desired satisfaction to the breadmaker appliance recipe. The inverse map allows to provide recommendations to the user given its preferences, while the direct map allows to evaluate a recipe predicting user satisfaction.

1 Introduction

There is an emerging view of social networks as information and knowledge repository at the service of the social agents to solve specific problems or to learn procedures relative to a shared domain of problems. Besides popular web service implementations, social networks have shown to be useful to spread educational innovations.

Social computing [1] may be defined as the result of social interaction when it is oriented towards information processing or decision making. Preliminary elaborations towards a taxonomy of social computing systems [2] include the term *subconscious intelligent social computing* [2–5] characterized by some hidden layer of intelligent processes that helps to produce innovative solutions to the problems posed by the social players. The social player asks for the solution

© Springer International Publishing Switzerland 2015
E. Onieva et al. (Eds.): HAIS 2015, LNAI 9121, pp. 16–25, 2015.
DOI: 10.1007/978-3-319-19644-2_2

of a problem, i.e. how to wash my laundry composed of items with some specific dirtiness and according to my preferences? The social framework provides solutions either from previous reported experiences of other social players or as innovation generated by the hidden intelligent layer.

Intuitive description of the system. In the framework of the Social and Smart (SandS) project[1] users are called eahoukers [6]. There are two repositories of knowledge in the SandS Social Network containing tasks to be carried on the appliances and the recipes solving them. When a user requires a task to be performed (blue dashed arrows) there are two possible situations, either the recipe solving the task is known or not. In the second case, the so called Networked Intelligence incorporating the hidden intelligent layer is in charge to produce a new recipe to solve the unknown task. In other words, it is in charge of achieving innovation (green arrow). The recipe found either way is returned to the appliance (black arrows). In the specific case of the breadmaker appliance, we do not have a proper task specification, because it is always the same. In some way it can be said that the specification of the desired satisfaction parameters, i.e. baking, crustines, softness, fragance, are the task specification. So, real life experiments give us pairs of (recipe, satisfaction) vector values, which are always the result of setting the breadmaker parameters and measuring the resulting bread. There is no way in real life to produce the data in the inverse way, setting the user satisfaction to see what is the resulting recipe. Therefore, this inverse map must be estimated from the data gathered in the direct experiments.

The SandS system simplified description introduces the fundamental questions that we are tackling in this paper by designing a prototype recommender system for a specific appliance, the breadmaker, and its validation.

- The first question is: how to build a recipe recommendation from the specification of the user satisfaction? That problem is addressed by building an Extreme Learning Machine[2] [7,8] from the experimental data that implements the inverse mapping.
- The second question is: how to decide that we need innovation? In other words, the inverse model may produce a recipe which in fact is far from solving the problem, so we need to create some new recipe outside the knowledge embedded in the mappings. How we detect that situation? The answer lies in the application of the direct mapping from recipes to satisfaction, and measuring the distance between the predicted satisfaction vector and the one specified by the user.
- The third question is: how to perform innovation? We need to build some generative process that achieves to create new recipes optimizing expected satisfaction. The solution proposed in [9] is a stochastic search process guided by the learned user satisfaction model, specifically an Evolutionary Strategy approach [17].

---

[1] http://www.sands-project.eu/.
[2] Source-code: http://www.ntu.edu.sg/home/egbhuang/elm_codes.html.

A critical issue is the lack of real life data supporting the design and validation of this architecture. The SandS project is currently building the framework that would allow users to experience this social interaction, but no actual data is being generated yet. So we have to resort to synthetic data.

Paper contribution. The contribution of this paper is a recommendation system for breadmaker recipes based on the know information about user satisfaction with past recipes tried, in the context of a social intelligence for appliance management. The system is composed of direct and inverse mappings between recipes and satisfaction evaluations, so it may produce a recipe recommendation from the specification of desired satisfaction parameter values given by the user. The direct mapping may be used for the satisfaction prediction on the recommended recipe, which may be used to decide if a random search innovation mechanism is required to produce a better suited recipe.

Contents of the paper. The paper is organized as follows: Sect. 2 reviews some ideas about recommender systems. Section 3 provides the precise specification of the problem and the description of the dataset synthesis, which has been used for the computational experiments. Section 4 reports results obtained on the synthetic dataset of recipes and satisfaction. Section 5 gives some conclusions of this paper.

2   Recommender Systems

Recommender systems [10] are taking a prominent role in the interaction with the virtual world incorporated by the miriad of webservices used on a daily basis by the common people. Early realizations included forms of collaborative filtering, however the advent of the Internet of Things will allow to use implicit, local and personal information gathered by the surrounding environment of smart objects. Recommender Systems are currently being applied in many different domains. Some example applications are: intelligent tourism [11], movie suggestions [12], electronic marketplaces [13], and university library research [14].

The State of the Art techniques involved in recommender systems deal with the problem of accurate representation and management of the user profile, requiring computational tools from many fields of Artificial Intelligence, such as Multi-agent systems, advanced optimization techniques, clustering of the users data to detect communities, and advanced knowledge representation and reasoning for the management of uncertainty.

Collaborative filtering social recommender systems [15] use social network information as additional input for improved recommendation accuracy. They define two categories of CF-based social recommender systems: matrix factorization based approaches and neighborhood based approaches, providing a comparison among algorithms.

In this paper we are concerned with the use of regression models trained with Extreme Learning Machines (ELM) to recommend a recipe from a given satisfaction, and also in the other way, to predict a satisfaction from a given recipe. Recipes are modeled as a feature vector of values from 0 to 1. Satisfaction is composed by associated models.

3 Problem Definition and Dataset Synthesis

In this section we give the specification of the recommendation problem that we try to solve. As there is not real life data to validate our proposal, we have had to build some models to generate a synthetic dataset with some degree of arbitrary complexity, so that if our approach succeeds on this dataset, it can be successful in real life experiments. The experiment context is the "SandS" European project (http://www.sands-project.eu/). In this project, Eahoukers (word that refers to easy house workers, in other words, users) provide a description of a problem dealing with household appliance usage to the social network. The system gives back a "recipe" that solves the proposed problem. These recipes are either proposed by the knowledge provided by other users or by the underlying intelligent layer [16]. Once that recipe is proposed, user can give the order to the system to execute it in the choosen appliance. Finally, users give a satisfaction of the recipe, this feedback is used to tune the intelligent layer and/or to personalize the system.

3.1 Specification of the Recommendation Problem

This paper is focused on the case of the breadmaker. It has some specific features that differentiate the way recommendations are generated. First, there is no task description per se. The user only gives the order to make the bread stating some expected satisfaction values with the result which are not stated beforehand. In other words, we only have the recipe and satisfaction pairs. The recommendation system then has two problems to solve, first it must learn the map from recipes to satisfaction, in order to predict the user satisfaction. Second, it must learn the inverse model from satisfaction to recipes in order to propose the best recipe for the user. It is also possible, once we have this inverse model, to tune the recipe to specific values of the predicted satisfaction. It may even possible to work with missing values, that is, to provide a recipe that matches some of the satisfaction parameters, when the other are left undefined. We have not touched this aspect in this paper.

Recipes. The baking operation consists of 5 steps carried sequentially: first leavening, second leavening, precooking, cooking and browning. Each step is specified by a pair $[Time, Temperature]$. Thus, in this case, the recipe consists in 10 variables $[r_1, ..., r_{10}]$.

Satisfaction. The user give a satisfaction feedback. For the breadmaker, the satisfaction consists in 4 parameters: $[fragance, softness, baking, crust]$. These parameters are represented in 4 variables $[s_1, ..., s_4]$.

Problem specification. The problems that we want to solve with this experiment are two:

- Direct prediction: What will be the satisfaction feedback obtained from the user for a given recipe?
- Inverse recommendation: Which is the recipe that I need to get a specific satisfaction?

Let us define:

- Let be R a recipe described by bread making variables, so $[r_1, ..., r_{10}] = R$. Thus, $R \in \mathbb{R}^{10}$ and each r_i is normalized in the range $[0..1]$
- Let be S a satisfaction described by $[s_1, .., s_4] = S$. Thus, $S \in \mathbb{R}^4$ and each s_j is a number in the set $\{0, 1, 2, 3, 4, 5\}$

To answer these questions, we define:

- A direct mapping $\phi(R) = S$ to predict the satisfaction of the user with the quality of the bread resulting from a proposed recipe (first question) $\phi : \mathbb{R}^{10} \longrightarrow \mathbb{R}^4$
- The inverse mapping $\phi^{-1}(S) = R$ that looks for the recipe that would provide the desired satisfaction parameter values (second question) $\phi^{-1} : \mathbb{R}^4 \longrightarrow \mathbb{R}^{10}$

We model the experiment with the numbers and parameters defined before but numbers and set of variables could be adapted to any other context of similar experimentation. These mappings are built by ELM because of the quick learning time which allows frequent updates when the experience of the users increase the database for learning. Notice that we only have information about experiments going in the direct prediction sense, i.e. we can try a recipe and ask the user its satisfaction. It is not possible to obtain experimental data in the other direction.

The first learning experiment is to calculate the regression of satisfaction values from given recipes. We denote this experiment as $\phi(R) \rightarrow S_j$. The second experiment is to calculate the regression o f recipe valuesfrom a given satisfaction, i.e. to create the recommendation. We denote this experiment as $\phi^{-1}(S) \rightarrow R_i$. We divided the dataset in several datasets according to the application requirements of the 10-fold cross-validation technique. Figure 1 is the pipeline which summarizes the process of the experiment.

3.2 Dataset Generation

We generate a dataset of 100,000 instances of recipe satisfaction pairs taking into consideration the following:

- We consider that there is a non-linear map that models the contribution from each recipe parameter to each satisfaction parameter value. For the experimental works in this paper, we have created arbitrary maps which are shown in Fig. 2. The idea is that if we can approximate these models with ELMs then we can approximate almost anything. Each entry (i, j) in the table is a map randomly generated relating recipe parameter r_i with each satisfaction parameter s_j. Thus, we have 40 models.

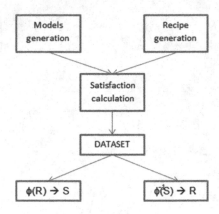

Fig. 1. Pipeline of experiment

– We consider that the satisfaction value is a linear combination of the contributions of the recipe parameters. If a_{ij} is the satisfaction value in variable s_j induce from a given value from recipe variable r_i, then:

$$s_j = \frac{\sum_{r=1}^{10} \alpha_i * a_{ij}}{r'}$$

using α_i as weighting factor of recipe variable and being r' the normalizing value to obtain the weighted average. If result has decimal part, we round the number to the nearest natural one. We have choosen the value of the α_i arbitrarily for the experiments reported here.

Once we have models, we are able to generate a synthetic dataset according with models. To generate a database we generate randomly 100,000 instances of $[r_1, ..., r_{10}]$ then, we use the models to calculate the satisfaction.

As example, we show in Table 1 the first row of the dataset.

Table 1. Example of the content of Dataset

	r1	r2	r3	r4	r5	r6	r7	r8	r9	r10	s1	s2	s3	s4
#1	0.6	0.3	0.4	0.2	1	0	0.4	0.8	0.3	0.4	2	2	2	2
#i	...	...	...	...	...	...	...	...	...	...	...	...	...	...

4 Experimental Results

Experiments are carried out using ELM standar code in Matlab[3]. We select Sine ('sin') activation function for executions. We test results with 1 hidden unit until

---

[3] Source-code: http://www.ntu.edu.sg/home/egbhuang/elm_codes.html.

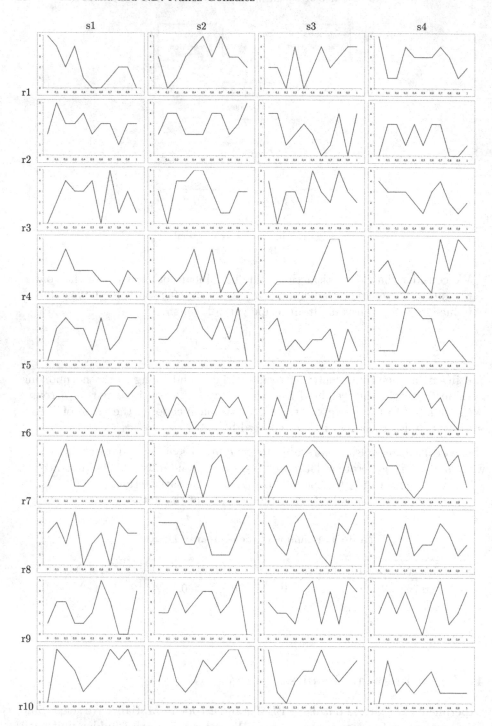

Fig. 2. Maps specifying the influence of the recipe parameters into the satisfaction parameters. Each entry relates a pair of recipe-satisfaction variables. Each plot has horizontal axis in the range $[0, 1]$ and the vertical axis in the set $\{0, 1, 2, 3, 4, 5\}$.

525 hidden units that are the maximum hidden units allowed without raising a memory exception. Increasing neurons, square error decreases significantly. Table 2 shows the average regression error for the direct mapping regression for each satisfaction parameter obtained in a 10-fold cross-validation experiment for the two extreme ELM sizes. The best result is equivalent to a relative error, computed dividing the regression error by the variable range which is 5 for all satisfaction values, is below 0.01. Table 3 shows the average regression error for the inverse mapping regression for each recipe parameter obtained in a 10-fold cross-validation experiment for the two extreme ELM sizes. The best relative error, computed dividing the regression error by the variable range which is 1 for all satisfaction values, is below 0.2, still too high for the practical purposes of this paper.

Table 2. Average cross-validation error results of satisfaction prediction for given recipes: $\phi(R) \rightarrow S_j$

	1 hidden unit	525 hidden units
s1	1.4490	0.4972
s2	1.7756	0.4790
s3	1.6259	0.5639
s4	1.1084	0.4832

Table 3. Average cross-validation error results of recipe recommendation for desired satisfactions: $\phi^{-1}(S) \rightarrow R_i$

	1 hidden unit	525 hidden units
r1	0.4382	0.2816
r2	0.3910	0.2887
r3	0.4298	0.2919
r4	0.4080	0.2659
r5	0.4433	0.2923
r6	0.4063	0.2837
r7	0.3936	0.2903
r8	0.4743	0.2885
r9	0.4308	0.2911
r10	0.4456	0.2688

5   Conclusions

We propose the application of regression ELM to build a breadmaker recommender system which is an instance of the social intelligence in the Internet of

Things framework of the SandS european project. We have proposed a dataset synthesis procedure to carry the experimental validation of the system, due to the lack of real-life data. The experimental results are quite good for the direct mapping from recipes to satisfaction evaluations, but not so good for the inverse mapping, which will require a more careful tuning for the practical application. Further work will be addressing the computational experiments on real life data, once it is available from the breadmaking experiments being carried out by other project partners. It is also possible to open the experimentation to the general public by the implementation of a social network of breadmaking "aficionados". This implementation would be a real test of the idea of subconscious social intelligence, which in this setting will encompass the application of both direct an inverse mappings.

Acknowledgements. This research has been partially funded by EU through SandS project, grant agreement no 317947. The GIC has been supported by grant IT874-13 as university research group category A.

References

1. Vannoy, S.A., Palvia, P.: The social influence model of technology adoption. Commun. ACM **53**(6), 149–153 (2010)
2. Graña, M., Marqués, I., Savio, A., Apolloni, B.: A domestic application of intelligent social computing: the sandsproject. In: Herrero, Á., et al. (eds.) International Joint Conference SOCO'13-CISIS'13-ICEUTE'13. AISC, vol. 239, pp. 221–228. Springer, Heidelberg (2013)
3. Graña, M.: Subconscious social computational intelligence. In: Krishnan, G.S.S., Anitha, R., Lekshmi, R.S., Kumar, M.S., Bonato, A., Graña, M. (eds.) Computational Intelligence, Cyber Security and Computational Models, Proceedings of ICC3. Advances in Intelligent Systems and Computing, vol. 246, pp. 15–21. Springer, India (2013)
4. Graña, M., et al.: Social and smart: towards an instance of subconscious social intelligence. In: Iliadis, L., Papadopoulos, H., Jayne, C. (eds.) EANN 2013, Part II. CCIS, vol. 384, pp. 302–311. Springer, Heidelberg (2013)
5. Grana, M., Rebollo, I.: Instances of subconscious social intelligent computing. In: 2013 Fifth International Conference on Computational Aspects of Social Networks (CASoN), pp. 74–78, August 2013
6. Apolloni, B., Fiasche, M., Galliani, G., Zizzo, C., Caridakis, G., Siolas, G., Kollias, S., Grana Romay, M., Barriento, F., San Jose, S.: Social things - the sands instantiation. In: IoT-SoS 2013. IEEE (2013)
7. Huang, G.B., Zhu, Q.Y., Siew, C.K.: Extreme learning machine: theory and applications. Neurocomputing **70**, 489–501 (2006)
8. Huang, G., Zhu, Q., Siew, C.: Extreme learning machine: a new learning scheme of feedforward neural networks. In: IEEE International Conference on Neural Networks - Conference Proceedings, vol. 2, pp. 985–990 (2004). Cited By (since 1996):113
9. Marques, I., Graña, M., Kamińska-Chuchmała, A., Apolloni, B.: An experiment of subconscious intelligent social computing on household appliances. Neurocomputing (2014, in press)

10. Bobadilla, J., Ortega, F., Hernando, A., GutiÃrrez, A.: Recommender systems survey. Knowl.-Based Syst. **46**, 109–132 (2013)
11. Borras, J., Moreno, A., Valls, A.: Intelligent tourism recommender systems: a survey. Expert Syst. Appl. **41**(16), 7370–7389 (2014)
12. Briguez, C.E., Budan, M.C., Deagustini, C.A., Maguitman, A.G., Capobianco, M., Simari, G.R.: Argument-based mixed recommenders and their application to movie suggestion. Expert Syst. Appl. **41**(14), 6467–6482 (2014)
13. Christidis, K., Mentzas, G.: A topic-based recommender system for electronic marketplace platforms. Expert Syst. Appl. **40**(11), 4370–4379 (2013)
14. Tejeda-Lorente, A., Porcel, C., Peis, E., Sanz, R., Herrera-Viedma, E.: A quality based recommender system to disseminate information in a university digital library. Inf. Sci. **261**, 52–69 (2014)
15. Yang, X., Guo, Y., Liu, Y., Steck, H.: A survey of collaborative filtering based social recommender systems. Comput. Commun. **41**, 1–10 (2014)
16. Graña, M., Nuñez-Gonzalez, J.D., Apolloni, B.: A discussion on trust requirements for a social network of eahoukers. In: Pan, J.-S., Polycarpou, M.M., Woźniak, M., de Carvalho, A.C.P.L.F., Quintián, H., Corchado, E. (eds.) HAIS 2013. LNCS, vol. 8073, pp. 540–547. Springer, Heidelberg (2013)
17. Gonzalez, A.I., Graña, M., Ruiz Cabello, J., D'Anjou, A., Albizuri, F.X.: Experimental results of an evolution-based adaptation strategy for VQ image filtering. Inf. Sci. **133**(3–4), 249–266 (2001). http://dx.doi.org/10.1016/S0020-0255(01)00088-3

Random Forests and Gradient Boosting for Wind Energy Prediction

Álvaro Alonso, Alberto Torres, and José R. Dorronsoro[✉]

Departamento de Ingeniería Informática e Instituto de Ingeniería del Conocimiento,
Universidad Autónoma de Madrid, Madrid, Spain
jose.dorronsoro@uam.es

Abstract. The ability of ensemble models to retain the bias of their learners while decreasing their individual variance has long made them quite attractive in a number of classification and regression problems. Moreover, when trees are used as learners, the relative simplicity of the resulting models has led to a renewed interest on them on Big Data problems. In this work we will study the application of Random Forest Regression (RFR) and Gradient Boosted Regression (GBR) to global and local wind energy prediction problems working with their high quality implementations in the Scikit–learn Python libraries. Besides a complete exploration of the RFR and GBR application to wind energy prediction, we will show experimentally that both ensemble methods can improve on SVR for individual wind farm energy prediction and that at least GBR is also competitive when the interest lies in predicting wind energy in a much larger geographical scale.

1 Introduction

Among the many possibilities available when designing hybrid artificial intelligence systems, ensembles, i.e., the aggregation of suitable independent base models, is certainly one of the simplest and potentially most powerful approaches. In fact, ensemble models have the very attractive potential of being able to decrease the variance of their individual learners while retaining the small bias achievable if these learners are powerful enough. Random Forest Regression (RFR) achieves this using regression trees as learners and exploiting the combination of the sample randomness derived from bagging and the feature randomness applied in their construction. In Gradient Boosted Regression (GBR) a number of regression trees are also built but now under a boosting perspective in which, to the sample and feature randomness just mentioned, boosting contributes with a bias decrease. Besides their promise of variance and (partially) bias reduction, RFR and GBR models add their relatively simple structure and, in the RFR case, their highly parallelizable construction. Because of this, they are receiving a large attention in Big Data contexts, further enhanced by their very good performance in several benchmark problems, such as the 2013 competition jointly organized by the American Meteorological Society (AMS) and

© Springer International Publishing Switzerland 2015
E. Onieva et al. (Eds.): HAIS 2015, LNAI 9121, pp. 26–37, 2015.
DOI: 10.1007/978-3-319-19644-2_3

Kaggle [10] where the goal was to predict daily aggregated radiation at a number of weather stations in Oklahoma and in which the best submission was based on GBR.

In this work we will apply both RFR and GBR to the problem of predicting wind energy production. Currently wind energy is almost impossible to store but, on the other hand, its very high penetration in countries like Spain, among the world leaders in wind energy, makes it very important to provide accurate forecasts, both at the individual farm level and also at the scale in which transmission system operators (TSO) work, Red Eléctrica de España (REE) in Spain's case. Just as an example, February 2015 was a record month for wind energy in Spain, that met well above 20 % of the country's total electricity demand for that month.

Clearly, a very high penetration and difficult storage can only be compensated by adequate planning which, in turn, requires accurate enough forecasting methods. Machine learning (ML) has a very strong presence in wind energy forecasting with multilayer perceptrons (MLPs) and support vector regression (SVR) being the approaches most often used. In general, the prediction models are built using as input patterns the forecasts provided by numerical weather prediction (NWP) systems such as the ECMWF [3] (which we will use here) or the GFS [6]. Usually they provide forecasts of several weather variables given at the points of a rectangular grid that covers the areas under study. This grid is derived from an orographic model that smooths out the actual physical orography under a certain resolution (0.25° here).

Wind energy prediction becomes then, in general, a non–linear regression problem to be solved by some ML model; RFR, GBR and SVR in our case. We will work both at the scale of an individual farm, namely the Sotavento wind farm, and also at the much larger scale of the total wind energy production of peninsular Spain. We point out that while ensemble methods are a natural choice in regression problems, their use in wind energy has been so far done, to the best of our knowledge, considering only ensembles of strong learners, such as neural networks [7] or SVR [9]. Therefore, ours seems to be one of the first works where RFR and GBR are used for wind energy prediction. This is thus an initial contribution, to which we may add:

- A review of RFR and GBR from a practical point of view linked to the Scikit–learn [12] Python libraries that provide very good implementations of RFR and GBR and include in some cases parallelization tools to speed up model training.
- An exploration of their application to the problems of local and large scale wind energy prediction.
- Experimental results that show both ensemble methods and, particularly, GBR, to be very competitive with SVR, possibly the current state of the art of ML based wind energy prediction.

The rest of the paper is organized as follows. In Sect. 2 we briefly review the basic theory of RFR and GBR and Sect. 3 contains a succinct description of the framework for wind energy prediction over NWP inputs, a description of our experimental setup and the prediction results for both the Sotavento wind farm and the entire wind energy prediction over peninsular Spain that is overseen by REE. Finally, in Sect. 4 we briefly discuss our results and offer pointers to further work.

2   Random Forest and Gradient Boosting Regression

In the following subsections we will briefly review the construction of RFR and GBR models largely following [8].

2.1   Random Forest for Regression

Assume a sample $S = \{(X_p, t_p) : 1 \leq p \leq N\}$ with $X_p \in R^d$. To build a Regression Tree (RT) we have to partition the input space in rectangular regions R_j, $j = 1, \ldots, M$ and, once these M rectangles are selected and if square error minimization is our goal, the response of a tree that minimizes that error is $T(X) = \sum_j \gamma_j I_{R_j}(X)$, where $I_{R_j}(X)$ is the indicator function of the rectangle R_j and γ_j is given by the locally expected target value, i.e.

$$\gamma_j = \frac{1}{|R_j|} \sum_{R_j} t_p = E[t_p | X_p \in R_j].$$

The standard approach to find the R_j is CART [1], probably the most popular method for building RTs. CART performs binary splits along successive variables j according to concrete split values s, doing so in a greedy way. The depth of the final tree can be controlled but, in general, the successive splits could lead to a large tree; to avoid overfitting, the tree is pruned (see below). In more detail ([8], Sect. 9.2), splitting the variable j in terms of an s value yields two left–right regions $R_{j,s}^L = \{X : x_j \leq s\}$, $R_{j,s}^R = \{X : x_j > s\}$. An optimal choice of j, s should solve

$$\min_{j,s} \left[\min_{c_L} \left\{ \sum_{X_p \in R_{j,s}^L} (t_p - c_L)^2 \right\} + \min_{c_R} \left\{ \sum_{X_p \in R_{j,s}^R} (t_p - c_R)^2 \right\} \right].$$

Assuming again square error to be minimized, the optimal c_L^*, c_R^* are given by $c_L^* = E[t_p | x_p \in R_{j,s}^L]$, $c_R^* = E[t_p | x_p \in R_{j,s}^R]$ and, since increasing s just "moves" points from R^R to R^L, the first split j_1, s_1 can be quickly obtained exploring in this way the x_j variables. This is successively applied to the regions $R_{j_1,s_1}^L, R_{j_1,s_1}^R$ and so on, and splitting stops when a rectangular region (then called a leaf) containing a prefixed small number of points is reached.

This way we arrive at a possibly very large tree T_0 which we prune in such a way that cost (i.e., error) and complexity (i.e., tree size) are balanced. Assuming T is a subtree of T_0 with $|T|$ leaves associated to the regions R_j, we set

$$N_j = |R_j|, \quad c_j = \frac{1}{N_j} \sum_{X_p \in R_j} t_p, \quad Q_j(T) = \frac{1}{N_j} \sum_{X_p \in R_j} (t_p - c_j)^2,$$

and define for $\alpha > 0$ the cost-complexity criterion function $C_\alpha(T) = \alpha|T| + \sum_1^{|T|} N_j Q_j$. In [1] it is shown that for each α there is a unique smallest subtree T_α of T_0 that minimizes $C_\alpha(T)$. This T_α, that will be the final RT, can be found by *weakest link pruning*, where the leaves of the nodes that produce the smallest increase in $\sum_j N_j Q_j(T)$ are successively collapsed until the entire tree contracts to its root. It is also shown in [1] that the sequence of subtrees built this way must contain the minimizing T_α tree, which can thus be identified during the pruning procedure. When $\alpha = 0$, the full tree T_0 that has single pattern leaves clearly minimizes $C_0(T)$ but with a large overfitting and the largest possible complexity $|T_0| = N$. Increasing α tunes the trade-off between tree size and goodness of fit; hence, α acts as a regularization parameter.

RTs are likely to have a small bias but possibly a large variance. An obvious first way to reduce it is to apply bootstrap averaging, i.e., bagging, to build an RT family $T_m, 1 \leq m \leq M$, over M bootstrapped subsamples of S and then average them. A second way is to consider a random subset of the d features instead of all of them when deciding the splitting feature at each new node. Bagging ensures that the RTs are i.d. and have small bias. If, moreover, the T_m are i.i.d. with the same variance σ^2, the average's variance will be σ^2/M, decreasing with M. However, if they have a pairwise correlation $\rho > 0$, the average's variance will become $\rho\sigma^2 + \frac{1-\rho}{M}\sigma^2$, with the first term being independent of M ([8], p. 603). This is why to reduce pairwise correlation, in Random Forests (RFs) bootstrap subsampling is paired with the random selection of the variable subsets to be split. Typical values for the number p of variables retained are $\sqrt{d}$, $\lfloor d/3 \rfloor$ or even 1; we will use the Scikit–klearn option to consider as p a fraction of pattern dimension. The random forest (regression) predictor rf_M is the average

$$rf_M(X) = \frac{1}{M} \sum_1^M T_m(X)$$

of the M such trees $T_m(X)$ built this way.

It follows from the preceding that several hyper–parameters may be adjusted in RFR. The routine `RandomForestRegressor` in the Scikit–learn Python library [12] will be use in our experiments; in Sect. 3 we discuss how to choose concrete values of the most relevant hyper–parameters involved.

2.2 Gradient Boosted Regression

In general, boosting methods iteratively combine weak learners by repeatedly focusing in the errors resulting in the previous iteration until a suitable strong learner is obtained. One general approach to boosting is based on functional gradient descent [11]. Assume once more a sample $S = \{(X_p, t_p) : 1 \leq p \leq N\}$; if we want to fit some model $F(X)$ over S using a loss function $L(y, F)$ a natural option is to consider the variational cost function $L(F) = E_{X,t}[L(t, F(X))]$ and then try to find a g that would cause the greatest cost reduction on $L(F + \rho g)$ along the "half line" ρg, $\rho > 0$, defined by g. Since at first order we have $L(F +$

$\rho g) = L(F) + \rho \nabla L(F) \cdot g$, it is natural to choose a g that minimizes $\nabla L(F) \cdot g$, that is, to take g as the minus (variational) gradient $-\nabla L(F)$.

While computing $\nabla L(F)$ may be out of the question, we can simply follow a sample based approximation. In fact, $L(F)$ can be approximated by $L(\mathcal{F}) = \sum_p L(t_p, F(X_p))$, with $\mathcal{F} = (F(X_1), \ldots, F(X_N))^t$ being the vector of values of the unknown F at the sample points X_p. Then, to optimize $L(\mathcal{F}) = \sum_p L(t_p, F(X_p))$ over $\mathcal{F}$, we may start at some h_0 and follow a steepest descent approach in which we take $h_m = -\rho_m g_m$, where $g_m(X)$ is the gradient of $L(\mathcal{F})$ at the current vector $\mathcal{F}_{m-1}$, i.e.,

$$g_m(X_p) = \left[\frac{\partial L(\mathcal{F})}{\partial \mathcal{F}_p}\right]_{\mathcal{F}=\mathcal{F}_{m-1}} = \frac{\partial L(\mathcal{F}_{m-1})}{\partial F_{m-1}(X_p)} = \frac{\partial L}{\partial F}(t_p, F_{m-1}(X_p)).$$

We can next derive the step length ρ_m as the solution of $\rho_m = \arg\min_\rho L(\mathcal{F}_{m-1} - \rho g_m)$ and, finally, we update $\mathcal{F}_{m-1}$ to $\mathcal{F}_m = \mathcal{F}_{m-1} - \rho_m g_m = \mathcal{F}_{m-1} + h_m$.

However, since we are considering only sample points, we need to make it possible to work with other, out of sample points. In a boosting context it is natural to approximate the sample valued–only $-g_m$ by a weak learner $h(X; \Theta_m)$ parameterized by Θ_m, which we can do by least squares, solving

$$\Theta_m = \arg\min_\Theta \sum_1^N (-g_m(X_p) - h(X_p; \Theta))^2.$$

The optimal step ρ_m is then computed as before $\rho_m = \arg\min_\rho L(\mathcal{F}_{m-1} + \rho h(\cdot; \Theta_m))$ and the new update is $\mathcal{F}_m(X) = \mathcal{F}_{m-1}(X) + \rho_m h(X; \Theta_m)$. This is essentially the approach proposed by J.H. Friedman in [4], where regression trees $T_m(X) = T(X; \Theta_m)$ are used as weak learners and where the updating h_m would have the form $h_m(x, \rho, \Theta) = \rho \sum_1^{J_m} \beta_j^m I_{R_j^m}(x)$. Here again, the features to be considered when splitting a node are randomly selected. However, in [5] Friedman slightly changes this overall approach by retaining only the leaves' rectangles $R_1^m, \ldots, R_{J_m}^m$ of T_m, discarding the ρ and β_m coefficients and fitting instead individual values γ_j^m at the R_j^m by solving

$$\gamma_j^m = \arg\min_{\gamma \in R^{J_m}} \sum_{X_p \in R_j^m} L(t_p, \mathcal{F}_{m-1}(X_p) + \gamma)$$

with γ^m an J_m–dimensional vector, and arriving finally at the GBR updates

$$\mathcal{F}_m(X) = \mathcal{F}_{m-1}(X) + \sum_1^{J_m} \gamma_j^m I_{R_j^m}(X_p).$$

In principle, the GBR hyper–parameters are similar to those in RFR, namely the number M of iterations to be performed (i.e., the number of trees to be built) and the RT hyper–parameters. Given that only the rectangle leaves of the RTs are used, some hyper–parameter shortcuts could be possible. For instance, and as discussed at the end of Sect. 10.11 in [8], values in the range $4 \le J \le 8$ for the number of leaves J_m work well in practice while it is unlikely that larger values $J > 10$ are required. Also, we could follow a shrinkage-based regularization approach to decide on M instead of applying, say, cross validation, in which one works with updates of the form

$$\mathcal{F}_m(X) = \mathcal{F}_{m-1}(X) + \nu \sum_1^{J_m} \gamma_j^m I_{R_j^m}(X_p)$$

where the parameter ν, $0 < \nu < 1$, "shrinks" the contribution of the new RT to be added. It has been observed in [4] that smaller values of ν lead to larger M values and usually a better performance. On the other hand, a smaller ν implies obviously longer training times and there is thus a trade-off between M and ν. The usual strategy, which we will largely follow, is to fix a small ν around 0.1 and then choose M using a validation subset. In any case, we have used the GradientBoostingRegressor implementation in Scikit–learn in our experiments and select the most relevant hyper–parameters using a validation subset, as we discuss in the following section.

3   Experiments

In this section we will apply Random Forest and Gradient Boosting Regression to the problem of predicting wind energy production first over peninsular Spain and then on the Sotavento wind farm, situated in Galicia (northwestern Spain) which makes its wind energy data publicly available on its web site, www.sotaventogalicia.com. We describe first the experimental data and then how model parameters were selected and test results obtained.

3.1   NWP and Production Data

We will work with the Numerical Weather Prediction (NWP) system of the European Centre for Medium-Range Weather Forecasts (ECMWF). It currently provides variable forecasts over a global world grid with a 0.125° resolution although we will work on a 0.25° one. To predict wind energy of peninsular Spain we consider a 57×35 rectangular sub–grid that covers entirely the Iberian Peninsula; for Sotavento we will use a 15×9 rectangular sub grid approximately centered on the Sotavento site (43.34° N, 7.86° W). The ECMWF meteorological variable forecasts used will be the following:

- P, the pressure at surface level.
- T, the temperature at 2 m.
- U_s, the x wind component at surface level.
- V_s, the y wind component at surface level.
- v_s, the wind norm at surface level.
- U_{100}, the x wind component at 100 m height.
- V_{100}, the y wind component at 100 m.
- v_{100}, the wind norm at 100 m.

We point out that surface and 100 m height refer to the geopotential of the grid point for which these variables are provided; in turn, the grid node geopotential is that of the concrete orography model used, which may or may not coincide with the actual geographical point with the same coordinates. Input dimensions for Sotavento are thus quite large, $15 \times 9 \times 8 = 1,080$, while for peninsular Spain are even larger $57 \times 35 \times 8 = 15,960$. We will work with data for the years 2011, 2012 and 2013. As mentioned, wind energy data for Sotavento can be obtained through their web site; wind energy values for peninsular Spain were kindly provided by Red Eléctrica de España (REE). In both cases we normalize productions to the $[0, 100]$ interval by dividing them by the rate power of Sotavento (i.e., the maximum power the farm would provide) and total installed wind power of Peninsular Spain. In other words, at each hour we will work with the percentage of energy actually produced with respect to the maximum possible values. While hourly values are available for wind energy, NWP forecasts are available only every three hours, starting at UTC hour 00. Thus, in every year we will approximately have $(24/3) * 365 = 2,920$ patterns. In what follows we will refer to these as the Sotavento and REE problems respectively.

3.2   RFR Models

In all our experiments we will work with the RFR and GBR models available in the Scikit Python library. For RFR the main model hyper–parameters are the number of regression trees to be built ($RFRnumRT$), the minimum number of samples in a tree leaf ($RFRminSL$), the minimum number of samples in a node for it to be split ($RFRminSN$), the maximum number of features to be randomly selected at a node ($RFRmaxV$) given as a fraction of the total pattern dimension and the maximum tree depth. Of these, the minimum numbers of leaf patterns and the tree's depth are loosely related. Thus, to minimize computational cost while estimating optimal hyper–parameters, we shall only consider $RFRnumRTs, RFRminSL, RFRminSN$ and $RFRmaxV$.

In order to select the hyper–parameters for both the RFR and GBR models (as well as for the SVR ones) we applied a simplified cross–validation (CV) procedure, namely, we explored the combinations of predetermined values of each model's relevant hyper–parameters (listed below) using as training data the year 2011 and applying the resulting models to 2012 with the Mean Absolute Error (MAE), that is,

$$MAE = \frac{1}{N} \sum_{n=1}^{N} |T(x_n; P) - y_n|,$$

as the validation merit function; here $T(x; P)$ denotes the value on pattern x of the RFR model T built using the hyper–parameter set P. We use the MAE instead of the more often used squared error as it is the measure of choice in renewable energy since it gives a direct estimate of a model deviation and, thus, of the energy to be shed or obtained from other generation sources. Moreover, it corresponds to the `lad` option as the RFR loss function in Scikit–learn.

The hyper–parameters finally selected for each model were those giving the smallest MAE in that year and these hyper–parameters were then used to train all the models in the six train-test combinations that we will report below. Notice that, in a strict sense, this is not actually cross–validation, as we do not split a given set into a number of train-test folds but it is a very natural option for this problem given the time structure of the data. The discrete hyper–parameter search for Sotavento was done over all the combinations of the following values

- $\{100, 200, 300, 400, 500, 600\}$ for $RFRnumRT$,
- $\{1, 2, 4, 8\}$ for $RFRminSL$,
- $\{2, 4, 8, 16\}$ for $RFRminSN$ and
- $\{0.2, 0.3, 0.4, 0.5, 0.6\}$ for $RFRmaxV$.

The total number of possible hyper–parameter selections is thus 480 and the resulting optimal hyper–parameters were $RFRnumRT = 300$, $RFRminSL = 4$, $RFRminSN = 4$ and $RFRmaxV = 0.4$. Similarly, the hyper–parameter values for REE were

- $\{100, 250, 500, 750, 1000\}$ for $RFRnumRT$,
- $\{1, 2, 5, 10\}$ for $RFRminSL$,
- $\{5, 10, 20, 30, 40\}$ for $RFRminSN$ and
- $\{0.2, 0.3, 0.4, 0.5, 0.6\}$ for $RFRmaxV$.

The total number of possible hyper–parameter selections is now 500 and the resulting optimal REE hyper–parameters were $RFRnumRT = 750$, $RFRminSL = 5$, $RFRminSN = 10$ and $RFRmaxV = 0.3$. As mentioned, once these hyper–parameters are obtained, we will use as train–test pairs all 6 combinations of any two of the three data years, and report the averages of the 6 train and test MAE values. In all cases we normalize the train subset to zero mean and 1 standard deviation component–wise and apply the same normalizing parameters (i.e., the component mean and standard deviation) to the corresponding test subset.

3.3 GBR Models

We follow essentially the same strategy for the GBR models although with some variants in hyper–parameter optimization linked to the implementation of `GradientBoostingRegressor` in Scikit–learn. Here we will analyze again the number of trees to be built ($GBRnumGT$), the minimum number of samples in a node for it to be split ($GBRminSN$), the minimum number of samples in a tree leaf ($GBRminSL$) and the maximum number of features to be randomly selected at a node ($GBRmaxV$); moreover, we will also consider now the maximum tree depth $GBRmaxD$. Other relevant hyper–parameter here that was not present for RFR is the learning rate for which we take the default value of 0.1. Again, we use the `lad` option as the loss function. The hyper–parameter search for Sotavento was done on the following values

- $\{200, 400, 600, 800\}$ for $GBRnumRT$,
- $\{1, 2, 4\}$ for $GBRminSL$,
- $\{2, 4, 8\}$ for $GBRminSN$,
- $\{0.3, 0.4, 0.5, 0.6\}$ for $GBRmaxV$ and
- $\{6, 9, 20, 40\}$ for $GBRmaxD$.

The total number of possible hyper–parameter selections is thus 576 and the resulting optimal hyper–parameters were $GBRnumRT = 600$, $GBRminSL = 4$, $GBRminSN = 4$, $GBRmaxV = 0.4$ and $GBRmaxD = 20$. In the REE case we left $GBRmaxD$ fixed at a value of 3 and, instead, explored the learning rate $GBRlR$. The GBR hyper–parameter values considered here were

- $\{600, 900, 1, 200\}$ for $GBRnumRT$,
- $\{1, 2, 4\}$ for $GBRminSL$,
- $\{2, 4, 8\}$ for $GBRminSN$,
- $\{0.4, 0.5, 0.6\}$ for $GBRmaxV$ and
- $\{0.05, 0.1, 0.15\}$ for $GBRlR$.

The number of possible hyper–parameter choices is now 243 and the resulting optimal REE hyper–parameters were $GBRnumRT = 900$, $GBRminSL = 1$, $GBRminSN = 4$, $GBRmaxV = 0.4$ and $GBRlR = 0.1$.

3.4   Results and Discussion

Besides the preceding RFR and GBR models, we will also consider for comparison purposes a Gaussian SVR model using the very well known and used LIBSVM library [2], whose optimal hyper–parameters C, γ and ϵ have been established by a grid search; their final values are C=128.0, $\gamma = 3.0518 \times 10^{-5}$ and $\epsilon = 6.25$ for Sotavento and C=128.0, $\gamma = 12.2078 \times 10^{-5}$ and $\epsilon = 1.0$ for REE.

Table 1. Train and test MAE values for the Sotavento and REE problems.

Method	Sotavento		REE	
	Train	Test	Train	Test
RFR	2.91	7.01	1.34	3.83
GBR	2.43	7.09	1.12	3.46
SVR	6.14	7.25	1.08	3.40

The results of the preceding RFR, GBR and SVR models are summarized in Table 1. As it can be seen, in Sotavento both RFR and GBR clearly outperform SVR, with RFR slightly ahead. This can be partially seen in the error histograms in Fig. 1 that corresponds to 2013 test errors of models built over 2012 data. Those of RFR and GBR are slightly less spread and have a sharper value at 0 than the SVR histogram. On the other hand, SVR is the winner for REE but

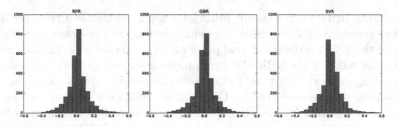

Fig. 1. Test error histograms for Sotavento.

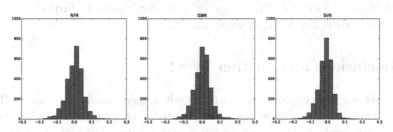

Fig. 2. Test error histograms for REE.

with GBR very close and RFR farther away. This can also be appreciated on the error histograms in Fig. 2, where the SVR histogram is the sharpest and the RFR one is slightly more spread than the one for GBR.

A first reason for this may be an inadequate hyper–parameter search. It must be pointed out that while the hyper–parameter structure of SVR is fairly straightforward, that of RFR and GBR is much more complicated, with several hyper–parameters having a potential interplay that may need further attention. A clear case is the minimum number of samples in leaves and the maximum depth of the tree: if this depth is taken to be a relatively small value, leaves must have a sizeable number of samples. Notice that in our case sample size is $2,920 = 365 \times 8$ and a binary tree of, say, depth 6 must have at least 2^6 leaves, with an average of 46.6 samples per leave.

The characteristics of the wind energy problems may also have an effect on the different performance of RFR and GBR on the Sotavento or REE problems in contrast to that of SVR. First, the REE problem's dimensionality is very high, $15,960$, 15 times larger than that of Sotavento. Besides, while the Sotavento NWP sub–grid is relatively tight with respect to the concrete wind farm location, the NWP grid for REE covers a much larger area than that where wind farms actually exist, as it includes the entirety of Portugal, a sizeable part of the Mediterranean, parts of North Africa and, also, several regions in Spain with either none or a very small number of wind farms. In other words, Sotavento patterns may have many more relevant features for wind energy than the REE patterns. Moreover, in the REE case this is likely to affect less to GBR than to RFR models.

In fact, the latter will repeatedly build individual independent trees according to random selections of featuressubsets, which may or may not capture a sizeable number of the NWP variables at grid points close to actual wind farm locations. On the other hand, while GBR also randomly selects feature subsets, it does so on a boosting context that tries to improve the previous predictions. In other words, among the trees selected by GBR, those built on a random subset with more relevant features for the REE problem are more likely to have a better performance and be given a stronger role on the overall GBR tree family.

In any case, the better performance of RFR and GBR in Sotavento and GBR being so close to SVR for REE suggests it is worthwhile to further study the application of RFR and GBR in wind energy.

4   Conclusions and Further Work

In this work we have explored the application of tree based ensemble methods, namely Random Forest Regression, (RFR), and Gradient Boosting Regression (GBR) to the problem of predicting wind energy production at the farm level (the Sotavento problem) and also on the much wider area of peninsular Spain (the REE problem), comparing their performance with that of Support Vector Regression (SVR), which may represent the current state of the art in machine learning based wind energy forecasting.

We have shown that both RFR and GBR outperform SVR at the wind farm level while on peninsular Spain GBR performs very closely to SVR while RFR falls behind. In any case, further work is to be done. A first line in the REE problem is the selection of a NWP grid that fits better with the areas in Spain where wind farms are located. Recall that both RFR and GBR make a random selection of the features they will consider, which will work much better if feature relevance is similar across all variables; on the other hand, NWP forecasts in areas without wind farms won't be as important as those for areas with them. This may explain the better performance of RFR and GBR for Sotavento, for which grid points are in general close to the wind farm actual position. Along this line it is also clear that some of the NWP variables considered, such as wind speeds at 100 m will have a greater influence than, say, surface pressure. All this makes likely that a suitable pre–selection of grid points and/or features will enhance RFR and GBR results.

Another area of further work is to better understand the influence on the behavior of the RFR and GBR models of the several parameter choices that they require to be made, as well as the workings of the trees finally built. In principle an advantage of tree–based methods is their interpretability, but this is rather hard on the very high dimensional problems we have worked with. However, issues such as the variables chosen in the better performing trees or the sample distribution on a tree's leaves may yield useful information on the most relevant variables or on the grouping of NWP patterns with a similar effect. We are currently pursuing these questions.

Acknowledgments. With partial support from Spain's grants TIN2013-42351-P (MINECO) and S2013/ICE-2845 CASI-CAM-CM (Comunidad de Madrid), and the UAM–ADIC Chair for Data Science and Machine Learning. The first author is kindly supported by the UAM–ADIC Chair for Data Science and Machine Learning and the second author by the FPU-MEC grant AP-2012-5163. We gratefully acknowledge the use of the facilities of Centro de Computación Científica (CCC) at UAM and thank Red Eléctrica de España for kindly supplying wind energy production data.

References

1. Breiman, L., Friedman, J., Olshen, R., Stone, C.: Classification and Regression Trees. Wadsworth and Brooks, Monterey (1984)
2. Chang, C., Lin, C.: LIBSVM: a library for support vector machines. ACM Trans. Intell. Syst. Technol. **2**, 27:1–27:27 (2011). http://www.csie.ntu.edu.tw/cjlin/libsvm
3. ECMWF: European Center for Medium-range Weather Forecasts (2005). http://www.ecmwf.int/
4. Friedman, J.: Greedy function approximation: a gradient boosting machine. Ann. Stat. **29**, 1189–1232 (2001)
5. Friedman, J.: Stochastic gradient boosting. Comput. Stat. Data Anal. **38**, 367–378 (2002)
6. GFS: NOAA Global Forecast System (2014). http://www.emc.ncep.noaa.gov/
7. Han, S., Liu, Y., Yan, J.: Neural network ensemble method study for wind power prediction. In: 2011 Asia-Pacific Power and Energy Engineering Conference (APPEEC), pp. 1–4 (2011)
8. Hastie, T., Tibshirani, R., Friedman, J.: The Elements of Statistical Learning. Springer, New York (2009)
9. Heinermann, J., Kramer, O.: Precise wind power prediction with SVM ensemble regression. In: Wermter, S., Weber, C., Duch, W., Honkela, T., Koprinkova-Hristova, P., Magg, S., Palm, G., Villa, A.E.P. (eds.) ICANN 2014. LNCS, vol. 8681, pp. 797–804. Springer, Heidelberg (2014)
10. Kaggle-American Meteorological Society: Kaggle-AMS 2013–2014 Solar Energy Prediction Contest (2013). www.kaggle.com/c/ams-2014-solar-energy-prediction-contest
11. Mason, L., Baxter, J., Bartlett, P., Frean, M.: Boosting algorithms as gradient descent in function space. In: NIPS (1999)
12. Pedregosa, F., Varoquaux, G., Gramfort, A., Michel, V., Thirion, B., Grisel, O., Blondel, M., Prettenhofer, P., Weiss, R., Dubourg, V., Vanderplas, J., Passos, A., Cournapeau, D., Brucher, M., Perrot, M., Duchesnay, E.: Scikit-learn: machine learning in Python. J. Mach. Learn. Res. **12**, 2825–2830 (2011)

Agent-Based Web Resource Acquisition System for Scientific Knowledge Base

Adam Omelczuk and Piotr Andruszkiewicz[✉]

Institute of Computer Science, Warsaw University of Technology, Warsaw, Poland
Omelczuk.A@gmail.com, P.Andruszkiewicz@ii.pw.edu.pl

Abstract. The paper presents the summary of design, development, and deployment of the Web Resource Acquisition System as a mean to gather knowledge and scientific resources for common University Knowledge Base. This module was designed and developed under the SYNAT research project. The module uses common logical data interface developed for this purpose and is integrated with the user presentation layer of the Knowledge Base from the Warsaw University of Technology. The work emphasizes on the usage of definition and strategies in the context of Knowledge Delivery problem. Presented solution can be interpreted as an alternative to web crawlers when it comes to general problem of browsing through the Internet data. In particular, the effort was put on in-depth coverage of requested domain of knowledge when specifying query. At the same time, integration with the semi-automatic classification module was performed to support assessment of the retrieved resources with respect of their types. That resulted in development of Multi Agent System for universal resource delivery. Heterogeneous knowledge sources as Bing, Google, CiteSeer, etc. were used to provide wide-ranging input data from the Internet.

Keywords: Agents · Multiagent system · Knowledge delivery · Knowledge Base · Web Resource Acquisition · Information retrieval

1 Introduction

We exist in a world of enormous amount of information. This amount currently doubles about every two years. In those circumstances, the important issue arises: How to organize it, how to ensure the quality and keep the information up to date in the system?

The solution for the aforementioned issue consists of three sub-areas: (1) Knowledge delivery; (2) Knowledge classification and analysis; (3) Knowledge presentation.

This work was supported by the National Centre for Research and Development(NCBiR) under Grant No. SP/I/1/77065/10 devoted to the Strategic scientific research and experimental development program: 'Interdisciplinary System for Interactive Scientific and Scientific-Technical Information'.

© Springer International Publishing Switzerland 2015
E. Onieva et al. (Eds.): HAIS 2015, LNAI 9121, pp. 38–49, 2015.
DOI: 10.1007/978-3-319-19644-2_4

In this paper we discuss Knowledge Delivery issue and present a solution in terms of a system design for handling this problem. The emphasis is put on the usage of definitions and strategies in the context of accomplishing this task.

This paper does not include query optimization itself. It focuses only one research on passing, requesting and delivering queries and then providing web resources.

The system is designed to facilitate information resource delivery processes for complex systems that require continuous information feed. It is designed and developed in the form of agent-based system. The system focuses on knowledge delivery within the domain of science.

Resource acquisition functionalities considered in this project are implemented as software agents interacting with selected software artefacts and various knowledge sources.

The main purpose of developing the system in question is to implement selected vital functionalities which are necessary to complete pre-specified work scenarios for information retrieval within SYNAT project. The scope of the work is limited to the domain of scientific information. However, it has to be noted, that it could be easily extended to other domains in terms of information resource delivery, as it is generic in that sense. The limitation is also due to the usage scenarios of University Knowledge Base at the Warsaw University of Technology.

The system is designed to obtain URL and a type of a desired resource. It is extended with an automatic classification module and can be assigned to any domain of analyzed knowledge. The main language is English, this language is used both in the user interface and targeted domain of resources to be found and stored.

2 Theoretical Background - Problem Analysis

The described system utilizes MAS architecture paradigm; let us shortly remind its vital characteristics.

2.1 Multi Agent System

As the complexity of current software systems expands, as the systems are becoming more tightly coupled than ever, the need of reliability and responsiveness increases. Thus, the new ways of building software are necessary. Researchers are striving for more effective techniques. One of the emerging technologies that can support this pursuit is Agent Based software development [1].

An agent is a software entity, capable of acting with a certain degree of autonomy as its goal can be defined as accomplishing tasks on behalf of its user.

Fard describes *'Multi-agent systems as an emerging sub field of artificial intelligence concern with interaction of agents to solve a common problem.'* [2].

MAS is a system that consists of society of agents collaborating with each other within an environment, together to execute specific goal(s). It manifests relatively high level of self-organization and self-awareness, including controlling and developing complex behaviors. For comprehensive modeling description please refer to [1–3].

2.2   Information Retrieval

Crawler, Web Spider. *Web spider*, also called *web crawler* is a program designed to follow web pages using links found at previous pages for their content retrieval. Their capabilities include browsing, updating their information about web content, indexing of the data stored or just validate hyperlinks.

Information Retrieval – Current Research Review. Search engines operating on Web are one of the most commonly used tools on the Internet. Unfortunately, the exponential growth rate and the high variability of the Web pages content, makes it very hard to extract all relevant information just in time. In fact, the issue of crawling the Web pages is perhaps one of the greatest bottlenecks for search engines [4].

Research issues related to the challenges of the Internet exploration include the following problems [2, 4–6]:

1. Maintaining the knowledge domain fresh and complete, means continuous browsing and analysis of web resources.
2. Identifying and accessing high quality content. Internet is full of low quality content both in terms of syntax and semantics. That includes unreliable, noisy and contradictory data found on different knowledge sources. Therefore, another problem is how much an Internet resource site can be trusted.
3. Semantic data (difficulty with semantic data usage in modern web pages, or rather the lack of it, with only rare exceptions). This also includes supplementing web resources with metadata, including modeling relationships based on ontological description of desired knowledge domain, complementing with contexts, such as genre or time, with defined relations between them.

Distributed Information Retrieval – Problem Analysis. Let us focus on information retrieval challenges and present current approaches to this issue in this section.

In [2], Fard et al. describe the idea of distributed information retrieval in the following way: '*The goal of distributed information retrieval (DIR) is to provide a single search interface that provides access to the available databases (. . .) choosing which databases to search for particular information, and merging retrieved results into a single result list*'. They point out the main issues in DIR. The first issue is that knowledge is dispersed across different databases. Second is the need to provide a single interface for these different databases. Third is the process of merging results from different databases. The fact that the number of data providers is continuously increasing makes DIR more complicated.

In order to perform the whole DIR process, one needs to solve the following challenges:

1. adequate resource description – how to learn and describe the domain of knowledge covered by each different database,
2. resource selection according to particular needs – how to select a precise set of resources when provided with a query and a knowledge source to search,
3. query translation depending on a knowledge source – means designing the adequate mapping from one information representation to another representation,
4. result merging – when sets of results are returned from the selected knowledge sources, algorithm for merging those results should be executed to integrate them into a single list (perhaps according to some explicit criteria) [2].

All of which were taken into account while developing the presented solution.

3   System design

General System Architecture of Ψ^R. The main purpose of the Platform for Scientific Information Retrieval (called Ψ^R) is to gather scientific information from different data sources and store it in the database in a structuralized form.

The high level architecture of designed system is presented in Fig. 1. Information collected by the platform comes from the Internet. Web Resource module (here also called Web Resource Acquisition System – WRAS) retrieves possible resources from the Internet based on requests. The retrieved resources are passed to reviewers (users that accept the retrieved resources). Then users or an automatic classification module decide whether a given resource is of a desired type. Sets of these retrieved and accepted results are stored in the university database.

We focused on looking for all resources that contain information about the objects related to the scientific world. Our target was to create semi-automatically a set of rules and queries that provide adequate description of the domain of our interest. A manual definition and initialization of the custom searching process is also possible.

In order to describe resources gathered by the WRAS system, the system *ontology* is used [7,8], which itself is the central point of the platform. The system *ontology* contains concepts related to scientific community and its activities, e.g., scientists, their activities, scientific documents, academic organizations, scientific events. It counts 472 classes and 296 properties.

URLs of web resources of a specific type are collected and passed to *Information extraction module,*where additional extraction occurs. Furthermore, *Information extraction module* is capable of searching on its own for new information on the Internet. Then, the extracted information is integrated and stored in the *Knowledge Base*, in a form of a structured data base conforming with the design of the *system ontology*. The Knowledge Base content consists of objects that are instances of semantic concepts from the system *ontology*. Relations between particular instances of those objects are stored in the Knowledge Base as well. Analyzing types of objects considered in the information extraction stage, we

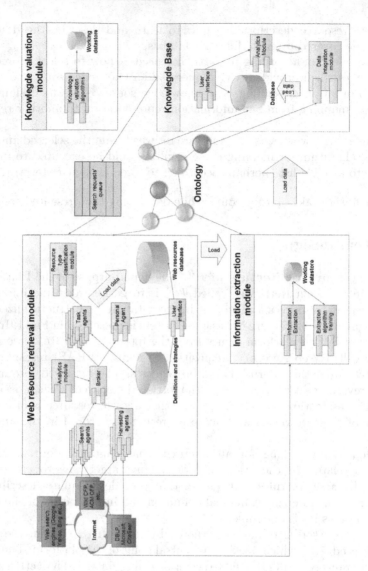

Fig. 1. General system architecture of Ψ^R, source: [7].

decided to define a static mapping between types of objects that are the results of the information extraction process and concepts in the *ontology*. The static mapping means that an object is represented in the Knowledge Base as an instance of a concept that is prescribed to that type of object. In the other words, there is a list of all types of objects and concepts related to them, where one type of objects has a concept or a group of concepts associated with it. When an object is inserted into the Knowledge Base, all instances of related concepts are created. For more information, please refer to [7].

The process of evaluation of scientific publications and authors is performed in the *knowledge valuation module*, it is based on gathered knowledge, i.e., publications and their impact factors of a given researcher, etc. Moreover, social networks of given researchers are also analyzed [7].

The modules of Ψ^R are only mentioned to provide full context of the purpose of SYNAT project. In the following sections of this paper we focus on WRAS module and its integrated components.

3.1   Web Resource Acquisition System

The main parameters while designing and developing the system were: scalability, efficiency, and reliability for delivering large amount of data - everything in terms of resources that covers domain of scientific knowledge as accurately and completely as possible. One of considered solutions was to use data crawlers or spiders running on given sets of URLs, another was exploitation of existing databases by direct pull of resources to final database, however, in this case, the main issue was that none of knowledge sources accessible on the Internet provide proper quality and amount of resources within desired domain. Some databases would have to be merged. Moreover, quite often knowledge pulled down would be unnecessary or semantically incorrect. In any case, this could not assure the complete coverage of newest resources, additionally some sub-areas of resource space could be hidden from our search in the case when the initial set of base links was incomplete or out of date.

Given the described problems and considerations, the new approach was developed: (a) to fulfil those expectations (b) to fit exactly with SYNAT project assumptions and be fully under developers' control.

The proposed solution is to solve described problem by a further decomposition into two sub-problems:

(1) knowledge domain identification and adequate coverage of search space;
(2) keeping data up to date, with continuous refreshing of outdated resources as time flows and data changes on the Internet, all by possibly lowest cost in terms of querying, data throughput and computational power.

We proposed a three-phase solution:

$$\text{Strategy} + \text{Definition} \rightarrow \text{Search queries} \rightarrow \text{Resources}$$

In the next subsections, it is described in more detail.

Definition. As an alternative solution to web crawlers, we proposed browsing a knowledge space using well prepared queries for pre-defined area of knowledge that is of our interest. That again should consist of the following parts: adjusting a query to a specific knowledge source and defining a meta-content of the query itself. We believe that this proposed approach helps to solve the problem of knowledge domain identification and adequate coverage of a search space.

Strategy. Assurance of holding up-to-date resources in the data-base should be provided by defining time intervals when specific queries should be executed, based on analyzed resource domain and the expectation of variability of data. Moreover, resource acquisition should be performed with best-adjusted domain of knowledge for requested resource with respect to true domain of database. This could be achieved by: (a) explicit definition of such preferred knowledge sources based on types of resources and (b) admin/user description and a possibility to choose the optimal database(s) to be searched in order to obtain a set of resources for a given query. This solution is designed to solve the second sub-problem and to further optimize the results.

Classifiers. To increase the number of automatic solutions at the general level of the system, we proposed to include classification (i.e. resource quality assessment) module into the system. Classification process should be executed on retrieved results, obtained from databases with respect to their types and requested domain. Automatic classification system will significantly decrease the workload put on human – the administrator of the system, as the human will have to only review the results and to act upon inconsistencies, not upon all the results delivered.

3.2 Data Model

Let us define *Resource* (*Information Resource* or *Web Resource*) as an object found in some database or search engine that contains some kind of information about the object related with the scientific world, with a valid URL descriptor as mandatory property. Of course, *Resource* can contain other descriptive metadata (and will) in case when particular Knowledge Source or Database can provide it. In most cases it could contain: snippet information about resource, name, knowledge source etc., possibly extended by any other type of data that user will find interesting to retrieve.

We defined the following pre-specified types of *Resources* in the system: Person, University, Faculty, Institute, Division, Conference, Publisher, Digital library, Digital library of conferences, Digital library of universities, Other digital libraries, Journal, Publication, Any.

3.3 Technologies Used

The programming language used to create Web Resource Acquisition System is SCALA [9] with Scala Actors framework [10]. A particular Search Agents connects to different interfaces of the following web information sources: Google (by Google API), Bing (by Bing API), CiteSeer (by CiteSeer API).

4 Experimental Results

In this section, we present simulation scenario, summary of retrieved data and the conclusions drawn from these initial experiments.

4.1   Simulation Scenario - Conference List - Acquisition

Let us describe one of the pre-specified scenarios of the system usage.

The goal is to collect representative sample of resources from scientific conferences domain, to cover domain of knowledge for conferences; that is, to find a website for a given conference and year.

Resource type: Conference;
Input data: conference list retrieved from the University Knowledge Base [11], consisting of 1000 international conferences within the domain of Computer Science,

Defined queries that are issued in order to find a website of a conference:

```
parametric / generic search query:   ''\{Acronym\} OR \{Full Name\}
[Previous Year] international conference''
```

```
parametric / generic search query:   ''\{Full Name\} [Current Year]
international conference''
```

```
parametric / generic search query:   ''\{Full Name\} [Following Year]
international conference''
```

The following search queries are designed for a single conference: (1) a query for full name of the conference, (2) a query for abbreviation. Of course, only when both data are available, otherwise only one parameter is filled and therefore one search query is executed.

Example:

```
Full Name = Computer Science and Information Systems; Acronym = ComSIS;
Current Year = 2013;
```

```
''ComSIS 2013 international conference''
''Computer Science and Information Systems 2013 international conference''
''ComSIS OR Computer Science and Information Systems 2013 international
conference''
...
```

4.2   Experimental Results

During the time of initial testing, over 50 000 resources were gathered in total, including different data types and scenarios. In particular: data traffic, quality of resources, reliability of the system and search providers were tested.

In order to present the results in details, one testing scenario was chosen. There were defined approximately 1000 entries for Conferences within Computer Science domain, inserted into CSV file, uploaded as Generic Definition and initialized the Strategy to execute them; that is, search for a website of a conference in a given year. Based on that input data, the experiment began. It was possible to perform searches of about 800 out of 1000 samples. As a result, 15203 resources, candidate websites, were retrieved for Conference type from Google and Bing Providers, this data is analysed in more detail. Below, a sample of generic definition file content (compliant with CSV file) is presented:

```
name; shortName
AAAI Spring Symposium on Answer Set Programming;
ACIS International Workshop on Self-Assembling Wireless Networks;
ACM/IEEE International Conference on Compilers, Architecture
and Synthesis for Embedded Systems;
...
```

Coverage of Knowledge Domain. In Fig. 2, Knowledge Domain is depicted in the scope of our possible interest (big circle), and particular search requests (Request 1–4) that could be mapped as sub-areas of the whole search space. Each of them covers both specific and different part that possibly overlaps of the knowledge domain in that we are interested in.

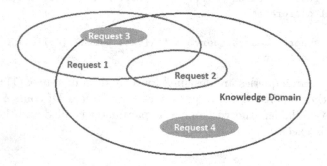

Fig. 2. Sample of knowledge domain coverage.

The sizes of the shapes correspond with the amount of possible data hits. Thus we can approximate that more results come from a *broader search* – that means better coverage of search space. However, it takes much more time to classify and process all of the resources.

As Bing Search Provider delivers maximum 50 results per search, it is possible to cover greater subspace area (it is depicted as Request 1 and Request 2 in Fig. 2). On the other hand, Google Search Provider returns less results, therefore it is possible to deliver more accurate and less dispersed data (Requests 3 and 4).

Resource Quality Comparison. In this section, quality of results will be analyzed with respect to initial assumptions of resource delivery process. Classifier accuracy itself is out of the scope of this research, thus, we can only quote its quality results and assume that they are valid.

The aim of the conference classifier is to recognize if a given website is a website of some conference. In order to test the classifier the data set with 1681 websites was prepared. It contained 993 positive examples; that is, conference websites and 688 examples that were not conference websites. The classifier was

Table 1. Quality of conference classifier. Quality means % of samples correctly assigned to each class.

Class	Quality
Positive	95%
Negative	93%

Table 2. Resource class comparison statistics.

Class	Total	Ratio
positive	3460	31,43%
negative	7547	68,57%
	11007	

used to classify these examples. Theoretical quality of the classifier for Conference is presented in Table 1. Quality measure shows the percentage of websites for a given class of examples that were correctly identified as such. In our experiments there were two classes, positive - conference websites and negative - websites that were not websites of conferences. The quality measure for both classes was high, values above 90%. Thus, the classifier had very good quality and could be used for identifying conference websites. For more details about the conference classifier, please refer to [12].

Below, we present results gathered during initial experiments with respect to distinct knowledge providers. The gathered resources were used in calculating statistics presented further in this section.

Google
  Number of queries to Google Search Agent: 457
  Resources retrieved from Google Search Agent: 3943
  Number of resources that were classified by Classification Module: 800
BING
  Number of queries to Bing Search Agent: 333
  Resources retrieved from Bing Search Agent: 11260
  Number of resources that were classified by Classification Module: 10207

Table 2 presents particular class assignment of retrieved results. This data is based on automatic classification process. System classified over 68% of received resources as negative for a given type of request. Based on that, we can see how much we can decrease the amount of work necessary for human to review all of them by hand, in comparison to utilizing those results directly from search engines.

In Table 3 we can see the classifier current capability at the 72,40% level. This means that not all of resources were classified. One of the reasons behind this behaviour is that Search Providers returned many of the *.pdf and *.doc documents that classifiers were unable to process properly. Because of varying

Table 3. Resource classification statistics.

Total retrieved results	Total classified	Classifier capability
15203	11007	72,40 %

maximal resource retrieval number, the choice of search provider influences directly work for human reviewer and indirectly area of search space discussed previously. Based on this experiment, there was retrieved almost 3 500 resources possibly valid for further investigation and at the same time (automatically) rejected over 11 500 as negative (or invalid) cases.

5   Possible Extensions and Future Work

The presented system is easily extendable, i.e., it was designed to easily add new agent entities, roles and features or extend capabilities of already existing roles in the future. This could require adjusting some of already existing roles, but creates possibility to further extend system features, especially in terms of resource analysis and optimization of search queries or network traffic. It is also easy to connect the new knowledge sources of Web Resources as the infrastructure for that already exist, including direct harvesting resources from digital libraries and databases. In order to achieve that, it is only necessary to develop an interface between them and the Brokering system. As we are providing set of possible extensions, one of them is being already developed, Definition Optimizer Agent, which is an additional module wrapped with the Agent interface. It will include two additional agents, Definition Optimizer Module, that will provide function of analysis of query texts for the purpose of optimization in terms of correctness, validity and importance. Second, which is designed to be a modified Task Agent to provide interface of resource delivery directly to Optimizer Module, and to meet its specific needs, possibly with further customization of search queries with respect to different search engines.

Another issue is extending the set of classifiers to cover all of the predefined types in the system. Ultimately, more detailed analysis in terms of their quality should be performed in order to increase their specialization and efficiency.

At this point there is also a need for performing larger scale efficiency tests on University infrastructure with higher number of users involved. At the same time, there is a need for increasing efficiency and speed of processing new resources. More detailed analysis of each components should be carried out in order to discover bottlenecks which should be eventually optimized.

6   Conclusions

In this paper we proposed the system for web resources delivery based on the requirements of SYNAT project. We proved validity of a design of the system proposed herein. It utilizes an agent technology based on SCALA Actors to build a Multi Agent System for Information Retrieval.

This modern software engineering paradigm was used to provide technical solution for challenges we encountered and the usage of well defined search queries and search engines was proposed as a approach to web crawlers and web spiders, which are currently widely used in those situations.

Based on defined queries and strategies, it is possible to retrieve knowledge resources about a specific domain. The incorporation of the presented solution into the real University Knowledge Base and integration with existing search providers have been demonstrated.

References

1. Jennings, N.R.: An agent-based approach for building complex software systems. Commun. ACM **44**(4), 35–41 (2001)
2. Fard, A.M., Kahani, M., Ghaemi, R., Tabatabaee, H.: Multi-agent data fusion architecture for intelligent web information retrieval. Int. J. Intell. Syst. Technol. **2**(3), 201–205 (2007)
3. Zambonelli, F., Jennings, N.R., Wooldridge, M.: Developing multiagent systems: the gaia methodology. ACM Trans. Softw. Eng. Methodol. **12**(3), 317–370 (2003)
4. Baeza-Yates, R.A.: Information retrieval in the web: beyond current search engines. Int. J. Approx. Reasoning **34**(2–3), 97–104 (2003)
5. Barraza, A.P., Carrillo-Ramos, A.: Basic requirements to keep in mind for an ideal agent-based web information retrieval system in ubiquitous environments. In: Proceedings of the 12th International Conference on Information Integration and Web-based Applications & Services. iiWAS 2010, pp. 550–557. ACM, New York (2010)
6. Henzinger, M.R., Motwani, R., Silverstein, C.: Challenges in web search engines. In: Proceedings of the 18th International Joint Conference on Artificial Intelligence. IJCAI 2003, pp. 1573–1579. Morgan Kaufmann Publishers Inc., San Francisco (2003)
7. Andruszkiewicz, P., Gambin, T., Kryszkiewicz, M., Kozlowski, M., Lieber, K., Matusiak, A., Miedzinski, E., Morzy, M., Nachyla, B., Omelczuk, A., Rybinski, H., Skonieczny, L.: Synat - report 4, b11 stage. Technical report (2012)
8. SYNAT system ontology. https://wizzar.ii.pw.edu.pl/passim-ontology/
9. SCALA. http://www.scala-lang.org/
10. Scala Actors tutorial. http://docs.scala-lang.org/overviews/core/actors.html
11. Koperwas, J., Skonieczny, Ł., Rybiński, H., Struk, W.: Development of a university knowledge base. In: Bembenik, R., Skonieczny, Ł., Rybiński, H., Kryszkiewicz, M., Niezgódka, M. (eds.) Intell. Tools for Building a Scientific Information. SCI, vol. 467, pp. 97–110. Springer, Heidelberg (2013)
12. Adamczyk, T., Andruszkiewicz, P., Kozlowski, M., Kryszkiewicz, M., Lieber, K., Miedzinski, E., Nachyla, B., Omelczuk, A., Rybinski, H.: Synat - report 5, b11 stage. Technical report (2013)

An Efficient Nearest Neighbor Method for Protein Contact Prediction

Gualberto Asencio-Cortés$^{(\boxtimes)}$, Jesús S. Aguilar-Ruiz,
and Alfonso E. Márquez-Chamorro

School of Engineering, Pablo de Olavide University, Sevilla, Spain
{guaasecor,aguilar,amarcha}@upo.es

Abstract. A variety of approaches for protein inter-residue contact prediction have been developed in recent years. However, this problem is far from being solved yet. In this article, we present an efficient nearest neighbor (NN) approach, called PKK-PCP, and an application for the protein inter-residue contact prediction. The great strength of using this approach is its adaptability to that problem. Furthermore, our method improves considerably the efficiency with regard to other NN approaches. Our NN-based method combines parallel execution with k-d tree as search algorithm. The input data used by our algorithm is based on structural features and physico-chemical properties of amino acids besides of evolutionary information. Results obtained show better efficiency rates, in terms of time and memory consumption, than other similar approaches.

Keywords: k-nearest neighbor · k-d tree · Protein inter-residue contact prediction

1 Introduction

Protein inter-residue contact prediction has been an important and relevant topic in bioinformatics and computational biology in last decades. The prediction of inter-residue contacts represents an important previous step to solve the protein structure prediction problem (PSP). Predicting the structure of a protein from its amino acid sequence is the main key to cure those diseases which are related with the anomalous formation of proteins, *e.g.* Alzheimer. Computational methods represent a faster and more economic way to solve the PSP problem, than experimental methods, *e.g.* X-ray crystallography.

The nearest neighbor (NN) algorithm is an adequate computational approach to address the problem of protein structure prediction, due to the knowledge that proteins which share a high degree of similarity in their sequences, should have similar 3D structures. In protein contact prediction problem, NN methods find the K-closest protein sequence profiles from a database of known protein structures, according to a distance measure, and predict the corresponding class (contact or non-contact).

Previously, nearest neighbor algorithms have been presented in the PSP literature. Abu-doleh *et al.* [1] predicts contact maps using an inference system

© Springer International Publishing Switzerland 2015
E. Onieva et al. (Eds.): HAIS 2015, LNAI 9121, pp. 50–60, 2015.
DOI: 10.1007/978-3-319-19644-2_5

based on a fuzzy-neural network and nearest neighbor approach. The algorithm employs 5 windows of amino acids and performs an attribute selection according to negative matrix factorization. Colubri *et al.* [7] performs a homology-based method using torsion angles. The algorithm analyses propensities of the different types of amino acids and secondary structures. Similar structures search is carried out using a simulated annealing approach. Davies *et al.* [8] implements a case based reasoning method which predicts protein contact maps. The method obtains secondary structure from the contact maps and from the geometric knowledge about alpha-helix contacts. Finally, Glasgow and Davies [10] proposes a contact map predictor using sequence data. Case representation includes protein name, protein sequence, assignment of secondary structure to residues, structure class and protein contact map. The solution consists of a 3D backbone model of the protein structure computed from the contact map.

All these algorithms constitute a part of ensemble methods. In this article we have developed a method exclusively based on a NN approach for the contact prediction. A protein contact is established according to the geometrical distance of each pair of amino acids of a sequence. If this distance is lower than a determined threshold in angstroms, a contact is defined. We highlight that the performance efficiency of our method, in terms of execution time and computer memory used, is better than other NN implementations. A parallel implementation of the algorithm and the incorporation of k-d trees [5] as search algorithm contributes to the improvement of these measures. On the other hand, we have employed as encoding features, physico-chemical properties of residues (hydrophobicity, polarity and net charge), structural features, such as secondary structure and solvent accessibility, and evolutionary information, in the form of position specific scoring matrices (PSSM). This encoding shares the assumption that the prediction of the 3D structure of a protein can be based on characteristics of the amino acids [14].

The remainder of this paper is organized as follows. Section 2 introduces our methodology. Section 3 presents the experimentation and obtained results. Finally, Sect. 4, includes some conclusions and possible future works.

2 Methods

2.1 Overview

Our prediction system, named PKK-PCP, is able to predict contacts between amino acids in protein structures from protein sequences. Our system takes, as input data, the hydrophobicity, polarity and charge of residues. It also uses as input, external predictions for secondary structure and solvent accessibility. Furthermore, evolutionary profiles (PSSM) of residues are also employed as input.

Our system returns a contact probability value for each pair of amino acids. PKK-PCP is based on the classic nearest neighbour algorithm. The system uses k-d trees to optimize the neighbour search. Moreover, our system is implemented in C++, parallelized and optimised for 64 bits architecture.

The methodology carried out to build profiles for each residue pair is detailed in Sect. 2.2. Then we explain the prediction process based on nearest neighbour approach in Sect. 2.3. In Sect. 2.4 we detail several important implementation notes of our predictor. Finally, we define the evaluation measures used for effectiveness and efficiency in Sect. 2.5.

2.2 Profile Construction

From input protein sequences, our system takes each pair of amino acids as usual in PSP methods [1,4]. Formally, we represent an amino acid sequence of length L as $s_1 \ldots s_L$. Then we consider amino acid pairs (s_i, s_j) such that $1 \le i < j \le L$.

For each amino acid pair, PKK-PCP builds a profile that contains 50 attributes. We define the profile for each pair (s_i, s_j) as shown in Eq. 1.

$$[H_{i,j}^*, P_{i,j}^*, SS_i, SS_j, SA_i, SA_j, PSSM_i, PSSM_j] \in \mathbb{R}^{50} \qquad (1)$$

The components $H_{i,j}^*$ and $P_{i,j}^*$ measure the average of hydrophobicity and polarity between residues (i, j) and they are defined in Eq. 2, where H_i and H_j are the hydrophobicities of amino acids i and j respectively. P_i and P_j are the polarities of amino acids i and j respectively.

$$H_{i,j}^* = \frac{H_i + H_j}{2} \in [0, 1]$$
$$P_{i,j}^* = \frac{P_i + P_j}{2} \in [0, 1] \qquad (2)$$

We used the scale proposed by Black and Mould [6] for hydrophobicity and the scale proposed by Radzicka and Wolfenden [16] for polarity. We found that the hydrophobicity average of amino acids i and j ($H_{i,j}^*$) produces better predictions than separated hydrophobicities H_i and H_j into the profile, and it reduces the profile size. Same conclusions are applied to polarity.

We included into the profile the predicted secondary structure of amino acids i and j (SS_i and SS_j respectively). These predictions are returned by PSI-PRED [11] as commonly used by PSP methods in literature.

The SS values are encoded using three values for three secondary states: $\{0.5, 0, 0\}$ for alpha helix, $\{0, 0.5, 0\}$ for beta sheet and $\{0, 0, 0.5\}$ for random coil. Thus, the Euclidean distance between SS attributes is 0 or 1 depending whether amino acids have the same secondary structure or not, respectively. Therefore, SS_i and SS_j have 3 attributes each.

The components SA_i and SA_j of the profile are the predicted solvent accessibility of amino acids i and j respectively. For this purpose we used the predictor proposed by Rost and Sander [17] as in the work of Bacardit et al. [4]. We used a 5-state representation for SA, ranging from 0 to 4, where lower values mean a buried state and higher values represent exposed states.

Finally we included into the profile the evolutionary information ($PSSM_i$ and $PSSM_j$ for amino acids i and j) from PSI-BLAST [2] as widely used in PSP and bioinformatics literature. $PSSM_i$ and $PSSM_j$ have 20 attributes each.

All values in the profile are normalized between 0 and 1 in order to provide an equal contribution to distance calculation among profiles in further nearest neighbour search scheme, as we show in the next subsection.

2.3 Residue Contact Prediction

PKK-PCP begins with an initial set of proteins, it builds the profiles as we have explained in the previous subsection and divides the protein set into training and test folds according to a cross-validation scheme.

For each profile within the test fold, PKK-PCP assess the Euclidean distance between that profile and each profile in the training fold, in order to find the K training profiles with the lowest distances (most similar training profiles).

Then, the contact probability returned by our system for amino acids i and j of the test profile is calculated as the number of contacts in most similar training profiles divided by K.

In order to improve the performance, a pruning in the neighbour search is applied for all the methods in comparison. This pruning is based on the charge of amino acids i and j of the test sequence. Specifically, this means that given a test profile, if the net charge [12] of amino acid i or j is distinct to 0 (at least one amino acid is positive or negative charged), then the contact probability is 0 and the neighbour search is omitted.

This pruning is in line with the results obtained by Márquez-Chamorro et al. [13] in the Fig. 10. In that work the percentage of contacts between charged amino acids is close to 0 and they could be rejected. This pruning is introduced with the aim of providing a comparison using a high number of proteins in a reasonable time. Moreover, this pruning has a low impact to the effectiveness of methods in comparison, as we show in the experimentation section.

2.4 Predictor Implementation

The system PKK-PCP is implemented in Microsoft C++ 2012 using the release configuration for 64 bits and was built for multithreading architecture. PKK-PCP is based on the ANN library of David Mount [3] for nearest neighbor searching using k-d trees. We have adapted that library for parallel execution, cross validation and protein contact evaluation. That evaluation was designed to measure the protein inter-residue contact prediction, which is a classification problem with a binary class.

2.5 Effectiveness and Efficiency Evaluation

The effectiveness and efficiency of PKK-PCP are assessed using several measures. Regarding the effectiveness, we computed accuracy (Acc) and coverage (Cov), defined as shown in Eqs. 3 and 4 respectively. These measures are widely used by PSP methods in literature [1,4]. The reason is that these measures are focused in prediction of positive cases of contacts between amino acids, and these cases are quite less frequent than negative ones, as it is shown in Table 1.

$$Acc = \frac{TP}{TP + FP} \tag{3}$$

$$Cov = \frac{TP}{NumContacts} \tag{4}$$

TP are true positives and FP are false positives. $NumContacts$ are the number of real contacts. The accuracy is the ratio of predicted contacts that are presented in the native structure. The coverage is the ratio of native contacts that are predicted to be contacts.

In this work, we used a cut-off value of 8 angstroms in order to define a contact between two amino acids, which is commonly used in literature [9,19].

Regarding the efficiency, we computed the elapsed time during the prediction process and the space consumed in computer memory.

3   Experimentation

This section presents the experimentation followed and the results obtained by our method. The aim of this experimentation consists on providing an analysis of the effectiveness and efficiency of our system for different sizes of protein sets. The results have been compared with Weka IBk algorithm [18] with $K = 1$ using both linear and k-d tree search algorithms.

3.1   Datasets

Protein datasets used in our experimentation were selected from the dataset of Bacardit *et al.* [4]. This dataset is derived from PDB-REPRDB [15] and consists of 3,262 protein chains with sequence identity lower than 30 %, a resolution smaller than 2Å and a crystallographic R factor lower than 20 %.

We have randomly extracted from this dataset several subsets: DS25, DS50, DS75, DS100, DS200, DS300. We used them for our experimentation, where the number included in their names indicates the number of proteins in each subset. The aim of using incremental size of subsets is to test the efficiency of our approach in terms of time and memory consumption. Table 1 shows the main characteristics of each dataset used in the experimentation.

Table 1. Number of proteins, minimum, maximum and average length of protein sequences, number of contacts and non-contacts between residues and their ratio for each dataset employed in the experimentation.

Dataset	#	min	max	avg	contacts	non-contacts	ratio(c:nc)
DS25	25	54	405	123.08	4,871	282,692	1:58
DS50	50	54	405	119.20	11,114	646,518	1:58
DS75	75	53	405	120.77	17,852	1,167,011	1:65
DS100	100	53	405	124.02	23,750	1,497,252	1:63
DS200	200	53	602	169.78	48,809	3,075,366	1:63
DS300	300	50	822	195.53	84,203	7,122,243	1:84

Table 2. Comparative study of efficiency (time in hours and memory in megabytes) of PKK-PCP and Weka IBk algorithm using the charge-based pruning. Weka IBk uses linear search (Weka column) and k-d tree (Weka-KDT column) as search algorithms. The effectiveness (accuracy and coverage) is also shown.

Dataset	Measure	Weka	Weka-KDT	PKK-PCP
DS25	Acc	0.797	0.797	0.797
	Cov	0.689	0.689	0.689
	Time	38.12	9.31	1.07
	Mem	6259	7140	505
DS50	Acc	0.788	0.788	0.788
	Cov	0.682	0.682	0.682
	Time	312.07	29.25	3.04
	Mem	8522	10,832	935
DS75	Acc	0.798	0.798	0.798
	Cov	0.691	0.691	0.691
	Time	744.52	63.72	6.26
	Mem	9,425	11,974	1,340
DS100	Acc	0.795	0.795	0.795
	Cov	0.690	0.690	0.690
	Time	–	92.11	10.47
	Mem	10,054	12,720	1,859
DS200	Acc	0.791	0.791	0.791
	Cov	0.685	0.685	0.685
	Time	–	183.42	44.72
	Mem	13,289	16,542	4,597
DS300	Acc	0.789	0.789	0.789
	Cov	0.690	0.690	0.690
	Time	–	295.04	114.11
	Mem	17,254	20,358	7,362

3.2 Configuration

All the experiments were run on a 64-bit workstation, a Dell Precision T7400, with 2x Intel Xeon X5482 3.2 GHz (2x4 cores), 32 GB DDR2 RAM, SATA2 7200rpm HD and Windows 7 Ultimate.

As we mentioned before, our algorithm returns a contact probability for each test instance. We determine a contact if this probability is higher than 0.5. We also set the number of neighbors to $K = 1$. A 10-fold cross-validation with 5 runs per fold was applied.

To evaluate the predictions, we have obtained a coverage and accuracy value for each test protein, instead for each data point. Since Weka does not obtain

Table 3. Comparative study of efficiency (time in hours and memory in megabytes) of PKK-PCP and Weka IBk algorithm without using the charge-based pruning. Weka IBk uses linear search (Weka column) and k-d tree (Weka-KDT column) as search algorithms. The effectiveness (accuracy and coverage) is also shown.

Dataset	Measure	Weka	Weka-KDT	PKK-PCP
DS25	Acc	0.803	0.803	0.803
	Cov	0.712	0.712	0.712
	Time	54.35	13.27	1.45
	Mem	6259	7140	505
DS50	Acc	0.811	0.811	0.811
	Cov	0.709	0.709	0.709
	Time	447.21	41.33	4.27
	Mem	8522	10832	935
DS75	Acc	0.817	0.817	0.817
	Cov	0.719	0.719	0.719
	Time	1,055.64	90.68	8.81
	Mem	9,425	11,974	1,340
DS100	Acc	0.812	0.812	0.812
	Cov	0.716	0.716	0.716
	Time	–	130.85	14.45
	Mem	10,054	12,720	1,859

Table 4. Number of pruning applied for each dataset in a 10-fold cross validation and number of false negatives incurred when the pruning are applied.

Dataset	Instances	Pruning	FN
DS25	287,563	123,105(42.8%)	7,521(6.1%)
DS50	657,632	286,201(43.5%)	17,085(5.9%)
DS75	1,184,863	508,424(42.9%)	31,624(6.2%)
DS100	1,521,002	647,946(42.6%)	43,477(6.7%)
DS200	3,124,175	1,377,761(44.1%)	84,456(6.1%)
DS300	7,206,446	3,124,066(43.3%)	200,252(6.4%)

these measures for each protein, we have implemented an external evaluator in order to evaluate the Weka predictions for each test protein using exactly the same training instances as in our approach.

Furthermore, the Weka IBk algorithm (with both linear and k-d tree search) was modified to include the charge-based pruning mentioned in Sect. 2.3, in order to perform a fair comparison between PKK-PCP and Weka IBk algorithm (linear and k-d tree) in terms of efficiency.

3.3   Results

The time and memory consumed were analysed comparing PKK-PCP to Weka IBk method, using both linear and k-d tree search algorithms implemented in Weka. The effectiveness (accuracy and coverage) is also shown, but these values are the same for all the methods because they share the same training nearest neighbours and the comparison is focused in their efficiency.

As we can see in Table 2, the execution time of our method widely improves the Weka IBk k-d tree results. In the worst case (for dataset DS25), PKK-PCP used only the 11.5 % of the time employed by Weka with k-d tree (with a difference of 8.24 h). The optimized implementation of nearest neighbors approach inside PKK-PCP and its parallel execution contributes to this efficiency improvement.

Table 3 is included in order to appreciate the impact of removing the charge-based pruning to the effectiveness and efficiency of methods in comparison. Table 3 shows the accuracy, coverage, time in minutes and memory in megabytes of the three methods in comparison with no pruning in the neighbour search. Only datasets DS25, DS50, DS75 and DS100 are presented in Table 3. Note that the differences with and without pruning, in terms of times and memory consumption, are high (around 43 % faster with the charge-based pruning). However, the differences of accuracy and coverage are slight (around 0.15 of accuracy and 0.21 of coverage better without pruning). This low difference in effectiveness due to pruning is explained by the values shown in Table 4. According to values shown in Table 4, it is remarkable the low number of false negatives incurred despite the high number of pruning performed (up to 6.7 % false negatives with respect to the total of pruning, in the worst case DS100). The high number of instances to tackle, when the number of proteins on datasets increases, leads to

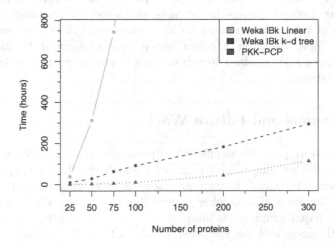

Fig. 1. Evolution of execution time (in hours) of Weka IBk with linear search, Weka IBk with k-d tree and PKK-PCP for each dataset of proteins.

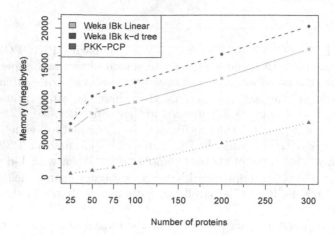

Fig. 2. Evolution of computer memory (in megabytes) used by Weka IBk with linear search, Weka IBk with k-d tree and PKK-PCP for each dataset of proteins.

using some type of pruning like we have used. In our case, the selected pruning gains an important benefit in terms of performance with a low decrement of effectiveness.

Figure 1 shows a chart which represents the execution times of PKK-PCP and Weka IBk (with linear and k-d trees search algorithms) for the different datasets. While k-d trees provides a complexity order of $NlogN$ to nearest neighbor approach, Weka IBk with linear search belongs to a quadratic order N^2. However, as we can see in Fig. 1, the execution time of our method remains in lower values than Weka k-d tree method for all studied datasets.

Figure 2 presents the memory used by PKK-PCP and Weka-IBk for different datasets. Our method obtains lower rates of memory consuming due to the optimization of the data structures we have introduced in our implementation. PKK-PCP achieved a memory consumption improvement of $10,494 \pm 1,990$ megabytes (mean and standard deviation values) with respect to Weka IBk (k-d tree) for all datasets.

4   Conclusions and Future Work

The presented work provides an efficient implementation of K-NN approach and a labelling rule for pruning nearest neighbour search specific for the protein contact prediction problem. A faster and a low memory consumption method is presented to handle a high number of proteins in a reasonable time. The use of our charge-based pruning has allowed, on the one hand, to improve considerably the efficiency, and, on the other hand, to loose the minimum degree of effectiveness.

The efficiency of our approach, in terms of execution time and memory used, was shown in comparative terms, and we have found that our system achieved times and memory consumption much better than Weka IBk with k-d tree. This seems to be a wide improvement of efficiency in nearest neighbor approach applied to protein inter-residue contact prediction.

The low memory consumption achieved by PKK-PCP allows to include more number of attributes than classical nearest neighbors approaches for a predetermined time horizon. For that reason, as future work, we will consider the addition of two amino acid windows to represent the environments of the target residues in the profiles, and also include more physico-chemical properties of amino acids like residue volume, accessible surface area or molecular weights.

Acknowledgments. This research was supported by the Spanish MEC under project TIN2011-28956-C02-01.

References

1. Abu-doleh, A., Al-jarrah, O., Alkhateeb, A.: Protein contact map prediction using multi-stage hybrid intelligence inference systems. J. Biomed. Inf. **45**, 173–183 (2012)
2. Altschul, S., Madden, T., Schffer, A., Zhang, J., Zhang, Z., Miller, W., Lipman, D.: Gapped BLAST and PSI-BLAST: a new generation of protein database search programs. Nucleic Acids Res. **25**(17), 3389–3402 (1997)
3. Arya, S., Mount, D., Netanyahu, N., Silverman, R., Wu, A.: An optimal algorithm for approximate nearest neighbor searching fixed dimensions. J. ACM **45**(6), 891–923 (1998)
4. Bacardit, J., Widera, P., Márquez-Chamorro, A., Divina, F., Aguilar-Ruiz, J., Krasnogor, N.: Contact map prediction using a large-scale ensemble of rule sets and the fusion of multiple predicted structural features. Bioinformatics **28**(19), 2441–2448 (2012)
5. Bentley, J.: Multidimensional binary search trees used for associative searching. Commun. ACM **18**(9), 509–517 (1975)
6. Black, S., Mould, D.: Development of hydrophobicity parameters to analyze proteins which bear post or cotranslational modifications. J. Anal. Biochem. **193**, 72–82 (1991)
7. Colubri, A., Jha, A., Shen, M., Sali, A., Berry, R., Sosnick, T., Freed, K.: Minimalist representations and the importance of nearest neighbor effects in protein folding simulations. J. Mol. Biol. **363**, 835–857 (2006)
8. Davies, J., Glasgow, J., Kuo, T.: Visio-spatial case-based reasoning: a case estudy in prediction of protein structure. Comput. Intel. **22**, 194–207 (2006)
9. Fariselli, P., Casadio, R.: A neural network based predictor of residue contacts in proteins. Protein Eng. **12**, 15–21 (1999)
10. Glasgow, J., Kuo, T., Davies, J.: Protein structure from contact maps: a case-based reasoning approach. Inf. Sys. Front **8**, 29–36 (2006)
11. Jones, D.: Protein secondary structure prediction based on position-specific scoring matrices. J. Mol. Biol. **292**, 195–202 (1999)
12. Klein, P., Kanehisa, M., DeLisi, C.: Prediction of protein function from sequence properties: discriminant analysis of a data base. J Biochim. Biophys. **787**, 221–226 (1984)

13. Márquez-Chamorro, A., Asencio-Cortés, G., Divina, F., Aguilar-Ruiz, J.: Evolutionary decision rules for predicting protein contact maps. In: Pattern Analysis and Applications, September 2012, pp. 1–13 (2012)
14. Márquez-Chamorro, A.E., Divina, F., Aguilar-Ruiz, J.S., Bacardit, J., Asencio-Cortés, G., Santiesteban-Toca, C.E.: A NSGA-II algorithm for the residue-residue contact prediction. In: Giacobini, M., Vanneschi, L., Bush, W.S. (eds.) EvoBIO 2012. LNCS, vol. 7246, pp. 234–244. Springer, Heidelberg (2012)
15. Noguchi, T., Matsuda, H., Akiyama, Y.: PDB-REPRDB: a database of representative protein chains from the protein data bank (PDB). Nucl. Acids Res. **29**(1), 219–220 (2001)
16. Radzicka, A., Wolfenden, R.: Comparing the polarities of the amino acids: sidechain distribution coefficients between the vapor phase, cyclohexane, 1-octanol, and neutral aqueous solution. J. Biochem. **27**, 1664–1670 (1988)
17. Rost, B., Sander, C.: Conservation and prediction of solvent accessibility in protein families. Proteins **20**(3), 216–26 (1994)
18. Witten, I., Frank, E., Hall, M.: Data Mining: Practical Machine Learning Tools and Techniques. Morgan Kauffman, San Francisco (2011)
19. Zhang, G., Huang, D., Quan, Z.: Combining a binary input encoding scheme with RBFNN for globulin protein inter-residue contact map prediction. Pattern Recognit. Lett. **26**, 1543–1553 (2005)

Interface for Composing Queries for Complex Databases for Inexperienced Users

Rodolfo A. Pazos R.[✉], Alan G. Aguirre L., Marco A. Aguirre L., and José A. Martínez F.

Instituto Tecnológico de Cd. Madero, Tecnológico Nacional de México,
Cd. Madero, Mexico
r_pazos_r@yahoo.com.mx, li.aguirre.lam@hotmail.com,
marco.aguirre@itcm.edu.mx, jose.mtz@gmail.com

Abstract. In most business activities, decision-making has a very important role, since it may benefit or harm the business. Nowadays decision-making is based on information obtained from databases, which are only accessible directly by computer experts; however, the end-user that requires information from a database is not always a computer expert, so the need arises to allow inexperienced users to obtain information directly from a database. To this end, several tools are commercially available such as visual query building and natural language interfaces to databases (NLIDBs). However, the first kind of tools requires at least a basic level of knowledge of some formal query language, while NLIDBs, despite the fact that users do not require training for using the interface, have not obtained the desired performance due to problems inherent to natural language processing. In this paper an intuitive interface is presented, which allows inexperienced users to easily compose queries in SQL, without the need of training on its operation nor having knowledge of SQL.

1 Introduction

Natural interfaces allow users to access information in a database by a query formulated in natural language (NL) or by multimodal interfaces. Examples of such interfaces are described in [1, 2]. However, the use of natural language to formulate a query to a DB can lead to some problems concerning the process of translating the query to SQL [3], which could cause that users could not obtain the desired result.

An alternative to NLIDBs are the tools for query composition for databases, which aim at obtaining information from a DB by formulating an SQL query by using a friendly graphical interface. They also facilitate the composition of an SQL query using various methods of composition; however, they require users to have some degree of knowledge of SQL and the database schema; as a result, such interfaces are difficult to use for inexperienced users.

This paper presents a human-computer interface that facilitates mid and higher managers to compose an SQL query to obtain information from a database, which is necessary for their decision-making tasks. Unlike other interfaces, the design of this interface allows composing a query without the need to have any knowledge of neither SQL nor the database schema. The design of the interface involves two major aspects:

© Springer International Publishing Switzerland 2015
E. Onieva et al. (Eds.): HAIS 2015, LNAI 9121, pp. 61–72, 2015.
DOI: 10.1007/978-3-319-19644-2_6

the human-computer interaction, which is presented in this paper; and the semantic information dictionary, which is based on a semantically enriched database model (described in [4]).

This interface has been customized for and tested with Spanish-speaking users, but its design allows its customization for other European languages: English, French, Italian, Portuguese.

2   Related Work

As mentioned in Sect. 1, there are a large number of interfaces that allow the composition of SQL queries, such as COBASE [5], WYSIWYM [6], TAICHI [7] and Query by Example of Microsoft Access,[1] among others.

Table 1 shows a comparison of the characteristics of the interfaces mentioned before and those of the interface described in this paper. As shown, most interfaces require a degree of knowledge of SQL, which could lead the user to face difficulties in using these interfaces. Furthermore, none of the interfaces explains the contents of the database to the user, so the user can not be sure that the information that he/she needs is in the database.

Table 1. Characteristics of some interfaces for query composition

Interface	Domain independence	Method of query composition	Explanation of the DB contents	Need of SQL knowledge	Used in complex DBs
CoBase	✓	Selection	×	✓	×
WYSIWYM	×	• NL • Templates	×	×	✓
TAICHI	✓	• NL • Drag & Drop	×	✓	×
MS Access	✓	• Drag & Drop • SQL templates	×	✓	✓
Proposed interface	✓	Selection	✓	×	✓

Unlike the interfaces presented in Table 1, a NLIDB requires the user to formulate a NL query in order to generate an SQL query. Such task requires a semantic processing of the NL query. An example of a semantic processing is presented by Agrawal [2] in 2013. Unfortunately, while using a NLIDB, sometimes the user may request information that is not stored in the database, this may happen because the user does not know the database schema; moreover, the user may think that the NLIDB can answer any questions, which is not so.

---

[1] http://products.office.com/en-us/access.

3   Description of the Query Composition Interface

The proposed interface aims at allowing an inexperienced user to compose SQL queries through a three-step composition process: selection of the topic of interest, selection of the elements of interest, and specification of the search conditions.

The graphical interface contains controls that most users are familiar with; therefore, the composition of a query does not require the user to receive training to use the interface, as the experimental results show (Sect. 5).

To this end, the interface uses a classification of tables that belong to the database and builds a graphic structure (composition tree) to represent the database schema based on the classification of tables and the relations between them.

In addition, the interface displays descriptions of the tables and columns of the DB keeping their names hidden, thus the user can get a better idea of what is stored in the database than by just looking at the names of tables and columns.

In the next subsections the classification of tables and the composition tree are explained, which are two of the most important aspects of the interface.

3.1   Classification of Tables

The classification of tables allows the interface to group tables of the database according to their level of relevance to query composition. In addition, the classification of tables is used to build the query tree.

Table 2 shows the different types of tables proposed for classification, they are listed in decreasing order of relevance to query composition.

Table 2. Classification of tables

Type of table	Description
1. Base tables	Main tables that store information that is frequently used for querying the database.
2. Views	Virtual tables that are obtained from a Select statement that involves base tables and are used for providing information that can not be directly obtained from base tables.
2. Catalogs	Tables that are used mainly for obtaining a NL description for a key or ID.
3. M-to-N relations	Tables that contain foreign keys that belong to other tables (T_i and T_j) and are used for implementing M-to-N relations between T_i and T_j.
4. Satellite tables	Tables that are disconnected from the rest of the tables. These tables are used by internal processes of the applications that use the database.

In query composition, base tables have the highest relevance, also views and catalogs are highly likely to be used for composition, while tables that implement M-to-N relations are only used for the construction of the composition tree; finally, satellite tables are seldom used for query composition.

3.2   Composition Tree

The composition tree is the most important component of the interface. It is used by the user for selecting the columns belonging to the tables of the database that will be used in query composition.

In the composition tree, a fragment of the DB (tables and columns) is presented using NL descriptions instead of names. Each table is represented as an expandable node, while the columns of each table are represented with simple nodes, which can not be expanded and are the only nodes that can be selected by the user.

The construction of the composition tree is carried out by the interface in the second step of the query composition process (selection of the elements of interest) from a table selected by the user in the first step.

Algorithm 1 shows the pseudocode for the construction of the composition tree, where CT is the composition tree, n is the relation node (of the composition tree) that represents a table, and R is a set of tables that are related with table t. The construction consists of initializing CT by inserting the root table T_r and applying the recursive function shown at line 1, which requires a table t as input. Subsequently, the interface obtains a set R of related tables of t, and for each table r in R its type is evaluated as follows:

- If the related table is a base table, it applies the recursive function to insert the columns and relations in the composition tree CT (line 8).
- If the related table is a catalog table, the nodes corresponding to the columns of this table are inserted into the parent node (line 11).
- If the related table is an M-to-N relation, the table related to this one is obtained (line 14), and the function to insert related tables is applied (line 15), thus, hiding the M-to-N relation table.

Algorithm 1. Pseudocode for constructing a composition tree

```
 1:   insertRelations(t)
 2:       p //Parent node of t
 3:       n ← insertRelationNode(CT_p, t)
 4:       insertColumnNode(CT_n, t)
 5:       R ← getRelatedTables(t)
 6:       for each r from R do
 7:           if isBaseTable (r)
 8:               insertRelations(r)
 9:           endif
10:           if isCatalog(r)
11:               insertColumnNodes(CT_n, r)
12:           endif
13:           if isMtoN (r)
14:               r' ← getRelatedTable(r)
15:               insertRelations(r')
16:           endif
17:       endfor
18:   end
```

3.3 Query Composition Process

The query composition process is performed by the user using the interface. This process consists of three steps: selection of the topic of interest, selection of the elements of interest, and specification of the search conditions.

In the step of selection of the topic of interest, the interface displays the tables in the database grouped by the classification shown in Table 2. In this step, the interface starts displaying the tables commonly used for composition and, at the end, those tables that are used less frequently.

For example, the classification of tables proposed for the ATIS database is shown in Table 3, which shows table descriptions in Spanish (along with their translation to English). In this case, the interface would show first the base tables, then the catalog tables, next the M-to-N relation tables, and finally the satellite tables.

Table 3. Proposed classification of tables for the ATIS database

Base tables	Catalogs	Relations M-to-N	Satellite tables
Avión (Aircraft)	Clase de servicio	Vuelo – Tarifa	Descripción de código
Aerolínea (Airline)	(Class of service)	(Flight – Fare)	(Code description)
Aeropuerto (Airport)	Servicio de comida	Restricción de	Día (Day)
Servicios de	(Food service)	empresa (Airline	Días de vuelo
aeropuerto	Clase de restricción	restriction)	(Flight days)
(Airport service)	(Class of restriction)	Segmento de	Nombres de mes
Ciudad (City)	Estado (State)	conexión	(Month names)
Clase compuesta	Zona horaria	(Connection leg)	Intervalo de tiempo
(Compound class)	(Time zone)	Empresa doble	(Time interval)
Tarifa (Fare)	Servicio de transporte	(Dual carrier)	
Vuelo de un	del aeropuerto (Transport	Servicio terrestre	
aeropuerto a	service of the airport)	(Ground service)	
otro (Flight from an		Parada (Stop)	
airport to another)			
Conexión de vuelo			
(Flight connection)			

In this step, the selected table will be used to build the composition tree. This table represents the main topic of which the user is interested in finding information.

After choosing the topic of interest of the query, the user will be directed to the selection of the elements of interest, where the interface displays the composition tree and asks the user to select the elements that he/she wants to be displayed as the result of the query. In this step the interface obtains the information needed to build the Select clause of the query.

For each element that the user wants to know in the database, he/she must add it to a list containing the elements of interest. Next, the interface stores a vector of tree nodes that represents the path from the root of the tree to the selected element. Each node is represented as a vector with four positions, where the first position stores the description of the table to which the node belongs, the second stores the description of the column representing the node, the third stores the relation between the previous node and the current node, and the fourth represents the type of table to which the node belongs. Figure 1 shows how the information concerning the generation of a path is stored.

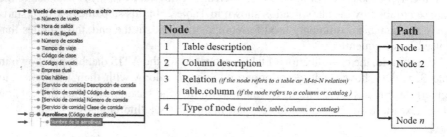

Fig. 1. Generation of the path information for a selected node

Once the user has finished adding items to the list of elements of interest, the interface will have a set of vectors representing the paths of each element of interest. This set of paths is stored in a vector with m positions, where m is the total number of elements added by the user, as shown in Fig. 2.

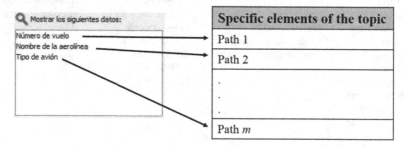

Fig. 2. Information of the paths of the elements of interest

Once the user has defined the elements of interest, if the user wants to obtain a dataset with specific information, he/she can use the interface to enter the search conditions to discriminate the data and get a result with specific characteristics. In this step the interface obtains the information needed to construct the Where clause of the query.

The information obtained by the interface concerning the search conditions is shown in Fig. 3. This figure shows that the information of a search condition is constituted by a column node or catalog, a comparison operator (=, <, >, <=, > =, <>), the description of the comparison operator, the value of the search condition, and the path from the root node to the selected node (see Fig. 1). After the user has finished defining search conditions, the interface will have a list of search conditions.

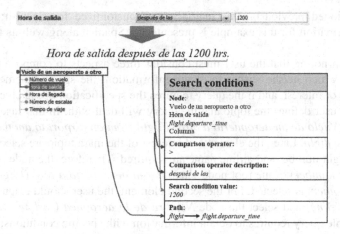

Fig. 3. Definition of a search condition

Once the three steps of the composition process have been completed, the interface will be able to generate the SQL expression from the elements of interest and search conditions already defined. The query is constructed as follows:

- Select clause. From the list of elements of interest, for each element, the last node of the path (the column selected by the user) is obtained and defined as an element of the clause.
- Where clause. From the list of search conditions, for each condition specified by the user, the name of the column, the comparison operator and the value of the condition are taken to build a condition of the clause. Subsequently the joins between tables are defined from the paths of all the elements of the list of elements of interest and the paths from the list of search conditions.

4   Composition Example

Considering the classification of tables proposed in Subsect. 3.1, the following types of queries that the user could compose using the interface were considered:

- Queries that involve one base table.
- Queries that involve two base tables.
- Queries that involve three base tables.
- Queries that involve two base tables and one M-to-N table.

To illustrate the composition of a query, consider the next query that involves two base tables directly connected:

> *Dame el número de vuelo y nombre de aerolínea de los vuelos que salen antes de las 1500 h*
> *(Give me the flight and airline name of the flights departing before 1500 h).*

As mentioned previously, this interface was customized for Spanish; thus, the relevant information for this example is presented in Spanish along with its translation to English.

It is worth noting that the user must consider three aspects to compose the query: the topic on which he/she wishes to obtain information, the specific elements of the topic that are of interest, and if the query requires the specification of search conditions.

First, the user defines the topic that the query will deal with. In this case, the topic of interest is *Vuelo de un aeropuerto a otro* (*Flight from an airport to another*), which involves table *flight*. Later, the elements of interest of the main topic are selected. In the example a flight number and airline name are required. Therefore, the node *Número de vuelo* (*Flight number*) of the root node *Vuelo de un aeropuerto a otro* (*Flight from an airport to another*) is selected. For the second element, the user should extend the node *Aerolínea* (*Airline*) and select the node *Nombre de la aerolínea* (*Airline name*).

The sample query requires to obtain information with specific conditions; therefore, the search conditions are defined. For this example, it is required that the flight departs before 1500 h, then, the node *Hora de salida* (*Departure time*) is selected from the node *Vuelo de un aeropuerto a otro* (*Flight from an airport to another*). For the selected node, it is necessary to specify the description of the comparison operator *antes de las* (*before*) and the value *1500* without the measurement unit (*hrs*). Finally, the interface will display the SQL query and its result as a table whose columns are *Número de vuelo* (*flight number*) and *Nombre de aerolínea* (*Airline name*).

5 Experimental Results

The experiments performed on the composition interface aim at measuring the ease of use in conjunction with its functionality. This is done in order to determine if the interface is friendly and functional enough to compose the queries mentioned in Sect. 4 to a complex database. For this purpose, the following parameters are measured:

- Amount of time that a user spends in composing a query.
- Number of attempts by a user to compose a query correctly.

Considering the abovementioned parameters, information can be obtained on the difficulty involved in composing a query for a specific type of query.

5.1 Description of the Experimental Setting

The experiments were conducted in a one-hour session with 17 students majoring in engineering in computer science. They were provided a user manual with one day in advance that details how the composition interface is used. The users were given a set of 20 natural language queries related to the ATIS database sorted by level of difficulty, which are separated in groups of five queries, ordered as follows:

- Queries from 1 to 5. Queries that involve one base table.
- Queries from 6 to 10. Queries that involve two base tables.
- Queries from 11 to 15. Queries that involve three base tables.

- Queries from 16 to 20. Queries that involve two base tables and one M-to-N relation table.

It is worth mentioning that the students were never provided with a diagram of the database schema nor the correct SQL statement for each query; moreover, some of them were not familiar with the domain of the database.

5.2 Results

The experimental results are shown in Table 4. These results were obtained from 20 queries composed by 17 users, discarding the attempts of queries that were not composed correctly.

Table 4. Experimental results for each query

Query No.	Attempts			Times			No. of correct compositions
	Minimum	Maximum	Average	Minimum (sec.)	Maximum (sec.)	Average (min.)	
1	1	10	2.35	42	609	2.78	17
2	1	6	1.47	43	343	1.55	17
3	1	3	1.25	27	303	1.49	16
4	1	2	1.12	31	73	0.76	17
5	1	7	1.59	28	285	1.17	17
6	1	2	1.06	24	105	0.71	17
7	1	1	1.00	20	85	0.59	16
8	1	5	2.00	24	280	1.36	17
9	1	1	1.00	27	57	0.59	17
10	1	6	2.15	41	514	2.55	13
11	1	1	1.00	34	97	0.83	17
12	1	2	1.06	39	123	0.98	16
13	1	2	1.06	46	182	1.23	16
14	1	4	1.24	24	185	0.91	17
15	1	4	1.18	55	257	1.63	17
16	1	1	1.00	19	75	0.49	17
17	1	2	1.06	31	99	0.82	17
18	1	2	1.24	26	110	0.84	17
19	1	3	1.25	25	237	1.30	16
20	1	8	4.64	90	970	6.93	11
Average			**1.48**			**1.47**	

The meaning of the columns of Table 4 is explained next. The first column indicates the number of query, the second column indicates the minimum number of attempts it took to compose the query, the third column indicates the maximum number of attempts, the fourth column shows the average number of attempts. The fifth column indicates the minimum time in seconds that was spent in composing the query, the sixth column indicates the maximum time, the seventh column shows the average time in

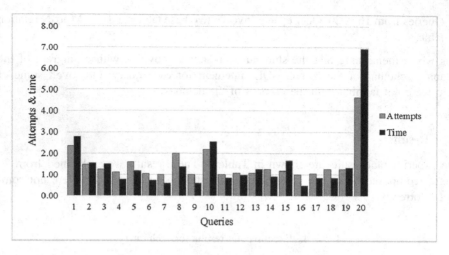

Fig. 4. Average attempts for each query

minutes; finally, the eighth column shows the number of users that were able to correctly compose the query.

As shown in the plot of Fig. 4, most of the queries could be answered by the users in one or two attempts in less than 2 min. However, for query number 1 a higher average of attempts and time occurs. This is so because it is the first query that the users must compose and they face the learning process of the operation of the interface. Later, the attempts and the average time were declining because users got used to the operation of the interface. It is important to remark that by the fourth query, the users have already learned to operate the interface.

The queries from number 4 to 19 were composed by most users in the first attempt, except for queries 8 and 10, and the average time for this set of queries was 55 s.

Query number 10 (*Dame los códigos de clase de tarifa y tipos de tarifa de temporada de la clase de servicio con rango 12 – Give me the codes of fare class and the types of season fare of the service class with rank 12*) required a larger number of attempts because the query requires that the user has more knowledge about the topic at hand.

Additionally, query number 20 has a high number of attempts because it involves a large number of tables (three base tables and one M-to-N relation table), and the required information by the query needs to be searched in the deepest levels of the composition tree.

In summary, the experiments indicate that users can compose a query of any type in about one minute with an average of approximately 1.5 attempts.

Some comments left by the users about the interface were the following: "At first, it was hard to understand how to use it. However, it became easier to use it by just using it". "It works just fine for me". "As you use it, it becomes easier to get the queries right". As noted, the comments about the interface were mostly positive and some of them confirm the conclusions drawn from the experimental results.

6 Conclusions

The experiments carried out on the composition interface show that users require to use the query composition interface a small number of times (about three) to learn how to compose queries quickly and efficiently. This is so because the interface is intuitive enough for users that do not know the schema and domain of the DB so as to allow composing queries in about one minute.

Note that a third party designed the natural language queries used in these experiments. Therefore, the interface will perform better when a user devises his/her own queries, because the user knows specifically what information he/she needs from the DB.

Table 4 shows that the average number of attempts is 1 to 2 per query and that a user takes an average of 1.47 min per query, indicating that the interface allows users to compose queries properly in a reasonable time.

One of the main aspects that enable the good performance of the interface is the use of the composition tree. This mechanism allows displaying a fragment of the database schema (specifically, the fragment of interest for each particular query), so the users can make use of several tables at once without this being a problem to compose queries. Therefore, the number of tables involved in a query does not greatly increase the difficulty of the composition of a query when using the composition tree.

In summary, the proposed interface has proven useful for the composition of queries that include three different types of tables. This is because the interface allows the user to view a section of the database schema through the composition tree, which provides information about each element of the database schema using natural language descriptions that are easy to understand.

The results in Table 4 show that from a total of 20 queries, 13 could be correctly composed by all of the 17 users. In addition, another 5 queries were composed correctly by 16 users, leaving 2 queries with 13 and 11 correct compositions respectively. This shows that most of the queries could be composed correctly by the users. Additionally, the low number of correct compositions for queries number 10 and number 20 was due to the lack of knowledge about the domain of the database by the users.

It is important to point out that 11 out of 17 users composed correctly all the queries showing that the interface can be used for composing queries by most of the users. This is remarkable considering that neither a diagram of the database schema nor the correct SQL statements were provided to the users involved in these experiments.

References

1. Chai, J., Pan, S., Zhou, M.: MIND: a context-based multimodal interpretation framework in conversational systems. In: Van Kuppevelt, J.C.J., Dybkjær, L., Bernsen, N.O. (eds.) Advances in Natural Multimodal Dialogue Systems Text, Speech and Language Technology, vol. 30, pp. 265–285. Springer, Netherlands (2005)

2. Agrawal, A., Kakde, O.: Semantic analysis of natural language queries using domain ontology for information access from database. Int. J. Intell. Syst. Appl. **5**, 81–90 (2013)
3. Pazos, R., Aguirre, M., Gonzalez, J., Carpio, J.: Features and pitfalls that users should seek in natural language interfaces to databases. In: Castillo, O., Melin, P., Pedrycz, W., Kacprzyk, J. (eds.) Studies in Computational Intelligence, vol. 547, pp. 617–630. Springer, Heidelberg (2014)
4. Pazos, R., González, J., Aguirre, M.: Semantic model for improving the performance of natural language interfaces to databases. In: Batyrshin, I., Sidorov, G. (eds.) MICAI 2011. LNCS, vol. 7094, pp. 227–290. Springer, Heidelberg (2011)
5. Zhang, G., Chu, W., Meng, F., Kong, G.: Query formulation from high-level concepts for relational databases. In: User Interfaces to Data Intensive Systems, pp. 64–74. IEEE Computer Society, Los Alamitos, CA (1999)
6. Hallet, C., Scott, D., Power, R.: Composing questions through conceptual authoring. Computational linguistics **33**(1), 105–133 (2007)
7. Pan, S., Zhou, M., Houck, K., Kissa, P.: Natural language aided visual query building for complex data access. In: 22nd Innovative Applications of Artificial Intelligence Conference (IAAI-10), pp. 1821–1826. Association for the Advancement of Artificial Intelligence, Palo Alto, CA (2010)

A Structural Pattern Mining Approach for Credit Risk Assessment

Bernardete Ribeiro[1]([envelope]), Ning Chen[2],
and Alexander Kovačec[3]

[1] CISUC, Department of Informatics Engineering, University of Coimbra,
Coimbra, Portugal
bribeiro@dei.uc.pt

[2] College of Computer Science and Technology (Software College),
Henan Polytechnic University, 2001 Century Avenue, Jiaozuo 454003, Henan,
People's Republic of China
nchenyx@outlook.com

[3] Department of Mathematics, University of Coimbra, Coimbra, Portugal
kovacec@mat.uc.pt

Abstract. In recent years graph mining took a valuable step towards harnessing the problem of efficient discovery of substructures in complex input data that do not fit into the usual data mining models. A graph is a general and powerful data representation formalism, which found widespread application in many scientific fields. Finding subgraphs capable of compressing data by abstracting instances of the substructures and identifying interesting patterns is thus crucial. When it comes to financial settings, data is very complex and in particular when risk factors relationships are not taken into account it seriously affects the goodness of predictions. In this paper, we posit that risk analysis can be leveraged if structure can be taken into account by discovering financial motifs in the input graphs. We use gBoost which learns from graph data using a mathematical linear programming procedure combined with a substructure mining algorithm. An algorithm is proposed which has shown to be efficient to extract graph structure from feature vector data. Furthermore, we empirically show that the graph-mining model is competitive with state-of-the-art machine learning approaches in terms of classification accuracy without increase in the computational cost.

Keywords: Graph mining · Classification · Financial applications

1 Introduction

Nowadays, data is naturally structured in form of trees or graphs, which are structures that may convey important information. The awareness of big data together with the poor understanding of the processes that generate data has enforced techniques to extract frequent structural patterns from such data [1]. Graph mining techniques are sought for a class of problems lying on the crossroads of several research topics including graph theory, data sensing, data mining and data visualization.

© Springer International Publishing Switzerland 2015
E. Onieva et al. (Eds.): HAIS 2015, LNAI 9121, pp. 73–84, 2015.
DOI: 10.1007/978-3-319-19644-2_7

Graphs are very important mathematical structures that can represent information in many real world domains such as chemistry, biology and, web and text processing. Examples are protein interactions and phylogenetic trees [2], molecular graphs [3], computer networks [4], hypertextual and XML documents, social networks, mobile call networks, among other important data [5].

Pattern mining takes essentially two approaches: statistical learning and structural. In the statistical learning, patterns are represented by feature vectors $\mathbf{x} = (x_1, \cdots, x_n) \in \mathbb{R}^n$ of n measurements. It has two main drawbacks: first, the vectors uphold a predefined set of features, despite the size and complexity of the objects they represent; second, the binary relationships among (parts of) objects cannot be captured. The above pitfalls, size constraints and lack of ability to represent relationships, might prevent to expose better models. In the structural approach, patterns are represented by graphs that can overcome above limitations with their inherent structure. Yet the complexity increases, for instance, it takes exponential time for finding the isomorphism between two graphs while linear time is needed for the similarity of two features vectors [6].

In this paper, in the settings of a financial risk analysis problem we take a structural pattern mining approach. We propose a graph construction algorithm on the basis of a qualitative data set of financial statements to gain further insights on the data structure, and then a graph-based model for pattern mining is generated via gBoost [7], a frequent subgraph discovery technique on the grounds of mathematical programming and gSpan algorithm [8]. This pattern-growth method uses Dept-First Search (DFS) and is able to find financial motifs in the graph data rendering the risk estimation very successful. We empirically show that the performance evaluation is competitive to the statistical learning algorithms such as Naive Bayes, Decision Trees and Support Vector Machines when unstructured dimensional feature vectors are used, without a substantial increase in the computational cost. Our case study encompasses a graph-based methodology that enables to unravel structural subtleties otherwise hidden in the data.

In the next section we will review the literature and background for the work. The graph classification model is explained in detail in Sect. 3. In Sect. 4 an algorithm is proposed for extracting graphs from feature vectors aiming at gathering the graph data. In the context of financial credit risk, we present in Sect. 5 the experiments including the research design and discussion of results. The paper will end with the conclusions and future work in Sect. 6.

2   Related Work

2.1   Financial Credit Risk Assessment

The financial credit risk indicates the risk associated with financing, in other words, a borrower cannot pay the lenders, or goes into default. Accordingly, financial credit risk assessment intends to solve the problem stated as follows: given a number of companies labeled as bad / good credit or bankrupt / healthy, and a set of financial variables that describe the situation of a company over a given period, predict the probability that the company may belong to a high risk group or become bankrupt during the following years.

In the literature, a wide range of methods that can be divided into parametric methods, semi-parametric methods, and non-parametric methods have approached this problem from the viewpoint of model structure specification. Parametric methods (mainly referred to statistical methods) specify definitely the model structure and modeled process. Non-parametric methods that includes Artificial Neural Networks (ANNs), Fuzzy Set Theory (FST), Decision Trees (DTs), Case-Based Reasoning (CBR), Support Vector Machines (SVMs), Rough Set Theory (RST) among other intelligent methods, determine the model structure from the data. Semi-parametric methods define the modeled process with flexible structure [9,10].

When dealing with real world financial credit risk problems, there are usually characterized by large scale of data and high-dimensional representation. The key financial ratios comprise financial information (operational performance, financial liquidity, risk return, sustainable growth etc.) and non-financial information (government policy, economic environment marking reports, customers screening etc.) [11]. These performance key indicators are well fit to establish the relationships between nodes of financial companies.

Although many successful approaches have been used rarely the structural component has been endorsed in the literature review. It becomes important to provide structural performance data mining techniques in financial domain where a large-scale complex data is produced today.

2.2   Graph-Based Pattern Mining

Graph classification can be investigated from two perspectives: graph classification (between graph) and vertex classification (within graph). In the former we aim at classifying individual graphs and in the latter we are interested in the classification of individual vertices within a graph. Either way, our focus is to find non-trivial characteristics (e.g. pattern subgraphs) that can determine class membership, that is, to assign a class label.

Classification of graphs has many applications. An obvious example are molecular structures that can be represented by graphs and classification is used to predict properties of molecules such as toxicity [3]. Another example comprises computer network traffic where the problem representation is embedded in graphs. Network traffic traces can represent the network behavior exposing better visual and structural differences among nodes and capturing many interesting patterns of node interactions [4].

Graph-based pattern mining took a new breed of approaches since the introduction of frequent pattern mining in [12]. In particular, many subgraph mining algorithms have been developed such as Apriori based methods like AGM [13], FSG [14], or pattern-growth methods like gSpan [8] and Gaston [15]. A major challenge in subgraph mining is the subgraph isomorphism, which is an NP-complete problem [8]. In gSpan, Dept-First Search (DFS) is employed to reduce the search space significantly making possible to check whether between two graphs an isomorphism exists. Its purpose is to enumerate all connected frequent subgraphs from graph representation of patterns. gBoost [7] is an extension of boosting for graphs which uses gSpan. Apart from the mathematical graph theory based approaches, a few other can be considered for graph mining such as: greedy search-based approaches, inductive programming logic and inductive database approaches.

3   gBoost Classifier

gBoost [7] is an extension of boosting for graphs and comprises a mathematical programming tool [16] that progressively collects "informative" frequent patterns to use as features for classification and regression. Furthermore, this tool uses linear program (LP) approaches to boosting providing an efficient solution using LPBoost, a column generation based simplex method [16]. The problem is formulated as if all possible weak hypotheses had already been generated, where the labels produced by the weak hypotheses become the new feature space of the problem. The boosting consists of constructing a learning function in the label space that minimizes misclassification error and maximizes the soft margin.

It is also considered a frequent subgraph mining technique similar to gSpan in frequent subgraph mining [8]. gBoost uses first gSpan method [8] which finds frequent subgraphs and constructs a canonical search space in the form of a Depth-First Search (DFS) which is an algorithm for traversing or searching tree or graph data structures. With the proviso for achieving an optimal search the tree structure and the DFS code are necessary.

Let $\{g_t\}_{t=1}^{T}$ denote a set of frequent subgraphs generated from gSpan. Given the learning graphs $\{(G_n, y_n)\}_{n=1}^{N}$ where G_n is a training graph and $y_n \in \{+1, -1\}$ is the associated class label. Let $\mathcal{T}$ the set of all patterns (subgraphs) included in at least one training graph. Each graph G_n can be encoded as a $|\mathcal{T}|$ dimensional vector $\mathbf{x}_n$ through an indicator function $\mathcal{I}(\cdot)$ as indicated below:

$$\mathbf{x}_{n,t} = \mathcal{I}(t \subseteq G_n) \ \forall t \in \mathcal{T} \tag{1}$$

The hypotheses or individual stumps are defined as:

$$h(\mathbf{x}_n, g_t) = \begin{cases} +1 \ \text{if} g_t \in \mathbf{x}_n \\ -1 \ \text{if} g_t \notin \mathbf{x}_n \end{cases} \tag{2}$$

where we simplified the notation for $\mathbf{x}_n$. Given training data $\{(\mathbf{x}_n, y_n)\}_{n=1}^{N}$ directly solving the optimization problem is intractable. Therefore, the equivalent dual problem below is solved instead which can be expressed as follows:

$$\begin{aligned} &\underset{\alpha,\gamma}{\text{minimize}} && \gamma \\ &\text{subject to} && \sum_{n=1}^{N} \lambda_n y_n h(\mathbf{x}_n, g_t) \leq \gamma \ \ s = 1, 2, \cdots, T \\ & && \sum_{n=1}^{N} \lambda_n = 1, 0 \leq \lambda_n \leq D \ \ s = 1, 2, \cdots, T, \end{aligned} \tag{3}$$

where $D = \frac{1}{cN}, c \in (0,1)$ is the cost classification parameter controlling the misclassification errors [7,16]. After solving the dual optimization problem, the primal solution α is obtained from the Lagrange multipliers. It has a limited number of variables and an intractably number of constraints. Therefore, gBoost algorithm uses a methodology based on the column generation [17]. The algorithm sets up a maximum number of columns to add at each iteration. Then rather than considering all the constraints, the subgraph g_s whose corresponding constraint is violated the most is selected. At the k iteration the constraints are formulated as

$$\sum_{n=1}^{N} \lambda_n^{(k)} y_n h(\mathbf{x}_n, gt) \leq \gamma^{(k)}, \ t \in \mathcal{T}^{(k)} \tag{4}$$

As defined aboveAs defined above $\mathcal{T}$ gathers the index number of the selected subgraphs. At the start of this procedure, $\mathcal{T}^{(0)}$ is set to empty and $\alpha_n(0) = \frac{1}{N}$. Following, the optimal solutions $\alpha_n^{(k)}$ and $\gamma^{(k)}$ for solving the restricted dual optimization problem are updated iteratively. In the sequel, the subgraph that violates the constraint the most (corresponding to the largest margin) is selected:

$$t^* = \arg\max_{t=1,2,\cdots,T} \sum_{n=1}^{N} \lambda_n^{(k)} y_n h(\mathbf{x}_n, g_t) \tag{5}$$

The set $\mathcal{T}^{(k)}$ is updated by adding the new index number $t^* : \mathcal{T}^{(k+1)} = \mathcal{T}^{(k)} \cup \{t^*\}$.

The iterative procedure proceeds until the criteria based on the satisfaction of all constraints are met. For a specific test graph $\mathbf{x}$ the prediction rule is a convex combination of simple classification stumps $h(\mathbf{x}, g_t)$ and takes the form:

$$y = \text{sign} \left(\sum_{t \in \mathcal{T}^{(K)}} \alpha_t h(\mathbf{x}, g_t) \right) \tag{6}$$

A test graph is labeled in the positive class if $y = 1$ and in the negative class if $y = -1$.

4   Graph Construction Algorithm

The algorithm to build the graph data takes feature vectors from the data collection and constructs graphs to be used as inputs in the gBoost classifier. The main focus is to set up the nodes and edges for the data, running over all the data samples in the dataset. Depending on the problem the relationships between nodes should be taken into account for setting up the edges to link the nodes among graph 'points'.

The proposed algorithm is presented in Algorithm 1 and will be used in the next section with the benchmark qualitative data. We have coded the algorithm in Matlab for easiness of use with gBoost package. Each sample of the data is a graph with a set of nodes corresponding to the features in the feature dimensional space. The edges are assigned during graph construction and represent the relationships between nodes. The graph samples are connected, undirected and labeled graphs. The overall graph data samples were further partitioned to find the training and test graphs for further use in the gBoost classifier.

More specifically, the algorithm cycles over the N rows of the feature dimensional vectors matrix data, assigns the nodes of each graph and updates the edges as shown in Algorithm 1. The assessment of the gBoost classifier has been performed with the classification accuracy and test AUC performance metrics.

Algorithm 1. Graph Construction from Feature Vector Data

Input: For each collection of data $\mathcal{D}$, $\mathcal{X} = \{x_1, \cdots, x_n\}$ with labels
$\{y_n \in \{+1, -1\} \quad n = 1, 2, \cdots N\}$
/*Cycle over N rows*/
for all $n \leftarrow 1, \cdots, N$ **do**
    Initializations
    /* Cycle over the first row */
    for all $j \leftarrow 1, \cdots, NumNodes - 1$ **do**
        Detects the transition of weights
        Update Edges
    end for
    Makes the connection with last element of index array
    /* Find Dangling Nodes in the Graph */
    if *Dangling Nodes exist* **then**
        Find the node closest Weight Distance
        Adjust Weight Connections
    end if
    /* Find disconnected Components in the graph */
    if *Subgraphs remain to be connected* **then**
        Connect subgraphs
    end if
end for**Output**: Get connected learning graphs $\{(G_n, y_n)\}_{n=1}^{N}$ where G_n is a training graph and $y_n \in \{+1, -1\}$ is the associated class label

---

In the next section we will present the experimental setting, describe the research design including the dataset, the evaluation metrics and the empirical analysis.

5 Experiments

5.1 Dataset

The Qualitative Bankruptcy (QB) dataset can be download from https://archive.ics.uci.edu/ml/datasets/Qualitative_Bankruptcy. The attributes and samples of the dataset are from [18] where a rule-based approach was presented.

Table 1. QB Dataset: the attributes are qualitative (Positive, Average, Negative) and the assigned class is (B, NB).

	Financial indicators	Qualitative attributes
1	Industrial risk	{P,A,N}
2	Management risk	{P,A,N}
3	Financial flexibility	{P,A,N}
4	Credibility	{P,A,N}
5	Competitiveness	{P,A,N}
6	Operating risk	{P,A,N}
7	Class	{B,NB}

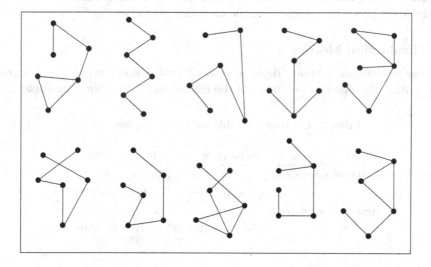

Fig. 1. Motifs for 6 node graph financial samples.

The sample size is 250 and the number of attributes is 6 each corresponding to Qualitative Parameters in Bankruptcy, namely, Industrial Risk, Management Risk, Financial Flexibility, Credibility, Competitiveness, and Operating Risk. The attribute information is nominal (P-Positive, A-Average, N-Negative) and there are two classes (B-Bankruptcy, NB-Non-Bankruptcy). The dataset is unbalanced being composed by 143 samples pertaining to the class NB and 107 samples pertaining to the class B. We assigned B to the positive class and NB to the negative class. The dataset is briefly described in Table 1. For example, sample #1 = (P, P, A, A, A, P) is assigned to class B while sample #250 = (P, N, N, N, A, A) pertains to the other class NB.

After running the Algorithm 1 we built the training data $train_G$ with 143 graphs for training and the test data $test_G$ with 107 graphs for test with identical distribution of positive and negative samples as in the whole original dataset. Each graph has 6 nodes. For easiness of handling the data we decided to assign a corresponding weight to each qualitative value (for example, we assigned 2 to Positive, 1 to Average and 3 to Negative). From the labels of the qualitative data set (B, NB) we assigned the label $(+1, -1)$ to the positive and negative class, respectively, for use in the gBoost algorithm. According to the partition in train and test we, respectively, built the label vectors $train_Y$ and $test_Y$ with the same size as the train and test graph samples.

5.2 Financial Motifs

In Fig. 1 examples of data samples found in the qualitative data are represented for better illustration of the financial motifs built by the graph construction algorithm. These motifs are 6 node graphs (each node is an attribute of the qualitative data illustrated in Table 1) that play a decision role on the overall classification procedure influencing the classifier prediction.

5.3 Evaluation Metrics

In order to evaluate a binary decision task we first define a contingency matrix representing the possible outcomes of the classification, as shown in Table 2.

Table 2. Contingency table for binary classification.

	Class positive	Class negative
Assigned positive	tp	fp
	(True positives)	(False positives)
Assigned negative	fn	tn
	(False negatives)	(True negatives)

Several measures have been defined based on the contingency Table 2, such as, error rate ($\frac{fp+fn}{tp+fp+tn+fn}$), accuracy $\frac{tp+tn}{tp+fn+fp+tn}$ which measures the overall effectiveness of a classifier and AUC (Area Under the Curve)$\frac{1}{2}\left(\frac{tp}{tp+fn} + \frac{tn}{tn+fp}\right)$ which captures the classifier's capability to avoid false classification.

AUC captures a single point on the Reception Operating Characteristic (ROC) curve. It is also known as ROC curve, and is a graphical plot that illustrates the performance of a binary classifier system as its discrimination threshold is varied. Plotting the true positive rate against the false positive rate at various threshold settings creates the curve. AUC is sometimes referred as balanced accuracy.

5.4 Empirical Analysis

In this section we present several algorithms spanning over machine learning and data mining methods using the open source Weka Toolbox[1].

---

[1] http://www.cs.waikato.ac.nz/ml/weka/ [19].

Support Vector Machines (SVMs) belong to the maximum margin classifiers aiming to find an optimal separating hyperplane, which maximizes the margin between two classes of data in kernel, induced feature space. SVMs use the structural risk minimization principle to avoid overfitting. Since the introduction to the area of financial risk analysis [20], SVMs have gained wide popularity owing to the good generalization on a small amount of high-dimensional data [21]. Apart from SVM, we also used Neural Networks, Naive Bayes, Decision Trees, fuzzy grid, and random committee for comparison. J48 constructs a decision tree well adapted to the training data and then prunes the tree structure to avoid over-fitting. Naive Bayes (NB) estimates the probability of each class under the assumption of feature independence. Multi-Level Perceptron (MLP) and RBF network are artificial neural networks for machine learning. The former is a multi-layer, feed-forward neural network, trained iteratively to adjust the connection weights via back-propagation algorithm. The latter has only one hidden layer, each node of which implements a normalized Gaussian radial basis function with the center and width as parameters. Fuzzy grid method partitions the input and output data into grids and extracts the fuzzy rules for data classification. Random committee builds an ensemble of randomized base classifiers to improve the classification accuracy. Since we are interested to compare the two categories of methods - unstructured versus structured - the model selection for each case was not so important. Therefore, we let the default parameters in all the algorithms tested.

Table 3. Classifier methods vs Accuracy ratio (%)

Classifier method	Accuracy ratio (%)	Classifier method	Accuracy ratio (%)
SVM	98.13	MLP	93.46
Naive Bayes	93.46	RBF	97.19
J48	95.32	Fuzzy grid	96.26
gBoost	98.13	Rand committee	96.26

In Table 3 the performance accuracy of various machine learning methods including SVM, J48, Naive Bayes and neural networks (Multi-Layer Perceptron (MLP) and radial Basis Functions (RBF)), fuzzy grid, and random committee are illustrated. The gBoost outperforms neural networks, decision trees and many other machine learning algorithms, while showing competitive performance as compared to SVM.

The test ROC AUC for gBoost found was 99.06 (see Fig. 3) while for the SVM the test ROC AUC was 98.1. Although these are preliminary results graph mining can boost classification in this financial setting via a small size dataset with low dimensionality. In the prediction phase the algorithm takes a test graph $\mathbf{x}$ and outputs a classification result as indicated in Eq. 6 by the convex combination of simple classification stumps $h(\mathbf{x}, g_t)$.

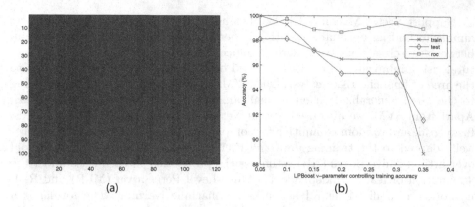

(a)   (b)

Fig. 2. (a) Graph test data $test_G$; (b) ν parameter controlling training accuracy.

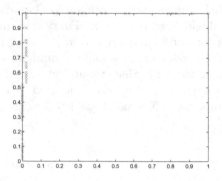

Fig. 3. ROC curve

For gBoost, the maximum pattern size, which in our case corresponds to the maximum number of nodes in a subgraph, was constrained up to 6, since we have 6 attributes defining the financial indicators. The regularization parameter ν is chosen from $\{0.05, 0.1, 0.15, 0.2, 0.25, 0.3, 0.35\}$.

In Fig. 2 results from running gBoost on the dataset are illustrated (a) Graph Test Data $test_G$ and (b) performance of gBoost by varying ν parameter controlling training accuracy. This parameter is used in the graph optimization process LPBoost for finding frequent subgraphs [16]. The convergence tolerance ϵ used in the runs was set to 0.05. For a short range of the parameter ν the results are encouraging and outperform well-known classifier methods as illustrated in Table 3.

The classification algorithm gBoost takes into account the structure embedding information that is advantageous as compared to the traditional two-dimensional feature vectors framework. As such, it incorporates relations among the entities that integrate extra knowledge capable of better models, which fosters the goodness of predictions.

6   Conclusion and Future Work

The combination of the formalism of graphs with a powerful frequent pattern mining algorithm such as gBoost evidenced that the structure is able to effectively capture knowledge essential to attain good predictions in financial settings.

In this work we developed an algorithm for graph construction on the grounds of the binary relationships found on qualitative data from a credit risk problem. Furthermore we used gBoost classifier to mine specific sampled graphs that are able to predict the samples category in either bankrupt or non-bankrupt. The structure pattern mining methodology can be simply extended to other kind of data.

Despite the myriad of statistical learning models able to tackle this problem we empirically showed that by using structural approaches the performance results can be enhanced in particular if graphs to cast data are carefully built.

Future work will trace the performance of this approach while spanning over the historic data in a real-world data set. Another future issue will be to check the scalability to large graph data.

References

1. Martino, G.D.S., Sperduti, A.: Mining structured data. IEEE Comput. Intell. Mag. **5**(1), 42–49 (2010)
2. Pimentel, C., Van Der Straeten, D., Pires, E., Faro, C., Rodrigues-Pousada, C.: Characterization and expression analysis of the aspartic protease gene family of cynara cardunculus l. FEBS J. **274**(10), 2523–2539 (2007)
3. Borgelt, C., Berthold, M.: Mining molecular fragments: finding relevant substructures of molecules. In: Proceedings of the IEEE International Conference on Data Mining, ICDM 2002, pp. 51–58, December 2002
4. Iliofotou, M., Pappu, P., Faloutsos, M., Mitzenmacher, M., Singh, S., Varghese, G.: Network monitoring using traffic dispersion graphs (tdgs). In: Dovrolis, C., Roughan, M. (eds.) Internet Measurement Conference, pp. 315–320. ACM (2007)
5. Saigo, H., Uno, T., Tsuda, K.: Mining complex genotypic features for predicting HIV-1 drug resistance. Bioinformatics **23**(18), 2455–2462 (2007)
6. Bunke, H., Riesen, K.: Recent advances in graph-based pattern recognition with applications in document analysis. Pattern Recogn. **44**(5), 1057–1067 (2011)
7. Saigo, H., Nowozin, S., Kadowaki, T., Kudo, T., Tsuda, K.: gBoost: a mathematical programming approach to graph classification and regression. Mach. Learn. **75**(1), 69–89 (2009)
8. Yan, X., Han, J.: gspan: graph based substructure pattern mining. In: IEEE International Conference on Data Mining, Maebashi City, Japan, pp. 721–724, December 2002
9. Cheng, K.F., Chu, C.K., Hwang, R.: Predicting bankruptcy using the discrete-time semi-parametric hazard model. Quant. Finance **10**(9), 1055–1066 (2010)
10. Hwang, R.C., Chung, H., Chu, C.K.: Predicting issuer credit ratings using a semiparametric method. J. Empirical Finance. **17**(1), 120–137 (2010)
11. Ribeiro, B., Silva, C., Chen, N., Vieira, A., das Neves, J.C.: Predicting issuer credit ratings using a semiparametric method. Expert Syst. Appl. **39**, 10140–10152 (2012)

12. Agrawal, R., Imielinski, T., Swami, A.: Mining association rules between sets of items in large databases. In: Proceedings of the 1993 ACM SIGMOD International Conference on Management of Data, SIGMOD 1993, pp. 207–216. ACM Press, New York, NY, USA(1993)

13. Inokuchi, A., Washio, T., Motoda, H.: An apriori-based algorithm for mining frequent substructures from graph data. In: Zighed, D.A., Komorowski, J., Żytkow, J.M. (eds.) PKDD 2000. LNCS (LNAI), vol. 1910, pp. 13–23. Springer, Heidelberg (2000)

14. Kuramochi, M., Karypis, G.: Frequent subgraph discovery. In: Proceedings of the IEEE International Conference on Data Mining, ICDM 2001, pp. 313–320 (2001)

15. Nijssen, S., Kok, J.N.: The Gaston tool for frequent subgraph mining. Electron. Notes Theor. Comput. Sci. **127**(1), 77–87 (2005). Proceedings of the International Workshop on Graph-Based Tools (GraBaTs 2004) Graph-Based Tools 2004

16. Demiriz, A., Bennett, K.P., Shawe-Taylor, J.: Linear programming boosting via column generation. Mach. Learning **46**(1–3), 225–254 (2002)

17. Luenberger, D.G.: Optimization by Vector Space Methods Decision and Control. Wiley, New York (1969)

18. Kim, M.J., Han, I.: The discovery of experts' decision rules from qualitative bankruptcy data using genetic algorithms. Expert Syst. Appl. **25**(4), 637–646 (2003)

19. Hall, M., Frank, E., Holmes, G., Pfahringer, B., Reutemann, P., Witten, I.H.: The weka data mining software: an update. SIGKDD Explor. newsl. **11**(1), 10–18 (2009)

20. Min, J.H., Lee, Y.C.: Bankruptcy prediction using support vector machine with optimal choice of kernel function parameters. Expert Syst. Appl. **28**(4), 603–614 (2005)

21. Yang, Z., You, W., Ji, G.: Using partial least squares and support vector machines for bankruptcy prediction. Expert Syst. Appl. **38**(7), 8336–8342 (2011)

Video and Image Analysis

A Novel Technique for Human Face Recognition Using Fractal Code and Bi-dimensional Subspace

Benouis Mohamed[⊠]

Computer Science Department, University of Oran, Oran, Algeria
mhbenouis@yahoo.com

Abstract. Face recognition is considered as one of the best biometric methods used for human identification and verification; this is because of its unique features that differ from one person to another, and its importance in the security field. This paper proposes an algorithm for face recognition and classification using a system based on WPD, fractal codes and two-dimensional subspace for feature extraction, and Combined Learning Vector Quantization and PNN Classifier as Neural Network approach for classification. This paper presents a new approach for extracted features and face recognition. Fractal codes which are determined by a fractal encoding method are used as feature in this system. Fractal image compression is a relatively recent technique based on the representation of an image by a contractive transform for which the fixed point is close to the original image. Each fractal code consists of five parameters such as corresponding domain coordinates for each range block. Brightness offset and an affine transformation. The proposed approach is tested on ORL and FEI face databases. Experimental results on this database demonstrated the effectiveness of the proposed approach for face recognition with high accuracy compared with previous methods.

Keywords: Biometric · Face recognition · 2DPCA · 2DLDA · DWT · PNN · WPD · IFS · Fractal codes · LVQ

1 Introduction

The security of persons, goods or information is one of the major concerns of the modern societies. Face recognition is one of the most commonly used solutions to perform automatic identification of persons. However, automatic face recognition should consider several factors that contribute to the complexity of this task such as the occultation, changes in lighting, pose, expression and structural components (hair, beard, glasses, etc.) [1].

Several techniques have been proposed in the past in order to solve face recognition problems. Each of them evidently has their strengths and weaknesses, which, in most of the cases, depend on the conditions of acquiring information. Recently, several efforts and research in this domain have been done in order to increase the performance of the recognition, such as support vector machine (SVM), Markov hidden model (HMM), probabilistic methods (Bayesian networks) and artificial neural networks. This latter

© Springer International Publishing Switzerland 2015
E. Onieva et al. (Eds.): HAIS 2015, LNAI 9121, pp. 87–98, 2015.
DOI: 10.1007/978-3-319-19644-2_8

has attracted researchers because of its effectiveness in detection and classification of shapes, which has been adopted in new face recognition systems [2].

2 Face Recognition System

A face recognition system is a system used for the identification and verification of individuals, which checks if a person belongs to the system's database, and identifies him/her if this is the case.

The methods used in face recognition based on 2D images are divided into three categories: global, local and hybrid methods.

- Local or analytical facial features approaches. This type consists on applying transformations in specific locations of the image, most frequently around the features points (corners of the eyes, mouth, nose,). They therefore require a prior knowledge of the images…
- Global approaches use the entire surface of the face as a source of information without considering the local characteristics such as eyes, mouth, etc.
- Hybrid methods associate the advantages of global and local methods by combining the detection of geometrical characteristics (or structural) with the extraction of local appearance characteristics.

This article is organized as follows: Basic notions concerning Two-dimensional subspace, wavelet transform theory are provided in Sect. 2. Fractal codes features are presented in Sect. 3. Feature vectors results from two-dimensional subspaces is applied to a Combined LVQ and PNN classifier are described in Sect. 4. Section 5 provides face recognition system based on PNN, LVQ, the experimental results and Comparison between the serval's types of features obtained using WPD, DWT, IFS, 2DPCA and 2DLDA. A comparison with other approaches is also done in Sect. 6. Conclusion and future works are presented in Sect. 7.

2.1 Two-Dimensional Principal Component Approach Analysis (2DPCA)

Proposed by Yang in 2004 [3], 2DPCA is a method of feature extraction and dimensionality reduction based on Principal Component Analysis (PCA) that deals directly with face images as matrices without having to turn them into vectors like as the traditional global approach.

2.2 The Steps of Face Recognition by 2DPCA

Considering a training set S of N face images, the idea of this technique is to project a matrix X of size (n × m) via a linear transformation like that:

$$Y_i = X . R_i \tag{1}$$

where Y_i is the principal component vector of size (n × 1), and R_i is the base projection vector of size (m × 1). The optimal vector R_i of the projection is obtained by maximizing the total generalized variance criterion

$$J(R) = R^T . G_t . R \tag{2}$$

Where G_t is the covariance matrix of size (m × m) given by:

$$G_t = \frac{1}{M} \sum_{j=1}^{M} (X_j - \bar{X})^T (X_j - \bar{X}) \tag{3}$$

With X_j: The jth image of the training set
$\bar{X}$: The average image of all the images in the training set.

$$\bar{X} = \frac{1}{M} \sum_{j=1}^{M} X_j \tag{4}$$

In general, one optimal projection axis is not enough. We must select a set of projection axes like:

$$\{R_1, R_2, \ldots, R_d\} = arg\, max\, J(R) \tag{5}$$

$$R_i^T . R_j = 0,\ i \neq j,\ i, j = 1, \ldots, d$$

These axes are the eigenvectors of the covariance matrix corresponding to the largest "d" Eigenvalues. The extraction of characteristics of an image using 2DPCA is as follows

$$Y_k = X . R_k\ ; k = 1 \ldots d \tag{6}$$

Where $[R_1, R_2, \ldots \ldots, R_d]$ is the projection matrix and $[Y_1, Y_2, \ldots \ldots, Y_d]$ is the features matrix of the image X.

2.3   The 2DLDA Approach

In 2004, Li and Yuan [4] have proposed a new two-dimensional LDA approach. The main difference between 2DLDA and the classic LDA is in the data representation model. Classic LDA is based on the analysis of vectors, while the 2DLDA algorithm is based on the analysis of matrices.

2.4   Face Recognition Using 2D LDA

Let X be a vector of the n-dimensional unitary columns. The main idea of this approach is to project the random image matrix of size $(m \times n)$ on X by the following linear transformation:

$$Y_i = A_j X \qquad (7)$$

Y: the m-dimensional feature vector of the projected image A.

Let us suppose L: class numbers.

M: The total number of training images

The training image is represented by a matrix $m \times n A_j (j = 1, \ldots, M)$

$\bar{A}_i$ (i = 1...L): The mean of all classes

N_i: Number of samples in each class

The optimal vector projection is selected as a matrix with orthonormal columns that maximizes the ratio of the determinant of the dispersion matrix of the projected inter-class images to the determinant of the dispersion matrix of the projected intra-class images;

$$J_{FLD}(X_{opt}) = \arg\max_W \frac{|X^T S_b X|}{|X^T S_w X|} \qquad (8)$$

$$P_b = \text{trace}(S_b)$$

$$P_w = \text{trace}(S_w)$$

The unitary vector X maximizing J(X) is called the optimal projection axis. The optimal projection is chosen when X_{OPT} maximizes the criterion, as the following equation:

$$X_{OPT} = argmax_X J(X) \qquad (9)$$

If S_W is invertible, the solution of optimization is to solve the generalized eigenvalue problem.

$$S_b X_{opt} = \lambda S_W X_{opt} \qquad (10)$$

Like that λ is the maximum Eigenvalues of $S_W^{-1} S_b$.

In general, it is not enough to have only one optimal projection axis. We need to select a set of projection axes, $x_1, x_2, \ldots, x_d$ under the following constraints:

$$\{x_1, x_2, \ldots, x_d\} = argmax_X J(X) \qquad (11)$$

Indeed, the optimal projection axes $x_1, x_2, \ldots, x_d$ are orthonormal eigenvectors of $S_W^{-1} S_b$ corresponding to the best first "d" eigenvalues permitting to create a new projection matrix X, which is a matrix of size $n \times d : X = [x_1, x_2, \ldots, x_d]$.

We will use the 2DLDA optimal projection vectors $x_1, x_2, \ldots, x_d$ to extract the image features; we use the Eq. (8).

3 Discrete Wavelet Transform

Discrete wavelet transform (DWT) is a well-known signal processing field tool; it is widely used in feature extraction and compression and de-noising applications.

The discrete wavelet transform has been used in various face recognition studies. The main advantage of the wavelet transform over the Fourier transform is the time-scale location. Mallat [6] shows that the DWT may be implemented using a filters bank including a low-pass filter (PB) and a high-pass filter (PH).

Discrete Wavelet Package Decomposition (D-WPD) is a wavelet transform where signal is passed through more filters that the Discrete Wavelet Transform (DWT). In the DWT, each level is calculated by passing only the previous approximation coefficients through low and high pass filters. However in the D-WPD, both the detail and approximation coefficients are decomposed [5, 6] (Fig. 1).

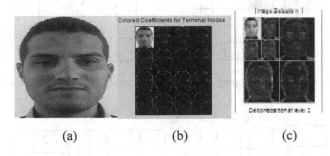

(a)   (b)   (c)

Fig. 1. Wavelet decomposition at different levels (a) Original image (b) 2-level wavelet decomposition using WPD (c) 2-levels wavelet decomposition using DWT

4 Fractal Theory Codes

Fractal theory of iterated contractive transformation has been used in several areas of image processing and computer vision. In this method, similarity between different parts of an image is used for representing of an image by a set of contractive transforms on the space of images, for which the fixed point is close to the original image. This concept was first proposed by Barnsley [7, 8]. Jacquin was the first to publish an implementation of fractal image coding in [9]. Despite the number of researchers and the proposed methods, several factors can significantly affect face recognition performances, such as the pose, the presence/absence of structural components, facial expressions, occlusion, and illumination variations. Different image compression methods have been focused for a long time to reduce this massive information, but fractal image compression is a relatively recent technique based on representation of an image by contractive transforms, for which the fixed point is close to original image.

Suppose we are dealing with a 64*64 binary image in which each pixel can have on of 256 levels (ranging from black to white). Let R_1, R2,....., R_{256} be 4*4 non-overlapping sub-squares of the image (range blocks); and let D be the collection of all 8*8 pixel overlapping sub-squares of the image (Domain blocks) as depicted in Fig. 2.

The collection D contains 57*57 = 3249 squares. For each R block, search through all of D blocks a $D_i \in D$ which minimizes Eq. (11). There 8 ways to map one square onto another. Each square can be rotated to 4 orientations or flipped and rotated into 4 other orientations as shown in Fig. 3 having 8 different affine transformations means comparing 8*3249 = 25992 domain squares with each of the 256 range squares (Fig. 2).

$$collage\, Error = min\|R_i - w(D_i)\|^2 \tag{12}$$

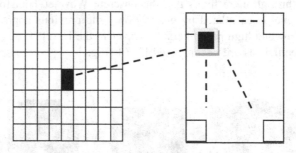

Fig. 2. One of the block mapping in partitioned function systems representation (IFS)

1	2
3	4

4	3
2	1

3	4
1	2

2	1
4	3

4	2
3	1

2	4
1	3

3	1
4	2

1	3
2	4

Fig. 3. Eight different affine transformations

As mentioned before, a D_i block has 4 times as many pixels as an R_i, so we must either sub-sample (choose 1 from each 2*2 sub-square of D_i) or average the 2*2 sub-squares corresponding to each pixel of R when we minimize Eq. (12). Minimizing equation means two things. First it means finding a good choice for Di second, it means finding a good contrast and brightness setting S_i and O_i for W_i. In Eq. (11)

$$w_i \begin{bmatrix} x \\ y \\ z \end{bmatrix} = \begin{bmatrix} a_i & b_i & 0 \\ c_i & d_i & 0 \\ 0 & 0 & s_i \end{bmatrix} \begin{bmatrix} x \\ y \\ z \end{bmatrix} + \begin{bmatrix} c_i \\ f_i \\ o_i \end{bmatrix} \tag{13}$$

A choice of D_i, along with a corresponding S_i and O_i determines a map W_i. The type of image partitioning used for the range blocks can be so different. A wide variety of partitions have been investigated, the majority being composed of rectangular blocks. Different types of range block partitioning were described in [10, 11]. In this research we used the simplest possible range partition consists of the size square blocks, that is called fixed size square blocks (FSSB) partitioning. The procedure for finding a fractal model for a given image is called encoding; compression; or searching for a fractal image representation. After finding the best match, fractal elements which of 6 real numbers (a, b, c, d, e, f) are selected as follows. (a, b, c, d) are (x, y) coordinates of the D block and its corresponding R block respectively. (e) is the index of affine transformation that makes the best match. (it is a number between 1 and 8), (f) is the intensity is a number between 0 and 256 (Fig. 4).

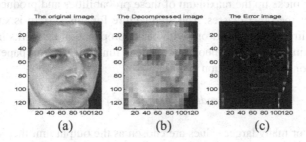

Fig. 4. Decoding algorithm results (IFS) (a) Original image (b) Decoded image after 8 iteration for N = 8 (c) The error image

In this paper, fractal code is introduced in order to extract the face features from the normalized face image based WPD. After fractal coding, where each domain is compared with all regions of the image, we obtain a set of transformations which can approximate the face image. Each transformation is represented by parameters of contrast S_i, brightness O_i, spatial coordinates of Range/Domain, and rotation W_i. The output of fractal code is the feature matrix with 2D-dimension used as a database of face which is applied two-dimensional subspace for reduction, discrimination and speed time.

5 Face Classification Using Neural Networks

Several studies have shown improved face recognition systems using a neural classification compared to classification based on Euclidean distance measure [12].

5.1 Probabilistic Neural Networks

The probability neural network is proposed by D.F. Specht for solving the problem of classification in 1988 [13]. The theoretical foundation is developed based on Bayes decision theory, and implemented in feed-forward network architecture.

PNN represent mathematically by the following expression

$$a = radbas(\|IW - x\|b) \tag{14}$$

$$y = compet(LW\alpha) \tag{15}$$

The structure PNN: The PNN architecture consists of two layers [13, 14]:

The first layer computes distances from input vector to the input weights (IW) and produces a vector whose elements indicate how close the input is to the IW.

The second layer sums these contributions for each class of inputs to produce as its net output a vector of probabilities. Finally a complete transfer function on the output of the second layer picks up the maximum of these probabilities and produces a 1 for that class and a 0 for the other classes. The architecture for this system is shown above.

The probability of neural network with backs propagation networks in each hidden unit can approximate any continuous non linear function. In this paper, we use the Gaussian function as the activation function:

$$radbas = \exp\left[(-n^2)\right] \tag{16}$$

Finally, one or many larger values are chosen as the output unit that indicates these data points are in the same class via a competition transfer function from the output of summation unit [9], i.e.

$$compet(n) = e_i = [0000_1 0. \ldots . .0_i], n(I) = MAX(n).$$

5.2 Linear Vector Quantization (LVQ)

The vector quantization technique was originally evoked by Tuevo Kohonen in the mid 80's [13, 15]. Both Vector quantization network and self organizing maps are based on the Kohonen layer, which is capable of sorting items into appropriate categories of similar objects. Such kinds of networks find their application in classification and segmentation problems.

LVQ network comprises of three layers: Input layer, Competitive layer and Output layer [15]. The number of neurons in each layer depends on the input data and the class of the system. The input neurons are as many as the input matrix features of the training pattern, and the number of the output neurons is equal to the number of person's to which face patterns are classified. The number of hidden neurons is heuristic. In order to implement a face recognition system by our approach, we follow this methodology:

- stage pre-processing using technique WPD
- coding image using fractal code
- feature extraction using 2DPCA/2DLDA
- classification using LVQ and PNN network.

6 Results and Discussion

In order to evaluate and test our approach described for face recognition system, we chose three databases: ORL, FEI [16, 17] and our database of our laboratory. All experiences were performed in Matlab installed on a laptop with a dual core processor T5870 with 2.03 GHz and 2 GB of RAM.

To evaluate the performance of our proposed approach, we chose two test databases: ORL and FEI. The global performance of algorithms tested on the FEI database is not as better as that of the ORL database. There are two main reasons:

- The image quality of the ORL database is better than that of the FEI database.
- The FEI database is more complex due to variations in the face details and head orientations.
- After a series of experiences, we chose the best values of parameters in order to fix the choice of Eigenvalues, which give a better recognition rate.

(a)Salt&pepper Noise (b) Gaussian Noise (c) Gaussian Noise m=0,v=0.01 m=0, v=0.04

(a)Salt&pepper Noise (b) Gaussian Noise (c) Gaussian Noise m=0,v=0.01 m=0, v=0.04

Fig. 5. Adding Noise (database face ORL &FEI)

Adding Some Effects: it is wanted to test our system with and without added noisy in the two data base in order to evaluate robustness of these approaches namely 2DPCA, 2DLDA, DWT, WPD, fractal codes combined by using two classifier LVQ and PNN.

Noise: Two types of noise are used in this simulation: the Salt and Pepper type noise with a noise density a = 0.06 (Fig. 5(a)) and Gaussian noise with mean m = 0, variance v = 0.04. Figure 5 illustrates these effects which are obtained as follows.

The Pre-processing Stage: we proposed to add a preprocessing stage in order to improve our system's performance in speed by reducing the size and eliminating redundant information from the face images by the means of the DWT and WPD technique, and in other hand reduce the memory and compute of our neural network-training algorithm (PNN) and LVQ.

We performed face recognition analysis through WPD and DWT with various wavelet series: Daubechies, Gabor, Coiflets, Symlets and Gauss. In order to select a best wavelet to enhance a rate recognition.

The fractal code is used on WPD and DWT coefficients, derived from WPD to generate detailed high frequency features of animation which forms Feature set one. In order to have fractal feature vectors with the same length, the size of the face must be normalized (32×32). The normalized image is coded by 64 transformations using fractal code. Consequently, we obtained 320 fractal features as each transformation is coded on 5 parameters, as already explained in Sect. 3. Table 2 shows the performance of our system using fractal features for the two databases.

Feature Extraction Using 2DPCA/2DLDA: After reducing the dimensional of the face images using IFS. We used the 2DPCA and 2DLDA feature extraction approaches in order to extract the weight images (Features images in the new space) which must be converted into vectors before implementing the classifier network (LVQ and PNN).

Choice of the Number of Eigenvalues: Two dimensional methods do not escape this problem, and the choice of the appropriate number depends on the used method and faces database. In our experiences, we have selected the best eigenvalues corresponding to the best variance values (eigenvectors).

Selection Parameters and Architecture System Classifier
PNN: our neural network training algorithm used in system face recognition is not require many parameters compared other neural networks (MLP, BP, LVQ, etc..), that only parameter that is needed for performance of the network is the smoothing parameter σ. Usually, the researchers need to try different σ in a certain range to obtain one that can reach the optimum accuracy [14, 15].

To get a higher recognition rate, we have made a series of experiments to choose the best smoothing parameter σ used in PNN.

The probabilistic Neural Network used in our system is composed of two layers:

Input Layer: The first layer is the input layer and the number of hidden unit is the number of independent variables and receives the input data (number of feature extraction for each approach used in this paper).

Output Layer: gives the number of faces used in the Database training (ex: ORL 200 person's).

LVQ: The changes of LVQ classifier parameters have a high effect on the classification results. In this paper, we found that the best learning rate increases the recognition rate of the system whereas the learning rate is a critical parameter that affected in the recognition process. We use a different number of learning rate (0.1, 0.2, 0.3, and 0.6) with 500 epochs and 80 hidden Neurons experiments.

Discussion: After these series of experiments, we clearly see the superiority of the two-dimensional methods combined with a probabilistic neural classifier combining those of a LVQ classifier (Table 1).

Table 1. The recognition rate obtained by different methods on the database ORL with added noisy

Type classifier	DWT-2DPCA	DWT-2DLDA	WPD-2DPCA	WPD-2DLDA
LVQ	93 %	94 %	**94 %**	**96 %**
PNN	94.8 %	95 %	**96 %**	**98 %**

Table 2 The recognition rate obtained by different methods on the database FEI with added noisy

Type of classifier	WPD-2DPCA	WPD-2DLDA	WPD/IFS-2DPCA	WPD/IFS-2DLDA
LVQ	90 %	92.8 %	**95 %**	**96 %**
PNN	95 %	96 %	**99 %**	**99 %**

Table 3 The running time (s) obtained by different methods on the database FEI with added noisy

	DWT-2DPCA	WPD-2DLDA	WPD&IFS-2DPCA	WPD&IFS-2DLDA
PNN	1.20	1.25	**2.10**	**2.05**
LVQ	1.25	1.45	**2.08**	**1.98**

In Table 2, we present the recognition rate obtained when using all fractal features, and those reduced by the bi-dimensional subspace analysis. There is trade -off between encoding time and average of recognition rate because when N(domain range decreases, size of features vector will increase so LVQ and PNN learns more details and its generalization ability become weak. As feature extraction is faster for N = 8 and average of recognition rate is also fair so we encoded input faces with this R blocks size. The classification results for face is shown in Table 2 for N = 8.

We also note that the choice of optimal component and the choice smoothing parameter, which represents a better recognition, rate for methods, 2DPCA and 2DLDA and accuracy of classification PNN and LVQ.

In Table 3, we present the running time obtained when using fractal codes. computational complexity of fractal encoding is the disadvantage of fractal features in our system which can be improving by adaptive search to speed-up fractal image compression.

7 Conclusion

In this paper, we propose an approach for face recognition based on the combination of two approaches, one used for the reduction of space and feature extractions in two dimensions and the other for classification and decision.

A hybrid approach is introduced in which, through the bi-dimensional subspace analysis, the most discriminating wavelet fractal features are extracted and used as the input of a neural network (LVQ, PNN). The performance of our method is both due to the fidelity of fractal coding for representing images, the WPD algorithm to speed up the features extraction step, and the 2DPCA and 2DLDA which highlights all discriminating features.

As a perspective, we propose to use this approach in an uncontrolled environment (video surveillance) based on video sequences (dynamic images) in order to make the task of face recognition more robust.

References

1. Jain, A.K., Flynn, P.J., Ross, A. (eds.): Handbook of Biometrics. Springer, Heidelberg (2007). ISBN:978-0-387-71040-2
2. Pato, J.N., Millett, L.I. (eds.): Biometric recognition challenges and opportunities. Whither Biometrics Committee Computer Science and Telecommunications Board Division on Engineering and Physical Sciences. The National Academy of Sciences (2010)
3. Nguyen, N., Liu, W., Venkatesh, S.: Random subspace two-dimensional PCA for face recognition. In: Ip, H.H.-S., Au, O.C., Leung, H., Sun, M.-T., Ma, W.-Y., Hu, S.-M. (eds.) PCM 2007. LNCS, vol. 4810, pp. 655–664. Springer, Heidelberg (2007)
4. Yang, J., Zhang, D.: Two-dimensional PCA: a new approach to appearance-based face representation and recognition. IEEE Trans. Pattern Anal. Mach. Intell. 26(1), 131–137 (2004)
5. Mallat, S.: A theory of multiresolution signal decomposition: the wavelet representation. IEEE Trans. Pattern Anal. Mach. Intell. 11(7), 674–693 (1989)
6. Feng, G.C., Yuen, P.C., Dai, D.Q.: Human face recognition using PCA on wavelet subband. SPIE J. Electron. Imaging 9(2), 226–233 (2000)
7. Barnsley, M.: Fractals Everywhere. Academic Press, San Diego (1988)
8. Jacquin, A.E.: Fractal image coding: a review. Proc. IEEE 81, 1451–1465 (1993)
9. Jacquin, A.E.: A fractal theory of iterated markov operators with applications to digital. Dissertation, Georgia Institute of Technology (1989)
10. Jacquin, A.E.: A fractal theory of iterated Markov operators with applications to digital image coding. Ph.D. dissertation, Georgia Institute of Technology (1989)
11. Fisher, Y.: Fractal Image Compression: Theory and Application. Springer-Verlag Inc., New York (1995)
12. Nazish et al.: Face recognition using neural networks. In: Proceedings IEEE INMIC 2001, pp. 277–281 (2007)
13. Specht, D.F.: Probabilistic neural network and the polynomial adaline as complementary techniques for classification. IEEE Trans. Neural Netw. 1(1), 111–121 (1990)
14. Demuth, H., Beale, M., Hagan, M: Neural network toolbox user's guide. The MathWorks. Inc., Natrick, USA (2009)
15. Sumathi, S., Paneerselvam, S.: Computational intelligence paradigms: theory & applications using MATLAB. Taylor and Francis Group, LLCCRC Press is an imprint of Taylor & Francis Group, An Informa Business International Standard Book Number: 978-1-4398-0902-0 (2010)
16. ORL: The ORL face database at the AT&T (Olivetti) Research Laboratory. http://www.uk.research.att.com/facedatabase.html (1992)
17. FEI: The FEI face database at the Artificial Intelligence Laboratory of FEI in São Bernardo do Campo, São Paulo, Brazil (June 2005 and March 2006) http://fei.edu.br/~cet/facedatabase.htmt

A Platform for Matching Context in Real Time

Andrei Olaru[✉] and Adina Magda Florea

University Politehnica of Bucharest, 313 Splaiul Independentei,
060042 Bucharest, Romania
cs@andreiolaru.ro, adina.florea@cs.pub.ro

Abstract. Context-awareness is a key feature of Ambient Intelligence
and future intelligent systems. In order to achieve context-aware behavior, applications must be able to detect context information, recognize
situations and correctly decide on context-aware action. The representation of context information and the manner in which context is detected
are central issues. Based on our previous work in which we used graphs to
represent context and graph matching to detect situations, in this paper
we present a platform that completely handles context matching, and
does so in real time, in the background, by deferring matching to a component that acts incrementally, relying on previous matching results. The
platform has been implemented and tested on an AAL-inspired scenario.

Keywords: Graph matching · Context matching · Context patterns ·
Software agents

1 Introduction

Ambient Intelligence – or AmI – is one of the current priorities in the world of
intelligent distributed systems. In order to appear as truly intelligent, and in
order to provide the user with the appropriate information at the right time,
or with the appropriate, non-intrusive assisting action [21], AmI relies on several essential features, such as system distribution, fusion of information from a
large number of sensors, detection of context and context-aware action. Context-
awareness [20] is the ability of a system or application to correctly identify the
situation of the user based on a large quantity of information, and to take appropriate action in that situation.

This work has as framework the <u>AmIciTy</u>[1] initiative to build a software
infrastructure for Ambient Intelligence. The initiative relies on two key features.
One is the use of agent technology as an enabler of individual autonomy and
of distributed, reliable behavior for the system. The other is a representation of
context information that is adequate for a distributed system, allowing both an

---

This work has been funded by the Sectoral Operational Programme Human
Resources Development 2007-2013 of the Ministry of European Funds through the
Financial Agreement POSDRU/159/1.5/S/134398.

[1] See more details at http://aimas.cs.pub.ro/amicity.

© Springer International Publishing Switzerland 2015
E. Onieva et al. (Eds.): HAIS 2015, LNAI 9121, pp. 99–110, 2015.
DOI: 10.1007/978-3-319-19644-2_9

efficient management of context information at the system level, and context-awareness at the individual level, without the mandatory presence of context servers and other centralized components.

In the architecture of the AmIciTy system [19], context information is handled in a distributed manner by persistently storing in each agent the context information that is relevant to its activity. Agents also exchange between them information that is potentially relevant to other agents. Context information is stored in agents as *context graphs* (or CGs), that are very much like semantic networks – graphs having concepts as nodes and relations as edges. Each agent also stores a set of *context patterns* (or, in short, Patterns), that describe situations as graphs with generic (wildcard) nodes. Agents detect the current situation by matching patterns against the CG and take action as indicated by the matching pattern(s). This is what we call *context matching*.

Although graphs are a great way to visually and comprehensively represent information, the drawback of our method is that the general problem of graph matching is NP-complete [9]. However, we have shown in the past that since most of the nodes and edges in context graphs are labeled, the computational effort of matching the graphs is greatly reduced, by using a purpose-built algorithm that starts from single-edge matches and grows them to reach the maximum common subgraph (MCS).

This paper deals with how to perform context matching in an efficient, timely fashion, even when context changes very quickly. In this work we describe the architecture and implementation of a context matching platform that increases the efficiency of matching by relying on two facts: first, changes in the context graph are incremental, even if they are rapid; second, the context patterns remain quasi constant throughout the operation of the system – they are added or removed relatively rarely. This means that, at the expense of keeping part of the (partial) matches in memory, new matches can be obtained quickly when the context graph changes, based on the partial matches stored in memory.

The proposed platform is able to handle rapid changes in the context graph while performing matching in the background. It uses queues of transactions to follow changes in the sequence in which they happened. Matches that are detected in the background are notified to the host process through a mechanism of notifications. This paper not only introduces these new features of platform, but also makes a comprehensive, focused presentation of the whole architecture, in order to allow, together with the open source implementation[2], the use and replication of these results by other researchers.

After discussing some related work, we present the formalism of context graphs in Sect. 3, followed by the introduction of the Continuous Context Matching Platform and related concepts in Sect. 4. Section 5 shows some experimental results and the last section draws the conclusion.

---

[2] The implementation is freely available under a GPLv3 license at https://github.com/andreiolaru-ro/net.xqhs.Graphs.

2 Related Work

Modeling of context information uses representations that range from tuples to logical, case-based and ontological representations [4]. The most popular approaches are ontologies for representing situations and rules for reasoning, coupled with propositional or predicate logic to represent current context information. We have previously advocated context graphs as an appropriate method to represent context, that couples a simple theoretical formalism with a visual representation and powerful algorithms for graph matching [18]. Ontologies are used in many projects to describe potential situations or situation elements and to establish the relations among the elements of context. Several ontologies have been created specifically for use in context-aware computing (e.g. SOUPA [8]). The main criticism regarding ontologies is a lack of support for temporal relations, the lack of dynamicity, and the large space and temporal complexity required for ontological reasoning [5]. The mechanisms we propose are directed towards system distribution, local storage of context information and local reasoning. The work of Turner et al. shows how context-mediated behavior (CMB) [22] can be used to adapt behavior to cases that have not been encountered before, but share similarities with existing cases, much like we use patterns for context recognition. Our research is somewhat similar in behavior but we use structures that are easy to represent graphically and to visualize.

In terms of using graphs, in their works in 2004 and 2014 respectively, Conte and Foggia [9,13] analyze the use of graphs in pattern matching in the last 40 years. Graph matching has gained traction since the beginning of the millennium, as computational power increased and NP-complete problems became more approachable. It is notable that in every application domain where graphs are used there are specific challenges related to the process of pattern matching, but algorithms are customized starting from classical, generic graph-matching algorithms, such as the ones enumerated in the rest of this section. None of those fields has, however, the same particular constraints as our problem, therefore in this and previous work, algorithms had to be adapted to solve it.

We may classify graph matching algorithms in two major categories: exact matching, when the reference structure must be found entirely in the examined structure; and inexact matching, when a match might be valid even if the two entities are different to a certain extent. Among the most important algorithms for matching of unlabeled graphs are tree-search algorithms [10] and algorithms for the matching of a graph against a library of graphs [17]. Some algorithms, especially those for inexact matching [3], are based on powerful mathematical instruments – such as expectation maximization [15] and learning of assignment coefficients [7].

We have previously adapted several popular algorithms for graph matching in order to observe their behavior on context matching problems [11]. The algorithms that we have focused on were algorithms that can be adapted to the problem of context matching: they rely on label comparison and can be adapted to deal with generic edges and nodes. Among them, algorithms using incremental matching by exploring the entire state space (McGregor's algorithm [16]);

algorithms using the equivalence between finding a maximal clique and finding the maximum common subgraph (algorithms by Bron-Kerbosch [6], Durand-Pasari [12], Akkoyunlu [1] and Balas-Yu [2]); and algorithms using the equivalence with the maximal clique, but considering an extended modular product of the edges, not of the nodes (Koch's [14]). While we have found that some of these algorithms have certain advantages with respect to our problem, there was room for improvement. While testing algorithms for matching a pattern to a graph, the algorithm we have developed in previous work was by far the most efficient for all test cases.

While connected with, and sometimes inspired by related research, this work is innovative not only due to the approach we have to using graph matching for context awareness, but especially due to the purpose-built algorithms and methods that we have developed in order to make context matching viable in a distributed setup of resource-constrained devices.

3   Formal Model

In an Ambient Intelligence system, each agent should have a representation of the information that is interesting to it, and also the means of detecting what information is interesting to it from the stream of information that it receives [18]).

Each agent A has a *Context Graph* $CG_A = (V, E)$ that contains the information that is currently relevant to its function. Considering a global set of *Concepts* (strings or URIs) and a global set of *Relations* (strings, URIs or the empty string, for unnamed relations), we have:

$CG_A = (V, E)$, where $V \subseteq Concepts$
$E = \{edge(from, to, value, persistence) \mid from, to \in V, value \in Relations\}$

In order to implement *forgetting* information, or limited validity of information, edges feature an element of persistence. They can be permanent, or they may have an 'expiration time', after which they are removed. The persistence of edges is set when they are added to the graph, according to settings in the pattern that generated the edge (see below).

In order to detect relevant information, or to find potential problems, an agent has a set of patterns that it matches against graph CG_A. These patterns describe situations that are relevant to its activity. A pattern s is defined by a graph G_s^P. We will use the " P " superscript to mark structures that support generic elements, such as generic nodes:

$G_s^P = (V_s^P, E_s^P)$
$V_s^P \subseteq Concepts \cup \{?\}$
$E_s^P = \{edge(from, to, value) \mid from, to \in V_s^P, value \in Relations \cup \{\lambda\}\}$

We have used λ as a notation for the empty string. Examples of a pattern and a graph are shown in Fig. 1.

By using graph matching algorithms – matching a pattern from the agent's set of patterns against the agent's context graph – an agent is able to detect interesting information and is able to decide on appropriate action to take.

(a)   (b)

Fig. 1. Example of context graph and pattern. The pattern 3-matches the context graph.

The pattern G_s^P *matches* the subgraph $G_A' = (V', E')$, *iff* there exists an injective function $f_v : V_s^P \rightarrow V'$, so that the following conditions are met simultaneously:

(1) $\forall v^P \in V_s^P, v^P = ?$ or $v^P = f(v^P)$ (same value)
(2a) $\forall edge(v_i^P, v_j^P, rel) \in E_s^P, edge(f(v_i^P), f(v_j^P), value) \in E', value \in \{rel, \lambda\}$
(2b) $\forall edge(v_i^P, v_j^P, \lambda) \in E_s^P, \exists value \in Relations, edge(f(v_i^P), f(v_j^P), value)$
        $\in E'$

That is, every non-? vertex in the pattern matches (has the same label) a different vertex from G_A' (f_v is injective), and every edge in the pattern matches (same label for the edge and vertices) an edge from G_A'. Subgraph G' should be minimal (no edges that are not matched by edges in the pattern). One pattern may match various subgraphs of the context graph.

We allow partial matches. A pattern G_s^P *k-matches* a subgraph G' of G, if conditions (2) above are fulfilled for $m_s - k$ edges in E_s^P, $k \in \{1..m_s - 1\}$, $m_s = ||E_s^P||$ and G' remains connected and minimal. The k number of a match is the number of edges in the pattern that have not been found in the graph. For a complete match, k is null.

Partial matches are useful because, depending on a set threshold for k, they indicate actionable cases. A small k indicates that the user is indeed in the situation described by the pattern. A strictly positive k indicates however that there is something missing. Depending on the settings of the pattern, this either indicates that the agent should issue a notification about the missing edge(s), or, if the missing edges are *actionable*, the agent may add them to the graph, with a certain persistence.

We have also developed a formalism, called *timelines*, for higher-level patterns which match a certain temporal sequence of pattern matches. While the context matching platform currently supports the detection of timelines, the focus of this paper is on efficiently matching individual patterns.

4   Platform Architecture

The architecture of the platform that is presented in this paper has been designed specifically for the problem of context matching. More precisely, having a context graph, presumably quite large, and a number of context patterns (this number

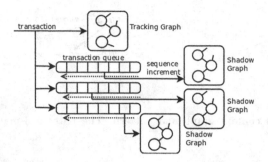

Fig. 2. Shadow graphs take transactions from transaction queues to which the tracking graph appends operations.

depends on the complexity of the functionality of the device / agent), that have a relatively small size compared to the graph, we desire to obtain notifications when a match is found between the current CG and a Pattern (the k is chosen by the user), and also when a previously reported match disappears.

Performance-wise, we desire that the notification comes in a timely fashion (while allowing some small delay), and that no changes are overlooked. For instance, if, as a result of a perception, an edge appears in the CG, and then immediately disappears, and that edge completes a match, we wish that match to not be missed, even if before these events the system worked on obtaining other computationally intensive matches.

The challenges in developing the platform were, on the one hand, to not miss any changes, and on the other hand, to obtain reasonable performance at the expense of some memory space.

The platforms relies on an algorithm developed in previous work [18], that is limited to matching one pattern to one graph. In short, the algorithm grows and merges matches. It starts with creating one potential match for each pair of matching edges in the graph and in the pattern (same edge label and matching labels for adjacent vertices). For each match a set of candidates for merger is computed, based on common frontier vertices in the two matches and on the fact that matches should not overlap. Matches that share a common frontier are 'immediate' merger candidates. Matches that are compatible, but not adjacent, are 'outer' merger candidates. In the second phase of the algorithm, using these two candidate sets for each match, matches are merged incrementally with immediate candidates. The gist is that compatibility between matches does not need to be checked in the second phase, because it is insured by computing new candidate sets as set operations between the candidate sets of the merged matches. For instance, the resulting outer candidate set is the intersection between the outer candidate sets of the merged matches – that is, candidates that were compatible (not overlapping) with, but not immediate merge candidates for any of the two merged matches.

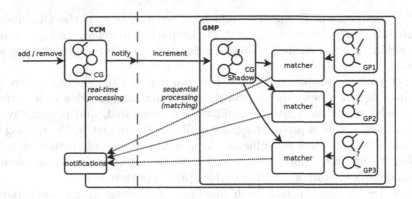

Fig. 3. Architecture of the Continuous Context Matching Platform. The dotted line separates the part that works in real time from the components that do matching sequentially, in the order of transactions applied to the context Graph.

4.1 Tracking Changes

In order to correctly track changes in the context graph, we have created a special structure called a *tracking graph*. As the normal operations in a graph are addition and removal of nodes and edges, the tracking graph is modified by means of *transactions*. A transaction contains any number of operations, each of the operations being the addition or removal of a node or edge. The only condition is that the same transaction does not simultaneously contain the addition and the removal of the same graph component. Whenever a transaction is *applied* to a tracking graph, the operations in the transaction are applied immediately. A transaction is considered atomic – there is no state in which only part of the operations in a transaction are applied.

However, a tracking graph may have any number of *shadow graphs* (see Fig. 2). When it is created, a shadow graph is a snapshot of the tracking graph (they are identical). Whenever a transaction is applied to the tracking graph, it is added to the transaction queue of each shadow graph. Shadow graphs only update their state when an *increment* operation is invoked. One increment invocation causes the shadow graph to take one transaction from the queue and apply it to the graph.

This way, the matching process can be safely performed on the shadow graph, regardless of what changes happen in the tracking graph in the mean time. When the matching is finished, and if changes have occurred, the shadow graph is incremented and the matching process is started again.

4.2 Incremental Matching

When using the algorithm presented at the beginning of the section, whenever the context graph changes, the matching process must be done again completely, wasting resources even if, for instance, an edge has been added that cannot be found in any pattern. Resources could be saved, because, if the CG changes only slightly, for every pattern most of the partial matches, and potentially the matching process entirely, remain unchanged with respect to the previous matching.

It is therefore possible to remember partial matches that have been created previously. When a new edge is added, and it matches an edge in a pattern, a single-edge match is created, candidates are computed, and potentially the match is merged with a pre-existing, hopefully maximal, match. Computing the candidate sets is not even too difficult: the match is compatible with all matches that do not contain the pattern edge, and it can be immediately compatible only with candidates containing neighbor edges (in the pattern).

Of course, it may be that with modifications in the graph, some partial matches that are stored become invalid. Therefore an index is stored of what edges in the graph are part of which matches. Whenever an edge is removed, all matches that it was part of are removed as well.

4.3   Continuous Context Matching Platform

The CCM platform (see Fig. 3) completely deals with the matching of a set of patterns against a context graph. At any time, the context graph can be modified. The CCM platform uses, internally, a component that is called a Graph Matching Platform (GMP). The GMP is capable of obtaining all matches of a set of patterns against a context graph. An incremental process, called a Matching Process, is attached to each of the Patterns. When there are changes in the CG, Matching Processes are executed by a pool of threads, giving priority to the patterns which are closest to the changed edges (simple label comparison is performed). Matching Processes work on shadows of the CG.

A Matching Process holds two indexes of matches – for each edge in the graph, the list of matches containing that edge, and for each in the pattern, the list of matches containing it. When an edge in the graph is removed, all matches containing that edge are declared invalid and will be removed whenever they are iterated over. When an edge is added to the graph, initial matches are created (against matching edges from the pattern) and merge candidates are added from among the matches of the neighbor pattern edges.

4.4   Complexity Considerations

While the matching of graphs with unlabeled nodes and edges is an NP-complete problem, labels greatly improve the performance of the process. This section extends our previous analysis [18] but focuses on real-time matching.

Since a certain number of matches are kept in memory and the matching is done incrementally, the largest computational effort is when the initial matches are created, that is when new Patterns are added. Later, matching processes are executed whenever an edge is added or removed in the CG. When an edge is added, It is first matched against all edges in the pattern in an attempt to create a single-edge match. For all patterns, this means one label comparison for each pattern

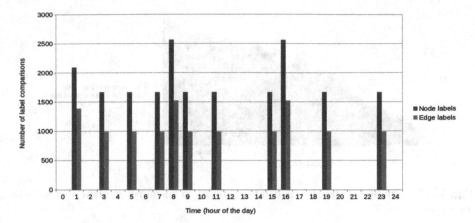

Fig. 4. The number of label comparisons for nodes and edges in every hour-long interval.

edge. Next, the candidate sets are computed for each resulting single-edge match, which is done in $O(\overline{m_n})$, where $\overline{m_n}$ is the mean number of neighbor edges for an edge in the pattern. As seen in Sect. 5.2, only single-edge matches are significant computationally. Practically, the computational effort is proportional to the number and size of patterns, but also to the branching factor of patterns. Thanks to indexing, removing an edge from the CG is done in $O(1)$ for each pattern.

From the point of view of memory consumption, results show that storing partial matches consists mostly in single-edge matches. For a CG and a pattern with no labeled edges and nodes, there is a maximum of $m \times m^P$ matches, but when edges and vertices are labeled, there is one single-edge match per pair of CG edge and pattern edge with the same label and matching vertices. Practically, performance is better when the pattern is less ambiguous.

5   Experiments with Matching Context

The Continuous Context Matching Platform was implemented[2] in Java, so it can be executed on workstation platforms as well as on Android devices. The tested scenario, taken from the AAL domain, takes place in the home of an elderly woman named Emily. Emily is aged 87 and lives alone in a small apartment. Motion sensors in the home track Emily. The system, running on a limited piece of hardware, must be able to promptly detect the current activity of Emily, based solely on location detection.

5.1   Experimental Setup

Each experiment is a simulation using an automatically generated scenario which takes place over 24 h – one day in Emily's life.

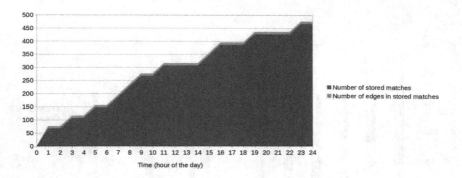

Fig. 5. The number of matches and labels stored in memory to allow incremental matching.

Emily's apartment is consists of a living room, a hall, a kitchen and a bathroom. Each of the first three rooms is equipped with a motion detector, and there is a detector to know whether someone is near the bathroom door. There are no sensors in the bathroom. The context graph of the system contains nodes referring to the current state of Emily, the layout of the rooms, food in the fridge, etc. (about 50 nodes).

Emily sleeps between 10 PM and 7 AM. During the day, she eats two or three times, goes to the bathroom, and may take a shower. At times she wanders around the house and spends time in the kitchen without eating anything, just sitting down and looking out of the window.

In order to generate a 24 h long scenario, we use a generator that inserts various activities (one of sleeping, having a meal, going to the bathroom, taking a shower, wandering around the house, and doing nothing) at various moments of time, using a distribution of probability for each type of activity. For example, if Emily just ate, she will not eat again for the following 3 or 4 h, but after that the probability of her deciding to eat will increase with time. Depending on their type, some activities may have variable durations.

5.2   Results

We have executed the Continuous Context Matching Platform on 24-h long scenarios in compressed time. We have mapped every second in simulation time to a millisecond in real time, but the platform had no problem completing the matches in that millisecond, even on older, slower, machines.

Incremental matches mean that the number of operations is very low at any given time. In Fig. 4 a chart is shown of the number of label comparisons, for nodes and for edges, for every hour of simulated time. We have chosen to show label comparisons because they are the most computationally intensive operation while performing the matching.

Of course, incremental matching brings performance at the expense of memory consumption. In order to evaluate the tradeoff, we have monitored how the number of stored matches evolves over time. We have also inspected the total number of edges in stored matches. These results are shown in Fig. 5, in the context in which no optimization of memory space was done (e.g. activating a strategy in which some partial matches are removed in time).

A first observation would be that the number of matches grows steadily with time and does not reach a very high number. The matches can be stored even on devices with low capabilities. Secondly, it is interesting to observe that the difference between the number of matches and the total number of edges stored in matches is very small. Basically, all matches are single-edge matches. The platform could therefore be optimized to keep only larger (much fewer) matches and recreate less used single-edge matches, in case memory is constrained and the device handles many patterns.

6 Conclusion

Although the problem of graph matching is computationally difficult, using graph for representing context is an approach that is flexible, easy to understand, and suitable to detecting context by matching patterns against a graph. This paper presents a platform for graph matching that uses tracking graphs in order not to miss any rapid sequences of operations, and uses incremental matching, at the expense of some memory, to keep the useful results in the matching process for future matchings.

An implementation is currently underway for a set of tools that allows working in a uniform manner with varied datasets of activity data, some very large. The presented platform will be deployed against such datasets in the near future. On the medium term, our goal is to build a large experiment in which context matching will be used by a large number of agents, on the same machine, so as to full understand the impact of the performance and memory tradeoffs that exist in the implementation.

As a long term goal, the deployment of AmIciTy on multiple machines and platforms (such as smartphones) will enable us to apply machine learning to improve patterns and learn new patterns by tracking the user's activity.

References

1. Akkoyunlu, E.: The enumeration of maximal cliques of large graphs. SIAM J. Comput. **2**(1), 1–6 (1973)
2. Balas, E., Yu, C.S.: Finding a maximum clique in an arbitrary graph. SIAM J. Comput. **15**(4), 1054–1068 (1986)
3. Bengoetxea, E., Larrañaga, P., Bloch, I., Perchant, A., Boeres, C.: Inexact graph matching by means of estimation of distribution algorithms. Pattern Recogn. **35**(12), 2867–2880 (2002)
4. Bettini, C., Brdiczka, O., Henricksen, K., Indulska, J., Nicklas, D., Ranganathan, A., Riboni, D.: A survey of context modelling and reasoning techniques. Pervasive Mob. Comput. **6**(2), 161–180 (2010)

5. Bolchini, C., Curino, C., Quintarelli, E., Schreiber, F., Tanca, L.: A data-oriented survey of context models. ACM SIGMOD Rec. **36**(4), 19–26 (2007)
6. Bron, C., Kerbosch, J.: Algorithm 457: finding all cliques of an undirected graph. Commun. ACM **16**(9), 575–577 (1973)
7. Caetano, T., McAuley, J., Cheng, L., Le, Q., Smola, A.: Learning graph matching. IEEE Trans. Pattern Anal. Mach. Intell. **31**(6), 1048–1058 (2009)
8. Chen, H., Finin, T., Joshi, A.: The SOUPA ontology for pervasive computing. In: Cranefield, S., Finin, W.T., Willmott, S., Tamma, V. (eds.) Ontologies for Agents: Theory and Experiences, pp. 233–258. Birkhäuser Basel, Basel (2005)
9. Conte, D., Foggia, P., Sansone, C., Vento, M.: Thirty years of graph matching in pattern recognition. Int. J. Pattern Recogn. Artif. Intell. **18**(3), 265–298 (2004)
10. Cordella, L., Foggia, P., Sansone, C., Vento, M.: A (sub) graph isomorphism algorithm for matching large graphs. IEEE Trans. Pattern Anal. Mach. Intell. **26**(10), 1367–1372 (2004)
11. Dobrescu, A., Olaru, A.: Graph matching for context recognition. In: Dumitrache, I., Florea, A.M., Pop, F. (eds.) In: Proceedings of CSCS 19, 19th International Conference on Control Systems and Computer Science, pp. 479–486. IEEE Xplore, Romania, 29–13 May 2013
12. Durand, P.J., Pasari, R., Baker, J.W.: An efficient algorithm for similarity analysis of molecules. Internet J. Chem. **2**(17), 1–16 (1999)
13. Foggia, P., Percannella, G., Vento, M.: Graph matching and learning in pattern recognition in the last 10 years. Int. J. Pattern Recog. Artif. Intell. **28**(01), 1554–1585 (2014)
14. Koch, I.: Enumerating all connected maximal common subgraphs in two graphs. Theoret. Comput. Sci. **250**(1), 1–30 (2001)
15. Luo, B., Hancock, E.: Structural graph matching using the EM algorithm and singular value decomposition. IEEE Trans. Pattern Anal. Mach. Intell. **35**, 1120–1136 (2001)
16. McGregor, J.J.: Backtrack search algorithms and the maximal common subgraph problem. Softw. Pract. Experience **12**(1), 23–34 (1982)
17. Messmer, B., Bunke, H.: Efficient subgraph isomorphism detection: a decomposition approach. IEEE Trans. Knowl. Data Eng. **12**(2), 307–323 (2000)
18. Olaru, A.: Context matching for ambient intelligence applications. In: Björner, N., Negru, V., Ida, T., Jebelean, T., Petcu, D., Watt, S., Zaharie, D. (eds.) In: Proceedings of SYNASC 2013, 15th International Symposium on Symbolic and Numeric Algorithms for Scientific Computing, pp. 265–272. IEEE CPS, Romania, 23–26 September 2013
19. Olaru, A., Florea, A.M., El Fallah Seghrouchni, A.: A context-aware multi-agent system as a middleware for ambient intelligence. Mob. Netw. Appl. **18**(3), 429–443 (2013)
20. Perera, C., Zaslavsky, A., Christen, P., Georgakopoulos, D.: Context aware computing for the internet of things: a survey. IEEE Commun. Surv. Tutorials **16**(1), 414–454 (2013)
21. Sadri, F.: Ambient intelligence: a survey. ACM Comput. Surv. **43**(4), 36 (2011)
22. Turner, R.M.: Context-mediated behavior. In: Brézillon, p, Gonzalez, A.J. (eds.) Context in Computing, pp. 523–539. Springer, New York (2014)

Motion Capture Systems for Jump Analysis

Sendoa Rojas-Lertxundi[1]([✉]), J. Ramón Fernández-López[2], Sergio Huerta[1],
and Pablo García Bringas[1]

[1] DeustoTech - University of Deusto, Av. Las Universidades 24,
48007 Bilbao, Bizkaia, Basque Country, Spain
srojas@deusto.es
http://www.deustotech.deusto.es
[2] KIROLENE Public Centre for Sports Education, San Ignazio Auzunea, 5,
48200 Durango, Bizkaia, Basque Country, Spain
http://www.kirolene.net

Abstract. This paper presents several methods used in motion capture
to measure jumps. The traditional systems to acquire jump information
are force plates, but they are very expensive to most people. Amateur
sports enthusiasts that want to improve their performance, do not have
enough money to spend in professional systems (±20.000 EUR). The
price reduction of electronic devices, specifically the inertial measurement units (IMU), are generating new methods of motion capture. In
this paper we present the state-of-art motion capture systems for this
purpose, from the classical force plates to latest released IMUs. Noise
reduction techniques, as an inherent part of motion capture systems,
will be reviewed.

Keywords: Motion capture · Accelerometers · Inertial measurement
units · Force plate · Jump · Noise reduction

1 Introduction

Motion Capture (Mocap for short) is the process or technique of recording patterns of movement digitally, and the goal is transforming a live performance into
a digital performance. The subject is usually a person, an animal or a machine. It
is used in military [1], films [2], video games [3], sports [4], medical applications
[5], and robotics [6]. In health and sports, human motion capture is frequently
used to study musculoskeletal biomechanics and clinical problems, as well as to
provide an improve sport techniques.

The price of this systems is so high, that most people can not access even
to use it. Their use is restricted to films and video game producers, hospitals,
military or prestigious sports team and players. With mocap systems we can
create a film character [7] simulating his movements to real world, estimate
patient injuries and their evolution [8], and improve the performance of athletes,
evaluating their biomechanical variables [9].

© Springer International Publishing Switzerland 2015
E. Onieva et al. (Eds.): HAIS 2015, LNAI 9121, pp. 111–124, 2015.
DOI: 10.1007/978-3-319-19644-2_10

The jump is one of the most popular test in all the application areas; specially in sports and medicine, due to the relevant information about the explosive force, the footprint or the gait. The jump establishes an excellent workbench for testing mocap's performance. We present in this paper a review of the actual mocap systems focusing in the jump analysis problematic. The main mocap systems are cameras, force plates and inertial measurement units.

Once data is captured it is necessary to filter it to reduce the noise raw data comes with. This step unavoidable for the subsequent data analysis step performed to convert this data into valuable knowledge. Several filters might be used, of which Kalman's and Butterworth's are the most common ones.

The remainder of this paper is organized as follows. In Sect. 2 the jump and its main features are described. In Sect. 3 various mocap systems are introduced giving special attention to the main ones: force platforms, cameras and inertial sensors. Section 4 present a compilation of filters used in the literature to reduce noise in capture process for biomechanics applications. In Sect. 5 we conclude the paper.

2   Jump Description

There exist several standard jumps used in literature and in the practice of jump analysis. The basic ones are:

- Countermovement Jump (CMJ): The subject performs a short initial descent followed by a jump.
- Squat Jump (SJ): The subject performs a jump from a semi-squatted position.
- Drop Jump (DJ): A vertical jump that is started from a surface higher (30–100 cm) than ground level. The subject jumps to the ground and the springs up as high as he can in one motion.

Data given by all sensors is necessary to quantify the information from a jump. Firstly, a graphical representation of the jump is constructed. The graphics that can be obtained are: Ground Reaction Force (GRF)-time, Acceleration-time, Velocity-time, Displacement-time, Force-displacement. The most significant information can be given by the first one (GRF-time). With this graphical representation the following representative points, given by Linthorne [10] at the Fig. 1, are calculated.

These kind of vertical jumps have low differences between them, but they have common movements from point c to h represented in Fig. 1 that correspond from the lowest part of countermovement and the landing in a surface. In a squat jump the Linthorne points are:

- (a) - Start of jump
- (b) - Maximum downward acceleration of jumper's central of mass
- (c) - Maximum downward velocity

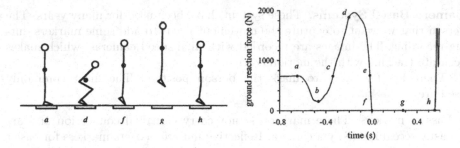

Fig. 1. Left: movement in a squat jump. Right: GRF-time graphic.

- (d) - Lowest point of countermovement
- (e) - Maximum upward velocity
- (f) - Instant of takeoff
- (g) - Peak of the jump
- (h) - Instant of landing

This information is useful for first inspection of any kind of vertical jump for all people. Gerrish [11] and Offenbacher [12] establish during the twentieth century the principle of measuring vertical jumps. In 2001 Linthorme [10] performs this analysis obtaining similar results applying new technologies.

3   Motion Capture Systems

The systems to capture the movement are organised in following groups.

- Inertial: Inertial Measurement Units (IMUs) senses and processes multiple degrees of freedom, acquiring data from gyroscope, accelerometer and magnetometer [13].
- Force/Pressure: Is a transducer that converts a mechanical force input into an electrical output signal [14].
- Fibre Optic: It is a small transducer that gives the extension of a body part. It is commonly used to measure the spine posture [15,16].
- Camera: Is an electronic device that captures pictures, movies or other visual images to digitalize them [17].
- Goniometer: It is a device that measures angles [18,19].
- Ultrasound: Electronic device that uses sound waves above 20 kHz. to obtain the outline of people [20].
- Ultra-Wide Band: They work in the same way as Ultrasound system but using waves above 500 MHz instead [21].

3.1   Main Types of Motion Capture Systems

The most commonly used systems to capture the movement in a jump are: cameras, force plates and inertial sensors.

Camera Based Systems. These systems have been used for many years. The person that we want to capture the movement needs to add some markers during recording. The images are recorded with high-speed cameras, which makes accurate tracking with the motion carried.

There are few ways to mark the person position. The most commonly used are:

- Passive markers: These markers do not carry electrical connection and are easily recognizable by a camera. Reflective material covers markers for easier identification. Painted suits are also considered as passive markers. These suits are usually black with few points in high contrast colour, such as white or yellow. They are widely used as we can see in [22–24].
- Active markers: This elements are electrically connected to illuminate the marker. The marker has a LED inside to increase the contrast for easier recognition of the camera. These kind of markers are frequently used in [25–27].
- Markerless: Do not use any kind of markers. Instead of them, a more complex image processing task is executed.

This type of capture has less precision and lower sampling speed than other systems. For easy motion capture can be used, for example [28–31] (Fig. 2).

Fig. 2. Passive markers

The necessary high speed cameras makes it an overpriced system. It is needed a minimum of 3 cameras with viewing angle of 120° to calculate accurately, by triangulating, the position in 3 axes. With a single camera we only could see the movement on one axis. Very high speed cameras can capture till 200K FPS at a cost of a lower resolution. Depending the object that we want to capture, is necessary to make a balance between sampling rate and resolution.

Microsoft has developed a system to use with Xbox videoconsole[1]. This has been used in motion capture in biomechanics. Staranowicz et al. [32] has used it to evaluate people with hip disease. Gabel et al. [33] captures all the body for gait analysis.

---

[1] http://www.xbox.com/en-US/xbox-one/accessories/kinect-for-xbox-one.

Force Plates. The force plates are systems that measure the weight exerted against the floor during a period of time. A person must be placed above the platform and do some exercise such as jump or walk on it.

Three main elements that composes a force plate are: housing, weighting system and data acquisition system.

- Housing: It is a plain surface where the person that we want to measure will be placed. The plate dimensions are limited by manufacturer recommendation because this size is calculated to measure equally in all the surface.
- Weighting System: Two type of weight transducers are used: piezoelectric devices and load cells.
  - Piezoelectric: Professional force plates used this type of transducer. These sensors generate a voltage based on the pressure being exerted. They are very accurate but the cost is very high.
  - Load cell: It is a resistive strip placed on a metal piece that measures the deformation when a weight is placed on it. Measuring this deformation we can obtain the weight. Its cost is really cheap comparing with piezoelectric devices, and performs jump tasks precisely enough.
- Data acquisition system: It is the system that transforms data given by trans- ducer (analogue signals) into information that we can send to a computer (digital signals) (Fig. 3).

Fig. 3. Force platform

In contrast with the rest of mocap systems, force platform give us directly the ground reaction force (GRF).

The application of these systems is very wide. It is frequently found in hos- pitals for making gait analysis, or in a sport centres to value the features of an athlete.

Inertial Measurement Unit. The IMUs have been in use for many years but they have not become affordable until this last years. These devices are placed in different parts of the body and autonomously are able to know the situation, where you are starting from a known point.

They are considered Microelectromechanical Systems (MEMS). They are very small devices that have inside 3 physical miniature ones, which are:

– Accelerometer: Measures the acceleration in 3 axes.
– Gyroscope: Measures the rotation speed in 3 axes.
– Magnetometer: Measures the magnetic field of the Earth in 3 axes (Fig. 4).

Fig. 4. Inertial Measurement Unit (IMU)

IMUs were commonly used in aeronautical navigation. But last years price reduction have made them to be used in other fields, such as mobile telephony. In medicine, specifically in biomechanics, is used to capture movement to analyse it. Sometimes those systems are used in combination with other to increase the precision.

Although their low cost, the noise is the biggest problem that IMUs have. Noise reduction becomes more relevant than with other mocap systems. The limited resolution to 16 bit is another disadvantage of this devices, depending on the task, it might be inadequate.

Xiang et al. [34] validates inertial system with Kinect.

3.2   Relation Between Systems

All the analysed systems register some information about the jump over the time. Cameras and wave based systems (Ultrasound or Ultra-wide band) obtain position-time graphic. IMUs obtain acceleration-time graphic, that can be converted into position-time with some additional information. Force plates gives GRF-time. Notice that while position-time and acceleration-time graphics are relative to the mass centre of the athlete, GRF-time is relative to the force exerted on the ground. Fiber optic and goniometer give quite different information, the angular momentum of joints of athlete. In Fig. 5 we can see a taxonomy of this relation.

The important information in a jump is the displacement in the vertical axis. The analysed systems can give information in 3 axes. IMUs give information directly in 3 axes. Cameras can give also 3 axes information combining several cameras with different view angles [35]. Even force platforms, that initially only

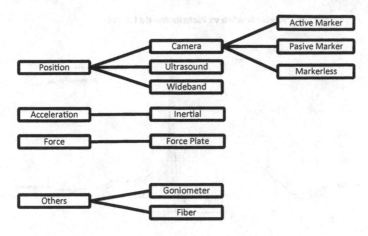

Fig. 5. Taxonomy of capture systems.

measures vertical force, but technology is achieving this issue and some manufacturers are producing triaxial force plates. In this article, we disregard the information of lateral displacements and we focus on a vertical axis movement.

Camera based systems and ultra-sounds gives the position in a moment of time. Those systems obtain a image of an athlete. With image processing techniques we can obtain a graphic with markers position versus time. Therefore, the mass centre of the athlete is calculated. The final result is a position-time graphic.

The motion capture systems based on accelerometer gives directly the acceleration time graphic. Orientation and angular speed information is neglected since it already was used to calculate the vertical axis. We can pass directly from position-time to acceleration-time, calculating the second derivative. This allow us have the same information as given by a camera based system. To obtain camera information from IMUs [36], we have to capture additional data. To achieve

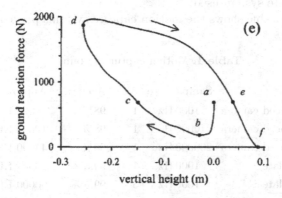

Fig. 6. Ground reaction force versus height graph.

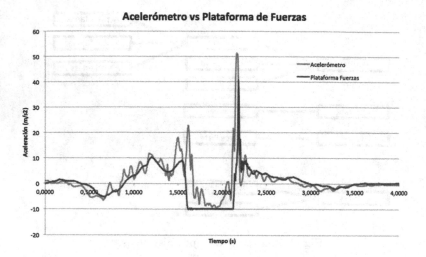

Fig. 7. Force plate and accelerometer graphs

the position, by integration, the initial position and speed are necessary. Initial speed is set up to 0. However, the initial position needed to be captured with other system. Given these observations, we can accept that cameras and IMUs give the same information.

The force platform gives GRF-time graphic. This information is quite different than previous because the reference point is not the mass centre of the athlete, it is the ground, instead. The Fig. 6 shows this fact. GRF-time is the graphic used in the application areas, a doctor can show the improvement of a patient in rehabilitation task [37], or can know the explosivility of athlete [38], and son on. Knowing the mass of the person being tested, Newton's Law $(F = ma)$ may be applied to transform the information given by accelerometers into the one given by a force platform, and reverse way, as we can see in Fig. 7.

All this post-processing of data allow us to analyse the jump regardless of the motion capture system used.

The following table shows the motion capture systems previously presented:

Table 1. Motion capture systems

Type	Sample rate	Axis	Accuracy	Approx. price
High speed camera	1000 Hz	1	98 %	5000 EUR
High speed camera	10000 Hz	1	98 %	12000 EUR
High speed camera	200000 Hz	1	98 %	44000 EUR
Force plate	1000 Hz	1	99,5 %	20000 EUR
Force plate	1000 Hz	3	99,5 %	60000 EUR
IMU	1000 Hz	3	90 %	2000 EUR

The most commonly sampling rate is 1000 Hz. There are morte expensive systems with higher precision in data and also higher speed. Knowing the precision that we need we can use several types of sensors with the data quality required. The most accurate system is the uniaxial or triaxial force platform. However, the commercial inertial sensors offer a acceptable precision with affordable cost (comparing with the rest of systems). All information given in Table 1 is form commercial devices. Nowadays there is a big community that makes his own systems, such as force plates and inertial sensor with great and even better result than commercial systems.

4 Noise Reduction Techniques

The graph shown on Fig. 1 is an ideal jump without noise. In real world the sensors produces noise and this could be high with higher sampling rates. During last years, scientific community is trying to reduce noise testing several techniques.

4.1 Low Pass Filter

A low-pass filter is a filter that passes signals with a frequency lower than a certain cutoff frequency and attenuates signals with frequencies higher than the cutoff frequency.

Kristianslund et al. [39] shows the effectiveness of this filter in inverse dynamics to show the implications for injury prevention.

4.2 Butterworth Filter

The Butterworth filter is a type of signal processing filter designed to have as flat a frequency response as possible in the passband. It is also referred to as a maximally flat magnitude filter. It was first described in 1930 by the British engineer and physicist Stephen Butterworth [40].

Fourth-order Butterworth low-pass filter is used by McEllean et al. [41], Huang et al. [42] and Malfait et al. [43] to reduce signal noise in their applications.

4.3 Kalman Filter

Kalman filter is an algorithm that uses a series of measurements observed over time, containing noise (random variations) and other inaccuracies, and produces estimates of unknown variables that tend to be more precise than those based on a single measurement alone. More formally, the Kalman filter operates recursively on streams of noisy input data to produce a statistically optimal estimate of the underlying system state. This kind of filter has successfully used in [44–46].

4.4 Chevyshv Filter

Chebyshev filters are analog or digital filters having a steeper roll-off and more passband ripple (type I) or stopband ripple (type II) than Butterworth filters. Chebyshev filters minimize the error between the idealized and the actual filter characteristic over the range of the filter. Moschas et al. [47] uses this filter to reduce noise given by a GPS and accelerometer, that is similar to our system

4.5 Elliptical (Cauer) Filter

An elliptic filter (also known as a Cauer filter) is a signal processing filter with equalized ripple behavior in both the passband and the stopband. The amount of ripple in each band is independently adjustable, and no other filter of equal order can have a faster transition in gain between the passband and the stopband, for the given values of ripple (whether the ripple is equalized or not). Alternatively, one may give up the ability to independently adjust the passband and stopband ripple, and instead design a filter which is maximally insensitive to component variations.

As the ripple in the stopband approaches zero, the filter becomes a type I Chebyshev filter. As the ripple in the passband approaches zero, the filter becomes a type II Chebyshev filter and finally, as both ripple values approach zero, the filter becomes a Butterworth filter.

Several publications uses it in their experiments such as Lugade et al. [48], Fletcher et al. [49] and Fortune et al. [50].

4.6 Gaussian Filter

Is a filter whose impulse response is an approximation Gaussian function. This filters have the properties of having no overshoot to a step function input while minimizing the rise and fall time. This behavior is closely connected to the fact that the Gaussian filter has the minimum possible group delay. It is considered the ideal time domain filter, just as the sinc is the ideal frequency domain filter. Gaussian filter modifies the input signal by convolution with a Gaussian function; this transformation is also known as the Weierstrass transform.

This filter is widely used in the biography, some of last publications that uses it are: Stone et al. [51], Alonge et al. [52] and Ng et al. [53].

4.7 Bessel Filter

Bessel filter is an analog linear filter with a maximally flat group/phase delay, which preserves the wave shape of filtered signals in the passband. This filter is quite similar to the Gaussian filter, and tends towards the same shape as filter order increases. Mouroy et al. [54] and Sala et al. [55] are using it for decreasing noise ir our input signals.

4.8   Small Comparative Between Filters

As literature shows, there are plenty of filters to apply to reduce the noise generated by the inertial sensors. According to realized test by several authors, the most commonly used filters are Kalman and Butterworth filters.

5   Concluding Remarks

There are different kinds of motion capture systems, depending the budget that we can spend on it. With a high budget we can access to professional system that permits capturing the movement with high precision. Camera based systems with passive markers have the advantage that markers are very cheap, but require more post-processing after. Active markers increase the price but also increases the resolution. With markerless we have slow speed, but the advantage of no having any kind of device that slow down the movement. Inertial systems, provide us much information but generated noise is elevated, so it is necessary to reduce it applying noise reduction techniques. Most commonly used filters are Kalman and Butterworth. The force plataforms are traditional systems most commonly used, but their cost is not accessible for all. The three systems are compatible and comparable between them. Combining them we have a precise and valuable information for research.

As future work is planned to realized a capture of a movement with the three systems at the same time, and analyse the filtering noise from the sample, with the filters named before.

References

1. Owens, B., Cameron, K., Duffey, M., Vargas, D., Duffey, M., Mountcastle, S., Padua, D., Nelson, B.: Military movement training program improves jump-landing mechanics associated with anterior cruciate ligament injury risk. J. Surg. Orthop. Adv. **22**(1), 66–70 (2012)
2. Kitagawa, M., Windsor, B.: MoCap for Artists: Workflow and Techniques for Motion Capture. Taylor & Francis, London (2008)
3. Bregler, C.: Motion capture technology for entertainment [in the spotlight]. IEEE Signal Process. Mag. **24**(6), 158–160 (2007)
4. Supej, M.: 3d measurements of alpine skiing with an inertial sensor motion capture suit and gnss rtk system. J. Sports Sci. **28**(7), 759–769 (2010)
5. Rychlik, M.: Application of mocap systems in medical diagnostic and ergonomic analysis of body movements of disabled persons. In: Proceedings of 13th International Conference on Biomedical Engineering, pp.194–199 (2009)
6. Stanton, C., Bogdanovych, A., Ratanasena, E.: Teleoperation of a humanoid robot using full-body motion capture, example movements, and machine learning. In: Proceedings of Australasian Conference on Robotics and Automation (2012)
7. Menache, A.: Understanding Motion Capture For Computer Animation. Elsevier, Burlington (2011)

8. Fern'ndez-Baena, A., Susin, A., Lligadas, X.: Biomechanical validation of upper-body and lower-body joint movements of kinect motion capture data for rehabilitation treatments. In: 2012 4th International Conference on Intelligent Networking and Collaborative Systems (INCoS), pp. 56–661. IEEE (2012)
9. Ashby, B.M., Heegaard, J.H.: Role of arm motion in the standing long jump. J. Biomech. **35**(12), 1631–1637 (2002)
10. Linthorne, N.P.: Analysis of standing vertical jumps using a force platform. Am. J. Phys. **69**(11), 1198–1204 (2001)
11. Gerrish, P.: A dynamical analysis of the standing vertical jump. Ph.D thesis, Teacher College, Columbia University (1934)
12. Offenbacher, E.L.: Physics and the vertical jump. Am. J. Phys. **38**(7), 829–836 (1970)
13. Chardonnens, J., Favre, J., Cuendet, F., Gremion, G., Aminian, K.: Measurement of the dynamics in ski jumping using a wearable inertial sensor-based system. J. Sports Sci. **32**(6), 591–600 (2014)
14. Owen, N.J., Watkins, J., Kilduff, L.P., Bevan, H.R., Bennett, M.A.: Development of a criterion method to determine peak mechanical power output in a counter-movement jump. J. Strength Conditioning Res. **28**(6), 1552–1558 (2014)
15. Roriz, P., Carvalho, L., Frazão, O., Santos, J.L., Simões, J.A.: From conventional sensors to fibre optic sensors for strain and force measurements in biomechanics applications: a review. J. Biomech. **47**(6), 1251–1261 (2014)
16. Cloud, B.A., Zhao, K.D., Breighner, R., Giambini, H., An, K.N.: Agreement between fiber optic and optoelectronic systems for quantifying sagittal plane spinal curvature in sitting. Gait Posture **40**(3), 369–374 (2014)
17. Perez-Sala, X., Escalera, S., Angulo, C., Gonzalez, J.: A survey on model based approaches for 2d and 3d visual human pose recovery. Sensors **14**(3), 4189–4210 (2014)
18. Argus, C.K., Chapman, D.W.: The effect of initial knee angle on the reliability of variables derived from a squat jump. Med. Sport **18**(4), 125–130 (2014)
19. Bergmann, J., Kumpulainen, S., Avela, J., Gruber, M.: Acute effects of motor imagery on performance and neuromuscular control in maximal drop jumps. J. Imag. Res. Sport Phys. Act. **8**(1), 45–53 (2013)
20. Weenk, D., Roetenberg, D., van Beijnum, B., Hermens, H., Veltink, P.: Ambulatory estimation of relative foot positions by fusingultrasound and inertial sensor data (2014)
21. Bryan, J., Kwon, J., Lee, N., Kim, Y.: Application of ultra-wide band radar for classification of human activities. IET Radar Sonar Navig. **6**(3), 172–179 (2012)
22. Mapelli, A., Zago, M., Fusini, L., Galante, D., Colombo, A., Sforza, C.: Validation of a protocol for the estimation of three-dimensional body center of mass kinematics in sport. Gait Posture **39**(1), 460–465 (2014)
23. Pàmies-Vilà, R., Font-Llagunes, J., Lugrís, U., Alonso, F., Cuadrado, J.: A computational benchmark for 2d gait analysis problems. In: Flores, P., Viadero, F. (eds.) New Trends in Mechanism and Machine Science, pp. 689–697. Springer, Switzerland (2015)
24. Carse, B., Meadows, B., Bowers, R., Rowe, P.: Affordable clinical gait analysis: an assessment of the marker tracking accuracy of a new low-cost optical 3d motion analysis system. Physiotherapy **99**(4), 347–351 (2013)
25. Kiernan, D., Walsh, M., O'Sullivan, R., Fitzgerald, D., OBrien, T.: Reliability of the coda cx1 motion analyser for 3-dimensional gait analysis. Gait Posture **39**, S99–S100 (2014)

26. Carroll, S., Owen, J., Hussein, M.: Reproduction of lateral ground reaction forces from visual marker data and analysis of balance response while walking on a laterally oscillating deck. Eng. Struct. **49**, 1034–1047 (2013)
27. Mayich, D.J., Novak, A., Vena, D., Daniels, T.R., Brodsky, J.W.: Gait analysis in orthopedic foot and ankle surgerytopical review, part 1 principles and uses of gait analysis. Foot Ankle Int. **35**(1), 80–90 (2013)
28. Sundaresan, A., Chellappa, R.: Markerless motion capture using multiple cameras. In: Conference on Computer Vision for Interactive and Intelligent Environment, 2005, pp. 15–26. IEEE (2005)
29. Rosenhahn, B., Brox, T., Kersting, U., Smith, A., Gurney, J., Klette, R.: A system for marker-less motion capture. Künstliche Intell. **1**(2006), 45–51 (2006)
30. Pierce, R., Heller, D., Moodie, N.: Comparison of kinetic and kinematic variables during jump station and markerless motion capture vertical jumps. In: Proceedings of International Conference on Journal of Exercise Science, vol. 11, p.16 (2014)
31. Moen, T.S.: Evaluation of a markerless motion capture system as a tool for sports movement analysis-implications for acl injury risk assessment (2014)
32. Staranowicz, A., Brown, G.R., Mariottini, G.L.: Evaluating the accuracy of a mobile kinect-based gait-monitoring system for fall prediction. In: Proceedings of the 6th International Conference on PErvasive Technologies Related to Assistive Environments, p. 57. ACM (2013)
33. Gabel, M., Gilad-Bachrach, R., Renshaw, E., Schuster, A.: Full body gait analysis with kinect. In: Proceedings of 2012 Annual International Conference of the Engineering in Medicine and Biology Society (EMBC), pp. 1964–1967. IEEE (2012)
34. Xiang, C., Hsu, H.H., Hwang, W.Y., Ma, J.: Comparing real-time human motion capture system using inertial sensors with microsoft kinect. In: 2014 7th International Conference on Ubi-Media Computing and Workshops (UMEDIA), pp. 53–58. IEEE (2014)
35. Park, H.S., Shiratori, T., Matthews, I., Sheikh, Y.: 3D reconstruction of a moving point from a series of 2d projections. In: Daniilidis, K., Maragos, P., Paragios, N. (eds.) ECCV 2010, Part III. LNCS, vol. 6313, pp. 158–171. Springer, Heidelberg (2010)
36. Wang, J.S., Hsu, Y.L., Liu, J.N.: An inertial-measurement-unit-based pen with a trajectory reconstruction algorithm and its applications. IEEE Trans. Ind. Electron. **57**(10), 3508–3521 (2010)
37. LeMoyne, R., Kerr, W., Mastroianni, T., Hessel, A.: Implementation of machine learning for classifying hemiplegic gait disparity through use of a force plate. In: 2014 13th International Conference on Machine Learning and Applications (ICMLA), pp. 379–382. IEEE (2014)
38. Hansen, K.T., Cronin, J.B., Newton, M.J.: The reliability of linear position transducer and force plate measurement of explosive force-time variables during a loaded jump squat in elite athletes. J. Strength Conditioning Res. **25**(5), 1447–1456 (2011)
39. Kristianslund, E., Krosshaug, T., van den Bogert, A.J.: Effect of low pass filtering on joint moments from inverse dynamics: implications for injury prevention. J. Biomech. **45**(4), 666–671 (2012)
40. Butterworth, S.: On the theory of filter amplifiers. Wirel. Eng. **7**(6), 536–541 (1930)
41. McLellan, C.P., Lovell, D.I., Gass, G.C.: The role of rate of force development on vertical jump performance. J. Strength Conditioning Res. **25**(2), 379–385 (2011)
42. Huang, C.Y., Hsieh, T.H., Lu, S.C., Su, F.C., et al.: Effect of the kinesio tape to muscle activity and vertical jump performance in healthy inactive people. Biomed. Eng. Online **10**, 70 (2011)

43. Malfait, B., Sankey, S., Azidin, R.M.F.R., Deschamps, K., Vanrenterghem, J., Robinson, M.A., Staes, F., Verschueren, S.: How reliable are lower-limb kinematics and kinetics during a drop vertical jump? Med. Sci. Sports Exerc. **46**(4), 678–685 (2014)
44. Zihajehzadeh, S., Loh, D., Lee, M., Hoskinson, R., Park, E.: A cascaded two-step kalman filter for estimation of human body segment orientation using mems-imu. In: 2014 36th Annual International Conference of the Engineering in Medicine and Biology Society (EMBC), pp. 6270–6273. IEEE (2014)
45. Ahmadi, A., Mitchell, E., Destelle, F., Gowing, M., OConnor, N.E., Richter, C., Moran, K.: Automatic activity classification and movement assessment during a sports training session using wearable inertial sensors. In: 2014 11th International Conference on Wearable and Implantable Body Sensor Networks (BSN), pp. 98–103. IEEE (2014)
46. Vishnoi, N., Mitra, A., Duric, Z., Gerber, N.L.: Motion based markerless gait analysis using standard events of gait and ensemble kalman filtering. In: 2014 36th Annual International Conference of the IEEE Engineering in Medicine and Biology Society (EMBC), pp. 2512–2516. IEEE (2014)
47. Moschas, F., Stiros, S.: Measurement of the dynamic displacements and of the modal frequencies of a short-span pedestrian bridge using GPS and an accelerometer. Eng. Struct. **33**(1), 10–17 (2011)
48. Lugade, V., Fortune, E., Morrow, M., Kaufman, K.: Validity of using tri-axial accelerometers to measure human movement part I: posture and movement detection. Med. Eng. Phys. **36**(2), 169–176 (2014)
49. Fletcher, I.M.: An investigation into the effect of a pre-performance strategy on jump performance. J. Strength Conditioning Res. **27**(1), 107–115 (2013)
50. Fortune, E., Lugade, V., Morrow, M., Kaufman, K.: Validity of using tri-axial accelerometers to measure human movement-part ii: step counts at a wide range of gait velocities. Med. Eng. Phys. **36**(6), 659–669 (2014)
51. Stone, E.E., Butler, M., McRuer, A., Gray, A., Marks, J., Skubic, M.: Evaluation of the microsoft kinect for screening acl injury. In: 2013 35th Annual International Conference of the IEEE Engineering in Medicine and Biology Society (EMBC), pp. 4152–4155. IEEE (2013)
52. Alonge, F., Cucco, E., D'Ippolito, F., Pulizzotto, A.: The use of accelerometers and gyroscopes to estimate hip and knee angles on gait analysis. Sensors **14**(5), 8430–8446 (2014)
53. Ng, H., Tan, W.H., Abdullah, J.: Multi-view gait based human identification system with covariate analysis. Int. Arab J. Inf. Technol. **10**(5), 519–526 (2013)
54. Mauroy, G., Schepens, B., Willems, P.: The mechanics of running while approaching and jumping over an obstacle. Eur. J. Appl. Physiol. **113**(4), 1043–1057 (2013)
55. Sala, M., Cunzolo, P., Barrettino, D.: Body sensor network for posturometric studies. In: Proceedings of 2014 IEEE International Conference on Instrumentation and Measurement Technology (I2MTC) , pp. 536–541. IEEE (2014)

Expert System for Handwritten Numeral Recognition Using Dynamic Zoning

David Álvarez[✉], Ramón Fernández, Lidia Sánchez, and José Alija

Department of Mechanical, Computer and Aerospace Engineerings,
University of León, León, Spain
{dalvl,ramon.fernandez,lidia.sanchez,jmalip}@unileon.es
http://www.unileon.es

Abstract. This paper introduces an expert system for handwritten digit recognition. The system considers that a numeric handwritten character can be decomposed into vertical and horizontal strokes. Then, the positions where horizontal strokes are connected to the vertical strokes are extracted as features using dynamic zoning. These features are laid into a representative string which is validated by a regular expression following a matching pattern. The knowledge base is constructed from a decision tree structure that stores all well-formatted representative strings with the digits definitions. Finally, the inference engine tries to match unknown digits with the trained knowledge base in order to achieve the recognition. The promising results obtained by testing the system on the well-known MNIST handwritten database are compared with other approaches for corroborating its effectiveness.

Keywords: Expert system · Digit recognition · Stroke segmentation · Inference engine · Knowledge base · MNIST database

1 Introduction

Pattern recognition covers a lot of topics as human face recognition [6], gesture recognition [14], speech recognition [5], etc. In the field concerning written recognition, many research efforts have been dedicated in word recognition [12], character recognition [26] or even in numerical recognition [7].

There are some stages required to achieve the recognition. After data acquisition, a pre-processing step is commonly used involving techniques such as thresholding [29], size normalization, slant correction [3] or noise reduction [8]. This pre-processing plays an important role in order to improve the final recognition results. After this, segmentation and normalization provide images suitable to be described by many kinds of features: graph-based features, moment-based features, geometrical features, projections, histograms, intersections [15,25], etc. Zoning algorithms use a grid that covers the input image and, hence, divides it into several zones where the information is extracted and evaluated. Impedovo et al. [10] distinguish between two zoning topologies: *static topologies*,

© Springer International Publishing Switzerland 2015
E. Onieva et al. (Eds.): HAIS 2015, LNAI 9121, pp. 125–135, 2015.
DOI: 10.1007/978-3-319-19644-2_11

with regular and non-regular grids; and *adaptive topologies*, that are obtained as the result of optimization problems. Following this step, a classifier assesses a feature vector in order to make a decision and identify the character. Expert systems [1] constitute an approach that uses a customized classification engine based on rules. Other methods such us Hidden Markov Models (HMM) [13] or k-nearest-neighbor (k-NN) classification [27] are in general considered. However, Neural Networks (NN) are the most commonly strategy used [19,22] and in particular, self-organized maps (SOM) approaches as unsupervised neural networks are regarded. For example, L. Bezerra Batista et al. [4] define a Growing Hierarchical Self-Organized Maps (GHSOM) where the size and the depth of the hierarchy is determined in training process. H. Shah-Hosseini [23], proposes another approach describing a Binary Tree Time Adaptive SOM (BTASOM) system where the levels of the tree and children are determined dynamically depending on input data. Fuzzy logic combined with neural networks are also purposed by [9] in order to achieve the recognition.

Nowadays, numeral recognition purposes are frequently focused in real data, for example, on reading amounts [21], dates on bank checks [18] as well as car plates [11] and so on, in order to automate the process and replace visual checking.

This paper is organized as follows: Sect. 2 presents the methodology exposed in HAIS 2012 [17] but deepening on numeral recognition. So, pre-processing steps, feature extraction by dynamic zoning and the knowledge base design for storing the features are described in greater detail. Well-known MNIST dataset is used in the experiments, detailed in Sect. 3, for comparing the obtained results with other authors. Finally, Sect. 4, discusses the conclusions and further work.

2   Methodology

This section will describe the expert system with all steps involved to achieve the recognition. After pre-processing, the image that represents a digit can be decomposed into vertical and horizontal strokes. Then, the location where these strokes are connected can be extracted by dynamic zoning. This feature is located into a representative string validated by a regular expression. The knowledge base stores all well-formatted strings for using by an Inference Engine to search new unknown digits. So, the next sections show in greater detail the pre-processing, stroke segmentation, feature extraction by dynamic zoning for generating the descriptors, knowledge base development and inference engine construction.

2.1   Pre-processing

In order to improve the input image, it is necessary to convert it into a binary format. N. Otsu thresholding method [20] is performed to ensure that all pixels of the input only take one possible value: 0 for black pixels and 1 for white ones.

So, in this way, a matrix $M = (X, Y)$ can be constructed applying the next function with a specific *thres* value over the input image:

$$M(x, y) = \begin{cases} 1 \ (x, y) \geq thres \\ 0 \ \text{otherwise} \end{cases}$$

Then, the matrix with thresholded values is slant normalized with the vertical. So, Changming Sun et al. [24] slant correction method is applied. The angles α considered to be corrected, range from $-\frac{\pi}{4}$ to $\frac{\pi}{4}$. Thus, for each angle a new matrix M_α is computed and consequently, the original pixels coordinates (x_s, y_s) will be moved to the new coordinates (x_α, y_α) as show Fig. 1 following the next equation:

$$\begin{bmatrix} x_\alpha \\ y_\alpha \end{bmatrix} = \begin{bmatrix} 1 & -tg(\alpha) \\ 0 & 1 \end{bmatrix} \times \begin{bmatrix} x_s \\ y_s \end{bmatrix} \tag{1}$$

Once all matrix M_α are calculated, the vertical projection is analyzed for each them [28] and compared with the each other. So, the matrix M_α which highest peak in its vertical projection will corresponds with the matrix for the unslanted digit.

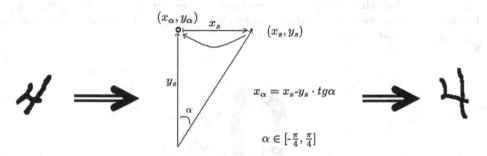

Fig. 1. Getting the distance to move pixels in digit '4'.

Due to the input digits are drawn with different stroke thickness, is also performed a thinning operation [16] to obtain all images with the same stroke width. Then, for improving the performance of our method, a dilation morphological operation is computed on the result to get a minimum stroke thickness of 5 pixels. All pre-processing operations can be resumed as show Fig. 2 with a selected digits.

2.2 Stroke Segmentation

Our system assumes that numeral handwritten characters can be decomposed into its vertical and horizontal strokes [2]. Vertical strokes are considered the leading strokes over horizontal strokes and therefore, only the connections between vertical strokes and their adjacent horizontal strokes are evaluated as main feature. Thus, for each pixel containing the stroke is calculated the width

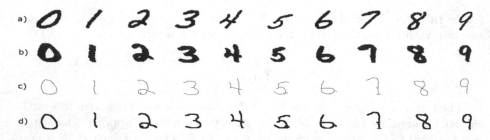

Fig. 2. (a): Original images. **(b):** Images with slant correction applied. **(c):** The result of performing thinning operation. **(d):** Final result after dilation operation.

and the height with the borders, and consequently, is labeled as v or h depending on the difference of the distances between width and height.

$$P(x, y) = \begin{cases} v \ width - distance \geq height - distance \\ h \ otherwise \end{cases}$$

Pixels with the same label are grouped with the purpose of creating a stroke with the label of that pixels. So, as vertical strokes are main, if any group of horizontal pixels overlaps a vertical stroke then this group is relabeled as v and they are included in that vertical stroke (see Fig. 3).

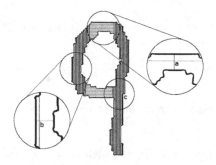

Fig. 3. Labeling pixels for digit '9'. Pixel located at a is labelled as h. However, pixel located at b is tagged as v. As vertical strokes are main, the group of pixels located in region c are relabeled as v.

2.3   Feature Extraction by Dynamic Zoning for Generating the Descriptors

Once labeling process is performed in the strokes involved in a numeric character, the connections of all vertical strokes with their adjacent horizontal strokes are evaluated. Therefore, a 4×3 grid is resized to match with the height of each vertical stroke. Thus, eight adjacency regions on both sides are identified starting by 1 on top left and following the counter-clockwise direction to 8 at top right (Fig. 4). In this way, the regions where horizontal strokes are attached can be identified.

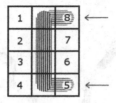

Fig. 4. Zoning based on 4×3 grid applied over a vertical stroke. The horizontal strokes are joined to this vertical stroke at 5 and 8 labeled zones.

Then, to save the extracted feature, each vertical stroke is included into a string as V followed by the number of the region where horizontal strokes are joined to that vertical stroke as show the Fig. 5. The final result is a string containing a representation of the number that is being identified.

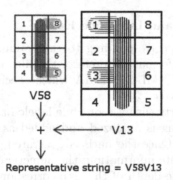

Fig. 5. The grids are scaled to vertical strokes. For number 9, two grid are used and the representative string is constructed from the result of applying both grids.

To verify the well-formatted representative string, a regular expression is used. The alphabet of the regular expression is composed by the characters defined for each zoning region along with the identification of a vertical stroke V. Then, for the defined alphabet and a set of rules, it is possible match representative strings with the next search pattern:

$$[V [1|11] | [2|22] | [3|33] | [4|44] | [5|55] | [6|66] | [7|77] | [8|88]] + \qquad (2)$$

If any representative string doesn't match with the search pattern then this will be rejected and not be considered as a valid representation of the numeric character involved.

As vertical strokes are analyzed separately, sometimes, representative strings for different numeric characters may be the same. It is due to horizontal strokes connects two vertical strokes in different positions. When this occurs, the ambiguity is solved by repeating the label of horizontal stroke that makes the connection as show Fig. 6.

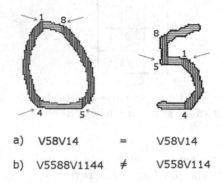

a)   V58V14   =   V58V14

b)   V5588V1144   ≠   V558V114

Fig. 6. (a): Numeric characters 0 and 5 can produce the same representative string. **(b):** The ambiguity is solved by repeating the label of the horizontal stroke involved.

2.4   Knowledge Base and Inference Engine

All representative strings corresponding to the training set, are stored in the knowledge base in XML format. Therefore, the file containing the knowledge base, is validated using a XML-SCHEMA which specifies the rules about how to construct the decision tree.

The tree structure starts with a root node labeled as V. Then, each element of the representative string is analyzed and added as a new node in the tree starting from root node. Once the path is generated, a leaf node is joined to the structure with the route information: the numeric character that represents that path. In this way, the depth of the tree corresponds to the number of the elements in the longest representative string stored.

The inference engine is developed to manage the trained knowledge base for achieving the recognition. When a new unknown digit is analyzed by inference engine, it tries to match the representative string of that unknown number with an entry of the trained knowledge base. If one path is located, the recognition is reached and the numeric character stored in the leaf of searched path is returned as a solution. Otherwise, a rejection is performed since a leaf node is not found at the final of the entrance.

3   Experiments and Results

To evaluate our methodology, the experiments have been performed using the well-known MNIST handwritten digit database offered by LeCun et al.[1].

---

[1] http://yann.lecun.com/exdb/mnist/.

It contains a training set of 60,000 images and a set of 10,000 images for testing purposes. The images are normalized in bilevel (black and white) format and centered into a 28×28 field.

For improving the results, MNIST database images were rescaled to 112×112 pixels at pre-processing in our methodology. Afterwards, in classification stage, two knowledge bases were generated for containing each training digit description. The first knowledge base stores the representation of the digit without unslant process and the second one, manages the representation of the deslanted digit. So, the Inference engine operates over these two knowledge bases to achieve the recognition in this way: firstly, it tries match an unknown digit in the knowledge base without slant process and if a rejection is produced, then tries match it at konwledge base with slant corrected digits.

In order to configure the best training sample from main MNIST training set for the experiments, 10,000 images were randomly selected as validation set. Then, from the remaining group of 50,000 images, it was selected a subset, firstly of 10,000 images and increasing by 10,000 until 50,000, to train the knowledge bases described above. After 10 tests, the best result was on a 40,000 images subset with 88.34 % accuracy rate.

Once trained the knowledge bases with the best training set, it is performed a final test using MNIST test set. The recognition accuracy obtained for each digit is reported in Table 1 as well as the error rate, including the confusion matrix with the other numbers, and the rejection rates.

MNIST database is also used for testing purposes by other authors whose approaches are based on self-organized maps. L. Bezerra Batista et al. [4] have developed a custom Growing Hierarchical SOM where the size and the depth of the hierarchy are modified along the unsupervised training process unlike generic model, where the hierarchy of the SOM must be defined prior to training.

Table 1. Confusion matrix obtained by testing our methodology using MNIST test set.

Digit	HIT %	MISS %										REJ. %
		0	1	2	3	4	5	6	7	8	9	
0	93.57	0	0	0.31	0.20	0	0.41	2.55	0.51	1.43	0.92	0.10
1	95.68	0.79	0	0.54	0.26	0.26	0.62	0.35	1.41	0.09	0	0
2	85.66	1.36	0.98	0	3.68	0.19	0.19	0.58	5.33	0.97	0.19	0.87
3	88.71	2.77	0.31	1.68	0	0	2.67	0.10	1.49	0.69	0.69	0.89
4	91.45	0.20	1.12	0.41	0	0	0	2.04	0.31	0.51	3.16	0.80
5	89.46	0.34	1.46	0	2.24	0.11	0	3.03	0.56	1.46	1.01	0.33
6	81.52	3.65	6.68	0.21	0	1.57	3.03	0	0.21	2.30	0.21	0.62
7	84.53	0.10	0.20	10.31	3.70	0.39	0.19	0	0	0.19	0.29	0.10
8	85.42	1.13	0.82	1.75	1.85	1.54	1.03	1.44	1.85	0	1.95	1.22
9	90.78	0.69	0.79	0.30	0.30	1.29	0.99	0.20	3.87	0.69	0	0.10
Total	88.77 %	10.73 %										0.50 %

Table 2. Comparison of the accuracy results for BTASOM, GHSOM and our work.

Digit	H. Shah-Hosseini (BTASOM)	L. Bezerra Batista et al. (GHSOM)	This work
0	93.16 %	96.63 %	93.57 %
1	96.65 %	96.24 %	95.68 %
2	85.27 %	87.18 %	85.66 %
3	80.69 %	77.06 %	88.71 %
4	74.03 %	67.62 %	91.45 %
5	83.30 %	79.24 %	89.46 %
6	93.53 %	89.65 %	81.52 %
7	87.45 %	78.55 %	84.53 %
8	78.34 %	79.73 %	85.42 %
9	79.98 %	83.44 %	90.78 %
Average	**85.24 %**	**83.53 %**	**88.77 %**

After resizing the 28×28 input gray level images for obtaining a new image of 16×16 pixels, they selected 2000 digits for training the classifier and 3000 for testing it. H. Shah-Hosseini [23] proposes a Binary Tree Time Adaptive SOM strategy where the levels of the tree and the number of its nodes dynamically grow depending on parameters defined by the user. The BTASOM experiments also require a previous resizing input image for getting a final image of 14×14 pixels. The resized training test is used for training the BTASOM tree. Finally, the trained BTASOM is tested with the 10,000 images from MNIST test set. Table 2 outlines the recognition accuracies (numbers zero to nine and the average) for BTASOM, GHSOM and our proposed method.

It can clearly be seen that our methodology, it is capable to obtain higher average accuracy, 88.77 %, than the average accuracy obtained by BTASOM and GHSOM approaches, 85.24 % and 83.53 %, respectively.

4   Conclusions and Further Works

This work presents a new approach for digit recognition. After pre-processing steps, a digit can be divided into vertical and horizontal strokes. Then, it is obtained the positions where these strokes are connected by dynamic zoning and, depending whether unslant process was applied on input digit, this feature is stored into two knowledge bases as a representative string checked by regular expression. Finally, an Inference Engine tries to seek in trained knowledge bases a new unknown digits in order to achieve the recognition. However, the algorithm for feature extraction still generates the same representative string for different digits. A wrong digit segmentation into its vertical and horizontal strokes causes a mistaken feature generated dynamic zoning. Our effort is focused in reducing the number of that digits are wrongly segmented to enhance the results.

MNIST database contains a large number digits written by 500 authors, but how these digits are written influence clearly in the recognition. So, there are still some recognition errors as show confusion Table 1. Our future work involves to improve the methodology with the purpose of minimize the impact of these errors affect the recognition rate.

Our expert system is capable to obtain higher average accuracy than others approaches based on self-organized map methods like BTASOM or GHSOM. However, our future work also involves performing statistical inference tests by studying how the population is distributed by our classifier in order to provide more accurate results.

Finally, on the whole, our further work will be rely on to try out other classification approaches such as a self-organized map, neural network or fuzzy systems for comparing the results with the obtained in this paper.

References

1. Ahmed, M., Ward, K.R.: An expert system for general symbol recognition. Pattern Recognit. **33**, 1975–1988 (2000)
2. Alonso, A., Fernández, R.A., García, I.: Recognition of merged characters based on vertical strokes and adjacency regions. V Congress of Hispalinux (2005)
3. Bertolami, R., Bertolami, R., Uchida, S., Uchida, S., Zimmermann, M., Zimmermann, M., Bunke, H., Bunke, H.: Non-uniform slant correction for handwritten text line recognition. In: ICDAR 2007, pp. 18–22 (2007). http://ieeexplore.ieee.org/lpdocs/epic03/wrapper.htm?arnumber=4378668
4. Batista, B.L., Gomes, M.H., Herbster, F.R.: Application of growing hierarchical self-organizing map in handwritten digit recognition. In: Brazilian Symposium on Computer Graphics and Image Processing, pp. 1539–1545 (2003)
5. Chen, W., Liao, Y., Chen, S.: Speech recognition with hierarchical recurrent neural networks. Pattern Recognit. **28**(6), 795–805 (1995). http://www.sciencedirect.com/science/article/pii/003132039400145C
6. De Marsico, M., Nappi, M., Riccio, D., Wechsler, H.: Robust face recognition after plastic surgery using region-based approaches. Pattern Recognit. **48**(4), 1261–1276 (2015). http://www.sciencedirect.com/science/article/pii/S0031320314003884
7. Ha, T.M., Zimmermann, M., Bunke, H.: Off-line handwritten numeral string recognition by combining segmentation-based and segmentation-free methods. Pattern Recognit. **31**(3), 257–272 (1998). http://www.sciencedirect.com/science/article/pii/S0031320397000502
8. Haji, M., Bui, T.D., Suen, C.Y.: Removal of noise patterns in handwritten images using expectation maximization and fuzzy inference systems. Pattern Recognit. **45**(12), 4237–4249 (2012). http://linkinghub.elsevier.com/retrieve/pii/S0031320312002439
9. Hanmandlu, M., Mohan, M.K., Chakraborty, S., Goyal, S., Choudhury, D.: Unconstrained handwritten character recognition based on fuzzy logic. Pattern Recognit. **36**(3), 603–623 (2003). http://www.sciencedirect.com/science/article/pii/S0031320302000699
10. Impedovo, D., Pirlo, G.: Zoning methods for handwritten character recognition: a survey. Pattern Recognit. **47**(3), 969–981 (2014). http://linkinghub.elsevier.com/retrieve/pii/S0031320313002458

11. Jiang, D., Mekonnen, T.M., Merkebu, T.E., Gebrehiwot, A.: Car plate recognition system. In: 2012 Fifth International Conference on Intelligent Networks and Intelligent Systems, pp. 9–12 (2012). http://ieeexplore.ieee.org/lpdocs/epic03/wrapper.htm?arnumber=6376472

12. Kessentini, Y., Paquet, T., Hamadou, A.: Off-line handwritten word recognition using multi-stream hidden markov models. Pattern Recognit. Lett. **31**(1), 60–70 (2010). http://www.sciencedirect.com/science/article/pii/S0167865509002232

13. Kundu, A., He, Y., Bahl, P.: Recognition of handwritten word: first and second order hidden markov model based approach. Pattern Recognit. **22**(3), 283–297 (1989). http://www.sciencedirect.com/science/article/pii/0031320389900769

14. Li, H., Greenspan, M.: Model-based segmentation and recognition of dynamic gestures in continuous video streams. Pattern Recognit. **44**(8), 1614–1628 (2011). http://www.sciencedirect.com/science/article/pii/S0031320310005807

15. Liu, C.L., Nakashima, K., Sako, H., Fujisawa, H.: Handwritten digit recognition: investigation of normalization and feature extraction techniques. Pattern Recognit. **37**(2), 265–279 (2004). http://linkinghub.elsevier.com/retrieve/pii/S0031320303002243

16. Lü, H.E., Wang, P.S.P.: A comment on a fast parallel algorithm for thinning digital patterns. Commun. ACM **29**(3), 239–242 (1986)

17. Álvarez, D., Fernández, R., Sánchez, L.: Stroke based handwritten character recognition. In: Corchado, E., Snášel, V., Abraham, A., Woźniak, M., Graña, M., Cho, S.-B. (eds.) HAIS 2012, Part I. LNCS, vol. 7208, pp. 343–351. Springer, Heidelberg (2012)

18. Morita, M., Letelier, E.: Recognition of handwritten dates on bank checks using an HMM approach. In: Proceedings of XIII Brazilian Symposium on Computer Graphics and Image Processing, pp. 113–120 (2000). http://ieeexplore.ieee.org/xpls/abs_all.jsp?arnumber=883903

19. Oh, I.S., Suen, C.Y.: A class-modular feedforward neural network for handwriting recognition. Pattern Recognit. **35**(1), 229–244 (2002). http://linkinghub.elsevier.com/retrieve/pii/S0031320300001813

20. Otsu, N.: A threshold selection method from gray-level histograms. IEEE Trans. Syst. Man Cybern. B Cybern. SMC **9**(1), 62–66 (1979). http://web-ext.u-aizu.ac.jp/course/bmclass/documents/otsu1979.pdf

21. Palacios, R., Gupta, A.: Training neural networks for reading handwritten amounts on checks. In: 2003 IEEE 13th Workshop on Neural Networks for Signal Processing, NNSP 2003, pp. 607–616 (2003)

22. Ping, Z., Lihui, C.: A novel feature extraction method and hybrid tree classification for handwritten numeral recognition. Pattern Recognit. Lett. **23**(13), 45–56 (2002). http://www.sciencedirect.com/science/article/pii/S0167865501000885

23. Shah-Hosseini, H.: Binary tree time adaptive self-organizing map. Neurocomputing **74**(11), 1823–1839 (2011). http://www.sciencedirect.com/science/article/pii/S0925231211000786

24. Sun, C., Si, D.: Skew and slant correction for document images using gradient direction. In: Proceedings of the Fourth International Conference on Document Analysis and Recognition, vol. 1, pp. 142–146 (1997)

25. Trier, D., Jain, A., Taxt, T.: Feature extraction methods for character recognition-a survey. Pattern Recognit. **29**(4), 641–662 (1996). http://www.sciencedirect.com/science/article/pii/0031320395001182

26. Vamvakas, G., Gatos, B., Perantonis, S.: Handwritten character recognition through two-stage foreground sub-sampling. Pattern Recognit. **43**(8), 2807–2816 (2010). http://www.sciencedirect.com/science/article/pii/S0031320310000968

27. Wakahara, T., Yamashita, Y.: k-nn classification of handwritten characters via accelerated GAT correlation. Pattern Recognit. **47**(3), 994–1001 (2014)
28. Zeeuw, F.: Slant correction using histograms. Bachelors thesis in Artificial Intelligence, pp. 1–10 (2006)
29. Zou, Y., Dong, F., Lei, B., Sun, S., Jiang, T., Chen, P.: Maximum similarity thresholding. Digit. Signal. Process. **1**, 1–16 (2014). http://linkinghub.elsevier.com/retrieve/pii/S1051200414000451

Arabic Handwriting Recognition Based on Synchronous Multi-stream HMM Without Explicit Segmentation

Khaoula Jayech[✉], Mohamed Ali Mahjoub,
and Najoua Essoukri Ben Amara

SAGE Research Unit, National Engineering School of Sousse,
University of Sousse, Sousse, Tunisia
jayech_k@yahoo.fr, medali.mahjoub@ipeim.rnu.tn,
najoua.benamara@eniso.rnu.tn

Abstract. In this study, we propose a synchronous Multi-Stream Hidden Markov Model (MSHMM) for offline Arabic handwriting word recognition. Our proposed model has the advantage of efficiently modelling the temporal interaction between multiple features. These features are composed of a combination of statistical and structural ones, which are extracted over the columns and rows using a sliding window approach. In fact, word models are implemented based on the holistic and analytical approaches without any explicit segmentation. In the first approach, all the words share the same architecture but the parameters are different. Nevertheless, in the second approach, each word has it own model by concatenating its character models. The results carried out on the IFN/ENIT database show that the analytical approach performs better than the holistic one and the MSHMMs in Arabic handwriting recognition is reliable.

Keywords: Arabic handwriting recognition · Multi-stream HMMs · OCR · Sliding window · Analytical approach

1 Introduction

In the last years, a great interest has been devoted to offline Arabic handwriting recognition, which has become a very popular topic of research. A review of the literature shows that the most studies, treated the Arabic handwritten word, are based on the Hidden Markov Models (HMMs) using the sliding window approach, which give good results when a relevant feature-extraction process is performed. Actually, Giménez et al. [1] presented an Arabic handwriting recognition system using windowed Bernoulli HMMs. In order to surmount the feature extraction and to ensure that no discriminative information was filtered out, they suggested to use columns of raw, binary image pixels, which were directly fed into the embedded Bernoulli HMM where the emission probabilities were modeled with the Bernoulli mixture. Using this approach, promising results were reported on the IFN/ENIT database. However, the HMMs are applied especially to model one dimensional signal. Consequently, to model bi-dimensional signals such as word image or multiple features, a solution consists in combining multi-classifiers, then a post-treatment selecting the best hypothesis is applied. In this context,

E. Onieva et al. (Eds.): HAIS 2015, LNAI 9121, pp. 136–145, 2015.
DOI: 10.1007/978-3-319-19644-2_12

Ramy El Hajj et al. [2] developed an offline Arabic handwritten recognition system by combining three HMM classifiers. In fact, the baseline-independent features and base-line-dependent ones were extracted using a sliding window with three successive angles of inclination (−a, 0, +a). For each direction, an HMM classifier was proposed to classify these features. After that, a combination of the results given by the three homogenous HMMs was done at the decision level. The results showed that this combination gives better results than a single HMM. Also, Kessentini et al. [3] suggested a multi-scripter handwriting recognition system based on the MSHMM. This approach combined two types of feature streams. The first stream modelled the density feature and the second one modelled the features computed from the upper and lower contours. That modelling allowed processing the different streams independently until they reached a constraint for re-synchronizing and combining their partial contribution. This approach was extended to model multiple feature streams.

In our study, we have developed an extension of the HMM in which the observation node has been decomposed in a number of observations that are considered independent, given the state. Thus, multiple observations can be modelled with a simple, efficient and synchronous manner. The main motivations to use these models are the following. First, the MSHMM can model the temporal interaction between multiple streams of observations to achieve a good discriminative power. Second, when there are many observation symbols, it minimizes significantly the number of parameters, hence requiring a few number of samples to train the model. Third, the topology of the MSHMM can be adapted to model two or more streams of features that can be continuous or/and discrete.

The rest of the paper is organized as follows. In the second section, we describe the architecture of the proposed recognition system. In the third section, we present the realized experimentation to adjust the model to data and discuss the obtained results. Finally, we finish by a conclusion and some perspectives for future works.

2 Word Recognition System

2.1 System Overview

The architecture of the developed system is illustrated by Fig. 1.

2.2 Preprocessing and Segmentation

In this step, we have applied the following preprocessing that were used later to extract some features: (i) Thinning: which consists in normalizing the line thickness to one pixel in order to reduce the number of pixels to the minimum necessary for the subsequent operation; (ii) Removing the vertical and horizontal spaces; (iii) Removing the horizontal elongation based on the vertical histogram projection; (iv) Baseline estimation based on the horizontal projection histogram.

In order to avoid the difficulty of segmenting an Arabic handwritten word, we have applied the sliding window technique [2, 3, 7]. Therefore, in this step, the feature vectors for each word image are performed by scanning the word image in two directions to obtain the characteristics over the lines and columns. Hence, we have

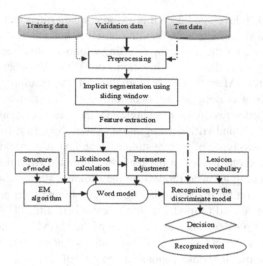

Fig. 1. Architecture of the developed system.

applied a right-to-left sliding window having the same height of the word image and a fixed width (determined empirically) to compute the characteristics over the columns. In the same way, we have used a top-to-bottom sliding window having the same width of the word image and a fixed height (determined empirically) to obtain the characteristics over the lines.

2.3   Feature Extraction and Vector Quantization

To minimize the intra-class and maximize the inter-class pattern variability, we have computed a combination of statistical and structural features as follows:

Statistical Features. *Hu invariant moment:* The features from f_1 to f_7 are computed from each window strip based on the seven invariant moments proposed by Hu and are normalized using this equation:

$$f(x) = \frac{x - min}{max - min} \tag{1}$$

Histogram chain code: The features from f_8 to f_{15} are computed from the chain code histogram. We have generated from this chain sequence representation of each window strip an histogram that represents the results of counting the occurrence N(i) for each possible digit $i \in \{0, 1, \ldots, 7\}$ as in (2).

$$I(i) = \left(\sum_{d=0}^{7} n_d\right)^{-1} n_i \tag{2}$$

Then we have normalized each possible value in the histogram I(i), which represents the intensity of a direction.

Topological features: Eight additional topological features from f_{16} to f_{23} based on pixel density have been computed from each window strip. To extract these features, a zoning has been applied to split each vertical window strip in two parts, above and below the baseline. Moreover, the upper and lower zones have been each divided in four zones. The same is for the horizontal window strips, but they are divided into eight equal zones. The feature vectors are representing the count of black pixels in each of the eight zones, normalized by the respective zone area.

Structural Features. Four structural features f_{24} to f_{27} have been computed from the thinned image as follows:

Feature points: They represent the black pixels in the word skeleton. We distinguish two types: (i) End points: They represent the beginning/ending of a line segment. (ii) Junction points: They correspond to the connection of two or more strokes. They are split into cross and branch points.

Inflexion points: They represent the curvature sign change in the word skeleton.

Loop: It represents the inner skeleton contours with the information reflecting their partiality or completeness including the window strip inside.

Vector Quantization. In our study, we have used the discrete MSHMMs which require discrete values. Accordingly, we have to generate for each continuous feature vector describing a window strip a discrete symbol. This generation is done by a Vector Quantization (VQ) process. Our VQ technique implements the LBG algorithm which is a variant of the K-means algorithm and has the advantage of being simple and not requiring an excessive computation. The choice of the codebook is made empirically and is fixed to 64, which yields to a high recognition accuracy.

2.4 Synchronous Multi-stream HMM

In order to model synchronous multi-streams, we investigate the use of MSHMM where the hidden state generates two or more observations. In our case, there are two streams of observations: O_V and O_H.

Description MSHMM. Let $O_V = \{o_{v1}, \ldots, o_{vT}\}$ and $O_H = \{o_{h1}, \ldots, o_{hT}\}$ be two sequences of feature vectors representing a handwritten word to be recognized. An MSHMM is a probability function of the form:

$$P(O_V, O_H | \lambda) = \sum_{q_1, \ldots, q_T} \prod_{t=0}^{T} a_{q_t q_{t+1}} \prod_{t=1}^{T} b_{q_t}(o_{vt}) b_{q_t}(o_{ht}) \tag{3}$$

where the sum is over all possible state sequences $q_0, \ldots, q_{T+1}$, such that $q_0 = I$ (start or initial state), $q_{T+1} = F$ (final state), $q_t, t \in \{1, \ldots, T\}$, with T being the number of regular states of the MSHMM. Therefore, for any regular state, the parameters of the model are: $a_{ij} = P(q_t = j | q_{t-1} = i)$ denoting the transition probability from i to j, and $b_j(k) = P(o_t = k | q_t = j)$ denoting the observation probability function at j. The initial and final non-emitting states are applied to indicate the probability of a given character/sub-character being followed or preceded by another character/sub-character.

Hence, they are used to produce the composite model applied for word recognition. As it is illustrated in Fig. 2, an MSHMM example for the character "ﺵ" is shown with a binary image.

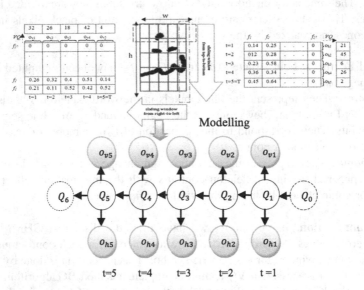

Fig. 2. Right-left MSHMM character model

Each character model has a right-left topology and has five hidden states and two observations generated from each hidden state. The two observations are assigned to model the vertical and horizontal frames. This frame-by-frame emission of feature vectors in a horizontal and vertical direction attempts to better model the horizontal and vertical distortions at the character level and the interaction between the two observation sequences in a synchronous manner.

Modelling. In this paper, our handwriting recognition system is built and trained at two levels. Firstly, we have used a holistic approach to extract the features from the word and training the whole word model, as shown in Fig. 3.

Secondly, we have retained another analytical approach at the character level, where the word is recognized by the concatenation of character models as shown in Fig. 4.

The first approach consists in creating a different MSHMM for each word from the samples labeled by the word identity. The models of all words share the same MSHMM architecture (empirically fixed), but their parameters are different and change from one class to another. In this approach, the MSHMM may suffer from poor discriminative abilities when there are poorly estimated class models due to insufficient training samples or insufficient complexity. For example, in the IFN/ENIT database, some words are well represented through a few hundreds of samples, whereas other words are poorly represented with three samples. So to surmount this problem, the

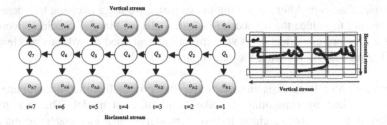

Fig. 3. MSHMM word model using implicit segmentation

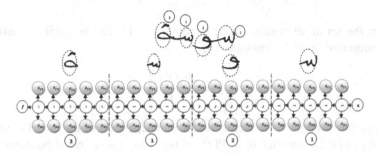

Fig. 4. MSHMM for the word "سوسة" using the analytical approach

second approach has occurred. It consists in following the analytical model training by performing character model training. In fact, in our database, we do not have letter samples; however, we dispose word samples. Thus, the training algorithm is not applied directly to letter models but to their concatenation corresponding to the words in the training set. This is known as embedded training [2, 3, 8]. This training algorithm is very efficient and has the following advantages. First, the explicit segmentation of words into characters is not necessary to perform the training. Second, the characters are modelled when being part of a word. Considering Fig. 4, an embedded MSHMM for the word "سوسة" is shown, which is the result of concatenating the MSHMM of the characters "س" ,"و" ,"س" and "ة" in that order. It is noted that the MSHMM for the different characters shares the same topology and characteristics, which are empirically determined and detailed in Sect. 3.2.

MSHMM Training. Training the MSHMM consists in estimating its parameters, i.e. the state transition probability, the emission probability, the optimal number of codebook and the optimal number of hidden states. It is independently performed model by model by applying the Expectation/Maximization (EM) algorithm which is an iterative approach of maximum likelihood estimators. The EM algorithm is used in a straightforward manner to train the set of parameters in two ways: either by whole model training or analytical model training using the embedded training [8].

Recognition Process. After feature extraction, we have proposed to process the classification of candidate words in two steps:

Pre-classification step: After computing the features, we use a decision tree based on a discrete feature to reduce the number of potential classes that the candidate word may belong to. This pre-classification is very important and used in order to accelerate the recognition process by reducing the search space.

Classification step: It consists in computing the probability that a candidate word belongs to a class by computing the likelihood of each model. The task may be formulated as the one of searching the word model λ^* that can reach the maximum posterior probability given a sequence of observation $O = (O_V, O_H)$:

$$\lambda^* = \text{argmax}_{\lambda \in \theta} P(\lambda|O) \qquad (4)$$

where θ is the set of all possible word hypotheses. This can be computed using the Bayes's theorem defined by this equation:

$$\lambda^* = \text{argmax} \frac{P(O|\lambda)P(\lambda)}{P(O)}$$

$P(O)$: is the observation probability and it is independent of the model λ, so it can be ignored from the calculation of λ^*. $P(\lambda)$: is assumed to be an equal prior probability $P(\lambda)$ for all possible word hypotheses.

Thus, the recognition process consists in determining the model λ^* that maximizes the likelihood $P(O|\lambda)$, which is maximizing the parameters in (3). This can be done using an exact inference algorithm based on the junction tree algorithm.

3   Experimental Results and Analysis

This section describes the IFN/ENIT database and presents the results obtained with the corresponding analysis and discussion.

3.1   IFN/ENIT Database Description

We have tested our MSHMM on the benchmark IFN/ENIT database. It contains 946 Tunisian town/village names. It is a widely used database to compare Arabic handwriting recognition systems.

3.2   Training and Recognition

The model training is based on the EM algorithm and the cross-validation process. The main focus of the cross-validation is to search and optimize the parameters of our model during the training process. The cross-validation is done over two sets of data: training and validation. Initially, for both the holistic approach and the analytical one, the training process has been done with different values of parameters until the best set of parameters has been determined. As first experiments, after the preprocessing phase, we have tried different values for the sliding window width dividing the image into a different number of window strips/frames.

As seen in Table 1, it is clear that increasing the number of frames improves the recognition rate until the system reaches its saturation. Precisely, the best results, 83.4 and 91.1, are recorded respectively for number of frames NF = 13 by the holistic approach and for number of frames per character NFC = 5 by the analytical approach. Based on these settings, a second series of experiments have been conducted. To find an optimal number of codebook for MSHMM, we compare the recognition rate under different codebook sizes varying from 8 to 128, and the results are summarized in Table 2a.

Table 1. Recognition rate in function of the number of frames

NF	Recognition rate recorded by the holistic approach	NFC	Recognition rate recorded by the analytical approach
5	63.5	2	85.1
7	68.6	3	88.9
9	73.8	4	90.2
11	78.5	5	91.10
13	83.4	6	91.15
15	83.5		

Table 2. (a) Recognition rate in function of codebook sizes (b) Recognition rate in function of a number of hidden states

Codebook size	Holistic approach	Analytical approach
8	81.11	88.74
16	82.30	89.39
32	82.41	90.23
64	83.42	91.02
128	83.44	91.13
Number of hidden state	Holistic approach	Analytical approach
6	79.51	88.14
12	80.01	89.24
18	81.24	89.73
24	83.32	91.12
30	83.38	91.16

As it is shown in Table 2a, a better recognition rate is yielded by increased codebook sizes. Besides, we can notice that a high recognition rate for both approaches is reached when the codebook size becomes 64 and more. As a result, an optimal codebook size is fixed to 64 to find a comprise between the high recognition rate and low time execution. In the same way, an optimal number of hidden states for both approaches are empirically determined. Possible numbers of hidden states are specified as 6, 12, 18, 24 and 30, and the results obtained are listed in Table 2b. We have seen that the recognition rate increases as the number of hidden states augments until the system reaches its saturation. The best recognition rate is reached at 24.

In all the performed tests and fixing the best parameters determined in the training process, we notice, as shown in Table 3, that the analytical model training technique is more efficient than the holistic one. This can be attributed to the insufficient training data for some classes. In fact some words are well represented in the data base. However, other words are represented by 3 samples−even missing. As a result, their models are poorly trained.

As it is shown by Table 4, the proposed analytical approach based on the MSHMM

Table 3. Recognition rate obtained by cross validation

Training set	Test set	Holistic approach	Analytical approach
abc	d	83.1	91.05
abd	c	82.1	92.20
acd	b	82.3	91.01
bcd	a	83.38	91.11
abcd	e	72.4	82.91
abcde	f	61.5	70.8
abcdf	s	50.06	65.4

with the combination of statistical and structural features achieves good results compared to other systems presented in the literature.

Most of the recognition errors of the developed system can be explained by the

Table 4. Comparison with other Arabic word recognition system

System	Technology	Recognition rate (%)			
		Set d	Set e	Set f	Set s
JU-OCR [11]	RF	75.49	63.75	63.86	49.75
RWTH-OCR [10]	HMM + NN	99.67	98.61	92.20	84.55
LITIS-MIRACL[3]	MSHMM	93.04	85.46	82.09	74.51
UPV PRHLT [1]	HMM	99.38	98.03	92.20	84.62
AI2A [4]	HMM	97.02	91.68	89.42	76.66
REGIM [9]	HMM	94.12	86.62	79.03	68.44
UOB-ENST[2]	HMM	92.38	83.92	81.93	69.93
Proposed system	MSHMM	91.1	82.91	70.8	65.4

poor quality of some writers' writing. Consequently, some words are badly written. Furthermore, the vector quantization procedure which searches to quantize the extracted continuous features can reduce their discrimination. Therefore, this can alter the discriminative power of the recognizers. To reduce these errors and ameliorate the performance of the developed system, the feature extraction process can be enhanced by computing other relevant features which can be suitable to describe the Arabic characters. In addition, instead of using synchronous 2-stream HMMs, the model can be generalized by applying n-stream HMMs. Also, to avoid the quantization process and keep the natural aspect of our features, a multivariate Gaussian HMM can be used.

4 Conclusion

Our work presents a recognizer system for the offline recognition of an Arabic handwritten word based on the discrete synchronous MSHMM. We have used the sliding window approach to compute a combination of statistical and structural features according to the columns and lines. Then two-word-model trainings are achieved: the whole model training and the analytical model training using the embedded training. The results show the effectiveness of the analytical approach and the reliability of the MSHMMs in Arabic handwriting recognition. As a future work, we plan to conduct experiments to assess the recognition rate of models using n-streams of observations. Furthermore, we will use a multivariate Gaussian HMM to avoid the quantization process and keep the natural aspect of our features.

References

1. Giménez, A., Khoury, I., Andrés-Ferrer, J., Juan, A.: Handwriting word recognition using windowed Bernoulli HMMs. Patt. Recog. Lett. **35**, 149–156 (2014)
2. El-Hajj, R., Likforman-Sulem, L., Mokbel, C.: Combining slanted-frame classifiers for improved HMM-based Arabic handwriting recognition. IEEE Trans. Patt. Anal. Mach. Intell. **31**, 1165–1177 (2009)
3. Kessentini, Y., Paquet, T., Hamadou, A.B.: Off-line handwritten word recognition using multi-stream hidden Markov models. Patt. Recog. Lett. **31**, 60–70 (2010)
4. Menasri, F., Vincent, N., Augustin, E., Cheriet, M.: Un système de reconnaissance de mots Arabes manuscrits hors ligne sans signes diacritiques. In: Proceeding of CIFED, pp.121–126, 2008
5. Jayech, K., Mahjoub, M.A., Essoukri Ben Amara, N.: Arabic handwritten word recognition based on dynamic bayesian network. Int. Arab J. Inform. Technol. (IAJIT) **13**(3) (2016) (To appear)
6. Jayech, K., Trimech, N., Mahjoub, M.A., Essoukri Ben Amara, N.: Dynamic Hierarchical Bayesian Network for Arabic Handwritten Word Recognition. In: IEEE 4th International Conference on ICT & Accessibility, 24–26 Oct 2013
7. Mahjoub, M.A., Ghanmy, N., Jayech, K., Miled, I.: Multiple models of Bayesian networks applied to offline recognition of Arabic handwritten city names. Int. J. Imaging Robot. **9**(1) (2013)
8. Rabiner, LR.: A tutorial on hidden Markov model and selected applications in speech recognition. In: Readings in Speech Recognition, pp. 267–296, San Mateo (1990)
9. Elbaati, A., Kherallah, M., El Abed, H., Ennaji, A., Alimi, A.M.: Arabic handwriting recognition using restored stroke chronology. In: Proceeding of ICDAR, (2009)
10. Dreuw, P., Heigold, G., Ney, H.: Confidence-based discriminative training for model adaptation in offline Arabic handwriting recognition. In: Proceeding of ICDAR (2009)
11. Abandah, G., Jamour, F.: Recognizing handwritten Arabic script through efficient skeleton-based grapheme segmentation algorithm. In: Proceedings of ISDA, pp. 977–982 (2010)

Image Segmentation Based on Hybrid Adaptive Active Contour

Amira Soudani[(⊠)] and Ezzeddine Zagrouba

Equipe de recherche SIIVA, Laboratoire RIADI,
Institut Supérieur d'Informatique, Université de Tunis El Manar,
2 Rue Abou Rayhane Bayrouni, 2080 Ariana, Tunisia
amira.soudani@gmail.com, ezzeddine.zagrouba@fsm.rnu.tn

Abstract. In this paper, we focus on segmentation based active contour model. In fact, we present an hybrid adaptive active contour segmentation algorithm. In this approach, we merge a global and an adaptive local based active contour models in order to segment images. The proposed energy is then minimized based on level set method. Experiments shows the good segmentation results provided by the proposed method.

Keywords: Segmentation · Active contour · Region based method · Level set methods

1 Introduction

Since the publication of Kass *et al.* [1], deformable models have become a very important issue for image processing. In fact, the active contour (AC) are applied in numerous areas such as pattern recognition, image segmentation, tracking object, etc. due to their ability to deform like snakes. This technique aims to segment an object by deforming iteratively an edge until it attempts the border of the object through the minimization of an energy computed based on different criteria. The minimization process moves the points of the curve until it attempts the border of the target object. The proposed works based on active contour are divided into three categories: edge based methods, region based methods and hybrid approaches.

At first, we cite the edge based active contour methods take into consideration the information on the target object's edge [1–4]. The principle idea is to move the points along the AC to make them closer to high gradient area while pertaining properties such as curvature and elasticity of the curve. This kind of models requires initialization of the curve in the immediate vicinity of the contours of the object of interest. The criterion used to characterize the more the contours is their the image gradient. The major drawback of the edge based approaches which take into consideration only local information is the quite sensitivity to noise. Thus, by minimizing the energy functional, it is likely to fall in a local minima.

© Springer International Publishing Switzerland 2015
E. Onieva et al. (Eds.): HAIS 2015, LNAI 9121, pp. 146–156, 2015.
DOI: 10.1007/978-3-319-19644-2_13

Secondly, we cite the region based active contour methods [5–11] which identify the region of interest using a descriptor for guiding the movement of the AC. These models are often based on the assumption that the image intensities are homogeneous on the region of interest. In [8], a local region based active contour is proposed. Local energies are constructed at each point of the curve based on the local neighborhoods which are divided into local interior and local exterior. Then, they extend the proposed framework to allow multiple object segmentation based on the idea of competing regions. In fact, the energy update equation is considered as having two competing components: retreat and advance. The advance force of the current edge is compared to retreat forces of all adjacent contours and similarly, the retreat force is compared to adjacent advance forces. Despite the significant improvement in accuracy for segmenting heterogeneous images, the method has limitations such as its increased sensitivity to initialization and the non automation of the radius value. In [9], authors propose a model which is based on the use of local image intensities that are described using gaussian distribution with different means and variances. A local energy is first defined to characterize the fitting of the local gaussian distribution to image data around a point neighborhood. Then, this energy is integrated over the whole image in order to obtain the local gaussian distribution fitting (LGDF) energy that will be incorporated into a variational level set formulation. Authors in [11] define an energy functional that integrates a local clustering criterion. In fact, they define a local clustering criterion function for the intensities in a neighborhood of each pixel. An interleaved process of level set evolution is then adopted to minimize the energy functional.

The last category consists on hybrid methods which exploit the advantages of the edge and region based AC approaches [12,13]. Authors in [13] proposed a geodesic intensity fitting model that incorporates the Chan-Vese model [6] and an edge-based active contour model. They proposed two models: global geodesic intensity fitting model is for images with intensity homogeneity and local geodesic intensity fitting model for images with intensity inhomogeneity. In [12], authors use the local region-based force of the localizing region-based active contour method [8] in conjunction with the smoothing force of the geodesic active contour method [14] to propose the energy functional. The method can handle the heterogeneous texture objects and able to reach into deep concave shapes.

In our work, we focus on hybrid based active contour methods. In fact, we propose an energy model based on the association of a global and an adaptive local based active contour energy terms. This allows us to capitalize on advantages of the two models (global and local). Then, the proposed energy is minimized based on level set representation.

The rest of the paper is organized as follows. Section 2 outlines the proposed approach. In Sect. 3, experimental results are shown followed by the conclusion in Sect. 4.

2   Proposed Approach

In the proposed method, the energy functional is composed of a local and a global region based energy terms. In fact, global region based active contour methods present a major limitation in case of intensity inhomogeneities present in the image which prevent these methods from correctly segmenting objects while the local region based methods can handle with such cases.

Let's denote by I an image on the domain Ω and Γ a closed contour. The proposed energy is expressed as

$$E_{hybrid}(\Gamma) = \alpha E_{global}(\Gamma) + (1 - \alpha)E_{local}(\Gamma). \tag{1}$$

where E_{global} and E_{local} are respectively the global and the local energy terms, α is a positive user fixed constant such that $\alpha \in]0..1[$.

In order to keep the curve smooth during the evolution, we add a regularization term, which penalizes the arc length of the contour. Then, the final energy term is a follows:

$$E_{hybrid}(\Gamma) = \alpha E_{global}(\Gamma) + (1 - \alpha)E_{local}(\Gamma) + \gamma|\Gamma|. \tag{2}$$

where $|\Gamma|$ is the length of the contour and γ is a positive fixed constant such that $\gamma \in]0..1[$.

2.1   Global Energy

We first present E_{global} which is based on the work presented in [6]. Let's denote by u and v the means intensities inside and outside Γ respectively. Then, E_{global} is expressed as follows:

$$E_{global}(\Gamma) = \lambda_1 \int_{inside(\Gamma)} |I(x) - u|^2 dx + (1 - \lambda_1) \int_{outside(\Gamma)} |I(x) - v|^2 dx. \tag{3}$$

where x is a point of I, $inside(\Gamma)$ and $outside(\Gamma)$ are respectively the areas inside and outside Γ, λ_1 is a positive constant such that $\lambda_1 \in]0..1[$. In order to solve the minimization problem, level set representation is used [15]. Hence, the closed contour Γ is represented as the zero level set of a signed function ϕ which is null for pixels on Γ, strictly positive for pixels inside Γ and strictly negative otherwise. Thus the energy functional is reformulated in terms of level set function ϕ:

$$E_{global}(\phi) = \lambda_1 \int_{\Omega} (H(\phi(x)))|I(x) - u|^2 dx + (1 - \lambda_1) \int_{\Omega} (1 - H(\phi(x)))|I(x) - v|^2 dx. \tag{4}$$

where $H(.)$ is an approximation of the Heaviside function.

$$u = \frac{\int_{\Omega} I(x)H(\phi(x))dx}{\int_{\Omega} H(\phi(x))dx}, v = \frac{\int_{\Omega} I(x)(1 - H(\phi(x)))dx}{\int_{\Omega}(1 - H(\phi(x)))dx}. \tag{5}$$

2.2   Local Energy

We associate to the input image I an edge map computed based on gradient information. It is represented by the function $\Psi(.)$ (Fig. 1(a)) such as for all points $x \in I$, $\Psi(x) = 1$ for $x \in \Gamma$ and null otherwise. We denote by ξ the smallest ellipse that includes Γ with minor and major axis length a and b respectively (Fig. 1(b)).

In order to compute local statistics, we will represent rectangular masks centered at each point $x \in \Gamma$ (Fig. 1(c)) of side length l_x by the function $M_x(.)$ where $M_x(y) = 1$ for all pixels $y \in \Omega$ inside the mask and null otherwise. We deduced that the masks side lengths have a high impact on the convergence process.

Thus, we propose an adaptive side length that will be updated at each iteration automatically, so $l_x = \upsilon * a$ where $\upsilon = 1$ if $\Psi(x) = 0$ and $\upsilon \in]0 \ldots 1[$ otherwise. This allows us to judge whether the pixel is close to the object boundaries. The side length of this mask will be maximum for pixels which coordinates don't coincide with the detected edge. Therefore, the weighting coefficient decreases as the pixel is closer to object's boundaries. Parameters are updated at each iteration until reaching the final contour.

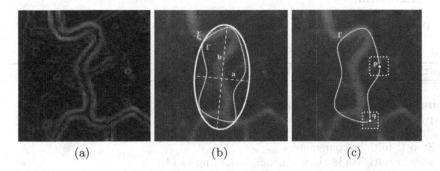

Fig. 1. (a) Edge Map. (b) Ellipse determination. (c) Masks extraction.

The local energy (4) is then reformulated as follows:

$$E_{local}(\phi) = \lambda_2 \int_\Omega \int_\Omega M_x(y) \cdot H(\phi(x))(I(x) - u_x)^2 dx dy$$

$$+ (1 - \lambda_2) \int_\Omega \int_\Omega M_x(y) \cdot (1 - H(\phi(x)))(I(x) - v_x)^2 dx dy. \qquad (6)$$

where:

$$u_x = \frac{\int_\Omega M_x(y) I(y) H(\phi(y)) dy}{\int_\Omega M_x(y) H(\phi(y)) dy}, v_x = \frac{\int_\Omega M_x(y) I(y)(1 - H(\phi(y))) dy}{\int_\Omega M_x(y)(1 - H(\phi(y))) dy}. \qquad (7)$$

2.3   Final Model

Now, we can rewritten the final energy as

$$E_{hybrid}(\phi) = \alpha E_{global}(\phi) + (1 - \alpha)E_{local}(\phi) + \gamma \int_{\Omega} \delta(\phi(x))|\nabla\phi(x)|. \quad (8)$$

where δ is a smoothed version of the Dirac Delta defined as the derivative of H. In order to solve the minimization problem, we use the Euler-Lagrange equations. Then, the level set function can be updated by gradient descent method. The evolution equation is expressed as

$$\frac{\partial \phi}{\partial t}(x) = \delta(\phi(x))(\lambda_1(I(x) - v)^2 - (1 - \lambda_1)(I(x) - u)^2)$$

$$+ \delta(\phi(x)) \int_{\Omega} M_x(y) \cdot \delta(\phi(y)) \cdot (\lambda_2(I(y) - v_x)^2 - (1 - \lambda_2)(I(y) - u_x)^2) dy$$

$$+ \delta(\phi(x))\left(\gamma \, divergence\left(\frac{\nabla\phi(x)}{|\nabla\phi(x)|}\right)\right). \quad (9)$$

2.4   Algorithm

The proposed algorithm can be summarized as follow[1]:

Algorithm 1. Algorithm of the proposed method

Input: Initial contour, Edge map
Output: Final contour

- Step 1: Initialize parameters;
- Step 2: Initialize level set function according to (4);
- Step 3: Initialize level set function according to (6);
- Step 4: Update the level set function according to (9);
- Step 5: Update parameters;
- Step 6: Return to step 2 until convergence condition is checked.

---

3   Experiments

In this section, we will evaluate the effectiveness and performance of the proposed method by using a series of medical, synthetical and real-world images. The choice of the images is due to the presence of intensity inhomogeneity and surrounding nearby clutter. Experiments are implemented under Matlab7.4 in a

---

[1] The evolution of the detected contour is less than a fixed threshold or the maximum number of iteration is reached.

personal computer with a processor Intel Core i5-3210M, 250 GHZ, Windows7. The parameters are set as follows: $\lambda_1 = \lambda_2 = 0.5$, $\alpha = 0.3$ and $\gamma = 0.02$.

We fist present results on medical images. In Fig. 2 we show the results of the segmentation of medical images. In fact, $Row1$ to $Row3$ show brain images with different initial contours. We deduce that better results are given by the proposed method. Otherwise, results provided by [8] in column(c) and [9] in column(d) fail to extract the desired object boundaries while the methods proposed in [6,11] in columns(b, e) respectively, converge to a global result by detecting even not desired regions due to inhomogeneity present in the hole image.

In $Row4$, we segment a vessel image, we obtain good results by the global method of [6] and our algorithm comparing to the other segmentation results. In $Row5$ we show that [8,9] retrieve an empty boundary whereas [6,11] extract undesired boundary and the proposed method gives the best segmentation result. We report in Table 1 the execution time and number of iteration associated to

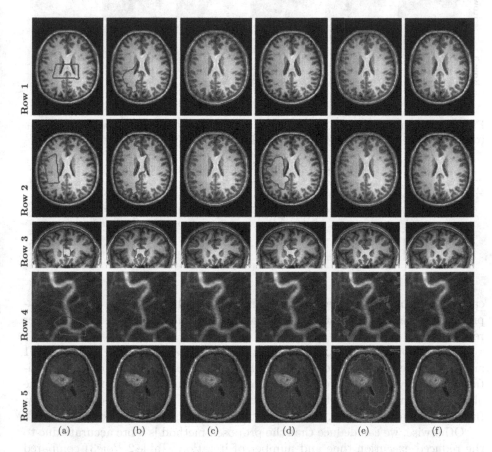

Fig. 2. Comparative results: (a) Initial contours. Results of: (b) Lankton et al. [8]. (c) Chan et al. [6]. (d) Wang et al. [9]. (e) Li et al. [11]. (f) The proposed method.

Table 1. CPU time for medical images

Id	Lankton et al. [8]		Chan et al. [6]		Wang et al. [9]		Li et al. [11]		Proposed	
	Iter. Nb	CPU(s)	Iter. Nb	CPU(s)	Iter. Nb	CPU(s)	Iter. Nb	CPU(s)	Iter. Nb	CPU(s)
Row1	1000	183	1000	21.19	821	208	200	14	85	29.88
Row2	319	35.12	1000	20.77	314	52.66	200	13.69	90	29.56
Row3	360	62.97	1000	11.58	31	40.32	100	18.41	128	69.04
Row4	1000	133	1000	9.46	995	144	200	7	212	37.2
Row5	14	1.51	1000	10.31	100	70.15	200	11.09	46	11.15

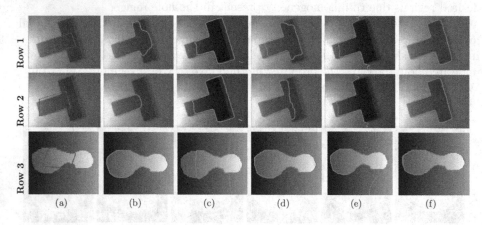

Fig. 3. Comparative results: (a) Initial contours. Results of: (b) Lankton et al. [8]. (c) Chan et al. [6]. (d) Wang et al. [9]. (e) Li et al. [11]. (f) The proposed method.

Table 2. CPU time for synthetical images

Id	Lankton et al. [8]		Chan et al. [6]		Wang et al. [9]		Li et al. [11]		Proposed	
	Iter. Nb	CPU(s)	Iter. Nb	CPU(s)	Iter. Nb	CPU(s)	Iter. Nb	CPU(s)	Iter. Nb	CPU(s)
Row1	1000	104.48	1000	9.47	1000	163.39	200	7.29	251	34.14
Row2	1000	115.87	1000	9.45	1000	193.8	200	7.04	247	34.88
Row3	273	11.08	1000	6.16	240	40.97	200	4.33	90	3.94

each algorithm, we deduce that the proposed method provides a good compromise between segmentation results and execution time regarding the other results.

Then, we present comparative results on synthetical images in Fig. 3. In *Row*1 and *Row*2, the proposed method in the last column provides the better segmentation results whereas [8] in column(b) and [9] in column(d) detect partially the object. In columns(c, e), methods of [6, 11] can't detect well the object's boundary. In *Row*3, the methods of [6, 11] fail to extract object boundaries (columns(c, e)).

Otherwise, we can deduce that the proposed method is more accurate due to the reduced execution time and number of iteration (Table 2 *Row*3) compared to the methods what succeed to segment well the target object [8, 9].

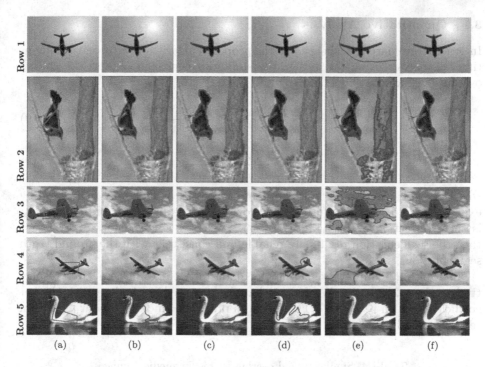

Fig. 4. Comparative results: (a) Initial contours. Results of: (b) Lankton et al. [8]. (c) Chan et al. [6]. (d) Wang et al. [9]. (e) Li et al. [11]. (f) The proposed method.

Table 3. CPU time for real images

Id	Lankton et al. [8]		Chan et al. [6]		Wang et al. [9]		Li et al. [11]		Proposed	
	Iter. Nb	CPU(s)	Iter. Nb	CPU(s)	Iter. Nb	CPU(s)	Iter. Nb	CPU(s)	Iter. Nb	CPU(s)
Row1	1000	201	1000	24.16	1000	185	200	15.06	156	31
Row2	1000	59.44	1000	7.43	362	43.36	100	14.60	89	7.73
Row3	299	89.35	1000	27.02	390	406.59	200	21.87	105	32.70
Row4	188	56.44	1000	27.722	1000	1055	200	17.82	55	29.41
Row5	156	63.52	1000	27.58	99	1323.1	200	19.66	143	72.74

Finally, in Fig. 4 we use real images to evaluate the proposed method. In *Row*1, *Row*3 and *Row*4 results provided by our algorithm and by [6] in respectively column(f) and column(c) show the better segmentation results while [11] always fails to extract well the object's boundary in column(e). In *Row*2, [9] and our method detect well the bird's boundary the image (column(d, f)). In *Row*5, results shows the good results provided by the proposed method whereas [6,11] fail to detect correct boundary due to presence of shadow in the image. Otherwise, as reported in Table 3, we deduce that the proposed method provides good results in reasonable execution time and number of iteration (Table 3).

3.1 Quantitative Analysis

In order to evaluate the efficiency of the proposed algorithm, we propose a quantitative analysis using two terms: the similarity coefficient S and the spatial overlap O expressed as follows [16]:

$$S = 1 - \frac{\mid I_{truth} - I_{algorithm} \mid}{\mid I_{truth} \mid} \tag{10}$$

$$O = \frac{2 * I_{intersection}}{I_{truth} + I_{algorithm}} \tag{11}$$

where I_{truth} is the ground truth segmentation which is manually segmented by experts, $I_{algorithm}$ is the segmentation provided by the algorithm and $I_{intersection}$ is the intersection of I_{truth} and $I_{algorithm}$. If those coefficients are close to 1 then the segmentation results are reliable and consistent with the ground truth segmentation.

In Tables 4, 5 and 6 we represent the quantitative analysis associated respectively to Figs. 2, 3 and 4. We deduce that the proposed method gives the higher coefficients which reach 0.97. Those results prove the efficiency of our algorithm regarding methods of state of art.

Table 4. Similarity and overlap scores for medical images

		Lankton et al. [8]	Chan et al. [6]	Wang et al. [9]	Li et al. [11]	Proposed
Row1	S	0.108	0.555	0.057	0.301	**0.770**
	O	0.246	0.818	0.167	0.741	**0.987**
Row2	S	0.443	0.567	0.182	0.318	**0.779**
	O	0.630	0.822	0.311	0.745	**0.900**
Row3	S	0.092	0.697	0.069	−0.210	**0.919**
	O	0.169	0.863	0.129	0.603	**0.959**
Row4	S	0.010	0.697	0.037	0.042	**0.748**
	O	0.003	0.823	0.354	0.623	**0.859**
Row5	S	0	−1.354	0	−6.641	**0.881**
	O	0	0.340	0	0.202	**0.937**

Table 5. Similarity and overlap scores for synthetical images

		Lankton et al. [8]	Chan et al. [6]	Wang et al. [9]	Li et al. [11]	Proposed
Row1	S	0.696	0.622	0.542	−0.357	**0.919**
	O	0.827	0.818	0.697	0.595	**0.960**
Row2	S	0.455	0.656	0.513	−0.344	**0.923**
	O	0.637	0.837	0.682	0.597	**0.976**
Row3	S	**0.944**	−0.256	**0.942**	−0.027	**0.933**
	O	**0.968**	0.518	**0.967**	0.655	**0.966**

Table 6. Similarity and overlap scores for real images

		Lankton et al. [8]	Chan et al. [6]	Wang et al. [9]	Li et al. [11]	Proposed
Row1	S	0.634	**0.981**	0.275	−7.445	**0.950**
	O	0.776	**0.990**	0.432	0.191	**0.975**
Row2	S	0.345	0.653	0.809	0.438	**0.826**
	O	0.513	0.828	0.896	0.758	**0.906**
Row3	S	0.399	0.860	0.505	−1.039	**0.866**
	O	0.570	0.924	0.671	0.465	**0.928**
Row4	S	0.373	0.697	0.449	−0.682	**0.7084**
	O	0.544	0.822	0.689	0.476	**0.829**
Row5	S	0.357	0.783	0.314	0.439	**0.827**
	O	0.526	0.883	0.523	0.752	**0.905**

4 Conclusion and Outlines

In this paper, we propose an hybrid region based active contour model for image segmentation. Experiments underscore that the merge of a global and a local energy with the use of an adaptive side length updated automatically in the minimization process yield to the improvement of segmentation results. Furthermore, experiments shows the weak sensitivity of the proposed method to initialization and its ability to deal with intensity inhomogeneity compared to other region based active contour methods.

References

1. Kass, M., Witkin, A., Terzopoulos, D.: Snakes: active contour models. Int. J. Comput. Vision **1**(4), 321–331 (1988)
2. Vasilevskiy, A., Siddiqi, K.: Flux maximizing geometric flows. IEEE Trans. Pattern Anal. Mach. Intell. **24**(12), 1565–1578 (2002)
3. Melonakos, J., Pichon, E., Angenent, S., Tannenbaum, A.: Finsler active contours. IEEE Trans. Pattern Anal. Mach. Intell. **30**(3), 412–423 (2008)
4. Hahn, J., Lee, C.-O.: Geometric attraction-driven flow for image segmentation and boundary detection. J. Vis. Commun. Image Represent. **21**(1), 56–66 (2010)
5. Yezzi Jr., A.Y., Tsai, A., Willsky, A.: A fully global approach to image segmentation via coupled curve evolution equations. J. Vis. Commun. Image Represent. **13**(12), 195–216 (2002)
6. Chan, T.F., Vese, L.A.: Active contours without edges. IEEE Trans. Image Process. **10**(2), 266–277 (2001)
7. Zhu, S.C., Yuille, A.: Region competition: unifying snakes, region growing, and bayes/mdl for multiband image segmentation. IEEE Trans. Pattern Anal. Mach. Intell. **18**(9), 884–900 (1996)
8. Lankton, S., Tannenbaum, A.: Localizing region-based active contours. IEEE Trans. Image Process. **17**(11), 2029–2039 (2008)
9. Wang, L., He, L., Mishra, A., Li, C.: Active contours driven by local gaussian distribution fitting energy. Signal Process. **89**(12), 2435–2447 (2009)

10. Wang, H., Huang, T.-Z., Xu, Z., Wang, Y.: An active contour model and its algorithms with local and global gaussian distribution fitting energies. Inf. Sci. **263**, 43–59 (2014)
11. Li, C., Huang, R., Ding, Z., Gatenby, C., Metaxas, D.N., Gore, J.C.: A level set method for image segmentation in the presence of intensity inhomogeneities with application to mri. IEEE Trans. Image Process. **20**(7), 2007–2016 (2011)
12. Srikham, M.: Active contours segmentation with edge based and local region based. In: 21st International Conference on Pattern Recognition (ICPR), pp. 1989–1992. IEEE (2012)
13. Xu, H., Liu, T., Wang, G.: Hybrid geodesic region-based active contours for image segmentation. Comput. Electr. Eng. **40**(3), 858–869 (2014). special Issue on Image and Video Processing
14. Caselles, V., Kimmel, R., Sapiro, G.: Geodesic active contours. Int. J. Comput. Vision **22**(1), 61–79 (1997)
15. Osher, S., Fedkiw, R.P.: Level Set Methods and Dynamic Implicit Surfaces. Applied Mathematical Science. Springer, New York (2003)
16. Zheng, Q., Dong, E., Cao, Z., Sun, W., Li, Z.: Modified localized graph cuts based active contour model for local segmentation with surrounding nearby clutter and intensity inhomogeneity. Signal Process. **93**(4), 961–966 (2013)

Particle Swarm Optimizer with Finite Velocity of Information Transmission

Miguel Cárdenas-Montes[1]($\boxtimes$) and Miguel A. Vega-Rodríguez[2]

[1] Department of Fundamental Research, Centro de Investigaciones Energéticas
Medioambientales y Tecnológicas, Madrid, Spain
miguel.cardenas@ciemat.es
[2] Department Technologies of Computers and Communications,
University of Extremadura, ARCO Research Group, Cáceres, Spain
mavega@unex.es

Abstract. Particle Swarm Algorithm is based on the capacity of the particles which integrate the swarm to share and to communicate relevant information about the best positions visited: *localbest* and *globalbest*. Independently of the position of the particles, all particles know the best position visited by any other particle in the same time-step when it is reached. However, in real world, information transmission has to take some time to travel between two particles positions. In this paper, the effect of a finite velocity for information transmission on the performance of the Particle Swarm Algorithm is analysed. Two scenarios appear in this context; first at all, when the velocity of information transmission is almost equal to the maximum velocity of the particles; and the second one, when it is much larger. This study clarifies the role played by a finite velocity of information transmission in the performance of the algorithm, specially when it is almost equal to the maximum velocity of the particles.

Keywords: Particle swarm optimizer · Performance · Optimization

1 Introduction

Particle Swarm Algorithm emerged as a powerful mechanism to find good solutions in complex problems. The Particle Swarm Optimizer Algorithm (PSO) [1–5] is based on the capacity of the particles to learn from their self experience and from the experience of the other particles integrating the swarm. These terms are usually called *cognitive term* and *social term*.

The social term of the PSO algorithm allows the particles to know about good solutions found by other particles. As early as one particle finds a good solution, information about this position is transmitted to the other particles. The transmission of this critical information is instantaneously done. In the same step that this information is known, it is cast away; simultaneously arriving to all particles; independently of their positions. So that, there is an assumption that the velocity of information transmission is infinite, or at least, much larger than the maximum velocity of the particles.

© Springer International Publishing Switzerland 2015
E. Onieva et al. (Eds.): HAIS 2015, LNAI 9121, pp. 157–169, 2015.
DOI: 10.1007/978-3-319-19644-2_14

However, information transmission at infinite velocity does not exit. The highest limit of the velocity of information transmission is the speed of light, $c = 299,792,458\,\text{m/s}$. If a finite velocity for information transmission is applied to PSO, then a best position found by any particle can not be reported in the same time-step when it is reached. Instantaneous information transmission is forbidden. Information propagation has to take some time in order to propagate throughout the search space.

At every time step, any particle knows information about the best position visited by itself, as well as a mixture of best positions visited by the other particles in different steps in the past. With this information, each particle must compose its own *global best known*.

With this modification, at each time-step all particles cast information about their present position, *localbest fitness* and *localbest position*. This information wave travels throughout the search space with finite velocity. A key element in this schema is the value of this velocity in relation to the maximum velocity of the particles. Two scenarios are significant: when the information velocity is much larger than the maximum velocity of the particles; and when both velocities are comparable.

The case with information velocity much larger than maximum velocity of the particles is equivalent to a classic formulation of PSO algorithm, at the same time it is equivalent to the classic kinematics. In this case, all the particles share a very similar information. The social term is relevant in the movement of the particles because each particle has updated information of the latest best position visited by any particle: information travels much faster than particles.

On the other hand, when both velocities are similar, it is equivalent to relativistic kinematics. In this second case, particles receive information from the past, and with this information plus the information of best position visited by itself the particle composes its strategy to move in the search space. In this case, the social term of each particle greatly differs among them. So that, the cognitive term becomes more relevant, since the social term holds information from the past of other particles. This allows to the particle a more intensive exploration of the local space around its position.

In order to establish a clear distinction between the two extreme cases — relativistic and non-relativistic—, the Lorentz's Factor, γ, can be used (Eq. 1). This factor is widely used in the Theory of Relativity to indicate when the relativistic effects become relevant.

$$\gamma = \frac{1}{\sqrt{1 - \frac{u^2}{c^2}}} \tag{1}$$

- The first case corresponds when the velocity of the particles (u) is similar to the velocity of information transmission (c); i.e. $u = 0.995\,c$. Using the Lorentz Factor, this case can be illustrated as:

$$\gamma = \frac{1}{\sqrt{1 - \frac{u^2}{c^2}}} = \frac{1}{\sqrt{1 - (0.995)^2}} \simeq 10 >> 1 \tag{2}$$

In this work, this case is termed *relativistic PSO*, RPSO.

- The second case corresponds when the velocity of the particles (u) is much lower than the velocity of information transmission, $u \ll c$. Then the Lorentz Factor is:

$$\gamma = \frac{1}{\sqrt{1 - \frac{u^2}{c^2}}} \simeq \frac{1}{\sqrt{1 - 0}} \simeq 1 \tag{3}$$

When the Lorentz factor approaching to one, the results of the proposed modification (RPSO) asymptotically tend to the results of standard PSO (SPSO). In SPSO the velocity of information transmission is much higher than the maximum velocity of the particles. Due to this, particles know about the best position visited by any particle in the same time-step when it is visited.

Grid computing has emerged as a powerful paradigm in e-Science, providing to the researchers an immense volume of computational resources distributed along diverse institutions. This paradigm [6,7] has made proof of being able to cover the requirements of a lot of scientific communities. The computing capabilities delivered by this paradigm have increased the generation of new science. For these reasons, a platform of grid computing has been selected for the present work. The infrastructure of ES-NGI (Spanish Grid Initiative) with gLite as middleware and GridWay as metascheduler has been used to support the production.

The rest of the paper is organized as follows: Sect. 2 summarizes the Related Work and previous efforts done. Section 3.1 makes short remarks about PSO algorithm. In Sect. 3.2, the most relevant details about the RPSO implementation are presented. The benchmark functions and the configurations used to evaluate the new approach are presented in Sect. 3.3. The Results and the Analysis are displayed in Sect. 4. Finally, the Conclusions are presented in Sect. 5.

2   Related Work

Many articles are published every year with works related to Particle Swarm Optimizer, mainly in the areas of adaptation for solving complex problems, and improvements or hybridizations of PSO for avoiding the stagnation of the solutions. For the sake of conciseness, few of them are cited in this section.

From the first works describing the foundations of the algorithm [1–3], it must be underlined the contributions describing the weaknesses of PSO. In [5,8] it is demonstrated that the particles in SPSO oscillate in damped sinusoidal waves until they converge to new positions. These new positions are between the *globalbest* position and the previous best position of the particle. During this oscillation, new positions are visited, and they can have better fitness than its previous *localbest*, so that this reactivates the oscillation. This movement is continuously repeated by all particles until the convergence is reached or any stop criterion is met.

However, in some cases, where the global optimum has not a direct path between current position and the local minimum already reached, the convergence is prevented. In this case, the efficiency of the algorithm diminishes. From the computational point of view, a lot of CPU-time is wasted exploring areas of suboptimal solutions already discovered.

In order to avoid this pernicious effect, diverse alternatives to PSO formulation have been proposed. Frequently, these enhancements are based on effects present in the nature, enforcing the image of the PSO algorithm as a bio-inspired algorithm. Among them: the Inertial Weight in which the previous velocity of the particle is progressively reduced [4], PSO with Massive Extinction which allows removing stagnant groups [9], Fitness Distance Ratio Based Particle Swarm Optimization which proposes that particles are also able to learn from the experience of the neighbouring particles having a better fitness that itself spite of it is not the *globalbest* [10], Dissipative PSO in which the stagnation is prevented by a negative entropy at the same time that some additional randomness is introduced [11], a Diversity-Guide PSO which through a measure of the diversity of the swarm, attractive and repulsive phases are switched [12], MeanPSO in which an alternative equation for the movement of the particles is proposed [13]. The MeanPSO replaces the role of the *globalbest* and the *localbest* by the half of their addition and the half of their difference.

Besides, it can be cited the works aimed to evaluate the relative performance of the previous approaches [14].

Our work is well aligned with this set of works: modification of the SPSO in order to improve its performance. To the authors' knowledge, no similar modifications of PSO have been proposed and analysed.

3   Methodology

In the PSO technique, each particle is represented as a point inside of a N-dimensional space. The dimension (N) of the problem is the number of variables of the problem to be evaluated.

Initially, a set of particles are created randomly. During the process, each particle keeps track of its coordinates in the problem space that are associated with the best solution it has achieved so far. This value is called *localbest*. Not only the best historical position of each particle is kept, also the associated fitness is stored. Other best value that is tracked and stored by the global version of the particle swarm optimizer is the overall best value, and its location, obtained so far by any particle in the population. This location is called *globalbest*.

The PSO concept consists in, at each time step, changing the velocity (accelerating) each particle toward its *localbest* and the *globalbest* locations (in the global version of PSO). Acceleration is weighted by a random term, with separate random numbers being generated for acceleration toward *localbest* and *globalbest* locations.

3.1   Standard Particle Swarm Optimization

The process for implementing the SPSO is as follows:

1. Creation of a random initial population of particles. Each particle has a position vector and a velocity vector on N dimensions in the problem space.

2. Evaluation of the desired (benchmark function) fitness in N variables for each particle.
3. Comparison of the each particle fitness function with its *localbest fitness*. If the current value is better than the recorded *localbest fitness*, it is replaced. Additionally, if replacement occurs, the current position is recorded as *localbest position*.
4. For each particle, comparison of the present fitness with the global best fitness, *globalbest*. If the current fitness improves the *globalbest* fitness, it is replaced, and the current position is recorded as *globalbest position*.
5. Updating the velocity and the position of the particle according to Eqs. 4 and 5 (where c_1 and c_2 are learning factors):

$$v_{id}(t + \delta t) \leftarrow v_{id}(t) + c_1 \cdot Rand() \cdot (x_{id}^{localbest} - x_{id}) +$$
$$c_2 \cdot Rand() \cdot (x_{id}^{globalbest} - x_{id}) \qquad (4)$$

$$x_{id}(t + \delta t) \leftarrow x_{id}(t) + v_{id} \qquad (5)$$

6. If neither stop criterion – fitness threshold or number of generations– is met, back to the step 2.

3.2   Implementation of RPSO

The main modification carried out for implementing RPSO is the inclusion of a finite velocity of information transmission. Thus, in each time-step the particles cast a spherical N-dimensional signal (Fig. 1). The signal embodies information about the best position visited by the particle, its *localbest fitness* and its current position.

The signals travel throughout the search space with finite velocity. At each time-step, the particles are receiving and processing information cast at different time-steps in the past from the other particles (Fig. 2).

Since the information held by each particle is different, the concept of a *global best position* known by all particles of the swarm disappears. Consequently, the different information about the position visited by the rest of the swarm that each particle holds, makes impossible to compose it for creating the *globalbest*.

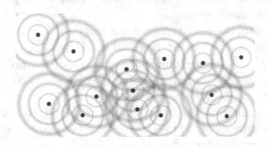

Fig. 1. Example of swarm casting information waves at diverse time steps (concentric circles).

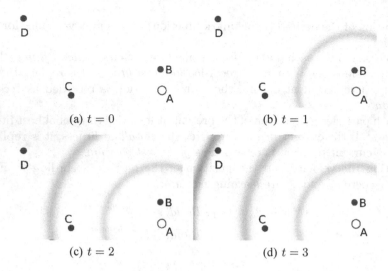

Fig. 2. Example of mechanism of information propagation. At $t = 0$, particle A casts information about the best position visited by itself. At $t = 1$, the information wave cast by the particle A in the previous time-step has arrived at particle B, but not to the particles C and D. Later at $t = 2$, the wave cast by A at $t = 0$ has also arrived to the particle C, whereas a second wave cast by A at $t = 1$ has arrived to B. At $t = 2$, neither information has arrived to D. At $t = 3$, the wave cast by A at $t = 0$ has arrived to particle D.

Otherwise, each particle can compose *a global best known by itself*. The proposed schema does not modify the *localbest* concept.

The concept termed as *a global best known by itself* substitutes to the *globalbest* in the fundamental equation of movement of particles in the PSO algorithm (Eq. 4). By replacing the *globalbest* by the *global best known by itself*, no modifications affect to the fundamental equations (Eqs. 4 and 5) of the PSO algorithm, being them still valid. Moreover, the calculation of the *localbest* by each particle is not modified either. A schema of the pseudocode of RPSO is shown at Algorithm 1.

Other aspect to underline is how many waves have to be stored in order to keep all relevant information. For each particle, the number of past waves has to be enough to be able to cross the longest path. This longest path is the longest diagonal, LD, in the search space.

In our configuration, the search space has a length of $L = 10$ in arbitrary units by dimension. Therefore, the longest diagonal is $LD^2 = \sum_{i=1}^{dimension} L^2 = D \cdot L^2$; then $LD = L \cdot \sqrt{D}$. The higher dimensionality, D, of the problem, the longer is the longest diagonal. The extreme case will be for $D = 20$, then the longest diagonal will be $LD = 10 \cdot \sqrt{20} \simeq 45$.

As the velocity of information transmission in the relativistic case is $c = 2$ (equal to maximum velocity of the particles), then the number of past waves necessary to store all relevant information is $\frac{longest\ path}{transmition\ velocity} = \frac{45}{2} = 22.5 \simeq 23$.

Algorithm 1. The Relativistic PSO Algorithm pseudocode.

---

initialization;
while *not done do* **do**
   foreach *Particle* **do**
      calculate which wave have reached the position;
      if *yes* **then**
         use this information to calculate the globalbest known;
         calculate the localbest;
         update Velocity();
         new Position();
         calculate Fitness;
         upgrade the wave information;

Table 1. Benchmark functions used in this work. They include multimodal and monomodal functions, separable and non-separable functions

Expression	Optimum
$f_1 = \sum_{i=1}^{D}[sin(x_i) + sin(\frac{2 \cdot x_i}{3})]$	$\simeq -1.90596 \cdot D$
$f_2 = \sum_{i=1}^{D-1}[sin(x_i \cdot x_{i+1}) + sin(\frac{2 \cdot x_i \cdot x_{i+1}}{3})]$	$-2 \cdot D + 2$
$f_3 = \sum_{i=1}^{D}[(x_i + 0.5)^2]$	0
$f_4 = \sum_{i=1}^{D}[(x_i)^2 - 10 \cdot cos(2\pi x_i) + 10]$	0
$f_5 = \sum_{i=1}^{D}[(x_i)^2]$	0
$f_6 = \sum_{i=1}^{D}[x_i \cdot sin(10 \cdot \pi \cdot x_i)]$	$\simeq -5 \cdot D$
$f_7 = 20 + 20 \cdot exp(-20 \cdot exp(-0.2\sqrt{\frac{\sum_{i=1}^{D} x_i^2}{D}})) - exp(\sum_{i=1}^{D} \frac{cos(2\pi x_i)}{D})$	0
$f_8 = 418.9828 \cdot D - \sum_{i=1}^{D}[x_i \cdot sin(\sqrt{|x_i|})]$	0
$f_9 = \sum_{i=1}^{D-1}[100 \cdot (x_{i+1} - x_i^2)^2 + (x_i - 1)^2]$	0
$f_{10} = \sum_{i=1}^{D}[i \cdot (x_i)^2]$	0
$f_{11} = \sum_{i=1}^{D}[(x_i)^2] + [\sum_{i=1}^{D}(\frac{i}{2} \cdot x_i)]^2 + [\sum_{i=1}^{D}(\frac{i}{2} \cdot x_i)]^4$	0

3.3 Production Setup

The empirical study was conducted using a set of benchmarks, with diverse functions widely used in these cases [15–17]. These functions were selected in order that the set has a mixture of multimodal and monomodal functions, separable and non-separable. For each benchmark function, a set of identical configurations was executed; including the relativistic ($c = 2, \gamma >> 1$) and non-relativistic cases ($c = 20, \gamma \simeq 1$). These configurations show the most characteristic values of dimensionality ($D = 3, 10, 20$), population ($P = 10, 20$) size and number of generations ($G = 10^2, 10^3, 10^4$). The benchmark functions selected are presented in Table 1.

For each benchmark function and configuration, 600 tries have been executed. In order to support this large set of executions, a grid infrastructure is used.

To manage the complexity of the problem, involving several benchmark functions and the set of configurations; the grid jobs were created with 50 tries of each configuration. This structure assures the optimization of the execution time for the grid environment. Several runs were executed to reach the statistical relevance desired.

Each job is composed by a shellscript that handles the execution, and a tarball containing the source code of the program and the configuration files. When the job arrives to the Worker Node, it executes the instructions of the shellscript: to roll-out the tarball, to compile the source code and to execute the 50 tries of each configuration for a benchmark function, and finally to tarball the results files. When the job finishes, it recuperates the results tarball.

Both PSO algorithms, the standard (SPSO) and the relativistic (RPSO) versions share some common parameters, such as, $c_1 = c_2 = 1$ in Eq. 4, and the maximum velocity, $V_{max} = 2$. Furthermore, for the configuration values of dimensionality (3, 10, 20), population size (10, 100) and number of cycles (10^2, 10^3, 10^4) were established. As pseudorandom number generator, a subroutine based on Mersenne Twister has been used [18].

The whole production takes a total of 521.52 h, taking 43.46 h by run. The number of jobs executed to complete the production was 28,512 –with 12 runs by function–; and, taking into consideration the number of tries by each configuration, then the number of tries was 237,600.

4   Results and Dicussion

In Tables 2, 3 and 4, a resume of the mean fitness obtained for each fitness function, configuration and PSO implementation is presented. However, these data are not enough to state if the new implementation outperforms in certain benchmark function the SPSO.

For the sake of conciseness, similar tables but presenting the minimum reached for each case for the RPSO and SPSO have been omitted. The analysis of the minima' results shows a similar number of best results for both algorithms: RPSO (73) and SPSO (94). This equality stems from the capacity of RPSO to find as good solutions as SPSO.

In spite of these results, the analysis of the results requires of their statistical analysis based on non-parametric tests.

In this work, the usual statistical analysis in the numerical optimization works has been followed [19,20]. The analysis is based on non-parametric tests, such as: Wilcoxon signed-rank tests. In-depth description of the statistical tests is beyond of the scope of this paper. This analysis has been performed using only 50 randomly selected results per case.

At Table 5, the p-value for the Wilcoxon signed-rank test is presented. Only the cases with statistically significant differences for a confidence level of 95 % (p-value under 0.05) are presented. This means that the differences are unlikely to have occurred by chance with a probability of 95 %.

Table 2. Mean fitness of benchmark functions f_1, f_2, f_3 and f_4 after 600 tries

D	P	G	f_1		f_2		f_3		f_4	
			c = 2	c = 20	c = 2	c = 20	c = 2	c = 20	c = 2	c = 20
			$\gamma \gg 1$	$\gamma \simeq 1$	$\gamma \gg 1$	$\gamma \simeq 1$	$\gamma \gg 1$	$\gamma \simeq 1$	$\gamma \gg 1$	$\gamma \simeq 1$
3	10	10^2	−5.569	−5.575	−3.720	−3.707	0.057	0.058	2.878	2.733
		10^3	−5.700	−5.695	−3.894	−3.901	0.013	0.013	1.083	1.097
		10^4	−5.689	−5.707	−3.950	−3.951	0.003	0.003	0.322	0.316
	20	10^2	−5.631	−5.596	−3.874	−3.874	0.036	0.033	2.274	2.383
		10^3	−5.689	−5.686	−3.965	−3.960	0.007	0.007	1.061	1.070
		10^4	−5.710	−5.707	−3.996	−3.996	0.001	0.001	0.328	0.311
10	10	10^2	−14.082	−12.575	−9.718	−9.687	1.542	1.549	41.804	42.165
		10^3	−15.084	−14.435	−11.595	−11.451	1.539	1.516	38.144	37.016
		10^4	−16.270	−15.960	−12.695	−12.829	1.424	1.405	30.428	30.353
	20	10^2	−14.933	−14.439	−10.325	−10.238	1.405	1.399	32.987	33.429
		10^3	−16.404	−16.276	−11.865	−11.757	1.237	1.227	27.609	27.191
		10^4	−17.854	−17.863	−13.454	−13.510	0.867	0.852	19.093	18.520
20	10	10^2	−27.925	−18.408	−14.457	−14.165	3.990	4.053	103.741	103.266
		10^3	−28.031	−20.879	−16.988	−16.865	3.882	3.993	99.802	99.150
		10^4	−28.590	−24.018	−18.791	−18.348	3.985	4.000	95.065	93.958
	20	10^2	−28.398	−22.822	−15.129	−15.003	4.051	4.201	84.294	85.661
		10^3	−28.430	−24.994	−17.367	−17.296	4.118	4.188	82.535	83.864
		10^4	−29.682	−28.663	−19.823	−19.843	4.201	4.180	82.606	83.445

As can be appreciated (Table 5), in many cases both algorithms similarly perform. The results do not show significant differences among those cases[1]. Besides, for some functions f_3, f_4, f_5, f_7, f_8, f_9, f_{10} and f_{11} the number of cases where one of the approaches outperforms to other is less than 3 (over a total of 18 cases per benchmark function).

On the other hand, for f_6 RPSO clearly outperforms SPSO. It produces significant better results for 10 cases, where no cases of better results of SPSO are produced for this function. For the functions f_1 and f_2 the inverse scenario is produced, SPSO outperforms RPSO (13 cases versus 1 case for f_1, 7 cases versus 3 cases for f_2).

In summary, on a total of 198 cases, the cases where the differences are significant and RPSO outperforms SPSO are 23 cases, whereas the opposite performance is produced in 36 cases, obtaining (by both algorithms) similar results in 139 cases.

---

[1] For these cases, where significant differences between both implementations are not found, no figure of p-value is shown at Table 5.

Table 3. Mean fitness of benchmark functions f_5, f_6, f_7 and f_8 after 600 tries

D	P	G	f_5		f_6		f_7		f_8	
			$c=2$	$c=20$	$c=2$	$c=20$	$c=2$	$c=20$	$c=2$	$c=20$
			$\gamma \gg 1$	$\gamma \simeq 1$	$\gamma \gg 1$	$\gamma \simeq 1$	$\gamma \gg 1$	$\gamma \simeq 1$	$\gamma \gg 1$	$\gamma \simeq 1$
3	10	10^2	0.038	0.038	−9.595	−9.596	17.289	17.288	1245.799	1245.691
		10^3	0.009	0.008	−9.834	−9.968	17.282	17.282	1245.336	1245.259
		10^4	0.002	0.002	−11.508	−11.653	17.282	17.282	1245.186	1245.184
	20	10^2	0.029	0.030	−10.523	−10.719	17.286	17.286	1245.837	1245.870
		10^3	0.005	0.005	−14.131	−14.207	17.282	17.282	1245.474	1245.525
		10^4	0.001	0.001	−14.848	−14.848	17.282	17.282	1245.309	1245.286
10	10	10^2	1.068	1.048	−19.422	−19.692	17.700	17.702	4162.078	4161.962
		10^3	1.011	1.020	−28.565	−28.895	17.498	17.493	4160.598	4160.314
		10^4	0.937	0.855	−39.678	−40.220	17.361	17.360	4158.343	4158.421
	20	10^2	0.901	0.975	−19.315	−19.608	17.540	17.537	4161.690	4161.979
		10^3	0.725	0.724	−22.705	−22.986	17.436	17.438	4159.911	4159.996
		10^4	0.385	0.373	−27.814	−28.287	17.331	17.331	4156.726	4156.804
20	10	10^2	2.887	2.923	−27.383	−27.930	17.958	17.959	8331.031	8331.355
		10^3	2.932	2.852	−39.586	−40.332	17.833	17.815	8329.989	8329.929
		10^4	2.892	2.805	−46.959	−46.299	17.656	17.662	8327.494	8327.663
	20	10^2	2.664	2.651	−27.643	−28.171	17.713	17.713	8330.039	8330.365
		10^3	2.715	2.786	−31.605	−31.761	17.671	17.680	8327.013	8327.501
		10^4	2.832	2.737	−36.101	−36.147	17.605	17.591	8323.511	8323.071

Table 4. Mean fitness of benchmark functions f_9, f_{10} and f_{11} after 600 tries

D	P	G	f_9		f_{10}		f_{11}	
			$c=2$	$c=20$	$c=2$	$c=20$	$c=2$	$c=20$
			$\gamma \gg 1$	$\gamma \simeq 1$	$\gamma \gg 1$	$\gamma \simeq 1$	$\gamma \gg 1$	$\gamma \simeq 1$
3	10	10^2	2.177	2.119	0.073	0.070	0.662	0.660
		10^3	0.592	0.557	0.015	0.015	0.241	0.248
		10^4	0.086	0.076	0.003	0.003	0.087	0.100
	20	10^2	1.476	1.455	0.054	0.051	0.800	0.778
		10^3	0.479	0.510	0.009	0.010	0.210	0.196
		10^4	0.090	0.087	0.002	0.002	0.044	0.041
10	10	10^2	109.944	110.773	5.195	5.241	15.784	16.477
		10^3	110.105	105.326	5.279	5.312	11.597	11.067
		10^4	104.625	100.953	5.073	4.642	8.338	8.131
	20	10^2	96.016	96.630	4.785	4.771	12.482	13.777
		10^3	76.931	73.147	3.850	3.647	7.478	7.281
		10^4	47.930	46.534	2.256	2.313	4.169	4.125
20	10	10^2	344.920	368.145	28.994	27.967	73.179	71.691
		10^3	338.426	352.895	28.231	28.666	53.017	52.825
		10^4	367.202	384.586	27.917	28.007	43.376	42.033
	20	10^2	347.703	336.548	26.708	26.428	56.396	61.217
		10^3	342.324	331.502	27.037	27.566	45.872	44.744
		10^4	335.593	344.042	27.062	27.368	35.628	35.968

Table 5. Wilcoxon signed-rank test value for all cases

D	P	G	f_1	f_2	f_3	f_4	f_5	f_6	f_7	f_8	f_9	f_{10}	f_{11}
3	10	10^2								0.010			
		10^3	0.015	0.008				0.014		4.8e-06			
		10^4	0.041					0.0008					
	20	10^2	4.8e-05			0.025	0.048	0.009					
		10^3		0.023				0.003	0.015	0.041			
		10^4								0.041			
10	10	10^2	0.0					0.017					
		10^3	0.0	0.019		0.026				0.006			
		10^4	3.9e-05	0.015			0.012	0.033				0.012	
	20	10^2	8.9e-12	0.022			0.012	0.002		0.035			0.019
		10^3	0.004	0.010							0.044	0.035	
		10^4		0.023		0.035		1.6e-05					
20	10	10^2	0.0	0.0				0.0002					
		10^3	0.0						0.0008				
		10^4	0.0	2.9e-06									
	20	10^2	0.0	0.012	0.002			1.6e-05					0.017
		10^3	0.0						0.039	0.006			
		10^4	0.0				0.022		0.0005	0.010			

5   Conclusions

In this paper, a modification for Particle Swarm Optimizer has been proposed and evaluated. The new approach modifies the infinite velocity for information transmission inherent in the standard implementation of PSO by a finite velocity for information transmission. This modification is evaluated with a wide set of benchmark functions, which include separable and non-separable, monomodal and multimodal functions; as well as for a wide set of configurations.

As a consequence of this modification, the existence of an unique *globalbest* for all particles is replaced by a new concept termed *globalbest known* for each particle. Furthermore, the fact that the particles are receiving and processing information cast by other particles in past, makes more relevant the cognitive term of the PSO movement equation in contrast to the social term. This allows a better exploration of the local area of the particles rather than jumping to the best position of other particles of the swarm.

The statistical analysis of the results obtained indicates that on a total of 198 cases, the new approach, RPSO, outperforms the standard PSO in 23 cases. Oppositely the PSO implementation outperforms the RPSO in 36 cases; whereas, in 139 cases the statistical analysis indicates that the differences are not significant.

As final conclusion it can be stated that the new approach can be incorporated to the portfolio of modifications proposed to the standard PSO to tackle optimization problems.

Acknowledgment. The research leading to these results has received funding by the Spanish Ministry of Economy and Competitiveness (MINECO) for funding support through the grant FPA2013-47804-C2-1-R, together with the European Community's Seventh Framework Programme (FP7/2007-2013) via the project EGI-InSPIRE under the grant agreement number RI-261323.

References

1. Eberhart, R., Kennedy, J.: A new optimizer using particle swarm theory. In: Proceedings of the Sixth International Symposium on Micro Machine and Human Science, MHS 1995, pp. 39–43 (1995)
2. Kennedy, J., Eberhart, R.C.: Particle swarm optimization. In: Proceedings of the IEEE International Conference on Neural Networks, vol. IV, pp. 1942–1948 (1995)
3. Eberhart, R.C., Shi, Y., Kennedy, J.: Swarm Intelligence. Artificial Intelligence, 1st edn. Morgan Kaufmann, San Francisco (2001)
4. Eberhart, R.C.: Computational Intelligence: Concepts to Implementations. Morgan Kaufmann Publishers Inc., San Francisco (2007)
5. Clerc, M., Kennedy, J.: The particle swarm - explosion, stability, and convergence in a multidimensional complex space. Trans. Evol. Comp 6(1), 58–73 (2002)
6. Kesselman, C., Foster, I.: The Grid: Blueprint for a New Computing Infrastructure. Morgan Kaufmann Publishers, San Francisco (1998)
7. Li, M., Baker, M.: The Grid Core Technologies. John Wiley & Sons, London (2005)
8. Ozcan, E., Cad, S., No, T.S., Mohan, C.K.: Particle swarm optimization: surfing the waves. In: Proceedings of the Congress on Evolutionary Computation, pp. 6–9. IEEE Press (1999)
9. Xie, X.F., Zhang, W.J., Yang, Z.L.: Hybrid particle swarm optimizer with mass extinction. In: IEEE 2002 International Conference on Communications, Circuits and Systems and West Sino Expositions, vol. 2, pp. 1170–1173, June 2002
10. Peram, T., Veeramachaneni, K., Mohan, C.K.: Fitness-distance-ratio based particle swarm optimization. In: Proceedings of IEEE on Swarm Intelligence Symposium, pp. 174–181, April 2003
11. Xie, X.F., Zhang, W.J., Yang, Z.L.: Dissipative particle swarm optimization. In: Proceedings of the Congress on Evolutionary Computation on 2002, CEC 2002, Washington, DC, USA, pp. 1456–1461. IEEE Computer Society (2002)
12. Riget, J., Vesterstroem, J.: A diversity-guided particle swarm optimizer - the ARPSO. Technical Report no. 2002–02, Aarhus Universitet (2002)
13. Deep, K., Bansal, J.C.: Mean particle swarm optimisation for function optimisation. Int. J. Comput. Intell. Stud. 1(1), 72–92 (2009)
14. Cárdenas-Montes, M., Vega-Rodríguez, M.A., Gómez-Iglesias, A., Morales-Ramos, E.: Empirical study of performance of particle swarm optimization algorithms using grid computing. In: González, J.R., Pelta, D.A., Cruz, C., Terrazas, G., Krasnogor, N. (eds.) NICSO 2010. SCI, vol. 284, pp. 345–357. Springer, Heidelberg (2010)
15. Liang, J., Qu, B., Suganthan, P.: Problem definitions and evaluation criteria for the CEC 2014 special session and competition on single objective real-parameter numerical optimization. Technical report, Technical Report 201311, Computational Intelligence Laboratory, Zhengzhou University, Zhengzhou China and Technical Report, Nanyang Technological University, Singapore (2013)

16. Tang, K., Li, X., Suganthan, P.N., Yang, Z., Weise, T.: Benchmark functions for the CEC 2010 special session and competition on large-scale global optimization. Technical report, Nature Inspired Computation and Applications Laboratory (NICAL), School of Computer Science and Technology, University of Science and Technology of China (USTC), Electric Building No. 2, Room 504, West Campus, Huangshan Road, Hefei 230027, Anhui, China (2009)
17. Tang, K., Yao, X., Suganthan, P.N., MacNish, C., Chen, Y.P., Chen, C.M., Yang, Z.: Benchmark functions for the CEC 2008 special session and competition on large scale global optimization. Technical report, Nature Inspired Computation and Applications Laboratory, USTC, China (2007)
18. Matsumoto, M., Nishimura, T.: Mersenne twister: a 623-dimensionally equidistributed uniform pseudo-random number generator. ACM Trans. Model. Comput. Simul. **8**(1), 3–30 (1998)
19. García, S., Molina, D., Lozano, M., Herrera, F.: A study on the use of nonparametric tests for analyzing the evolutionary algorithms' behaviour: a case study on the CEC'2005 special session on real parameter optimization. J. Heuristics **15**(6), 617–644 (2009)
20. García, S., Fernández, A., Luengo, J., Herrera, F.: A study of statistical techniques and performance measures for genetics-based machine learning: accuracy and interpretability. Soft Comput. **13**(10), 959–977 (2009)

Bio-inspired Models
and Evolutionary Computation

Cryptanalysis of Simplified-AES Using Intelligent Agent

Rania Saeed[✉] and Ashraf Bhery

Computer Science Subdivision, Faculty of Science,
Ain Shams University, Cairo, Egypt
`rania_saeed@sci.asu.edu.eg`

Abstract. Software agent technology is a rapidly developing area of research. In this paper, we introduce a new application of an agent system, called *cryptanalytic-agent* system whose behaviour will be intelligent enough to attack Simplified Advance Encryption Standard (S-AES) block cipher. Our results confirm the versatility of our proposed approach.

Keywords: Intelligent agent · Cryptography · Cryptanalysis

1 Introduction

Simplified Advance Encryption Standard, S-AES, was developed by Professor Edward Schaefer of Santa Clara University and several of his students [1] in 2003. It is an encryption algorithm to help cryptographers and cryptanalysts to better understanding the concepts behind the real Advance Encryption Standard, AES [2]. It has a good mathematical structure, such as AES.

Artificial agents, subsuming both robots and software agents, represent a new paradigm in Software Engineering and Artificial Intelligence. Depending on the technologies used in their implementation, they may exhibit various characterstics. In particular, they may act more or less *autonomously*, they may be able to *learn* and to *adapt* with a changing environment. They may be able to achieve their goals *pro-actively* [3–5]. Due to these unique characteristics developing agent systems has been a very challenging task for agent researches and application developers. In this paper, we introduce a new application of agent system, called *cryptanalytic-agent*[1] system whose behaviour will be intelligent enough to attack S-AES. To do this, firstly, the S-AES encryption algorithm is translated into an equivalent formula that is conjunctive normal form, denoted by E-CNF. This formula is obtained using a set of rules presented in this paper. Variables in our E-CNF formula will be plaintext bits, ciphertext bits, cipher key bits, and an auxiliary variables that are used in the translation. Our cryptanalytic attack is the known plaintext attack. Then, we propose a cryptanalytic agent to interact with the E-CNFformula and use his initial knowledge about

---

[1] The type of agent, that we focus on, is the autonomous, pro-active behaviour of a single agent, that is situated in a particular environment.

© Springer International Publishing Switzerland 2015
E. Onieva et al. (Eds.): HAIS 2015, LNAI 9121, pp. 173–187, 2015.
DOI: 10.1007/978-3-319-19644-2_15

ciphertext and plaintext to deduce the original cipher key bits. This method can led to design a better cryptanalytic attack on real AES [2].

In the previous work, Musa et al. [1], attacked S-AES for the first time using linear and differential cryptanalysis. Linear and differential cryptanalysis is applied for one round S-AES. From their results, 109 plaintext and corresponding ciphertext pair were required. Mansoori et al. [6], attacked S-AES against linear cryptanalysis. Linear cryptanalysis is applied using the known plaintext attack. To break the first round 116 plaintexts were required and 548 plaintexts were required to break the second round. Simmons [7], attacked S-AES using Algebraic cryptanalysis. More number of plaintext and ciphertext pair is required for this type of attack. Valarmathi and Vimalathithan [8] attacked S-AES using Particle Swarm Optimization and used ciphertext-only attack, More number of ciphertext is required for this type of attack. But the proposed approach allows to find the cipher key by using only one plaintext and its corresponding ciphertext.

The rest of the paper is structured as follows. In Sect. 2, we describe briefly the main transformations of S-AES encryption process. In Sect. 3, we show the used method in the transformation S-AES encryption into an equivalent E-CNF formula. In Sect. 4, an encryption model of E-CNF, its validity, and the key-equivalent of two encryption models are defined. In Sect. 5, the construction related issues of the proposed cryptanalytic agent system are discussed. The results are given in Sect. 6. Finally, the conclusion is presented in Sect. 7.

2   Simplified AES (S-AES)

S-AES [9] is a non-feistel block cipher, which means that each transformation or group of transformations must be invertible. It takes 16 bit plaintext and 16 bit cipher key as input and generates 16 bit ciphertext as output. The 16 bit input plaintext are treated as matrix of 4 nibbles (a nibble is 4 bits), called state. Figure 1 shows encryption and decryption algorithms for S-AES.

2.1   S-AES Transformations

For ease of explanation of these transformations, the 16 bit plaintext block, $P = (p_0p_1p_2p_3 \; p_4p_5p_6p_7 \; p_8p_9p_{10}p_{11} \; p_{12}p_{13}p_{14}p_{15})$ are expressed as a matrix of 4 nibbles as follows:

$$\begin{bmatrix} p_0p_1p_2p_3 & p_8p_9p_{10}p_{11} \\ p_4p_5p_6p_7 & p_{12}p_{13}p_{14}p_{15} \end{bmatrix}$$

SubNibbles (S-box). The first transformation, SubNibbles, is used at the encyrption process. Only one table is used for transformations of every nibble. To substitute a nibble, we interpret the nibble as 4 bits. The left 2 bits define the row and the right 2 bits define the column of the substitution table. The hexadecimal digit at the junction of the row and the column is the new nibble. Figure 2 shows the idea and also shows the SubNibbles table (S-box) for the SubNibbles transformation.

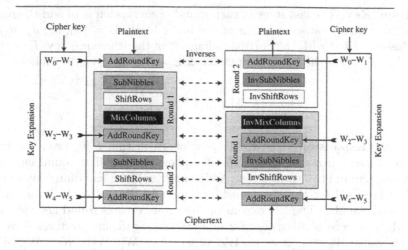

Fig. 1. S-AES encryption and ecryption

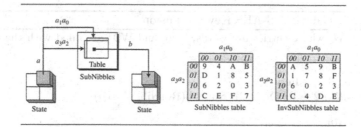

Fig. 2. SubNibbles transformation

ShiftRows. The second transformation, ShiftRows, is used at the encyrption process and the shifting is done at the nibble level and to the left. The order of the bits in the nibble is not changed. The number of shifts depends on the row number(0, 1) of the state matrix. This means row 0 is not shifted at all and row 1 is shifted 1 nibble.

MixColumns. The MixColumns transformation operates at the column level; it transforms each column of the state into a new column. The transformation is actually the matrix multiplication of a state column by a constant square matrix. The nibbles in the state column and constants matrix are interpreted as polynomials with coefficients in Galois Field GF(2). Multiplication of bytes is done in $GF(2^4)$ with modulus (x^4+x+1) [10]. Addition is the same as XORing of 4-bit words. The mixcolumns transformation defined by the following matrix multiplication on the state matrix:

$$\begin{bmatrix} S'_{0,0} & S'_{0,1} \\ S'_{1,0} & S'_{1,1} \end{bmatrix} = \begin{bmatrix} 1 & 4 \\ 4 & 1 \end{bmatrix} \begin{bmatrix} S_{0,0} & S_{0,1} \\ S_{1,0} & S_{1,1} \end{bmatrix}$$

AddRoundKey. The last stage of each round of encryption is to add the round key. AddRoundKey causes each bit of the input block, D = (d_0, d_1, d_2, d_3) to be exclusived-ORed with the corresponding bit of the ith round key, $K_i = (k_0, k_1, k_2, k_3)$ to obtain the 16 bit output block E = (e_0, e_1, e_2, e_3) as follows:

$$\begin{bmatrix} e_0 \ e_2 \\ e_1 \ e_3 \end{bmatrix} = \begin{bmatrix} d_0 \ d_2 \\ d_1 \ d_3 \end{bmatrix} \oplus \begin{bmatrix} k_0 \ k_2 \\ k_1 \ k_3 \end{bmatrix}$$

S-AES KeyExpansion. The KeyExpansion Algorithm 1 [6] produces three 16 bit round keys from one single 16 bit cipher key. The first round key (K_0) is used for preround transformation (AddRoundKey); the remaining round keys (K_1, K_2) are used for the last transformation (AddRoundKey) at the end of round 1 and round 2. The key expansion algorithm creates round keys word by word, where a word is an array of 2 nibbles, the algorithm produces 6 words, which are called $W_0, W_1, W_2, \ldots, W_5$. Where $K_0 = W[0]W[1]$, $K_1 = W[2]W[3]$, $K_2 = W[4]W[5]$.

Algorithm 1. Calculate S-AES Key Expansion

//An array W, whose entries are words, W[0] and W[1] are filled with the original key in order.
for $2 \le i \le 5$ **do**
   if $i \equiv 0 (\mod 2)$ **then**
      W[i] = W[i-2]$\oplus$ RCON(i/2)$\oplus$SubNib(RotNib(W[i-1]))
   else
      W[i] = W[i-1]$\oplus$W[[i-2]
   end if
end for

In Algorithm 1, RCON[i] = RC[i]0000, where RC[i] is defined as RC[i] = $x^{i+2} \in$ GF(2^4) so RC[1] = x^3 = 1000 and RC[2] = x^4 = x +1 = 0011. If N_0 and N_1 are nibbles, then their concatenation denoted as N_0N_1. The function RotNib is defined to be RotNib(N_0N_1) = N_1N_0 and the function SubNib to be SubNib(N_0N_1)= S-box(N_0) S-box(N_1).

3   Converting S-AES Encryption into Conjunctive Normal Form Formula (CNF)

In this section, we convert the S-AES encryption algorithm into an equivalent Conjunctive Normal Form formula[2] (denoted by E-CNF). A propositional formula F is in Conjunctive Normal Form (CNF) if it is a conjunction (AND, $\land$) of clauses, where each clause is a disjunction (OR, $\lor$) of literals, and each literal

---

[2] This form is used widely for describing SAT and MAXSAT problems.

is either a variable or its negation (NOT, ¬). The set of all variables occurring in a formula F is denoted as VAR(F). In the following, we give a procedure that used to convert the S-AES encryption algorithm into an equivalent CNF formula. This conversion is based on rules about logical equivalences [11] and the other rules as in Fig. 3.

Rule No	RULE	Equivalent RULE in CNF
1	¬(a ∧ b)	(¬a∨¬b)
2	(a ∨(b∧ c))	((a ∨b)∧(a ∨c))
3	a⇒b	(¬a ∨ b)
4	a=b	((¬a∨b)∧(¬b∨a))
5	c=a∧b=ab	(¬ c∨ a)∧ (¬ c∨ b)∧ (c∨¬ a∨¬ b)
6	c=a⊕ b	(¬ c∨a∨ b)∧(c∨ ¬a∨b)∧(c∨ a∨ ¬b)∧ (¬c∨ ¬b∨ ¬a)

Fig. 3. General rules about logical equivalences

For transferring to CNF, each individual transformation SubNibbles, ShiftRows, MixColumns, and AddRoundKey of S-AES is converted into an equivalent CNF formula. From Sect. 2, the transformations ShiftRows and AddRoundKey can be transfered easily into an equivalent CNF formula by using rules in Fig. 3. The CNF formula corresponding to SubNibbles and MixColumns transformations are shown in the following subsections.

3.1   CNF of S-box

In [7], the authors generate the S-box as a system of polynomials. This is done by constructing an ordered list of four polynomials each of which accepts 4-bit input and returns one bit of output. The four ordered bits of output are the four bits of the S-box output. By using rules 5 and 6 in Fig. 3, we can transfer these polynomials into CNF formula.

$$b'_1 = b_1b_2 \oplus b_1b_3b_4 \oplus b_1b_4 \oplus b_1 \oplus b_2b_3b_4 \oplus b_3b_4 \oplus b_4 \oplus 1,$$
$$b'_2 = b_1b_2b_4 \oplus b_1b_2 \oplus b_1b_3 \oplus b_1 \oplus b_2b_3b_4 \oplus b_2b_3 \oplus b_2 \oplus b_3b_4 \oplus b_4,$$
$$b'_3 = b_1b_2b_3 \oplus b_1b_2b_4 \oplus b_1b_2 \oplus b_1b_3b_4 \oplus b_1 \oplus b_2x_3 \oplus b_3,$$
$$b'_4 = b_1b_2b_3 \oplus b_1b_2b_4 \oplus b_1b_3b_4 \oplus b_1b_3 \oplus b_1b_4 \oplus b_1 \oplus b_2b_3b_4 \oplus b_2b_4 \oplus b_3 \oplus b_4 \oplus 1.$$

3.2   CNF of MixColumns

The basic operations employed in MixColumn transformation are addition and multiplication elements of $GF(2^4)$, with $x^4 + x + 1$ as polynomial for the field multiplication. Addition consists of a simple bitwise exclusive-or, while multiplication is the vital calculation module. Various architectures have been proposed for the implementation of the multiplication in GF (2^n) [12]. By applying the multiplication architecture presented in [10], we get the four ordered bits $(c_3\ c_2\ c_1\ c_0)$ output of multiplication are defined as in Eq. (1), where $(a_3\ a_2\ a_1\ a_0)$ and $(b_3\ b_2\ b_1\ b_0)$ are the inputs.

$$c_0 = a_0b_0 \oplus a_1b_3 \oplus a_3b_1 \oplus a_2b_2$$
$$c_1 = a_0b_1 \oplus a_1b_0 \oplus a_1b_3 \oplus a_3b_1 \oplus a_2b_2 \oplus a_2b_3 \oplus a_3b_2$$
$$c_2 = a_1b_1 \oplus a_0b_2 \oplus a_2b_0 \oplus a_2b_3 \oplus a_3b_2 \oplus a_3b_3$$
$$c_3 = a_0b_3 \oplus a_1b_2 \oplus a_2b_1 \oplus a_3b_0 \oplus a_3b_3$$

$$(1)$$

By using rules in Fig. 3, we can get the CNF formula for the multiplication.

Finally, for the full-version of S-AES, the CNF representation has been obtained by adding intermediate literals during the conversion of main transformations for S-AES. As a result, we obtained a system of 2200 clauses in 645 variables with at most 3 literals per clause.

4   An Encryption Model of E-CNF

The boolean satisfiability problem (SAT) [13] is defined as follows: given a boolean formula, check whether an assignment of Boolean values to the propositional variables in the formula exists, such that the formula evaluates to true. If such an assignment exists, the formula is said to be satisfiable; otherwise, it is unsatisfiable. The complexity of such problems is known to be NP-hard [14]. Unfortunately, SAT approach does not provide a model(or a solution) for the E-CNF formula that obtained from Sect. 3. So, we focus on the MAX-SAT, an optimization version of SAT which consists of finding a truth assignment that satisfies the maximum number of clauses in a CNF formula. Therefore, we may seek to find values for a subset of the E-CNF variables that satisfy the constraint $(E_K(P) = C$ or $D_K(C) = P)$, where E and D are the S-AES encryption and decryption algorithms, P, C, and K are the plaintext, ciphertext, and cipher key. Hence, in the following, we formalizes the notion of "An encryption model" of E-CNF, its validity, and the key-equivalent of two encryption models.

Definition 1. *Let F be a E-CNF formula. A vector is an assignment σ: $Var(F) \rightarrow \{0, 1, ?\}$. The symbol $?$ denotes that a variable is undetermined. A vector is total if every variable is determined. (i.e., it is assigned a value from $\{0, 1\}$).*

A vector that restricted to the set of all plaintext variables is called *plain-vector*. Similarly, we have *cipher-vector, cipher key-vector, extended cipher key-vector* and *auxiliary-vector*.

Definition 2. *Let F be a E-CNF formula. An encryption model of F, denoted by M, is defined as a tuple (PV, CV, KV), where PV is the plain-vector, CV is the cipher-vector, and KV is the cipher key-vector.*

Definition 3. *Let F be a E-CNF formula and $M = (PV, CV, KV)$ be an encryption model of F. We say that M is valid model iff PV, CV, and KV are totals vectors and $(E_{V(KV)}(V(PV)) = V(CV) \vee D_{V(KV)}(V(CV)) = V(PV))$, where $V(x)$ denoted the ordered value assigned to x, E and D are the S-AES encryption and decryption algorithms.*

Definition 4. *Let F be a E-CNF formula. Two encryption models $M = (PV, CV, KV)$ and $M' = (PV, CV, KV')$ of F are said to be key-equivalent iff M and M' are valid models.*

5   Cryptanalytic Agent of S-AES

In this section, we introduce a new intelligent agent-based cryptanalytic model called *cryptanalytic-agent* for attacking S-AES. The main function of the proposed cryptanalytic-agent system is to deal with E-CNF and to use its knowledge about ciphertext and plaintext in order to find a valid encryption model in the system. The architecture that serves as a basis for the proposed cryptanalytic agent in this paper is the *rule-based agent* architecture [15]. The following concepts are essential to rule-based systems.

- A fact base stores information about the state of the world in the form of facts.
- A rule base stores rules which represent the knowledge of how to process certain facts stored in fact base. The rule base consists of a condition part (called left-hand side, LHS) and an action part (called right-hand side, RHS).
- An Inference Engine controls the inference process by selecting and processing the rules which can fire on the basis of certain conditions. This can be done in a forward-chaining or backward-chaining manners.

5.1   Cryptanalytic-Agent: Fact Base

In this section, we will model an agent's knowledge about the world as a 4-tuple $S = (C, A, X, AK)$, where

- C is the E-CNF state. The state of E-CNF is either C or new(C) or old(C)
- A is a vector restricted to the set of all E-CNF variables, initialy each variable in A is undetermined. The vector A represents what knowledge can be computed from E-CNF.
- X is a sequence of vectors, initialy empty and is denoted by <>.
- AK is an agent's knowledge about the plaintext, ciphertext, and the cipher key. This knowledge is modeled as Agent Knowledge System (AK-System) which explain in the following.

Agent Knowledge System (AK-System). We propose a deduction system called the Agent Knowledge System (or the *AK-System*). In AK-system, we will model an agent's knowledge about the plaintext, ciphertext, and the cipher key as an encryption model M, and model the derivation of new knowledge by an agent as an inference process in this encrypted model M. An AK-System consists of a triple $(M, \Sigma, \vdash_{AK})$, where:

1. M is an encryption model,
2. Σ is the set of AK-inference rules which explain in the following. Each AK-inference rule has zero or more premises and a conclusion.
3. $\vdash_{AK}$ is the AK-derivation relation, which is defined using a sequence of applications of AK-inference rules. We write the formula $M \vdash_{AK} \phi$ if formula ϕ can be derived from model M using set of Ak-inference rules Σ.

AK-Inference Rules. In the following, we define the set of AK-inference rules. Each AK-inference rule is represented in the form of $\frac{premises}{conclusion}$, where the premises are a set of terms and a conclusion is a term. This means that from the premises, we can derive a conclusion. In the following AK-inference rules, we use p, k, and c to denote meta-variables over PV, KV, and CV respectively. We use x and y to denote meta-variables over PV, KV, CV, and their concatenations. The notation $M \models x$ is used to indicate that agent knows x from the model M. If the agent does not know x from the model M, then we write $M \not\models x$.

1. $$\frac{}{M \models p} \quad \text{(for each } p \in PV)$$
   The cryptanalytic-agent knows all the plaintext variables in the model M.

2. $$\frac{}{M \models k} \quad \text{(for each } k \in KV),$$
   The cryptanalytic-agent knows all the cipher key variables in the model M.

3. $$\frac{}{M \models c} \quad \text{(for each } c \in CV),$$
   The cryptanalytic-agent knows all the ciphertext variables in the model M.

4. $$\frac{M \models x \quad \text{determined(x)}}{M \models V(x)}$$
   The cryptanalytic-agent knows the value of x in the model M.

5. $$\frac{M \models x \quad \text{undetermined(x)}}{M \not\models V(x)}$$
   The cryptanalytic-agent knows that it does not know the value of x in the model M.

6. $$\frac{M \models V(x) \wedge M \models V(y)}{M \models V(x,y)}$$
   The cryptanalytic-agent knows the value of pattern x, y if it knows the value of x and also knows the value of y in the model M.

7. $$\frac{M \not\models V(x) \vee M \not\models V(y)}{M \not\models V(x,y)}$$
   The cryptanalytic-agent knows that it does not know the value of pattern x, y if it does not know the value of either x or y in the model M.

8. $$\frac{M \models V(x,y)}{M \models V(x) \wedge M \models V(y)}$$
   If the cryptanalytic-agent knows the value of pattern x, y, then it knows the value of x and also knows the value of y in the model M.

9. $$\frac{M \not\models V(x,y) \wedge M \models V(x)}{M \not\models V(y)}$$
   If the cryptanalytic-agent knows that it does not know the value of pattern x, y and it knows the value of x, then it knows that it does not know the value of y in the model M.

10. $$\frac{M \not\models V(x,y)}{M \not\models V(y,x)}$$
    If the cryptanalytic-agent knows that it does not know the value of pattern x, y, then it knows that it does not know the value of pattern y, x in the model M.

11. $\dfrac{M \models V(x,y)}{M \models V(y,x)}$

If the cryptanalytic-agent knows the value of pattern x,y, then it knows the value of pattern y, x in the model M.

12. $\dfrac{M \models V(PV) \wedge M \models V(KV) \wedge M \models V(CV)}{M \models valid}$ $\qquad Valid(PV,\ KV,\ CV)$

13. $\dfrac{M \not\models V(PV) \vee M \not\models V(KV) \vee M \not\models V(CV)}{M \models invalid}$

14. $\dfrac{M \models V(PV) \wedge M \models V(KV) \wedge M \models V(CV)}{M \models invalid}$ $\qquad \neg(Valid(PV,\ KV,\ CV))$

The cryptanalytic-agent knows that the encryption model M is either valid as in rule 12 or invalid as in rules 13 and 14.

Definition 5. *Consider S_1, S_2 and S_3 are meta variables range over statement, $\vdash_{AK}$ is defined inductively as follows.*

1. *Base case. If the AK-inference rule of the form $\overline{M \models S_1}$, then $M \vdash_{AK} S_1$ is a AK-derivation.*
2. *Induction case: if we have AK-derivation $M \vdash_{AK} S_1, M \vdash_{AK} S_2$, and there is an AK-inference rule of the form $\frac{M \models S_1, M \models S_2}{M \models S_3}$ (or of the form $\frac{M \models S_1}{M \models S_3}$), then $M \vdash_{AK} S_3$ is a AK-derivation.*

5.2 Cryptanalytic-Agent: Rule Base

The rule base contains the action rules[3] that available to our cryptanalytic-agent system. Each action rule has the form $\Phi \Rightarrow Act$, where Φ is a mental state condition[4] and Act is an action. Our cryptanalytic-agent is capable of performing a set of actions Acts $= \{Simplify(t),\ Maxsat(C),\ Revise(t,M),\ Choose(t),\ Undo(t),\ Reverse(t,M)\}$, where t is a vector. The actions Simplify(), Maxsat() and Undo() are external, while the actions Revise(), Choose() and Reverse() are internal. For the formula E-CNF, the action Simplify(t) denotes the simplified formula E-CNF' that obtained by replacing the variables appearing in t with their specified values then removing all clauses with at least one TRUE literal, and deleting all occurrences of FALSE literals from the remaining clauses. The action Maxsat(C) computes an assignment which maximizes the number of satisfied C clauses. The cryptanalytic-agent has ability to select the vector t from his knowledge base using the action Choose(t). The action Revise(t, M) gives the ability of our cryptanalytic-agent to update his own knowlege base according the vector t in model M. In addition, the action undo(t) gives the ability of the cryptanalytic-agent to return to the E-CNF prior to the execution of the last action. Finally, the action Reverse(t, M) gives the ability of the cryptanalytic-agent to reverse the value of vector t in model M.

---

[3] These action rules give a new strategy for known plaintext attack of S-AES.

[4] A mental state condition determines the states in which *Act* may be executed.

1. $M \vdash_{AK}$ invalid $\wedge$ NEW(C) $\Rightarrow$ $Maxsat(C)$
2. IN(new(t, V(t)), X) $\Rightarrow$ $Simplify(t)$
3. $(M \vdash_{AK}$ invalid $\wedge$ NEW(A) $\wedge$ Check-key(M, Key(A)) $\vdash_{AK}$ valid) $\vee$
   $(\exists k \subseteq KV, \forall p \in PV, \forall c \in CV :$ IN(old(p, V(p)), X) $\wedge$ IN(old(c, V(c)), X) $\wedge$
   NEW(A) $\wedge$ IN (V(k),A)$\wedge M \not\vdash_{AK}$ $V(k))$ $\Rightarrow$ $Revise(Key(A), M)$
4. $\exists$ k $\subset$ KV : IN(old(k, V(k)), X) $\wedge$ LAST(k) $\wedge$ NEW(A) $\wedge$ Check-key(M, Key(A)) $\vdash_{AK}$ invalid $\Rightarrow$ $Undo(k)$
5. $M \vdash_{AK}$ invalid $\wedge M \vdash_{AK}$ V(t) $\wedge \neg$ IN(old(t, V(t)), X)) $\wedge \neg$ IN(new(t, V(t)), X)) $\Rightarrow$ $Choose(t)$
6. $M \vdash_{AK}$ valid $\Rightarrow$ $Validkey$
7. $\forall k \in KV :$ IN(old(k, V(k)), X) $\wedge$ M$\vdash_{AK}$ invalid $\Rightarrow$ $Reverse(KV, M)$

In the cryptanalytic-agent action rules, we use the symbols new and old to stand for state (for example, new(t) means that the state of t is new), and we use IN, NEW, OLD, and LAST to stand for predicates. The predicate NEW(t) checks if the state of t is new or not. Similarly, the predicate OLD(t) checks if the state of t is old or not. The predicate IN(new(t, V(t)), X) checks if the vector t exists in X and its state is new or not. The predicate LAST(t) checks if t is the last vector that simplified with it in E-CNF or not. We use the symbols Key and Check-key to stand for functions, where Key(A) function used to extract the values of the key from the assign A and the function Check-key(M,Key(A)) used to check the key from an assign A with a model M to derive the model M is valid or not. Finally, we explain the effect of each action rule that defines what happens in the environment when a possible action is fired as in Fig. 4.[5]

Action Rule No	Current State	Effect
1	(new(C), old\<A\> , X, AK) or (new(C), < > , X, AK)	**(old(C), new\<A\>** , X, AK)
2	(C, new\<A\>, X U new(t,V(t)), AK)	**(new(C), old\<A\>, X U old(t,V(t))**, AK)
3	(C, A , X U old(PV,CV), AK)	(C, A , X U old(PV,CV), **(AK)'**) where **(AK)'**: an agent knowledge after adding the result key
4	(C, new(A), X U old(k,V(k)), AK)	**(C', old(A)**, X U old(k,V(k)), AK) where **C'** : the CNF before simplified with k
5	(C, A, X , AK)	(C, A, **X U new(t,V(t))**, AK)
6	VALID MODEL	**valid key**
7	(C, A, X U old(k,V(k)), AK)	(C, A, X U old(k,V(k)), **(AK)'**) reverse all bits of KV in a model M

Fig. 4. Effect of action rules

---

[5] The bold components in column effect are the components that effected by the applied rule.

5.3   Cryptanalytic-Agent: Inference Engine

The inference engine controls the inference process by selecting and processing the action rules which can fire on the basis of certain conditions. Given the contents of the fact base, the inference engine determines the set of rules which can be *fired*. These are the rules for which the conditions are satisfied. The set of rules which can be fired is called the *conflict set*. Out of the rules in the conflict set, the inference engine selects one rule based on some predefined criteria (This process is called *conflict resolution strategy*). There are several different strategies used to handle this situation [15]. In this paper, we can consider a conflict set as a list of sets and fire the last set in the list. If the last set contains more than one rule, then fire the rule with the highest priority (The priority is taken according to the order of rules that stated in Sect. 5.2). For example, if the conflict set contains sets $\{3, 5\}$, $\{2, 3, 4\}$, then fire rule 2.

6   Results

The cryptanalytic-agent's results are based on the used MAXSAT action. Semantically, the agent has used the SAT4J MAXSAT Solver [16] which is an open-source tool rewarded in different SAT competitions. Cryptanalytic-agent can achieve the required goal according to the following steps.

1. First we calculate a ciphertext c from a chosen plaintext p with a known key k. Then we give only the pair (p, c) to Cryptanalytic-agent (i.e. an encryption model say, $M1=(PV, CV, ?)$[6] is constructed). By applying agent action rules

Cryptanalytic-agent			
#iteration	Fact Base	Conflict set	Rule fired
0	(C,< >,< >,(PL,CI,K))	{{5}}	5
1	(C,< >,< >, (PL,CI,K)), (C,< >,X={new(PL,CI)},(PL,CI,K))	{{5},{2}}	2
2	(C,< >,< >, (PL,CI,K)), (C,< >,X={new(PL,CI)},(PL,CI,K)), (new(C),< >,X={old(PL,CI) },(PL,CI,K))	{{5},{2},{1}}	1
3	(C,< >,< >, (PL,CI,K)), (C,< >,X={ new(PL,CI) },(PL,CI,K)), (new(C),< >,X={old(PL,CI)},(PL,CI,K)), (old(C),new<A>,X={ old(PL,CI)},(PL,CI,K))	{{5},{2},{1},{3}}	3
4	(C,< >,< >, (PL,CI,K)), (C,< >,X={ new(PL,CI) },(PL,CI,K)), (new(C),< >,X={old(PL,CI)},(PL,CI,K)), (old(C),new<A>,X={ old(PL,CI)},(PL,CI,K)), (old(C),new<A>,X={ old(PL,CI) },(PL,CI,KV))	{{5},{2},{1},{3},{6}}	6
5	(C,< >,< >, (PL,CI,K)), (C,< >,X={ new(PL,CI) },(PL,CI,K)), (new(C),< >,X={old(PL,CI)},(PL,CI,K)), (old(C),new<A>,X={ old(PL,CI)},(PL,CI,K)), (old(C),new<A>,X={ old(PL,CI) },(PL,CI,KV)), Valid key	{{5},{2},{1},{3},{6},HALT}	HALT

Fig. 5. Example for attacking S-AES using cryptanalytic-agent

---

[6] The symbol ? denotes that the key vector KV is undetermined.

5.2 and inference rules 5.1, the cryptanalytic-agent has ability to find a valid encryption model (i.e. finds the valid key (k')). This valid key may be either an original key (k) or an equivalent key (k')(see definition 4). The following example will explain how our cryptanalytic-agent work.

Example 1. *Suppose that the plain-vector, the cipher-vector, and the cipher key-vector are as follows.*

$PL = (pl_0, 0),\ (pl_1, 1),\ (pl_2, 0),\ (pl_3, 1),\ (pl_4, 1),\ (pl_5, 1),\ (pl_6, 0),\ (pl_7, 0),$
$(pl_8, 1),\ (pl_9, 1),\ (pl_{10}, 1),\ (pl_{11}, 0),\ (pl_{12}, 1),\ (pl_{13}, 0),\ (pl_{14}, 1),\ (pl_{15}, 0)$

$CI = (ci_0, 1),\ (ci_1, 0),\ (ci_2, 0),\ (ci_3, 1),\ (ci_4, 1),\ (ci_5, 1),\ (ci_6, 0),\ (ci_7, 1),$
$(ci_8, 1),\ (ci_9, 0),\ (ci_{10}, 0),\ (ci_{11}, 0),\ (ci_{12}, 1),\ (ci_{13}, 0),\ (ci_{14}, 0),\ (ci_{15}, 0)$

$K = (k_0, ?),\ (k_1, ?),\ (k_2, ?),\ (k_3, ?),\ (k_4, ?),\ (k_5, ?),\ (k_6, ?),\ (k_7, ?),\ (k_8, ?),$
$(k_9, ?),\ (k_{10}, ?),\ (k_{11}, ?),\ (k_{12}, ?),\ (k_{13}, ?),\ (k_{14}, ?),\ (k_{15}, ?)$

At the beginning (iteration 0), the fact base is written in row 0. The conflict set is calculated and written in the same row. The agent will apply rule (5) according to his conflict resolution strategy to get the new fact base[7]. The new fact base is written in row 1. The new conflict set is then calculated and written in the same row (1). According to his conflict resolution strategy, the agent applies a new rule (2). This new rule is written in the same row (row 1). Figure 5 describes the next iterations by the same way until the agent halts and gets the valid Model. In this example, the agent halts with the key-vector $KV = (kv_0, 1),\ (kv_1, 0),\ (kv_2, 1),\ (kv_3, 0),\ (kv_4, 0),\ (kv_5, 0),\ (kv_6, 1),\ (kv_7, 1),$ $(kv_8, 0),\ (kv_9, 0),\ (kv_{10}, 0),\ (kv_{11}, 1),\ (kv_{12}, 0),\ (kv_{13}, 1),\ (kv_{14}, 0),\ (kv_{15}, 1).$ Notice that the figure contains not only the new fact base in the ith iteration but it also contains the history.

2. In order that, the cryptanalytic-agent can distinguish between the original key (k) and the equivalent key (k'), it needs to another input pair $(p',\ c')$ (i.e. another model, say M2 $= (PV',\ CV',\ ?)$) to add to his fact base, where $(p,\ c)$ and $(p',\ c')$ are encrypted with the same key. Therefore, we need to extend AK-Inference Rules 5.1 by the following rules to determine whether the key is an original key or an equivalent key.

(a) $$\frac{M1 \vdash_{AK} valid \wedge M2 \vdash_{AK} V(PV', CV')}{M1, M2 \vdash_{AK} Original(KV)} \qquad Valid(PV',\ KV,\ CV')$$

(b) $$\frac{M1 \vdash_{AK} valid \wedge M2 \vdash_{AK} V(PV', CV')}{M1, M2 \vdash_{AK} Equivalent(KV)} \qquad \neg(Valid(PV',\ KV,\ CV'))$$

In the following figure, the results of some examples are given to show how cryptanalytic-agent uses the above inference rules to check whether the key is an original key or an equivalent key.

---

[7] The bold components in column fact base are the components that effected by the fired rule.

3. In case of equivalent key, it has ability to find the original key by extending the preconditions of action rules 5.2 by the following new extended rules. The notation $\Vdash_{AK}$ is another derivation that uses to determine whether the valid key is an original or an equivalent.

   (a) M1, M2 $\Vdash_{AK}$ Equivalent(KV) $\wedge$ NEW(C) $\Rightarrow$ $Maxsat(C)$
   (b) IN(new(t), X) $\Rightarrow$ $Simplify(t)$
   (c) $\exists$ k $\subset$ KV : LAST(k) $\wedge$ M1, M2 $\Vdash_{AK}$ Equivalent(KV) $\wedge$ NEW(A) $\wedge$ Check-key'[8](M2, Key(A), k) $\vdash_{AK}$ valid $\Rightarrow$ Revise(Key(A),M1)
   (d) $\exists$ k $\subset$ KV : IN(old(k,V(k)), X) $\wedge$ LAST(k) $\wedge$ NEW(A) $\wedge$ Check-key'(M2, Key(A), k) $\vdash_{AK}$ invalid $\Rightarrow$ $Undo(k)$
   (e) M1, M2 $\Vdash_{AK}$ Equivalent(KV)) $\wedge$ $M1 \vdash_{AK}$ V(k) $\wedge \neg$ IN(old(k,V(k)),X)) $\wedge \neg$ IN(new(k,V(k)),X)) $\Rightarrow$ $Choose(k)$
   (f) M1, M2 $\Vdash_{AK}$ Original(KV) $\Rightarrow$ $Goal$
   (g) $\forall k \in KV$: IN(old(k,V(k)), X) $\wedge$ M1,M2 $\Vdash_{AK}$ Equivalent(KV) $\Rightarrow$ $Reverse(KV, M1)$

Input		Output	Another input		Check A Valid Key	
plain text	cipher text	valid key	plain text	cipher text	original key	equivalent key
0101 0011 1010 1101	1011 0010 0001 1100	1111 0011 1011 1111	1111 0001 0011 0110	0111 0010 1100 0001	—	✓
0101 1100 1110 1010	1001 1101 1000 1000	1010 0011 0001 0101	1110 0001 0000 1111	0101 1110 1110 0111	✓	—
1001 1000 1010 0101	1010 0010 0010 0101	0010 0011 1111 0011	1000 0010 0101 0001	0000 0000 0111 0011	✓	—
0011 0001 0111 1011	0100 1101 1001 1011	1011 1101 0011 0101	1011 1100 0001 1111	1001 0000 1101 1100	✓	—
0001 0011 1111 1110	1100 0111 0111 0001	0000 0010 1110 1100	0010 0111 0001 0011	0001 1001 0001 1000	—	✓
1010 0000 0011 1110	1001 0100 0001 0100	0010 0011 0101 0111	0011 0001 0111 0101	1100 0110 1000 0100	✓	—
1101 0101 0010 0011	0111 0111 0011 1111	0111 0010 0011 0101	1010 1100 1011 0001	0101 0001 0110 1001	✓	—
1110 0111 1010 0101	0011 1010 0001 1111	0111 1011 0011 0101	1101 0011 1111 0010	1110 0110 0001 1010	✓	—
1010 1101 1110 0101	0000 0110 1000 0101	1111 1101 1111 0100	0101 1110 1101 1100	1011 0111 1010 0100	—	✓
0110 1111 0011 0000	1100 1100 1001 1110	1101 1111 1110 0010	0000 1111 0001 1011	1011 0100 0110 1000	—	✓

Fig. 6. Sample of results

Examples in Fig. 7 will explain how cryptanalytic-agent deals with the equivalent key in order to obtain the original key through applying the above extended agent action rules. The agent has applied the new extended rules only to those examples in Fig. 6 which have equivalent key.

We have 2^{16} different blocks for the plaintext. Out of these blocks we have chosen 3200 arbitrary block, and 3200 arbitrary key and then we calculated in each case the corresponding cipher block. As a result for applying the cryptanalytic-agent on these 3200 examples, we found that the result key is either an original key or an equivalent key. In the case of equivalent key, the cryptanalytic-agent will apply the extended agent action rules to obtain the original key from the equivalent key.

---

[8] The function 'Check-key' used to check the key from an assign A with k in a model M2 to derive the model M2 is valid or not.

Input		Output	Check a valid key		How to obtain original key from equivalent key			
plain text	cipher text	valid key	Original key	Equivalent key	Equivalent key	inverse equivalent key	Which bit can be discover an original key?	original key
0101 0011 1010 1101	1011 0010 0001 1100	11110011 10111111	—	✓	11110011 10111111		16	11111100 01010111
00010011 11111110	11000101 01100001	00000010 11101100	—	✓	00000010 11101100	11111101 00010011	4	00110101 10101011
10101101 11100101	00000110 10000101	11111101 11110100	—	✓	11111101 11110100		1	10111101 00100111
01101111 00110000	11001100 10011110	11011111 11100010	—	✓	11011111 11100010	00100000 00011101	1	00011011 01001011

Fig. 7. How to get the original key from the equivalent key

7   Conclusion

A new approach has been proposed in this paper for attacking simplified-AES using Rule-Based Intelligent Agent that breaks the key successfully using known plaintext attack with only one plaintext and its corresponding ciphertext. At the same time, we propose a new application of the agent system in cryptanalysis. Our results confirm the versatility of our proposed approach. In a future work, we aim to design a better cryptanalytic agent on real AES.

References

1. Musa, M.A., Schaefer, E.R., Wedig, S.: A simplified AES algorithm and its linear and differential cryptanalyses. Cryptologia **27**(2), 148–177 (2003)
2. Daemen, J., Rijmen, V.: The Design of Rijndael: AES The Advanced Encryption Standard. Springer, Heidelberg (2002)
3. Wooldridge, M.: An Introduction to MultiAgent Systems. 1 edn. John Wiley & Sons, Chichester (2002)
4. Wooldridge, M., jennings, N.R.: Intelligent agents: theory and practice. Knowl. Eng. Rev. **10**(2), 115–152 (1995)
5. Russel, S., Norving, P.: Artificial Intelligence-A Modern Approach, 2nd ED. Prentice Hall, Upper saddle river (2003)
6. Mansoori, S.D., Bizaki, H.K.: On the vulnerability of simplified aes algorithm against linear cryptanalysis. Int. J. Comp. Sci. Netw. Secur. **7**(7), 257–263 (2007)
7. Simmons, S.: Algebraic cryptanalysis of simplified AES. Cryptologia **33**(4), 305–314 (2009)
8. Valarmathi, M.L., Vimalathithan, R.: Cryptanalysis of simplified-aes using particle swarm optimisation. Defence Sci. J. **62**(2), 117–121 (2012)
9. Forouzan, B.A.: Cryptography and Network Security. McGraw-Hill Company, Boston (2007)
10. Paar, C.: A new architecture for a parallel finite field multiplier with low complexity based on composite fields. IEEE Trans. Comput. **45**(7), 856–861 (1996)
11. Tseitin, G.S.: On the complexity of derivation in the propositional calculus. In Slisenko, A.O., (ed.) Studies in Constructive Mathematics and Mathematical Logic, Part II, pp. 115–125. Springer, New York (1970)
12. Christof, P., Fleischmann, P., Roelse, P.: Efficient multiplier architectures for galois fields. IEEE Trans. Comput. **47**, 70–162 (1998)

13. Cook, S.A.: The complexity of theorem proving procedures. In: Proceedings of the Third Annual ACM Symposium on the Theory of Computing, pp. 151–158. ACM (1971)
14. Biere, A., Heule, M., Van Maaren, H., Walsh, T.: Handbook of Satisfiability. IOS Press, Amsterdam (2009)
15. Hill, E.F.: Jess in Action: Java Rule-Based Systems. Manning Publications Co., Greenwich (2003)
16. Argelich, J., Li, C.-M., Manyà F., Planes, J.: The first and second Max-SAT evaluations. Journal on Satisfiability, Boolean Modeling and Computation 4, 251–278 (2008)

A Discrete Bat Algorithm for the Community Detection Problem

Eslam A. Hassan[1,3], Ahmed Ibrahem Hafez[2,3], Aboul Ella Hassanien[1,3(✉)], and Aly A. Fahmy[1]

[1] Faculty of Computers and Information, Cairo University, Giza, Egypt
eslam.ali@fci-cu.edu.eg, {aboitcairo,aly.fahmy}@gmail.com
http://www.egyptscience.net
[2] Faculty of Computer and Information, Minia University, Minya, Egypt
ah.hafez@gmail.com
[3] Scientific Research Group in Egypt (SRGE), Giza, Egypt

Abstract. Community detection in networks has raised an important research topic in recent years. The problem of detecting communities can be modeled as an optimization problem where a quality objective function that captures the intuition of a community as a set of nodes with better internal connectivity than external connectivity is selected to be optimized. In this work the Bat algorithmwas used as an optimization algorithm to solve the community detection problem. Bat algorithm is a new Nature-inspired metaheuristic algorithm that proved its good performance in a variety of applications. However, the algorithm performance is influenced directly by the quality function used in the optimization process. Experiments on real life networks show the ability of the Bat algorithm to successfully discover an optimized community structure based on the quality function used and also demonstrate the limitations of the BA when applied to the community detection problem.

Keywords: Community detection · Community structure · Social networks · Bat algorithm · Nature-inspired algorithms

1 Introduction

A social network can be modeled as a graph composed of nodes that are connected by one or more specific types of relationships, such as friendship, values, work. The purpose of community detection in networks is to recognize the communities by only using the information embedded in the network topology. Many methods have been developed for the community detection problem. These methods use tools and techniques from different disciplines like physics, chemistry, applied mathematics, and computer and social sciences [1]. One of the main interests in social network analysis is discovering community structure. A Community is a group of nodes that are tightly connected to each other and loosely connected with other nodes. Community detection is the process of network clustering into similar groups or clusters. Community detection has many

© Springer International Publishing Switzerland 2015
E. Onieva et al. (Eds.): HAIS 2015, LNAI 9121, pp. 188–199, 2015.
DOI: 10.1007/978-3-319-19644-2_16

applications including visualization, detecting communities of special interest, realization of the network structure [2], etc. [3]. One of the recent techniques in community detection is Girvan-Newman (GN) algorithm [4]. Girvan-Newman is a divisive method that uses the edge betweenness as a measure to discover the boundaries of communities. This measure detects the edges between communities through counting the number of shortest paths between two specific nodes that passes through a special edge or node. Later on Girvan and Newman introduced a new technique called Modularity [5]. Modularity measures the community strength of a partition of the network, where high Modularity means strong community structure that has dense inter-connections between the community's nodes, Thus the problem of community detection can be viewed as a Modularity Maximization problem. Finding the optimal Modularity is an NP-Complete problem, many heuristic search algorithms have been investigated to solve this problem such as genetic algorithm (GA), simulated annealing, artificial bee colony optimization (ABC) [1]. The remainder of this paper is organized as follows. In Sect. 2 we formulate the community detection problem and show the objective function used in the research. In Sect. 3 we illustrate The Basic Bat algorithm. In Sect. 4 we illustrate our proposed algorithm. Section 5 shows our experimental result on real life social networks. Finally we provide conclusions in Sect. 6.

2 The Community Detection Problem

A social network can be viewed as a graph $G = (V, E)$, where V is a set of nodes, and E is a set of edges that connect two nodes of V. A community structure S in a network is a solution to the problem which is a set of communities of nodes that have a bigger density of edges among the nodes and a smaller density of edges between different sub-groups. The problem of detecting m communities in a network, where the number m is unknown can be formalized as finding a clustering of the nodes in m subsets that can best satisfy a given quality measure of communities $F(S)$. The problem can be formalized as an optimization problem where one usually wants to optimize the given fitness measure $F(S)$ [6].

The objective function has a significant role in the optimization process; it's the "steering wheel" in the process that leads to good solutions. A lot of objective functions have been introduced to capture the intuition of communities, and there does not exist a direct method to compare those objective functions based on their definitions [7–9]. Network Modularity [5] is one of the most used quality measure of communities in the literature. Modularity measures the number of within-community edges relative to a null model of a random graph with the same degree distribution. We use community Modularity as our objective function in the Bat algorithm.

3 Bat Algorithm

The Bat Algorithm (BA), that was presented by Xin-She Yang [10], is a new meta-heuristic optimization algorithm derived by simulating the echolocation system of bats. It is becoming a promising method because of its good performances in solving many problems [11].

Biological Inspiration. In nature, the echolocation behavior of bats used for hunting and navigation, where a bat emits ultrasound pulses to the surrounding environment, then listens back to the echoes in order to locate and identify preys and obstacles as shown in Fig. 1. Each bat in the swarm can find the more nutritious area by individual search or moving forward towards a more nutritious location in the swarm. The basic idea of the BA is to imitate the echolocation behavior of bats with local search of bat individual for achieving the global optimum.

At the beginning of the search, each individual bat emits pulses with low frequency but with greater loudness in order to cover bigger area in the search space, later on when a bat approaches from its prey, it increases its pulse emission rate and decreases the pulse loudness, this frequency/loudness adjustment process can control the balance between the exploration and the exploitation operations of the algorithm.

3.1   Bat Movements Description

Applying the algorithm to the optimization problem, generally a 'bat' represents an individual in a population. The environment in which the artificial bat lives is mainly the solution space and the states of other artificial bats. Its next movement depends on its current state, velocity and its environmental state (including the quality and state of the best bats in the swarm).

Let the state vector of an artificial bat x composed of n variables such that $x = (x_1, x_2, \ldots, x_n)$, and the velocity vector of artificial bat v composed of n variables such that $v = (v_1, v_2, \ldots, v_n)$, f_i is the current frequency that moves between f_{min} and f_{max}, v_i^t is a new velocity selected according to Eq. 2 and x_i^t a new state selected as in Eq. 3.

Where $\beta \in [0, 1]$ is a random vector drawn from a uniform distribution, x^* is the current best global solution that is determined after selecting the best solutions between all the n bats in the current population, Because the product $\lambda_i f_i$ is the increase in velocity, then we can either use f_i (or λ_i) to modify the velocity while fixing the other parameter according to the problem type.

$$f_i = f_{min} + (f_{max} - f_{min}) * \beta \tag{1}$$

$$v_i^t = v_i^{t-1} + (x_i^t - x^*) * f_i \tag{2}$$

$$x_i^t = x_i^{t-1} + v_i^t \tag{3}$$

We chose $f_{min} = 0$ and $f_{max} = 1$, and draw initial frequency of each virtual bat from a uniform distribution $f_0 \in [f_{min}, f_{max}]$.

Performing a local search, one of the best solutions in the current population is selected randomly, then a new solution is produced using 4, Where $\epsilon \in [0, 1]$ is random number, and $A_t = \langle A_i^t \rangle$ is the average loudness of all bats in the current population.

$$x_{new} = x_{old} + \epsilon A^t \tag{4}$$

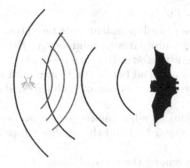

Fig. 1. Shows the echolocation behavior of an Artificial Bat approaching its prey

3.2   Pulse Emission Rate and Loudness Description

Moreover, the pulse emission rate r and the loudness A of each virtual bat must be updated when a new population generated, As soon as the bat found its prey, its loudness decreases and pulse emission rate increases according to Eqs. 5 and 6

$$A_i^{t+1} = \alpha A^t \tag{5}$$

$$r_i^{t+1} = r_i^0[1 - exp(-\gamma t)] \tag{6}$$

where α and γ are constants, after performing some experiments we chose $\alpha = 0.99$, $\gamma = 0.02$, $r_i^0 = 0.01$ and $A_i^0 = 0.99$, Also we can notice that $A_i^t \leftarrow 0$, $r_i^t \leftarrow r_i^0$ as the virtual bat gets closer to its prey $t \leftarrow \infty$, which is rational since a bat has just reached its prey and stops emitting any sound.

This update process will only occur when a new better solution generated, which imply that this bat moves towards an optimal solution.

4   Proposed Algorithm

It is not possible to directly apply the Bat algorithm to the problem of community detection. First the algorithm should be redesigned. In the current section we illustrate the modified Bat algorithm so it can be applied to the community detection problem. The algorithm is outlined in listing 1.

4.1   Parameters Redesign

The first step of modifying a BA for solving the problem of community detection, To provide an appropriate scheme of representation of an individual artificial bat in a population. The locus-based adjacency encoding scheme [12,13] is selected to represent the solution. In that representation, each artificial bat state x composed of n elements $(x_1, x_2, \ldots, x_n)$ and each element can take a value j in the range $[1 .. n]$. A value j set to the ith element is translated as an association between

Input: A Network $G = (V, E)$
Output: Community membership assignments for network's nodes
1 Initialize the parameters: pulse rates r_i, loudness A_i, Swarm size np, the maximum number of iterations $Max\_Iterations$
2 Randomly initialize each artificial bat in the swarm with a random possible solution as its current state, the velocity of each bat, and calculate its fitness
3 **repeat**
4   Generate new solutions by adjusting frequency, and updating velocities and locations/solutions [Eqs. 2 to 4 and the modified Eqs. 7 and 8]
5   **if** $rand > r_i$ **then**
6   Select a solution among the best solutions
7   Generate a local solution around the selected best solution
8   **end**
9   **if** $rand < A_i$ and $f(x_i) < f(x_*)$) **then**
10   Accept the new solutions
11   Increase r_i and decrease A_i
12   **end**
13      $t \leftarrow t + 1$
14 **until** $t > Max\_Iterations$;
15 **return** *the best solution achieved*

Algorithm 1. Bat algorithm

node i and node j. Which means that, in the community structure detected, nodes i and j will exist in the same community.

Normally the bat swarm will contain np artificial bats (AB). The bat current state represents a solution in the search space and the fitness value of the solution represents the amount of food resource at that location. The food condensation in the location of an artificial bat is formulated as $y_i = f(x_i)$, Where y_i is the fitness function value associated with x_i calculated using Modularity quality measure.

4.2 Bat Movement

Bat movement are described in Eqs. 1–3. In a discrete problem representation such equations can not be applied directly. First the difference operator between to bat position will be calculated using Eq. 7; where $g(x_i)$ is the group assignment of node i in the solution represented by bat position x.

$$d_i = (x_i - x_i^*) = \begin{cases} 1 \ if \ g(x_i) \neq g(x_i^*) \\ -1 \ if \ g(x_i) = g(x_i^*) \end{cases} \tag{7}$$

Now Eq. 3 will be considered as uniform crossover between (x, x^*) using velocity vector v as the mixing ratio controller, so the new position value will be updated using Eq. 8.

$$x_i^{new} = \begin{cases} x_i^* \ if \ v_i \geq 1 \\ x_i \ otherwise \end{cases} \tag{8}$$

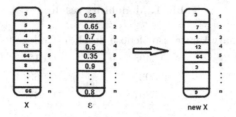

Fig. 2. Shows how a new solution is generated using ϵ and the old solution X when the average loudness $A^t = 0.6$.

4.3 Local Search

In order to create a new solution using Eq. 4, First ϵ should be converted into a vector of size n of uniformly distributed random numbers between 0 and 1, then perform the generation process by selecting a new element from one of the neighbors of the ith node when $\epsilon_i > A^t$, otherwise keep the old neighbor as illustrated in Fig. 2.

4.4 Current Global Best

The Basic Bat algorithm uses x^* the current global best solution in updating all VB in the swarm, which will lead to moving all bats to the same location. In optimization problems this will might lead to trap the algorithm in a local optima. To overcome this problem instead of using one global best, we select η top bats according to their fitness value, then for each VB update a randomly selected VB from the current η top best is used. η is set 10 % of the population size np by trail and error.

Since the algorithm employs stochastic process to find optimal solution, it may converge to different solutions (non-deterministic). It is therefore not uncommon to run the algorithm multiple T times i.e. number of restarts, starting with initial different population in each iteration (chosen randomly) and then returning the best solution found across all runs according to the objective function used in the optimization process.

5   Experimental Results

In the section we tested our algorithm on a real life social networks for which a ground truth communities partitions is known. To compare the accuracy of the resulting community structures; we used Normalized Mutual Information (NMI) [14] to measure the similarity between the true community structures and the detected ones. Since Modularity is a popular community quality measure used extensively in community detection, we used it as a quality measure for the result community structure of all other objectives.

Table 1. Modularity result

	Zachary karate	Bottlenose dolphin	College football	Facebook
Modularity	0.4696	0.5498	0.612	0.753
Ground truth	0.4213	0.395	0.563	0.7234
NMI	0.6873	0.5867	0.84786	0.67374

We applied our algorithm on the following social networks datasets:

- **The Zachary Karate Club:** which was first analyzed in [15], contains the community structure of a karate club. The network consists of 34 nodes. Due to a conflict between the club president and the karate instructor, the network is divided into two approximately equal groups. The network consists of 34 nodes and 78 edges.
- **The Bottlenose Dolphin network:** was compiled by Lusseau [16] and is based on observations over a period of seven years of the behaviour of 62 bottlenose dolphins living in Doubtful Sound, New Zealand. The network split naturally into two large groups.
- **American College football network:** [4] represent football games between American colleges during a regular season in Fall 2000, nodes in the graph represent teams and edges represent regular-season games between the two teams they connect. Games are more frequent between members of the same conference than between members of different conferences, the network is divided into 12 conferences.
- **Facebook Dataset:** Leskovec [17] collects some data for the Facebook website -10 ego networks. The data was collected from survey participants using a Facebook application [7]. The ago network consist of a user's –the ego node– friends and their connections to each other. The 10 Facebook ego networks from [17] are combined into one big network. The result network is undirected network which contain 3959 nodes and 84243 edges. Despite there is no clear community structure for the network, a ground truth structure was suggested in [18].

For each dataset; we applied the Bat algorithm 10 restarts and calculated the NMI and Modularity value of the best solution selected. This process was repeated 10 times and average NMI and average Modularity is reported. The Bat algorithm was applied with the following parameters values; number of VB in the population $np = 100$ and the maximum number of iterations $Max\_Iterations = 100$.

Table 1 summarizes the average NMI and Modularity for the result obtained using the Bat algorithm. We observed that the result for the each network is better that its ground truth in term of Modularity.

The detected community structures for each network is visualized in Fig. 3. Figure 3a shows a visualization of the result for the Zachary network. The original division of the network is indicated by the vertical line and the detected structure is indicated by the nodes' colors. As we can observe that the detected community structure contains 4 communities with a high Modularity value = 0.4696 in which the top level is similar to the original division of the network, however in the detected structure each group is farther divided into two groups. Thus the NMI of comparing the detected structure with the ground truth of Zachary network is 0.6873 i.e. 68 % of similarity between the two structures. Despite that the NMI value is somehow low, it is not a major judgmental criteria of result for two reasons. First the major quality criteria is Modularity value, since the algorithm is optimizing Modularity objective. Second the know ground truth of the network from the original study [15] might not be the optimal one and it is possible that there is a more modular structure that the ground truth.

Figure 3b visualizes the result for the Bottlenose Dolphin network. As before the original division of the network is indicated by the curved line and the detected structure is indicated by the nodes' colors. The original division of the Bottlenose Dolphin network is divided into 2 groups with Modularity value of 0.395. The detected community structure by the Bat algorithm is divided into 5 groups and has a higher Modularity value of 0.5498. Regarding the College football network; the original division of the network into conferences is highlighted in Fig. 3c; only edges between nodes from the same group are shown and nodes' color refer to which groups they belong to. From Fig. 3c we can observe that some nodes never played any match with other nodes from their group. The detected community structure for this network is shown in Fig. 3d which contains 10 communities with a more modular structure than the one shown in Fig. 3c.

Figure 3e shows a visualization of the largest 12 communities from the detected community structure of the Facebook dataset. As we can observe that each group show a dense connection between nodes from the same group and spare or low interactions between nodes from different groups except for a few nodes that has a large edge degree cross different groups such as nodes {1750, 476 and 294} which make group membership assignment a hard process for the algorithm.

5.1   Comparison Analysis

Now we compare the result obtained by Bat algorithm with other methods in the literature which are AFSA community detecton [19], Infomap [20], Fast greedy [21], Label propagation [22], Multi-level or Louvain [23], Walktrap [24] and leading Eignvector [25]. Each method is run 10 times for each dataset and the average NMI and Modularity of the result community structure is reported.

Figure 4 summarize the NMI and Modularity values for all methods. As we can observe that in term of NMI; Bat algorithm produces a good result compared to other methods as shown in Fig. 4a. In term of Modularity; Bat algorithm is very competitive with other methods as shown in Fig. 4b. For the small size data set we can observe the Bat algorithm produce a community structure with a high Modularity value compared to all other methods. Regarding the Facebook

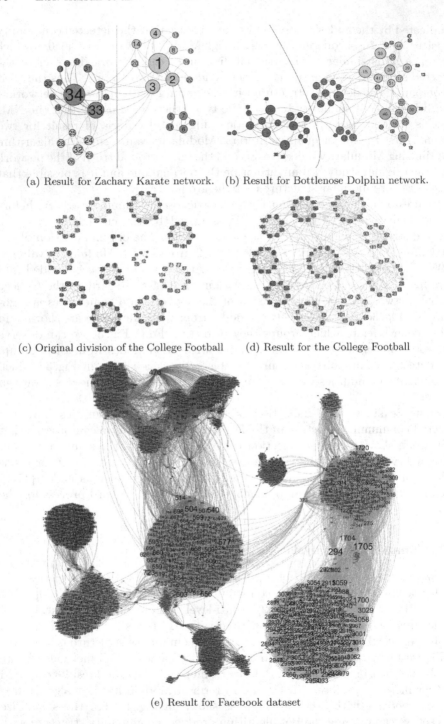

(a) Result for Zachary Karate network.   (b) Result for Bottlenose Dolphin network.

(c) Original division of the College Football   (d) Result for the College Football

(e) Result for Facebook dataset

Fig. 3. Visualizations of the result obtained by Bat Algorithm on each social network dataset.

datasets; Bat algorithm failed to produce a result with high Modularity value compared to the other methods.

5.2 Discussion

As observed from our experimental result that the Bat algorithm performance is promising for small size networks, however for a large networks Bat algorithms performance is degraded compared to other CD algorithms. From our initial analysis, we found there is no much diversity in the VB swarm over the search space and the Bat algorithm does not explore a large region in the search space for the following reasons:

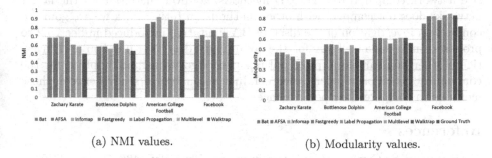

(a) NMI values.　　　　　　　　　(b) Modularity values.

Fig. 4. Average NMI and Modularity values of the result community structure obtained by each algorithm.

- All the population is moving toward one position (Current global best x^*). Over iterations this will lead to all VBs will move/evolve to similar solutions. Despite that we overcome this problem using η top global best, it decreased its impact but did not eliminate it.
- There is no operator/behavior that allow the VB to escape a local optima or jump/explore new random regions in the search space. For example in Genetic algorithm there exist a mutation operation that allow such behavior even a simple mutation in the current solution could cause a large diversity in the current population. Despite that Bat algorithm performance in other application [11] that are continues in nature is very promising, however for the community detection problem (discrete case) Bat algorithm performance has some limitations.
- The local search and Bat difference operator that we proposed for the community structure Sects. 4.2 and 4.3 are not optimal and it is not clear if they are efficient in exploring the search space. It is possible for another design to cause a significant improvement to the algorithm performance.
- Accepting criteria for new solution has some limitation. The basic Bat algorithm accept new solution only if it is better than the current global best. This may constrain the number of moves that a bat can perform.

6 Conclusions and Future Work

A discrete Bat algorithm is introduced for finding community structure in social network. The locus-based adjacency encoding scheme is applied to represent a community structure. The locus-based adjacency encoding scheme has a major advantage that it enables the algorithm to deduce the number of communities k without past knowledge about it. The BA uses Modularity Quality measure as the fitness function in the optimization process. Experimental results demonstrate that the performance of the bat algorithm is quite promising in terms of accuracy and successfully finds an optimized community structure based on the Modularity quality function for small size networks, however the performance is degraded for large size networks. BA algorithm produce good result for the small size network compared to other CD methods, however the result for the larger networks does not compete with other methods. In future work we are going to conduct an investigation of the discrete BA limitation introduced in Sect. 5.2 to propose a new enhanced BA for the community detection problem and investigate other popular bio-inspired optimization algorithms, and apply it for the community detection problem, then conduct an analytical study between those methods to compare their performance.

References

1. Fortunato, S.: Community detection in graphs. Phys. Rep. **486**, 75–174 (2010)
2. Ali, A.S, Hussien, A.S, Tolba, M.F, Youssef, A.H.: Visualization of large time-varying vector data. In: 2010 3rd IEEE International Conference on Computer Science and Information Technology (ICCSIT), vol. 4, pp. 210–215. IEEE (2010)
3. Masdarolomoor, Z., Azmi, R., Aliakbary, S., Riahi, N.: Finding community structure in complex networks using parallel approach. In: 2011 IFIP 9th International Conference on Embedded and Ubiquitous Computing (EUC), pp. 474–479, October 2011
4. Girvan, M., Newman, M.E.J.: Community structure in social and biological networks. Proc. Nat. Acad. Sci. **99**, 7821–7826 (2002)
5. Newman, M.E.J., Girvan, M.: Finding and evaluating community structure in networks. Phys. Rev. E **69**, 026113 (2004)
6. Shi, C., Zhong, C., Yan, Z., Cai, Y., Wu, B.: A multi-objective approach for community detection in complex network. In: IEEE Congress on Evolutionary Computation (CEC), pp. 1–8. IEEE (2010)
7. Leskovec, J., Lang, K.J, Mahoney, M.: Empirical comparison of algorithms for network community detection. In: Proceedings of the 19th International Conference on World Wide Web, pp. 631–640. ACM (2010)
8. Shi, C., Yu, P.S., Cai, Y., Yan, Z., Wu, B.: On selection of objective functions in multi-objective community detection. In: Proceedings of the 20th ACM International Conference on Information and Knowledge Management, pp. 2301–2304. ACM (2011)
9. Hafez, A.I., Al-Shammari, E.M., ella Hassanien, A., Fahmy, A.A.: Genetic algorithms for multi-objective community detection in complex networks. In: Pedrycz, W., Chen, S.-M. (eds.) Social Networks: A Framework of Computational Intelligence. Studies in Computational Intelligence, pp. 145–171. Springer, Heidelberg (2014)

10. Yang, X.-S.: A new metaheuristic bat-inspired algorithm. In: González, J.R., Pelta, D.A., Cruz, C., Terrazas, G., Krasnogor, N. (eds.) NICSO 2010. SCI, vol. 284, pp. 65–74. Springer, Heidelberg (2010)

11. Yang, X.-S., He, X.: Bat algorithm: literature review and applications. Int. J. Bio-Inspired Comput. 5(3), 141–149 (2013)

12. Shi, C., Wang, Y., Wu, B., Zhong, C.: A new genetic algorithm for community detection. In: Zhou, J. (ed.) Complex 2009. LNICST, vol. 5, pp. 1298–1309. Springer, Heidelberg (2009)

13. Pizzuti, C.: GA-Net: a genetic algorithm for community detection in social networks. In: Rudolph, G., Jansen, T., Lucas, S., Poloni, C., Beume, N. (eds.) PPSN 2008. LNCS, vol. 5199, pp. 1081–1090. Springer, Heidelberg (2008)

14. Danon, L., Diaz-Guilera, A., Duch, J., Arenas, A.: Comparing community structure identification. J. Stat. Mech Theor. Exp. 9, 9008 (2005)

15. Zachary, W.W.: An information flow model for conflict and fission in small groups. J. Anthropol. Res. 33, 452–473 (1977)

16. Lusseau, D.: The emergent properties of dolphin social network. Proc. Roy. Soc. Lond. Ser. B Biol. Sci. 270, S186–S188 (2003)

17. McAuley, J.J., Leskovec, J.: Learning to discover social circles in ego networks, pp. 548–556 (2012)

18. Hafez, A.I., Hassanien, A.E., Fahmy, A.A.: Testing community detection algorithms: a closer look at datasets. In: Panda, M., Dehuri, S., Wang, G.-N. (eds.) Social Networking. ISRL, vol. 65, pp. 87–102. Springer, Heidelberg (2014)

19. Hassan, E.A., Hafez, A.I., Hassanien, A.E., Fahmy, A.A.: Community detection algorithm based on artificial fish swarm optimization. In: Filev, D., et al. (eds.) Intelligent Systems 2014. AISC, pp. 509–521. Springer International Publishing, Heidelberg (2015)

20. Rosvall, M., Axelsson, D., Bergstrom, C.T.: The map equation. Eur. Phy. J. Spec. Top. 178(1), 13–23 (2009)

21. Clauset, A., Newman, M.E.J., Moore, C.: Finding community structure in very large networks. Phys. Rev. E 70(6), 066111 (2004)

22. Raghavan, U.N., Albert, R., Kumara, S.: Near linear time algorithm to detect community structures in large-scale networks. Phys. Rev. E 76(3), 036106 (2007)

23. Blondel, V.D., Guillaume, J.-L., Lambiotte, R., Lefebvre, E.: Fast unfolding of communities in large networks. J. Stat. Mech. Theor. Exp. 2008(10), 10008 (2008)

24. Pons, P., Latapy, M.: Computing communities in large networks using random walks (long version 12 (2005). ArXiv Physics e-prints

25. Newman, M.E.J.: Finding community structure in networks using the eigenvectors of matrices. Phys. Rev. E 74(3), 036104 (2006)

Emergence of Cooperation Through Simulation of Moral Behavior

Fernanda Monteiro Eliott[(✉)] and Carlos Henrique Costa Ribeiro

Computer Science Division - Aeronautics Institute of Technology,
Praça Marechal Eduardo Gomes 50, São José dos Campos, Brazil
fernandaeliott@gmail.com

Abstract. Human behavior can be analysed through a moral perspective when considering strategies for cooperation in evolutionary games. Presuming a multiagent task performed by self-centered agents, artificial moral behavior could bring about the emergence of cooperation as a consequence of the computational model itself. Herein we present results from our MultiA computational architecture, derived from a biologically inspired model and projected to simulate moral behavior through an Empathy module. Our testbed is a multiagent game previously defined in the literature such that the lack of cooperation may cause a cascading failure effect ("bankruptcy") that impacts on the global network topology via local neighborhood interactions. Starting with sensorial information originated from the environment, MultiA transforms it into basic and social artificial emotions and feelings. Then its own emotions are employed to estimate the current state of other agents through an Empathy module. Finally, the artificial feelings of MultiA provide a measure (called well-being) of its performance in response to the environment. Through that measure and reinforcement learning techniques, MultiA learns a mapping from emotions to actions. Results indicate that strategies relied upon simulation of moral behavior may indeed help to decrease the internal reward from selfish selection of actions, thus favoring cooperation as an emergent property of multiagent systems.

1 Introduction

At first glance, we may associate *cooperation* to an action mostly motivated by willing. Under an evolutionary perspective, morality is conceivable as a form of cooperation, as the association of skills and reasons for cooperation would provide the emergence of morality [1]. In this sense, cooperation would require the equalization of the self-interest of the individual with that of others or its suppression. In [2], cooperation is thought as something that sews up the interactions among the members of a group, but in general — especially in utility-based computational approaches — it is not easily modelled. For the sake of illustration, consider public goods (goods that are public and not wasted through consumption) that have to be sustained by the group (e.g. through taxes). If public lighting is freely available, what would endorse other strategy than

© Springer International Publishing Switzerland 2015
E. Onieva et al. (Eds.): HAIS 2015, LNAI 9121, pp. 200–212, 2015.
DOI: 10.1007/978-3-319-19644-2_17

free riding? In fact, public goods games are a metaphor to describe trivial relations in natural societies and generalize the Prisoner's Dilemma Game (PDG) to an arbitrary number of individuals (see [3]). Not unusually, commitment is required to accomplish the best social outcome: individuals must keep choices that only as a group will render the best outcome. Then it emerges the dilemma between individual's self-interest and the group. In general, cooperators support costs while benefiting the group, and defectors just use common resources [4]. With regard to artificial agents, it can be a challenge to accomplish a task by coordinating activities and priorities. The prospect can become more complex if there is no possibility of sharing data [5] and when dealing with agents designed to be rational, thus following a best-response policy [6]. With respect to social interactions and to the balance of homeostatic goals, [7] emphasizes the relevance of social emotions and feelings as empathy. In [8] we outlined the artificial neural networks (ANN) from [9], modeled to classify cases with moral sense, and the LIDA model [10,11], expected to be able to deal with moral decisions. As a computational and conceptual model of human cognition, LIDA is described as a cognitive architecture designed to select an action after dealing with ethically pertinent information.

In [12], emotions and feelings are described as crucial on helping humans to make faster and more intelligent decisions. We propose the MultiA computational architecture designed from reflections over the relevance of moral behavior in the search for a rational *and cooperative* biologically-inspired artificial agent. We hypothesize that the simulation of emotions and moral behavior aiding the computational architecture to make decisions favours cooperation even in face of high reinforcements to selfish behavior. The analogy with moral behavior is implemented through simulation of empathy, thus the agent can have the ability to select actions that may not be the best selfish option, but that help to enhance the interactions among agents. Therefore, through the application of its empathy feeling, MultiA rudimentarily mimics moral behavior [8]. MultiA resulted from transformations over the Alec computational architecture, developed in [13,14]. Alec is applicable to the context of a single agent and is grounded on from [12], such as considerations of emotions and feelings taking part on filtrating data and as an attentional mechanism; and on the implementation of artificial homeostasis — hence the agent has to accomplish homeostatic goals in order to maintain its internal variables within a threshold to keep its internal balance. MultiA also has homeostatic goals, meaning that selecting actions may not increase the level of the empathy. MultiA also uses a set of its own emotions to provide itself a prospect about the current situation of other agents. In [8] we detail the biological motivation for designing MultiA, including the concept of mirror neurons [15,16]. Although there is some controversy about it (see for instance [17]), we used mirror neurons as inspiration on the mechanism for projecting MultiA own emotions to mirror other agents' situation, avoiding explicit data sharing among local agents. Actions related to high empathy are designed to be avoided, since it is considered that when an agent rouses high empathy it is because the agent itself may be disturbing the performance of the others. For the design of the Empathy module, we used the utilitarian calculus from [18] as guideline. This way, MultiA agents have the empathy more accessible for agents whose interactions have resulted in positive reinforcements. Furthermore, if a MultiA agent has been receiving a high number of positive reinforcements, it is also more susceptible to cooperate.

2   The MultiA Architecture

MultiA consists of three main systems (Fig. 1): the Perceptive System (PS), the Cognitive System (CS) and the Decision System (DS). As input to the PS, MultiA receives artificial sensations that are triggered by reinforcements, and by an identifying index for the agent it is interacting with. Interactions occur only among neighboring agents. Each agent has an identifying index $i = \{1, ..., N\}$. Also, the neighbors relating to each agent i also have an identifying index $p = \{1, ..., M\}$, a given value of p refers to a particular neighbor that is interacting with i. Action selection results from sensations triggered by the environment. As consequence of those actions, the environment triggers new sensations, and so on. The artificial sensations feed emotions, feelings and, subsequently, through a weighted sum of the feelings, the general perspective of MultiA (so-called Well-Being, W_i) about its own performance. More specifically, W_i informs how suitable has been the action selection (from DS) regarding the reinforcements received by the agent itself as well as the remaining feelings, as empathy ($S_{4,i}p$, Sect. 2.3). The empathy was designed to represent the impact of the action selection of MultiA agent on its neighbors, thus, the higher the empathy for a particular neighbor p, the lower is W_i, all the remaining variables that affect W_i kept constant. That means the agent may not have been choosing its actions properly, since it may be causing negative impacts on this particular neighbor p. That way the selected actions of MultiA are considered good when they generate positive reinforcements but, at the same time, when they do not provoke high empathy: in fact, if p arouses high empathy, p may be receiving low reinforcements and therefore its neighbors should revise their actions. Two requirements must exist in order to rise the empathy: p is expected to be receiving low reinforcements, and the emotion $E_{4,i}^s p$ of MultiA for p is high. The CS provides to the PS the current number of neighbors for each agent, a history of the reinforcements acquired in the environment and, when there is an interaction with neighbor p, the number of times interacting with p resulted in positive reinforcements. Before the DS selects an action, the CS has access to the current emotions and produces $W_p i$: an expectation about the current situation of p (see Sect. 2.3). The mechanism for providing $W_p i$ was inspired by the idea of mirror-neurons internally mirroring the current situation of another agent. Once it is intended to use as little external information as possible, the own emotions of the MultiA agent are used to mimic another agent p (before interacting with it) and provide $W_p i$. The CS sends $W_p i$ to the PS, where it will influence the particular emotion $E_{4,i}^s p$, thus impacting the empathy feeling $S_{4,i}p$. The PS will then calculate its artificial emotions, feelings and W_i.

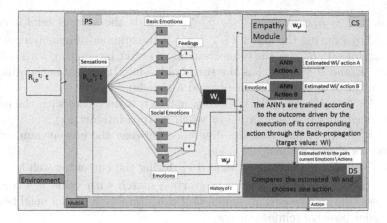

Fig. 1. The general scheme of MultiA.

2.1 Cognitive and Decision Systems (*CS* and *DS*)

The *CS* uses three-layer feed-forward artificial neural networks (ANNs), one for each action, and the Q-Learning algorithm [19] to estimate the resulting Well-Being (value provided from the single output unit) if, face to the current emotions (input space from *PS*) and bias, the corresponding action is to be executed. Each ANN is trained according to the outcome driven by the execution of its corresponding action [20] through the Backpropagation algorithm [21] employing W_i as the target value. The *CS* will then provide the outputs from all ANNs to the *DS* to consider and choose an action: the *DS* will choose the action with the highest output (if the outputs have the same value, selection will be random). However, observe that during the beginning of a simulation, the *DS* will apply a high exploration rate for the state(emotion)-action space. The generating process of the artificial empathy feeling will be detailed next.

2.2 Perceptive System (*PS*)

We consider a model where reinforcements are non negative. Sensations fall in the range $[0, 1]$ and, together with the history provided by the *CS*, give rise to artificial emotions. There are basic emotions $= \{E_{1,i}^b, E_{2,i}^b, ..., E_{n,i}^b\}$ and social emotions $= \{E_{1,i}^s, E_{2,i}^s, ..., E_{n,i}^s\}$, all normalized to the range $[-1, 1]$. The basic emotions are related to the MultiA agent itself:

- $E_{1,i}^b = -1 + 2*(m_i^t/V_i^1)$, where t is the time index for the (possibly unfinished) current match, V_i^1 is the initial number of neighbors of agent i at the first match and m_i^t is the number of concluded interactions of i during current match t. $E_{1,i}^b$ increases with the number of interactions of i in the same match (i.e. while i does not interact again with the same neighbor). Interactions are always in order w.r.t. neighboring agent index.

- $E_{2,i}^b = r_i^{t-1} - R_0$, where $r_i^{t-1} = \sum_{j=1}^{V_i^{t-1}} R_{i,j}^{t-1}$ is the sum of reinforcements received by i during the match $t-1$, V_i^{t-1} is the number of neighbors of agent i at match $t-1$, $R_{i,j}^{t-1}$ is the reinforcement of i after interacting with neighbor j at $t-1$, and $0 \le R_0 \le 1$ is the threshold value. It indicates the difference between the sum of reinforcements and a threshold value.
- $E_{3,i}^b = 1 - 2 * ((V_i^1 - V_i^t)/V_i^1)$. At each match t, it decreases with the number of lost neighbors (a neighbor is lost when it stops interacting).
- $E_{4,i}^b = r_i^t - R_0$. It indicates the difference between the current sum of reinforcements r_i^t and a threshold value.
- $E_{5,i}^b = -1 + (2 * r_i^t)$ is the normalized r_i^t during the current match t.
- $E_{6,i}^b = E_{6,i}^b - 2 * (1/V_i^1)$. It always starts a match with value $= 1$ and only decreases (during the current match t) if the interaction with a neighbor does not render positive reinforcements.

In contrast with basic emotions, social emotions are driven by the neighbors and by the influence of the MultiA agent on those neighbors:

- $E_{1,i}^s$: emphasizes behaviors relating to the social context that did not originate positive outcomes to i but, still and in minor degree, increases together with positive reinforcements of the agent. That way, $E_{1,i}^s$ increases at any change on $E_{5,i}^b$ (then: $Es_{1,i} = E_{1,i}^s + s$) and, in a greater degree, at any change on $E_{6,i}^b$ (then: $Es_{1,i} = E_{1,i}^s + (2/V_i^1)$). It always starts a match with value $= -1$; and $s < (2/V_i^1)$ is a weight used to establish the importance of $E_{5,i}^b$.
- $E_{2,i}^s$: is the average number of variations of $E_{5,i}^b$ per iteration, normalized to the range $[-1, 1]$, from the first match until the current one. It starts with zero;
- $E_{3,i}^s p = -1 + (2 * M_i p)$, is the average number of variations of $E_{5,i}^b$ per iteration with neighbor p. $M_i p$ is the average number of variations of $E_{5,i}^b$ (i.e., average number of increases in r_i^t) per interaction with neighbor p.
- $E_{4,i}^s p$: is fed both by the expectation about neighbor p (provided by the CS), and by the empathy feeling $S_{4,i} p^{t-1}$ by p right after the last interaction with p (during last match at $t-1$), a residual value from the past influencing the current emotion. Formally, $E_{4,i}^s p = (c_a * S_{4,i} p^{t-1}) + ((1 - c_a) * Y_i p)$, where $0 \le c_a \le 1$ is a weight for the importance of residual values of $S_{4,i} p^{t-1}$. The calculation of $Y_i p$ of agent i for p takes into account $M_i p$. Thus, if $M_i p < 0.5$, $Y_i p$ is calculated according to Table 1, and according to Table 2 otherwise. The CS provides three possible classificatory values for $W_p i = \{-1, 0, 1\}$ (Sect. 2.3). Positive ($W_p i = 1$) means the neighbor p is probably achieving high reinforcements; uncertain ($W_p i = 0$): the situation of p is inaccessible; negative ($W_p i = -1$): p is probably receiving low reinforcements from the environment.

The artificial feelings $= \{S_{1,i}, S_{2,i}, ..., S_{n,i}\}$ fall in the range $[-1, 1]$ and arise through a weighted sum of emotions. The weights are set according to the relevance of each emotion to the domain. Table 3 presents the set of emotions that

Table 1. The Calculation of Y_ip: If $M_ip < 0.5$

W_pi	Y_ip	Description
1	-1	p may be achieving positive reinforcements because it is producing low reinforcements to i. Thus Y_ip of i for p should be minimum
0	$M_ip - 1$	p is producing low reinforcements to i *but* it is uncertain if p is achieving or not positive reinforcements
-1	$M_ip - 0.5$	p may be only producing low reinforcements to i in response to low reinforcements from environment

Table 2. The Calculation of Y_ip: If $M_ip >= 0.5$

W_pi	Y_ip	Description
1	$M_ip - 0.5$	p is producing high reinforcements to i and also may be achieving positive reinforcements
0	M_ip	p is producing high reinforcements to i, but its situation is uncertain
-1	1	p is producing high reinforcements to i, even though it may be achieving low reinforcements

feed each feeling ($E^b_{1,i}$ does not feed any feeling). Because of its feeding set of emotions, the only feeling that adapts to the interacting neighbor p is $S_{4,i}p$. The well-being W_i uses feelings to internally represent the general situation of agent i. It is calculated with normalizing weights so that the final value falls in the range $[-1, 1]$: $W_i = \sum_{j=1}^{n} a_j S_{j,i}$, where n is the number of feelings. The weights a_j are set respecting the relevance of each feeling to the domain. For simplification, the p index of $S_{4,i}p$ is omitted from the sum. W_i measures the performance of MultiA agent i in the environment, considering the empathy for p. If the empathy reaches high levels, W_i will be low: probably the last selected actions may be causing bad outcomes to p; therefore the well-being W_i of agent i should be low, even though its reinforcements may be high.

2.3   Empathy Module and Mirror Neurons Inspiration

We used a biological inspiration to simulate moral behavior through a computational implementation of an empathy feeling that diminish the importance of selfish actions and bring up the emergence of cooperation. To be more or less sensitive to other agents, MultiA simulates the process of mirroring another agent p by using its own emotions to establish an expectation (W_pi) about the current situation of the interacting neighbor p. The usage of MultiA's i emotions assumes that, if the environment provides high reinforcements to i, probably it will do the same to its neighbors. The expectation fits in one of three classificatory values $W_pi = \{-1, 0, 1\}$. The CS keeps two sets of values ($I = \{\{I_P\}, \{I_N\}\}$) of the four

Table 3. Set of emotions that feed each Artificial Feeling

	$S_{1,i}$	$S_{2,i}$	$S_{3,i}$	$S_{4,i}p$
Fed by Emotion	$E_{2,i}^b$ and $E_{3,i}^b$	$E_{4,i}^b$, $E_{5,i}^b$ and $E_{6,i}^b$	$E_{1,i}^s$ and $E_{2,i}^s$	$E_{3,i}^s p$ and $E_{4,i}^s p$

emotions: $E_{2,i}^b$, $E_{3,i}^b$, $E_{2,i}^s$ and $E_{3,i}^s p$. Those emotions were selected because they provide a basic and social overview about the reinforcements of the MultiA agent and the number of neighbors. If all four emotional variables present maximum values, i will have excellent performance ($I_P = \{1; 1; 1; 1\}$). On the contrary, if all present minimum values, i will have poor performance ($I_N = \{-1; -1; -1; -1\}$). The classification is determined by using the Euclidean Distance of the current values of those four emotions from I_P and I_N. If the longest distance of the current values of emotions is from I_P, $W_p i = -1$ (the current reinforcements of p are probably low). On the contrary, if the longest distance is from I_N, $W_p i = 1$ (the current reinforcements of p are probably high). But if the distances from I_P and I_N are too close, $W_p i = 0$. Finally, the CS sends $W_p i$ to the PS, where it will feed the emotion $E_{4,i}^s p$ (see Tables 1 and 2) and, consequently the empathy.

3   Experimental Setting

Wang *et al.* [22] present a generalized PDG model applied to a two-dimensional lattice with four neighbors for each node (called 2D4n) and discuss related results that show the emergence of cascading failures. Each node in the network adopts a particular strategy (to defect or to cooperate) that is followed right through the end of each game match. Before the beginning of a simulation, the strategies of the nodes are already established, but once each match ends, there is a probability of each node imitating the strategy of a neighbor, provided that the strategy resulted in higher final reinforcement. Immediately before that, there is elimination of nodes that did not get enough cooperative actions from neighbors, and the network topology changes accordingly. The higher the value of defection when the neighbor cooperates, the higher is the probability of a cooperating node imitating a defective neighbor. A defecting strategy can easily spread to the whole network, causing a cascading failure effect: cooperative nodes being eliminated and their elimination provoking the elimination of its neighbors, and so forth.

The parameters defined herein consider that each agent has initially 4 neighbors (2D4n lattice as in [22]) and reinforcements are normalized to $[-1, 1]$. The reinforcement for mutual cooperation is $B_{c,c} = 0.25$; for defection when the neighbor cooperates is $B_{d,c}$; for mutual defection is $B_{d,d} = 0$ and finally, for cooperation vs. defection is $B_{c,d} = 0$. The value of $B_{d,c}$ is a design parameter, but $B_{d,c} > B_{c,c}$. The terms used to describe the results are:
1. Game: a set of interactions among agents as defined in the PDG by [22].
2. Match: every agent will interact (choose to defect or cooperate) only once with each and all of its neighbors - always in the same order. Once all neighbors have

interacted, the match ends. 3. Simulation: a predetermined number of matches played in sequence. 4. Elimination: at the end of each match, the individual sum of reinforcements of every agent is compared to T_i (after each match, the minimum individual sum of reinforcements required to persist in the network). If one agent fails (ends a match with $r_i^t < T_i$), the agent itself and all its connections are eliminated from the network. T_i falls in the range $[0; 1]$: from no elimination to all neighbors cooperating to prevent elimination. For all MultiA agents, the value of R_0 is the same as T_i. 5. In our simulated games, $V_i^1 = 4$ for every agent i. If all neighbors of i choose to cooperate (and none of them has been eliminated) and i is a cooperator, the maximum possible value for r_i^t is $B_{c,c} * V_i^1$, and as we set $B_{c,c} = 0.25$, then $r_i^t = 1$). Thus, if $T_i = 0.5$, the cooperative agent i will need 2 cooperative neighbors to prevent elimination in each match. We call χ_c this minimum number of cooperative neighbors a cooperative agent needs to prevent elimination in each match. On the other hand, if i is a defector, the maximum possible r_i^t is $B_{d,c} * V_i^1 = B_{d,c} * 4$. Thus, if $T_i = 0.5$ and $B_{d,c} >= 0.5$, the defective agent will need a single cooperative neighbor. We call χ_d this minimum number of cooperative neighbors a defective agent needs to prevent elimination in each match. The actual value of $B_{d,c}$ has to be set before the beginning of each simulation. 6. ρ_c is the percentage of cooperators in the final network, and ρ_d the percentage of defectors. The percentage of remaining (not eliminated) agents from the original network is ρ_f. 7. The set parameters for the ANNs (in the CS) are: the hidden and output units use the Logarithmic activation function; for learning, we used a learning rate of 0.001 and a momentum term of 0.9. The DS applies a 10 % exploration rate.

3.1   Results

For each simulation we used $1,000$ MultiA agents and the results were collected until the size of the network stopped changing (t^F matches). Each experiment consists of 20 simulations, results were averaged over these simulations. To prevent a massive elimination of agents during exploration, no elimination takes place in the first t^B matches. Still, we calculate which agents should be eliminated: then, its neighbors receive the information about agents elimination, even though that never happens in this initial phase. Notice that the information about the loss of neighbors is not followed by lower reinforcements. The elimination process actually begins in match t^{B+1}. It is also important to emphasize that there is no local agent access to neighbor reinforcements: the Empathy module tries to mirror the neighbors current state before the DS selects an action. The successive interactions among agents will impact on the PS, *ergo* on the whole MultiA architecture, and the action selection (both in the same match and from a match to another) will be influenced by previous interactions. Information that defection weakens the network (by causing agents elimination) only presents itself when a neighbor is eliminated (or considered to be eliminated, in the first t^B matches) from the network. But the cause-consequence (neighbors elimination through defection) can be shadowed by the game dynamics itself, as:

1. Once there is elimination, not only the defecting agent that caused it will loss its neighbors, but also the cooperative agent. Thus the bad outcome in response to defection will impact on both agents PS, since the two of them will lose a neighbor. 2. During a match t, each agent interacts with all its neighbors and only at the beginning of the next match $(t + 1)$ they will have access to the number of eliminated neighbors in t; 3. If $\chi_c = 1$, the cooperative agent can have several defecting neighbors, since at least one of its neighbors keeps following the cooperative strategy. Depending on the values of T_i and $B_{d,c}$, if $\chi_c > \chi_d$, defectors will be more resilient; 4. Once the network has stabilized and the elimination process has ended, the remaining defecting agents will stop having access to the neighbors bad effect of that strategy, namely neighbors elimination.

On two experiments we varied the value of T_i (for $B_{d,c} = 0.5$ and $B_{c,c} = 0.25$). Experiment 1 (Exp. 1) has $T_i = 0.5$, thus $\chi_c = 2$ and $\chi_d = 1$. The value of T_i establishes that each cooperator must have at least half of its neighbors cooperating to avoid elimination and a possible cascading failure. Hence, cooperators must be clustered to avoid elimination. Moreover, as $\chi_c > \chi_d$, defectors are more resilient: being connected to a single cooperator is enough to be kept in the network. Experiment 2 (Exp. 2) has $T_i = 0.25$, thus $\chi_c = 1$ and $\chi_d = 1$, i.e., defectors and cooperators need a single cooperating neighbor to avoid elimination, even though $B_{d,c} > B_{c,c}$. The corresponding results of three groups of simulations are in Table 4 and Fig. 2 for Exp. 1, and in Table 5 and Fig. 3 for Exp. 2. We compared the simulations of MultiA agents against two variations, both determined by different ways of calculating W_i. The first group $G1$ of simulations maximizes current reinforcements by making $W_i = E^b_{5,i}$. The second group $G2$ has $W_i = S_{4,i}p$ so we can better analyze the functioning of $S_{4,i}p$. There was also the possibility of using $W_i = E^b_{3,i}$ to prevent neighbors elimination, but that was rejected since agents would not take into account their own reinforcements. Besides, once a necessary number of agents (χ_c) has learned to cooperate and prevent elimination, the strategy of the remaining agents becomes unimportant (specially for small χ_c). That is due to the fact that some of the agents would learn to maximize the number of neighbors (by cooperating), thus ending the elimination process. Then, the remaining agents would not have anything to maximize through W_i, since regardless the strategy, no neighbor would be eliminated.

Agents from $G1$ maximize reinforcements. As a result, in both experiments agents become defectors (since $B_{d,c} > B_{c,c}$) and are continuously eliminated.

Table 4. Experiment 1: $T_i = 0.5$.

	MultiA	G2	G1
ρ_f	86%	55%	5%
ρ_d	39%	42%	58%
ρ_c	61%	58%	42%

Table 5. Experiment 2: $T_i = 0.25$.

	MultiA	G2	G1
ρ_f	97%	86%	36%
ρ_d	47%	48%	65%
ρ_c	53%	52%	35%

Even when agents form clusters of defectors during the elimination process, the consequence of weak reinforcements $(B_{d,d} = 0)$ is that some of the agents learn to cooperate. As it can be seen in Table 4 for Exp. 1 and in Table 5 for Exp. 2, as temptation to defect is high $(B_{d,c} = 0.5)$, there is massive agents elimination and $\rho_d > \rho_c$. In the case of $G2$, $W_i = S_{4,i}p$ produces $\rho_d < \rho_c$ and the final ρ_f is larger than in $G1$. Since MultiA agents have got $S_{4,i}p$ as part of W_i, $G2$ is used to provide the individual functioning of $S_{4,i}p$ and its interference on measuring actions utility. Because of that, for MultiA and $G2$, at the end of each match t, we summed up the final reinforcements r_i^t received by each remaining agent (not given as eliminated by t^B and not eliminated from t^{B+1}). The sum of reinforcements was then divided by the total number of remaining agents. We made that for all simulations, providing the mean agent reinforcement, $\overline{R}$: in Fig. 2 for Exp. 1 and in Fig. 3 for Exp. 2.

Agents from $G2$ maximize the empathy feeling. When agent i has high levels of $S_{4,i}p$ for agent p, its actions are taken as generating low outcomes — i may be causing low reinforcements to neighbor p, and are taken as generating high outcomes otherwise. As the empathy is more sensitive to neighbors that have been generating high reinforcements, agents from $G2$ indirectly maximize reinforcements and have a better final ρ_f than $G1$. As $G2$ agents learn to cooperate, $\overline{R}$ decreases $(B_{d,c} > B_{c,c})$. Observe that indirectly maximizing reinforcements is not so successful as, in the case of MultiA, directly maximizing them (through the use of all feelings in W_i). Thus, during t^B, $G2$ has $\overline{R}$ similar to MultiA, but there are more eliminated agents due to the absence of the other feelings on the calculation of W_i. From the absence of $S_{2,i}$, for example, multiple defections $(B_{d,d} = 0)$ occur. And from the absence of $S_{1,i}$, neighbors elimination is frequent. Then, the final $\overline{R}$ is lower than that of MultiA. In fact, $\rho_f = 55\%$, 45% of agents from $G2$ were eliminated and the remaining agents ended up with fewer neighbors — therefore weaker reinforcements — than MultiA.

Regarding MultiA agents, during the learning stage they have to learn that neighbors elimination is related to the defection strategy. They change their strategies to prevent neighbors elimination and guarantee reinforcements but, at the same time, high $S_{4,i}p$ reduces the relevance of reinforcements on W_i, because the selected actions of agent i may be causing low reinforcements to neighbor p. Thus, MultiA agents may present low W_i even after receiving high reinforcements. Hence, there is more time to learn the long-term impact of actions that rendered high reinforcements, such as losing a neighbor after defecting and receiving a high reinforcement from that. When a neighbor p does not produce high levels of $S_{4,i}p$, MultiA agents emphasize their own reinforcements (through all the feelings used to calculate W_i). Once the defection strategy ceases causing elimination on the network (because the cooperators already have the minimum $\chi_c = 2$), more agents shall maximize reinforcements and follow the defecting strategy. MultiA agents were able to learn to cooperate to prevent neighbors elimination providing at least the minimum χ_c and, once that was accomplished, the remaining MultiA agents $(V_i^1 - \chi_c)$ could learn to maximize reinforcements. Associated to high $B_{d,c}$ (high temptation to defect), this helped to increase the number of defectors in the network, resulting on $\rho_d = 39\%$. From all groups, MultiA presented the better results, with $\rho_f = 86\%$ and $\rho_c = 61\%$.

Regarding Exp. 2, as in Exp. 1, $G2$ was not as successful as MultiA on handling the game dynamics, but both learned to cooperate. As $\chi_c = 1$, few agents need to learn the cooperative strategy to keep the neighborhood. Because of that, ρ_f for $G2$ and MultiA was better on Exp. 2 than on Exp. 1. But, for the same reason, ρ_c in Exp. 1 was better than ρ_c in Exp. 2 for MultiA and $G2$. However, due to the absence of the other feelings on the calculation of W_i, $G2$ had more eliminated agents and defections than MultiA. By comparing MultiA results from Exps. 1 and 2, we observe that the first resulted in smaller final population and fewer defecting agents, and thus it seems that it should have a lower $\overline{R}$ than Exp. 2. But as Figs. 2 and 3 show, that is not the case, because the lower value of χ_c on Exp. 2 allows more combinations of mutual defection than on Exp. 1.

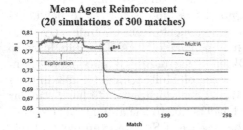

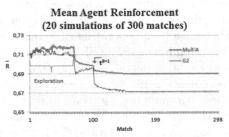

Fig. 2. Mean agent reinforcement during the simulations of Table 4, $T_i = 0.5$.

Fig. 3. Mean agent reinforcement during the simulations of Table 5, $T_i = 0.25$.

4   Final Remarks and Future Work

As analyzed in [2], on the game described in [22] cooperation works to keep the nodes connected. Depending on the temptation to defect, the network can suffer a cascading failure effect, losing nodes and connections. MultiA agents, from the internalization of the required cooperation on its Perceptive System and through the exercise of its empathy, are able to cooperate, even after facing high temptation to defect. Once MultiA agent stop correlating its actions to bad effects on its neighborhood, the empathy reduces its impact and MultiA focuses on maximizing the other feelings, specially the ones influenced by high reinforcements. Thus the cooperation strategy works in consonance with the empathy feeling, the consequence is that there is no full adhesion to the cooperation strategy. During a joint task, should the artificial moral agents be morally hybrid: immoral toward agents that disturb in achieving the task and moral otherwise? Thereby we ponder upon defection as a manner of getting profit or/and of detaching someone from the group. Hence regarding the moral, immoral and amoral patterns of morality, we plan to use different weights on the perceptive system: according to those patterns, our intention is to frame MultiA's exercise of empathy through its action policy. For the amoral version, we intend to neutralize social emotions and feelings, and then compare its performance with that of MultiA to provide more results on the feasibility of the artificial empathy model. We also plan to examine the functioning of MultiA in different game dynamics and under different network topologies.

Acknowledgment. The authors thank CNPQ and FAPESP for the financial support.

References

1. Tomasello, M., Vaish, A.: Origins of human cooperation and morality. Annu. Rev. Psychol. **64**, 231–255 (2013)
2. Tomasello, M.: Human culture in evolutionary perspective. Adv. Cult. Psychol. **1**, 5–51 (2011)
3. Wakano, J.Y., Hauert, C.: Pattern formation and chaos in spatial ecological public goodsgames. J. Theor. Biol. **268**(1), 30–38 (2011)
4. Wardil, L., Hauert, C.: Origin and structure of dynamic cooperative networks. Sci. Rep. **4**, 1–6 (2014)
5. Matignon, L., Laurent, G., Le Fort-Piat, N., et al.: Independent reinforcement learners in cooperative markov games: a survey regarding coordination problems. Knowl. E. Rev. **27**(1), 1–31 (2012)
6. Bowling, M., Veloso, M.: Convergence of gradient dynamics with a variable learning rate. In: ICML, pp. 27–34 (2001)
7. Damásio, A.: Looking for Spinoza: Joy, Sorrow, and the Feeling Brain. Random House, New York (2004)
8. Eliott, F., Ribeiro, C.: A computational model for simulation of moral behavior. In: Proceedings of the International Conference on Neural Computation Theory and Applications (NCTA-2014), pp. 282–287. SCITEPRESS (Science and Technology Publications) (2014)
9. Guarini, M.: Moral cases, moral reasons, and simulation. AISB/IACAP World Congr. **21**(4), 22–28 (2012)
10. Franklin, S., Madl, T., D'Mello, S., Snaider, J.: LIDA: a systems-level architecture for cognition, emotion, and learning. IEEE Trans. Auton. Ment. Dev. **6**, 19–41 (2014)
11. Faghihi, U., Estey, C., McCall, R., Franklin, S.: A cognitive model fleshes out Kahneman's fast and slow systems. Biol. Inspired Cogn. Architect. **11**, 38–52 (2015)
12. Damásio, A.: Descartes' Error. Putnam, New York (1994)
13. Gadanho, S., Custódio, L.: Asynchronous learning by emotions and cognition. In: Proceedings of the Seventh International Conference on Simulation of Adaptive Behavior on From Animals to Animats, pp. 224–225. MIT Press (2002)
14. Gadanho, S.: Learning behavior-selection by emotions and cognition in a multi-goal robot task. J. Mach. Learn. Res. **4**, 385–412 (2003)
15. Di Pellegrino, G., Fadiga, L., Fogassi, L., Gallese, V., Rizzolatti, G.: Understanding motor events: a neurophysiol. study. Exp. Brain Res. **91**(1), 176–180 (1992)

16. Rizzolatti, G., Fadiga, L., Gallese, V., Fogassi, L.: Premotor cortex and the recognition of motor actions. Cogn. Brain Res. **3**(2), 131–141 (1996)
17. Hickok, G.: The Myth of Mirror Neurons: The Real Neuroscience of Communication and Cognition. WW Norton & Company, New York (2014)
18. Bentham, J.: An Introduction to the Principles of Morals and Legislation. Courier Dover Publications, New York (2007 (1789))
19. Watkins, C.J.: Learning from delayed rewards. Ph.D. thesis, Kings College, UK (1989)
20. Lin, L.: Reinforcement learning for robots using neural networks. Technical report, DTIC Document (1993)
21. Werbos, P.J.: Beyond regression: new tools for prediction and analysis in the behavioral sciences. Ph.D. thesis, Harvard (1974)
22. Wang, W.X., Lai, Y.C., Armbruster, D.: Cascading failures and the emergence of cooperation in evolutionary-game based models of social and economical networks. Chaos: an Interdisciplinary. J. Nonlin. Sci. **21**(3), 033112–033112 (2011)

MC-PSO/DE Hybrid with Repulsive Strategy – Initial Study

Michal Pluhacek[1(✉)], Roman Senkerik[1], Ivan Zelinka[2],
and Donald Davendra[2]

[1] Faculty of Applied Informatics, Tomas Bata University in Zlin,
Nam T.G. Masaryka 5555, 760 01 Zlin, Czech Republic
{pluhacek, senkerik}@fai.utb.cz
[2] Faculty of Electrical Engineering and Computer Science,
Technical University of Ostrava, 17. Listopadu 15, 708 33 Ostrava,
Poruba, Czech Republic
{ivan.zelinka, donald.davendra}@vsb.cz

Abstract. In this initial study it is described the possible hybridization of advanced Particle Swarm Optimization (PSO) modification called MC-PSO and the Differential evolution (DE) algorithm. The advantage of hybridization of various evolutionary techniques is the shared benefit from various advantages of these methods. The motivation came from previous studies of the MC-PSO performance and behavior. The performance of the proposed method is tested on IEEE CEC 2013 benchmark set and compared with both PSO and DE.

Keywords: Particle swarm optimization · PSO · Differential evolution · DE

1 Introduction

The Particle Swarm Optimization (PSO) [1–4] and Differential Evolution (DE) [5, 6] are two most prominent representatives of evolutionary computational techniques (ECTs). Many more algorithms belong into the ECTs such as Ant Colony Optimization (ACO) [7] or SOMA [8] however the PSO and DE are the most popular and regularly used with great results in various tasks.

Given the popularity of PSO and DE and the focus of the researching community on the improvement of these methods, the hybridization of PSO and DE was an inevitable step [9, 10]. The performance of DE and PSO on certain types of optimization problems is often very different. Thru the process of hybridization it is possible to achieve good results on very broad spectrum of optimization tasks.

In this paper it is investigated a novel approach for PSO and DE hybridization based on recently proposed modification of PSO called the Multiple-Choice PSO (MC-PSO) [11, 12]. Further inspiration was taken from the diversity guided PSO (ARPSO) [13] to improve the performance of the proposed algorithm. The IEEE CEC 2013 Benchmark [15] is used in this initial study to show that it is possible in several cases to outperform both PSO and DE by the proposed hybridization method and to achieve good results on the whole benchmark set.

© Springer International Publishing Switzerland 2015
E. Onieva et al. (Eds.): HAIS 2015, LNAI 9121, pp. 213–220, 2015.
DOI: 10.1007/978-3-319-19644-2_18

In the next two sections the original PSO and DE algorithms are shortly described. Following is the description of proposed hybrid method. The experiment is designed and results presented in following sections.

2 Particle Swarm Optimization Algorithm

Original PSO takes the inspiration from behavior of fish and birds. The knowledge of global best found solution (typically noted *gBest*) is shared among the particles in the swarm. Furthermore each particle has the knowledge of its own (personal) best found solution (noted *pBest*). Last important part of the algorithm is the velocity of each particle that is taken into account during the calculation of the particle movement. The new position of each particle is then given by (1), where x_i^{t+1} is the new particle position; x_i^t refers to current particle position and v_i^{t+1} is the new velocity of the particle.

$$x_i^{t+1} = x_i^t + v_i^{t+1} \tag{1}$$

To calculate the new velocity the distance from pBest and gBest is taken into account alongside with current velocity (2).

$$v_{ij}^{t+1} = w \cdot v_{ij}^t + c_1 \cdot Rand \cdot (pBest_{ij} - x_{ij}^t) + c_2 \cdot Rand \cdot (gBest_j - x_{ij}^t) \tag{2}$$

Where:

v_{ij}^{t+1} - New velocity of the ith particle in iteration $t + 1$. (component j of the dimension D).
w - Inertia weight value.
v_{ij}^t - Current velocity of the ith particle in iteration t. (component j of the dimension D).
$c_1, c_2 = 2$ - Acceleration constants.
$pBest_{ij}$ - Local (personal) best solution found by the ith particle. (component j of the dimension D).
$gBest_j$ - Best solution found in a population. (component j of the dimension D).
x_{ij}^t - Current position of the ith particle (component j of the dimension D) in iteration t.
$Rand$ - Pseudo random number, interval (0, 1).

Finally the linear decreasing inertia weight [2, 4] is used. The dynamic inertia weight is meant to slow the particles over time thus to improve the local search capability in the later phase of the optimization. The inertia weight has two control parameters w_{start} and w_{end}. A new w for each iteration is given by (3), where t stands for current iteration number and n stands for the total number of iterations. The typical values used in this study were $w_{start} = 0.9$ and $w_{end} = 0.4$.

$$w = w_{start} - \frac{((w_{start} - w_{end}) \cdot t)}{n} \tag{3}$$

3 Differential Evolution

Similarly to PSO the DE is a population-based optimization method that works on real-number-coded individuals [5]. For each individual $\vec{x}_{i,G}$ in the current generation G, DE generates a new trial individual $\vec{x}'_{i,G}$ by adding the weighted difference between two randomly selected individuals $\vec{x}_{r1,G}$ and $\vec{x}_{r2,G}$ to a randomly selected third individual $\vec{x}_{r3,G}$. The resulting individual $\vec{x}'_{i,G}$ is crossed-over with the original individual $\vec{x}_{i,G}$. The fitness of the resulting individual, referred to as a perturbed vector $\vec{u}_{i,G+1}$, is then compared with the fitness of $\vec{x}_{i,G}$. If the fitness of $\vec{u}_{i,G+1}$ is greater than the fitness of $\vec{x}_{i,G}$, then $\vec{x}_{i,G}$ is replaced with $\vec{u}_{i,G+1}$; otherwise, $\vec{x}_{i,G}$ remains in the population as $\vec{x}_{i,G+1}$. DE is quite robust, fast, and effective, wi th global optimization ability. It does not require the objective function to be differentiable, and it works well even with noisy and time-dependent objective functions. Please refer to [5, 6] for the detailed description of the used DE/rand/1/bin strategy (4) as well as for the complete description of all other strategies.

$$u_{i,G+1} = x_{r1,G} + F \cdot \left(x_{r2,G} - x_{r3,G}\right) \tag{4}$$

The full schematic of DE algorithm is given in Fig. 1.

1. Input: $D, G_{max}, NP \geq 4, F \in (0,1+), CR \in [0,1]$, and initial bounds: $\vec{x}^{(lo)}, \vec{x}^{(hi)}$.

2. Initialize: $\begin{cases} \forall i \leq NP \wedge \forall j \leq D : x_{i,j,G=0} = x_j^{(lo)} + rand_j[0,1] \bullet \left(x_j^{(hi)} - x_j^{(lo)}\right) \\ i = \{1,2,...,NP\}, \ j = \{1,2,...,D\}, \ G = 0, \ rand_j[0,1] \in [0,1] \end{cases}$

3. While $G < G_{max}$

    4. Mutate and recombine:

        4.1 $r_1, r_2, r_3 \in \{1,2,....,NP\}$, randomly selected, except: $r_1 \neq r_2 \neq r_3 \neq i$

        4.2 $j_{rand} \in \{1,2,...,D\}$, randomly selected once each i

$\forall i \leq NP$ 4.3 $\forall j \leq D, u_{j,i,G+1} = \begin{cases} x_{j,r_3,G} + F \cdot (x_{j,r_1,G} - x_{j,r_2,G}) \\ \qquad \text{if } (rand_j[0,1] < CR \vee j = j_{rand}) \\ x_{j,i,G} \ \text{ otherwise} \end{cases}$

    5. Select

      $\vec{x}_{i,G+1} = \begin{cases} \vec{u}_{i,G+1} & \text{if } f(\vec{u}_{i,G+1}) \leq f(\vec{x}_{i,G}) \\ \vec{x}_{i,G} & \text{otherwise} \end{cases}$

$G = G + 1$

Fig. 1. DE schematic

4 MC-PSO/DE Hybrid with Repulsive Strategy

The MC-PSO as the new hybrid method proposed in this paper is mostly based on the original PSO. The algorithm is similar to PSO as presented in Sect. 2 with one exception. In the original MC-PSO [11, 12] four different velocity calculation formulas are defined. Afterwards the particle is randomly assigned one the pre-defined formulas in each iteration. The particle can either: stay in its current position, follow randomly chosen particle, follow its own pBest or follow the gBest. The probability of selection of particular behavior is given by three numbers b_1, b_2 and b_3. These numbers represent border values for different behavior rules and they follow the pattern: $b_1 < b_2 < b_3$. Afterwards during the calculation of new velocity of each particle a random number r is generated from the interval $< 0, 1 >$. For further details (including full pseudocode of the original MC-PSO) refer to [12].

For the purposes of hybridization two changes were introduced into the original MC-PSO. Firstly the DE/rand/1/bin is performed on stationary particles. Secondly to prevent fast premature convergence the gBest is used as a repulsive point. The repulsive strategy was firstly introduced in [13] and it is implemented here in such manner that the gBest is repulsing the particles instead of attracting them (See (8)).

For clarity the selection process of new velocity calculation formula and the DE implementation can be described as follows.

During the new velocity and position calculation a random number r is generated:

If $r \leq b1$ DE/rand/1/bin is performed for the particle and the new velocity of particle is given by (5):

$$v(t + 1) = 0 \tag{5}$$

If $b1 < r \leq b2$ the new velocity of particle is given by (6):

$$v(t + 1) = w \cdot v(t) + c \cdot Rand \cdot (x_r(t) - x(t)) \tag{6}$$

If $b2 < r \leq b3$ the new velocity of particle is given by (7):

$$v(t + 1) = w \cdot v(t) + c \cdot Rand \cdot (pBest - x(t)) \tag{7}$$

If $b3 < r$ the new velocity of particle is given by (8):

$$v(t + 1) = w \cdot v(t) - c \cdot Rand \cdot (gBest - x(t)) \tag{8}$$

Where $x_r(t)$ is the position of randomly chosen particle and $c = 2$.

5   Results and Discussion

In this initial study the performance of the newly proposed hybrid method was tested on the IEEE CEC 2013 benchmark set [15] for dimension setting $(dim) = 10$. According to the benchmark rules 51 separate runs were performed for each algorithm and the maximum number of cost function evaluations (CFE) was set to 100000. The population size was set to 40. Other controlling parameters of the PSO and DE were set to typical values as follows:

For PSO:

$$c_1, c_2 = 2;$$
$$w_{start} = 0.9;$$
$$w_{end} = 0.4;$$
$$v_{max} = 0.2;$$

For DE:

$$CR = 0.9;$$
$$F = 0.5;$$

The mean results of PSO, MC-PSO/DE and DE are presented in the following Table 1. The best results are given in bold numbers.

Table 1. Mean results comparison, $dim = 10$, max. CFE = 100000

Function	f min	PSO	MC-PSO/DE	DE
f_1^u	−1400	**−1.400E + 03**	**−1.400E + 03**	**−1.400E + 03**
f_2^u	−1300	2.449E + 05	**2.565E + 03**	6.033E + 03
f_3^u	−1200	1.862E + 06	**−1.167E + 03**	−1.018E + 03
f_4^u	−1100	−5.202E + 02	−9.276E + 02	**−9.448E + 02**
f_5^u	−1000	**−1.000E + 03**	**−1.000E + 03**	**−1.000E + 03**
f_6^m	−900	−8.936E + 02	−8.966E + 02	**−8.971E + 02**
f_7^m	−800	−7.961E + 02	−7.999E + 02	**−8.000E + 02**
f_8^m	−700	**−6.797E + 02**	**−6.797E + 02**	−6.796E + 02
f_9^m	−600	−5.968E + 02	−5.969E + 02	**−5.992E + 02**
f_{10}^m	−500	−4.996E + 02	**−4.999E + 02**	**−4.999E + 02**
f_{11}^m	−400	−3.982E + 02	−3.898E + 02	**−3.993E + 02**
f_{12}^m	−300	−2.868E + 02	−2.886E + 02	**−2.920E + 02**
f_{13}^m	−200	−1.802E + 02	−1.871E + 02	**−1.898E + 02**
f_{14}^m	−100	5.719E + 01	9.090E + 02	**−2.769E + 00**
f_{15}^m	100	**8.445E + 02**	1.073E + 03	1.405E + 03
f_{16}^m	200	**2.009E + 02**	2.011E + 02	2.010E + 02
f_{17}^m	300	**3.142E + 02**	3.289E + 02	3.144E + 02
f_{18}^m	400	4.320E + 02	4.323E + 02	**4.308E + 02**
f_{19}^m	500	**5.007E + 02**	5.013E + 02	5.008E + 02
f_{20}^m	600	6.026E + 02	6.033E + 02	**6.021E + 02**
f_{21}^c	700	**1.083E + 03**	1.096E + 03	1.100E + 03
f_{22}^c	800	9.715E + 02	1.899E + 03	**9.024E + 02**
f_{23}^c	900	**1.809E + 03**	2.072E + 03	1.859E + 03
f_{24}^c	1000	1.205E + 03	**1.195E + 03**	1.200E + 03
f_{25}^c	1100	1.303E + 03	**1.299E + 03**	1.300E + 03
f_{26}^c	1200	1.357E + 03	**1.322E + 03**	1.324E + 03
f_{27}^c	1300	1.669E + 03	1.606E + 03	**1.602E + 03**
f_{28}^c	1400	**1.687E + 03**	1.688E + 03	1.692E + 03

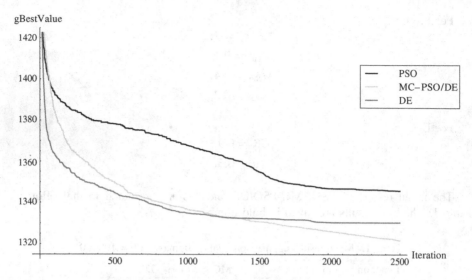

Fig. 2. Mean best value history comparison – f_{26}

Furthermore as an example the mean history of the best found solution during the optimization in given in Fig. 2.

In the Table 1 the benchmark functions are divided into unimodal (noted with ^{u}), basic multimodal (noted with ^{m}) and composite functions (noted with ^{c}). The performance of the proposed method on the unimodal functions is very promising. The MC-PSO/DE managed to obtain the best result in 4 of 5 cases. This brings evidence of fast convergence capability of the method.

The results for basic multimodal are overall comparable with both PSO and DE. This supports the claim that the hybrid method successfully combines the advantages of both PSO and DE. Finally the performance of this initial design on the composition functions is very encouraging. Under closer investigation (Fig. 2.) is clear that the design is able of fast initial convergence but is robust enough to prevent premature convergence in local extremes. Based on this observation, it will be further investigated the possibility of increasing the speed of initial convergence of this method.

6 Conclusion

In this initial study the hybridization of MC-PSO and DE/rand/1/bin was proposed. The results presented in this work support the claim that in some cases the hybridization could lead to significantly improved performance. In many cases where the original methods outperformed each other (one achieved superb results second not good) the hybrid managed to achieve very good results. These results support the idea of using hybrid algorithms when dealing with very broad spectrum of problems or unknown optimization task. The DE was used here to improve the performance of MC-PSO and the repulsive strategy was implemented in order to prevent the algorithm from fast premature convergence. This is the first step in the research of this approach and will be followed with more detailed studies and extensive performance testing.

Acknowledgements. This work was supported by Grant Agency of the Czech Republic - GACR P103/15/06700S, further by financial support of research project NPU I No. MSMT-7778/2014 by the Ministry of Education of the Czech Republic. Also by the European Regional Development Fund under the Project CEBIA-Tech No. CZ.1.05/2.1.00/03.0089, partially supported by Grant of SGS No. SP2015/142 and SP2015/141, VŠB - Technical University of Ostrava, Czech Republic and by Internal Grant Agency of Tomas Bata University under the project No. IGA/FAI/2015/057.

References

1. Kennedy, J., Eberhart, R.: Particle swarm optimization. In: Proceedings of the IEEE International Conference on Neural Networks, pp. 1942–1948 (1995)
2. Shi, Y., Eberhart, R.: A modified particle swarm optimizer. In: Proceedings of the IEEE International Conference on Evolutionary Computation (IEEE World Congress on Computational Intelligence), pp. 69–73 I. S (1998)
3. Kennedy, J.: The particle swarm: social adaptation of knowledge. In: Proceedings of the IEEE International Conference on Evolutionary Computation, pp. 303–308 (1997)
4. Nickabadi, A., Ebadzadeh, M.M., Safabakhsh, R.: A novel particle swarm optimization algorithm with adaptive inertia weight. Appl. Soft Comput. **11**(4), 3658–3670 (2011). ISSN 1568-4946
5. Price, K.V.: An introduction to differential evolution. In: Corne, D., Dorigo, M., Glover, F. (eds.) New Ideas in Optimization, pp. 79–108. McGraw-Hill Ltd., Maidenhead (1999)
6. Price, K.V., Storn, R.M., Lampinen, J.A.: Differential Evolution - A Practical Approach to Global Optimization. Natural Computing Series. Springer, Berlin Heidelberg (2005)
7. Dorigo, M., Gambardella, L.M., Birattari, M., Martinoli, A., Poli, R., Stützle, T.: ANTS 2006. LNCS, vol. 4150. Springer, Heidelberg (2006)
8. Zelinka, I.: SOMA — Self-Organizing Migrating Algorithm. New Optimization Techniques in Engineering. Studies in Fuzziness and Soft Computing, vol. 141, pp. 167–217. Springer, Berlin Heidelberg (2004)
9. Pant, M., Thangaraj, R., Grosan, C., Abraham, A.: Hybrid differential evolution - Particle swarm optimization algorithm for solving global optimization problems. In: Third International Conference on Digital Information Management, ICDIM 2008, pp. 18-24 13–16 Nov 2008
10. Yu, X., Cao, J., Shan, H., Zhu, L., Guo, J.: An adaptive hybrid algorithm based on particle swarm optimization and differential evolution for global optimization. The Scientific World Journal **2014**, 16 (2014). doi:10.1155/2014/215472. Article ID 215472
11. Pluhacek, M., Senkerik, R., Zelinka, I.: Multiple choice strategy – a novel approach for particle swarm optimization – preliminary study. In: Rutkowski, L., Korytkowski, M., Scherer, R., Tadeusiewicz, R., Zadeh, L.A., Zurada, J.M. (eds.) ICAISC 2013, Part II. LNCS, vol. 7895, pp. 36–45. Springer, Heidelberg (2013)
12. Pluhacek, M., Senkerik, R., Zelinka, I.: Investigation on the performance of a new multiple choice strategy for PSO Algorithm in the task of large scale optimization problems. In: 2013 IEEE Congress on Evolutionary Computation (CEC), pp. 2007-2011 20–23 June 2013

13. Riget, J., Vestterstrom, J.S.: A diversity-guided particle swarm optimizer - the ARPSO. Technical report, EVAlife, Dept. of Computer Science, University of Aarhus, Denmark (2002)
14. Liang, J.J., Qu, B.-Y., Suganthan, P.N., Hernández-Díaz, A.G.: Problem definitions and evaluation criteria for the cec 2013 special session and competition on real-parameter optimization. Technical Report 201212, Computational Intelligence Laboratory, Zhengzhou University, Zhengzhou, China and Technical Report, Nanyang Technological University, Singapore (2013)

OVRP_ICA: An Imperialist-Based Optimization Algorithm for the Open Vehicle Routing Problem

Shahab Shamshirband[1], Mohammad Shojafar[2($\boxtimes$)],
Ali Asghar Rahmani Hosseinabadi[3], and Ajith Abraham[4,5]

[1] Department of Computer System and Technology,
Faculty of Computer Science and Information Technology,
University of Malaya, Kuala Lumpur, Malaysia
shamshirband@um.edu.my
[2] Department of Information Engineering Electronics
and Telecommunications (DIET), University Sapienza of Rome, Rome, Italy
shojafar@diet.uniroma1.it
[3] Young Research Club, Behshahr Branch,
Islamic Azad University, Tehran, Iran
a.r.hosseinabadi@iaubs.ac.ir
[4] Machine Intelligence Research Labs (MIR Labs),
Scientific Network for Innovation, and Research Excellence, Auburn, AL, USA
ajith.abraham@ieee.org
[5] IT4Innovations - Center of Excellence,
VSB - Technical University of Ostrava, Ostrava, Czech Republic

Abstract. Open vehicle routing problem (OVRP) is one of the most important problems in vehicle routing, which has attracted great interest in several recent applications in industries. The purpose in solving the OVRP is to decrease the number of vehicles and to reduce travel distance and time of the vehicles. In this article, a new meta-heuristic algorithm called OVRP_ICA is presented for the above-mentioned problem. This is a kind of combinatorial optimization problem that can use a homogeneous fleet of vehicles that do not necessarily return to the initial depot to solve the problem of offering services to a set of customers exploiting the imperialist competitive algorithm. OVRP_ICA is compared with some well-known state-of-the-art algorithms and the results confirmed that it has high efficiency in solving the above-mentioned problem.

Keywords: Metaheuristic algorithms · Open vehicle routing problem (OVRP) · Imperialist competitive algorithm (ICA) · Combinatorial optimization problem

1 Introduction

The OVRP involves finding one of the best routes for a set of vehicles that must offer services to a set of customers. Every route in OVRP includes a sequence of customers that starts at the initial depot and ends at one of the customers [1]. The usual limitations of the OVRP are that all vehicles must have the same capacity, and each customer must

© Springer International Publishing Switzerland 2015
E. Onieva et al. (Eds.): HAIS 2015, LNAI 9121, pp. 221–233, 2015.
DOI: 10.1007/978-3-319-19644-2_19

be visited by only one vehicle to receive the required service. The total requests of all the customers in a route should not exceed the total capacity of the vehicles. In some problems, the time limit is considered together with the distance limit in covering the specific route: the distance traveled and the travel time spent of vehicle for the route must not exceed the permissible limits [2]. Lowering the number of vehicles, decreasing the distance traveled in the routes, and reducing travel time are among the main purposes of solving this problem.

The OVRPs are different and their most important difference is that there are Hamiltonian routes and Hamiltonian cycles in them, respectively. Hamiltonian routes start from one point and end in another Hamiltonian cycles finally return to the initial point [2]. Therefore, one of the main features of OVRP is that vehicles do not necessarily return to the initial depot after servicing to the customers, and if they do return to the initial depot, they will visit the same customers [3]. The OVRP is an NP-hard problem and its solution is considered a scientific challenge. In traditional studies, the OVRP was solved by assuming definite answers to the requests of all customers on the routes. Moreover, researchers have introduced various methods based on innovative and meta-heuristic methods for solving the OVRP, a few of which will be described here. Brandao [3] used Tabu Search to solve the VRP with limitations on vehicle capacity and on maximum travel distance in routes. Authors [4] introduced an algorithm to solve the OVRP for managing open routes. Fleszar et al. [5] implemented the variable neighborhood search technique for the OVRP with the purpose of reducing the number of vehicles and of decreasing travel time, and travel distance in the routes. Erbao and Mingyong [6] dealt with the OVRP by considering the fuzzy demands and combined the improved differential evolution algorithm and random simulation to solve the problem. In [7], a combination in the form of (GA + TS), in which the parallel computational power, the global optimization GA, and the rapid local search TS were used with the purpose similar to that of the above mentioned methods, was used for solving the OVRP. Repoussis et al. [8] introduced a combinatorial evolution strategy for the OVRP with the purpose of reducing the number of vehicles in the fleet and of decreasing the travel distance in the routes. Furthermore, Tabu Algorithms [9] and improved Tabu Algorithms [10] were implemented by Huang and Liu with the purpose of reducing the number of vehicles and travel costs for OVRP. Based on results of simulations, the introduced algorithm can decrease the number of required vehicles and reduce travel costs. Considering the slow rate of convergence and the weak search ability of the traditional genetic algorithm, the combinatorial genetic algorithm (which has greater convergence rate and rapid search ability) can be used to simplify the problem and improve its search efficiency [11, 12]. Authors in [13] introduced an algorithm that was based on genetic rules in order to upgrade the optimal performance of particle swarm and of differential evolution for solving the OVRP. In their algorithm, all members had dominant and recessive characters, optimization of particle swarm took place by the dominant character and differential evolution by the recessive one, and if the proportionality of the dominant character was smaller than that of the recessive one, the recessive character replaced the dominant one. In [14], the concepts of variable neighborhood search and evolutionary algorithms were used for optimization of the OVRP. This method could offer solutions with acceptable quality. Zachariadis and Kiranoudis [15] introduced a new search method for solving the

OVRP that could investigate an extensive solution space to reduce the number of routes and decrease routing costs. Marinakis and Marinaki have introduced a new version of the BBMO algorithm for solving the OVRP problem [16], among the main parts of which is the replacement of outward movement by a local search that makes the proposed algorithm more effective for solving combinatorial optimization problems. They presented a special decoding method for implementing the PSO in which a vector including customers' positions was produced in a descending order and then each customer was assigned to a specific route based on his/her position and, finally, a one-unit mutation was applied on all produced routes. This was an effective method for solving the problem because it allowed for studying the feasibility of the routes and for investigating the quality of the answers. The problem, and the in/equalities are defined in Sect. 2. Section 3 introduces the proposed algorithm which is based on imperialist competitive algorithms, and Sect. 4 explains in detail the results of algorithm simulations. Finally, conclusions are presented in Sect. 5.

2 Problem Definition and Notation

The OVRP is a kind of the classic vehicle routing problem (VRP) in which the vehicles do not necessarily return to the initial depot after servicing to the customers. The OVRP applies in cases where either the company does not have the required vehicles or there are not enough vehicles in the company to distribute the product among the customers. In both cases, the company will rent a number of vehicles, and when these vehicles carry out their tasks, they do not return to the initial depot. This is one of the class 3PL problems [17]. In this research, the following assumptions were made in solving the OVRP. n is taken to be the number of customers, $N = \{1, 2, \ldots, n\}$ the set of n customers, and $V = \{0, 1, \ldots, n\}$ the set of customers and the starting point, where 0 represents the starting point, q_i the request of customer $i \in V - \{0\}$, and Q is the capacity of each vehicle. It is assumed that K is the maximum number of available vehicles, and c_{ij} the cost for the sequence of customers from i to j and a scale equivalent to the appropriate adjustments. Moreover, the cost w_k is considered for each travel of the vehicle k. Therefore, the OVRP will involve finding the minimum number of required vehicles and determining a route for each vehicle in a way that all customer requests are satisfied and each customer is visited exactly by one vehicle and no vehicle exceeds its capacity [16, 18]. Mathematical modeling of the OVRP requires two groups of variables, the first group for modeling a sequence in which customers are visited by vehicles and is defined as follows [16]:

$$x_{ij}^k = \begin{cases} 1 & \textit{if customer } i \textit{ precedes customer } j \textit{ visited by vehicle } k \\ 0 & \textit{otherwise} \end{cases} \tag{1}$$

The second group of variables (shown as z_k) is a binary variable and defined in

$$z_k = \begin{cases} 1 & \textit{if vehicle } k \textit{ is active} \\ 0 & \textit{otherwise} \end{cases} \tag{2}$$

If the same vehicle services at least one customer, it will be considered active [16]. Using the considered parameters and variables, we can express the OVRP problem in this way [16]:

$$min \sum_{k=1}^{k} \sum_{i=0}^{n} \sum_{j=o}^{n} c_{ij} x_{ij}^{k} + \sum_{k=1}^{k} w_k z_k \qquad (3)$$

Subject to

$$\sum_{k=1}^{k} \sum_{j=1}^{n} x_{ij}^{k} = 1, \forall j = 1, 2, \ldots, n \qquad (4)$$

$$\sum_{k=1}^{k} \sum_{j=1}^{n} x_{ij}^{k} = 1, \forall i = 1, 2, \ldots, n \qquad (5)$$

$$x_{ij}^{k} \le z_k, \quad \forall k = 1, \ldots, K, \quad \forall i = 1, 2, \ldots, n, \quad \forall j = 1, 2, \ldots, n \qquad (6)$$

$$\sum_{i=0}^{n} x_{iu}^{k} - \sum_{j=1}^{n} x_{uj}^{k} = 0, \forall k = 1, 2, \ldots, K, \forall u = 1, 2, \ldots, n \qquad (7)$$

$$\sum_{(i,j)\in s \times s} x_{ij}^{k} \le |S| - 1, \quad \forall S \subseteq V : 1 \le |S| \le n, \quad k \qquad (8)$$

$$\sum_{j=1}^{n} q_j \left(\sum_{i=0}^{n} x_{ij}^{k} \right) \le Q, \quad \forall k = 1, 2, \ldots, K \qquad (9)$$

$$\sum_{j=1}^{n} x_{0j}^{k} \le 1, \quad \forall k = 1, 2, \ldots, K \qquad (10)$$

$$\sum_{i=1}^{n} x_{i0}^{k} \le 0, \forall k = 1, 2, \ldots, K \qquad (11)$$

$$x_{ij}^{k} \in \{0, 1\}, \forall k = 1, 2, \ldots, K, \forall i = 1, \ldots, n, \forall j = 1, \ldots, n \qquad (12)$$

$$z_k \in \{0, 1\}, \forall k = 1, 2, \ldots, K \qquad (13)$$

The objective function in (3) will create equilibrium between the travel cost and the vehicle. Equation (4) represents the connectivity of all routes taken by all vehicles after they move from the initial point and the cost of the first part of each route too. Equations (5) and (6) guarantee the arrival to and departure of exactly one car to/from each customer. Equation (6) is related to variables x and z and indicates that all customers receive services from active vehicles. Equation (7) exhibits the continuity of each route, and (8) the identifier of the sub-tours. Inequality in (9) shows the maximum vehicle capacity, and inequalities in (10) and (11) indicate that only one vehicle must start its tour from the starting point to give service to a sequence of customers and that none of the vehicles returns to the starting point. Equations (12) and (13) are definitions for the variables x and z for each vehicle k [16]. There are some limitations considered in the problem: (1) All vehicles must be of the same capacity; (2) Travel time for each vehicle must be less than the threshold time considered; (3) The sum of the requests of the customers in each route must be less than the capacity of the vehicle assigned to the route; (4) Each customer is visited only once and by only one of the vehicles for his/her request to be satisfied. Put it simply, the purpose of OVRP is to reduce the number of vehicles considered for giving service to customers, and to decrease travel distance and time of the vehicles in the routes [4, 19, 20]. We use the ICA algorithm [21] to improve the consumed resources of an OVRP. ICA considers the algorithm has little information such as search space and definition of feasible answers for the problems, it can move toward finding better answers and progress as well as possible in the search space by creating random answers.

3   OVRP_ICA Algorithm

The following six basic steps are taken to apply the proposed algorithm to the OVRP (which is one of the most frequently met problems in transportation). In the first step, the feasible answers (the initial countries) are defined. It must be noted that this is a very important step because these countries must be defined in a way that they have the necessary coordination with the structure of the problem. Therefore, in this step a two-part array is used as shown in Fig. 1. This array is prepared in such a way that customers met are ordered in turn from left to right in the first part of the array, and the number of customers visited by each vehicle is shown in the second part. It must be kept in mind that the number of the elements in the second part is equal to the total number of the vehicles. Moreover, in this figure, the first vehicle visits five customers, the second four, and, finally, the third vehicle visits two customers. It must be noted that the number of the customers allocated to each vehicle must not exceed its capacity.

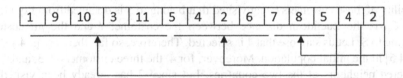

Fig. 1. One country in the OVRP_ICA algorithm

In the OVRP_ICA, a determined and variable number P of random initial answers are produced and the values of the f_m objective function are calculated for each member in $m = 1,...,P$. These answers are then placed in the D matrix together with their values (every row of this matrix shows one initial feasible answer, or one initial country, together with the related objective function). The use of a random structure in this step causes the obtained answers to have various structures in the feasible region.

In the second step, values of the objective function for each county are compared, and the I number of countries that have lower objective function values are considered as independent countries (because OVRP is a minimization problem). By replacing the countries in the matrix, rows from 1 to I of the initial population in the D matrix are given to the independent countries. To determine the sphere of influence of each independent country, the number of dependent countries is allocated to the jth independent country according to Eq. (14) so that I empires are created

$$k_j = int\left(\frac{1/f_j}{\sum_{i=1}^{I} 1/f_i}\cdot(P-I)\right) \quad j = 1,\ldots,I \tag{14}$$

Equation (14) shows the number of dependent countries allocated to the jth independent country. It must be added that, according to this relation, each independent country that has a lower objective function value will acquire a larger number of dependent countries and a larger empire will be formed. Moreover, the $int(.)$ function in Eq. (14) is the integer part function that causes each empire to be allocated an integer number of dependent countries. On the other hand, because the $int(.)$ function is used, there may be some countries left in the end that have not been assigned to any of the empires. In this case, these countries are allocated to the most powerful independent country (which has the lowest objective function value). It must be noted that Eq. (14) determines only the number of countries allocated randomly to each empire.

In step three, after the empires have formed, the dependent countries in each empire increases their quality by using the independent countries that have the role of local optimums. The noteworthy point is that, since a large number of dependent countries are combined with one independent country in each empire, some kind of an assimilation function having the random concept must be used so that similar answers are not produced. To achieve this, a modified nearest neighbor method is used in this step. For example, consider the two feasible answers [5 2 4 3 1 6 8 9 7 11 10| 3 3 5] as the independent country and the [2 6 5 3 1 11 9 6 8 10 4|2 4 5] as the dependent country. Now, start to move from 2, that is the first customer of the dependent country, and consider the two countries that are neighbors of 2 (that is, 4, 5, and 6) and have not been visited so far and put them in the S set. According to the modified nearest neighbor method, the probability of those customers being visited that belong to S is obtained from Eq. (15), in which C_{ij} is the Euclidean distance between the customer I and the jth customer belonging to S. Let us suppose that 4 is selected. Therefore, so far, there are [2 4 - - - - - - - - -|2 4 5] in the initial population. Moreover, for 4, the three customers 2, 3, and 10 are considered neighbors of the two countries, but since 2 has already been visited, the nearest possible neighbor is selected from 3 and 10 that form the new S set. This process continues until the rest of the customers in [2 4 - - - - - - - - -|2 4 5] are found, and it continues for all dependent countries. It must be noted that, in this method, all customers are selected only once, so that the obtained answer will be a feasible answer in this respect. The only thing that must be investigated is whether the capacity of each vehicle is less than the total capacities of the customers allocated to the vehicle which puts in s according to Eq. (15). If the answer is affirmative (i.e., accepted), the new answer replaces the old one; otherwise, the previous answer remains unchanged.

$$s = \frac{1/c_{ij}}{\sum_{j\int s} 1/c_{ij}} \tag{15}$$

Moreover, in this step, with the changed status of ρ percent of the dependent countries, the empires will have sufficient diversity. As in the previous step the first part of the answers were examined and upgraded according to the possible nearest neighbor algorithm, the second part in the vector of feasible answers will be studied in this step. For this purpose, one of the members is randomly selected and one unit is added to it. For example, let us consider the feasible answer [2 11 8 9 10 6 5 3 7 1 4|2 4 5]. Suppose 4 is selected from part 2 and one unit is added to it. Now, consider the neighbors of 4 (that are 2 and 5). As one unit was added to 4, therefore, one unit is deducted from one of the neighbors at random. For example, one unit is deducted from 5 and the new answer will be [2 11 8 9 10 6 5 3 7 1 4|2 4 5]. Here, again, the condition of the feasibility of the answer and its application within the limitations of the problem are examined.

After calculating the answer and the new ρ value (ρ is the percentage of dependent countries), these countries may have greater power compared to the independent country in the empire. Therefore, a dependent country with the best value in each empire is selected and replaces the independent country. Care must be taken so that, if several dependent countries have the same objective function, to randomly select one of them, to compare it with the independent country in the empire and, if needed, to replace the independent country with this dependent one.

In step four, since until the end of an iteration of the algorithm no other changes take place in the objective function, it is necessary to store the best answer and the value of the objective function. Therefore, in all iterations, after the replacement of independent countries takes place, the best answer among the independent countries is selected as the best current answer and, if it is better compared to previous answers, a local search is conducted on it and the new answer replaces the previous answer and value. The local search used in this step is based on omission of customer from the problem and on entering it in the appropriate position. This change is accepted if the new answer, besides applying within the limitations of the problem, is of higher quality compared to the previous answer. It must be noted that the customer is randomly selected, is tested for all entrance sites, and the best state is selected. Up to this step of the algorithm, the purpose is to conduct a global search to find good answers for important regions.

Now, in the next step, these regions must be identified, and countries must converge towards them, so that important regions are more extensively examined, and the algorithm can find better answers. Therefore, in step five, the powers of the empires are compared by using Eq. (16). h_j, f_i, S_i, and λ represent the total power (the value of the objective function) of each empire, the power of each independent country, the mean power of the dependent countries in the jth empire, and the influence coefficient, respectively. The influence coefficient has values from zero to 1 and determines the importance of the mean power of the dependent countries compared to the power of the independent country in an empire. Now, the weaker empire gives its weakest dependent country to one of the empires. It must be kept in mind that if a weaker empire does not have a dependent country, it will be destroyed and its independent country will be allocated to the most powerful empire.

$$h_j = f_i + \lambda(S_j) \quad j = 1, \ldots, I \tag{16}$$

In step six, the final condition will be examined, and if it is satisfied, the algorithm ends; otherwise, the algorithm will return to step three and repeat its operation. To end the algorithm, the two conditions of iterating the algorithm a determined T times or having only one empire left are used, and these two conditions are simultaneously examined at the end of each algorithm iteration. Either of the two conditions that are satisfied sooner will end the algorithm, and the best answer and value obtained until that time will be introduced as the final answer for the problem. Finally, the main steps in the OVRP_ICA are summarized in the pseudocode shown in Algorithm 1.

Algorithm 1. OVRP_ICA
1: **Input:** N, V, Q, ICA parameters
2: **Output:**   minimum distance traveled N on V
3: **Begin:**
6: Randomly generate initial population of countries and initial empires
7: Move colonies toward to the relevant empires(Assimilation)
8: Randomly select some colonies and change the value of colonies(Revolution)
9: If position a is better than the imperialist, exchanges position of colony and imperialist
10: Compute total cost of each empire
11 Peak the weakest colony from the weakest empire. Other imperialists compete to take possession of colonies.
12: If an empire loses all colonies, collapse it
13: If the stop condition is satisfied, stop, if not go to line 5
15: **End Algorithm**

4   Performance Evaluation

In this section, we describe the test beds dataset and the show simulation results in small-scale and large-scale test problems.

4.1   Setup for Benchmark Data Sets

The proposed method was tested on the famous data set of Christofide et al. [22], Fisher [23], and Li et al. [1]. In Fisher's model, there are $C1$ to $C14$ problems [23]. The numbers of customers in both sets were in the interval of 50 to 199, with Cartesian coordinates and Euclidean distance [23]. Among them, the limitations of route length (L) and service time (e) were considered for all customers. We Use problems which are specified as 8 problems ($C1$ to $C8$) introduced by Christofide et al. [22] and Fisher [23]. Among these problems, namely $C6$–$C8$, consider route length restrictions (180, 144, 207) and a uniform service time for all customers (10 for all), simultaneously. The maximum route length, compared to the VRP model, was a factor of 0.9 because the lengths considered in the VRP model are not suitable. The last column, in which K_{min} (the total requests of the customers divided by the capacity of each vehicle), represents the lower limit. Moreover, the set of large-scale data of Li et al. [1] was also considered. The second case includes 8 problems in the form of $O1$–$O8$ with 200–480 customers without any limitations regarding route length. Each problem has a geometric symmetry and the customers are in a circle around the depot.

4.2   Computational Results

Results of simulations conducted to solve the OVRP are presented in this section. To test the efficiency of the proposed algorithm on OVRP, and to compare it with other meta-heuristic algorithms, the proposed algorithm was tested on two classes of standard examples taken from [24]. Implementation took place in the C#.NET programming language and the programs were executed on a computer with 2.06 GHz Pentium-IV processor and 6 GB RAM. Results of simulations of the proposed algorithm (OVR-P_ICA) were compared with several samples of various algorithms including HTS [9], ITS [10], DHPD [13] and Hybrid (1 + 1) ES [14] for small-scale and TR [1], HES [9], BLSA [15] and BBMOOVRP [17] for large-scale of problems which will be helpful in industries. Considering the steps mentioned in the previous section, results of outputs are presented in the following tables. In these tables, the k_min column shows the number of vehicles, the Fitness column the travel distance of the vehicle, and the Time column the time taken to solve the problem and to find the best answer. Results of the comparison indicate that the proposed algorithm is superior to the algorithms it was compared with respect to the time taken to solve the problem and the minimum number of vehicles, and with respect to the minimum travel distance of each vehicle.

Small-Scale Test Problems: In Table 1, while the number of vehicles increase, the result of of fitness function which is calculated according to the aforementioned algorithm provide better (i.e., lower fitness values) results compared to HTS [9] and ITS [10]. In detail, it is better than HTS and ITS due to convergent and finding appropriate colony in each step and it search the problem space globally rather than Tabu searching which search the system locally. Also, OVRP_ICA total travel distacne is about 50 % less than other methods in medium and smooth restriction as are shown in rows C6 and C8 but it has approcimetely 1 % higher travel distance compared to the least one in C7.

Table 1. Results of comparisons among OVRP_ICA, HTS [9] and ITS [10] methods for minimizing the total travel distance and time of the vehicle and the number of vehicles (small-scle)

OVRP_ICA		ITS [10]		HTS [9]		The input			Problem
Time (s)	Fitness	Time	Fitness	Time	Fitness	K_{min}	Q	N	
63.429	**409.68**	14.9	461.37	16. 1	451.59	5	160	50	C1
131.758	**557.14**	26.7	663.28	28.3	649.38	10	140	75	C2
254.385	**629.74**	218.4	954.34	2 12.5	928.41	8	200	100	C3
350.132	**716.73**	531.5	1247.52	542.7	1201.95	12	200	150	C4
563.876	**902.45**	253.1	1059.47	268.6	1018.56	16	200	199	C5
85.12	**411.87**	61.4	890.63	68.3	870.06	5	160	50	C6
91.67	587.76	17.9	602.71	18.6	**586.64**	10	140	75	C7
576.23	**634.52**	553.1	1261.39	562.8	1254.28	8	200	100	C8

In next Table, we compare our approach with ES [14] and DHPD [13] methods in the same problems to evaluate our approach with PSO-based and integrated neighborhood based methods for small-scale problems to minimize the total travel distance and time of the vehicle and the number of vehicles. As we seen in Table 2, our approach is able to minimize the total travel distance while the number of the customers and vehicles capacity increase well compared with the ES and DHPD [13] even with rising the restrictions (i.e., C6 an C8), but when the restriction is too tight DHPD [13] provide better result rather than others.

Table 2. Results of comparisons among OVRP_ICA, ES [14] and DHPD [13] methods (small-scale)

OVRP_ICA		Hybrid (1 + 1) ES [14]		DHPD [13]		The input			Problem
Time	Fitness	Time	Fitness	Time	Fitness	K_{min}	Q	N	
63.429	409.68	–	412.95	–	**408.5**	5	160	50	C1
131.758	**557.14**	–	564.06	–	567.14	10	140	75	C2
254.385	629.74	–	639.25	–	**617.0**	8	200	100	C3
350.132	**716.73**	–	733.13	–	733.13	12	200	150	C4
563.876	**902.45**	–	**868.44**	–	897.93	16	200	199	C5
85.12	**411.87**	–	412.95	–	412.96	5	160	50	C6
91.67	587.76	–	566.93	–	**552.87**	10	140	75	C7
576.23	**634.52**	–	**640.89**	–	644.63	8	200	100	C8

Large-Scale Test Problems: The OVRP contains eight large-scale problems that have no limitations regarding travel distance. Therefore, solving them is difficult and time-consuming. In this research, the vehicle routing problem with large-scale as solved by Li et al. [1] was considered. Eight problems with 200–480 customers and no limitations regarding route distance were selected. Each of the problems had a geometrical symmetry and the customers were on a circular orbit around the depot. Each problem showed a geometrical symmetry that made it possible to estimate an answer. Tables 3 and 4 list the obtained results, the time spent in OVRP_ICA runs and the values related to answers estimated by the other algorithms. As can be seen in the tables, standard data and much more complex problems were used to compare the three methods of solving the OVRP. Results obtained showed the proposed algorithm could find considerably better answers compared to the other algorithms.

Table 4 shows that the proposed method provides better results compared with two other methods in all huge problems except O7 even with lower execution time. This happens because while we fix the maximum capacity to 900 and increase slightly the active vehicles and customers the colonies increases and produce some new regin/ colony and the ICA unable to find precise imperialist somehow and the final result increases. On the other hand, ICA feels it finds proper imperlaist sooner than expected and the run time decreases with faster rate.

Table 3. Comparison among ORTR [1] and HES[8] methods with the proposed method in 8 problems wirh huge customers (large-scale problems).

OVRP_ICA		ORTR [1]		HES [8]		The input			Problem
Time	Fitness	Time	Fitness	Time	Fitness	K_{min}	Q	N	
331.14	**6016.98**	365	6018.52	452	6018.52	5	900	200	O1
438.35	**4572.40**	439	4584.55	613	4583.70	9	550	240	O2
492.76	**7730.95**	**492**	7732.85	736	7733.77	7	900	280	O3
573.98	**7158.36**	**573**	7291.89	833	7271.24	10	700	320	O4
765.43	**9112.67**	**766**	9197.61	1365	9254.15	8	900	360	O5
971.29	**9743.72**	977	9803.80	1213	9821.09	9	900	400	O6
933.74	10484.49	935	10374.97	1547	10363.40	10	900	440	O7
1125.21	**12412.56**	1126	12429.56	1653	12428.20	10	1000	480	O8

Table 4. Comparison among refrences [15, 17] methods with the proposed method for huge customers.

OVRP_ICA		Reference [17]		BLSA [15]		The input			Problem
Time	Fitness	Time	Fitness	Time	Fitness	K_{min}	Q	N	
331.14	**6016.98**	2.51	6021.11	612	6018.52	5	900	200	O1
438.35	4572.40	3.05	**4557.38**	774	**4557.38**	9	550	240	O2
492.76	**7730.95**	3.17	7735.14	681	7731.00	7	900	280	O3
573.98	**7158.36**	3.27	7267.18	957	7253.20	10	700	320	O4
765.43	**9112.67**	3.42	9198.25	1491	9193.15	8	900	360	O5
971.29	**9743.72**	4.06	9798.19	1070	9793.72	9	900	400	O6
933.74	10484.49	4.21	10351.18	1257	**10347.70**	10	900	440	O7
1125.21	**12412.56**	4.41	12418.57	1512	12415.36	10	1000	480	O8

5 Conclusion

In this research, a meta-heuristic algorithm called OVRP_ICA is presented for solving the OVRP. The advantages of this algorithm include its minimum traveling distance for the vehicles, the time needed for its execution, the low number of required evaluators for small-scale and large-scale problems, simultaneously. In detail, OVRP_ICA reduces the execution time, to find the shortest route between the customers and reduce the number of vehicles. Its efficiency was compared with those of eight different algorithms in small and large scale benchmark problems. This algorithm has a competitive structure compared to other meta-heuristic algorithms and could obtain reasonable and suitable answers for standard examples of this problem especially for small-scale problem with approximately 50 % lower traveling distances. It seems use of other meta-heuristic algorithms such as Tabu Search or ant colony optimization in combination with this algorithm can result in finding better answers for OVRP, especially in large and very large examples due to covering locally the search space. On the other hand, this algorithm can be used for other OVRP expansions such as the vehicle routing problem together with receiving and delivering goods. The use of such combinations of algorithms and work on these suggestions will be studied in future articles.

Acknowledgement. This work was also supported in the framework of the IT4 Innovations Centre of Excellence project, reg. no. CZ.1.05/1.1.00/02.0070 by operational programme 'Research and Development for Innovations' funded by the Structural Funds of the European Union and state budget of the Czech Republic, EU.

References

1. Li, F., Golden, B., Wasil, E.: The open vehicle routing problem: Algorithms, large-scale test problems, and computational results. COR **34**, 2918–2930 (2007)
2. Fleszar, K., et al.: A variable neighborhood search algorithm for the open vehicle routing problem. EJOR **195**, 803–809 (2009)
3. Sariklis, D., Powell, S.: A heuristic method for the open vehicle routing problem. JORS **51**, 564–573 (2000)
4. Reza, C.M.F.S., Mekhilef, S.: Online stator resistance estimation using artificial neural network for direct torque controlled induction motor drive. In: IEEE 8th ICIEA, pp. 1486–1491 (2013)
5. Cao, E., Lai, M., Yang, H.: Open vehicle routing problem with demand uncertainty and its robust strategies. ESWA **41**, 3569–3575 (2014)
6. Cao, E., Lai, M., Yang, H.: The open vehicle routing problem with fuzzy demands. Exp. Sys. Apps. **37**, 2405–2411 (2010)
7. Yu, Sh, Ding, Ch., Zhu, K.: A hybrid GA–TS algorithm for open vehicle routing optimization of coal mines material. ESWA **38**, 10568–10573 (2011)
8. Repoussisa, P.P., Tarantilis, C.D., Braysy, O., Ioannou, G.: A hybrid evolution strategy for the open vehicle routing problem. Comp. Oper. Res. **37**, 443–455 (2010)
9. Huang, F., Liu, C.: A hybrid tabu search for open vehicle routing problem. CCTAE **1**, 132–134 (2010)
10. Huang, F. Liu, C.: An improved tabu search for open vehicle routing problem. In: Management and Service Science (MASS), pp. 1–4 (2010)
11. Shamshirband, Sh., et al.: OSGA: genetic-based open-shop scheduling with consideration of machine maintenance in small and medium enterprises. ANOR, pp. 1–16. Springer, New York (2015)
12. Shamshirband, Sh., et al.: A solution for multi-objective commodity vehicle routing problem by NSGA-II. IEEE HIS **2014**, 12–17 (2014)
13. Hu, F., Wu, F.: Diploid hybrid particle swarm optimization with differential evolution for open vehicle routing problem. In: WCICA, pp. 2692–2697 (2010)
14. Schneider, H., Reinholz, A.: Integrating Variable Neighborhood Search into a Hybrid Evolutionary Strategy for the Open Vehicle Routing Problem. In: EU/MEeting 2008 pp. 1–6. Troyes, France (2008)
15. Zachariadis, E.E., Kiranoudis, ChT: An open vehicle routing problem metaheuristic for examining wide solution neighborhoods. COR **37**, 712–723 (2010)
16. MirHassani, S.A., Abolghasemi, N.: A particle swarm optimization algorithm for open vehicle routing problem. ESWA **38**, 11547–11551 (2011)
17. Marinakis, Y., Marinaki, M.: A bumble bees mating optimization algorithm for the open vehicle routing problem. Swarm Evol. Comp. **15**, 80–94 (2014)
18. Rababah A.M.: Taylor theorem for planar curves. AMS **119**, 803–810 (1993)
19. Atabani, A.E., et al.: A comprehensive review on biodiesel as an alternative energy resource and its characteristics. RSER **16**(4), 2070–2093 (2012)

20. Rababah A.M.: High order approximation method for curves. Com. Aid. Geom. Des. **12**, 89–102 (1995)
21. Atashpaz-Gargari, E., Lucas, C.: Imperialist competitive algorithm: an algorithm for optimization inspired by imperialistic competition. In: IEEE ICEC, pp. 4661–4667 (2007)
22. Toth, P., Vigo, D.: The Vehicle Routing Problem. Society for Industrial and Applied Mathematics, Philadelphia (2001)
23. Fisher, M.: Optimal solution of vehicle routing problems using minimum k-trees. Oper. Res. **42**, 626–642 (1994)
24. Site: www.branchandcut.org/VRP/data/

New Adaptive Approach for Multi-chaotic Differential Evolution Concept

Roman Senkerik[1(✉)], Michal Pluhacek[1], Donald Davendra[2],
Ivan Zelinka[2], and Jakub Janostik[1]

[1] Faculty of Applied Informatics, Tomas Bata University in Zlin,
Nam T.G. Masaryka 5555, 760 01 Zlin, Czech Republic
{senkerik, pluhacek, janostik}@fai.utb.cz
[2] Faculty of Electrical Engineering and Computer Science,
Technical University of Ostrava,
17. listopadu 15, 708 33 Poruba, Ostrava, Czech Republic
{donald.davendra, ivan.zelinka}@vsb.cz

Abstract. This research deals with the hybridization of the two soft computing fields, which are the chaos theory and evolutionary computation. This paper aims on the investigations on the adaptive multi-chaos-driven evolutionary algorithm Differential Evolution (DE) concept. This paper is aimed at the embedding and adaptive alternating of set of two discrete dissipative chaotic systems in the form of chaotic pseudo random number generators for the DE. In this paper the novel adaptive concept of DE/rand/1/bin strategy driven alternately by two chaotic maps (systems) is introduced. From the previous research, it follows that very promising results were obtained through the utilization of different chaotic maps, which have unique properties with connection to DE. The idea is then to connect these two different influences to the performance of DE into the one adaptive multi-chaotic concept with automatic switching without prior knowledge of the optimization problem and without any manual setting of the "switching point". Repeated simulations were performed on the IEEE CEC 13 benchmark set. Finally, the obtained results are compared with state of the art adaptive representative jDE.

Keywords: Differential evolution · Deterministic chaos · jDE

1 Introduction

This research deals with the hybridization of the two softcomputing fields, which are chaos theory and evolutionary computation. This paper is aimed at investigating the novel adaptive control scheme for multi-chaos driven Differential Evolution algorithm (DE) [1]. Although a number of DE variants have been recently developed, the focus of this paper is the further development of ChaosDE concept, which is based on the embedding of chaotic systems in the form of Chaos Pseudo Random Number Generators (CPRNG) into the DE.

A chaotic approach generally uses the chaotic map in the place of a pseudo random number generator [2]. This causes the heuristic to map unique regions, since the chaotic

© Springer International Publishing Switzerland 2015
E. Onieva et al. (Eds.): HAIS 2015, LNAI 9121, pp. 234–243, 2015.
DOI: 10.1007/978-3-319-19644-2_20

map iterates to new regions. The task is then to select a very good chaotic map as the pseudo random number generator.

The focus of our research is the direct embedding of chaotic dynamics in the form of CPRNG for evolutionary algorithms. The initial concept of embedding chaotic dynamics into the evolutionary algorithms is given in [3]. Later, the initial study [4] was focused on the simple embedding of chaotic systems in the form of chaos pseudo random number generator (CPRNG) for DE and Self Organizing Migration Algorithm (SOMA) [5] in the task of optimal PID tuning. Also the PSO (Particle Swarm Optimization) algorithm with elements of chaos was introduced as CPSO [6]. The concept of ChaosDE proved itself to be a powerful heuristic also in combinatorial problems domain [7]. At the same time the chaos embedded PSO with inertia weigh strategy was closely investigated [8], followed by the introduction of a PSO strategy driven alternately by two chaotic systems [9].

And based on the promising experimental results with PSO algorithm driven adaptively by two different chaotic systems, the idea was to extend this approach also on DE algorithm.

Firstly, the motivation for this research is proposed. The next section is focused on the description of evolutionary algorithm DE. The core of methodology of your presented research, which is the concept of adaptive chaos driven DE is explained in section four, followed by the experiment description. Results and conclusion follow afterwards.

2   Related Work and Motivation

This research is an extension and continuation of the previous successful initial experiments with multi-chaos driven PSO and DE algorithms [10, 11]. Recent research [12–14] shows that chaos driven heuristics applied to many interdisciplinary problems have better overall performance than canonical (original) versions of such heuristics. Furthermore there exist many possible approaches for hybridization, injection and control of chaotic complex dynamics into the heuristics.

In this paper the novel adaptive control concept for DE/rand/1/bin strategy driven alternately by two chaotic maps (systems) is introduced. From the aforementioned previous research it follows, that very promising experimental results were obtained through the utilization of different chaotic dynamics. And at the same time it was clear that different chaotic systems have different effects on the performance of the algorithm. The idea was then to connect these two different influences to the performance of DE into the one multi-chaotic concept. The previous research was aimed at the determining of the switching time (certain number of generations/iterations) between different chaotic systems. Such a "manual" approach proved to be successful, but also many open issues have arisen (i.e. when to start the switching, how many times, etc.). The novelty of the proposed adaptive approach is that, the chaotic pseudorandom number generators are switched over automatically without prior knowledge of the optimization problem and without any manual setting of the "switching point".

3 Differential Evolution

DE is a population-based optimization method that works on real-number-coded individuals [1, 15]. DE is quite robust, fast, and effective, with global optimization ability. A schematic of the canonical DE strategy is given in Fig. 1. There are essentially five sections to the code depicted in Fig. 1.

1. Input: $D, G_{max}, NP \geq 4, F \in (0,1+), CR \in [0,1]$, and initial bounds: $\bar{x}^{(lo)}, \bar{x}^{(hi)}$.

2. Initialize: $\begin{cases} \forall i \leq NP \wedge \forall j \leq D : x_{i,j,G=0} = x_j^{(lo)} + rand_j[0,1] \bullet \left(x_j^{(hi)} - x_j^{(lo)}\right) \\ i = \{1,2,...,NP\}, \quad j = \{1,2,...,D\}, \quad G = 0, \quad rand_j[0,1] \in [0,1] \end{cases}$

3. While $G < G_{max}$

    4. Mutate and recombine:

        4.1 $r_1, r_2, r_3 \in \{1,2,....,NP\}$, randomly selected, except: $r_1 \neq r_2 \neq r_3 \neq i$

        4.2 $j_{rand} \in \{1,2,...,D\}$, randomly selected once each i

$\forall i \leq NP$ 4.3 $\forall j \leq D, u_{j,i,G+1} = \begin{cases} x_{j,r_3,G} + F \cdot (x_{j,r_1,G} - x_{j,r_2,G}) \\ \quad \text{if } (rand_j[0,1] < CR \vee j = j_{rand}) \\ x_{j,i,G} \text{ otherwise} \end{cases}$

    5. Select

        $\bar{x}_{i,G+1} = \begin{cases} \bar{u}_{i,G+1} & \text{if } f(\bar{u}_{i,G+1}) \leq f(\bar{x}_{i,G}) \\ \bar{x}_{i,G} & \text{otherwise} \end{cases}$

$G = G + 1$

Fig. 1. DE schematic

Section 1 describes the input to the DE. D is the size of the problem, G_{max} is the maximum number of generations, NP is the total number of solutions, F is the scaling factor, CR is the factor for crossover, $x^{(lo)}$ and $x^{(hi)}$ represents the initial bounds of the solutions. F and CR together make the internal tuning parameters for the heuristic.

Section 2 in Fig. 1 outlines the initialization of the heuristic, i.e. creation of the initial population. Each solution $x_{i,j,G=0}$ is created randomly between the two bounds $x^{(lo)}$ and $x^{(hi)}$. The parameter j represents the index to the values within the solution and parameter i indexes the solutions within the population. So, to illustrate, $x_{4,2,0}$ represents the fourth value of the second solution at the initial generation.

After initialization, the population is subjected to repeated iterations in Sect. 3.

Section 4 describes the conversion routines of DE. Initially, three random numbers r_1, r_2, r_3 are selected, unique to each other and to the current indexed solution i in the population in 4.1. Henceforth, a new index j_{rand} is selected in the solution. j_{rand} points to the value being modified in the solution as given in 4.2. In 4.3, two solutions, $x_{j,r1,G}$ and $x_{j,r2,G}$ are selected through the index r_1 and r_2 and their values subtracted. This value is then multiplied by F, the predefined scaling factor. This is added to the value indexed by r_3.

However, this solution is not arbitrarily accepted in the solution. A new random number is generated, and if this random number is less than the value of CR, then the new value replaces the old value in the current solution. The fitness of the resulting solution, referred to as a perturbed vector $u_{j,i,G}$, is then compared with the fitness of $x_{j,i,G}$. If the fitness of $u_{j,i,G}$ is greater than the fitness of $x_{j,i,G}$, then $x_{j,i,G}$ is replaced with $u_{j,i,G}$; otherwise, $x_{j,i,G}$ remains in the population as $x_{j,i,G+1}$. Hence the competition is only between the new *child* solution and its *parent* solution.

4 The Concept of Adaptive Multi-chaotic DE

The general idea of ChaosDE and CPRNG is to replace the default pseudorandom number generator (PRNG) with the discrete chaotic map. As the discrete chaotic map is a set of equations with a static start position, we created a random start position of the map, in order to have different start position for different experiments (runs of EA's). This random position is initialized with the default PRNG, as a one-off randomizer. Once the start position of the chaotic map has been obtained, the map generates the next sequence using its current position.

In this research, direct output iterations of the chaotic maps (iteration x or y – see Sect. 5) were used for the generation of real numbers in the process of crossover based on the user defined CR value and for the generation of the integer values used for selection of individuals.

Previous successful initial experiments with multi-chaos driven PSO and DE algorithms [10, 11] have manifested that very promising experimental results were obtained through the utilization of Delayed Logistic, Lozi, Burgers and Tinkerbelt maps. The last two mentioned chaotic maps have unique properties with connection to DE: strong progress towards global extreme, but weak overall statistical results, like average cost function (CF) value and std. dev., and tendency to premature stagnation. While through the utilization of the Lozi and Delayed Logistic map the continuously stable and very satisfactory performance of ChaosDE was achieved. The above described influences around switching point (500 or 1500 generations) are visible from the Fig. 2, which depicts the illustrative example of time evolution of average CF values for all 50 runs of four combinations of Multi-Chaotic DE and canonical DE/rand/1/bin strategies.

To maximize the benefit from the influences of different chaotic dynamics a new adaptive control approach was developed. It does not require any prior knowledge of the optimization problem and any manual setting of the one ore more "switching points". The exact transition point is determined by following simple rule: If the change of global best value between two subsequent generations is less than 0.001 over more than 1 % of total number of generations, the chaotic systems used as the CPRNGs are alternated.

5 Chaotic Maps

This section contains the description of discrete dissipative chaotic maps used as the chaotic pseudo random generators for DE. Following chaotic maps were used: Burgers (1), and Lozi map (2).

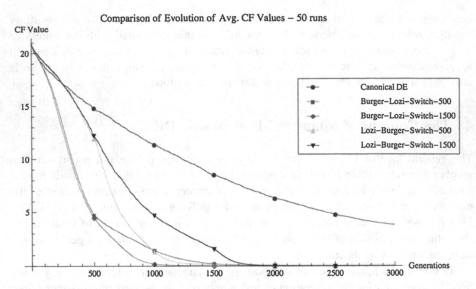

Fig. 2. Comparison of the time evolution of avg. CF values for the all 50 runs of Canonical DE, and all four versions of Multi-ChaosDE; shifted Ackley's original function, $D = 30$.

The Burgers mapping is a discretization of a pair of coupled differential equations which were used by Burgers [16] to illustrate the relevance of the concept of bifurcation to the study of hydrodynamics flows. The map equations are given in (1) with control parameters $a = 0.75$ and $b = 1.75$ as suggested in [17].

$$X_{n+1} = aX_n - Y_n^2$$
$$Y_{n+1} = bY_n + X_nY_n$$
(1)

The Lozi map is a discrete two-dimensional chaotic map. The map equations are given in (2). The parameters used in this work are: $a = 1.7$ and $b = 0.5$ as suggested in [17]. For these values, the system exhibits typical chaotic behavior and with this parameter setting it is used in the most research papers and other literature sources.

$$X_{n+1} = 1 - a|X_n| + bY_n$$
$$Y_{n+1} = X_n$$
(2)

6   Results

IEEE CEC 2013 benchmark set [18] was utilized within this experimental research for the purpose of performance comparison of Multi-Chaotic DE and state of the art adaptive representative jDE.

Experiments were performed in the combined environments of Wolfram Mathematica and C language; jDE therefore used the built-in C language pseudo random

Table 1. Parameter set up for ChaosDE, multi-Chaos DE and jDE

DE Parameter	Value
Popsize	75
F	0.4
CR	0.4
Dim	30
Max. Generations	1500
Max Cost Function Evaluations (CFE)	112500

Table 2. Final average CF values: Performance comparison for ChaosDE, Multi-Chaos DE and jDE on CEC 13 Benchmark Set, *dim* = 30, max. Generations = 1500

DE version/ function	f min	ChaosDE Lozi	ChaosDE Burgers	Multi-chaos DE Lozi-Bur	Multi-chaos DE Bur-lozi	jDE
f1	−1400	*−1400*	−1396,27	*−1400*	−1396,11	*−1400*
f2	−1300	8.26E07	**4.42 E06**	7.76E06	5.19E06	1.20 E07
f3	−1200	4.02 E05	5.89 E07	**3.94 E05**	4.35 E07	2.27 E06
f4	−1100	54253,37	44554,04	53146,18	43651,36	**24176.48**
f5	−1000	*−1000*	−976,96	*−1000*	−924,734	*−1000*
f6	−900	−879,406	−837,74	−879,877	−837,617	**−883.662**
f7	−800	−794,683	−785,823	**−794,907**	−785,744	−787.59
f8	−700	−679,014	−679,024	−679,011	−679,011	**−679.031**
f9	−600	−559,911	−566,911	−560,081	**−568,102**	−565.196
f10	−500	−499,703	−493,783	**−499,793**	−489,324	−498.97
f11	−400	−283,176	−367,734	−282,657	**−368,74**	−365.637
f12	−300	−110,399	−123,585	−109,368	−117,521	**−134.237**
f13	−200	−13,4393	**−24,4889**	−14,8037	−21,165	−22.0975
f14	−100	5208,844	4263,938	5212,473	3925,126	**2120.024**
f15	100	7525,375	7596,434	7514,516	7550,981	**7340.324**
f16	200	**202,661**	202,7216	202,7273	202,7534	202.6974
f17	300	457,0986	433,8154	455,6688	429,3077	**385.4481**
f18	400	617,938	603,0269	619,7844	**604,9512**	620.9147
f19	500	514,2732	747,2032	514,1383	512,6819	**507.8474**
f20	600	612,4499	612,0908	612,4901	**612,0437**	612.5353
f21	700	**976,2085**	1061,987	984,6014	1071,636	1015.886
f22	800	6109,917	5137,034	6185,512	4970,348	**3610.891**
f23	900	8682,76	**8527,86**	8717,706	8557,785	8575.498
f24	1000	*1200,494*	1214,893	*1200,494*	1214,61	1208.364
f25	1100	1409,554	1355,86	1408,71	**1354,989**	1398.31
f26	1200	1416,277	1434,2	1405,164	1407,463	**1400.423**
f27	1300	1670,244	1722,026	**1662,702**	1747,692	1886.461
f28	1400	*1700*	1711,01	*1700*	1747,365	*1700*

number generator Mersenne Twister C representing traditional pseudorandom number generators in comparisons. All experiments used different initialization, i.e. different initial population was generated in each run.

Within this research, one type of experiment was performed. It utilizes the maximum number of generations fixed at 1500 generations, Population size of 75 and dimension $dim = 30$. This allowed the possibility to analyze the progress of all studied DE variants within a limited number of generations and cost function evaluations.

The parameter settings (see Table 1) for Multi-Chaos DE were obtained based on numerous experiments and simulations. ChaosDE requires lower values of CR and F for almost any CPRNG and benchmark test function. The same settings was used also for the jDE, except values of mutation and crossover control parameters F and CR (see Sect. 3), which are not required, since they are adaptively tuned during the run of the algorithm.

Table 3. Best solutions - minimal CF values: Performance comparison for ChaosDE, Multi-Chaos DE and jDE on CEC 13 Benchmark Set, $dim = 30$, max. Generations = 1500

DE version/ function	f min	ChaosDE Lozi	ChaosDE Burgers	Multi-chaos DE Lozi-Bur	Multi-chaos DE Bur-lozi	jDE
f1	−1400	*−1400*	*−1400*	*−1400*	*−1400*	*−1400*
f2	−1300	5.16 E07	1.35 E06	4.70 E07	**1.25 E06**	3.88 E06
f3	−1200	**−1165,34**	2177953	−653,822	2969479	175895,6
f4	−1100	36762,6	34658,47	35599,14	22393,15	**17535,48**
f5	−1000	*−1000*	−999,966	*−1000*	−999,96	*−1000*
f6	−900	−883,984	−882,853	−884,208	−882,963	**−884,505**
f7	−800	−798,224	−798,612	**−798,772**	−797,954	−795,117
f8	−700	−679,132	**−679,249**	−679,158	−679,134	−679,145
f9	−600	−564,836	**−592,694**	−562,608	−591,792	−569,265
f10	−500	**−499,995**	−499,361	−499,99	−499,464	−499,158
f11	−400	−309,348	−390,523	−302,912	**−393,035**	−371,654
f12	−300	−133,452	−153,452	−139,953	−140,463	**−161,821**
f13	−200	−49,4624	**−52,423**	−40,1887	−48,0608	−49,5397
f14	−100	4571,05	2656,683	4587,607	**244,2955**	1490,476
f15	100	6508,819	7167,982	**6488,74**	6965,063	6880,111
f16	200	**201,7184**	201,7998	202,0703	201,7819	202,134
f17	300	436,168	387,3263	433,179	376,9962	**371,9252**
f18	400	588,5691	**572,2911**	599,705	583,1972	599,8971
f19	500	511,9499	506,9294	512,1244	**503,2695**	505,9997
f20	600	611,4797	**611,3011**	611,7701	611,3222	611,8896
f21	700	*900*	900,6238	*900*	900,0088	*900*
f22	800	5238,421	2006,774	4986,105	**1335,865**	3149,514
f23	900	**7734,353**	7981,328	8075,904	7964,318	8024,026
f24	1000	**1200,273**	1205,897	1200,23	1203,53	1203,392
f25	1100	1354,924	1315,61	1379,102	**1310,948**	1383,773
f26	1200	1403,552	1400,055	1402,663	**1400,042**	1400,212
f27	1300	**1606,48**	1626,16	1607,371	1641,696	1717,833
f28	1400	*1700*	*1700*	*1700*	*1700*	*1700*

To track the influence of adaptive multi-chaotic approach, an experiment encompasses three groups:

- Two versions of ChaosDE with Lozi map or Burgers map (i.e. single chaos approach – no alternation).
- Two versions of adaptive Multi-Chaos DE: Initialized with Lozi map or Burgers map.
- State of the art adaptive representative jDE.

The results of the experiments are shown in Tables 2 and 3. Table 2 contains the final average CF values, whereas Table 3 shows the minimum found CF values representing the best individual solution for all 50 repeated runs of ChaosDE, Multi-Chaos DE and jDE. Finally the Table 4 shows the overall performance comparison for aforementioned three groups of DE versions. Within Tables 2 and 3, the bold values represent the best performance, italic equal. Detailed results analysis is present in the conclusion section.

Table 4. Overall statistical performance comparison

	ChaosDE	Multi-chaos DE	jDE
Average CF value	5+, 4=, 19−	9+, 4=, 15−	10+, 3=, 15−
Min. CF value	11+, 4=, 13−	9+, 4=, 15−	4+, 4=, 20−

7 Conclusion

The primary aim of this work is to use and test the hybridization of natural chaotic dynamics with evolutionary algorithm as the multi-chaotic pseudo random number generator. In this paper the novel adaptive concept of DE/rand/1/bin strategy driven alternately by two chaotic maps (systems) is introduced. These two different influences to the performance of DE were connected here into the one adaptive multi-chaotic concept with automatic switching without prior knowledge of the optimization problem and without any manual setting of the "switching point". Repeated simulations were performed on the IEEE CEC 13 benchmark set. The obtained results were compared with the original predecessor ChaosDE and state of the art adaptive representative jDE. The findings can be summarized as follows:

- The high sensitivity of the DE to the internal dynamics of the chaotic PRNG is fully manifested.
- When comparing simple ChaosDE and adaptive Multi-Chaos DE, the both multi-chaotic versions have kept stable performance for both average and minimal observed final CF values. While through the utilization of simple ChaosDE, the aforementioned different influences of two chaotic dynamics have been revealed. Both versions of ChasoDE have outperformed all other studied heuristic in the case of min CF value (i.e. the best individual solution founded). Nevertheless in case of average results, the performance was the worst. This supports the claim, that adaptive multi chaotic approach suppresses the weak spots of particular CPRNGs,

which are the weak overall statistical results, like average CF value and std. dev.; and tendency to stagnation; thus that adaptive multi chaotic approach connects such strong progress towards global extreme with stable searching process without premature stagnation issues given by particular CPRNGs.

- When comparing the adaptive Multi-Chaos DE and adaptive jDE, the performance is comparable in case of final average CF values; whereas in case of min. CF values the chaos driven heuristic has outperformed the adaptive jDE.
- Based on the previous point, we can assume that in case of differential evolution, the sensitivity to the adaptive changes of internal chaotic dynamics driving the selection of individuals and crossover process may be higher than sensitivity to the adaptive tuning of control parameters. Nevertheless this will be more experimentally investigated in future work and research experiments.
- Furthermore the direct embedding of chaotic dynamics into the evolutionary/swarm based algorithms is advantageous, since it can be easily implemented into any existing algorithm or strategy. Also there are no major adjustments in the code required (instead of calling function Rand(), one iteration of chaotic system is taken).

Acknowledgements. This work was supported by Grant Agency of the Czech Republic - GACR P103/15/06700S, further by financial support of research project NPU I No. MSMT-7778/2014 by the Ministry of Education of the Czech Republic and also by the European Regional Development Fund under the Project CEBIA-Tech No. CZ.1.05/2.1.00/03.0089, partially supported by Grant of SGS No. SP2015/142 and SP2015/141 of VSB - Technical University of Ostrava, Czech Republic and by Internal Grant Agency of Tomas Bata University under the projects No. IGA/FAI/2015/057 and IGA/FAI/2015/061.

References

1. Price, K.V.: An introduction to differential evolution. In: Corne, D., Dorigo, M., Glover, F. (eds.) New Ideas in Optimization, pp 79–108. McGraw-Hill Ltd., London (1999)
2. Aydin, I., Karakose, M., Akin, E.: Chaotic-based hybrid negative selection algorithm and its applications in fault and anomaly detection. Expert Syst. Appl. **37**(7), 5285–5294 (2010)
3. Caponetto, R., Fortuna, L., Fazzino, S., Xibilia, M.G.: Chaotic sequences to improve the performance of evolutionary algorithms. IEEE Trans. Evol. Comput. **7**(3), 289–304 (2003)
4. Davendra, D., Zelinka, I., Senkerik, R.: Chaos driven evolutionary algorithms for the task of PID control. Comput. Math Appl. **60**(4), 1088–1104 (2010)
5. Zelinka, I.: SOMA — Self-Organizing Migrating Algorithm. In: Zelinka, I. (ed.) New Optimization Techniques in Engineering. Studies in Fuzziness and Soft Computing, vol. 141, pp. 167–217. Springer, Heidelberg (2004)
6. Coelho, L., Mariani, V.C.: A novel chaotic particle swarm optimization approach using Hénon map and implicit filtering local search for economic load dispatch. Chaos, Solitons Fractals **39**(2), 510–518 (2009)
7. Davendra, D., Bialic-Davendra, M., Senkerik, R.: Scheduling the lot-streaming flowshop scheduling problem with setup time with the chaos-induced enhanced differential evolution. In: 2013 IEEE Symposium on Differential Evolution (SDE), 16–19 April 2013, pp. 119–126 (2013)

8. Pluhacek, M., Senkerik, R., Davendra, D., Kominkova Oplatkova, Z., Zelinka, I.: On the behavior and performance of chaos driven PSO algorithm with inertia weight. Comput. Math Appl. **66**(2), 122–134 (2013)
9. Pluhacek, M., Senkerik, R., Zelinka, I., Davendra, D.: Chaos PSO algorithm driven alternately by two different chaotic maps - an initial study. In: 2013 IEEE Congress on Evolutionary Computation (CEC), 20–23 June 2013, pp. 2444–2449 (2013)
10. Senkerik, R., Pluhacek, M., Davendra, D., Zelinka, I., Oplatkova, Z.K.: performance testing of multi-chaotic differential evolution concept on shifted benchmark functions. In: Polycarpou, M., de Carvalho, A.C., Pan, J.-S., Woźniak, M., Quintian, H., Corchado, E. (eds.) HAIS 2014. LNCS, vol. 8480, pp. 306–317. Springer, Heidelberg (2014). doi:10. 1007/978-3-319-07617-1_28
11. Pluhacek, M., Senkerik, R., Zelinka, I., Davendra, D.: New adaptive approach for chaos PSO algorithm driven alternately by two different chaotic maps – an initial study. In: Zelinka, I., Chen, G., Rössler, O.E., Snasel, V., Abraham, A. (eds.) Nostradamus 2013: Prediction, Modeling and Analysis of Complex Systems. AISC, vol. 210, pp. 77–87. Springer, Heidelberg (2013). doi:10.1007/978-3-319-00542-3_9
12. Coelho, L.D.S., Ayala, H.V.H., Mariani, V.C.: A self-adaptive chaotic differential evolution algorithm using gamma distribution for unconstrained global optimization. Appl. Math. Comput. **234**, 452–459 (2014)
13. Coelho, L.D.S., Mariani, V.C.: Firefly algorithm approach based on chaotic Tinkerbell map applied to multivariable PID controller tuning. Comput. Math. Appl. **64**(8), 2371–2382 (2012)
14. Lu, P., Zhou, J., Zhang, H., Zhang, R., Wang, C.: Chaotic differential bee colony optimization algorithm for dynamic economic dispatch problem with valve-point effects. Int. J. Electr. Power Energy Syst. **62**, 130–143 (2014)
15. Price, K.V., Storn, R.M., Lampinen, J.A.: Differential Evolution - A Practical Approach to Global Optimization. Natural Computing Series. Springer, Heidelberg (2005)
16. ELabbasy, E., Agiza, H., EL-Metwally, H., Elsadany, A.: Bifurcation analysis, chaos and control in the burgers mapping. Int. J. Nonlinear Sci. **4**(3), 171–185 (2007)
17. Sprott, J.C.: Chaos and Time-Series Analysis. Oxford University Press, Oxford (2003)
18. Liang, J.J., Qu, B.-Y., Suganthan, P.N., Hernández-Díaz, A.G.: Problem definitions and evaluation criteria for the CEC 2013 Special session and competition on real-parameter optimization. Technical Report 201212, Computational Intelligence Laboratory, Zhengzhou University, Zhengzhou China and Technical Report, Nanyang Technological University, Singapore (2013)

Automatic Design of Radial Basis Function Networks Through Enhanced Differential Evolution

Dražen Bajer, Bruno Zorić, and Goran Martinović[(✉)]

Faculty of Electrical Engineering, J.J. Strossmayer University of Osijek,
Kneza Trpimira 2b, 31000 Osijek, Croatia
{drazen.bajer,bruno.zoric,goran.martinovic}@etfos.hr

Abstract. During the creation of a classification model, it is vital to keep track of numerous parameters and to produce a model based on the limited knowledge inferred often from very confined data. Methods which aid the construction or completely build the classification model automatically, present a fairly common research interest. This paper proposes an approach that employs differential evolution enhanced through the incorporation of additional knowledge concerning the problem in order to design a radial basis neural network. The knowledge is inferred from the unsupervised learning procedure which aims to ensure an initial population of good solutions. Also, the search space is dynamically adjusted i.e. narrowed during runtime in terms of the decision variables count. The results obtained on several datasets suggest that the proposed approach is able to find well performing networks while keeping the structure simple. Furthermore, a comparison with a differential evolution algorithm without the proposed enhancements and a particle swarm optimization algorithm was carried out illustrating the benefits of the proposed approach.

Keywords: Differential evolution · Initial population · k-means · Neural network · Radial basis function

1 Introduction

When confronting a classification problem, it is often difficult to select adequate model parameters. The selection procedure includes tedious steps of selecting the parameters and then testing the model on available data. This is especially true for classifiers with a large number of parameters, such as neural networks. The approach proposed in this paper aims to relieve this burden of parameter selection for a radial basis function network (RBFN) [2,13] classifier through automatic parameter determination. In general, RBFNs represent a kind of artificial neural networks often used in classification problems. Initial step of the network training process is selecting the activation (kernel) function for the hidden neurons. Among various kernel functions such as the logistic, cubic, inverse

© Springer International Publishing Switzerland 2015
E. Onieva et al. (Eds.): HAIS 2015, LNAI 9121, pp. 244–256, 2015.
DOI: 10.1007/978-3-319-19644-2_21

multiquadratic etc., the Gaussian kernel function is most widely used [13]. These networks are then usually trained in a two step procedure. The first step consists of selecting parameters for the hidden layer neurons and the second step is performed by finding the values of the hidden to output weights. Evolutionary and swarm intelligence algorithms, and unsupervised learning methods are commonly proposed for the first step, while for the second step methods such as gradient descent, the pseudo-inverse method and again computational intelligence methods are employed.

As can be observed, this area of research is active with various methods being proposed for automatic model creation. Here we briefly review some computational intelligence approaches. For example, Qin *et al.* [11] proposed a particle swarm optimization (PSO) algorithm for automatic RBFN model generation. In the proposed approach each particle is composed of the centers, associated widths and activation flags for each of the aforementioned. The weights are calculated using the pseudo-inverse method and the quality/fitness of each particle is evaluated based on Akaike's information criterion. Furthermore, Korürek and Doğan [5] employed a non-automatic version of the aforementioned approach for ECG beat classification. They also tested a version in which only the network's centers are evolved, while the widths (equal for every neuron) were determined heuristically based on a scaled maximum distance between two centers. Ince *et al.* [4] also proposed the utilization of PSO for automatically determining RBFN model parameters (that is, centers and widths). The remaining parameters, connection weights and biases, are calculated via a backpropagation algorithm. Several other approaches and combinations for RBFN structure and parameter determination are described in e.g. [3,14], including differential evolution (DE), genetic algorithm, orthogonal least squares algorithm and ant system.

Although various automatic selection methods for obtaining a good network structure already exist in the literature, we hope to show that the process of parameter pre-selection through unsupervised learning aids the search for adequate centers and associated widths, which in turn leads to easier network structure search and better classification results. Furthermore, by narrowing the search space dynamically during runtime, focus around more prominent and simpler network structures is achieved.

The rest of the paper is organized as follows. Section 2 introduces and briefly describes the related fundamental concepts—radial basis function networks and differential evolution. The proposed algorithm for the automatic design of RBFNs for classification needs is presented in Sect. 3. The setup and results of the conducted experimental analysis are given and discussed in Sect. 4. Finally, in Sect. 5 the drawn conclusions are stated.

2 Fundamental Concepts

Next, an overview of the essential concepts is given where the basic terms and working principles concerning RBFN and DE are introduced. The concepts covered are the key components on which the proposed approach is based upon.

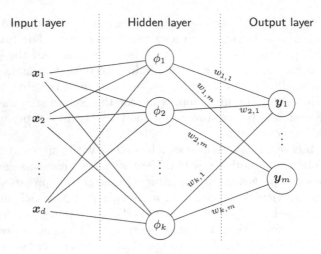

Input layer   Hidden layer   Output layer

Fig. 1. Common radial basis function network structure

2.1 Radial Basis Function Networks

The structure of a typical RBFN, which is also used in this paper (Fig. 1) can be
fully described through the number of hidden neurons, each with a corresponding
kernel function, and a weights array. The output can be calculated as

$$y^j = \sum_{i=1}^{k} \phi_i w_i^j, \quad \phi_i = \exp\left(-\frac{\|\,x - c^i\,\|^2}{\sigma^i}\right), \quad j = 1, \ldots, m, \tag{1}$$

where ϕ_i represents the Gaussian kernel function, described with centers c^i and
widths σ^i, and w^j is the weight array which represents the connections between
the hidden and the corresponding output neuron. Parameters to be tuned during
the training procedure are the centers of the basis functions, widths i.e. the
spread of the centers influence (if Gaussian function is observed it is notable
that the influence of a center decreases with the distance from the center) and
the weights connecting the hidden neurons and the output neurons, as mentioned
earlier. The number of hidden neurons is also subject to tuning, since according
to [2], the number of centers to be used depends on the complexity of the dataset,
and not on the number of instances it contains. The main difference between
RBFN and the most widely used kind of neural network that is the Multilayer
Perceptron (MLP), according to [13], is the fact that the activation responses
are of local nature in RBFN, and of global nature in MLP. This generally leads
to RBFN having better training speed, while MLPs having better generalization
capabilities.

2.2 Differential Evolution

Differential evolution [10,12] is a simple yet effective method originally proposed
for continuous optimization problems. It has been successfully applied for many

different global optimization problems (e.g. [7–9]). As other common evolutionary algorithms, it utilizes crossover and mutation for the creation of new individuals and the selection for choosing a new generation. The modus operandi of the classic/canonical DE (usually denoted as DE/rand/1/bin [12]) can be described as follows.

The DE population consists of NP real vectors $\boldsymbol{v}^j = (v_1^j, \ldots, v_d^j) \in \mathbb{R}^d$, $j = 1, \ldots, NP$. The initial population is usually created randomly within a designated space $[\boldsymbol{x}^L, \boldsymbol{x}^U]$, where $\boldsymbol{x}_i^L$ and $\boldsymbol{x}_i^U$ for $i = 1, \ldots, d$, represent the lower and upper bound for the i-th component of each vector, respectively. In each generation/iteration a new population is created of size NP through the mutation and crossover of individuals, i.e. the vectors contained in the current population. For each of the target vectors $\boldsymbol{v}^j$, mutation creates a corresponding mutant or donor

$$\boldsymbol{u}^j = \boldsymbol{v}^{r1} + F \cdot (\boldsymbol{v}^{r2} - \boldsymbol{v}^{r3}), \tag{2}$$

where $\boldsymbol{v}^{r1}$, $\boldsymbol{v}^{r2}$ and $\boldsymbol{v}^{r3}$ are population vectors selected at random, such that $j \neq r1 \neq r2 \neq r3$. Vector $\boldsymbol{v}^{r1}$ is called the base vector which is perturbed by the difference vector representing the difference between $\boldsymbol{v}^{r2}$ and $\boldsymbol{v}^{r3}$. The parameter $F \in [0, \infty)$ is the scale factor that determines the mutation step size. Furthermore, mutant $\boldsymbol{u}^j$ and target vector $\boldsymbol{v}^j$ are crossed over thus creating the trial vector

$$t_i^j = \begin{cases} u_i^j, & \text{if } \mathcal{U}[0,1) \leq CR \text{ or } i = r_j \\ v_i^j, & \text{else} \end{cases}, \quad i = 1, \ldots, d, \tag{3}$$

where $\mathcal{U}[0,1)$ is a uniformly distributed random variable in $[0,1)$, parameter $CR \in [0,1)$ is the crossover-rate, while r_j is a randomly chosen number from the set $\{1, \ldots, d\}$. After the trial vector population is created, its individuals transfer to the next generation only if they are equal or better (in terms of the objective/fitness function) than the corresponding target vectors.

3   Proposed Approach

The proposed algorithm/approach (hereinafter referred to as EDE) searches for an optimal number of centers and their locations along with the corresponding widths, and is outlined in Algorithm 1. In order to achieve this, the candidate solutions are encoded as shown in Fig. 2. Each candidate solution $\boldsymbol{v} = (F, C, \Sigma)$ consists of three parts; the activation flags $f^1, \ldots, f^{k_{max}} \in [0, 1]$, a set of centers $c^1, \ldots, c^{k_{max}} \in \mathbb{R}^d$ and their associated widths $\sigma^1, \ldots, \sigma^{k_{max}} \in \mathbb{R}$. The activation flags determine whether a given center and the corresponding width should be used in the solution, more specifically if $f^r \geq 0.5$ then the c^r and the corresponding σ^r should be used, while in the opposite case they should be omitted. Furthermore, in order to obtain a whole network, it is necessary to determine the weights, which was in this paper achieved by the pseudo-inverse method.

Algorithm 1. Outline of the proposed algorithm (EDE)

1: set NP, F and $CR = 0.9$
2: set k_{min} and k_{max}
3: initialize population using Algorithm 2
4: **for** $t := 1 \rightarrow t_{max}$ **do**
5:     **for** $j := 1 \rightarrow NP$ **do**   *%Create trial vector population*
6:         create mutant vector $\boldsymbol{u}^j$ (Eq. (2))
7:         cross over $\boldsymbol{v}^j$ and $\boldsymbol{u}^j$ to create trial vector $\boldsymbol{t}^j$ (Eq. (3))
8:     **end for**
9:     **for** $j := 1 \rightarrow NP$ **do**   *%Select new generation*
10:         **if** $f(\boldsymbol{t}^j) \le f(\boldsymbol{v}^j)$ **then**
11:             $\boldsymbol{v}^j := \boldsymbol{t}^j$
12:         **end if**
13:     **end for**
14:     **if** $t \in \{(\frac{1}{4}, \frac{1}{2}, \frac{3}{4}) \cdot t_{max}\}$ **then**   *%Adjust exploration window and crossover-rate*
15:         increase k_{min} by 20 %
16:         decrease k_{max} by 20 %
17:         decrease CR by 25 %
18:     **end if**
19: **end for**

Along with determining the manner of solution encoding, an important factor is their evaluation. This paper employs the following objective/fitness function

$$f(\boldsymbol{v}) = \text{MSE} + \lambda \cdot k, \tag{4}$$

where $\lambda = \frac{1}{2m} 0.01$, k represents the number of active centers and corresponding widths, while the mean squared error is given as

$$\text{MSE} = \frac{\sum_{i=1}^{n} \| \boldsymbol{y} - \boldsymbol{o} \|^2}{n \cdot m}, \tag{5}$$

where $\boldsymbol{y}$ is the network output, $\boldsymbol{o}$ the desired output, n the total number of training patterns, and m the number of outputs (classes in the dataset).

Besides the upper bound on the number of centers and corresponding widths k_{max}, a lower bound k_{min} is also introduced. Accordingly, each valid candidate solution must satisfy the lower bound. To ensure the aforementioned, before the evaluation, each candidate solution is tested against the given bound. If the number of active centers and corresponding widths is lower than k_{min}, randomly selected activation flags are set to the value of $\mathcal{U}[0.5, 1)$ while this condition is not met.

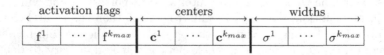

Fig. 2. Representation of DE candidate solutions

Considering that the size of the search space directly depends on the values of the bounds k_{min} and k_{max}, after each quarter of executed iterations, the values of the bounds are reconsidered and updated. More precisely, k_{min} and k_{max} are increased and decreased by 20 %, respectively. This is done for the purpose of reducing the search space which in the end should lead to finding better solutions. It must be noted that the upper bound k_{max} decreases much faster than the lower k_{min}, thus smaller networks are favored. Neither k_{min} nor k_{max} are allowed to overstep the size of the best-so-far solution. Besides the aforementioned, the crossover-rate is decreased in the same fashion in order to enable a finer exploration as the search progress goes on.

By introducing the solutions of relatively high quality into the initial population, convergence speed can be significantly increased and better solutions can be obtained with a lower number of fitness function evaluations, since the exploration is directed from the very start around more promising areas [6]. Considering the computational intensity of the fitness function evaluation, the stated represents a desirable enhancement. The initial population containing solutions of high quality may be created by using a simple method for solving the given problem. Therefore, in this paper the introduction of the well-known k-means algorithm [13] is proposed for initial center search and a heuristic rule for width calculation. The proposed approach for creating the initial population is outlined in Algorithm 2, and can be described as follows.

For randomly selected values of k, k-partitions and corresponding centers are found by the k-means algorithm, and the associated widths are calculated as the scaled distances to the nearest neighbor

$$\sigma^i = \tau \min_{\substack{r = 1, \ldots, k \\ i \neq r}} \{\| \, c^i - c^r \, \|\}, \quad i = 1, \ldots, k, \tag{6}$$

where $\tau = \mathcal{U}[1, 2)$ and it determines the overlap intensity. Setting τ to a random value contributes to population diversity and removes the burden of fixed value selection, while the mean is $\tau \approx 1.5$. After the centers and the associated widths are determined for a given value of k, for the corresponding individual v the first k flags are set as $\hat{f} = \mathcal{U}[0.5, 1)$, and the remaining ones as $\bar{f} = \mathcal{U}[0, 0.5)$. By analogy, the centers and their widths are also set, where the first k centers are set as $\hat{c}$ determined by the k-means algorithm, and the other ones are set as randomly generated centers $\bar{c}$. Accordingly, the first k widths are set as $\hat{\sigma}$ calculated by (6), and the remaining ones are set as $\bar{\sigma}$ which are randomly generated. Once this procedure is completed, the remainder of the population is generated completely in a random fashion.

4   Experimental Analysis

For the purpose of evaluating the effectiveness and shortcomings of the proposed algorithm, an experimental analysis was conducted on several well known

---

Algorithm 2. Outline of the proposed population initialization method

---

1: Set $j = 0$
2: **while** $j \neq \frac{1}{2}NP$ **do**
3:     set k to a randomly selected value form the set $\{k_{min}, \ldots, k_{max}\}$
4:     find centers $\hat{c}^1, \ldots, \hat{c}^k$ (k-means)
5:     calculate associated widths $\hat{\sigma}^1, \ldots, \hat{\sigma}^k$ (Eq. (6))
6:     $\boldsymbol{v}^j = (\hat{f}^1, \ldots, \hat{f}^k, \bar{f}^{k+1}, \ldots, \bar{f}^{k_{max}}, \hat{c}^1, \ldots, \hat{c}^k, \bar{c}^{k+1}, \ldots, \bar{c}^{k_{max}},$
        $\hat{\sigma}^1, \ldots, \hat{\sigma}^k, \bar{\sigma}^{k+1}, \ldots, \bar{\sigma}^{k_{max}})$
7:     $j := j + 1$
8: **end while**
9: Initialize the remaining $\frac{1}{2}NP$ individuals randomly

---

Table 1. Characteristics of datasets, used

Dataset	#instances	#features	#classes
Banknote authentication	1372	4	2
Image segmentation	2310	18	7
Ionosphere	351	34	2
Iris	150	4	3
Parkinsons	195	22	2
Seeds	210	7	3
Thyroid	215	5	3
Wine	178	13	3

datasets obtained from the UCI machine learning repository [1]. The characteristics of those datasets can be seen in Table 1. All used datasets were preprocessed and normalized into the space $[0, 1]^d$ in order to eliminate the possible influence of different feature value ranges.

4.1   Experiment Setup

The efficiency of the proposed method EDE is compared with the PSO algorithm for automatic RBFN design proposed in [11] (described in Sect. 1). As mentioned before, a non-automatic variant of the same approach has been applied successfully for ECG beat classification in [5]. In order to evaluate the influence of the proposed enhancements, a comparison is conducted with a DE, in which the population is initialized randomly and without adjustments of the exploration window and crossover-rate. All listed algorithms were implemented in the C# programming language. The parameters of the algorithms are reported in Table 2. All parameters besides the population size were taken from the literature [7,11,12], while the size of the population was determined empirically and was kept the same for all in order to remove bias and to enable comparison. The execution terminating condition was equal for all algorithms. More precisely, the execution is terminated after 1000 performed iterations, which proved to

Table 2. Algorithm parameter values, used

Algorithm	Parameter values
EDE	$NP = 30,\ F = 0.5$
DE	$NP = 30,\ CR = 0.9,\ F = 0.5$
PSO	$NS = 30,\ w = 0.9 \rightarrow 0.4,\ c_1 = 2,\ c_2 = 2$

be enough to make conclusions about performances without introducing unnecessary computational burden. In this manner fairness is maintained, since the number of function evaluations remains the same for all algorithms. Furthermore, k_{min} and k_{max} were set for all algorithms to the values of 2 and 20, respectively.

4.2 Results and Discussion

A concise overview of the achieved results is presented in Table 3, all of which are based on 30 independent algorithm runs for each of the datasets used. The algorithm performances are compared based on several parameters, including average misclassification rate (MCR), its standard deviation (σ), best and worst achieved MCR and the kappa statistic/score. The average network size is also reported along with its standard deviation in order to discuss the achieved results in the light of network complexity.

Regarding the MCR, the proposed approach shows promising results. This is most notable on sets such as Ionosphere, Iris and Parkinsons where it outperforms the DE and PSO algorithms in terms of classification accuracy. On several datasets where it does not achieve the best result, it matches the results of the other two algorithms very closely. It is also notable that the best and worst results are in favor of the proposed approach. Across all datasets, both the best and the worst solutions are the lowest among the tested algorithms. The achieved results suggest that the good overall performances have resulted from the proposed enhancements, considering that the difference in the DE and EDE results is rather significant. It should be noted that the proposed improvements affected primarily the MCR, and to a far lesser extent the network structure complexity reduction. It is highly questionable, considering the achieved network sizes, that further reductions in network size would lead to comparable, let alone better results.

The network complexity is the second important factor to consider and the results should be viewed through the prism of hidden layer size. The proposed approach takes into consideration the search process itself and the knowledge it provides through the best solutions found during the search space exploration. In this manner it achieves the smallest network on average. In the cases where the proposed approach did not find the smallest network structure, it did achieve the highest classification accuracy (e.g. Parkinsons and Iris). The difference in network sizes between the PSO approach and the EDE approach is significant, which can be seen in basically all datasets. Either the MCR difference is small

Table 3. Obtained experimental results

Dataset	Algorithm	Best	Mean ± σ	Worst	$k_{avg} \pm \sigma$	κ score
Banknote	EDE	0	1.248 ± 0.864	3.273	3.433 ± 0.559	0.975
	DE	0	1.042 ± 0.750	2.909	3.567 ± 0.559	0.979
	PSO	0	0.073 ± 0.173	0.727	19.133 ± 0.991	0.999
Img. seg.	EDE	4.978	7.670 ± 1.389	10.173	10.700 ± 0.936	0.911
	DE	6.277	8.629 ± 1.105	11.039	12.200 ± 1.376	0.899
	PSO	5.844	7.929 ± 1.120	10.39	19.333 ± 1.043	0.907
Ionosphere	EDE	1.408	6.150 ± 2.558	11.268	6.667 ± 1.193	0.866
	DE	2.817	8.216 ± 3.394	16.901	5.500 ± 1.232	0.818
	PSO	1.408	7.136 ± 3.148	15.493	15.500 ± 1.727	0.844
Iris	EDE	0	2.778 ± 2.992	10	4.000 ± 1.000	0.958
	DE	0	6.444 ± 3.645	13.333	4.533 ± 0.846	0.903
	PSO	0	4.333 ± 4.230	16.667	15.467 ± 2.077	0.935
Parkinsons	EDE	2.5	10.083 ± 4.495	17.5	5.433 ± 1.257	0.706
	DE	2.5	12.083 ± 4.522	20	4.900 ± 1.35	0.665
	PSO	2.5	11.667 ± 4.758	27.5	11.300 ± 3.143	0.671
Seeds	EDE	0	5.317 ± 3.116	11.905	5.400 ± 0.841	0.920
	DE	0	5.238 ± 2.910	9.524	5.567 ± 1.055	0.921
	PSO	0	6.667 ± 3.956	14.286	15.267 ± 2.25	0.900
Thyroid	EDE	0	3.876 ± 2.640	11.628	4.467 ± 0.921	0.915
	DE	0	4.341 ± 2.734	9.302	3.933 ± 0.929	0.907
	PSO	0	3.798 ± 2.718	9.302	15.933 ± 1.632	0.917
Wine	EDE	0	1.892 ± 1.584	5.405	3.833 ± 0.898	0.971
	DE	0	2.523 ± 2.199	8.108	5.433 ± 1.383	0.962
	PSO	0	2.252 ± 1.857	5.405	17.067 ± 1.843	0.966

with a much simpler network provided by the EDE (e.g. Banknote and Thyroid), or the final result favors the EDE while also maintaining significantly smaller and thus simpler networks (e.g. Ionosphere, Parkinsons and Seeds). The Thyroid dataset highlights this fact in particular. The proposed approach achieves a better result than the DE used for comparison while maintaining a network comparable in size. This suggests a better exploration, and perhaps that further improvements based on the proposed approach could increase this gap even further. It is worth noting that among all of the datasets used in this comparison, the proposed approach achieved the best results between the considered algorithms on those sets which have the highest MCR rates (e.g. Ionosphere and Parkinsons).

In order to assess the behavior of the proposed approach throughout the algorithm run, a separate experiment was conducted where the cost (in terms of the used fitness function) of the current-best solution and the hidden layer

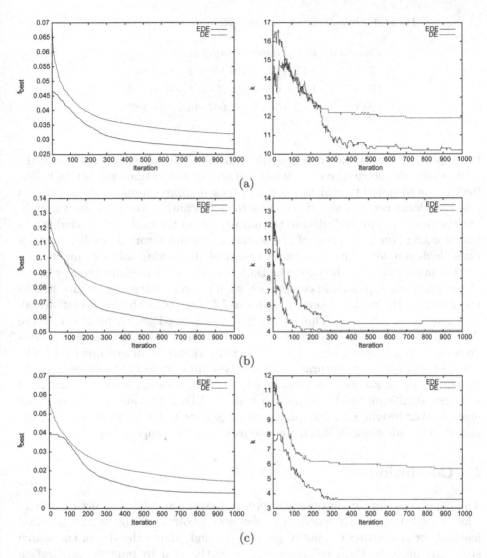

Fig. 3. Convergence data on the best solution cost and network size for (a) Img. seg., (b) Parkinsons, and (c) Wine datasets

size was recored. The results are shown in Fig. 3, and are based on 10 additional independent runs per dataset. The PSO algorithm was excluded since it employs a different objective/fitness function. Firstly, it can be easily observed that the proposed approach EDE has a considerable advantage at the start of the search. This suggests that the proposed population initialization method is able to introduce solutions of relatively high quality which does indeed provide a good starting point for the search. The aforementioned advantage is kept throughout the whole search process, resulting in a considerably lower solution cost compared to

Table 4. Overall average of the obtained experimental results

Algorithm	Best	Mean	Worst	k_{avg}	κ score
EDE	1.111	4.877	10.144	5.492	0.903
DE	1.449	6.065	11.390	5.704	0.882
PSO	1.625	5.565	12.697	16.3	0.887

the approach without the proposed enhancements. This observation would make EDE a suitable choice when the number of objective function evaluations is limited. It can be noted that although the proposed approach may start out with a relatively large network size it manages to significantly reduce its size throughout the run. This can be linked to the adjustment of the exploration window. As stated earlier, the narrowing of the search space and favoring smaller network sizes yields simpler solutions without negatively impacting solution quality.

The overall averages are shown in Table 4. These serve to give a broader image of the proposed approach in comparison with the remaining algorithms used in the analysis. It can be observed that the EDE gives both the lowest overall best and worst solutions. This means that the focused search provided by the directed exploration gives good results. It fails to find the worst solutions, which do occur in other algorithms. The average network size is comparable to the DE, but a smaller and more accurate network structures are found by employing the proposed enhancements. The difference in network sizes between EDE and PSO is rather significant, and goes in favor of the EDE. The average kappa score gives further insight into the quality of constructed classification models, and this statistic additionally illustrates the merits of the proposed approach.

5   Conclusion

The paper considers an automatic approach towards an RBFN structure design. The proposed approach based on differential evolution utilizes unsupervised learning for generating the initial population, and adapts the size of the search space dynamically. Both enhancements have the goal to improve exploration and exploitation of the search space. The performance analysis is conducted on several well known datasets obtained from a public repository and the results are compared to a version of DE without the proposed enhancements and an approach available in literature based on PSO. The presented results show the advantages of the designed approach, the fact that it finds good network structures and parameters, while keeping the network complexity on a lower level than its adversaries. This approach is susceptible to further improvements to remove its deficiencies, which could include further reductions in both network complexity and MCR. The steps described earlier could also be modified and additionally explored to find the best combination of preprocessing and penalty. Other forms of learning could be introduced, such as maintaining of an archive of prominent solutions and using them for final solution determination. The application of the proposed method for other classifiers and its impact on their performances should be considered in future work.

Acknowledgments. This work was supported by research project grant No. 165-0362980-2002 from the Ministry of Science, Education and Sports of the Republic of Croatia.

References

1. Bache, K., Lichman, M.: UCI machine learning repository (2013). http://archive.ics.uci.edu/ml
2. Bishop, C.M.: Neural Networks for Pattern Recognition. Oxford University Press Inc., New York (1995)
3. Huang, C.M., Hsieh, C.T., Wang, Y.S.: Evolution of radial basic function neural network for fast restoration of distribution systems with load variations. Electr. Power Energy Syst. **33**(4), 961–968 (2011)
4. Ince, T., Kiranyaz, S., Gabbouj, M.: Evolutionary RBF classifier for polarimetric SAR images. Expert Syst. Appl. **39**(5), 4710–4717 (2012). http://dx.doi.org/10.1016/j.eswa.2011.09.082
5. Korürek, M., Doğan, B.: ECG beat classification using particle swarm optimization and radial basis function neural network. Expert Syst. Appl. **37**(12), 7563–7569 (2010)
6. Martinović, G., Bajer, D.: Impact of NNA implementation on GA performance for the TSP. In: 5th International Conference on Bioinspired Optimization Methods and their Applications, pp. 173–184. Jožef Štefan Institute, Ljubljana, Slovenia (2012)
7. Martinović, G., Bajer, D.: Data clustering with differential evolution incorporating macromutations. In: Panigrahi, B.K., Suganthan, P.N., Das, S., Dash, S.S. (eds.) SEMCCO 2013, Part I. LNCS, vol. 8297, pp. 158–169. Springer, Heidelberg (2013). http://dx.doi.org/10.1007/978-3-319-03753-0_15
8. Martinović, G., Bajer, D., Zorić, B.: A differential evolution approach to dimensionality reduction for classification needs. Int. J. Appl. Math. Comput. Sci. **24**(1), 111–122 (2014). http://dx.doi.org/10.2478/amcs-2014-0009
9. Naveen, N., Ravi, V., Rao, C.R., Chauhan, N.: Differential evolution trained radial basis function network: application to bankruptcy prediction in banks. Int. J. Bio-Inspired Comput. **2**(3/4), 222–232 (2010). http://dx.doi.org/10.1504/IJBIC.2010.033090
10. Price, K., Storn, R.M., Lampinen, J.A.: Differential Evolution: A Practical Approach to Global Optimization. Springer-Verlag New York Inc., Secaucus (2005)
11. Qin, Z., Chen, J., Liu, Y., Lu, J.: Evolving RBF neural networks for pattern classification. In: Hao, Y., Liu, J., Wang, Y.-P., Cheung, Y., Yin, H., Jiao, L., Ma, J., Jiao, Y.-C. (eds.) CIS 2005. LNCS (LNAI), vol. 3801, pp. 957–964. Springer, Heidelberg (2005). http://dx.doi.org/10.1007/11596448_142
12. Storn, R., Price, K.: Differential evolution - a simple and efficient heuristic for global optimization over continuous spaces. J. Glob. Optim. **11**(4), 341–359 (1997). http://dx.doi.org/10.1023/A:1008202821328

13. Theodoridis, S., Koutroumbas, K.: Pattern Recognition, 4th edn. Academic Press, New York (2008)
14. Zheng, S., Li, Z., Wang, H.: A genetic fuzzy radial basis function neural network for structural health monitoring of composite laminated beams. Expert Syst. Appl. **38**(9), 11837–11842 (2011). http://dx.doi.org/10.1016/j.eswa.2011.03.072

Performance Evaluation of Ant Colony Systems for the Single-Depot Multiple Traveling Salesman Problem

Raluca Necula[1(✉)], Mihaela Breaban[1], and Madalina Raschip[2]

[1] Alexandru Ioan Cuza University, Iasi, Romania
{raluca.necula,pmihaela}@info.uaic.ro
[2] University of Neuchatel, Neuchatel, Switzerland
{madalina.raschip}@unine.ch

Abstract. Derived from the well-known Traveling Salesman problem (TSP), the multiple-Traveling Salesman problem (multiple-TSP) with single depot is a straightforward generalization: several salesmen located in a given city (the depot) need to visit a set of interconnected cities, such that each city is visited exactly once (by a single salesman) while the total cost of their tours is minimized. Designed for shortest path problems and with proven efficiency for TSP, Ant Colony Systems (ACS) are a natural choice for multiple-TSP as well. Although several variations of ant algorithms for multiple-TSP are reported in the literature, there is no clear evidence on their comparative performance. The contribution of this paper is twofold: it provides a benchmark for single-depot-multiple-TSP with reported optima and performs a thorough experimental evaluation of several variations of the ACS on this problem.

Keywords: Multiple-TSP · Ant colony optimization · Clustering

1 Introduction

The traveling salesman problem (TSP) is one of the most famous combinatorial optimization problems. The multiple traveling salesman problem (multiple-TSP) is an extension of this well-known problem that involves further a new parameter - the number of salesmen. It can accommodate easily related real-world problems, especially routing and scheduling problems. The problem is NP-hard and is difficult to solve. One solution is to transform the problem, with m salesmen and n cities, into a TSP with $n + m - 1$ cities by adding $m - 1$ artificial depots $n + 1, ..., n + m - 1$. The resulting TSP is highly degenerate and more difficult to solve than an ordinary TSP with the same number of cities.

There are various approaches in literature to solve variants of the multiple-TSP. A detailed overview of the problem's variants and methods used for solving them is available in [1]. Exact algorithms, like cutting planes [2] or branch and bound [3] were developed, but they can obtain optimal solutions only for small size instances in acceptable time. Due to the combinatorial complexity

© Springer International Publishing Switzerland 2015
E. Onieva et al. (Eds.): HAIS 2015, LNAI 9121, pp. 257–268, 2015.
DOI: 10.1007/978-3-319-19644-2_22

of the problem, heuristics to solve real-world instances were also employed. For large dimensions of the problem, heuristic approaches like k-opt approach [4], or metaheuristics like Tabu Search [5], Genetic Algorithms [6–9], Ant Colony Optimization [10], Neural Networks [11] are necessary to solve it. In [12] two new swarm intelligence based metaheuristics, artificial bee colony and invasive weed optimization, are proposed for solving the single depot multiple-TSP. Another approach, relying on a market-based solution, is employed in [13] for a multiple-TSP with multiple depots, where agents and tasks operate in a market to achieve near-optimal solutions.

With a proven efficiency on the standard TSP, ant algorithms were also adapted for the multiple-TSP. In [14] the ant colony optimization is used to solve the multiple-TSP with the ability constraint. The problem imposes that the number of cities which are traveled by each salesman to be upper bounded by a value. The problem was converted to TSP. In [10] two objectives were considered: minimizing the total tour length of all the salesmen and minimizing the maximum tour length of each salesman. The ACO algorithm follows the MAX-MIN Ant System scheme and integrates a local improvement procedure. In [15] is presented an algorithm based on multiple artificial ant colonies, that cooperate by means of frequent pheromone exchanges in order to find a competitive solution to the multiple-TSP. A multi-depot variant of multiple-TSP is considered in [16], where lower and upper bounds are imposed on the number of cities visited in a tour and the objective is to minimize the total distance traveled by all the salesmen.

Another criterion, much less addressed, but important in real-world applications is the balancing of workloads amongst salesmen. Such a criterion is addressed in [17], where a team of ants construct in parallel solutions to the multiple-TSP with MinMax objective. In order to achieve balanced tours, the moving member of a team is chosen as being the one with the minimum route length. In [18], the authors present a comparison of evolutionary computation algorithms and paradigms for the euclidean multiple traveling salesman problem. The authors are concerned with the first level of optimization, the optimal subdivision of cities into groups. To this end, the chromosome representation makes use of the neighborhood attractor schema which is a variation of k-means. The shrink-wrap algorithm is used to determine the circuit path lengths. Another clustering approach to solve the multiple-TSP is proposed in [19]. The clustering algorithm minimizes the variation of distances traveled within each cluster. A good balance of workloads among clusters is achieved.

The current paper aims at proposing and evaluating several variations of the Ant Colony System (ACS) for the single-depot multiple-TSP. The paper is structured as follows. Section 2 defines the problem as an integer linear program (ILP) that can be solved to optimality with dedicated software. Section 3 reviews the standard formulation of the Ant Colony System. A number of 5 variants of the standard ACS adapted for the single-depot multiple-TSP problem are subsequently described in Sect. 4. Experiments and results are presented in Sect. 5.

2   The Single-Depot Multiple Traveling Salesman Problem

There are several integer linear programming formulations for the multiple-TSP. We have used the variant that restricts the minimal number of nodes that a salesman may visit [20]. Such restrictions appear in real-life applications where the purpose is to have a good balance of workloads for the salesmen.

Let $G = (V, A)$ be a directed graph where V is the set of nodes and A is the set of arcs and $C = (c_{ij})$ is the cost (distance) matrix associated with each arc $(i, j) \in A$. Let n be the number of cities and m be the number of salesmen. All salesmen are located at the depot city 1. They start and end at the same depot, and each other node is located in only one tour. The number of nodes a salesman can visit lies within a predetermined interval. The problem is to find the tours of each salesman such that the previous restrictions are satisfied and the overall cost of visiting all nodes is minimized.

The problem is formulated as the following:

$$\min \quad \sum_{(i,j) \in A} c_{ij} x_{ij} \tag{1}$$

$$\text{s.t.} \quad \sum_{j=2} x_{1j} = m \tag{2}$$

$$\sum_{j=2} x_{j1} = m \tag{3}$$

$$\sum_{i=1}^{n} x_{ij} = 1, \; j = 2, .., n \tag{4}$$

$$\sum_{j=1}^{n} x_{ij} = 1, \; i = 2, .., n \tag{5}$$

$$u_i + (L - 2)x_{1i} - x_{i1} \leq L - 1, \; i = 2, .., n \tag{6}$$

$$u_i + x_{1i} + (2 - K)x_{i1} \geq 2, \; i = 2, .., n \tag{7}$$

$$x_{1i} + x_{i1} \leq 1, \; i = 2, .., n \tag{8}$$

$$u_i - u_j + Lx_{ij} + (L - 2)x_{ji} \leq L - 1, \; 2 \leq i \neq j \leq n \tag{9}$$

$$x_{ij} \in \{0, 1\}, \; \forall (i, j) \in A. \tag{10}$$

where x_{ij} is a binary variable that is equal to 1 if the arc (i, j) is contained in the optimal solution and 0 otherwise. u_i denotes the number of nodes visited on that salesman's path from the origin to node i, for any salesman, i.e. the position of node i in a tour. L is the maximum number of nodes a salesman may visit, and K the minimum number of nodes a salesman must visit.

Constraints (2) and (3) ensure that exactly m salesmen depart from and return to the depot. Constraints (4) and (5) are the degree constraints, i.e. exactly one tour enters and exits each node. Constraints (6) and (7) are bounding constraints, their corresponding inequalities serve as upper and lower bound constraints on the number of nodes visited by each salesman. Inequality (8) forbids a vehicle from visiting only a single node. The inequalities from (9) ensure that $u_j = u_i + 1$ if and only if $x_{ij} = 1$. Constraints (9) are the classical subtour elimination constraints that prevent the formation of any subtour between nodes in $V \setminus \{1\}$. The formulation is valid if $2 \leq K \leq \lfloor (n-1)/m \rfloor$ and $L \geq K$. Constraint (8) becomes redundant when $K \geq 4$.

3   The Ant Colony System

The fundamental idea of the ant colony algorithms is inspired by the way the natural ants succeed in finding food. The ants communicate via the pheromone trails in order to find the shortest paths from the nest to the food sources.

The algorithms investigated in this paper are based on the original version of the Ant Colony System designed by Dorigo and Gambardella for the Traveling Salesman problem [21]. In this section we review the main steps of the standard algorithm for solving TSP, leaving the presentation of its variations for multiple-TSP for the next section.

3.1   Route Selection

Each ant builds a route by iteratively selecting a node it has not visited yet. At each step in this process, the nodes not selected yet form the candidate set. The node to be added to the current route is chosen relative to the current position of the ant, in a probabilistic manner, from the candidate set. The probability assigned to a node s in the candidate set C, considering that node r is the current position of the ant, is computed with Eq. (11):

$$p(r, s) = \frac{\tau(r, s) \cdot \eta^\beta(r, s)}{\sum_{u \in C} \tau(r, u) \cdot \eta^\beta(r, u)} \tag{11}$$

where τ is the pheromone, η is the inverse of the cost measure (distance) $\delta(r, s)$, and β is a parameter that specifies the relative importance of pheromone vs. distance. The product $\tau(r, s) \cdot \eta^\beta(r, s)$ can be viewed as the fitness of node s, while the probabilistic selection based on the probabilities defined in Eq. (11) corresponds to the *roulette wheel* selection in genetic algorithms. The selection of the next node for tour construction in ACS can be synthesised by the following equation:

$$s = \begin{cases} \arg\max_{s \in C} \tau(r, s) \cdot \eta^\beta(r, s), & \text{if } rand(0, 1) < q_0 \\ S, & \text{otherwise} \end{cases}$$

where q_0 is a parameter and S is a random variable with the probability distribution given by Eq. (11).

3.2   Local Pheromone Update

Each time an ant builds a route, it changes the pheromone level on each edge it traverses. The pheromone of each edge traversed is updated by Eq. (12):

$$\tau(r, s) = (1 - \rho) \cdot \tau(r, s) + \rho \cdot \Delta\tau(r, s) \tag{12}$$

where $\rho \in (0,1)$ is a local pheromone decay parameter. The purpose of the local pheromone update is to ensure that the same links are not included again and again forming very similar tours.

3.3   Global Pheromone Update

Usually, ants search for food in a neighborhood of the best tour. In order to make the search more directed, after all ants have completed their tours, the globally updating phase of the pheromone follows. Only the edges included in the best global solution receive pheromone in this phase. The pheromone level is updated by applying the following rule:

$$\tau(r,s) = (1-\alpha) \cdot \tau(r,s) + \alpha \cdot \Delta\tau(r,s) \tag{13}$$

where

$$\Delta\tau(r,s) = \begin{cases} (L_{gb})^{-1}, & \text{if } (r,s) \in \text{global-best-tour} \\ 0, & \text{otherwise} \end{cases}$$

where $\alpha \in (0,1)$ is the pheromone decay parameter and L_{gb} is the length of the globally best tour encountered. By this rule, only the edges that belong to the globally best tour receive reinforcement.

4   Algorithms Investigated for Multiple-TSP

4.1   Problem Decomposition with k-Means Followed by ACS for TSP (kM-ACS)

One possible approach to tackle the multiple-TSP problem is to decompose the problem instance into a number of small subproblems equal to the number of salesmen; subsequently, each subproblem can be solved by the standard ACS resulting in one (near)optimal subtour for the corresponding salesman. The problem decomposition can be performed by means of clustering algorithms, with the aim to group closely interconnected cities. Among the popular clustering algorithms, k-Means seems to be the most appropriate choice due to its reduced time and space complexity and, more important, due to the fact that it is known to generate groups of equal volumes. The latter characteristic is desirable for the multiple-TSP problem, where we aim to obtain balanced subtours.

To split one single-depot multiple-TSP instance into several TSP instances, we need to adapt the k-Means algorithm. Our problem formulation necessitates that the depot should be included in each of the TSP subproblems generated. Since k-Means is a crisp-clustering algorithm, when applied the multiple-TSP instance, it will generate disjoint sets of cities. To obtain an optimal clustering of the cities where all groups share the depot city, the assignment step is changed in k-Means: at every iteration in k-Means, all the cities are assigned to the cluster based on their distances to the centroids, with the exception of the depot which is assigned to every cluster; thus, all the centroids will be biased towards the location of the depot. This modification discourages the clustering algorithm from forming isolated groups, at far distances from the depot. After the cities are clustered into m groups (where m is the number of salesmen), m independent runs of the ACS are performed, one for each group; in this step, m smaller TSP instances are practically solved. The final solution for the multiple-TSP problem is obtained by aggregating the solutions obtained in the ACS runs, as subtours to be assigned to the m salesmen. This version of the algorithm is denoted in the experimental section by $kM - ACS$.

4.2   ACS with Global-Solution Pheromone Update (g-ACS)

Several salesmen can compete towards building the subtours in one run of the ACS, idea found also in [14]. In such an approach, for a problem instance with m salesmen, m salesmen are placed at the depot location - each ant corresponding to a team of m salesmen. At each step, one salesman is chosen at random (selection with replacement). The selected salesman chooses the next city in its subtour in agreement with the route selection mechanism in ACS, detailed in Sect. 3.1; the candidate set of nodes consists of the nodes that are not selected in any of the m subtours under construction. This process is repeated until a complete solution is obtained (when the candidate set of nodes is empty). Each traversed edge receives the quantity of pheromone computed with Eq. (12), regardless of which salesman traverses it.

At each iteration of the algorithm, several groups of salesmen, each of size m, build complete solutions as explained above. From these solutions, the one with the smallest cost - measured as the sum of the costs of the m subtours - is considered to be the global best at the given iteration. The best-so-far solution (global best - the best solution encountered during the run) is updated if necessary. Then, the edges encountered in the subtours of the global best solution are updated with Eq. (13), where L_{gb} is the total cost of the global solution. This version of the ACS algorithm is denoted in the experimental section as $g - ACS$.

4.3   ACS with Subtour Pheromone Update (s-ACS)

Another version we propose, denoted as $s - ACS$, is a small variation of the previous algorithm. The difference between the two consists only in the third phase of the ACS algorithm - the global pheromone update. $s - ACS$ does not use the same pheromone quantity on each edge, but differentiates the edges based on the subtour to which they are assigned. Thus, we refine/update Eq. (13) by including subtour information as follows:

$$\tau(r, s) = (1 - \alpha) \cdot \tau(r, s) + \alpha \cdot \Delta\tau(r, s) \tag{14}$$

where

$$\Delta\tau(r, s) = \begin{cases} (L_k)^{-1}, & \text{if } (r, s) \in \text{subtour k in global-best-tour} \\ 0, & \text{otherwise} \end{cases}$$

According to the new equation, each edge included in the best solution encountered so far (the global best solution) receives a quantity of pheromone inverse proportional with the cost of the subtour to which it belongs.

4.4 ACS with Global-Solution Pheromone Update and Bounded Tours (gb-ACS)

Another variation we propose, is to enforce within the $g - ACS$ algorithm the bounds imposed by the problem with regard to the number of cities to be included in each subtour. Although in the phase of solution construction, the salesman designated to add one more city to its subtour is uniformly drawn at random (i.e. each salesman has the same probability), experimental studies showed that the solution built is sometimes highly unbalanced with regard to the number of cities included in the subtours. This is justified, since the law of large numbers from statistics is not applicable to the size of the problems we deal with. The bounds on the size of each subtour are imposed by changing the way salesmen are selected when constructing the solution. Here, we use a selection strategy without replacement: in a first step, the lower bound K on the number of cities to be included in each subtour is guaranteed by sampling at random from a population of size $K \cdot m$ without replacement, consisting of K instances of each of the m salesmen. When this sampling procedure ends (all instances are used during solution construction), all m subtours consist of the minimum number of cities allowed. A similar salesman selection scheme begins (without replacement) with a population of size $(L-K) \cdot m$ ($L-K$ instances of each of the m salesmen) to guarantee that the maximum bound imposed on the size of each subtour is not exceeded. This sampling phase ends when a complete solution is built. This variant of the $g - ACS$ algorithm where bounds are enforced, is called gb-ACS.

4.5 ACS with Subtour Pheromone Update and Bounded Tours (sb-ACS)

The bounds on the size of the subtours are imposed in the same manner in the ACS algorithm with pheromone updates based on the cost of the subtours ($s - ACS$). This leads to new variant denoted as $sb - ACS$.

5 Experiments

5.1 Problem Instances

Although multiple-TSP is, by its formulation, only one step away from the standard TSP problem which provides very popular benchmarks such as TSPLIB[1], there is no freely available benchmark for multiple-TSP at this moment to test

---

[1] http://comopt.ifi.uni-heidelberg.de/software/TSPLIB95/.

the performance of various heuristics. To fill this gap, we formulate several problem instances for multiple-TSP and provide exact solutions by solving them in CPLEX[2]. The problem instances we propose are based on the TSPLIB benchmark. Specifically, we extracted from TSPLIB four instances of various size and distribution and we transformed them in multiple-TSP instances by setting the number of salesmen to be, by turn, 2, 3, 5 and 7. The selected TSPLIB instances were chosen so that to reflect different distributions of cities and different positions of the depot city. These settings generate from each TSPLIB instance, 4 multiple-TSP instances. The depot, for each instance, is considered to be the first city in the file. The problem instances along with the distribution of cities and position of depot city, the optimal solutions and their visualisations are publicly available as multiple-TSPLIB.[3]

As stated in Sect. 2, we impose bounds on the number of cities each salesman needs to visit. If considered as a problem with a single objective - that of minimising the total cost of visiting all the cities - and no bounds are imposed on the number of cities to be visited by each salesman, the multiple-TSP with single depot is an ill-posed problem: the optimal solution is obtained when one salesman visits all the cities while the rest do not have assigned any work. This is obvious by comparing the total costs obtained on the same TSPLIB instance with different numbers of salesmen: when increasing the number of salesmen, the total cost increases.

The use of several salesmen in practice for single-depot-multiple-TSP does not aim to obtain better costs compared to the case when a single salesman is used, but aims at shortening the time needed to serve all the clients or is triggered by the limited capacity of each agent - problem closely related to the Capacitated Vehicle Routing. From the first point of view, single-depot-multiple-TSP is inherently a bi-objective optimization problem: the total cost should be minimized while maintaining the subtours as balanced as possible; the bi-objective formulation will be the scope of our future studies. In fact, imposing bounds on the number of cities visited by each salesman, increases significantly the complexity of the multiple-TSP problem being solved. Obtaining with CPLEX the optimal solution for MTSPLIB instances, when no bounding constraints were considered, lasted at most 17 min. This is a major difference compared with the time required by CPLEX to solve MTSPLIB instances when these bounding constraints are included; the reported solution for the rat99-m7 problem instance was obtained with CPLEX after 14 h. All the runs were performed on a PC with 8 GB RAM, processor Intel Core i5-4590S 3.00 GHz using 4 processing units (multi-threaded implementation of CPLEX). In comparison, one run of any ACS variant described in this paper required on average 1 s and 11 ms in a single-threaded implementation.

With the aim of obtaining balanced solutions, we chose to set the bounds (L and K) on the number of cities to be included in each subtour, by running

---

[2] http://www-01.ibm.com/software/commerce/optimization/cplex-optimizer/.

[3] The address where it can be visualized the multiple-TSP instances is www.infoiasi. ro/~mtsplib.

30 times k-Means clustering algorithm, on the same problem instance to split the cities in m groups; the partition with the lowest sum of the within-cluster variances was used to set K equal to the size of the smallest cluster and L equal to the size of the largest cluster.

5.2   Parameters Setup

The standard ACS algorithm introduces some numerical parameters which, usually, are empirically optimized. As suggested in [21], we set $q_0 = 0.9$, $\alpha = 0.1$, $\rho = 0.1$, $\beta = 2.0$ in all tested algorithms. The number of ants in $kM - ACS$ was set to 10 for each TSP subproblem (corresponding to each of the m clusters), corresponding to a total of $10 \cdot m$ ants used to solve each of the multiple-TSP problem instances. The number of ants used in all the other versions is also set to $10 \cdot m$ in the following way: at each iteration of these algorithms 10 groups of ants, each of size m, build in parallel, independently, 10 complete candidate solutions. Each algorithm is ran for 1 400 iterations for the problem instances with 51 and 52 cities, 1 800 iterations for eil76 problem instances and 2 200 iterations for rat99 problem instances.

5.3   Results

We provide results for each investigated algorithm regarding both the total cost of the solutions and the balancing degree of the subtours. For all algorithms, we report the average cost of the solutions over 50 runs.

In order to evaluate the balancing degree, for each solution returned at the end of a run we compute the amplitude of the costs of its subtours as the difference between the cost of the longest subtour and the cost of the shortest subtour of the solution. We report the average amplitude over 50 runs for each algorithm. Please note that the amplitude is computed taking into account subtour costs and not subtour cardinalities (the number of cities in each subtour), because the two criteria are not equivalent.

Figure 1 illustrates the evolution of the best cost (best solution) during the run of the algorithms for the eil76-m5 problem; the curves are obtained as averages over 10 runs for each algorithm. As anticipated, kM-ACS shows the highest convergence rate, because it solves in parallel several smaller and simpler problems. However, the performance with regard to the best solution it can achieve is limited, because of the problem decomposition scheme which imposes rigid boundaries on the candidate solution space; in this regard, the non-deterministic character of k-Means introduced by random initializations is an advantage. The best performance on this problem instance is recorded by gb-ACS - the bounded version of g-ACS which uses the cost of the global solution (and not of the individual subtours) for pheromone update.

Table 1 report the costs of the optimal solutions and their corresponding amplitudes, as obtained with CPLEX, and the performance of all the ACS variants we propose - as averages over 50 runs. For each problem instance and ACS variant, along with the average cost we also report the standard error of the

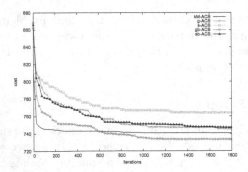

Fig. 1. Evolution of the cost of the best solution during the run of the algorithms for eil76-m5, averaged over 10 runs.

mean multiplied with the 0.975 quantile of the Student's t distribution (used to compute confidence intervals). Where CPLEX was stopped before finding the optimal solution, both the upper (corresponding to the best known solution) and the lower bound on the cost are given; the amplitude in this case is computed on the best known solution. In each table, the best value from a row was highlighted with boldface. Similar graphics for berlin52, eil76 and rat99 instances can be found at this address[4]. They weren't included here due to page limits.

Table 1. The performance of the ACS variants for the eil51 instance

m	measure	optimum	kM-ACS	g-ACS	s-ACS	gb-ACS	sb-ACS
2	cost	**442.32**	454.30 ± 0.84	452.66 ± 1.77	454.96 ± 2.04	452.22 ± 1.48	453.81 ± 1.63
	amplitude	**14.18**	57.69	72.29	47.54	30.42	28.79
3	cost	**464.11**	500.00 ± 0.24	485.73 ± 3.44	489.64 ± 3.59	479.51 ± 3.37	483.39 ± 3.75
	amplitude	41.78	**25.97**	98.47	98.68	49.41	47.51
5	cost	**[519.10, 529.70]**	563.58 ± 0.52	582.36 ± 3.58	590.63 ± 4.64	585.76 ± 4.34	598.61 ±5.16
	amplitude	62.19	114.35	104.65	99.11	58.09	**57.45**
7	cost	**[584.02, 605.21]**	634.47 ± 0.04	674.78 ± 4.32	680.38 ± 3.84	688.26 ± 3.57	699.47 ± 4.34
	amplitude	86.17	77.44	100.19	**62.13**	70.01	68.27

Figure 2 illustrate, for eil51 problem, the distribution of the costs and the amplitudes of subtour costs for the solutions obtained in 50 runs of each algorithm. On each chart corresponding to a TSP instance, 4 groups are emphasized, corresponding to the 4 distinct settings of the number of salesmen (2, 3, 5 and 7). The increase in the total cost with the increase of parameter m is evident. For each of the four groups in each chart, we have 6 sets of solutions: corresponding to the best known solution - obtained with CPLEX (this behaves as lower bound for the ACS-based algorithms), to $kM - ACS$, to the two versions of ACS adapted for multiple-TSP that do not enforce bounds on the size of the subtours and the two ACS versions with bounds. Similar figures along with the

---

[4] www.infoiasi.ro/~mtsplib.

representation of the confidence intervals for the mean of the costs can be found at this address[5]. They weren't included here due to page limits.

Evident in the boxplots but also from the size of the confidence intervals, kM-ACS is the most stable algorithm. With a quick convergence, this algorithm even achieves on some problem instances (eil51-m5, eil76-m7, rat99-5, rat99-7) the best cost (proven by statistical tests on the means). It seems that this algorithm is a good choice for very large instances, with high number of cities and many salesmen. Among the two bounded variants - $gb-ACS$ and $sb-ACS$ - $gb-ACS$ converges more quickly, achieving at the same time better solutions. Comparing the two unbounded variants - $g-ACS$ and $s-ACS$ - the same conclusion can be drawn: the version laying equal pheromone quantities on the edges of the best solutions (irrespective of the cost of the subtour) achieves better costs. However, $g-ACS$ returns solutions which are highly unbalanced compared to $s-ACS$ and this is a real concern for its applicability in practice.

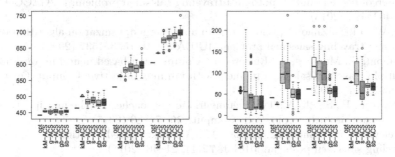

Fig. 2. Results obtained in 50 runs for eil51: (a) total cost, (b) amplitude of the costs of subtours; the groups correspond to different settings for m: 2, 3, 5, 7

6   Conclusions

Inspired by the ant colonies behavior in nature, the Ant Colony System proved to be an efficient approach for searching for an optimal path in a graph. As shown in our study, this meta-heuristic can be easily adapted for the multiple traveling salesman problem. For real world, large instances of multiple-TSP, which become untractable with exact deterministic algorithms, the ant colony system is a viable solution. Future work will be conducted towards studying the bi-objective formulation of multiple-TSP, by means of ACSs.

References

1. Bektas, T.: The multiple traveling salesman problem: an overview of formulations and solution procedures. Omega **34**(3), 209–219 (2006)

---

[5] www.infoiasi.ro/~mtsplib.

2. Laporte, G.G., Nobert, Y.A.: Cutting planes algorithm for the m-salesmen problem. J. Oper. Res. Soc. **31**, 1017–1023 (1980)
3. Ali, A., Kennington, J.L.: Exact solution of multiple traveling salesman problems. Discrete Appl. Math. **13**, 259–276 (1986)
4. Russell, R.A.: An effective heuristic for the m-tour traveling salesman problem with some side conditions. Oper. Res. **25**(3), 517–524 (1977)
5. Ryan, J.L., Bailey, T.G., Moore, J.T., Carlton, W.B.: Reactive Tabu search in unmanned aerial reconnaissance simulations. In: WSC 1998, pp. 873–880 (1998)
6. Yuan, S., Skinner, B., Huang, S., Liu, D.: A new crossover approach for solving the multiple travelling salesmen problem using genetic algorithms. EJOR **228**, 72–82 (2013)
7. Singh, A., Baghel, A.S.: A new grouping genetic algorithm approach to the multiple traveling salesperson problem. Soft Comput. **13**(1), 95–101 (2009)
8. Li, J., Sun, Q., Zhou, MC., Dai, X.: A new multiple traveling salesman problem and its genetic algorithm-based solution. In: SMC 2013, pp. 627–632 (2013)
9. Andrade, C.E., Miyazawa, F.K., Resende, M.G.C.: Evolutionary algorithm for the k-interconnected multi-depot multi-traveling salesmen problem. In: GECCO 2013, pp. 463–470 (2013)
10. Liu, W., Li, S., Zhao, F., Zheng, A.: An ant colony optimization algorithm for the multiple traveling salesmen problem. ICIEA **2009**, 1533–1537 (2009)
11. Somhom, S., Modares, A., Enkawa, T.: Competition-based neural network for the multiple travelling salesmen problem with minmax objective. Comput. Oper. Res. **26**, 395–407 (1999)
12. Venkatesh, P., Singh, A.: Two metaheuristic approaches for the multiple traveling salesperson problem. Appl. Soft. Comput. **26**, 74–89 (2015)
13. Kivelevitch, E., Cohen, K., Kumar, M.: A market-based solution to the multiple traveling salesmen problem. JIRS J. **72**(1), 21–40 (2013)
14. Junjie, P., Dingwei, W.: An ant colony optimization algorithm for multiple travelling salesman problem. In: ICICIC 2006, vol. 1, pp. 210–213 (2006)
15. Salas, Y.J.C., Ledn, R.A., Machado, N.I.C., Now, A.: Multi-type ant colony system for solving the multiple traveling salesman problem. Rev. Tc. Ing. Univ. Zulia **35**(3), 311–320 (2012)
16. Ghafurian, S., Javadian, N.: An ant colony algorithm for solving fixed destination multi-depot multiple traveling salesmen problems. Appl. Soft. Comput. **11**(1), 1256–1262 (2011)
17. Vallivaara, I.: A team ant colony optimization algorithm for the multiple travelling salesmen problem with minmax objective. In: MIC 2008, pp. 387–392 (2008)
18. Sofge, D.A., Schultz, A., De Jong, K.A.: Evolutionary computational approaches to solving the multiple traveling salesman problem using a neighborhood attractor schema. In: Cagnoni, S., Gottlieb, J., Hart, E., Middendorf, M., Raidl, G.R. (eds.) EvoIASP 2002, EvoWorkshops 2002, EvoSTIM 2002, EvoCOP 2002, and EvoPlan 2002. LNCS, vol. 2279, pp. 153–162. Springer, Heidelberg (2002)
19. Chandran, N., Narendran, T.T., Ganesh, K.: A clustering approach to solve the multiple traveling salesmen problem. IJISE **1**(3), 372–387 (2006)
20. Kara, I., Bektas, T.: Integer linear programming formulations of multiple salesman problems and its variations. EJOR **174**(3), 1449–1458 (2006)
21. Dorigo, M., Gambardella, L.M.: Ant colony system: a cooperative learning approach to the traveling salesman problem. IEEE Trans. Evol. Comput. **1**(1), 53–66 (1997)

A Metaheuristic Hybridization Within a Holonic Multiagent Model for the Flexible Job Shop Problem

Houssem Eddine Nouri$^{(\boxtimes)}$, Olfa Belkahla Driss, and Khaled Ghédira

Stratégies d'Optimisation et Informatique intelligentE (SOIE),
Higher Institute of Management of Tunis, Tunis, Tunisia
houssemeddine.nouri@gmail.com,
{olfa.belkahla,khaled.ghedira}@isg.rnu.tn

Abstract. The Flexible Job Shop scheduling Problem (FJSP) is an extension of
the classical Job Shop scheduling Problem (JSP) that allows to process operations on one machine out of a set of alternative machines. It is an NP-hard
problem consisting of two sub-problems which are the assignment and the
scheduling problems. This paper proposes a hybridization of a genetic algorithm
with a tabu search within a holonic multiagent model for the FJSP. Firstly, a
scheduler agent applies a Neighborhood-based Genetic Algorithm (NGA) for a
global exploration of the search space. Secondly, a cluster agents set uses a local
search technique to guide the research in promising regions. Numerical tests are
made to evaluate our approach, based on two sets of benchmark instances from
the literature of the FJSP: Brandimarte and Hurink. The experimental results
show the efficiency of our approach in comparison to other approaches.

Keywords: Scheduling · Flexible job shop · Genetic algorithm · Local search ·
Holonic multiagent

1 Introduction

The Job Shop scheduling Problem (JSP), which is among the hardest combinatorial
optimization problems [15], is a branch of the industrial production scheduling problems. The Flexible Job Shop scheduling Problem (FJSP) is an extension of the classical
JSP that allows to process operations on one machine out of a set of alternative
machines. Hence, the FJSP is more computationally difficult than the JSP, presenting
an additional difficulty caused by the machine assignment problem. This problem is
known to be strongly NP-Hard even if each job has at most three operations and there
are two machines [6].

To solve this problem, some authors used the metaheuristics to find near-optimal
solutions for the FJSP with acceptable computational time. [2] proposed a hierarchical
algorithm based on Tabu Search metaheuristic for routing and scheduling with some
known dispatching rules to solve the FJSP. [10] developed a Tabu Search procedure for
the job shop problem with multi-purpose machines. [14] used Tabu Search techniques
and presented two neighborhood functions allowing an approximate resolution for the
FJSP. [5] adapted a hybrid Genetic Algorithm (GA) and a Variable Neighborhood

© Springer International Publishing Switzerland 2015
E. Onieva et al. (Eds.): HAIS 2015, LNAI 9121, pp. 269–281, 2015.
DOI: 10.1007/978-3-319-19644-2_23

Descent (VND) for FJSP. The GA used two vectors to represent a solution and the disjunctive graph to calculate it. Then, a VND was applied to improve the GA final individuals. [1] presented a Tabu Search approach based on a new golf neighborhood for the FJSP. A new model for low-carbon scheduling in the FJSP is proposed by [16] combining the original Non-dominated Sorting Genetic Algorithm II (NSGA-II) with a Local Search algorithm based on a neighborhood search technique. Furthermore, distributed artificial intelligence techniques were used for this problem, such as the multiagent model proposed by [3] composed by three classes of agents, job agents, resource agents and an interface agent. This model is based on a local search method which is the tabu search to solve the FJSP. Also, [9] proposed a multiagent model based on a hybridization of two metaheuristics, a local optimization process using the tabu search to get a good exploitation of the good areas and a global optimization process integrating the Particle Swarm Optimization (PSO) to diversify the search towards unexplored areas.

In this paper, we propose a hybridization of two metaheuristics within a holonic multiagent model for the flexible job shop scheduling problem. This new approach follows two principal hierarchical steps, where a genetic algorithm is applied by a scheduler agent for a global exploration of the search space. Then, a local search technique is used by a set of cluster agents to guide the research in promising regions. Numerical tests were made to evaluate the performance of our approach based on two literature data sets for the FJSP, completed by comparisons with other approaches.

The rest of the paper is organized as follows. In Sect. 2, we define the formulation of the FJSP with its objective function and a simple problem instance. Then, in Sect. 3, we detail the proposed hybrid approach with its holonic multiagent levels. The experimental and comparison results are provided in Sect. 4. Finally, Sect. 5 ends the paper with a conclusion.

2 Problem Formulation

The Flexible Job Shop scheduling Problem (FJSP) could be formulated as follows. There is a set of n jobs $J = \{J_1,..., J_n\}$ to be processed on a set of m machines $M = \{M_1,...,M_m\}$. Each job J_i is formed by a sequence of n_i operations $\{O_{i,1}, O_{i,2},..., O_{i,ni}\}$ to be performed successively according to the given sequence. For each operation $O_{i,j}$, there is a set of alternative machines $M(O_{i,j})$ capable of performing it. The main objective of this problem is to find a schedule minimizing the end date of the last operation of the jobs set which is the makespan. The makespan is defined by $Cmax$ in Eq. (1), where C_i is the completion time of job J_i.

$$Cmax = max_{1 \leq i \leq n}(C_i) \tag{1}$$

To explain the FJSP, a sample problem of three jobs and five machines is shown in Table 1, where the numbers present the processing times and the tags "-" mean that the operation cannot be executed on the corresponding machine.

Table 1. A simple instance of the FJSP

Job	Operation	M1	M2	M3	M4	M5
J1	O_{11}	2	9	4	5	1
	O_{12}	-	6	-	4	-
J2	O_{21}	1	-	5	-	6
	O_{22}	3	8	6	-	-
	O_{23}	-	5	9	3	9
J3	O_{31}	-	6	6	-	-
	O_{32}	3	-	-	5	4

3   Hybrid Metaheuristics Within a Holonic Multiagent Model

Glover and Kelly [8] elaborated a study about the nature of connections between the genetic algorithm and tabu search metaheuristics, searching to show the existing opportunities for creating a hybrid approach with these two standard methods to take advantage of their complementary features and to solve difficult optimization problems. After this pertinent study, the hybridization of these two metaheuristics has become more well-known in the literature, which has motivated many researchers to try to adapt it for the resolution of different complex problems in several areas.

Ferber [4] defined a multiagent system as an artificial system composed of a population of autonomous agents, which cooperate with each other to reach common objectives, while simultaneously each agent pursues individual objectives. [12] gave the first definition of the term "holon" in the literature, by combining the two Greek words "hol" meaning whole and "on" meaning particle or part. He said that almost everything is both a whole and a part at the same time. In fact, a holon may be viewed as a sort of recursive agent, which is a super-agent composed by a sub-agents set, where each sub-agent has its own behavior as a complementary part of the whole behaviour of the super-agent. Holons are agents able to show an architectural recursiveness [7].

In this work, we propose a hybrid metaheuristic approach processing two general steps: a first step of global exploration using a genetic algorithm to find promising areas in the search space and a clustering operator allowing to regroup them in a set of clusters. In the second step, a tabu search algorithm is applied to find the best individual solution for each cluster. The global process of the proposed approach is implemented in two hierarchical holonic levels adopted by a recursive multiagent model, named a hybrid Genetic Algorithm with Tabu Search within a Holonic Multiagent model (GATS + HM), see Fig. 1. The first holonic level is composed by a Scheduler Agent which is the Master/Super-agent, preparing the best promising regions of the search space, and the second holonic level containing a set of Cluster Agents which are the Workers/Sub-agents, guiding the search to the global optimum solution of the problem. Each holonic level of this model is responsible to process a step of the hybrid metaheuristic approach and to cooperate between them to attain the global solution of the problem.

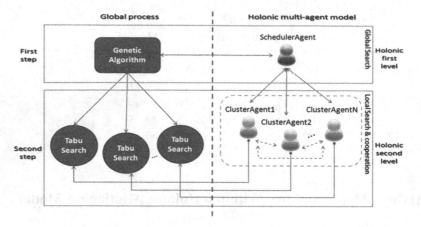

Fig. 1. A metaheuristic hybridization within a holonic multiagent model

In fact, the choice of this new metaheuristic combination is justified by that the standard metaheuristic methods use generally the diversification techniques to generate and to improve many different solutions distributed in the search space, or by using local search techniques to generate a more improved set of neighbourhood solutions from an initial solution. But they did not guarantee to attain promising areas with good fitness converging to the global optimum despite the repetition of many iterations, that is why they need to be more optimized. So, the novelty of our approach is to launch a genetic algorithm based on a diversification technique to only explore the search space and to select the best promising regions by the clustering operator. Then, applying the intensification technique of the tabu search allowing to relaunch the search from an elite solution of each cluster autonomously to attain more dominant solutions of the search space.

In addition, the use of a multiagent system gives the opportunity for distributed and parallel treatments which are very complimentary for the second step of the proposed approach. Indeed, our combined metaheuristic approach follows the paradigm of "Master" and "Workers" which are two recursive hierarchical levels adaptable for a holonic multiagent model, where the Scheduler Agent is the Master/Super-agent of its society and the Cluster Agents are its Workers/Sub-agents.

3.1 Scheduler Agent

The Scheduler Agent (SA) is responsible to process the first step of the combined approach by using a genetic algorithm called NGA (Neighborhood-based Genetic Algorithm) to identify areas with high average fitness in the search space. In fact, the goal of using the NGA is only to explore the search space, but not to find the global solution of the problem. Then, a clustering operator is integrated to divide the best identified areas by the NGA in the search space to different parts where each part is a cluster $CL_i \in CL$ the set of clusters, where $CL = \{CL_1, CL_2, ..., CL_N\}$. In addition, this agent plays the role of an interface between the user and the system (initial parameter inputs and final result outputs). According to the number of clusters N obtained after the integration of the clustering operator, the SA creates N Cluster Agents (CAs) preparing the passage to the next step of the global process. After that, the SA remains in a waiting state until the reception of the best solutions found by the CAs. Finally, it finishes the process by displaying the final solution of the problem.

Individual's Solution Presentation. The flexible job shop problem is composed by two sub-problems: the machine assignment problem and the operation scheduling problem, that is why the chromosome representation is encoded in two parts: Machine Assignment part (MA) and Operation Sequence part (OS). The first part MA is a vector V_1 with a length L equal to the total number of operations and where each index represents the selected machine to process an operation indicated at position pos, see Fig. 2(a). For example $pos = 2$, $V_1(2)$ is the selected machine M_4 for the operation $O_{1,2}$. The second part OS is a vector V_2 having the same length of V_1 and where each index represents an operation $O_{i,j}$ according to the predefined operations of the job set, see Fig. 2(b). For example the operation sequence $1 - 2-1 - 3-2 - 3-2$ can be translated to: $(O_{1,1}, M_5) \rightarrow O_{2,1}, M_1) \rightarrow (O_{1,2}, M_4) \rightarrow (O_{3,1}, M_3) \rightarrow (O_{2,2}, M_3) \rightarrow (O_{3,2}, M_1) \rightarrow (O_{2,3}, M_2)$.

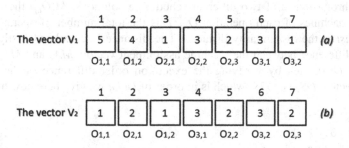

Fig. 2. The chromosome representation

To convert the chromosome values to an active schedule, we used the priority-based decoding of [5]. This method considers the idle time which may exist between operations on a machine m, and which is caused by the operation precedence constraints belonging to the same job i. Let $S_{i,j}$ is the starting time of an operation $O_{i,j}$ (starting only after processing its precedent operation $O_{i,(j-1)}$) with its completion time $C_{i,j}$. In addition, we have an execution time interval $[t^S_m, t^E_m]$ starts form t^S_m and ends at t^E_m on a machine m to allocate an operation $O_{i,j}$. So, if $j = 1$, $S_{i,j}$ takes t^S_m, else if $j \geq 2$, it takes $max\{t^S_m, C_{i,(j-1)}\}$. In fact, the availability of the time interval $[t^S_m, t^E_m]$ for an operation $O_{i,j}$ is validated by verifying if there is a sufficient time period to complete the execution time p_{ijm} of this operation, see Eq. (2):

$$
\begin{cases}
t^S_m + p_{ijm} \, t^E_m & \text{if } j = 1 \\
max\{t^S_m, C_{i,(j-1)}\} + p_{ijm} \, t^E_m & \text{if } j \geq 2
\end{cases}
\tag{2}
$$

The used priority-based decoding method allows in each case to assign each operation to its reserved machine following the execution order of the operation sequence vector V_2. Also, to schedule an operation $O_{i,j}$ on a machine m, the fixed idle time intervals of the selected machine are verified to find an available period to its execution. So, if a period is found, the operation $O_{i,j}$ is executed there, else it is moved to be executed at the end of the machine m.

Noting that the fitness of each chromosome *Fitness(i)* is calculated by Eq. (3), where *Cmax(i)* is its makespan value, $i \in \{1,..., P\}$ and P is the population size.

$$Fitness(i) = \frac{1}{Cmax(i)} \tag{3}$$

Population Initialization. The initial population is generated randomly following a uniform law and based on a neighborhood parameter to make the individual solutions more diversified and distributed in the search space. In fact, each new solution should have a predefined distance with all the other solutions to be considered as a new member of the initial solution. The used method to determinate the neighborhood parameter is inspired from [1], which is based on the permutation level of operations to obtain the distance between two solutions. Let *Chrom1(MA₁, OS₁)* and *Chrom2(MA₂, OS₂)* two chromosomes of two different scheduling solutions, $M(O_{i,j})$ the alternative number of machines of each operation $O_{i,j}$, L is the total number of operations of all jobs and *Dist* is the dissimilarity distance. The distance is calculated firstly by measuring the difference between the machine assignment vectors MA_1 and MA_2 which is in order of $O(n)$, then by verifying the execution order difference of the operation sequence vectors OS_1 and OS_2 which is in order of $O(1)$, we give here how to proceed:

```
Begin
  Dist=0, k=1
  For k from 1 to L
    If Chrom1(MA₁(k)) ≠ Chrom2(MA₂(k))
      Dist = Dist + M(Oᵢ,ⱼ)
    End if
    If Chrom1(OS₁(k)) ≠ Chrom2(OS₂(k))
      Dist = Dist + 1
    End if
  End for
  Return Dist
End
```

Noting that *Dist_max* is the maximal dissimilarity distance and it is calculated by Eq. (4), representing 100 % of difference between two chromosomes.

$$Dist\_max = \sum_{i,1}^{i,ni} [M(Oi,j)] + L \tag{4}$$

Selection Operator. The selection operator is used to select the best parent individuals to prepare them to the crossover step. This operator is based on a fitness parameter allowing to analyze the quality of each selected solution. But progressively the fitness values will be similar for the most individuals. That is why, we integrate the neighborhood parameter, where we propose a new combined parent selection operator named Fitness-Neighborhood Selection Operator (FNSO) allowing to add the dissimilarity distance criteria to the fitness parameter to select the best parents for the crossover step. The FNSO chooses in each iteration two parent individuals until engaging all the population to create the next generation. The first parent takes successively in each case a solution i, where $i \in \{1,..., P\}$ and P is the total population size. The second parent obtains its solution j randomly by the roulette wheel selection method based on the two Fitness and Neighborhood parameters relative to the selected first parent, where $j \in \{1,..., P\}\backslash\{i\}$ in the P population and where $j \neq i$. In fact, to use this random method, we should calculate the Fitness-Neighborhood total FN for the population, see Eq. (5), the selection probability sp_k for each individual I_k, see Eq. (6), and the cumulative probability cp_k, see Eq. (7). After that, a random number r will be generated from the uniform range [0,1]. If $r \leq cp_1$ then the second parent takes the first individual I_1, else it gets the kth individual $I_k \in \{I_2,..., I_P\}\backslash\{I_i\}$ and where $cp_{k-1} < r \leq cp_k$. For Eqs. (5–7), $k = \{1, 2,..., P\}\backslash\{i\}$.

- The Fitness-Neighborhood total for the population:

$$FN = \sum_{k=1}^{P} [1/(Cmax[k] \times Neighborhood[i][k])] \tag{5}$$

- The selection probability sp_k for each individual I_k:

$$sp_k = \frac{1/(Cmax[k] \times Neighborhood[i][k])}{FN} \tag{6}$$

- The cumulative probability cp_k for each individual I_k:

$$cp_k = \sum_{h=1}^{k} p_h \tag{7}$$

Crossover Operator. The crossover operator has an important role in the global process, allowing to combine in each case the chromosomes of two parents in order to obtain new individuals and to attain new better parts in the search space. In this work, this operator is applied with two different techniques successively for the parent's chromosome vectors MA and OS. For the machine vector crossover, a uniform crossover is used to generate in each case a mixed vector between two machine vector parents, Parent1-MA1 and Parent2-MA2, allowing to obtain two new children, Child1-

MA1′ and Child2-MA2′. This uniform crossover is based on two assignment cases, if the generated number is less than 0.5, the first child gets the current machine value of parent1 and the second child takes the current machine value of parent2. Else, the two children change their assignment direction, first child to parent2 and the second child to parent1. For the operation vector crossover, an improved precedence preserving order-based on crossover (iPOX), inspired from [13], is adapted for the parent operation vector OS. This iPOX operator is applied following four steps, a first step is selecting two parent operation vectors (OS_1 and OS_2) and generating randomly two job sub-sets Js_1/Js_2 from all jobs. A second step is allowing to copy any element in OS_1/OS_2 that belong to Js_1/Js_2 into child individual OS'_1/OS'_2 and retain them in the same position. Then the third step deletes the elements that are already in the sub-set Js_1/Js_2 from OS_1/OS_2. Finally, fill orderly the empty position in OS'_1/OS'_2 with the reminder elements of OS_2/OS_1 in the fourth step.

Mutation Operator. The mutation operator is integrated to promote the children generation diversity. In fact, this operator is applied on the chromosome of the new children generated by the crossover operation. Also, each part of a child chromosome MA and OS has separately its own mutation technique. The machine mutation operator uses a random selection of an index from the machine vector MA. Then, it replaces the machine number in the selected index by another belonging to the same alternative machine set. The operation mutation operator selects randomly two indexes index1 and index2 from the operation vector OS. Next, it changes the position of the job number in the index1 to the second index2 and inversely.

Replacement Operator. The replacement operator has an important role to prepare the remaining surviving population to be considered for the next iterations. This operator replaces in each case a parent by one of its children which has the best fitness in its current family.

Clustering Operator. By finishing the last iteration of the genetic algorithm, the Scheduler Agent applies a clustering operator using the hierarchical clustering algo-rithm of [11] to divide the final population into N Clusters, to be treated by the Cluster Agents in the second step of the global process. The clustering operator is based on the neighbourhood parameter which is the dissimilarity distance between individuals. The clustering operator starts by assigning each individual $Indiv(i)$ to a cluster CL_i, so if we have P individuals, we have now P clusters containing just one individual in each of them. So, for each case, we fixe an individual $Indiv(i)$ and we verify successively for each next individual $Indiv(j)$ from the remaining population (where i and j ∈ {$1,...,P$}, i ≠ j) if the dissimilarity distance $Dist$ between $Indiv(i)$ and $Indiv(j)$ is less than or equal to a fixed threshold $Dist\_fix$ (representing a percentage of difference X% relatively to $Dist\_max$, see Eq. (8)) and where $Cluster(Indiv(i)) ≠ Cluster(Indiv(j))$. If it is the case, $Merge(Cluster(Indiv(i)),Cluster(Indiv(j)))$, else continue the search for new combina-tion with the remaining individuals. The stopping condition is by browsing all the population individuals, where we obtained at the end N Clusters.

$$Dist\_fix = Dist\_max \times X\% \tag{8}$$

3.2 Cluster Agents

Each Cluster Agent CA_i is responsible to apply successively to each cluster CL_i a local search technique which is the Tabu Search algorithm to guide the research in promising regions of the search space and to improve the quality of the final population. In fact, this local search is executed simultaneously by the set of the CAs agents, where each CA_i starts the research autonomously from an elite solution of its cluster searching to attain new more dominant individual solutions separately in its assigned cluster CL_i. The used Tabu Search algorithm is based on an intensification technique allowing to start the research from an elite solution in a cluster CL_i in order to collect new sequence minimizing the makespan. Let E the elite solution of a cluster CL_i, $E' \in N(E)$ is a neighbor of the elite solution E, GL_i is the Global List of each CA_i to receive new found elite solutions by the remaining CAs, each CL_i plays the role of the tabu list with a dynamic length and $Cmax$ is the makespan of the obtained solution. So, the search process of this local search starts from an elite solution E using the *move and insert* method of [14], where each Cluster Agent CA_i changes the position of an operation $O_{i,j}$ from a machine m to another machine n belonging to the same alternative machine set of this selected operation $O_{i,j}$, searching to generate new scheduling combination $E' \in N(E)$. After that, verifying if the makespan value of this new generated solution $Cmax$ (E') dominates $Cmax(E)$ $(Cmax(E') < Cmax(E))$, and if it is the case CA_i saves E' in its tabu list (which is CL_i) and sends it to all the other CAs agents to be placed in their Global Lists $GLs(E', CA_i)$, to ensure that it will not be used again by them as a search point. Else continues the neighborhood search from the current solution E. The stopping condition is by attaining the maximum allowed number of neighbors for a solution E without improvement. We give here how to proceed:

```
Begin
  E ← Elite(CL_i)
  While N(E) ≠ ∅
    E' ← {Move and insert(E) | E' ∈ N(E) | E' ∉ GL_i}
    If Cmax(E') < Cmax(E) and E' ∉ CL_i
      E ← E'
      CL_i ← E'
      Send_to_all(E',CA_i)
    End if
  End while
  Return E
End
```

By finishing this local search step, the CAs agents send their last elite solutions to the SA agent, which considers the best one of them the global solution for the FJSP.

4 Experimental Results

4.1 Experimental Setup

The proposed GATS + HM is implemented in Java language on a 2.10 GHz Intel Core 2 Duo processor and 3 Gb of RAM memory, using the *eclipse* IDE to code the approach and the multiagent platform *Jade* to create the holonic multiagent model. To evaluate its efficiency, numerical tests are made based on two sets of benchmark instances from the literature of the FJSP: the *Brandimare data* [2] consists of 10 problems considering a job set ranging from 10 to 20 and an operation set ranging from 55 to 240, processed by a machine set ranging from 4 to 15. The *Hurink edata* [10] consisting of 40 problems (la01-la40) inspired from classical job shop instances where three test problems are generated: rdata, vdata and edata which is used in this paper. Due to the non-deterministic nature of the proposed approach, we run it five independent times for each one of the two instances in order to obtain significant results.

The used parameter settings for our approach are adjusted experimentally and presented as follow: Crossover probability = 1.0, Mutation probability = 1.0, Maximum number of iterations = 1000. The population size ranged from 15 to 400 depending on the complexity of the problem.

The computational results are presented in the Tables 2 and 3, where the first column is the name of each instance, the second column is the size of each instance ($n \times m$) with n jobs and m machines, and the remaining columns detail the experimental results in terms of the best makespan (*Best*), the average of makespan (*Avg Cmax*), the average of CPU time in seconds (*Avg CPU*), and the standard deviation of makespan (*Dev %*) which is calculated by Eq. (9). The Mk**o** is the makespan obtained by **O**ur approach and Mk**c** is the makespan of an approach that we chose to **C**ompare to. The bold values in the tables signify the best obtained results.

$$\text{Dev} = [(\text{Mkc} - \text{Mko})/\text{Mkc}] \times 100\% \qquad (9)$$

Table 2. Results of the Brandimarte data instances

Instance	Problem n×m	TS		MATSLO+		MATSPSO		GATS+HM		
		Best	Dev (%)	Best	Dev (%)	Best	Dev (%)	Best	Avg Cmax	Avg C.P.U (in seconds)
Mk01	10×6	42	4,761	40	0	**39**	-2,564	40	40,80	0,93
Mk02	10×6	32	15,625	32	15,625	**27**	0	**27**	27,80	1,18
Mk03	15×8	211	3,317	207	1,449	207	1,449	**204**	204,00	1,55
Mk04	15×8	81	20,987	67	4,477	65	1,538	**64**	65,60	4,36
Mk05	15×4	186	6,989	188	7,978	174	0,574	**173**	174,80	8,02
Mk06	10×15	86	24,418	85	23,529	72	9,722	**65**	67,00	110,01
Mk07	20×5	157	8,280	154	6,493	154	6,493	**144**	144,00	19,73
Mk08	20×10	**523**	0	**523**	0	**523**	0	**523**	523,00	11,50
Mk09	20×10	369	15,718	437	28,832	340	8,529	**311**	311,80	79,68
Mk10	20×15	296	25	380	41,578	299	25,752	**222**	224,80	185,64

Table 3. Results of the Hurink edata instances

Instance	Problem n×m	LB Best	LB Dev (%)	N1-1000 Best	N1-1000 Dev (%)	MATSLO+ Best	MATSLO+ Dev (%)	GATS+HM Best	GATS+HM Avg Cmax	GATS+HM Avg C.P.U (in seconds)
la01	10×5	609	0	611	0,327	609	0	609	609,00	24,64
la02	10×5	655	0	655	0	655	0	655	655,00	4,65
la03	10×5	550	-3,091	573	1,047	575	1,391	567	567,40	10,67
la04	10×5	568	0	578	1,730	579	1,900	568	569,60	22,13
la05	10×5	503	0	503	0	503	0	503	503,00	10,22
la16	10×10	892	0	924	3,463	896	0,446	892	909,60	73,14
la17	10×10	707	0	757	6,605	708	0,141	707	709,60	116,58
la18	10×10	842	-0,119	864	2,431	845	0,237	843	848,60	34,98
la19	10×10	796	-1,005	850	5,412	813	1,107	804	813,40	36,88
la20	10×10	857	0	919	6,746	863	0,695	857	859,80	70,36

4.2   Experimental Comparisons

To show the efficiency of our GATS + HM approach, we compare its obtained results from the two previously cited data sets with other well known algorithms in the literature of the FJSP. The chosen algorithms are the TS of [2], the N1-1000 of [10], the MATSLO + of [3] and the MATSPSO of [9].

By analyzing the Table 2, it can be seen that our approach GATS+HM obtains nine out of ten best results for the Brandimarte instances. In fact, our approach outperforms the TS in nine out of ten instances. Moreover, for the comparison with MATSLO+, our GATS+HM outperforms it in eight out of ten instances. Furthermore, the MATSPSO attained the best result for the MK01 instance, but our approach obtains a set of solutions better than it for the remaining instances. By solving this second data set, our GATS+HM attains the same results obtained by some approaches such as the MK01 for MATSLO+, the MK02 for MATSPSO and the MK08 for all methods.

From Table 3, the comparison results show that the GATS+HM obtains seven out of ten best results for the Hurink edata instances (la01–la05) and (la16–la20). Indeed, our approach outperforms the N1-1000 in eight out of ten instances. Moreover, our GATS+HM outperforms the MATSLO+ in seven out of ten instances. For the comparison with the literature lower bound LB, the GATS+HM attains the same results for the la01, la02, la04, la05, la16, la17 and la20 instances, but it gets slightly worse result for the la03, la18 and la19 instances. Furthermore, by solving this second data set, our GATS+HM attains the same results obtained by the chosen approaches such as in the la01 for the MATSLO+ ; in the la02 for the N1-1000 and the MATSLO+ ; in the la05 for the N1-1000 and the MATSLO+. By analyzing the comparison results, we can distinguish the efficiency of the new proposed GATS +HM relatively to the literature of the FJSP. This efficiency is explained by the flexible selection of the promising parts of the search space by the clustering operator after the genetic algorithm process and by applying the intensification technique of the tabu search allowing to start from an elite solution to attain new more dominant solutions.

5 Conclusion

In this paper, a new combination of two metaheuristics within a holonic multiagent model, called GATS + HM, is proposed for the flexible job shop scheduling problem (FJSP). In this approach, a genetic algorithm is adapted by a scheduler agent for a global exploration of the search space and a local search technique is applied by a cluster agents set to guide the research in promising regions. To measure its performance, numerical tests are made using two well known data sets from the literature of the FJSP. The experimental results show that the proposed approach is efficient in comparison to others approaches. In the future work, we will integrate new constraints of other extensions of the FJSP, such as the transportation resources. So, we will make improvements to our approach to adapt it to this new transformation and study its effects on the makespan.

References

1. Bozejko, W., Uchronski, M., Wodecki, M.: The new golf neighborhood for the flexible job shop problem. In: The International Conference on Computational Science, pp. 289–296 (2010)
2. Brandimarte, P.: Routing and scheduling in a flexible job shop by tabu search. Ann. Oper. Res. **41**(3), 157–183 (1993)
3. Ennigrou, M., Ghédira, K.: New local diversification techniques for the flexible job shop problem with a multi-agent approach. Auton. Agent. Multi-Agent Syst. **17**(2), 270–287 (2008)
4. Ferber, J.: Multi-agent Systems: An Introduction to Distributed Artificial Intelligence. Addison-Wesley Longman Publishing, Boston (1999)
5. Gao, J., Sun, L., Gen, M.: A hybrid genetic and variable neighborhood descent algorithm for flexible job shop scheduling problems. Comput. Oper. Res. **35**(9), 2892–2907 (2008)
6. Garey, M.R., Johnson, D.S., Sethi, R.: The complexity of flow shop and job shop scheduling. Math. Oper. Res. **1**(2), 117–129 (1976)
7. Giret, A., Botti, V.: Holons and agents. J. Intell. Manuf. **15**(5), 645–659 (2004)
8. Glover, F., Kelly, J.P., Laguna, M.: Genetic algorithms and tabu search: Hybrids for optimization. Comput. Oper. Res. **22**(1), 111–134 (1995)
9. Henchiri, A., Ennigrou, M.: Particle swarm optimization combined with tabu search in a multi-agent model for flexible job shop problem. In: Tan, Y., Shi, Y., Mo, H. (eds.) ICSI 2013, Part II. LNCS, vol. 7929, pp. 385–394. Springer, Heidelberg (2013)
10. Hurink, J., Jurisch, B., Thole, M.: Tabu search for the job-shop scheduling problem with multi-purpose machines. Oper. Res. Spektr. **15**(4), 205–215 (1994)
11. Johnson, S.C.: Hierarchical clustering schemes. Psychometrika **32**(3), 241–254 (1967)
12. Koestler, A.: The Ghost in the Machine. Hutchinson, London (1967)
13. Lee, K., Yamakawa, T., Lee, K.M.: A genetic algorithm for general machine scheduling problems. In: The second IEEE International Conference on Knowledge-Based Intelligent Electronic Systems, pp. 60–66 (1998)
14. Mastrolilli, M., Gambardella, L.: Effective neighbourhood functions for the flexible job shop problem. J. Sched. **3**(1), 3–20 (2000)

15. Sonmez, A.I., Baykasoglu, A.: A new dynamic programming formulation of (nm) flow shop sequencing problems with due dates. Int. J. Prod. Res. **36**(8), 2269–2283 (1998)
16. Zhang, C., Gu, P., Jiang, P.: Low-carbon scheduling and estimating for a flexible job shop based on carbon footprint and carbon efficiency of multi-job processing. J. Eng. Manuf. **39** (32), 1–15 (2014)

Quantum Evolutionary Methods for Real Value Problems

Jonathan Wright and Ivan Jordanov[(✉)]

School of Computing, University of Portsmouth, Portsmouth, UK
{jonathan.wright,ivan.jordanov}@port.ac.uk

Abstract. We investigate a modified Quantum Evolutionary method for solving real value problems. The Quantum Inspired Evolutionary Algorithms (QIEA) are binary encoded evolutionary techniques used for solving binary encoded problems and their signature feature follows superposition of multiple states on a quantum bit. This is usually implemented by sampling a binary chromosome string, according to probabilities stored in an underlying probability string. In order to apply this paradigm to real value problems, real QIEAs (rQIEA) were developed using real encoding while trying to follow the original quantum computing metaphor. In this paper we report the issues we encounter while implementing some of the published techniques. Firstly, we found that the investigated rQIEAs tend to stray from the original quantum computing interpretation, and secondly, their performance on a number of test problems was not as good as claimed in the original publications. Subsequently, we investigated further and developed binary QIEA for use with real value problems. In general, the investigated and designed quantum method for real-value problems, produced better convergence on most of the examined problems and showed very few inferior results.

Keywords: Global optimization · Quantum evolutionary methods · Estimation of distribution algorithms · Real value problems · Multimodal functions

1 Introduction

About a decade ago a new class of optimisation algorithm was presented, that took inspiration from quantum computing [1]. These Quantum Inspired Evolutionary Algorithms (QIEA) were binary encoded evolutionary optimisation techniques, used to solve binary encoded problems [1, 2]. Their signature feature follows superposition of multiple states on a quantum bit (Qbit). This is usually implemented by sampling a binary chromosome string, according to probabilities stored in an underlying probability string, for every generation of the evolutionary process. As determined in [2], this process places QIEA into the class of techniques called estimation of distribution algorithms (EDAs) [3].

In order to apply QIEA to real value problems, real QIEAs (rQIEAs) were developed using real encoding while trying to follow the original quantum computing metaphor. As discussed later in this paper, some issues were found when trying to implement published rQIEA. Of specific concern was, for example, the implementation [4],

© Springer International Publishing Switzerland 2015
E. Onieva et al. (Eds.): HAIS 2015, LNAI 9121, pp. 282–293, 2015.
DOI: 10.1007/978-3-319-19644-2_24

which made claims of superior performance to an optimization algorithm that was later found to not perform as well as claimed previously [5]. Another implemented by us algorithm, presented in [6], performed very poorly and produced disappointing results. The proposed method in [7] was substantially outperformed by the method published in [8] (and so, we have included this technique in this study for comparison purposes. However, we found that the rQIEAs tended to stray from the original quantum computing interpretation. This led us to further investigate and develop binary QIEA for use with real value problems. At the same, we are mindful that optimisation algorithms exist to solve practical problems, and therefore we include comparisons to a successful rQIEA, highlighting those areas where the different versions are more successful. A number of variations of QIEAs have been published in the literature [11], including a variety of hybrid algorithms [9, 10].

2 Binary QIEA (bQIEA)

This section presents the original QIEA and a variant from the literature. We then present an examination into the evolution properties when applying them to real value problems, and in doing so highlight a premature convergence problem. In response, we present modifications to the original algorithm, designed the directly address these problems, and conclude this section with further strategies to avoid premature convergence.

2.1 Original (oQEA) and Versatile Quantum Evolutionary Algorithm (vQEA)

The original QIEA was first published in [1] and contains the core properties of QIEA – Qbit sampling and the rotation gate operator. Unlike a traditional binary evolutionary algorithm, the oQEA stores a string of probability values called Qbits. Each Qbit value gives the probability of sampling a 0 or 1. Through repeated sampling of generations, the same Qbit value can be used to sample a sequence of binary values. If a Qbit has a value of 0.5, both 1 and 0 have an equal chance of being sampled. A Qbit value near 1.0 favours sampling of 1 s, and a value close to 0.0 favours sampling 0 s.

Even in the absence of evolution of the chromosomes, the oQEA will continue to produce different candidates for the fitness function. This is in contrast to a traditional evolutionary algorithm. The combination of probability and sampling is likened to the quantum computing principal of superposition (the ability of a Qbit to hold multiple states simultaneously).

While random sampling allows the solution space to be searched, the Qbits need to be changed in order to localise and refine the search. By interpreting the Qbit probability as an angle, a quantum logic gate called a rotation gate can be used. This simply shifts the angle, and therefore the probability one way or the other. By using the best solution found so far, this rotation can be made to rotate towards a position that reinforces the best solution probabilities, if it is still the best solution, or away if the candidate was better. The rotation is governed by Eq. 1.

The versatile (vQEA) algorithm, first presented in [2], makes a simple change to the oQEA. After making the comparison between candidate and attractor, the attractor is always replaced. By removing the attractor elitism, the algorithm effectively makes a series of pair-wise comparisons, between the last generation and the current generation. The authors demonstrated superior performance on some binary value problems and suggested that vQEA achieved this by reducing premature convergence.

$$Q_{i,t+1} = \theta_{i,t+1} = \begin{cases} \min\left(\theta_{i,t} + \Delta, \frac{\pi}{2}\right), & \Delta > 0 \\ \max\left(\theta_{i,t} + \Delta, 0\right), & \Delta < 0 \end{cases} \tag{1}$$

where Δ is the size and direction of rotation.

2.2 Application to Real Value Problems

An initial investigation was performed to apply oQEA and vQEA to real value problems. Mapping was done as described later in Sect. 4, and optimisation was performed on the Shekel family functions. Both versions of the bQIEA were able to approximately find the global minimum for a reasonable percentage of runs. However, convergence to the precise minima could have been better. We produced plots of Qbit evolution for the Shekel 5 optimisation process (a typical plot is shown in Fig. 1a). The plot shows that the least significant Qbits were saturating before the most significant Qbits. Once a Qbit saturates, it will no longer evolve because sampling will continuously produce ones or zeros, depending on which end of the scale the Qbit has saturated to. This means that the LSBs had randomly fixed relatively early on in the optimisation (which prevents fine scale optimization).

For reasonably smooth search spaces, the early stages of search should focus on finding the general locations of extrema, rather than refining solutions to a precise position. During this time, the fitness function will be affected more by large movements than by small ones. With a binary representation, this will manifest in the MSBs dominating the search, as changes to them are likely to find larger improvements to the fitness, than changes to the LSBs. In other words, MSBs could be associated with the exploration, and the LSBs with the exploitation phases of the search.

Therefore, in the early stages, the LSBs provide little optimisation pressure, and so random values for these bits will be tolerated, while the MSBs are optimised. The early evolution of the LSBs can therefore be modelled as a random walk process. We would therefore expect several bits to have deviated substantially from the neutral middle probability position. Also, the process is reinforced. As an attractor adopts a solution, shifts in the random walks will make producing a zero or one more likely. This will lead to the random walk being attracted to a probability of zero or one respectively. By the time the MSBs have been optimised, it is likely therefore, that the LSBs have saturated their probabilities. In the following sub-sections, we present modifications to the binary algorithms that are designed to address this problem.

2.3 Limiting to Neighbouring Bits

To directly address the issue of the LSBs prematurely converging, we first propose the Limit to significant neighbour QEA (LSNQEA). It limits the range of each Qbit so that it cannot be evolved (rotated) to a more extreme position than its more significant adjacent Qbit (Eq. 2). This forces the algorithm to rotate the MSBs more before the LSBs do (the LSBs can only evolve as the MSBs become more saturated). The modified saturation behaviour is shown in Fig. 1b.

$$Q_{i,t+1} = \theta_{i,t+1} = \begin{cases} \min\left(\theta_{i,t} + \Delta, 0.25\pi + \left|\theta_{i-1,t} - 0.25\pi\right|\right), & \Delta > 0 \\ \max\left(\theta_{i,t} + \Delta, 0.25\pi - \left|\theta_{i-1,t} - 0.25\pi\right|\right), & \Delta < 0 \end{cases}, \text{ and } i > 0 \quad (2)$$

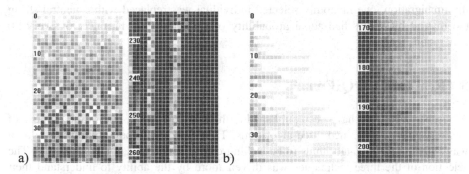

Fig. 1. Evolution of Qbit probabilities on Shekel 5 using (a) oQEA and (b) LSNQEA. Bits for one real value are shown, with most significant bits to the left. Early in the evolution, all squares are pale (mid-range). Later on, for oQEA, the least significant bits (to the right) are all saturated while several of the most significant bits are paler and still undergoing evolution. For LSNQEA however, limiting saturation of a Qbit to be no more than the current value of the immediately more significant neighbour, prevents the least significant bits from saturating before the most significant bits.

$$Q_{i,t+1} = \theta_{i,t+1} = \begin{cases} \min\left(\theta_{i,t} + \Delta, \ 0.25\pi + \left|\theta_{j,t} - 0.25\pi\right|\right), & \Delta > 0 \\ \max\left(\theta_{i,t} + \Delta, \ 0.25\pi - \left|\theta_{j,t} - 0.25\pi\right|\right), & \Delta < 0 \end{cases} \quad (3)$$

where i > 0, j = floor(i/2).

In the initial tests, it appeared the LSNQEA may have been too aggressive in delaying LSB convergence, and therefore may delay convergence overall. To address this, we present a modification where instead of using the immediately more significant bit as a limit, the bit that was placed half way along compared to the bit undergoing limitation. We call this version half significant neighbour QEA (HSNQEA). With bit zero being the most significant, this modification is shown in Eq. 3.

A simpler modification is to simply limit bit rotation to a small, inside the $(0, \pi)$, interval. For example, oQEA and vQEA can be modified as follows:

$$Q_{i,t+1} = \theta_{i,t+1} = \begin{cases} \min\left(\theta_{i,t} + \Delta, \, 0.49\pi\right), & \Delta > 0 \\ \max\left(\theta_{i,t} + \Delta, \, 0.01\pi\right), & \Delta < 0 \end{cases} \tag{4}$$

Desaturated versions of vQEA and HSNQEA were investigated and labelled vQEAd and HSBQEAd respectively.

2.4   Additional Variants – Mutation and Immigration

The final modifications we present are to investigate all of the bQIEAs with the addition of mutation or immigration. For mutation, all Qbits were mutated with probability 0.01. Mutation simply meant replacing that Qbit with a random value. For the immigration, one randomly selected individual was replaced with a neutral string (so that all bit values had equal probability of sampling 0 or 1), once for every 20 generations.

3   Real QIEA (rQIEA)

A number of rQIEAs have been published in the literature [6–8], but for the purpose of this research we examined three algorithms. This appeared to be a difficult task, as it was common for the algorithms to be lacking clarity and details at the same time. The selection of the three techniques was driven more by the ability to understand their description (and reproduce them), rather than any other consideration. Of the three algorithms explained below, Simple rQIEA performed very badly, RQEA was better but was substantially outperformed by RCQIEA. Therefore, we decided to use RCQIEA to compare against our investigation of bQIEAs.

In general, we interpret these rQIEA to be further away from the original concept of QIEAs than their binary cousins. This was a major reason for our decision to investigate bQIEAs for real-value problems. With the exception of the Simple rQIEA, the real algorithms have a definite real-encoded solution, which is then mutated. This emulates superposition, whereas the bQIEAs directly implement superposition through sampling. This issue is discussed more in Sect. 5.3.

In the Simple rQIEA [6], the stored angles are used to directly produce a real-value α^2 or $1 - \alpha^2$, each with probability 0.5. A rotation gate is used to update the values, and a cross-over operator is periodically applied.

The RQEA [7], stores a solution as a set of real values, and then generates a family of neighbouring solutions using two different mutation operators. The first operator uses creep mutation from the parent to produce a set of offspring. The second operator does the same, but then remaps the set of real values to between the corresponding values in the best solution found by the family so far, and in the best solution found across the whole population so far. If any of the new children are found to be better than the best in the population, the parent values are adjusted using the standard rotation gate operator.

Unlike RQEA, the RCQIEA [8], stores candidate values and angle variables. The angles are used to specify the variance of a creep mutation operator. A set of candidate children are produced for each parent, using both course and fine mutations. Any superior candidates instantly replaced the stored solution. Angles are then updated using the rotation gate operator. A cross-over operator is also applied during the evolution. For our investigation, we applied it four times during the course of each evolution.

4 Methods Analysis

Real values were encoded using 24bit binary strings and the MSB was assigned a value of 0.5 if one, the next bit 0.25, the next bit 0.125, etc.... This gave a value in the interval $[0, 1]$ which was then mapped to the domain of the test function.

In this investigation, every algorithm was tested over 100 runs for each population configuration and test function. A run was terminated when it reached a particular generation number. The length of a run was either fixed to 1000 generations or adjusted to maintain a fixed number of function evaluations. Best fitness results were recorded to an accuracy of 6 s.f.

Success rates were measured by seeing how many runs achieved a fitness that was sufficiently close enough to the best value found at any time by any algorithm. The threshold of fitness was calculated using the median fitness score across all algorithms and runs, according to: success if: $f_r \leq 0.99 f_B + 0.01\tilde{f}$, where f_r is the best fitness for the run, f_b is the best fitness found at any time, and $\tilde{f}$ is the median fitness across the whole investigation.

The optimisation functions were tested on a range of real fitness functions. They were selected based on previous author experience [12] and choices made in other QIEA research. Some were later added to further explore trends described in the results sections, relating properties of the fitness functions to the relative performance of the various investigated methods. For some of the functions we offset the input values so that the global minimum was no longer at the origin. This was done because some algorithms appeared to be overly capable of finding the minimum when it was at the origin.

5 Results and Discussion

Many optimisation runs were performed to explore the properties of the investigated algorithms, on a range of fitness functions (real valued). In this section, we first present an exploration of the effect of population size and generation limit. Secondly, we investigate the ability of the algorithms to find best solutions. Finally, we present data on how often the algorithms produced acceptable results, using the success threshold outlined in Sect. 4.

We first tested the algorithms across a range of population sizes (5, 10, 20, 50 and 100 individuals), where the number of function evaluations was kept constant. This was done by adjusting the number of generations. By keeping the total number of function evaluations constant, we were establishing the best configurations for a given amount of computing time. However, when comparing between different algorithms, it should

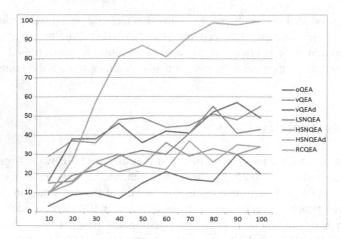

Fig. 2. An example of the effect of population size on algorithm performance, based on the percentage of successful runs. QIEA performance when the number of generations was kept constant and population varied is shown, with results for Shubert 2. This exhibited approximately linear increase with population, with some flattening for higher population sizes for some algorithms.

be noted that the bQIEAs took more processing for their optimisation algorithms than the rQIEAs and the rQIEAs were substantially faster. If fitness function evaluation is intensive (for example, through simulation), then the difference in algorithm computing time will be less relevant, and a comparison with equal total function evaluations will be valid.

Table 1. Best, and second best, population sizes for each algorithm, determined by success rates. Total number of function evaluations was kept to a constant 10000.

Algorithm	Best pop	2nd best	Algorithm	Best pop	2nd best
oQEA D0	50	20	LSNQEA D1	5	10
oQEA D1	20	10	LSNQEA D2	10	5
oQEA D2	50	10	HSNQEA D0	10	5
vQEA D0	20	10	HSNQEA D1	5	20
vQEA D1	100	50	HSNQEA D2	10	5
vQEA D2	20	50	HSNQEAd D0	10	5
vQEAd D0	20	10	HSNQEAd D1	10	5
vQEAd D1	20	50	HSNQEAd D2	10	5
vQEAd D2	20	50	GA	10	5
LSNQEA D0	5	10	RCQEA	5	20

Success rates were taken using the criterion given in Sect. 4. The LSNQEA algorithm had the best performance with population sizes of 5 or 10, with an abrupt drop-off, while RCQIEA was best with a population size of 5 or 20, with a flatter success rate/population size relationship. Although the best configuration varied between fitness functions, we have determined an overall best configuration by looking for those that were best more often, and underperformed less than others. This analysis is summarized in Table 1.

We next investigated increasing population size while keeping the number generations fixed. In general, this led to an increase in the success rate (Fig. 2). The relationship was often linear in the lower population range, and then either linearly increasing in the top range, or largely flat (indicating diminishing returns with greater population size). Some algorithms produced poor results for low population sizes, and then crossed a threshold where they increased more strongly.

5.1 Best Solutions Found

The first assessment of the algorithms that we performed was to see how often they could equal the best solution found for that fitness function, during the whole analysis by any algorithm. Evaluation was performed for each algorithm, upon every fitness function, using population sizes of 5, 10, 20, 50 and 100. These results were then either summed across the different population configurations, or the best single configuration was selected. When summing across all configurations, RCQEA found the best solution for the largest number of fitness functions (Fig. 3a), followed by standard oQEA, and oQEA with immigration. When seeing how often they equaled the best solution in a batch of runs, RCQEA and oQEA with immigration performed best (Fig. 3b) followed by standard oQEA. Only the vQEA and LSNQEA variants failed to outperform the other algorithms for any fitness function.

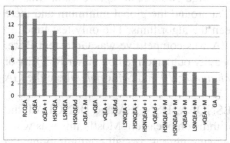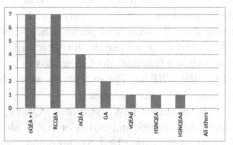

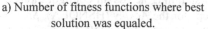

| a) Number of fitness functions where best solution was equaled. | b) Number of fitness functions for which algorithm was the best, or joint best. |

Fig. 3. Ability of algorithms to find the best solution for each fitness function, when summed across all population configurations. In a) the number of functions for which the best solution was equaled is given for each algorithm, and in b) the number of functions for which each algorithm was the best, or equal best, performer, with regards to success rates.

When only the best configuration was selected for each algorithm, for each fitness function, all had at least one best position. Overall, RCQEA performed best (eight), followed by standard oQEA (six), and then oQEA with immigration, standard

HSNQEA and GA jointly (three). The RCQEA algorithm performed best when other algorithms struggled (when the median fitness was a sizeable distance away from the minimum), with the exception of *De Jong 5* function. The oQEA with immigration performed above the others when, in general, the algorithms were closer in performance. The exception to this was for the *Shekel* functions where, like RCQEA, the oQEA with immigration performed well while other algorithms were more variable.

One extra observation to note is that, when matching the best solutions for the *Shekel* test functions, the newly presented algorithms, and immigration modification to oQEA, outperformed the plain oQEA, vQEA and vQEAd. This gives evidence that, when testing the *Shekel* functions, premature LSB convergence was a problem.

5.2   Success Rates

We counted the number of times the algorithms had successful runs, using population sizes of 5, 10, 20, 50 and 100. When summing across all the configurations, RCQEA was the most successful algorithm, outperforming the other algorithms for 13 of the test functions. This was followed by six top performances for oQEA with immigration. The only other top performers were two wins for GA and one win for plain oQEA. When taking only the single best configuration, RCQEA again outperformed the other algorithms most often (13 wins). However, the best performances for other test functions were spread around more, the oQEA with immigration was second best with four best performances. Then plain vQEAd, plain HSNQEA, HSNQEAd with immigration and GA all scored two wins.

Although the RCQEA comes out as the best performer overall, there were occasions for which it was outperformed by the bQIEAs. These were *Beale, Branin, Rosenbrock 2*, and when taking the single best configuration, *Sum Square Sum*. Most of these functions have the properties of being flat around the global minimum and there being a small variance of performance between the algorithms. The only test function that shared these properties, for which RCQEA was competitive was Goldstein Price. For each test function, the GA tended to be heavily outperformed by either RCQEA or one of the bQIEAs. The exceptions were *Michalewicz 10* and *Schwefel*, where the GA produced the only successes.

The presented new algorithms vQEAd, LSNQEA, HSNQEA and HSNQEAd, did outperform the original oQEA or vQEA algorithms on occasion. Mostly this was when looking at the single best configuration. When summing across all configurations, the best bQIEA was always an oQEA variant except for the *Ackley* (HSNQEA), *Sum and product* (vQEA), and *Rosenbrock 5* (vQEAd). The very best bQIEA variant, when summed across all configurations, was oQEA with immigration, with 12 top performances. The next best was the other two oQEA variants which jointly achieved two top performances.

When taking the single best configuration, oQEA with immigration and plain vQEAd achieved the best performances (for the bQIEA) with four hits each. However, all algorithms were top performers for at least one test function with one or more of their variants. Looking at both the summed configuration performances, and single best configuration performances, the presented new algorithms did have successes, but mostly for their single best configuration. This suggests they are more configuration sensitive than the competing algorithms. When summed across all configurations, there were times when one of them was the best bQIEA, and there were times when one or more of them outperformed RCQEA and GA, but they could never outperform all the other algorithms at the same time.

5.3 Discussion

The RCQIEA was the best overall performer. When generalising across all population size configurations, it found acceptable solutions for all but two of the test functions, outperforming the other algorithms. It particularly excelled for test functions where there was a big variation in performance across the algorithms. When the algorithm performances were similar, and especially when the fitness landscape was quite flat around the global minimum, the bQIEA often produced the best results. Overall, these results suggest RCQIEA is better at finding minima, but possibly has some convergence issues, when compared to bQIEA. However, across all the test-functions, several of the tested algorithms had their moments of success.

One other issue to consider is how much the real variants of QIEAs continue to effectively follow the quantum computing metaphor. The Qbit inspiration is inherently binary in nature, but in RCQIEA, a string of these bits is replaced with a single real value. By producing a set of alternative candidates through neighbour selection, RCQIEA has an equivalent to the sampling procedure of the bQIEA. Nevertheless, there is an underlying real value which also represents the best solution found for that dimension. In bQIEAs the Qbits are simply a probability specification for generating more sampled values. For RCQIEA, the procedure can be likened to Simulated Annealing, where the rotation gate metaphor gives a method for controlling neighbour selection, by changing the variance of the distribution used in a mutation operator. In contrast, the Qbits for bQIEAs partition to search space of each dimension. The probability values for each Qbit have the effect of both localising and reducing the variance of the search for each binary partition.

For bQIEAs then, there is a natural convergence to some solution as the probability values become more saturated towards zero or one for each of the bits. This may suggest why RCQIEA was more successful in multi-modal tests, where other algorithms struggled. The bQIEA may have prematurely converged to local minima, but when the search area around the global minimum was quite flat, the bQIEA often performed well (with respect to RCQIEA). Local convergence for bQIEA was expected to be poor because of premature convergence of the least significant bits. Although the results for the *Shekel* functions support this, the plain oQEA algorithm still performed remarkably well. The newly presented algorithms LSNQEA, HSNQEA, and HSNQEAd did directly address LSB convergence, and did have some successes when compared to the other algorithms. However, overall they were not as successful as oQEA. It may be that they replace premature convergence with difficulty to converge. This is supported by the less aggressive HSNQEA and HSNQEAd algorithms slightly outperforming LSNQEA.

The presented modification of immigration was very beneficial and for both finding the best solution across the entire investigation, and the success rates, immigration improved the oQEA consistency, reflected in higher figures when summarising across the population configurations. For the best solo configuration, the picture was mixed but for some test functions immigration was also beneficial (occasionally for HSNQEAd). In contrast, mutation provided little added benefit.

6 Conclusion and Future Work

In summary, this investigation demonstrates that bQIEA can be successfully applied to real-value problems, often outperforming a standard GA (Fig. 3). In general, RCQIEA, which was designed for real-value problems, produced better results and rarely disappointing performances, in addition to the faster computing of each function evaluation. However, for those interested in exploring the quantum computing metaphor for optimisation, and perhaps implementation in a quantum computer, the bQIEA are a truer reflection of the original inspiring quantum principles, especially with regard to the Qbit implementation.

To improve bQIEA performance, we recommend the addition of immigration. The scheme used here was very simple, so it is feasible that alternative versions may perform even better. The presented schemes that directly addressed premature LSB convergence did not outperform the other algorithms often enough to be worthwhile. Looking at the results as a whole, it would appear that the bQIEA are quite sensitive to the exploration/exploitation balancing, and that simpler strategies, such as immigration, are useful to add to the original oQEA algorithm.

Finally, it is our intention, in future work, to examine modifications to the RCQIEA, in order to improve upon those areas for which it did not perform as well as some of the other algorithms. Such modifications may include optimizing the algorithm parameters, modifications to the algorithm itself, and combining it with another strategy for a hybrid approach.

References

1. Han, K.-H., Kim, J.-H.: Quantum-inspired evolutionary algorithm for a class of combinatorial optimization. IEEE Trans. Evol. Comput. **6**, 580–593 (2002)
2. Platel, M.D., Schliebs, S., Kasabov, N.: Quantum-inspired evolutionary algorithm: a multimodel EDA. IEEE Trans. Evol. Comput. **13**, 1218–1232 (2009)
3. Zhang, Q., Muhlenbein, H.: On the convergence of a class of estimation of distribution algorithms. IEEE Trans. Evol. Comput. **8**(2), 127–136 (2004)
4. Chaoyong, Q., Yongjuan, L., Jianguo, Z.: A real-coded quantum-inspired evolutionary algorithm for global numerical optimization. In: IEEE Conference on Presented at the Cybernetics and Intelligent Systems 2008, pp. 1160–1164 (2008)
5. Tu, Z., Lu, Y.: Corrections to "a robust stochastic genetic algorithm (StGA) for global numerical optimization". IEEE Trans. on Evol. Comput. **12**, 781 (2008)

6. Zhang, G., Rong, H.: Real-observation quantum-inspired evolutionary algorithm for a class of numerical optimization Problems. In: Shi, Y., van Albada, G.D., Dongarra, J., Sloot, P.M. (eds.) ICCS 2007, Part IV. LNCS, vol. 4490, pp. 989–996. Springer, Heidelberg (2007)

7. Babu, G.S., Das, D.B., Patvardhan, C.: Real-parameter quantum evolutionary algorithm for economic load dispatch. Gener. Transm. Distrib. IET **2**, 22–31 (2008)

8. Zhang, R., Gao, H.: Real-coded Quantum evolutionary algorithm for complex functions with high-dimension. In: International Conference on Mechatronics and Automation, ICMA 2007, pp. 2974–2979 (2007)

9. Hossain, M.A., Hossain, M.K., Hashem, M.M.A.: A generalized hybrid real-coded quantum evolutionary algorithm based on particle swarm theory with arithmetic crossover. Int. J. Comput. Sci. Inf. Technol. **2**(4), 172–187 (2010)

10. Xiao, J., Xu, J., Chen, Z., Zhang, K., Pan, L.: A hybrid quantum chaotic swarm evolutionary algorithm for DNA encoding. Comput. Math Appl. **57**(11–12), 1949–1958 (2009)

11. Grosan, C., Abraham, A.: Evolutionary algorithms. In: Grosan, C., Abraham, A. (eds.) Intelligent Systems. ISRL, vol. 17, pp. 345–386. Springer, Heidelberg (2011)

12. Georgieva, A., Jordanov, I.: A hybrid meta-heuristic for global optimisation using low-discrepancy sequences of points. Comput. Oper. Res. **37**(3), 456–469 (2010)

A Modified Wind Driven Optimization Model for Global Continuous Optimization

Abdennour Boulesnane[1,2(✉)] and Souham Meshoul[1]

[1] Computer Science Department, Constantine 2 University, Constantine, Algeria
abdennour.boulesnane@gmail.com,
souham.meshoul@univ-constantine2.dz
[2] MISC Laboratory, Constantine 2 University, Constantine, Algeria

Abstract. Metaheuristics have been proposed as an alternative to mathematical optimization methods to address non convex problems involving large search spaces. Within this context a new promising metaheuristic inspired from earth atmosphere phenomena and termed as Wind Driven Optimization (WDO) has been developed by Bayraktar. WDO has been successfully applied to solve continuous optimization problems. However it requires tuning several parameters and it may lead to premature convergence. In this paper the basic WDO is modified in a way to improve the search capabilities of the algorithm and to reduce the number of tunable parameters. In the proposed variant of WDO, the original model equation is modified by introducing a pressure based term to replace the rank based term. Furthermore, the value of the gravitational term is automatically and adaptively set. The performance of the proposed modified WDO has been assessed using several benchmarks in numerical optimization. The obtained results show that the modified WDO outperforms the original WDO in most test problems from both accuracy and robustness.

Keywords: Global optimization · Wind driven optimization · Continuous optimization · Hybrid-metaheuristic

1 Introduction

Optimization problems are ubiquitous. Most real world problems in various fields such as engineering, communication systems, control systems design among many others are concerned with maximizing some profit/utility function and or minimizing some cost/loss function. Basically, an optimization problem can be defined by a set of decision variables, one or many objective functions and some constraint functions. Solving an optimization problem can be viewed as the task that aims at finding the values of the decision variables that optimize (maximize or minimize) the objective function while satisfying the problem constraints if any. Several variants of optimization problems can be defined depending on the type of decision variables (discrete/continuous), the number of the objective functions (one/many) and the type of the problem functions (linear/nonlinear). The problem can be as well constrained or unconstrained depending on whether some constraints need to be satisfied. This variety of problems has been translated into a plethora of optimization methods proposed in the

E. Onieva et al. (Eds.): HAIS 2015, LNAI 9121, pp. 294–304, 2015.
DOI: 10.1007/978-3-319-19644-2_25

literature. A comprehensive review can be found in [1]. Traditional methods proposed for mathematical optimization such as linear and nonlinear programming succeeded in solving efficiently some classes of problems. However, they cannot be applied to all kinds of problems and they are not appropriate when large search spaces are involved. These limitations have guided research toward nature-inspired meta-heuristics for global optimization in order to solve non-convex problems in high dimensional spaces.

Many natural biological and naturel systems have served as inspiration sources for this purpose among which genetics, the bird flocking behavior and the ant's foraging behavior leading to a variety of search strategies to define various variants of genetic algorithms (GAs) [2, 3], particle swarm optimization (PSO) [4] and Ant colony optimization (ACO) [5] and others. A good review about these metaheuristics can be found in [6]. Despite the large number of these optimization methods, there is still a need to achieve a good balance between the exploration and the exploitation of the search abilities in order to prevent premature convergence and to improve the outcomes of the algorithms in terms of accuracy and robustness. None of the developed optimization metaheuristics has been shown to be the best for all kinds of problems and with respect to all these requirements. Given these challenges, research efforts are spent towards either developing hybrid methods to get benefit from the merits of each of these methods or towards developing novel metaheuristics.

Joining these research direction, a new metaheuristic inspired from earth atmosphere phenomena and termed as Wind Driven Optimization (WDO) has been developed by Bayraktar to solve electromagnetic problems. As the name suggests, the dynamics of wind and more precisely the motion of air parcels in the earth atmosphere has been translated into a computational model to explore the search space of an optimization problem. Like PSO, air parcels in WDO are abstracted as particles defined by a position vector and a velocity vector. Particles undergo an iterative optimization process during which velocities and positions are updated. The difference with PSO lies in the equation that governs the update of velocities and that is derived from the physical model. From this physical model four forces have been abstracted and translated into terms in the WDO model namely the pressure gradient force, the gravitational force, the friction force and the Coriolis force. The pressure at each air parcel is related to the quality of the solution. WDO has been successfully applied in electromagnetics field and extended to dynamic optimization [9].

However, WDO suffers from two shortcomings: it is easy to be trapped in local optima and five parameters need to be set besides the swarm size. In this paper, a modified version of WDO is proposed, termed as Modified Wind Driven Optimization (MWDO) to improve the performance of the basic WDO by addressing both issues. We propose reducing the number of tunable parameters by automatically and adaptively setting the gravitational parameter. Furthermore, we propose introducing a pressure based term instead of a rank based term in the model equation to further enhance the search abilities of the algorithm.

The rest of this paper is organized as follows: Sect. 2 presents the original WDO algorithm. The proposed Modified WDO is described in Sect. 3. Section 4 is devoted to the experimental study. Finally, conclusions and perspectives are given in Sect. 5.

2   Wind Driven Optimization Technique

Recently, a new approach to deal with multi-dimensional and multi-modal optimization problems has been proposed by Bayraktar [7] and termed as Wind Driven Optimization. As the name suggests, WDO is inspired by the earth's atmosphere in the Troposphere layer and more specifically by the contribution of wind in the equalization of horizontal imbalances in the air pressure. In his study, Bayraktar [8] used the physical equations that govern atmospheric motion. This later is generally described by the movement of air which is a consequence of pressure gradient due to temperature differences. It is observed that wind blows from a high pressure zone to low pressure zone with a velocity proportional to the pressure gradient force. In addition to this force, there are three other major forces that cause the movement of the wind in a certain direction or deflect it from its path, including: the friction force, the gravitational force which becomes in N-dimensional space an attractive force that pulls towards the origin of the coordinate system and the Coriolis force that is caused by the rotation of the earth, and deflects the path of the wind from one dimension to another, in WDO, it is implemented as a motion in one dimension that affects the velocity in another. Particles in WDO refer to small air parcels that are assumed dimensionless and weightless for simplification. The trajectories of these parcels are defined according to the Newton's second law of motion. The pressure at each air parcel is used as information about the related solution quality. Updating positions and velocities of air parcels is governed by the following equations where the variable i refers to the particle and the variable t to iteration [8].

$$u_{t+1}^i = (1 - \alpha)u_t^i - gx_t^i + \left(RT\left|\frac{1}{r} - 1\right|(x_{opt} - x_t^i)\right) + \left(\frac{cu_t^{other\ dim}}{r}\right) \qquad (1)$$

$$x_{t+1}^i = x_t^i + u_{t+1}^i \qquad (2)$$

where u_t^i and u_{t+1}^i are the current and the new velocity of the air parcel respectively, x_{opt} is the global best position, x_t^i and x_{t+1}^i are the current and the new positions of the air parcel, parameters α, g, R, and T are related respectively to the friction coefficient, gravity, universal gas constant and temperature in the physical model. The variable r represents the rank of the air parcel where all air parcels are ranked in descending order based on their pressure. An in-depth description WDO is available at [8].

Like Particle Swarm Optimization (PSO) [4], these air parcels are described by a position and a velocity that refer to a candidate solution and the amount of position displacement respectively. However, WDO exploits additional terms in the velocity update equation such as gravitation and Coriolis forces (the second and the fourth terms respectively).The gravitational force provides a helping perturbation at air parcels to prevent them from being trapped at the boundary for long periods of time and to pull them back into the search space. On the other hand, in the Coriolis force, a dimension of a given air particle is influenced by a different dimension of another population member. Therefore, the WDO model equations can be viewed as an abstraction of these forces. WDO has been designed for continuous optimization problems where real valued decision variables need to be optimized over an objective function.

3 Proposed Modified Wind Driven Optimization

WDO is a promising approach to solve optimization problems and we believe that the improvement of the abstraction of the physical model it is inspired from has great potential to lead to effective search strategies. WDO algorithm has some demerits that may affect his performance. The first one is related to the number of parameters $[\alpha, g, c, RT]$ to set as shown on Eq. (1). There is no general rule for their setting which problem specific. The second shortcoming is that the representation of the pressure in the velocity update equation using a rank based term can be particularly inappropriate in some cases where the number of particles large which will negatively influence the fourth term (the Coriolis force) in Eq. (1). Moreover, the gravitational force is defined as the force pulling an air parcel from its current location towards the center of the coordinate system [8], which can cause a premature convergence if a local optimum is located at the center of the coordinate system. Otherwise, this force can influence the rapidity of convergence by making unnecessary perturbation. By addressing these issues, we propose MWDO a variant of WDO.

Our motivation is that in nature several factors influence the atmospheric pressure such as temperature, humidity and altitude. These factors impact raising and lowering the air pressure according to the spatial distribution and topography on the surface of the earth. This leads to the formation of high pressure regions and low pressure regions and the gradient of the pressure force gives rise to air motion. As shown in Eq. (1) of WDO model, the influence of pressure on velocity of air parcels is not expressed in terms of actual values of pressure but is implicitly represented in the third and fourth terms by the rank of the particle among other particles based on their objective function values. By another side, it is known that altitude is inversely proportional to pressure. Moreover, one natural way to establish analogy between optimization and atmospheric models is to relate altitude to objective function. Therefore, the matter is how to express in a convenient manner the relationship between pressure and objective function. In [10], Chao et al. proposed a Tropical Cyclone-based Method (TCM), for solving global optimization problems with box constraints. Inspired from their work, we propose expressing the relationship between the pressure p_i of a particle i and its objective function value $f(x_i)$ as follows:

$$p_i = exp\left(-D * \frac{f(x_i) - f_{worst}}{sum}\right) \tag{3}$$

$$\text{And } sum = \sum_{j=1}^{N} (f(x_j) - f_{worst}) + (f_{best} - f_{worst}) \tag{4}$$

where f_{best} represents the best value of objective function achieved so far, $f_{worst} = \max (\max (f(x_1), \ldots, f(x_N)), f_{best})$(max: case of minimization) represents the worst value of test function achieved so far, N is the number of particles and D the problem dimension.

According to Eq. (3), a particle with a higher objective function value possesses a lower pressure, and the pressure is scaled to be 1 at x_{worst}. Therefore, in the modified WDO we propose to use the value of pressure as given by Eq. (3) instead of the rank of the particle to better reflect the influence of pressure on velocities. In other words, the optimal value of pressure and the parameter r in Eq. (1) is replaced by the parameters p_{best} and p_i respectively as shown in Eq. (5):

$$u_{t+1}^i = (1 - \alpha)u_t^i - gx_t^i + \left(RT \left| \frac{p_{best}}{p_i} - 1 \right| (x_{opt} - x_t^i) \right) + \left(\frac{cu_t^{other\ dim}}{p_i} \right) \qquad (5)$$

The optimal value of pressure p_{best} found so far, is updated iteratively according to the change in the value f_{best} as shown in Eq. (3).

It is known that, in several algorithms which implement the concept of velocity, the updated velocities of each particle are limited to a maximum value per iteration, within the predefined interval $[-V_{max}, V_{max}]$, depending on the problem being solved. In our case, this maximum value will be reduced depending on the state of quality improvement. In this way, the algorithm could start with high velocity value to converge rapidly toward the global optimum. Whilst, in each time this interval reduces we will obtain more accurate values as shown in the following pseudo code:

```
for each iteration t do
    if (f_best(t-1) == f_best(t)) then
        count++;
    else
        count :=0;
    end if
    if (count==5) then // no improvement after a predefined
number of successive iterations
        new_V_max := V_max/2;
        count :=0;
    end if
end for
```

As explained previously, the presence of the gravitational force introduces perturbations into the movements of particles within the search space which can be beneficial especially in the case where these particles are trapped in a local optimum. In our model, we propose introducing this force via the gravitational parameter g when all particles converge to the same point and no improvement of objective function could occur in the future, that is formally expressed. This situation can be depicted when the sum of the difference between objective function values and f_{worst} calculated using Eq. (4) is the same in two successive iterations $(t - 1)$ and t (i.e. $sum_{t-1} = sum_t$). In this case the value of the parameter g is chosen randomly in the range $[0, 1]$. Therefore, the convergence point can be optimal, then this perturbation can improve the quality of solution. Else, this perturbation will help the algorithm to avoid undesirable cases such as the premature convergence problem.

Finally, the proposed MWDO algorithm can be outlined as follows:

```
for each particle i do
  Initialize f_best;
  Initialize population: random x_i, v_i;
  evaluate  f(x_i);
  if f(x_i) < f_best then   // Case of minimization
    f_best := f(x_i);
    x_opt := x_i;
  end if
end for
calculate p_i , p_best using (3) and (4);
Do
  for each particle i do
    Update the velocity by (5) within [-new_V_max, new_V_max];
    Update the position using (2);
    evaluate  f(x_i);
  end for
  calculate sum using (4);
  if (sum_old== sum) then
    g := rand[0,1]; // gravitational parameter
    new_V_max := V_max;
  else
    g := 0;  // gravitational parameter
    calculate p_i , p_best using (3);
  end if
  sum_old= sum;
  for each particle i do
    if f(x_i) < f_best then
      f_best := f(x_i);
      x_opt := x_i;
      p_best := p_i;
    end if
  end for
Until the stop criterion is satisfied
```

4 Experimental Study

4.1 Experimental Settings

To compare the performance of WDO vs MWDO, six benchmark test functions are used in our experiments as described in Table 1 namely Sphere, Trid10, Ackley, Michalewicz, Shubert and Easom. The dimension of the problem, the range of decision variables and the known optimal solutions for each test function are given on Table 2.

The values of the common parameters used in each algorithm such as swarm size and maximum number of iterations were chosen to be the same. Swarm size was set to 100 and maximum number of iterations was set to 1000.

Table 1. Benchmark functions used in experimental study.

Function	Description
Sphere	$F_{SPH}(x) = \sum_{i=1}^{N} (x_i - 5)^2$
Trid10	$F_{TRI}(x) = \sum_{i=1}^{N} (x_i - 1)^2 - \sum_{i=2}^{N} x_i x_{i-1}$
Ackley	$F_{ACK}(x) = 20 + e - 20\exp\left(-0.2\sqrt{\frac{1}{N}\sum_{i=1}^{N}(x_i - 5)^2}\right)$ $- \exp\left(\frac{1}{N}\sum_{i=1}^{N}\cos(2\pi(x_i - 5))\right)$
Michalewicz	$F_{MCH}(x) = -\sum_{i=1}^{N}\left(\sin(x_i)(\sin(ix_i^2/\pi))^{2m}\right)$ $m = 10$
Shubert	$F_{SHU}(x) = \left(\sum_{i=1}^{5} (i\cos((i+1)x_1 + i))\right)$ $\left(\sum_{i=1}^{5} (i\cos((i+1)x_2 + i))\right)$
Easom	$F_{ESM}(x) = -\cos(x_1)\cos(x_2)\exp(-(x_1 - \pi)^2 - (x_2 - \pi)^2)$

The other specific parameters α, g, c, RT and V_{max} have been set as follows:

1. WDO: the parameters have been set as adopted in [8] to allow a fair comparison. In [8] several experiments have been performed to find the suitable values. Therefore, the values of α, g, c, RT and V_{max} are set to 0.8, 0.6, 0.7, 1.0 and 0.3 respectively.
2. MWDO: In our proposed algorithm, the experiments done to find the settings lead to the following values for α, c, RT and V_{max}. For all test functions, these parameters are set to 0.1, 0.2, 5.0 and 4 respectively.

Table 2. Initial configuration for the benchmark functions.

Function	Initialization range and dimension	Optimum value
Sphere	$x_i \in [-100, 100]$, N = 30	$F_{SPH}(x^*) = 0$
Trid10	$x_i \in [-100, 100]$, N = 10	$F_{TRI}(x^*) = -210$
Ackley	$x_i \in [-32, 32]$, N = 30	$F_{ACK}(x^*) = 0$
Michalewicz	$x_i \in [0, \pi]$, N = 10	$F_{MCH}(x^*) = -9.6602$
Shubert	$x_i \in [-10, 10]$, N = 2	$F_{SHU}(x^*) = -186.73$
Easom	$x_i \in [-100, 100]$, N = 2	$F_{ESM}(x^*) = -1$

4.2   Experimental Results

WDO and MWDO algorithms have been run 100 times. The obtained results over these runs are summarized in terms of mean value, standard deviation, worst and best values in Table 3.

As shown in Table 3, MWDO outperforms WDO in many orders of magnitude in all test functions and with regard to all statistics except for Michalewicz function where the results are close to some extent. Furthermore, the best values for each test function achieved by MWDO are close to the true optimal values reported in Table 2. This shows the good performance of MWDO regarding accuracy given the standard deviations obtained by MWDO.

For the purpose of comparison in terms of performance, Boxplot analysis is carried out for all the considered algorithms. The empirical distribution of data is efficiently represented graphically by the boxplot analysis tool [11]. The Boxplots for mean test function of all benchmark functions of MWDO and WDO are shown in Figs. 1, 2, 3, 4, 5 and 6. It is clear from these figures (except in Fig. 4) that MWDO is better than WDO as Interquartile range and Median are low for this algorithm i.e. MWDO.

Table 3. Results over 100 runs obtained by WDO and MWDO algorithms, Mean: mean of the best values, Std: standard deviation of the best values, Best: the optimal test function value, Worst: the worst test function value (best results in bold).

Function		WDO	MWDO
Sphere	Mean	4.37e+02	**2.42e-16**
	Std	8.6995322	**6.9e-17**
	Worst	637.4829	**4.7046e-15**
	Best	230.5757	**4.6e-19**
Trid10	Mean	−36.400	**−210**
	Std	2.08166251	**−210**
	Worst	−3.2193	**−210**
	Best	−93.6193	**−210**
Ackley	Mean	11.3000	**1.5710**
	Std	0.08493237	**0.1003371**
	Worst	12.9698	**3.8362**
	Best	7.8368	**1.75e-10**
Michalewicz	Mean	−5.4400	**−5.5787**
	Std	0.05427748	**0.0878379**
	Worst	−4.1168	**−3.6748**
	Best	−7.3039	**−7.8349**
Shubert	Mean	−169	**−186.7309**
	Std	3.06698850	**2.36e-05**
	Worst	−66.7568	**−186.7295**
	Best	−186.7207	**−186.7309**
Easom	Mean	−0.9510	**−1**
	Std	0.0061562	**1.041e-08**
	Worst	−0.6789	**−0,99999983**
	Best	−0.9999	**−1**

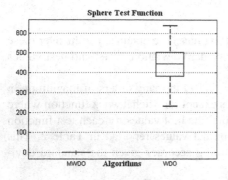

Fig. 1. Boxplot graph for Mean test function of F_{SPH}.

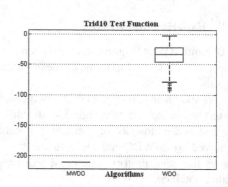

Fig. 2. Boxplot graph for Mean test function of F_{TRI}.

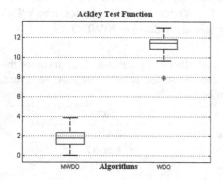

Fig. 3. Boxplot graph for Mean test function of F_{ACK}.

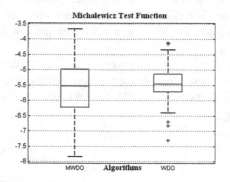

Fig. 4. Boxplot graph for Mean test function of F_{MCH}.

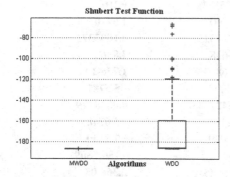

Fig. 5. Boxplot graph for Mean test function of F_{SHU}.

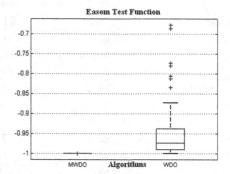

Fig. 6. Boxplot graph for Mean test function of F_{ESM}.

For testing the significance of the results (SR) the Wilcoxon Rank Sum Test was used to compare the results of the 100 test runs for MWDO and WDO algorithms. We performed the significance tests at a significance level $\delta = 0.05$. Note that here '+' indicates the significant difference (or the null hypothesis is rejected) at δ (i.e., $p < \delta$), whilst '−' implies that there is no significant difference (i.e., $p > \delta$) for each pair of algorithms. It is observed from Table 4 that significant differences observed in 5 comparisons out of 6 comparisons. Therefore, it can be concluded that results of MWDO is significantly different from the basic WDO algorithm.

Table 4. The Wilcoxon rank sum test results of comparing MWDO with WDO for different benchmark functions, where "+" means significant difference and "−" means no significant difference.

	Sphere	Trid10	Ackley	Michalewicz	Shubert	Easom
p	2.56e-34	5.64e-39	2.53e-34	0.4379	1.08e-34	1.81e-37
SR	+	+	+	−	+	+

5   Conclusion and Future Work

In this paper, a modified WDO algorithm is proposed to improve the performance of the basic WDO algorithm. The proposed algorithm introduces new terms exactly at the velocity equation to improve the quality of solution. In addition, this algorithm reduces the number of tunable parameters to simplify the basic WDO. MWDO has been shown to address properly the issues raised by the WDO model. The obtained experimental results show the significant improvements brought by our suggestions.

Future work will focus on optimizing the performance of the MWDO. In addition, extensive study of the applications in more complex practical optimization problems is necessary to fully investigate the properties and evaluate the performance of MWDO.

References

1. Chong, E., Zak, S.: An Introduction to Optimization, 3rd edn. Wiley, Hoboken (2008)
2. Xing, L., Chen, Y., Cai, H.: An intelligent genetic algorithm designed for global optimization of multi-minima functions. Appl. Math. Comput. **178**, 355–371 (2006)
3. Tsoulos, I.G.: Modifications of real code genetic algorithm for global optimization. Appl. Math. Comput. **203**, 598–607 (2008)
4. Kennedy, J.: Stereotyping: improving particle swarm performance with cluster analysis. In: Proceedings of IEEE Congress on Evolutionary Computation, pp. 1507–1512 (2000)
5. Dorigoand, M., Stutzle, T.: Ant Colony Optimization. MIT Press, Cambridge (2004)
6. Leguizamon, G., Blum, C., Alba, E.: Evolutionary computation. In: Gonzalez, T. (ed.) Handbook of Approximation Algorithms and Metaheuristics, pp. 24.1–24.X. CRC Press, Boca Raton (2007)
7. Bayraktar, Z., Komurcu, M., Werner, D.H.: Wind driven optimization (WDO): a novel nature-inspired optimization algorithm and its application in electromagnetics. In: IEEE International Symposium on Antennas and Propagation Society, pp. 1–4 (2010)

8. Bayraktar, Z., Komurcu, M., Bossard, J.A., Werner, D.H.: The wind driven optimization technique and its application in electromagnetics. IEEE Trans. Antennas Propag. **61**(5), 2745–2757 (2013)
9. Boulesnane, A., Meshoul, S.: A new multi-region modified wind driven optimization algorithm with collision avoidance for dynamic environments. In: Tan, Y., Shi, Y., Coello, C.A. (eds.) ICSI 2014, Part II. LNCS, vol. 8795, pp. 412–421. Springer, Heidelberg (2014)
10. Chao, C.W., Fang, S.C., Liao, C.J.: A Tropical Cyclone-Based Method For Global Optimization. J. Ind. Manage. Optim. **8**, 103–115 (2012)
11. Williamson, D.F., Parker, R.A., Kendrick, J.S.: The box plot: a simple visual method to interpret data. Ann. Intern. Med. **110**(11), 916 (1989)

Learning Algorithms

Input Filters Implementing Diversity
in Ensemble of Neural Networks

Eva Volna[✉], Martin Kotyrba[✉], and Vaclav Kocian

Department of Informatics and Computers,
University of Ostrava, Ostrava, Czech Republic
{eva.volna,martin.kotyrba,vaclav.kocian}@osu.cz

Abstract. This paper discusses possibilities how to use input filters to improve performance in ensemble of neural-networks-based classifiers. The proposed method is based on filtering of input vectors in the used training set, which minimize demands on data preprocessing. Our approach comes out from a technique called boosting, which is based on the principle of combining a large number of so-called weak classifiers into a strong classifier. In the experimental study, we verified that such classifiers are able to sufficiently classify the submitted data into predefined classes without knowledge of details of their significance.

Keywords: Neural networks · Input filters · Diversity of classifiers · Ensemble of classifiers

1 Introduction

Recently, ensembles of classifiers (multiple classifier systems, mixtures of experts, committees of learners, etc.) have become the most important research directions in machine learning and pattern recognition. Ensemble learning has been shown as an effective solution for classification tasks. Ensemble learning is to generate a set of base classifiers and then combine their outputs to classify new samples. An ensemble is often more accurate than any of its base classifiers. However, two main problems should be improving a good performance of ensemble: how to generate accurate and diverse base classifiers and how to choose classifiers for combine effectively.

The two most popular methods for creating ensembles are boosting [7] and bagging [1]. Both of them modify set of training examples to achieve diversity of weak learners in ensemble. There have been examined several methods to improve performance of boosting [3]. As alternative methods we can mention combining ensemble with decision tree to boost the results [10]. This method provides better performance than a single model. Ensemble techniques with neural networks are shown in [9], where ensemble technique helps to improve the efficiency of the model. The overview of existing ensemble techniques is shown in [6].

We have provided an experimental study which was aimed to explore the possibility of using neural network as the base algorithms for weak classifiers. We were inspired by the possibility of using neural networks in place of commonly used

© Springer International Publishing Switzerland 2015
E. Onieva et al. (Eds.): HAIS 2015, LNAI 9121, pp. 307–318, 2015.
DOI: 10.1007/978-3-319-19644-2_26

decision trees [10]. The main idea of our approach comes out from the idea that it is more efficient to create a number of imperfectly adapted networks, which are small in their topology than one perfectly adapted a sophisticated network. We have also proposed a sloppy neural networks adaptation, where each neural network was adapted by only one pass through the training set. We have generated experimental ensembles of weak classifiers based on various neural networks. We have proposed filtering of input as the new diversity-achieving method. We have tested this method in common with more traditional approaches.

2   Diversity in Ensemble of Classifiers

The goal of ensemble learning methods is to construct a collection (an ensemble) of individual classifiers that are diverse and yet accurate. If this can be achieved, then highly accurate classification decisions can be obtained by voting the decisions of the individual classifiers in the ensemble. A typical ensemble method for classification tasks contains the following building blocks [6]:

1. Training set. A labelled dataset used for ensemble training. The training set can be described in a variety of languages. Most frequently, the instances are described as attribute - value vectors. We use the notation A to denote the set of input attributes containing n attributes: $A = \{a_1, ..., a_i, ..., a_n\}$ and y to represent the class variable or the target attribute.
2. Base Inducer. The inducer is an induction algorithm that obtains a training set and forms a classifier that represents the generalized relationship between the input attributes and the target attribute. Let I represent an inducer. We use the notation $M = I\ (S)$ for representing a classifier M which was induced by inducer I on a training set S.
3. Diversity Generator. This component is responsible for generating the diverse classifiers.
4. Combiner. The combiner is responsible for combining the classifications of the various classifiers.

The success of an ensemble system rests on the diversity of the classifiers that make up the ensemble. The ensemble has ability to correct errors of some of its members. Each individual classifier in the ensemble system allows generating different decision boundaries. If proper diversity is achieved, a different error is made by each classifier, strategic combination of which can then reduce the total error. Figure 1 graphically illustrates this concept, where each classifier - trained on a different subset of the available training data - makes different errors (shown as instances with dark borders), but the combination of the three classifiers provides the best decision boundary.

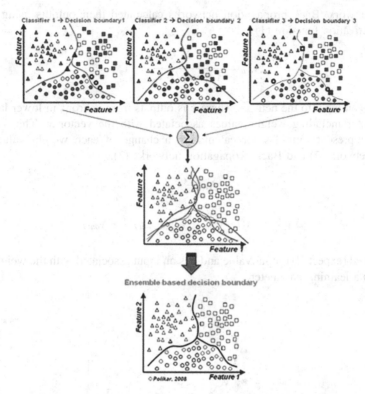

Fig. 1. Combining an ensemble of classifiers for reducing classification error (adapted from http://shareengineer.blogspot.cz/2012/09/ensemble-learning-and-model-selection.html)

3 Sloppy Adaptation of Classifiers

Sloppy adaptation of neural networks represents a method of learning in which the neural networks were not fully, nor well adapted. One of the basic properties of neural networks is the fact that a very major part of neural networks' adaptation is performed during the first pass. It was also confirmed during our experimental study. Figure 2 shows a typical evolution of a neural network error during adaptation, where the first iteration is marked in each graph. This approach uses only the power of the neural network adaptation rule in the early stages of its work and thus time is not lost due to a full adaptation of the classifier. We have utilized this property and used neural networks as generators of weak classifiers in the proposed ensemble system. For weak classifiers, their diversity is more important than their accuracy.

During the experimental study, we used two different types of networks in three configurations: a Hebbian network, a Back propagation neural network with 5 hidden neurons and a Back propagation neural network with 20 hidden neurons. All used neural networks worked with bipolar values. Formula for calculating a neuron output value (activation function) $y_{out} = \varphi(y_{in})$ is represented by identity in the case of a

Hebbian network. Back propagation networks calculated their outputs using bipolar sigmoid activation function (1):

$$y_{out} = \frac{2}{1 + \exp(-y_{in})} - 1 \qquad (1)$$

$y_{in} = \boldsymbol{x} \cdot \boldsymbol{w}$ is an input to the neuron, where $\boldsymbol{x}$ is outputs from neurons in lower layer and $\boldsymbol{w}$ is a vector including weight values associated with the vector $\boldsymbol{x}$. The following equations represent formulas for calculating a change of each weight value, i.e. a Hebbian network (2) and Back propagation networks (3).

$$\Delta w = x \cdot t \qquad (2)$$

$$\Delta w = \alpha \cdot x(t - y_{out}) \frac{1}{2}(1 + y_{out})(1 - y_{out}), \qquad (3)$$

t is a required (expected) output value and x is an input associated with the weight value w and α is a learning parameter.

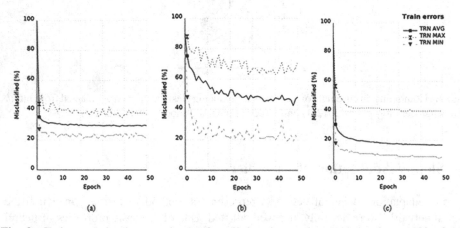

(a)   (b)   (c)

Fig. 2. Train error development in the first 50 learning cycles. Statistics from 1000 of (a) Hebbian networks; (b) Back propagation networks with 5 neurons in the hidden layer, and (c) Back propagation networks with 20 neurons in the hidden layer. The first iteration is always marked.

We tested 1000 instances of each configuration. The acquired data is plotted in graphs, see Fig. 2. They provide values from the first 50 cycles of each neural network adaptation only. We have monitored minimal, maximal and average error in each cycle. From Fig. 2, we can see that the main deal of the adaptation work is done during the first epoch of learn. This means that the neural network is adapted through one cycle only. In the first cycle, the 'exploitation' of classifier is unambiguously the highest. Back propagation network with 20 hidden neurons has achieved about 75 % successfulness in the first cycle. The graph analysis is the following:

- Almost each tested classifier has its error significantly smaller than a random classifier after the first iteration. Exceptions were related to Back propagation classifier only.
- In the next iterations, a remarkable improvement in performance of a classifier occurs for Back propagation classifier only.
- Some instances of Back propagation classifier achieve success of around 80 % in the first iteration.
- 'Constricted' form of Hebb graph implies that the diversity of the linear classifier is less than at multilayer Back propagation networks. In fact, the diversity of Hebb classifier in the basic configuration equals zero because the adaptation rule has no random parameters. In the graph in Fig. 2, we can see diversity obtained exclusively by filtering which is described further in the text.
- Sloppy adaptation works with all neural network based classifiers. The sloppy adaptation makes it possible to utilize the sophisticated Back propagation neural networks in the ensembles of classifiers. The method does not affect the classifier's algorithm. It only exploits an observed property of the Back propagation neural network.

4   The Proposed Neural-Networks-Based Classifiers

The most significant experimental part of the article focused on dealing with text (machine readable) in particular. However, we were not limited to printed text. The experiment has been conducted over the MNIST database of handwritten digits [5], MNIST database is commonly used for training various image processing systems. MNIST is also widely used for training and testing in the field of machine learning and pattern recognition methods on real-world data while spending minimal efforts on preprocessing and formatting. The reasons for testing on text data are as follows:

- Recognition, especially of handwritten text, is a very complex task and it is expected that the found procedures can be applicable to other problem domains with only slight modifications of parameters.
- Used text data can be easily obtained by scanning the original.
- Quality assessment for text classification is simple and does not require cooperation with a domain expert (as when working with inputs from technological processes). Everybody who can read the language in which the processed text is written can be considered as a domain expert.

We have used a total of five types of neural networks in the study as well as AdaBoost [7] that is a method for improving the accuracy of a learning algorithm (a.k.a. base learner). This is achieved by iteratively calling the base learner on re-sampled training data, and by combining the so-produced hypothesis functions together to form ensemble classifiers. Each ensemble always used a specific base of algorithms. In fact, generating different classifiers using random feature subsets is known as the random subspace method [5]. Just the approach we have used in our work.

4.1   Parameters of Classifiers

Here, the classifier is an alias for an instance of a neural network. A base of algorithms is a set of neural networks whose instances form the ensemble. We used neural networks only, no other types of classifiers. In total, we used five different types of neural networks. In the text we use codes N1–N5 for them. Networks N1–N4 have been single-layer, N5 has been a two-layer. All the single-layer neural networks shared a common topology shown in Fig. 3.

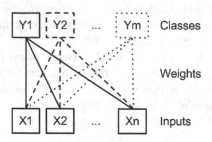

Fig. 3. Common topology of single-layer neural networks – m classifiers over n inputs.

The proposed ensembles of neural-networks-based classifiers are basically a set of m classifiers. All the m classifiers work with the same set of n inputs. Each of the m classifiers tries to learn to recognize objects of one class in the input patterns of size n. Details about the parameters of the networks are shown in Table 1.

Table 1. Parameters of classifiers used in the experiment

Type	Values	Activation function φ	Δw	Anotation
N1	Bipolar	*Identity*	$\alpha \cdot x \cdot \left(\frac{2}{1+\exp(y_{in}-t)} - 1 \right)$	modified Adaline rule
N2	Binary	$\frac{1}{1+\exp(-y_{in})}$	$\alpha \cdot x \cdot (t - y_{out})$	Delta rule
N3	Bipolar	*Identity*	$x \cdot t$	Hebb rule
N4	Bipolar	*Identity*	$\alpha \cdot x \cdot t$	Perceptron learning rule
N5	Binary	$\frac{1}{1+\exp(-y_{in})}$	$\alpha \cdot x(t - y_{out})y_{out}(1 - y_{out})$	Back propagation rule

Adaline did not perform well with the basic learning rule $\alpha x(t - y_{in})$, see [2]. We assume that the cause lays in the relatively big number of patterns and inputs and therefore possibly the big value of $(t - y_{in})$. That is, why we have normalized value of $(t - y_{in})$ by the sigmoid function.

4.2   Adaptation Strategy

Each classifier was created separately and adapted by only one pass through the training set. All the neural networks used the *winner-takes-all strategy* for output neurons $(Y_1, \ldots, Y_m)$ when they worked in the active mode [8]. So only one output neuron with the highest y_{out} value could be active. The Y_i is considered the winner if and only if $\forall j : y_j < y_i \bigvee (y_j = y_i \bigwedge i < j)$, i.e. the winner is the neuron with the highest output value y_i. In the case that more neurons have the same output value, the winner is considered the first one in the order. All these neural networks used the algorithm for an elimination of irrelevant inputs as proposed in [4]. Principles of the method are simple:

- Before adaptation, algorithm walks through the training set and identify as irrelevant all the items, whose value in all patterns is the same.
- Weights of connections related to the irrelevant items are ignored during the adaptation.
- Thanks to that, such weights remain '0'.

Algorithm that marks irrelevant items can be written as follows:

1. Mark all items as irrelevant.
2. Load input vector of the first pattern and remember values of its items.
3. Repeat with all successive patterns:
   (a)   Load input vector.
   (b)   Mark every irrelevant item as relevant in case that its actual value differs from that in the first pattern.
4. End.

For purpose of our experiment we have defined an ensemble as a group of 100 classifiers generated over the same set of algorithms with the same configuration of the generator. A total of six sets of ensembles were created. Each set of ensembles has been generated over another subset of available algorithms. One set of ensembles has been made over all available algorithms, the other five sets always used only one of the algorithms. We have used six bases of algorithms in total, see Table 1: N1 represents Adaline, N2 represents delta rule, N3 represents Hebbian network, N4 represents perceptron, N5 represents Back propagation network and the sixth base N1–N5 represents all ensembles contain 20 specific instances of a specific type.

Classifiers were generated as instances of N1–N5 algorithms during the experiment. The accuracy of each generated classifier was verified on both the test and the training set. The results achieved by each classifier were stored in a database and evaluated at the end of the experiment. Twelve different configurations have been tested within each set. Each configuration was tested 50 times in every set of ensembles.

The experiment was conducted over the data from the MNIST database [5], as was mentioned above. Therefore the training contains 60000 patterns and the testing contains 10000 patterns. Patterns are stored in the database as a 28×28 pixel images with 256 grayscale. As the examples represent digits, it is obvious, that they can be divided into 10 classes. Therefore all the tested neural networks had a total of 10 output neurons. The highest number of input neurons was $28 \times 28 = 784$. Actual number depended on the current teaching strategy (see description of proposed filters below).

The number of neurons in the hidden layer of the Back propagation network was determined experimentally.

5 Input Filters as Tools of Diversity Enhancing

In the experimental study, we try to increase diversity of classifiers using input filters. The main idea of the input filter is, that classifier 'sees' only a part of the input. It forces the classifier to focus its attention only on certain features (parts of pattern). It should increase the diversity of individual classifiers generated. Input filter is represented by a bitmap of the same size as the original pattern. Topology of classifier always reflects the current filter, i.e. the number of pixels that are visible to classifier. It implies that the topology of classifiers when using a non-blank filter is smaller than the topology of classifiers when using the original pattern. However, it is also clear that the classification of filtered patterns is less accurate because the classifier cannot see the whole pattern, but only a part of it. We have used the three modes of the input filters:

- Blank
- Random (white noise)
- Random Streak. In this mode, vertical or horizontal filter was picked-up with the same probability of 0.5.

Figure 4 shows the example of application of different filters to the pattern representing the number '8' resulting in a reduction of the size of the input vector. Pixels which are hidden by the filter (white filter pixels) are not processed. The four different filters in the figure reduce the original input vector's size by 0 %, 68 %, 75 % and 66 %.

We have used the diversity of classifiers in the ensembles as the criterion for judging the success of algorithms and configurations. Moreover, we have focused mainly on performance at the test set of patterns. We have expressed the *diversity* as the reciprocal of the count of patterns, which were not correctly classified by any of the classifiers in the ensemble. The smaller number of unrecognized patterns means the more successful ensemble as well as the more successful configuration and base of algorithms. Experiment results with the input filters are shown in Figs. 5 and 6, which present boosting results only with two very different neural networks, e.g. Hebb network and Back propagation network. As we have expected, the more classifiers was in the ensemble, the more difficult it was to find another sufficient classifier. This difficulty tended to grow exponentially fast and together with the growing training set it made the adaptation process very slow.

The effectiveness of a quality of *ensembles with and without filtering* was verified experimentally. Each calculation was run 50 times, to achieve statistically significant results. There were recorded values of the error function of neural networks, which is the squared error for all particular training patterns [2]. Figure 7 shows the influence of different filters on the ensembles behaviour. The filtering method put the ensemble's performance forward in both the average error and the generalization capabilities. We can also see that the streak filter performs significantly better than the random one. G/T (GAvg/TAvg) represents generalization capabilities of ensembles by used base algorithm. The higher value indicates the higher overfitting. So the smaller number means the

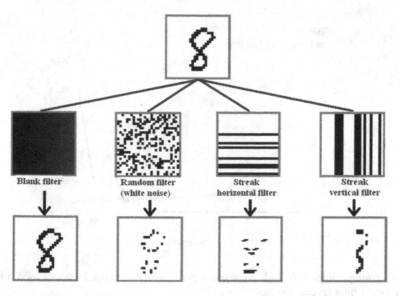

Fig. 4. Example of use of different filters on the input pattern with the image number '8'. In the top row we can see four different filter matrices, in the bottom row there are the results of the filtration (what the classifier can see). Through the blank filter (left) the original shape of the pattern is visible. Displayed filters from the left: the blank filter, the random filter, the horizontal streak filter, the vertical streak filter.

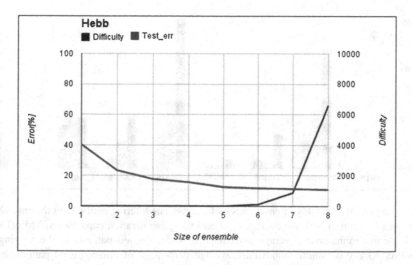

Fig. 5. Boosting results with Hebb network over a filter (average values)

higher quality of the classifier. The values of G/T > 1 indicates the typical behaviour when an ensemble performs better on the train set then on the test one. A value of 1 would indicate that the ensemble performed same on both the train and the test set. The value of

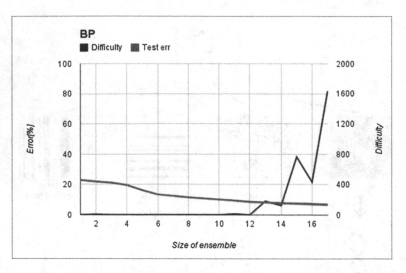

Fig. 6. Boosting results with Back propagation network; the network instances used 5 hidden neurons over a filter (average values)

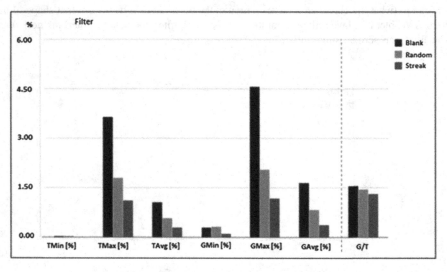

Fig. 7. Comparison of quality of ensembles by filtering. The filtering method put the ensembles' performance forward in both the average error and the generalization capabilities. TMin/TMax/ TAvg is minimum/maximum/average percentage of unrecognized patterns in the training set GMin/GMax/GAvg is minimum/maximum/average percentage of unrecognized patterns in the test set. G/T means GAvg/TAvg an error ratio.

G/T < 1 would indicate really 'intelligent' and unlike behaviour - the better performance on the test set than on the train one. If the diversity on the testing set was remarkably worse than the diversity on the training set, we have experienced over-fitting.

6 Conclusion

We have verified the statistical significance of differences between the results with and without various filtering methods during both phases of adaptation and testing. The obtained values were compared by Two tailed T-test with a significance level of $\alpha = 0.05$. Differences between *quality of ensembles with and without filtering* (ensembles are represented by their error function E) is statistically significant, therefore we can reject the null hypothesis H_o ($\mu_{with\_filtering} = \mu_{without\_filtering}$). Results representing processes of adaptation and testing belonging to ensembles with and without filtering are shown in Table 2.

Table 2. Statistical significance of the results representing processes of adaptation and generalization belonging to ensembles with and without filtering

	t-value	p-value	t-critic (2-sides)	H_o - rejection
Random filter: Adaptation - Training	7,0796	0,0000	2	Yes
Streak filter: Adaptation - Training	9,4253	0,0000	2	Yes
Random filter: Test - Generalization	6,4303	0,0000	2	Yes
Streak filter: Test - Generalization	9,5374	0,0000	2	Yes

The experimental study demonstrated that input filters increase the diversity of the neural networks. As the method reduces the size of input vector, it also increases the speed of the classifier in both the learning and the classifying. During experiments the method reduced the size of the neural networks by 0–80 % depending on used input filter (Fig. 4). It is obvious that filters can reduce accuracy of the classifier, but this fact is not vital as the classifiers are used in the boosted ensembles.

Acknowledgments. The research described here has been financially supported by University of Ostrava grant SGS17/PRF/2015. Any opinions, findings and conclusions or recommendations expressed in this material are those of the authors and do not necessarily reflect the views of the sponsors.

References

1. Breiman, L.: Bagging predictors. Mach. Learn. **24**, 123–140 (1996)
2. Fausett, L.V.: Fundamentals of Neural Networks. Prentice-Hall Inc., Englewood Cliffs (1994)
3. Iwakura, T., Okamoto, S., Asakawa, K.: An adaboost using a weak-learner generating several weak hypotheses for large training data of natural language processing. IEEJ Trans. Electron. Inf. Syst. **130**, 83–91 (2010)

4. Kocian, V., Volná, E.: Ensembles of neural-networks-based classifiers. In: Proceedings of the 18th International Conference on Soft Computing, Mendel 2012, Brno, pp. 256–261 (2012)
5. LeCun, Y., Cortes, C., Burges, C.: The MNIST Database. http://yann.lecun.com/exdb/mnist/. Accessed March 2014
6. Rokach, L.: Ensemble-based classifiers. Artif. Intell. Rev. **33**(1-2), 1–39 (2010)
7. Schapire, R.E.: A brief introduction to boosting. In: Proceedings of IJCAI 1999, pp. 1401–1406. Morgan Kaufmann Publishers Inc., San Francisco (1999)
8. Volna, E., Kocian, V., Kotyrba, M.: Boosting of neural networks over MNIST data. In: Proceedings of NCTA 2014, pp. 256–263. SCITEPRESS, Portugal (2014)
9. Wang, J., Yang, J., Li, S., Dai, Q., Xie, J.: Number image recognition based on neural network ensemble. In: Proceedings of the Third International Conference on Natural Computation, vol. 1. IEEE Computer Society (2007)
10. Yao, Y., Fu, Z., Zhao, X., Cheng, W.: Combining classifier based on decision tree. In: ICIE, 2009 WASE International Conference on Information Engineering, vol. 2, pp. 37–40 (2009)

Learning-Based Multi-agent System for Solving Combinatorial Optimization Problems: A New Architecture

Nasser Lotfi[✉] and Adnan Acan

Computer Engineering Department, Eastern Mediterranean University,
Famagusta, North Cyprus, Cyprus
{nasser.lotfi, adnan.acan}@emu.edu.tr

Abstract. Solving combinatorial optimization problems is an important challenge in all engineering applications. Researchers have been extensively solving these problems using evolutionary computations. This paper introduces a novel learning-based multi-agent system (LBMAS) in which all agents cooperate by acting on a common population and a two-stage archive containing promising fitness-based and positional-based solutions found so far. Metaheuristics as agents perform their own method individually and then share their outcomes. This way, even though individual performance may be low, collaboration of metaheuristics leads the system to reach high performance. In this system, solutions are modified by all running metaheuristics and the system learns gradually how promising metaheuristics are, in order to apply them based on their effectiveness. Finally, the performance of LBMAS is experimentally evaluated on Multiprocessor Scheduling Problem (MSP) which is an outstanding combinatorial optimization problem. Obtained results in comparison to well-known competitors show that our multi-agent system achieves better results in reasonable running times.

Keywords: Multi-agent systems · Metaheuristics · Agents · Combinatorial optimization · Multiprocessor scheduling

1 Introduction

Due to NP-complete computational complexity, solving hard combinatorial optimization problems using exhaustive search methods is not computationally feasible. Hence, metaheuristics like evolutionary algorithms are applied to reach a near optimal solution within reasonable running times. Like evolutionary algorithms, other nature- and bio-inspired metaheuristics have been developed and their success for the solution of difficult combinatorial optimization problems is demonstrated through experimental evaluations.

This paper presents a novel multi-agent system in which a number of metaheuristic agents act cooperatively through sharing their individual experiences gained individually and the overall multi-agent system favors those agents based on their performance in search for good solutions. The proposed learning-based multi-agent system (LBMAS) is supported by a two-stage external memory archive such that the first stage

© Springer International Publishing Switzerland 2015
E. Onieva et al. (Eds.): HAIS 2015, LNAI 9121, pp. 319–332, 2015.
DOI: 10.1007/978-3-319-19644-2_27

stores promising solutions based on their fitness values whereas the second stage keeps promising solutions that are apart from each other based on a defined dissimilarity measure. Individual metaheuristics act one at a time and average improvement achieved by each individual agent in fitness function is recorded. Then, to decide which metaheuristic is best to employ for the next turn, individual average improvement of each agent is taken as its fitness and the agent selection is carried out using roulette-wheel selection method. The proposed multi-agent system also contains dedicated coordination agents for data and message transfer among agents, retrieval of common population and the common archive elements, and initialization of algorithm parameters. A detailed architectural description the proposed multi-agent system is presented in Sect. 3.

The seven metaheuristics implemented within the framework of the proposed approach are Genetic Algorithms (GAs) [1], Differential Evolution (DE) [3, 4], Simulated Annealing (SA) [5], Ant Colony Optimization (ACO) [6], Great Deluge Algorithm (GDA) [7], Tabu Search (TS) [8], and the Cross Entropy (CE) [9] method. Detailed descriptions of these metaheuristics can be found in the associated references. The other four agents implemented within the proposed system are Problem Agent initializing the parameters of the input problem, Solution Pool Agent handling all transactions with the common population, Archive agent handling retrieval and update operations associated with the common two-stage archive and the Manager Agent that handles coordination and performance based employment of individual agents.

The rest of this paper is organized as follows: Sect. 2 presents a review of state-of-the-art in multi-agent systems for optimization. Section 3 introduces a detailed description of the proposed multi-agent system of metaheuristic agents. Experimental results in solving a well-known combinatorial optimization problem are given in Sect. 4. Finally, Sect. 5 covers the conclusions and the future research directions.

2   State-of-the-Art in Multi-agent Systems for Optimization

Multi-agent systems including metaheuristics as individual agents are widely used to provide cooperative frameworks for optimization. Many efforts have been done on this field and there exist some outstanding literature in this context [10, 11]. It has already been shown through several implementations that multi-agent systems with metaheuristic agents provide effective strategies for solving difficult optimization problems. Meignan et al. proposed an organizational multi-agent framework to hybridize metaheuristics algorithms [11]. Their agent metaheuristic framework (AMF) is fundamentally developed for hybridization of metaheuristic based on an organizational model. In this model, each metaheuristic is given a role among the tasks of intensification, diversification, memory and adaption. This organizational model is named as RIO (Role Interaction Organization) and an illustrative description of its architectural model is given in Fig. 1.

The authors exploited the ideas and basic concepts of adaptive memory programming (AMP) [12] developed a hybrid algorithm, called the coalition–based metaheuristic (CBM), as a multi-agent system. CBM is used for the solution of vehicle routing problem and the obtained results exhibited that even though CBM is not as good as its

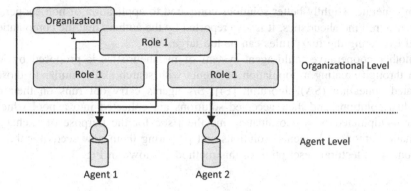

Fig. 1. The RIO model of a multi-agent system of metaheuristics proposed in [11].

competitors in terms of solution quality, it provides close to optimal solutions in significantly small computation times.

Cadenas et al. introduced a multi-agent system of cooperative metaheuristics in which each metaheuristic is implemented as an agent and they try to solve a problem in cooperation with each other. A coordinating agent monitors and modifies the behavior of other agents based on their performance in improving the solution quality [13]. Individual agents communicate using a common blackboard part of which is controlled by each agent and they record their best solution found so far on the blackboard. The blackboard is monitored by the coordinator agent to decide on the performance of agents to derive conclusions on how to modify their behavior. The coordinator agent uses a fuzzy rule from which inferences are derived based on the performance data of individual agents. A block diagram description of this multi-agent system is presented in Fig. 2.

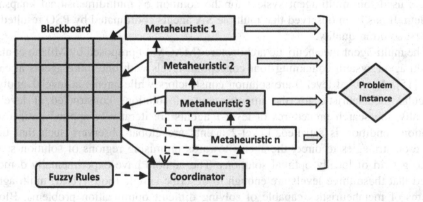

Fig. 2. The multi-agent system architecture proposed in [13].

The authors applied the above-mentioned multi-agent system for the solution 0/1 knapsack problems and experimental results showed that the proposed cooperative system generates slightly better solutions compared to application of non-cooperative nature-inspired metaheuristics. It is also reported by the authors that the computational cost of extracting the fuzzy rules can be too large.

Another cooperative multi-agent system of metaheuristics is proposed by M.E. Aydin through creating a population of agents with search skills similar to those of simulated annealing (SA) algorithm [14]. SA agents carry out runs on their own individual solutions and their accepted solutions are collected into a pool which is further manipulated by a coordinating metaheuristic for the purpose of exchanging information among SA agents' solutions and preparing them new seeds for the next iteration. Architectural description of this method is shown in Fig. 3.

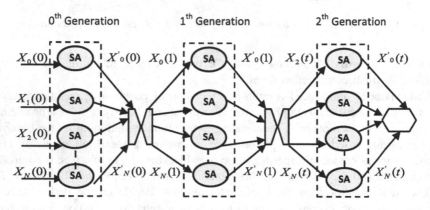

Fig. 3. Multi-agent system based on coordination of population of SA agents [14].

The coordinating metaheuristics considered in this approach are evolutionary simulated annealing, bee colony optimization, and particle swarm optimization. The authors used this multi-agent system for the solution of multidimensional knapsack problem. It has been observed that multiple SA agents coordinated by PSO resulted in the best solution quality.

The multi-agent metaheuristic architecture (MAGMA) proposed by Milano et al. is a multi-agent system containing four conceptual levels with one more agents at each level [15]. Agents at level-0 are solution constructors while agents at level-1 apply a particular metaheuristic for the improvement of solutions constructed at level-0. Basically, the search procedures of level-1 agents are iteratively applied until a termination condition is satisfied. Level-2 agents are global observers such that they decide on strategies to direct the agents towards promising regions of solution space and to get rid of locally optimal solutions. The authors have experimentally demonstrated that these three levels are enough to describe simple (non-hybrid) multi-agent systems of metaheuristics capable of solving difficult optimization problems. Block diagram description of MAGMA is given in Fig. 4.

The level-3 shown in Fig. 5 represents the presence of coordinating agents that are responsible for communication and synchronization. Implementation of this level aims the development of high-level cooperative multi-agent systems in which hybridization

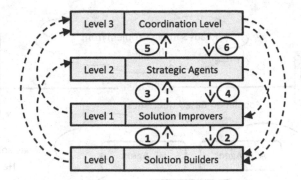

Fig. 4. Conceptual description of levels in MAGMA [15].

of multiple metaheuristics is possible. Multilevel structure and the multi-agent system organization of MAGMA allow all direct communications between all levels, however only some of them are implemented in [15]. The authors used iterated local search (ILS) within MAGMA framework for the solution MAXSAT problems with 1000 variables and 10000 clauses and their results exhibited that the resulting system achieved the best solutions with higher frequency compared to random restart ILS method.

The multi-agent system (MAS) proposed in this paper possesses novel properties compared to the above pioneering implementations. It includes several metaheuristics as problem solving agents acting on a common population and it also maintains a two-stage common archive keeping the promising solutions in fitness value and in spatial distribution. The proposed MAS approach runs in consecutive sessions and each session includes two phases: in the first phase a particular metaheuristic is selected based on its fitness value in terms of its improvements achieved in objective function value and the second phase lets the selected metaheuristic conduct its particular search procedure until some termination criteria are satisfied. In all phases and iterations of the proposed framework, all agents use the same population and archive in conducting their search procedures. This way, agents cooperate by sharing their search experiences through accumulating them in a common population and common archive. The proposed MAS includes dedicated agents to initialize parameters, retrieve data from common population and archive, and control communication and coordination of agents' activities. The resulting MAS framework is used to solve a hard combinatorial optimization problem and analysis of the obtained results showed that the objectives on the design of the proposed MAS are almost all achieved.

3   The Proposed Multi-agent System for Solving Combinatorial Optimization Problems

This section introduces the proposed learning-based multi-agent system (LBMAS) and agent interaction mechanism for solving a single objective combinatorial optimization problem, namely the multiprocessor scheduling problem. The proposed multi-agent

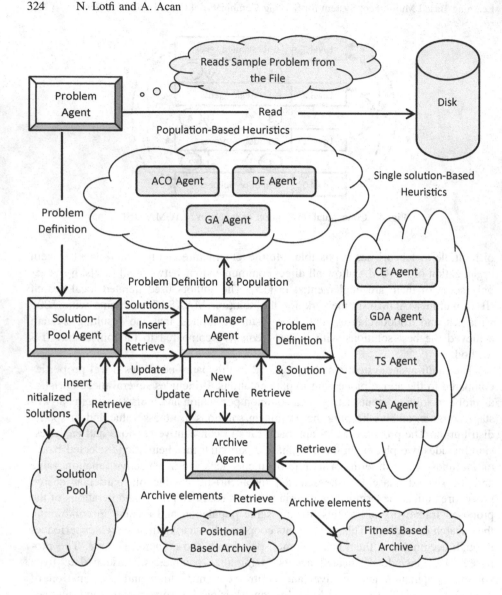

Fig. 5. Architectural description of LBMAS concerning its metaheuristic agents and the four functional agents.

system allows collaboration of metaheuristic agents over a common population and a two-stage common archive in such a way that promising solutions are searched over different regions of the search space using the currently most effective agent. In order to achieve the objectives of the proposed multi-agent system, agents responsible from initialization, data retrieval, archive management and agent coordination are also maintained within the system. Figure 5 illustrates the architectural components and functional interactions within the proposed system.

As briefly mentioned above, this multi-agent framework includes 7 metaheuristic agents and 4 system agents. When selected, each metaheuristic agent applies its own search strategy and returns its discovered solutions to the manager agent. Consequently, the manager agent distributes this data to solution pool agent and archive agent that update the common population and common archive respectively. Selection of metaheuristics is carried out using roulette-wheel selection principle where fitness values of metaheuristics are taken as their level of improvements in objective function. Initially all metaheuristics have the same rate of being selected and these improvement rates are increased or decreased based on performance of individual agents. In this respect, when the average fitness improvement achieved by particular agent is positive, its improvement rate is increased proportional to the improvement. On the other hand, if the agent's average improvement in fitness is not above a predefined percentage threshold, then its improvement rate is decreased by a constant amount. However, the improvement rates are not reduced below a lower limit. A second important component of the proposed system, that is very effective on the overall performance of the proposed system, is the two-stage external memory architecture which is first proposed in [2]. In this architecture the first level acts as a short term memory keeping the promising solutions considering their fitness values. Hence, elements of the first stage are frequently updated each time a solution better than the worst element is extracted. The second stage archive acts as a long term memory that is updated only after the first stage archive is updated for a predefined number of times. Furthermore, elements of the second stage archive are selected so that they are mutually dissimilar based on a similarity measures. In the proposed system, hamming distance is taken as similarity measure and elements of second stage archive are required to be dissimilar in at least half of their elements. This way, exploitation of promising solutions from different regions of the solution space is achieved, that is a very important issue for multimodal optimization problems.

As illustrated in Fig. 5, the seven metaheuristic agents implemented within the framework of the proposed approach are GAs, DE, SA, ACO, GDA, TS, and CE. The other four agents implemented within the proposed system are as follows: Problem Agent that handles all initialization procedures including the parameter settings, update rules, and variable ranges. Solution Pool Agent handles all transactions with the common population and associated communications with other agents. Archive agent performs retrieval and update operations associated with the common two-stage archive and the Manager Agent coordinates activities of agents and carries out the performance based selection of individual agents. Most of the critical operations for stable running of the proposed system are performed by the Manager Agent.

4 Experimental Results

This section presents experimental evaluation of the proposed method for the solution of multiprocessor scheduling problem that is a hard combinatorial optimization problem (MSP) [16, 17].

MSP is represented as a directed acyclic graph (DAG) consisting of a set of vertices and a set of directed edges between the vertices. Vertices demonstrate the parallel code partitions as tasks in which each task has its own execution time. Meanwhile, each directed edge indicates the execution order and the required time to make communication between tasks. This problem is aiming to schedule a DAG to a set of homogeneous fully connected processors. The objective is to find an optimal scheduling with minimum total completion time to run the task graph on multiprocessors [16, 17]. Figure 6 represents a sample task graph representing a particular MSP [16]. Entry and finish points of this task graph are t_0 and t_{18} respectively.

Solutions for MSP problem can be represented using simple data structure like Arrays. Figure 7 illustrates a sample solution for the task graph in Fig. 6 [27]. In this representation, processors are assigned to tasks in which t_i is assigned to p_j. Meanwhile, the tasks order should be feasible in the sense that for generating feasible solutions, they are chosen randomly among the tasks which are ready to be executed. Once a task is finished, its successors which don't have other unfinished predecessors can be added to the ready list.

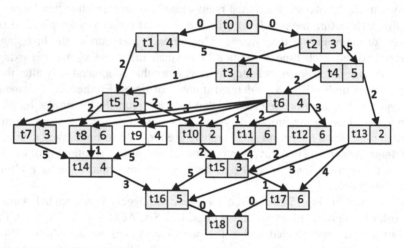

Fig. 6. A sample task graph representing a particular MSP [16].

t_0	t_2	t_3	t_1	t_4	t_5	t_6	t_{11}	t_{13}	t_{12}	t_9	t_{10}	t_8	t_7	t_{14}	t_{15}	t_{16}	t_{17}	t_{18}
p_0	p_1	p_2	p_0	p_1	p_2	p_1	p_1	p_1	p_1	p_1	p_0	p_0	p_2	p_0	p_1	p_0	p_1	p_1

Fig. 7. Solution representation for task graph in Fig. 6.

Algorithmic parameters for metaheuristics used within the proposed multi-agent system are given in Table 1. It should be noticed that, even though the metaheuristics within the multi-agent system are executed several times, they are run in small population size to reduce total computation time.

Table 2 presents completion time of the MSP mentioned in Fig. 6 using LBMAS and 6 existent deterministic methods. The computed result is compared to well-known deterministic methods including MCP [18], LAST [19], HLFET [20], ETF [21], EZ [22] and LC [23].

Table 1. Algorithmic parameters for metaheuristics.

Metaheuristic agent	Algorithm parameters
GA	|Pop| = 50, PC = 0.7, Pm = 0.1, Selection_method: Tournament Selection
ACO	|Pop| = 50, Decay-Factor = 0.1, Heuristic-Coefficient = 2.5, Local-Pheromone-Factor = 0.1, Greediness-Factor = 0.9
DE	|Pop| = 50, PC = 0.8, Pm = 0.2, CR = 0.7, F = 1.0
CE	Learning-Rate = 0.7
TS	Stopping-criteria = 200 iterations without solution change.
SA	T0 = 150, α = 0.2, Tmin = 0.1
GDA	Level = Fitness(Initial-sol), No-Improvement-Length limit= Level-Decay = (Fitnesss(Initial-sol) - Estimated_Best) /Max Iterations

Table 2. Completion time of task graph shown in Fig. 6 for all algorithms.

Algorithm	LC	EZ	HLFET	ETF	LAST	MCP	LBMAS
Completion time	39	40	41	41	43	40	39

Figure 8 presents the visual comparison of LBMAS to its competitors to provide a better quantitative evaluation.

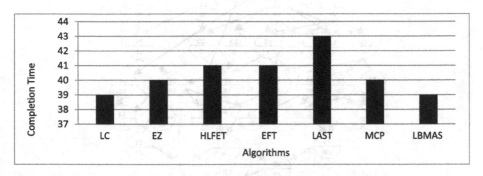

Fig. 8. Comparison of LBMAS to other deterministic algorithms.

It can be seen that, the completion time found by LBMS is 39. That means that the total running time of task graph shown in Fig. 6 over 3 multiprocessors system is 39 units. It is clearly seen that LBMAS produced better scheduling than most of its competing algorithms. In particular, identical results are obtained with LC, however, LC assumes that the number of processors is unlimited, whereas LBMAS assumes only 3 processors.

We continue the evaluation of LBMAS over two other useful benchmarks of MSP, namely Fast Fourier Transformation (FFT) and Internal Rate of Return (IRR) [24]. FFT graph has three types of edge weights, so we deal with three problems FFT1, FFT2 and FFT4. Figure 9 presents the FFT and IRR task graphs [24].

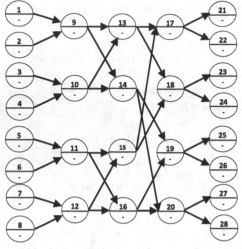

Vertex#	FFT-1	FFT-2	FFT-4
1 – 8	1	60	20
9 – 12	20	50	20
13 – 16	30	5	30
17 – 20	20	5	20
21 - 28	1	5	5

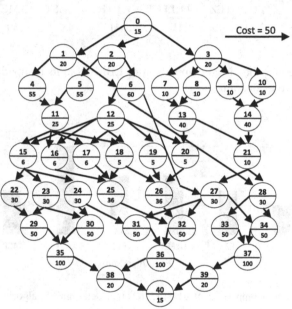

Fig. 9. FFT (Up) and IRR (Down) task graphs [24].

Table 3 shows the experimental results of LBMAS compared to two existing remarkable evolutionary methods, namely BCGA [25], CGL [26], and the MCP algorithm. LBMAS generated better scheduling for FFT and IRR graphs. In this experiment the number of processors is assumed to be four.

Also, below in Table 4 we compare LBMAS to three more competing algorithms, namely DLS [28], MH [29] and SES [30].

In Tables 3 and 4, LBMAS is evaluated upon four task graphs with certain number of nodes (Tasks) and edges. Also, the serial running time of these graphs on a single

Table 3. Completion time of applying MCP,CGL, BSGA and LBMAS on FFT and IRR graphs

Graph	Serial time	Nodes #	Edges #	MCP	CGL	BCGA	LBMAS
FFT1	296	28	32	148	152	124	124
FFT2	760	28	32	205	270	240	193
FFT4	480	28	32	710	260	255	195
IRR	1330	41	69	600	600	580	475

Table 4. Completion time of applying DLS, MH, SES and LBMAS on FFT and IRR graphs

Graph	Serial time	Nodes #	Edges #	DLS	MH	SES	LBMAS
FFT1	296	28	32	175	175	173	124
FFT2	760	28	32	275	280	255	193
IRR	1330	41	69	600	710	650	475

processor are given in the tables. It can be seen that, the completion time of scheduling discovered by LBMAS for FFT1 is 124 which is equal to BCGA and better than others. Also, LBMAS achieves better completion time for FFT2, FFT4 and IRR in comparison to all competitors. In other words, LBMAS is able to find a scheduling of IRR on a set of four processors with completion time of 475, while the total completion times found by MCP, CGL, BCGA, DLS, MH and SES are 600, 600, 580, 600, 710 and 650 respectively.

Figure 10 shows the improvement rate values for the problems FFT4 (up) and IRR (down) adjusted by LBMAS during the execution. According to the Fig. 10, TS and GA metaheuristics have larger values as improvement rates for FFT4 and IRR respectively, means that their chance to be selected is more than others. Five meta-heuristics are applied for solving multiprocessor Scheduling Problem. Improvement rate cannot be lower than 10, in order to give small chance to worst metaheuristics to be selected. This way, Roulette Wheel Selection mechanism will not cause damaging convergence.

As mentioned in previous sections, in LBMAS, metaheuristics are run several times according to their improvement rates. Metaheuristics are executed in small sizes, because they are supposed to run more times. This way, multi-agent system will be quick without any time complexity problems. Figure 11 below shows the reliability of LBMAS and demonstrates that our LBMAS obtains almost same results in 20 different runs for FFT4 graph. In this figure, the vertical axis values shows the completion time of FFT4 graph and the horizontal values indicates the run number which is totally 20 independent runs. It can be seen that in 12 runs out of 20 different runs, the system reaches to 195 and in other 8 runs the obtained value is very close to 195. Therefore, the system is reliable without any outstanding fluctuation.

Finally, below in Fig. 12, the evolution of solutions during applying metaheuristics on IRR graph is illustrated. It can be seen that the completion time of the best solution is reducing until the 475 is reached. In this figure, the vertical axis values present the completion time of IRR and the horizontal axis values show the sample number in which the total number of samples is 80. This figure shows that in the early samples the speed of evolution is outstanding and then it is gradually converged to 475.

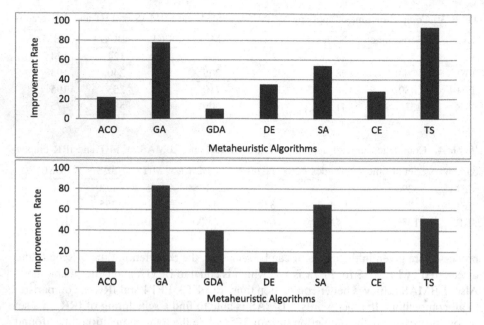

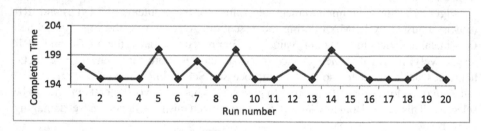

Fig. 10. Improvement rate values for FFT4 (Up) and IRR (Down).

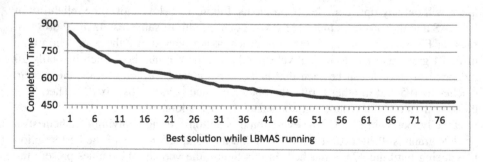

Fig. 11. Reliability of LBMAS in 20 different runs.

Fig. 12. Evolution of solutions.

5   Conclusions

This paper presents a learning-based multi-agent system (LBMAS) of metaheuristics for solving combinatorial optimization problems. Its effectiveness is tested using the well-known multiprocessor scheduling problem (MSP) in comparison to existing famous algorithms. Experimental results obtained using the proposed method exhibit good improvements and showed that the search capability achieved is better than most the competitors and is at least as good as a few of the others.

Further works are planned to use the proposed LBMAS with enhanced learning algorithms and use the resulting systems to solve other types of optimization problems. Also, we are aiming to extend our multi-agent system to deal with multi-objective optimization problems. In addition to this, LBMAS is appropriate to be implemented on parallel processor environments.

References

1. Goldberg, D.E.: Genetic Algorithms in Search, Optimization and Machine Learning. Addison-Wesley Longman Publishing Co., Boston (1989)
2. Acan, A., Unveren, A.: A two-stage memory powered Great Deluge algorithm for global optimization. J. Soft Comput. (2014)
3. Price, K.V.: An introduction to differential evolution. In: Corne, D., Dorgio, M., Glover, F., Dasgupta, D., Moscato, P., Poli, R., Price, K.V. (eds.) New Ideas in Optimization. McGraw-Hill, London (1999)
4. Storn, R., Price, K.: Differential evolution - a simple and efficient heuristic for global optimization over continuous spaces. J. Global Optim. **11**(4), 341–359 (1997)
5. Bertsimas, D., Tsitsiklis, J.: Simulated annealing. Stat. Sci. **8**(1), 10–15 (1993)
6. Dorigo, M., Caro, G.D., Lotfi, N.: The ant colony optimizationmeta-heuristic. In: Corne, D., Dorgio, M., Glover, F., Dasgupta, D., moscato, P., Poli, R., Price, K.V. (eds.) New Ideas in Optimization, pp. 11–32. McGraw-Hill, New York (1999)
7. Dueck, G.: New optimization heuristics, the great deluge algorithm and the record-to-record travel. J. Comput. Phys. **104**(1), 86–92 (1993)
8. Chelouah, R., Siarry, P.: Tabu search applied to global optimization. Eur. J. Oper. Res. **123** (2), 256–270 (2000)
9. Naeem, M., Xue. S., Lee, D.C.: Cross-entropy optimization for sensor selection problems: communications and information technology. In: ISCIT 2009, pp. 396–401, September 2009
10. Sycara, K.P.: Multi-agent systems: american association for artificial intelligence. AI Mag. **19**(2), 79–92 (1998)
11. Meignan, D., Creput, J.C., Koukam, A.: An organizational view of metaheuristics. In: Proceedings of First International Workshop on Optimization on Multi-agent Systems, pp. 77–85 (2008)
12. Taillard, E.D., Gambardella, L.M., Gendrau, M., Potvin, J.Y.: Adaptive memory programming: a unified view of metaheuristics. Eur. J. Oper. Res. **135**, 1–16 (2001)
13. Cadenas, J.M., Garrido, M.C., Munoz, E.: Construction of a cooperative metaheuristic system based on data mining and soft-computing: methodological issues. In: Proceedings of IPMU 2008, pp. 1246–1253 (2008)

14. Aydin, M.E.: Coordinating metaheuristic agents with swarm intelligence. J. Intell. Manuf. **23**(4), 991–999 (2013)
15. Milano, M., Roli, A.: MAGMA: a multi-agent architecture for metaheuristics. IEEE Trans. Syst. Man Cybern. B Cybern. **33**(2), 925–941 (2004)
16. Al-Mouhamed, M.A.: Lower bound on the number of processors and time for scheduling precedence graphs with communication costs. IEEE Trans. Softw. Eng. **16**(12), 1390–1401 (1990)
17. Wu, A.S., Yu, H., Jin, S., Lin, KCh., Schiavone, G.: An incremental genetic algorithm approach to multiprocessor scheduling. IEEE Trans. Parallel Distrib. Syst. **15**(9), 824–834 (2004)
18. Wu, M.Y.: MCP Revisited. Department of Electrical and Computer Engineering. University of New Mexico (2000)
19. Baxter, J., Patel, J.H.:The last algorithm: a heuristic-based static task allocation algorithm. In: Proceeding of International Conference on Parallel Processing, vol. 2, pp. 217–222 (1989)
20. Coffman, E.G.: Computer and Job-Shop Scheduling Theory. Wiley, New York (1976)
21. Hwang, J.J., Chow, Y.C., Anger, F.D., Lee, C.Y.: Scheduling precedence graphs in systems with inter-processor communication times. SIAM J. Comput. **18**(2), 244–257 (1989)
22. Kim, S.J., Browne, J. C.: A general approach to mapping of parallel computation upon multiprocessor architectures. In: Proceeding Of International Conference on Parallel Processing, Vol. 2 pp. 1–8 (1988)
23. Sarkar, V.: Partitioning and Scheduling Parallel Programs for Multiprocessors. MIT Press, Cambridge (1989)
24. McCreary, C.L., Khan, A.A., Thompson, J.J., McArdle, M.E.: A comparison of heuristics for scheduling dags on multiprocessors. In: Proceedings of the 8th International Parallel Processing Symposium, pp. 446–451 (1994)
25. Rinehart, M., Kianzad, V., Bhattacharyya, SH.S.: A Modular Genetic Algorithm for Scheduling Task Graphs. Department of Electrical and Computer Engineering, and Institute for Advanced Computer Studies, University of Maryland, College Park (2003)
26. Correa, R.C., Ferreira, A., Rebreyend, P.: Scheduling multiprocessor tasks with genetic algorithms. IEEE Trans. Parallel Distrib. Syst. **10**(8), 825–837 (1999)
27. Parsa, S., Lotfi, S., Lotfi, N.: An evolutionary approach to task graph scheduling. In: Beliczynski, B., Dzielinski, A., Iwanowski, M., Ribeiro, B. (eds.) ICANNGA 2007. LNCS, vol. 4431, pp. 110–119. Springer, Heidelberg (2007)
28. Sih, G.C., Lee, E.A.: Scheduling to account for inter-processor communication within interconnection-constrained processor network. In: 1990 International Conference on Parallel Processing, pp. 9–17, August 1990
29. El-Rewini, H., Lewis, T.G.: Scheduling parallel program tasks onto arbitrary target machines. J. Parallel Distrib. Comput. **9**(2), 138–153 (1990)
30. Ahmad, E., Dhodhi, M.K., Ahmad, I.: Multiprocessor scheduling by simulated evolution. J. Softw. **5**(10), 1128–1136 (2010)

A Novel Approach to Detect Single and Multiple Faults in Complex Systems Based on Soft Computing Techniques

Imtiez Fliss[✉] and Moncef Tagina

COSMOS Laboratory, National School of Computer Sciences,
Manouba University, Manouba, Tunisia
{Imtiez.Fliss,Moncef.Tagina}@ensi.rnu.tn

Abstract. To ensure complex systems reliability and to extent their life cycle, it is crucial to properly and timely correct eventual faults. In this context, this paper propose an intelligent approach to detect single and multiple faults in complex systems based on soft computing techniques. This approach is based on the combination of fuzzy logic reasoning and Artificial Fish Swarm optimization. The experiments focus on a simulation of the three-tank hydraulic system, a benchmark in the diagnosis domain.

Keywords: Fault detection · Soft computing · Fuzzy logic · Artificial fish swarm algorithm

1 Introduction

Soft Computing consists of several computing paradigms, including fuzzy logic, neural networks, and evolutionary algorithms, which can be used to produce powerful hybrid intelligent systems for solving real problems like the diagnosis of complex systems. In fact, with the spread and the omnipresence of complex systems there is a great need for more accuracy and reliability. The complex system should be inspected to properly diagnose faults and to allow timely actions to be taken to eliminate or reduce the frequency of future similar faults.

Diagnosis is the process of detecting an abnormality in the system behavior and isolating the cause or the source of this abnormality. These faults can be single (meaning that there is a unique fault in the system to monitor) or multiple (meaning that there are several faults that have simultaneous effects on variables. Essentially two cases of multiple faults can be considered:independant multiple faults and dependent multiple faults). Multiple independent faults mean that many faults are detected at a given time, and each produces a single malfunction on one component. On the other hand, multiple dependent faults mean that all detected faults are the result of the propagation of a single fault. There is necessarily a causal link between the corresponding components. It is possible to identify the original fault by browsing the associated causal link.

Several Soft computing techniques are used to produce powerful solutions to diagnose faults in complex systems [1–4]. An individual method can be excellent

© Springer International Publishing Switzerland 2015
E. Onieva et al. (Eds.): HAIS 2015, LNAI 9121, pp. 333–344, 2015.
DOI: 10.1007/978-3-319-19644-2_28

in approximate reasoning and modeling uncertainty but may not be good at learning with experiential data or may not be good at adapting in an unknown environment. Thus, a combined approach with computational intelligence techniques and their implementation is of importance for overall performance, computation cost, convenience and accuracy of diagnosis.

In this context, we propose in this paper a new approach based on synergism of fuzzy systems and Artificial Fish Swarm Algorithm to detect the presence of faults (single and multiple as well).

In fact, fuzzy reasoning [5] have attracted growing interest of researchers in various scientific and engineering areas [6–8]. The advantage of a fuzzy reasoning is that it works using approximate information and it represents knowledge in a linguistic form, which resembles human-like reasoning. For efficiency, an optimal design of membership functions is desired. Therefore, we choose Artificial Fish Swarm Algorithm [9,10] as an optimization technique to adjust the parameters of the inputs and outputs fuzzy membership functions as it is one of the best methods of optimization according to [11]. This algorithm is inspired by the collective movement of the fish and their various social behaviors. Based on a series of instinctive behaviors, the fish always try to maintain their colonies and accordingly demonstrate intelligent behaviors. This algorithm has many advantages including high convergence speed, flexibility, fault tolerance and high accuracy.

After detecting the presence of eventual faults, we display the result as a colored causal graph representing the state of system variables through a gradual colored palette from the green nominal state to the red faulty state.

This paper is organized as follows: while the second section introduce the intelligent approach that we propose, the third section is devoted to present simulation results. Finally, some concluding remarks will be made.

2   The New Intelligent Approach to Detect Faults in Complex Systems

Faults detection consists in deciding if the physical process is faulty or not regardless of disturbances. Early detection of faults in processes can help to avoid abnormal event progression and reduce productivity loss. Thus many works have be interested in faults in complex systems. Several detection approaches have been proposed: thresholds [12], Statistical Decision [13], fuzzy decision [14–16], interval model decision [17,18].

In this context, we rely on the study, we conducted in [15] and choose the fuzzy logic decision for detection step to avoid instable decisions in case of uncertainties and disturbances. In fact, it is an efficient tool for the conversion of uncertain and inaccurate information. It can take into account the uncertainties by the gradual nature of belonging to a fuzzy set. Fuzzy logic detection module consists of three phases: fuzzification, fuzzy inference and deffuzzification.

Fuzzy logic fault detection consists in interpreting the residuals by generating a value of belonging the faulty state (class Faulty) between 0 and 1 as shown in Fig. 1.

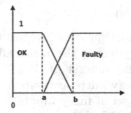

Fig. 1. Output fuzzy partitions

Where:
a: maximum value of the system variable in fault-free case.
b: minimum value of the system variable in fault case.

2.1 Fuzzification

Fuzzification module transforms the crisp inputs into fuzzy values. In fact, actual input values are mapped into fuzzy membership functions and each input's grade of membership in each membership function is evaluated. Then, these values are processed in the fuzzy domain by inference system, which, is based on the rule base provided by the Knowledge Base (KB).

The inputs of our fuzzy logic detection module are residuals which are representing the numerical evaluation of consistency indicators between recorded measures observations (system behavior). These residuals are equal to zeros in normal functioning mode, negative or positive otherwise. Thus, the linguistic set N, Z, P meaning negative, zero and positive respectively describes the inputs as shown in Fig. 2. The supports of the membership functions of the inputs are as the following: With β a domain characteristic variable which is obtained from experts' knowledge.

Symmetrical trapezoidal membership functions are used for the input fuzzy partitions. In fact, in the absence of a fault, residuals are zero, and positive or negative faults have the same importance. The symmetry also leads to a simple parametrization of the residual value fuzzy partition with only two parameters: ai1 and ai2 (instead of four) corresponding to the trapezoid boundaries.

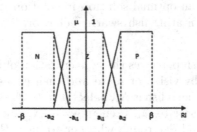

Fig. 2. Input fuzzy partitions

2.2   Fuzzy Inference System

The second step in the fuzzy logic process involves the inference of the residual values. The fuzzy inference system is the responsible for drawing conclusions from the knowledge-based fuzzy rule set of IF-THEN linguistic statements. In case of faults detector, the fuzzy inference system infers variables' states from a set of residuals. In fact, the set of fuzzy inputs (corresponding to the N Analytical Redundancy Relations) with their respective membership functions form the premise part of a fuzzy logic analysis. A fuzzy rule set (linguistic if-then statements) is then used to form "judgment" on the fuzzy inputs derived from the N residuals to get the system variables' states. All fuzzy rules are determined according to the system functioning analysis.

2.3   Defuzzification

After determining the relationship between residuals and system variable states and creating the fuzzy connections between the two, the final step is to defuzzify these sets. Defuzzification is then the process of converting the fuzzy information into crisp values. The system variable states are finally defuzzified into an index of a color map from green (normal state) to red (faulty state) and are displayed through a causal graph. The causal graph show the eventual state of each component of the system (system variables).

2.4   Optimization of Fuzzy Membership Functions

To identify fuzzy sets, we can refer to the opinion of several experts, or through statistical analysis, or by means of learning systems based on fuzzy logic [19]. However, the definition of the optimal fuzzy sets is a better manner. In this context, we choose to optimize the fuzzy sets. As it is one of the best methods of optimization among the swarm intelligence algorithms according to [11], we have chosen it to optimize the membership parameters.

The artificial fish swarm algorithm (AFSA), which was proposed in [9] and is sometimes called the artificial fish school algorithm, is loosely based on the swarming behavior of fish. In water areas, following other fish, a fish can always find food at a place where there are a lots of food, hence generally the more food, the more fish. According to this phenomenon, AFSA builds some artificial fish (AF), which search an optimal solution in solution space (the environment in which AF live) by imitating fish swarm behavior. Three basic behaviors of AF are:

1. Prey behavior: The fish perceives the concentration of food in water to determine the movement by vision or sense and then chooses the tendency. Supposed the state of artificial fish is X_i, Select a state X_j within its sensing range randomly. If X_j superior to X_i, then move to X_j; on the contrary, selected randomly state X_j and determine whether to meet the forward conditions, repeated several time, if still not satisfied forward conditions, then move one step randomly.

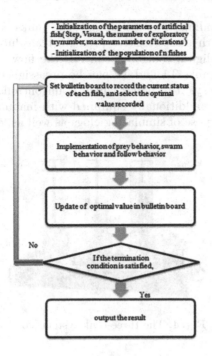

Fig. 3. Flow-Chart of the artificial fish swarm algorithm

2. Swarm behavior: The fish will assemble in groups naturally in the moving process, which is a kind of living habits in order to guarantee the existence of the colony and avoid dangers.
3. Follow behavior: In the moving process of the fish swarm, when a single fish or several fish find food, the neighborhood partners will trail and reach the food quickly.

The structure of artificial fish swarm algorithm can be described as given in Fig. 3.

3   Validation of the Proposed Approach

To validate the proposed approach, we refer to the three-tank hydraulic. This system is an experimental laboratory system called DTS 200 from a benchmark designed by Amira GmbH [20].

3.1   System Presentation

The system consists, as shown in Fig. 4, of three plexiglass cylinders T1, T2 and T3 with the cross-sectional area A which are interconnected in series by two connecting pipes. The liquid (distilled water) leaving T2 is collected in a reservoir from which pumps 1 and 2 supply the tanks T1 and T2. All three tanks are equipped with piezo-resistive pressure transducer for measuring the level of the liquid. A digital controller controls the flow rate Q1 and Q2 such that the levels in the tanks T1 and T2 can be preassigned independently. The level in tank T3 is always a response which is uncontrollable. The connecting pipes and the tanks are additionally equipped with manually adjustable valves and outlets for the purpose of simulating clogs as well as leaks.

Fig. 4. The three-tank system [20]

The global purpose of the three- tank system is to keep a steady fluid level in the Tank 3, the one in the middle. Msf1 and Msf2, corresponding to volume flows applied to the system, are the two inputs of the process. We put five sensors: effort sensors De_1, De_2 and De_3 to measure pressure of tank1, tank3 and tank2 and flow sensors Df_1 and Df_2 measuring flow level of the valve 1 and valve 2.

3.2   System Residuals'

This step consists in calculating the residuals which are consistency indicators between recorded measures observations (system behavior) and the model behavior. To generate residuals, we use, in this work, we rely on Bond Graph modeling [21, 22]. Bond Graph is a powerful multidisciplinary tool for modeling, analysis and residual generation. The Bond Graph model of the three- tank system is the given in Fig. 5.

– Tanks and valves are modeled as fluid capacitances (C) and resistances (R) respectively.
– 0- and 1- junctions represent the common effort (i.e., pressure) and common flow (i.e., flow rate) points in the system, respectively.
– Measurement points, shown as De_i and Df_i components, are connected to junctions.

The system residuals' are the following:
R1:
$$\frac{1}{sC_1}MSf_1 - \left(1 + \frac{1}{R_1C_1s}\right)De_1 - \frac{1}{C_1s}Df_1 = 0 \,(1)$$

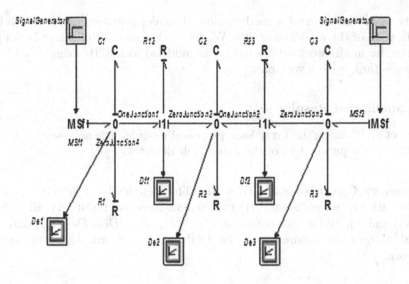

Fig. 5. The three-tank system Bond Graph model

R2:

$$\frac{1}{sC_2}Df_1 - \left(1 + \frac{1}{R_2C_2s}\right)De_2 + \frac{1}{C_2s}Df_2 = 0 \,(2)$$

R3:

$$\frac{1}{C_3s}MSf_2 - \frac{1}{C_3s}Df_2 - \left(1 + \frac{1}{R_3C_3s}\right)De_3 = 0 \,(3)$$

R4:

$$\frac{De_3 - De_2}{R_{23}} - Df_2 = 0 \,(4)$$

R5:

$$\frac{De_1 - De_2}{R_{12}} - Df_1 = 0 \,(5)$$

3.3 Experiment Choices'

Disturbance Modeling. Disturbance is an important criterion for testing the performance of detection techniques. Through our tests, we disturb the parameters R and C with a Gaussian white noise.

Fault Modeling. There are two ways to model faults. The first one assumes that faults are modeled by parasite signal inputs. This is known as additive faults. The second way assumes that faults modify the system model. This change usually takes the form of a modification of model parameters, more rarely, a modification of the model structure. We referred to as multiplicative faults [23]. We consider in our work additional faults modeled as additive signals added to the three- tank system variables.

3.4   Simulation Results

To detect faults using the fuzzy logic proposed module, it is necessary first of all to optimize the parameters of the fuzzy fault detector.

Parameters Optimization's Results. The membership functions' parameters are [ai1, ai2] for each input (in this case we have five inputs R1, R2, R3, R4 and R5) and [aj, bj] for each output Msf_1, Msf_2, De_1, De_2, De_3, Df_1 and Df_2.

Table 1 lists the parameters of the Artificial Fish Swarm Algorithm used in our work.

Table 1. The used parameters of Artificial Fish Swarm Algorithm

Population Size	120
Visual range	3.1
Initial Step	0.34
Trynumber	3
Number of Iterations	10000
ai1	[0,2]
ai2	[2,5]
aj with i $\in$ [|1 . . 5|]	[0,0.4]
bj with j $\in$ [|1 . . 7|]	[0.4,1]

After the evolution process of the Artificial Fish Swarm Algorithm, the optimal input and the output membership functions, we get are given in Figs. 6 and 7.

Once the parameters of membership functions are adjusted, we use fuzzy reasoning to determine the status of the system: normal or faulty displaying the results as a colored causal graph representing the state of the different variables through a gradual palette of colors from the green nominal state to the red faulty state.

Fuzzy Inference Results. To test the performance of the presented approach, we use a total number equal to forty faults scenarios. The considered scenarios concern: injecting single and multiple faults. For each type of injected faults, we perform a series of twenty tests. At each test scenario, we note the rate of correct

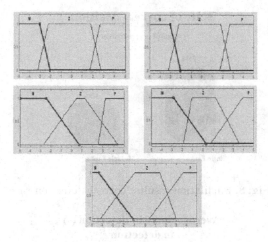

Fig. 6. The input membership functions optimized using the Artificial Fish Swarm Algorithm

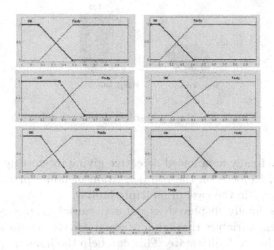

Fig. 7. The output membership functions optimized using the Artificial Fish Swarm Algorithm

decision and the delay in detection. The Simulation results we get are summed up in Figs. 8 and 9.

The detection results are interesting. In fact, in the case of the forty considered scenarios, we get the proper decision in 37/40 of cases (19/20 in case of single faults and 18/20 in case of multiple faults). The detection delay is also promising (0.46 s in case of injecting single faults and 1.23 s in case of injecting multiple faults).

The proposed approach detects faults in 95 % of single injected faults and in 90 % of multiple injected faults as presented in Fig. 8. Most variables that are

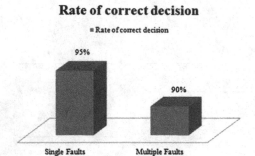

Fig. 8. Simulation results: correct detection rate

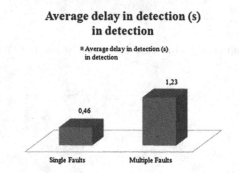

Fig. 9. Simulation results: detection delay

actually faulty are finally announced defective giving interesting proper decision rates but we need to focus on the compensation of faults presented in 10 % of incorrect diagnosing (in the case of multiple faults).

The results as finally displayed as colored causal graphs representing the state of the different variables through a gradual palette of colors from the green nominal state to the red faulty state. This can help the human operator to make the adequate corrective actions. For instance, results we get in case of injecting multiple faults on De2 and Msf2 and in the case of injecting faults in De2, Msf1 and Msf2 are given in Figs. 10 and 11:

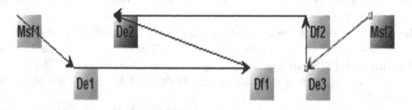

Fig. 10. Result of injecting Msf2 and De2 using the fuzzy fault detection module

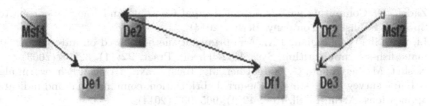

Fig. 11. Result of injecting Msf1, Msf2 and De2 using the fuzzy fault detection module

4   Conclusion

Hybrid intelligent systems that combine several soft computing techniques are needed due to the complexity and high dimensionality of real-world problems. We considered in this paper the case of fault detection problem. We proposed a new hybrid intelligent approach to detect single and multiple faults in complex systems. The proposed approach is based on the combination of fuzzy logic and Artificial Fish Swarm Algorithm. In fact, fuzzy systems are efficient solution for detecting faults. The major drawback of the fuzzy logic systems is insufficient analytical technique design (like parameterizations of the membership functions). Therefore, an optimization of the proposed fuzzy detection module using Artificial Fish Swarm Algorithm is proposed in order to adjust the membership functions' parameters. Finally, a simulation of the three-tank system (a benchmark in fault diagnosis field) is made. This simulation proves that detection solution gives interesting results. Thus, we intend in future works to highlight the potential of using such a diagnosis solution for real complex systems.

References

1. Patton, R., Uppal, F., Lopez-Toribio, C.: Soft computing approaches to fault diagnosis for dynamic systems: a survey. In: 4th IFAC Symposium on Fault Detection supervision and Safety for Technical Processes, pp. 198–211 (2000)
2. Calado, J., Korbicz, J., Patan, K., Patton, R.J., Da Costa, J.S.: Soft computing approaches to fault diagnosis for dynamic systems. Eur. J. Control **7**(2), 248–286 (2001)
3. Witczak, M.: Modelling and Estimation Strategies for Fault Diagnosis of Nonlinear Systems: from Analytical to Soft Computing Approaches, vol. 354. Springer Science and Business Media, Ottawa (2007)
4. Chen, J., Patton, R.J.: Robust Model-based Fault Diagnosis for Dynamic Systems, Incorporated. Springer Publishing Company, New York (2012)
5. Yager, R.R., Zadeh, L.A.: An Introduction to Fuzzy Logic Applications in Intelligent Systems. Kluwer Academic Publishers, Norwell (1992)
6. Pourghasemi, H.R., Pradhan, B., Gokceoglu, C.: Application of fuzzy logic and analytical hierarchy process (ahp) to landslide susceptibility mapping at haraz watershed, iran. Nat. Hazards **63**(2), 965–996 (2012)
7. Berhan, E., Abraham, A.: Hierarchical fuzzy logic system for manuscript evaluation. Middle-East J. Sci. Res. **19**(9), 1235–1245 (2014)

8. Zadeh, L.: Computing with Words: Principal Concepts and Ideas, Incorporated. Springer Publishing Company, Berlin (2014)

9. Li, X.I., Shao, Z.J., Qian, J.X.: An optimizing method based on autonomous animats: fish-swarm algorithm. Syst. Eng. Theory Pract. **22**(11), 32–38 (2003)

10. Neshat, M., Sepidnam, G., Sargolzaei, M., Toosi, A.N.: Artificial fish swarm algorithm: a survey of the state-of-the-art, hybridization, combinatorial and indicative applications. Artifi. Intell. Rev. **42**(4), 965–997 (2014)

11. Neshat, M., Adeli, A., Sepidnam, G., Sargolzaei, M., Toosi, A.N.: A review of artificial fish swarm optimization methods and applications. Int. J. Smart Sens. Intell. Syst. **5**(1), 107–148 (2012)

12. Hofling, T., Isermann, R.: Fault detection based on adaptive parity equations and single-parameter tracking. Control Eng. Pract. **4**(10), 1361–1369 (1996)

13. Basseville, M.: Segmentation de signaux: introduction. Traitement du Sig. **9**(1), 115–119 (1992)

14. Frank, P., Kiupel, N.: Fuzzy supervision and application to lean production. Int. Syst. Sci. **24**(10), 1935–1944 (1993)

15. Fliss, I., Tagina, M.: Multiple faults model-based detection and localisation in complex systems. J. Decis. Syst. **20**(1), 7–31 (2011)

16. Fliss, I., Tagina, M.: Hybrid intelligent approach to diagnose multiple faults in complex systems, In: 14th International Conference on Hybrid Intelligent Systems (HIS 2014), December 14–16, 2014, Kuwait (2014)

17. Janati-Idrissi, H., Adrot, O., Ragot, J.: Residual generation for uncertain models. In: 40th Conference on Decision and control, Orlando, Etats-Unis (2001)

18. Heim, B.: Approche Ensembliste et par Logique Floue pour le diagnostic causal de procedes de raffinage. Application un pilote FCC. Ph.D. thesis, Institut Polytechnique de Grenoble (2003)

19. Albusac, J., Castro-Schez, J., Vallejo, D., Jimenez-Linares, L.: Learning maximal structure rules with pruning based on distances between fuzzy sets. In: Proceedings of the Information Processing and Management of Uncertainty in Knowledge-based Systems, IPMU, vol. 8, pp. 441–447 (2008)

20. AmiraGmbH: Amira-DTS200 Laboratory Setup Three Tank System, Bismarckstra. D-47057 Duisburg, Germany (2002)

21. Dauphin-Tanguy, G.: Les Bond Graph. Hermes Sciences Publications, Paris (2000)

22. Borutzky, W.: Bond Graph Modelling of Engineering Systems. Springer, New York (2011)

23. Gentil, S.: Supervision des Procedes Complexes. Hermes Science Publication, Paris (2007)

Using Mouse Dynamics to Assess Stress During Online Exams

Davide Carneiro[1]([⊠]), Paulo Novais[1], José Miguel Pêgo[2,3], Nuno Sousa[2,3], and José Neves[1]

[1] Algorimti Centre, University of Minho, Braga, Portugal
{dcarneiro,pjon,jneves}@di.uminho.pt
[2] School of Health Sciences, Life and Health Sciences Research Institute (ICVS),
University of Minho, Braga, Portugal
{jmpego,njcsousa}@ecsaude.uminho.pt
[3] ICVS/3B's - PT Government Associate Laboratory, Braga/Guimarães, Portugal

Abstract. Stress is a highly complex, subjective and multidimensional phenomenon. Nonetheless, it is also one of our strongest driving forces, pushing us forward and preparing our body and mind to tackle the daily challenges, independently of their nature. The duality of the effects of stress, that can have positive or negative effects, calls for approaches that can take the best out of this biological mechanism, providing means for people to cope effectively with stress. In this paper we propose an approach, based on mouse dynamics, to assess the level of stress of students during online exams. Results show that mouse dynamics change in a consistent manner as stress settles in, allowing for its estimation from the analysis of the mouse usage. This approach will allow to understand how each individual student is affected by stress, providing additional valuable information for educational institutions to efficiently adapt and improve their teaching processes.

Keywords: Stress · Human-computer interaction · e-Learning · Mouse dynamics

1 Introduction

Modern life can be often assume a frenetic rhythm, caused by competitiveness, social judgement, productivity demands, information overload and many other modern sources of pressure. This exerts a significant and constant pressure on individuals, driving them to a constant attempt to perform more and better. There are environments which constitute particularly "good" examples of this reality. The workplace, for one, is a milieu currently associated to stress, competition, demanding working conditions and even certain illnesses. The classroom is another one in which individuals, from early in their lives, are confronted with frequent evaluations of their performance and the pressure that stems from its impact on their future and from the social judgement of their peers [3].

© Springer International Publishing Switzerland 2015
E. Onieva et al. (Eds.): HAIS 2015, LNAI 9121, pp. 345–356, 2015.
DOI: 10.1007/978-3-319-19644-2_29

Higher education, in particular, is a period of the individual's educational path that is especially prone to result in added pressure [4]. It is so because it constitutes a transition period before students reach the working environment, combining the fears and the pressure of both environments. Students are subjected to increasing periods of work with a progressive focus on autonomy and continuous assessment as mandated by current educational policies. The increasing workload is perceived as stressful and commonly leads to mental disorders and perception that their cognitive performance is bellow their expected standards [5]. This is corroborated by the high prevalence of anxiety disorders among higher education students.

Assessment is a fundamental phase in the training and certification process that a higher education student is submitted to. It is also one of the strongest stress factors due to the high-stake implications in the academic progress and self-perceived image. Stress is a risk factor for anxiety and may lead to worsening of performance in assessment tasks [7,13].

This paper focuses on this kind of specific moments, which may be extremely important in the individuals' lives and, therefore, extremely stressful. Specifically, the paper discusses how a group of medical students was monitored in order to study the effect of stress/anxiety in the performance of high demand tasks. Students were monitored in terms of the efficiency of their interaction patterns with the computer, an approach that can be included in the so-called behavioural biometrics.

Results show that, in a general way, the performance of the interaction increases with stress. However, the study carried out also points out that not all students behave alike and that individual behavioural models should be developed for increased accuracy.

The main aim of this line of research is to provide additional sources of contextual information about students during evaluation tasks that can allow the educational institution to design better and more individualized teaching strategies.

The remaining of the paper is organized as follows. Section 2 briefly presents some related work on the field of Behavioral Biometrics. Section 3 details the experimental study carried out, followed by a statistical analysis of the data in Sect. 4. Section 5 details the training of classifiers for stress assessment and Sect. 5 is dedicated to the discussion of the results and the future work.

2   Related Work

Biometrics consist of the use of individual's characteristics (usually physical or physiological), generally for the purpose of user identification or access control. These characteristics include fingerprints, facial recognition, retina or iris recognition or even DNA analysis [8]. More recently research started in the so-called behavioural biometrics, which is based on behavioural traits of the individual, including interaction or movement patterns, speech rhythm or movement patterns.

A general and thorough review of behavioural biometrics, addressing several fields of applications, was conducted by Yampolskiy et al. [9]. One of the most common fields of application is for security-related purposes. Shen et al. detail a system for identifying and authenticating the user of a computer based on his usage of the mouse [10]. Other similar systems are detailed in [8]. Our own research team has developed work in the past to assess attention and fatigue from behavioural biometrics [1].

Specifically, the use of the mouse, known as Mouse Dynamics, has been used with success in numerous approaches [11,12] and has shown that it can produce a wide range of different features. In this paper we also make use of Mouse Dynamics, proposing a set of 10 different features to characterize the interaction of medical students with the computer while taking exams.

3 Study Design

The purpose of this work is to determine if increasing levels of stress on medical students have a significant effect on mouse dynamics while they participate in high stake exams using a computer. For this purpose, a group of 53 students was selected. The participation in the study did not imply any change in their routines, i.e., these students needed to perform exactly the same tasks as those not taking part in the study.

In this kind of exams, when students enter the room, they are indicated their seats. At the designated time they log in the exam platform using their personal credentials and the exam begins. During the exam, which consists mostly of single-best-answer multiple choice questions [6], students use mostly the mouse as an interaction means. When the exam ends, students are allowed to leave the room.

The collection of the interaction data is completely transparent from the point of view of the student. It is performed by a previously developed application described in [1] which runs in the background, capturing all system events related to interaction. Subsections 3.1 and 3.2 describe, respectively, the process of data collection and its transformation into useful behavioural features.

3.1 Data Collection

The data collection tool, which is installed locally in each computer, runs in the background and listens to all the system events related to the use of the mouse. As the events happen it continuously builds a log that is sent to a centralized server, allowing a posterior analysis of the data. The log includes the following events and the respective information:

– MOV, timestamp, posX, posY
  An event describing the movement of the mouse, in a given time, to coordinates (posX, posY) in the screen;

- MOUSE_DOWN, timestamp, [Left|Right], posX, posY
  This event describes the first half of a click (when the mouse button is pressed down), in a given time. It also describes which of the buttons was pressed (left or right) and the position of the mouse in that instant;
- MOUSE_UP, timestamp, [Left|Right], posX, posY
  An event similar to the previous one but describing the second part of the click, when the mouse button is released;
- MOUSE_WHEEL, timestamp, dif
  This event describes a mouse wheel scroll of amount dif, in a given time;
- KEY_DOWN, timestamp, key
  Identifies a given key from the keyboard being pressed down, at a given time;
- KEY_UP, timestamp, key
  Describes the release of a given key from the keyboard, in a given time.

The following example depicts a brief log that starts with some mouse movement (first two lines), contains a click with a little drag (lines 3–5) and ends with some more movement (last two lines).

```
MOV,    635296941683402953,  451,  195
MOV,    635296941684123025,  451,  197
MOUSE_DOWN,  635296941684443057,  Left ,  451,  199
MOV,    635296941685273140,  452,  200
MOUSE_UP,  635296941685283141,  Left ,  452,  200
MOV,    635296941685723185,  452,  203
MOV,    635296941685803193,  454,  205
```

3.2   Extraction of Behavioural Features

The individual logs build by the aforementioned application are then processed in order to compile information that can efficiently characterize the behaviour of students while interacting with the computer. This subsection details the features extracted from the logs of the students detailed in Sect. 3.2.

It is important to note that these features aim at quantifying the students' performance. Taking as example the movement of the mouse, one never moves it in a straight line between two points, there is always some degree of curve. The larger the curve, the less efficient the movement is. An interesting property of these features is that, except for mouse velocity and acceleration, an increasing value denotes a decreasing performance (e.g. longer click $\Rightarrow$ poorer performance, larger average excess of distance $\Rightarrow$ poorer performance). Concerning mouse velocity and acceleration, the relationship is not straightforward. While up to a certain point they might indicate better performance, after that point people have a smaller degree of control, i.e., less precision. For that reason, and given that the focus of this work is on assessing performance, these two features will not be considered in the data analysis.

The following features are considered:

Absolute Sum of Angles (ASA)

UNITS - degrees

This feature seeks to find how much the mouse "turned", independently of the direction to which it turned (Fig. 1(a)). In that sense, it is computed as the absolute of the value returned by function $degree(x1, y1, x2, y2, x3, y3)$, as depicted in Eq. 1.

$$rCls\_angle = \sum_{i=0}^{n-2} \mid degree(posx_i, posy_i, posx_{i+1}, posy_{i+1}, posx_{i+2}, posy_{i+2}) \mid$$

$$(1)$$

Average Distance of the Mouse to the Straight Line (ADMSL)

UNITS - pixels

This feature measures the average distance of the mouse to the straight line defined between two consecutive clicks. Let us assume two consecutive MOUSE_UP and MOUSE_DOWN events, mup and mdo, respectively in the coordinates $(x1, y1)$ and $(x2, y2)$. Let us also assume two vectors $posx$ and $posy$, of size n, holding the coordinates of the consecutive MOUSE_MOV events between mup and mdo. The sum of the distances between each position and the straight line defined by the points $(x1, y1)$ and $(x2, y2)$ is given by Eq. 2, in which $ptLineDist$ returns the distance between the specified point and the closest point on the infinitely-extended line defined by $(x1, y1)$ and $(x2, y2)$. The average distance of the mouse to the straight (Fig. 1(b)) line defined by two consecutive clicks is this given by s_dists/n.

$$s\_dists = \sum_{i=0}^{n-1} ptLineDist(posx_i, posy_i)$$

$$(2)$$

Average Excess of Distance (AED)

UNITS - pixels

This feature measures the average excess of distance that the mouse travelled between each two consecutive MOUSE_UP and MOUSE_DOWN events. Let

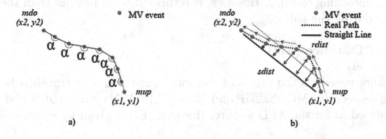

Fig. 1. (a) The sum of the angles of the mouse's movement is given by summing all the angles between each two consecutive movement vectors. (b) The average distance at which the mouse is from the shortest line between two clicks is depicted by the straight dashed line.

us assume two consecutive MOUSE_UP and MOUSE_DOWN events, mup and mdo, respectively in the coordinates $(x1, y1)$ and $(x2, y2)$. To compute this feature, first it is measured the distance in straight line between the coordinates of mup and mdo as $s\_dist = \sqrt{(x2 - x1)^2 + (y2 - y1)^2}$. Then, it is measured the distance actually travelled by the mouse by summing the distance between each two consecutive MOUSE_MV events. Let us assume two vectors $posx$ and $posy$, of size n, holding the coordinates of the consecutive MOUSE_MV events between mup and mdo. The distance actually travelled by the mouse, $real\_dist$ is given by Eq. 3. The average excess of distance between the two consecutive clicks (Fig. 2(a) is thus given by r_dist/s_dist.

Click Duration (CD)
UNITS - milliseconds
Measures the timespan between two consecutive MOUSE_UP and MOUSE_DOWN events.

Distance Between Clicks (DBC)
UNITS - pixels
Represents the total distance travelled by the mouse between two consecutive clicks, i.e., between each two consecutive MOUSE_UP and MOUSE_DOWN events. Let us assume two consecutive MOUSE_UP and MOUSE_DOWN events, mup and mdo, respectively in the coordinates $(x1, y1)$ and $(x2, y2)$. Let us also assume two vectors $posx$ and $posy$, of size n, holding the coordinates of the consecutive MOUSE_MOV events between mup and mdo. The total distance travelled by the mouse is given by Eq. 3.

$$r\_dist = \sum_{i=0}^{n-1} \sqrt{(posx_{i+1} - posx_i)^2 + (posy_{i+1} - posy_i)^2} \tag{3}$$

Distance of the Mouse to the Straight Line (DMSL)
UNITS - pixels
This feature is similar to the previous one in the sense that it will compute the s_dists between two consecutive MOUSE_UP and MOUSE_DOWN events, mup and mdo, according to Eq. 2. However, it returns this sum rather than the average value during the path.

Excess of Distance (ED)
UNITS - pixels
This feature measures the excess of distance that the mouse travelled between each two consecutive MOUSE_UP and MOUSE_DOWN events. r_dist and s_dist are computed as for the AED feature. However, ED is given by $r\_dist - s\_dist$

Mouse Acceleration (MA)
UNITS - pixels/milliseconds^2
The velocity of the mouse (in pixels/milliseconds) over the time (in milliseconds). A value of acceleration is computed for each interval defined by two consecutive

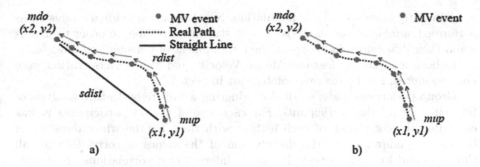

Fig. 2. (a) A series of MOV events, between two consecutive clicks of the mouse. The difference between the shortest distance (sdist) and distance actually travelled by the mouse (rdist) is depicted. (b) The real distance travelled by the mouse between each two consecutive clicks is given by summing the distances between each two consecutive MOV events.

MOUSE_UP and MOUSE_DOWN events, using the intervals and data computed for the Velocity.

Mouse Velocity (MV)
UNITS - pixels/milliseconds
The distance travelled by the mouse (in pixels) over the time (in milliseconds). The velocity is computed for each interval defined by two consecutive MOUSE_UP and MOUSE_DOWN events. Let us assume two consecutive MOUSE_UP and MOUSE_DOWN events, mup and mdo, respectively in the coordinates $(x1, y1)$ and $(x2, y2)$, that took place respectively in the instants $time_1$ and $time_2$. Let us also assume two vectors $posx$ and $posy$, of size n, holding the coordinates of the consecutive MOUSE_MOV events between mup and mdo. The velocity between the two clicks is given by $r\_dist/(time_2 - time_1)$, in which r_dist represents the distance travelled by the mouse and is given by Eq. 3.

Time Between Clicks (TBC)
UNITS - milliseconds
The timespan between two consecutive MOUSE_UP and MOUSE_DOWN events, i.e., how long did it took the individual to perform another click.

4 Data Analysis

After the collection and transformation of the data, work continued to the analysis of the collected data. The first phase of this analysis, in which statistical methods are used to obtain preliminary conclusions, is described in this section. The second phase, in which machine learning methods are used to model the students' response to stress, is described in Sect. 5.

Data was analysed in two different ways. First, a general analysis was carried out with the aim of searching for group trends, i.e., behaviours common to a significantly large slice of the population. Secondly, an individual analysis was performed, aiming at the analysis of each student at a time, in order to understand their differences and support the development of personalized models.

In both analysis the features Mouse Velocity and Mouse Acceleration were not considered, for the reasons pointed out in Sect. 3.2.

Group performance was studied conducting a feature-by-feature analysis of the data, for all the participants. For each one of the 53 participants it was computed the correlation of each feature with time, for the whole duration of the exam. Figure 3 shows the distribution of the values of correlation for all the users and for each feature. It can be inferred that correlations are mostly negative (with the exception of mouse velocity and acceleration). This provides a first hint towards the trend that most of the students increase their performance with stress.

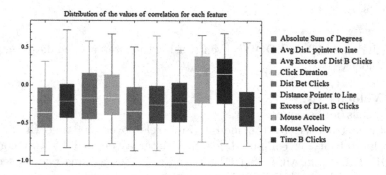

Fig. 3. Distribution of the participant's values of correlation with time, for each feature.

Indeed, most of the participants evidence this negative correlation for most of the features. Figure 4 shows the values of the features during the exam, for three arbitrary participants. It can be seen that, despite variations in the values of correlation, they are mostly negative.

Having established that performance tends to increase with time, the next step was to partition the data in intervals, so as to compare, for instance, the distributions of the first and the last interval in order to determine if there are statistically significant differences between them. Five intervals were defined, of equal length. Data from all features were divided accordingly. From this we concluded that the average value in each part tends to decrease with time for all the features (Table 1).

The last column of Table 1 shows the percentage of participants, for each feature, for whom the differences of the data between Part 1 and Part 5 are statistically significant. For this purpose, the Mann-Whitney test was used, with a p-value of 0.05.

The group analysis performed showed that a certain trend of improving performance for the group of participants can be found in the data. However, the

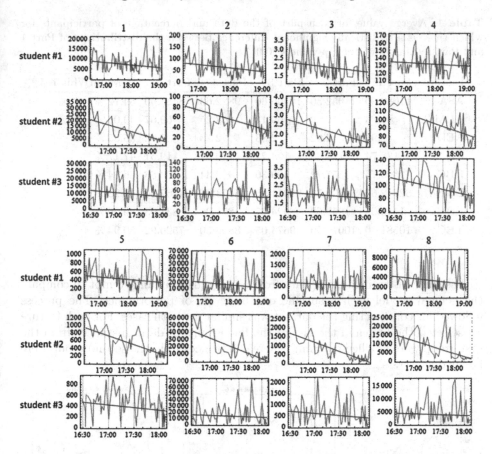

Fig. 4. Time plot of the features for three arbitrary students. The negative correlation with time is visible for all features. Lines depict three different students. Columns depict the following eight features: 1 - ASA, 2 - ADMSL, 3 - AED, 4 - CD, 5 - DBC, 6 - DMSL, 7 - ED, 8 - TBC.

collected data also shows that not all students behave alike: there are cases in which correlation is stronger/weaker and there are cases in which correlation is positive for some features.

Indeed, as the results presented further ahead show, individually trained classifiers perform better than a general one. Figure 5 details time plots for a specific student. The negative correlation in all the features is clearly visible. The values of correlation for the plots in the Figure are, respectively, -0.926177, -0.819893, -0.789006, -0.534707, -0.863852, -0.861359, -0.895728 and -0.685151.

5   Classifying Stress from the Interaction with the Mouse

The data collected and already detailed in the previous sections was used to train two classifiers. The first was trained with data from all the participants.

Table 1. Averge value for each part of the data and percentage of participants for which there is a statistically significant difference between the distributions of Part 1 and Part 5 (Mann-Whitney, p-value < 0.05).

Feature	Part 1	Part 2	Part 3	Part 4	Part 5	% MannWhit 1–5
ASA	11689.00	11052.30	10496.60	9822.63	8488.60	54.72%
ADMSL	81.93	76.02	69.13	68.25	69.67	49.06%
AED	2.99	2.92	2.83	2.73	2.82	35.85%
CD	126.74	125.85	124.21	120.92	119.51	47.17%
DBC	600.76	557.72	499.30	442.34	403.83	66.04%
DMSL	32812.60	31001.50	29811.20	25013.90	24667.60	45.28%
ED	1143.04	1052.62	924.77	871.06	831.93	49.06%
TBC	10581.80	10079.50	9674.05	8896.50	7526.92	50.94%

The second was trained using data from a single user, in an attempt to compare the general model with a specific one in terms of performance. The process followed for constructing the dataset was similar for both cases. For each feature we selected the first and the last of the five groups of data. Instances from the first group were labelled as 'calm' whereas instances from the second group were labelled as 'stress'.

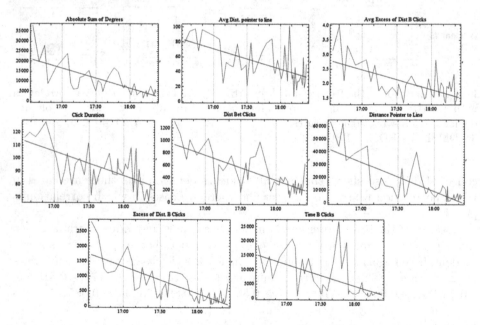

Fig. 5. Plot of the data of all features of a particular student. Negative correlations are visible. Features, from bottom to top and left to right: 1 - ASA, 2 - ADMSL, 3 - AED, 4 - CD, 5 - DBC, 6 - DMSL, 7 - ED, 8 - TBC.

The first dataset contains a total of 2438 instances whereas the second one contains a total of 162 instances. In both cases a Naive Bayes Classifier was used, with 10-fold cross-validation [2]. This is a classification algorithm that resulted from the combination of Decision Trees and Naive Bayes based algorithms. It generally outperforms these algorithms alone and tends to scale better to large databases.

The model trained with the general dataset resulted in a tree of size 13, with 7 leaves. The number of correctly classified instances amounts to 1575 (64.6 %), which is not an especially satisfying value. We must however recall that this includes data from all the students, integrating and blurring all their individual differences.

Indeed, individually trained classifiers tend to have much more satisfying results. Taking as example the case depicted in Fig. 5, the percentage of correctly classified instances rises to 86.4 % (140 out of 162 instances).

6   Discussion and Future Work

This work allows drawing some interesting conclusions about students and their behaviour during exams. First of all, it shows that stress actually influences students' interaction patterns with the computer during high-stake exams. This could open the door to the development of new approaches for assessing and managing stress, especially in the context of superior education. It also shows that it is possible to train classifiers that can carry out this task in real-time. Moreover, it is our conviction that this kind of approaches can be extended to other domains, namely the workplace. Nonetheless, this calls for the carrying out of new studies since the characteristics of these milieus are imminently different.

There are, however, many issues still to address. The first is to understand why some students improve their general performance with stress while others do not. Knowing which factors influence this might allow higher education institutions to implement individualized coping strategies with the aim to mitigate negative stress effects. This will be addressed in future work, by comparing the extensive profile of students maintained by the School of Health Sciences with the performance features.

We will also improve the training of the classifiers by selecting the most significant features only. Moreover, using clustering techniques, we will try to identify groups of students that behave alike. The main advantages that we expect from this are twofold. (1) We will be able to train group classifiers that have performances similar to the ones trained for individual students. (2) Students who are participating for the first time, for whom there is still not a model trained, can be assigned to a known group with a similar behavioural pattern, thus using the model of that group for classifying his own behaviour.

Acknowledgments. This work is part-funded by ERDF - European Regional Development Fund through the COMPETE Programme (operational programme for competitiveness) and by National Funds through the FCT (Portuguese Foundation for Science and Technology) within project FCOMP-01-0124-FEDER-028980 (PTDC/EEI-SII/1386/2012) and project PEst-OE/EEI/UI0752/2014.

References

1. Pimenta, A., Carneiro, D., Novais, P., Neves, J.: Detection of distraction and fatigue in groups through the analysis of interaction patterns with computers. In: Camacho, D., Braubach, L., Venticinque, S., Badica, C. (eds.) Intelligent Distributed Computing VIII. SCI, vol. 570, pp. 29–40. Springer, Heidelberg (2014)
2. Kohavi, R.: Scaling up the accuracy of naive-bayes classifiers: a decision-tree hybrid. In: Proceedings of the Second International Conference on Knowledge Discovery and Data Mining (1996)
3. Dyrbye, L.N., Thomas, M.R., Shanafelt, T.D.: Systematic review of depression, anxiety, and other indicators of psychological distress among US and Canadian medical students. Acad. Med. **81**(4), 354–373 (2006)
4. Goebert, D., Thompson, D., Takeshita, J., Beach, C., Bryson, P., Ephgrave, K., Kent, A., Kunkel, M., Schechter, J., Tate, J.: Depressive symptoms in medical students and residents: a multischool study. Acad. Med. **84**(2), 236–241 (2009)
5. Strous, R.D., Shoenfeld, N., Lehman, A., Wolf, A., Snyder, L., Barzilai, O.: Medical students' self-report of mental health conditions. Int. J. Med. Educ. **3**, 1 (2012)
6. Case, S.M., Swanson, D.B.: Constructing Written Test Questions for the Basic and Clinical Sciences. National Board of Medical Examiners, Philadelphia (1998)
7. McEwen, B.S.: Brain on stress: how the social environment gets under the skin. Proc. Natl. Acad. Sci. **109**, 17180–17185 (2012)
8. Jain, A.K., Ross, A., Prabhakar, S.: An introduction to biometric recognition. IEEE Trans. Circuits Syst. Video Technol. **14**(1), 4–20 (2004)
9. Yampolskiy, R.V., Govindaraju, V.: Behavioral biometric: a survey and classification. Int. J. Biometrics **1**(1), 81–113 (2008)
10. Shen, C., Cai, Z., Guan, X., Du, Y., Maxion, R.A.: User authentication through mouse dynamics. IEEE - Inf. Forensics Secur. **8**(1), 16–30 (2013)
11. Ahmedand, A.A.E., Traore, I.: Anomaly intrusion detection based on biometrics. In: Proceedings of IEEE Information Assurance Workshop, pp. 452–453, West Point (2005)
12. Aksari, Y., Artuner, H.: Active authentication by mouse movements. In: Proceedings of 24th International Symposium on Computer and Information Science, pp. 571–574, Guzelyurt (2009)
13. Soares, J.M., Sampaio, A., Ferreira, L.M., Santos, N.C., Marques, F., Palha, J.A., Cerqueira, J.J., Sousa, N.: Stress-induced changes in human decision-making are reversible. Transl. psychiatry **2**(7), e131 (2012)

Modeling Users Emotional State for an Enhanced Human-Machine Interaction

David Griol$^{(\boxtimes)}$ and José Manuel Molina

Computer Science Department, Carlos III University of Madrid,
Avda. de la Universidad, 30, 28911 Leganés, Spain
{david.griol,josemanuel.molina}@uc3m.es

Abstract. Spoken conversational agents have been proposed to enable a more natural and intuitive interaction with the environment and human-computer interfaces. In this paper, we propose a framework to model the user's emotional state during the dialog and adapt the dialog model dynamically, thus developing more efficient, adapted, and usable conversational agents. We have evaluated our proposal developing a user-adapted agent that facilitates touristic information, and provide a detailed discussion of the positive influence of our proposal in the success of the interaction, the information and services provided, as well as the perceived quality.

Keywords: Conversational agents · Spoken interaction · User modeling · Emotion recognition · Adaptation

1 Introduction

As an attempt to enhance and ease human-computer interaction, in the last years there has been an increasing interest in simulating human-to-human communication, employing spoken conversational agents [1]. A conversational agent is an automatic system that engages the user in a dialog that aims to be similar to that between humans.

Speech and natural language technologies allow users to access applications in which traditional input interfaces cannot be used (e.g. in-car applications, access for disabled persons, etc.). Also speech-based interfaces work seamlessly with small devices and allow users to easily invoke local applications or access remote information.

In human conversation, speakers adapt their message and the way they convey it to their interlocutors and to the context in which the dialog takes place. Most studies in the literature focus only on external context, one of the most popular is location information [2]. However, external and users internal context are intimately related, as it happens in representative examples like service context and proactive systems [3]. In addition, although much work emphasize the importance of taking into account context information not only to solve the tasks presented to the conversational agent by the user, but also to enhance the system

© Springer International Publishing Switzerland 2015
E. Onieva et al. (Eds.): HAIS 2015, LNAI 9121, pp. 357–368, 2015.
DOI: 10.1007/978-3-319-19644-2_30

performance in the communication task, this information is not usually considered when designing a dialog model [4].

In this paper, we propose a method for modeling users emotional state and then integrate this valuable information in the dialog management process to decide the next system response. To do so, we propose a user emotional state prediction module that can be easily incorporated in the architecture of a conversational agent. The information provided by this recognizer is considered as an additional input for the dialog manager of the conversational agent.

This way, depending on the user's emotional state, the system can inform the user about the anticipated benefits of changing, sets goals for the user to achieve, or suggests solutions to overcome barriers to prevent relapse. Our proposal reduces the computational cost required by other proposal in the state of the art by recognizing negative emotions that might discourage users from employing the system again or even lead them to abort an ongoing dialog.

We also describe the practical application of our proposal for the development of the *Enjoy Your City* information system, which provides context-aware tourist information. We have evaluated the developed system and assessed the influence of the predicted user emotional state in the quality of the acquired dialogs and the information provided. The results of this evaluation show that the users emotional state prediction improves system performance as well as its perceived quality.

After this introduction, the remainder of the paper is organized as follows. Section 2 describes existing approaches for the recognition of emotions and the development of affective systems. Section 3 describes the proposed methodology to model users emotional state. Section 4 describes the practical application of our proposal to the *Enjoy Your City* system. This section also presents and discuss the results of the evaluation of this practical application. Section 5 presents the conclusions and suggests some future work guidelines.

2   State of the Art

Although emotion is receiving increasing attention from the dialog systems community, most research described in the literature is devoted exclusively to emotion recognition. For example, a comprehensive and updated review can be found in [5].

In this area, emotion has been used for several purposes, as summarized in the taxonomy of applications proposed by [6]. In some application domains, it is fundamental to recognize the affective state of the user to adapt the systems behavior. For example, in emergency services [7] or intelligent tutors [8], it is necessary to know the user emotional state to calm them down, or to encourage them in learning activities. For other applications domains, it can also play an important role in order to solve stages of the dialog that cause negative emotional states, avoid them and foster positive ones in future interactions.

Emotions affect the explicit message conveyed during the interaction. They change people voices, facial expressions, gestures, and speech speed; a phenomenon addressed as emotional coloring [9,10]. This effect can be of great importance for the interpretation of user input, for example, to overcome the Lombard effect in the case of angry or stressed users [11], and to disambiguate the meaning of the user utterances depending on their emotional state [12].

Emotions can also affect the actions that the user chooses to communicate with the system. According to [13], emotion can be understood more widely as a manipulation of the range of interaction affordances available to each counterpart in a conversation. Riccardi and Tür studied the impact of emotion temporal patterns in user transcriptions, as well as semantic and dialog annotations of the *How May I help you?* system [14]. In their study, the representation of the user state was defined only in terms of dialog act or expected user intent. They found that emotional information can be useful to improve the dialog strategies and predict system errors, but it was not employed in their system to adapt dialog management.

Emotions have also been considered as a very important factor of influence in decision making processes. For instance, a context-aware model of emotions that can be used to design intelligent agents endowed with emotional capabilities is described in [15]. The study is complemented by also modeling personalities and mood [16].

Very recently, other authors have developed affective dialog models which take into account both emotions and dialog acts. The dialog model proposed by [17] combined three different submodels: an emotional model describing the transitions between user emotional states during the interaction regardless of the data content, a plain dialog model describing the transitions between existing dialog states regardless of the emotions, and a combined model including the dependencies between combined dialog and emotional states. Then, the next dialog state was derived from a combination of the plain dialog model and the combined model.

Bui et al. [18] based their model on Partially Observable Markov Decision Processes (POMDP) [19] that adapt the dialog strategy to the user actions and emotional states, which are the output of an emotion recognition module. Their model was tested in the development of a route navigation system for rescues in an unsafe tunnel in which users could experience five levels of stress. In order to reduce the computational cost required for solving the POMDP problem for dialog systems in which many emotions and dialog acts might be considered, the authors employ decision networks to complement POMDP. As will be described in Sect. 3, we propose an alternative to this statistical modeling which can also be used in realistic conversational agents and evaluate it in a less emotional application domain in which emotions are produced more subtly.

3   Our Proposal to Model Users Emotional State

As our architecture has been designed to be highly modular, different emotion recognizers could be employed within it. We propose to use an emotion recognizer based solely in acoustic and dialog information because in most application

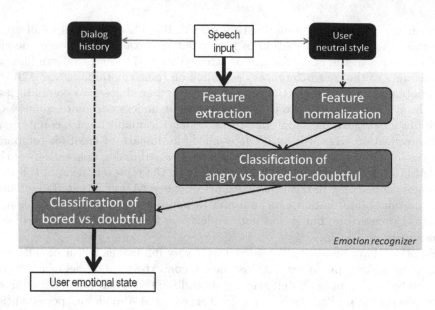

Fig. 1. Schema of the emotion recognizer

domains the user utterances are not long enough for the linguistic parameters to be significant for the detection of emotions.

Our recognition method, based on the previous work described in [20], firstly takes acoustic information into account to distinguish between the emotions which are acoustically more different, and secondly dialog information to disambiguate between those that are more similar. We are interested in recognizing negative emotions that might discourage users from employing the system again or even lead them to abort an ongoing dialog. Concretely, we have considered three negative emotions: *anger*, *boredom* and *doubtfulness*, where the latter refers to a situation in which the user uncertain about what to do next.

Following the proposed approach, our emotion recognizer employs acoustic information to distinguish anger from *doubtfulness* or *boredom* and dialog information to discriminate between *doubtfulness* and *boredom*, which are more difficult to discriminate only by using phonetic cues.

This process is shown in Fig. 1. As can be observed, the emotion recognizer always chooses one of the three negative emotions under study, not taking neutral into account. This is due to the difficulty of distinguishing neutral from emotional speech in spontaneous utterances when the application domain is not highly affective. This is the case of most information providing spoken dialog systems, in which a baseline algorithm which always chooses "neutral" would have a very high accuracy, which is difficult to improve by classifying the rest of emotions, that are very subtlety produced. Instead of considering neutral as another emotional class, we calculate the most likely non-neutral category and then the dialog manager employs this category to decide whether to take the user input as emotional or neutral.

The first step for emotion recognition is feature extraction. The aim is to compute features from the speech input which can be relevant for the detection of emotion in the users' voice. We extracted the most representative selection from the list of 60 features shown in Table 1. The feature selection process is carried out from a corpus of dialogs on demand, so that when new dialogs are available, the selection algorithms can be executed again and the list of representative features can be updated. The features are selected by majority voting of a forward selection algorithm, a genetic search, and a ranking filter using the default values of their respective parameters provided by Weka [21].

The second step of the emotion recognition process is feature normalization, with which the features extracted in the previous phase are normalized around the user neutral speaking style. This enables us to make more representative classifications, as it might happen that a user 'A' always speaks very fast and loudly, while a user 'B' always speaks in a very relaxed way. Then, some acoustic features may be the same for ='A' neutral as for 'B' angry, which would make the automatic classification fail for one of the users if the features are not normalized.

The values for all features in the neutral style are stored in a user profile. They are calculated as the most frequent values of the user previous utterances which have been annotated as neutral. This can be done when the user logs in to the system before starting the dialog. If the system does not have information about the identity of the user, we take the first user utterance as neutral assuming that he is not placing the telephone call already in a negative emotional state.

Once we have obtained the normalized features, we classify the corresponding utterance with a multilayer perceptron (MLP) into two categories: *angry* and *doubtful_or_bored*. If the utterance is classified as *doubtful_or_bored*, it is passed through an additional step in which it is classified according to two dialog parameters: depth and width. The precision values obtained with the MLP are discussed in detail in [20], where we evaluated the accuracy of the initial version of this emotion recognizer and compare the use of the MLP with other definitions of the classification function.

Dialog context is considered for emotion recognition by calculating depth and width. Depth represents the total number of dialog turns up to a particular point of the dialog, whereas width represents the total number of extra turns needed throughout a subdialog to confirm or repeat information. This way, the recognizer has information about the situations in the dialog that may lead to certain negative emotions, e.g. a very long dialog might increase the probability of *boredom*, whereas a dialog in which most turns were employed to confirm data can make the user angry.

The computation of depth and width is carried out according to the dialog history, which is stored in log files. Depth is initialized to 1 and incremented with each new user turn, as well as each time the interaction goes backwards (e.g. to the main menu). Width is initialized to 0 and is increased by 1 for each user turn generated to confirm, repeat data or ask the system for help.

Then, the dialog manager tailors the next system answer to the user state by changing the help providing mechanisms, the confirmation strategy and the

Table 1. Features employed for emotion detection from the acoustic signal [22–25]

Groups	Features	Physiological changes related to emotion
Pitch	Minimum value, maximum value, mean, median, standard deviation, value in the first voiced segment, value in the last voiced segment, correlation coefficient, slope, and error of the linear regression	Tension of the vocal folds and the sub glottal air pressure
First two formant frequencies and their bandwidths	Minimum value, maximum value, range, mean, median, standard deviation and value in the first and last voiced segments	Vocal tract resonances
Energy	Minimum value, maximum value, mean, median, standard deviation, value in the first voiced segment, value in the last voiced segment, correlation, slope, and error of the energy linear regression	Vocal effort, arousal of emotions
Rhythm	Speech rate, duration of voiced segments, duration of unvoiced segments, duration of longest voiced segment and number of unvoiced segments	Duration and stress conditions

interaction flexibility. The conciliation strategies adopted are, following the constraints defined in [26], straightforward and well delimited in order not to make the user loose the focus on the task. They are as follows:

- If the recognized emotion is *doubtful* and the user has changed his behavior several times during the dialog, the dialog manager changes to a system-directed initiative and adds at the end of each prompt a help message describing the available options. This approach is also selected when the user profile indicates that the user is non-expert (or if there is no profile for the current user), and when his first utterances are classified as *doubtful*.
- In the case of *anger*, if the dialog history shows that there have been many errors during the interaction, the system apologizes and switches to DTMF (Dual-Tone Multi-Frequency) mode. If the user is assumed to be angry but the system is not aware of any error, the system's prompt is rephrased with more agreeable phrases and the user is advised that they can ask for help at any time.
- In the case of *boredom*, if there is information available from other interactions of the same user, the system tries to infer from those dialogs what the most likely objective of the user might be. If the detected objective matches the

predicted intention, the system takes the information for granted and uses implicit confirmations.
- In any other case, the emotion is assumed to be neutral, and the next system prompt is decided only on the basis of the user intention and the user profile (i.e., considering his preferences, previous interactions, and expertise level).

4 Case Application: The *Enjoy Your City* System

We have applied our proposal to develop and evaluate the adaptive system *Enjoy Your City*, which provides user-adapted tourist information in natural language in Spanish. The information provided by the system includes places of interest, weather forecast, hotel booking, restaurants and bars, shopping, street guide and "how to get there" functionalities, cultural activities (cinema, theater, music, exhibitions, literature and science), sport activities, festivities, and public transportation. The information offered to the user is extracted from different web pages and several databases are also used to store this information and automatically update the data that is included in the application. A total of 115 system actions (dialog acts) were defined taking into account the information that is required by the system to provide the requested information.

For comparison purposes, we have also developed a baseline system [27] using industry-wide standards and protocols such as VoiceXML [28], for which the definition of a dialog strategy is based on scripted Finite State Machines. The system prompts and the grammars for automatic speech recognition are also implemented in VoiceXML-compliant formats (e.g., Java Speech Grammar Format or JSGF, and Speech Recognition Grammar Specification or SRGS); and the VoiceXML files include each specific system prompt defined for the system and a reference to a grammar that defines the valid user's inputs for the corresponding prompt.

To assess the benefits of our proposal to include user-adaptation, we have evaluated the *Enjoy Your City* system for the specific scenario of the city of Granada (Spain) and compared it to the baseline for the same city. In order to do so, 150 recruited users have followed a set of scenarios that specifies a set of objectives that must be fulfilled by the user at the end of the dialog and are designed to include the complete set of functionalities previously described for the system. A total of 600 dialogs were recorded from the interactions of the 150 users, 75 users employed the baseline version of the system and 75 users employed the user-adapted system.

To compare the baseline and user-adapted versions of the *Enjoy Your City* system we computed the mean value for the evaluation measures extracted from different studies [29, 30].

By means of high-level dialog features, we evaluate the duration of the dialogs, how much information is transmitted in individual turns, and how active the dialog participants are. These dialog features cover the following statistical properties: (i) Dialog length, measured as the mean and shape of the distribution of the number of turns per task, the number of turns of the shortest dialog, the number of turns of the longest dialog, and the number of turns of the most frequent dialog; (ii) Average rates corrected and uncorrected errors by the dialog manager. Only errors that modify the values of the attributes provided by the users are considered; (iii) Percentage of different dialogs in each corpus and the number of repetitions of the most frequent dialog; (iv) Turn length, measured by the number of actions per turn; and (v) Participant activity as a ratio of system and user actions per dialog. Table 2 shows the comparison of the different high-level measures for the baseline and user-adapted versions of the system.

Table 2. Results of the high-level dialog features defined for the comparison of the baseline and user-adapted systems

	Baseline	User-adapted System
Dialog success rate	85 %	89 %
Average number of corrected errors per dialog	0.83	0.90
Average number of uncorrected errors per dialog	0.18	0.09
Error correction rate	81 %	92 %
Average number of turns per dialog	12.2	10.1
Percentage of different dialogs	79 %	77 %
Number of repetitions of the most seen dialog	8	5
Number of turns of the most seen dialog	9	7
Number of turns of the shortest dialog	7	5
Number of turns of the longest dialog	17	15

As can be observed, on the one hand the success rate for the user-adapted system (89 %) is higher than the obtained for the baseline (85 %). On the other hand, the error correction rates were also improved in absolute values by using the user-adapted system. Both results are explained by the fact that we have not designed a specific strategy to improve the recognition or understanding processes and decrease the error rate, but rather our proposal for adaptation to the user emotional state overcomes these problems during the dialog once they are produced.

Regarding the number of dialog turns, the user-adapted system produced shorter dialogs (10.1 turns in average) compared to the number of turns of the baseline system (12.2). As shown in Table 2, this general reduction in the number of turns is generalized also to the case of the longest, shortest and most seen dialogs for the user-adapted system. This might be because users have to explicitly provide and confirm more information using the baseline system, whereas the user-adapted system automatically adapted the dialog to the user and the dialog history. This way, users have more variability in order to provide the different information that is needed to access the different services.

In fact, the dialogs acquired with the baseline system have a higher standard deviation (3.67) given that the proportion of number of turns per dialog is more

Table 3. Proportions of dialog spent on-goal directed actions, ground actions and other possible actions

	Baseline	User-adapted System
Goal directed actions	66.37 %	71.16 %
Grounding actions	32.34 %	27.39 %
Rest of actions	1.29 %	1.45 %

disperse. The dialogs gathered with the user-adapted system have a smaller deviation (3.09) since the successful dialogs are usually those which require the minimum number of turns to achieve the objective(s) predefined in the scenarios.

Dialog style and cooperativeness measures analyze the frequency of different speech acts and reflect the proportion of actions that are goal-directed (i.e. not indexed in dialog formalities). For dialog style features we grouped all user and system actions into three categories: "goal directed" (actions to provide or request information), "grounding" (confirmations and negations), and "other". Table 3 shows a comparison between these categories. As can be observed, the dialogs provided by the user-adapted system have a better quality, as the proportion of goal-directed actions is higher.

In addition, we asked the recruited users to complete a questionnaire to assess their subjective opinion about system performance. The questionnaire had five questions: (i) Q1: How well did the system understand you?; (ii) Q2: How well did you understand the system messages?; (iii) Q3: Was it easy for you to get the requested information?; (iv) Q4: Was the interaction rate adequate?; (v) Q5: If the system made errors, was it easy for you to correct them? The possible answers for each one of the questions were the same: Never/Not at all, Seldom/In some measure, Sometimes/Acceptably, Usually/Well, and Always/Very Well. All the answers were assigned a numeric value between one and five (in the same order as they appear in the questionnaire).

Table 4 shows the average results obtained with respect to the subjective evaluation carried out by the recruited users. As can be observed, both systems correctly understand the different user queries and obtain a similar evaluation regarding the user observed easiness in correcting errors made by the ASR module. However, the user-adapted system has a higher evaluation rate regarding the user observed easiness in obtaining the data required to fulfill the complete set of objectives defined in the scenarios, as well as the suitability of the interaction rate during the dialog.

Table 4. Results of the subjective evaluation of the baseline and user-adapted systems with real users (1=worst, 5=best evaluation)

	Q1	Q2	Q3	Q4	Q5
Baseline	4.6	3.6	3.8	3.4	3.2
User-adapted System	4.8	3.9	4.3	4.2	3.3

5 Conclusions and Future Work

In this paper, we have combined different aspects from the areas of knowledge representation, natural language processing, user modeling and intelligent information retrieval to facilitate a personalized and more natural access to information and services by means of speech interaction. In order to do this, we have contributed a framework to predict users emotional state, which can be used to develop adaptive spoken conversational agents.

Our recognition method obtains the user emotional state from the acoustics of his utterance as well as the dialog history. Two phases are followed to firstly distinguish between the emotions which are acoustically more different, and secondly disambiguate between those that are more similar. Our proposal is focused on the recognition of negative emotions that might discourage users from employing a conversational agent again or even lead them to abort an ongoing dialog.

We have provided a practical implementation of our proposal in the *Enjoy Your City* system, which provides personalized tourist information. To develop this system we have defined the complete requirements for the task and developed the different modules, and the necessary information to be incorporated in the users emotional state prediction. From a set of dialogs acquired with recruited users we have studied the influence of the adaptation on the quality of the services that are provided by the system.

The results show that our proposal not only allows a higher success rate in the provision of the adapted services. By means of the user-adapted system, the time required to provide the information can be reduced. In addition, the quality of the interaction between the user and the system is increased, as user-adapted dialogs present a better ratio of goal-directed actions selected by the system to successfully provide the different services. This way, actions that might discourage users (e.g., confirmations or re-request of information) are also reduced.

For future work we plan to apply the proposed technique to other tasks in order to see whether it can be used for comparison between several user intention models and dialog management techniques. We also want to combine our proposal for emotion recognition with other proposals within the field of Sentiment Analysis. We also want to consider the neutral state in our classifier by studying different proposals related to imbalanced classification. Finally, we also intend to extend the assessment of the developed system considering additional user satisfaction measures that complement the described evaluation.

Acknowledgements. This work was supported in part by Projects MINECO TEC2012-37832-C02-01, CICYT TEC2011-28626-C02-02, CAM CONTEXTS (S2009/TIC-1485).

References

1. Pieraccini, R., Rabiner, L.: The Voice in the Machine: Building Computers That Understand Speech. MIT Press, Cambridge (2012)

2. Osland, P., Viken, B., Solsvik, F., Nygreen, G., Wedvik, J., Myklbust, S.: Enabling context-aware applications. In: Proceedings of the International Conference on Convergence in Services, Media and Networks (ICIN 2006), pp. 1–6 (2006)
3. Strauss, P., Minker, W.: Proactive Spoken Dialogue Interaction in Multi-Party Environments. Springer, US (2010)
4. Kartakis, S.: A design-and-play approach to accesible user interface development in ambient intelligence environments. J. Comput. Ind. **61**(4), 318–328 (2010). Elsevier
5. Schuller, B., Batliner, A., Steidl, S., Seppi, D.: Recognising realistic emotions and affect in speech: state of the art and lessons learnt from the first challenge. Speech Commun. **53**(9–10), 1062–1087 (2011). Elsevier
6. Batliner, A., Burkhardt, F., van Ballegooy, M., Nöth, E.: A taxonomy of applications that utilize emotional awareness. In: Proceedings of the 1st International Language Technologies Conference (IS-LTC 2006), pp. 246–250 (2006)
7. Bickmore, T., Giorgino, T.: Some novel aspects of health communication from a dialogue systems perspective. In: Proceedings of AAAI Fall Symposium on Dialogue Systems for Health Communication, pp. 275–291 (2004)
8. Litman, D., Forbes-Riley, K.: Recognizing student emotions and attitudes on the basis of utterances in spoken tutoring dialogues with both human and computer tutors. Speech Commun. **48**(5), 559–590 (2006). Elsevier
9. Khalifa, O., Ahmad, Z., Gunawan, T.: SMaTTS: standard malay text to speech system. Int. J. Comput. Sci. **2**(4), 285–293 (2007). JARCS
10. Acosta, J., Ward, N.: Responding to user emotional state by adding emotional coloring to utterances. In: Proceeding of 10th Annual Conference of the International Speech Communication Association (Interspeech 2009), pp. 1587–1590 (2009)
11. Boril, H., Hansen, J.: Unsupervised equalization of Lombard effect for speech recognition in noisy adverse environments. IEEE Trans. Audio Speech Lang. Process. **28**(6), 1379–1393 (2010). IEEE
12. Bosma, W., Andre, E.: Exploiting emotions to disambiguate dialogue acts. In: Proceedings of 9th International Conference on Intelligent User Interface, pp. 85–92 (2004)
13. Wilks, Y., Catizone, R., Worgan, S., Turunen, M.: Some background on dialogue management and conversational speech for dialogue systems. Comput. Speech Lang. **25**(2), 128–139 (2011). Elsevier
14. Riccardi, G., Hakkani-Tür, D.: Grounding emotions in human-machine conversational systems. In: Maybury, M., Stock, O., Wahlster, W. (eds.) INTETAIN 2005. LNCS (LNAI), vol. 3814, pp. 144–154. Springer, Heidelberg (2005)
15. Marreiros, G., Santos, R., Ramos, C., Neves, J.: Context-aware emotion-based model for group decision making. IEEE Intell. Syst. **25**(2), 31–39 (2010). IEEE
16. Santos, R., Marreiros, G., Ramos, C., Neves, J., Bulas-Cruz, J.: Personality, emotion, and mood in agent-based group decision making. IEEE Intell. Syst. **26**(6), 58–66 (2011). IEEE
17. Pittermann, J., Pittermann, A., Minker, W.: Emotion recognition and adaptation in spoken dialogue systems. Int. J. Speech Technol. **13**, 49–60 (2010). Springer
18. Bui, T., Poel, M., Nijholt, A., Zwiers, J.: A tractable hybrid DDN-POMDP approach to affective dialogue modeling for probabilistic frame-based dialogue systems. Nat. Lang. Eng. **15**(2), 273–307 (2009). Cambridge University Press
19. Williams, J., Young, S.: Partially observable Markov decision processes for spoken dialogue systems. Comput. Speech Lang. **21**, 393–422 (2007). Elsevier
20. Callejas, Z., López-Cózar, R.: Influence of contextual information in emotion annotation for spoken dialogue systems. Speech Commun. **50**(5), 416–433 (2008). Elsevier

21. Witten, I., Frank, E.: Data Mining: Practical Machine Learning Tools and Techniques. Morgan Kaufmann, San Francisco (2005)
22. Hansen, J.: Analysis and compensation of speech under stress and noise for environmental robustness in speech recognition. Speech Commun. **20**(2), 151–170 (1996). Elsevier
23. Ververidis, D., Kotropoulos, C.: Emotional speech recognition: resources, features and methods. Speech Commun. **48**, 1162–1181 (2006). Elsevier
24. Morrison, D., Wang, R., Silva, L.: Ensemble methods for spoken emotion recognition in call-centers. Speech Commun. **49**(2), 98–112 (2007). Elsevier
25. Batliner, A., Steidl, S., Schuller, B., Seppi, D., Vogt, T., Wagner, J., Devillers, L., Vidrascu, L., Aharonson, V., Kessous, L., Amir, N.: Whodunnit - searching for the most important feature types signalling emotion-related user states in speech. Comput. Speech Lang. **25**(1), 4–28 (2011). Elsevier
26. Burkhardt, F., van Ballegooy, M., Engelbrecht, K., Polzehl, T., Stegmann, J.: Emotion detection in dialog systems - usecases, strategies and challenges. In: Proceedings of International Conference on Affective Computing and Intelligent Interaction (ACII 2009), pp. 1–6 (2009)
27. Griol, D., García-Jiménez, M.: Development of interactive virtual voice portals to provide municipal information. Adv. Intell. Soft Comput. **151**, 161–172 (2012). Springer
28. Will, T.: A Simple Guide to IBM SPSS: For Version 20.0. Akademiker Verlag (2012)
29. Ai, H., Raux, A., Bohus, D., Eskenazi, M., Litman, D.: Comparing spoken dialog corpora collected with recruited subjects versus real users. In: Proceedings of the 8th SIGdial Workshop on Discourse and Dialogue, pp. 124–131 (2007)
30. Schatzmann, J., Georgila, K., Young, S.: Quantitative evaluation of user simulation techniques for spoken dialogue systems. In: Proceedings of the 6th SIGdial Workshop on Discourse and Dialogue, pp. 45–54 (2005)

Hybrid Intelligent Systems for Data Mining and Applications

Predicting PM_{10} Concentrations Using Fuzzy Kriging

Jan Caha[1($\boxtimes$)], Lukáš Marek[2], and Jiří Dvorský[3]

[1] Institute of Geoinformatics, VSB-Technical University of Ostrava, 17. listopadu 15,
708 33 Ostrava-Poruba, Czech Republic
{jan.caha,jiri.dvorsky}@vsb.cz
[2] Department of Geoinformatics, Faculty of Science, Palacký University in Olomouc,
17. listopadu 50, 771 46 Olomouc, Czech Republic
lukas.marek@upol.cz
[3] Department of Computer Science, VSB-Technical University of Ostrava,
17. listopadu 15, 708 33 Ostrava-Poruba, Czech Republic

Abstract. The prediction of meteorological phenomena is usually based on the creation of surface from point sources using the certain type of interpolation algorithms. The prediction standardly does not incorporate any kind of uncertainty, either in the calculation itself or its results. The selection of the interpolation method, as well as its parameters depend on the user and his experiences. That does not mean the problem necessarily. However, in the case of the spatial distribution modelling of potentially dangerous air pollutants, the inappropriately selected parameters and model may cause inaccuracies in the results and their evaluation. In this contribution, we propose the prediction using fuzzy kriging that allows incorporating the experts knowledge. We combined previously presented approaches with optimization probabilistic metaheuristic method simulated annealing. The application of this approach in the real situation is presented on the prediction of PM10 particles in the air in the Czech Republic.

Keywords: Fuzzy surface · Fuzzy kriging · PM_{10} · Uncertainty

1 Introduction

Spatial predictions of values of PM_{10} (particulate matter with diameter of $10\,\mu m$ or smaller) is lately an important topic [3,7,12,13,22]. It is because PM_{10} is one of the most hazardous air pollutants. Previous studies showed that there is no safe level of PM_{10} concentration and every rise by $10\,\mu g/m^3$ can be linked to increase chance of lung cancer [20]. In [13] it is specified that the problematic concentrations starts at around $30\,\mu g/m^3$ and concentrations higher than $50\,\mu g/m^3$ are identified as hazardous level. The measurements of PM_{10} concentrations are only performed at monitoring sites, and spatial interpolation methods are later used to predict the concentrations at locations without measurement. Amongst these interpolation techniques, the most commonly used is kriging [3,7,12,13,22].

© Springer International Publishing Switzerland 2015
E. Onieva et al. (Eds.): HAIS 2015, LNAI 9121, pp. 371–381, 2015.
DOI: 10.1007/978-3-319-19644-2_31

The process of calculation of predictions by kriging is significantly dependant on the suitable determination of a theoretical variogram (its type and parameters) [17]. As shown in [17] the selection of slightly different parameters of the variogram may result in distinct predictions, as different spatial trends can be identified in the dataset. A theoretical variogram is fitted either by an automatic method (usually by means of regression analysis) or manually by the user [6]. In both cases, there is significant amount of epistemic uncertainty in the theoretical variogram. In most applications, the fitting of a theoretical variogram is done manually, and the user incorporates not only hard data but also his knowledge about the dataset in the variogram. This step is generally considered as useful as there can be factors affecting the variogram that are not apparent from the data [2]. However, due to the fact that the selection of the theoretical variogram type and particularly its parameters is partially subjective process that depends on user's knowledge and experience [2,17], the fitted variogram contains some amount of epistemic uncertainty. Besides that, there are other factors affecting the certainty of the empirical variogram. The most important is the fact that data used to construct empirical variogram are only a sample. If more data would be available, it is possible that the empirical variogram would be different, which would lead to the fitting of different theoretical variogram [1,17]. To overcame these problems fuzzy kriging was proposed [2]. The method is based on a soft computing technique where the parameters of kriging are specified as fuzzy numbers, and this epistemic uncertainty about the values of parameters is propagated through the calculation into predictions [17]. The predicted surface is not precise (as in the case of classic kriging) but it contains uncertainty. This uncertainty is modelled as fuzzy numbers that provides mainly the information about modal, minimal and maximal value of the estimates at each location. Fuzzy kriging allows the user to acknowledge his uncertainty about spatial dependencies in the data which is rather important especially if there is no simple fit of a theoretical variogram through an empirical variogram [2].

The utilization of possibility theory is necessary in order to extract information about exceedance of particular thresholds by the fuzzy kriging estimation. Examples of this procedure were provided in [10] and [4]. Notably the vague queries described in [4] allow comparison of fuzzy surface to thresholds that can not be specified exactly. A fuzzy number can model such threshold. As mention previously, the significant concentration of PM_{10} can not be specified precisely, which makes this particular threshold appropriate for being modelled as vague query.

In the presented article monthly average of PM_{10} concentration for October 2013 in Czech republic are interpolated by means of fuzzy kriging. The obtained results are then queried in order to identify areas where threshold is exceeded by the predicted concentration. The Sects. 2 and 3 provide brief introduction about fuzzy prediction models and fuzzy kriging; Sect. 4 provides theory for querying fuzzy surface. The Sects. 5 and 6 describe the case study and the Sect. 7 provides conclusions and further directions.

2   Fuzzy Prediction Models

Fuzzy models are usually considered if data and/or model parameters are vague, imprecise or ill-known [16]. Such uncertain values can be modelled as fuzzy numbers [9]. Even though, fuzzy numbers are special cases of fuzzy sets and have at least piecewise continuous membership function the calculations are often simplified into utilization of triangular fuzzy numbers [16,23]. Such definition of fuzzy number $\tilde{A}$ as triplet $[a^-, a^m, a^+]$ (representing minimal, modal and maximal value) is both easy and comprehensible for the user as well as less demanding in the process of calculation of results than utilization of other types of fuzzy numbers. The calculation of fuzzy predictions is usually done in order to obtain the modal value as the most likely result (the most likely result that equals also to the result of common crisp prediction) and the limit values with respect to uncertainty of data or/and parameters.

3   Fuzzy Kriging

Details about kriging calculation and a variogram estimation can be found in [6,11]. The discussion regarding the role of epistemic uncertainty on kriging is summarized in [2,17]. Fuzzy kriging is a special variant of kriging that accounts for uncertainty. According to [17], two main attitudes exist – Diamond's [8] and Bardossy's [2] fuzzy kriging. The method presented by Diamond [8] focuses on kriging with fuzzy numbers as input values and crisp (exact) variogram. Fuzzy kriging described by Bardossy et al. [1,2] handles both, the fuzzy data as well as fuzzy variogram. Since crisp data are consider to be special case of fuzzy data the method can also handle crisp data and fuzzy variogram. This property of kriging proposed in [2] is very useful for practical applications as usually only crisp (precise) data are available from real world measurements.

   In this paper, the variant of fuzzy kriging based on ideas originally presented in [1,2] that were further developed in [18,19] is considered and used. Bardossy et al. [1,2] describe a fuzzy variogram and its definition. A fuzzy variogram is a result of situation in which it is difficult to select model and parameters of a theoretical variogram based on existing empirical variogram. There maybe more than one applicable model and a range of values for one or more parameters [2]. Through this paper the variogram with fuzzy parameters is of interest.

   As described in [19], in the kriging framework, it is assumed that the prediction at any location is a linear combination of n input values at their respective locations $\mathbf{z} = \{z(x_i), i = 1, \ldots, n\}$. The estimation also depends on set of kriging weights $\Lambda_0 = \{\lambda_i(x_0), i = 1, \ldots, n\}$ that are estimated from the variogram [6,11]. The set of Λ_0 depends on the selected theoretical variogram. Variogram is usually specified by three variables – sill, range and nugget effect [6,11]. As such the variogram can be perceived as a function with p parameters $\mathbf{a} = \{a_1, \ldots, a_p\}$ [19].

   The estimated value of the variable $z^*(x_0)$ at location x_0 is calculated according to:

$$z^*(x_0) = \sum_{i=1}^{n} \lambda_i(x_0) z(x_i), \tag{1}$$

where $\lambda_i(x_0)$ is kriging weight that is calculated from a theoretical variogram for the location x_0 and value of variable $z(x_i)$ at location x_i. The kriging estimate can be rewritten in a form [19]:

$$z^*(x_0) = \sum_{i=1}^{n} \lambda_i(x_0) z(x_i) = f_0(\mathbf{a}, \mathbf{z}). \tag{2}$$

The function f_0 have $n + p$ variables. If $\mathbf{a}$ and $\mathbf{z}$ are fuzzy numbers $\tilde{\mathbf{a}}$ and $\tilde{\mathbf{z}}$ the function f_0 can be calculated using the extension principle [2,19] to obtain fuzzy prediction $\tilde{z}^*(x_0)$. The details regarding the calculation can be found in [1,2]. As mentioned by Loquin and Dubois [18,19] the papers [1,2] do not provide any computational method besides the direct usage of the extension principle which is often computationally and time demanding [14].

To overcome this problem the variant of fuzzy kriging based on interval analysis was proposed in [18,19]. This approach is common in solving complex computational problems involving fuzzy numbers as it significantly simplifies the calculation [14]. The input fuzzy numbers are divided into m α-cuts then for each alpha cut the calculation is performed and a resulting α-cut is obtained. From these α-cuts the resulting fuzzy number is obtained [14].

The whole process can be represented as calculation of arbitrary α-cut, that is repeated for the set of α-cuts. Determination of α-cut of fuzzy kriging can be than represented as twofold problem regarding uncertainty of function f_0 [19]:

$$\begin{cases} \underline{z}^0 = \min_{(\mathbf{a},\mathbf{z})=\in\underline{\mathbf{a}}\times\underline{\mathbf{z}}} f_0(\mathbf{a}, \mathbf{z}), \\ \overline{z}^0 = \max_{(\mathbf{a},\mathbf{z})=\in\underline{\mathbf{a}}\times\underline{\mathbf{z}}} f_0(\mathbf{a}, \mathbf{z}), \end{cases} \tag{3}$$

where $\underline{z}^0$ and $\overline{z}^0$ are interval limits of the prediction and $\underline{\mathbf{a}} \times \underline{\mathbf{z}}$ is a Cartesian product of domains $\underline{\mathbf{a}}$ and $\underline{\mathbf{z}}$ for the specific α-cut.

Since we are interested in variant of fuzzy kriging with only parameters of the variogram represented by fuzzy numbers ($\tilde{\mathbf{a}}$) the problem is even simpler in our case as $\mathbf{z}$ are crisp numbers:

$$\begin{cases} \underline{z}^0 = \min_{\mathbf{a}=\in\underline{\mathbf{a}}} f_0(\mathbf{a}, \mathbf{z}), \\ \overline{z}^0 = \max_{\mathbf{a}=\in\underline{\mathbf{a}}} f_0(\mathbf{a}, \mathbf{z}). \end{cases} \tag{4}$$

3.1   Optimisation Scheme

In order to calculate Eq. (4) it would be necessary to explore parameters domain $\underline{\mathbf{a}}$ and calculate kringing for every combination of $\mathbf{a}$ to obtain limits of prediction $- \underline{z}^0, \overline{z}^0$. The original approach by Bardossy et al. [2] does not propose any method to optimise the calculation. Loquin and Dubois [18,19] note that based on their empirical observation the limits of prediction are often reached for p-uplets formed by the bounds of $\underline{\mathbf{a}}$. Based on this observation authors suggest to calculate preliminary results by using 2^p variants of $\mathbf{a}$. Obtained values of $\underline{z}^0$,

$\overline{z}^0$ are with high possibility the true limits, however this preliminary calculation should be combined with probabilistic metaheuristic method – simulated
annealing, to explore the parameters domain $\overline{\underline{a}}$ with exhaustive combinatorial
method [18,19].

4   Fuzzy Surface Querying

The process of the information extraction from the surface that contains
uncertainty is usually more complicated than in common surfaces. Common
approaches determining whether the value exceeds the threshold are insufficient,
since there is a range of values with preference measurement instead of crisp
number [4]. However, procedures utilizing the possibility theory based on the
ranking of fuzzy numbers can be used [9]. This approach utilizes two measures -
possibility and necessity that allow a complex assessment of the comparison of
the fuzzy number to a threshold. Examples of utilization of possibility theory to
query fuzzy surfaces are presented in [4,10].

For the purpose of this research, we are interested obtaining the information,
if the prediction $\tilde{P}$ defined by triplet $[p^-, p^m, p^+]$ exceeds threshold t. That is a
classic query as we want to find out areas where concentration of PM$_{10}$ is higher
then specific value t.

The possibility of exceedance t by $\tilde{P}$ is defined as:

$$\Pi_{\tilde{P}>(t)} = \begin{cases} 1 & \text{if } t < p^m \\ \dfrac{p^+ - t}{p^+ - p^m} & \text{if } p^m \leq t \leq p^+ \\ 0 & \text{if } c < t \end{cases} \tag{5}$$

and the necessity of exceedance t by $\tilde{P}$:

$$\mathcal{N}_{\tilde{P}>(t)} = \begin{cases} 1 & \text{if } t < p^- \\ 1 - \dfrac{t - p^-}{p^m - p^-} & \text{if } p^- \leq t \leq p^m \\ 0 & \text{if } p^m < t \end{cases} . \tag{6}$$

Both indices takes values on interval $[0, 1]$ where 0 means no fulfilment, 1 means
complete fulfilment and values in between represent partial fulfilment. For further
details please see [4] and [10].

5   Data

The original dataset contains 182 measurement sites located in the Czech republic. However, several measurement sites do not provide average for October 2013,
and there are few duplicates (stations at the same location) that need to removed
from the dataset. After these steps, the data set of 155 measurements sites was
used for the interpolation. The concentrations of PM$_{10}$ are not normally distributed, which is rather common when dealing with spatial data [11]. This problem
is overcome by working with logarithm of the original values in the interpolation
meaning that results are later exponentiated to obtain correct prediction [6].

6   Predicted Fuzzy Surface

For the fuzzy predictions three values are of interest – the minimal, modal and maximal values of the fuzzy numbers. Modal value of the fuzzy prediction can be calculated as classic crisp prediction using the modal values of fuzzy variogram parameters. The minimal and maximal values of prediction are calculated according to Eq. (4) with respect to range of the fuzzy variogram parameters. Firstly, the optimisation scheme described in Sect. 3.1 is used and it is compared to the simulated annealing to determine the usefulness of the optimisation.

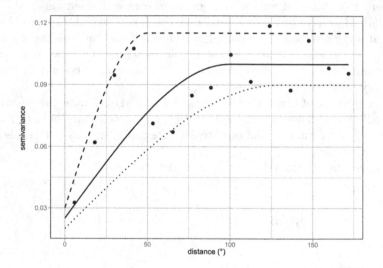

Fig. 1. Estimated fuzzy variogram (minimal, modal and maximal value) based on empirical variogram (black dots) of PM_{10}.

The prediction of PM_{10} concentration by fuzzy kriging is calculated on a grid covering the Czech republic with cell size $0.0125° \times 0.0125°$ (expressed in geographic coordinates). Based on empirical variogram (Fig. 1) a spherical variogram model was chosen. The variogram model is defined as [6,19]:

$$\gamma(h) = \begin{cases} s, & \text{if } h \leq s, \\ \eta + (s - \eta)\left(\frac{3h}{2r} - \frac{h^3}{2r^3}\right), & \text{otherwise.} \end{cases} \quad (7)$$

where η is nugget effect, s is sill and r range of the theoretical variogram. As visible from Fig. 1, the empirical variogram is rather complicated and selection of correct theoretical variogram with correct parameters is difficult. Solution to this problem is a specification of fuzzy variogram (Fig. 1). The parameters of fuzzy variogram are specified in Table 1.

The calculation of fuzzy surface was done by the optimisation scheme and also by simulated annealing. Range of each parameter was divided into l equally

Table 1. Parameters of fuzzy variogram and number of selected values for simulated annealing

Parameter	Minimum	Modal value	Maximum	Intervals SA
sill (s)	0.07	0.075	0.085	15
range (r)	50	100	130	32
nugget effect (η)	0.02	0.025	0.03	10

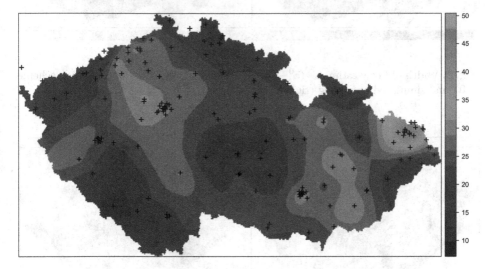

Fig. 2. Modal value of fuzzy surface with measurement locations (crosses).

distributed values (Table 1) and the calculation was done for all combinations. In this case, that meant 4800 calculations. Comparison amongst these two methods showed that in 60 % of estimates the simulated annealing provides lower predictions of $\underline{z}^0$ and higher predictions of $\overline{z}^0$. However, in only 8.56 % of cases the differences varied by more than 0.5 for $\underline{z}^0$. For $\overline{z}^0$ 16.38 % varied by at least 0.5. The spatial distribution of these differences is visible in Fig. 3. While the maximal width of estimates ($\overline{z}^0 - \underline{z}^0$) does not change amongst methods, there is a significant growth in areas with higher differences in results of simulated annealing. Based on this comparison, we conclude that in this particular case it is better to use results of simulated annealing. Even though the optimisation scheme provided results in much shorter time, it cannot be considered as complete. Modal value of fuzzy surface is visualized in Fig. 2 and limit values in Fig. 4.

6.1 Exceedance of Concentration 30 μg/m³ in prediction

Based on created fuzzy surface, the information about exceedance of limit concentration 30 μg/m³ (higher concentrations can be problematic for health [13])

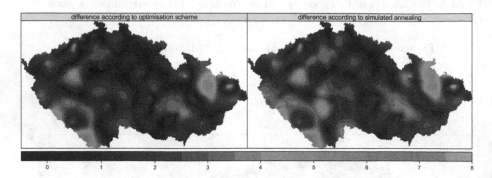

Fig. 3. Width of fuzzy estimates $(\overline{z}^0 - \underline{z}^0)$ for results calculated by optimisation scheme (left) and simulated annealing (right).

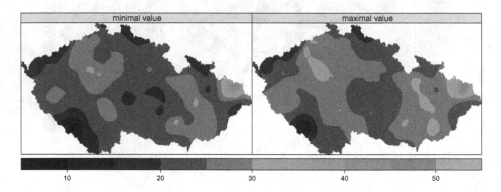

Fig. 4. Minimal (left) and maximal (right) values of fuzzy estimates.

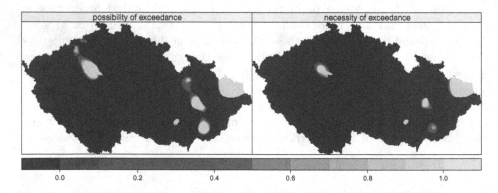

Fig. 5. Possibility (left) and necessity (right) of concentration PM_{10} exceeding $30 \ \mu g/m^3$.

can be done based on Eqs. (5, 6). Visualization of results is in Fig. 5. The results show that the areas that have possibly concentration higher than $30\,\mu g/m^3$ are larger than areas that have necessary concentration higher than $30\,\mu g/m^3$. The difference amongst areas with possibility and necessity of exceedance show the uncertainty associated with the particular threshold.

7   Conclusions

In this paper, the utilization of method that combines soft and hard computing to obtain spatial predictions is shown on the example of air the pollutant PM$_{10}$. Since this pollutant is one of the most hazardous ones it is necessary to examine new approaches towards modelling its spatial distribution and its patterns. Traditional methods of hard computing fail to acknowledge epistemic uncertainty related to user's knowledge about spatial dependence of data. This spatial dependence could have significant effect on the expected result. The difference amongst the limits in the presented example of fuzzy prediction are in range $[0, 8]$ (Fig. 3). Although these differences does not seem as significant, we must take into account the fact that the monthly average is interpolated. These differences for each day in a month could accumulate to a rather significant numbers. Because of this fact, there is clearly a difference amongst the predictions when thinking about exposure to this pollutant. The results provide important insight about the uncertainty of spatial interpolation caused by epistemic uncertainty of kriging parameters.

The influence of the difference is demonstrated on the query that is used to identify areas with higher concentrations of PM$_{10}$ (Sect. 6.1). The result of query show areas that have necessarily higher concentration higher then $30\,\mu g/m^3$ (Fig. 5) and also areas where this threshold might be exceed only possibly. The results of this query on soft data acknowledge the uncertainty of the fuzzy prediction, showing the range of results $[0, 1]$ for both possibility and necessity.

The presented research shows an example of interpolation technique that requires relatively simple inputs and extends simple or ordinary kriging. The approach can be extended towards more complex interpolation techniques such are cokriging [6], regression/hybrid kriging [15] or geographically weighted regression. These approaches would allow modelling of PM$_{10}$ concentration with respect to higher number of input parameters (e.g. terrain, distance from sources of pollution). However, such extensions are beyond the scope of this research, as the main objective was to evaluate benefits and usefulness of the fuzzy kriging proposed in [2, 18]. The obtained results should also be compared to predictions obtained from machine learning methods [5, 21] in order to assess the differences amongst these attitudes towards spatial interpolation.

The further research should focus on automatic determination of fuzzy parameters for variogram from the empirical variogram. The fuzzy surface could be also queried by a vague query (as described in [4]) in order to acknowledge the uncertainty about threshold value of PM$_{10}$ concentration. The determination of days with significant concentration of PM$_{10}$ based on daily measurements is also topic that could be analyzed.

8   Appendix

In order to ensure the reproducible research, authors decided to publish all the necessary data along with the used source code of analyses. The source code in **R** and data are available at https://github.com/JanCaha/Hais2015-paper.

Acknowledgement. The authors gratefully acknowledge the support by the Operational Program Education for Competitiveness - European Social Fund (project CZ.1.07/2.3.00/20.0170 of the Ministry of Education, Youth and Sports of the Czech Republic).

We would like to thank also to the Czech Hydrometeorological Institute for providing the up-to-date as well as summary data on their websites.

References

1. Bardossy, A., Bogardi, I., Kelly, W.E.: Imprecise (fuzzy) information in geostatistics. Math. Geol. **20**(4), 287–311 (1988)
2. Bardossy, A., Bogardi, I., Kelly, W.E.: Kriging with imprecise (fuzzy) variograms. I: theory. Math. Geol. **22**(1), 63–79 (1990)
3. Beelen, R., Hoek, G., Pebesma, E., Vienneau, D., de Hoogh, K., Briggs, D.J.: Mapping of background air pollution at a fine spatial scale across the European Union. Sci. Total Environ. **407**(6), 1852–1867 (2009)
4. Caha, J., Dvorský, J.: Querying on fuzzy surfaces with vague queries. In: Pan, J.-S., Polycarpou, M.M., Woźniak, M., de Carvalho, A.C.P.L.F., Quintián, H., Corchado, E. (eds.) HAIS 2013. LNCS, vol. 8073, pp. 548–557. Springer, Heidelberg (2013)
5. Champendal, A., Kanevski, M., Huguenot, P.-E.: Air pollution mapping using nonlinear land use regression models. In: Murgante, B., Misra, S., Rocha, A.M.A.C., Torre, C., Rocha, J.G., Falcão, M.I., Taniar, D., Apduhan, B.O., Gervasi, O. (eds.) ICCSA 2014, Part III. LNCS, vol. 8581, pp. 682–690. Springer, Heidelberg (2014)
6. Cressie, N.A.C.: Statistics for Spatial Data. John Wiley & Sons Inc, New York (1991)
7. Denby, B., Schaap, M., Segers, A., Builtjes, P., Horálek, J.: Comparison of two data assimilation methods for assessing PM10 exceedances on the European scale. Atmos. Environ. **42**(30), 7122–7134 (2008)
8. Diamond, P.: Fuzzy kriging. Fuzzy Sets Syst. **33**(3), 315–332 (1989)
9. Dubois, D., Prade, H.: Ranking fuzzy numbers in the setting of possibility theory. Inf. Sci. **30**(3), 183–224 (1983)
10. Fisher, P., Caha, J.: On use of fuzzy surfaces to detect possible elevation change. In: Stewart, K., Pebesma, E., Navratil, G., Fogliaroni, P., Duckham, M. (eds.) Extended Abstract Proceedings of the GIScience 2014, Department of Geodesy and Geoinformation, Vienna University of Technology, Vienna, Austria, pp. 215–220 (2014)
11. Goovaerts, P.: Geostatistics for Natural Resources Evaluation. Oxford University Press, New York (1997)
12. Gulliver, J., de Hoogh, K., Fecht, D., Vienneau, D., Briggs, D.: Comparative assessment of GIS-based methods and metrics for estimating long-term exposures to air pollution. Atmos. Environ. **45**(39), 7072–7080 (2011)

13. Guo, D., Guo, R., Thiart, C.: Predicting air pollution using fuzzy membership grade kriging. Comput. Environ. Urban Syst. **31**(1), 33–51 (2007)
14. Hanss, M.: The transformation method for the simulation and analysis of systems with uncertain parameters. Fuzzy Sets Syst. **130**(3), 277–289 (2002)
15. Hengl, T., Heuvelink, G., Stein, A.: A generic framework for spatial prediction of soil variables based on regression-kriging. Geoderma **120**(1–2), 75–93 (2004)
16. Ishibuchi, H., Nii, M.: Fuzzy regression using asymmetric fuzzy coefficients and fuzzified neural networks. Fuzzy Sets Syst. **119**(2), 273–290 (2001)
17. Loquin, K., Dubois, D.: Kriging and epistemic uncertainty: a critical discussion. In: Jeansoulin, R., Papini, O., Prade, H., Schockaert, S. (eds.) Methods for Handling Imperfect Spatial Information. STUDFUZZ, vol. 256, pp. 269–305. Springer, Heidelberg (2010)
18. Loquin, K., Dubois, D.: Kriging with Ill-Known Variogram and Data. In: Deshpande, A., Hunter, A. (eds.) SUM 2010. LNCS, vol. 6379, pp. 219–235. Springer, Heidelberg (2010)
19. Loquin, K., Dubois, D.: A fuzzy interval analysis approach to kriging with ill-known variogram and data. Soft Comput. **16**(5), 769–784 (2012)
20. Raaschou-Nielsen, O., et al.: Air pollution and lung cancer incidence in 17 European cohorts: prospective analyses from the European study of cohorts for air pollution effects (ESCAPE). Lancet Oncol. **14**(9), 813–822 (2013)
21. Robert, S., Foresti, L., Kanevski, M.: Spatial prediction of monthly wind speeds in complex terrain with adaptive general regression neural networks. Int. J. Climatol. **33**(7), 1793–1804 (2013)
22. Shad, R., Mesgari, M.S., Abkar, A., Shad, A.: Predicting air pollution using fuzzy genetic linear membership kriging in GIS. Comput. Environ. Urban Syst. **33**(6), 472–481 (2009)
23. Stein, A., Verma, M.: Handling spatial data uncertainty using a fuzzy geostatistical approach for modelling methane emissions at the island of java. In: Fisher, P.F. (ed.) Developments in Spatial Data Handling, pp. 173–187. Springer, Heidelberg (2005)

Neuro-Fuzzy Analysis of Atmospheric Pollution

Ángel Arroyo[1(✉)], Verónica Tricio[2], Emilio Corchado[3],
and Álvaro Herrero[1]

[1] Department of Civil Engineering, University of Burgos, Burgos, Spain
{aarroyop,ahcosio}@ubu.es
[2] Department of Physics, University of Burgos, Burgos, Spain
vtricio@ubu.es
[3] Departamento de Informática y Automática,
University of Salamanca, Salamanca, Spain
escorchado@usal.es

Abstract. Present study proposes the application of different soft-computing and statistical techniques to the characterization of atmospheric conditions in Spain. The main goal is to visualize and analyze the air quality in a certain region of Spain (Madrid) to better understand its circumstances and evolution. To do so, real-life data from three data acquisition stations are analysed. The main pollutants acquired by these stations are studied in order to research how the geographical location of these stations and the different seasons of the year are decisive in the behavior of air pollution. Different techniques for dimensionality reduction together with clustering techniques have been applied, in a combination of neural and fuzzy paradigms.

Keywords: Hybrid systems · Clustering techniques · Air quality · Statistical models · Artificial neural networks

1 Introduction

In recent years, our knowledge of atmospheric pollution and our understanding of its effects have advanced greatly. It has been accepted for some years now that air pollution not only represents a health risk. Other serious consequences may be mentioned such as acid rain, corrosion, climate change and global warming. Thus, all efforts that are directed towards studying these phenomena [1] may improve our understanding and help us to prevent the serious problematic nature of atmospheric pollution. Systematic measurements in Spain, which are usually taken within large cities, are fundamental due to the health risks caused by high levels of atmospheric pollution. Recent trends point to the benefits of continuing to extend the network of atmospheric pollution measurement stations. These measurement stations acquire data continuously. Thanks to the open data policy promulgated by the public institutions [2] these data are available for further study and analysis.

Dimensionality reduction techniques [3] do the transformation of high-dimensional data into a meaningful representation of reduced dimensionality. These techniques have been previously applied to the field of Environmental Conditions (EC) [4–6]. There is a wide range of dimensionality reduction techniques, such as Principal Component

© Springer International Publishing Switzerland 2015
E. Onieva et al. (Eds.): HAIS 2015, LNAI 9121, pp. 382–392, 2015.
DOI: 10.1007/978-3-319-19644-2_32

Analysis (PCA) [7], Local Linear Embedding (LLE) [8], Isometric Mapping (ISO-MAP) [9] and Cooperative Maximum Likelihood Hebbian Learning (CMLHL) [10], which have previously achieved very good results in the field of Environmental Conditions (EC) [11]. One characteristic of these techniques is that clusters are identified in the graphical representation with the naked eye, and there is not any label or assignment of each sample to a certain group of data. These techniques are very useful as pre-processors for the application of other machine learning paradigms, or as the final step in the visualization task.

On the other hand, clustering or grouping techniques [12] divide a given dataset into groups of similar objects, according to several different "similarity" measures. In most cases, the number of desired clusters and the function determines the assignment of each sample to a certain cluster is defined. These sets of techniques have been previously applied to EC [13, 14]. Most of the previous studies apply clustering techniques and only a few dimensionality reduction techniques. So, to the best of the authors' knowledge, this is the first time that those techniques are applied in unison, and its results are compared.

The main idea of present work is to analyse data describing air pollution from a case study associated to the region of Madrid (Spain). Firstly, some neural dimensionality reduction techniques are applied to project the data and get an intuitive visualization of the data structure. In a second step, clustering techniques are applied to the original data set in order to find the best possible clustering of data. For that, the output of first step is taken into account and fuzzy logic is applied for the clustering.

The rest of this study is organized as follows. Section 2 presents the techniques and methods that are applied to analyse the data. Section 3 details the real-life case study that is addressed in present work, while Sect. 4 describes the experiments and results. Finally, Sect. 5 sets out the conclusions and future work.

2 Techniques and Methods

In order to analyse data sets with atmospheric pollution information, several dimensionality reduction techniques and clustering methods are applied. Those methods are described in this section.

2.1 Neural Projection Techniques

To reduce the cost of the dimensionality of the representation space, the use of feature selection procedures was proposed [15], with the aim of reducing this dimensionality. The problem of dimensionality reduction can be expressed as follows: for each sample i determine a selection or transformation of attributes so that:

$$x_{ij} \longrightarrow y_{ik}, j = 1, \ldots, n; k = 1, \ldots, l, l < n \qquad (1)$$

where x_{ij} represent each vector in the input space, y_{ik} represent each vector in the output space, n and l are the number of dimensions in the input and output spaces, respectively.

From the wide range of neural projection techniques, two different ones have been applied in present work. Principal Component Analysis has been applied as a standard projection technique. At the same time, a more advanced technique (Cooperative Maximum Likelihood Hebbian Learning) is also applied for comparison purposes.

Principal Component Analysis. Principal Component Analysis (PCA) [16] is a well-known method that gives the best linear data compression in terms of least mean square error by addressing the data variance. Although it was proposed as an statistical method, it has been proved that it can be implemented by several Artificial Neural Networks [17, 18].

Cooperative Maximum Likelihood Hebbian Learning. Cooperative Maximum Likelihood Hebbian Learning (CMLHL) [19] is an extended version of Maximum Likelihood Hebbian Learning (MLHL) [20] that incorporates lateral connections, which have been derived from the Rectified Gaussian Distribution. The resultant net can find the independent factors of a data set but does so in a way that captures some type of global ordering in the data set.

Consider an N-dimensional input vector x, an M-dimensional output vector y and a weight matrix W, where the element W_{ij} represents the relationship between input x_j and output y_i, then as it is shown in [19], CMLHL can be carried out as a four-step procedure:

Feed-forward step, where outputs are calculated according to:

$$y_i = \sum_{j=1}^{N} W_{ij}x_j, \forall i \tag{2}$$

Lateral activation passing step, where lateral connections of output neurons are given by:

$$y_i(t + 1) = [y_i(t) + \tau(b - Ay)]^+ \tag{3}$$

Feedback step:

$$e_j = x_j - \sum_{i=1}^{M} W_{ij}y_i, \forall j \tag{4}$$

Weight update step, where the following learning rule is applied:

$$\Delta W_{ij} = \eta.y_i.sign(e_j)|e_j|^{p-1} \tag{5}$$

Where η is the learning rate, τ is the "strength" of the lateral connections, b the bias parameter, p a parameter related to the energy function, and A is a symmetric matrix used to modify the response to the data.

2.2   Clustering Techniques

Cluster analysis organizes data by abstracting underlying structure either as a grouping of individuals or as a hierarchy of groups. The representation can then be investigated to see if the data group according to preconceived ideas or to suggest new experiments [12]. Intuitively, two elements belonging to a valid cluster should be more similar to each other than those which are in different groups. As in the case of projection techniques, only two clustering methods, from the wide range of clustering techniques, have been applied in present work. The k-means method has been selected as a standard clustering technique and fuzzy c-means as a more advanced technique, comprising Fuzzy Logic, to compare clustering outputs.

K-means. The standard k-means [21] is an algorithm for grouping data points into a given number of clusters. Its application requires two input parameters: the number of clusters, k, and their initial centroids, which can be chosen by the user or obtained through some pre-processing. Each data element is assigned to the nearest group centroid, thereby obtaining the initial composition of the groups. Once these groups are obtained, the centroids are recalculated and a further reallocation is made. The process is repeated until the centroids do not change. Given the heavy reliance of this method on initial parameters, a good measure of the goodness of the grouping is simply the sum of the proximity Error Sums of Squares (SSE) that it attempts to minimize:

$$SSE = \sum_{j=1}^{k} \sum_{x \in G_j} \frac{p(x_i, c_j)}{n} \tag{6}$$

where p is the proximity function, k is the number of the groups, c_j are the centroids and n the number of rows.. In the case of working with Euclidean distance, the expression is equivalent to the global mean square error.

Fuzzy c-means. Conventional clustering approaches (such as k-means) assume that an object can belong to only one cluster. In practice, the separation of clusters is a fuzzy notion. Fuzzy clustering algorithms, that combine Fuzzy Logic and cluster analysis techniques, outperform conventional clustering algorithms by allowing each object to be assigned to one or more clusters. According to Fuzzy Logic, the membership function is not a crisp value (0, 1) but it is now defined as a percentage.

The c–means clustering algorithm [22] is a clustering method that lets one piece of data belong to two or more clusters. Let $X = [x_1, x_2, ..., x_m]$ be a set of numerical data in $\mathbf{R}^N$. Let c be an integer, $1 < c < M$. Given X, it can be said that c-fuzzy subsets $\{u_k: X \rightarrow [0, 1]\}$ are partitions of X if the following conditions are satisfied:

$$0 \leq u_{kj} \leq 1 \; \forall \, k, j \tag{7}$$

$$\sum_{k=1}^{c} u_{kj} = 1 \; \forall \, j \tag{8}$$

$$0 < \sum_{j=1}^{M} u_{kj} < n \, \forall \, k \tag{9}$$

Where $u_{kj} = u_k(X_j)$, $1 <= k <= c$ and $1 <= j <= M$.

3 Real-Life Case Study

This study is focused on the analysis of air pollution data recorded in the region of Madrid [23] and Madrid city (central Spain) [24].

Three reasons determine the selection of the stations under study: the same pollutants are acquired and these pollutants are the most interesting ones in order to study the atmospheric conditions [25]. The second reason is that the areas, where the stations are located, have strong differences, such as traffic density, population or protection of the vegetation. This fact is important for comparing the levels of air pollution between areas with high population density and others with low population density.

From the timeline point of view, data are selected from years 2007 and 2008 because that was the time for the beginning of the economic crisis in this country. This fact implies a significant variation in the levels of air pollution compared with other periods of time. Along these two years the economic activity in strategic fields like building, was significantly reduced. Further studies will compare these results with other ones from subsequent years.

The data was gathered in stations located in the following areas:

1. Aranjuez: this is an urban background station. The full station specification can be found in [23].
2. Atalaz: this is a vegetation protection station. Full station specification can be found in [23].
3. Madrid city center: it represents the average values for the stations located in the downtown area of the Madrid city. Full station specification can be found in [24].

There are a total of 72 samples for the twelve months of 2007 and 2008 and the 3 stations analyzed in this study, 12 samples for each station, one sample per month (monthly daily average). The following parameters (four air pollutants and two meteorological variables) were analyzed:

1. Nitric Oxide (NO) - $\mu g/m^3$, primary pollutant. NO is a colorless gas which reacts with ozone undergoing rapid oxidation to NO_2, which is the predominant in the atmosphere.
2. Nitrogen Dioxide (NO_2) - μ/m^3, primary pollutant. From the standpoint of health protection, nitrogen dioxide has set exposure limits for long and short duration.
3. Particulate Matter (PM10) - $\mu g/m^3$, primary pollutant. These particles remain stable in the air for long periods of time without falling to the ground and can be moved by the wind important distances.
4. Ozone (O_3) - $\mu g/m^3$, secondary pollutant. Ozone is an odorless, colorless gas composed of three oxygen atoms.

5. Wind Speed Module - m/s.
6. Air Temperature - °C.

4   Results and Discussions

As previously stated, many dimensionality reduction methods have been firstly applied. In this step a possible structure in the data is seek. PCA is the first technique applied in order to find a possible structure in the data. Figure 1 shows the two principal components of the data through which the whole dataset is projected.

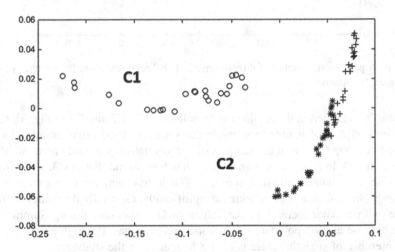

Fig. 1. PCA projection. Number of dimensions: 2. Label representation: '*' urban area, '+' vegetation protected area, 'o' madrid center.

In Fig. 1 data samples are depicted according to their geographical location (data acquisition station). PCA depicts two main groups of data (labeled in Fig. 1 as C1 and C2). Group **C1** comprises all the samples corresponding to the mean values of the stations located in the city center of Madrid. This area is related to the highest values of air pollution, given mainly by a very large increase of the values of NO. Group **C2** contains the samples corresponding to the urban area and vegetation protection area. So, data from these two stations are merged in the same group.

PCA projection is also depicted in Fig. 2 but, in this case, data are projected according to the season of the year they belong to (winter, spring, summer and autumn). The obtained projection is not as clear as the previous one (Fig. 1). Reviewing the original data set, it can be observed an evolution of the atmospheric pollution along the year, as Winter and Autumn data contains higher levels of air pollution in Madrid center (cluster C1). In cluster C2, it is also observed an increase of atmospheric pollution especially in the station of Atalaz (protected vegetation area).

Figure 3 shows the CMLHL projection where data are depicted according to their geographical location (place of the data acquisition station). Three main clusters of data

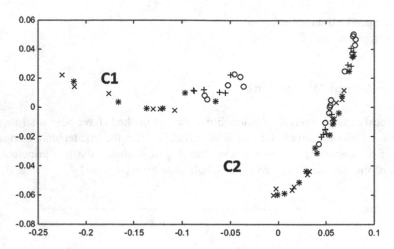

Fig. 2. PCA projection. Number of dimensions: 2. Label representation: '*' winter, '+' spring, 'o' summer, 'x' autumn.

can be easily identified in this projection (labelled as C1, C2 and C3 in Fig. 3). CMLH outperforms PCA as it is able to separate the samples of the urban area (all of them contained in group **C2**), from the samples of the vegetation protection area (all of them contained in **C3**). In a subsequent analysis, it has been found that in **C3**, where there is little traffic or pollutant emission sources of industrial activity in comparison with others areas, the pollution values decrease significantly, especially the values of the NO variable, with a major increase in the values of O_3, especially during Summer. This may be because the NO pollutant is an ozone precursor gas. For high air temperatures (in the presence of sunlight) there is ozone formation in the study area.

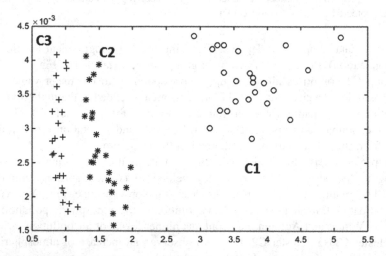

Fig. 3. CMLHL projection. Number of dimensions: 2, number of iterations: 1000, learning rate: 0.001, p parameter: 2.5, τ: 2.5. Label representation: '*' urban area, '+' vegetation protected area and 'o' madrid center.

As for PCA, Fig. 4 shows the CMLHL projection, where data samples are depicted according to associated season of the year. As for previous figure, CMLH projection outperforms that from PCA (Fig. 2) as in the three clusters (C1, C2 and C3), it is observed a clear direction in the data, being the seasons of Winter and Autumn those with higher levels of air pollution. **C1** groups the samples corresponding to the city of Madrid in the seasons of Winter and Autumn. This area offers the highest values of air pollution, given mainly by a very large increase of the values of NO, reaching values of 150 $\mu g/m^3$ in the autumn and winter seasons. **C1** also groups the samples of Madrid center in Summer and Spring, where the air pollution is still high. A certain ordering of the data (from north-west to south-east) can be identified in the group visualization through CMLH. **C2** groups the samples corresponding to Aranjuez (urban areas), these samples shows the highest values of air pollution in urban areas in season of Autumn and Winter and a decrease in the other two seasons of the year. In cluster **C3**, which groups the most of samples acquired in the protected vegetation area, the pollution values fall significantly, especially the values of NO variable, with a notable increase in the values of O_3. In this case, the pollution values have fallen significantly, especially in relation to values of NO variable, not significantly increasing its value in any season of the year. In the case of groups C2 and C3, a certain ordering of data can be seen as well: from top to bottom, data are ordered according to the season.

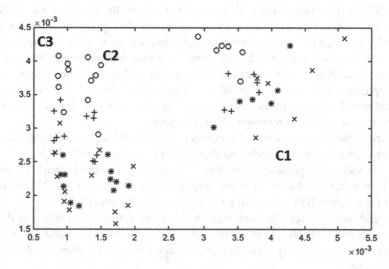

Fig. 4. CMLHL projection. Number of dimensions: 2, number of iterations: 1000, learning rate: 0.001, p parameter: 2.5, τ: 2.5. Label representation: '*' winter, '+' spring, 'o' summer and 'x' autumn.

In this first step two dimensionality reduction techniques are applied in order to visually identify the structure of data, that leads to an analysis of the environmental conditions in the case study. CMLHL obtains better graphical results in order to identify clusters of data. By applying these dimensionality reduction methods, several groups of data can be easily observed with the naked eye.

In a second step, some clustering methods are applied in order to compare the results of the two techniques and the validity of both techniques in this case of study. The results of such techniques are shown in Table 1.

Table 1. Clustering results for the atmospheric pollution dataset.

Method	K	Metric	Cluster samples allocation (%)		
			Madrid center	Atalaz	Aranjuez
K-means	2	0.1704	[100 0]	[0 100]	[0 100]
Fuzzy c-means	2	0.1443	[100 0]	[0 100]	[0 100]
K-means	3	0.1191	[100 0 0]	[0 75 25]	[0 0 100]
Fuzzy c-means	3	0.0854	[100 0 0]	[0 4 96]	[0 41 39]
K-means	4	0.0622	[0 0 29 71]	[80 20 0 0]	[4 96 0 0]
Fuzzy c-means	4	0.0432	[75 0 0 25]	[0 26 74 0]	[0 96 4 0]
K-means	5	0.0935	[100 0 0 0]	[0 33 0 0 67]	[0 0 41 59 0]
Fuzzy c-means	5	0.0285	[88 12 0 0 0]	[0 0 75 25 0]	[0 0 25 75 0]

In Table 1, column k represents the number of clusters specified for the algorithm in advance. Metric is the output value of the method to assess the quality of the clustering: in fuzzy c-means it is the distance from any given data point to a cluster center weighted by that data point's membership grade; in k-means it is the total quantization error for the data set. Columns Madrid center, Atalaz and Aranjuez represents the percentage of samples from this location that are allocated to each one the clusters. e.g. [100 0] represents 100 % of samples allocated in the first cluster and 0 % allocated in the second one. In fuzzy c-means is assumed that each data is assigned to the cluster that score for the highest percentage of membership.

Selected values for parameters of k-means are: method: 'seq', D: original dataset, k: number of clusters selected, epoch: number of iterations (max 100).

Selected values for parameters of fuzzy c-means are: method: 'seq', D: original dataset, k: number of clusters selected, exponent for the matrix U: 2.0, maximum number of iterations: 100, minimum amount of improvement: $1*e^{-5}$.

In Table 1, it can be seen that although PCA clearly defines two clusters of data, (in Figs. 1 and 2) and CMLHL clearly defines three clusters (in Figs. 3 and 4), clustering techniques give substantially more optimal values for higher values of clusters, see column 'metric'.

Analyzing the distribution of samples in clusters, it is observed that increasing the number of selected clusters, this subdivision of clusters of data occurs at the station of Aranjuez and to the station of Atalaz in a minor way, while most of the Madrid center samples stay in the same cluster. This fact reveals that Madrid city center has very particular atmospheric conditions and highly differentiated from the other two locations.

5 Conclusions and Future Work

Conclusions can be divided into two parts, firstly with regard to the analysis of air pollution in the analysed case study. On the other hand, the behaviour of the combined methods of clustering and dimensionality reduction in the process of data grouping.

The conclusions about the quality of the air pollution in Madrid in this case study reflects the fact that there are very high values of NO in the center of Madrid, especially during the Autumn and Winter seasons. This accounts for an increase in air pollution. The O_3 concentration and the wind speed are lower than in the other two seasons, which affects air quality in a negative way. Background urban areas and protected vegetation areas present much lower levels of NO and higher levels of O_3 in summer, especially in the protected vegetation areas. It is also possible to observe an evolution in the levels of air pollution throughout the year, showing higher values in parameters such as NO during the Autumn and Winter seasons. The air pollution observed in these three air quality monitoring stations does not suffer hardly any variation between 2007 and 2008.

Regarding the application of dimensionality reduction techniques, CMLH obtains excellent performance identifying structure of data. CMLHL gives us an easy visual representation of the data, finding internal structures in the data with the naked eye.

Finally, the clustering techniques find relationships between data in a more precise way. Cluster allocation for some of the data is clearly defined. The main disadvantage is the lack of the easy graphical representation of the results that neural projection techniques output. Comparing the two clustering methods applied, can conclude that both work in a correct way for this case study, providing similar results. However fuzzy c-means, thanks to its allocation percentages, gives a more precise answer giving the possibility of a fine adjustment in the allocation of samples to clusters.

In future work, will expand the years of study and methods used to draw new conclusions about the behavior of atmospheric conditions in selected areas of study, as well as the validity of these techniques in the case study.

References

1. San José, R., Pérez, J.L., González, R.M.: An operational real-time air quality modelling system for industrial plants. Environ. Model Softw. **22**, 297–307 (2007)
2. The Aporta project as a driver of the re-use of public sector information in Spain (2015). http://datos.gob.es/content/proyecto-aporta-como-impulsor-de-reutilizacion-de-informacion-del-sector-publico-espana
3. Corchado, E., Perez, J.C.: A three-step unsupervised neural model for visualizing high complex dimensional spectroscopic data sets. Pattern Anal. Appl. **14**, 207–218 (2011)
4. Corchado, E., Arroyo, A., Tricio, V.: Soft computing models to identify typical meteorological days. Logic J. IGPL **19**, 373–383 (2010)
5. Chattopadhyay, G., Chattopadhyay, S., Chakraborthy, P.: Principal component analysis and neurocomputing-based models for total ozone concentration over different urban regions of India. Theoret. Appl. Climatol. **109**, 221–231 (2011)

6. Glezakos, T.J., Tsiligiridis, T.A., Iliadis, L.S., Yialouris, C.P., Maris, F.P., Ferentinos, K.P.: Feature extraction for time-series data: an artificial neural network evolutionary training model for the management of mountainous watersheds. Neurocomputing **73**, 49–59 (2009)

7. Abdi, H., Williams, L.J.: Principal component analysis. Wiley Interdisciplinary Rev.: Comput. Stat. **2**, 433–459 (2010)

8. Li, X., Lin, S., Yan, S., Xu, D.: Discriminant locally linear embedding with high-order tensor data. IEEE Trans. Syst. Man, Cybern. Part B: Cybern. **38**, 342–352 (2008)

9. Shao, C., Hu, H.: Extension of ISOMAP for imperfect manifolds. J. Comput. **7**, 1780–1785 (2012)

10. Corchado, E., Han, Y., Fyfe, C.: Structuring global responses of local filters using lateral connections. J. Exp. Theor. Artif. Intell. **15**, 473–487 (2003)

11. Arroyo, A., Corchado, E., Tricio, V.: Atmospheric pollution analysis by unsupervised learning. In: Corchado, E., Yin, H. (eds.) IDEAL 2009. LNCS, vol. 5788, pp. 767–772. Springer, Heidelberg (2009)

12. Jain, A.K., Maheswari, S.: Survey of recent clustering techniques in data mining. J. Curr. Comput. Sci. Technol **3**, 72–78 (2013)

13. Kassomenos, P., Vardoulakis, S., Borge, R., Lumbreras, J., Papaloukas, C., Karakitsios, S.: Comparison of statistical clustering techniques for the classification of modelled atmospheric trajectories. Theoret. Appl. Climatol. **102**, 1–12 (2010)

14. Pires, J.C.M., Sousa, S.I.V., Pereira, M.C., Alvim-Ferraz, M.C.M., Martins, F.G.: Management of air quality monitoring using principal component and cluster analysis— Part I: SO2 and PM10. Atmos. Environ. **42**, 1249–1260 (2008)

15. Smola, A.J., Schölkopf, B.: A tutorial on support vector regression. Stat. Comput. **14**, 199–222 (2004)

16. Pearson, K.: On lines and planes of closest fit to systems of points in space. Philos. Mag. **2**, 559–572 (1901)

17. Oja, E.: Principal components, minor components, and linear neural networks. Neural Netw. **5**, 927–935 (1992)

18. Oja, E.: Neural networks, principal components, and subspaces. Int. J. Neural Syst. **1**, 61–68 (1989)

19. Corchado, E.F.C.: Connectionist techniques for the identification and suppression of interfering underlying factors. Int. J. Pattern Recognit Artif Intell. **17**, 1447–1466 (2003)

20. Corchado, E., MacDonald, D., Fyfe, C.: Maximum and minimum likelihood Hebbian learning for exploratory projection pursuit. Data Min. Knowl. Disc. **8**, 203–225 (2004)

21. Ding, C., He, X.: K-means clustering via principal component analysis, vol. 29 (2004)

22. Gao, X., Xie, W.: Advances in theory and applications of fuzzy clustering. Chin. Sci. Bull. **45**, 961–970 (2000)

23. Region of Madrid, Area Air Quality - Air Quality Network (2015). http://gestiona.madrid. org/azul_internet/html/web/ListaEstacionesAccion.icm?ESTADO_MENU=3_2

24. Council of Madrid, Air Quality (2015). http://www.mambiente.munimadrid.es/opencms/ opencms/calaire/ContaAtmosferica/portadilla.html

25. Snelder, T.H., Dey, K.L., Leathwick, J.R.: A procedure for making optimal selection of input variables for multivariate environmental classifications. Conserv. Biol. **21**, 365–375 (2007)

Improving Earthquake Prediction with Principal Component Analysis: Application to Chile

Gualberto Asencio-Cortés[1]($\boxtimes$), Francisco Martínez-Álvarez[1], Antonio Morales-Esteban[2], Jorge Reyes[3], and Alicia Troncoso[1]

[1] Department of Computer Science, Pablo de Olavide University, Seville, Spain
{guaasecor,fmaralv,ali}@upo.es
[2] Department of Building Structures and Geotechnical Engineering, University of Seville, Seville, Spain
ame@us.es
[3] NT2 Labs, Santiago, Chile
daneel@geofisica.cl

Abstract. Increasing attention has been paid to the prediction of earthquakes with data mining techniques during the last decade. Several works have already proposed the use of certain features serving as inputs for supervised classifiers. However, they have been successfully used without any further transformation so far. In this work, the use of principal component analysis to reduce data dimensionality and generate new datasets is proposed. In particular, this step is inserted in a successfully already used methodology to predict earthquakes. Santiago and Pichilemu, two of the cities mostly threatened by large earthquakes occurrence in Chile, are studied. Several well-known classifiers combined with principal component analysis have been used. Noticeable improvement in the results is reported.

Keywords: Earthquake prediction · Principal component analysis · Time series · Data mining

1 Introduction

Earthquake prediction is a task of utmost difficulty that involves many variables. Although many studies have identified several phenomena as earthquake precursors, they have not been reliably encountered all over the world.

The prediction of large magnitude earthquakes is of particular importance given its potential to cause loss of life. Earthquake prediction must be distinguished from earthquake forecasting (probabilistic assessment of earthquake hazard) and from earthquake warning systems (real-time warnings to specific areas once an earthquake has occurred). Since there is no practical method for successfully and systematically predicting earthquakes so far, it is needed to conducting research in this direction.

It is well-known that Chile is one of the countries with higher seismic activity across the world. This is evidenced by the large amount of earthquakes with

© Springer International Publishing Switzerland 2015
E. Onieva et al. (Eds.): HAIS 2015, LNAI 9121, pp. 393–404, 2015.
DOI: 10.1007/978-3-319-19644-2_33

magnitude larger than $7.5\,M_s$ encountered during the last centuries. Indeed, the largest earthquake ever occurred, known as *Earthquake of Valdivia, Chile* (May 22, 1960) reached a $9.5\,M_s$ magnitude and caused a 10 m high tsunami [6].

This work is focused on the application of supervised classifiers combined with principal component analysis (PCA) to improve earthquake prediction. It is based on the inputs proposed in previous works [12, 16, 21] and searches for datasets with different dimensionality and properties, constructed after the application of PCA. The problem of data dimensionality reveals that an excessive number of features usually lead to poorer results. For this reason PCA is a suitable methodology to create proper vector spaces with adequate number of coordinates.

The two most seismic Chilean zones described in [20], Santiago, the capital city of Chile, (Region #5) and Pichilemu (Region #4), have been subjected to analysis in order to assess the performance of such proposal. But, obviously, this study could be extended to any other active seismic zone.

It is important to highlight that this work is an attempt to simultaneously fulfil all the requirements demanded by the Seismological Society of America to make an accurate prediction [2]. In this sense it provides predictions for when (within the next five days), where (at a reduced surface of no more than $100 \times 100\,\mathrm{km}^2$ for Santiago, and no more than $50 \times 50\,\mathrm{km}^2$ for Pichilemu), and how large (magnitude larger than $4.5\,M_s$, which is an accepted threshold by the Scientific Community to determine that an earthquake is large enough to cause losses).

The remainder of the article is structured as follows. Section 2 reviews the state-of-the-art for earthquake prediction based on data mining. Section 3 describes the new methodology proposed here. The results for the two cities analyzed are shown in Sect. 4. Finally, the conclusions drawn from this study are summarized in Sect. 5.

2   Related Work

The prediction of earthquakes, due to the devastating effect they may cause in human activity, has been thoroughly studied as discussed by Panakkat and Adeli in 2008 [17] and, later in 2012, by Tiampo and Shcherbakov [23]. These two surveys reveal the vast number of approaches proposed based on geophysical assumptions and statistical procedures.

However, a new collection of techniques based on data mining are emerging as powerful tools nowadays as pointed out in recent reviews [3, 15].

The proposal of seismicity indicators as inputs for supervised classifiers were first proposed in [16]. The authors selected artificial neural networks as classifier to make predictions. The zone studied was South California. The same authors refined their own approach two years later and obtained even better results for the same location [18].

Another new set of seismicity indicators were proposed in [21]. This time most of them were based on the well-known Gutenberg-Ritcher's b-value [8], as well as on the Bath and Omori-Utsu laws. The zones under analysis were four Chilean cities and surroundings. The same set of seismicity indicators were used to predict earthquakes in the Iberian Peninsula [12] and even to discover seismic zoning in Croatia [13].

Another active zone, India, has been analyzed with supervised classifiers [5]. Also the tectonic regions of Northeast India have been explored [22]. The authors retrieved earthquake data from NOAA and USGS catalogues and proposed two non-linear forecasting models. Both approaches are stable and suggest the existence of certain seasonality in earthquake occurrence in this area.

Zamani et al. [24] also proposed a set of seismicity indicators but, this time, its performance was assessed before the Qeshm earthquake in South Iran. They used artificial neural networks and adaptive neural fuzzy inference system. The seismicity in Greece has also been studied [10]. In this work, the authors only used the magnitude of the previous earthquakes as input and obtained a high accuracy rate for medium earthquakes. However, the rate considerably decreased when major seismic events were considered. The northern Red Sea area is not an exception and has also been analyzed in [1]. The authors compared the performance of their approach to several Box-Jenkins models.

All the mentioned methods have obtained, in general terms, good results. However they all share a same feature: none of them questioned the quality of the sets they used or even they tried to transform. This gap in the literature justifies the conduction of this research study.

3   Methodology

This section describes the proposed approach to improve earthquake prediction methodologies used in [11, 21].

First of all, it is worth noting that a prediction problem has been turned into a binary classification one. That is, the labels assigned to every event have information about the future: a sample has been labeled with an *1* if an earthquake with a magnitude larger than a preset threshold has occurred within the next days; and with a *0* if not. The horizon of prediction has been set to five days for Chile [21]. The triggering thresholds are those that ensure balanced training sets [7, 9] as proposed in [12, 21], and are 4.5 for both cities.

Figure 1 illustrates the full process. Every task is described below:

1. Set of inputs #1 stands for the features proposed in [21] whereas set of inputs #2 are those introduced in [16]. Table 1 lists all these features. Note that OU stands for Omori-Utsu and GR for Gutenberg-Ritcher. For a deeper understanding, the reader should refer to the original works.
2. Principal component analysis (PCA). This step transforms original data into a new dataset with reduced dimensionality and different physical properties. Since the goal of this work is to evaluate its usefulness, a wide range of principal components will be generated in order to determine if PCA improves or not the prediction process.

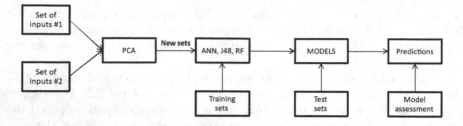

Fig. 1. Steps involved in the proposed methodology.

Table 1. Set of features used as inputs for classifiers.

Set	Feature	Description
Inputs #1	x_1	$b_i - b_{i-4}$
	x_2	$b_{i-4} - b_{i-8}$
	x_3	$b_{i-8} - b_{i-12}$
	x_4	$b_{i-12} - b_{i-16}$
	x_5	$b_{i-16} - b_{i-20}$
	x_6	OU's law
	x_7	Dynamic GR's law
Inputs #2	T	Elapsed time
	M_{mean}	Mean magnitude
	$dE^{1/2}$	Square root of seismic energy
	β	Slope of magnitude-log plot
	a	a−value from GR's law
	ΔM	Magnitude deficit
	η	Mean square deviation

3. Application of well-known classifiers. In order to make fair comparisons, artificial neural networks (ANN), classification trees (J48) and random forest (RF) algorithms have been used. The first two ones because they were used in the original works, and the third one because it has been found that provides even better results.

4. Evaluation of the generated results by means of a wide variety of quality parameters (see Sect. 4.1), typically used for assessing classifiers performance.

Please note that a prediction is made every time that an earthquake of magnitude larger than 3.0 occurs. In [21], it was shown that the cutoff magnitude for the earthquakes' database of Chile is 3.0 ($M_0 = 3.0$). Ought to the high seismic activity of the areas under study, a prediction is made almost daily.

4 Experimental Study

This section presents the results obtained. First, the quality measures used to assess the methodology's performance are introduced in Sect. 4.1. Section 4.2 describes the datasets used in this work. Then, the setup of all the algorithms used is reported in Sect. 4.3. Finally, the results themselves for Santiago and Pichilemu are exposed in Sect. 4.4.

4.1 Quality Measures

To assess the performance of the ANN's designed, several parameters have been used. In particular:

1. True positives (TP). The number of times that an upcoming earthquake has been properly predicted.
2. True negatives (TN). The number of times that neither the ANN triggered an alarm nor an earthquake occurred.
3. False positives (FP). The number of times that the ANN erroneously predicted the occurrence of an earthquake.
4. False negatives (FN). The number of times that the ANN did not trigger an alarm but an earthquake did occur.

The combination of these parameters leads to the calculation of:

$$NPV = \frac{TN}{TN + FN} \tag{1}$$

$$PPV = \frac{TP}{TP + FP} \tag{2}$$

where NPV denotes the well-known negative predictive value, and PPV the well-known positive predictive value.

Additionally, two more parameters that correspond to common statistical measures of supervised classifiers performance have been used to evaluate the performance of the ANN's. These two parameters, sensitivity or rate of actual positives correctly identified as such (denoted by S_n) and specificity or rate of actual negatives correctly identified (denoted by S_p), are defined as:

$$S_n = \frac{TP}{TP + FN} \tag{3}$$

$$S_p = \frac{TN}{TN + FP} \tag{4}$$

To globally take into consideration all these measures, an arithmetic mean will be calculated for all of these parameters. Obviously, this average could be weighted reinforcing, for instance, specificity (high reliability when no alarms are triggered) or PPV (high reliability when an alarm is triggered). However, this would pose several questions such as determining a subjective weight for each of them. For this reason, the authors have decided to calculate just the simple arithmetic average.

4.2   Datasets Description

This section describes the datasets used. Two cities of Chile especially affected by significant quakes have been analyzed. In particular, Santiago and Pichilemu earthquake data have been retrieved from a public repository, managed by the University of Chile's National Service of Seismology [4].

Analyzed cities and surroundings' surfaces are $1° \times 1°$ for Santiago and $0.5° \times 0.5°$ for Pichilemu, following with the description in [21]. Moreover, these cities are the main cities in seismic regions #5 and #4, as determined in [20]. This information is summarized in Table 2.

Table 2. Seismic Chilean areas analyzed.

Main city	Seismic area	Vertices	Dimensions
Pichilemu	#4	(34°S, 72.5°W), (34.5°S, 72°W)	$0.5° \times 0.5°$
Santiago	#5	(33°S, 71°W), (34°S, 70°W)	$1° \times 1°$

As for the length of the datasets, Santiago's training set contains the linearly independent vectors occurred from August 10th 2005 to March 31th 2010. Analogously, the test set included the vectors generated from April 1st 2010 to October 8th 2011. As for Pichilemu, the training set contains the linearly independent vectors occurred from August 10th 2005 to March 31st 2010. Its test set includes the vectors generated from April 1st 2010 to October 8th 2011.

4.3   Parameters Setup

The implementation of ANN, J48 and RF algorithms are those integrated in Weka 3.6 open source tool [14]. In particular, to make comparisons to original papers possible, default setup for these methods have been chosen. Table 3 summarizes such configuration.

Table 3. Setup for methods used combined with PCA to assess methodology's performance.

Method	Setup
ANN	numLayers = AUTO, learningRate = 0.2, momentum = 0.2
RF	maxDepth = 0, numFeatures = 0, numTrees = 10
J48	confidenceFactor = 0.25, minNumObject = 2, numFolds = 3, unpruned = FALSE

The PCA has been launched in the R environment [19]. In particular, the *Psych* package, version 1.4.2.3, has been used with Varimax rotation. The analysis has been carried out from two to thirteen principal components in order to evaluate the number of components that better transform the data. This number has been selected because the number of considered attributes is fourteen.

4.4 Study Cases: Santiago and Pichilemu

Results from the application of the proposed methodology to Santiago and Pichilemu are presented in this section. Table 4 summarizes the results for the city of Santiago. The best results have been obtained when original data have been transformed into eleven components prior to the application of the three selected classifiers: ANN, J48 and RF. The average result for the four quality parameters without previous PCA is 56.01 %, whereas a 63.98 % average result has been obtained when PCA has been used. That is, a relative improvement of 14.23 %. Figure 2 illustrates the degree of membership for the fourteen attributes listed in Table 1 (same order in the figure as listed in the table) for the eleven principal components generated.

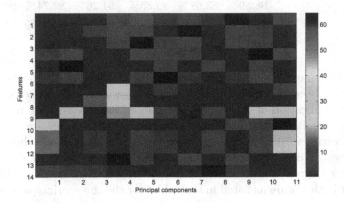

Fig. 2. Feature distribution into the eleven principal components for Santiago.

If a effectiveness ranking of methods is performed, with and without the application of previous PCA, it is noteworthy that RF without PCA obtained the best result: 74.09 %. However, this result is somewhat tricky since only one TP has been detected. This high average rate is justified due to the low number of real earthquakes existing in the test set, since RF tends to classify all samples as negative cases. Even if low false alarm rate is desirable, a 7.10 % sensitivity cannot be interpreted as a satisfactory result. On the contrary, the use of the PCA obtained the second, third and fourth best results, as wanted to be shown. Moreover, the results seem to be more stable, reaching higher sensitivity but maintaining acceptable specificity rates. Moreover, except for RF without PCA, the other best results have been all reached when PCA has been firstly applied.

Another indicator that shows that the use of PCA generates better results is the sum of FP and FN. Without PCA this value is 140 ($FP + FN = 140$) and with PCA is 50 ($FP + FN = 50$), a decrease of 64.28 %. That is, the use of PCA generates more reliable predictions since the false negative and positive rates are dramatically lower.

Table 4. Results for Santiago with and without previous PCA.

Quality paremeters	Without PCA			With PCA		
	ANN	J48	RF	ANN	J48	RF
TP	6	6	1	5	3	2
TN	64	41	108	94	105	107
FP	44	67	0	14	3	1
FN	8	8	13	9	12	11
S_n	42.90 %	42.90 %	7.10 %	35.71 %	14.29 %	21.43 %
S_p	59.26 %	37.96 %	100.00 %	87.04 %	97.22 %	99.07 %
PPV	12.00 %	8.20 %	100.00 %	26.32 %	40.00 %	75.00 %
NPV	88.89 %	83.67 %	89.26 %	91.26 %	89.74 %	90.68 %
Average	50.76 %	43.18 %	74.09 %	60.08 %	60.31 %	71.55 %

Table 5 summarizes the results for the city of Pichilemu. The best results, this time, have been obtained when PCA has been used with three components, prior to the application of ANN, J48 and RF, as proposed in the methodology. The average result for the four quality parameters without previous PCA is 64.08 %, whereas a 73.03 % average result has been obtained when PCA has been previously applied. That is, a relative improvement of 13.97 %. Figure 3 illustrates the degree of membership for the fourteen attributes listed in Table 1 (same order in the figure as listed in the table) for the three principal components generated.

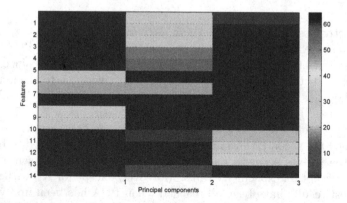

Fig. 3. Feature distribution into the three principal components for Pichilemu.

Table 5. Results for Pichilemu with and without previous PCA.

Quality paremeters	Without PCA			With PCA		
	ANN	J48	RF	ANN	J48	RF
TP	29	17	18	10	12	12
TN	6	79	68	88	89	90
FP	87	14	25	5	4	3
FN	0	12	11	19	17	17
S_n	100 %	58.60 %	62.10 %	34.48 %	41.38 %	41.38 %
S_p	6.45 %	84.95 %	73.12 %	94.62 %	95.70 %	96.77 %
PPV	25.00 %	54.80 %	41.90 %	66.67 %	75.00 %	80.00 %
NPV	100 %	86.81 %	86.08 %	82.24 %	83.96 %	84.11 %
Average	57.86 %	71.29 %	65.80 %	69.50 %	74.01 %	75.57 %

The best result has been obtained when RF has been applied after PCA with three components, with an average result of 75.57 %. Except for the J48 without PCA, again three out of four best results correspond to configurations with previous PCA. It is particularly remarkable the low number of FP that RF generated when PCA has been applied: 12 versus 126 generated without previous PCA. This fact is especially important because too many false alarms generally turn the predictions quite unreliable.

Again, the sum of FP and FN is significantly lower when PCA is applied. This number is 149 without PCA ($FP + FN = 149$) and 65 with PCA ($FP + FN = 105$), a value 56.38 % better. That is, the inclusion of PCA in the general scheme of prediction turns its outputs into more reliable results, admitting than less earthquakes are going to be detected.

Figures 4 and 5 illustrate the average results of applying PCA from two to thirteen components. It can be appreciated that the best results are achieved with eleven and three components for Santiago and Pichilemu, respectively. As for the rest of the values, it can be easily concluded that an adequate application of PCA may lead to major improvements in terms of accuracy, as wanted to be shown in this work. Even though the use of some particular number of components decreases the classifiers performance, it is undeniable that it can lead to much better results.

Additionally, in order to avoid possible smoothing in results when averaging all quality parameters, Figs. 6 and 7 depict the value of every parameter separately for the cities of Santiago and Pichilemu, respectively. It is noteworthy that S_n and NPV reach values verging on 90 % in both cases. In other words, the FP rate remains at a very low value which is a very desirable situation due to the social alarm that FP generally cause. By contrast, S_p and PPV are not as high as desired but higher enough to be considered satisfactory.

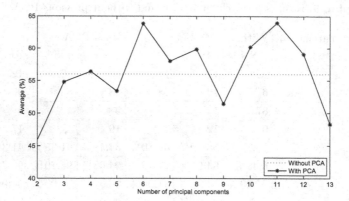

Fig. 4. Average results for Santiago, when PCA varies from 2 to 13 components.

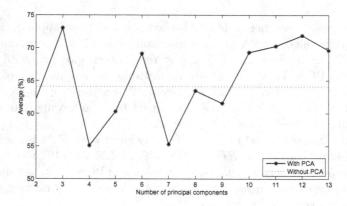

Fig. 5. Average results for Pichilemu, when PCA varies from 2 to 13 components.

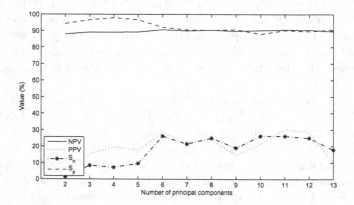

Fig. 6. Disaggregated results for Santiago for every quality parameter.

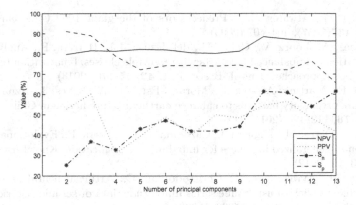

Fig. 7. Disaggregated results for Pichilemu for every quality parameter.

5 Conclusions

The use of PCA has been shown to be useful to improved earthquake prediction in Chile. By including this step in an existing methodology, the results obtained, in terms of average accuracy, have been significantly outperformed. In particular, artificial neural networks, classification trees and random forest algorithms have been successfully applied to Santiago and Pichilemu, two of the Chilean cities with the highest seismic activity. The results reported in this work suggest that this methodology could be applied to any other region in the world. As future work, given the imbalanced nature of data to be classified [7], these techniques are intended to be applied, especially when considering higher magnitude thresholds where the imbalance becomes more evident in the classes.

Acknowledgments. The financial support from the Junta de Andalucía, under project P12-TIC-1728, and from the Pablo de Olavide University of Seville, under help APPB813097, are acknowledged.

References

1. Alarifi, A.S.N., Alarifi, N.S.N., Al-Humidan, S.: Earthquakes magnitude predication using artificial neural network in northern Red Sea area. J. King Saud University - Sci. **24**, 301–313 (2012)
2. Allen, C.R.: Responsibilities in earthquake prediction. Bull. Seismol. Soc. Am. **66**, 2069–2074 (1982)
3. Azam, F., Sharif, M., Yasmin, M., Mohsin, S.: Artificial intelligence based techniques for earthquake prediction: a review. Sci. Int. **26**(4), 1495–1502 (2014)
4. Centro Sismológico Nacional. Universidad de Chile (2015). www.seismologia.cl
5. Chattopadhyay, G., Chattopadhyay, S.: Dealing with the complexity of earthquake using neurocomputing techniques and estimating its magnitudes with some low correlated predictors. Arab. J. Geosci. **2**(3), 247–255 (2009)

6. Cisternas, M., Atwater, B.F.: Predecessors of the giant 1960 Chile earthquake. Nature **437**(7057), 404–407 (2005)
7. Fernández, A., López, V., Galar, M., del Jesús, M.J., Herrera, F.: Analysing the classification of imbalanced data-sets with multiple classes: binarization techniques and ad-hoc approaches. Knowl.-Based Syst. **42**, 97–110 (2013)
8. Florido, E., Martínez-Álvarez, F., Morales-Esteban, A., Reyes, J., Aznarte, J.L.: Detecting precursory patterns to enhance earthquake prediction in Chile. Comput. Geosci. **76**, 112–120 (2015)
9. García, S., Derrac, J., Triguero, I., Carmona, C.J., Herrera, F.: Evolutionary-based selection of generalized instances for imbalanced classification. Knowl.-Based Syst. **25**(1), 3–12 (2012)
10. Moustra, M., Avraamides, M., Christodoulou, C.: Artificial neural networks for earthquake prediction using time series magnitude data or seismic electric signals. Expert Syst. Appl. **38**(12), 15032–15039 (2011)
11. Martínez-Álvarez, F., Reyes, J., Morales-Esteban, A., Rubio-Escudero, C.: Determining the best set of seismicity indicators to predict earthquakes. Two case studies: Chile and the Iberian Peninsula. Knowl.-Based Syst. **50**, 198–210 (2013)
12. Morales-Esteban, A., Martínez-Álvarez, F., Reyes, J.: Earthquake prediction in seismogenic areas of the Iberian Peninsula based on computational intelligence. Tectonophysics **593**, 121–134 (2013)
13. Morales-Esteban, A., Martínez-Álvarez, F., Scitovski, S., Scitovski, R.: A fast partitioning algorithm using adaptive Mahalanobis clustering with application to seismic zoning. Comput. Geosci. **73**, 132–141 (2014)
14. The University of Waikatu. WEKA: Data mining with open source machine learning software in Java. http://www.cs.waikato.ac.nz/ml/weka/
15. Otari, G.V., Kulkarni, R.V.: A review of application of data mining in earthquake prediction. Int. J. Comput. Sci. Inform. Technol. **3**(2), 3570–3574 (2012)
16. Panakkat, A., Adeli, H.: Neural network models for earthquake magnitude prediction using multiple seismicity indicators. Int. J. Neural Syst. **17**(1), 13–33 (2007)
17. Panakkat, A., Adeli, H.: Recent efforts in earthquake prediction (1990–2007). Natural Hazards Rev. **9**(2), 70–80 (2008)
18. Panakkat, A., Adeli, H.: Recurrent neural network for approximate earthquake time and location prediction using multiple sesimicity indicators. Comput. Aided Civil Infrastruct. Eng. **24**, 280–292 (2009)
19. R Development Core Team R: A Language and Environment for Statistical Computing. R Foundation for Statistical Computing, Vienna, Austria (2008). ISBN: 3-900051-07-0
20. Reyes, J., Cárdenas, V.: A Chilean seismic regionalization through a Kohonen neural network. Neural Comput. Appl. **19**, 1081–1087 (2010)
21. Reyes, J., Morales-Esteban, A., Martínez-Álvarez, F.: Neural networks to predict earthquakes in Chile. Appl. Soft Comput. **13**(2), 1314–1328 (2013)
22. Srilakshmi, S., Tiwari, R.K.: Model dissection from earthquake time series: a comparative analysis using nonlinear forecasting and artificial neural network approach. Comput. Geosci. **35**, 191–204 (2009)
23. Tiampo, K.F., Shcherbakov, R.: Seismicity-based earthquake forecasting techniques: ten years of progress. Tectonophysics **522–523**, 89–121 (2012)
24. Zamani, A., Sorbi, M.R., Safavi, A.A.: Application of neural network and ANFIS model for earthquake occurrence in Iran. Earth Sci. Inf. **6**(2), 71–85 (2013)

Detecting Anomalies in Embedded Computing Systems via a Novel HMM-Based Machine Learning Approach

Alfredo Cuzzocrea[1]([⊠]), Eric Medvet[2], Enzo Mumolo[2],
and Riccardo Cecolin[2]

[1] ICAR-CNR and University of Calabria, Rende, Italy
cuzzocrea@si.dimes.unical.it
[2] DIA Department, University of Trieste, Trieste, Italy
{emedvet,mumolo}@units.it

Abstract. Computing systems are vulnerable to anomalies that might occur during execution of deployed software: e.g., faults, bugs or deadlocks. When occurring on embedded computing systems, these anomalies may severely hamper the corresponding devices; on the other hand, embedded systems are designed to perform autonomously, i.e., without any human intervention, and thus it is difficult to debug an application to manage the anomaly. Runtime anomaly detection techniques are the primary means of being aware of anomalous conditions. In this paper, we describe a novel approach to detect an anomaly during the execution of one or more applications. Our approach describes the behaviour of the applications using the sequences of memory references generated during runtime. The memory references are seen as signals: they are divided in overlapping frames, then parametrized and finally described with Hidden Markov Models (HMM) for detecting anomalies. The motivations of using such methodology for embedded systems are the following: first, the memory references could be extracted with very low overhead with software or architectural tools. Second, the device HMM analysis framework, while being very powerful in gathering high level information, has low computational complexity and thus is suitable to the rather low memory and computational capabilities of embedded systems. We experimentally evaluated our proposal on a ARM9, Linux based, embedded system using the SPEC 2006 CPU benchmark suite and found that it shows very low error rates for some artificially injected anomalies, namely a malware, an infinite loop and random errors during execution.

1 Introduction

Embedded computing systems are extensively used in every-day life. Their use include automotive applications, consumer applications and particular domains such as industrial subsystems or military applications. Embedded systems share some important properties, namely the fact that their failures often result in severe consequences (whose degree of gravity depends on the specific application), the fact that it is hard or even impossible to interact with them, and the

© Springer International Publishing Switzerland 2015
E. Onieva et al. (Eds.): HAIS 2015, LNAI 9121, pp. 405–415, 2015.
DOI: 10.1007/978-3-319-19644-2_34

fact that the number of concurrent executions is limited and very often well known a-priori. Embedded system failures may be caused by software errors (bugs), faults, or by injection of new applications, including those deliberately designed to cause failures (malware), possibly coming from the network to which some embedded systems could be connected. All of these events could result in runtime anomalies: the ability to automatically detect these anomalies may allow preventing failures in embedded systems, and hence avoiding damages to the controlled systems.

Anomalies are events that differ from some standard or reference events. They can be detected explicitly, i.e., through pattern recognition which aims to classify patterns using a-priori knowledge or on statistical information extracted from the patterns [1]. Our anomaly detection technique establishes a behavior of the normal executions under examination, compare the observed behavior with the normal behavior, and signals when the observed behavior differs significantly from its normal profile. Since anomaly detection techniques signal all anomalies, false alarms are expected when anomalies are caused by behavioral irregularities.

In this paper, we propose a technique to build a profile of the behavior of a program and to detect deviations from this profile. The profile is based on a statistical model of the memory references generated during the execution. Our technique is designed to operate, for the detection phase, on embedded devices: its computational complexity is low and hence the overhead on the embedded device is limited. In particular, our prototypical implementation on an embedded device currently introduces an overhead lower than 35 %. However, it can easily speeded-up.

Our approach uses the memory address sequences generated by the applications during their execution, since these sequences contain a lot of information about the running applications. After an initial time period where the applications perform initialization tasks, we learn, for each application, a Hidden Markov Model of the execution. Then, we compute the likelihood that the sequences observed during the following execution is consistent with the HMM models and we use this figure to detect the anomalies.

This paper is organized as follows. In Sect. 2 we summarize some work done in embedded systems, and in Sect. 3 we report preliminary basic concepts used through the paper. Then, Sect. 4 describes the analysis algorithm and in Sect. 5 we show experimentally that the analysis framework gives good performances when applied to classification. In Sect. 6 we describe some detection experiments with artificial anomalies. In Sect. 7 some final remarks are reported.

2   Related Work

Anomaly detection, also called intrusion detection in networked systems, is a very important problem that has been widely studied in different areas and applications. Markovian techniques are one of the best methods for detecting anomalies in a sequence of discrete symbols [2]. Training a Markov model means learning the parameters of a probabilistic model of a sequence without anomalies; after training, the likelihood of unknown sequences are computed given the parameters of the learned model. In [3] Maxion and Tan present two methods for detecting anomalies in embedded systems, namely Markov and Stide (Sequence Time Delay Embedding). The Markov approach evaluates the probabilities of the transitions between events in a training set and uses these probabilities to see if they correspond to the transitions of the test set. The Stide approach builds templates of normal executions and compares the templates with unknown sequences. Other approaches, such as [4], use Markov Models of system call sequences. In some cases, better models can be obtained with Hidden Markov Models, which are widely used for sequence modeling. Wang et al. report in [5] a survey of HMM based techniques for intrusion detection. Despite their power, there are few papers dealing with the use of HMM for anomaly detection in embedded system. Sugaya et al. describe in [6] an anomaly detection system based on HMM modeling of resource consumption such as CPU, memory and network. In [7], Zandrahimi et al. propose two methods, a buffer-based and a probabilistic detector. The buffer based detector builds a cache formed with events considered as normal. During test stage, the method counts the cache misses. The probabilistic detector employs the probability of events to evaluate the testing sequence. The approaches are suitable for embedded systems because require lower memory size and can be easily implemented in hardware. Some authors, for example [8–10], consider the discrete sequences as signals, and use signal processing techniques to analyze them.

With respect to classical state-of-the-art proposals, our method has the specific merit of addressing embedded systems, which is very relevant at now. With respect to similar, few approach that make use of HMM for anomaly detection, our main contribution consists in specifically pointing memory references as the input of our analysis, contrary to others that make use of other parameters like CPU and network flows.

3 Preliminaries

3.1 Spectral Description of Memory References

The short-term Fourier transform, is a Fourier-related transform used to determine the sinusoidal frequency and phase content of local sections of a signal as it changes over time. It describe how the energy is distributed on a spectral range.

We show hereafter that memory references can be described with spectral parameters. In fact, important parts of a program are composed by loops, that becomes peaks in the spectral domain, as we point out shortly.

Let us consider for example a simple cycle of the type:

```
i=0;
while(i<N) {
    i++;
}
```

The virtual memory references sequence generated during the execution of this loop can be modeled with a sawtooth signal. Calling $F(\omega)$ the amplitude spectrum of a single ramp, the analytic form of the sawtooth spectrum is $F(\omega) \sum_n \delta(n - N)$ where N is the wideness of the cycle. The spectrum is therefore composed by a periodic series of peaks with decreasing amplitudes whose period is related to the loop width N.

As a more practical example, let us consider the code of a simple bubble sort, which is basically formed by inner cycles. After acquisition of the virtual memory sequence, a Short Time Fourier Transform (STFT) described in (1) is performed.

$$X(n) = \sum_{-\infty}^{\infty} x(n)w(n - m)e^{-j\omega n} \tag{1}$$

wherein: (i) $X(n)$ is the input signal to be transformed based on the STFT; (ii) $x(n)$ represents one of the chunks in which $X(n)$ is transformed; (iii) $w(n)$ is the *window function* on top of which chunks $x(n)$ are projected.

The sequence of memory addresses is divided into chunks or frames (which usually overlap each other, to reduce artifacts at the boundary). Each chunk is Fourier transformed, and the resulting amplitude spectrum over time is reported in Fig. 1. It is worth observing that the spectra peaks represent the wideness of the cycles in the code. Thus, the spectral patterns well characterize the executions. Indeed, spectral representation is obtained with Fast Discrete Cosine Transform.

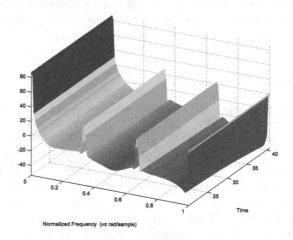

Fig. 1. Spectral representation of a Bubble sort.

3.2 Discrete Cosine Transform Representation

DCT [11] is a method to obtain spectral information, and it is used in this work instead of STFT, because it is fast and has a good energy compaction capability.

Energy compaction means the capability of the transform to redistribute signal energy into a small number of transform coefficients. It can be characterized by the fraction of the total number of signal transform coefficients that carry a certain (substantial) percentage of the signal energy. The lower this fraction is for a given energy percentage, the better the transform energy compaction capability is.

The principle advantage of DCT transformation is the removal of redundancy between neighboring addresses. This leads to uncorrelated transform coefficients which can be processed independently. Efficacy of a transformation scheme can be directly gauged by its ability to pack input data into as few coefficients as possible. This allows the quantizer to discard coefficients with relatively small amplitudes without introducing visual distortion in the reconstructed image.

4   The Proposed Algorithmic Anomaly Detection Framework and Its Implementation

4.1   Parametrization of Memory Reference Sequences

The initial part of the executions is normally devoted to initialization tasks, and is very different from the steady-state phase of the programs. For this reason, we simply blindly fast forward for 1 billion instructions before starting data analysis.

After that, each sequence of memory address references is divided into 1024 addresses blocks; on these blocks a spectral vector is computed with Discrete Cosine Transform (DCT) and from each vector the first sixteen coefficients are extracted. The following step is to perform Vector Quantization with 64 centroids [12] to reduce the 16-dimension vectors into 1 symbol; the final result is that each block of 1024 addresses is represented by a discrete symbol from 0 to 63. The sequences of memory addresses are then transformed in sequences of symbols which are called *Observations*.

Given N programs running in our system, we have thus N observations, O_1, O_2, ..., O_N, which are the sequences of symbols estimated from the memory reference sequences with DCT analysis and vector quantization.

The N observations are used to train a Hidden Markov Model (HMM) of each application, called λ_1, λ_2, ..., λ_N in the following. The training of the HMM models is performed as follows. For each observation, nine thousand blocks are randomly chosen within the first 20000 symbols (recall that each symbol corresponds to a block, which is composed of 1024 addresses) and the HMM parameters are computed with the Baum-Welch algorithm. Thus, we use 20 million addresses of each execution to train a HMM. It is worth recalling that the first billion of addresses is omitted from the training procedure because it is generally related to an initialization phase.

After HMM modeling, the observations are used to compute, with the forward-back-word algorithm [13], the $P(O|\lambda)$ likelihoods. The data used for computing the likelihoods is chosen into the subsequent billion memory addresses in the following way: twenty sub-sequences of 100 symbols are chosen randomly within the sequence corresponding to the billion addresses. The final value of likelihood is obtained by averaging all the computed likelihoods. It is worth recalling that the observations used to compute the $P(O|\lambda)$ are formed by sequences of 100 symbols.

In conclusion, the sequence of memory references is divided in sections of one billion addresses that we call *epochs*. For each epoch we compute the likelihoods by averaging the values obtained on twenty sets of 100 blocks of memory reference, each block is of 1024 addresses, chosen randomly. The analysis algorithm does not work continuously: as said before, during each epoch the algorithm acquires addresses, computes DCT coefficients and vector quantization and computes likelihoods by randomly sampling portions of data.

4.2 Anomaly Detection Algorithm

According to the previous discussion, during the execution of the programs, a series of likelihoods matrices, one for each epoch, are computed:

$$\cdots$$

$$L_{k-1} = \begin{vmatrix} P(O_1^{k-1}|\lambda_1) & P(O_2^{k-1}|\lambda_1) & \cdots & P(O_N^{k-1}|\lambda_1) \\ P(O_1^{k-1}|\lambda_2) & P(O_2^{k-1}|\lambda_2) & \cdots & P(O_N^{k-1}|\lambda_2) \\ \cdots \\ P(O_1^{k-1}|\lambda_N) & P(O_2^{k-1}|\lambda_N) & \cdots & P(O_N^{k-1}|\lambda_N) \end{vmatrix} \tag{2}$$

$$L_k = \begin{vmatrix} P(O_1^k|\lambda_1) & P(O_2^k|\lambda_1) & \cdots & P(O_N^k|\lambda_1) \\ P(O_1^k|\lambda_2) & P(O_2^k|\lambda_2) & \cdots & P(O_N^k|\lambda_2) \\ \cdots \\ P(O_1^k|\lambda_N) & P(O_2^k|\lambda_N) & \cdots & P(O_N^k|\lambda_N) \end{vmatrix} \tag{3}$$

$$\cdots$$

where $O_1^k, \ldots, O_N^k$ are the observations of the k-th epoch for process 1 to N and $P(O_i^k|\lambda_j)$ is the likelihood that the jth model generates the ith observation, at the kth time epoch.

Our monitoring algorithm is based upon the difference between the Observations. The distance between observation O_i and O_j at epoch k is given by (4):

$$d(O_i^k, O_j^k) = \sqrt{\sum_{n=1}^N [P(O_i^k|\lambda_n) - P(O_j^k|\lambda_n)]^2} \tag{4}$$

In the same way, we can compute the distance between observation O_i at epoch $k-1$ and O_j at epoch k. The key of the algorithm is that, in normal executions, the distance between O_i at epoch $k-1$ and O_i at epoch k should be lower than the distances between O_i at epoch $k-1$ and O_j at epoch k, for all the j different from i.

Using for simplicity a vector representation, that is calling $V_{k,i}$ the i-th column of the L_k matrix, $V_{k,i} = |P(O_i^k|\lambda_1), \ldots, P(O_i^k|\lambda_N)|^T$, the above mentioned condition means that, in normal conditions the Euclidean distance between $V_{k-1,i}$ and $V_{k,i}$ is less than the distances between $V_{k-1,i}$ and $V_{k,j}$, for $j \neq i$. However, if the execution of the application i is corrupted by an anomaly the condition is not true.

In other words, the algorithm must look if

$$\sqrt{V_{k-1,i} \cdot V_{k,i}^T} = \min_{j=1 \leq N \leq n} \sqrt{V_{k-1,i} \cdot V_{k,j}^T} \tag{5}$$

4.3   Runtime Implementation Using PIN

Tools capable of extracting and processing memory traces from running processes have been developed to monitor systems in real-time. We chosen Intel PIN as binary instrumentation framework, as it is freely available on both x86, x86_64 and ARM architectures under a Linux environment. Using the API of PIN [14], we developed a tool that attach to a running process, track memory accesses until requested then detach and let the monitored application continue its execution unharmed. Provided a rule set to detect processes to monitor (e.g. processes listening on a specific port, processes running as a specific user), standard system tools can be used to find matching process IDs (PID). PIDs will be used by training and tracking PIN tools to attach to each process and produce models or test workload resemblance as requested.

A tracking system daemon is devoted to run the testing tool at regular time intervals: the tool attaches to target process, dumps memory references and then detaches, so target process is able to keep running without any more overhead. Memory addresses are then processed and output is used to classify the tracked process as belonging to the claimed application or not.

5   Validation of the HMM-Based Machine Learning Approach

Before performing experimental evaluations of the detection tool, we performed extensive classification experiments to verify the described analysis framework. Namely, the HMM models computed from each observation are used to see if the observations with the higher likelihood correspond to the related model. To perform this classification, we use the programs contained in the suite CINT2006 of the SpecCPU2006 benchmark. The suite is composed by twelve programs with different inputs. Of course, a program with a different input generates different observations.

Classification results are reported in Fig. 2 for all the SPEC benchmarks: h264, gcc, perl, bzip, go, mcf, hmmer, sjeng, quantum, omnet, astar, xalanc.

It was impossible to perform this analysis using stored address traces, because of the extremely large amount of data required to perform the experiments, and the high processing time due to the reading operations. In fact, a single classification experiment may require to analyze several billion bytes. For this reason we developed a Valgrind tool, that we called Tracehmm, to perform on line all the described processing.

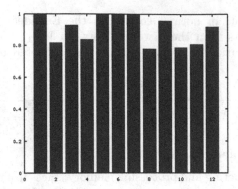

Fig. 2. The figure shows one bar for each application whose height corresponds to the classification accuracy for that application

5.1 Valgrind

Valgrind [15] is an instrumentation framework designed to give the possibility to perform dynamic analysis of software, i.e. analysis performed during the code execution. Valgrind is distributed with several tools designed to perform common analysis of memory, threading etc. Valgrind is available under the GNU GPLv2 licence; it is possible to modify the available tools and to modify also the code of the framework itself, i.e. Coregrind. Coregrind [16] has been designed to analyze already developed execution code. When the name of the executable file is given as input to Valgrind, the code itself is loaded in memory together with the related libraries. The instructions are translated into instructions of a RISC-like language, called VEX IR, and then executed on a virtual CPU.

The Tracehmm tool performs the DCT analysis and the HMM training using directly the memory addresses generated during execution. The direct porting of the off line analysis tools cannot be performed because Coregrind cannot use any library. For this reason, we rewrite all the writing/reading, memory allocation and memory copy functions of the standard library. Moreover, we rewrite also some necessary mathematical functions, namely cos(), sqrt() and log(). The tool is called from the command line as follows:

```
valgrind --tool=tracehmm [opt] prog & args
```

With this tool it is possible to perform the training of a new HMM model or the re-estimation of an already computed HMM model. It perform also the Viterbi test on a previously trained HMM model for computing the likelihood that the model λ may generate the execution sequence O.

6   Experimental Results

The tool based on PIN described above has been tested in three different experiments. In all the tests of this section, an embedded device equipped with an ARM9 at 500 MHz, 128 Mb RAM and a Debian Linux has been used.

6.1   Experiment 1 - Malware Detection

In this test, the PIN tool has been attached to two different processes, and the anomaly detector changes artificially its input at a given epoch. This test aims at simulating a malware affecting a process, that suddenly change its behavior becoming a different process. For this test 8 different models of SPEC CPU2006 benchmark (see Appendix for further details on the benchmarks) have been used, namely sjeng, omnet, astar, h264, xalanc, mcf, perl, quantum, changing this 8 execution suddenly into gcc, hmm, bzip_0, bzip_1, bzip_2, bzip_3, go_0, go_1, go_2, go_3, where for bzip and go different execution have been considered. Thus, 80 different anomalies has been tested. For example, in this test, at a given epoch, the execution of astar suddenly becomes gcc (or bzip_0, etc.). This behavioral change can be detected by the proposed algorithm.

Results shows that the algorithm can determine in an accurate way the epoch that has produced the error, with an error rate below 1 %.

6.2   Experiment 2 - Loop Bug Detection

In this experiment, an infinite loop substitutes the normal execution of the benchmark at a given epoch. This experiment shows if the proposed algorithm is capable to detect anomalies in programs that remain blocked in loops.

This test has been conducted using the following benchmarks: omnet, astar, h264, xalanc, mcf, perl, gcc, bzip. In all the 8 tested cases, the epoch in which the anomaly has occurred has been always correctly determined. In this test, the execution that introduces the anomaly has also been detected with an accuracy of 87.5 %.

6.3   Experiment 3 - Memory Reference Random Error Detection

In this experiment, the memory trace gathered using PIN has been modified by adding a white Gaussian noise. This experiment shows that energy differences in memory reference are detected as anomaly by the proposed program.

The results have been conducted on the same 8 benchmark of Experiment 2, namely: omnet, astar, h264, xalanc, mcf, perl, gcc, bzip, and the noise has been added to one benchmark at a time, resulting in 8 tests for each value of SNR. From 0 dB to 35 dB, all the anomalies where correctly detected, while if the sequence shows a SNR greater that 40 dB, which means really low injected noise, no anomalies were detected.

As a final remark, we observe that some experiments were conducted looking at the values of the single likelihoods $P(O|\lambda)$. Clearly, it can be expected that in presence of an anomaly, the value of the likelihood is modified with respect to the normal executions. However, this procedure leads to a very high number of false positive because it is impossible to set that right threshold. Using the procedure depicted in (5) no thresholds must be found; the false positive are limited by the fact that (5) measures the behaviour of all the applications with respect to the HMM models.

6.4   Overhead Analysis

Most of the complexity relies on the binary instrumentation method which is needed to extract the memory references. We experimentally evaluated that the instrumentation causes a slowdown of about 30 %. Our tool, each time a memory address is accessed by the instrumented application, executes a callback function in order to save the memory reference, hence introducing an overhead to the normal execution of the application. This is done for the strictly necessary number of references to provide good values of accuracy, then tool detaches from the application, which can continue its execution normally. Those memory references are shared with a tracking process, typically on a different machine on the same network, that will begin the analysis of the trace avoiding the instrumenting tool to slow down the application even more.

There are many other possibilities to reduce this overhead, from statistical methods to software tools to architectural methods: in the ARM architectures, for example, there is a register which furnish the running value of the program counter. The other task which requires high computation is the Baum-Welch algorithm, but it is computed once, at the beginning of the executions, to compute the HMM models. The other operations, namely DCT, Vector quantization, forward-backward are much less computationally intensive and it was evaluated that their overhead is less than 5 %.

7   Final Remarks and Conclusions

In this paper, we propose a technique to determine anomaly behaviors in programs based on a model built from memory reference sequences. We present a detailed modeling techniques based on spectral representation of memory reference sequences and Hidden Markov Models, and show that the executions epochs of each program can be clustered and represented using multidimensional scaling. This modeling technique is the base of the proposed algorithm for anomaly detection, that is capable of accurately determine the epoch where an anomaly has occurred. It is also capable to determine the program subject to the anomaly. In a multi-thread program, this technique should be extended to consider an aggregate model of all the different threads. In the scenario of monitoring programs running on a given embedded system this is not a problem, as typically the processes in such environments are single threaded.

The experimental evaluations of the algorithm reported in the paper is obviously preliminary, but, at the same, it has provided a clear vision of the potentialities offered by our proposed framework, and its reliability in effectively and efficiently supporting anomaly detection. Indeed, we obviously plan to further experimentally investigate the algorithm through extensive experiments with different faults and anomaly injections. In addition to this, we plan to extend our proposed framework to other classes of data, such as streaming data (e.g., [17]), and to study compression (e.g., [18]) and privacy (e.g., [19]) issues in order to catch other advanced features that may return to be useful in emerging Big Data (e.g., [20]) environments.

References

1. Maxion, R., Tan, K.: Anomaly detection in embedded systems. IEEE Trans. Comput. **51**(2), 108–120 (2002)
2. Chandola, V., Banerjee, A., Kumar, V.: Anomaly detection for discrete sequences: a survey. IEEE Trans. Knowl. Data Eng. **PP**(99), 1 (2010)
3. Maxion, R., Tan, K.: Benchmarking anomaly-based detection systems. In: Proceedings International Conference on Dependable Systems and Networks, DSN 2000, pp. 623–630 (2000)
4. Tan, X., Wang, W., Xi, H., Yin, B.: A markov model of system calls sequence and its application in anomaly detection. Comput. Eng. **43**, 189–191 (2002)
5. Wang, P., Shi, L., Wang, B., Wu, Y., Liu, Y.: Survay on HMM based anomaly intrusion detection using system calls. In: The 5th International Conference on Computer Science and Education, pp. 102–105, August 2010
6. Sugaya, M., Ohno, Y., van der Zee, A., Nakajima, T.: A lightweight anomaly detection system for information appliances. In: ISORC, pp. 257–266 (2009)
7. Zandrahimi, M., Zarandi, H., Mottaghi, M.: Two effective methods to detect anomalies in embedded systems. Microelectron. J. **43**, 77–87 (2012)
8. Moro, A., Mumolo, E., Nolich, M.: Ergodic continuous hidden markov models for workload characterization. In: Proceedings of 6th International Symposium on Image and Signal Processing and Analysis, ISPA 2009, pp. 99–104, September 2009
9. Moro, A., Mumolo, E., Nolich, M.: Workload modeling using pseudo2D-HMM. In: IEEE International Symposium on Modeling, Analysis Simulation of Computer and Telecommunication Systems, MASCOTS 2009, pp. 1–2, September 2009
10. Zadeh, M., Zein, M., Salem, M., Kumar, N., Cutulenco, G., Fischmeister, S.: SiPTA: signal processing for trace-based anomaly detection. In: Proceedings of the Conference on Embedded Software (EMSOFT), pp. 2–10, October 2014
11. Makhoul, J.: Fast cosine transform in one and two dimensions. IEEE Trans. Acoust. Speech Sig. Proc. **28**(1), 27–34 (1980)
12. Linde, Y., Buzo, A., Gray, R.M.: An algorithm for vector quantizer design. IEEE Trans. Commun. **1**, 702–710 (1980)
13. Devijver, P.A.: Baum's forward–backward algorithm revisited. Pattern Recogn. Lett. **3**, 369–373 (1985)
14. Intel: Pin tool. http://www.pintool.org/
15. Valgrind instrumentation framework. http://valgrind.org/
16. kcachegrind/coregrind. http://kcachegrind.sourceforge.net/html/Home.html
17. Cuzzocrea, A., Furfaro, F., Masciari, E., Saccà, D., Sirangelo, C.: Approximate query answering on sensor network data streams. In: Stefanidis, A., Nittel, S. (eds.) GeoSensor Networks, pp. 53–72. CRC Press, Boca Raton (2004)
18. Cuzzocrea, A., Saccá, D., Serafino, P.: A hierarchy-driven compression technique for advanced OLAP visualization of multidimensional data cubes. In: Tjoa, A.M., Trujillo, J. (eds.) DaWaK 2006. LNCS, vol. 4081, pp. 106–119. Springer, Heidelberg (2006)
19. Cuzzocrea, A., Saccà, D.: Balancing accuracy and privacy of OLAP aggregations on data cubes. In: Proceedings of the ACM 13th International Workshop on Data Warehousing and OLAP, DOLAP 2010, Toronto, Ontario, Canada, 30 October, pp. 93–98 (2010)
20. Cuzzocrea, A., Saccà, D., Ullman, J.D.: Big data: a research agenda. In: 17th International Database Engineering & Applications Symposium, IDEAS 2013, Barcelona, Spain, 09–11 October, pp. 198–203 (2013)

Using Dalvik Opcodes for Malware Detection on Android

José Gaviria de la Puerta[✉], Borja Sanz, Igor Santos,
and Pablo García Bringas

DeustoTech Computing, University of Deusto, Bilbao, Spain
{jgaviria,borja.sanz,isantos,pablo.garcia.bringas}@deusto.es

Abstract. Over the last few years, computers and smartphones have become essential tools in our ways of communicating with each-other. Nowadays, the amount of applications in the Google store has grown exponentially, therefore, malware developers have introduced malicious applications in that market. The Android system uses the Dalvik virtual machine. Through reverse engineering, we may be able to get the different opcodes for each application. For this reason, in this paper an approach to detect malware on Android is presented, by using the techniques of reverse engineering and putting an emphasis on operational codes used for these applications. After obtaining these opcodes, machine learning techniques are used to classify apps.

Keywords: Android · Malware · Opcodes · Detection · Machine learning

1 Introduction

As we all known, in the last few years, mobile terminals, also known as smartphones, have become very popular devices. Nowadays, many smartphones have more computing capabilities and memory than many computers that are only a few years old.

Like any personal device, the smartphone uses an operating system, which is usually pretty friendly for that the users do not have problems when using it. Throughout history, different operating systems to these devices have emerged. In an interview with Andy Rubin, former Android boss, he stated that "there should be nothing that users can access on their desktop that they cannot access on their cell phone" [1]. Thanks to this sentence, we can demonstrate the progress that these small computers are having. By its hardware, which consists of a wide range of sensors such as camera, accelerometer and GPS, we are provided a wealth of information and data, which put a number of additional requirements to mobile operating systems.

People use mobile devices for a wide range of purposes as if they were desktop computers: web browsing, social networking, online banking, and more. The so-called smartphones also offer features that are unique to mobile phones

© Springer International Publishing Switzerland 2015
E. Onieva et al. (Eds.): HAIS 2015, LNAI 9121, pp. 416–426, 2015.
DOI: 10.1007/978-3-319-19644-2_35

like, for instance, SMS messaging, location data constantly updated, and ubiquitous access. As a result of their popularity and functionality, smartphones are a growing target of malicious activity.

Today, one of the most common ways to perform malicious actions is by using malicious code or malware. The term *malware* comes from the Anglo-Saxon words *MALicious* and *softWARE*, which comes to mean malicious software. Typically, such software poses as legitimate applications to run its malicious actions without the user's knowledge. One of the primary objectives of the malware is to make enormous profit, whether economic or theft of information, for as long as possible. In order to achieve this goal, these malicious applications try to stay hidden in the system without the user to see an anomalous behaviour in the device.

It is well known that malware has grown in recent years and that is has become one of the biggest threats in recent times. According to Kaspersky Labs antivirus company, about 145,000 new malware samples for mobile devices appeared in 2013, tripling the samples detected in the previous year[1]. Lately, malware has increased exponentially, specially in the Android platform.

The Sect. 2 is a small state of the art with related researches of android systems that have been carried out by the scientific community. In Sect. 3 we present the scope of this experiment, and how we obtained the necessary information to perform it. Section 4 summarizes the different classifiers used for this experiment. Section 5 makes a statement of the results, and the parameters to consider with such experimental validation. Finally, the Sect. 6 shows the conclusions obtained by the experiment and some possible lines of future work to be carried out.

2 Related Work

The Android operating system is designed to run each application on its own virtual machine, Dalvik. This type of implementation makes the system more robust and limits the damage caused by bad programming [2].

In addition, the Android systems are supplied with a permission system that does not allow third party applications to access resources that should not be accessible. These permissions are assigned to the application at installation time but the user is the one that has to make that final decision. He or she is the person to choose to install the application or not, depending on the permissions that the application has. Malicious applications developers can request more permissions than they really need, for example, to obtain private user information [3]. Along this line, a research which was conducted by Sanz et al. [4] showed us that just by taking a look at the permissions that the app required, they could classify it as malicious or benign. Other authors have also used this feature in their researches [5,6]. Nevertheless, Android is a system that is constantly changing

---

[1] http://www.kaspersky.com/about/news/virus/2014/Mobile-malware-evolution-3-infection-attempts-per-user-in-2013?ClickID=c4azsxkfiallqkfvsvzavqvkz4ixn4q7fnqn.

and now takes groups of permissions. With those clusters, these approaches lose effectiveness.

A classical approach in mobile devices is to analyse the behaviour of different hardware components, such as the CPU or the battery, searching for anomalies [7,8]. However, even if it is true that these approaches can help us discover strange behaviour in the system, they have the problem of the complexity in the programming, and also, the constant updates that a program could have in a month. These problems can impact in these elements but not for that reason are malicious applications.

Meanwhile, Schmidt et al. [9] developed a framework that used system calls as a feature for the classification of benign and malicious applications in the Android system. Still, this type of classification has the problem that it is very expensive to get such information. Furthermore, depending on the number of calls, the performance of this approach may be very low.

Shabtai et al. [10] did some research using the decompiled files of an Android application. In this study, they managed to classify malware using extracted features, such as the classes used by the application, as well as some machine learning techniques. For this approach we need a very large number of features extracted from the applications to get a good ranking.

One of the techniques that is often used in the creation of *Android malware* is to use a legitimate application and include a malicious code in it. Along this line, Zhou et al. [11] did some research on third party app stores. A major limitation of this approach is the necessity of the legitimate application to see if malicious code is inserted into it.

3   Experimentation Scope

In this context, following the guidelines used for the detection of malicious code on desktops led by Santos et al. [12], the authors propose a study that consists of: (1) Capture of information on the operational codes used by an application, (2) malicious or benign classification of an application, by using machine learning techniques.

After obtaining all applications, the main objective of the research is the ability, through supervised learning techniques, to detect with the fewest false positives and false negatives, the malicious apps generated to be used within the Android platform.

In the next subsections, we define the methodology that has been used for modelling the applications, as well as its characteristics that will be used to present this proof of concept. This methodology uses all the possibilities of the application created by the University of Waikato, Weka[2], to employ different ranking algorithms.

---

[2] Weka: Data Mining Software is a collection of machine learning algorithms for automated data mining tasks: http://www.cs.waikato.ac.nz/ml/weka/.

3.1 Samples Collection

On the one hand, to obtain benign code samples, we used the Selenium[3] applica-tion for automating web browser. With this automation we use the application web APIfy[4] for downloading Android applications from different categories.

On the other hand, the samples of malicious code have been used throughout the dataset provided by *Android Genome Project* [13].

3.2 Information Gathering

This phase has proceeded to create a platform in the programming language C#. This platform has been implemented as a plugin for obtaining different opcodes used by an apk to execute their actions. Studying these opcodes, a particular one called *RSUB_INT* has been found. It is only published on benign code applications, specially in 639 applications.

4 Machine Learning and Supervised Classification

In this paper the authors present an experimental model that makes use of mod-eling techniques described above. The objective is to obtain the opcodes for such application that may be employed by some classifiers for classify applications.

In problems of machine learning and supervised classification, a phenomenon represented by a vector X in R^d which can be classified in K ways according to *label Y*, is studied.

To this end, we have $D_n = \{(X_i, Y_i)\}_{i=1}^{n}$ called *training set*, where X_i repre-sents the events corresponding to the phenomenon X while Y_i is the label that puts it in the category that the classifier takes as correct. For example, in the present case, we are talking about an application X_i defined by a set of opcodes that represent it, where Y_i the category assigned to that application as estimated by the classifier.

In this learning case, all classifiers were done using the method of represen-tation of «*vector space*» model for the representation as a vector of different frequencies of opcodes.

This method represents documents in natural language to a formal way using vectors in a multi-dimensional linear space. The basic form of this method is represented by the cosine of the angle between the two vectors generated for the similarity between the terms.

4.1 Classification Algorithms

In this research, we have chosen to compare the performance of different clas-sification algorithms given the occasionally notable differences in effectiveness that can be observed in similar experiments conducted in other areas [14].

---

[3] http://docs.seleniumhq.org/.
[4] http://apify.ifc0nfig.com/.

The algorithms used for the tests in Sect. 5 are the following: Random Forest, J48, Bayes Theorem-based algorithms, K-Nearest Neighbor (KNN), Sequential Minimal Optimization (SMO) and Simple Logistic.

– Random Forest. Random Forest is an aggregation classifier developed by Leo Breiman [15] which is formed by a bunch of decision trees considered in a way in which the introduction of a stochastic component improves de precision of the classifier, either in the construction of the trees or either in the training dataset.

– J48. J48 is an open source implementation for Weka of the C4.5 algorithm [16]. C4.5 creates decision trees given an amount of training information making use of the concept *information entropy* [17]. The training data consist of a group $S = s_1, s_2, ..., s_n$ of already classified samples $s_1 = x_1, x_2, ..., x_m$ in which $x_1, x_2, ..., x_m$ represent the attributes or characteristics of each sample. In each node of the decision tree, the algorithm will choose the attribute in the data that most efficiently divides the dataset in enriched choruses of a given class using the entropy difference or the already mentioned *normalized information gain* as selective criteria.

– Bayes Theorem-based algorithms. The Bayes Theorem, the base for the Bayesian inference, is a statistical method which determines, based on a number of observations, the probability of a certain hypotheses being true. For the classification needs here exposed, this is the most important capability of Bayesian networks: in our case, the probability of an app being malicious or benign The theorem is capable of adjusting the probabilities as soon as new observations are performed. Thus, Bayesian networks conform a probabilistic model that represents a collection of randomized variables and their conditional dependencies by means of a directed graph. We have trained our models with three different search algorithms: K2, Hill Climbing and TAN.

In this group we have also considered the inclusion of Naïve Bayes. The idea is that if the number of independent variables managed is too big, it does not make any sense to make probability tables [18]. Then, the reduced model with simplified datasets give to the algorithm the appellative of *Naïve*.

– K-Nearest Neighbor (KNN). The KNN algorithm is one of the most simple classification algorithms amongst all of those available for the machine learning techniques. It takes decisions based on the results of the k closest neighbours to the analysed sample in the experimental n-dimensional space ($\forall k \in \mathbb{N}$).

In this case, and taken into account the simplicity of the algorithm, we have explored even more values ($k = 1, 3, 5$) so as to determine if this enlargement would throw any kind of additional advantage.

– Sequential Minimal Optimization (SMO). SMO, invented by John Platt [19], is an iterative algorithm used for the solution of the optimization problems that appear when training *Support Vector Machines* (SVM). Basically, SMO divides the problem into a series of smaller subproblems which are analytically solved lately.

At this point, we have selected different kernels with these algorithms: a polynomial kernel, a normalized polynomial kernel, RBF and Pearson-VII.

– Simple Logistic. This algorithm is used to predict the result of a variable function of the independent variables, or predictor. The logistic regression formula is:

$$Y_i = \frac{1}{1 + e^{-(\beta_0 + \beta_1 X_{1,i} + \dots + \beta_d X_{d,i})}} \tag{1}$$

Being Y_i the classification to predict by the model, in our case it would be *goodware* or *malware*. The variable X is the vector with the opcodes generated for a specific application, finding that $X_{d,i}$ is the value assigned to an n-gram of opcodes in d enforcement position that is in row i. Parameters *beta* $_{ast}$ are determined by the algorithm in the training phase.

So, having a downloaded and validate, using the VirusTotal platform[5], dataset as goodware, and secondly, using the Android Genome Project [13] dataset with malicious applications, it has been easy to label the purpose of each of the applications as *goodware* or *malware* to generate the *training datasets* used in the Sect. 5.

5 Experimental Validation

Next step, we recollect the information stored in each of the apps. First of all, a total of 1,494 applications from *Google Play*[6] were downloaded. In particular we got them from the lists of "the most free downloaded", in "the most free downloaded in Spanish", applications that "have generated more revenue", those of "lifestyle" and those of "tools".

The choice of these lists for obtaining samples was completely random to have a heterogeneous applications dataset from Google's store. To verify that the samples do not contain malicious code, we have used the online platform VirusTotal. This platform uses 43 antivirus engines to scan the sample that previously has been sent. This analysis returns the total number of engines that have been detected as malicious and malware is for that engine. Since the experiment is desired to have all possible clean malware samples, it was decided that if only one antivirus engine detected it sample as malicious, it would be separated from the dataset. The ones that were detected as adware[7], were also separated from that dataset.

After the analysis with VirusTotal, we found that we had a 14.59 % of applications considered malware or adware in our dataset. Specifically there were 218 apps which, according to the metrics we have said before, could not be within the dataset itself benign code. Given that for the dataset of malicious code we used the one provided by the *Android Genome Project*, which consists of 1,259 samples, so our dataset benign still had to be reduced in 17 more samples to be balanced. These samples were selected randomly from the total, leaving the final data set with 2,518 samples applications, half benign and half malignant.

---

[5] https://www.virustotal.com/es/.

[6] https://play.google.com/store.

[7] Adware is a type of action hidden in applications, which send targeted advertisements to our device when you run an application.

For the information of the samples was done using the Dedexer tool, a disassembler for .dex files that is on the Android platform. Using this tool, we obtained the operational codes of the different samples analyzed. These codes are the minimum operating instructions means the Dalvik virtual machine to run applications on it. Figure 1 we see a sequence extracted from an Android application opcodes.

```
const-string        v0, aCursor
invoke-interface    v3, v0, <ref Map.get(ref)
                    imp. @ _def_ Map_get@LL>
move-result-object  v0
check-cast          v0, <t: String>
const-string        v1, aHasmore
invoke-interface    v3, v1, <ref Map.get(ref)
                    imp. @ _def_ Map_get@LL>
move-result-object  v1
check-cast          v1, <t: String>
const-string        v3, aTrue_0
invoke-virtual      v3, v1, <boolean String.equalsIgnoreCase(ref)
                    imp. @ _def_String_ equalsIgnoreCase@ZL>
move-result         v7
invoke-virtual      this, v0,
                    <boolean KiwiPurchaseUpdatesCommandTask.isNullOrEmpty(ref)
                    imp. @ _def_KiwiPurchaseUpdatesCommandTask_ isNullOrEmpty@ZL>
move-result         v1
if-eqz              v1, loc_ C1AD2
sget-object         v6, Offset_ BEGINNING
```

Fig. 1. Example of operational codes with variables used in an Android application.

With all the samples we have disassembled, we generated opcode files ranging from 10 KB to 32 MB for the goodware and from 5 KB to 20 MB in the case of malware. In these files we can meet the different operational codes used by both benign and malicious applications. From here there has been a Arff file for use with the Weka tool. For each of them, an experiment to demonstrate its validity as predictors using different classifiers detailed in Sect. 4.

Thus, this section will detail the results obtained when evaluating the different opcodes.

This evaluation will be performed according to the following parameters, usually employed to compare the performance of different algorithms in the field of machine learning:

- *True Positive Ratio* (*TPR*), which is calculated by dividing the number of bening apps correctly classified (*TP*) between the total samples taken (*TP* + *FN*).

$$TPR = \frac{TP}{(TP + FN)} \qquad (2)$$

- *False Positive Ratio* (*FPR*), which is calculated by dividing the number of samples corresponding to malicious app whose classification (*FP*) were missed by the total number of samples (*FP* + *TN*).

$$FPR = \frac{FP}{(FP + TN)} \qquad (3)$$

Table 1. Performance of classifiers when analyzed correctly categorize applications using opcodes.

Classifier	TPR	FPR	Precision (%)	ROC
IBk 1	0.94408	0.04217	95.761	0.97198
IBk 3	0.93558	0.04202	95.727	0.97924
IBk 5	0.93344	0.04432	95.495	0.98102
Simple Logistic	0.92177	0.05535	94.379	0.97839
NaiveBayes	0.83789	0.20294	80.561	0.88461
BayesNet K2	0.82057	0.19325	81.006	0.87881
BayesNet TAN	0.89365	0.09793	90.181	0.94768
SMO PolyKernel	0.92995	0.04916	95.022	0.94039
SMO Norm. PolyKernel	0.90985	0.04828	95.002	0.93078
J48	0.92581	0.05901	94.071	0.94434
RandomTree	0.91454	0.06147	93.749	0.92654
RandomForest I = 10	0.95147	0.05091	94.953	0.98879
RandomForest I = 50	0.94853	0.03645	96.322	0.99208
RandomForest I = 100	0.94829	0.032	96.758	0.99255

- *Precisión* (P), which is calculated by dividing the total hits by the total number of instances in the dataset.

$$P = \frac{TP + TN}{TP + FP + TN + FN} \qquad (4)$$

- *Area Under ROC Curve* (AUC) [14], that establishes the relationship amongst the false negatives and the false positives. The ROC Curve it is usually used to generate statistics that represent the performance or the effectiveness in a wider sense of a classifier.

As such, the results are displayed in Table 1. The best results have been obtained for the Random Forest classifier with the number of trees equal to 100, with a classification accuracy of 96.758 % and value of the area under the ROC curve of 0.99255.

In contrast, it has been observed that classifiers that have worked have been worse Naive Bayes (with an overall accuracy of 80.561 % and a value of *AURC* of 0.88461) and BayesNet with K2 algorithm (with a total accuracy of 81.006 % and a value of *AURC* of 0.87881).

In Table 2 we can see the results of classification of malicious applications using application permissions on our dataset, conducted by Sanz et al. [4]. In this table we can see one of the best classifiers using application permissions is Random Forest with number of trees equal to 100, which is taking the area under the ROC curve of 0.99382 and an accuracy of 95.423 %.

Table 2. Performance of classifiers when analyzed correctly categorize applications using permissions.

Classifier	TPR	FPR	Precision (%)	ROC
IBk 1	0.94615	0.04924	95.103	0.98597
IBk 3	0.93701	0.05281	94.717	0.98737
IBk 5	0.93312	0.05893	94.127	0.98709
Simple Logistic	0.96235	0.0587	94.288	0.9894
NaiveBayes	0.95392	0.21255	81.854	0.95679
BayesNet K2	0.96981	0.22208	81.463	0.96868
BayesNet TAN	0.97689	0.09284	91.378	0.98233
SMO PolyKernel	0.96616	0.05957	94.221	0.95329
SMO Norm. PolyKernel	0.9745	0.05433	94.751	0.96009
J48	0.95195	0.06457	93.686	0.96116
RandomTree	0.93178	0.06179	93.824	0.95412
RandomForest I = 10	0.961	0.04892	95.189	0.99148
RandomForest I = 50	0.95806	0.04551	95.511	0.99361
RandomForest I = 100	0.94829	0.04654	95.423	0.99382

We can also see that one of the worst is SMO classifiers using Normalized PolyKernel with an area under the ROC curve of 0.95329 and an accuracy of 94.751 %.

Comparing the two methods it can be seen that the two approaches follow the same trend roughly in values obtained. On the one hand we can see that the area under the ROC curve values tend to be 95 % or higher in most of the classifiers. On the other hand if you consider that the best classifier for both approaches is the Random Forest Tree number 100.

6   Conclusions and Future Work

The opcodes are instructions performed by an application. All Apps must use these codes to perform the activities for which they are scheduled. In this paper we use the operational codes with machine learning techniques for classification of malicious apps on the Android operating system, with a comparison with application permissions. To validate our approach, we collected 1,259 samples totally benign applications from Google Play and 1,259 Android malware samples obtained from the «*Android Genome Project*». After that, the operational codes were extracted and models were created to evaluate each configuration of classifiers by the area under the ROC curve.

As the application permissions are very quick to get, operational codes require more computation time, thus penalizing the performance of the approach. In contrast, nowadays there are no longer unique permissions as before, but there are groups of permissions, making this approach not so optimal. Therefore, today you can use this method as one of the first approaches to malware detection on Android.

As future work, the analysis of 639 samples containing the opcode «*RSUB_INT*» is proposed. By doing this we would be able to see why this opcode only appears in benign samples.

This study may result in the generation of a pattern. This would be used to detect unknown malware faster and it could also limit the amount of possible malicious codes in many applications.

References

1. Waters, D.: Google bets on Android future, February 2008. http://news.bbc.co.uk/2/hi/technology/7266201.stm
2. Enck, W., Octeau, D., McDaniel, P., Chaudhuri, S.: A study of android application security. In: USENIX Security Symposium (2011)
3. Fragkaki, E., Bauer, L., Jia, L., Swasey, D.: Modeling and enhancing android's permission system. In: Foresti, S., Yung, M., Martinelli, F. (eds.) ESORICS 2012. LNCS, vol. 7459, pp. 1–18. Springer, Heidelberg (2012)
4. Sanz, B., Santos, I., Laorden, C., Ugarte-Pedrero, X., Bringas, P.G., Álvarez, G.: PUMA: permission usage to detect malware in android. In: Herrero, Á., et al. (eds.) Int. Joint Conf. CISIS 2012-ICEUTE 2012-SOCO 2012. AISC, vol. 189, pp. 289–298. Springer, Heidelberg (2013)
5. Shin, W., Kiyomoto, S., Fukushima, K., Tanaka, T.: Towards formal analysis of the permission-based security model for android. In: Fifth International Conference on Wireless and Mobile Communications, ICWMC 2009, pp. 87–92. IEEE (2009)
6. Shin, W., Kiyomoto, S., Fukushima, K., Tanaka, T.: A formal model to analyze the permission authorization and enforcement in the android framework. In: 2010 IEEE Second International Conference on Social Computing (SocialCom), pp. 944–951. IEEE (2010)
7. Jacoby, G.A., Davis IV, N.J.: Battery-based intrusion detection. In: Global Telecommunications Conference, GLOBECOM 2004, vol. 4, pp. 2250–2255. IEEE (2004)
8. Buennemeyer, T.K., Nelson, T.M., Clagett, L.M., Dunning, J.P., Marchany, R.C., Tront, J.G.: Mobile device profiling and intrusion detection using smart batteries. In: Proceedings of the 41st Annual Hawaii International Conference on System Sciences, pp. 296–296. IEEE (2008)
9. Schmidt, A.D., Bye, R., Schmidt, H.G., Clausen, J., Kiraz, O., Yuksel, K.A., Camtepe, S.A., Albayrak, S.: Static analysis of executables for collaborative malware detection on android. In: IEEE International Conference on Communications, ICC 2009. pp. 1–5. IEEE (2009)
10. Shabtai, A., Fledel, Y., Elovici, Y.: Automated static code analysis for classifying android applications using machine learning. In: 2010 International Conference on Computational Intelligence and Security (CIS), pp. 329–333. IEEE (2010)
11. Zhou, W., Zhou, Y., Jiang, X., Ning, P.: Detecting repackaged smartphone applications in third-party android marketplaces. In: Proceedings of the Second ACM Conference on Data and Application Security and Privacy, pp. 317–326. ACM (2012)

12. Santos, I., Brezo, F., Sanz, B., Laorden, C., Bringas, P.G.: Using opcode sequences in single-class learning to detect unknown malware. IET Inf. Secur. 5(4), 220–227 (2011)
13. Zhou, Y., Jiang, X.: Dissecting android malware: characterization and evolution. In: 2012 IEEE Symposium on Security and Privacy (SP), pp. 95–109. IEEE (2012)
14. Singh, Y., Kaur, A., Malhotra, R.: Comparative analysis of regression and machine learning methods for predicting fault proneness models. Int. J. Comput. Appl. Technol. 35(2), 183–193 (2009)
15. Breiman, L.: Random forests. Mach. Learn. 45, 5–32 (2001). doi:10.1023/A:1010933404324
16. Quinlan, J.: C4. 5: Programs for Machine Learning. Morgan kaufmann, San Francisco (1993)
17. Salzberg, S.L.: C4.5: Programs for machine learning by J. Ross Quinlan. Morgan Kaufmann Publishers, Inc., 1993. Mach. Learn. 16, 235–240 (1994). doi:10.1007/BF00993309
18. Jiang, L., Wang, D., Cai, Z., Yan, X.: Survey of improving Naive Bayes for classification. In: Alhajj, R., Gao, H., Li, X., Li, J., Zaïane, O.R. (eds.) ADMA 2007. LNCS (LNAI), vol. 4632, pp. 134–145. Springer, Heidelberg (2007)
19. Platt, J.C.: Sequential minimal optimization: a fast algorithm for training support vector machines (1998)

A Method to Encrypt 3D Solid Objects Based on Three-Dimensional Cellular Automata

A. Martín del Rey$^{(\boxtimes)}$

Department of Applied Mathematics, Institute of Fundamental Physics and
Mathematics, University of Salamanca, Salamanca, Spain
`delrey@usal.es`

Abstract. In this work a novel encryption algorithm to assure the confidentiality of 3D solid objects is introduced. The encryption method consists of two phases: the confusion phase and the diffusion phase. In the first one a three-dimensional chaotic Cat map is applied N times, whereas in the diffusion phase a 2-th order memory reversible 3D cellular automata is evolved T times during M rounds. The encryption method is shown to be secure against the most important cryptanalytic attacks: statistical attacks, differential attack, etc.

Keywords: Encryption · 3D solid objects · 3D cellular automata · 3D chaotic Cat map · Reversibility

1 Introduction

Currently there is an increasing interest in the analysis and management of digitalized 3D objects, and the appearance of additive manufacturing (or 3D printing) has accelerated this fact. In this sense, a recent technical report by Gartner Inc. stated that the worldwide shipments of 3D printers grew 49% in 2013. Consequently, it is reasonable to suppose that in the next years there will be a great proliferation of 3D digital files and their applications to real life [12].

The 3D digitalized objects are defined by means of two types of 3D models: 3D solid models and 3D shell (boundary) models. A solid model defines the volume of the physical object that represents, whereas a shell model represents the surface, not the volume. Solid models are more realistic and they usually appear in medical and engineering applications, CAD and constructive solid geometry; on the other hand, shell models are mainly used in games and films.

This scenario makes necessary to design efficient protocols to safeguard the security of three-dimensional data (confidentiality, integrity, authenticity, etc.) There have been proposed few algorithms dedicated to this purpose and the majority of them are related to watermarking techniques [4,5,7,10], to hash algorithms [2,9], to authentication schemes [8] or to secret sharing protocols for 3D objects [1,6]. Unfortunately, any proposal related with the confidentiality of the 3D data (encryption algorithms) has not appeared in the literature. This is the challenge of this work: the design of a novel encryption method for

© Springer International Publishing Switzerland 2015
E. Onieva et al. (Eds.): HAIS 2015, LNAI 9121, pp. 427–438, 2015.
DOI: 10.1007/978-3-319-19644-2_36

3D objects. The proposed algorithm is focused on solid models adapting to a three-dimensional array the Fridrich's paradigm to cipher digital images [3]. This approach consists of two iterative phases: the confusion phase and the diffusion phase. In the confusion phase a chaotic map is used to permute the position of the pixels of the image, whereas in the diffusion phase the values of the pixels (the color) are modified sequentially in order to modify the statistical properties of the plain image by spreading the influence of each bit of the plain image all over the cipher image. To de-correlate the relationship between adjacent pixels there must be $N \geq 1$ permutation rounds in the confusion stage. The whole confusion-diffusion round repeats for a sufficient number of times M to achieve a satisfactory level of security. In our method, a 3D chaotic Cat map is used in the confusion phase, whereas the diffusion phase depends on the evolution of a reversible memory 3D cellular automata.

Roughly speaking, a cellular automaton is a simple model of computation [11] consisting of a discrete spatial lattice of sites called cells, each one endowed at each time with a state belonging to the finite state set $\mathbb{F}_2 = \{0, 1\}$. The state of each cell is updated in discrete steps of time according to a local transition function which depends on the states of the neighbor cells. As the lattice is finite some type of boundary conditions must be imposed: usually null and periodic boundary conditions are considered. 3D cellular automata are characterized by the three-dimensional arrangement of their cells.

The rest of the paper is organized as follows: In Sect. 2 the basic theory about three-dimensional Cat maps and 3D cellular automata is presented; in Sect. 3 the encryption algorithm is introduced, and its security analysis is shown in the Sect. 4. Finally, the conclusions are presented in Sect. 5.

2   Mathematical Background

2.1   The 3D Chaotic Cat Maps

The discretized 3D Arnold cat map is a three-dimensional chaotic map defined by the following matrix expression:

$$\begin{pmatrix} x^{t+1} \\ y^{t+1} \\ z^{t+1} \end{pmatrix} = C \cdot \begin{pmatrix} x^t \\ y^t \\ z^t \end{pmatrix} \pmod{n}, \quad C = \begin{pmatrix} c_{11} & c_{12} & c_{13} \\ c_{21} & c_{22} & c_{23} \\ c_{31} & c_{32} & c_{33} \end{pmatrix}, \tag{1}$$

where

$$c_{11} = 1 + a_1 a_3 b_2, \; c_{12} = a_3, \; c_{13} = a_2 + a_1 a_3 + a_1 a_2 a_3 b_2,$$
$$c_{21} = b_3 + a_1 b_2 + a_1 a_3 b_2 b_3, \; c_{22} = a_3 b_3 + 1,$$
$$c_{23} = a_2 b_3 + a_1 a_2 a_3 b_2 b_3 + a_1 a_3 b_3 + a_1 a_2 b_2 + a_1, \; c_{31} = a_1 b_1 b_2 + b_2,$$
$$c_{32} = b_1, \; c_{33} = a_1 a_2 b_1 b_2 + a_1 b_1 + a_2 b_2 + 1, \tag{2}$$

with $a_1, a_2, a_3, b_1, b_2, b_3 \in \mathbb{Z}^+$. This is an invertible map since $\mid C \mid = 1$ and it exhibits a chaotic behavior if its leading Lyapunov exponent is strictly larger than 0.

2.2 3D Cellular Automata

A 3D-cellular automaton (3D-CA for short) is a particular type of discrete dynamical system formed by $p \times q \times r$ memory units called cells that are arranged uniformly into a three-dimensional space called its cellular space.

Each cell is endowed with a state from the finite state set $\mathbb{F}_2 = \{0, 1\}$ at every step of time where $s_{ijk}^t \in \mathbb{F}_2$ stands for the state of the (i, j, k)-th cell at time t. The states of all cells change synchronously in discrete steps of time according to a local transition rule f, where its variables are the states of the m neighbor cells at the previous step of time: $s_{i_1 j_1 k_1}^{t-1}, s_{i_2 j_2 k_2}^{t-1}, \ldots, s_{i_m j_m k_m}^{t-1}$. As a consequence:

$$f : \mathbb{F}_2^m \to \mathbb{F}_2$$

$$\left(s_{i_1 j_1 k_1}^{t-1}, \ldots, s_{i_m j_m k_m}^{t-1} \right) \mapsto s_{ijk}^t = f\left(s_{i_1 j_1 k_1}^{t-1}, \ldots, s_{i_m j_m k_m}^{t-1} \right) \tag{3}$$

for every $1 \le i \le p, 1 \le j \le q, 1 \le k \le r$.

Usually, Moore neighborhoods are considered, that is, the neighborhood of the cell (i, j, k) is formed by the 27 nearest cells around it, including itself: $\{(i + \alpha, j + \beta, k + \gamma), (\alpha, \beta, \gamma) \in V\}$, where:

$$\begin{aligned}
V = \{ & (-1, -1, -1), (-1, 0, -1), (-1, 1, -1), (0, -1, -1), (0, 0, -1), (0, 1, -1), \\
& (1, -1, -1), (1, 0, -1), (1, 1, -1), (-1, -1, 0), (-1, 0, 0), (-1, 1, 0), \\
& (0, -1, 0), (0, 0, 0), (0, 1, 0), (1, -1, 0), (1, 0, 0), (1, 1, 0), (-1, -1, 1), \\
& (-1, 0, 1), (-1, 1, 1), (0, -1, 1), (0, 0, 1), (0, 1, 1), (1, -1, 1), \\
& (1, 0, 1), (1, 1, 1) \}.
\end{aligned} \tag{4}$$

As the cellular space is finite, null boundary conditions can be established in order to assure a well-defined evolution of the cellular automaton: $s_{ijk}^t = 0$ if the cell (i, j, k) is not in the cellular space. The configuration at time t of the 3D-CA is the boolean vector whose coordinates are the states of the cells of the 3D-CA at time t: $C^t = \left(s_{111}^t, s_{112}^t, \ldots, s_{pqr}^t \right) \in \mathbb{F}_2^{pqr}$. Note that the coefficients are ordered following the lexicographical ordering of their subindices. The global transition function of the 3D-CA is a transformation that yields the configuration at the next time step during its evolution, that is:

$$\Phi : \mathbb{F}_2^{pqr} \to \mathbb{F}_2^{pqr}, \quad C^{t-1} \mapsto C^t = \Phi\left(C^{t-1} \right).$$

A 3D-CA is reversible if it is possible to compute its inverse evolution by means of another cellular automaton called its inverse. If Φ is the global transition function of the main CA, Φ^{-1} is the global transition function of the inverse CA.

A 3D-CA is said to be a m-th order memory cellular automaton if the state of each cell at the step of time t not only depends on the state of its neighbor cells at the previous step of time $t - 1$, but also on the states of these neighbor cells at $t - 2, t - 3, \ldots, t - m$. In this case the global transition function is defined as follows:

$$\Phi : \mathbb{F}_2^{pqr} \times \ldots \times \mathbb{F}_2^{pqr} \to \mathbb{F}_2^{pqr} \tag{5}$$

$$\left(C^{t-1}, \ldots, C^{t-m} \right) \mapsto C^t = \Phi\left(C^{t-1}, \ldots, C^{t-m} \right)$$

The configurations $C^0, C^1, \ldots, C^{m-1}$ are called initial configurations of the m-th order memory 3D-CA.

Finally, note that a 3D object of dimension $p \times q \times r$ can be interpreted as a configuration of a 3D-CA where the state of the cell at position (i, j, k) is 1 if this position is occupied in the 3D object, and 0 if the position is free.

3   The Encryption Method

The 3D solid object of dimension $n \times n \times n$ to be ciphered can be interpreted as a 3D boolean array $Q_0 = \left(q^0_{ijk}\right)_{1 \leq i,j,k \leq n}$ of dimension $n \times n \times n$ such that $q^0_{ijk} = 1$ if the position (i, j, k) of the 3D solid object is occupied by a cuboid, and $q^0_{ijk} = 0$ if the position (i, j, k) is empty in the solid object.

The proposed encryption protocol consists of three phases: the key scheming, the confusion phase $\mathcal{C}$, and the diffusion phase $\mathcal{D}$.

Set W the three-dimensional array of dimensions $n \times n \times n$ associated to the encrypted 3D object. It is obtained from the following iterative process:

$$Q_i = \mathcal{D}\left(\mathcal{C}^N\left(Q_{i-1}, K_c\right), K_d\right), \, 1 \leq i \leq M, \quad W = Q_M,$$

where N and M are the number of rounds of the confusion and diffusion phases respectively. Moreover, K_c is the confusion key and K_d is the diffusion key.

3.1   Key Scheming

The secret key used in this protocol consists of two parts: K_c and K_d, each holding the parameters used in the confusion and diffusion phases.

The subkey K_c gives the number of iterations of the confusion phase N and the six parameters used to compute the coefficients of the matrix C of the chaotic 3D Cat maps: $a_1, a_2, a_3, b_1, b_2, b_3$.

The subkey K_d determines the number of iterations of the diffusion phase M, the number of iterations of the 3D-CA, T, and the pseudorandom coefficients $B = \{b_{\alpha\beta\gamma}, (\alpha, \beta, \gamma) \in V\}$ of the local transition function of the 3D-CA.

The computation of the parameters involved in the protocol is done by means of the pseudorandom bit generator ANSI X9.31 using AES with the 128-bit length seeds K_c and K_d.

3.2   The Confusion Phase

During this phase the positions of the bits of the three dimensional array $Q_l = \left(q^l_{ijk}\right)$, $0 \leq l \leq M - 1$, are permuted N times using the chaotic and discretized 3D Cat map defined in (1)–(2). Specifically, the bit q^l_{ijk} at the position (i, j, k), $1 \leq i, j, k \leq n$, of the three-dimensional array Q_l, $1 \leq l \leq M - 1$, moves to the position $\left(\bar{i}, \bar{j}, \bar{k}\right)$ where:

$$\left(\bar{i} \, \bar{j} \, \bar{k}\right)^T = C^N \cdot \left(i \, j \, k\right)^T (\bmod n). \tag{6}$$

3.3 The Diffusion Phase

Let P_l be the three-dimensional array obtained from the l-th confusion phase, $1 \leq l \leq M$, that is: $P_l = \mathcal{C}^N(Q_{l-1}, K_c) = (p_{ijk})_{1 \leq i,j,k \leq n}$. Its dimension is $n \times n \times n$ and consequently, it can be divided into two three-dimensional arrays $P_{l,1} = \left(p_{ijk}^1\right)_{1 \leq i,j \leq n, 1 \leq k \leq n/2}$, and $P_{l,2} = \left(p_{ijk}^2\right)_{1 \leq i,j \leq n, 1 \leq k \leq n/2}$ of dimension $n \times n \times \frac{n}{2}$ as follows:

$$p_{ijk}^1 = p_{ijk} \text{ if } 1 \leq k \leq \frac{n}{2}, \text{ with } 1 \leq i,j \leq n, \tag{7}$$

$$p_{ijk}^2 = p_{ijk} \text{ if } \frac{n}{2}+1 \leq k \leq n, \text{ with } 1 \leq i,j \leq n. \tag{8}$$

This phase is governing by means of a 2-th order memory reversible 3D cellular automaton endowed with Moore neighborhoods and local transition function defined as follows:

$$s_{ijk}^t = \bigoplus_{(\alpha,\beta,\gamma) \in V} b_{\alpha\beta\gamma} \cdot s_{i+\alpha,j+\beta,k+\gamma}^{t-1} \oplus s_{ijk}^{t-2}, \ 1 \leq i,j \leq n, 1 \leq k \leq \frac{n}{2}, \tag{9}$$

where $b_{\alpha\beta\gamma} \in \mathbb{F}_2$ for every $(\alpha, \beta, \gamma) \in V$.

The three-dimensional arrays $P_{l,1}$ and $P_{l,2}$ can be interpreted as the initial configurations of this 3D cellular automaton: $C^0 = P_{l,1}$ and $C^1 = P_{l,2}$. Then the output of the diffusion phase, $Q_{l+1} = \mathcal{D}(P_l, K_D)$, is a $n \times n \times n$ three-dimensional array which is formed by the union of the configurations of the 3D cellular automaton at times T and $T+1$: $C^T = \left(s_{ijk}^T\right)_{1 \leq i,j \leq n, 1 \leq k \leq n/2}, C^{T+1} = \left(s_{ijk}^{T+1}\right)_{1 \leq i,j \leq n, 1 \leq k \leq n/2}$, that is, Q_{l+1} is a three-dimensional array whose coefficient at position (i, j, k) is:

$$(Q_{l+1})_{ijk} = \begin{cases} s_{ijk}^T, & \text{if } 1 \leq k \leq \frac{n}{2} \\ s_{ijk}^{T+1}, & \text{if } \frac{n}{2}+1 \leq k \leq n \end{cases}. \tag{10}$$

3.4 Some Illustrative Examples

As an illustrative example, in Figs. 1 and 2 two plain 3D objects and their corresponding encrypted objects are presented. The key parameters used to obtain the encrypted 3D objects are shown in Table 1.

4 Security Analysis

The security analysis of the proposed encryption protocol is performed in this section. This analysis includes the most important cryptanalytic attacks: statistical attacks, differential attacks, etc. Several simulations have been done using different original 3D objects, and for the sake of simplicity only two examples will be introduced and studied here; nevertheless, all of them exhibit the same behavior and the results obtained are similar.

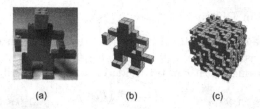

Fig. 1. (a) Real 3D object (robot). (b) Digitalized 3D object. (c) Encrypted 3D object.

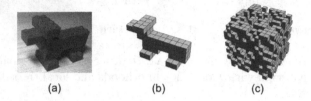

Fig. 2. (a) Real 3D object (dog). (b) Digitalized 3D object. (c) Encrypted 3D object.

4.1   Statistical Analysis

A statistical analysis has been performed in order to prove the confusion and diffusion properties of the proposed protocol, which allows it to strongly resists statistical attacks. Specifically the distribution of occupied positions in the original objects and their encrypted results are checked, the study of the balancedness of the configurations generated by the 3D cellular automaton and the distribution of bits in the neighborhood or every position are performed.

Distribution of Occupied Positions. In what follows it is studied the occupied positions of the 3D objects. Specifically, we are interested in the occupied positions per x-column, y-column and z-column of a three-dimensional lattice $Z = (z_{ijk})$. In this sense the matrices $\Lambda_x = (\lambda_x(j,k))_{1 \leq j,k \leq n}$, $\Lambda_y = (\lambda_y(i,k))_{1 \leq i,k \leq n}$ and $\Lambda_z = (\lambda_z(i,j))_{1 \leq i,j \leq n}$ are computed and their coefficients are defined as follows:

$$\lambda_x(j,k) = \sum_{i=1}^{n} z_{ijk}, \lambda_y(i,k) = \sum_{j=1}^{n} z_{ijk}, \lambda_z(i,j) = \sum_{k=1}^{n} z_{ijk}. \qquad (11)$$

The matrices obtained for the original objects to be ciphered and the encrypted objects are far different. Moreover, the distribution of the number of occupied positions per z-column in the original objects and the corresponding encrypted objects is shown in Fig. 3.

As a consequence, the distributions of occupied positions are far apart. In the case of the original objects some clusters appears, whereas in the case of encrypted objects the distribution seems to be homogeneously.

Table 1. Parameters used in the encryption protocol

	n	N	A	Lyapunov exponent	M	B	T
Robot	12	50	$\begin{pmatrix} 3 & 2 & 5 \\ 7 & 5 & 12 \\ 3 & 2 & 6 \end{pmatrix}$	3.6402	15	7ec33a1	40
Dog	11	77	$\begin{pmatrix} 9 & 10 & 1 \\ 2 & 1 & 2 \\ 8 & 3 & 5 \end{pmatrix}$	3.66169	42	256b330	23

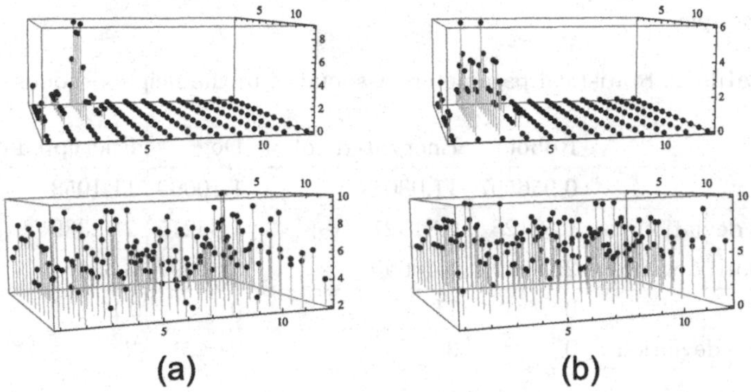

(a)   (b)

Fig. 3. Distribution of occupied positions per column. (a) Robot's example. (b) Dog's example.

Balancedness. The encrypted objects computed exhibit a balanced behavior, that is, the number of 1's in the associated CA configuration is approximately the 50 %. In Fig. 4-(a) the evolution of the number of 1's in the configurations is shown when robot's example is considered; in Fig. 4-(b) the same study is presented when dog's example is taken into account.

Neighbor Analysis. It is important to study the distribution of bits in the neighbor positions of a given one. In this sense, and taking into account Moore neighborhoods, the number of occupied positions around every one is computed and some statistical parameters are derived. As is shown in Table 2 below, the encrypted objects exhibit good statistical properties.

4.2 Key Space

The key space of an encryption scheme should be large enough to resist brute-force attacks. As is mentioned in the section introducing the key scheming, the secret key used in this method is formed by two subkeys: the confusion subkey K_c, and the diffusion subkey K_d, each one of them holding the parameters of confusion and diffusion phases, respectively.

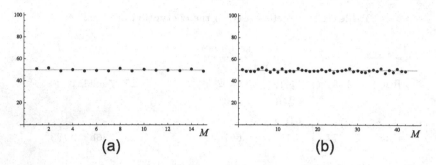

Fig. 4. Evolution of the number of 1's in the configurations. (a) Robot's example. (b) Dog's example.

Table 2. Statistical parameters associated to the neighborhoods

	Robot	Encrypted robot	Dog	Encrypted dog
Mean	0.956597	11.0804	1.10069	11.1053
Mean deviation	1.52126	2.81321	1.84215	2.72339
Standard deviation	2.25909	3.40695	3.06997	3.36411
Median	0	11	0	11
Median deviation	0	3	0	2

The confusion key gives the integer numbers $N, a_1, a_2, a_3, b_1, b_2, b_3$, and the diffusion subkey gives M, T, and the 27-bit sequence B. Consequently, $27 + 9 \log_2 n$ bits must be generated with both sub keys with total length 256 bits. Consequently, there are $2^{256} \simeq 1.15792 \cdot 10^{77}$, and the size of the key space is enormous enough to resist all kinds of brute-force attacks.

4.3   Sensitivity Analysis

A desirable property of the encryption method is that small changes in the secret key should result in a significant change in the encrypted 3D object. If we change only one bit in the sequence B of diffusion subkey K_d, the resulting encrypted object is far different from the encrypted object obtained using the original bit sequence B. For example, if we consider the example shown in Fig. 5 with the same parameters and the bit at position 13 in B is changed, the differences (different bits) between the two encrypted objects obtained are 50.8102 % (note that the ideal would be the 50 %). Furthermore, similar results are obtained in the case of the example given in Fig. 2: the percentage of different positions is 49.7106 %. The encrypted objects computed with the modified bit sequences are shown in Fig. 5.

Moreover, if a modified subkey K_d (for example, only one bit in B is changed) is used to decrypt the cipher objects given in Figs. 1-(c), and 2-(c), the decryption completely fails and the percentage of different bits between the original 3D object and the recovered object (see Fig. 6) is the 51.5625 % in the case of the robot, and the 50.5787 in the other case.

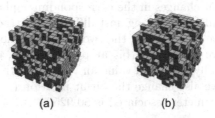

(a)   (b)

Fig. 5. (a) Robot's encrypted object obtained from a modified bit sequence B. (b) Dog's encrypted object obtained from a modified bit sequence B.

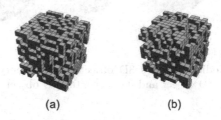

(a)   (b)

Fig. 6. (a) Robot's decrypted object obtained from a single-bit modified bit sequence B. (b) Dog's decrypted object obtained from a modified single-bit sequence B.

As a consequence, it can be concluded that the encryption protocol is sensitive to secret key, that is, a small change of the key yields a different deciphered 3D object and no information about the original one is obtained.

4.4 Differential Attack

In the differential attack, it is suppose that an opponent is capable to modify one single position/bit of the original 3D object and obtain the encrypted object; if this change results in a significant change in the encrypted result, the attack is considered to be inefficient. To check the influence of one single position change of the original 3D object, the $NPCR$ (that is, the number of positions change rate) parameter can be considered. The $NPCR$ measures the percentage of different positions numbers between two objects: Let $Q_1 = \left(q_{ijk}^1\right)_{1 \leq i,j,k \leq n}$ and $Q_2 = \left(q_{ijk}^2\right)_{1 \leq i,j,k \leq n}$ be two encrypted objects whose corresponding original objects differ in only one position. The $NPCR$ parameter is defined as follows:

$$NPCR = \frac{\sum_{i,j=1}^{n} q_{ijk}^1 \oplus q_{ijk}^2}{n^3} \times 100\,\%. \qquad (12)$$

As in the previous cases, several tests have been performed on the proposed scheme using different original objects with different sizes. For each pair, the $NPCR$ is computed and similar results are obtained: a small change in plain image creates significant changes in the corresponding cipher image, so the proposed algorithm is highly resistant against differential attack. As an illustrative example (see Fig. 7), we can consider the two examples shown before, using the same parameters. If we change the bit at position $(4, 4, 4)$ in the robot's 3D object, the experimentally measured value for $NPCR$ of the encrypted object is 49.0741; moreover, if we also change the bit at position $(4, 4, 4)$ of the dog's 3D object, the $NPCR$ parameter associated is 50.9259.

(a)   (b)

Fig. 7. (a) Single-bit modified robot's 3D object and its encrypted 3D object. (b) Single-bit modified dog's 3D object and its encrypted 3D object.

4.5   Other Cryptanalytic Attacks

Finally, we will study the robustness of the protocol against some specific cryptanalytic attacks which are initially designed for text-based encryption protocols. Specifically, they are cipher object-only attack, known-plain object attack and chosen-plain object attack. In the cipher object-only attack, an opponent must determine the secret key solely from an intercepted encrypted object. In the known-plain object attack, the opponent must deduce the secret key starting from several pairs of original objects and their corresponding encrypted objects; finally, in the chosen-plain object attack, the cryptanalyst is able to choose the plain objects and obtain the corresponding ciphered objects. If the encryption protocol is secure against the chosen-plain object attack, it is also secure against cipher object-only attack and known-plain object attack.

Suppose that the opponent chooses a plain object Q whose positions are all occupied by the same bit: 0 or 1. Then the encrypted object obtained does not reveal any information about the secret key. Moreover, any information about the original 3D object can be derived. As an illustrative example, we can see the Fig. 8 where a homogeneous solid 3D object (all positions are occupied by the bit 1) of dimension $12 \times 12 \times 12$ is encrypted using the proposed algorithm. The parameters used in the encryption protocol are $N = M = T = 15, B =$

1802a37 and the matrix of the 3D Cat map is the following:

$$C = \begin{pmatrix} 7 & 3 & 7 \\ 1 & 4 & 3 \\ 3 & 11 & 8 \end{pmatrix},$$ (13)

with Lyapunov exponent 3.87612. Note that the encrypted object is not homogeneous and the different positions between both objects are 49.1898 %.

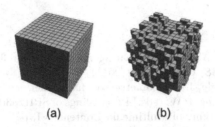

(a)   **(b)**

Fig. 8. (a) Homogeneous original 3D object. (b) Its encrypted 3D object.

Note that in this cases all bits of the three-dimensional lattices Q_l, $1 \leq l \leq M - 1$ obtained from the confusion phase are 0 or 1 and the confusion phase does not produce any effect, that is: $C^N(Q_l, K_c) = Q_l$ for every N and i. Then, the input in the first round of the diffusion phase is the own original object. In this phase, the 3D-CA defined by (9) is evolved starting from the initial configurations $C^0 = 0, C^1 = 0$ or $C^0 = 1, C^1 = 1$. A simple computation shows that in the first case we obtain $C^2 = C^3 = \ldots = C^T = C^{T+1} = 0$, and in the second case (when all the states of the initial configurations are 1) we obtain $C^2 = \left(\bigoplus_{(\alpha,\beta,\gamma) \in V} z_{\alpha\beta\gamma} + 1 \right)_{1 \leq i,j \leq n, 1 \leq k \leq n/2}$ and $C^3 = \ldots = C^T = C^{T+1} = 0$. Consequently any information about the secret key K_d can be obtained.

5   Conclusions

In this work a novel protocol to encrypt solid 3D objects constructed by the aggregation of elementary cuboids is shown. As far as we know, this is the first algorithm to encrypt 3D objects and it is based on the standard paradigm for chaotic image encryption stated by Fridrich.

Consequently, the method consists of two phases: the confusion phase and the diffusion phase, where original object to be ciphered is rendering into a three dimensional lattice. In the confusion phase a three-dimensional 3D Cat maps is considered whereas a reversible 2-th order memory 3D cellular automaton governs the diffusion phase.

This protocol is shown to be secure against the most important cryptanalytic attacks: statistical attacks, differential attack, chosen-plain object attack, etc.

The main drawback exhibited by this protocol is that it does not consider special characteristics of the cuboids that form the 3D object such as color, etc. In this sense, future work aimed at designing an improved method where this characteristics can be taken into account; it could be achieved by using cellular automata defined over different state sets.

Acknowledgement. This work has been supported by Gerencia Regional de Salud (Junta de Castilla y León, Spain) under grant number GES/SA01/14.

References

1. Elsheh, E., Hamza, A.B.: Secret sharing approaches for 3D object encryption. Expert Syst. Appl. **38**, 13906–13911 (2011)
2. Fernandes, E., Delaigle, J.F.: Geometric soft hash functions for 2D and 3D objects. In: Delp III, E.J., Wong, P.W. (eds.) Proceedings of SPIE 5306, Security, Steganography, and Watermarking of Multimedia Contents VI, p. 784. SPIE (2004)
3. Fridrich, J.: Symmetric ciphers based on two-dimensional chaotic maps. Int. J. Bifurcat. Chaos **8**, 1259–1284 (1998)
4. Lee, S.-H., Kwon, K.-R.: Robust 3D mesh model hashing based on feature object. Digit. Signal Process. **22**, 744–759 (2012)
5. Lee, S.-H., Kwon, K.-R., Hwang, W.-J., Chandrasekar, V.: Key-dependent 3D model hashing for authentication using heat kernel signature. Digit. Signal Process. **23**, 1505–1522 (2013)
6. Martín del Rey, A.: A multi-secret sharing scheme for 3D solid objects. Expert Syst. Appl. **42**, 2114–2120 (2015)
7. Montañola Sales, M., Rondão Alface, P., Macq, B.: 3D objects watermarking and tracking of their visual representations. In: Proceedings of the Third International Conferences on Advances in Multimedia, p. 111. IARIA (2011)
8. Nguyen, V.D., Chow, Y.-W., Susilo, W.: On the security of text-based 3D CAPTCHAs. Comput. Secur. **45**, 84–99 (2014)
9. Tarmissi, K., Ben Hamza, A.: Information-theoretic hashing of 3D objects using spectral graph theory. Expert Syst. Appl. **36**, 9409–9414 (2009)
10. Wang, K., Lavoué, G., Denis, F., Baskurt, A.: Three-dimensional meshes watermarking: review and attack-centric investigation. In: Furon, T., Cayre, F., Doërr, G., Bas, P. (eds.) IH 2007. LNCS, vol. 4567, pp. 50–64. Springer, Heidelberg (2008)
11. Wolfram, S.: A New Kind of Science. Wolfram Media Inc., Champaign (2002)
12. Zhang, S.: Handbook of D Machine Vision: Optical Metrology and Imaging. CRC Press, New York (2013)

Exemplar Selection Using Collaborative Neighbor Representation

F. Dornaika[1,2]($\boxtimes$), I. Kamal Aldine[1], and B. Cases[1]

[1] University of the Basque Country UPV/EHU, San Sebastian, Spain
[2] IKERBASQUE, Basque Foundation for Science, Bilbao, Spain
fadi.dornaika@ehu.es

Abstract. Retrieving the most relevant exemplars in image databases has been a difficult task. Most of exemplar selection methods were proposed and developed to work with a specific classifier. Research in exemplar selection is targeting schemes that can benefit a wide range of classifiers. Recently, *Sparse Modeling Representative Selection* (SMRS) method has been proposed for selecting the most relevant instances. SMRS is based on data self-representation in the sense that it estimates a coding matrix using a codebook set to the data themselves. The matrix coefficients are estimated using block sparsity constraint. In this paper, we propose a coding scheme based on a two stage Collaborative Neighbor Representation in the matrix of coefficients is estimated without any explicit sparse coding. For the second stage, we introduce two schemes for sample pruning in the second stage. Experiments are conducted on summarizing two video movies. We also provide quantitative performance evaluation via classification on the selected prototypes. To this end, one face dataset, one handwritten digits dataset, and one object dataset are used. These experiments showed that the proposed method can outperform state-of-the art methods including the SMRS method.

Keywords: Exemplar selection · Collaborative neighbor representation · Sample pruning · Classification · Video summarization

1 Introduction

Finding a subset of data points, known as representatives or exemplars, that can effectively describe the entire dataset, is an important issue in the analysis of scientific data, with a lot of application in machine learning, data recovery, signal processing, image processing, etc. The representatives can summarize datasets of images, videos, texts or Web documents. Finding a small number of examples which replaces the learning database has two main advantages: (i) reducing the memory space needed to store data and (ii) improving the computation time of classification algorithms. For example, the method of nearest neighbors (NN) is more efficient [1] when comparing test samples to the K representatives rather

---

This work was supported by the project EHU13/40.

E. Onieva et al. (Eds.): HAIS 2015, LNAI 9121, pp. 439–450, 2015.
DOI: 10.1007/978-3-319-19644-2_37

than to all the N training samples, with generally $K \ll N$. The problem of finding representative data has been well studied in the literature [2–7]. Like in feature selection, according to the strategy used for selecting instances, we can divide the instance selection methods in two groups: (i) Wrapper methods in which the selection criterion is based on the accuracy obtained by a classifier (commonly, those instances that do not contribute with the classification accuracy are discarded from the training set) (e.g. [8,9]), and (ii) Filter methods in which the selection criterion uses a selection function which is not based on a classifier (e.g., [10]).

Depending on the information that must be preserved by representatives, the filter algorithms used in this area can be divided into two categories. The first category finds representatives from data contained in one or several subspaces of reduced dimensionality [4–7,11,12]. The algorithm *Rank Revealing QR (RRQR)* [5,11] tries to select a few data points through finding a permutation of the data which gives the best conditioned submatrix. *Greedy* and *Randomized* algorithms have also been proposed in order to find a subset of columns in a reduced rank matrix [4,7].

The second group of algorithms finds representatives assuming there is a natural grouping of data collection based on an appropriate measure of similarity between pairs of data points [3,13,14]. Accordingly, these algorithms generally work on the similarity/dissimilarity between data points to be grouped. The *Kmedoids* algorithm, which can be considered as a variant of *Kmeans* [15], supposes that the data are located around several centers of classes, called medoids, which are selected from the data. Another algorithm based on the similarity/dissimilarity of data points is the *AP* (*Affinity propagation*) [3,14]. This algorithm tries to find representatives from the similarities between pairs of data points by using a message passing algorithm. Although AP has suboptimal properties and can find approximate solutions, it does not require any initialization (like Kmeans and Kmedoids) and has shown good performance in problems such as unsupervised image categorization [16]. In [17], the authors proposed Prototype Selection by Relevance (PSR) method for prototype selection. PSR selects the most relevant prototypes per class in a training set and through them some border prototypes are selected in order to preserve discrimination capability between classes.

Recently a new method, called *Sparse Modeling Representative Selection* (SMRS) [6] has been proposed in this area and is based on setting every data sample as a linear combination of the whole dataset. The computation of the combination coefficients has been solved by optimizing a criterion formed by two terms: the least square error of data self-representation, and (ii) a regularization term set to the $L_{1,q}$ norm of the coefficient matrix for imposing block sparsity. The instances are selected according to the norm of the estimated matrix rows where a row reflects the relevance of a given instance in the whole reconstruction. In this paper, we propose a Two phase Collaborative Neighbor Representation for estimating the coefficient matrix needed for instance selection. Our proposed scheme implicitly takes into account the locality and similarity among samples. Furthermore, our proposed scheme aims to compute a non-dense coefficient matrix. These two properties can lead to a better estimation of the coefficient matrix than that obtained with SMRS. Our proposal was first described in [18]. In the current work, we extend this proposal in two directions. First, we propose another variant in which the sample pruning will be based on the coding coefficients instead of the reconstruction errors. This variant will make the whole algorithm more flexible and accurate. Second, we provide more comparisons including real video summarization and object classification.

The remainder of the paper is structured as follows: in Sect. 2, we provide a brief review of the Sparse Modeling Representative Selection. In Sect. 3, we describe our proposed two phase Collaborative Neighbor Representation. Two different variants for the second phase are described. The experimental results are presented in Sect. 4. Section 5 gives some conclusions.

2   Review of Sparse Modeling Representative Selection (SMRS)

Consider a set of data points in $\mathbb{R}^m$ arranged as the columns of the data matrix $\mathbf{Y} = [\mathbf{y}_1, \ldots, \mathbf{y}_N]$. The key idea proposed by [6] is to set the coding dictionary to the original collection data $\mathbf{Y}$. This leads to the self-representativeness of data samples. The basic assumption is that every data sample can be set to a linear combination of the dataset. Mathematically, this assumption can be written as $\mathbf{y}_i = \mathbf{Y}\mathbf{b}_i$ where $\mathbf{b}_i$ is a vector of coefficients. The N equations, associated with the N samples, can be encapsulated in one single matrix equation:

$$\mathbf{Y} = \mathbf{Y}\mathbf{B}$$

where $\mathbf{B} = [\mathbf{b}_1, \ldots, \mathbf{b}_N]$. One likes to minimize the following criterion using some constraints on the coefficients:

$$\sum_{i=1}^{N} \|\mathbf{y}_i - \mathbf{Y}\mathbf{b}_i\|^2 = \|\mathbf{Y} - \mathbf{Y}\mathbf{B}\|_F^2$$

The SMRS method [6] proposes to estimate the coding matrix $\mathbf{B}$ by imposing some regularization on the unknown coefficients. Thus, the matrix $\mathbf{B}$ is estimated by minimizing the following criterion:

$$\mathbf{B} = \arg\min_{\mathbf{B}} \left(\frac{1}{2}\|\mathbf{Y} - \mathbf{Y}\mathbf{B}\|^2 + \lambda\|\mathbf{B}\|_{1,q} \right) \quad s.t. \quad \mathbf{1}^T\mathbf{B} = \mathbf{1}^T \tag{1}$$

The criterion has two terms. The first term is the Least square error associated with the self-representativeness of data. The second term is set to the $L_{1,q}$ norm of the matrix $\mathbf{B}$, i.e., $\|\mathbf{B}\|_{1,q} = \sum_j [|B_{(j,1)}|^q + \ldots + |B_{(j,N)}|^q]^{\frac{1}{q}}$. Thus, if $q = 2$, the regularization term is the sum of L_2 norm of the rows of $\mathbf{B}$. The $L_{1,2}$ norm imposes row sparsity.

The affine constraint $\mathbf{1}^T\mathbf{B} = \mathbf{1}^T$ makes the selection of representatives invariant with respect to a global translation of the data. The optimization of (1) can be carried out using the Alternating Direction Method of Multipliers (ADMM) technique [19]. As can be seen, SMRS provides a relevance score from the estimated coding matrix $\mathbf{B}$. Intuitively, if all elements of the ith row of $\mathbf{B}$ (or most of them) are non-null, this means that the ith sample has a significant contribution in reconstructing many samples. Hence, this i^{th} sample is a relevant instance. On the contrary, whenever the ith row contains zeros or very small values this means that the ith sample is not related to the rest of samples and hence can be considered as a non-relevant instance. Thus, the relevance score of the ith sample set to the L_2 norm of the ith row of $\mathbf{B}$.

The framework for this selection is summarized in Algorithm 1. It should be noticed that in supervised learning context the same framework of SMRS can be applied on each class separately in order to retrieve the most representative examples in each class.

Data: Dataset $\mathbf{Y} = [\mathbf{y}_1, \ldots, \mathbf{y}_N]$ and the desired number of representatives K

Result: Set of representatives $\{\mathbf{y}_1^*, \ldots, \mathbf{y}_K^*\}$

- Calculate the coding coefficients $\mathbf{B}$ using
$\mathbf{B} = \arg\min_{\mathbf{B}} \left(\frac{1}{2}\|\mathbf{Y} - \mathbf{Y}\mathbf{B}\|^2 + \lambda\|\mathbf{B}\|_{1,q}\right) s.t. \mathbf{1}^T\mathbf{B} = \mathbf{1}^T$;
- Compute the L_2 norms of the rows of $\mathbf{B}$ as $l_j = \|\mathbf{B}(j,:)\|, j = 1, \ldots, N$;
- Select the K samples that correspond to the largest K norms $\{\mathbf{y}_1^*, \ldots, \mathbf{y}_K^*\}$;
- $\mathbf{Y}_s = [\mathbf{y}_1^*, \ldots, \mathbf{y}_K^*]$;

Algorithm 1: Representative selection using SMRS.

3 Two Phase CNR-Based Instance Selection

In this section we propose a different methodology for constructing the matrix of coefficients. Our proposed scheme retrieves the coefficient matrix $\mathbf{B}$ from the data matrix $\mathbf{Y}$ using two phase Collaborative Neighbor Representation (CNR). By adopting our coding scheme both implicit similarity among samples and sparsity are imposed. This leads to a better estimation of the coefficient matrix than that obtained with SMRS. In this section, we first describe the one phase estimation, and then we describe the two phase estimation scheme. For the latter scheme, we introduce two variants for the second phase.

One Phase CNR. Collaborative Neighbor Representation or locality-constrained linear code is essentially a least square coding in which the regularization term contains individual weights [20]. Let $\mathbf{y}$ be the vector to be coded using $\mathbf{Y}$ as a dictionary. In our work, $\mathbf{y}$ will be one sample $\mathbf{y}_i$ and the dictionary will be the original data matrix from which the sample $\mathbf{y}_i$ is removed. For the sake of presentation simplicity, we present the principle using $\mathbf{Y}$ as a dictionary and $\mathbf{y}$ as the sample to be coded. CNR coding estimates the vector of coefficients, $\mathbf{b}$, by minimizing the following criterion:

$$\mathbf{b} = \arg\min_{\mathbf{b}} \frac{1}{2} \left(||\mathbf{y} - \mathbf{Y}\mathbf{b}||_2^2 + \sigma \sum_{j=1}^{N} w_j^2 b_j^2 + \lambda ||\mathbf{b}||^2 \right) \; s.t. \mathbf{1}^T \mathbf{b} = 1 \qquad (2)$$

where λ and σ are two small positive scalars, and w_j^2 is a positive weight associated with the coefficient b_j (or equivalently the sample $\mathbf{y}_j$). The solution to (2) will reconstruct the input signal $\mathbf{y}$ by a combination of the space spanned by $\mathbf{Y}$. In (2), the second term is the weighted regularized term. The linear constraint on the $\mathbf{b}$ can be included in the reconstruction error by appending the vector $\mathbf{y}$ and the matrix $\mathbf{Y}$ by 1 and $[1, \ldots, 1, 1]$, respectively. For the sake of simplicity, in the sequel, we will omit the linear constraint. The weights w_j are usually set to the Euclidean distance such that $w_j^2 = ||\mathbf{y} - \mathbf{y}_j||^2$. Let $\mathbf{W}$ denote a diagonal matrix formed by $W_{jj} = w_j = ||\mathbf{y} - \mathbf{y}_j||$.

The one phase CNR estimates the coefficient vector $\mathbf{b}$ by minimizing:

$$\mathbf{b} = \arg\min_{\mathbf{b}} \frac{1}{2} \left(||\mathbf{y} - \mathbf{Y}\mathbf{b}||_2^2 + \sigma ||\mathbf{W}\mathbf{b}||^2 + \lambda ||\mathbf{b}||^2 \right) \qquad (3)$$

After some algebraic manipulation, we get the solution to (3):

$$\mathbf{b} = \left(\mathbf{Y}^T \mathbf{Y} + \sigma \mathbf{W} + \lambda \mathbf{I} \right)^{-1} \mathbf{Y}^T \mathbf{y} \qquad (4)$$

where $\mathbf{I}$ is the identity matrix.

Each column in the matrix $\mathbf{B} = (\mathbf{b}_1, \ldots, \mathbf{b}_N)$ is estimated using Eq. (4) with an appropriate $\mathbf{y}$ and $\mathbf{Y}$. For estimating the ith column vector $\mathbf{b}_i$, $\mathbf{y}$ is set to the sample $\mathbf{y}_i$ and the dictionary $\mathbf{Y}$ is set to $[\mathbf{y}_1, \ldots, \mathbf{y}_{i-1}, \mathbf{y}_{i+1}, \ldots, \mathbf{y}_N]$. The diagonal elements of $\mathbf{B}$ are set to zero.

Two Phase CNR (First Variant). In this scheme, every column vector of coefficients, $\mathbf{b}_i$, is estimated in two consecutive stages. In the first stage, this vector is given by Eq. (4). In the second stage, we invoke another coding in which only a small dictionary is used. This dictionary is formed by the most relevant samples selected according to the sample contribution. Let us assume that the vector $\mathbf{b}$ is estimated using Eq. (4). In order to detect the most similar or relevant samples in the original dictionary, we will use the concept of contribution. The contribution of a given sample $\mathbf{y}_j$ (the jth column in the original dictionary) in constructing the test sample $\mathbf{y}$ is $b_j \mathbf{y}_j$. In order to evaluate the contribution of the samples $\mathbf{y}_j$ in representing the test sample, the following score is used:

$$e_j = ||\mathbf{y} - b_j \mathbf{y}_j||^2 \qquad (5)$$

A small score e_j means a large contribution. Based on this fact, we can estimate an automatic threshold given by the mean, $\overline{e_j}$, of all scores $e_j, j = 1, \ldots, N$. Let Th denote this threshold (i.e., $Th = \overline{e_j}$). We generate another dictionary $\mathbf{Y}_{sel}$ formed by all $\mathbf{y}_j$ whose contribution is large enough (small scores). In other words, we only keep the samples that satisfy $e_j < Th$.

Let $\mathbf{Y}_{sel}$ be the data matrix formed by the selected examples (the ones whose contribution is greater than the chosen threshold). Then, the vector $\mathbf{b}'$ associated with the selected examples will be solved using a formula similar to (4):

$$\mathbf{b}' = \left(\mathbf{Y}_{sel}^T \mathbf{Y}_{sel} + \sigma \mathbf{W}_{sel} + \lambda \mathbf{I} \right)^{-1} \mathbf{Y}_{sel}^T \mathbf{y} \tag{6}$$

The original N-vector $\mathbf{b}$ is set as follows. A non-selected sample $\mathbf{y}_j$ will have $b_j = 0$ and a selected one will have the corresponding coefficient in the vector $\mathbf{b}'$ estimated by (7).

Finally, each column vector in $\mathbf{B} = (\mathbf{b}_1, \ldots, \mathbf{b}_N)$ is estimated using the two phases described above (i.e., Eqs. (4) and (7)). The matrix $\mathbf{B}$ obtained by the two phase CNR is sparser than the one obtained with the one phase CNR since the columns contain a lot of zeros due to the introduced filtering scheme.

Two Phase CNR (Second Variant). By exploiting the fact that the coefficients obtained by the first phase can be used as a similarity measure between two samples, we propose a more flexible variant for the second phase that can naturally incorporate the similarity concept. In this variant, the new set of pruned samples is generated by eliminating samples having low similarities with the sample to be coded. We can estimate an adaptive sample-based threshold given by a statistical function of all scores $|b_j|, j = 1, \ldots, N$. Let Th' denote this threshold (i.e., $Th' = STAT(|b_j|, j = 1, \ldots, N)$. In our work, we used $Th' = MEAN + s.MAD$ where $MEAN$ is the mean values of the coefficients, MAD is the median of absolute differences of the coefficients, and s is a scale controlling the magnitude of the sample-based threshold. We generate another data matrix formed by all samples $\mathbf{y}_j$ whose coefficient is large enough (high similarities). In other words, we only keep the samples that satisfy $|b_j| > Th'$. Let $\mathbf{Y}'$ be the data matrix formed by these selected examples. Then, the coding vector $\mathbf{b}'$ associated with the selected examples will be solved using a formula similar to (4):

$$\mathbf{b}' = \left(\mathbf{Y}'^T \mathbf{Y}' + \sigma \mathbf{W}' + \lambda \mathbf{I} \right)^{-1} \mathbf{Y}'^T \mathbf{y} \tag{7}$$

4   Experimental Results

In this section, we evaluate the performance of the proposed algorithm for finding representatives of real datasets on two illustrative problems: video summarization (qualitative evaluation) and pattern classification (quantitative evaluation). Firstly, we demonstrate the applicability of our proposed algorithm for summarizing videos. Secondly, we evaluate the performance of our method as well as other algorithms for finding representatives that are used for image classification.

4.1   Qualitative Evaluation: Video Summarization

We consider a 4150-frame video retrieved from YouTube[1]. This video is called "They shall Have music". It consists of a series of continuous activities with a variable background (some frames are shown in Fig. 1). We apply the SMRS

---

[1] https://www.youtube.com/watch?v=fHP3sdnz-r4.

method and the proposed method in order to obtain 40 representative images among the 4150 images. Then, these 40 representatives are pruned such that very close representatives (in time) are merged into one single frame. Figure 1(b) and (c) show the final image representatives obtained by the SMRS method (11 representatives) and the proposed method (15 representatives), respectively. Here the coding of both the SMRS and the proposed method is performed on the whole 4150 frames. Note that the representatives obtained by the algorithms captured the main events of the video. We can observe that the representative images selected by the SMRS method and the proposed are not the same. Furthermore, we can see that the SMRS method obtained more close representatives than the proposed method since their final number is 11 images. Figure 2 show the final image representatives associated with a 27-minute video called "The Jack Benny Program - New Year's Eve"[2]. For both algorithms, the requested

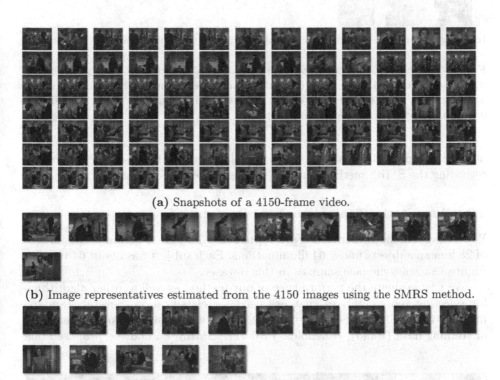

(a) Snapshots of a 4150-frame video.

(b) Image representatives estimated from the 4150 images using the SMRS method.

(c) Image representatives estimated from the 4150 images using the proposed method.

Fig. 1. Some frames of the They shall Have music video (a). The automatically computed representatives of the whole video sequence (4150 frames) using the SMRS method (b), and the proposed method (c). Depending on the amount of activities in each shot of the video and on the method used, we obtained one or a few representatives for that shot.

---

[2] http://www.youtube.com/watch?v=0-mStina7Xs.

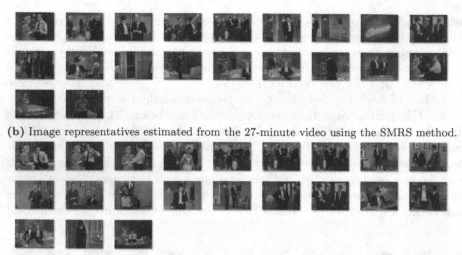

(b) Image representatives estimated from the 27-minute video using the SMRS method.

(c) Image representatives estimated from the 27-minute video using the proposed method.

Fig. 2. The automatically computed representatives of the whole video sequence (4150 frames) using the SMRS method (b), and the proposed method (c). Depending on the amount of activities in each shot of the video and on the method used, we obtained one or a few representatives for that shot.

number of representatives is 30. From the obtained results, a similar conclusion regarding the SMRS method and the proposed method can be drawn.

4.2   Quantitative Evaluation: Face Recognition

We considered the **Extended Yale - part B**[3] dataset. It contains the images of 28 human subjects under 64 illuminations. Each subject has about 64 images. Figure 3 shows some face samples in this dataset.

We now evaluate the performance of our method as well as other algorithms for selecting representatives that are used for classification. Several standard methods for finding representatives of datasets are used: simple random selection of training data (Rand), Kmedoids, PSR [17], SMRS [6], and the proposed one

Fig. 3. Some samples in Extended Yale dataset.

---

[3] http://vision.ucsd.eduleekc/ExtYaleDatabase/ExtYaleB.html.

phase CNR and two phase CNR (two variants). The first variant is denoted Two Phase CNR (V1) and the second variant is denoted Two Phase CNR (V2).

For the training data in each class, we find the representatives and use them as a reduced training dataset to perform classification. Ideally, if the representatives are informative enough about the original data, the classification performance using the representatives should be close to the performance using all the training data. Therefore, representatives not only summarize a dataset and reduce the data storage requirements, but also can be effectively used for tasks such as recognition and clustering.

Table 1 illustrates the recognition performance on the Extended Yale B face dataset after the selection of 12 representatives of the 48 training samples in each class. The number of test images is 12 images per class. The classifiers used are the Nearest Neighbor, Sparse Representation Classifier (SRC), and Support Vector Machines (SVM). As can be seen, the proposed Two Phase CNR variants have provided the best performance for the three classifiers used with a slight superior performance for the second variant (the one using the coefficients of the first phase).

Table 1. Classification accuracy (%) on the Extended Yale B face database using 12 representatives of the 51 training samples in each class. The selection methods used are: RAND, K-medoids, PSR, SMRS, One phase CNR, Two Phase CNR (two variants), and All data.

Selection method\Classifier	NN	SRC	SVM
Rand	60.9	82.2	82.5
K-medoids	67.8	90.0	92.2
PSR	70.3	83.7	83.9
SMRS	66.2	90.0	94.1
One phase CNR	71.2	87.5	86.0
Two Phase CNR (V1)	72.6	**91.4**	94.2
Two Phase CNR (V2)	**75.0**	90.8	**94.5**
All data	86.1	97.5	98.9

4.3   Quantitative Evaluation: Handwritten Digit Recognition

We consider the **USPS**[4] dataset. This Handwritten Digit dataset is composed of grayscale images of ten digits "0" through "9"; each class (digit) has 550 images. Table 2 illustrates the classification performance on the USPS dataset after the selection of 50 representatives of the 500 training samples in each class. The number of test images is 50 images per class. As can be seen, the proposed Two Phase CNR schemes have outperformed the other competing methods for all classifiers. We also notice that the second variant is superior to the first variant.

---

[4] http://www.cs.nyu.edu/roweis/data.html.

4.4   Quantitative Evaluation: Object Recognition

We consider the (Columbia Object Image Library) **COIL-20**[5] dataset: This dataset consists of 1440 images of 20 objects. Each object has underwent 72 rotations (each object has 72 images). The objects display a wide variety of complex geometry and reflectance characteristics. Table 2 illustrates the classification performance on the COIL-20 dataset after the selection of 10 representatives of the 62 training samples in each class. The number of test images is 10 images per class. As can be seen, the proposed Two Phase CNR schemes have outperformed the other competing methods for all classifiers. We also notice that the second variant is superior to the first variant (Table 3).

Table 2. Classification accuracy (%) on the USPS database using 50 representatives of the 500 training samples in each class. The selection methods used are: RAND, K-medoids, PSR, SMRS, One phase CNR, Two Phase CNR (two variants), and All data.

Selection method\Classifier	NN	SRC	SVM
Rand	88.6	92.1	92.4
K-medoids	88.8	92.6	93
PSR	82.6	85.4	80
SMRS	81.6	90.4	95.2
One phase CNR	83.2	87.4	90.2
Two phase CNR (V1)	89.6	93.2	95.2
Two phase CNR (V2)	**92.0**	**93.6**	**96.4**
All data	95.8	97.6	98.6

Table 3. Classification accuracy (%) on the COIL-20 database using 10 representatives of the 67 training samples in each class. The selection methods used are: RAND, K-medoids, PSR, SMRS, One phase CNR, Two Phase CNR (two variants), and All data.

Selection method\Classifier	NN	SRC	SVM
Rand	83.0	90.0	93.0
K-medoids	85.0	94.0	94.0
PSR	79.0	87.0	84.0
SMRS	84.0	94.0	94.0
One phase CNR	80.0	92.0	88.0
Two phase CNR (V1)	84.0	95.0	95.0
Two phase CNR (V2)	**88.0**	**96.0**	**96.0**
All data	98.0	100	100

---

[5] www.cs.columbia.edu/CAVE/software/softlib/coil-20.php.

5 Conclusion

We have proposed a Two phase Collaborative Neighbor Representation for finding a subset of representatives in a dataset. For the second phase of coding, we have introduced two schemes for sample pruning in order to get the final coding used by instance selection. We have compared our proposed schemes with several standard methods used in the domain: Kmedoids, simple random selection of training data (Rand), and the recent SMRS method. Qualitative and quantitative evaluations were performed on images through video summarization and classification. These experiments demonstrate the efficacy of the proposed approaches. They also show that sample pruning using the coefficients can give better results than that based on residual errors. Future work will investigate efficient schemes for large datasets (e.g., above 10 K of samples). Moreover, it will investigate an in depth statistical analysis by using more datasets and competing proposals.

References

1. Garcia, S., Derrac, J., Cano, R., Herrera, F.: Prototype selection for nearest neighbor classification: taxonomy and empirical study. IEEE Trans. Pattern Anal. Mach. Intell. **34**(3), 417–435 (2012)
2. Gu, M., Eisenstat, S.: Efficient algorithms for computing a strong rankrevealing QR factorization. SIAM J. Sci. Comput. **17**, 848–869 (1996)
3. Frey, B., Dueck, D.: Clustering by passing messages between data points. Sci. Mag. **315**, 972–976 (2007)
4. Tropp, J.: Column subset selection, matrix factorization and eigenvalue optimization. In: Proceedings of ACM-SIAM Symposium on Discrete Algorithms (SODA), pp. 978–986, January 2009
5. Boutsidis, C., Mahoney, M., Drineas, P.: An improved approximation algorithm for the column subset selection problem. In: Proceedings of ACM-SIAM Symposium on Discrete Algorithms (SODA), pp. 968–977, January 2009
6. Elhamifar, E., Sapiro, G., Vidal, R.: See all by looking at a few: sparse modeling for finding representative objects. In: Proceedings of IEEE Conference on Computer Vision and Pattern Recognition, pp. 1600–1607, June 2012
7. Bien, J., Xu, Y., Mahoney, M.: CUR from a sparse optimization viewpoint. In: Advances in Neural Information Processing Systems, pp. 217–225, December 2010
8. Czarnowski, I.: Cluster-based instance selection for machine classification. Knowl. Inf. Syst. **78**(3), 1–21 (2010)
9. Chen, J., Zhang, C., Xue, X., Liu, C.L.: Fast instance selection for speeding up support vector machines. Knowl.-Based Syst. **47**, 1–7 (2013)
10. Narayan, B., Murthy, C., Pal, S.: Maxdiff kd-trees for data condensation. Pattern Recogn. Lett. **27**, 187–200 (2006)
11. Chan, T.: Rank revealing QR factorizations. Linear Algebra Appl. **88–89**, 67–82 (1987)
12. Esser, E., Moller, M., Osher, S., Sapiro, G., Xin, J.: A convex model for nonnegative matrix factorization and dimensionality reduction on physical space. IEEE Trans. Image Process. **21**(7), 3239–3252 (2012)

13. Charikar, M., Guha, S., Tardos, A., Shmoys, D.: A constant-factor approximation algorithm for the k-median problem. J. Comput. Syst. Sci. **65**(1), 129–149 (2002)
14. Givoni, I., Chung, C., Frey, B.: Hierarchical affinity propagation. In: Conference on Uncertainty in Artificial Intelligence, July 2011
15. Duda, R., Hart, P., Stork, D.: Pattern Classification. WileyInterscience, U.S.A (2004)
16. Dueck, D., Frey, B.: Non-metric affinity propagation for unsupervised image categorization. In: Proceedings of International Conference in Computer Vision, pp. 1–8, October 2007
17. Olvera-López, J.A., Carrasco-Ochoa, J.A., Martínez-Trinidad, J.F.: Prototype selection via prototype relevance. In: Ruiz-Shulcloper, J., Kropatsch, W.G. (eds.) CIARP 2008. LNCS, vol. 5197, pp. 153–160. Springer, Heidelberg (2008)
18. Dornaika, F., Aldine, I.K.: Instance selection using two phase collaborative neighbor representation. In: Wermter, S., Weber, C., Duch, W., Honkela, T., Koprinkova-Hristova, P., Magg, S., Palm, G., Villa, A.E.P. (eds.) ICANN 2014. LNCS, vol. 8681, pp. 121–128. Springer, Heidelberg (2014)
19. Boyd, S., Parikh, N., Chu, E., Peleato, B., Eckstein, J.: Distributed optimization and statistical learning via the alternating direction method of multipliers. Found. Trends Mach. Learn. **3**(1), 1–122 (2011)
20. Waqas, J., Yi, Z., Zhang, L.: Collaborative neighbor representation based classification using l_2-minimization approach. Pattern Recogn. Lett. **34**(2), 201–208 (2013)

On Sentiment Polarity Assignment in the Wordnet Using Loopy Belief Propagation

Marcin Kulisiewicz, Tomasz Kajdanowicz[✉], Przemyslaw Kazienko, and Maciej Piasecki

Department of Computational Intelligence, Wroclaw University of Technology, Wroclaw, Poland
{marcin.kulisiewicz,tomasz.kajdanowicz,
przemyslaw.kazienko,maciej.piasecki}@pwr.edu.pl

Abstract. Sentiment analysis is a very active and nowadays highly addressed research area. One of the problem in sentiment analysis is text classification in terms of its attitude, especially in reviews or comments from social media. In general, this problem can be solved by two different approaches: machine learning methods and based on lexicons. Methods based on lexicons require properly prepared lexicons which usually are obtained manually from experts and it costs a lot in terms of time and resources. This paper aims at automatic lexicon creation for sentiment analysis. There are proposed the methods based on Loopy Belief Propagation that starting from small set of seed words with a priori known sentiment value propagates the sentiment to whole Wordnet.

Keywords: Sentiment analysis · Wordnet · Relational classification · Collective classification

1 Introduction

Knowledge about people's opinions and their attitude to specific subjects is highly desired in business, politics or media. Such aggregated information could be easily used to improve an election campaign or a strategy of creating brand. The simplest approach to posses this knowledge is to manually (by human) assign sentiment polarity for each opinion. The polarity of sentiment can be expressed in many different ways, for instance in 'likes' using 'Like it' on Facebook, ratings expressed in stars - as in IMDb or in continuous values as in SentiWordNet [3]. However, manually obtained sentiment polarity might cause high cost of application, both in terms of time and money. Alternative approach is an automatic sentiment analysis on opinions. Automatic sentiment analysis can be perform in general in two ways: (1) based on machine learning methods and (2) based on lexicons.

Machine learning classification methods are a well known approach to solve the problem of label assignment to a given text (e.g. opinion) based on the set of text features. Sentiment analysis can be also considered as a classification

© Springer International Publishing Switzerland 2015
E. Onieva et al. (Eds.): HAIS 2015, LNAI 9121, pp. 451–462, 2015.
DOI: 10.1007/978-3-319-19644-2_38

problem in which a label set represent three distinct classes: *positive, neutral, negative*. These three classes aggregate opinions with the same polarization from a certain text collection.

In order to perform useful sentiment classification, an appropriate dataset should be utilized to train the classifier. However, the complexity of natural language and the variance of the statements people use in their opinions, it can be intuitively suggested that the training set should be very extensive. Classification of opinion attitude is a very complex problem, even for human annotators. It comes from the fact that the analyzed text could have distinct sentiment polarity depending on the general context, e.g. *"an conservative approach"* can be seen either positively or negatively. Another complex problem that arise in sentiment analysis is how to extract an appropriate feature set from the text.

This paper is dedicated to the problem of how to create a general lexicons for sentiment assignment. For that purpose, a method for automatic sentiment polarity assignment in the WordNet by means of Loopy Belief Propagation algorithm (LBP) and its modification for multilayer networks are proposed, see Sect. 3. Another Sect. 4 contains the description of experimental studies together with their results and analysis. The paper is summarized in Sect. 5.

2   Related Work

Typically, sentiment is expressed by means of textual statements, remarks or opinions. Sentiment does not determine human emotion, but the overall attitude of author's statements towards a given subject. Dan Jurafsky in his publication [7] shows how to distinguish affective states using examples of Sherer Typology of Affective States. To express the sentiment, one of terms from a particular set of types can be used, for instance: *liking, loving, hating, valuing, desiring*. But in common use it is also polarity: *positive* and *negative*. More complex approach is using graded polarity: *strong positive, positive, neutral, negative* and *strong negative* which can be also expressed by stars or ranks from 1 to 5.

Sentiment assignment is a subject of wide research in social media domain. Numerous authors use tweets in their research e.g. [13]. Major part of tweets can be characterized in terms of sentiment polarity. J. McAuley and J. Leskovec in their research [11] derived a huge database of reviews from Amazon.com. They parsed 253,059 products and their reviews from 889,178 users and collect a set of 7,911,684 reviews. Each review has a score expressed in stars from 1 to 5 which is assumed to correspond to sentiment polarity in the review text. Another example can be a message board containing a lot of opinions about financial stock. V. Sehgal and C. Song in [14] used such relevant messages to predict stock values. Sentiment analysis faces a lot of problems. Researchers have to deal with difficult tasks such as properly prepared lexicon for sentiment polarity assignment, irony detection, spam detection [6], etc.

Sentiment Lexicons. Words' lexicon is a set of words in a particular language (in recent work it is English). Generally for sentiment analysis lexicons contain an information about sentiment value. Given a sentence or a text it can be considered as a set of words with assigned sentiment value that corresponds to the value from lexicon. It is expected that appropriate aggregation of this sentiment values gives a collective sentiment value for whole sentence. Selection of aggregation methods is presented in [9], where sentence decomposition is considered. The next paragraph briefly presents some of well known lexicons.

Existing Lexicons. In the past there were many researchers who worked on sentiment analysis using lexicons. Das and Chen [2] used a lexicon of hand-picked collection of finance words with scoring methods to classify a stock posting on investors bulletin. Also Huttner and Subasic [5] used manually created lexicon of words that were describing or were connected to some affects. Hu and Kiu in [4], Blair-Goldensohn and McDonald in [10] perform a propagation using connections between synsets in the WordNet. This approach will be extended within this paper.

WordNet. WordNet [1] can be used for lexicon creation. It is a large lexical database of English. Nouns, verbs, adjectives and adverbs are grouped into sets of cognitive synonyms (synsets), each expressing a distinct meaning. Synsets are interlinked by means of conceptual-semantic and lexical relations. In this paper WordNet refers to its 3.0 version. WordNet is used by researchers for natural language analysis and affective states analysis. A Valitutti et al. in [16] extracted a subset of WordNet synsets (named WordNet-Affect), that refers to emotional states.

3   Proposed Methods

The problem considered in this work lies in a foundation of sentiment analysis. Appropriate approach to determination of words sentiment polarity and its strength gives solid basement for sentiment analysis in various domains. Automatic methods are capable to prepared lexicon for number of domains with low cost in term of time and resources. This paper introduces a new automatic method for lexicon creation using an auxiliary information about the language - derived from the WordNet - that will provide an appropriate sentiment value for words.

3.1   WordNet 3.0 Usage

In this paper proposed methods base on a belief propagation approach are performed by using WordNet 3.0. Therefore, to apply developed methods to that lexical database, pre-processing is required. Generally, WordNet is a network of synsets. The purpose of experiments is to assess a sentiment value to words. To fulfil this assumption the WordNet has to be transformed in following way: synsets are divided to a set of pairs - a word and a synset. Words from each synset are connected to every other word from the same synset representing the relation of synonymy. Moreover, the newly created nodes, i.e. "word-synset" keep the links from the basic WordNet structure in the sense that the links between words from different synsets are kept and the same applies to the relation between synsets. This way of processing the WordNet creates a complex network of "word-synset" nodes, compatible with further proposed methods.

In this setting the WordNet is considered as a multiplex. Layers of this multiplex are defined in the following way: each type of existing connections forms one layer with varying density. Each of these layers has the same set of nodes but they differ by the set of edges. In total, the number of layers will be equal to the number of different relationships.

3.2　Proposed Methods for Sentiment Assignment

Propagation methods used in experiments are based on a typical loopy belief propagation algorithm (LBP) [12]. Generally, propagation method is an iterative process in which neighboring variables communicates with each other and pass messages.

First proposed algorithm is based on an original LBP method. It is applied to the uniplex derived from a reduced multiplex. Second approach considers the WordNet as a multilayer graph, computes propagation for each layer independently and fuses results from each layer into one result. Third method is a complex random walk method which considers the WordNet also as a multilayer graph but propagation is conducting in parallel in each layer. More details about these methods are presented below.

Sentiment Assignment by Layer Reduction. In this method the WordNet is considered as a uniplex. This kind of network can be represented as a tuple: set of nodes V and set of directed edges E, $\mathbf{G} = (\mathbf{V}, \mathbf{E})$, where $\mathbf{V} = \{v_1, v_2, ..., v_n\}$ represents the set of nodes and $\mathbf{E} = \{e_1, e_2, ..., e_n\}$ represents the set of edges, such that $\bigvee e \in \mathbf{E}, e = (v_i, v_j), v_i, v_j \in \mathbf{V}, v_i \neq v_j$.

Set of nodes can be divided to two separate subsets:

- X - a set of already classified (known) nodes
- Y - a set of nodes with unknown classes

In this setting the set of classes contains only two of classes: 1)positive polarization and 2) negative polarization of particular word. A class is represented by a continuous value in range [0-1] that describes how strongly a node belongs to each of available classes or in another words - probability that node is in particular class. Each of apriori known node has one dominant class for instance *positivity = 1.0, negativity = 0.0*. Unknown nodes have an equal distribution on class values - in this case *positivity = 0.5, negativity = 0.5*.

As it was mentioned transformed WordNet is a complex network which contains many layers. To use Layer Reduction methods WordNet needs to be flattened into a uniplex. All multiple edges between nodes are reduced to one edge. In graph theory it is called fusion at graph level.

Such prepared network is a base for running the LBP algorithm. In each step of that algorithm for each node its new sentiment polarity is computed in the following way:

$$P(v_i, c_k) = \frac{1}{n_i} \sum_{j=1}^{n_i} P(v_j, c_k) \tag{1}$$

where $P(v_i, c_k)$ is a probability that node v_i is in class c_k and n_i is a number of neighbors of node v_i.

In the beginning a matrix represents classes of each node is derived from network. Its dimensions are $[C * N]$, where C is a number of classes and N is a number of nodes in the network. Matrix field $[c_i, n_j]$ has a value from range [0,1] represents the probability that node n_j belongs to class c_i. Next, an adjacency matrix is derived from the network. That adjacency matrix has dimensions $[N * N]$, field $[n_i, n_j]$ has value 0 or 1 and represents the connection between node n_i and n_j.

The schema of layer reduction method is presented in Fig. 1.

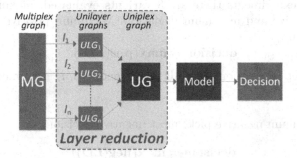

Fig. 1. Layer reduction schema.

Sentiment Assignment by Decision Fusion. An another approach - decision fusion - is computed in similar a way as Layer Reduction, because is also based on a typical LBP method. Multiplex can be separated into several independent networks - each network is based on one layer of multiplex - with the same set of nodes, differing by the set of edges.

On each layer a node can have different set of neighbours which influence it. Thus, on each layer the classification decision can be different. Decision fusion method aggregates these decisions and derives a final decision. Intuition of decision fusion method is presented in Fig. 2. There is several approach to perform decision fusion. In this work average fusion and max fusion in 3 variants will be used. Next few paragraphs will present this approaches.

Computing final decision by average is defined as follows:

$$\text{decision} = \frac{1}{N} \sum_{n=1}^{N} d(l_n) \tag{2}$$

where N is a number of layers and $d(l_n)$ is decision obtained from layer n.

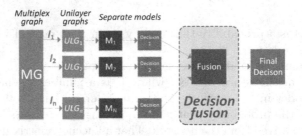

Fig. 2. Decision fusion schema.

An alternative fusion method - max fusion - picks maximum value from layers. In this experiments there are 3 variants evaluated: maximum positive, maximum negative and maximum deviation. Maximum positive chooses most positive decision:

$$\text{decision} = \max(\text{pos}(LD)), \tag{3}$$

where LD is set of decision from all layers and $pos(d)$ is a value *Positive* of decision d.

Similarly, maximum negative picks most negative decision:

$$\text{decision} = \max(\text{neg}(LD)) \tag{4}$$

where $neg(d)$ is value *Negative* of decision d. Maximum deviation pick most polarized decision:

$$\text{decision} = \max(\max(\text{neg}(LD)), \max(\text{pos}(LD))) \tag{5}$$

All fusion methods base on decisions obtained from each of layer. On each layer the propagation is computed by LBP, as presented above.

Sentiment Assignment by Random Walker. Last method proposed in this paper is Random Walker LBP, which can be located between two previous methods by means of the level of fusion. In simple terms it is a fusion inside model, where it is computed during propagation, in opposite to previous methods. Intuition of this method is presented in Fig. 3. The propagation is computed in similar way as in the Layer Reduction method - there are also two kinds of thresholds determining the stop condition. The only difference is in the way how new classes values are computed in each step. For each node in each step sentiment polarity is computed as follows:

$$P(v_i, c_k) = \sum_{l=1}^{|L|} \frac{\sum_{j=1}^{n_i^l} \frac{w_{ij}^l P(v_j, c_k)}{S_{il}}}{LP_l} \tag{6}$$

where:
$P(v_i, c_k)$ is a probability that node v_i belongs to in class c_k
$|L|$ represents a number of layers
n_i^l equals to a number of neighbours of node v_i in layer $l \in L$
w_{ij}^l is a weight of edge between node v_i and v_j in layer $l \in L$
LP_l represents the position of a layer

In this paper edge weight and layer position remain unused. It means that all layers are equally significant and all edges weights are set to 1.

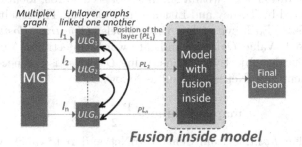

Fig. 3. Random Walker schema.

3.3   Seed Selection

One of the most important requirements in belief propagation methods is the selection of known nodes as a seed for propagation. In this work the seed is a set of word selected by Turney and Littman in 2003 [15]. It is a set of 14 words - 7 words paradigmatically positive (with sentiment values P=1, N=0) and 7 words paradigmatically negative (with sentiment values P=0, N=1). Paradigmatically positive words are: *good, nice, excellent, positive, fortunate, correct, superior* and paradigmatcally negative words are: *bad, nasty, poor, negative, unfortunate, wrong inferior.*

4   Experiments and Results

In this section, the details of experiment are explained. There are information of the experiment environment, used dataset and evaluation methods. At the end of the section results are presented and discussed.

4.1 Datasets

Datasets are used in experiment to evaluate proposed propagation methods. Each dataset is a words' lexicon with a sentiment value represented in different way. Chosen lexicons give a diverse basis for further evaluation.

General Inquirer Lexicon. General Inquirer - a lexicon created on Harvard contains over 11,000 words marked with 182 type of tags. From available categories, two of them have been chosen - *Positiv*, that covers 1,915 words, and *Negativ*, that covers 2,291 words. These categories are the basis to evaluate sentiment value. Disadvantage of these lexicon is a relatively small amount of tagged word by *Positiv* and *Negativ* tag and the lack of *Neutral* tag. General Inquirer version used in the experiment was merged in July 2000.

SentiWordNet 3.0. SentiWordNet 3.0 - an improved version of SentiWordNet 1.0 - is a word lexicon based on WordNet 3.0. SentiWordNet was created in a process of automatic sentiment annotation using glosses of WordNet synsets. Automatic annotation start with a small set of seed words, identical as used in this work, selected by Turney and Littman in 2003 [15]. The result is a network of marked synsets. Each synset has three labels: *Objective, Positive, Negative* that sum up to 1. Value *Objective* indicate words objectivity. Methods in this work do not consider objectivity. Thus, value *Objective* is not necessary. Triple of label from SentiWordNet is mapped as follow:

$$\mathbf{mappedValue} = \frac{\mathbf{p} - \mathbf{n}}{\mathbf{2}} + \frac{\mathbf{1}}{\mathbf{2}} \tag{7}$$

where **p** is value *Positive* from SentiWordNet and **n** is value *Negative* from SentiWordNet for particular synset. Such mapping is proper if the distribution of value in SentiWordNet comes from continuous uniform distribution.

4.2 Evaluation

The evaluation of propagation methods is based on comparison of the obtained results to values derived from lexicon. It is carried out in two ways and each way is based on another lexicon. In this work absolute mean error, squared mean error and F-score are chosen for evaluation. For evaluation on SentiWordNet, each pair $< word, synset >$ in evaluated network is linked to corresponding synset in SentiWordNet. Sentiment values of SentiWordNet synsets are mapped as expressed in Eq. 7. Such connected data is well prepared to compute absolute mean error and squared mean error.

Second source in the evaluation is a comparison to General Inquirer lexicon. Each word in lexicon was linked to all matched nodes in WordNet by words. As it was described in previous section General Inquirer contains words tagged by categories - in this work we use two of them: *Positiv* and *Negativ*. Other words which are not tagged by one of this categories are treated as *Neutral*. Thus, results of propagation also should be mapped to these categories. For these purpose 3 ranges have been adopted to map the sentiment values to categories:

- Negativ[0,0.45], Neutral(0.45,0.55), Positiv(0.55,1]
- Negativ[0,0.4], Neutral(0.4,0.6), Positiv(0.6,1]
- Negativ[0,0.2], Neutral(0.2,0.8), Positiv(0.8,1]

Such operations makes the evaluation available only for a subset of WordNet content. Each method was assessed in terms of precision, recall and f-score.

4.3 Experimental Scenarios

The experiment is conducted with following settings: (1) maximal number of LBP iterations set to 100, (2) stop threshold set to 0.001. Starting from selected seeds LBP assigned sentiment beliefs to each node. The obtained results were compared to values from General Inquire and SentiWordNet.

4.4 Results

In this section all gathered results are presented. Results of comparison to SentiWordNet are presented in Table 1. Results of comparison to General Inquirer are presented in Table 2.

Table 1. The results of propagation methods compared to SentiWordNet. LR - Layer Reduction, RW - Random Walker, DF - Decision Fusion, avg - fusion by average in DF, mp - fusion by maximal positive in DF, mn - fusion by maximal negative in DF and md - fusion by maximal deviation in DF

	LR	RW	DF avg	DF mp	DF mn	DF md
MAE	0,04536	0,04034	0,04970	0,05132	0,05113	0,05606
MSE	0,00206	0,00163	0,00247	0,00263	0,00261	0,00314

4.5 Discussion

The proposed propagation methods compared to lexicons gives some interesting but ambiguous results. First, the best method for SentiWordNet comparison is Random Walker. What is surprising is that the result of Layer Reduction is better then all Decision Fusion methods.

Evaluation using General Inquirer gives different results. The best method in this evaluation is Decision Fusion with maximum deviation fusion giving significantly better results than rest of the methods. In opposite to evaluation with SentiWordNet the worst method is Random Walker.

Table 2. The results of propagation methods compared to General Inquire lexicon, where LR - Layer Reduction, RW - Random Walker, DF - Decision Fusion, avg - fusion by average in DF, mp - fusion by maximal positive in DF, mn - fusion by maximal negative in DF and md - fusion by maximal deviation in DF.

		LR		RW		DF avg		DFmp		DFmn		DFmd	
		pos	neg	pos	neg	pos	neg	pos	neg	pos	neg	pos	neg
[0.45;0.1; 0.45]	prec.	0,436	0,490	0,395	0,576	0,475	0,579	0,456	0,562	0,454	0,586	0,452	0,583
	recall	0,011	0,010	0,004	0,004	0,017	0,026	0,033	0,016	0,018	0,028	0,047	0,028
	f-score	0,022	0,019	0,007	0,007	0,033	0,050	0,062	0,032	0,034	0,054	0,086	0,053
[0.4; 0.2; 0.4]	prec.	0,536	0,545	0,461	0,565	0,5	0,576	0,460	0,559	0,444	0,603	0,452	0,6
	recall	0,005	0,007	0,003	0,002	0,007	0,020	0,019	0,016	0,016	0,016	0,033	0,016
	f-score	0,011	0,014	0,006	0,005	0,014	0,039	0,036	0,032	0,031	0,031	0,062	0,030
[0.2; 0.6; 0.2]	prec.	0,444	0,485	0,2	0,428	0,454	0,555	0,468	0,558	0,438	0,6	0,449	0,6
	recall	0,001	0,003	0,0002	0,0005	0,001	0,015	0,005	0,015	0,015	0,005	0,020	0,005
	f-score	0,002	0,006	0,0005	0,0011	0,002	0,030	0,011	0,029	0,029	0,010	0,038	0,010

Additionaly, comparison of three methods: Layer Reduction, Decision Fusion by average and Random Walker is presented in Fig. 4. It can be observed that the best method is Random Walker.

It hard task to uniquely classify any the methods significantly better then other while considering differences of the results obtained on both evaluation sources. More lexicons should be used in order to provide statistically significant results. Also, each of them should cover more words then General Inquirer lexicon.

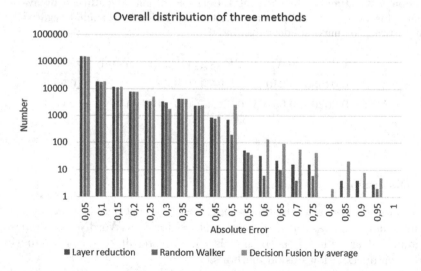

Fig. 4. The distribution of absolute error results for Layer Reduction (LR), Random Walker (RW) and Decision Fusion by average (DF avg) methods.

5 Conclusions and Further Work

5.1 Conclusions

This paper provide a comparison of the sentiment assignment performed by there propagation methods: Layer Reduction, Decision Fusion and Random Walker. The comparison was focused on accuracy and efficiency of the sentiment assignment.

Results obtained in experiments are ambiguous. An evaluation using Senti-WordNet revealed that Random Walker is better propagation method for sentiment assignment in WordNet than Layer Reduction and Decision Fusion. From the other hand, an evaluation by General Inquirer shows that Decision Fusion by maximum deviation is the best propagation method and the second best is decision fusion by maximum positive while Random Walker has the worst results. The observed difference is not significant statistically.

The results may encourage to rise the question - whether the WordNet is good base for sentiment propagation? The intuitive conclusion may lead to the statement that relations within WordNet do not reflect sentiment relation well. Whats more, foundations of defining such relations (at least most of it) between synsets is different from sentiment assumptions. However, the concept of automatic lexicons generation still seems to be reasonable idea and that may provide very useful methods for sentiment assignment.

5.2 Further Work

One of the possible improvements can be achieved by Random Walker method extension by means of additional parameters describing relations between layers. These parameters can be provided by experts or assessed by computational methods.

Another possible future development of sentiment assignment can be achieved by application of local conditional classification models, for instance ICA [8].

Nevertheless, the outcome of propagation methods presented in this paper provided a kind of lexicon that can be interesting for linguists and in multiple application areas. However, it has to be validated by appropriated examination and assessment provided by language specialists.

Acknowledgements.. The work was partially supported by European Union, the ENGINE grant, agreement no 316097 (FP7) and by The National Science Centre, the decision no. DEC-2013/09/B/ST6/02317. The work was partially financed as part of the investment in the CLARIN-PL research infrastructure funded by the Polish Ministry of Science and Higher Education.

References

1. http://wordnet.princeton.edu/ 2014. Accessed: 30 May 2014
2. Das, S., Chen, M.: Yahoo! for amazon: extracting market sentiment from stock message boards. Proc. Asia Pac. financ. Assoc. Ann. Conf. (APFA) **35**, 43 (2001)

3. Esuli, A., Sebastiani, F.: Sentiwordnet: a publicly available lexical resource for opinion mining. In: Proceedings of the 5th Conference on Language Resources and Evaluation LREC 2006, pp. 417–422 (2006)
4. Hu, M., Liu, B.: Mining and summarizing customer reviews. In: Proceedings of the Tenth ACM SIGKDD International Conference on Knowledge Discovery and Data Mining, pp. 168–177. ACM (2004)
5. Huettner, A., Subasic, P.: Fuzzy typing for document management. In: ACL 2000 Companion Volume: Tutorial Abstracts and Demonstration Notes, pp. 26–27 (2000)
6. Jindal, N., Liu, B.: Review spam detection. In: WWW 2007: Proceedings of the 16th International Conference on World Wide Web, pp. 1189–1190. ACM Press (2007)
7. Jurafsky, D., Manning, C.: Sentiment analysis, natural language processing. In: Coursera.com (2014)
8. Kazienko, P., Kajdanowicz, T.: Label-dependent node classification in the network. Neurocomput. 75(1), 199–209 (2012)
9. Kim, S.M., Hovy, E.: Extracting opinions, opinion holders, and topics expressed in online news media text. In: Proceedings of the Workshop on Sentiment and Subjectivity in Text, SST 2006, Association for Computational Linguistics pp. 1–8, Stroudsburg (2006)
10. Lerman, K., Blair-goldensohn, S., Mcdonald, R.: Sentiment summarization: evaluating and learning user preferences. In: Proceedings of the European Chapter of the Association for Computational Linguistics EACL, pp. 514–522 (2009)
11. McAuley, J.J., Leskovec, J.: From amateurs to connoisseurs: modeling the evolution of user expertise through online reviews. In: Proceedings of the 22nd International Conference on World Wide Web, pp. 897–908. International World Wide Web Conferences Steering Committee / ACM (2013)
12. Murphy, K.P., Weiss, Y., Jordan, M.I.: Loopy belief propagation for approximate inference: an empirical study. In: Proceedings of the Fifteenth Conference on Uncertainty in Artificial Intelligence, UAI 1999, pp. 467–475 (1999)
13. Raez, A.M., Martinez-Camara, E., Martin-Valdivia, M.T., Urena-Lopez, L.A.: Ranked wordnet graph for sentiment polarity classification in twitter. Comput. Speech Lang. 28(1), 93–107 (2014)
14. Sehgal, V., Song, C.: Sops: stock prediction using web sentiment. In: Seventh IEEE International Conference on Data Mining Workshops, ICDM Workshops 2007, pp. 21–26. IEEE (2007)
15. Turney, P.D., Littman, M.L.: Measuring praise and criticism: inference of semantic orientation from association. ACM Trans. Inf. Syst. 21(4), 315–346 (2003)
16. Valitutti, A., Strapparava, C., Stock, O.: Developing affective lexical resources. PsychNology J. 2(1), 61–83 (2004)

Classification and Cluster Analysis

Evaluation of Relative Indexes
for Multi-objective Clustering

Tomáš Bartoň[1,2](✉) and Pavel Kordík[1]

[1] Faculty of Information Technology, Czech Technical University
in Prague, Thakurova 9, Prague 6, Czech Republic
{tomas.barton,pavel.kordik}@fit.cvut.cz
http://www.fit.cvut.cz
[2] Institute of Molecular Genetics of the ASCR, V. V. I., Vídeňská 1083,
142 20 Prague 4, Czech Republic

Abstract. One of the biggest challenges in clustering is finding a robust
and versatile criterion to evaluate the quality of clustering results. In this
paper, we investigate the extent to which unsupervised criteria can be
used to obtain clusters highly correlated to external labels. We show that
the usefulness of these criteria is data-dependent and for most data sets
multiple criteria are required in order to identify the best performing
clustering algorithm. We present a multi-objective evolutionary clustering algorithm capable of finding a set of high-quality solutions. For the
real world data sets examined the Pareto front can offer better clusterings
than simply optimizing a single unsupervised criterion.

Keywords: Clustering · Evolution · Multi-objective clustering · Multi-
objective evolutionary algorithm

1 Introduction

Clustering is a popular data-mining technique which can lead to extracting new,
useful and understandable knowledge from data. Clustering has many practical applications in many fields, including biology, chemistry and social network
analysis. It is especially useful in cases when the categorization of elements is
unknown and unsupervised methods might discover interesting relationships and
reveal patterns in the data set. Clustering attempts to group together similar items based on certain criteria, such that similar items are placed in the
same cluster and dissimilar items are placed in different clusters. It is generally
acknowledged that clustering is an ill-defined problem, mainly due to its unsupervised nature, unclear quality measure and the lack of a precise definition of
what a cluster really is [1,2].

Traditional approaches to clustering, such as k-means [3] and agglomerative hierarchical clustering [4] optimize a single objective function to identify a
homogeneous structure in the data; whereas a heterogeneous structure in the
data could be found by approaches which use cluster ensembles [5]. However,

E. Onieva et al. (Eds.): HAIS 2015, LNAI 9121, pp. 465–476, 2015.
DOI: 10.1007/978-3-319-19644-2_39

selecting the optimal algorithm for a given data set is one of the main difficulties in cluster analysis [6]. Moreover, most of the available algorithms have many parameters which need to be fine tuned in order to obtain reasonable results.

In real-world applications, clustering can be misled by the assumption that it provides a unique solution. Noise, intrinsic ambiguity in the data and optimization models which are designed to maximize a fitness function could also reduce the quality of the result [7].

In this paper we present an advanced multi-objective optimization technique for clustering algorithms. Our objectives (unsupervised criteria) are carefully selected based on an analysis of their correlation with external criteria, tested on multiple data sets. We present visualizations that reveal the complexity of the problem. In spite of this complexity, the multi-objective optimization technique is capable of finding high-quality clusterings for most of the data sets in our experiments.

2   Background and Related Work

Many unsupervised criteria have been proposed to measure clustering quality, these indexes are usually called relative validity indexes. Another group of criteria was designed to compare the similarity of two clusterings. When external labels are available, we can use these indexes to validate results externally.

2.1   Relative Validity Indexes (Unsupervised Criteria)

One of the key issues in clustering is how we measure the quality of clusterings, since naturally we would like to know which algorithms produce better clusterings. However, creating a universal measure to compare any two clusterings seems to be an impossible task.

Many validation indexes have been proposed in the literature. An extensive survey of validation metrics is available in [8]. In [9] we evaluated several unsupervised criteria and measured their effects and similarities.

In this paper, we begin by comparing these different metrics' ability to sort clustering results. The idea behind clustering validation is simple, and most metrics express a ratio between cluster compactness and intra-cluster distances (separatedness).

An example of one such validation criterion is the C-index, which was introduced by Hubert and Levin [10] in 1976. It is computed as

$$p_{\text{c-index}}(\mathbb{C}) = \frac{d_w - \min(d_w)}{\max(d_w) - \min(d_w)} \tag{1}$$

where d_w is the sum of the intra-cluster distances. This index was found to exhibit excellent recovery characteristics by Milligan [11], who used the minimum value across the hierarchy levels to indicate the optimal number of clusters [12].

Deviation [13] minimizes the distances to a centroid within a cluster. It is defined as:

$$Dev(\mathbb{C}) = \sum_{C_k \in \mathbb{C}} \sum_{i \in C_k} \delta(i, \mu_k) \qquad (2)$$

where $\mathbb{C}$ is the set of all clusters, μ_k is the centroid of the cluster C_k and $\delta(.,.)$ is a chosen distance function (in our case Euclidean distance).

Connectivity [13] reflects the connectedness of items in a cluster. Clusterings with a low value of connectivity might have arbitrary shapes (non-spherical shapes), unlike solutions typically produced by algorithms like k-means. Connectivity evaluates the degree to which neighbouring data-points have been placed in the same cluster. It is computed as:

$$Conn(\mathbb{C}) = \sum_{i=1}^{N} \left(\sum_{j=1}^{L} x_{i,nn_{ij}} \right), \qquad (3)$$

where

$$x_{r,s} = \begin{cases} \frac{1}{j}, & \text{if } \nexists C_k : r \in C_k \wedge s \in C_k \\ 0, & \text{otherwise,} \end{cases}$$

nn_{ij} is the jth nearest neighbour of item i, N is the size of the data set and L is a parameter determining the number of neighbours that contribute to the connectivity measure.

The Davies-Bouldin index [14] combines two measures, one related to dispersion and the other to separation between different clusters. Mathematically,

$$p_{DB} = \frac{1}{k} \sum_{i=1}^{k} \max_{i \neq j} \left(\frac{\bar{d}_i + \bar{d}_j}{d(C_i, C_j)} \right) \qquad (4)$$

where $d(C_i, C_j)$ corresponds to the distance between the centre of clusters C_i and C_j, and $\bar{d}_i$ is the average within-group distance for cluster C_i.

$$\bar{d}_i = \frac{1}{|C_i|} \sum_{l=1}^{|C_i|} d(\mathbf{x}_i(l), \bar{\mathbf{x}}_i)$$

It is desirable for the clusters to have maximum separation from each other, therefore we seek clustering that minimizes the Davies-Bouldin index.

The Akaike information criterion [15] is typically used in supervised learning when trying to estimate model error. Essentially it attempts to estimate the optimism of the model and add it to the model error [16].

$$p_{AIC} = -2 \cdot \frac{\log(L_n(k))}{n} + 2 \cdot \frac{k}{n} \qquad (5)$$

where $L_n(k)$ is the maximum likelihood of a model with k parameters based on a sample of size n BIC (the Bayesian information criterion) works in a similar way.

2.2 External Validation

Another group of similarity measures consists of indices that can be used for comparing two clusterings, or a single clustering to external labels that were not used during the clustering process. Albatineh et al. [17] made a comprehensive list of 22 different indices of this type, and found that after a correction of chance some of those indices become equivalent. The most popular index seems to be the Adjusted Rand index [18], which was introduced by Hubert and Arabie in 1985. This index was also used for the evaluation of results in studies [13] and [19].

Yet another important group of measures is built upon fundamental concepts from information theory. The mutual information between two clusterings measures how much knowing one of these clusterings reduces our uncertainty about the other [20]. Kvalseth [21] introduced Normalized Mutual Information (NMI) which was later used by Strehl and Ghosh [5] and sometimes is referred as NMI_{sum}. This measure is more stable than the Adjusted Rand Index, especially when dealing with a higher number of clusters. This measure was also used in several follow-up works in the context of ensemble clustering [22,23].

2.3 Cluster Ensembles

The goal of ensemble methods is to find a consensus partition that agrees as much as possible with all the base partitions. Strehl and Ghosh [5] proposed three heuristics for solving the ensemble problem. The CSPA (Cluster-based Similarity Partitioning Algorithm) combines multiple clusterings based on their pairwise similarity. The HGPA (Hyper-Graph Partitioning Algorithm) partitions a hypergraph where hyperedges represent clusters. Lastly, the MCLA (Meta-CLustering Algorithm) identifies groups of clusters (meta-clusters) and consolidates them.

It is worth noticing that all these advanced algorithms still rely on traditional clustering algorithms, which can be very effective in revealing the type of structure they were designed for. A disadvantage of these ensemble methods is, however, that the final result is usually a single clustering.

2.4 Multi-objective Clustering

Multi-objective clustering usually optimizes two objective functions. Using more than a few objectives is not usual because the whole process of optimization becomes less effective.

The first multi-objective evolutionary clustering algorithm was introduced in 2004 by Handl and Knowles [24] and is called VIENNA (the Voronoi Initialized Evolutionary Nearest-Neighbour Algorithm).

Subsequently, in 2007 Handl and Knowles published a Pareto-based multi-objective evolutionary clustering algorithm called MOCK [13] (Multi-Objective Clustering with automatic K-determination). Each individual in MOCK is represented as a directed graph which is then translated into clustering. The genotype is encoded as an array of integers whose length is same as the number of instances in the data set. Each number is a pointer to another instance (an edge in the graph), since it is connected to the instance at a given index. This easily enables the application of mutation and crossover operations.

As a Multi-Objective Evolutionary Algorithm (MOEA) MOCK employs the Pareto Envelope-based Selection Algorithm version 2 (PESA-II) [25], which keeps two populations, an internal population of fixed size and a larger external population which is exploited to explore good solutions. Two complementary objectives, *deviation* and *connectivity*, are used as objectives in the evolutionary process.

A clear disadvantage of MOCK is its computation complexity, which is a typical characteristic of evolutionary algorithms. Nevertheless, the computation time spent on MOCK should be rewarded with high-quality solutions. Faceli et al. [19] reported that for some high-dimensional data it is not guaranteed that the algorithm will complete, unless the control front distribution has been adjusted for the given data set.

2.5 Multi-objective Ensembles

Faceli et al. [19] combined a multi-objective approach to clustering with ensemble methods and the resulting algorithm is called MOCLE (Muli-Objective Clustering Ensemble Algorithm). The objectives used in the MOCLE algorithm are the same as those used in MOCK [13]: deviation (Eq. 2) and connectivity (Eq. 3). Unlike MOCK, in this case the evolutionary algorithm used is NSGA-II [26].

MOCLE is capable of selecting clusterings with a high Adjusted Rand Index value, however it should be noted that the algorithm is initialized with high-quality partitions produced by carefully configured algorithms with a number of clusters close to the optimal value. In real world scenarios this kind of initialization is impossible especially when exploring an unknown data set.

3   Experiments

Our experiments are designed to investigate the state space of possible clustering algorithm configurations, the resulting clusterings and the usefulness of unsupervised criteria to navigate in the space towards high quality clusterings similar to the reference labels.

We use hierarchical clustering with Euclidean distance as a base algorithm. Other variants are generated by changing the linkage, standardization, dendrogram cutting method and relative index used for dendrogram cutting. Altogether this creates more than 3 thousand possible configurations, although the number of unique clusterings will be much lower.

3.1 Usefulness of Single Criteria

It is important to sort in a stable manner, not only for ensemble approaches or evolutionary algorithms, but generally for any cluster analysis where more than one result is produced. Using a brute-force approach we generated 250 unique clustering results using the Iris data set, which we sorted according to 21 unsupervised relative indexes. An ideal sorting criterion should be able to distinguish between good and bad results. As a reference for "correct" sorting we used external class labels that were not used during the clustering process.

A typical single-objective evolutionary algorithm sorts its population and rejects the lower half of the population. In case the average ranking error is close to 50 % of the list's length, it is very likely that the algorithm would reject many good individuals. We do not expect an evaluation function to find the best solution, nonetheless a decent sorting error is desirable.

Our clustering results were produced using a hierarchical agglomerative clustering algorithm with various settings and data preprocessing. The quality of the results is varied and the number of clusters ranges from 2 to 147 (where almost each instance is in a separate cluster). Figure 2 presents a visualization of the sorting results. Each bar represents a clustering result; the height of the bar is proportional to a supervised metric (Adjusted Rand Index or NMI), and its position on axis x corresponds to an unsupervised sorting. The best results should be towards the left, the worst results on the right.

A single objective function for sorting a set of clusterings is very hard to find for real-world data sets. Single criteria can only correlate with external criteria for simple data sets such as the Zoo data set, as can be observed for the Point-BiSerial criterion [27] (Fig. 1).

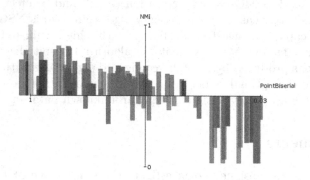

Fig. 1. Sorted clustering results of Zoo data set with Point-BiSerial criterion (Color figure online).

Figure 2a shows that Silhouette is quite a good estimator of both the Adjusted Rand Index (ARI) and NMI (Figure) external measures. However, some clusterings with higher Silhouette values do not have high supervised index values.

Sorting using the Davies-Bouldin index [14] (Fig. 2c) places clusterings with low ARI values next to items with high ARI values. Red bars signify incorrect placement, since the clusterings should be on the opposite side of the scale. This makes the Davies-Bouldin index unusable (at least for the Iris data set) because we can not distinguish between the good and the bad solutions.

A similar problem is found with AIC sorting (Fig. 2e); there are a few results among those on the left hand side which are false positive results, marked in red. Looking at Fig. 2f we notice that according to NMI the clusterings are not as bad as it would seem with ARI. Moreover, it should be noted that AIC does not project all results to a single value: the clusterings are almost evenly divided across the range.

C-index [10] produces slightly better results, as the first half of the clusterings produced would probably include a few high-quality clusterings. However, the best C-index values do not correlate with the best ARI or NMI values (Fig. 2g and h). A "golden standard" clustering (a hand made clustering based on class labels), marked yellow in the figure, is located in the middle of the C-index scale which might suggest that ideal clustering in the Iris data set is given by average C-index values.

Comparing different relative validation indexes is complicated for many reasons. First of all, the absence of a unanimous reference scale does not helping. Secondly, each index might be suitable for a different type of data. Our visualization illustrates this complexity, and demostrates that no single objective function for sorting a set of clusterings exists. Except for simple data sets, like Zoo data, we were not able to find any combination of internal and external criteria which are correlated.

4   Our Approach

In previous section we demostrated that a single objective function does not usually sort clusterings as perfectly. To overcome this issue we employed a multi-objective evolution algorithm which uses NSGA-II [26].

Our evolutionary algorithm operates on a meta-algorithm level. There are many parameters which can be adjusted in order to obtain reasonable clustering. It is difficult to decide which normalization will be better for a given data set before analysing the data. Therefore typical steps of data preprocessing are encoded in the individual. We use normalizations typically used in cluster analysis [28]: *z-score* formula, min-max normalization, division by the maximum value of that attribute (transforming the value into a value between -1 and 1) and standardized measurement (subtracting the mean value of the attribute and dividing by its mean absolute deviation) or no standardization. Another parameter determines whether to logarithmise the whole data set or not.

As a base clustering algorithm we use hierarchical agglomerative clustering with different linkage methods (single linkage, complete linkage, average linkage and Ward's linkage). After producing a dendrogram we applied a heuristic to convert a hierarchical structure into a flat partitioning. One heuristic is based on a hill-climbing algorithm. It cuts the dendrogram at each level and computes a relative validation index for each cut. When going to the next level would not improve the index, the algorithm stops.

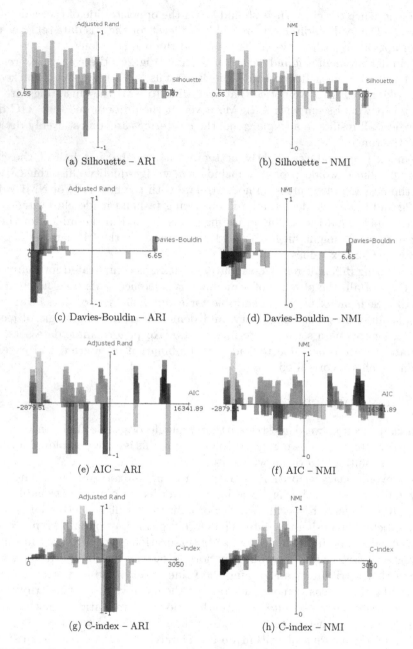

(a) Silhouette – ARI

(b) Silhouette – NMI

(c) Davies-Bouldin – ARI

(d) Davies-Bouldin – NMI

(e) AIC – ARI

(f) AIC – NMI

(g) C-index – ARI

(h) C-index – NMI

Fig. 2. Visualization of Iris data set clustering results sorted by internal validation index compared to external (supervised) validation index. The colour of the bar signifies its distance from ideal placement (green – correct, black – misplaced by half the scale, red – incorrect placement). Yellow bars represent ideal clustering performed using external labels (Color figure online).

Table 1. Comparison of the best clusterings found during multi-objective evolution with combination of two objectives. Best ARI is the value of the solution with the highest Adjusted Rand Index value found during evolution. *BF ARI* and *BF NMI* are Adjusted Rand Index values and Normalized Mutual Information values found by a brute-force algorithm which tried all possible settings of the given clustering algorithms.

Dataset	Best objectives	Best ARI	BF ARI	BF NMI
Iris	AIC/BIC & Calinski-Harabasz	0.88	0.88	0.86
	C-index & Deviation			
	C-index & Davies-Bouldin			
Glass	C-index & Hybrid Centroid Similarity	0.70	0.70	0.31
	AIC & PointBiserial	0.67		
	AIC/BIC & Sum of AVG parwise sim			
	Deviation & Sum of AVG parwise sim			
	AIC/BIC & Sum of squared errors			
Wine	C-index & min-max cut	0.90	0.95	0.93
	min-max cut & Sum of Centroid Sim	0.86		
	BIC & Silhouette	0.81		
	AIC & min-max cut			

An individual is encoded as an array of integers and each index in the genome is mapped to a certain parameter, which can have any range. All clustering parameters are nominal values. We used a polynomial mutation as it is implemented in the original NSGA-II and Simulated Binary Crossover (SBX). The probability of crossover was 50 % and mutation probability 20 %. For each dataset we evaluated

$$\binom{21}{2} = 210$$

combinations of two objective functions.

In Table 1 the best combinations of objectives for evolution of clusterings with two objectives are presented. Introducing AIC (or BIC) as one objective can significantly improve the results of multi-objective evolution. We managed to find a pair of objectives for each data set, whereby the final Pareto front with at most 10 individuals includes a solution matching the best solution found by the brute-force approach, or whose ARI value is very close to the optimum. Each evolution run was repeated 5 times; an example of a resulting Pareto front is shown in Fig. 3. Some objectives always converge to the same set of solutions, others produce very diverse results. We would like to examine these properties in our follow up work.

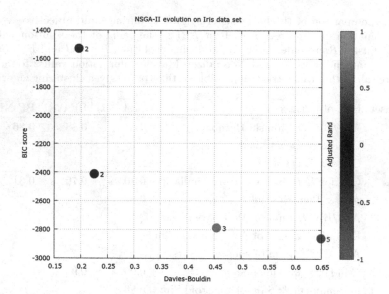

Fig. 3. Final Pareto front produced by NSGA-II algorithm (10 generations, population 20, crossover 50 %, mutation 20 %). Each dot represents a clustering result and is coloured according to the Adjusted Rand Index value. The number next to each result marks the number of clusters (Color figure online).

5   Conclusion

Mutating the parameters of clustering algorithms can lead to a very diverse set of clusterings. The purpose of this study was to find a set of unsupervised objectives and heuristics that can help locate a set of high quality clusterings instead of trying to find the best clustering possible. The best clustering is hard to define and clusterings labeled by external criteria are often disputable. Our unsupervised approach can locate high quality clusterings for diverse real-world data sets, whereas previous studies [13] showed partial success mostly on hand-crafted and generated (Gaussian) data sets.

Using our visualization methods, one can evaluate the usefulness of unsupervised criteria in comparison to supervised criteria.

AIC and BIC criteria proved to be beneficial for the multi-objective optimization and in combination with Silhouette, Calinski-Harabasz or C-index can successfully navigate the search for a set of high-quality clusterings.

Acknowledgements. We would like to thank Petr Bartůněk, Ph.D. from the IMG CAS institute for supporting our research and letting us publish all details of our work. This research is partially supported by CTU grant SGS15/117/OHK3/1T/18 New data processing methods for data mining and Program NPU I (LO1419) by Ministry of Education, Youth and Sports of Czech Republic.

References

1. Caruana, R., Elhawary, M., Nguyen, N., Smith, C.: Meta Clustering. In: Proceedings of the Sixth International Conference on Data Mining. ICDM 2006, pp. 107–118. IEEE Computer Society, Washington, DC (2006)
2. Law, M.H.C., Topchy, A.P., Jain, A.K.: Multiobjective Data Clustering. In: CVPR, vol. 2, pp. 424–430 (2004)
3. MacQueen, J.B.: Some Methods for Classification and Analysis of MultiVariate Observations. In: Cam, L.M.L., Neyman, J. (eds.) Proceedings of the fifth Berkeley Symposium on Mathematical Statistics and Probability, vol. 1, pp. 281–297. University of California Press (1967)
4. Lance, G.N., Williams, W.T.: A general theory of classificatory sorting strategies. Comput. J. 9(4), 373–380 (1967)
5. Strehl, A., Ghosh, J.: Cluster ensembles - a knowledge reuse framework for combining multiple partitions. J. Mach. Learn. Res. (JMLR) 3, 583–617 (2002)
6. Xu, R., Wunsch, I.: Survey of clustering algorithms. IEEE Trans. Neural Netw. 16(3), 645–678 (2005)
7. Bifulco, I., Fedullo, C., Napolitano, F., Raiconi, G., Tagliaferri, R.: Global optimization, meta clustering and consensus clustering for class prediction. In: Proceedings of the 2009 International Joint Conference on Neural Networks, IJCNN 2009, pp. 1463–1470. IEEE Press, Piscataway (2009)
8. Halkidi, M., Vazirgiannis, M., Batistakis, Y.: On clustering validation techniques. J. Intell. Inf. Syst. 17(2–3), 107–145 (2001)
9. Bartoň, T., Kordík, P.: Encoding time series data for better clustering results. In: Herrero, Á., Snášel, V., Abraham, A., Zelinka, I., Baruque, B., Quintián, H., Calvo, J.L., Sedano, J., Corchado, E. (eds.) Int. Joint Conf. CISIS 2012-ICEUTE 2012-SOCO 2012. AISC, vol. 189, pp. 467–475. Springer, Heidelberg (2013)
10. Hubert, L., Levin, J.: A general statistical framework for assessing categorical clustering in free recall. Psychol. Bull. 83(6), 1072 (1976)
11. Milligan, G.W.: A monte carlo study of thirty internal criterion measures for cluster analysis. Psychometrika 46(2), 187–199 (1981)
12. Milligan, G.W., Cooper, M.C.: An examination of procedures for determining the number of clusters in a dataset. Psychometrika 50(2), 159–179 (1985)
13. Handl, J., Knowles, J.: An evolutionary approach to multiobjective clustering. IEEE Trans. Evol. Comput. 11(1), 56–76 (2007)
14. Davies, D.L., Bouldin, D.W.: A cluster separation measure. IEEE Trans. Pattern Anal. Mach. Intell. 1(2), 224–227 (1979)
15. Akaike, H.: A new look at the statistical model identification. IEEE Trans. Autom. Control 19(6), 716–723 (1974)
16. Hastie, T., Tibshirani, R., Friedman, J., Corporation, E.: The Elements of Statistical Learning. Springer, Dordrecht (2009)
17. Albatineh, A., Niewiadomska-Bugaj, M., Mihalko, D.: On similarity indices and correction for chance agreement. J. Classif. 23(2), 301–313 (2006)
18. Hubert, L., Arabie, P.: Comparing partitions. J. Classif. 2(1), 193–218 (1985)
19. Faceli, K., de Souto, M.C.P., de Araujo, D.S.A., de Carvalho, A.C.P.L.F.: Multiobjective clustering ensemble for gene expression data analysis. Neurocomputing 72(13–15), 2763–2774 (2009)
20. Nguyen, X.V., Epps, J., Bailey, J.: Information theoretic measures for clusterings comparison: variants, properties, normalization and correction for chance. J. Mach. Learn. Res. 11, 2837–2854 (2010)

21. Kvålseth, T.O.: Entropy and correlation: some comments. IEEE Trans. Syst. Man Cybern. **17**(3), 517–519 (1987)
22. Tumer, K., Agogino, A.K.: Ensemble clustering with voting active clusters. Pattern Recogn. Lett. **29**(14), 1947–1953 (2008)
23. He, Z., Xu, X., Deng, S.: k-ANMI: A mutual information based clustering algorithm for categorical data. Inf. Fusion **9**(2), 223–233 (2008)
24. Handl, J., Knowles, J.D.: Evolutionary multiobjective clustering. In: Yao, X., Burke, E.K., Lozano, J.A., Smith, J., Merelo-Guervós, J.J., Bullinaria, J.A., Rowe, J.E., Tiňo, P., Kabán, A., Schwefel, H.-P. (eds.) PPSN 2004. LNCS, vol. 3242, pp. 1081–1091. Springer, Heidelberg (2004)
25. Corne, D., Jerram, N., Knowles, J., Oates, M.: PESA-II: region-based selection in evolutionary multiobjective optimization. In: Proceedings of the Genetic and Evolutionary Computation Conference (GECCO-2001) (2001)
26. Deb, K., Pratap, A., Agarwal, S., Meyarivan, T.: A fast and elitist multiobjective genetic algorithm: NSGA-II. IEEE Trans. Evol. Comput. **6**(2), 182–197 (2002)
27. Milligan, G.: An examination of the effect of six types of error perturbation on fifteen clustering algorithms. Psychometrika **45**(3), 325–342 (1980)
28. Milligan, G., Cooper, M.: A study of standardization of variables in cluster analysis. J. Classif. **5**(2), 181–204 (1988)

A Hybrid Analytic Hierarchy Process for Clustering and Ranking Best Location for Logistics Distribution Center

Dragan Simić[1(✉)], Vladimir Ilin[1], Ilija Tanackov[1], Vasa Svirčević[2], and Svetlana Simić[3]

[1] Faculty of Technical Sciences, University of Novi Sad,
Trg Dositeja Obradovića 6, 21000 Novi Sad, Serbia
dsimic@eunet.rs, {v.ilin, ilijat}@uns.ac.rs
[2] Lames Ltd., Jarački put bb, 22000 Sremska Mitrovica, Serbia
vasasv@hotmail.com
[3] Faculty of Medicine, University of Novi Sad,
Hajduk Veljkova 1–9, 21000 Novi Sad, Serbia
drdragansimic@gmail.com

Abstract. Facility location decisions play a critical role in the strategic design of supply chain networks. This paper discusses facility location problem with focus on logistics distribution center (LDC) in Balkan Peninsula. Methodological hybrid *Analytical Hierarchy Process* (AHP) and *k-means* method is proposed here and it is shown how such a model can be of assistance in analyzing a multi criteria decision-making problem. This research represents a continuation of two existing studies: (1) PROMETHEE II ranking method; and (2) combine Greedy heuristic algorithm and AHP. The experimental results in our research could be well compared with other official results of the feasibility study of the LDC located in Balkan Peninsula.

Keywords: Facility location · Logistics distribution center · Analytical hierarchy process · k-means clustering

1 Introduction

Facility location decisions play a critical role in the strategic design of supply chain networks. Typical application of facility location includes placement of manufacturing plants, storage facilities, depots, warehouses, schools, libraries, fire stations, hospitals and base stations for wireless services.

It is possible to consider the facility location problem with focus on logistics distribution center (LDC) in Balkan Peninsula (BP). This research for clustering, ranking and selecting the best location for logistics distribution center in BP is based on two existing studies [1, 2]. First study used PROMETHEE II ranking method and the second study used combined Greedy heuristic algorithm and *Analytical Hierarchy Process*. In the first study twenty criteria were used, but in the second there are extended on twenty-nine criteria divided in six criteria groups.

© Springer International Publishing Switzerland 2015
E. Onieva et al. (Eds.): HAIS 2015, LNAI 9121, pp. 477–488, 2015.
DOI: 10.1007/978-3-319-19644-2_40

In this research the hybrid *Analytical Hierarchy Process* (AHP) and *k-means* method for ranking, clustering and selection for the most suitable location for logistics distribution center in BP is proposed. This paper discusses five groups of criteria with appropriate 20 criteria and ten alternatives as the set of possible solutions to the cities in the BP. Experimental results show that it is possible to make a decision with lower number of features, combining hybrid method and solutions.

The rest of the paper is organized in the following way: Sect. 2 provides some approaches about facility location selection methods and related work. In Sect. 3 Official Studies selecting LDC in BP are presented. Section 4 proposes methodology of hybrid *Analytical Hierarchy Process* and *k-means* ranking and clustering method. Selection of a facility for LDC, criteria and facility rating with respect to established criteria are discussed in Sect. 5. An application of this hybrid model's experimental result and rank, the order of the facility location and selection of LDC in BP, are presented in Sect. 6. Finally, Sect. 7 gives concluding remarks.

2 Facility Location Problem and Related Work

Facility location is an important topic in logistic management. Different researches have discussed location problems with multiple attributes and various methods used for solving them. In [3] a fuzzy goal programming for locating a single facility with a given convex region is presented. Solving facility location problems using different solution approaches of fuzzy multi-attribute group decision making is presented in [4]. In [5] fuzzy AHP and fuzzy TOPSIS are used for the selection of facility location. In that particular research they compare results of the proposed methods. Fuzzy TOPSIS is proposed for selecting plant location in [6].

The system proposed in [7], integrates fuzzy set theory, factor rating system, and simple additive weighting and it is applied to deal with both qualitative and quantitative dimensions. A method to determine the optimal location of fire station facilities is discussed in [8]. The model is a combination of a fuzzy multi-objective programming and a genetic algorithm. TOPSIS method has become popular multiple criteria decision technique due to (1) its theoretical rigorousness [9], (2) a sound logic that represents the human rationale in selection [10], and (3) the fact that it has been provided in [11] as one of the most appropriate methods in solving traversal rank.

3 Choosing a Location for a Logistics Distribution Center in Balkan Peninsula – Official Studies

This research for clustering, ranking and selecting the best location for logistics distribution center in BP is based on two existing studies: (1) Decision on the logistics centers location, Case of the Balkan Peninsula [1]; and (2) The selection of logistic centers location using multi-criteria comparison: Case study of the Balkan peninsula [2]. First study, done in 2013, used PROMETHEE II ranking method. The second study, done in 2014, combined Greedy heuristic algorithm and *Analytical Hierarchy Process* used.

Our research relies on certain elements of the above mentioned studies, so processing of these potential sites with their advantages and disadvantages, confirmation or rejection of the final site selection for the development of logistics distribution center is in detailed discussed in new hybrid approach.

The Europe enlargement, outsourcing in economy, development of LDCs and their progressing towards Eastern European countries, as well as expansion of cargo flows between Western Europe and Asia, create new challenges for the BP region. As a consequence of permanently increasing cargo flows, there is a trend of building LDCs in BP to reduce transportation time and cost and to improve customer service and distribution network between Central Europe and Asia Minor region. This claim by a graphic presentation of the present LDCs in Europe and BP is confirmed on Fig. 1.

Fig. 1. Important LDCs in Europe – the basis of present logistic area model [1]

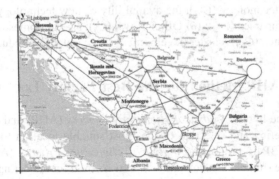

Fig. 2. Candidate sites for LDC locations on the Balkan peninsula countries

The information necessary for creating a map of LDCs, was taken from published papers and projects which contributed to the development of LDCs. Thus, the Center for Advanced Infrastructure and Transport [12] published a study in which all important LDCs with a strong influence on global transport are described. The project carried out under the European Commission (EC) called "Sutranet" [13], gave the list of the most influential LDCs in Europe in the final report. Candidate sites for LDC locations are the capital cities of BP countries, except Greece (Fig. 2).

Within this research, the limitation of the set of possible solutions to the cities in the BP is introduced: Serbia – Belgrade; Bulgaria – Sofia; Macedonia – Skopje; Romania – Bucharest; Greece – Thessaloniki; Montenegro – Podgorica; Albania – Tirana; BIH – Sarajevo, Croatia – Zagreb; Slovenia – Ljubljana. An illustrative example, in some novel research is the possibility of application of wider number of cities as set of new solution.

3.1 Data Collection

During evaluation of alternative location A_l, in the first study [1] twenty criteria and their usage are defined by PROMETHEE II method. On the other side, in the second study [2] six (6) groups criteria (C_i), which included 29 criteria (C_{ij}) are defined and analyzed by Greedy heuristic algorithm and AHP method. All 20 criteria in the first study are included in second study where 29 criteria are discussed.

The details for these group criteria are listed in the following way: **(1) Physical flows (C_1)**: road infrastructure (C_{11}), quality of railway infrastructure (C_{12}), development of a number of airports (C_{13}), development of ports (C_{14}), geografical position (C_{15}), infrastructure (energy) (C_{16}); **(2) Economics flows (C_2)**: facility of getting a bank credit (C_{21}), taxes and dues (C_{22}), inflation rate (C_{23}), salary and worker productivity (C_{24}), the presence of trade bariers (C_{25}); **(3) Institutional flows (C_3)**: Legal and judicial efficiency (C_{31}), safety in country (C_{32}), political stability (C_{33}), bribery and corruption (C_{34}), complesity of customs proced (C_{35}), bureaucracy (C_{36}); **(4) Goods flows (C_4)**: anti-monopoly politics (C_{41}), local competition of LDC (C_{42}), total country import (C_{43}), total country export (C_{44}), supply chain development (C_{45}); **(5) Information flows (C_5)**: telecomunication technology (C_{51}), the availability of new technology (C_{52}), Presence of distribution companies (C_{53}); **(6) Other flows (C_6)**: size of domestic suppliers (C_{61}), logistics competence (C_{62}), cluster development (C_{63}), quality of education (C_{64}).

4 A Hybrid AHP Method for the Best Facility Location

In this research the hybrid *Analytical Hierarchy Process* (AHP) and *k-means* method for ranking, clustering and selection of the most suitable location for logistics distribution center in BP is proposed. *Analytical Hierarchy Process* (AHP) is used for ranking alternative suitable location and *k-means* method for clustering, also with some external date for selection for the most suitable location of LDC in BP, takes the following algorithm depicted in Fig. 3.

4.1 Analytical Hierarchy Process

The AHP starts by decomposing a complex, multi-criteria problem into a hierarchy where each level consists of a few manageable elements (group criteria C_i) which are then decomposed into another set of elements (criteria C_{ij}). Later, these criteria (C_{ij}) are

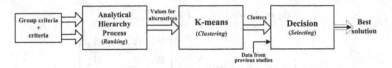

Fig. 3. Hybrid AHP and *k-means* method for ranking, clustering and selecting best solution

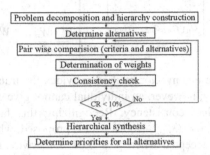

Fig. 4. Analytical Hierarchy Process methodology [14]

mutually compared in order to get the priority of each criterion in hierarchy. Finally, all alternatives are compared in relation to the set of criteria (C_{ij}) and in this way the comparison of alternatives (A_i) is obtained (Fig. 4).

In order to get the final result and in order to get gradation of influence for each criterion, it is first necessary to compare criteria mutually. The comparison of any two criteria C_i and C_j with respect to the goal is made using the questions of the type: of the two criteria C_i and C_j which is more important and how much. In original, it is suggested to use a nine-point scale to transform the verbal judgments into numerical quantities representing the values of C_{ij} [15]. During comparison of criteria Ci with criteria Cj by Saaty's scale, numerical coefficient aij is determined and set on position aij in matrix A. Matrix A is called a symmetrically reciprocal (SR) matrix and can be defined as:

$$A = [a_{ij}], \ i, j = 1, 2, 3 \ldots n. \tag{1}$$

$$a_{ij} > 0, \ a_{ij} = 1/a_{ij}, \ a_{ij} * a_{ji} = 1, \ for \ i \neq j \tag{2}$$

Here an entry a_{ij} from R^n represents a ratio, i.e., a_{ij} indicates the strength with which alternative A_i dominates alternative A_j with respect to a given criterion C_{ij}, $i,j = 1,2, \ldots,$ m. Such a matrix is called a pairwise comparison matrix (PCM) and is usually constructed by eliciting experts' judgments. The basic objective is to derive implicit weights (priority scores), $W_1, W_2, \ldots, W_m$, with respect to each criterion C_{ij}. A vector of the weights, $W = [W_i]$, $W_i > 0$, $i = 1, \ldots, n$, may be determined by using the eigenvalue formulation $\mathbf{AW} = \lambda \max \mathbf{W}$, λmax is the principal eigenvalue of the matrix $\mathbf{A}$. Since the single criteria are usually not equally important, therefore, a vector of the weighting factors of each criterion, $s = [s_{ij}]$, should also be determined, where s_{ij}, i, $j = 1,2, \ldots, m$ is often normalized so that $0 < s_{ij} < 1$.

$$a_{ij} = 1, \text{ for } i = j, \ i = 1, 2, 3\ldots n \tag{3}$$

$$A = \begin{bmatrix} a_{11} \, a_{12} \, a_{13} & a_{1n} \\ a_{21} \, a_{22} \, a_{23} & a_{2n} \\ \vdots \ \vdots \ \vdots & \vdots \\ a_{n1} \, a_{n2} \, a_{n3} & a_{nn} \end{bmatrix} = \begin{bmatrix} \dfrac{W_1}{W_1} \, \dfrac{W_1}{W_2} & \cdots & \dfrac{W_1}{W_n} \\ \dfrac{W_2}{W_1} \, \dfrac{W_2}{W_2} & \cdots & \dfrac{W_2}{W_n} \\ \vdots \ \vdots & & \vdots \\ \dfrac{W_n}{W_1} \, \dfrac{W_n}{W_2} & \cdots & \dfrac{W_n}{W_n} \end{bmatrix} \tag{4}$$

In the transitive case the eigenvector method provides the true relative dominance of the alternatives. In reality, however, an individual cannot give estimates such that they would conform to perfect consistency. Recognizing this fact, a measure for the inconsistency of a PCM: $\mu = (\lambda_{max} - n)/(n - 1)$ is proposed, where n is the matrix size [15]. Results might be accepted when $\mu \leq 0.08$. Otherwise the problem should be reconsidered and the associated PCM must be revised, as mentioned in [15].

4.2 *K-means* Clustering Method

Clustering is the process of organizing a set of data into groups in such a way that observations within a group are more similar to each other than they are to observations belonging to a different cluster. Many methods for grouping or clustering data can be found in various communities, such as statistics, machine learning, and data mining. Clustering is also known as unsupervised learning. However, several authors have pointed out the difficulty of formally defining such a term [16]. Most clustering methods assume some sort of structure or model for the cluster (spherical, elliptical). Thus, they find cluster of that type, regardless of whether they really are present in the data or not.

In this research, *k-means* clustering algorithm with the squared Euclidean distance measure and the *k-means* ++ algorithm for cluster center initialization is used. This structure is very strict with proximity defined as Euclidean distance given by:

$$\delta_{ij} = \sqrt{\sum_k \left(x_{ik} - x_{jk} \right)^2} \tag{5}$$

where: x_{ik} is the k-th element in the i-th observation.

5 Selecting Best Facility Location for LDC in Balkan Peninsula

This research continues two studies mentioned before [1, 2]. In the first study there are twenty (20) defined criteria, and in the second six (6) groups of criteria consisting of twenty-nine (29) criteria are defined. In this research, data set from the first study was used, twenty criteria for ten alternatives for LDC location. Those twenty criteria are classified in five groups, in the following way: The details for these group criteria are listed in the following way: **(1) Physical flows (C_1)**: road infrastructure (C_{11}), quality of railway infrastructure (C_{12}), development of a number of airports (C_{13}), development of ports (C_{14}), geografical position (C_{15}), infrastructure (energy) (C_{16}); **(2) Economics flows (C_2)**: facility of getting a bank credit (C_{21}), taxes and dues (C_{22}), inflation rate (C_{23}), salary and worker productivity (C_{24}), the presence of trade bariers (C_{25}); **(3) Institutional flows (C_3)**: Legal and judicial efficiency (C_{31}), safety in country (C_{32}), political stability (C_{33}), bribery and corruption (C_{34}), complexity of customs proced (C_{35}); **(4) Goods flows (C_4)**: antimonopoly politics (C_{41}), local competition of LDC (C_{42}), supply chain development (C_{45}); **(6) Other flows (C_6)**: size of domestic suppliers (C_{61}). In order to keep the consistency in all three papers, universal labeling has been used for group criteria and criteria. For that reason, in this research, group criteria: C_1, C_2, C_3, C_4 and C_6 are used. The basic structure of hierarchical structure AHP method for facility location problem implemented on LDC in BP is presented on Fig. 5.

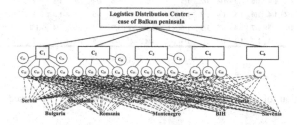

Fig. 5. A hierarchical structure for facility location problem LDC in Balkan peninsula

One of the goals of this research is to determine the minimal number of features, in this case minimal number of criteria to get best solution for LDC. Minimal number of features facilitates easier decision-making, for example: it is easier to calculate symmetrically reciprocal matrix with twenty (20) than with twenty-nine (29) criteria in AHP method. For twenty criteria, SR matrix has 400 elements, as opposed to SR matrix for 29 criteria which contains 841 elements, which is more than twice the number of elements of the first matrix. Of course, the measure for the inconsistency μ must be given, which might be accepted when $\mu \leq 0.08$.

The most important goal of this research is to find the minimal number of features and to get appropriate results. The experimental results of the inconsistency test of the comparison matrix, presented in Table 1 are: $\lambda_{max} = 20.73$, $\mu = 0.0384$, CR = μ/ RI = 0.0242. The measure for the inconsistency ($\mu = 0.0384$) is $\mu \leq 0.08$ indicating 'consistency' according with [15] and proposed model with reduced number – categories features can be used in further research (Table 2).

Table 1. Pairwise comparison matrix - evaluation of criteria C_{ij} based on the level of importance

Cij	C11	C12	C13	C14	C15	C16	C21	C22	C23	C24	C25	C31	C32	C33	C34	C35	C41	C42	C45	C61
C11	1	3	3	2	1/3	2	1	3	1/2	4	1/2	4	1/3	1/3	1	2	4	4	5	3
C12	1/3	1	2	1/3	1/5	1/2	1/3	2	1/4	3	1/4	3	1/5	1/5	1/3	1/5	3	3	4	1
C13	1/3	1/2	1	1/2	1/5	1/2	1/3	1	1/4	2	1/4	2	1/5	1/5	1/3	1/2	2	2	3	1
C14	1/2	3	2	1	¼	2	1/2	3	1/3	4	1/3	4	1/4	1/4	1/2	2	4	4	5	3
C15	3	5	5	4	1	4	3	5	1	6	1	6	1/2	1	3	4	6	6	7	5
C16	1/2	2	2	1/2	1/4	1	1/2	2	1/3	3	1/3	3	1/4	1/4	1/2	1	3	3	4	2
C21	1	3	3	2	1/3	2	1	3	1/2	4	1/2	4	1/3	1/3	1	2	4	4	5	3
C22	1/3	1/2	1	1/3	1/5	1/2	1/3	1	1/4	2	1/4	2	1/5	1/5	1/3	1/2	2	2	3	1
C23	2	4	4	3	1	3	2	4	1	5	1	5	1/2	1/2	2	3	5	5	6	4
C24	1/4	1/3	1/2	1/4	1/6	1/3	1/4	1/2	1/5	1	1/5	1	1/6	1/6	1/4	1/3	1	1	2	1/2
C25	2	4	4	3	1	3	2	4	1	5	1	5	1/2	1/2	2	3	5	5	6	4
C31	1/4	1/3	1/2	1/4	1/6	1/3	1/4	1/2	1/5	1	1/5	1	1/6	1/6	1/4	1/3	1	1	2	1/2
C32	3	5	5	4	2	4	3	5	2	6	2	6	1	2	3	4	6	6	7	5
C33	3	5	5	4	1	4	3	5	2	6	2	6	1/2	1	3	4	6	6	7	5
C34	1	3	3	2	1/3	2	1	3	1/2	4	1/5	4	1/3	1/3	1	2	4	4	5	3
C35	1/2	2	2	1/2	1/4	1	1/2	2	1/3	3	1/3	3	1/4	1/4	1/2	1	3	3	4	2
C41	1/4	1/3	1/2	1/4	1/6	1/3	1/4	1/2	1/5	1	1/5	1	1/6	1/6	1/4	1/3	1	1	2	1/2
C42	1/4	1/3	1/2	1/4	1/6	1/3	1/4	1/2	1/5	1	1/5	1	1/6	1/6	1/4	1/3	1	1	2	1/2
C45	1/5	1/4	1/3	1/5	1/7	1/4	1/5	1/3	1/6	1/2	1/6	1/2	1/7	1/7	1/5	1/4	1/2	1/2	1	1/3
C61	1/3	1/2	1	1/3	1/5	1/2	1/3	1	1/4	2	1/4	2	1/5	1/5	1/3	1/2	2	2	3	1

Table 2. Evaluation of criteria C_j for each alternative-country A_i based on the level of importance

Country / Criteria	SRB	BUL	MAC	ROM	GRE	MON	ALB	BIH	CRO	SLO
C_{32}	2.5	2.0	3.0	2.0	4.0	3.0	3.5	1.5	5.0	4.5
C_{33}	2.0	3.0	2.5	2.5	3.0	3.0	1.5	2.0	3.5	3.0
C_{15}	3.0	4.0	3.0	4.0	5.0	4.1	5.0	2.5	4.5	5.0
C_{23}	2.8	3.8	3.7	3.0	4.0	3.4	3.5	1.6	4.0	5.0
C_{25}	5.0	5.0	4.0	5.0	3.0	2.0	1.0	2.0	2.0	1.0
C_{11}	3.0	3.0	4.0	2.5	4.5	3.0	3.5	2.0	5.0	5.0
C_{21}	2.5	3.0	2.0	2.5	2.5	3.5	2.5	2.0	2.5	3.0
C_{34}	3.0	3.0	5.0	2.0	2.0	3.0	2.0	3.0	3.0	3.0
C_{14}	1.0	4.0	5.0	3.0	4.0	3.0	4.0	5.0	4.0	5.0
C_{16}	3.5	4.0	4.0	4.5	3.0	4.0	5.0	3.0	3.5	4.0
C_{35}	4.5	4.0	4.5	5.0	5.0	5.0	5.0	4.0	5.0	5.0
C_{12}	2.5	3.0	3.0	2.9	3.0	4.0	4.0	2.0	3.0	4.0
C_{13}	4.0	3.5	4.0	4.0	4.0	5.0	4.5	4.0	4.5	5.0
C_{61}	2.0	2.0	3.0	2.0	2.0	3.5	3.0	2.0	2.0	3.0
C_{22}	3.5	3.5	4.5	4.5	3.5	4.0	4.0	3.5	4.0	5.0
C_{24}	3.5	3.5	4.5	4.0	4.0	4.5	4.0	3.5	4.0	5.0
C_{31}	3.0	3.5	4.0	4.0	4.0	4.0	3.5	3.0	4.0	5.0
C_{41}	4.0	4.5	4.5	5.0	5.0	4.0	4.0	3.5	4.0	5.0
C_{42}	3.0	3.0	3.5	3.0	3.5	4.0	3.0	3.0	3.0	4.5
C_{45}	4.5	4.5	5.0	4.5	4.5	4.5	4.0	4.0	4.5	5.0

6   Experimental Results

According to the input data, pairwise comparison matrix, presented in Table 1 evaluation of criteria C_{ij} based on the level of importance can be defined. The most influential and the least influential criteria could be presented. Gradations of influence for all criteria calculated in AHP hybrid model and gradations of influence by decision maker in study [1] and differences between them are shown below in Table 3. Safety and stability in country (C_{32}) represent the most influential criteria, as in [1], while supply chain development (C_{45}) represents the least influential, as in [1]. Gradations of influence and difference for all criteria are presented in Table 3.

Table 3. Gradient of influence – Weight coefficient

| | Level of importance | | | Difference |
| | Weight coefficient | | | |
	Hybrid	< = >	[1]	%
C_{11}	0.0569	<	0.0800	−40.60
C_{12}	0.0302	=	0.0300	0.66
C_{13}	0.0229	>	0.0200	12.66
C_{14}	0.0473	>	0.0400	15.43
C_{15}	0.1113	=	0.1100	1.17
C_{16}	0.0362	>	0.0300	17.13
C_{21}	0.0569	=	0.0600	−5.45
C_{22}	0.0226	>	0.0150	33.63
C_{23}	0.0878	=	0.0800	8.88
C_{24}	0.0147	>	0.0050	65.99
C_{25}	0.0878	<	0.1100	−25.28
C_{31}	0.0147	>	0.0050	65.99
C_{32}	**0.1353**	=	**0.1500**	−10.86
C_{33}	0.1201	<	0.1400	−16.57
C_{34}	0.0569	=	0.0600	−5.45
C_{35}	0.0362	>	0.0300	17.13
C_{41}	0.0147	>	**0.0050**	65.99
C_{42}	0.0147	>	**0.0050**	65.99
C_{45}	**0.0104**	>	**0.0050**	51.92
C_{61}	0.0226	=	0.0200	11.50

Experimental results could be presented after inserting the responses of ten locations, five groups of criteria by twenty criteria. According to the presented AHP method, the resulting weights of suggested alternatives are determined in Table 4, by summing the weights throughout the hierarchy in Table 3.

When three previous results are compared, it could be concluded that Slovenia alternative has the highest value, and as such, it will represent the country which offers the most suitable conditions for logistics distribution center in BP (Table 5).

Table 4. The experimental results of given alternatives for weight coefficients

Group crite.	Criteria	Weight	Serbia	Bulgaria	Macedonia	Romania	Greece	Montenegro	Albania.	B I H	Croatia	Slovenia
	C_{11}	0.0569	0.1423	0.1138	0.1707	0.1138	0.2276	0.1707	0.1992	0.0854	0.2845	0.2561
	C_{12}	0.0302	0.0604	0.0906	0.0755	0.0755	0.0906	0.0906	0.0453	0.0604	0.1057	0.0906
C_1	C_{13}	0.0229	0.0687	0.0916	0.0687	0.0916	0.1145	0.0939	0.1145	0.0573	0.1031	0.1145
	C_{14}	0.0473	0.1324	0.1797	0.1750	0.1419	0.1892	0.1608	0.1656	0.0757	0.1892	0.2365
	C_{15}	0.1113	0.5565	0.5565	0.4452	0.5565	0.3339	0.2226	0.1113	0.2226	0.2226	0.1113
	C_{16}	0.0362	0.1086	0.1086	0.1448	0.0905	0.1629	0.1086	0.1267	0.0724	0.1810	0.1810
	C_{21}	0.0569	0.1423	0.1707	0.1138	0.1423	0.1423	0.1992	0.1423	0.1138	0.1423	0.1707
	C_{22}	0.0226	0.0678	0.0678	0.1130	0.0452	0.0452	0.0678	0.0452	0.0678	0.0678	0.0678
C_2	C_{23}	0.0878	0.0878	0.3512	0.4390	0.2634	0.3512	0.2634	0.3512	0.4390	0.3512	0.4390
	C_{24}	0.0147	0.0515	0.0588	0.0588	0.0662	0.0441	0.0588	0.0735	0.0441	0.0515	0.0588
	C_{25}	0.0878	0.3951	0.3512	0.3951	0.4390	0.4390	0.4390	0.4390	0.3512	0.4390	0.4390
	C_{31}	0.0147	0.0368	0.0441	0.0441	0.0426	0.0441	0.0588	0.0588	0.0294	0.0441	0.0588
	C_{32}	0.1353	0.5412	0.4736	0.5412	0.5412	0.5412	0.6765	0.6089	0.5412	0.6089	0.6765
C_3	C_{33}	0.1201	0.2402	0.2402	0.3603	0.2402	0.2402	0.4204	0.3603	0.2402	0.2402	0.3603
	C_{34}	0.0569	0.1992	0.1992	0.2561	0.2561	0.1992	0.2276	0.2276	0.1992	0.2276	0.2845
	C_{35}	0.0362	0.1267	0.1267	0.1629	0.1448	0.1448	0.1629	0.1448	0.1267	0.1448	0.1810
	C_{41}	0.0147	0.0441	0.0515	0.0588	0.0588	0.0588	0.0588	0.0515	0.0441	0.0588	0.0735
C_4	C_{42}	0.0147	0.0588	0.0662	0.0662	0.0735	0.0735	0.0588	0.0588	0.0515	0.0588	0.0735
	C_{45}	0.0104	0.0312	0.0312	0.0364	0.0312	0.0364	0.0416	0.0312	0.0312	0.0312	0.0468
C_6	C_{61}	0.0226	0.1017	0.1017	0.1130	0.1017	0.1017	0.1017	0.0904	0.0904	0.1017	0.1130

Table 5. Comparison results of alternative significance

Alternatives	Serbia	Bulgaria	Macedonia	Romania	Greece	Montenegro	Albania	B I H	Croatia	Slovenia
Results	-0.338	-0.288	0.118	-0.115	0.011	0.323	0.079	-0.527	0.185	0.552
Rank [1]	9	8	4	7	6	2	5	10	3	1
Results	0.049	0.069	0.092	0.088	0.099	0.146	0.094	0.055	0.106	0.202
Rank [2]	10	8	6	7	4	2	5	9	3	1
Rank [AHP+k]	3.21	3.41	3.79	3.49	3.58	3.71	3,46	2.93	3.68	4.02
Rank [A+k]	9	8	2	6	5	3	7	10	4	1

Now, we will continue with our model and make clusters of alternatives usage by *k-means* clustering methods. The experimental results are presented in Table 6.

The alternatives are first clustered in 3 clusters. The most important cluster is cluster 3 which includes: Macedonia, Montenegro, Croatia and Slovenia. In the next step, when the number of clusters is 4, this cluster doesn't change the number of elements. But, in the third step when 5 clusters are created, this cluster is divided in two. One cluster (number 5 in Table 6) includes Macedonia, Montenegro, and Croatia. The second cluster (number 3) includes only Slovenia, and in Slovenia, the city of Ljubljana is ranked by 1, the best solution for logistics distribution centre in BP.

Final step in our methodology is Decision (Selecting). According to the presented methods: (1) PROMETHEE II; (2) Greedy heuristic algorithm and AHP (29 criteria); (3) AHP (20 criteria); (4) *k-means* clustering algorithm; (5) ranking after clustering, and calculating vector as result of all values gathered by mentioned methods, it could be concluded that Slovenia, the city of Ljubljana is the best solution for logistics distribution centre in Balkan Peninsula.

Table 6. Clustering and ranking the alternatives

Alternatives	Number of clusters			Rank
	3	4	5	
Serbia	1	1	1	5
Bulgaria	2	2	2	4
Macedonia	3	3	5	2
Romania	2	4	4	4
Greece	2	4	5	2
Montenegro	3	3	5	2
Albania	2	4	4	3
BIH	1	1	1	5
Croatia	3	3	5	2
Slovenia	3	3	3	1

7 Conclusion and Future Work

This paper presents the hybrid *Analytical Hierarchy Process* and *k-means* method for ranking, clustering and selection for the most suitable location for logistics distribution center in Balkan Peninsula. This research continues two existing studies.

The proposed hybrid AHP + *k-means* method is described and implemented on real-world data sets presented in previously mentioned studies. The first thing that can be concluded is that twenty criteria used in first study instead of twenty-nine criteria used in the second study is quite enough. Our research and experimental results very convincingly confirm this claim. On the other side, using the *Analytical Hierarchy Process* and *k-means* method shows that, Slovenia, the city of Ljubljana to be more precise, is the best solution for logistics distribution centre in Balkan Peninsula.

Experimental results encourage further research. Using the smaller number of features enables easier decision-making and it is easer to calculate symmetrical reciprocal matrix with lower number of criteria in AHP method.

Acknowledgments. The authors acknowledge the support for research project TR 36030, funded by the Ministry of Science and Technological Development of Serbia.

References

1. Tomić, V., Memet, A., Milosavljević, M., Milisavljević, S.: Decision on the logistics centers location, case of the Balkan peninsula. Ann. Oradea Univ. Fascicle Manage. Technol. Eng., Issue 2, pp. 330–338 (2013)
2. Tomić, V., Marinković, D., Marković, D.: Using multi-criteria comparison: case study of the Balkan peninsula. Acta Polytech. Hung. **11**(10), 97–113 (2014)
3. Bhattacharya, B.K., Sen, S.: On a simple, practical, optimal, output-sensitive randomized planar convex hull algorithm. J. Algorithms **25**(1), 177–193 (1997)
4. Kahraman, C., Ruan, D., Dogan, I.: Fuzzy group decision-making for facility location selection. J. Inf. Sci. **157**(1), 135–153 (2003)
5. Ertugrul, I., Karakasoglu, N.: Performance evaluation of Turkish cement firms with fuzzy analytic hierarchy process and TOPSIS methods. Expert Syst. Appl. **36**(1), 702–715 (2009)
6. Chu, T.C.: Selecting plant location via a fuzzy TOPSIS approach. Int. J. Adv. Manuf. Technol. **20**(11), 859–864 (2002)
7. Chou, C.C.: The canonical representation of multiplication operation on triangular fuzzy numbers. Comput. Math Appl. **45**(10–11), 1601–1610 (2003)
8. Yang, L., Jones, B.F., Yang, S.H.: A fuzzy multi-objective programming for optimization of fire station locations through genetic algorithms. Eur. J. Oper. Res. **181**, 903–915 (2007)
9. Deng, H., Yeh, C.H., Willis, R.J.: Inter-company comparison using modified TOPSIS with objective weights. Comput. Oper. Res. **27**(10), 963–973 (2000)
10. Shih, H.S., Shyur, H.J., Lee, E.S.: An extension of TOPSIS for group decision making. Math. Comput. Model. **45**(7–8), 801–813 (2007)
11. Zanakis, S.H., Solomon, A., Wishart, N., Dublish, S.: Multi-attribute decision making: a simulation comparison of select methods. Eur. J. Oper. Res. **107**(3), 507–529 (1998)
12. Boile, M., Theofanis, S., Wieder, A.: Feasibility of Freight Villages in the NYMTC Region, Center for Advanced Infrastructure and Transport, New Jersey (2008)
13. Bentzen, K., Laugesen M., Cerneckyte, V.: Transport and Logistics Centres, SUTRANET – Sustainable Transport Research & Development Network in the North Sea Region, Aalborg (2007)
14. Sharma, M.J., Moon, I., Bea, H.: Analytic hierarchy process to assess and optimize distribution network. Appl. Math. Comput. **202**(1), 256–265 (2008)
15. Saaty, T.L.: Analytic Hierarchy Process, Planning, Priority Setting, Resource Allocation. McGraw Hill Inc., New York (1980)
16. Everitt, B.S., Landau, S., Leese, M., Stahl, D.: Cluster Analysis. Wiley, Hoboken (2011)

Resampling Multilabel Datasets by Decoupling Highly Imbalanced Labels

Francisco Charte[1]($\boxtimes$), Antonio Rivera[2], María José del Jesus[2],
and Francisco Herrera[1]

[1] Department of Computer Science and Artificial Intelligence, University of Granada,
Granada, Spain
{fcharte,herrera}@ugr.es
http://sci2s.ugr.es
[2] Department of Computer Science, University of Jaén, Jaén, Spain
{arivera,mjjesus}@ujaen.es
http://simidat.ujaen.es

Abstract. Multilabel classification is a task that has been broadly studied in late years. However, how to face learning from imbalanced multilabel datasets (MLDs) has only been addressed latterly. In this regard, a few proposals can be found in the literature, most of them based on resampling techniques adapted from the traditional classification field. The success of these methods varies extraordinarily depending on the traits of the chosen MLDs.

One of the characteristics which significantly influences the behavior of multilabel resampling algorithms is the joint appearance of minority and majority labels in the same instances. It was demonstrated that MLDs with a high level of concurrence among imbalanced labels could hardly benefit from resampling methods. This paper proposes an original resampling algorithm, called REMEDIAL, which is not based on removing majority instances nor creating minority ones, but on a procedure to decouple highly imbalanced labels. As will be experimentally demonstrated, this is an interesting approach for certain MLDs.

Keywords: Multilabel classification · Imbalanced learning · Resampling · Label concurrence

1 Introduction

While in traditional classification the models get a set of input attributes aiming to predict only one output, whether it is binary (binary classifiers) or not (multiclass classifiers), in multilabel classification (MLC) [1] the algorithms have to figure out several outputs from the same set of inputs. There are many real-world applications for MLC, including automatic email classification [2], semantic annotation of music [3], and object recognition in images [4].

The imbalance problem [5], which has been profoundly studied in non-MLC, is also present in MLC. Actually, almost all MLDs suffer from imbalance. Some

© Springer International Publishing Switzerland 2015
E. Onieva et al. (Eds.): HAIS 2015, LNAI 9121, pp. 489–501, 2015.
DOI: 10.1007/978-3-319-19644-2_41

labels are scarcely represented (minority labels), while others are very frequent (majority labels). The use of resampling techniques is a common approach in non-MLC [6]. Therefore, when it came to face this problem in MLC, a clear path was adapting existent resampling methods to work with MLDs.

Since 2012 several ways to deal with imbalance in MLC have been proposed, including oversampling [7–9] algorithms, undersampling [10,11] algorithms, and ensemble based solutions [12]. As was stated in [13], the success of some resampling techniques is highly influenced by the concurrence of minority and majority labels in the same instances. The level of concurrence in an MLD can be computed with a measure called *SCUMBLE* (*Score of ConcUrrence among iMBalanced LabEls*), also proposed in [13]. The higher the *SCUMBLE* the harder it will be for a resampling algorithm to balance the labels distribution.

MLC raises new challenges, since MLDs exhibit traits unseen in traditional datasets. Therefore, new solutions have to be considered, specific to these traits. This is the goal of REMEDIAL (*REsampling MultilabEl datasets by Decoupling highly ImbAlanced Labels*). REMEDIAL evaluates the concurrence among imbalance labels of each sample in an MLD, by means of the aforementioned *SCUMBLE* measure, and splits those with a high level, decoupling minority and majority labels. As will be experimentally demonstrated, this is by itself an interesting approach for certain MLDs. However, the goal of REMEDIAL is not so much to compete with oversampling or undersampling techniques, but to facilitate the work of those methods.

The remainder of this paper is divided into four sections. In Sect. 2 a brief introduction to MLC is provided, along with a description on how learning from imbalanced MLDs has been tackled until now. Section 3 defines the problem of concurrence among imbalanced labels in MLDs, introducing the assessment of this concurrence with the *SCUMBLE* measure and how REMEDIAL addresses it. In Sect. 4 the experimental framework is described, and the results obtained are discussed. Finally, in Sect. 5 some conclusions are yield.

2   Background

This section provides a concise presentation of MLC, describing as well how learning from imbalanced MLDs has been recently tackled.

2.1   Introducing MLC

Many real world classification problems have an intrinsic multilabel nature. Some of them have been mentioned above [2–4]. Additionally, tasks as protein classification [14], gene functional classification [15], and automatic code assignment to medical texts [16] have to predict not a class label for each instance, but a group of them. D being an MLD, L the full set of labels in D, D_i the i-th instance, and $Y_i \subseteq L$ the subset of labels relevant to D_i, a multilabel classifier aims to predict a subset $Z_i \subseteq L$ which is as closer to Y_i as possible.

There have been plenty of MLC algorithm proposals during the last decade. Most of them follow one of two main approaches:

- **Data Transformation:** Addresses the task by converting the MLD into one or more traditional datasets. Although there are several transformation algorithms documented in the literature [1], the best known ones are called BR (*Binary Relevance*) [17] and LP (*Label Powerset*) [18]. BR generates one binary dataset for each label in the MLD, while LP produces a multiclass dataset using each label combination as class. Both have been used as foundation for designing different ensemble based algorithms, such as CC [19] and HOMER [20].
- **Method Adaptation:** Attempts to adapt existent non-MLC algorithms to work with MLDs natively, without transforming them. There are proposals of MLC classifiers based on kNN [21], SVMs [15], trees [22], and ANNs [23], among others. A description of many of them can be found in [24], a recently published review.

In addition to new algorithms, MLC also needed new measures to assess both MLDs characteristics and classification results. Many of them are described in [1,24]. The best known characterization measures are *Card* (*label cardinality*), calculated as the average number of labels in the instances of an MLD, and a dimensionless measure known as *label density*, computed as $Card/|L|$.

2.2   MLC and Imbalanced Datasets

The imbalance problem is well known in the context of non-MLC. Essentially, during training most classifiers tend to be biased to the most frequent class, since they are designed to maximize a global performance measure, such as precision or accuracy. This problem has been tackled mainly by means of resampling techniques [25,26] and algorithmic adaptations [27], as well as through a mix of both methods called *cost-sensitive classification* [28].

As stated in [9], where specific measures to assess the imbalance levels in MLDs were proposed, imbalance is usually present in most MLDs, and the imbalance levels tend to be higher than those in traditional datasets. Learning from imbalanced MLDs has been faced through algorithmic adaptations in [29–31], and there is also some ensemble-based studies [12], as well as several proposals which have chosen the resampling approach [8–10].

Resampling is a classifier independent approach, therefore it can be applied in a broader spectrum of cases than adapted classifiers. Moreover, undersampling and oversampling algorithms have proven to be effective in many scenarios [6]. However, the specificities of MLDs can be a serious obstacle for these algorithms. The most noteworthy are the huge differences in imbalance levels between labels, and the join appearance of minority and majority labels in the same instances.

The imbalance ratio for each label in an MLD, as well as the mean imbalance ratio, can be determined as proposed in [7]. The first measure suggested is *IRLbl*, shown in Eq. 1. Its goal is to assess the imbalance ratio for an individual label. The rarer a label is the higher its *IRLbl* will be. The value 1 will correspond to the most frequent label, whereas the least frequent one will have the largest *IRLbl*. The second measure, called *MeanIR* (see Eq. 2), provides a global estimate of how imbalanced an MLD is. In both equations D stands for any MLD, L the full set of labels in D, l the label being assessed, and Y_i the labelset of the *i-th* sample in D.

$$IRLbl(y) = \frac{\underset{l'=L_1}{\overset{L_{|L|}}{\text{argmax}}}(\sum_{i=1}^{|D|} h(l', Y_i))}{\sum_{i=1}^{|D|} h(l, Y_i)}, \quad h(l, Y_i) = \begin{cases} 1 & l \in Y_i \\ 0 & l \notin Y_i \end{cases}. \tag{1}$$

$$MeanIR = \frac{1}{|L|} \sum_{l=L_1}^{L_{|L|}} (IRLbl(l)). \tag{2}$$

In order to know the extent to which minority and majority labels jointly appear in the same instances in an MLD, a measure called *SCUMBLE* was presented in [13]. As can be seen in Eq. 3, *SCUMBLE* relies on the *IRLbl* measure previously mentioned. First the concurrence level for each instance ($SCUMBLE_{ins}$) is obtained, then the mean *SCUMBLE* for the whole MLD is computed in Eq. 4. The value of *SCUMBLE* is normalized in the range $[0, 1]$, denoting a higher value a larger concurrence of imbalanced labels.

$$SCUMBLE_{ins}(i) = 1 - \frac{1}{IRLbl_i}(\prod_{l=1}^{|L|} IRLbl_{il})^{(1/|L|)} \tag{3}$$

$$SCUMBLE(D) = \frac{1}{|D|} \sum_{i=1}^{|D|} SCUMBLE_{ins}(i) \tag{4}$$

3 Multilabel Resampling with REMEDIAL

In this section the context in which the proposed algorithm, REMEDIAL, has been developed is depicted. First, how multilabel resampling has been confronted until now is reviewed. Then, the REMEDIAL approach, as a specific method for MLDs with concurrence of highly imbalanced labels, is described.

3.1 Related Work

In general, resampling methods aimed to work with non-MLDs can be divided into two categories, oversampling algorithms and undersampling algorithms. The former technique produces new samples with the minority class, while the latter removes instances linked to the majority class. The way in which the samples to be removed or reproduced are chosen can also be grouped into two categories, random methods and heuristic methods. Since this kind of datasets use only one class per instance, the previous techniques effectively balance the distribution of classes. However, this is not always true when dealing with MLDs. Moreover, most MLDs have more than one minority and one majority label.

The preceding approaches have been migrated to the multilabel scenario at some extent, giving as result proposals such as the following:

- **Random Undersampling:** Two multilabel random undersampling algorithms are presented in [9], one of them based on the LP transformation (LP-RUS) and another one on the *IRLbl* measure (ML-RUS). The latter determines what labels are in minority, by means of their *IRLbl*, and avoids removing samples in which they appear.
- **Random Oversampling:** The same paper [9] also proposes two random oversampling algorithms, called LP-ROS and ML-ROS. The former is based on the LP transformation, while the latter relies on the *IRLbl* measure. Both take into account several minority labels, and generate new instances cloning the original labelsets.
- **Heuristic Undersampling:** In [10] a method to undersample MLDs following the ENN (*Edited Nearest Network*) rule was presented. The instances are not randomly chosen, as in LP-RUS or ML-RUS, but carefully selected after analyzing their *IRLbl* and the differences with their neighborhood.
- **Heuristic Oversampling:** The procedure proposed in [8] is based on the original SMOTE algorithm. First, instances of an MLD are chosen using different criteria, then the selected samples are given as input to SMOTE, producing new samples with the same labelsets.

A major disadvantage of these algorithms is that they always work over full labelsets, cloning the set of labels in existent samples or completely removing them. Although this approach can benefit some MLDs, in other cases the result can be counterproductive depending on the MLD traits.

3.2 The Label Concurrence Problem

Since each instance in an MLD has two or more labels, it is not rare that some of them are very common ones while others are minority labels. This fact can be depicted using an interaction plot as the shown in Fig. 1[1]. The top half of this plot corresponds to two MLDs with a high level of concurrence between imbalanced labels, denoted by a *SCUMBLE* above of 0.1. As can be seen, the minority labels (on the right side) are entirely linked with some majority labels.

In some MLDs the concurrence between majority and minority labels is low, as shown in the bottom half of Fig. 1. In these cases the level of *SCUMBLE* is below 0.1, and as can be seen there are many arcs between minority labels, denoting interactions between them but not with the majority ones.

The aforementioned multilabel resampling algorithms will not have an easy work while dealing with MLDs which have a high *SCUMBLE*. Undersampling

---

[1] Visualizing all label interactions in an MLD is, in some cases, almost impossible due to the large number of labels. For that reason, only the most frequent labels and the most rare ones for each MLD are represented in these plots. High resolution version of these plots can be found at http://simidat.ujaen.es/remedial and they can be generated using the `mldr` R package [32].

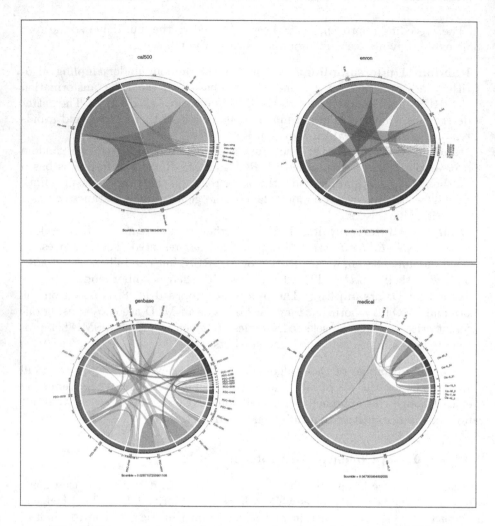

Fig. 1. Concurrence among minority and majority labels in four MLDs.

algorithms can produce a loss of essential information, as the samples selected for removal because majority labels appear in them can also contain minority labels. In the same way, oversampling algorithms limited to cloning the labelsets, such as the proposals in [8,9], can be also increasing the presence of majority labels. These facts were empirically demonstrated in [13].

3.3   Algorithm Description

As its name suggests, REMEDIAL (*REsampling MultilabEl datasets by Decoupling highly ImbAlanced Labels*) is a method specifically designed for MLDs which suffer from concurrence between imbalanced labels. In this context, *highly imbalanced labels* has to be understood as labels with large differences in their *IRLbls*. This is a fact assessed with the *SCUMBLE* measure, thus REMEDIAL is directed to MLDs with a high *SCUMBLE* level.

When the few samples in which a minority label is present also contain one or more majority labels, whose frequency in the MLD is much higher, the power of the input features to predict the labels might be biased to the majority ones. Our hypothesis is that, in a certain way, majority labels are masking the minority ones when they appear together, a problem that could be solved to some extent by decoupling the labels in these instances.

REMEDIAL is a resampling algorithm. It could be seen as an oversampling method, since it produces new instances in some cases. At the same time it also modifies existent samples. In short, REMEDIAL is an editing plus oversampling algorithm, and it is an approach which has synergies with traditional resampling techniques. The method pseudo-code is shown in Algorithm 1.

Algorithm 1. REMEDIAL algorithm.

1: **function** REMEDIAL(MLD D, Labels L)
2:     $IRLbl_l \leftarrow$ calculateIRLbl(l in L)   ▷ Calculate imbalance levels
3:     $IRMean \leftarrow \overline{IRLbl}$
4:     $SCUMBLEIns_i \leftarrow$ calculateSCUMBLE(D_i in D)   ▷ Calculate SCUMBLE
5:     $SCUMBLE \leftarrow \overline{SCUMBLEIns}$
6:     **for each** *instance* i **in** D **do**
7:         **if** $SCUMBLEIns_i > SCUMBLE$ **then**
8:             $D_i' \leftarrow D_i$ ▷ Clone the affected instance
9:             $D_i[labels_{IRLbl<=IRMean}] \leftarrow 0$ ▷ Maintain minority labels
10:            $D_i'[labels_{IRLbl>IRMean}] \leftarrow 0$ ▷ Maintain majority labels
11:            $D \leftarrow D + D_i'$
12:        **end if**
13:    **end for**
14: **end function**

The *IRLbl*, *IRMean* and *SCUMBLE* measures are computed in lines 2–5. $SCUMBLE_{Ins_i}$ is the concurrence level of the D_i instance. The mean *SCUMBLE* for the MLD is obtained by averaging the individual *SCUMBLE* for each sample.

Taking the mean *SCUMBLE* as reference, only the samples with a *SCUMBLEIns > SCUMBLE* are processed. Those instances, which contain minority and majority labels, are decoupled into two instances, one containing only the majority labels and another one with the minority labels. In line 8 D_i, a sample affected by problem at glance, is cloned in D_i'. The formula in line 9 edits the original D_i instance by removing the majority labels from it. Majority labels are considered as those whose *IRLbl* is equal or below to *IRMean*. Line 10 does the opposite, removing from the cloned D_i' the minority labels. D_i belongs to the D MLD, but D_i' has to be added to it (line 11).

4   Experimental Analysis

This section describes the experimental framework used to test the proposed algorithm, then presents the obtained results, and finally analyzes them.

4.1   Framework

To check the influence of REMEDIAL in classification results six MLDs have been chosen (see Table 1). These are the MLDs used in [13] with *SCUMBLE* values above 0.1, which were the more problematic to process with classic resampling methods, and two more with low *SCUMBLE* levels. These MLDs are given as input, before and after preprocessing them with REMEDIAL, to three different MLC algorithms: BR [18], HOMER [20] and IBLR [33]. These are representatives of three main approaches to MLC classification, ensembles of binary classifiers, ensembles of label powerset classifiers, and instance based classifiers.

Table 1. Datasets used in experimentation.

Category	Dataset	SCUMBLE	max(MeanIR)	MeanIR	Ref
High SCUMBLE > 0.1	cal500	0.3369	133.1917	21.2736	[3]
	corel5k	0.3932	896.0000	168.7806	[4]
	enron	0.3023	657.0500	72.7730	[2]
	yeast	0.1044	53.6894	7.2180	[15]
Low SCUMBLE < 0.1	genbase	0.0283	136.8000	32.4130	[14]
	medical	0.0465	212.8000	72.1674	[16]

A 5×2 fold cross validation has been used. Classification results are evaluated using three usual multilabel measures: HammingLoss (HL), Macro-FMeasure (MacroFM) and Micro-FMeasure (MicroFM). HL (see Eq. 5) is a global sample based measure. It assesses differences between Z_i, the predicted labelset, and Y_i, the real one, without distinction among labels. The lower the HL the better the predictions are. MacroFM and MicroFM are label based measures. As can be seen in Eqs. 6 and 7, in MacroFM the *F-measure* is evaluated independently for each label and then is averaged, while in MicroFM the counters for all labels are aggregated and then used for calculating the *F-measure*. The former approach is more sensitive to performance classifying minority labels.

$$HammingLoss = \frac{1}{|D|} \sum_{i=1}^{|D|} \frac{|Y_i \Delta Z_i|}{|L|}. \tag{5}$$

$$MacroFM = \frac{1}{|L|} \sum_{i=1}^{|L|} F\text{-}measure(TP_i, FP_i, TN_i, FN_i) \tag{6}$$

$$MicroFM = F\text{-}measure(\sum_{i=1}^{|L|} TP_i, \sum_{i=1}^{|L|} FP_i, \sum_{i=1}^{|L|} TN_i, \sum_{i=1}^{|L|} FN_i) \tag{7}$$

The results obtained from each classifier over the datasets, before and after preprocessing, are the shown in Table 2. Best results are highlighted in bold.

Table 2. Results before and after applying REMEDIAL

		BR		HOMER		IBLR	
	Dataset	Before	After	Before	After	Before	After
HL	cal500	0.1630	**0.1496**	0.1888	**0.1794**	0.2340	**0.2125**
	corel5k	0.0098	**0.0094**	0.0132	**0.0118**	0.0242	**0.0148**
	enron	**0.0522**	0.0524	0.0583	**0.0560**	**0.0572**	0.0573
	yeast	0.2505	**0.2240**	0.2632	**0.2433**	0.1942	0.2139
	genbase	**0.0012**	0.0084	**0.0016**	0.0062	**0.0022**	0.0092
	medical	**0.0107**	0.0131	**0.0108**	0.0125	0.0198	0.0198
MacroFM	cal500	**0.2934**	0.2516	0.3316	**0.3358**	**0.2772**	0.2597
	corel5k	0.1774	**0.1826**	0.1916	**0.1924**	0.1059	**0.1432**
	enron	0.4029	**0.4190**	0.3790	**0.3793**	**0.3458**	0.3114
	yeast	0.4341	**0.5204**	0.4334	**0.4626**	**0.4944**	0.4156
	genbase	0.9890	**0.9924**	**0.9780**	0.9697	**0.9655**	0.8450
	medical	**0.8166**	0.8013	**0.7942**	0.7780	**0.6404**	0.6216
MicroFM	cal500	**0.3488**	0.2506	0.3978	**0.4008**	**0.3184**	0.2934
	corel5k	**0.1096**	0.0782	**0.1744**	0.1627	**0.0542**	0.0530
	enron	**0.5334**	0.4745	**0.5265**	0.5036	**0.4561**	0.3541
	yeast	0.5787	**0.5898**	0.5763	**0.5974**	**0.6502**	0.5546
	genbase	**0.9867**	0.9012	**0.9820**	0.9284	**0.9768**	0.8902
	medical	**0.8006**	0.7350	**0.7994**	0.7582	**0.6324**	0.5830

4.2 Analysis

Beginning with the two MLDs which have low *SCUMBLE* values, the results produced by REMEDIAL are not good almost in any case. Although some differences are quite small, in general the decoupling of labels has worsened classification performance. As a consequence a clear guideline follows from these results, REMEDIAL should not be used with MLDs with low *SCUMBLE* levels, since it is an algorithm specifically designed to face the opposite casuistic. The analysis of results from the other four MLDs can be divided into two parts, depending on where the focus is.

Looking at the results by evaluation measure, it is clear that REMEDIAL is benefiting minority labels, with better MacroFM values, and has a good overall behavior, denoted by the HL values after resampling. There are mixed results when MicroFM is used, as for some MLDs the results are improved while for others there is a worsening.

Going through the results by classifier, that REMEDIAL works better with BR and HOMER than with IBLR can be observed. Binary relevance based algorithms train a classifier for each label, taking as positive the instances containing it and as negative the remainder samples. When a majority label is being processed, all the instances in which it appears jointly with a minority label are processed as positive, disregarding the fact that they contain other labels. The decoupling of these labels tends to balance the bias of each classifier. LP based algorithms, such as HOMER, surely are favored by REMEDIAL, since the decoupling produces simpler labelsets. Moreover, the number of distinct labelsets is reduced after the resampling. The influence of REMEDIAL on instance based classifiers, such as IBLR, is easy to devise. The attributes of the decoupled samples do not change, so they will occupy exactly the same position with respect to the instance which is taken as reference for searching nearest neighbors. Therefore, the classifier will get two samples at the same distance but with disjoint labelsets, something that can be confusing depending on how the algorithm predicts the labelset of the reference sample.

Overall, REMEDIAL would be a recommended resampling for MLDs with high *SCUMBLE* levels and when BR or LP based classifiers are going to be used. In these cases the prediction of minority labels would be improved, and the global performance of the classifiers would be better. These are the benefits brought by itself, but REMEDIAL could be used as a first step aimed to ease the work of traditional resampling techniques.

5   Conclusions

In this paper REMEDIAL, a new resampling algorithm aimed to boost multilabel imbalanced learning, has been presented. This algorithm is specifically devised for MLDs with a high concurrence between minority and majority labels, a trait that can be assessed with a measure called *SCUMBLE*. REMEDIAL looks for instances with a high *SCUMBLE* level and decouples minority and majority labels, producing new instances.

The conducted experimentation has proven that REMEDIAL is able to improve classification results when applied to MLDs with a high *SCUMBLE*, although the chosen classifier also influences the obtained outputs.

Those results could be improved joining REMEDIAL with some of the existent resampling methods. Once the labels have been decoupled, traditional oversampling and undersampling algorithms would find less obstacles to do their work. Thus, this a potential path for future research into the imbalanced treatment for MLDs.

Acknowledgments. F. Charte is supported by the Spanish Ministry of Education under the FPU National Program (Ref. AP2010-0068). This work was partially supported by the Spanish Ministry of Science and Technology under projects TIN2011-28488 and TIN2012-33856, and the Andalusian regional projects P10-TIC-06858 and P11-TIC-7765.

References

1. Tsoumakas, G., Katakis, I., Vlahavas, I.: Mining multi-label data. In: Maimon, O., Rokach, L. (eds.) Data Mining and Knowledge Discovery Handbook, Ch. 34, pp. 667–685. Springer, Boston (2010). doi:10.1007/978-0-387-09823-4_34

2. Klimt, B., Yang, Y.: The enron corpus: a new dataset for email classification research. In: Boulicaut, J.-F., Esposito, F., Giannotti, F., Pedreschi, D. (eds.) ECML 2004. LNCS (LNAI), vol. 3201, pp. 217–226. Springer, Heidelberg (2004). doi:10.1007/978-3-540-30115-8_22

3. Turnbull, D., Barrington, L., Torres, D., Lanckriet, G.: Semantic annotation and retrieval of music and sound effects. IEEE Audio Speech Lang. Process. 16(2), 467–476 (2008). doi:10.1109/TASL.2007.913750

4. Duygulu, P., Barnard, K., de Freitas, J.F.G., Forsyth, D.: Object recognition as machine translation: learning a lexicon for a fixed image vocabulary. In: Heyden, A., Sparr, G., Nielsen, M., Johansen, P. (eds.) ECCV 2002, Part IV. LNCS, vol. 2353, pp. 97–112. Springer, Heidelberg (2002). doi:10.1007/3-540-47979-1_7

5. Chawla, N.V., Japkowicz, N., Kotcz, A.: Editorial: special issue on learning from imbalanced data sets. SIGKDD Explor. Newsl. 6(1), 1–6 (2004). doi:10.1145/1007730.1007733

6. García, V., Sánchez, J., Mollineda, R.: On the effectiveness of preprocessing methods when dealing with different levels of class imbalance. Knowl. Based Syst. 25(1), 13–21 (2012). http://dx.doi.org/10.1016/j.knosys.2011.06.013

7. Charte, F., Rivera, A., del Jesus, M.J., Herrera, F.: A first approach to deal with imbalance in multi-label datasets. In: Pan, J.-S., Polycarpou, M.M., Woźniak, M., de Carvalho, A.C.P.L.F., Quintián, H., Corchado, E. (eds.) HAIS 2013. LNCS, vol. 8073, pp. 150–160. Springer, Heidelberg (2013). doi:10.1007/978-3-642-40846-5_16

8. Giraldo-Forero, A.F., Jaramillo-Garzón, J.A., Ruiz-Muñoz, J.F., Castellanos-Domínguez, C.G.: Managing imbalanced data sets in multi-label problems: a case study with the SMOTE algorithm. In: Ruiz-Shulcloper, J., Sanniti di Baja, G. (eds.) CIARP 2013, Part I. LNCS, vol. 8258, pp. 334–342. Springer, Heidelberg (2013). doi:10.1007/978-3-642-41822-8_42

9. Charte, F., Rivera, A.J., del Jesus, M.J., Herrera, F.: Addressing imbalance in multilabel classification: Measures and random resampling algorithms, Neurocomputing to be published

10. Charte, F., Rivera, A.J., del Jesus, M.J., Herrera, F.: MLeNN: a first approach to heuristic multilabel undersampling. In: Corchado, E., Lozano, J.A., Quintián, H., Yin, H. (eds.) IDEAL 2014. LNCS, vol. 8669, pp. 1–9. Springer, Heidelberg (2014). doi:10.1007/978-3-319-10840-7_1

11. Tahir, M.A., Kittler, J., Yan, F.: Inverse random under sampling for class imbalance problem and its application to multi-label classification. Pattern Recogn. 45(10), 3738–3750 (2012). doi:10.1016/j.patcog.2012.03.014

12. Tahir, M.A., Kittler, J., Bouridane, A.: Multilabel classification using heterogeneous ensemble of multi-label classifiers. Pattern Recogn. Lett. 33(5), 513–523 (2012). doi:10.1016/j.patrec.2011.10.019

13. Charte, F., Rivera, A., del Jesus, M.J., Herrera, F.: Concurrence among imbalanced labels and its influence on multilabel resampling algorithms. In: Polycarpou, M., de Carvalho, A.C.P.L.F., Pan, J.-S., Woźniak, M., Quintian, H., Corchado, E. (eds.) HAIS 2014. LNCS, vol. 8480, pp. 110–121. Springer, Heidelberg (2014)
14. Diplaris, S., Tsoumakas, G., Mitkas, P.A., Vlahavas, I.P.: Protein classification with multiple algorithms. In: Bozanis, P., Houstis, E.N. (eds.) PCI 2005. LNCS, vol. 3746, pp. 448–456. Springer, Heidelberg (2005). doi:10.1007/11573036_42
15. Elisseeff, A., Weston, J.: A kernel method for multi-labelled classification. In: Dietterich, G., Becker, S., Ghahramani, Z. (eds.) Advances in Neural Information Processing Systems 14, vol. 14, pp. 681–687. MIT Press, Cambridge (2001)
16. Crammer, K., Dredze, M., Ganchev, K., Talukdar, P.P., Carroll, S.: Automatic code assignment to medical text. In: Proceedings of the Workshop on Biological, Translational, and Clinical Language Processing, BioNLP 2007. Prague, Czech Republic, pp. 129–136 (2007)
17. Godbole, S., Sarawagi, S.: Discriminative methods for multi-labeled classification. In: Dai, H., Srikant, R., Zhang, C. (eds.) PAKDD 2004. LNCS (LNAI), vol. 3056, pp. 22–30. Springer, Heidelberg (2004). doi:10.1007/978-3-540-24775-3_5
18. Boutell, M., Luo, J., Shen, X., Brown, C.: Learning multi-label scene classification. Pattern Recogn. 37(9), 1757–1771 (2004). doi:10.1016/j.patcog.2004.03.009
19. Read, J., Pfahringer, B., Holmes, G., Frank, E.: Classifier chains for multi-label classification. Mach. Learn. 85, 333–359 (2011). doi:10.1007/s10994-011-5256-5
20. Tsoumakas, G., Katakis, I., Vlahavas, I.: Effective and efficient multilabel classification in domains with large number of labels. In: Proceedings of the ECML/PKDD Workshop on Mining Multidimensional Data, MMD 2008. Antwerp, Belgium, pp. 30–44 (2008)
21. Zhang, M., Zhou, Z.: ML-KNN: a lazy learning approach to multi-label learning. Pattern Recogn. 40(7), 2038–2048 (2007). doi:10.1016/j.patcog.2006.12.019
22. Clare, A.J., King, R.D.: Knowledge discovery in multi-label phenotype data. In: Siebes, A., De Raedt, L. (eds.) PKDD 2001. LNCS (LNAI), vol. 2168, p. 42. Springer, Heidelberg (2001). doi:10.1007/3-540-44794-6_4
23. Zhang, M.-L.: Multilabel neural networks with applications to functional genomics and text categorization. IEEE Trans. Knowl. Data Eng. 18(10), 1338–1351 (2006). doi:10.1109/TKDE.2006.162
24. Zhang, M., Zhou, Z.: A review on multi-label learning algorithms. IEEE Trans. Knowl. Data Eng. 26(8), 1819–1837 (2014). doi:10.1109/TKDE.2013.39
25. Chawla, N.V., Bowyer, K.W., Hall, L.O., Kegelmeyer, W.P.: SMOTE: synthetic minority over-sampling technique. J. Artif. Intell. Res. 16, 321–357 (2002). doi:10.1613/jair.953
26. Kotsiantis, S.B., Pintelas, P.E.: Mixture of expert agents for handling imbalanced data sets. Ann. Math. Comput. Teleinformatics 1, 46–55 (2003)
27. López, V., Fernández, A., García, S., Palade, V., Herrera, F.: An insight into classification with imbalanced data: empirical results and current trends on using data intrinsic characteristics. Inf. Sci. 250, 113–141 (2013). doi:10.1016/j.ins.2013.07.007
28. Provost, F., Fawcett, T.: Robust classification for imprecise environments. Mach. Learn. 42, 203–231 (2001). doi:10.1023/A:1007601015854
29. He, J., Gu, H., Liu, W.: Imbalanced multi-modal multi-label learning for subcellular localization prediction of human proteins with both single and multiple sites. PloS one 7(6), 7155 (2012). doi:10.1371/journal.pone.0037155

30. Li, C., Shi, G.: Improvement of learning algorithm for the multi-instance multi-label rbf neural networks trained with imbalanced samples. J. Inf. Sci. Eng. **29**(4), 765–776 (2013)
31. Tepvorachai, G., Papachristou, C.: Multi-label imbalanced data enrichment process in neural net classifier training. In: IEEE International Joint Conference on Neural Networks, IJCNN 2008, pp. 1301–1307 (2008). doi:10.1109/IJCNN.2008.4633966
32. Charte, F., Charte, F.D.: How to work with multilabel datasets in R using the mldr package. doi:10.6084/m9.figshare.1356035
33. Cheng, W., Hüllermeier, E.: Combining instance-based learning and logistic regression for multilabel classification. Mach. Learn. **76**(2–3), 211–225 (2009). doi:10.1007/s10994-009-5127-5

Creating Effective Error Correcting Output Codes for Multiclass Classification

Wiesław Chmielnicki[✉]

Faculty of Physics, Astronomy and Applied Computer Science,
Jagiellonian University, Krakow, Poland
wieslaw.chmielnicki@uj.edu.pl
http://www.fais.uj.edu.pl

Abstract. The error correcting output code (ECOC) technique is a genesral framework to solve the multi-class problems using binary classifiers. The key problem in this approach is how to construct the optimal ECOC codewords i.e. the codewords which maximize the recognition ratio of the final classifier. There are several methods described in the literature to solve this problem. All these methods try to maximize the minimal Hamming distance between the generated codewords. In this paper we are showing another approach based both on the average Hamming distance and the estimated misclassification error of the binary classifiers.

Keywords: Error correcting output codes · Support vector machine · Statistical classifiers · Multiclass classifiers

1 Introduction

Most of the classification tasks in the real-world applications are involving more than two classes. We call them the multi-class problems. However some classifiers are defined as binary. So to use such classifier we have to reduce the multi-class problem to the set of the binary subproblems. There are many methods of decomposition such a task into the set of the smaller classification problems involving two classes only.

Even if we can use the classifier which is able to deal with more than two classes it might be a good choice to decompose the problem to the two-class version and employ the set of the binary classifiers. Benefits obtained from the decomposition of the multi-class task have been addressed by many authors for example in [1, 23, 26].

Additionally some interesting review considering this topic can be found in [19]. We can also look at the problem of the decomposition from the efficiency point of view [7] or we can investigate how the problem properties can be employed to the construction of the decomposition scheme [20].

There are many methods of the decomposition of the multi-class problems into the set of the binary classification problems described in the literature. We

© Springer International Publishing Switzerland 2015
E. Onieva et al. (Eds.): HAIS 2015, LNAI 9121, pp. 502–514, 2015.
DOI: 10.1007/978-3-319-19644-2_42

can list some most popular such as OVR (One-Versus-Rest), OVO (One-Versus-One) strategies, DAG (Directed Acyclic Graph), ADAG (Adaptive Directed Acyclic Graph) methods [17,25], BDT (Binary Decision Tree) approach [14], DB2 method [31], PWC (PairWise Coupling) [16] or ECOC (Error-Correcting Output Codes) [2,9].

The last method has been successfully applied to solve a range of different multi-class tasks. However still ongoing problem is how to construct efficient ECOC codes i.e. codes which maximize the result obtained by the final classifier. There are four strategies described by Dietterich [9] in the paper introducing this technique and several others presented in the literature [6,12,18]. The new approach based both on the average Hamming distance and the estimated misclassification error of the binary classifiers is proposed in this work.

The algorithm have been tested on several different databases using the support vector machine (SVM) classifier. The obtained results show that this solution is promising achieving the best recognition ratio on all tested databases.

The rest of this paper is organized as follows: Sect. 2 describes the ECOC technique, Sect. 3 presents the base methods of constructing ECOC codes, Sect. 4 introduces proposed method, Sect. 5 is dedicated the experiments conducted to test the solution, Sect. 6 shows experimental results and finally in Sect. 7 conclusions are discussed.

2   The ECOC Approach

The error correcting output codes framework is a powerful tool to deal with the multi-class problems proposed by Dietterich and Bakiri [9]. The method is robust with the respect to the changes in the size of the training sample and the assignment of distributed representations to particular classes. Some other papers also show that this technique can improve the generalization performance of the classifier [1,32].

The technique consists of two distinct steps: coding and decoding. At the coding step we design a codeword for each class based on the different binary problems and at the decoding step we make a classification decision for a given test sample based on the values from the set of binary classifiers defined by these codewords.

The first step to use ECOC technique is to create the binary output code for each of the N classes. Let's assume that we create the codes of the length L constructing the matrix C of the size NxL. Each code consists of the sequence of 0 s and 1s. The codes should be unique and moreover they should be as much different from each other as possible. We can express it in a more formal way:

Definition 1. *The Hamming distance $d(u,v)$ between two codewords of the same length u and v is equal to the number of symbol places in which the codewords differ from one another.*

Remark 1. We can easily spot that:

(1) $d(u,v) = 0$ when $u = v$

(2) $d(u, v) = d(v, u)$ and
(3) $d(u, w) \leq d(u, v) + d(v, w)$

So constructing the codewords for the classes we should use the sequences 0s and 1s that are most distant in a sense of the Hamming distance. However if we maximize the Hamming distance between the codewords representing two pairs of the classes, let's say between u, v and between v, w then the distance between u and w could be very low - even it could be equal to zero. It means we have to define another measure:

Definition 2. *The minimum Hamming distance of the code matrix C denoted by $d(C)$ is the minimum Hamming distance between any two distinct codewords c_i, c_j of C. That is,*

$$d(C) = \min_{c_i, c_j \in C, c_i \neq c_j} d(c_i, c_j), \tag{1}$$

Let's assume that the minimum Hamming distance of the code matrix C is equal to D. Then we can see that even if we made some errors transmitting the codeword c_i then we will be able to correctly identify it as long as we made less than $\lfloor (D-1)/2 \rfloor$ mistakes. So the code matrix C with the maximized minimum Hamming distance $d(C)$ seems to be a good candidate to use in our classification task.

In this approach we look at the recognition process as a kind of communication system in which the sample represented by a feature vector is transmitted over a channel. The errors made by the classifiers are treated as the transmission errors and the ECOC codes with an error correcting property help us to classify the sample to the correct class.

Table 1. An example of the ECOC code matrix

class	columns
1	1 1 1 1 1 1 1 1 1 1 1 1 1 1 1
2	0 0 0 0 0 0 0 0 1 1 1 1 1 1 1
3	0 0 0 0 1 1 1 1 0 0 0 0 1 1 1
4	0 0 1 1 0 0 1 1 0 0 1 1 0 0 1
5	0 1 0 1 0 1 0 1 0 1 0 1 0 1 0

If we look at the ECOC code matrix, see the Table 1, we can see that each column of the matrix creates a partition of the classes into two subsets. Some classes are marked as "0" other as "1". Each column define the binary classifier which can be used to recognize the samples. For example the first two columns of the matrix presented in the Table 1 define the binary classifiers 1 vs 2, 3, 4, 5 and 1, 5 vs 2, 3, 4.

After constructing the code matrix C of the size NxL we are ready to start the next step of the ECOC method. First we have to train L binary classifiers defined by the columns of the code matrix then each sample is tested against them. Every classifier assigns a label 0 or 1 for the sample building the binary codeword representing it. Finally we compare this codeword with the codewords representing all the classes. It is clear that if the all L binary classifiers made less than $\lfloor (D-1)/2 \rfloor$ errors then the sample will be correctly classified.

3   Construction of the ECOC Codewords

It is nontrivial task to construct the optimal codewords for the classes. We can see that every binary classifier works on the same set of the samples. The only difference is a label that is assigned to each sample. So, if some of the columns are the same or similar, errors committed on this sample will be repeated many times by the classifier.

In order to prevent this effect, the Hamming distance between columns should be maximized to avoid correlation between the single base classifiers. However the Hamming distance between the rows must be also maximized in order to achieve good classification ratio at the decoding phase.

Less obvious is the condition that the Hamming distance between a column and its complementary column should also be considered by the constructing algorithm. When the two columns are complementary, the outputs of their corresponding classifiers are also complementary, therefore they are identical. All classes labelled as 0s become 1s and all classes labelled as 1s become 0s. In fact these columns define the same binary classifier. It is obvious if we consider two binary classifiers, for example $1, 5$ vs $2, 3, 4$ and $2, 3, 4$ vs $1, 5$. Due to these constraints there are four different kind of methods proposed in the literature:

– Exhaustive codes – problems with $3 \leq N \leq 7$.
– Column selection from Exhaustive codes – problems with $8 \leq N \leq 11$.
– Randomized Hill Climbing – problems with $N > 11$.
– BCH codes – problems with $N > 11$.

Each column of the code matrix can be considered as a binary problem which divides two subsets of the classes. However, some of these subsets are hard to separate. The binary classifier makes a lot of mistakes i.e. has big misclassification error. These columns should be avoided when constructing our code matrix. The method using a ranking list of the binary classifiers has been proposed in our earlier paper [6]. The solution turns out to achieve better recognition ratio for the tested database even though the generated codewords were closer in the sense of the Hamming distance.

4   Proposed Method

Maximizing the minimal Hamming distance improve the efficiency of the multi-class classifier because the binary classifiers can make more errors and still we can correctly classify the sample. However in this approach we assume that the

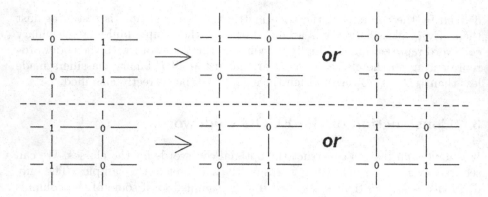

Fig. 1. The improving the rows separation

errors are made randomly, but in fact they are connected with the partition of the classes generated by the column of the code matrix. The code matrix with a very high minimum Hamming distance may generate partitions and then binary classifiers which make a lot of classification errors.

Moreover when we focus on the maximizing the distance between two worst codewords representing two classes then if we cannot improve it we cannot improve the minimal Hamming distance for the whole matrix although increasing the distance between the other codewords also improves the separability of the classes. As a matter of fact the average distance between the codewords may be even of more importance than the minimum Hamming distance when we consider the problem with very high number of the classes.

Considering above drawbacks of the methods we propose another approach. In this solution we focus on improving the average Hamming distance between the codewords however we don't forget about the misclassification error of the binary classifiers defined by the generated columns of the code matrix. Below we show the draft of the proposed algorithm:

```
1) Generate a random code matrix C size NxL
2) Avg = Average(d(C))
3) find rows u, v which d(u, v) < Average(d(C))
4) improve d(u, v) considering the binary classifiers
5) if it is not possible then go to 3
6) if all u, v has been checked then stop
7) go to 2
```

The algorithm needs some explanations. In the step 3 we can search for the rows scanning through all possible combinations one by one or we can choose the rows at random. We find this second solution better although it needs additional care not to check the same combinations twice. The procedure which try to improve the Hamming distance $d(u, v)$ between the rows in the step 4 is of much importance. It tries to change the bits in the columns in the selected rows as in the original RHC algorithm, see Fig. 1. However it will switch the bits only when the two newly generated binary classifiers have the same or lower misclassification error.

Summarizing, the algorithms which focus on maximizing the minimum Hamming distance between the codewords generate more optimal ECOC codes. However they assume that the errors made by the binary classifiers are completely random. It is true when we consider the transmitter and the receiver in the telecommunication system. In the classification task focusing on the average Hamming distance and considering the recognition ratio of the binary classifiers defined by the columns of the code matrix leads to much better results.

Described procedure tends to generate very close columns because if one binary classifier has very small misclassification error then if we change assignment of the one class only then usually the result obtained by this new classifier will be also very good. In our algorithm we demanded that the Hamming distance between the columns cannot be less than some constant value H. This value is defined in the next section.

The computational complexity of each iteration of the algorithm is quite high. First, we have to train the binary classifiers defined by the columns of the code matrix which are crossing with our rows u and v. The cost is at leat quadratic with respect to the number of the training examples (which is proportional to the number of classes). In every pair of rows we have to consider $O(M^2)$ pairs of bits when we try to improve the distance between them where M is the length of the codeword.

The stopping criteria for the algorithm is to check all possible combinations of the rows and not to find the possibility to improve the distance between them. It is visible that there is $N * (N - 1)/2$ possible pairs of classes (then the same number pairs of rows). The procedure of improving the distance between them is also very demanding as we discussed it in the paragraph above.

This procedure can be very inefficient especially when the number of the classes is very high. So the maximum number of the iterations could be considered as an optional stopping criteria of the algorithm. The maximum number of the classes in our experiments was 50, so we are able to use the criteria *"no possibility to improve the distance between any combinations of the rows u, v such as $d(u, v) < Average(d(C))$ has been found"*.

5   Experiments

Several experiments has been conducted to test the proposed method. We decided to use the support vector machine (SVM) classifier because it is very effective in the high dimensional feature spaces. It is also known to be quite resistant to overfitting and robust to the noise. The SVM classifier is shortly described below.

The Support Vector Machine (SVM) is a well known large margin classifier proposed by Vapnik [30]. The basic concept behind the SVM classifier is to find an optimal separating hyperplane, which separates two classes. The decision function of the binary SVM is:

$$f(x) = sign\left(\sum_{i=1}^{N} \alpha_i y_i K(x_i, x) + b \right) , \qquad (2)$$

where $0 \leq \alpha_i \leq C, i = 1, 2, \ldots, N$ are nonnegative Lagrange multipliers, C is a cost parameter, that controls the trade-off between allowing training errors and forcing rigid margins, x_i are the support vectors and $K(x_i, x)$ is the kernel function.

Before we could start with our experiments we have to choose some parameters. We can find them using training data set. However, to avoid overfitting, the cross-validation procedure must be used. We use k-fold cross-validation with k = 7, because there are at least seven samples of each class in the training data set (in the protein database).

In our experiments we used an SVM classifier with the RBF kernel, so the parameters C and γ must be chosen. It has been done using a cross-validation procedure on the training data set. We used a grid-search algorithm with the values of $C = 2^0, 2^1 \ldots, 2^{10}$ and $\gamma = 2^{-10}, 2^{-9}, \ldots, 2^0$ The best recognition ratios were achieved using parameters from the Table 2.

Additionally the all values of the feature vectors are scaled to the range $[-1; +1]$ before using an SVM classifier to avoid attributes in greater numeric ranges dominating those in smaller numeric ranges.

Table 2. C and γ parameters used in the experiments

database	C	γ
Gestures IITIS	4	2^{-10}
ISOLET	2	2^{-6}
Proteins	128	2^{-6}
Leafs	1024	2^{-5}
ACRS	64	2^{-10}

We need several databases with different characteristics to test our solution. Some of the databases we find in the UCI Machine Learning Repository [29]: leafs database [28], ACRS [27], ISOLET [13]. We also used a gesture database [15] and the protein database described in [10,11]. In the Table 3 we show the number of the classes and the size of the feature vector for all databases used.

On each database the four algorithms has been tested i.e. standard one-verus-one (OVO) from LibSvm library [4], ECOC-RHC algorithm described in [9], our previous ECOC MDCRL algorithm [6] and the algorithm Maximize Average Hamming Distance (MAHD) proposed in this paper. All these algorithms has been tested using SVM classifiers with the parameters shown in the Table 2. The

Table 3. The databases used in the experiments

database	Number of		
name	classes	samples	features
Gestures IITiS	22	1 320	256
ISOLET	26	7 797	617
Proteins	27	698	126
Leafs	36	340	13
ACRS	50	1 500	10 000

results are presented in the Tables 4 and 5. We used the binary classifiers from LibSvm to create combined multi-class ECOC classifiers.

It is visible that the length of the ECOC code influences the Hamming distance between the codewords and therefore the final result of the classifier. Generally increasing the length of the codeword will improve the result of the classifier. However when the length of the code is too big then another factor (the number of the errors made by the binary classifiers) deteriorate the result. We made several experiments using different code lengths and we find out that the length longer than 128 bits may only slightly improve the results or even may worsen it [6].

Some more thoroughly analysis should be conducted especially considering the number of the classes but for the purpose of this paper we decided to use two code lengths only: 64 and 128 bit. Generally the more classes then the length of the code should be longer but you have to remember that the length of the code impacts also the algorithm complexity. Even for a quite limited number of the columns (128) our algorithm runs several hours. Of course we are saying about the training phase but still it should be considered.

The last problem we have to consider is the Hamming distance between the columns and the complement columns. As we explained in the Sect. 3 the outputs of the classifiers defined by close columns are correlated so such columns should be avoided. In our solution we define a constant H which restrain the algorithm from using columns which Hamming distance is less than this value.

It is clear that we should aim at the high value of H, but if this value will be too high it limits the ability of the algorithm to generate good codewords i.e. codewords distant in the mean of the Hamming distance. The maximum value of H is the number of the classes N. We set the value of $H = \lfloor N/6 \rfloor$, however some deeper analysis is needed to find the optimal value of H constant.

6 Results

The Tables 4 and 5 show the results obtained by our algorithm. We can see that the proposed method achieves better results than the original RHC algorithm even though the minimum Hamming distance between the codewords is worse in

Table 4. The results using SVM classifier, code length = 64

Database	Method			
name	OVO	RHC	MDCRL	MAHD
Gestures	81.1%	72.7%	83.0%	84.3%
ISOLET IITIS	96.5%	87.1%	87.8%	88.1%
Proteins	57.2%	57.1%	60.8%	61.2%
Leafs	79.1%	61.3%	63.2%	63.9%
ACRS	73.2%	43.2%	48.3%	52.5%

our approach, see Table 6. It is visible that this effect is achieved by using better binary classifiers. We can also see that the average Hamming distance between rows of the code matrix is also better in our algorithm, see Table 6.

Table 5. The results using SVM classifier, code length = 128

Database	Method			
name	OVO	RHC	MDCRL	MAHD
Gestures IITIS	81.1%	81.6%	82.0%	82.7%
ISOLET	96.5%	96.6%	96.9%	97.1%
Proteins	57.2%	53.5%	61.9%	62.4%
Leafs	79.1%	77.5%	82.7%	83.9%
ACRS	73.2%	68.2%	74.5%	76.1%

The procedure of the k-crossvalidation has been used to avoid biased results. We use $k = 7$ in our experiments. Only the average value of the k-crossvalidation has been shown in the tables. We can observe that our solution overcomes all other algorithms on all tested databases.

Let us examine the Table 6. It shows the minimal and the average Hamming distances obtained using different methods. The RHC method generally obtain the best minimal Hamming distances. The codewords are nearly optimal, but as we can see the overall results are worse than MDCRL and MAHD strategies which give less optimal codewords. Let us consider this experimental result. In RHC method the codewords are nearly optimal, but we use classifiers which produce very large number of the mistakes.

The average recognition ratio of the binary classifiers using the RHC algorithm is about 65% (using protein database) since in the MDCRL method it is 77% and in MAHD method is even 79%. The similar results we can see for a gesture database. When RHC method use binary classifiers with the average recognition ratio about 88% then MCDRL method 92% and MAHD method even 94%.

Table 6. The Hamming distances between the rows of the code matrix obtained using different strategies and different sizes of the codewords: (average - minimum)

Database	code	Method		
name	length	RHC	MDCRL	MAHD
Proteins	64	32.5 - 27	29.4 - 13	32.2 - 21
Proteins	128	65.4 - 59	60.9 - 42	62.4 - 52
ACRS	64	21.7 - 15	16.5 - 7	22.1 - 13
ACRS	128	47.3 - 42	43.2 - 27	46.2 - 39
Leafs	64	19.4 - 14	15.1 - 7	19.0 - 12
Leafs	128	48.7 - 43	44.7 - 29	48.0 - 41
Gestures IITIS	64	33.1 - 26	28.9 - 12	34.5 - 23
Gestures IITIS	128	64.9 - 56	61.7 - 29	65.1 - 55
ISOLET	64	34.8 - 28	26.9 - 11	34.7 - 25
ISOLET	128	69.0 - 60	57.8 - 39	65.2 - 51

If we look closer we see that the MAHD method can be improved for example by increasing the number of the iterations when in the MDCRL method we are limited by the number of the columns in the ranking list. Moreover many columns from the ranking list are defining binary classifiers with very low recognition ratios. For example in our experiments the last column in the ranking list defined the binary classifier with recognition ratio equal to 50.48 % (for protein database). We avoid considering such classifiers in MAHD method. Additionally when we use MDCRL method all the classifiers from the ranking list have to be tested before we start looking for the ECOC codewords. In MAHD method we test only these classifiers which are candidates for improving the average Hamming distance between the codewords.

We observe that the minimal Hamming distance is better in RHC method (in MDCRL and MAHD it is comparable), but the usage of better binary classifiers cause that the final results obtained by these two methods is higher (Table 7).

Table 7. The average recognition ratio of the binary classifiers

Database	Method		
name	RHC	MDCRL	MAHD
Gestures IITIS	88.2 %	92.3 %	94.1 %
ISOLET	97.8 %	98.2 %	98.6 %
Proteins	65.2 %	77.3 %	79.2 %
Leafs	88.6 %	89.9 %	91.2 %
ACRS	84.1 %	87.1 %	87.8 %

7   Conclusions

The results achieved using the proposed strategies are promising. The recognition ratios obtained using the algorithm are comparable or better than those described in the literature. For example for the proteins database our algorithm achieves 62.4 % when the algorithms we found in the literature get (48.8 % - 61.2 %) [3,5,8,10,21,22,24]

The crucial problem in our method is how to obtain the optimal code matrix i.e. with large average Hamming distance between the codewords. As we can see in the Table 6 the coding matrix created using an MDCRL and MAHD strategies have smaller values of the minimal Hamming distance between codewords. However we can see that the overall recognition ratios are quite good. It is because the average Hamming distance between codewords has more importance when we are dealing with the large number of the classes.

In this paper we propose the new strategy to create the ECOC codewords. This strategy focuses on the minimizing the misclassification error of the individual binary classifiers and on increasing the average Hamming distance between the codewords instead of maximizing the minimal Hamming distance. We show that this strategy gives better results than simple RHC strategy and it is slightly better than the MDCRL method.

There are some open questions still remained for the future research. The size of the codewords, the the stopping condition of the algorithm for improving the average Hamming distance between the codewords, the value of the H constant. However the proposed solution seems to be good way to improve the results obtained by the final classifier.

References

1. Allwein, E., Schapire, R., Singer, Y.: Reducing multiclass to binary: a unifying approach for margin classifiers. J. Mach. Learn. Res. **1**, 113–141 (2002)
2. Alpaydin, E., Mayoraz, E.: Learning error-correcting output codes from data. In: International Conference on Artificial Neural Networks (ICANN99), pp. 743–748 (1999)
3. Bologna, G., Appel, R.D.: A comparison study on protein fold recognition. In: Proceedings of the ninth ICONIP, vol. 5, pp. 2492–2496, Singapore, 18–22 November 2002
4. Chang, C.C., Lin, C.J.: LIBSVM: a library for support vector machines (2001). Software available at http://www.csie.ntu.edu.tw/cjlin/libsvm
5. Chmielnicki, W., Stapor, K.: Protein fold recognition with combined SVM-RDA classifier. In: Graña Romay, M., Corchado, E., Garcia Sebastian, M.T. (eds.) HAIS 2010, Part I. LNCS, vol. 6076, pp. 162–169. Springer, Heidelberg (2010)
6. Chmielnicki, W., Stapor, K.: A new approach to multi-class SVM-based classification using error correcting output codes. In: Burduk, R., Kurzyński, M., Woźniak, M., Żołnierek, A. (eds.) Computer Recognition Systems 4. AISC, pp. 499–506. Springer, Heidelberg (2011)
7. Chmielnicki, W., Roterman-Konieczna, I., Stapor, K.: An improved protein fold recognition with support vector machines. Expert Syst. **20**(2), 200–211 (2012)

8. Chung, I.F., Huang, C.D., Shen, Y.H., Lin, C.T.: Recognition of structure classification of protein folding by NN and SVM hierarchical learning architecture. In: Kaynak, O., Alpaydin, E., Oja, E., Xu, L. (eds.) ICANN/ICONIP 2003. LNCS, vol. 2714, pp. 1159–1167. Springer, Heidelberg (2003)
9. Dietterich, T.G., Bakiri, G.: Solving multiclass problems via error-correcting output codes. J. Artif. Intell. Res. **2**, 263–286 (1995)
10. Ding, C.H., Dubchak, I.: Multi-class protein fold recognition using support vector machines and neural networks. Bioinformatics **17**, 349–358 (2001)
11. Dubchak, I., Muchnik, I., Kim, S.H.: Protein folding class predictor for SCOP: approach based on global descriptors. In: Proceedings ISMB (1997)
12. Escalcera, S., Pujol, O., Radeva, P.: Error-correcting output code library. J. Mach. Learn. Res. **11**, 661–664 (2010)
13. Fanty, M., Cole, R.: Spoken letter recognition. In: Advances in Neural Information Processing Systems 3 (1991)
14. Fei, B., Liu, J.: Binary tree of SVM: a new fast multiclass training and classification algorithm. IEEE Trans. Neural Netw. **17**(3), 696–704 (2006)
15. Glomb, P., Romaszewski, M., Opozda, S., Sochan, A.: Choosing and modeling the hand gesture database for a natural user interface. In: Efthimiou, E., Kouroupetroglou, G., Fotinea, S.-E. (eds.) GW 2011. LNCS, vol. 7206, pp. 24–35. Springer, Heidelberg (2011)
16. Hastie, T., Tibshirani, R.: Classification by pairwise coupling. Ann. Stat. **26**(2), 451–471 (1998)
17. Kijsirikul, B., Ussivakul, N.: Multiclass support vector machines using adaptive directed acyclic graph. In: Proceedings of the International Joint Conference on Neural Networks, pp. 980–985 (2002)
18. Kuncheva, L.I.: Using diversity measures for generating error-correcting output codes in classifier ensembles. Pattern Recogn. Lett. **26**, 83–90 (2005)
19. Lorena, A.C., Carvalho, A.C., Gama, J.M.: A review on the combination of binary classifiers in multiclass problems. Artif. Intell. Rev. **30**(1–4), 19–37 (2008)
20. Lorena, A.C., Carvalho, A.C.: Building binary-tree-based multiclsss classifiers using separability measures. Neurocomputing **73**(16–-18), 2837–2845 (2010)
21. Nanni, L.: A novel ensemble of classifiers for protein fold recognition. Neurocomputing **69**, 2434–2437 (2006)
22. Okun, O.: Protein fold recognition with k-local hyperplane distance nearest neighbor algorithm. In: Proceedings of the Second European Workshop on Data Mining and Text Mining in Bioinformatics, pp. 51–57, Pisa, 24 September 2004
23. Ou, G., Murphey, Y.L.: Multi-class pattern classification using neural networks. Pattern Recogn. **40**, 4–18 (2006)
24. Pal, N.R., Chakraborty, D.: Some new features for protein fold recognition. In: Kaynak, O., Alpaydın, E., Oja, E., Xu, L. (eds.) ICANN 2003 and ICONIP 2003. LNCS, vol. 2714. Springer, Heidelberg (2003)
25. Platt, J.C., Cristianini, N., Shawe-Taylor, J.: Large margin DAGs for multiclass classification. In: Proceedings of Neural Information Processing Systems, pp. 547–553 (2000)
26. Sáez, J.A., Galar, M., Luengo, J., Herrera, F.: A first study on decomposition strategies with data with class noise using decision trees. In: Corchado, E., Snášel, V., Abraham, A., Woźniak, M., Graña, M., Cho, S.-B. (eds.) HAIS 2012, Part II. LNCS, vol. 7209, pp. 25–35. Springer, Heidelberg (2012)
27. Sanya, L., Zhi, L., Jianwen, S., Lin, L.: Application of synergic neural network in online writeprint identification. Int. J. Digital Technol. Appl. **5**(3), 126–135 (2011)

28. Silva, P.F.B., Marçal, A.R.S., da Silva, R.M.A.: Evaluation of features for leaf discrimination. In: Kamel, M., Campilho, A. (eds.) ICIAR 2013. LNCS, vol. 7950, pp. 197–204. Springer, Heidelberg (2013)
29. UCI machine learning repository (2014). http://archive.ics.uci.edu/ml/datasets. html
30. Vapnik, V.: The Nature of Statistical Learning Theory. Springer, New York (1995)
31. Vural, V., Dy, J.G.: A hierarchical method for multi-class support vector machines. In: Proceedings of the twenty-first ICML, pp. 831–838 (2004)
32. Windeatt, T., Ghaderi, R.: Coding and decoding for multi-class learning problems. Inf. Fusion 4(1), 11–21 (2003)

FM3S: Features-Based Measure of Sentences Semantic Similarity

Mohamed Ali Hadj Taieb[(✉)], Mohamed Ben Aouicha,
and Yosra Bourouis

MIRACL Laboratory, Sfax University, Sfax, Tunisia
{mohamedali.hadjtaieb,benaouicha.mohamed,yosra.
bourouis}@gmail.com

Abstract. The investigation of measuring Semantic Similarity (SS) between sentences is to find a method that can simulate the thinking process of human. In fact, it has become an important task in several applications including Artificial Intelligence and Natural Language Processing. Though this task depends strongly on word SS, the latter is not the only important feature. The current paper presents a new method for computing sentence semantic similarity by exploiting a set of its characteristics, namely Features-based Measure of Sentences Semantic Similarity (FM3S). The proposed method aggregates in a non-linear function between three components: the noun-based SS including the compound nouns, the verb-based SS using the tense information, and the common word order similarity. It measures the semantic similarity between concepts that play the same syntactic role. Concerning the word-based semantic similarity, an information content-based measure is used to estimate the SS degree between words by exploiting the WordNet "is a" taxonomy. The proposed method yielded into competitive results compared to previously proposed measures with regard to the Li's benchmark, showing a high correlation with human ratings. Further experiments performed on the Microsoft Paraphrase Corpus showed the best F-measure values compared to other measures for high similarity thresholds. The results displayed by FM3S prove the importance of syntactic information, compound nouns, and verb tense in the process of computing sentence semantic similarity.

Keywords: Semantic similarity · Sentence similarity · Word similarity · Compound nouns · Verb tense · WordNet

1 Introduction

The semantic similarity between words, sentences, texts, and documents is widely studied in various fields, including natural language processing, document semantic comparison, artificial intelligence, semantic web, and semantic search engines. In the sentence context, Jiang and Conrath [1] presented an approach for measuring semantic similarity/distance between words and concepts wherein a lexical taxonomy structure is combined with corpus statistical information. Lin [2] introduced the idea of measuring the similarity between two objects based on an information-theoretical approach. Turney [3] described Latent Relational Analysis (LRA), a method for measuring

© Springer International Publishing Switzerland 2015
E. Onieva et al. (Eds.): HAIS 2015, LNAI 9121, pp. 515–529, 2015.
DOI: 10.1007/978-3-319-19644-2_43

semantic similarity based on the semantic relations between two pairs of words. Li et al. [4] also presented an algorithm that takes account of semantic information and word order information implied in the sentences. The semantic similarity of two sentences is calculated using information from a structured lexical database and from corpus statistics.

Corley and Mihalcea [5] and Mihalcea et al. [6] presented a method for measuring the semantic similarity of texts, using corpus based and knowledge-based measures of similarity. Hliaoutakis et al. [7] investigated approaches to computing the semantic similarity between general terms using WordNet[1] and between medical terms using MeSH.[2] Islam and Inkpen [8] reported on a Semantic Text Similarity (STS) measure using a corpus-based measure for semantic word similarity and a modified version of the Longest Common Subsequence (LCS) string matching algorithm. Ramage et al. [9] proposed an algorithm that aggregates relatedness information via a random walk over a graph constructed from WordNet. Gad and Kamel [10] proposed a semantic similarity based model (SSBM) that computes semantic similarities by exploiting WordNet. Furthermore, Madylova and Öğüdücü [11] outlined a method for calculating semantic similarities between documents which is based on the calculation of cosine similarity between concept vectors of documents obtained from an "*is a*" taxonomy. Pedersen [12] presented a through comparison between similarity measures for concept pairs based on Information Content[3] (IC). Oliva et al. [13] reported on a method, called SyMSS, for computing short-text and sentence semantic similarity. The method considers that the meaning of a sentence is made up of the meanings of its separate words and the structural way the words are combined.

Batet et al. [14] proposed a measure based on the exploitation of the taxonomical structure of a biomedical ontology. Bollegala et al. [15] suggested an empirical method to estimate semantic similarity using page counts and text snippets retrieved from a web search engine for two words. Furthermore, Lintean and Rus [16] exploited word-to-word semantic similarity metrics for estimating the semantic similarity at sentence level. Šaric et al. [17] described have also presented a system consisting of two major components for determining the semantic similarity of short texts using a support vector regression model with multiple features measuring word-overlap similarity and syntax similarity.

In this paper, we present a model for estimating the semantic similarity between sentences based, firstly, on the semantic similarity of their words through the separate processing of verbs and nouns and secondly on the common words order. The present approach is the first which exploits an IC-based semantic similarity measure in the quantification of noun and verb semantic similarity. Also, it is the first which includes the compound nouns and verb tense in the design of semantic similarity measure between two sentences.

---

[1] http://wordnet.princeton.edu/.

[2] http://www.ncbi.nlm.nih.gov/mesh.

[3] Information content-based approach quantifies the similarity between concepts as a function of the Information Content (IC) that both concepts have in common in a given ontology. The basic idea is that general and abstract entities found in a discourse present less IC than more concrete and specialized ones.

The rest of paper is organized as follows: Sect. 2 describes the proposed model and its different components. Section 3 presents the benchmarks used for studying the performance of the FM3S measure. Section 4 presents and interprets the obtained results using the Li et al. dataset and Microsoft Paraphrase Corpus. Section 5 provides a conclusion and perspectives for future research.

2 FM3S: Features-Based Measure of Sentences Semantic Similarity

A sentence is a set of words that, in principle, tells a complete thought and is grouped meaningfully to express a statement. Accordingly, the proposed FM3S measure aggregates between three modules, namely noun similarity, verb similarity and common words order.

2.1 Noun Semantic Similarity

In this module, compound and simple nouns are extracted from the sentence pair (S_1, S_2) using the syntactic analyzer Stanford.[4] Empty words are removed using a stop list formed by 678 words. Moreover, compound nouns are determined using the tag (NP) provided by Stanford in the form of a syntactic tree structure. WordNet is then used to check whether each expression is a compound noun.

Furthermore, a morphological analysis is applied to transform each noun from plural into singular and radicalize it to obtain its representative canonical form. We then check its presence in WordNet. However, it would be interesting to consider the idea of compound nouns because it was not treated in previous works as in [4, 13].

Semantic similarity is computed using the intrinsic quantification method of information content described by Hadj Taieb et al. [18] coupled with the similarity measure of Lin [2]. This measure is based on the WordNet noun "is a" taxonomy where each noun N_i is represented by a set of vertices $Syn(N_i)$ called synsets. Each synset includes a specific meaning of the noun N_i. The similarity computation function between the nouns assigned to sentences S_1 and S_2 is defined as follows:

$$SS_{Nouns}(S_1, S_2) = \frac{\sum_{N_i \in Nouns(S_1)} \max_{N_j \in Nouns(S_2)} SemSim(N_i, N_j)}{\max(|Nouns(S_1)|, |Nouns(S_2)|)} \quad (1)$$

where $Nouns(S_i)$ refers to the set of simple and compound nouns in sentence S_i.

The semantic similarity between two nouns N_i and N_j is computed as follows:

$$SemSim(N_i, N_j) = \max_{(c_1, c_2) \in Syn(N_i) \times Syn(N_j)} SimSem(c_1, c_2) \quad (2)$$

---

[4] http://nlp.stanford.edu/.

where $SimSem(c_1, c_2)$ is defined as follows:

$$SemSim(c_1, c_2) = \frac{2 \times IC(LCS(c_1, c_2))}{IC(c_1) + IC(c_2)} \tag{3}$$

where $LCS(c_1, c_2)$ is a function that return the lowest common subsumer to the concept pair (c_1, c_2) into the WordNet "*is a*" taxonomy. Concerning the function $IC(c_i)$, it returns the information content of the concept c_i using the quantification method of Hadj Taieb et al. [18].

Table 1 shows the computing process of $SS_{Nouns}(S_1, S_2)$ using the following example:

S_1 = "*When you make a **journey**, you travel from one **place** to another.*"

S_2 = "*A **car** is a **motor vehicle** with **room** for a small **number** of **passengers**.*"

Table 1. Example of computing $SS_{Nouns}(S_1, S_2)$

N_j $\diagdown$ N_i	journey	place	$\max\limits_{N_j \in Nouns(S_2)} SemSim(N_i, N_j)$
car	0.0	0.246	0.246
motor	0.0	0.249	0.249
vehicle	0.0	0.767	0.767
motor vehicle	0.0	0.114	0.114
room	0.043	0.314	0.314
number	0.219	0.407	0.407
passenger	0.0	0.188	0.188
$SS_{Nouns}(S_1, S_2) =$		$\dfrac{0.246 + 0.249 + 0.767 + 0.114 + 0.314 + 0.407 + 0.188}{7} = 0.326$	

2.2 Verb Semantic Similarity

This module focuses on the quantification of the verbs contribution in the final semantic similarity between two sentences. The computation process also takes the verb tense into consideration. This idea is considered original because it has not been employed in former works in the literature. The process starts by extracting the set of verbs using Stanford. It then moves to convert each verb into its infinitive form by means of the morphological Stanford analyzer. After that, the semantic similarity between a couple of verbs is calculated based on the IC quantification method of Hadj Taieb et al. [18] together with the Lin [2] measure.

The use of verb tense into a sentence is integrated in the computing process as described below. The Stanford analyzer is employed to extract verb tense using the tense tags such as *VBD* for the past and *VBZ* for the present with the singular pronoun. The verbs component of the semantic similarity between two sentences S_1 and S_2 is computed as follows:

$$SS_{Verbs}(S_1, S_2) = \frac{\sum_{V_i \in Verbs(S_1)} \max\limits_{V_j \in Verbs(S_2)} SemSim(V_i, V_j)}{\max(|Verbs(S_1)|, |Verbs(S_2)|)} \tag{4}$$

where $Verbs(S_i)$ is the set of verbs included within the sentence S_i.

The semantic similarity between two verbs V_i and V_j is computed as follows:

$$SemSim\left(V_i, V_j\right) = \begin{cases} \max\limits_{(v_1,v_2)\in Syn(V_i)\times Syn(V_j)} SimSem(v_1, v_2) \ if\ Tense(V_i) = Tense\left(V_j\right) \\ 0 \qquad\qquad\qquad\qquad\qquad\qquad\qquad\qquad\qquad\quad else \end{cases} \tag{5}$$

where $Syn(V_i)$ refers to the set of synsets representing the verb V_i in the verbal "*is a*" taxonomy of WordNet, and $Tense(V_i)$ designates the verb tense within the concerned sentence. The verbs are exploited in their infinitive form. Furthermore, $SimSem(v_1, v_2)$ is defined as follows:

$$SemSim(v_1, v_2) = \frac{2 \times IC(LCS(v_1, v_2))}{IC(v_1) + IC(v_2)} \tag{6}$$

where $LCS(v_1, v_2)$ is a function that returns the lowest common subsumer to the verb pair (v_1, v_2) within the verbal WordNet "*is a*" taxonomy. $IC(v_i)$ returns the information content of the concept v_i using the quantification method [18]. Using the illustrative example below, Table 2 shows the computing mode of $SS_{Verbs}(S_1, S_2)$:

S_1 = "*those **involved** were allegedly **told** to never **speak** of the incident again, according to the letter*".

S_2 = "*the letter said staff was **told** to never **speak** of the incident*"

The verbs "*were, according, said, was*" are eliminated because they are considered as stop words.

Table 2. Example of computing $SS_{Verbs}(S_1, S_2)$

	Told	Speak	$\max\limits_{V_j \in Verbs(S_2)} SemSim\left(V_i, V_j\right)$
Involved	0.0	0.0	0.0
Told	1.0	0.752	1.0
Speak	0.752	1.0	1.0
$SS_{Verbs}(S_1, S_2) = \frac{0+1+1}{3} = 0.66$			

2.3 Computing Information Content

Hadj Taieb et al. [18] proposed a method that quantifies the concept's IC based on the subgraph of ancestors (view Fig. 1).

This quantification is based mainly on the contribution of each ancestor according to its depth and descendants' number. The IC value of a concept C is computed as follows:

$$IC(C) = \left(\sum_{c \in Hyper(C)} Score(c)\right) \times AverageDepth(C) \tag{7}$$

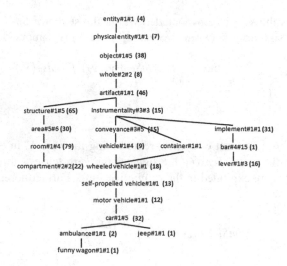

Fig. 1. WordNet "*is a*" taxonomy fragment. The number in parentheses refers to the number of direct hyponyms of each concept including itself. The notation *w#i#j* refers to the synset number *i* of the word *w* among its *j* synsets.

where *Score(c)* indicates the contribution of each ancestor pertaining to the set *Hyper (C)* that represents the ancestors of the concept *C*. This score is computed as follows:

$$Score(c) = \left(\sum_{c' \in DirectHyper(c)} \frac{Depth(c')}{|Hypo(c')|} \right) \times |Hypo(c)| \tag{8}$$

where *c* and *c'* are concepts, *DirectHyper(c)* is the set of directs parents of *c*, and *Hypo (c)* is the set of direct and indirect descendants, including the concept *c*.

AverageDepth(C) is exploited to express the vertical distribution of the subgraph modeling the IC of a concept *C*.

$$Average\ Depth(C) = \frac{1}{|Hyper(C)|} \times \sum_{c \in Hyper(C)} Depth(c) \tag{9}$$

2.4   Common Word Order Similarity

The shared words and their order within the two candidate sentences have an impact on the computing of semantic similarity. This module tries to quantify the Common Word Order (CWO). In fact, the CWO is treated in two steps: simple $SS_{CWO1}(S_1, S_2)$ and $SS_{CWO2}(S_1, S_2)$. Firstly, the stop words and special and punctuation characters are removed. The common words are then represented by their order indexes according to each sentence. After that, the similarity is computed based on the indices of simple and successive words independently. Finally, a linear aggregation is defined to combine between the two components.

Concerning the simple common words, the term is defined as follows:

$$SS_{CWO1}(S_1, S_2) = \frac{|\{w_i \backslash Order(w_i, S_1) = Order(w_i, S_2) \text{ with } w_i \in S_1 \cap S_2\}|}{|S_1 \cap S_2|} \quad (10)$$

where $Order(w_i, S_i)$ is a function that returns the order of the word $w_i \in S_1 \cap S_2$ within S_i. Regarding the successive common words, the term is defined as follows:

$$SS_{CWO2}(S_1, S_2) = \frac{|\{w_i \backslash Order(w_iw_{i+1}, S_1) = Order(w_iw_{i+1}, S_2) \text{ with } (w_i, w_{i+1}) \in S_1 \cap S_2\}|}{|S_1 \cap S_2|} \quad (11)$$

The aggregation between the two components is determined as follows:

$$SS_{CWO}(S_1, S_2) = \beta \times SS_{CWO1}(S_1, S_2) + (1 - \beta) \times SS_{CWO2}(S_1, S_2) \quad (12)$$

Where β is a tuning parameter pertaining to the interval $[0, 1]$. For example:

S_1 = "An implement is an instrument tool or other piece of equipment"

S_2 = "A tool is any instrument or simple piece of equipment that you hold in your hands and use to do a particular kind of work"

$SS_{CWO}(S_1, S_2)$ is computed as follows:

- Common words are {instrument, tool, piece, equipment}, the orders of shared words are {1, 2, 3, 4} for S_1 and {2, 1, 3, 4} for S_2.
- $SS_{CWO1}(S_1, S_2)$ = 0.5, $SS_{CWO2}(S_1, S_2)$ = 0.25, and for β = 0.6 we obtain $SS_{CWO}(S_1, S_2)$ = 0.4

2.5 The Aggregation of SS_{Noms}, SS_{Verbs} and SS_{CWO}

The semantic similarity between two sentences S_1 and S_2 is based on the aggregation of the three components defined above, namely SS_{Noms}, SS_{Verbs} and SS_{CWO}. The aggregation combines between them in a non-linear function using the tuning parameter $\alpha \in [0, 1]$ to turn the contribution of each component into the final score:

$$SemSim(S_1, S_2) = \frac{SS_{Nouns}(S_1, S_2)^\alpha + (SS_{Verbs}(S_1, S_2) + SS_{CWO}(S_1, S_2))^{\alpha - \alpha^2}}{1 + SS_{Nouns}(S_1, S_2)^\alpha} \quad (13)$$

As Eq. 13 clearly shows, the component SS_{Nouns} has the main contribution in the final score because $\alpha \geq \alpha - \alpha^2 \forall \alpha \in [0, 1]$. As presented in Fig. 2, the aggregate function $SemSim(S_1, S_2)$ provides values in the interval $[0, 1.2]$.

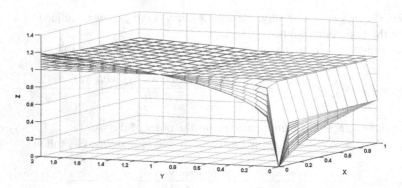

Fig. 2. Curves of Eq. 13 through the variation of the parameter α, where $X=SS_{Nouns}(S_1, S_2)$, $Y = (SS_{Verbs}(S_1, S_2) + SS_{CWO}(S_1, S_2))$, and $Z = \left(X^\alpha + Y^{\alpha - \alpha^2}\right)/1 + X^\alpha$

Accordingly, the final semantic similarity degree between S_1 and S_2 is:

$$FM3S(S_1, S_2) = \left\{ \begin{array}{ll} SemSim(S_1, S_2), & if \ SemSim(S_1, S_2) \leq 1 \\ 1 & , else \end{array} \right\} \tag{14}$$

We present below an example using $\beta = 0.6$ and $\alpha = 0.6$ and including the sentence pair:

S_1 = "*An autograph is the signature of someone famous which is specially written for a fan to keep.*"

S_2 = "*Your signature is your name, written in your own characteristic way, often at the end of a document to indicate that you recorded the document or that you agree with what it says*"

Each component is computed as follows:

- SS_{Nouns}: the set *Nouns(S_1)* = {*autograph, signature*} and *Nouns(S_2)* = {*signature, document*}. Using the Eq. 1, $SS_{Nouns}(S_1, S_2)$ = 0.955
- SS_{Verbs}: the set *Verbs(S_1)* = {*written*} and *Verbs(S_2)* = {*written, indicate, recorded, agree*}. Using the Eq. 4, $SS_{Verbs}(S_1, S_2)$ = 0.25
- SS_{CWO}: The common words are {*signature, written*}, $SS_{CWO}(S_1, S_2)$ = 0.8

So, *SemSim(S_1, S_2)* = 1.02, then *FM3S(S_1, S_2)* = 1.

3   Assessment Benchmarks

The sentence similarity measure is evaluated through two methods. The first method involves the study of the correlation between the similarity values assigned to sentence pairs judged by experts and the automatically provided ones. The second involves the integration of the measure in a specific application such as paraphrase determination.

3.1 Benchmarks

- Li et al. dataset.
  Li et al. [4] collected human ratings for the similarity of sentence pairs using a panel of 32 native speakers of English. Li et al. replaced 30 word couples of Rubenstein and Goodenough [19] by their definitions from the Collins Cobuild dictionary. The participants were asked to rate the similarity of meaning of the sentence pairs on the scale from 0.0 (minimum similarity) to 4.0 (maximum similarity)
- MicroSoft Paraphrase Corpus (MSPC).
  The FM3S method is used to identify automatically whether or not two sentences are paraphrases. Therefore, MSPC [20], consisting of 4,076 training pairs and 1,725 test pairs, is used to determine the number of correctly identified paraphrase pairs in the corpus to assess the proposed measure.

3.2 Evaluation Metrics

The metrics used to evaluate the performance of our measure according to:

- Li et al. dataset are:

Pearson coefficient: It indicates how well the results of a measure resemble human judgments. Pearson's r is calculated as follows:

$$r = \frac{n(\sum x_i y_i) - (\sum x_i)(\sum y_i)}{\sqrt{n(\sum x_i^2)(\sum x_i)^2}\sqrt{n(\sum y_i^2)(\sum y_i)^2}} \quad (15)$$

where x_i refers to the ith element in the list of human judgments, y_i to the corresponding i^{th} element in the list of SS computed values, and n to the number of sentence pairs.

Spearman coefficient: The ranking produced on the basis of the measure is compared to the one produced on the basis of human judgments. Spearman's ρ is computed as follows:

$$\rho = 1 - \frac{6\sum d_i^2}{n(n^2 - 1)} \quad (16)$$

The parameter d_i is the difference between the ranks of x_i and y_i.

- Corpus MSPC are:

Recall: It is the number of the determined relevant paraphrases divided by the existing number of paraphrases:

$$Recall = \frac{Number\ of\ pairs\ correctly\ annotated\ as\ paraphrases\ by\ the\ measure}{Number\ of\ paraphrases\ in\ the\ dataset} \quad (17)$$

Precision: It is the number of the determined relevant paraphrases divided by the number of returned paraphrases:

$$Precision = \frac{Number\ of\ pairs\ correctly\ annotated\ as\ paraphrases\ by\ the\ measure}{Number\ of\ pairs\ annotated\ as\ paraphrases\ by\ the\ measure}.$$

(18)

F-measure: it is the geometric mean of precision and recall and expresses a trade-off between those two measures:

$$F - mesure = 2 \times \frac{Precision * Recall}{Precision + Recall}$$

(19)

4 Experiments and Results

This section presents the results obtained for the employed benchmarks, Li et al. and MSRPC. All experiments are performed using the $\beta = 0.6$ and $\alpha = 0.6$ parameters, which are empirically determined with respect to Eqs. 12 and 13.

4.1   Li et al. Dataset

Table 3 shows the correlation coefficients Pearson (r) and Spearman (ρ) obtained from different measures on the Li et al. dataset. The results obtained by the proposed FM3S approach are competitive compared to the other measures and are noted to exceed the Sy-MSS measure. This can be explained by the fact that 28 sentence pairs in the dataset contain only the verb "*to be*", which affect negatively the contribution of the SS_{Verbs} component to the final similarity score.

Table 3. Results obtained using the Li et al. dataset

Measure	Li et al.	STS	SyMSS	FM3S
Ref	[4]	[8]	[13]	
r	0.81	0.85	0.76	**0.76**
ρ	0.81	0.83	0.71	**0.79**

4.2   MicroSoft Paraphrases Corpus: MSPC

The determination of whether or not a sentence pair is a paraphrase depends on the interpretation of $FM3S(S_1, S_2)$.

In other words, if the provided value is superior or equal to a threshold $\theta \in [0, 1]$, then (S_1, S_2) are considered as paraphrase; otherwise they are not paraphrase. Very satisfactory results are obtained for most of the data (Trial and Test). Figure 3 presents a comparison between the *STS* approach [8] and our approach. The results show that our approach is very competitive according to the results of the "*STS*" approach.

Due to the absence of published works presenting results on the MSPC dataset, our approach is compared only to "*STS*" [8]. Figure 3 illustrates the variation of the F-measure rate according to the similarity threshold θ for "*Training*" and "*Test*" data. Accordingly, using the FM3S approach for $\theta = 0.4$, we note that the F-measure value is 0.8028. This value is the same value found via the "*STS*" approach. However, and as clearly shown in Fig. 3, our approach provides the best results for $\theta \in [0.7, 1.0]$. For example, while with $\theta = 0.4$ our approach yielded into an F-measure value of 0.5472 for the Training data and 0.5204 for the Test data, the F-measure values obtained with the "*STS*" approach for the same interval tend towards 0. This provides further support for the advanced efficiency of our approach.

The results illustrated in Figs. 4 and 5 show the precision and the recall of the proposed measure, respectively. In fact, precision reached peak with $\theta = 0.9$, showing a value of 0.69 for the Training and Test datasets. This demonstrates that the sentence pairs judged as highly similar by our measure are qualified as paraphrases in the MSPC dataset.

Figure 4 demonstrates that the curve describing the precision has nearly a constant behavior. In fact, the proposed measure provides high values of similarity between

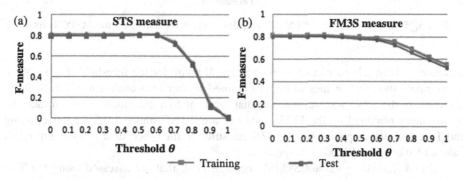

Fig. 3. Comparison between STS (a) and FM3S (b) approaches using F-measure values and varying the threshold θ on MSPC corpus.

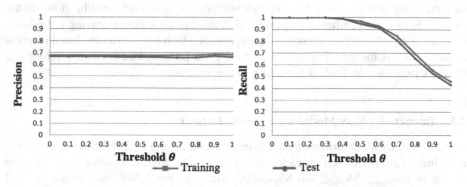

Fig. 4. Precision and Recall curves of FM3S measure applied the MSPC corpus.

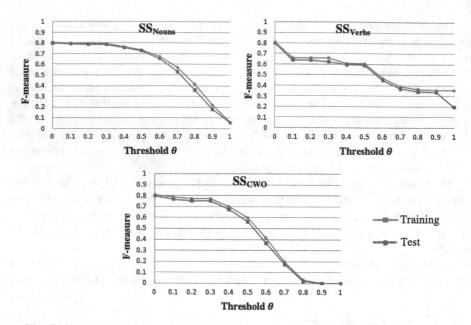

Fig. 5. F-measures curves of FM3S' modules applied separately on the MSPC corpus.

sentences, which allows us to obtain good recall value for the threshold $\theta = 1$. When we compare the recall values in Fig. 4 obtained by our measure for $\theta = 1$ with those obtained by the *STS* measure, we note that those of *STS* are much lower. In fact, the recall values obtained by the FM3S measure are 0.4557 and 0.4285 for the Training and Test datasets, respectively. The *STS* measure, on the other hand yielded into recall values of 0.0054 and 0.0044, respectively.

Table 4, including variant SyMSS measure [13], that are assessed using the Test dataset of the MSPC corpus. It specifies the threshold value for each triple (Recall, Precision and F-measure). In Table 4, we three rows for our method according to the thresholds ($\theta = 0.6, 0.8, 1$). In fact, the well-functioning of a method through the MicroSoft Paraphrase Corpus is related to good F-measure values for high θ-values. In fact, the computed similarity between two paraphrased sentences must be closer to the value 1. For example, when choosing $\theta = 0.2$, the pair of sentences having a similarity superior or equal to 0.2 are considered paraphrases which leads to a significant increase of the recall. So, the most important is to have good performance for high θ-values like the ones presented in Table 4 according to our proposal.

4.3   Impact of FM3S Modules on MSPC Dataset

In order to study the contribution of each module composing the propsosed measure, the experiments are performed on each module separately. Figure 5 shows the F-measure curves of SS_{Nouns}, SS_{Verbs} and SS_{CWO} according to the MSPC dataset and a fixed threshold θ.

Table 4. Comparison between the results of sentence similarity measures using the test dataset of the MSPC corpus.

Approach	θ	Recall	Precision	F-Measure	Ref
SyMSS-PATH	0.35	0.8982	0.7194	0.7989	[13]
SyMSS-RES	0.45	0.8982	0.7323	0.8068	[13]
SyMSS-HSO	0.55	0.8171	0.7047	0.7567	[13]
SyMSS-LIN	0.35	0.8943	0.7318	0.8049	[13]
Islam and Inkpen	0.6	0.8913	0.7465	0.8125	[8]
Mihalcea et al.	0.5	0.977	0.696	0.813	[6]
Random		0.50	0.683	0.578	[13]
Vector-based	0.5	0.795	0.716	0.753	[13]
FM3S	**0.6**	**0.9937**	**0.670**	**0.770**	
	0.8	**0.92.41**	**0.670**	**0.6564**	
	1	**0.7304**	**0.665**	**0.5204**	

The better result is found with SS_{Nouns} such as 0.58 with $\theta = 0.7$ for the training dataset. For the same threshold, F-measures values are 0.41 and 0.20 for respectively SS_{Verbs} and SS_{CWO}. Therefore, we assign to the module of noun semantic similarity the main factor in the nonlinear function ($\alpha > \alpha - \alpha^2$, with $\alpha \in [0, 1]$). In second place, the verbs module has less important contribution than that viewed with the nouns. When comparing the behavior of SS_{Nouns} and SS_{Verbs} in relation with $\theta \in [0.8, 1]$, we remark that the second one outperforms the first module (such the F-scores 0.34 and 0.19 for $\theta = 0.9$). This explains well the importance of the verbs and their tense like features in the calculation of the semantic similarity.

5 Conclusion and Future Work

The proposed measure determines the similarity of two sentences from the semantic and syntactic information they contain. The aggregate function *FM3S(S₁, S₂)*, defined in Eq. 14, combines the nouns, verbs and common word order in a non-linear way. The FM3S measure is based on the word semantic similarity of nouns and verbs. It exploits the IC quantifying method of [18] coupled with the Lin [2] measure and WordNet "*is a*" taxonomies. The IC computing method employs the topological parameters of the "*is a*" taxonomy, such as the depth, ancestors and descendants, to numerically express the sense of a concept. The proposed approach also takes, for the first time, the verb tense into consideration while computing $SS_{Verbs}(S_1, S_2)$. Our FM3S approach yields into an excellent Spearman correlation coefficient for the Li et al. dataset ($\rho = 0.79$). For the paraphrase recognition task, our proposed FM3S approach outperforms other measures, mainly for high thresholds of $\theta \in [0.7, 1]$. These results provide strong support for the utility of a number of sentence features, such as compound nouns, verb tense, common word order, and nominal and verbal WordNet taxonomies in the process of computing of semantic similarity. Considering the promising performance of this measure, further studies, some of which are underway in our laboratory are needed, to investigate its potential application on other languages, such as Arabic and French, using their WordNet versions.

References

1. Jiang, J.J., Conrath, D.W.: Semantic similarity based on corpus statistics and lexical taxonomy. CoRR cmp-lg/9709008 (1997)
2. Lin, D.: An information-theoretic definition of similarity. In: Proceedings of the Fifteenth International Conference on Machine Learning, pp 296–304. Morgan Kaufmann Publishers Inc., San Francisco (1998)
3. Turney, P.D.: Measuring semantic similarity by latent relational analysis. In: Proceedings of the 19th International Joint Conference on Artificial Intelligence, pp 1136–1141. Morgan Kaufmann Publishers Inc., Edinburgh, Scotland (2005)
4. Li, Y., McLean, D., Bandar, Z.A., O'Shea, J.D., Crockett, K.: Sentence similarity based on semantic nets and corpus statistics. IEEE Trans. Knowl. Data Eng. 18, 1138–1150 (2006)
5. Corley, C., Mihalcea, R.: Measuring the semantic similarity of texts. In: Proceedings of the ACL Workshop on Empirical Modeling of Semantic Equivalence and Entailment, pp 13–18. Association for Computational Linguistics, Ann Arbor, Michigan (2005)
6. Mihalcea, R., Corley, C., Strapparava, C.: Corpus-based and knowledge-based measures of text semantic similarity. In: Proceedings of the 21st National Conference on Artificial Intelligence, vol. 1, pp 775–780. AAAI Press, Boston, Massachusetts (2006)
7. Hliaoutakis, A., Varelas, G., Voutsakis, E., Petrakis, E.G.M., Milios, E.: Information retrieval by semantic similarity. Int. J. Semant. Web Inf. Syst. (IJSWIS) 3(3), 55–73 (2006). Special Issue of Multimedia Semantics
8. Islam, A., Inkpen, D.: Semantic text similarity using corpus-based word similarity and string similarity. ACM Trans. Knowl. Discov. Data 2, 10:1–10:25 (2008)
9. Ramage, D., Rafferty, A.N., Manning, C.D.: Random walks for text semantic similarity. In: Proceedings of the 2009 Workshop on Graph-based Methods for Natural Language Processing, pp 23–31. Association for Computational Linguistics, Suntec, Singapore (2009)
10. Gad, Walaa K., Kamel, Mohamed S.: New semantic similarity based model for text clustering using extended gloss overlaps. In: Perner, Petra (ed.) MLDM 2009. LNCS, vol. 5632, pp. 663–677. Springer, Heidelberg (2009)
11. Madylova, A., Öğüdücü, S.G.: A taxonomy based semantic similarity of documents using the cosine measure. In: ISCIS, pp 129–134. IEEE (2009)
12. Pedersen, T.: Information content measures of semantic similarity perform better without sense-tagged text. In: Human Language Technologies: The 2010 Annual Conference of the North American Chapter of the Association for Computational Linguistics, pp 329–332. Association for Computational Linguistics, Los Angeles, California (2010)
13. Oliva, J., Serrano, J.I., del Castillo, M.D., Iglesias, Á.: SyMSS: a syntax-based measure for short-text semantic similarity. Data Knowl. Eng. 70, 390–405 (2011)
14. Batet, M., Sánchez, D., Valls, A.: An ontology-based measure to compute semantic similarity in biomedicine. J. Biomed. Inf. 44, 118–125 (2011)
15. Bollegala, D., Matsuo, Y., Ishizuka, M.: A web search engine-based approach to measure semantic similarity between words. IEEE Trans. Knowl. Data Eng. 23, 977–990 (2011)
16. Lintean, M.C., Rus, V.: Measuring semantic similarity in short texts through greedy pairing and word semantics. In: FLAIRS Conference (2012)

17. Šaric, F., Glavaš, G., Karan, M., Šnajder, J., Bašic, B.D.: TakeLab: systems for measuring semantic text similarity. Proceedings of the First Joint Conference on Lexical and Computational Semantics - Volume 1: Proceedings of the Main Conference and the Shared Task, and Volume 2: Proceedings of the Sixth International Workshop on Semantic Evaluation, pp 441–448. Association for Computational Linguistics, Montréal, Canada (2012)
18. Hadj Taieb, M.A., Ben Aouicha, M., Ben Hamadou, A.: A new semantic relatedness measurement using WordNet features. Knowl. Inf. Syst. **41**, 467–497 (2014)
19. Rubenstein, H., Goodenough, J.B.: Contextual correlates of synonymy. Commun. ACM **8**, 627–633 (1965)
20. Dolan, B., Quirk, C., Brockett, C.: Unsupervised construction of large paraphrase corpora: exploiting massively parallel news sources. In: Proceedings of the 20th International Conference on Computational Linguistics. doi:10.3115/1220355.1220406

Improving Enzyme Function Classification Performance Based on Score Fusion Method

Alaa Tharwat[1,5]([✉]), Mahir M. Sharif[2,5]([✉]), Aboul Ella Hassanien[3,4,5],
and Hesham A. Hefeny[2]

[1] Faculty of Engineering, Suez Canal University, Ismailia, Egypt
engalaatharwat@hotmail.com
[2] Institute of Statistical Studies and Researches (ISSR),
Cairo University, Giza, Egypt
mahiralsharif@yahoo.com
[3] Faculty of Computers and Information, BeniSuef University, Beni Suef, Egypt
[4] Faculty of Computers and Information, Cairo University, Giza, Egypt
[5] Scientific Research Group in Egypt (SRGE), Cairo, Egypt
http://www.egyptscience.net

Abstract. Enzymes are important in our life and it plays a vital role
in the most biological processes. Computational classification of the enzyme's function is necessary to save efforts and time. In this paper, an
information fusion-based approach is proposed. The unknown sequence
is classified through aligning it with all labelled sequences using local
pairwise sequence alignment based on different score matrices. The outputs of all pairwise sequence alignment processes are represented by a set
of scores. The scores of alignment processes are combined using simple
fusion rules. The results of the fusion-based approach achieved results
better than all individual sequence alignment processes.

Keywords: Enzyme · Classification · Enzyme function classification ·
Local sequence alignment · Score fusion · Fusion rules

1 Introduction

An enzyme is a particular and important type of protein. Enzymes play a vital
role in the most biological processes in living organisms and catalyze biochemi-
cal reactions and play an important role in metabolic pathways. The enzyme or
protein sequences contained in various organisms are very easy to determine, but
to find experimentally the function of a protein remains a tedious and expensive task because it needs faster and more cost-effective manner [1]. Thus, the
biologists are interested and more urgent need in automatic approaches that
can help them to filter among the numerous possibilities, and so with the aid
of computational methods for the development of models to classify and predict
the functions of various enzymes based on similarities between their sequences
and/or their spatial structures [2,3].

© Springer International Publishing Switzerland 2015
E. Onieva et al. (Eds.): HAIS 2015, LNAI 9121, pp. 530–542, 2015.
DOI: 10.1007/978-3-319-19644-2_44

Generally there are three famous approaches using to classify and predict the enzymes and proteins include protein's structure, protein's features, and sequence alignment, and the last one that is used in this paper "sequence alignment" [4,5].

Enzyme functions are classified into six main classes such as (I) oxidoreductase, catalysing oxidation-reduction reactions; The systematic enzyme name is in the form donor: acceptor oxidoreductase.; (II) transferase, transferring a chemical group from one substrate (the donor) to another (the acceptor) according to the general reaction: $XY + Z = X + Y - Z$; (III) hydrolase, These enzymes catalyse the hydrolytic cleavage of bonds such as C-O, C-N, C-C and some other bonds, including phosphoric anhydride bonds; (IV) lyase, catalysing the nonhydrolytic and cleave C-C, C-O, C-N and other bonds by means other than hydrolysis or oxidation; (V) isomerase, catalysing geometrical or structural changes within one molecule.; (VI) ligase, catalysing the joining together of two molecules coupled with hydrolysis of a pyrophosphate bond in ATP or a similar triphosphate. The recommended name often takes the form A-B ligase [6].

Many studies conducted classification and predictions of enzymes based on sequence alignment approach, e.g. Francois Coste et al., proposed a classifier based on the identification of common subsequence blocks between known enzymes and new enzymes and the search of formal concepts built on the cross product of blocks and sequences for each class [2]. Peter Busk and Lene Lange [6], developed a simple algorithm, Peptide Pattern Recognition (PPR), that can divide proteins into groups of sequences that share a set of short conserved sequences, they achieved results with high precision (91 %–97 %) by finding short conserved motifs in their sequences. Clark and Predrag in [7], present a model called FANN-GO which abbreviation to Functional Annotator Neural Network Gene Ontology. Their proposed model is based on aligning a target sequence to a database of experimentally annotated proteins and calculating the i-score alignment that the protein is associated with each functional term. These scores were then used as inputs to an ensemble of multi-output neural networks that were trained to predict the probability that the protein is associated with each function. Des Jardins et al. [8], proposed a novel approach to predicting the function of a protein from its amino acid sequences, they achieved performance better than famous algorithms, e.g. Basic Local Alignment Sequence Tools (BLAST) and Support Vector Machine (SVM) in case using a small dataset. Faria et al. [4], developed a machine learning model called Peptide Program (PPs) that achieved a high accuracy when used small dataset. Mohammed and Guda proposed a model [9], reviewed a group of studies, which used a number of computational approaches to predict and classify enzymes based on the extracted features, e.g. molecular weight, Polar, etc. Bum et al., proposed new PNPRD features representing global and/or local differences in sequences, based on positively and/or negatively charged residues, to assist in predicting protein function, and useful feature subset for predicting the function of various proteins [10].

The proposed model aims to calculate the pairwise alignment between the unknown enzyme sequence and all the training sequences based on many local sequence similarity alignments due to its robustness against global alignment technique [11]. In the proposed model, the local sequence alignment is used based on different score matrices. The output of each local sequence alignment is represented by a set of scores (vector of scores). Each vector has the scores, which represent the similarity between the unknown sequence and all labelled sequences. All vectors of scores are combined using simple fusion rule into one vector. In this model, different fusion rules are used to combine the vectors of scores. The output of each fusion rule represents the class label or the function of the unknown sequence.

The rest of the paper is organized as follows, in Sect. 2 theoretical framework of the proposed model is explained; Sect. 3 introduces the steps of the proposed model; In Sect. 4 two different experiments are introduced; Discussions of the experiments are presented in Sect. 5; In Sect. 6 conclusions and future work of the proposed model are introduced.

2   Preliminaries

This section explains the theoretical framework of the proposed model. First, the sequence alignment technique is introduced including how to align two sequences and the types of score matrices. Moreover, the local sequence alignment technique is explained briefly. Second, the information fusion-based technique, including score fusion method is explained.

2.1   Sequence Alignment

The process of arranging two sequences of characters to determine the region of similarity and similarity score between these two sequences called sequence alignment.

Given two sequences X and Y, where $X \equiv x_1 x_2 \ldots x_m, Y \equiv y_1 y_2 \ldots y_n$, where x_i and y_i are letters chosen from the alphabet. Calculating distance or similarity score between two sequences (e.g. X and Y) is called sequence alignment. In each sequence, gaps are an arbitrary number of null characters or spaces (represented by dashes) may be placed. In sequence alignment process, the alignment of a character with null is called indel. Indel may be understood as insertion of a character into one sequence or deletion of a character from the other one [11].

The score of the alignment or similarity is then measured after aligning the two sequences. Calculating the scores or similarity of alignment depends on the scoring or substitution matrix, which is represented by a set of values representing the likelihood of one residue being substituted by another. Since, the proteins composed of 20 amino acid, the scoring matrices for proteins are 20×20 matrix, where the $((i, j)^{th})$ entry in the matrix is equal to the probability of the ith amino acid being substituted by the jth amino acid. Two well-known scoring matrices for proteins are Point Accepted Mutation or Percent Accepted Mutation (PAM) and BLOck SUbstitutions Matrices (BLOSUM). The alignment score is the sum of the scores for aligning pairs of letters (alignment of two letters) and gap scores (alignment of gap with letter). Global and local sequence alignment techniques are the most two famous pairwise sequence alignment techniques [11].

Local Alignment. The first algorithm that used local alignment to measure the similarity between different sequences was proposed by Smith-Waterman and it is expressed as in Eq. (1). Local alignment is useful when sequences are not similar in length or characters, but it finds the most similar regions in two sequences being aligned [12]. Thus, local alignment isolates regions in the sequences; hence it is easy to detect repeats.

$$SIM(i,j) = max \begin{cases} SIM(i-1,j-1) + s(x_i, y_i), & match \ or \ mismatch; \\ SIM(i-1,j) + g, & InsertionGap; \\ SIM(i,j-1) + g, & DeletionGap; \\ 0; \end{cases}$$

(1)

where $SIM(i,j)$ represents the maximum similarity score between the two sequences X and Y; and $1 \leq i \leq m$ and $1 \leq j \leq n$, where m and n represents the length of the two sequences X and Y, respectively. The insertion and deletion are represented using gap scoring g and $s(x_i, y_i)$ represents the match or mismatch score between the two letters (x_i and y_i).

2.2   Information Fusion

Information fusion technique is based on collecting information from many sources or experts and combine them to get the final decision. The accuracy of the information fusion decisions depends on many factors such as the independence of information resources and the combination methods that used to combine this information. Moreover, the combination methods depend on the type of data (e.g. abstract decisions, ranked lists, or score) [13,14]. In this study, a score fusion method is used to determine the function of the unknown enzyme.

Combining Sequence Alignment Scores. Given L pairwise sequence alignments (SA), each has different score matrix. Each sequence alignment process is used to align the unknown sequence (T) with the labelled or training sequences ($Z = \{z_1, z_2, \ldots, z_n\}$), where z_i represents the ith sequence in the labelled sequences and n represents the total number of labelled sequences. The output of each sequence alignment is represented by a set or a vector of scores $S = \{s_1, s_2, \ldots, s_n\}$, where s_i represents the similarity scores between the unknown sequence and the ith labelled sequence (z_i). To calculate the final decision, the output of all sequence alignment processes are combined as shown in Figs. 1 and 2. There are many different combination rules that can be used to combine scores such as sum, minimum, maximum, product, median, and mean rules as shown in Eqs. (2, 3, 4, 5, 6). The results of score fusion is better than combining ranks or abstract decisions because scores have a lot of data and when converting scores to the ranked lists or abstract decisions many of this information are lost [15]. To combine all scores, the following simple rules are used.

- **Sum rule:** This rule is applicable when there is a high-level of noise leading to ambiguity in the classification problem [16].

$$S_{fusion}(x) = arg\ max_j \sum_{i=1}^{L} S_{i,j}(x) \tag{2}$$

- **Product rule:** This rule is used when the sources are independent [16].

$$S_{fusion}(x) = arg\ max_j \prod_{i=1}^{L} S_{i,j}(x) \tag{3}$$

- **Max rule:** The max rule approximates the mean of the posteriori probabilities by the maximum value [16].

$$S_{fusion}(x) = arg\ max_j\ max_i\ S_{i,j}(x) \tag{4}$$

- **Min rule:** The min rule is similar to Max rule, but it calculates the minimum value [16].

$$S_{fusion}(x) = arg\ max_j\ min_i S_{i,j}(x) \tag{5}$$

- **Mean rule:** The mean or average rule calculates the average of all scores of the same training instance [16].

$$S_{fusion}(x) = arg\ max_j\ \frac{1}{L} \sum_{i=1}^{L} S_{i,j}(x) \tag{6}$$

where $S_{i,j}$ represents the similarity score between the unknown sequences and the ith labelled sequence in the jth pairwise sequence alignments (SA_j) process. In the sum rule, the fusion of all scores are calculated by adding all scores of the same labelled sequence as shown in Table 1. In our study, the output of the sequence alignment represents the similarity not distance, so the function of the nearest labelled sequence (i.e. maximum similarity) to the unknown sequence is assigned to the unknown sequence. By similarity, all rules are calculated and the maximum similarity is used in all rules.

Example: let L is the number of sequence alignment processes (each sequence alignment is based on different score matrix) as shown in Fig. 1. The output of each sequence alignment is represented by a set of scores $S = s_1, s_2, \ldots, s_n$. The scores of each sequence alignment process are normalised to make the sum of all scores equal to one.

Assume that for a certain unknown sequence T, the output of each sequence alignment process (SA) is represented by one row as shown in Table 1. Applying the simple rules in Eqs. (2, 3, 4, 5, 6) on each column to obtain the final decisions as shown in Table 1. For example, using the sum rule, the scores of each column is added. As shown in Eq. (2), the final decision when using the sum rule, is the maximum value; since the outputs of all sequence alignment processes represent similarity, not distance. In our example, the maximum value equal to 2.5, which represents the second labelled sequence. Thus, the function of the second sequence is assigned to the unknown sequences (T).

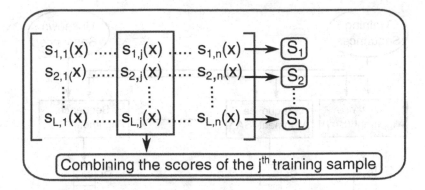

Fig. 1. An example of combining or fusion different vectors of scores

Table 1. Example of the proposed fusion-based method

Type of sequence alignment (single or fused)		Alignment with three samples			Decision
		1st sample	2nd sample	3rd sample	
Single sequence alignment	Sequence 1	0.2	0.5	0.3	0.5 (2nd sample)
	Sequence 2	0.0	0.0	1.0	1.0 (3rd sample)
	Sequence 3	0.1	0.5	0.4	0.5 (2nd sample)
	Sequence 4	0.0	0.7	0.3	0.7 (2nd sample)
	Sequence 5	0.0	0.8	0.2	0.8 (2nd sample)
Combined sequence alignment	Sum rule	0.3	**2.5**	2.2	2.5 (2nd sample)
	Min rule	0.0	0.0	**0.2**	0.2 (3rd sample)
	Max rule	0.2	0.8	**1.0**	1.0 (3rd sample)
	Product rule	0.0	0.0	**0.0072**	0.0072 (3rd sample)
	Mean rule	0.06	**0.5**	0.44	0.5 (2nd sample)

3   The Proposed Enzyme Function Classification Model

The proposed model is shown in Fig. 2 and it consists of two phases. In the first phase, different pairwise sequence similarity alignments are used to align the unknown sequence and all other training or labelled sequences. In the proposed model, the local sequence alignment is used to calculate the similarity between the unknown sequence and all other training sequences. Different pairwise alignments are calculated based on different scoring matrices (e.g. PAM, BLOSUM, etc.). As shown in Fig. 2, the sequence alignment process is denoted by SA_i. The output from each pairwise alignment is represented by a vector or a set of scores $S_i, i = 1, 2, \ldots, n$.

In the second phase of the proposed model, all score vectors S_i that are calculated in the first phase are fused using one of the fusion rules that mentioned in Sect. 2 (see Fig. 1), the final vector after fusion is denoted by, S_{fusion}. As shown in Fig. 2, all sets or vectors of scores that represent the results of the first phase are combined using different fusion rules as in Eqs. (2, 3, 4, 5, 6). The output of any combination rule is represented by a vector S_{fusion}. The final decision (i.e.

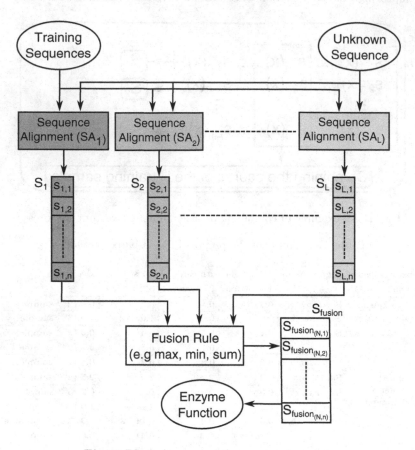

Fig. 2. Block diagram of the proposed model.

enzyme function) is the label of the sequence that has the maximum value (i.e. maximum similarity or score). The details of the proposed steps are summarized in Algorithm 1.

4   Experimental Results and Discussion

In this section, two experimental scenarios are designed to test the proposed model. In all experiments, one against all approach is used or, in other words, the similarity is calculated between the unknown sequence with all other labelled sequences in the dataset.

4.1   Dataset

The dataset, which is used in all experiments was obtained from SWISS-PROT enzyme database which consists of 6923 sequences of enzymes from [17], the details of each class are shown in Fig. 3. To save the time and memory storage,

---

Algorithm 1. Enzyme function classification Based on score fusion

---

1: **Input:** Given a set of labelled sequences as follows, $Z_i, i = 1, 2, \ldots, n$ where n represents the total number of labelled or training sequences. Each sequence has a function or a label $\Omega_i, i = 1, 2, \ldots, n$

2: Given Unknown sequences T.

3: Align the unknown sequence T with all labelled sequences Z using local pairwise alignment technique based on different score matrices.

4: **for all** $i = 1$ **to** L **do**

5:   **for all** $j = 1$ **to** n **do**

6:     Align the unknown sequence T with the jth labelled sequence. The output of each alignment process is represented by a similarity score $(S_{i,j})$.

7:   **end for**

8: **end for**

9: Combine all scores $S_{i,j}$ using fusion rules. The output of any fusion rule is represented by a set of values S_{fusion} (vector).

10: Assign the class label (i.e. enzyme function) Ω_i of the ith element, which has the maximum fused score $(\max_i S_{fusion})$ to the unknown sequence T.

---

we used a subset of the whole dataset which represents approximately a half $(\frac{3470}{6923} = 50.12\%)$ of the total number of all sequences.

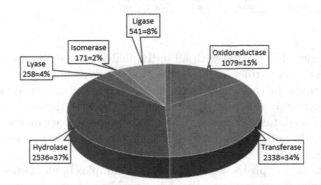

Fig. 3. Distribution of sequences in all classes in SWISS-PROT enzyme dataset (the percentages are rounded to the nearest integer)

4.2   Experimental Scenarios

In this section, two experiments are presented. In the first experiment, the unknown sequence alignment is aligned with all training or labelled sequences based on local sequence alignment technique. The alignment process is repeated for many times with different score matrices as shown in Table 2. In this experiment, the proposed fusion model is conducted to investigate the accuracy of

Table 2. A comparison between the accuracy (in %) of the single sequence alignment processes using different score matrices and the fusion of all single sequence alignment processes using sum fusion rule

Type of fusion	Type of score matrix	First experiment (unbalanced data)	Second experiment (balanced data)
Single sequence alignment method	BLOSUM62	89.8	88.8
	BLOSUM100	89.9	88.7
	BLOSUM30	88.9	88.9
	PAM10	89.3	86.7
	PAM100	90.3	86.9
	DAYHOFF	90.7	88.3
	GONNET	90.9	89.3
Fusion	Fusion of all scores (proposed model)	**93.9**	**92.2**

Table 3. Accuracy (in %) of the individual sequence alignment processes and the proposed fusion model using unbalanced dataset (first experiment)

Classes	No. of Sequences	Individual Sequence Alignment							Fusion-Based		
		BLOSUM62	BLOSUM100	BLOSUM30	PAM10	PAM100	DAYHOFF	GONNET	Sum	Max	Product
C1	540	490	489	482	486	490	493	492	510	507	511
C2	1170	1054	1055	1046	1051	1060	1060	1064	1111	1112	1110
C3	1270	1170	1172	1162	1162	1163	1166	1166	1212	1206	1202
C4	130	101	101	98	100	109	111	112	109	106	111
C5	90	65	66	62	63	70	69	68	68	62	65
C6	270	236	234	235	237	241	244	248	248	245	247
Total	3470	3116 ≈89.8	3117 ≈89.8	3085 ≈88.9	3099 ≈89.3	3133 ≈90.3	3143 ≈90.6	3150 ≈90.8	3258 ≈93.9	3238 ≈93.3	3246 ≈93.6

the proposed model compared with all individual sequence alignment processes. Three different fusion rules are used in this experiment, namely, sum, max, and product rules. In this experiment, the distribution of the sequences in all classes are completely different (the samples of the first three classes represent $\frac{2980}{3470} \approx 86\,\%$ of all dataset samples), which has a good impact on the classes that has a large number of samples and bad impact on the other classes. The results of this experiment are summarized in Tables 2 and 3.

In all classification problems, the number of samples in all classes is preferred to be approximately the same to avoid the problem of unbalanced distribution of the data, which gives high accuracy for the classes that have large number of samples than the other. In the second scenario, all classes have the same number of samples, 171 samples (Because 171 represents the number of samples of the fifth class, which represents the minimum number of samples as shown in Fig. 3). In this experiment, the same fusion rules that used in the first experiment are used (sum, max, and product rules). The results of this experiment are summarized in Tables 2 and 4.

5   Discussion

In all research experiments, the performance of the proposed model is evaluated using the accuracy, which represents the percentage of the total number

Table 4. Accuracy (in %) of the individual sequence alignment processes and the proposed fusion model using balanced dataset (second experiment)

Classes	No. of Sequences	Individual Sequence Alignment							Fusion-Based		
		BLOSUM62	BLOSUM100	BLOSUM30	PAM10	PAM100	DAYHOFF	GONNET	Sum	Max	Product
C1	171	144	148	147	145	145	146	145	155	152	153
C2	171	162	161	160	158	156	159	162	166	159	161
C3	171	162	166	163	160	160	162	165	169	167	168
C4	171	152	150	149	149	145	151	151	153	151	152
C5	171	141	142	144	137	137	139	140	141	143	142
C6	171	150	153	149	140	149	149	153	162	160	162
Total	1026	911 ≈88.8	920 ≈89.7	912 ≈88.9	889 ≈86.7	892 ≈86.9	906 ≈88.3	916 ≈89.3	946 ≈92.2	932 ≈90.8	938 ≈91.4

of predictions that were correct as follows, $Accuracy = \frac{N_t}{N_t + N_f}$, where N_t and N_f represent the total number of correct and total number of false for all test or unknown sequences respectively, and the total number of sequences is represented by $N = N_t + N_f$. All results are rounded to the nearest hundred.

As shown in Tables 2 and 3 many remarks are noticed. First, the results of the fusion-based model are better than all individual or single pairwise sequence alignment processes since the accuracy of the fusion-based model ranged from 93.3 % to 93.9 %, while the maximum individual pairwise sequence alignment is equal to 90.9 %. Second, the accuracies of each class using the sum rule fusion-based model are as follows, 94.4 %, 94.95 %, 95.4 %, 83.84 %, 75.55 %, and 91.85 %, which reflects the high accuracy in the first three classes because they have a large number of samples while the other three classes have a small number of samples. In other words, the dataset is unbalanced, which reflects a big variation in the accuracy of all classes. For this reason, the second experiment is performed to test the proposed model using balanced dataset. Third, the sum rule achieved the best accuracy while max rule achieved the worst accuracy. To conclude, the proposed fusion-based model achieved results significantly better than all other single pairwise alignments, which reflects the robustness of the proposed fusion model against all individual pairwise single alignments.

As shown in Tables 2 and 4 many remarks are noticed. First, the proposed fusion model achieved accuracy ranged from 90.8 % to 92.2 % compared with all other accuracies of the single pairwise sequence alignment processes, which achieved accuracy ranged from 86.7 % to 89.7 %, which reflects the robustness of the proposed fusion-based model against the single pairwise sequence alignment processes. The improvement of the accuracy results from combining different and independent outputs of single pairwise alignment processes. Second, as shown in Tables 3 and 4 we note that, the accuracy of different classes in each single sequence alignment are different, which reflects the independence of each single pairwise alignment. Moreover, the accuracies of all classes in the unbalanced data (i.e. the first experiment) are ranged from 68.9 % to 95.4 % (i.e. variation equal to 26.5 %). On the other hand, the accuracies of all classes in the balanced data ranged from 80.12 % to 98.8 %, which have a significantly lower variation=18.7 %, compared with the unbalanced data. Furthermore, the sum rule achieved the best accuracy and the max rule achieved the worst accuracy. In general, if all

Table 5. Comparison between the proposed model and the state of the art models

Reference	Method	Accuracy (in %)
[18]	Fuzzy-kNN	92.1
[19]	SVM + Wavelet	91.9
[20]	Functional Domain + Pseudo Position-Specific Scoring Matrix	93.7
Proposed model		93.9

classes have the same number of samples, there is no big discrimination between the accuracy of all classes, and the misclassified samples are distributed over all classes.

To conclude, the proposed model achieved a reasonable classification accuracy reached to 93.9 % when the dataset was unbalanced and 92.2 % when the data are balanced. Moreover, the distribution of the number of samples has a big impact on the accuracy of each class. The classification accuracy using the unbalanced data achieved a big variation between the accuracy of all classes, and the classes which have a large number of samples have a high probability to achieve accuracy better than the other classes. On the other hand, the variation in the accuracy of all classes in balanced data is much lower than in unbalanced data, and all classes have an equal probability to achieve high accuracy, which reflects that, the misclassification samples are distributed well over all classes. Moreover, the sum rule achieved a good results compared with the other two rules (i.e. max and product rules). Finally, our result is still much better than a lot of other models (see Table 5) and approaches that have been made for 6-class predictors, which reflects the robustness of our proposed model to classify enzyme functions.

6   Conclusions and Future Work

In this paper, an enzyme sequence function classification model based on scores fusion technique is proposed. In the proposed model, the outputs of seven pairwise local sequence alignment processes using different score matrices are represented by a vector of scores. All vectors are combined to determine the final vector of scores. The function or class label of the unknown sequence is the function of the candidate or element that has the maximum score. The proposed model achieved a reasonable classification accuracy reached to 93.9 % when the dataset was unbalanced. While the accuracy of the proposed model achieved 92.2 % when the dataset is balanced. The results of the proposed model achieved results better than in our experiment in [11] and the results in [18–20]. To conclude, the results which achieved by the proposed model are very promising and opens prospects for the future development.

References

1. Tseng, Y.Y., Li, W.H.: Classification of protein functional surfaces using structural characteristics. Proc. Natl. Acad. Sci. **109**(4), 1170–1175 (2012)
2. Coste, F., Garet, G., Groisillier, A., Nicolas, J., Tonon, T.: Automated enzyme classification by formal concept analysis. In: Glodeanu, C.V., Kaytoue, M., Sacarea, C. (eds.) ICFCA 2014. LNCS (LNAI), vol. 8478, pp. 235–250. Springer, Heidelberg (2014)
3. Kumar, C., Choudhary, A.: A top-down approach to classify enzyme functional classes and sub-classes using random forest. EURASIP J. Bioinform. Syst. Biol. **2012**(1), 1–14 (2012)
4. Faria, D., Ferreira, A.E., Falcão, A.O.: Enzyme classification with peptide programs: a comparative study. J. BMC Bioinform. **10**(1), 1–9 (2009)
5. Brown, D.P., Krishnamurthy, N., Sjölander, K.: Automated protein subfamily identification and classification. PLoS Comput. Biol. **3**(8), e160 (2007)
6. Busk, P.K., Lange, L.: Function-based classification of carbohydrate-active enzymes by recognition of short, conserved peptide motifs. Appl. Environ. Microbiol. **79**(11), 3380–3391 (2013)
7. Clark, W.T., Radivojac, P.: Analysis of protein function and its prediction from amino acid sequence. Proteins: Struct. Funct. Bioinform. **79**(7), 2086–2096 (2011)
8. des Jardins, M., Karp, P.D., Krummenacker, M., Lee, T.J., Ouzounis, C.A.: Prediction of enzyme classification from protein sequence without the use of sequence similarity. In: Proceedings of the 8th International Conference on Intelligent Systems for Molecular Biology, vol. 5, pp. 92–99 (1997)
9. Mohammed, A., Guda, C.: Computational approaches for automated classification of enzyme sequences. J. proteomics Bioinform. **4**, 147–152 (2011)
10. Lee, B.J., Shin, M.S., Oh, Y.J., Oh, H.S., Ryu, K.H.: Identification of protein functions using a machine-learning approach based on sequence-derived properties. Proteome Sci. **7**(1), 7–27 (2009)
11. Sharif, M.M., Thrwat, A., Amin, I.I., Ella, A., Hefeny, H.A.: Enzyme function classification based on sequence alignment. In: Mandal, J.K., Satapathy, S.C., Sanyal, M.K., Sarkar, P.P., Mukhopadhyay, A. (eds.) Information Systems Design and Intelligent Applications. AISC, vol. 340, pp. 409–418. Springer, Heidelberg (2015)
12. Xiong, J.: Essential Bioinformatics, 1st edn. Cambridge University Press, Cambridge (2006)
13. Olsson, B., Nilsson, P., Gawronska, B., Persson, A., Ziemke, T., Andler, S.F.: An information fusion approach to controlling complexity in bioinformatics research. In: Computational Systems Bioinformatics Conference, Workshops and Poster Abstracts, pp. 299–304. IEEE (2005)
14. Ibrahim, A., Tharwat, A.: Biometric authenticationmethods based on ear and finger knuckle images. Int. J. Comput. Sci. Issues (IJCSI) **11**(3), 134–138 (2014)
15. Kuncheva, L.I.: Combining Pattern Classifiers: Methods and Algorithms. Wiley, New York (2004)
16. Jain, A., Nandakumar, K., Ross, A.: Score normalization in multimodal biometric systems. Pattern Recogn. **38**(12), 2270–2285 (2005)
17. Bairoch, A.: The enzyme database in 2000. J. Nucleic Acids Res. **28**(1), 304–305 (2000). doi:10.1093/nar/28.1.304. http://www.expasy.ch/enzyme/
18. Huang, W.L., Chen, H.M., Hwang, S.F., Ho, S.Y.: Accurate prediction of enzyme subfamily class using an adaptive fuzzy k-nearest neighbor method. BioSystems **90**(2), 405–413 (2007)

19. Qiu, J.D., Huang, J.H., Shi, S.P., Liang, R.P.: Using the concept of chou's pseudo amino acid composition to predict enzyme family classes: an approach with support vector machine based on discrete wavelet transform. Protein Pept. Lett. **17**(6), 715–722 (2010)
20. Shen, H.B., Chou, K.C.: Ezypred: a top-down approach for predicting enzyme functional classes and subclasses. Biochem. Biophys. Res. Commun. **364**(1), 53–59 (2007)

A Low-Power Context-Aware System for Smartphone Using Hierarchical Modular Bayesian Networks

Jae-Min Yu and Sung-Bae Cho[⊠]

Department of Computer Science, Yonsei University, Seoul, South Korea
{yjam,sbcho}@yonsei.ac.kr

Abstract. Various applications using sensors and devices on smartphone are being developed. However, since limited battery capacity does not allow to utilize the phone all the time, studies to increase use-time of phone are very active. In this paper, we propose a hybrid system to increase the longevity of phone. User's context is recognized through hierarchical modular Bayesian networks, and unnecessary devices are inferred through device management rules. Inferring the user's context using sensor data, and considering device status, context inferred and user's tendency, we determine the device which is consuming the battery most. In the experiments with the real log data collected from 28 people for six months, we evaluated the proposed system resulting in the accuracy of 85.68 % and the improvement of battery consumption of about 6 %.

1 Introduction

The most serious concern in mobile user is the duration of battery, according to the technical document of Qualcomm in 2013. Despite the improvement of battery capacity and various applications, most of the users have spare battery.

The data collected by sensors and devices of smartphone are used for inferring context of user and developing applications with appropriate services. However, because battery of the smartphone has not been improved significantly for all day use, user's demand for long use-time is increasing, so that it stimulates the active relevant research.

In this paper, we propose a low-power device management system for smartphone using hierarchical Bayesian networks which can infer unnecessary device and user's context. The proposed system infers the user's context using Bayesian network. Considering the user's context, tendency inferred and the status of devices, we can infer the unnecessary device which can consume battery excessively. As a result, the proposed system can improve the duration of battery. In order to reveal the usefulness of the proposed system, we evaluated the inference accuracy of unnecessary device by real data collected from 28 people. The usefulness of the proposed system is confirmed by comparing with the alternatives.

© Springer International Publishing Switzerland 2015
E. Onieva et al. (Eds.): HAIS 2015, LNAI 9121, pp. 543–554, 2015.
DOI: 10.1007/978-3-319-19644-2_45

2 Backgrounds

2.1 Related Works

Moghimi performed user's context-aware in smartphone, proposed method to manage devices. In this research, to reduce complexity of context-aware, he used fuzzy inference model [6]. Zhuang adjusted update-time-gap to gain location information [10]. Herrman proposed low-power system which can adjust state of sensor device according to context [12]. Previous works define static situation for low-power platform, and adjust limited-sensor device (Table 1).

Table 1. Related works on low-power platform

Author	Method		Description
	Context-aware	Device adjustment	
Moghimi et al. (2013) [13]	O	X	Fuzzy inference model of low computation complexity considering context-aware of user in smartphone
Herrmann et al. (2012) [12]	X	Sensor device	Low-power system adjusting power consumption of sensor device according to context of user
Weiss et al. (2011) [8]	O	X	Analysis of correlation of context-aware of user using accelerometer sensor in smartphone for 70 people
Zhuang et al. (2010) [10]	X	GPS	Adjustment of update-time-gap of location information about static state of user
Bettini et al. (2007) [7]	X	Power consumption	Investigated power consumption of built-in sensor such as accelerometer, microphone, GPS, Wi-Fi, and Bluetooth

2.2 Device Management Application

The previous applications for low-power system did not take account for the use pattern of users, and had a problem that user cannot configure the setting directly. Applications considering user pattern have problem of cold-start which takes a long time to recognize the pattern and has few data sample. In order to fix this problem, we propose a device management application which can adjust appropriate device for user through context inference. The proposed system supports the automatic adjustment of battery-saving mode in accordance with each situation. This system can improve the accuracy of situation inference through learning of user patterns. Table 2 shows the commercial low-power device management applications.

Battery Guru developed by Qualcomm can grasp use-pattern and optimizes the device function of smartphone. This application leads to decreasing battery consumption. But these previous applications have a problem which takes a long time to recognize pattern or relies only on user's configuration.

Table 2. Commercial device management applications

Application	Saving mode	Configuration	Use pattern
Battery Guru	2	O	O
Battery Doctor	3	X	X
King of Energy Saving	3	O	X
2 Battery	2	O	X
Green Power	2	O	X
MX Battery Saver	4	X	O
DU Battery Saver	3	O	X
Battery Saver 2	2	X	X

3 The Proposed System

3.1 Structure Overview

In this paper, we analyze the correlation between situation and tendency of user and devices to develop low-power platform through related works and data collected. The sensor data are processed by decision tree and rules to provide input to Bayesian network. It is simple to implement rules and decision tree which have advantage of high accuracy when processing information such as acceleration data. As a movement of user, we distinguish state (walk, run, and stop) using acceleration sensor. As a posture of user, we distinguish posture (sit, stand, and lie) using orientation sensor, and distinguish user location of indoor and outdoor based on rules as information of GPS. In order to design Bayesian networks, we have to collect data and analyze the correlation.

Situation of user can be inferred by using modular Bayesian networks with tree structure using low-level data after preprocessing. Bayesian network is a good model for handling with uncertain input in smartphone environment. Because they are designed as tree structure, they can infer situation with low calculation complexity compared to the conventional Bayesian network. It has an effect on making low resource use of CPU. As network can be a powerful model through cumulated massive data learning, researchers are investigating the learning data in real time.

In order to process decision tree algorithm in mobile environment in real time, we implement it in C language and used Android application through NDK. In case of implementing in C, it can recognize fast because it does not use Java virtual machine, and decision tree has advantage of fast learning time (Fig. 1).

Figure 2 shows variation of sensor data according to state of user. This shows that we can classify data using time series sensor data on movement of user. In this paper, we extract movement of user from sensor data using decision tree. To detect movement state of user, we need to extract feature value as input of decision tree first. Sensor data used in decision tree are from acceleration, magnetic and orientation sensors. We use the equations below for these data.

$$sum\_X = \sum_{i=1}^{N} |x_i - x_{i-1}| \tag{1}$$

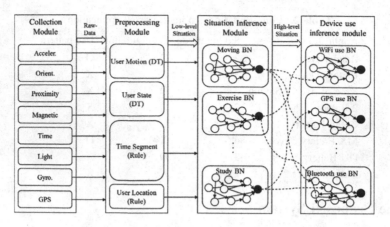

Fig. 1. The overall system structure

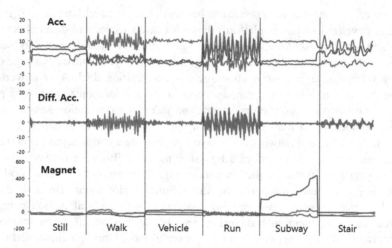

Fig. 2. An example of sensor data for each movement state

$$mean\_X = \frac{\sum\limits_{i=1}^{N} \sqrt{(x_{i+1} - x_i)^2}}{N} \qquad (2)$$

$$std\_X = \sqrt{\left(\sum \sqrt{(x_{i+1} - x_i)^2} - mean\_X\right)^2} \qquad (3)$$

$$SMA\_X = \sum_{1}^{N} (|x_i|) + (|y_i|) + (|z_i|) \qquad (4)$$

Here, X represents sensor, x means the value at present time of i, and N means the total data of amount in a window. Basically, we use 4 as feature value for each sensor. Table 3 is the list of total feature value used for decision tree.

Table 3. Feature value used for decision tree

Feature value	Description
sum_accX	Summation of X-axis acceleration
sum_accY	Summation of Y-axis acceleration
sum_accZ	Summation of Z-axis acceleration
std_accX	Standard deviation of X-axis acceleration
std_accY	Standard deviation of Y-axis acceleration
std_accZ	Standard deviation of Z-axis acceleration
sum_orientation	Summation of orientation
sum_pitch	Summation of pitch
sum_roll	Summation of roll
std_orientation	Standard deviation of orientation
std_pitch	Standard deviation of pitch
std_roll	Standard deviation of roll
sum_magX	Summation of X-axis magnetic field
sum_magY	Summation of Y-axis magnetic field
sum_magZ	Summation of Z-axis magnetic field
std_magX	Standard deviation of X-axis magnetic field
std_magY	Standard deviation of Y-axis magnetic field
std_magZ	Standard deviation of Z-axis magnetic field
SMA	Signal magnitude area

The proposed system consists of data collection module, preprocessing module, situation inference module, and device use inference module. Data collection module collects mobile sensor data and status of device. In preprocessing module, in order to decrease the time complexity, we preprocess the data using decision tree and rule-based method as shown in Table 4. Situation inference module infers user's context using the input data preprocessed. Considering the tendency of user, battery status, and inferred situation, device use inference module can infer unnecessary device and adjust automatically.

Table 4. The result of preprocessed sensor data

Method	Type	Use pattern
Decision tree	Acceleration, direction	Walk, run, stop
	Magnetic, Gyro	Sit, stand, lie
Rules	Light	Very bright, bright, normal, dim, very dim
	Time	Morning, afternoon, evening, dawn
	GPS	School, home, library, theatre, cafeteria
	Battery amount	Low, normal, high

Input:

    User situation, tendency of user, mobile state

Output:

    State of devices unnecessary

    Device =$\{d_1, d_2, \ldots, d_i\}$

    Select inference module through the state of devices;

    Configure the input value for each module;

    Calculate linearly probability;

    Decide the state of unnecessary device based on critical value;

    Repeated for selected inference module;

Fig. 3. Inference algorithm of unused devices

3.2   Hierarchical Probabilistic Model

Our previous work proposed to recognize low-power situation of user using linear inference [3]. We recognized situation of rest, sleep, dining, exercise, work, shopping and lesson using the proposed modular situation inference. According to the criteria of situation classification of National Statistical Office, we define 8 situations. Unnecessary device was not being utilized. Because this device is turned on, this can consume battery. For example, in outdoor, if Wi-Fi device is turned on, we did not use Wi-Fi. But that device always can try to search access point or Wi-Fi connection nearby. The inference technology proposed in this paper figures out unnecessary state of each device hierarchically considering the tendency of user and present mobile state. This technology reuses the result of user situation inference as evidence value. We use the tendency of user as Big-five tendency model proposed by McCrae and John [5]. Table 5 is the definition of I/O of probability model of each device.

3.3   Inference and Management of Unnecessary Device

When we infer unnecessary device, we calculate as the Eq. (5) based on linear inference algorithm by Das considering only coincidence of state value about cause-and-effect relationship of output value.

$$P(S) = \sum_{j=1}^{n} \omega_i p\left(S | Comp(I_j = i_j^{S_{ij}})\right) \tag{5}$$

$Comp\left(I_j = i_j^{s_j}\right)$ is the value of CPT on coincidence situation of node i. W_i means node i influence to the final situation.

Table 5. Input and output of inference Bayesian network of unnecessary device

Classification	Type	Description
Input	Sleeping	We consider co-relationship between the result of situation inference of user and device use based on the situation classification of National Statistical Office
	Dining	
	Work	
	Lesson	
	Watching	
	Exercising	
	Moving	
	Rest	
	Battery state	Considering usable device or not via battery state
	Screen state	Considering the state of screen be turned on or off
	Extroversion	We consider co-relationship with the tendency of user based on Big-five model
	Openness	
	Congeniality	
	Sincerity	
	Faithfulness	
Output	Device	Wi-Fi, GPS, Bluetooth, Data synchronized device

Figure 3 shows the inference algorithm to find unnecessary devices. First, we choose the inference module in order to understand the state of device d_i. We configure evidence value of input node of smartphone and the tendency and situation of user which is needed for inference module, and calculate probability value of unnecessary node. Next, we calculate conditional probability value and intermediate node. Finally, calculate probability value of result node which means the state of unnecessary device, and decide the unnecessary state of device based on a threshold. This process is repeated for device management inference module. Through the repeated result, we carry out device management. Figure 4 shows the graphic user interface of device management for each situation. GUI is designed to configure battery-saving level, and user can confirm to configure setting and working system.

To show the usefulness of the developed application in low-power environment, we designed a scenario which is effective for battery-saving and utilizing device management application. The scenario aims to show the effect of device management application through situation inference and alteration of state of device in addition to situation and tendency of user.

4   Experimental Results

4.1   Evaluation of Performance

The performance of decision tree to identify the type of transportation is evaluated first. User's movement state can be classified into stop, run and walk. The type of transportation is classified into vehicle, subway, train and taxi. As input value, we use sensor value of acceleration, magnetic, and orientation. After preprocessing, the accuracy of

Fig. 4. Device management application

10-fold cross validation is used for classification of decision tree with the input of the variation of axis of sensor, standard deviation and SMA. Tables 6 and 7 show the result of accuracy of 10-fold cross validation.

Table 6. Accuracy of classifying the state of movement

Class	TP rate	FP rate	Precision	Recall	F-measure	ROC area
Staying	0.947	0.014	0.957	0.947	0.952	0.984
Walking	0.908	0.079	0.912	0.908	0.91	0.96
Running	0.848	0.042	0.828	0.848	0.838	0.966
(Avg.)	0.901	0.045	0.899	0.901	0.9	0.97

Table 7. Accuracy of classifying the type of transportation

Class	TP rate	FP rate	Precision	Recall	F-measure	ROC area
Train	0.873	0.052	0.885	0.873	0.879	0.957
Car	0.928	0.072	0.841	0.928	0.883	0.96
Subway	00762	0.051	0.863	0.762	0.809	0.914
Bus	0.91	0.02	0.833	0.91	0.87	0.969
(Avg.)	0.86	0.054	0.861	0.86	0.859	0.946

Tables 8 and 9 show the confusion matrix of the type of transportation and the state of movement using decision tree algorithm. In Table 8, the state of walking has higher performance compared with the other movement states. For the type of transportation, subway and train may be confused.

Table 8. Confusion matrix for movement state

	a	b	c
a = Staying	1020	43	7
b = Walking	45	1032	46
c = Running	0	69	746

Table 9. Confusion matrix for type of transportation

	a	b	c	d
a = Train	1038	47	94	10
b = Car	22	1024	32	25
c = Subway	105	130	860	34
d = Bus	8	16	10	345

Figure 5 shows the performance of each classifier for the type of transportation. We compared the classifiers such as decision tree, SVM, Multi-layer perceptron and RBF network. In Fig. 5, running time of decision tree is more stable and faster than the other classifiers.

4.2 Inference Accuracy of Unnecessary Device

In order to evaluate the inference accuracy of unnecessary device of the proposed system, we collected data of 6985 for 28 university students during 14 days. In total 8

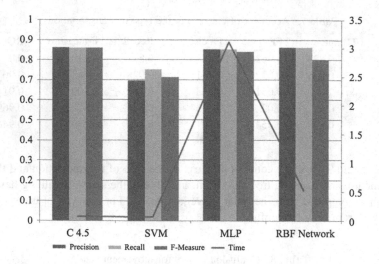

Fig. 5. Comparison of the accuracy and runtime for classifying the type of transportation

situations such as sleeping, dining, work, lesson, watching, moving and rest, we collected GPS, Wi-Fi, data synchronization, Bluetooth and state of battery. We investigate the tendency of users using NEO-RI-R survey. Using the collected data, we measure the accuracy comparing to result of inferred network of unnecessary device. Figure 6 presents average of 85.68 % accuracy. One of devices which have the highest accuracy is Bluetooth because of the definite usage distribution of data. Also, because GPS device is related in various situations, the accuracy was low.

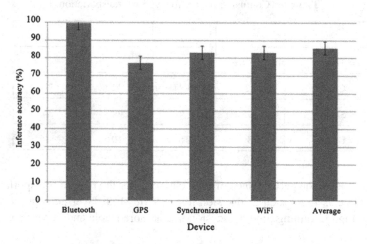

Fig. 6. Accuracy of inferring unnecessary devices

4.3 Comparing with Battery Level

In order to evaluate the performance of the proposed device management system, we compared the battery level for 1 day in environment with two Galaxy S4 smartphones.

One S4 device installed the proposed application. Figure 7 compares the battery level, resulting in the decrease of battery consumption about 6 % compared to existing one. This induced to increase the use time for about two hours.

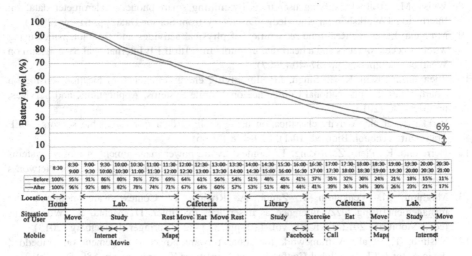

Fig. 7. Comparing battery levels

5   Concluding Remarks

In this paper, in order to increase the longevity of using smartphone through device management, we proposed a device management system based on hierarchical Bayesian networks inferring unnecessary devices and user's situations. In the experiments, we measured the accuracy of inference of the proposed system, compared the battery consumption, and confirmed the increased longevity.

Future works can be divided into short-term and long-term research. In the short-term, we need to incorporate a number of wearable devices and develop user-customized services based on them. In the long-term, we have to improve the context recognition model by learning larger data of more users.

References

1. Qualcomm, Designing mobile devices for low power and thermal efficiency. Qualcomm Technologies Report, pp. 1–13 (2013)
2. Qualcomm, BatteryGuru. (2014). https://play.google.com/
3. Yang, K.-M., Cho, S.-B.: A low-power consumption contet-aware system using modular Bayesian network with linear inference algorithm. In: Proceedings of the 41th KCC Conference, pp. 1370–1372 (2014)
4. National Statistical Office, Life style research (2010). http://kostat.go.kr/
5. McCrae, R.R., John, O.P.: An introduction to the five-factor model and its applications. J. Pers. **60**(2), 175–215 (1992)

6. Susi, M., Renaudin, V., Lachapelle, G.: Motion mode recognition and step detection algorithms for mobile phone users. Sensors **13**(2), 1539–1562 (2013)
7. Bettini, C., et al.: Anonymity in location-based services: towards a general framework. In: International Conference on Mobile Data Management, pp. 69–76 (2007)
8. Weiss, M., et al.: Identifying user traits by mining smart phone accelerometer data. In: International Workshop on Knowledge Discovery from Sensor Data, pp. 61–69 (2011)
9. Munguia, E., et al.: Real-time recognition of physical activities and their intensities using wireless accelerometers and a heart rate monitor. In: 11th IEEE International Symposium on Wearable Computers, pp. 37–40 (2007)
10. Zhenyun, Z., Kim, K.-H., Singh, J.P.: Improving energy efficiency of location sensing on smartphones. In: International Conference on Mobile Systems, Applications, and Services, pp. 315–330 (2010)
11. Parkka, J., et al.: Activity classification using realistic data from wearable sensors. IEEE Trans. Inf. Technol. Biomed. **10**(1), 119–128 (2006)
12. Herrmann, R., Piero, Z., Rosing, T.: Context aware power management of mobile systems for sensing applications. In: Conference on Information Processing in Sensor Networks (2012)
13. Moghimi, M., Venkatesh, J., Zappi, P., Rosing, T.: Context-aware mobile power management using fuzzy inference as a service. In: Uhler, D., Mehta, K., Wong, J.L. (eds.) MobiCase 2012. LNICST, vol. 110, pp. 314–327. Springer, Heidelberg (2013)
14. Yashiro, T., et al.: A framework for context-aware power management on embedded devices. In: IEEE 1st Global Conference on Consumer Electronics, pp. 588–592 (2012)
15. Zhao, X., et al.: A system context-aware approach for battery lifetime prediction in smart phones. In: Proceedings of the 2011 ACM Symposium on Applied Computing, pp. 641–646 (2011)
16. Nishihara, K., Kazuhisa, I., Sakai, J.: Power saving in mobile devices using context-aware resource control. In: International Conference on Networking and Computing, pp. 220–226 (2010)
17. Nishkam, R., et al.: Context-aware battery management for mobile phones. In: IEEE International Conference on Pervasive Computing and Communications, pp. 224–233 (2008)

HAIS Applications

A Parallel Meta-heuristic for Solving a Multiple Asymmetric Traveling Salesman Problem with Simulateneous Pickup and Delivery Modeling Demand Responsive Transport Problems

E. Osaba[✉], F. Diaz, E. Onieva, Pedro López-García, R. Carballedo, and A. Perallos

Deusto Institute of Technology (DeustoTech), University of Deusto, Av. Universidades 24, 48007 Bilbao, Spain
{e.osaba,fernando.diaz,enrique.onieva,p.lopez, roberto.carballedo,perallos}@deusto.es

Abstract. Transportation is an essential area in the nowadays society. Due to the rapid technological progress, it has gained a great importance, both for business sector and citizenry. Among the different types of transport, one that has gained notoriety recently is the transportation on-demand, because it can affect very positively the people quality of life. There are different kinds of on-demand transportation systems, being the Demand Responsive Transit (DRT) one of the most important one. In this work, a real-life DRT problem is proposed, and modeled as a Rich Traveling Salesman Problem. Specifically, the problem presented is a Multiple Asymmetric Traveling Salesman Problem with Simultaneous Pickup and Delivery. Furthermore, a benchmark for this new problem is also proposed, and its first resolution is offered. For the resolution of this benchmark the recently developed Golden Ball meta-heuristic has been implemented.

Keywords: On demand transportation · Demand responsive transport · Traveling salesman problem · Golden ball · Meta-heuristic · Combinatorial optimization

1 Introduction

Transportation is an important issue for the society these days, both for citizens and the business sector. Regarding the transportation in the business world, the rapid advance of technology has made the logistic increasingly important in this area. The fact that anyone in the world can be well connected has led transport networks to be very demanding, something that was less important in the past. Today, a competitive logistic network can make the difference between some companies and others.

On the other hand, public transport is used by almost all the population and it affects the life quality of the people. In addition, there are different kinds of

© Springer International Publishing Switzerland 2015
E. Onieva et al. (Eds.): HAIS 2015, LNAI 9121, pp. 557–567, 2015.
DOI: 10.1007/978-3-319-19644-2_46

public transportation systems, each one with its own characteristics. Nonetheless, all of them share the same disadvantages, which are the finite capacity of the vehicles, the geographical area of coverage, and the service schedules and frequencies.

With the intention of addressing these drawbacks the concept of Transportation-On-Demand (TOD) arises [1]. This concept is related with the transportation of goods or passengers between specific origins and destinations at the request of customers. Almost all the TOD systems are characterized by sharing the following three conflicting objectives: minimizing operating costs, maximizing the number of requests served, and minimizing clients inconveniences.

There are several kind of TOD problems, being the Demand Responsive Transport, or Demand Responsive Transit (DRT) one of the most important [2]. This problem is characterized by flexible routing and scheduling of small/medium vehicles operating in shared-ride mode between pick-up and drop-off locations according to passengers needs. A DRT system can be applicable in situations where passengers are transported between concrete origins and destinations. One common application of these kinds of systems is the transport service in areas of low passenger demand, where a regular transport service is not economically viable. Another typical application is the door-to-door services for handicapped or elderly people. In this context, users formulate two different related requests: an outbound request from home to a destination, and an inbound request for the return trip. This kind of transport has a great social interest since, above all, it helps to ensure welfare of people with special needs.

DRT and other kind of on-demand problems are the focus of many studies nowadays [3,4]. In addition, many sophisticated on-demand systems have been implemented in several major cities across the world, as Bristol (United Kingdom)[1], Cape Town[2], or London[3].

The objective of this research is to address one DRT problem. To achieve this goal, the DRT problem has been modeled as a Rich Traveling Salesman Problem (R-TSP), also known as Multi-Attribute Traveling Salesman Problem. Nowadays, these rich or multi-attribute problems, as well as the multi-attribute vehicle routing ones, are a hot issue in the literature [5]. These sorts of problems are specific cases of routing problems, with complex formulations and multiple restrictions. Furthermore, they have a great scientific interest because of their complexity of resolution, which represents a scientific challenge, and their applicability to real-world situations, which is greater than the conventional routing problems.

In this work an R-TSP is presented, to be more accurate, a Multiple Asymmetric Traveling Salesman Problem with Simultaneous Pickup and Delivery. Furthermore, the first benchmark for this problem is also detailed in this paper, and its first ever resolution is offered. To deal with this problem the recently proposed Golden Ball (GB) meta-heuristic has been implemented [6].

---

[1] http://www.bristoldialaride.org.uk/.

[2] https://www.capetown.gov.za/en/Transport/Pages/AboutDialaRide.aspx.

[3] https://www.tfl.gov.uk/modes/dial-a-ride/.

The remainder of this work is structured as follows: In the following section the proposed MA-TSP-SPD is described and formulated. In Sect. 3 the benchmark used for the presented problem is detailed. In Sect. 4 the technique implemented for the resolution of this benchmark is depicted. Additionally, the experimentation carried out is described in Sect. 5. Finally, conclusions and future work are explained in Sect. 6.

2 Description of the Proposed MA-TSP-SPD

As has been introduced in the previous section, an R-TSP is proposed in this paper, with the aim of addressing different kind of DRT problems. The principal feature of a R-TSP problem is its complex formulation, which is composed by multiple constraints. This feature directly leads to an increased complexity of resolution, which entails to a major scientific challenge at the same time. DRT problems are important because they model many real world problems and, therefore, efficient solving techniques for that kind of problems can be useful in many interesting practical applications. The problem presented in this research is a MA-TSP-SPD, which has three main characteristics.

1. *Multiple Vehicles:* This is a typical feature of the often studied Multiple Traveling Salesman Problem [7]. In this way, a fleet K composed by a finite and fixed k number of vehicles is available in the proposed MA-TSP-SPD. These k vehicles have to be employed to meet the customers needs. Additionally, there is a central depot in which all the vehicle routes have to begin and end. This feature requires the problem to plan exactly k paths, one for each available vehicle. Besides, each vehicle cannot plan a route composed by more than a fixed q nodes.
2. *Asymmetry:* The traveling costs in the proposed MA-TSP-SPD are asymmetric. This means that the traveling cost from any i node to another j node is different from the reverse trip cost. This feature is not common in most routing problems that can be found in the literature, and it brings realism and complexity to the problem. Anyway, asymmetric costs has been applied previously in the literature [8,9]. Because of the realism it brings, it noteworthy that this feature is very valuable in DRT situations.
3. *Simultaneous Pickup and Delivery:* This property is an adaptation of the often used pickup and delivery system of some routing problems [10,11]. Basically, this system consists in the existence of two types of nodes, the *delivery nodes* and the *pickup nodes*. The first ones are those points in where the peoples leave the vehicle. On the other hand, in *pickup nodes* is where the people who have requested the transportation access to the vehicle.
   In addition, it is important to highlight that, due to the simultaneous nature of this feature, in one concrete node more than one customer can leave or take the vehicle. This fact leads to the generation of routes in which the number of delivery nodes is greater than the amount of pickup nodes, and vice versa. Furthermore, the depot, mimicking the behavior of a central bus station, can also act as a pickup or delivery node.

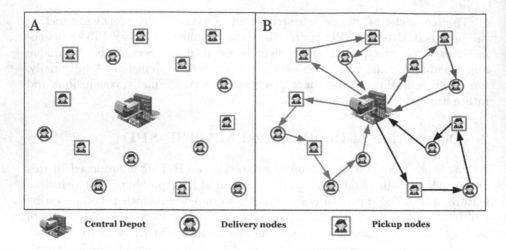

Fig. 1. A 15-noded and $k=4$ possible instance of the MA-TSP-SPD, and a possible solution

This feature is important in many DRT problems, as for example, the door-to-door transportation of elderly people.

Therefore, the proposed MA-TSP-SPD is a rich routing problem with asymmetric costs, in which the objective is to find exactly k number of different routes, each one with a maximum length of q nodes, minimizing the total cost of the complete solution.

In Fig. 1(a) an example of a MA-TSP-SPD instance with 15 nodes, and $k=4$ is depicted. Furthermore, in Fig. 1(b) a possible solution for this instance is shown.

In this manner, the presented MA-TSP-SPD can be defined on a complete graph $G = (V, A)$ where $V = \{v_0, v_1, v_2, \ldots, v_n,\}$ is the set of vertexes which represents the nodes of the system. On the other hand, $A = \{(v_i, v_j) : v_i, v_j \in V, i \neq j\}$ is the set of arcs which represents the interconnection between nodes. Each arc has an associated distance cost d_{ij}. Due to the asymmetry feature $d_{ij} \neq d_{ji}$. Furthermore, the vertex v_0 represents the depot, and the rest are the visiting points. In addition, with the aim of facilitating the problem formulation, the set of customers V can be separated into two different subsets, the first one for the *pickup nodes* $PN = \{pn_1, pn_2, \ldots, pn_n\}$, and the second one for the *delivery nodes* $DN = \{dn_{n+1}, dn_{n+2}, \ldots, dn_{n+m}\}$.

Additionally, the permutation codification has been used for the representation of the solutions. Thus, each solution X is encoded by a permutation of numbers, which represents the different routes that compose that solution. Besides, with the aim of distinguishing the routes in one solution, they are separated by zeros. For example, supposing a set of six *pickup nodes* $PN = \{pn_1, pn_2, pn_3, pn_4, pn_5, pn_6\}$, and seven *delivery nodes* $DN = \{dn_7, dn_8, dn_9, dn_{10}, dn_{11}, dn_{12}, dn_{13}\}$. One possible solution with $k=3$ would be $X = (pn_2, pn_5, dn_7, dn_9, \mathbf{0}, pn_4, dn_{12}, dn_{11}, pn_6, dn_{13}, \mathbf{0}, pn_1, dn_{10}, pn_3, dn_8)$.

Finally, the proposed MA-TSP-SPD can be mathematically formulated in the following way:
Minimize:

$$\sum_{i=0}^{n+m} \sum_{j=0}^{n+m} \sum_{r=1}^{k} d_{ij} x_{ij}^r \tag{1}$$

Where:

$$x_{ij}^r \in \{0,1\}, \quad i,j = 0, \ldots, n+m, i \neq j; r = 1 \ldots k \tag{2}$$

Subject to constraints:

$$\sum_{i=0}^{n+m} \sum_{r=1}^{k} x_{ij}^r = 1, \quad i = 0, \ldots, n+m; i \neq j \tag{3}$$

$$\sum_{j=0}^{n+m} \sum_{r=1}^{k} x_{ij}^r = 1, \quad j = 0, \ldots, n+m; j \neq i \tag{4}$$

$$\sum_{i=0}^{n+m} \sum_{j=0}^{n+m} x_{ij}^r \leq q, \quad r = 1 \ldots k \tag{5}$$

$$\sum_{j=0}^{n+m} \sum_{r=1}^{k} x_{0j}^r = k \tag{6}$$

$$\sum_{i=0}^{n+m} \sum_{r=1}^{k} x_{i0}^r = k \tag{7}$$

$$\sum_{i=0}^{n+m} x_{ij}^r - \sum_{l=0}^{n+m} x_{jl}^r, \quad j = 0, \ldots, n+m; r = 1 \ldots k \tag{8}$$

$$\sum_{j=0}^{n+m} x_{ij}^r - \sum_{l=0}^{n+m} x_{li}^r, \quad i = 0, \ldots, n+m; r = 1 \ldots k \tag{9}$$

The first clause represents the objective function, which is the sum of the costs of all routes of the solution, and it must be minimized. The formula 2 depicts the nature of the binary variable x_{ij}^k , which is 1 if the vehicle k uses the arc (i, j), and 0 otherwise. Functions 3 and 4 assure that all the nodes are visited exactly once. Besides, sentence 5 guarantees that all routes are shorter than the maximum allowed length q. On the other hand, constraints 6 and 7 ensure that the total amount of vehicles leaving the depot, and the number of vehicles that return to it is the same. In addition, that number has to be k, i.e., the total amount of available vehicles. Finally, the correct flow of each route is ensured thanks to functions 8 and 9 functions.

3   Description of the Used Benchmark

As it is well-known, the use of a benchmark to study how good a technique is at solving an optimization problem is a crucial factor. In this way, the benchmark presented in this work for the proposed MA-TSP-SDP is the same as presented in the work [12], which is a modification of the ATSP Benchmark that can be found in the TSPLib Benchmark [13].

In this way, 19 different instances have been used for the experimentation, which have from 17 to 443 nodes. It is noteworthy that the first node of each instance is the depot. Additionally, a parameter called $type_i$ suggests if the node i is a *delivery node* or a *pickup node*. This parameter has been set using the following procedure:

$$type_i = pickup\ node, \quad \forall i \in \{1, 3, 5, \ldots, n\}$$

$$type_i = delivery\ node, \quad \forall i \in \{2, 4, 6, \ldots, n\}$$

Furthermore, the number of vehicles available for each instance has been established in $k=4$. Besides, the maximum length of each route has been set in $q = n/3$, where n is the total number of nodes of the instance.

With the aim of allowing the replication of this experimentation, the benchmark developed is available under request to the corresponding author of this paper.

4   The Proposed Golden Ball

The problem proposed in this paper is applicable to real-world situations, this is the reason why it has been opted for a meta-heuristic with a great robustness and quick execution. Robustness is the ability of providing always similar results, leading to a small standard deviation. This feature, along with the quick execution, is very appreciated in real-world applications. The algorithm selected to deal with the presented MA-TSP-SPD, the Golden Ball, is a recently proposed technique which meets these two requirements. The first complete version of the GB, and its practical use for solving complex problems have been presented in 2014 by Osaba, Diaz and Onieva [6].

The main characteristics of the GB can be summarized as follows. The GB is a multiple-population based meta-heuristic inspired by some concepts of soccer sport. First, in the initialization phase, the whole population of solutions (called players) is randomly created. Then, these created players are randomly divided among a fixed number of subpopulations (called team). Each team has its own training method (or coach), which is randomly assigned in this first phase. This training is the way in which each player in the team individually evolves along the execution. One training function could be, for example, the well-known 2-opt [14]. Another important training is the called Custom Training. In this training, a player which is trapped in a local optimum receives a special training in cooperation with the best player of its team. One custom training function could be, for example, the well-known Order Crossover [15].

Algorithm 1. Pseudocode of the GB algorithm
1   Initialization of the initial population;
2   Division of players into different teams;
3   **repeat**
4   Competition league is restarted **for** *each matchday* **do**
5   **for** *each team t_i in the system* **do**
6   Training phase for t_i;
7   Custom training session for t_i;
8   Calculation of the quality of t_i;
9   **end**
10   Matchday in which matches are played;
11   **end**
12   Period of transfers;
13 **until** *termination criterion reached*;
14 Return the fitness of best player of the system;

Once the initialization phase is finished, the competition phase starts. This second step is divided in seasons, composed by weeks. Every week all the teams train independently, and they face each other creating a competition league. At the end of every season, a transfer procedure takes place. In this procedure the players and coaches can switch teams. The competition phase is repeated iteratively until the termination criterion is reached.

The execution of the GB is briefly schematized in Algorithm 1. For further information about the GB, the reading of [6] is highly recommended.

5   Experimentation

In this section the conducted experimentation is detailed, and it is divided into two different subsections. In the first one (Sect. 5.1), the parametrization used

Table 1. Summary of the characteristics of GB

Number of teams (TN)	4
Number of players per team (PT)	12
Number of trainings without improvement for a *custom training*	6
Number of trainings without improvement for a *special transfers*	12
Conventional training functions	2-opt, Insertion, Swapping Routes, & Insertion Routes
Custom training function	Random Route Crossover

Table 2. Results obtained by the GB for the proposed MA-TSP-SPD. For each instance results average, standard deviation, median, interquartile range and time average are shown

Instance	Avg	S. dev.	Median	I. R.	Time
MA-TSP-SPD_br17	66.1	1.4	65	2.2	0.71
MA-TSP-SPD_ftv33	1652.2	88.4	1575	149.2	1.35
MA-TSP-SPD_ftv35	1828.8	93.3	1765	123.5	1.46
MA-TSP-SPD_ftv38	1883.7	77.5	1813	120.7	1.64
MA-TSP-SPD_p43	5888.5	19.2	5873	24.7	1.69
MA-TSP-SPD_ftv44	2063.5	142.2	1896	260.7	1.83
MA-TSP-SPD_ftv47	2214.3	517.2	2235	186.0	2.23
MA-TSP-SPD_ry48p	18160.2	604.7	17784	601.5	3.09
MA-TSP-SPD_ft53	8614.5	444.8	8303	655.0	4.21
MA-TSP-SPD_ftv55	2239.6	141.6	2204	156.7	3.77
MA-TSP-SPD_ftv64	2505.9	145.1	2385	196.0	3.31
MA-TSP-SPD_ftv70	2720.5	136.7	2598	256.7	3.75
MA-TSP-SPD_ft70	44460.3	809.9	43717	1199.0	4.49
MA-TSP-SPD_kro124p	48277.6	2036.4	46407	3028.0	13.41
MA-TSP-SPD_ftv170	5482.5	309.6	5261	320.7	21.12
MA-TSP-SPD_rbg323	1851.3	59.8	1797	112.7	72.54
MA-TSP-SPD_rbg358	1856.3	72.6	1800	122.2	81.29
MA-TSP-SPD_rbg403	2859.2	50.6	2807	88.0	87.25
MA-TSP-SPD_rbg443	3121.4	55.7	3110	91.2	136.59

for the GB is described. On the other hand, in Sect. 5.2 the obtained results obtained are depicted.

5.1 Parameters of the GB

The population size used for the GB is 48, which has been divided into 4 teams of 12 players each. In addition, the number of trainings without improvement needed to perform a custom training and a special transfer are, respectively, 6 and 12. The well-known *2-opt* and *Insertion* functions have been used as conventional training functions. These operators are intra-route functions [16], i.e., they work within a specific route. Additionally, two inter-route functions have been developed:

– *Swapping Routes:* This operator selects randomly two nodes of two randomly selected routes. These nodes are swapped.
– *Insertion Routes:* This function selects and extracts one random node from one random route. After that, this node is re-inserted in a random position in another randomly selected route.

Table 3. Best solutions found by the GB for the proposed problem

Instance	Fitness	Evaluations	Time
MA-TSP-SPD_br17	65	40	0.65
MA-TSP-SPD_ftv33	1515	3783	1.72
MA-TSP-SPD_ftv35	1703	1939	1.71
MA-TSP-SPD_ftv38	1800	6351	2.28
MA-TSP-SPD_p43	5850	3421	1.53
MA-TSP-SPD_ftv44	1872	8887	3.57
MA-TSP-SPD_ftv47	2202	5047	2.07
MA-TSP-SPD_ry48p	17394	5157	2.14
MA-TSP-SPD_ft53	7901	8028	3.97
MA-TSP-SPD_ftv55	2001	5757	2.92
MA-TSP-SPD_ftv64	2323	7867	3.82
MA-TSP-SPD_ftv70	2540	16719	6.35
MA-TSP-SPD_ft70	43563	14190	5.26
MA-TSP-SPD_kro124p	45991	31664	13.85
MA-TSP-SPD_ftv170	5054	30779	21.20
MA-TSP-SPD_rbg323	1795	62850	80.72
MA-TSP-SPD_rbg358	1773	87121	112.56
MA-TSP-SPD_rbg403	2801	44375	81.67
MA-TSP-SPD_rbg443	3044	86175	163.57

It is noteworthy that all these functions take into account both the vehicles capacity, and the class of the nodes demands, never making infeasible solutions. Furthermore, the Random Route Crossover has been used as custom training function [6]. Finally, the configuration used for GB is summarized in Table 1.

5.2   Results

All the tests have been performed on an Intel Core i5 2410 laptop, with 2.30 GHz and a RAM of 4 GB. All the instances described in Sect. 3 has been used in the experimentation. The name of each instance has a number that represents the number of nodes it has. 30 executions have been run for each instance, and five different parameters are shown: average fitness value and its standard deviation, the median, the interquartile range and the average runtime (in seconds). These results can be observed in Table 2.

Besides, the fitness of the best solution found for each instance is shown in Table 3. Furthermore, the amount of objective function evaluations needed to reach these solutions are also represented, as well as the runtime.

6   Conclusions and Future Work

In this research a new multi-attribute TSP has been proposed, with the aim of addressing different sort of DRT problems. Concretely, the presented problem is a Multiple Asymmetric Traveling Salesman Problem with Simultaneous Pickup and Delivery. The objective of this problem is to find and exact number of routes, visiting all the nodes once, and only once, and minimizing the total traveling cost. Furthermore, it is noteworthy that these traveling costs are asymmetric, and that two kinds of nodes coexist in the system: *delivery nodes* and *pickup nodes*.

Additionally, the recently proposed Golden Ball meta-heuristic has been used to solve the proposed benchmark composed by 19 instances. This benchmark is an adaption of the well-known ATSP benchmark that can be found in the TSPLib, and it has been previously used to solve other R-TSP problems. Finally, the solutions offered for the mentioned benchmark are considered the best ones, since it is the first time that the MA-TSP-SPD has been dealt in the literature.

As further work, it is intended to find another real-life situation, with a great social interest, with the aim of modeling them as a multi-attribute vehicle routing problem, and addressing them.

Acknowledgement. The authors would like to thank the Entornos inteligentes ubicuos aplicados a la trazabilidad en el sector de transportes y vehiculares project (UBI-TRACE PC2013-71A) for its support in the development of this work.

References

1. Cordeau, J.F., Laporte, G., Potvin, J.Y., Savelsbergh, M.W.: Transportation on demand. Transp. Handb. Oper. Res. Manage. Sci. **14**, 429–466 (2004)
2. Brake, J., Nelson, J.D., Wright, S.: Demand responsive transport: towards the emergence of a new market segment. J. Transp. Geogr. **12**(4), 323–337 (2004)
3. Ritzinger, U., Puchinger, J., Hartl, R.F.: Dynamic programming based metaheuristics for the dial-a-ride problem. Ann. Oper. Res. **228**, 1–18 (2014)
4. Paquette, J., Cordeau, J.F., Laporte, G., Pascoal, M.: Combining multicriteria analysis and tabu search for dial-a-ride problems. Transp. Res. Part B: Methodol. **52**, 1–16 (2013)
5. Vidal, T., Crainic, T.G., Gendreau, M., Prins, C.: Heuristics for multi-attribute vehicle routing problems: a survey and synthesis. Eur. J. Oper. Res. **231**(1), 1–21 (2013)
6. Osaba, E., Diaz, F., Onieva, E.: Golden ball: a novel meta-heuristic to solve combinatorial optimization problems based on soccer concepts. Appl. Intell. **41**(1), 145–166 (2014)
7. Bektas, T.: The multiple traveling salesman problem: an overview of formulations and solution procedures. Omega **34**(3), 209–219 (2006)
8. Laporte, G., Mercure, H., Nobert, Y.: An exact algorithm for the asymmetrical capacitated vehicle routing problem. Networks **16**(1), 33–46 (1986)
9. Toth, P., Vigo, D.: A heuristic algorithm for the symmetric and asymmetric vehicle routing problems with backhauls. Eur. J. Oper. Res. **113**(3), 528–543 (1999)

10. Montané, F.A.T., Galvao, R.D.: A tabu search algorithm for the vehicle routing problem with simultaneous pick-up and delivery service. Comput. Oper. Res. **33**(3), 595–619 (2006)
11. Bianchessi, N., Righini, G.: Heuristic algorithms for the vehicle routing problem with simultaneous pick-up and delivery. Comput. Oper. Res. **34**(2), 578–594 (2007)
12. Osaba, E., Onieva, E., Diaz, F., Carballedo, R., Lopez, P., Perallos, A.: An asymmetric multiple traveling salesman problem with backhauls to solve a dial-a-ride problem. In: IEEE International Symposium on Applied Machine Intelligence and Informatics, pp. 151–156. IEEE (2015)
13. Reinelt, G.: TSPLIBA traveling salesman problem library. ORSA J. Comput. **3**(4), 376–384 (1991)
14. Lin, S.: Computer solutions of the traveling salesman problem. Bell Syst. Tech. J. **44**(10), 2245–2269 (1965)
15. Davis, L.: Applying adaptive algorithms to epistatic domains. In: Proceedings of the international joint conference on artificial intelligence, vol. 1, pp. 161–163 (1985)
16. Savelsbergh, M.W.: The vehicle routing problem with time windows: minimizing route duration. ORSA J. Comput. **4**(2), 146–154 (1992)

Self-Organizing Maps Fusion: An Approach to Different Size Maps

Leandro Antonio Pasa[1,2]([⊠]), José Alfredo F. Costa[2],
and Marcial Guerra de Medeiros[2]

[1] Federal University of Technology – Paraná, UTFPR, Medianeira, Brazil
pasa@utfpr.edu.br
[2] Federal University of Rio Grande Do Norte, UFRN, Natal, Brazil
{jafcosta,marcial.guerra}@gmail.com

Abstract. A set of neural networks working in an ensemble can lead to better classification results than just one neural network could. In the ensemble, the results of each neural network are fused resulting in a better generalization of the model. Kohonen Self-Organizing Maps is known as a method for dimensionality reduction, data visualization and also for data classification. This work presents a methodology to fuse different size Kohonen Self-Organizing Maps, with the objective of improving classification accuracy. A factorial experiment was conducted in order to test some variables influences. Computational simulations with some datasets from the UCI Machine Learning Repository and from Fundamental Clustering Problems Suite demonstrate an increase in the accuracy classification and the proposed method feasibility was evidenced by the Wilcoxon Signed Rank Test.

Keywords: Fusion · Self-organizing maps · Validity index

1 Introduction

An ensemble consists of an individual classifiers collection which has differences between each other and leads to a higher generalization than when working separately, a decrease in variance model and higher noise tolerance when compared to a single component [1]. Each classifier operates independently of the others and generates a solution that is combined by the ensemble, producing a single output. The study of ensembles started with Hansen and Salamon's researches [2], combining artificial neural networks, with separate training, resulting in a better system generalization capability.

One of the basic requirements for a successful outcome of the ensemble is that components generalize differently, there is no point combining models that adopt the same procedures and assumptions to solve a problem, it is essential that the errors introduced by each component are uncorrelated [3].

For Kohonen Self-Organizing Maps, this task is relatively simple because different networks can be trained from the same set of feature vectors - varying some

© Springer International Publishing Switzerland 2015
E. Onieva et al. (Eds.): HAIS 2015, LNAI 9121, pp. 568–579, 2015.
DOI: 10.1007/978-3-319-19644-2_47

training parameters - or different training sets, for example. The main difficulty is related to the combination of these maps to generate a single output. The ensemble of Kohonen Maps can be obtained by merging the neurons of the maps to be fused. These neurons must represent the same region of the data input space, in other words, the weight vectors to be fused should be quite similar.

This work presents a methodology to fuse different size Kohonen Self-Organizing Maps, with the objective of improving classification accuracy.

The paper is organized as follows: Sect. 2 presents concepts about this subject. In Sect. 3, it was described the new methodology to fuse Kohonen Maps with different sizes. Section 4 shows and discuss the results. Finally, Sect. 5 presents the conclusions and some proposals for future works.

2 Background

2.1 Self-Organizing Maps

The Self-Organizing Maps (SOM) [4] is an artificial neural network with competitive and unsupervised learning, performing a non-linear projection of the input space $\Re^p$, with $p \gg 2$, in a grid of neurons arranged in an usually two-dimensional array.

The SOM has only an input and an output layer. The network inputs x, correspond to the p-dimensional vector space. The neuron i of the output layer is connected to all the inputs of the network, being represented by a vector of synaptic weights, also in p-dimensional space, $w_i = [wi_1, wi_2, ..., wi_p]^T$. These neurons are connected to adjacent neurons by a neighbourhood relation that describes the topological structure of the map.

In training phase, every time an input pattern x is presented and compared to the neurons of the output layer in a random sequence. A winning neuron, called BMU (Best Match Unit), is chosen through the Euclidean distance criterion and will represent the weight vector with the smallest distance to the input pattern. In other words: the BMU has a great similarity with the input vector.

Assigning the winner neuron index by c, the BMU can be formally defined as the neuron according to the Eq. 1.

$$\|x - w_c\| = argmin_i \|x - w_i\| \tag{1}$$

The weights of the BMU and the neighboring neurons are adjusted according to the Eq. 2.

$$w_i(t+1) = w_i(t) + h_{ci}(t)[x(t) - w_i(t)] \tag{2}$$

where t indicates the iteration of the training process, $x(t)$ is the input pattern and $h_{ci}(t)$ is the nucleus of neighbourhood around the winner neuron c.

2.2 Adapted Cluster Validity Indexes

The cluster validity indexes (CVI) are used to evaluate the clustering algorithm's results, assisting in decision making about the definition of the correct number of clusters formed from a dataset.

Considering that the majority of cluster validation indexes have high computational complexity, which can be a complicating factor in applications involving large data volumes, Gonçalves [5] proposed a modification in the validity indexes calculations using a vector quantization produced by Kohonen Map. His research presents the equations for the modified validity indexes used in this work. The synaptic weight vectors (prototypes) are used instead of the original data. Thus, it causes the decrease of the amount of data and therefore the computational complexity for calculating the validity index decreases too. Also to avoid possible differences between the values calculated with all data and only the prototypes, the author proposed that hits should be used in conjunction with the prototypes.

The cluster validity indexes use some calculation related to distance. The modification proposed changes the way these processes are performed. The following example illustrates the proposed change in the calculation of the distance between two clusters, C_i and C_j:

$$\delta_{i,j} = \frac{1}{|C_i|\,|C_j|} \sum_{x \in C_i, y \in C_j} d(x,y) \tag{3}$$

In Eq. 3, $d(x,y)$ is a distance measure, and $|C_i|\,e\,|C_j|$ refers to the clusters' amount of points C_i and C_j, respectively. When the amount of those points is high, the computational complexity is also high. Equation 4 shows the proposed modification:

$$\delta_{i,j}^{SOM} = \frac{1}{|C_i|\,|C_j|} \sum_{w_i \in W_i, w_j \in W_j} h(w_i) \cdot h(w_j) \cdot d(w_i, w_j) \tag{4}$$

where W_i and W_j are the SOM prototype sets that represent the clusters C_i e C_j, respectively; $d(x,y)$ is the same distance measure type (Euclidian, for example) of Eq. 3, $h(w_i)$ is the prototype's hits w_i belonging to W_i and $h(w_j)$ is the prototype's hits w_j belonging to W_j.

The Eq. 4 presents a lower computational cost, since the quantities involved, w_i and w_j are lower than C_i and C_j. The inclusion of the prototypes' hits $h(.)$ leads to error minimization caused by the vector quantization that Kohonen Map produces, since it introduces in the calculation the approach for the points density in the input space, here represented by prototypes.

2.3   Related Work

The interest in ensemble methods applications have grown rapidly. It is possible to find variations in implementations and their applications in diverse knowledge areas.

In the approach of Georgakis et al. [6], they compared merged maps with the traditional SOM for document organization and retrieval. As a criterion for combining maps, the Euclidean distance between neurons was used in order to select the neurons were aligned (allowing the merger), working with two maps each time, until all maps are fused into one. The ensemble of SOM obtained a better result than the traditional application.

In work presented in [7], the fusion of neurons was named *Fusion*-SOM and it is based on Voronoi polygons - regions of the input space to which the neurons of the Kohonen map can be associated. The proposed method outperforms the performance of the SOM in MSQE (Mean Square Quantization Error) and topology preservation, by effectively locating the prototypes and relating the neighbour nodes.

Corchado [8] used a weighted voting process, called WeVoS-ViSOM, which purpose was the preservation of the map topology, in order to obtain the most truthful visualization of datasets. This algorithm was used in a hybrid system to predict business failure [9]. This methodology does not outperform single models classification accuracy or quantization error, but it succeeds in reducing the distortion error of single models.

It is possible to find variations in implementations of SOM ensemble methods and their applications in several areas of knowledge as image segmentation [10], robotic [11], identification and characterization of computer attacks [12], unsupervised analysis of outliers on astronomical data [13] and financial distress model [14], among others.

3   Proposed Fusion Method

In this work a novel method to fuse self-organizing maps is presented. The aim is to improve the classification accuracy fusing maps with different sizes. Figure 1 shows the fusion process steps, explained in the following.

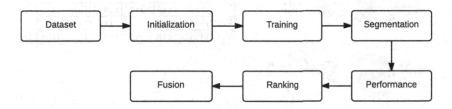

Fig. 1. Fusion process.

1. **Dataset.** In this step, the dataset is split in train and test data.
2. **Initialization.** The first map (called here as Base Map) has the dimensions, x and y, proportional to the two largest covariance matrix eigenvalues of the of the data: λ_1 e λ_2 [4]:

$$\frac{x}{y} \approx \sqrt{\frac{\lambda_1}{\lambda_2}} \tag{5}$$

The remaining maps size will have derived dimensions from x and y values from the first map. In this work was defined a permutation of three values up and down, related to first map dimensions. For example, if the first map size was 10×10, others maps will have rows and columns value varying between 7 and 13, i.e. 7×7, 7×8, ... 7×13, 13×12, 13×11, ... 13×7, resulting in 49 different size maps, as show in Fig. 2.

3. **Training.** The SOM was applied to each map.
4. **Segmentation.** The maps were segmented with k-means clustering. Due to random initialization, k-means is repeated 10 times and it is selected the result with the smallest sum of squared errors.
5. **Performance.** After maps segmentation, the five cluster validity indexes (CVI) and the MSQE were calculated. All maps were ranked by these indexes (called map performance).
6. **Ranking.** The maps were sorted according to the map performance, from the best value to the worst. All maps were sorted by these six different criteria: MSQE and five SOM adapted CVI: Generalized Dunn, Davies-Bouldin, CDbw, PBM and Calinski and Harabasz.
7. **Fusion.** Explained in the next subsection.

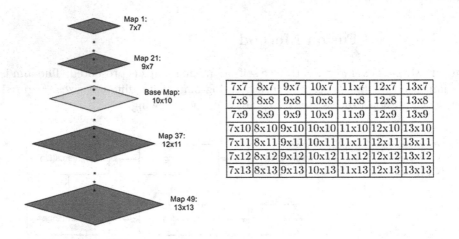

7x7	8x7	9x7	10x7	11x7	12x7	13x7
7x8	8x8	9x8	10x8	11x8	12x8	13x8
7x9	8x9	9x9	10x9	11x9	12x9	13x9
7x10	8x10	9x10	10x10	11x10	12x10	13x10
7x11	8x11	9x11	10x11	11x11	12x11	13x11
7x12	8x12	9x12	10x12	11x12	12x12	13x12
7x13	8x13	9x13	10x13	11x13	12x13	13x13

Fig. 2. Maps' sizes to be fused.

3.1   Maps Fusion

As not all components will contribute to the overall ensemble performance, it is necessary to identify and discard these components, since the inclusion of all candidates in the ensemble may degrade its performance [15].

By definition, the base map is the first component of ensemble. All 48 other maps candidates to be ensemble components shall be tested according to their ranked performances.

The fusion occurs between two neurons that have the minimum Euclidean distance between them, indicating that they represent the same region of the input space. In this study, in order to avoid the influence of neurons without hits and as the maps are merged in pairs, the Eq. 6 was used to find out each neuron weight vector.

$$w_c = \frac{w_i \cdot h_i \cdot VI_i + w_j \cdot h_j \cdot VI_j}{h_i \cdot VI_i + h_j \cdot VI_j} \tag{6}$$

where w_c represents each neuron of fused map, w_i and w_j, h_i and h_j are the prototype's hits and VI_i and VI_j are the Cluster Validity Index for each SOM map to be fused.

It begins with the base map being fused with the best performance map, according with performance value (CVI or MSQE) considered in this work, among the other 48 maps. If the performance criteria of the resulting fused map has improved, this fusion is maintained. Otherwise, it is discarded and the next map, with the second best performance, is fused to the base map. Each time the fusion improves the considered performance, the next map (in descending order of performance) is fused to the resulting fused map and so on, until all 48 questions are tested.

The different approaches explored in this work, are explained in Sect. 3.2.

3.2 Approaches

In this work it was defined four distinct approaches to maps fusion, as a combination between ranked maps and maps fusion criteria. The ranking was based in five CVI and MSQE and the maps' fusion was based in five CVI and MSQE improvement criteria:

1. Maps ranked by CVI and fused by MSQE improvement criterion.
2. Maps ranked by MSQE and fused by CVI improvement criterion.
3. Maps ranked by CVI and fused by CVI improvement criterion.
4. Maps ranked by MSQE and fused by MSQE improvement criterion.

The MSQE indicates how well the units of the map approximate the data on the dataset [8], i.e. it can be employed to evaluate the quality of adaptation to the data [7]. The cluster validity indexes evaluated was CDbw [16], Calinski-Harabasz [17], generalized Dunn [18], PBM [19] and Davies-Bouldin [20], however, all of them modified for use with SOM, proposed by Gonçalves [5].

In the first approach the maps were ranked by five CVI, but the fused maps was controlled by MSQE improvement of the fused map. In the second approach the maps were ranked by MSQE and the fusion process was validated by the CVI improvement. In third approach, maps were ranked by each CVI and the fusion was controlled by these CVI increase. At last, in the fourth approach the maps were ranked by MSQE and fused by MSQE improvement. Figure 3 shows the fusion process general view.

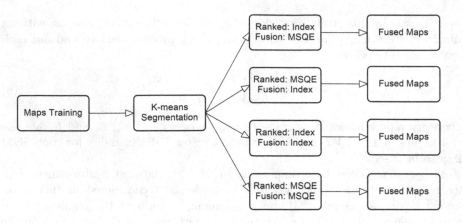

Fig. 3. Block diagram of the experiment.

3.3 Maps Fusion Requirement

In order to better evaluate the hits and BMUs variation influence in fusion process, the percentage of these measures was varied from 10 % to 100 %, with a step of 10 %.

The hits percentage can be interpreted in this manner: each neuron of the base map has a number of hits (how many times that neuron was the winner - BMU). When this neuron is fused to another neuron (from another map), it will take into the account of the minimum hits quantity (in percentage) that this neuron must have compared to the base map neuron. This percentage was varied from 10 % to 100 %.

The limitation of BMUs percentage is the heart of different size maps fusion method. In the fusion process, the maps are evaluated in pairs. The neurons of these maps are also evaluated in pairs too, by Euclidean distance. When the base map has smaller dimensions than the map to be merged with it, there will be more neurons in the second map than in the base map. For example, considering that the base map has dimensions of 10×10 and the map to be fused has dimensions of 12×12, there will be 100 neurons in the base map and 144 on the other map. Thus, the fusion will be limited to 100 % of the neurons of the base map, that is, only 100 of the 144 neurons will be evaluated in the fusion process.

4 Experimental Results

4.1 Datasets

The proposed method was applied to datasets from the UCI Repository [21] and from Fundamental Clustering Problems Suite (FCPS) [22]. Their characteristics are shown in Table 1. Lines with missing values were removed from the datasets. In all experiments the datasets were split into 80 % for training and 20 % for testing.

Table 1. Datasets.

Dataset	Repository	Instances	Attributes	Classes
BC Wisconsin	UCI	699	9	2
Column	UCI	310	6	2
Heart	UCI	303	75	2
Hepatitis	UCI	155	19	2
Ionosphere	UCI	351	34	2
Seeds	UCI	210	7	3
Wine	UCI	178	13	3
Chainlink	FCPS	1000	3	2
Lsun	FCPS	400	2	3
Tetra	FCPS	400	3	4
TwoDiamonds	FCPS	800	2	2
Wingnut	FCPS	1070	2	2

4.2 Results

Table 2 shows the best experimental results for each dataset, i.e. which approach and which CVI resulted in the best accuracy value for each dataset. The column Approach refers to the way the maps were ranked and fused, as specified in Sect. 3.2. Approaches 1 and 2 produced the bests results in this experiment.

The column Index shows which of the indexes was the best for each dataset (DB means Davies-Bouldin index and CH means Calinski and Harabasz index). In approach 1, the index was used for ranking and in approach 2, the indexes was used as fusion criteria. The column Map Size refers to a map size defined by the Eq. 5. The Hits and BMUs percentage columns (explained in Sect. 3.3), shows the value of these variables to achieve the maximum accuracy value.

The fusion accuracy results for each dataset was compared with the accuracy results for a single Self-Organizing Map in the last two columns. As can be observed, for all tested datasets (except the tetra dataset), the classification accuracy of the proposed model was higher than the accuracy obtained with a single map.

The Fig. 4 summarizes the accuracy results for this proposed method. The red line in red represents the single SOM accuracy, while green line shows the accuracy results for fused maps.

The non-parametric Wilcoxon signed rank test [23] was employed in order to evaluate the statistical significance of the fusion results, i.e. if the accuracies values was statistically different from a single map. The null hypothesis, H_0, was that there is no difference between the accuracies of a Single SOM and the Fused Maps. The Wilcoxon Test rejected the null hypothesis, (there was no equality

Table 2. Experimental results.

Dataset	Approach	Index	Map Size	Hits (%)	BMUs (%)	Fusion accuracy	Single SOM accuracy
BC Wisconsin	1	Dunn	22 × 6	10	100	**0.9629**	0.9407
Chainlink	2	DB	14 × 11	30	50	**0.7550**	0.7100
Column	1	CH	13 × 7	10	100	**0.7742**	0.7419
Heart	1	CDbw	11 × 8	100	100	**0.8305**	0.8136
Hepatitis	1	CDbw	8 × 5	10	80	**0.8667**	0.6000
Ionosphere	1	CH	13 × 7	10	80	**0.7429**	0.7143
Lsun	1	CDbw	11 × 9	80	90	**0.7750**	0.7500
Seeds	1	CDbw	14 × 5	50	90	**0.9762**	0.9524
Tetra	1	CDbw	11 × 9	100	100	1	1
Two Diamonds	2	CDbw	14 × 10	80	100	1	0.9875
Wine	2	Dunn	11 × 6	60	90	1	0.9118
Wingnut	1	CH	16 × 10	20	100	**0.8218**	0.7723

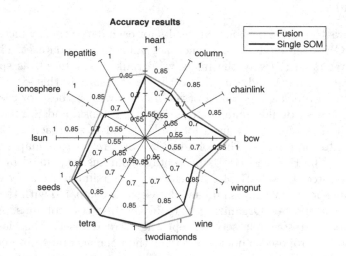

Fig. 4. Accuracy results

between the accuracies). The proposed method accuracy was higher than the Single Kohonen Map for all dataset tested.

The Figs. 5, 6, 7, 8, 9, 10, 11, 12, 13, 14, 15, and 16 and shows a contour graphic relating the Hits and BMUs percentages to the accuracy achieved with the fusion method proposed in this paper.

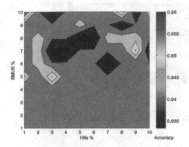

Fig. 5. BC Wisconsin - contour

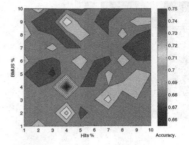

Fig. 6. Chainlink - contour

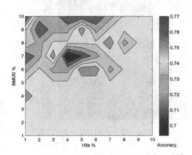

Fig. 7. Column - contour

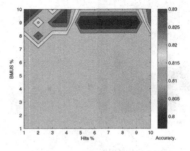

Fig. 8. Heart - contour

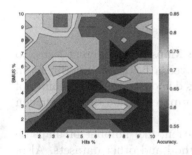

Fig. 9. Hepatitis - contour

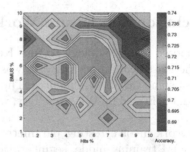

Fig. 10. ionosphere - contour

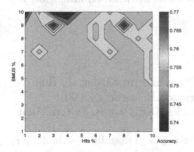

Fig. 11. Lsun - contour

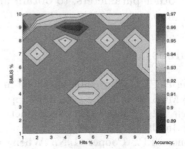

Fig. 12. seeds - contour

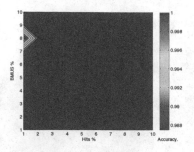

Fig. 13. Tetra - contour

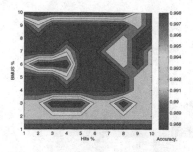

Fig. 14. twodiamonds - contour

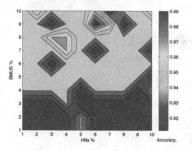

Fig. 15. Wine - contour

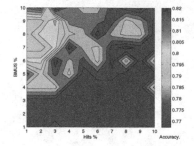

Fig. 16. wingnut - contour

5   Conclusion and Future Work

It was proposed a methodology to fuse Kohonen Maps with different sizes, to increase the classification accuracy. It was employed a factorial experiment in order to test some variables influences. The results demonstrate the feasibility of the method, confirmed by Wilcoxon Test, when compared with a single Kohonen Map.

Future work involve testing parameters variation, like number of maps to be fused, SOM training mode, segmentation method and other datasets. Also, besides increasing the classification accuracy, it is expected, with variations on these and other parameters, to obtain an improvement in data visualization in the fused map.

References

1. Dietterich, T.G.: Ensemble methods in machine learning. In: Kittler, J., Roli, F. (eds.) MCS 2000. LNCS, vol. 1857, pp. 1–15. Springer, Heidelberg (2000)
2. Hansen, L.K., Salamon, P.: Neural network ensembles. IEEE Trans. Pattern Anal. Mach. Intell. **12**, 10 (1990)
3. Perrone, M.P., Cooper, L.N.: When networks disagree: ensemble methods for hybrid neural networks. In: Mammone, R.J. (ed.) Neural Networks for Speech and Image Processing, pp. 126–142. Chapman and Hall, Boca Raton (1993)

4. Kohonen, T.: Self-Organized Maps, 2nd edn. Springer, Berlin (1997)
5. Gonçalves, M.L., De Andrade Netto, M.L., Costa, J.A.F., Zullo, J.: Data clustering using self-organizing maps segmented by mathematic morphology and simplified cluster validity indexes: an application in remotely sensed images. In: IJCNN 2006, International Joint Conference on Neural Networks, pp. 4421–4428 (2006)
6. Georgakis, A., Li, H., Gordan, M.: An ensemble of SOM networks for document organization and retrieval. In: International Conference on Adaptive Knowledge Representation and Reasoning (2005)
7. Saavedra, C., Salas, R., Moreno, S., Allende, H.: Fusion of self organizing maps. In: Sandoval, F., Prieto, A.G., Cabestany, J., Graña, M. (eds.) IWANN 2007. LNCS, vol. 4507, pp. 227–234. Springer, Heidelberg (2007)
8. Corchado, E., Baruque, B.: WeVoS-ViSOM: an ensemble summarization algorithm for enhanced data visualization. Neurocomputing 75, 171–184 (2012)
9. Borrajo, M.L., Baruque, B., Corchado, E., Bajo, J., Corchado, J.M.: Hybrid neural intelligent system to predict business failure in small-to-medium-size enterprises. Int. J. Neural Syst. 21(04), 277–296 (2011)
10. Jiang, Y., Zhi-Hua, Z.: SOM ensemble-based image segmentation. Neural Process. Lett. 20(3), 171–178 (2004)
11. Low, K.H., Wee, K.L., Marcelo, H.A.: An ensemble of cooperative extended kohonen maps for complex robot motion tasks. Neural Comput. 17, 1411–1445 (2005)
12. DeLooze, L.L.: Attack characterization and intrusion detection using an ensemble of self-organizing maps. In: 2006 IEEE In Information Assurance Workshop, pp. 108–115 (2006)
13. Fustes, D., Dafonte, C., Arcay, B., Manteiga, M., Smith, K., Vallenari, A., Luri, X.: SOM Ensemble for unsupervised outlier analysis. application to outlier identification in the gaia astronomical survey. Expert Syst. Appl. 40(5), 1530–1541 (2013)
14. Tsai, C.-F.: Combining cluster analysis with classifier ensembles to predict financial distress. Inf. Fusion 16, 46–58 (2014)
15. Zhou, Z.-H., Wu, J., Tang, W.: Ensembling neural networks: many could be better than all. Artif. Intell. 137(1–2), 239–263 (2002)
16. Halkidi, M., Vazirgiannis, M.: A density-based cluster validity approach using multi-representatives. Pattern Recogn. Lett. 29, 773–786 (2008)
17. Milligan, G.W., Cooper, M.C.: An examination of procedures for determining the number of clusters in a data set. Psychometrika 50, 159–179 (1985)
18. Bezdek, J.C., Pal, N.R.: Some new indexes of cluster validity. IEEE Trans. Syst. Man Cybern. B 28, 301–315 (1998)
19. Pakhira, M.K., Bandopadhyay, S., Maulik, U.: Validity index for crisp and fuzzy clusters. Pattern recogn. 37(3), 487–501 (2004)
20. Davies, D.L., Bouldin, D.W.: A cluster separation measure. IEEE Trans. Pattern Anal. Mach. Intell. PAMI 1(2), 224–227 (1979)
21. Bache, k., Lichman, M.: Machine Learning Repository. University of California, Irvine, School of Information and Computer Sciences (2013). http://archive.ics. uci.edu/ml
22. Ultsch, A.: Clustering with SOM: U*C. In: Proceedings Workshop on Self-Organizing Maps (WSOM 2005), pp. 75–82 (2005)
23. Demšar, J.: Statistical comparisons of classifiers over multiple data sets. J. Mach. Learn. Res. 7, 1–30 (2006)

Cloud Robotics in FIWARE: A Proof of Concept

F. Herranz[✉], J. Jaime, I. González, and Á. Hernández

Ikergune at Etxe-Tar Group, Elgoibar, Bilbao, Spain
{fherranz,jjaime,igonzalez,ahernandez}@ikergune.com

Abstract. Novel Cloud infrastructures and their extensive set of resources have potential to help robotics to overcome its limitations. Traditionally, those limitations have been related with the number of sensors that are equipped in the robots and their computational power. The drawbacks of these limitations can be reduced by using the benefits of cloud architectures such as cloud computing, Internet of Things (IoT) sensing and cloud storage. FIWARE is an open platform which integrates cloud capabilities and Generics Enablers (GE) to interact with the cloud. This paper proposes the development of a Robotics GE and it presents the integration of the new GE into the FIWARE architecture. Two are the main goals behind this integration, first to bring all the benefits that FIWARE provides to robotics, and second to facilitate the development of robotics applications to non-expert robotics developers. Finally, a real example of the integration is shown by means of a parking meter application that combines context information, robotics, and cloud computing of vision algorithms.

Keywords: Robotics · FIWARE · Cloud

1 Introduction

Traditionally, robots have been identified as individual systems that attempted to solve complex problems in spite of their limited intelligence. That limitation was mainly due to the fact that robots were equipped with a limited number of sensors (cameras, laser, etc.) and limited computational power. Nowadays, novel cloud architectures are emerging [1] and will help to overcome the robot's limitations, starting therefore, a revolution in the robotics field. Robotics will benefit from important cloud aspects such as cloud computing, storage, and communications resources to process and share information from various robots or entities (smart phones, IoT sensors, humans, etc.).

The cloud robotics approach opens a new scenario where it is possible to build lightweight, low cost, smarter robots that have their brains in the cloud. This cloud brain consists of components such as data centers, knowledge base, task planners, deep learning, information processing, environment models and communication support [2]. The cloud robotics approach also involves the software and hardware abstraction of each robot, and presenting general purpose

© Springer International Publishing Switzerland 2015
E. Onieva et al. (Eds.): HAIS 2015, LNAI 9121, pp. 580–591, 2015.
DOI: 10.1007/978-3-319-19644-2_48

interfaces to ease its management and deployment. The benefits of this approach are clear for non robotics experts that can now develop programs without
knowing the specific robot architecture, simply by using the provided interfaces.

This work aims at facilitating the development of robotics applications to
non-expert robotics developers and bringing all the benefits of cloud architectures to Robotics. To do so, this paper presents an architecture of cloud robotics based on the novel FIWARE [3] architecture (www.fiware.org) and the well
known Robot Operating System (ROS) [4] (www.ros.org). FIWARE is an open
platform which integrates advanced OpenStack-based Cloud capabilities and
a library of applications called Generic Enablers (GE) that make it easier to
develop cloud applications. The GEs cover areas such as connection to the IoT,
Context Management, Media stream processing, Open Data publication, Big
Data analysis or the cross-selling and co-creation of applications. From the point
of view of cloud robotics, FIWARE provides a set of toolboxes and communication mechanisms that allows us to easily develop a cloud of robots with a large
number of capabilities [5], such as the following ones:

- Big Data: access to remote maps, trajectories, and object data.
- Cloud Computing: access to parallel grid computing on demand for statistical
  analysis, learning, and motion planning.
- Collective Robot Learning: robots sharing trajectories, control policies, and
  outcomes.
- Human computation: using crowd-sourcing access to remote human expertise
  for analyzing images, classification, learning, and error recovery.
- Context information: access to information of the environment by means of
  IoT and human interaction.

The integration of a cloud of robots within FIWARE opens a new scenario in
robotics since we consider two types of users, the FIWARE developers and the
robotics developers. Developers, that build FIWARE-based applications, do not
usually have any specific knowledge about robotics and may only concern about
an easy way to use robots. Hence, they think about the robot as a black box. On
the other hand, robotics developers have a deep knowledge of robots, sensors and
algorithms but lack of cloud computing or web developing abilities. Typically,
robotics algorithms are very time consuming tasks in terms of computational
power and they cannot be executed in real time. Robotics developers have a need
for distributed computation which can be performed in the cloud but usually do
not know about cloud protocols. Thus, both kinds of users need an abstraction
layer that allows them an easy access to the integration of robots on the FIWARE
platform, creating a real robotics cloud.

In order to obtain software and hardware abstraction of robots and FIWARE,
this paper introduces a new GE within the FIWARE ecosystem. The Robotics
GE follows the open source philosophy of ROS and FIWARE, and brings the
communities a novel and easy way to manage and interact with robots by means
of REST petitions and JSON format. Hence, this work presents the development
of the FIROS component that allows the Robotics GE to connect FIWARE and
ROS worlds. FIROS can be considered a communications translator between

FIWARE and ROS but it also provides high-level functionalities such as watch-dog and database services. Hence, FIROS provides an abstraction layer between FIWARE and the cloud of robots.

The following sections of this paper are organized as follows: Sect. 2 describes the related work in this area; Sect. 3 presents the proposed architecture of the cloud of robots and FIWARE; Sect. 4 shows the test bed; and finally, in Sect. 5 some conclusions and future work are presented.

2   Related Work

During the past few years, cloud computing for robotics has got the focus of some researches. The DAvinCi Project [6] used ROS in combination with Hadoop cluster parallelizing the FastSLAM algorithm. The ubiquitous network robot platform (UNR-PF) [7] established a network between robots, sensors, and mobile devices by means of a cloud architecture. The RoboEarth project [2] provided a network and database cloud approach where robots could share information and learn from each other about their behavior and environment. The rosbridge package [8], an open source project, focuses on the external communication between a robot and a single ROS environment in the cloud; it is a HTTP and Javascript interface to ROS messaging. This convenience is appropriate for certain use cases but is unsuitable for robotics cloud with a large number of robots because it could saturate the network due to the number of simultaneous WebSockets that are needed to establish the connections.

FIWARE platform has been used in a number of applications such as IoT applications [3,5], smart homes, [9] and mobile learning and games [10].

The Robotics GE and FIWARE combination aims at solving some of the robotics clouds that are still open. Multi-robot configurations can be easily achieved by sharing the robot's context information in the Context Broker GE. Data structures are standardized within the Context Broker using the NGSI standard [11], which focuses on new requirements and API extensions for server-to-server based third party services. Robotics GE's communications are based on HTTP connections instead of WebSockets-based ones. This allows the system to make a more efficient use of the network since the connections do not need to be constantly open.

3   Robotics Generic Enabler Architecture

The Robotics GE consists of the robot manager (ROS), FIROS which communicates the cloud with the robotics domain, a set of communication protocols and a set of data structures to represent the robot's information. Figure 1 presents a schema of the Robotics GE architecture and the connection of the Robotics GE with the Context Broker GE. This connection allows an application to communicate with a set of robots by means of the Context Broker and Robotics GEs.

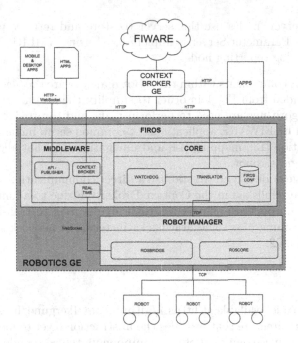

Fig. 1. Robotics GE architecture

3.1 Robot Manager

The robot manager is a ROS-based framework [4] which provides standard operating system services such as hardware abstraction, low-level device control, implementation of commonly used functionality, message-passing between processes, and package management. This framework uses the concept of nodes, topics, messages and services. A node is an executable program that performs any task and sends information through messages to other nodes. Messages always travel via special channels called topics. A node which sends messages on a topic is called a publisher and the receiving node has to subscribe the topic to receive that message, hence it is called a subscriber.

The robot manager is in charge of accessing the robot's sensors and actuators, processing their raw information and commanding the robot to execute tasks. One of the key components within the robot manager is the so-called "roscore", which is a collection of nodes that are needed to executed any other application in ROS. Roscore by default starts the following nodes:

– ROS Master: that provides naming and registration services to the rest of the nodes in the ROS system. It tracks publishers and subscribers to topics as well as services. The role of the Master is to enable individual ROS nodes to locate one another. Once these nodes have located themselves, they communicate with each other peer-to-peer. The ROS Master is implemented using XMLRPC [12].

– Parameter Server: nodes use this server to store and retrieve parameters at runtime. The Parameter Server is implemented using XMLRPC [12].
– Rosout node: log reporting node.

Other important components within the robot manager are the algorithms which have been excluded from Fig. 1 in order to simplify the graph. In the proposed architecture, algorithms are used to perform tasks and to provide services that can be initiated by FIWARE applications. A common setup includes algorithms such as localization [13], mapping [14] and navigation [15] that allows FIWARE users to command a robot.

The rosbridge node is used to establish a direct communication for large data, which cannot be published in the Context Broker GE due to a limited data size of 1 MB. In the proposed architecture, rosbridge is used to transfer data such as images overcoming also some drawbacks in terms of network saturation, as mentioned in Sect. 2.

3.2   FIROS

FIROS (source code available at https://github.com/Ikergune/firos) is the component in the architecture that provides the abstraction layer to integrate robots within FIWARE. It is composed of two components the core and a middleware. The main task of the core is the translation of ROS information to FIWARE GEs and vice versa. To do so, it uses a watchdog, a translator and a FIROS configuration database.

Watchdog: The watchdog checks the robot's status and notifies FIROS in case of disconnections or technical issues. It is based on Nagios [16] which is an open source computer system monitoring, network monitoring and infrastructure monitoring software application. The watchdog works as follows:

– Checks that the nodes of the robots are properly configured.
– Checks the connectivity with the robots.
– Checks the connectivity of FIROS with the rest of the components in the architecture as well as the Context Broke GE.
– In case there is an unexpected issue and a component is disconnected, the watchdog tries to reset the component. If the watchdog cannot set up the component, it sends an emergency stop command to the robots and notifies the rest of components.
– In case there is an error with a robot, the watchdog tries to reconnect the robot. If it fails reconnecting the robot, the watchdog notifies the rest of components.

Translator: The translator is a ROS node that dynamically parses ROS messages into FIWARE's GE messages. To do so, this component requires to know its role, defined in the FIROS configuration database, within the communication process (publisher or subscriber). If a ROS message is being sent to FIWARE, the translator subscribes to the ROS topic, translates the message and sends it to FIWARE. If the message is received from FIWARE, the translator receives the message from FIWARE, translates it and publishes it in the ROS topic. Additionally, the translator needs to know the structure of ROS messages, that are defined by "msg files", to translate them into JSON structures and vice versa. JSON structures are the kind of structures that are used in the FIWARE context. Codes 1.1 and 1.2 show an example of the message translation.

Code 1.1 presents the structure of a common ROS message like the Twist message, which expresses velocity in free space broken into its linear and angular parts.

Code 1.1. ROS Twist message

```
geometry_msgs/Vector3 linear
   float64 x
   float64 y
   float64 z
geometry_msgs/Vector3 angular
   float64 x
   float64 y
   float64 z
```

Code 1.2 the conversion of the Twist message into JSON notation. It decomposes the Twist message into the linear and angular structures and adds a stamp field called "firosstamp" to discard duplicated messages.

Code 1.2. JSON Twist message

```
{
    "linear": {
        "x": 0.0,
        "y": 0.0,
        "z": 0.0
    },
    "angular": {
        "x": 0.0,
        "y": 0.0,
        "z": 0.0
    },
    "firosstamp": 0.0
}
```

In order to send the JSON messages to the Context Broker, it is needed to create a HTTP petition as code 1.3 shows.

Each contextElement is associated to an entity that additionally contains a list of attributes elements. Each attribute provides the value for a given attribute of the entity (identified by name and type). The "id" attribute defines the identity of the entity, "type" defines that the entity is a robot, "isPattern" defines that the "id" of the robot is not a regular expression. The "COMMAND" attribute defines the ROS topic that is going to be translated. Finally, the JSON message is sent as an attribute by defining the topic name (e.g. *cmd_vel*) and the message type (e.g. *geometry_msgs.msg.Twist*).

Code 1.3. HTTP petition

```json
{
   "contextElements": [
      {
         "id":"robot_ID",
         "type":"ROBOT",
         "isPattern":"false",
         "attributes": [
            {
               "name":"COMMAND",
               "type":"COMMAND",
               "value": [
                  "TOPIC"
               ]
            },
            {
               "name":"TOPIC",
               "type":"MESSAGE_TYPE",
               "value":"JSON_MESSAGE"
            }
         ]
      }
   ],
   "updateAction":"APPEND"
}
```

FIROS Configuration Database: The configuration database stores information about the robots in the system such as the robot name, the topics and the kind of messages that travel through the topics. In addition, it informs FIROS about its role when transferring the messages topics by means of the "type" attribute. Code 1.4 shows an example of the configuration of a robot using a JSON string.

Code 1.4. FIROS robot configuration

```json
{
   "robot1":{
      "topics": {
         "cmd_vel_mux/input/teleop": {
            "msg":"geometry_msgs.msg.Twist",
            "type":"publisher"
         },
         "move_base/goal": {
            "msg":"move_base_msgs.msg.MoveBaseActionGoal",
            "type":"publisher"
         },
         "move_base/result": {
            "msg":"move_base_msgs.msg.MoveBaseActionResult",
            "type":"subscriber"
         }
      }
   }
}
```

Middleware: The middleware is used to provide a direct access to FIROS and the Context Broker from web applications. It provides channels for real time communications of large messages, such as video. This interface supports transportation of binary blob because sometimes it is more efficient to transport messages as a binary blob instead of using their corresponding ROS message type encoded as a JSON string.

4   Experimental Test Bed

This section presents a real experiment to demonstrate the feasibility of the robotics cloud in the FIWARE context. The experiment consists in a robotized parking meter that moves around a street while checking the all car plates to find out if a car has violated the parking laws. To do so, the application uses the Robotics GE to manage the robot, the Context Broker GE to store the context information of the robot and the Kurento GE [17]. Kurento is a WebRTC media server that provides a set of computer vision algorithms that are executed in the cloud. The robot that has been used in the test-bed is a Turtlebot platform equipped with a Kinect sensor and a laptop. The laptop is an old Asus EEE PC with a 1.6 GHz processor and 1 GB of RAM running Ubuntu 14.04. We have chosen this laptop to demonstrate the feasibility of the proposal with low-power laptops due to the fact that the computation power is in the cloud. Figure 2 shows the architecture of the proposed experiment.

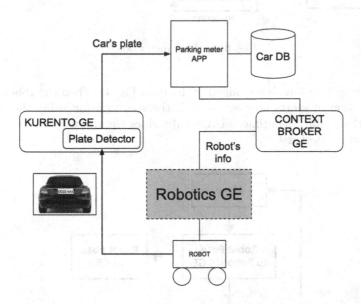

Fig. 2. Parking meter architecture

Figure 3 shows the application flow. First, the parking meter application commands the robot to move around the parking spots. To do so, the Robotics GE is configured with localization and navigation algorithms (it is explained in detail below) allowing the application to command the robot by means of FIROS and the Context Broker GE. When the robot navigates, it uses a WebRTC client to establish a video channel with Kurento. Kurento receives the video streaming and uses the plate detector algorithm to recognize a license plate. After recognizing the license plate, Kurento sends the information to the parking meter application on FIWARE. The parking meter application stores the car information in the database and monitors the cars to launch an alarm every time a car stays in a parking spot for longer than it should.

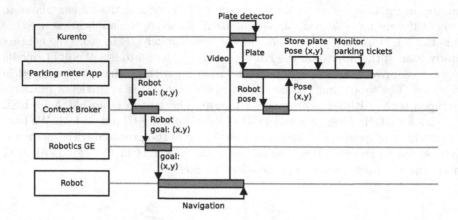

Fig. 3. Parking meter flow

The navigation flow is explained in detail in Fig. 4. When the robot receives a goal position, it starts moving to reach the goal location using the amcl and A^* algorithms [13]. Meantime, FIROS subscribes the robot's pose and sends it to the Context Broker GE.

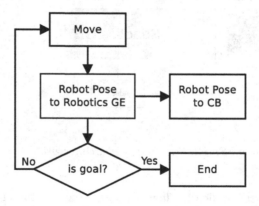

Fig. 4. Navigation flow

Figure 5 presents the robot navigating through the environment, the robot's path is shown in Fig. 5(a) as a green line. Figure 5(b) shows the perception of the robot where there is a car in a parking spot and it is possible to distinguish the plate of the car.

(a) Robot's Path   (b) Robot's perception

Fig. 5. Robot Navigation

Figure 6 shows the detection of a car's plate when the robot is close to the car. It can be seen the image that the robot is acquiring, in the case a blue car, and the message that the application displays to about the plate number.

Fig. 6. Plate detection

5   Conclusions

This paper has described the design and integration of the Robotics GE with the FIWARE platform. The Robotics GE was based on two key components FIROS and the Robot manager which allow the cooperation between FIWARE and robotics. By doing this, we accomplished the two main goals of this work: robotics are benefiting from FIWARE cloud components and general developers are able to develop robotics applications without a deep robotics knowledge. The paper has described in detail the connections between FIWARE and the Robotics GE and the way the messages are parsed. Finally, a experimental parking meter application has been presented to show the integration of the Robotics GE with other GEs such as the Context Broker GE and Kurento GE.

In the near future, we plan to take advantage of the modular design of the Robotics GE and integrate it with other robotics operating systems and other cloud platforms. By doing this, we pursue to introduce robotics to other communities independently the tools they use.

Acknowledgment. This work is being partially supported by the EU co-funded IST projects FI-WARE: Future Internet Core Platform (GA 285248) and FI-CORE: Future Internet - Core (GA 632893), as part of the European Commissions Future Internet Public-Private Partnership (FI-PPP) initiative.

References

1. Dinh, H.T., Lee, C., Niyato, D., Wang, P.: A survey of mobile cloud computing: architecture, applications, and approaches. Wirel. Commun. Mob. Comput. **13**(18), 1587–1611 (2013)
2. Hunziker, D., Gajamohan, M., Waibel, M., D'Andrea, R.: Rapyuta: the roboearth cloud engine. In: 2013 IEEE International Conference on Robotics and Automation (ICRA), pp. 438–444. IEEE (2013)
3. Usländer, T., Berre, A.J., Granell, C., Havlik, D., Lorenzo, J., Sabeur, Z., Modafferi, S.: The future internet enablement of the environment information space. In: Hřebíček, J., Schimak, G., Kubásek, M., Rizzoli, A.E. (eds.) ISESS 2013. IFIP AICT, vol. 413, pp. 109–120. Springer, Heidelberg (2013)
4. Quigley, M., Conley, K., Gerkey, B., Faust, J., Foote, T., Leibs, J., Wheeler, R., Ng, A.Y.: ROS: an open-source robot operating system. In: ICRA Workshop on Open Source Software, vol. 3, p. 5 (2009)
5. Ramparany, F., Marquez, F.G., Soriano, J., Elsaleh, T.: Handling smart environment devices, data and services at the semantic level with the FI-WARE core platform. In: 2014 IEEE International Conference on Big Data (Big Data), pp. 14–20. IEEE (2014)
6. Arumugam, R., Enti, V.R., Bingbing, L., Xiaojun, W., Baskaran, K., Kong, F.F., Kumar, A.S., Meng, K.D., Kit, G.W.: DAvinCi: a cloud computing framework for service robots. In: 2010 IEEE International Conference on Robotics and Automation (ICRA), pp. 3084–3089. IEEE (2010)
7. Sato, M., Kamei, K., Nishio, S., Hagita, N.: The ubiquitous network robot platform: common platform for continuous daily robotic services. In: 2011 IEEE/SICE International Symposium on System Integration (SII), pp. 318–323. IEEE (2011)
8. Crick, C., Jay, G., Osentoski, S., Jenkins, O.C.: ROS and rosbridge: roboticists out of the loop. In: Proceedings of the Seventh Annual ACM/IEEE International Conference on Human-Robot Interaction, pp. 493–494. ACM (2012)
9. Bellabas, A., Ramparany, F., Arndt, M.: Fiware infrastructure for smart home applications. In: O'Grady, M.J., Vahdat-Nejad, H., Wolf, K.-H., Dragone, M., Ye, J., Röcker, C., O'Hare, G. (eds.) AmI Workshops 2013. CCIS, vol. 413, pp. 308–312. Springer, Heidelberg (2013)

10. Gordillo, A., Gallego, D., Barra, E., Quemada, J.: The city as a learning gamified platform. In: Frontiers in Education Conference, pp. 372–378. IEEE (2013)
11. Bauer, M., Kovacs, E., Schulke, A., Ito, N., Criminisi, C., Goix, L.W., Valla, M.: The context API in the OMA next generation service interface. In: 2010 14th International Conference on Intelligence in Next Generation Networks (ICIN), pp. 1–5. IEEE (2010)
12. Cerami, E.: Web services essentials: distributed applications with XML-RPC, SOAP, UDDI & WSDL. O'Reilly Media, Inc. (2002)
13. Thrun, S., Burgard, W., Fox, D.: Probabilistic Robotics. MIT press, Cambridge (2005)
14. Grisetti, G., Stachniss, C., Burgard, W.: Improved techniques for grid mapping with rao-blackwellized particle filters. IEEE Trans. Robotics **23**(1), 34–46 (2007)
15. Elfes, A.: Using occupancy grids for mobile robot perception and navigation. Computer **22**(6), 46–57 (1989)
16. Barth, W.: Nagios: System and Network Monitoring. No Starch Press, New York (2008)
17. Lopez Fernandez, L., Paris Diaz, M., Benitez Mejias, R., Lopez, F., Santos, J.: Kurento: a media server technology for convergent www/mobile real-time multimedia communications supporting webrtc. In: 2013 IEEE 14th International Symposium and Workshops on a World of Wireless, Mobile and Multimedia Networks (WoWMoM), pp. 1–6. June 2013

Comparing Measurement and State Vector Data Fusion Algorithms for Mobile Phone Tracking Using A-GPS and U-TDOA Measurements

Ayalew Belay Habtie[1(✉)], Ajith Abraham[2,3], and Dida Midekso[1]

[1] Department of Computer Science, Addis Ababa University,
Addis Ababa, Ethiopia
{ayalew.belay,dida.midekso}@aau.edu.et
[2] Machine Intelligence Research Labs (MIR Labs), Washington 98071, USA
ajith.abraham@ieee.org
[3] IT4Innovations - Center of Excellence, VSB - Technical University of Ostrava,
Ostrava, Czech Republic

Abstract. Multi-Sensor Data Fusion (MSDF) becomes one research area in different disciplines including science and engineering. To enhance reliability and accuracy of sensor measurements' multisensory data fusion techniques are applied. The aim of this paper is to evaluate estimation performance of measurement fusion and state vector fusion algorithms in tracking a moving mobile phone along all journey of a vehicle. These two algorithms based on Kalman Filter are implemented in the tracking system. Performance evaluation is computed using MATLAB and the analysis show position and velocity estimation accuracy of measurement fusion algorithm is better than state vector fusion algorithm.

Keywords: Measurement fusion · State vector fusion · Kalman filter · Mobile phone positioning · A-GPS · U-TDOA

1 Introduction

Data fusion (DF) or multi-sensor data fusion (MSDF), according to Rao [1], is the process of combining or integrating measured or pre-processed data or information originating from different active or passive sensors or sources to produce a more specific, comprehensive, and unified dataset about an entity or event of interest that has been observed. MSDF enhances quality of the information output in a process in several ways like increasing robustness and reliability during sensor failure, extend parameter coverage, increase dimensionality of the measurement, improve resolution, reduce uncertainty and reduction of measurement time and possibly cost [2].

Data fusion is applicable in the estimation of target position or kinematic information from multiple measurements of single or multiple sensors. It enables to combine different target localization techniques (named hybrid localization methods) and optimize accuracy, coverage, availability and decrease latency of location delivery [3]. The widely applied and best known state estimator algorithm is Kalman Filter [4].

© Springer International Publishing Switzerland 2015
E. Onieva et al. (Eds.): HAIS 2015, LNAI 9121, pp. 592–604, 2015.
DOI: 10.1007/978-3-319-19644-2_49

This recursive algorithm gives a linear, unbiased, and minimum error variance. KF optimally estimate the unknown state of a linear dynamic system from Gaussian distributed noisy observations.

In this paper two different data fusion algorithms are considered and employed in tracking a moving in-vehicle mobile phone. The performance analysis of the algorithms is performed and the numerical results from simulation experiment are reported descriptively. The reminder of this paper is organized as follows. In Sect. 2, review of literatures on MSDF is presented. MF and SF data fusion algorithms together with their generic model are discussed in Sect. 3. Section 4 is about the technical and mathematical representation of A-GPS and U-TDOA positioning methods which are used to collect mobile phone location measurements. The simulation and numerical results are discussed in Sect. 5 and finally, the conclusion is presented in Sect. 6.

2 Related Literature

In the past few decades, sensor-data fusion has been researched and has added developments for many fields such as science and technology. And most of these researches are based on Kalman filter Algorithm that filter noise and recover signal. The work of Bahador Khaleghi et al. [5], for example, presented detail review of multi-sensor data fusion state of the art. The methods and the problems in using multi-sensor data fusion are described in [6]. The wide applications of MSDF in military, biomedical fields, engineering and its future research directions are described in [7]. Qiang and Chris [8] compared Kalman filter based measurement and state vector data fusion algorithms and their theoretically proof showed the superior of measurement data fusion algorithms. Similarly Mosallae and Salahshoor [9] discussed measurement and state vector data fusion algorithms based on UKF algorithm for fault diagnosis and simulation result revealed that measurement fusion is better than state vector fusion algorithm. The work of Anitha et al. [10] discusses the different data fusion algorithms based on KF and experimentally compared the performance of the algorithms using IR and Radar sensors which are with linear characteristics. The numerical result of the experimentation shows the superiority of state vector fusion over measurement fusion. This is due to the fact that the sensors are with linear process, which will not affect KF. However, for non-linear process sensors, KF will be inconsistent and measurement fusion is recommended [8, 11, 12]. In this work measurements based on A-GPS and U-TDOA as sensor to locate a moving mobile phone is applied to compare performance of the data fusion algorithms.

3 Data Fusion Algorithms

3.1 State Vector Fusion

State Vector Fusion (SVF) is KF based fusion. In this algorithm, a group of Kalman filters are used to obtain individual sensor based state estimates which are then fused to obtain an improved joint state estimate and the associated covariance. At the fusion center, track-to-track correlation is applied [1] as shown in Fig. 1.

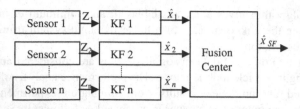

Fig. 1. State vector fusion

In this research work, we are interested to locate a mobile phone moving in all journey of a vehicle in 2D using A-GPS and U-TDOA UMTS positioning standards. The state-space model representing the continuous-time dynamics of the mobile phone is described as continuous White Noise Acceleration (WNA) model [13]. In this model the state vector of the mobile phone is defined as:

$$X(t) = [x(t)\ y(t)\ \dot{x}(t)\ \dot{y}(t)]^T \tag{1}$$

The slight changes of the velocity of the mobile phone are modelled by continuous-time zero-mean white acceleration v (t) which is given as:

$$\ddot{x}(t) = \ddot{y}(t) = v(t), \quad E[v(t)v^T(\tau)] = Q_c \delta(t-\tau) \tag{2}$$

Where Q_c is power spectrum density

The continuous-time state equation of the model is expressed as:

$$\dot{x}(t) = A\,x(t) + v(t) \tag{3}$$

The discrete-time state equation form of Eq. (3) at sample time ΔT is given by:

$$X(k) = F X(k-1) + V(K-1) \tag{4}$$

The corresponding measurement equation is defined as:

$$Z(k) = H X(k) + W(K) \tag{5}$$

Where k represents discrete-time index, X(k) is state vector, Z(k) is measurement vector, F is state transition matrix, H is observation transition matrix, v (k–1) and w(k) zero-mean white Gaussian noise with covariance matrices Q(k) and R(k) respectively.

The KF provided recursive solution for state estimation of the linear system and the optimal state estimation with minimum variance as derived in [14, 15] is given as:

Priori estimate $\left(\hat{X}_K^-\right)$ at time K is, $\quad \hat{X}_K^- = F\hat{X}_{k-1}^+ \tag{6}$

Priori covariance $\left(P_K^-\right)$ is, $\quad P_K^- = FP_{K-1}^+ F^T + Q \tag{7}$

$$\text{Kalman Gain } (K_K) \text{ is,} \quad K_k = P_K^- H^T (HP_K^- H^T + R)^{-1} \tag{8}$$

$$\text{Posteriori estimate } (\hat{X}_K^+) \text{ at time K is,} \quad \hat{X}_K^+ = \hat{X}_K^- + K_K(Z_K - H\hat{X}_K^-) \tag{9}$$

$$\text{Posteriori covariance } (P_K^+) \text{ is,} \quad P_K^+ = (I - K_K H)P_K^- \tag{10}$$

3.2   Measurement Fusion

Measurement fusion (MF) algorithm directly fuses the sensor measurements in the fusion center and use a single Kalman filter [8] to obtain the final state estimate based upon the fused observation as shown in Fig. 2.

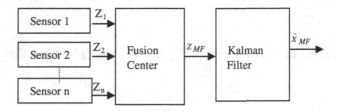

Fig. 2. Measurement fusion

Measurement fusion can be done either by simply merging the sensor measurements (augmentation) or using minimum-mean-square-error estimate criterion. In this work minimum-mean-square-error based fusion is used as it is more efficient than the first one due to the similarity of dimensions of the acquired measurements based on A-GPS and U-TDOA positioning techniques [8]. Hence the fused measurement Z_{MF} and the associated measurement noise covariance matrix $\hat{R}_{MF}$ are defined as:

$$
\begin{aligned}
Z_{MF}(k) &= Z_{A-GPS}(K) + \hat{R}^{A-GPS}(\hat{R}^{A-GPS} + \hat{R}^{U-TDOA})^{-1}(Z_{U-TDOA}(K) \\
&\qquad - Z_{A-GPS}(K)) \\
&= \frac{\hat{R}^{A-GPS} X_{U-TDOA}(K) + \hat{R}^{U-TDOA} X_{A-GPS}(K)}{\hat{R}^{A-GPS} + \hat{R}^{U-TDOA}}
\end{aligned} \tag{11}
$$

$$\hat{H}_{MF} = \left[(\hat{R}^{A-GPS})^{-1} + (\hat{R}^{U-TDOA})^{-1}\right]^{-1} * \begin{bmatrix} (\hat{R}^{A-GPS})^{-1} H_{A-GPS} + \\ (\hat{R}^{U-TDOA})^{-1} H_{U-TDOA} \end{bmatrix} \tag{12}$$

$$\hat{R}_{MF} = \left[(\hat{R}^{A-GPS})^{-1} + (\hat{R}^{U-TDOA})^{-1}\right]^{-1} \tag{13}$$

Where $X_{A-GPS}(K)$ is A-GPS measurement at time index k, $X_{U-TDOA}(K)$ is U-TDOA measurement at time index k, $\hat{R}^{A-GPS}$ is A-GPS measurement noise covariant matrix,

$\hat{R}^{U-TDOA}$ is U-TDOA measurement noise covariant matrix, H_{U-TDOA} is U-TDOA measurement transition matrix, H_{A-GPS} is A-GPS measurement transition matrix.

The KF algorithm is computed and the state and corresponding covariance time propagation is given as follows.

$$\text{Priori fused estimate } \left(\hat{X}_K^{f-}\right) \text{ at time K is,} \quad \hat{X}_K^{f-} = F\hat{X}_{k-1}^{f+} \tag{14}$$

$$\text{Priori fused covariance } \left(P_K^{f-}\right) \text{ is,} \quad P_K^{f-} = FP_{K-1}^{f+}F^T + Q \tag{15}$$

$$\text{Fused Kalman Gain } \left(K_k^f\right) \text{ is,} \quad K_k^f = P_K^{f-}\hat{H}_{MF}^T(\hat{H}_{MF}P_K^{f-}\hat{H}_{MF}^T + \hat{R}_{MF})^{-1} \tag{16}$$

$$\text{Posteriori fused estimate } \left(\hat{X}_K^{f+}\right) \text{ at time K is,} \quad \hat{X}_K^{f+} = \hat{X}_K^{f-} + K_K^f(Z_{MF_K} - \hat{H}_{MF}\hat{X}_K^{f-}) \tag{17}$$

$$\text{Posteriori fused covariance } \left(P_K^{f+}\right) \text{ is,} \quad P_K^{f+} = (I - K_K^f\hat{H}_{MF})P_K^{f-} \tag{18}$$

4   A-GPS and U-TDOA Measurements

In this section, facts about U-TDOA estimation and A-GPS based mobile phone location measurement collection in the real world are discussed.

4.1   A-GPS

In this work Java Specification Request 179 (JSR 179) Location Application Programming Interface (API) [16] is utilized to periodically request location updates from A-GPS mobile phone. We conducted several field tests on Samsung android A-GPS mobile phone moving along all journey of a vehicle. The location updates sent to java application on the central server include latitude and longitude coordinates with their accuracy, the timestamp and speed of the mobile phone. The horizontal accuracy is the root mean square error (RMSE) of easting and northing errors (in meters, 1-sigma standard deviation).

4.2   U-TDOA

The U-TDOA based mobile positioning system determines the position of the mobile based on hyperbolic lateration. Hyperbolic lateration mobile phone position method is accomplished in two steps. The first one is the estimation of the time difference of arrival (TDOA) between receivers (NodeBs) through the use of time delay estimation technique. And TDOAs are then transformed in to range difference measurements between NodeBs to define hyperbolic curves which are then intersected to obtain an estimation position location of the user equipment. As it is illustrated in [17], the accuracy and performance of U-TDOA positioning method is influenced by factors like Signal to Noise Ratio (SNR), signal bandwidth, multipath, Geometric Dilution Of Precision (GDOP), number of measurement and integration time.

4.3 Hyperbolic Lateration Using U-TDOA

U-TDOA mobile phone position estimation method is based on the estimation of the time difference in the arrival signal from the mobile (source) to multiple NodeBs (receivers). Assuming that the mobile phone and NodeBs are coplanar, the intersection of hyperbolas obtained as range difference of U-TDOA between mobile phone and NodeBs results position location estimate of the mobile.

Assume $NodeB_1$ received the transmitted signal and is the one controlling the call. And let $(X_{U\text{-}TDOA}, Y_{U\text{-}TDOA})$ be the location of the mobile and (X_i, Y_i) be the known location of the ith NodeB, where i = 2, 3, ... M. A general model for the two dimension (2D) position location estimate for a mobile phone using M NodeBs is the squared range distance between the ith NodeB and the mobile phone and defined as [18]:

$$R_i = \sqrt{(X_i - X_{U-TDOA})^2 + (Y_i - Y_{U-TDOA})^2} \tag{19}$$

The range difference between NodeBs with respect to $NodeB_1$ where the signal arrives first $(R_{i,1})$ is given as:

$$R_{i,1} = cd_{i,1} = R_i - R_1$$
$$= \sqrt{(X_i - X_{U-TDOA})^2 + (Y_i - Y_{U-TDOA})^2} - \sqrt{(X_1 - X_{U-TDOA})^2 + (Y_1 - Y_{U-TDOA})^2} \tag{20}$$

Where c is the signal speed (3×10^8 m/s), $R_{i,1}$ is the range difference distance between $NodeB_1$ and the ith NodeB, R_1 is the distance between $NodeB_1$ and the mobile phone, and $d_{i,1}$ is the estimated U-TDOA between the $NodeB_1$ and the ith NodeB. This defines the set of non-linear hyperbolic equations whose solution gives the 2-D coordinates of the mobile. To solve the non-linear hyperbolic Eq. (20), many methods have been proposed. But Chan's algorithm is the best available option to solve U-TDOA equation [18] and it is employed to locate the mobile phone using U-TDOA measurement. The linearized form of Eq. (20) is as follows:

$$R_{i2} = (R_{i,1} + R_1)^2 \tag{21}$$

Based on Eqs. (19) and (21) can be written as:

$$R_i^2 = R_{i,1}^2 + 2R_{i,1}R_1 + R_1^2$$
$$= X_i^2 + Y_i^2 - 2X_iX_{U-TDOA} - 2Y_iY_{U-TDOA} + X_{U-TDOA}^2 + Y_{U-TDOA}^2 \tag{22}$$

When we subtract Eq. (19) putting i = 1 from Eq. (22), the resulting equation is:

$$R_{i,1}^2 + 2R_{i,1} R_1 = X_i^2 + Y_i^2 - 2X_{i,1}X_{U-TDOA} - 2Y_{i,1}Y_{U-TDOA} - (X_1^2 + Y_1^2) \qquad (23)$$

Where $X_{i,1}$ is (X_i-X_1) and $Y_{i,1}$ equals (Y_i-Y_1). Eq. (23) is a set of linear equation with the unknown mobile phone location $(X_{U\text{-}TDOA}, Y_{U\text{-}TDOA})$ and R_1 is the distance between the mobile phone and NodeB$_1$ to be solved. Following Chan's method [19], for a three NodeB systems (M = 3), producing two U-TDOA's, $X_{U\text{-}TDOA}$ and $Y_{U\text{-}TDOA}$ can be solved in terms of R_1 from Eq. (23). The solution is in the form of:

$$\begin{bmatrix} X_{U-TDOA} \\ Y_{U-TDOA} \end{bmatrix} = - \begin{bmatrix} X_{2,1} Y_{2,1} \\ X_{3,1} Y_{3,1} \end{bmatrix}^{-1} \times \left\{ \begin{bmatrix} R_{2,1} \\ R_{3,1} \end{bmatrix} R_1 + \frac{1}{2} \begin{bmatrix} R_{2,1}^2 - K_2 + K_1 \\ R_{3,1}^2 - K_3 + K_1 \end{bmatrix} \right\} \qquad (24)$$

Where $K_1 = X_1^2 + Y_1^2$, $K_2 = X_2^2 + Y_2^2$, $K_3 = X_3^2 + Y_3^2$ When (24) is inserted into (19), with i = 1, a quadratic equation in terms of R_1 is produced. Substituting the positive root back into (24) results in the final solution.

For four or more NodeB systems (M $\geq$ 4) there will be more measurements of U-TDOA's than number of unknowns. Hence the original set of nonlinear U-TDOA equations are transformed in to another set of linear equations with extra variables. While applying weighted linear least square method repeatedly, the error vector ϕ using U-TDOA noise can be derived from (23) and represented as:

$$\phi = h - G_a Z_a^0 \qquad (25)$$

Where $Z_a^0 = [X_{U-TDOA}\ Y_{U-TDOA}\ R_1]^T$ which is noise free value.

$$h = \frac{1}{2} \begin{bmatrix} R_{2,1}^2 - X_2^2 - Y_2^2 + X_1^2 + Y_1^2 \\ R_{3,1}^2 - X_3^2 - Y_3^2 + X_1^2 + Y_1^2 \\ \vdots \quad \vdots \quad \vdots \\ R_{M,1}^2 - X_M^2 - Y_M^2 + X_1^2 + Y_1^2 \end{bmatrix} \qquad G_a = - \begin{bmatrix} X_{2,1} & Y_{2,1} & R_{2,1} \\ X_{3,1} & Y_{3,1} & R_{3,1} \\ \vdots & \vdots & \vdots \\ X_{M,1} & Y_{M,1} & R_{M,1} \end{bmatrix}$$

and the error vector ϕ is assumed to be normally distributed Gaussian random vector with covariance matrix ψ given by:

$$\psi = E[\phi\phi^T] = c^2 BQB \qquad (26)$$

Where $B = diag\{ R_2^0, R_3^0, ..., R_M^0 \}$, $Q = \hat{R}^{U-TDOA} = diag\{\sigma_{2,1}^2, \sigma_{3,1}^2, \cdots, \sigma_{M,1}^2\}$ U-TDOA measurement noise covariant matrix. Still Eq. (25) is nonlinear because of elements of Z_a and solving this equation gives:

$$Z_a = \arg\min \{(h - G_a Z_a)^T \psi^{-1}(h - G_a Z_a) \\ = (G_a^T \psi^{-1} G_a)^{-1} G^T \psi^{-1} h \qquad (27)$$

Z_a is a generalized LS solution of (25). To make Eq. (27) solvable further approximation is necessary and an approximation of (27) is:

$$Z_a \approx (G_a^T Q^{-1} G_a)^{-1} G^T Q^{-1} h \tag{28}$$

The solution given by (27) assumes X_{U-TDOA}, Y_{U-TDOA} and R_1 are independent. However they are related by (19). Hence incorporating this relationship enables to get improved estimate and defined as:

$$Z_a' = \left\{ \begin{bmatrix} 1 & 0 \\ 0 & 1 \\ 1 & 1 \end{bmatrix}^T (\psi')^{-1} \begin{bmatrix} 1 & 0 \\ 0 & 1 \\ 1 & 1 \end{bmatrix} \right\}^{-1} \begin{bmatrix} 1 & 0 \\ 0 & 1 \\ 1 & 1 \end{bmatrix}^T (\psi')^{-1} \begin{bmatrix} Z_{a,1}^2 \\ Z_{a,2}^2 \\ Z_{a,3}^2 \end{bmatrix} \tag{29}$$

Where

$$\psi' = E[\phi\phi^T] = 4 \begin{bmatrix} z_{a,1} \\ & z_{a,2} \\ & & z_{a,3} \end{bmatrix} \text{cov}(Z_a) \begin{bmatrix} z_{a,1} \\ & z_{a,2} \\ & & z_{a,3} \end{bmatrix} \tag{30}$$

The result $Z_a' = [X_{U-TDOA} \ Y_{U-TDOA} \ R_1]^T$ represents the mobile phone position estimation.

5 Simulation Results

To compare the performance of the proposed data fusion algorithms using A-GPS and U-TDOA location measurements of a moving in-vehicle mobile phone, random vehicle route/trajectory on a typical urban area is generated on MATLAB based on the dynamic model represented by Eq. (3). Observation of real vehicle speeds in urban traffic road reveal that the model is practical and motion of vehicles can be modelled as Gaussian Process [13]. Considering typical vehicle motion in urban traffic road, average speed of 54 km/h. (15 m/s) and mean acceleration of 1 m/s^2 are applied in the simulation. And according to McGuire and Plataniotis [13], the mobile phone acceleration process is a zero-mean Gaussian process with variance σ^2 in both x-and y-coordinate directions with magnitude of Rayleigh distributed random variable with mean of $\sigma\sqrt{\pi/2}$. Hence the value of σ^2, i.e., Qc in Eq. (2) is estimated as $2 * \bar{a}^2/\pi$.

To generate mobile phone position estimations based on U-TDOA positioning technique, a network of 7 NodeBs, which include serving NodeB and other 6 neighbouring NodeBs, is created in a hexagonal cells with radius 1 km as depicted in Fig. 2 (a). The position coordinates of NodeBs are (0,0), (1500,866), (1500,−866), (0,−1732), (−1500,−866), (−1500,866) and (0,1732). Then true position estimate of mobile phone is generated at every 1000 Monte Carlo run and with the assumption of U-TDOA based estimation noise is unbiased Gaussian, location estimation error, the squared distance of the estimation to the true mobile phone location is calculated using Root Mean Square Error (RMSE) which is computed as [20]:

$$\text{RMSE} = \sqrt{\frac{1}{mc} \sum_{k=1}^{mc} (Pos_k^{U-TDOA} - Pos_k^{True})^T (Pos_k^{U-TDOA} - Pos_k^{True})} \qquad (31)$$

Where mc is total number of Monte Carlo performed, $Pos_k^{U-TDOA} = [X^{U-TDOA} \ Y^{U-TDOA}]^T$ and for each grid point 1000 independent Monte Carlo runs are computed.

To determine position estimate of mobile phone, different number of NodeBs ranging from 4 to 7 are chosen to perform mobile phone positioning simulation as shown in Fig. 2(b). Assuming signal and noise at each NodeBs is white random process [19], the RMSE of U-TDOA estimation is obtained at noise values of 39 m, 78 m and 117 m which are 0.5, 1 and 1.5 chip periods in UMTS networks respectively [21]. And as it can be seen in Fig. 2(b), positioning accuracy increases with an increase of participating NodeBs. In the case of 7NodeBs, the mobile phone position accuracy is the highest.

But RMSE of 78.1 m (as it is indicated in Fig. 3(b) where 6NodeBs are hearable with U-TDOA noise of 100 m is selected in this simulation. This is because U-TDOA timing measurement accuracy is 3.84 Mchips/s which is 78.125 m [21] and measurements in [22] demonstrated that at this estimation noise the positioning accuracies for the probability of 67 % and 95 % of the calls meet the requirement of E-911.

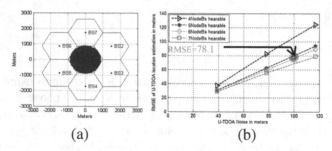

(a)   (b)

Fig. 3. U-TDOA based mobile phone position estimation, (a) mobile network cell regions and mobile phone distribution (b) influence of NodeBs number in mobile phone positioning accuracy

The mobile phone position based on A-GPS positioning method is collected directly from filed test using java application developed utilizing J2ME location API (JSR 179) as described in Sect. 4.1. The location of A-GPS based in-vehicle mobile is collected in 13 min trip in urban area of Addis Ababa and total of 158 valid location updates were measured with in a time rate of 5 s in a sample trajectory shown in Fig. 4.

The positioning error of A-GPS based mobile phone positioning method is obtained from the field test in the form of horizontal and vertical accuracy. The horizontal and vertical accuracy collected at each mobile phone location sample is the RMS composed of the northing (σ_N) and Easting (σ_E) standard deviations [22]. Assuming the circular case ($\sigma_N = \sigma_E$), A-GPS based mobile phone location error is generated as Gaussian noise with variance $\sigma = (Acc_k/\sqrt{2})^2$, where **Acc** represents the recorded horizontal accuracy at time t_k. Hence using variances of U-TDOA based mobile phone position

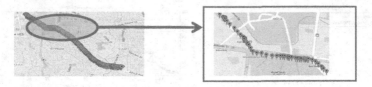

Fig. 4. Sample trajectory for moving in-vehicle mobile phone used to collect its location based on A-GPS positioning method

estimation and A-GPS based mobile phone location measurement sample mobile phone trajectory together with the generated noisy U-TDOA based mobile phone estimation and A-GPS based mobile phone measurement are generated as depicted in Fig. 5.

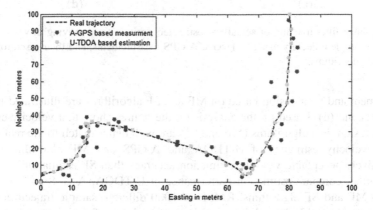

Fig. 5. Real mobile phone track vs. the generated A-GPS, and U-TDOA based locations.

To perform the tracking activity based on the two data fusion algorithms, initial conditions for KF are determined. According to McGuire and Plataniotis [13], good selection of initial condition for filters is essential for tracking algorithms. Accordingly, the position estimates are initialized by first locations measurements of A-GPS and U-TDOA based mobile phone positioning. The initial velocity estimates are zeros as at t_0 there is no location information. Initial variances for U-TDOA is based on Cramer-Rao Lower Bound (CRLB) which is derived from [19], for A-GPS based estimates it is the statistical mean from accuracy of test data and for velocity estimates the initial variance is taken based on the fact that initial velocity is between ± 15 m/s. Filtering on a sample trajectory, the position estimation results are depicted along the trajectory as shown in Figs. 6(a), (b), (c) and (d).

It can be seen from Fig. 6, KF based tracking of MF algorithm, Fig. 6(c), and SF algorithm, Fig. 6(d), shows better match to the real sample trajectory than the individual measurements. However, MF algorithm has better proximity to the real trajectory than SF algorithm as it is shown in the zoomed figures of Fig. 6(c) and (d).

The mobility model applied is White Noise Acceleration (WNA) as described in Sect. 3, Kalman Filter of real and estimated velocities for each of the noisy

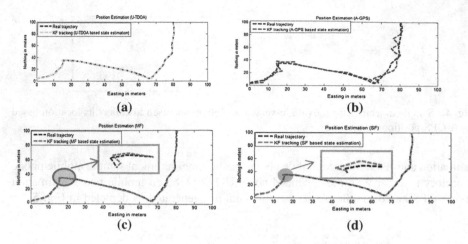

Fig. 6. Kalman filter tracking of actual and estimated position for a moving in-vehicle mobile phone on a sample trajectory using U-TDOA, A-GPS measurements, and their fused form using MF and SF algorithms.

measurement and their fusion based on MF and SF algorithms are illustrated in Fig. 7 (a), (b), (c) and (d). Based on the analysis on the figures show that velocity estimates based on fusion data algorithms (MF and SF) are with better match to the real velocity than the velocity estimates of U-TDOA and A-GPS and MF algorithm provides comparatively acceptable velocity estimation accuracy than SF estimation.

To further compare estimation performance of U-TDOA, A-GPS and their fusion based on MF and SF algorithms, RMSE of 1000 different sample trajectories where each is filtered at 158 Kalman Filter steps is computed, used for performance metrics is defined as [23]:

$$\text{RMSE}_{\text{position}} = \sqrt{\frac{1}{kf} \sum_{k=1}^{kf} [(X_k - \hat{X}_k)^2 + (Y_k - \hat{Y}_k)^2]} \tag{32}$$

$$\text{RMSE}_{\text{velocity}} = \sqrt{\frac{1}{kf} \sum_{k=1}^{kf} [(\dot{X}_k - \hat{\dot{X}}_k)^2 + (\dot{Y}_k - \hat{\dot{Y}}_k)^2]} \tag{33}$$

Where kf is total number of Kalman filter steps, $[X_k \quad Y_k \quad \dot{X}_k \quad \dot{Y}_k]^T$ and $[\hat{X}_k \quad \hat{Y}_k \quad \hat{\dot{X}}_k \quad \hat{\dot{Y}}_k]^T$ are real and state estimation at filter step k respectively.

The sample mean (μ_{RMSE}) from RMSE of position and velocity is calculated on these 1000 different sample trajectories generated and filtered with 158 filter steps each. And as it is shown in Table 1, position and velocity estimation accuracy of MF algorithm is better from SF algorithm.

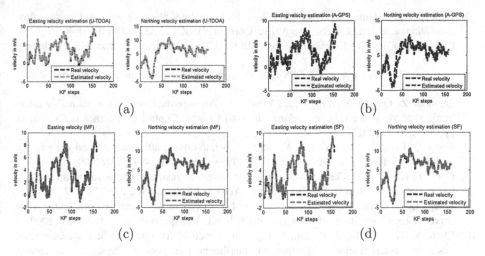

Fig. 7. Kalman filter tracking of actual and estimated velocities for a moving in- vehicle mobile phone on a sample trajectory uses U-TDOA, A-GPS measurements and their fused form using MF and SF algorithms.

Table 1. Sample mean of position and velocity estimation using RMSE

Generated sample trajectories N = 1000	U-TDOA	A-GPS	MF	SF
	μ_{RMSE}	μ_{RMSE}	μ_{RMSE}	μ_{RMSE}
RMSE$_{position}$	22.9695	48.1372	19.5369	21.4497
RMSE$_{velocity}$	3.4611	7.5482	2.7244	2.9871

6 Conclusion

The measurements obtained from A-GPS or U-TDOA has accuracy and reliability problem. To improve the accuracy and reliability of the information data fusion algorithms is applied. Commonly there are two types of data fusion algorithms:- measurement fusion (MF) and state vector fusion (SF) algorithms. In this research KF based MF and SF algorithms are implemented in tracking position of a moving mobile phone located in vehicle road. And from performance analysis made, MF algorithm is better than SF algorithm in estimating position as well as velocity of the mobile phone.

Acknowledgement. This work was also supported in the framework of the IT4 Innovations Centre of Excellence project, reg. no.CZ.1.05/1.1.00/02.0070 by operational programme 'Research and Development for Innovations' funded by the Structural Funds of the European Union and state budget of the Czech Republic, EU.

References

1. Raol, J.R.: Multi-Sensor Data Fusion with MATLAB. CRC Press, Boca Raton (2010)
2. Mitchell, H.B.: Multi-Sensor Data Fusion: An Introduction. Springer, Heidelberg (2007)

3. Habtie, A.B., Ajith, A., Dida, M.: In-vehicle mobile phone-based road traffic flow estimation: a review. J. Netw. Innovative Comput. (JNIC) **2**, 331–358 (2013)
4. Chui, C.K., Chen, G.: Kalman Filtering with Real-Time Applications. Springer, Heidelberg (2009)
5. Quiroga, C.A.: An integrated GPS-GIS methodology for performing travel time studies (1997)
6. Qiankun, Z., Qingjie, K., Yingjie, X., Yuncai, L.: An improved method for estimating urban traffic state via probe vehicle tracking. In: 30th Chinese Control Conference (CCC 2011), pp. 5586–5590 (2011)
7. Kong, Q.-J., Li, Z., Chen, Y., Liu, Y.: An approach to urban traffic state estimation by fusing multisource information. IEEE Trans. Intell. Transp. Syst. **10**, 499–511 (2009)
8. Gan, Q., Harris, C.J.: Comparison of two measurement fusion methods for Kalman-filter-based multisensor data fusion. IEEE Trans. Aerosp. Electron. Syst. **37**, 273–279 (2001)
9. Kong, Q.-J., Chen, Y., Liu, Y.: A fusion-based system for road-network traffic state surveillance: a case study of Shanghai. IEEE Intell. Transp. Syst. Mag. **1**, 37–42 (2009)
10. Chen, Y., Gao, L., Li, Z.-P., Liu, Y.-C.: A new method for urban traffic state estimation based on vehicle tracking algorithm. In: Intelligent Transportation Systems Conference, ITSC 2007. IEEE, pp. 1097–1101 (2007)
11. Cipriani, E., Gori, S., Mannini, L.: Traffic state estimation based on data fusion techniques. In: 2012 15th International IEEE Conference on Intelligent Transportation Systems (ITSC), pp. 1477–1482 (2012)
12. Yadaiah, N., Singh, L., Bapi, R.S., Rao, V.S., Deekshatulu, B.L., Negi, A.: Multisensor data fusion using neural networks. In: International Joint Conference on Neural Networks, IJCNN 2006, pp. 875–881 (2006)
13. McGuire, M., Plataniotis, K.N.: Dynamic model-based filtering for mobile terminal locationestimation. IEEE Trans. Veh. Technol. **52**, 1012–1031 (2003)
14. Simon, D.: Optimal state estimation: Kalman, H infinity, and nonlinear approaches. Wiley (2006)
15. Kremer, S.C.: Spatiotemporal connectionist networks: a taxonomy and review. NeuralComput. **13**, 249–306 (2001)
16. JCP, Java Specification Request (JSR) 179: Location API for J2METM (2011)
17. Hamdy, Y.R., Mawjoud, S.A.: Performance assessment of U-TDOA and A-GPSpositioning methods. In: 2012 InternationalConference on Future Communication Networks (ICFCN), pp. 99–104 (2012)
18. Senturk, H.: Performance Evaluation of Hyperbolic Position Location Technique in CellularWireless Networks. DTIC Document (2002)
19. Chan, Y., Ho, K.: A simple and efficient estimator for hyperbolic location. IEEE Trans. Sig. Proc. **42**, 1905–1915 (1994)
20. Bar-Shalom, Y., Li, X.R., Kirubarajan, T.: Estimation with applications to tracking andnavigation: theory algorithms and software. Wiley (2004)
21. Zhang, J.: C-curves: an extension of cubic curves. Comput. Aided Geom. Des. **13**, 199–217 (1996)
22. Guan, W., Deng, Z., Ge, Y., Zou, D.: A practical TDOA positioning method for CDMA2000mobile network. In: 2010 IEEE International Conference on Wireless Communications, Networking and Information Security (WCNIS),pp. 126–129 (2010)
23. Tao, S., Manolopoulos, V., Rodriguez, S., Ismail, M., Rusu, A.: Hybrid vehicle positioningand tracking using mobile phones. In: 2011 11th InternationalConference on ITS Telecommunications (ITST), pp. 315–320 (2011)

Hybrid U-TDOA and A-GPS for Vehicle Positioning and Tracking

Ayalew Belay Habtie[1(✉)], Ajith Abraham[2,3], and Dida Midekso[1]

[1] Department of Computer Science, Addis Ababa University,
Addis Ababa, Ethiopia
{ayalew.belay,dida.midekso}@aau.edu.et
[2] Machine Intelligence Research Labs (MIR Labs), Auburn, WA 98071, USA
ajith.abraham@ieee.org
[3] IT4Innovations - Center of Excellence, VSB - Technical University of Ostrava,
Ostrava, Czech Republic

Abstract. Due to the current emergent interests in location-based services, 3G and 4G cellular networks provide a key facility to locate the user equipment (UE). Vehicle positioning and tracking using the UE traveling on-board the vehicle is one of the value added location-based services enabled by this feature and has been studied by different researchers. However, there is no single standard on UE positioning technique that can provide better accuracy and coverage. To address this problem, we proposed to use measurement fusion based hybrid UE positioning method-combining measurements collected from A-GPS mobiles and simulated estimates of U-TDOA. Kalman Filter based filtering of positions and velocities as well as accuracy values determined based on measurement errors demonstrate that the proposed hybrid UE positioning method is effective in localizing a moving vehicle with better accuracy.

Keywords: User equipment positioning · A-GPS · U-TDOA · Measurment fusion · UE

1 Introduction

User Equipment (UE) positioning technologies have drawn a significant amount of attention over the past few years. Different types of location-based services utilizing UE positioning technologies have been proposed and studied, including the emergency 911 subscriber safety services and application to intelligent transport system. In addition to the high interest of network operators and subscribers on location-based services, the 3G and 4G cellular networks also provide a key facility to locate the UE utilizing the network service. Road traffic information based on the UE traveling on-board the vehicle is one of the value added location-based services studied by different researchers. However, no research has recommended a UE positioning technique with best accuracy and coverage for vehicle position and velocity estimation. Hence, tracking the position and velocity of in-vehicle UE along the journey with appropriate accuracy and coverage is a challenge. And this paper aims to address this problem, which will then be used for future research to estimate real-time urban traffic flow condition.

© Springer International Publishing Switzerland 2015
E. Onieva et al. (Eds.): HAIS 2015, LNAI 9121, pp. 605–619, 2015.
DOI: 10.1007/978-3-319-19644-2_50

Different types of location-based services require different position technologies based on position accuracy and according to 3GPP specifications, each positioning technology has its own positioning logic. Despite their numerous variations, these standardized methods can be classified as network-based and handset-based (terminal-based) positioning technology [1].

Among the four standard positioning methods supported in UMTS Terrestrial RAN [2], A-GPS UE positioning method provides excellent location accuracy, especially in open-space. Moreover, A-GPS phones gained significant market share in the mobile handset and personal computer markets, and this trend is expected to continue in the near future [3, 4]. Nevertheless, the best positioning accuracy for A-GPS is achieved in rural environment but in urban areas it is affected by shadow of high buildings. Hence supplementing A-GPS with inexpensive positioning method is preferable.

In relation to this, different authors conducted research on hybrid mobile positioning methods aiming to complement downside of one method with another to provide better performance measure [5–7]. But, they still recommend for further investigation as most of the researches are based on 2G cellular network location techniques not 3G standard location methods, most aim to address problem of the old GPS performance not the recent A-GPS and they hardly target vehicle location applications which will make difference in performance requirements. In this paper a hybrid of U-TDOA and A-GPS for moving vehicle position estimation and tracking is presented. This paper is organized as follows. Section 2 discusses the proposed hybrid scheme, technique used to gather location of moving in-vehicle UE based on A-GPS and U-TDOA and fusion and tracking algorithms. Section 3 discusses simulation results and finally Sect. 4 presents the conclusion.

2 Hybrid Positioning and Tracking Scheme

Mobile positioning technologies in cellular networks can be either Handset-based or Network-based positioning. To improve positioning accuracy, coverage and communication latency of positioning technologies, combination of Handset-based and Network-based positioning techniques has been proposed [5–7].

To combine different UE positioning methods Data Fusion algorithms are applied. Generally, there are two approaches for multi-sensor data fusion: measurement fusion and state vector fusion. Measurement fusion methods directly fuse the sensor measurements to obtain a weight or combined measurement and use a single Kalman filter to obtain the final state estimate but state vector fusion method uses a group of Kalman filters to obtain individual sensor based state estimates.

Comparing measurement fusion and state vector fusion, state vector fusion methods are consistent only when Kalman filters are consistent [8]. However many realistic applications like navigation and target tracking, which are with non-linear processes, when using Kalman filters (which utilize linearized process model like Taylor series) will be inconsistent. Hence when Kalman filter is applied for such kind of practical situations, measurement fusion methods generally provides better overall estimation performance than state vector fusion methods [10–12].

Due to the fact that real-time vehicle positioning and tracking is with non-linear process and Kalman Filter is used for in-vehicle UE position and velocity tracking, measurement fusion based on minimum mean square error estimate is applied as shown in Fig. 1. And the components of the proposed hybrid scheme are described as follows.

2.1 Measurements Based on A-GPs and U-TDOA

In this sub section, facts about U-TDOA estimation and A-GPS based UE location measurement collection in the real world are discussed.

A-GPS: According to 3GPP TS 25.305, in UE based A-GPS location method, the UE is the primary entity that computes mobile phone position and send the location data to a central server to update road traffic system with real-time position information. In this work, Java Specification Request 179 (JSR 179) Location Application Programming Interface (API) [13] is utilized to periodically request location updates from A-GPS UE. We conducted several field tests on Samsung Android A-GPS phone moving along all journey of a vehicle. The location updates sent to java application on the central server are two-dimensional (2D) geographic coordinates of the mobile position m_p in terms of latitude and longitude coordinates together with horizontal accuracy e_p, the timestamp and speed of the mobile phone. The horizontal accuracy is the root mean square error (RMSE) of easting and northing errors (in meters, 1-sigma standard deviation).

U-TDOA: Uplink Time Difference Of Arrival (U-TDOA) User Equipment (UE) positioning method is considered as network based positioning system that can provide positioning service to all kind of mobiles (legacy or modern) supported by the operator. The U-TDOA system determines the position of the UE based on hyperbolic lateration. As it is illustrated in [14], the accuracy and performance of U-TDOA positioning method is influenced by factors like Signal to Noise Ratio (SNR), signal bandwidth, multipath, Geometric Dilution Of Precision (GDOP), number of measurement and integration time.

2.2 Location Estimation and Noise Variance

The geographic coordinates of the UE position $m_p = [p_{lat} \ p_{lon}]^T$ are converted to the Cartesian coordinate $Z_{A\text{-}GPS} = [x_{lat} \ y_{lon}]^T$. The horizontal accuracy e_p is related to the variance $R_{A\text{-}GPS}$ of measurement noise. The time measurement using U-TDOA is converted in to hyperbolic equations and these equations are solved using Chan's Algorithm to get mobile location estimation result $Z_{U\text{-}TDOA} = [x_{U\text{-}TDOA} \ y_{U\text{-}TDOA}]^T$. The variance $R_{U\text{-}TDOA}$ represents the estimation uncertainty.

Hyperbolic Lateration Using U-TDOA: U-TDOA UE position estimation method is based on the estimation of the time difference in the arrival signal from the UE (source) to multiple NodeBs (receivers). Assuming that the UE and NodeBs are coplanar, the intersection of hyperbolas obtained as range difference of U-TDOA between UE and

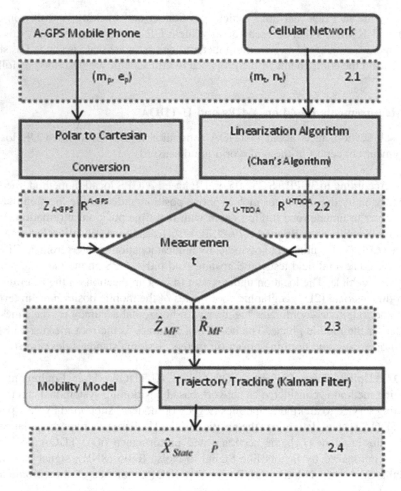

Fig. 1. Hybrid of U-TDOA and A-GPS positioning and tracking scheme.

NodeBs results position location estimate of the UE. The hyperbolic lateration is named to be trilateration [15] or hyperbolic position location [16] when the number of NodeBs is three.

Assume NodeB$_1$ received the transmitted signal and is the one controlling the call. And let $(X_{U\text{-}TDOA}, Y_{U\text{-}TDOA})$ be the location of the UE and (X_i, Y_i) be the known location of the ith NodeB, where $i = 2, 3, \ldots M$. A general model for the two dimension (2D) position location estimate for a UE using M NodeBs is the squared range distance between the ith NodeB and the UE and defined as [16]:

$$R_i = \sqrt{(X_i - X_{U-TDOA})^2 + (Y_i - Y_{U-TDOA})^2} \tag{1}$$

The range difference between NodeBs with respect to $NodeB_1$ where the signal arrives first ($R_{i,\ 1}$) is given as:

$$R_{i,1} = cd_{i,1}$$
$$= R_i - R_1 \sqrt{(X_i - X_{U-TDOA})^2 + (Y_i - Y_{U-TDOA})^2}$$
$$- \sqrt{(X_1 - X_{U-TDOA})^2 + (Y_1 - Y_{U-TDOA})^2} \tag{2}$$

where c is the signal speed (3×10^8 m/s), $R_{i,1}$ is the range difference distance between $NodeB_1$ and the ith NodeB, R_1 is the distance between $NodeB_1$ and the UE, and $d_{i,1}$ is the estimated U-TDOA between the $NodeB_1$ and the ith NodeB. This defines the set of non-linear hyperbolic equations whose solution gives the 2-D coordinates of the UE.

To solve the non-linear hyperbolic Eq. (2), many methods have been proposed. For example, Hamdey and Mawjoud [14] have compared three algorithms- Taylor-series expansion, Fang's Algorithm and Chan's Algorithm based on complexity, accuracy and their performance limitations. Accordingly, Chan's algorithm gives exact solution and has better accuracy, less complex, faster and suitable for real-time implementation than Taylor-series and Fang's algorithm [17]. Hence Chan's algorithm is the best available option to solve U-TDOA Eq. (16) and it is employed to locate the UE using U-TDOA measurement. The linearized form of Eq. (2) is as follows:

$$R_{i2} = (R_{i,1} + R_1)^2 \tag{3}$$

Based on Eq. (3), Eq. (1) can be written as:

$$R_i^2 = R_{i,1}^2 + 2R_{i,1}R_1 + R_1^2$$
$$= X_i^2 + Y_i^2 - 2X_iX_{U-TDOA} - 2Y_iY_{U-TDOA} + X_{U-TDOA}^2 + Y_{U-TDOA}^2 \tag{4}$$

When we subtract Eq. (1) putting i = 1 from Eq. (4), the resulting equation is:

$$R_{i,1}^2 + 2R_{i,1}R_1 = X_i^2 + Y_i^2 - 2X_{i,1}X_{U-TDOA} - 2Y_{i,1}Y_{U-TDOA} - (X_1^2 + Y_1^2) \tag{5}$$

where $X_{i,\ 1}$ is ($X_i - X_1$) and $Y_{i,1}$ equals ($Y_i - Y_1$).

Equation (5) is a set of linear equation with the unknown UE location (X_{U-TDOA}, Y_{U-TDOA}) and R_1 is the distance between the UE and NodeB1 to be solved.

Following the Chan's method [17], for a three NodeB systems (M = 3), producing two U-TDOA's, X_{U-TDOA} and Y_{U-TDOA} can be solved in terms of R_1 from Eq. (5). The solution is in the form of:

$$\begin{bmatrix} X_{U-TDOA} \\ Y_{U-TDOA} \end{bmatrix} = - \begin{bmatrix} X_{2,1} Y_{2,1} \\ X_{3,1} Y_{3,1} \end{bmatrix}^{-1} \times \left\{ \begin{bmatrix} R_{2,1} \\ R_{3,1} \end{bmatrix} R_1 + \frac{1}{2} \begin{bmatrix} R_{2,1}^2 - K_2 + K_1 \\ R_{3,1}^2 - K_3 + K_1 \end{bmatrix} \right\} \tag{6}$$

where $K_1 = X_1^2 + Y_1^2$, $K_2 = X_2^2 + Y_2$, $K_3 = X_3^2 + Y_3^2$ When (6) is inserted into (1), with i = 1, a quadratic equation in terms of R_1 is produced. Substituting the positive root back into (6) results in the final solution.

For four or more NodeB systems ($M \geq 4$) there will be more measurements of U-TDOA's than number of unknowns. Applying weighted linear least square method repeatedly, the error vector φ using U-TDOA noise can be derived from (5) and represented as:

$$\varphi = h - G_a Z_a^0 \tag{7}$$

where $Z_a^0 = [X_{U-TDOA} \quad Y_{U-TDOA} \quad R_1]^T$ which is noise free value.

$$h = \frac{1}{2} \begin{bmatrix} R_{2,1}^2 - X_2^2 - Y_2^2 + X_1^2 + Y_1^2 \\ R_{3,1}^2 - X_3^2 - Y_3^2 + X_1^2 + Y_1^2 \\ \vdots \quad \vdots \quad \vdots \\ R_{M,1}^2 - X_M^2 - Y_M^2 + X_1^2 + Y_1^2 \end{bmatrix} \qquad G_a = - \begin{bmatrix} X_{2,1} & Y_{2,1} & R_{2,1} \\ X_{3,1} & Y_{3,1} & R_{3,1} \\ \vdots & \vdots & \vdots \\ X_{M,1} & Y_{M,1} & R_{M,1} \end{bmatrix}$$

and the error vector φ is assumed to be normally distributed Gaussian random vector with covariance matrix Ψ given by:

$$\psi = E[\varphi \varphi^T] = c^2 BQB \tag{8}$$

where $B = \mathrm{diag}\{R_2^0, R_3^0, \ldots, R_M^0\}$, $Q = \hat{R}^{U-TDOA} = \mathrm{diag}\{\sigma_{2,1}^2, \sigma_{3,1}^2, \cdots, \sigma_{M,1}^2\}$ U-TDOA measurement noise covariant matrix.

Still Eq. (7) is nonlinear because of elements of Z_a and solving this equation is possible after applying two step procedures and the result is given as:

$$Z_a = \arg\min \{(h - G_a Z_a)^T \psi^{-1} (h - G_a Z_a) \tag{9}$$

To make Eq. (9) solvable further approximation is necessary and an approximation of (9) is:

$$Z_a \approx (G_a^T Q^{-1} G_a)^{-1} G^T Q^{-1} h \tag{10}$$

The solution given by (9) assumes that X_{U-TDOA}, Y_{U-TDOA} and R_1 are independent. However they are related by (1). Hence incorporating this relationship enables to get improved estimate and defined as:

$$Z_a' = \left\{ \begin{bmatrix} 1 & 0 \\ 0 & 1 \\ 1 & 1 \end{bmatrix}^T (\psi')^{-1} \begin{bmatrix} 1 & 0 \\ 0 & 1 \\ 1 & 1 \end{bmatrix} \right\}^{-1} \begin{bmatrix} 1 & 0 \\ 0 & 1 \\ 1 & 1 \end{bmatrix}^T (\psi')^{-1} \begin{bmatrix} Z_{a,1}^2 \\ Z_{a,2}^2 \\ Z_{a,3}^2 \end{bmatrix} \tag{11}$$

where $\psi' = E[\varphi \varphi^T] = 4 \begin{bmatrix} Z_{a,1} & & \\ & Z_{a,2}^2 & \\ & & Z_{a,3}^2 \end{bmatrix} \mathrm{cov}(Z_a) \begin{bmatrix} Z_{a,1} & & \\ & Z_{a,2}^2 & \\ & & Z_{a,3}^2 \end{bmatrix} \tag{12}$

The result $Z_a' = [X_{U-TDOA} \ Y_{U-TDOA} \ R_1]^T$ represents the position estimation.

2.3 Fusion of the Measurement

Centralized measurement fusion is done by fusing the measurements $Z_{A\text{-GPS}}$ and $Z_{U\text{-}TDOA}$ as presented in [18] to new fused measurement $\hat{Z}_{MF} = [\hat{x}_{MF}\ \hat{y}_{MF}]^{T}$. Weighted least square criterion is applied to determine the measurement fusion result as well as the fused covariance $\hat{R}_{MF}$. The fused measurement $\hat{Z}_{MF}$ and the associated measurement noise covariance matrix $\hat{R}_{MF}$ are defined as:

$$\hat{Z}_{MF}(k) = \frac{\hat{R}^{A-GPS}X_{U-TDOA}(K) + \hat{R}^{U-TDOA}X_{A-GPS}(K)}{\hat{R}^{A-GPS} + \hat{R}^{U-TDOA}} \tag{13}$$

$$\hat{R}_{MF} = \left[(\hat{R}^{A-GPS})^{-1} + (\hat{R}^{U-TDOA})^{-1}\right]^{-1} \tag{14}$$

where $Z_{A\text{-}GPS}(K)$ is A-GPS measurement at time index k, $Z_{U-TDOA}(K)$ is U-TDOA measurement at time index k, $\hat{R}^{A-GPS}$ is A-GPS measurement noise covariant matrix, $\hat{R}^{U-TDOA}$ is U-TDOA measurement noise covariant matrix.

2.4 Position and Velocity State Estimation

This subsection discusses location and velocity estimations of the moving in-vehicle UE using Kalman Filter (KF) from the fused measurement $\hat{Z}_{MF}$. To determine all possible states of the moving in-vehicle UE on the road network the mobility model applied is also described.

Mobility Models: Mobility models represent a state-space model that describes the motion of user equipment located in a road vehicle. A state-space model represents the time evolution of the system state of the user equipment in terms of differential equation in continuous-time but inputs change at discrete-time observed (measured) instances which are modelled as sample-data systems [19]. In general a state-space representation of continuous-time dynamics can be written as:

$$\dot{x}(t) = A(t)x(t) + B(t)u(t) + v(t) \tag{15}$$

where x is state vector, u is input control, v is process noise vector, A is transition/ system vector matrix and B is input gain at continuous-time.

Vehicle Motion Kinematics: Kinematic state models are defined by setting certain derivative of the position zero and if there is no random input, the motion is characterized by a polynomial in time [20]. Several kinematic models are available for tracking manoeuvring and non-manoeuvring targets. However, simplified state estimation kinematic models like White Noise Acceleration (WNA), the Wiener process acceleration (WPA), and the Keplerian State (KPS) model are preferable for state estimation [21].

Both WNA and WPA models are widely used in estimating state of moving targets because of the less complexity compared to KPS model [21]. But WNA is commonly used for tracking non-manoeuvring targets whose motions deviate little from the straight line path and with low initial measurement accuracy, WNA and WPA models are very consistent when compared to KPS [22]. Hence in this research work, the moving user equipment located in a road vehicle is modelled as a dynamic linear system driven by continuous white noise acceleration. Assuming the user equipment located in a vehicle is moving in 2D Cartesian coordinate system, the state vector of the moving user equipment is defined as:

$$X(t) = [x(t) \quad y(t) \quad \dot{x}(t) \quad \dot{y}(t)]^T \tag{16}$$

where $x(t)$ and $y(t)$ are user equipment locations, $\dot{x}(t)$ and $\dot{y}(t)$ are velocities of the moving user equipment.

The motion of the moving UE is described as continuous White Noise Acceleration (WNA) model [20]. In this model the velocity, although assumed constant, has slight changes and it can be modelled by continuous-time zero-mean white acceleration $v(t)$ as:

$$\ddot{x}(t) = \ddot{y}(t) = v(t), \ E[v(t)v^T(\tau)] = Q_c\delta(t - \tau) \tag{17}$$

where Q_c is power spectrum density.

The continuous-time state equation of the model is expressed as:

$$\dot{x}(t) = A x(t) + v(t) \tag{18}$$

After discretization, the discrete-time state equation with sampling period ΔT in the sample-data system is given as:

$$X(k+1) = F X(k) + V(K) \tag{19}$$

With the transition matrix

$$F = e^{A\Delta t} = \begin{bmatrix} 1 & 0 & \Delta T & 0 \\ 0 & 1 & 0 & \Delta T \\ 0 & 0 & 1 & 0 \\ 0 & 0 & 0 & 1 \end{bmatrix} \tag{20}$$

and the process noise vector $V(K) = [0 \ 0 \ v(k) \ v(k)]^T$ has a covariance given as

$$Q = E[V(k)V(k)^T] = \begin{bmatrix} \frac{1}{3}\Delta T^3 & 0 & \frac{1}{2}\Delta T^2 & 0 \\ 0 & \frac{1}{3}\Delta T^3 & 0 & \frac{1}{2}\Delta T^2 \\ \frac{1}{2}\Delta T^2 & 0 & \Delta T & 0 \\ 0 & \frac{1}{2}\Delta T^2 & 0 & \Delta T \end{bmatrix} Q_c \tag{21}$$

Where Q_c is process noise intensity whose choice should follow the guideline that the changes in the velocity over a sampling period T are of the order $\sqrt{Q_{22}} = \sqrt{Q_c T}$ and should be small relative to the actual velocity level [20].

Measurement Models: The discretized version of the state vector (16) is related to the location observation Z (k) by the measurement equation defined by

$$Z(k) = HX(k) + W(K), \text{ Where } H = \begin{bmatrix} 1 & 0 & 0 & 0 \\ 0 & 1 & 0 & 0 \end{bmatrix}, \tag{22}$$

which takes the measurement observation not the velocity and the measurement noise vector W(k). The measurement noise can be modelled as:

$$W(k) = \begin{bmatrix} w(k) \\ w(k) \end{bmatrix} \sim N\left(\begin{bmatrix} 0 \\ 0 \end{bmatrix}, \begin{bmatrix} R & 0 \\ 0 & R \end{bmatrix} \right),$$

Where, $R = \delta x = \delta y$ is the measurement error variance. It is assumed that the variances in both x and y directions are the same and independent.

Kalman Filter: To Track the user equipment moving in the entire journey with the vehicle at real-time, discrete-time Kalman filter (KF) is used for A-GPS and U-TDOA based noisy location measurements. The KF provided recursive solution for state estimation of the linear system described by (18) and (23) and written as:

$$X_k = FX_{k-1} + V_{k-1}, V_{k-1}N(0,Q), \quad Z_k = HX_k + W_k, W_k \sim N(0,R) \tag{23}$$

Where, Q and R are covariance matrices for process nose vector V_{k-1} and the measurement noise vector Wk respectively. The optimal state estimations with minimum variance as derived in [19, 20] are given as follows.

Priori fused estimate $\left(\hat{X}_K^{f-} \right)$ at time K is, $\hat{X}_K^{f-} = F\hat{X}_{k-1}^{f+}$ (24)

Priori fused covariance $\left(P_K^{f-} \right)$ is $P_K^{f-} = FP_{K-1}^{f+}F^T + Q$ (25)

Fused Kalman Gain $\left(K_K^f \right)$ is, $K_k^f = P_K^{f-} \hat{H}_{MF}^T (\hat{H}_{MF} P_K^{f-} \hat{H}_{MF}^T + \hat{R}_{MF})^{-1}$ (26)

Posteriori fused estimate $\left(\hat{X}_K^{f+} \right)$ at time K is, $\hat{X}_K^{f+} = \hat{X}_K^{f-} + K_K^f(Z_{MF_k} - \hat{H}_{MF}\hat{X}_K^{f-})$

   (27)

Posteriori fused covariance $\left(P_K^{f+} \right)$ is, $P_K^{f+} = (I - K_K^f\hat{H}_{MF})P_K^{f-}$ (28)

The matrices F, Q, H and R are defined before tracking the moving user equipment starts. Hence Eqs. (25), (26) and (28) can be evaluated offline and this feature favoured a real-time moving user equipment tracking application.

3 Simulation Results

The proposed hybrid vehicle positioning and tracking scheme depicted in Fig. 1 is evaluated using simulation of typical vehicle motion in urban area on MATLAB. In the simulation first a random vehicle route/trajectory is generated based on the dynamic model represented by Eq. (18). And based on observation of real vehicle speeds in urban traffic road, the model is practical and motion of vehicles can be modelled as Gaussian Process [23]. Considering typical vehicle motion in urban traffic road, average speed of 54 km/hr. (15 m/s) and mean acceleration of 1 m/s^2 are applied in the simulation. And according to McGuire and Plataniotis [23], the UE acceleration process is a zero-mean Gaussian process with variance σ^2 in both x-and y-coordinate directions with magnitude of Rayleigh distributed random variable with mean of $\sigma\sqrt{\pi/2}$. Hence the value of $\sigma^2 = Qc$ in Eq. (22) is given as $2 * \bar{a}^2/\pi$.

To generate UE position estimations based on U-TDOA positioning technique, a network of 7 NodeBs which include serving NodeB and other 6 neighbouring NodeBs is created in a hexagonal cells with radius 1 km on MATLAB as depicted in Fig. 2(a). The position coordinates of NodeBs are (0, 0), (1500, 866), (1500, −866), (0, −1732), (−1500, −866), (−1500, 866) and (0, 1732). Then true position estimate of UE is generated at every 1000 Monte Carlo run and with the assumption of U-TDOA based estimation noise is unbiased Gaussian, location estimation error, the squared distance of the estimation to the true UE location is calculated using Root Mean Square Error (RMSE) which is computed as [24]:

$$\text{RMSE} = \sqrt{\frac{1}{mc}\sum_{k=1}^{mc}(Pos_k^{U-TDOA} - Pos_k^{True})^T(Pos_k^{U-TDOA} - Pos_k^{True})} \qquad (29)$$

Where $Pos_k^{U-TDOA} = [X^{U-TDOA}\ Y^{U-TDOA}]^T$, mc IS number of Monte Carlo performed and for each grid point 1000 independent Monte Carlo runs are computed.

To determine position estimate of UE, different number of NodeBs ranging from 4 to 7 are chosen to perform UE positioning simulation as shown in Fig. 2(b). Assuming signal and noise at each NodeBs is white random process [17], the RMSE of U-TDOA estimation is obtained at noise values of 39 m, 78 m and 117 m which are 0.5, 1 and 1.5 chip periods in UMTS networks [25]. And as it can be seen in Fig. 2(b), positioning accuracy increases with an increase of participating NodeBs.

But RMSE of 78.1 m (as it is indicated in Fig. 2-b) where 6NodeBs are hearable with U-TDOA noise of 100 m is selected in this simulation. This is because U-TDOA timing measurement accuracy is 3.84 Mchips/sec which is 78.125 m [25] and measurements in [26] demonstrated that at this estimation noise the positioning accuracies for the probability of 67 % and 95 % of the calls meet the requirement of E-911.

The location of A-GPS based in-vehicle mobile is collected in 13 min trip in urban area of Addis Ababa and total of 158 valid location updates were measured with in a time rate of 5 s in a sample trajectory shown in Fig. 3.

The positioning error of A-GPS based UE positioning method is obtained from the field test in the form of horizontal and vertical accuracy. The horizontal and vertical

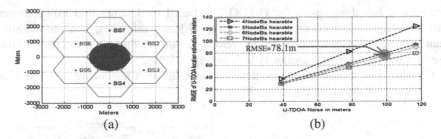

Fig. 2. U-TDOA based UE position estimation, (a) Mobile Network Cell Regions

accuracy collected at each UE location sample is the RMS composed of the northing (σ_N) and Easting (σ_E) standard deviations [27]. Assuming the circular case ($\sigma_N = \sigma_E$), A-GPS based UE location error is generated as Gaussian noise with variance $\sigma = (Acc_k/\sqrt{2})^2$, where Acc represents the recorded horizontal accuracy at time t_k.

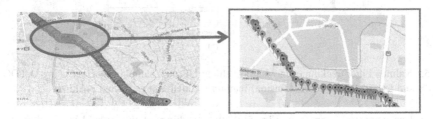

Fig. 3. Sample trajectory for moving in-vehicle UE used to collect its location

Hence using variances of U-TDOA based UE position estimation, A-GPS based UE location measurement and the fusion measurement, sample UE trajectory together with the generated noisy U-TDOA based UE estimation, A-GPS based UE measurement and their Fusion measurement using the described model are generated as depicted in Fig. 4.

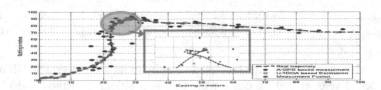

Fig. 4. Real UE track vs. the generated A-GPS, U-TDOA and MF based locations.

Discrete Kalman filter (described in Sect. 3) is applied to truck the moving in-vehicle UE at real-time for each of the noisy location measurements. And according to McGuire and Plataniotis [23], good selection of initial condition for filters is essential for tracking algorithms. Accordingly in this simulation for the KF, the position estimates are initialized by first locations measurements of A-GPS and U-TDOA based UE positioning. The initial velocity estimates are zeros as at t_0 there is no location information. Initial variances for U-TDOA is based on Cramer-Rao Lower Bound (CRLB) which is derived from [17], for A-GPS based estimates, it is the statistical mean from accuracy of test data and for velocity estimates the initial variance is taken based on the fact that initial velocity is between ±15 m/s.

Filtering on a sample trajectory, the position estimation results are depicted along the trajectory as shown in Fig. 5(a), (b) and (c).

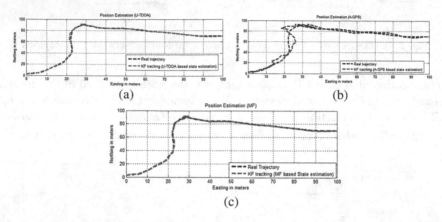

(a)   (b)

(c)

Fig. 5. Kalman Filter tracking of moving in-vehicle UE on a sample trajectory using U-TDOA, A-GPS and hybrid (Measurement Fusion) methods, actual and estimated position.

And as it can be seen from Fig. 5(c), the tracking of the hybrid state estimation, shows better match to the real sample trajectory (numeric values are to be provided later at Table 1). And Kalman Filter of real and estimated velocities for each noisy measurement is illustrated in Fig. 6(a), (b) and (c).

Table 1. Sample mean and standard deviation of position and velocity estimation

Generated sample trajectories N = 1000	U-TDOA		A-GPS		Hybrid (MF)	
	μ_{RMSE}	σ_{RMSE}	μ_{RMSE}	σ_{RMSE}	μ_{RMSE}	σ_{RMSE}
RMSE$_{position}$	24.1355	3.2589	47.9638	3.6992	21.9301	2.9142
RMSE$_{velocity}$	3.5592	0.5016	7.1873	0.6478	3.3089	0.4493

As it is shown in Fig. 6(c), the estimated velocity of moving in-vehicle UE matches with the actual velocity and we can say the hybrid positioning method (MF) is better from U-TDOA and A-GPS UE positioning methods. To compare the estimation accuracy of U-TDOA, A-GPS and the Hybrid (MF) methods, RMSE of 1000 different sample trajectories with 158 Kalman Filter each is computed and totally took 6 min. The sample mean (μRMSE) and standard deviation (σRMSE) from RMSE of position and velocity is calculated based on 1000 different sample trajectories generated and filtered with 158 filter steps each. And as it is shown in Table 1 the performance of the Hybrid (MF) UE positioning method is better from A-GPS and U-TDOA methods with minimum estimation error of position and velocity and the error is less dispersed.

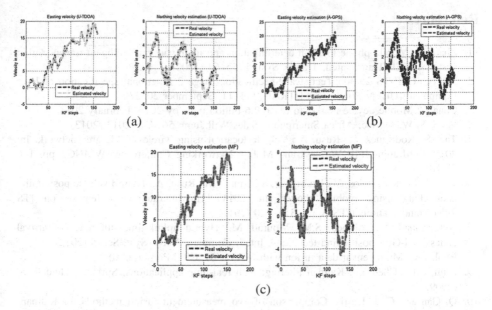

(a)

(b)

(c)

Fig. 6. Kalman Filter tracking of moving in-vehicle UE on a sample trajectory using U-TDOA, A-GPS and hybrid (Measurement Fusion) methods, actual and estimated velocities.

4   Conclusion

In this paper, hybrid UE-based Vehicle position and tracking based on the UE moving along all journey of the vehicle has been proposed. The proposed hybrid method, which combines the measurements from both U-TDOA and A-GPS, utilized a measurement fusion approach to get fused results of UE position measurements from the U-TDOA and A-GPS. Dynamic white Noise Acceleration (WNA) model is applied in generating noisy location measurements along a sample trajectory based on U-TDOA, A-GPS and MF measurement noise variances. Kalman filter is used to track the position and velocity state estimations of U-TDOA, A-GPS and MF based measurements and MF based measurements are with better match to real trajectory than the individuals. Moreover, computing RMSE of estimation errors with 1000 independent sample trajectories with a filter of 158 filter points each revealed that MF based UE position estimations are with less sample mean estimation error and less dispersed than U-TDOA as well as A-GPS based positioning methods.

Acknowledgement. This work was also supported in the framework of the IT4 Innovations Centre of Excellence project, reg. no. CZ.1.05/1.1.00/02.0070 by operational programme 'Research and Development for Innovations' funded by the Structural Funds of the European Union and state budget of the Czech Republic, EU.

References

1. Zhao, Y.: Mobile phone location determination and its impact on intelligent transportation systems. IEEE Trans. Intell. Transp. Syst. **1**, 55–64 (2000)
2. 3GPP: 3GPP TS 25.305 Technical Specification Stage 2 functional specification of User Equipment (UE) positioning in UTRAN, vol. 11, September 2012
3. Canalys: Mobile device market to reach 2.6 billion units by 2016, February 2013
4. W. S. S. W. service: Africa Smartphone Sales Will Jump 56 % in 2013 (2013)
5. Tao, S., Rodriguez, S., Rusu, A.: Vehicle location using wireless wide area network. In: 2010 Third Joint IFIP Wireless and Mobile Networking Conference (WMNC), pp. 1–6 (2010)
6. Tao, S., Manolopoulos, V., Rodriguez, S., Ismail, M., Rusu, A.: Hybrid vehicle positioning andtracking using mobile phones. In: 2011 11th InternationalConference on ITS Telecommunications (ITST), pp. 315–320 (2011)
7. Abo-Zahhad, M., Ahmed, S.M., Mourad, M.: Hybrid uplink-time difference of arrival andassisted-GPS positioning technique. Int. J. Commun. Netw. Syst. Sci. **5** (2012)
8. Raol, J.R.: Multi-sensor data fusion with MATLAB, CRC Press (2010)
9. Chui, C.K., Chen, G.: Kalman filtering: with real-time applications, Springer, Heidelberg (2009)
10. Q. Gan and C. J. Harris, Comparison of two measurement fusion methods for Kalman-filterbasedmultisensor data fusion. IEEE Trans. Aerosp. Electron. Syst. **37**, 273–279 (2001)
11. Cipriani, E., Gori, S., Mannini, L.: Traffic state estimation based on data fusiontechniques. In: 2012 15th International IEEEConference on Intelligent Transportation Systems (ITSC), pp. 1477–1482 (2012)
12. Yadaiah, N., Singh, L., Bapi, R.S., Rao, V.S., Deekshatulu, B.L., Negi, A.: Multisensor datafusion using neural networks. In: International JointConference on Neural Networks, IJCNN 2006, pp. 875–881 (2006)
13. JCP, Java Specification Request (JSR) 179: Location API for J2METM (2011)
14. Hamdy, Y.R., Mawjoud, S.A.: Performance assessment of U-TDOA and A-GPSpositioning methods. In: 2012 InternationalConference on Future Communication Networks (ICFCN), pp. 99–104 (2012)
15. Axel, K.: Location-Based Services: Fundamentals and Operation. Wiely, New York (2005)
16. Senturk, H.: Performance Evaluation of Hyperbolic Position Location Technique in CellularWireless Networks, DTIC Document (2002)
17. Chan, Y., Ho, K.: A simple and efficient estimator for hyperbolic location. IEEE Transactions on Signal Processing **42**, 1905–1915 (1994)
18. Naidu, V.: Fusion of radar and IRST sensor measurements for 3D target tracking usingextended Kalman filter. Defence Sci. J. **59**, 175–182 (2009)
19. Simon, D.: Optimal state estimation: Kalman, H infinity, and nonlinear approaches. Wiley (2006)
20. Bar-Shalom, Y., Li, X.R., Kirubarajan, T.: Estimation with applications to tracking andnavigation: theory algorithms and software. Wiley (2004)
21. Tian, X., Chen, G., Blasch, E., Pham, K., Bar-Shalom, Y.: Comparison of three approximatekinematic models for space object tracking. In: 2013 16thInternational Conference on Information Fusion (FUSION), pp. 1005–1012 (2013)
22. Kim, J., Menon, P., Ohlmeyer, E.: Motion models for use with the Maneuvering Ballistic Missile tracking estimators. In: AIAA Guidance, Navigation, and Control Conference, pp. 2–5 (2010)

23. McGuire, M., Plataniotis, K.N.: Dynamic model-based filtering for mobile terminal locationestimation. IEEE Trans. Veh. Technol. **52**, 1012–1031 (2003)
24. Kaune, R.: Accuracy studies for TDOA and TOA localization. In: 2012 15th International Conference on Information Fusion(FUSION), pp. 408–415 (2012)
25. Zhao, Y.: Standardization of mobile phone positioning for 3G systems. IEEE Commun. Mag. **40**, 108–116 (2002)
26. Guan, W., Deng, Z., Ge, Y., Zou, D.: A practical TDOA positioning method for CDMA2000mobile network. In: 2010 IEEE International Conference on Wireless Communications, Networking and Information Security (WCNIS),pp. 126–129 (2010)
27. NOVATEL. Statistics and its relationship to accuracy measure in GPS (2003)

Parallelizing NSGAII for Accelerating the Registration Areas Optimization in Mobile Communication Networks

Víctor Berrocal-Plaza[(⊠)], Miguel A. Vega-Rodríguez, and Juan M. Sánchez-Pérez

Department of Computers and Communications Technologies, University of Extremadura Escuela Politécnica, Campus Universitario S/N, 10003 Cáceres, Spain
{vicberpla,mavega,sanperez}@unex.es

Abstract. In this work, we propose a parallel version of our adaptation of the Non-dominated Sorting Genetic Algorithm II (NSGAII) with the aim of reducing its execution time when solving the Registration Areas Planning Problem (RAPP), a problem that describes one of the most popular strategies to manage the subscribers' movement in a mobile communication network. In this problem, the use of mobile activity traces is a good choice that allows us to assess the Registration Areas strategy in an accurate way. However and due to the huge number of mobile subscribers, a mobile activity trace of a current network could contain several millions of events, which leads to a large execution time. That is the reason why we propose to parallelize our version of NSGAII in a shared memory system, using for that the OpenMP Application Program Interface. The quality and efficiency of our approach is shown by means of an experimental study.

Keywords: OpenMP · Non-dominated Sorting Genetic Algorithm II · Mobile location management · Registration Areas

1 Introduction

Public Land Mobile Networks (PLMNs), as their name suggests, are the networks that provide mobile communications to the public. This kind of networks is being widely used throughout the world. As reported by the GSM Association, approximately the half of the world population will use mobile communications in 2017[1]. In a PLMN, the coverage area is arranged in several smaller land regions known as cells. The main reason of the cell division of the coverage area is to distribute and reuse the different radio-resources, and in this way, be able to cope with such huge service demand. However, a direct consequence of this cell-based architecture is that a mobile station (i.e. the subscriber's terminal) can be in any cell at any time, and hence, the network must have a procedure to

---

[1] GSM Association (GSMA): The Mobile Economy (2013).

© Springer International Publishing Switzerland 2015
E. Onieva et al. (Eds.): HAIS 2015, LNAI 9121, pp. 620–631, 2015.
DOI: 10.1007/978-3-319-19644-2_51

automatically detect the cell in which the callee's terminal is located in order to properly redirect the incoming call. For it, every PLMN has a system that tracks the subscribers' movement: the Location Management System. In relation with the mobility management, this system controls two main tasks: the subscribers' location update and the paging [1].

The location update is the procedure by means of which the mobile stations report to the network that their location (in terms of network cells) should be updated in the databases of the Core Network. In the literature, we can find several strategies of location update: periodic, movement-based, distance-based, cell-based, and area-based [2]. On the other hand, there are also several strategies of paging, mainly classified into two groups: simultaneous paging (in where all the network cells that have to be paged are polled simultaneously) and sequential paging (in where the network cells that have to be paged are grouped into two or more paging areas, which are sequentially polled). In this work, we study the location update strategy based on Registration Areas (an area-based strategy) because it is widely used in current mobile communication networks [3]. Moreover, the paging scheme used is the simultaneous paging.

In a location update strategy based on Registration Areas (RAs), the main challenge consists in finding the configurations of Registration Areas that minimize the number of location updates and the number of paging messages simultaneously (see Sect. 3). This optimization problem (called Registration Areas Planning Problem) is a multiobjective optimization problem that can be classified as NP-hard [4]. We propose to solve this problem by using a multiobjective genetic algorithm; and more specifically, an adaptation of the Non-dominated Sorting Genetic Algorithm II [5].

The main contribution of this work is the use of parallelism techniques for reducing the large execution time that results when the Registration Areas Planning Problem (RAPP) is optimized by using mobile activity traces. For definition, a mobile activity trace is a chronological list of events related to the subscribers' call and mobility patterns [6]. The use of mobile activity traces is a good choice because it allows us to study any mobility management strategy in an accurate way. However and considering that a current mobile network might have several thousands of subscribers, the assessment of a mobile activity trace increases considerably the execution time because it could have several millions of events. This is the reason why we propose a parallel version of our adaptation of the Non-dominated Sorting Genetic Algorithm II (NSGAII), a well-known multiobjective evolutionary algorithm proposed by K. Deb et al. in [5]. To the best of the authors' knowledge, this manuscript is the first one in the literature in which parallelism techniques are applied to RAPP.

The paper is organized as follows. The related work is discussed in Sect. 2. The Registration Areas strategy is explained in Sect. 3. Some basic concepts of multiobjective optimization, our adaptation of NSGAII, and a comparison with the NSGAII available in Matlab are presented in Sect. 4. The motivations for using parallelism in RAPP are discussed in Sect. 5, in where we also explain how we have parallelized NSGAII. The scalability study accomplished to evaluate the efficiency of our approach is shown in Sect. 6. Finally, our conclusions and future work are discussed in Sect. 8.

2   Related Work

There are several papers in the literature in which very different optimization techniques are applied to solve the Registration Areas Planning Problem (RAPP). P. R. L. Gondim is one of the first authors to study this problem with a Genetic Algorithm (GA) [4]. In his work, the RAPP is classified as an NP-hard optimization problem due to the huge size of the objective space. Afterwards, P. Demestichas et al. propose three metaheuristics (Simulated Annealing (SA), Tabu Search (TS), and GA) to analyze the Registration Areas strategy in different environments [7]. I. Demirkol et al. study in [8] the behavior of an optimization algorithm based on the SA but considering the paging cost as a constraint. J. Taheri and A. Y. Zomaya analyze in their research the suitability of several single-objective metaheuristics for solving the RAPP: Hopfield Neural Network (HNN) [9], SA [10], GA [11], and different combinations of the HNN with the GA [12]. Recently, S. M. Almeida-Luz et al. have proposed the use of the Differential Evolution [13] and the Scatter Search [14]. The main weakness of these papers is that they all propose the use of single-objective metaheuristics for solving a problem which is in essence a multiobjective optimization problem (as will be shown in Sect. 3). That is the reason why we research the suitability of different multiobjective optimization techniques [15,16]. Furthermore, with a multiobjective approach, we avoid the problems associated with the linear aggregation of the objective functions (all of them related to the proper value of the weight coefficients). On the other hand, the network information used in these related work [9–14] is very compressed and simplified (they only consider three attributes per cell: number of incoming calls, number of incoming users, and number of outgoing users), which is not enough for studying advanced mobility management strategies.

In our latest work on Registration Areas [16], we studied the mobile activity trace developed by J. Jannink and Y. Cui in [6]. During the course of that work, we could notice that the execution time of our optimizers was much higher than their execution time when solving the simplified test networks proposed and/or studied in previously published works [9–14]. That is the reason why we consider the use of parallelism techniques. To our best knowledge, this is the first time that parallelism techniques are applied to RAPP.

3   Registration Areas Planning

In a location update strategy based on Registration Areas (see Fig. 1), the network cells are arranged in continuous and non-overlapped groups (where every group of cells is a Registration Area) with the aim of partially tracking the subscribers' movement [2]. For it, the mobile stations must report to the network

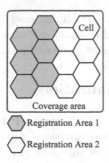

Fig. 1. Registration Areas strategy

that their location should be updated whenever they move from one Registration Area to another. Therefore, and considering that the network knows the location of its subscribers at a Registration Area level, a callee's terminal must only be searched in the cells inside the last visited Registration Area (for the mobile station in question).

The main challenge of this location update strategy consists in finding the configurations of Registration Areas that minimize simultaneously the number of location updates (or location update cost, LU) and the number of paging messages (or paging cost, PA). Formally, these two objective functions can be described by Eqs. 1 and 2 respectively:

$$\mathbf{f}_1 = \min \left\{ \mathrm{LU} = \sum_{t=T_{\mathrm{ini}}}^{T_{\mathrm{fin}}} \sum_{i=1}^{N_{\mathrm{user}}} \gamma_{t,i} \right\}, \tag{1}$$

$$\mathbf{f}_2 = \min \left\{ \mathrm{PA} = \sum_{t=T_{\mathrm{ini}}}^{T_{\mathrm{fin}}} \sum_{i=1}^{N_{\mathrm{user}}} \rho_{t,i} \cdot \mid \mathrm{RA}_{t,i} \mid \right\}. \tag{2}$$

where $[T_{\mathrm{ini}}, T_{\mathrm{fin}}]$ is the time interval during which the Registration Areas strategy is evaluated. N_{user} is the number of subscribers. $\gamma_{t,i}$ is a binary variable which is equal to 1 when the mobile station i crosses the border between two Registration Areas in the time t. $\rho_{t,i}$ is a binary variable which is equal to 1 when the mobile station i has an incoming call in the time t. $\mid \mathrm{RA}_{t,i} \mid$ is the number of cells inside the last visited Registration Area for the mobile station i.

It should be noticed that these two objective functions are conflicting, and therefore, the Registration Areas Planning Problem can be classified as a multi-objective optimization problem. Firstly, observe that the location update cost is maximized when every network cell belongs to a different Registration Area (in this case, the mobile stations update their location whenever they move from one network cell to another). However, the paging cost is minimum in this configuration of Registration Areas because the network knows the exact cell in where every mobile station is located (i.e. $\mid \mathrm{RA}_{t,i} \mid = 1 \ \forall t,i$). On the other hand, the location update cost is minimum when all the network cells are grouped into the same Registration Area (i.e. the mobile stations never update their location,

$\gamma_{t,i} = 0$ $\forall t,i$). But in that case, the paging cost is maximum because a mobile station should be searched in the whole network whenever it has an incoming call (i.e. $|$ $RA_{t,i}$ $|= N_{cell}$ $\forall t,i$, where N_{cell} is the number of network cells).

4   Multiobjective Optimization

For definition, a Multiobjective Optimization Problem is the problem in which two or more conflicting objective functions must be optimized under certain constraints [17]. In this kind of optimization problems, the challenge consists in finding the best possible set of non-dominated solutions, i.e. the solutions related to a specific trade-off among objectives. Commonly, this set of non-dominated solutions is referred as Pareto set (its image in the objective space is known as Pareto front). In the following and without loss of generality, we assume a bi-objective minimization problem (as the problem addressed in this manuscript). According to this assumption and given a pair of solutions $\mathbf{x}^i$ and $\mathbf{x}^j$, the solution $\mathbf{x}^i$ is said to dominate the solution $\mathbf{x}^j$ (expressed as $\mathbf{x}^i \prec \mathbf{x}^j$) if and only if:

$$\forall k \in [1,2], \mathbf{z}_k^i = \boldsymbol{f}_k(\mathbf{x}^i) \leq \mathbf{z}_k^j = \boldsymbol{f}_k(\mathbf{x}^j) \land \exists k \in [1,2] : \mathbf{z}_k^i < \mathbf{z}_k^j. \tag{3}$$

With the aim of finding the best possible set of non-dominated solutions, we use our adaptation of the Non-dominated Sorting Genetic algorithm II (NSGAII) [5]. NSGAII is a multiobjective evolutionary algorithm that uses the evolutionary operators of biological systems (recombination of parents or crossover, mutation, and natural selection) in order to iteratively improve a set of initial solutions. Furthermore, NSGAII is a population-based algorithm, which means that it deals simultaneously with a set of solutions (every individual of the population is an encoded solution of the problem). We have chosen a multiobjective evolutionary algorithm due to its suitability for solving multiobjective optimization problems [17].

Algorithm 1 presents the pseudo-code of NSGAII. As we can see in this pseudo-code, the first step in NSGAII is to initialize the first population of N_{pop} parents (line 3 (L3) of the pseudo-code). For it, every individual is randomly generated. Then, we evaluate the objective functions (L4) and the fitness function (L7) for these solutions. NSGAII has its own fitness function to estimate the quality of a solution in the multiobjective context. In this fitness function, firstly, we arrange the solutions in fronts by using the dominance concept. Then, the crowding distance is evaluated to discriminate among solutions of the same front. For further information about the fitness function of NSGAII, please consult [5]. After the initialization, the evolutionary operators are iteratively applied with the aim of improving this set of initial solutions (L9 - L26). Firstly, the crossover is used to generate a new population of N_{pop} individuals (the offspring) by recombining the individuals stored in the parent population with probability P_C (L12). In this work, we use an elitist crossover based on the binary tournament [17] in where the number of crossover points is randomly selected in the range $[1,4]$. Afterwards, the gene information of the offspring is slightly changed by means of the mutation operator, which is applied with probability P_M (L16).

Algorithm 1. Pseudo-code of NSGAII

```
1:  % Initialize and evaluate the parent population
2:  for p=1 to p=N_pop do
3:      Ind(p) ← Initialization();
4:      Ind(p) ← ObjectiveFunctionsEvaluation ( Ind(p) );
5:  end for
6:  % Evaluate the fitness function
7:  Ind ← FitnessEvaluation ( Ind, N_pop);
8:  % Main loop
9:  while stopping condition ≠ TRUE do
10:     % Crossover operation
11:     for p=N_pop + 1 to p=2·N_pop do
12:         Ind(p) ← Crossover ( Ind, P_C, N_pop );
13:     end for
14:     % Mutate the offspring
15:     for p=N_pop + 1 to p=2·N_pop do
16:         Ind(p) ← Mutation( Ind, P_M, N_pop);
17:     end for
18:     % Evaluate the offspring
19:     for p=N_pop + 1 to p=2·N_pop do
20:         Ind(p) ← ObjectiveFunctionsEvaluation ( Ind(p) );
21:     end for
22:     % Evaluate the fitness function
23:     Ind ← FitnessEvaluation ( Ind, 2·N_pop);
24:     % Natural selection
25:     Ind ← NaturalSelection ( Ind, N_pop);
26: end while
```

We have implemented two mutation operations. In the first one, the smallest RA is merged with its smallest neighboring RA. And in the second, a randomly selected border cell (i.e. a cell which is border among RAs) is merged with its smallest neighboring RA. After the mutation operation, the offspring is evaluated (L20 and L23) and finally, the natural selection is applied with the aim of selecting the best N_{pop} individuals as the parent population for the next generation (the best individuals will be those that have better fitness [5]). This iterative method is applied until reaching the stopping condition. In this work, we use the number of generations (N_G) as stopping condition.

The quality of our implementation of NSGAII has been already checked in our previous work [15,16], in where we showed that our proposal is able to surpass other metaheuristics developed by other authors [9–14]. In this manuscript, we extend our previous work with a comparison with the standard NSGAII available in Matlab. In order to perform a fair comparison, both algorithms use the same population size ($N_{pop} = 248$) and the same number of generations ($N_G = 3000$). The other parameters of our NSGAII have been configured by means of an experimental study of 30 independent runs per experiment. We have chosen the configuration that maximizes the Hypervolume: $P_C = 0.90$ and $P_M = 0.25$. The Hypervolume (I_H) is a multiobjective indicator which associates the quality of a Pareto front with the area of the objective space that is dominated by these non-dominated solutions, and is bounded by the reference points [17]. In the optimization problem addressed in this manuscript, these reference points can be easily obtained from the two extreme configurations of RAs: when all the cells belong to the same RA ($[LU_{min}, PA_{max}]$), and when each cell belongs to a different RA

Table 1. Comparison with the standard NSGAII available in Matlab

		Test Network 1	Test Network 2	Test Network 3	Test Network 4
Reference points					
LU_{min}		0	0	0	0
LU_{max}		5,675	8,770	13,284	19,860
PA_{min}		1,483	2,029	2,774	3,575
PA_{max}		37,075	71,015	135,926	225,225
Hypervolume indicator (I_H)					
Our NSGAII	$\bar{I}_H$	76.33	80.86	83.65	84.15
	σ_{I_H}	0.01	0.01	0.08	0.04
Standard NSGAII (Matlab)	$\bar{I}_H$	64.99	65.95	67.71	68.58
	σ_{I_H}	8.08	12.73	11.94	11.25

Table 2. Mean execution time per test network

	Test Network 1	Test Network 2	Test Network 3	Test Network 4
$\bar{T}(s)$	1119.73	1566.50	2271.80	3184.48

($[LU_{max}, PA_{min}]$). With this multiobjective indicator, the Pareto front A is said to be better than the Pareto front B when $I_H(A) > I_H(B)$.

The comparison with the standard NSGAII is performed over a set of four Test Networks of different complexity: Test Network 1 (TN1, a test network of 25 cells), Test Network 2 (TN2, a test network of 35 cells), Test Network 3 (TN3, a test network of 49 cells), and Test Network 4 (TN4, a test network of 63 cells). The results of this comparison are gathered in Table 1, where we present the reference points of each test network and statistical data of the Hypervolume indicator (we have performed 30 independent runs): mean ($\bar{I}_H$) and standard deviation (σ_{I_H}). This table reveals that our NSGAII obtains better and more stable results than the standard algorithm. A representation of the Pareto fronts associated with the mean I_H can be shown in Fig. 2. In this figure, we can see that our implementation of NSGAII is able to obtain more solutions and to explore better the objective space.

5 The Need for Parallelism

As stated in Sect. 1, the use of mobile activity traces allows the detailed study of any mobility management strategy. However, this choice considerably increases the execution time because a huge number of activity events should be analyzed per each evaluation of the objective functions. The mean execution time of our optimizer in each test network is presented in Table 2, in where we can see that the execution time of our implementation of NSGAII when solving the more complex test network (TN4) is about 53 min. If we extrapolate these data to a problem instance of several hundreds of cells (a common scenario in a current mobile network), the execution time of our proposal could be of several days. That is the reason why the use of parallelism techniques in the optimization problem addressed in this manuscript is an interesting research line.

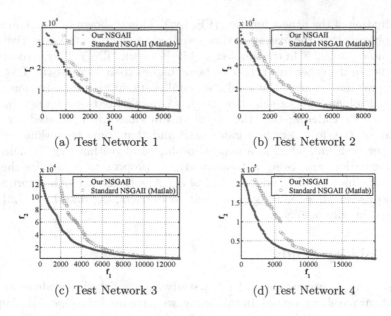

Fig. 2. Pareto fronts associated with the mean Hypervolume (Color figure online)

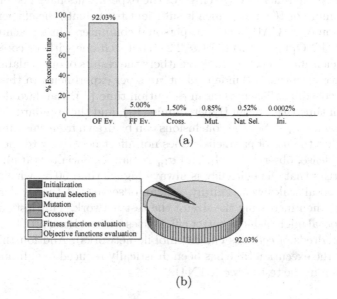

Fig. 3. Test Network 1. Mean execution time per operation (Color figure online)

With the aim of determining the percentage of time spent in calculating the objective functions, we have measured the execution time of every operation inside NSGAII: initialization procedure (Ini.), crossover (Cross.), mutation (Mut.), natural selection (Nat. Sel.), evaluation of the objective functions (OF. Ev.), and evaluation of the fitness function (FF. Ev.). This is shown in Fig. 3, in where we can observe that the execution time required to evaluate the objective functions is more than 92 % in the simplest mobile network (TN1). This percentage is even higher in the other test networks, being higher than 95 % for the TN4.

Once we have shown the need for parallelism in the Registration Areas Planning Problem, we explain how we have parallelized our implementation of NSGAII. Considering that the objective functions are evaluated for every new solution (i.e. for every new individual) and that some operations are performed per each individual in a population-based algorithm (e.g. initialization of the population, crossover, and mutation), we propose to parallelize the code between the lines L2 - L5 and L11 - L21 of the Algorithm 1. Furthermore and in order to prevent unnecessary synchronization barriers, the lines L11 - L21 have been fused in only one loop.

6   Scalability Study

In this section, we present the scalability study accomplished to evaluate the efficiency of our parallel proposal. In this study, we have used the OpenMP Application Program Interface because it is considered as a de facto standard for parallel computing in shared-memory systems. All the experiments have been performed up to a maximum of 16 cores (which is sufficient to evaluate the efficiency of our parallel version of NSGAII in current personal computers) in a machine with: 2 processors AMD Opteron(tm) 6174 @ 2.2 GHz (each one with 12 cores), 64-GB RAM, and Scientific Linux 6.1. Table 3 gathers the results of our scalability study, where we have performed 10 independent runs per experiment. In this table, we present: the speedup, efficiency, mean execution time ($\bar{T}$), standard deviation of the execution time (σ_T), mean Hypervolume ($\bar{I}_H$), and the standard deviation of the Hypervolume (σ_{I_H}). Several conclusions can be drawn from this table. Firstly, we observe that the use of parallelism does not affect negatively to the quality of our results (please, observe that $\bar{I}_H$ and σ_{I_H} remain essentially static). Secondly, it is noteworthy that the efficiency is always higher than 50 %, which indicates that our proposal scales well. Thirdly, we can observe that the acceleration factor increases when increasing the size of the test network. This last could mean that our proposal might achieve better efficiencies when solving problem instances of several hundreds of cells (as current mobile networks). And fourthly, we can observe that the execution time has been drastically reduced (e.g. from 53 min to less than 5 min in the test network TN4).

7   Comparison with Other Optimization Techniques

As stated in Sect. 4, the quality of our proposal has been already checked in our previous works [15, 16]. Nonetheless and with the aim of making the paper self-contained, this section presents a comparison with the metaheuristics proposed by other authors [9–14]. It should be noted that these previous metaheuristics are single-objective optimization techniques. In order to perform a comparison

Table 3. Scalability study

		Test Network 1	Test Network 2	Test Network 3	Test Network 4
2 cores	Speedup	1.87	1.92	1.90	1.90
	Efficiency(%)	93.49	96.04	94.87	94.78
	$\bar{T}(s)$	598.88	815.52	1197.31	1679.91
	σ_T	0.09	0.26	0.38	0.51
	$\bar{I}_H(\%)$	76.32	80.83	83.65	84.07
	σ_{I_H}	0.01	0.02	0.05	0.07
4 cores	Speedup	3.34	3.51	3.54	3.58
	Efficiency(%)	83.39	87.80	88.42	89.54
	$\bar{T}(s)$	335.68	446.06	642.37	889.11
	σ_T	0.11	0.19	0.18	0.34
	$\bar{I}_H(\%)$	76.32	80.84	83.62	84.11
	σ_{I_H}	0.01	0.02	0.05	0.06
8 cores	Speedup	5.54	6.03	6.27	6.51
	Efficiency(%)	69.19	75.31	78.35	81.33
	$\bar{T}(s)$	202.30	259.99	362.43	489.47
	σ_T	0.08	0.17	0.10	0.14
	$\bar{I}_H(\%)$	76.32	80.83	83.65	84.09
	σ_{I_H}	0.01	0.02	0.05	0.09
16 cores	Speedup	8.20	9.33	10.15	10.89
	Efficiency(%)	51.23	58.31	63.46	68.05
	$\bar{T}(s)$	136.60	167.90	223.75	292.46
	σ_T	0.08	0.13	0.08	0.11
	$\bar{I}_H(\%)$	76.33	80.83	83.62	84.12
	σ_{I_H}	0.01	0.03	0.08	0.04

Table 4. Comparison with other optimizers by other authors

	NSGAII	HNN [9]	SA [10]	GA [11]	GA-HNN1 [12]	GA-HNN2 [12]	GA-HNN3 [12]	DE [13]	SS [14]
TN1	26,990	27,249	26,990	28,299	26,990	26,990	26,990	26,990	26,990
TN2	39,832	39,832	42,750	40,085	40,117	39,832	39,832	39,859	39,832
TN3	60,685	63,516	60,694	61,938	62,916	62,253	60,696	61,037	60,685
TN4	89,085	92,493	90,506	90,318	92,659	91,916	91,819	89,973	89,085

with these optimizers, we have searched in our Pareto fronts the solutions that best optimize the aggregated objective function used in [9–14]. Furthermore and with the aim of performing a fair comparison, our proposal has been configured with the same population size ($N_{pop} = 250$) and the same number of generations ($N_G = 5000$). The results of this comparison are shown in Table 4, in where we can observe that our proposal is very competitive because it is able to obtain the minimum value found by these single-objective metaheuristics in all the test networks.

8 Conclusions and Future Work

Registration Areas Planning Problem is an important problem in the current mobile networks. The huge number of mobile users around the world makes that the efficient solution of this problem is a very important topic. This work addresses the use of parallelism techniques in shared-memory systems with the aim of reducing the execution time in the Registration Areas Planning Problem. The need for parallelism in this optimization problem arises when considering the network information in form of mobile activity traces (i.e. chronological lists of events related to the subscribers' call and mobility patterns). With mobile activity traces, we can study detailedly any mobility management strategy. Nonetheless, the use of mobile activity traces increases considerably the execution time because a lot of events should be analyzed per each evaluation of the objective functions. In fact, we have shown in Sect. 5 that the time required to evaluate the objective functions is more than 92 % of the total execution time. That is the reason why we have used the OpenMP Application Program Interface for implementing a parallel version of our adaptation of the Non-dominated Sorting Genetic Algorithm II (NSGAII, a well-known multiobjective evolutionary algorithm). We have chosen the OpenMP Application Program Interface because it is considered as a de facto standard for parallel computing in shared-memory systems. By means of a scalability study, we have shown the good efficiency of our parallel proposal (always higher than 50 %), which leads to a drastic reduction in the execution time of our optimizer. Furthermore, we have observed that the efficiency increases when increasing the size of the test network, which could indicate that we might obtain better results when solving real (or realistic) mobile networks (of several hundreds of cells). It is also noteworthy that the quality of our Pareto fronts (and the corresponding Hypervolume values) are clearly better than those obtained by the standard NSGAII (implemented in Matlab). This shows the advantages of our adaptation of NSGAII. As a future work, we propose to evaluate our proposal in more complex problem instances (with several hundreds of cells).

Acknowledgments. This work was partially funded by the Spanish Ministry of Economy and Competitiveness and the ERDF (European Regional Development Fund), under the contract TIN2012-30685 (BIO project). The work of Víctor Berrocal-Plaza has been developed under the Grant FPU-AP2010-5841 from the Spanish Government.

References

1. Kyamakya, K., Jobmann, K.: Location management in cellular networks: classification of the most important paradigms, realistic simulation framework, and relative performance analysis. IEEE Trans. Veh. Technol. **54**(2), 687–708 (2005)
2. Mukherjee, A., Bandyopadhyay, S., Saha, D.: Location Management and Routing in Mobile Wireless Networks. Artech House mobile communications series. Artech House, Boston (2003)

3. Lescuyer, P., Lucidarme, T.: Evolved Packet System (EPS): The LTE and SAE Evolution of 3G UMTS. Wiley Publishing, New York (2008)
4. Gondim, P.R.L.: Genetic algorithms and the location area partitioning problem in cellular networks. In: Procedings of the IEEE 46th Vehicular Technology Conference on Mobile Technology for the Human Race, vol. 3, pp. 1835–1838 (1996)
5. Deb, K., Pratap, A., Agarwal, S., Meyarivan, T.: A fast and elitist multiobjective genetic algorithm: NSGA-II. IEEE Trans. Evol. Comput. **6**(2), 182–197 (2002)
6. Jannink, J., Cui, Y.: Stanford University Mobile Activity TRAces (SUMATRA) (accessed in 2014). http://infolab.stanford.edu/sumatra
7. Demestichas, P., Georgantas, N., Tzifa, E., Demesticha, V., Striki, M., Kilanioti, M., Theologou, M.E.: Computationally efficient algorithms for location area planning in future cellular systems. Comput. Commun. **23**(13), 1263–1280 (2000)
8. Demirkol, I., Ersoy, C., Çaglayan, M.U., Deliç, H.: Location area planning and cell-to-switch assignment in cellular networks. IEEE Trans. Wireless Commun. **3**(3), 880–890 (2004)
9. Taheri, J., Zomaya, A.Y.: The use of a hopfield neural network in solving the mobility management problem. In: Proceedings of The IEEE/ACS International Conference on Pervasive Services, pp. 141–150 (2004)
10. Taheri, J., Zomaya, A.Y.: A simulated annealing approach for mobile location management. In: Proceedings of the 19th IEEE International Parallel and Distributed Processing Symposium, pp. 194–194 (2005)
11. Taheri, J., Zomaya, A.Y.: A genetic algorithm for finding optimal location area configurations for mobility management. In: Proceedings of the IEEE Conference on Local Computer Networks 30th Anniversary, pp. 568–577 (2005)
12. Taheri, J., Zomaya, A.Y.: A combined genetic-neural algorithm for mobility management. J. Math. Model. Algorithms **6**(3), 481–507 (2007)
13. Almeida-Luz, S.M., Vega-Rodríguez, M.A., Gómez-Púlido, J.A., Sánchez-Pérez, J.M.: Differential Evolution for solving the mobile location management. Appl. Soft Comput. **11**(1), 410–427 (2011)
14. Almeida-Luz, S.M., Vega-Rodríguez, M.A., Gómez-Pulido, J.A., Sánchez-Pérez, J.M.: Applying scatter search to the location areas problem. In: Corchado, E., Yin, H. (eds.) IDEAL 2009. LNCS, vol. 5788, pp. 791–798. Springer, Heidelberg (2009)
15. Berrocal-Plaza, V., Vega-Rodríguez, M.A., Sánchez-Pérez, J.M.: Solving the location areas management problem with multi-objective evolutionary strategies. Wireless Netw. **20**(7), 1909–1924 (2014)
16. Berrocal-Plaza, V., Vega-Rodríguez, M.A., Sánchez-Pérez, J.M.: On the use of multiobjective optimization for solving the location areas strategy with different paging procedures in a realistic mobile network. Appl. Soft Comput. **18**, 146–157 (2014)
17. Coello, C.A.C., Lamont, G.B., Veldhuizen, D.A.V.: Evolutionary Algorithms for Solving Multi-Objective Problems (Genetic and Evolutionary Computation). Springer-Verlag New York Inc., Secaucus (2006)

Improving Hotel Room Demand Forecasting with a Hybrid GA-SVR Methodology Based on Skewed Data Transformation, Feature Selection and Parsimony Tuning

R. Urraca[1](✉), A. Sanz-Garcia[2], J. Fernandez-Ceniceros[1],
E. Sodupe-Ortega[1], and F.J. Martinez-de-Pison[1]

[1] EDMANS Group, University of La Rioja, La Rioja, Spain
ruben.urraca@unirioja.es, edmans@dim.unirioja.es
http://www.mineriadatos.com
[2] Division of Biosciences, University of Helsinki, Helsinki, Finland
andres.sanz-garcia@helsinki.fi

Abstract. This paper presents a hybrid methodology, in which a KDD-scheme is optimized to build accurate parsimonious models. The methodology tries to find the best model by using genetic algorithms to optimize a KDD scheme formed with the following stages: feature selection, transformation of the skewed input and output data, parameter tuning, and parsimonious model selection. In this work, experiments demonstrated that optimization of these steps significantly improved the model generalization capabilities in some UCI databases. Finally, this methodology was applied to create room demand parsimonious models using booking databases from a hotel located in a region of Northern Spain. Results proved that the proposed method was useful to create models with higher generalization capacity and lower complexity to those obtained with classical KDD processes.

Keywords: Genetic algorithms · Soft computing · Hotel room demand forecasting · Feature selection · Parsimony criterion · Support vector machines

1 Introduction

Since the 1980s, data management systems termed revenue management (RM) have been widely developed and implemented in the hotel industry at varying levels of refinement [1]. A RM system focuses on supporting decisions in room pricing policies, under the opposing drives to reduce cost and maximize profit. Accurate room booking forecasting methods are essential since room prices are directly adjusted according to estimated demand [2].

Numerous websites specialized in on-line hotel booking have cropped up over the last two decades. These websites offer greater transparency and more

© Springer International Publishing Switzerland 2015
E. Onieva et al. (Eds.): HAIS 2015, LNAI 9121, pp. 632–643, 2015.
DOI: 10.1007/978-3-319-19644-2_52

detailed information, but also compare different products and prices. In fact, customers seem to appreciate the simplicity of usage of these websites and the swift nature of the purchase transaction. And so, customers' preferences are shifting in favor of on-line booking, which also encourages greater price scrutiny [3,4]. Customers can gather information simultaneously with just one click from different hotels at their travel destinations. Therefore, now that everyone can easily compare various alternatives, there is strong tendency to make last-minute on-line reservations [5].

In the last years, more and more websites like these are appearing, including hotel advertisements and other websites that collect information about hotel rates worldwide. This newfound behavior of customers is generating a significant impact on hotel pricing strategies, and also on customer's choice, which has led to a more complex pattern for the forecasting process [6]. The issues raised above suggest the importance of estimating hotel arrivals more accurately in order to adequately determine room charges. It is crucial to obtain more precise prediction models that take into account this new situation, and new alternatives are also required for hotel room booking forecasting by a given capacity for service over the long haul [7].

This study presents a method for creating parsimonious models in order to improve the estimation of hotel room booking with skewed information and high dimensional databases. The heart of every RM system is a prediction model, and its accuracy is the key to the RM success [8]. The use of parsimonious models represents a promising approach that has already achieved satisfactory results [9–12], and may also be considered a more robust solutions against perturbations, noise or skewed data. For this purpose, this hybrid proposal is focused primarily on the use of genetic algorithms (GA) to optimize a KDD-scheme based on parameter tuning (PT), parsimonious model selection (PMS), feature selection (FS), and transformation of density distribution (TDD) of skewed predictors and dependent variables.

The article is organized as follows: in Sect. 2 the hybrid methodology is presented. Section 3 shows the results of the proposal applied to nine UCI datasets with different configurations. In the next point, Sect. 4, experimental results in hotel room demand forecasting are discussed. And finally, Sect. 5 shows the conclusions and suggestions for further research.

2 Hybrid Methodology

A hybrid methodology based on GA is designed to improve a novel KDD-scheme which combines PT, PMS, FS, and TDD of the descriptors and the response. In particular, the main objective is to automatically search the best parsimonious model for the prediction of the target, *hotel room demand*, by adjusting the relevant steps of the KDD process.

Support vector machines (SVM) for regression (SVR) [13] with radial basis kernel were selected as modeling technique. SVR is a SVM version for regression tasks based on the Vapnik's concepts [14] able to avoid local minima offering high generalization capacity. Setting SVR parameters are: the penalty coefficient C, γ of RBF kernel and the insensitive loss parameter ε.

2.1 Hybrid Methodology Based on GA for PT, PMS, FS and TDD

It is well known that the model accuracy depends on the database characteristics and the SVR training settings. Thus, a fine tuning of the model parameters is essential to achieve satisfactory results. At the same time, models should be as simple as possible in terms of number of attributes, according to the *Parsimony Principle*. By following this principle, the generalization capacity of the model and its interpretability improve when a model selection is constructed by using complexity as second criterion. But also, transforming the input and output variables prior to the training process may be fundamental to reduce the effect of skewed information. For this purpose, the density distribution of the predictors and the response could be transformed in order to improve the modeling process.

Achieving the above-mentioned objectives involves an iterative KDD procedure traditionally based on trial-and-error. However, in order to automate the process, a hybrid GA-optimization of a KDD-scheme is proposed that includes PT, PMS, FS, and TDD in the optimization process (Fig. 1).

GA Chromosome Representation. A strategy is created to integrate FS, PT and TDD in the GA process. The representation for each individual (i) and generation (g) is a chromosome $\lambda_g^i = [C, \gamma, \varepsilon, Q, E, k]^T$ where C, γ, and ε are the specific SVR parameters of each i individual. Besides, Q is a binary-coded array that includes the selected inputs, and, E is a vector of exponents for transforming the input data by using $x_j^* = x_j^{e_j}$, where x_j is the predictor j raised by the exponent e_j. Finally, k is the exponent to transform the skewed dependent variable in a similar way, $y^* = y^k$.

In this case, this TDD is a power procedure similar to Box-Cox transformation [15] where the exponent is λ:

$$x^* = \begin{cases} x^{\lambda-1}/\lambda, & \lambda \neq 0 \\ log(x), & \lambda = 0 \end{cases} \tag{1}$$

but the TDD is simplified by removing the denominator because the database is previously normalized between 0 and 1 and, as a consequence, the range of the distribution does not change. Also, minus one is removed and $log(x)$ is never used because the search of the optimal exponents are established above zero in a range of 0.20 to 1.79.

In this way, input data and output variable are respectively raised by the exponents E and k to transform their density distribution (DD) before the modeling process. Figure 2 displays a DD-example of the original skewed hotel room demand (left) and its transformation when an exponent of $k = 0.45$ was applied (right). Finally, in order to revert the TDD after the model training process, outcome predicted values are raised by $\frac{1}{k}$ to obtain the untransformed room demand prediction.

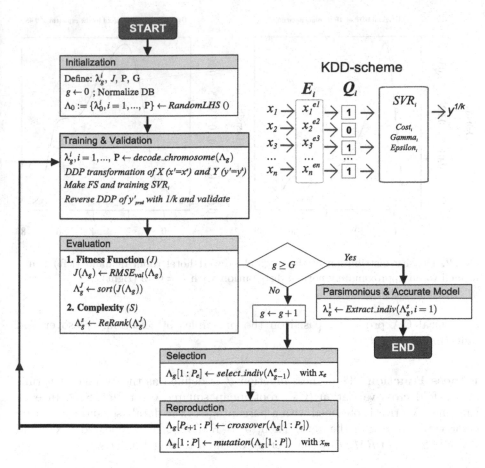

Fig. 1. Flowchart of the hybrid methodology based on GA optimization of a KDD-scheme with PT, PMS, FS, and TDD of input and output data.

Methodology Flowchart. The complete GA-based proposal is illustrated in Fig. 1. During the initialization process and, to accelerate convergence, *Latin Hypercube Sampling* (LHS) is used to define the first generation. The idea is to ensure a uniform distribution of the initial individuals. Next, after the normalization and transformation of data, GA iterative process continues the training and validation stage for each individual. In the evaluation phase, the proposal includes a standard ranking step based on a fitness function J. However, this methodology includes a second PMS step to rearrange models according to their complexity when the difference of J is not significant. To this end, two individuals sorted by J and with similar fitness values, change their positions when the first one is more complex than the second one (in the flowchart this procedure is named *ReRank*). As a result, this PMS procedure aims to rearrange equally accurate models by a parsimony criterion. After the evaluation process,

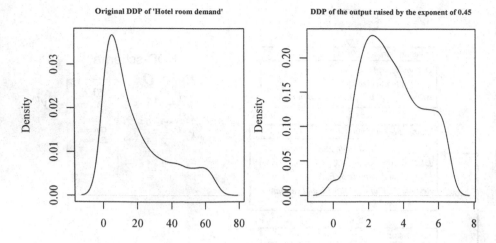

Fig. 2. Density distribution of the original skewed hotel room demand (left) transformed to an approximately normal distribution with $k = 0.45$ (right).

a classical GA procedure based on the principles of selection, crossover and mutation is conducted.

Fitness Function. The fitness function J is defined as the average of n runs of a k-fold cross validation (CV) root mean squared error ($RMSE$). In each run, the CV error is obtained with a percentage of the database, and the testing error with the rest of the data. Then, $J = RMSE_{val}$ is a repeated n x k-fold CV $RMSE$, and $RMSE_{tst}$ the average of the n testing $RMSEs$.

Complexity Measure. J of individuals are compared against a threshold μ. Then, when consecutive individuals have an absolute difference of J under μ, are re-ranked according to their model complexity. In our case, model complexity is based on the concept of generalized degrees of freedom (GDF) that may be applicable to any modeling technique. According to Ye [16], highly complex models would easily fit perturbed data against more simple models. Then, GDF are defined as the sum of sensitivities of fitted values to perturbations with respect to the observed values. In practice, GDF approach consists of three easy steps [17]: generation of a perturbed signal by adding random noise to the output variable; training the model with new data; assessment of the difference in model behavior between the original output variable and the perturbed signal. In particular:

$$GDF = \sum_{i=1}^{n} \frac{\Delta \tilde{y}_i}{\Delta y_i} = \frac{\tilde{y}_{i,pert} - \tilde{y}_i}{y_{i,pert} - y_i} \tag{2}$$

where n is the number of instances of the training dataset, $y_{i,pert}$ and y_i are, respectively, the perturbed and original output for the i-th instance; and $\tilde{y}_{i,pert}$

and $\tilde{y}_i$ the predicted values. The process is repeated with m_{gdf} random signals and the sensitivity of each instance is evaluated by fitting a linear regression (LR) model to $\Delta \tilde{y}_i$ vs. Δy_i. The mean of the slopes of all LR models represents the GDF.

GA Operators. Regarding the GA operators, *heuristic blending* is selected as crossover operation [18]. Moreover, a random uniform operator is utilized for selection. Finally, a random mutation is applied to the population, except for the best two individuals.

3   Testing Methodology with UCI Datasets

First, methodology was tested with nine UCI datasets. To this purpose, ten runs of the process were accomplished for each dataset and with five different configurations:

– *Base.* Basic configuration that includes *PT* and *PMS*.
– *Base + FS*

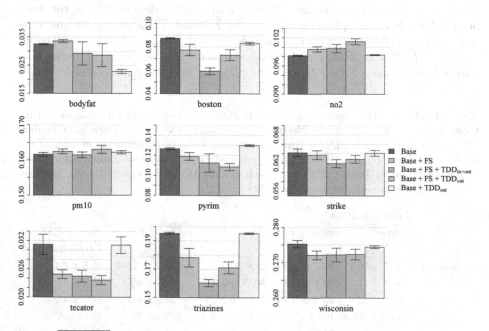

Fig. 3. $\overline{RMSE_{tst}}$ of the best models obtained in 10 runs for each datasets and 5 different configurations, where PT = Parameter Tuning, FS = Feature Selection, TDD = Transformation of Density Distribution of inputs (*in*), outputs (*out*) or inputs and outputs (*in + out*) and *Base* is the basic configuration that includes Parameter Tuning (*PT*) and Parsimonious Model Selection (*PMS*). Whiskers represent the 95 % confidence interval.

- $Base + FS + TDD_{in+out}$
- $Base + FS + TDD_{out}$
- $Base + TDD_{out}$

GA settings were the following: $P = 64$ individuals of population size, $J = RMSE_{val}$ obtained with a repeated 5x4-fold CV $RMSE$ of the 70 % of each database, threshold error $\mu = 0.5\%$, $m_{gdf} = 10$, elitism percentage of 25 %, *random uniform* for selection and *heuristic blending* for crossing as GA operators, and mutation percentage of 10 % with the two best individuals of each generation not mutated. Also, SVR parameters were defined according to the following ranges: base-10 logarithm of the complexity parameter C within the interval $[-3.\hat{9}, 1.4\hat{9}]$, and the same range $[10^{-6}, 0.\hat{9}]$ for ε and γ of RBF kernel. Finally, maximum number of generations was $G = 200$ but an early stopping procedure was established if J did not improve in $G_{early} = 20$ generations.

The statistical software for programming and testing all the experiments was R[19] with svm() function of e1071 package. All experiment were carried out with a dual quad-core processor computer (AMD Athlon^{TM} 64 X2 @ 1.8 GHz) with 8GB RAM memory.

Figure 3 depicts the $RMSE_{tst}$ mean of ten runs for the best individuals $(\overline{RMSE_{tst}})$. Results are showed for nine UCI datasets and with different configurations. Obviously, results were highly dependent on the type of problem. For example, the addition of FS and TDD of inputs and outputs to the basic configuration $(Base + FS + TDD_{in+out})$ improved significantly $\overline{RMSE_{tst}}$ in *boston* and *triazines* datasets. Also, error of *pyrim* was reduced with $Base + FS + TDD_{out}$ configuration, and *bodyfat* decreased without

Table 1. Mean of the execution time (min) with 95 % confidence intervals in 10 runs for each dataset and with the 5 different configurations, where PT = Parameter Tuning, FS = Feature Selection, TDD = Transformation of Density Distribution of inputs (*in*), outputs (*out*) or inputs and outputs (*in+out*) and *Base* is the base configuration which includes Parameter Tuning (PT) and Parsimonious Model Selection (PMS). Smallest execution times in each database are in bold

	Configurations				
	Base	*Base + FS*	*Base + TDD_{out}*	*Base + FS + TDD_{out}*	*Base + FS + TDD_{in+out}*
bodyfat	49.9 ± 16.8	38.7 ± 20.8	66.8 ± 37.7	$\mathbf{28.8 \pm 16.7}$	31.5 ± 7.4
boston	38.4 ± 11.3	82.3 ± 59.0	$\mathbf{30.5 \pm 0.2}$	87.7 ± 62.1	46.2 ± 3.8
no2	25.5 ± 0.1	$\mathbf{23.8 \pm 0.1}$	117.8 ± 56.9	24.9 ± 0.1	27.3 ± 4.0
pm10	$\mathbf{71.8 \pm 60.4}$	198.1 ± 56.3	96.0 ± 45.8	78.4 ± 57.1	122.3 ± 65.9
pyrim	32.1 ± 17.9	14.2 ± 3.5	$\mathbf{9.9 \pm 0.6}$	11.4 ± 2.1	14.8 ± 4.7
strike	85.6 ± 71.8	202.7 ± 65.3	57.6 ± 53.8	$\mathbf{39.7 \pm 18.7}$	66.5 ± 54.1
tecator	196.9 ± 92.6	57.9 ± 3.2	139.9 ± 66.1	$\mathbf{47.4 \pm 6.4}$	67.5 ± 14.9
triazines	$\mathbf{23.7 \pm 6.3}$	49.3 ± 20.9	30.6 ± 7.1	77.8 ± 37.0	75.4 ± 27.8
wisconsin	26.6 ± 6.4	44.6 ± 30.2	31.8 ± 26.9	$\mathbf{20.8 \pm 5.9}$	28.0 ± 21.2

including feature selection $(Base + TDD_{out})$. Otherwise, in the other datasets there were not significant improvements.

Table 1 shows the mean execution time with the 95 % confidence intervals. The values obtained proved that $Base + FS + TDD_{out}$ configuration was the fastest one regarding the mean execution times in 4 out of 9 datasets. This implies that adding more steps to the methodology, such as FS or TDD, did not significantly increased the overall execution time. What is more, the execution time was mainly influenced by the complexity of models being computed, and it was substantially reduced by selecting features or by transforming the density distribution of inputs and outputs.

4 Experiments in Hotel Room Demand Forecasting

4.1 Problem Definition and Database

In today's hospitality market, hotel managers must be able to accurately estimate rooms demand so that they can offer the most competitive prices. In this way, hotels can advertise special offers to attract potential customers during those dates when there is little expected demand. As a result of this need, the principal aim of this study is to create a robust and accurate model for hotel room demand forecasting employing soft computing (SC) techniques to select the best attributes, model parameters and data transformation procedures.

The case study presented herein concerns a hotel located in a small village of La Rioja region, in northern Spain. The database used to create the models was directly extracted from historical booking data provided by the aforementioned hotel. In addition, useful information regarding variables affecting room demand forecasting was also obtained from meteorological and sociological databases, as well as from the Spanish National Institute of Statistics (INE). Once the information was preprocessed, the next step consisted of establishing a set of indicators to describe the historical room booking information. These indicators comprise the macro-economic temporal situation, social patterns, meteorological data and local and regional holidays, among others. At the end of this process, 119 attributes were selected by the experts.

The number of attributes was still too large to obtain accurate predictive models. Therefore, several scatter-plots and matrix correlations were utilized to identify high dependencies between the input variables. As a result, the final dataset contained 22 attributes which define the basic characteristics of each day: month, day of the week, season, regional holidays in cities located near the hotel, daily average temperatures, etc. Additionally, the target variable y was the *hotel room demand* that corresponded to the number of reservations per day. Greater detail regarding the hotel is not presented herein because of our confidentiality agreement with the company in question.

After selecting the most significant attributes, a thorough search was undertaken to develop a methodology capable of generating accurate room-demand calendars for forecasting purposes. To this end, databases were obtained from booking data from the past six years to train and validate the predictive models.

A test dataset was also created from data extracted from between January and July of the actual year.

4.2   Results

In this section, hotel room demand forecasting results obtained with seven different configurations of the proposed hybrid methodology:

- *Base*. Basic configuration that includes PT and PMS.
- *Base* + *FS*
- *Base* + *FS* + TDD_{in+out}
- *Base* + *FS* + TDD_{out}
- *Base* + TDD_{out}
- *Base* + TDD_{in}
- *Base* + TDD_{in+out}

Figure 4 displays one example of elitist individuals $RMSE_{val}$ and $RMSE_{tst}$ evolution with the $Base + FS + TDD_{in+out}$ configuration, which stopped in the $37th$ generation. White box-plots represent $RMSE_{val}$ evolution whereas $RMSE_{tst}$ is depicted by gray box-plots. Continuous and dashed-dotted lines are respectively $RMSE_{val}$ and $RMSE_{tst}$ of the best individual of each generation. The evolution of the number of features N_{FS} is also represented in the same plot. The shaded area delimits the maximum and minimum N_{FS} of the elitism population and the dashed line depicts the N_{FS} of the best individual.

Figure 5 compares the mean and $CI_{95\%}$ of the predicted hotel room demand $\overline{RMSE_{val}}$ and $\overline{RMSE_{tst}}$ for the best models obtained through all configurations and with ten runs.

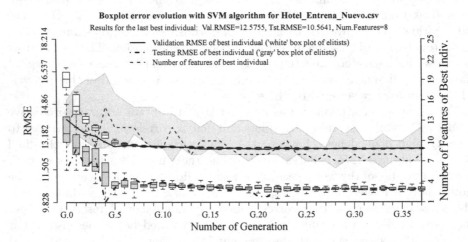

Fig. 4. Evolution of elitist individuals with $Base + FS + TDD_{in+out}$ configuration. White box-plots represent the evolution of $RMSE_{val}$ and grey filled box-plots, the $RMSE_{tst}$ of elitist individuals. The range of N_{FS} for elitist individuals is illustrated by the shaded area and the dashed line is the N_{FS} of the best individual.

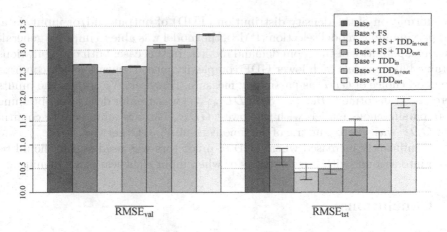

Fig. 5. Hotel room demand $\overline{RMSE_{val}}$ and $\overline{RMSE_{tst}}$ for 10 runs with 7 different configurations, where PT=Parameter Tuning, FS=Feature Selection, TDD=Transformation of Density Distribution of inputs (in), outputs (out) or inputs and outputs ($in + out$) and $Base$ is the basic configuration which includes Parameter Tuning (PT) and Parsimonious Model Selection (PMS). Whiskers represent the 95 % confidence interval.

Table 2. Hotel room demand forecasting results with 7 configurations. Values are the mean and $\pm CI_{95\%}$ of 10 runs. Best similar values are in bold.

Configuration	$\overline{Gen}$	$\overline{Time_{min}}$	$\overline{RMSE_{val}}$	$\overline{RMSE_{tst}}$	$\overline{GDF}$	$\overline{N_{FS}}$
$Base$	$\mathbf{27.6 \pm 7.0}$	$\mathbf{199.3 \pm 48.6}$	13.48 ± 0.004	12.49 ± 0.012	0.143 ± 0.003	25 ± 0.0
$Base + FS$	$\mathbf{32.1 \pm 7.5}$	$\mathbf{179.3 \pm 39.1}$	12.70 ± 0.010	10.75 ± 0.170	0.105 ± 0.003	$\mathbf{7.3 \pm 0.8}$
$Base + FS+$ TDD_{in+out}	72.0 ± 33.2	381.2 ± 170.3	$\mathbf{12.55 \pm 0.019}$	$\mathbf{10.42 \pm 0.159}$	$\mathbf{0.089 \pm 0.004}$	8.9 ± 0.6
$Base + FS+$ TDD_{out}	$\mathbf{30.9 \pm 2.7}$	$\mathbf{178.6 \pm 15.7}$	$\mathbf{12.65 \pm 0.010}$	$\mathbf{10.49 \pm 0.110}$	$\mathbf{0.095 \pm 0.002}$	7.4 ± 0.7
$Base + TDD_{in}$	71.8 ± 28.3	531.2 ± 209.4	13.08 ± 0.034	11.36 ± 0.170	0.150 ± 0.004	25 ± 0.0
$Base+$ TDD_{in+out}	62.2 ± 37.5	460.3 ± 278.7	13.08 ± 0.025	11.11 ± 0.157	0.103 ± 0.004	25 ± 0.0
$Base + TDD_{out}$	81.0 ± 51.3	574.0 ± 362.7	13.32 ± 0.016	11.86 ± 0.098	0.125 ± 0.003	25 ± 0.0

Additionally, Table 2 presents a summary of the results for ten runs and with the seven different configurations (first column). GA settings were similar than Sect. 3 but with $\mu = 0.1\%$ and $J = $ 5x8-fold CV $RMSE$.

Values of the other columns correspond to mean and confidence interval at 95 percent ($CI_{95\%}$) of ten runs. Second and third columns show the number of GA generations used ($\overline{Gen}$) and the elapsed time in minutes ($\overline{Time_{min}}$). Columns fourth to seventh present errors and complexity measures for the best individuals: $\overline{RMSE_{val}}$, $\overline{RMSE_{tst}}$, the GDF complexity metric ($\overline{GDF}$), and the number of input features ($\overline{N_{FS}}$).

From Table 2, it can be observed that $Base + FS + TDD_{in+out}$ and $Base + FS + TDD_{out}$ clearly outperform $\overline{RMSE_{tst}}$ of other configurations. Thus, using new proposal which combines feature selection (FS), parameter tuning (PT), transformation of the density distribution (TDD) of output and/or input data, and parsimonious model selection (PMS), the model was able to improve generalization capabilities of the room demand models. In this case, both configurations obtained also models with lower GDF complexity measurements which confirms the good choice of $\overline{GDF}$ as parsimony measure. However, $\overline{N_{FS}}$ when the inputs were also transformed $(Base+FS+TDD_{in+out})$ was greater despite of obtaining more parsimonious models with the lowest $\overline{GDF}$. These results seem to confirm that $\overline{GDF}$ was a better metric of parsimony than $\overline{N_{FS}}$. Otherwise, $\overline{Time_{min}}$ and $\overline{Gen}$ significantly increased when TDD of predictors was used and it should be taken into account with large datasets or when input skewness is not significant.

5   Conclusions

This article presents a hybrid methodology based on optimizing with GA a KDD-scheme for seeking models with high accuracy and generalization capabilities. The proposal was capable of obtaining good parsimonious models from high dimensional and skewed datasets by combining parameter tuning (PT), parsimonious model selection (PMS), feature selection (FS), and transformation of density distribution (TDD) of skewed predictors and dependent variables.

The performance of the proposal presented herein was tested with nine UCI datasets and with different configurations. Experiments demonstrated that our proposal was able to select the best features and to obtain parsimony models with high generalization capacities in some databases. However, improvement of model accuracy was highly dependent on the type of dataset and configuration selected. In particular, the usage of $Base + FS + TDD_{in+out}$ and $Base + FS + TDD_{out}$ configurations can be especially recommended when the skewness of data or/and the number of features are high.

Finally, this methodology was applied to a hotel room demand dataset with 22 attributes and a highly skewed dependent target. As a result, given the difficulty and high randomness inherent to this case, models achieved by the proposed methodology predicted expected room reservations with a better degree of accuracy in comparison with other previous models. However, other experiments are needed with more databases and with other modeling techniques to obtain better conclusions about the methodology. Also, future work will try to fuse other meta-heuristic methods to improve optimization performance.

Acknowledgements. We are greatly indebted to *Banco Santander* for the PROFAI-13/06 fellowship, and to the *Agencia de Desarrollo Económico de La Rioja* for the ADER-2012-I-IDD-00126 (CONOBUILD) fellowship and to the *Instituto de Estudios Riojanos* (IER) for funding parts of this research. We would also like to convey our gratitude to the European Union for its continuous encouragement through the 7th Framework Programme on the project VINEROBOT. And, one of the authors, ASG, would also like to acknowledge research founding No. 273689 (FINSKIN) and the mobility grant No. 276371 (VATURP) from the Academy of Finland.

References

1. Weatherford, L.R., Kimes, S.E.: A comparison of forecasting methods for hotel revenue management. Int. J. Forecast. **19**(3), 401–415 (2003)
2. Zickus, J.: Forecasting for airline network revenue management: Revenue and competitive impacts (1998)
3. Aziz, H.A., Saleh, M., Rasmy, M.H., ElShishiny, H.: Dynamic room pricing model for hotel revenue management systems. Egypt. Inf. J. **12**(3), 177–183 (2011)
4. Anjos, M.F., Cheng, R.C., Currie, C.S.: Optimal pricing policies for perishable products. Eur. J. Oper. Res. **166**(1), 246–254 (2005)
5. Sparks, B.A., Browning, V.: The impact of online reviews on hotel booking intentions and perception of trust. Tour. Manag. **32**(6), 1310–1323 (2011)
6. Cantoni, L., Fans, M., Inversini, A., Passini, V.: Hotel websites and booking engines: a challenging relationship. In: Law, R., Fuchs, M., Ricci, F. (eds.) Information and Communication Technologies in Tourism 2011 (Proceedings of the Int Conf. in Innsbruck, Austria), pp. 241–252. Springer, New York (2011)
7. Lai, K.K., Ng, W.L.: A stochastic approach to hotel revenue optimization. Comput. Oper. Res. **32**(5), 1059–1072 (2005)
8. Haensel, A., Koole, G.: Booking horizon forecasting with dynamic updating: a case study of hotel reservation data. Int. J. Forecast. **27**, 942–960 (2011)
9. Yang, Y.Y., Mahfouf, M., Pnoutsos, G.: Development of a parsimonious ga-nn ensemble model with a case study for charpy impact energy prediction. Adv. Eng. Softw. **42**, 435–443 (2011)
10. Sanz-Garcia, A., Fernández-Ceniceros, J., Fernández-Martínez, R., Martínez-De-Pisón, F.J.: Methodology based on genetic optimisation to develop overall parsimony models for predicting temperature settings on annealing furnace. Ironmak. Steelmaking **41**(2), 87–98 (2014)
11. Yang, Y., Linkens, D., Talamantes-Silva, J.: Roll load prediction - data collection, analysis and neural network modelling. J. Mater. Process. Technol. **152**(3), 304–315 (2004)
12. Helle, M., Saxen, H., Kerkkonen, O.: Assessment of the state of the blast furnace high temperature region by tuyere core drilling. ISIJ Int. **49**(2), 203–209 (2009)
13. Drucker, H., Chris, K.B.L., Smola, A., Vapnik, V.: Support vector regression machines. In: Advances in Neural Information Processing Systems 9, vol. 9, pp. 155–161 (1997)
14. Vapnik, V.N.: Statistical Learning Theory, 1st edn. Wiley, New York (1998)
15. Box, G.E.P., Cox, D.R.: An analysis of transformations. J. Roy. Stat. Soc.: Ser. B (Methodol.) **26**(2), 211–252 (1964)
16. Ye, J.: On measuring and correcting the effects of data mining and model selection. J. Am. Stat. Assoc. **93**(441), 120–131 (1998)
17. Seni, G., Elder, J.: Ensemble Methods in Data Mining: Improving Accuracy Through Combining Predictions. Morgan and Claypool Publishers, Chicago (2010)
18. Michalewicz, Z., Janikow, C.Z.: Handling constraints in genetic algorithms. In: ICGA, pp. 151–157 (1991)
19. R Core Team: R: A Language and Environment for Statistical Computing. R Foundation for Statistical Computing, Vienna, Austria (2013)

A Survey of Hybrid Artificial Intelligence Algorithms for Dynamic Vehicle Routing Problem

Vladimir Ilin, Dragan Simić$^{(\boxtimes)}$, Jovan Tepić, Gordan Stojić,
and Nenad Saulić

University of Novi Sad, Faculty of Technical Sciences, Trg Dositeja Obradovića
6, 21000 Novi Sad, Serbia
{v.ilin,jovan.tepic,gordan,n.saulic}@uns.ac.rs,
dsimic@eunet.rs

Abstract. In a Dynamic Vehicle Routing Problem (DVRP) new customer orders and changes of existing orders continually arrive and thus disrupt the optimal routing plan. This paper presents a survey of some of the recent hybrid artificial intelligence algorithms suitable for efficient optimization and re-optimization of different DVRPs. An artificial ant colony 2-OPT hybrid algorithm, a hybrid neighborhood search algorithm, and a hybrid heuristic algorithm are explained in detail. Particular interest is focused towards local improvement heuristic algorithms, such as 2-OPT algorithm and OR's algorithm, which are regularly used in hybrid approaches for intra-route and inter-route improvements.

Keywords: Dynamic Vehicle Routing Problem · Hybrid artificial intelligence algorithms · Improvement heuristic algorithms · Metaheuristic algorithms

1 Introduction

Straightforward development of Information and Communication Technologies (ICT) has enabled companies and individual customers to track their products from source to target. Also, ICT boom has facilitated the emergence of new trade environments, such as Business-to-Customer (B2C) environment, in which the process of buying, selling and exchanging products is done on the Internet [1]. ICT support allows companies to collect large amount of real-time information which can be used as competitive advantage. The Dynamic Vehicle Routing Problem (DVRP) is an example of a distribution context where intelligent use of real-time information can differentiate one company from another by means of superior on-time service [2].

The DVRP is the dynamic counterpart of the generic Vehicle Routing Problem (VRP). In the VRP problem the objective is generally to minimize the travel cost for several vehicles that must visit and service a certain number of customers. It is noteworthy that the VRP heuristic approach was derived from the Travelling Salesman Problem (TSP), which solved the problem of a single delivery carrier [3]. The existing vehicle routing algorithms are best for solving problems where orders are planned and repeated. In DVRP environment route optimizations are required to be instant, which means that the existing DVRP solutions need to be fast and precise. However, there is

© Springer International Publishing Switzerland 2015
E. Onieva et al. (Eds.): HAIS 2015, LNAI 9121, pp. 644–655, 2015.
DOI: 10.1007/978-3-319-19644-2_53

still a gap of high quality DVRP solutions with a short execution time in the literature. Therefore, hybrid artificial intelligence algorithms are constantly developing to speed up optimization and re-optimization processes.

The lack of variety of high quality solutions in DVRP environment was the motivation for writing this paper. The main idea was to perform a survey of some of the most up-to date hybrid artificial intelligence algorithms suitable for solving DVRPs. Six recently contributed hybrid approaches are selected from the literature and described in detail: (1) self-organizing map with an evolutionary algorithm hybrid model, (2) parallel tabu search hybrid model, (3) a particle swarm optimization algorithm and variable neighborhood search hybrid model, (4) an artificial ant colony 2-OPT hybrid model, (5) a hybrid neighborhood search model, and (6) a hybrid heuristic model. Local improvement heuristic algorithms such as 2-OPT algorithm and OR's algorithm, are regularly used in hybrid approaches for intra-route and inter-route improvements. Therefore, they are explained and illustrated as well.

The rest of the paper is organized in the following way. Section 2 introduces brief preconditions of technological environment. Section 3 describes the dynamic vehicle routing problem. Section 4 explains some of the most frequently used local search improvement heuristics algorithms. Section 5 shows hybrid DVRP models and applications. Concluding remarks and future work follow in Sect. 6.

2 Technological Environment

The communication directions vehicle drivers-dispatching center and communication center-customers are essential for maintaining the most up-to date information into the routing system (Fig. 1). A simple vehicle positioning strategy is to have the driver report back to the dispatching center every time a customer has been serviced. Also, dispatching center needs to operate with the latest changes in orders' size or new customers. Ideally, the dispatching center will dispose with the information regarding vehicle's position at all times. Global Positioning System (GPS), Global System for Mobile Communications (GSM), Geographical Information System (GIS), and web server are key ICT systems in a DVRP environment.

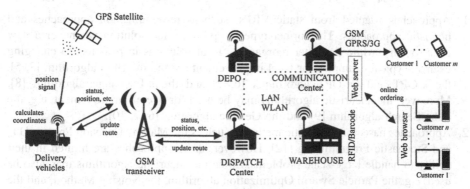

Fig. 1. Information flows in DVRP environment (Source: [2], p. 202, adapted by authors)

The insertion of immediate customer requests into already planned routes is usually a complicated task that leads to either partial or full re-planning of the non- visited parts of the routes. The complexity of a routing problem directly affects the difficulty of inserting dynamic customer.

3   The Dynamic Vehicle Routing Problem

In the DVRP, vehicles must serve two types of requests: (1) advance requests and (2) immediate requests. The former are requests of static customers that have placed them before the routing process begun. The latter requests are received from dynamic customers and arise in real-time during the day of operations. To better understand what dynamic means, an illustration of simple VRP is given (Fig. 2). While vehicles execute their routes, two new customers (X and Y) arrive at some point which triggers re-routing mechanism.

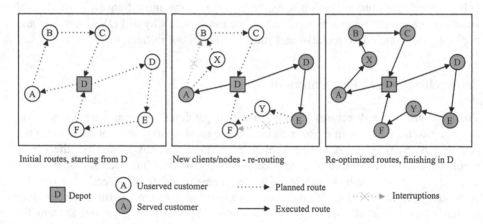

Initial routes, starting from D   New clients/nodes - re-routing   Re-optimized routes, finishing in D

Fig. 2. An example of dynamic vehicle routing (Source: [4], p. 3, adapted by authors)

Two main types of approaches have been adopted to solve DVRPs [3, 5]:

1. Approaches adapted from static VRPs, such as re-optimization approaches and heuristic approaches. The former type re-optimizes the solution whenever a new event occurs, while the latter reorganizes local solutions in response to changing events. Typical examples for local improvement are the Insertion algorithm [3, 5], the k-OPT and Or-OPT algorithms [6, 7] and the λ-Exchange algorithm [8]. Moreover, metaheuristic algorithms may be used for overall improvement, e.g. the Tabu Search algorithm [9] and the Genetic algorithm [6, 7, 10].
2. Approaches based on stochastic methods, such as the Markov Decision Process [11] and Stochastic Programming [12]. However, these approaches are limited in their ability to handle large-scale problems. Some metaheuristic algorithms may also be used, e.g. the Particle Swarm Optimization algorithm, the Noising Method, and the Simulated Annealing algorithm [8].

4 Heuristic Approaches for Dynamic Vehicle Routing Problem

A common strategy for solving DVRPs is to apply a static algorithm to already known data, and to update the current solution whenever new information becomes known [13]. The well-known concept is application of local search improvement heuristic approaches which initially compute a feasible starting solution, usually by some of the insertion operations, and then apply various improvement algorithms. Metaheuristics are also used as an improvement tool to search for the most promising region of the solution space.

4.1 Local Search Improvement Heuristics

The local search improvement heuristics are iterative search procedures that start from an initial feasible solution which is progressively improved by applying a series of local modifications called moves [14, 15]. Insertion procedure and improvement procedure along with several examples are discussed.

- Insertion Procedure builds a solution by determining the least expensive insertion of a node into a route. In some cases it may end up with sub-routes. Some of the examples are Nearest insertion, Cheapest insertion, Quick insertion, Farthest insertion and the Convex hull insertion algorithms [16, 17].
- Improvement Procedure explores the neighborhood of the identified initial solution and tries to transform it into possibly improved feasible solution. If no improvement can be made the initial solution is considered to be optimal [18]. Improvement heuristics may operate on a single route - intra-route improvement or on several routes - inter-route improvement. Some of the examples are 2-OPT and 3-OPT method [19, 20], Lin-Kernighan algorithm [21] and OR's algorithm [22]. OR's algorithm and 2-OPT algorithm are regularly used in hybrid approaches as local improvement heuristics. Therefore, a simple TSP is illustrated [23] to show how OR's algorithm and 2-OPT algorithm operate (Fig. 3).

The presented problem is symmetric which means that there are no one-way streets. In cases when VRP problem is observed, it is necessary to include, into optimization, vehicles' capacity and demand in every node.

The OR's algorithm can be implemented in the following way: (1) Construct a convex polygon from available nodes. This represents an initial route. (2) Select each node (named k) out of the initial route individually and perform calculation with all arc's (i, j) from the initial route, such as $[d(i, k) + d(k, j) - d(i, j)] \times \left[\frac{d(i,k)+d(k,j)}{d(i,j)}\right] \rightarrow min$. (3) Include node k with the lowest value into initial route between nodes i and j. (4) Repeat steps 2-3 until there are no available nodes for further calculation. Figure 4 illustrates application of OR's algorithm in presented example.

The 2-OPT algorithm can be implemented in the following way: (1) Construct initial route using some of the construction procedures. (2) Let initial route be:

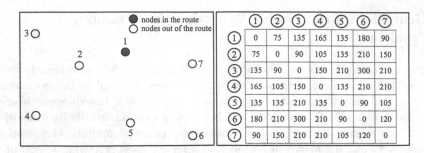

Fig. 3. An example of TSP with corresponding distances between nodes (Source: [23], p. 119)

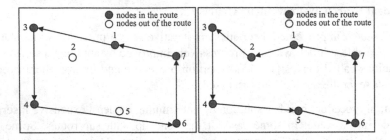

Fig. 4. Route created by OR's heuristic algorithm (Source: [23], p. 142)

$(a1, a2, \ldots, an, a1)$. Let D be the length of the initial route. Let $i = 1$. (3) Let $j = i + 1$. (4) Remove arcs $(ai, ai + 1)$ and $(aj, aj + 1)$ and construct new route: $(a1, a2, \ldots, ai, aj, \ldots, ai + 1, aj + 1, aj + 2, \ldots, a1)$. If the new route is shorter than the initial route memorize new route and return to the step 2. Otherwise, proceed to the next step. (5) Let $j = j + 1$. In case when $j \leq n$ return to the step 4; Otherwise, $i = i + 1$. In case $i \leq n - 2$ return to the step 3. Otherwise, finish with the algorithm. Table 1 illustrates how 2-OPT algorithm works in presented example.

Table 1. 2-OPT algorithm flow (Source: [23], p. 145)

Removing arcs	New route	Route length	Removing arcs	New route	Route length
(1,2), (3,4)	(1,3,2,4,5,6,7,1)	765	(2,3), (7,1)	(1,2,7,4,5,6,3,1)	1095
(1,2), (4,5)	(1,4,3,2,5,6,7,1)	840	(3,4), (5,6)	(1,2,3,5,4,6,7,1)	930
(1,2), (5,6)	(1,5,3,4,2,6,7,1)	1020	(3,4), (6,7)	(1,2,3,6,5,4,7,1)	990
(1,2), (6,7)	(1,6,3,4,5,2,7,1)	1140	(3,4), (7,1)	(1,2,3,7,5,6,4,1)	945
(1,2), (7,1)	(1,7,3,4,5,6,2,1)	960	(4,5), (6,7)	(1,2,3,4,6,5,7,1)	810
(2,3), (4,5)	(1,2,4,3,5,6,7,1)	840	(4,5), (7,1)	(1,2,3,4,7,6,5,1)	870
(2,3), (5,6)	(1,2,5,4,3,6,7,1)	1005	(5,6), (7,1)	(1,2,3,4,5,7,6,1)	855
(2,3), (6,7)	(1,2,6,4,5,3,7,1)	1140			

The initial rout is created using Nearest insertion algorithm with the total length of 750 [23]. Table 1, shows that the length of initial route cannot be improved, which means that the vehicle cannot travel less distances than it is initially proposed. This implies that initial route is 2-optimal.

4.2   Metaheuristics

Metaheuristics are usually used as a method for the fine tuning phase. Fine tuning means that improved initial routes from intra-route and inter-route improvement need to be revised once more. Metaheuristics offer global search strategies for exploring the solution spaces. The Tabu Search (TS) algorithm [24], the Simulated Annealing (SA) algorithm [25], the Genetic algorithm [26], and the Artificial Ant Colony (AAC) algorithm [27] are particularly suitable approaches for the fine tuning phase.

5   Hybrid DVRP Models and Applications

Dynamic problems have usually been solved using re-optimization or fast insertion techniques depending on the amount of time available for reacting to new events [13]. One of the earliest works presenting in re-optimization based hybrid metaheuristic in the dynamic vehicle routing context is the algorithm which combines a Dynamic Programming (DP) algorithm and a Genetic Algorithm (GA) for the single-vehicle Pickup and Delivery with time windows and capacity constraints [28]. The dynamic programming component is executed for a certain amount of time. It will either return an optimal solution or multiple partially constructed routes. Those partial solutions are used as initial population of a genetic algorithm. The hybrid approach was able to improve the results of the non-hybrid methods.

5.1   SOM-EA Hybrid Model

A novel approach combining a Self-Organizing Map (SOM) with an Evolutionary Algorithm (EA) for solving the VRP with dynamic requests has been proposed in [29]. The SOM approach is described as a center-based clustering algorithm preserving the density and the topology of the data distribution. The approach is based on applying SOM procedure to the TSP. The SOM plays the role of a local search by adjusting the network shape to the demand. To address the VRP, SOM has been extended to become an operator embedded into an evolutionary algorithm. The structure of the algorithm is similar to the memetic algorithm, which is an evolutionary algorithm incorporating a local search. New customers are added to the existing routes by simple insertion satisfying the relative route duration constraints. A vehicle can change its direction at any moment to deal with new demands or to follow a better schedule returned by the optimizer. The communication protocol between company and optimizer is an asynchronous. On one hand, the company receives new orders from the environment and communicates with the vehicles, on the other, the company communicates with the optimizer using mailboxes to exchange information. The company sends the updated route plans to the vehicles. Extensive computational results have shown the advantages of the presented approach. SOM-EA hybrid model has shown better results with respect to solution quality than the Multiple Ant Colony System - Vehicle Routing Problem with Time Windows approach (MACS-VRPTW), a Genetic algorithm, and Multi-agent oriented approach.

5.2   Parallelization Approaches

Alternative promising hybridization techniques for dynamic problems are various parallelization variants. Several variants of a parallel Tabu Search (TS) heuristic for the dynamic multivehicle dial-a-ride problem (DARP) are proposed in [30]. Dynamic and parallel DARP algorithms work as follows: a static solution is constructed based on already known requests. The parallel TS approach is applied to generate a starting solution. When a new request arrives, the algorithm performs a feasibility check, meaning that it searches for a feasible solution including the new service request. Once it has been decided whether the new request can be accepted or not, the algorithm performs a post-optimization. The fast insertion procedure is performed randomly inserting the new request in the current solution for every thread. If a feasible solution is found, the insertion is possible. If this is not the case the parallel TS with independent thread is run with parameters set to focus on feasibility. The presented computational experiments show that parallelization significantly increases the amount of served requests in real-world instances.

Another promising parallelization approach is developed in [31]. A Particle Swarm Optimization Algorithm (PSO) and Variable Neighborhood Search (VNS) for the resolution of the DVRP are presented. Two different hybrid solutions are created using 2-OPT improvement procedure in TSP and VRP environment. In addition to parallelization a low-level hybridization scheme (LRH) using 2-OPT as local improvement heuristic is implemented. To achieve a better response to environment changes a dynamic adaptive particle swarm optimization (DAPSO) is proposed. This mechanism allows the algorithm to restart the search from the best solutions found. VNS is based on the principle of systematically changing neighborhoods to escape a local optimal solution. The neighborhoods are defined in the following way: (1) $N_1(s)$ is the set of solutions which are results of swapping any 2 customers in the solution s. (2) $N_2(s)$ is the set of solutions which are result of λ-exchange operator with [1,0] and [1,1] moves. (3) $N_3(s)$ is the set of solutions which are results of applying 2-OPT to any sub-route of the solution s. (4) $N_4(s)$ is the set of solutions which are results of using 2-OPT to any two sub-route of the solution s. The results of the novel approach imply that PSO shows better results in smaller instances, whereas VNS outperforms PSO in the biggest ones.

5.3   An Artificial Ant Colony - 2-OPT Hybrid Algorithm

The most of recent hybrid algorithms combine local search improvement algorithms with metaheuristic background optimization methods. An Artificial Ant Colony algorithm based on 2-OPT local search (AAC-2-OPT) has been developed in [32].

An Artificial Ant Colony (AAC) approach is based on the way real ants find good paths to food sources. In their search for food sources, ants initially look around in a random manner. When they find a path, they come back to the nest and lay down an aromatic substance on the ground, known as pheromone. The amount of pheromone is related to the quality of the food source. The ants that come afterwards will thus search in a less random fashion, as they will be attracted by the pheromone trails. Ultimately, all ants will be attracted to the best path [33].

A hybrid solution aims to efficiently optimize dynamic pickup and delivery VRP. The basic processing steps in AAC-2-OPT hybrid algorithm are summarized in the following way: (1) Initialization (2) Route construction (3) Memorize the BESTSOL found (4) Local pheromone update (5) Local search, 2-OPT algorithm (6) Global pheromone update and (7) Stop criterion.

In the AAC metaheuristic, a set of agents (ants) build solutions to the given problem cooperating through pheromone-update. The success principles of AAC consist in an intelligent exploitation of the problem structure and in an effective interplay between the search space and the solution space elaborating with the local search. According to this method, the ants dynamically build a route in which they add a new customer while inserting it into any place of the already partial constructive route. In this manner, it is possible to dynamically change the route, caused by the insertion of other customers later in the solution construction. The insertion of new customer is difficult at this point because the vehicle is started to serve the customers and it is very hard to find the advantage place to insert the new customer. During the phase of solution construction, the ant can carry out some update of the values of the pheromone array, typically along the path that it is just following. The first update is a local pheromone update which occurs after an ant completes its solution. This update evaporates the pheromone values along the customers visited by the ant in order to allow the succeeding ants to explore other customers. Once ants complete their solution construction phase, local search algorithms can be used to refine their solutions. The 2-OPT local search algorithm has been used for intra-route improvement. The 2-OPT approach is incorporated in AAC before the update of a global pheromone for each iteration. The second update is the global pheromone update. The pheromone values of an objective are updated by the iteration's best route after local search with respect to that objective. The best solution is used for the global pheromone update. A constructive solution is stored in the pheromone trail matrix to generate a new solution by the next ants. Hybrid AAC-2-OPT algorithm has provided competitive and high quality solutions.

5.4   A Hybrid Neighborhood Search Algorithm

A Decision Support System (DSS) for optimizing dynamic courier routing operations has been proposed in [34]. In the dynamic operational environment of courier service, new customer orders and order cancellations arrive continually and thus disrupt originally designed optimal routing schedule.

The DSS aims to provide a flexible and interactive tool to simultaneously solve offline and online problems. The DSS has been designed as a distributed intelligent system that is composed of an Intranet Server End and a Mobile Client End. The Intranet Server End is responsible for assisting the fleet manager to schedule and re-schedule the courier routing plan, while the Mobile Client End is deployed on the courier's mobile devices to receive the routing information from the Intranet Server End. The DSS integrates a Hybrid Neighborhood Search (HNS) algorithm to solve the offline and online routing problems arising in courier service.

The HNS algorithm is designed for tackling a Dynamic Courier Routing problem with Order Cancellation and Fuzzy Time Windows (DCR-OCFTW) model. Fuzzy time windows are formulated in the DVRP model to quantify the service level and explore the service efficiency. The HNS algorithm has four phases and the first two phases are designed to solve the offline problems, while the last two phases are developed to solve the online problem. The hybrid algorithm is following: (1) initial solution generation, (2) static solution refinement, (3) removal and reinsertion, and (4) parallel neighborhood search-based re-optimization. A greedy heuristic algorithm has been proposed to create the initial solution, while the Variable Neighborhood Search (VNS) based neighborhood search algorithm has been proposed to improve the initial solution. The neighborhood structure is hybrid as the neighbors are generated by a series of different intra-route and inter-route operators, such as 2-OPT operator, Or-OPT operator, couple-exchange operator, double-bridge operator, exchange operator, relocate operator, and cross operator. Basically, the previous procedures are randomly used to find a neighbor of the current solution. Third and fourth phases are event-driven phases, which are performed if online customer requests are received in real-time. The basic idea of the parallel approach is to transform the sequential process of the algorithm into a parallel process and distribute the computational tasks to multiple cores of computation process units, through which the computation time of the algorithm can be largely reduced.

5.5   A Hybrid Heuristic Algorithm

A dynamic capacitated location-routing problem with fuzzy demands (DCLRP-FD) has been considered in this chapter. In the DCLRP-FD, facility location problem and vehicle routing problems are solved. Decisions regarding facility locations are permitted to be made only in the first time period of the planning process but, the routing decisions may be changed in each time period. The vehicles and depots have a known capacity to serve the customers with altering demands during each time period. Furthermore, it is assumed that the demands of customers are fuzzy variables [35].

A hybrid heuristic algorithm (HHA) is proposed to solve the DCLRP-FD. HHA is consisting of four phases: (1) establishing the depots, (2) clustering the customers, (3) allocating clusters to depot or depots, and (4) routing (Fig. 5). In the first phase (Fig. 5 (a)), the depots are selected between the candidate depots sites based on the coordination of customers. First, the sum of distances between the locations of customers and each potential depot and the capacities and the fixed costs are calculated. After that, the depots are sorted in descending order and ranked. The top-ranked potential depot is selected to be established. In the second phase (Fig. 5(b)), customers are clustered using a greedy search algorithm. The customers are grouped considering their intra distance, their fuzzy demands and the capacity of the vehicles. To form a cluster, a customer is selected randomly from the set of non-clustered customers. Then, the algorithm searches for the nearest customer to the last selected customer of the current cluster. The nearest customer is not assigned to the cluster if its demand exceeds the remaining capacity of the vehicle.

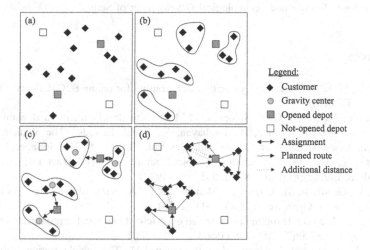

Fig. 5. Illustration of a HHA procedure in each period (Source: [35], p. 463)

In the third phase (Fig. 5(c)), the clusters are allocated to the opened depot or depots considering the distance between the depots and the gravity center of the clusters as well as the capacity of the depots. In the fourth phase (Fig. 5(d)), Ant Colony System (ACS) is proposed for the creation of the feasible route between each cluster and depot. The stochastic simulation is used to determine the demands of customers and a local search method is applied to evaluate the opened depot or depots in the first phase. In order to decrease the solving time of evaluation of the opened depots, half of the closed depots sorted in the first phase are used as a neighborhood in the local search method. Although, the HHA algorithm has shown good results, there is no similar research in the literature, so far, of the DCLRP-FD to compare results with.

6 Conclusion and Future Work

This paper has highlighted some of the recent hybrid solutions in a DVRP environment. The DVRP environment is highly dynamic which instigates engineers to develop efficient and fast algorithms for the optimization and re-optimization of routes. Different computational calculations allow the selection of the best combination of existing algorithms for routing vehicles ever more efficiently. Although computational power may present significant limitation in situations when solution is required instantly, constant expansion of ICT field increasingly favors and encourages the use of hybrid approaches.

Future research can be focused on systematic evaluation and numerical comparison of various hybrid solutions in a DVRP environment. Lack of hybrid algorithms in B2C environment shouldn't be neglected as well.

Acknowledgment. The authors acknowledge the support for research project TR 36030, funded by the Ministry of Science and Technological Development of Serbia.

References

1. Du, T.C., Li, E.Y., Chou, D.: Dynamic vehicle routing for online B2C delivery. Omega **33** (1), 33–45 (2005)
2. Larsen, A., Madsen, B.G.O., Solomon, M.M.: Recent developments in dynamic vehicle routing systems. In: Golden, B., Raghavan, S., Wasil, E. (eds.) The Vehicle Routing Problem: Latest Advances and New Challenges, vol. 43, pp. 199–218. Springer, US (2008)
3. Laporte, G.: The traveling salesman problem: an overview of exact and approximate algorithms. Eur. J. Oper. Res. **59**(2), 345–358 (1992)
4. Pillac, V., Gendreau, M., Guéret, C., Medaglia, A.L.: A review of dynamic vehicle routing problems. Eur. J. Oper. Res. **225**(1), 1–11 (2013)
5. Laporte, G.: The vehicle routing problem: an overview of exact and approximate algorithms. Eur. J. Oper. Res. **59**(2), 231–248 (1992)
6. Potvin, J.Y., Kervahut, T., Garcia, B.L., Rousseau, J.M.: The vehicle routing problem with time windows, Part I: Tabu search. INFORMS J. Comput. **8**(2), 158–164 (1996)
7. Potvin, J.Y., Bengio, S.: The vehicle routing problem with time windows, part II: genetic search. INFORMS J. Comput. **8**(2), 165–172 (1996)
8. Chiang, W.C., Russell, R.A.: Simulated annealing metaheuristics for the vehicle routing problem with time windows. Ann. Oper. Res. **63**(1), 3–27 (1996)
9. Liao, T.Y., Hu, T.Y.: An object-oriented evaluation framework for dynamic vehicle routing problems under real-time information. Expert Syst. Appl. **38**(10), 12548–12558 (2011)
10. Filipec, M., Skrlec, D., Krajcar, S.: An efficient implementation of genetic algorithms for constrained vehicle routing problem. Proceedings of 1998 IEEE International Conference on Systems, Man, and Cybernetics, pp. 2231–2236. IEEE Press, San Diego (1998)
11. Bertsimas, D.J., Ryzin, G.: Stochastic and dynamic vehicle routing in the euclidean plane with multiple capacitated vehicles. Oper. Res. **41**(1), 60–76 (1993)
12. Shen, Y., Potvin, J.Y., Rousseau, J.M., Roy, S.: A computer system for vehicle dispatching with learning capabilities. Ann. Oper. Res. **61**(1), 189–211 (1995)
13. Ritzinger, U., Puchinger, J.: Hybrid metaheuristics for dynamic and stochastic vehicle routing. In: Talbi, El-Ghazali (ed.) Hybrid Metaheuristics. SCI, vol. 434, pp. 81–100. Springer, Heidelberg (2013)
14. Anbuudayasankar, S.P., Ganesh, K., Mohapatra, S.: Models for Practical Routing Problems in Logistics. Springer International Publishing Switzerland (2014)
15. Tarantilis, C.D., Ioannou, G., Prastacos, G.: Advanced vehicle routing algorithms for complex operations management problems. J. Food Eng. **70**(3), 455–471 (2005)
16. Gendreau, M., Hertz, A., Laporte, G.: New insertion and post optimization procedures for the traveling salesman problem. Oper. Res. **40**(6), 1086–1094 (1992)
17. Foisy, C., Potvin, J.Y.: Implementing an insertion heuristic for vehicle routing on parallel hardware. Comput. Oper. Res. **20**(7), 737–745 (1993)
18. Salari, M., Toth, P., Tramontani, A.: An ILP improvement procedure for the Open vehicle routing problem. Comput. Oper. Res. **37**(12), 2106–2120 (2010)

19. Lin, S.: Computer solutions of the traveling salesman problem. Bell Syst. Tech. J. **44**, 2245–2269 (1965)
20. Alfa, A.S., Heragu, S.S., Chen, M.: A 3-opt based simulated annealing algorithm for vehicle routing problem. Comput. Ind. Eng. **21**(1–4), 635–639 (1991)
21. Lin, S., Kernighan, B.: An effective heuristic algorithm for the traveling salesman problem. Oper. Res. **21**(2), 498–516 (1973)
22. Or, I.: Traveling salesman type combinatorial problems and their relation to the logistics of blood banking. Ph.D thesis, Department of Industrial Engineering and Management Science, Northwestern University, Evanston, IL (1976)
23. Teodorović, D.: Transportation Networks (Transportne mreže). Faculty of transport and traffic engineering, Belgrade (2007)
24. Glover, F.: Tabu search Part I. ORSA J. Comput. **1**(3), 190–206 (1989)
25. Baykasoglu, A., Gindy, N.N.: A simulated annealing algorithm for dynamic layout problem. Comput. Oper. Res. **28**(14), 1403–1426 (2001)
26. Potvin, J.Y., Bengio, S.: The vehicle routing problem with time windows, Part II: genetic search. INFORMS J. Comput. **8**(2), 165–172 (1996)
27. Dorigo, M., Maniezzo, V., Colorni, A.: Ant system: optimization by a colony cooperation agents. IEEE Trans. Syst. Man. Cybern. Part B **26**(1), 29–41 (1996)
28. Jih, W.-R., Yung-Jen Hsu, J.: Dynamic vehicle routing using hybrid genetic algorithms. In: Proceedings of 1999 IEEE International Conference on Robotics and Automation, pp. 453–458. IEEE Piscataway, Detroit (1999)
29. Créput, J.-C., Hajjam, A., Koukam, A., Kuhn, O.: Self-organizing maps in population based metaheuristic to the dynamic vehicle routing problem. J. Comb. Optim. **24**(4), 437–458 (2012)
30. Attanasio, A., Cordeau, J.-F., Ghiani, G., Laporte, G.: Parallel tabu search heuristics for the dynamic multi-vehicle dial-a-ride problem. Parallel Comput. **30**(3), 377–387 (2004)
31. Khouadjia, M.R., Sarasola, B., Alba, E., Jourdan, L., Talbi, E.-G.: A comparative study between dynamic adapted PSO and VNS for the vehicle routing problem with dynamic requests. Appl. Soft Comput. **12**(4), 1426–1439 (2012)
32. Euchi, J., Yassine, A., Chabchoub, H.: The dynamic vehicle routing problem: Solution with hybrid metaheuristic approach. Swarm Evolutionary Computation. (in press, 2015)
33. Simić, D., Simić, S.: Hybrid artificial intelligence approaches on vehicle routing problem in logistics distribution. In: Corchado, E., Snášel, V., Abraham, A., Woźniak, M., Graña, M., Cho, S.-B. (eds.) HAIS 2012, Part I. LNCS, vol. 7208, pp. 208–220. Springer, Heidelberg (2012)
34. Lin, C., Choy, K.L., Ho, G.T.S., Lam, H.Y., Pang, G.K.H., Chin, K.S.: A decision support system for optimizing dynamic courier routing operations. Expert Syst. Appl. **41**(15), 6917–6933 (2014)
35. Nadizadeh, A., Nasab, H.H.: Solving the dynamic capacitated location-routing problem with fuzzy demands by hybrid heuristic algorithm. Eur. J. Oper. Res. **238**(2), 458–470 (2014)

A Straightforward Implementation of a GPU-accelerated ELM in R with NVIDIA Graphic Cards

M. Alia-Martinez, J. Antonanzas, F. Antonanzas-Torres, A. Pernía-Espinoza, and R. Urraca[✉]

EDMANS Group, University of La Rioja, Logroño, Spain
ruben.urraca@unirioja.es, edmans@dim.unirioja.es
http:www.mineriadatos.com

Abstract. General purpose computing on graphics processing units (GPGPU) is a promising technique to cope with nowadays arising computational challenges due to the suitability of GPUs for parallel processing. Several libraries and functions are being released to boost the use of GPUs in real world problems. However, many of these packages require a deep knowledge in GPUs' architecture and in low-level programming. As a result, end users find trouble in exploiting GPGPU advantages. In this paper, we focus on the GPU-acceleration of a prediction technique specially designed to deal with big datasets: the extreme learning machine (ELM). The intent of this study is to develop a user-friendly library in the open source R language and subsequently release the code in https://github.com/maaliam/EDMANS-elmNN-GPU.git. Therefore R users can freely implement it with the only requirement of having a NVIDIA graphic card. The most computationally demanding operations were identified by performing a sensitivity analysis. As a result, only matrix multiplications were executed in the GPU as they take around 99 % of total execution time. A speedup rate up to 15 times was obtained with this GPU-accelerated ELM in the most computationally expensive scenarios. Moreover, the applicability of the GPU-accelerated ELM was also tested with a typical case of model selection, in which genetic algorithms were used to fine-tune an ELM and training thousands of models is required. In this case, still a speedup of 6 times was obtained.

Keywords: ELM · GPU · gputools · CUDA · R Software · Big data · Optimization techniques

1 Introduction

In this day and age, data creation is steadily increasing at rates nobody could envision few years ago. Sources of data in society are diverse, from social media to machines, sensing or transactions [1]. This new phenomenon is commonly referred as *big data* and it emerges as one of the most challenging topics in our days. A vast amount of data has to be processed at the same rate it is recorded

© Springer International Publishing Switzerland 2015
E. Onieva et al. (Eds.): HAIS 2015, LNAI 9121, pp. 656–667, 2015.
DOI: 10.1007/978-3-319-19644-2_54

to obtain valuable information given the existing computing limitations. What is more, high computational demands can still arise when processing relatively-small databases but thousands of operations have to be executed. A typical case is the automation of the model selection process. In order to obtain a fine-tuned predictive model, both model parameter optimization (MPO) and feature selection (FS) are usually executed simultaneously. The problem basically consists on minimizing a loss function by applying different iterative meta-heuristics, which are optimization techniques that imply the computation of hundreds or even thousands of models. For instance, [2] tuning an extreme learning machine (ELM) for classification purposes by using genetic algorithms (GAs), setting both the population size and the number of generations to 100 and implementing 10-CV to obtain a more robust error measurement. As a consequence, 100,000 ELMs had to be computed.

Any of the above-mentioned situations entails too large execution times for practical applications. A huge effort is being made in the development of new processing techniques as well as more powerful computational tools to cope with these challenges. For instance, one of most basic and well-known solutions is the use of parallel computing with multi-core processors, which is commonly available in any commercial software. More advanced solutions exist in the context of different fields such as high performance computing (HPC) and supercomputers. Some applications are the use of computer clusters, computer grids or cloud computing among others. In this study, we focus in one of these emerging solutions: the use of the graphics processing unit (GPU) instead of the traditional central processing unit (CPU) to run computationally demanding computations.

GPUs are evolving at faster rates than the traditional CPUs [3]. Though they were initially built to manage the graphic display in computers, their multi-core structure with usually more than 200 units makes them adequate for parallel processing. The release of compute unified device architecture (CUDA) software from NVIDIA first enabled their use for running non-graphical computations, also known as general purpose computing on graphics processing units (GPGPU). Afterwards, several libraries for CUDA users have been released as well as software for other GPU developers, such as FireStream for AMD or the more general OpenCL. Nevertheless, most of these applications require an extensive knowledge on GPU structure and parallel processing in some specific programming languages such as C or Python. On the contrary, typical end users are researchers on the fields of statistics, chemistry, biology or finance, who posses limited programming abilities in more friendly interfaces such as Matlab, Mathematica or R. Consequently, there is still a need of developing user-friendly tools and functions, so these end users are able to fully exploit the advantages of GPGPU.

In this line, this study is focused on accelerating ELMs, an appropriate technique to deal with big datasets [4]. ELM major operations are simple matrix-matrix multiplications, inversions and transposes, so consequently they present an adequate structure to perform parallel processing. Some previous works exist related to the GPU-acceleration of ELMs [5], but they require high programming skills, as most of them are based on programming in C language. Therefore, our proposal is implemented in the open source R language [6], widely extended in data analysis field. A new library is freely released at https://github.com/maaliam/EDMANS-elmNN-GPU.git for future implementations. Computations were run with NVIDIA GPUs in order to take advantage of the numerous CUDA-related libraries available, such as the R package `gputools` [7].

2   Methodology

2.1   ELM

ELM [8] implements a simplification of traditional learning algorithms used in a Single-Hidden Layer Feedforward Network (SLFN) [9]. Instead of using an iterative procedure, ELM proposes a straightforward solution to the optimization problem behind a SLFN, while keeping its generalization capacity.

Mathematically, the algorithm is described as follows. An ELM predicts an output variable t_i given a training set (x_i, t_i) with $x_i \in \mathbb{R}^d, t_i \in \mathbb{R}, i = 1, ..., N$, where x_i is the set of inputs, d is the dimension of the input feature space, and N the number of instances. Random values are assigned to the weight vector w_i between the inputs and the hidden layer, and to the bias b_i. As a consequence, the hidden-layer output matrix H is directly obtained:

$$H(x_i) = \begin{bmatrix} h(x_1) \\ ... \\ h(x_N) \end{bmatrix} = \begin{bmatrix} g(w_1x_1 + b_1) & ... & g(w_Lx_1 + b_L) \\ ... & \ddots & ... \\ g(w_1x_N + b_1) & ... & g(w_Lx_N + b_L) \end{bmatrix} \tag{1}$$

where L is the number of neurons in the hidden layer and g is the activation function. Initially, the algorithm essentially maps the set of points from the d-dimensional feature space to a L-dimensional neurons space. Once matrix H is obtained, the problem is reduced to calculate the weight vector β between the hidden layer and the outputs ($H\beta = T$). This typical optimization problem is solved by using the minimal norm Least-Square method, in which the Moore-Penrose generalized inverse ($H^\dagger$) of matrix H has to be computed:

$$\beta = H^\dagger T \tag{2}$$

In this study, a variation of the traditional methods to compute this inverse is utilized. Following the theory explained at [10], a regularization parameter is included. This approach is strongly recommended for dealing with databases with high number of samples.

$$\beta = \left(\frac{I}{C} + H^T H \right)^{-1} H^T T \tag{3}$$

where C stands for the cost parameter. Based on the ridge regression theory, the addition of a positive value to the diagonal term of matrix $H^T H$ improves the robustness of the model.

2.2 GPU-acceleration

The original ELM functions of package `elmNN` [11] were used as baseline to develop the GPU-accelerated ELM. Two functions from this package were modified:

- `elmtrain.default()`, a method of the general function `elmtrain()`.
- `predict.elmNN()`, a method of the general function `predict()`.

In both functions, an additional argument labeled `GPU` has been included. The default value set to `GPU=FALSE` run the computations in the CPU and when the argument is turned into `GPU=TRUE` the GPU-accelerated version is activated.

First, a sensitivity study was performed (Subsect. 3.1) in order to detect the most demanding operations in each function. The nomenclature used is based on the package `elmNN`. According to this package, all matrices and vectors are transposed compared to the traditional theoretical explanation of Subsect. 2.1.

The training function based on `elmtrain.default()` computes the weight vector β given (x_i, t_i) and following the equations described in Subsect. 2.1. This function is comprised by ten different R instructions:

```
#1  tempH <- inpweight
#2  biasMatrix <- matrix(rep(biashid, ncol(P)), nrow=nhid,
ncol=ncol(P), byrow = F)
#3  tempH <- tempH + biasMatrix
#4  H <- 1 / (1 + exp(-1*tempH))
#5  H.Prod <- H
#6  C.Mat <- diag(ncol(H.Prod))/C + H.Prod
#7  inverse<-solve(C.Mat)
#8  mult<-inverse
#9  outweight <-mult
#10 Y <- t(t(H)
```

The predict function `predict.elmNN()` computes the output vector t_i based on the set of input samples x_i and on the previously calculated weight vector β. The function is comprised by six instructions:

```
#11 TV.P <- t(x)
#12 tmpHTest<-inpweight
#13 biasMatrixTE <- matrix(rep(biashid, ncol(TV.P)), nrow=nhid,
ncol=ncol(TV.P), byrow = F)
#14 tmpHTest <- tmpHTest + biasMatrixTE
#15 HTest <- 1 / (1 + exp(-1*tmpHTest))
#16 TY <- t(t(HTest)
```

Time spent by each instruction was recorded to establish the influence of each operation in the overall execution time. Preliminary trials (Subsect. 3.1) indicated that matrix-matrix multiplications where the most cost demanding operations, so they were the only executed in the GPU (instructions # 1, #

5, # 8 and # 12). These multiplications were implemented using the gpuMat-Mult() function of package `gputools`. Basically, this function is a wrapper for the cublasDgemm function of NVIDIA CUDA Basic Linear Algebra Subroutines (cuBLAS) library. The remaining operations were still implemented in the CPU.

3 Experiments

3.1 Sensitivity Analysis

Initially, the computational cost of each instruction using the CPU was compared with the proposed GPU-accelerated ELM. A two-dimensional grid of databases was designed to perform the comparisons by varying the number of samples N and features d. Besides, the main parameter of a ELM, the number of neurons in the hidden layer L, was also altered. Consequently, a three-dimensional grid of models was created with the following ranges and intervals of parameters:

- Number of samples N: from 5,000 to 50,000 in 5,000 samples interval.
- Number of neurons in the hidden layer L: from 100 to 1,000 in 100 neurons interval.
- Number of features d: 10, 100 and 1,000.

All databases were randomly generated using numbers from 0 to 1 as the only goal was to evaluate the execution times. Therefore, cost parameter C was held constant and equal to 1. To perform an even comparison, just exactly the same randomly generated bias b_i and input weight vector w_i were used in both types of ELMs.

Computations were performed in a workstation with the following hardware specifications: NVIDIA GeForce GTX650 with 384 cores and 2 Gb DDR5, a dual core processor (AMD Athlon^{TM}64 X2 @ 1.8 GHz) and a 4 GB RAM memory.

3.2 Case of Study: Estimation of Daily Global Solar Irradiation

The efficiency of GPU-accelerated ELM was further analyzed with a real case. Solar global irradiation was predicted given thirteen meteorological variables as inputs related to rainfall, temperature, extraterrestrial irradiation, wind speed and humidity. Daily measurements recorded at 4 different locations of southern Spain (Cordoba, Jaen, Nijar and Puebla Rio) from 2009 to 2013 were used. After spurious cleaning, a database composed by 6,605 samples was obtained. The period 2009–2012 was used for training (5249 samples) whilst 2013 samples were used for testing (1356 samples).

This case of study is a practical example where high computational resources are required with a relatively-small database, as running a vast amount of models is required to perform model selection. Genetic algorithms were used to simultaneously execute MPO and FS. Therefore, a hybrid chromosome was utilized, where a binary part models the set of input variables chosen and a real-coded part stands for the parameters of the model [12]. The population size and the number of generations were set to 64 and 20 respectively. Individuals were first ranked according to a fitness function J that accounts for error prediction ($J = MAE_{val}$) and they were subsequently re-ranked according to the model complexity. The re-rank works as follows. First, the complexity of each individual was evaluated based on the generalized degrees of freedom (GDF) theory [13]. Using GDF, complexity is defined as the sensitivity of each fitted value y_{ie} to a randomly perturbed target value y_i. In this case, the "horizontal" estimate with 10 repetitions and Gaussian noise $N(0, 0.05)$ was utilized as described in [14]. Then, models inside the same error interval (relative difference between errors less than 0.1 %) were re-ranked according to this complexity value. The 16 best individuals (25 % elitism) were selected as parents for the next generations. A mutation rate of 10 % was chosen but the best individual was not muted.

GA computations were run in the workstation described in Subsect. 3.1. When working only with the CPU, only one core was used in order to carry out an equal comparison and, consequently, only one model was computed at each time.

4 Results and Discussion

Table 1 depicts the execution time in seconds taken by each instruction in train and predict functions, when only the CPU was used to run the computations.

Table 1. Execution time in seconds taken by each instruction using the CPU. Results of the three-dimensional (neurons, samples, features) grid of models are summarized in three blocks. In each block, the variation of one parameter was individually studied while averaging the other two.

| | | elmtrain.default() | | | | | | | | | predict.elmNN() | | | | | |
		#1	#2	#3	#4	#5	#6	#7	#8	#9	#10	#11	#12	#13	#14	#15	#16
Features	10	0.44	0.74	0.16	1.49	35.78	0.01	1.26	35.43	0.14	0.44	0.00	0.43	0.74	0.16	1.48	0.43
	100	4.43	0.73	0.16	1.49	35.81	0.01	1.28	35.37	0.14	0.45	0.02	4.43	0.74	0.16	1.48	0.44
	1,000	50.82	0.74	0.16	1.49	35.79	0.01	1.28	35.39	0.14	0.44	0.35	50.84	0.73	0.15	1.64	0.50
Neurons	100	3.46	0.13	0.02	0.27	1.02	0.00	0.01	0.68	0.03	0.07	0.12	3.46	0.13	0.02	0.26	0.07
	200	6.75	0.26	0.05	0.54	3.87	0.00	0.03	2.70	0.05	0.15	0.12	6.75	0.26	0.05	0.54	0.15
	300	10.04	0.41	0.09	0.81	8.56	0.00	0.11	8.37	0.08	0.23	0.12	10.04	0.41	0.09	0.81	0.23
	400	13.34	0.53	0.11	1.08	15.08	0.00	0.28	14.84	0.10	0.31	0.12	13.36	0.53	0.11	1.08	0.31
	500	16.65	0.66	0.14	1.35	23.36	0.00	0.54	23.10	0.12	0.39	0.12	16.63	0.66	0.14	1.35	0.39
	600	19.99	0.80	0.18	1.62	33.52	0.01	0.93	33.24	0.15	0.47	0.12	19.95	0.80	0.17	1.62	0.47
	700	23.30	0.96	0.21	1.89	45.52	0.01	1.46	45.22	0.17	0.56	0.12	23.41	0.95	0.21	1.89	0.56
	800	27.29	1.07	0.23	2.16	59.31	0.01	2.14	59.04	0.20	0.64	0.12	27.31	1.06	0.22	2.21	0.66
	900	30.67	1.20	0.26	2.45	75.02	0.01	3.06	74.63	0.22	0.73	0.12	30.68	1.20	0.26	2.61	0.83
	1,000	34.16	1.33	0.29	2.75	92.67	0.02	4.17	92.14	0.25	0.88	0.12	34.12	1.33	0.28	2.99	0.93
Samples	5,000	3.38	0.13	0.03	0.27	6.49	0.01	1.27	6.43	0.03	0.06	0.02	3.37	0.13	0.02	0.27	0.06
	10,000	6.75	0.27	0.05	0.54	13.00	0.01	1.27	12.93	0.05	0.15	0.05	6.76	0.27	0.05	0.54	0.15
	15,000	10.16	0.41	0.09	0.81	19.50	0.01	1.27	19.36	0.08	0.23	0.06	10.13	0.41	0.09	0.82	0.23
	20,000	13.47	0.53	0.11	1.08	26.05	0.01	1.27	25.70	0.10	0.31	0.09	13.48	0.53	0.11	1.09	0.32
	25,000	16.85	0.66	0.14	1.37	32.53	0.01	1.27	32.20	0.12	0.39	0.10	16.87	0.66	0.14	1.36	0.40
	30,000	20.22	0.80	0.17	1.63	39.07	0.01	1.27	38.65	0.15	0.48	0.14	20.26	0.80	0.17	1.64	0.49
	35,000	23.63	0.95	0.21	1.90	45.56	0.01	1.27	45.05	0.17	0.56	0.14	23.60	0.95	0.20	1.92	0.57
	40,000	26.99	1.06	0.23	2.16	52.09	0.01	1.28	51.48	0.20	0.67	0.20	27.02	1.07	0.23	2.27	0.69
	45,000	30.38	1.20	0.26	2.44	58.57	0.01	1.28	57.87	0.22	0.74	0.19	30.40	1.20	0.26	2.55	0.77
	50,000	33.81	1.33	0.29	2.72	65.08	0.01	1.28	64.29	0.25	0.84	0.25	33.80	1.33	0.28	2.91	0.91

Table 2. Execution time in seconds taken by each instruction using the GPU. Results of the three-dimensional (neurons, samples, features) grid of models are summarized in three blocks. In each block, the variation of one parameter was individually studied while averaging the other two.

		elmtrain.default()										predict.elmNN()					
		#1	#2	#3	#4	#5	#6	#7	#8	#9	#10	#11	#12	#13	#14	#15	#16
Features	10	0.13	0.74	0.16	1.48	1.10	0.01	1.26	0.84	0.08	0.37	0.00	0.12	0.74	0.16	1.49	0.37
	100	0.23	0.73	0.16	1.48	1.10	0.01	1.28	0.84	0.08	0.37	0.02	0.22	0.74	0.16	1.48	0.37
	1,000	1.20	0.74	0.16	1.49	1.10	0.01	1.27	0.84	0.08	0.37	0.63	1.25	0.73	0.15	1.52	0.39
Neurons	100	0.24	0.13	0.02	0.26	0.09	0.00	0.00	0.05	0.02	0.06	0.12	0.14	0.13	0.02	0.26	0.06
	200	0.22	0.26	0.05	0.54	0.23	0.00	0.03	0.13	0.03	0.13	0.12	0.22	0.26	0.05	0.54	0.12
	300	0.31	0.41	0.09	0.81	0.40	0.00	0.11	0.26	0.04	0.20	0.12	0.31	0.41	0.09	0.81	0.20
	400	0.39	0.53	0.11	1.08	0.59	0.00	0.28	0.41	0.06	0.26	0.12	0.39	0.53	0.11	1.08	0.26
	500	0.47	0.66	0.14	1.35	0.82	0.00	0.54	0.59	0.07	0.33	0.12	0.47	0.66	0.14	1.35	0.32
	600	0.55	0.80	0.17	1.62	1.08	0.01	0.93	0.81	0.09	0.40	0.12	0.55	0.80	0.17	1.62	0.39
	700	0.63	0.96	0.20	1.89	1.37	0.01	1.45	1.06	0.10	0.47	0.12	0.62	0.95	0.21	1.89	0.47
	800	0.71	1.07	0.23	2.15	1.70	0.01	2.14	1.33	0.11	0.54	0.12	0.72	1.06	0.22	2.16	0.55
	900	0.81	1.20	0.26	2.43	2.15	0.01	3.04	1.70	0.13	0.61	0.34	0.96	1.20	0.26	2.50	0.64
	1,000	0.89	1.33	0.29	2.71	2.58	0.02	4.15	2.05	0.15	0.73	0.85	0.95	1.33	0.28	2.75	0.72
Samples	5,000	0.19	0.13	0.02	0.26	0.18	0.01	1.27	0.15	0.02	0.05	0.02	0.09	0.13	0.02	0.27	0.05
	10,000	0.19	0.27	0.05	0.54	0.40	0.01	1.27	0.31	0.03	0.13	0.05	0.19	0.27	0.05	0.54	0.13
	15,000	0.28	0.41	0.09	0.81	0.60	0.01	1.27	0.46	0.04	0.20	0.06	0.28	0.41	0.09	0.81	0.20
	20,000	0.37	0.53	0.11	1.08	0.81	0.01	1.27	0.61	0.06	0.28	0.09	0.37	0.53	0.11	1.08	0.27
	25,000	0.46	0.66	0.14	1.35	1.00	0.01	1.27	0.76	0.07	0.34	0.10	0.46	0.66	0.14	1.35	0.34
	30,000	0.55	0.80	0.17	1.63	1.21	0.01	1.27	0.91	0.09	0.41	0.14	0.57	0.80	0.17	1.64	0.41
	35,000	0.65	0.95	0.21	1.89	1.40	0.01	1.27	1.07	0.10	0.47	0.14	0.65	0.95	0.20	1.90	0.48
	40,000	0.74	1.06	0.23	2.15	1.60	0.01	1.27	1.22	0.12	0.54	0.20	0.86	1.07	0.23	2.17	0.55
	45,000	0.83	1.20	0.26	2.43	1.80	0.01	1.27	1.37	0.13	0.61	0.92	0.86	1.20	0.26	2.44	0.61
	50,000	0.93	1.33	0.29	2.70	2.01	0.01	1.27	1.52	0.15	0.69	0.47	0.97	1.33	0.28	2.74	0.69

Results proved that most time-consuming operations were matrix-matrix multiplications: operations # 1, # 5 and # 8 in `elmtrain.default()` and instruction # 12 in `predict.elmNN()`.

Operations #1 and # 12 are eventually the same, as both compute matrix H based on the randomly generated input weight vector w_i and the set of input variables x_i:

$$H[L \times N] = w_i[L \times d]x_i[d \times N] \tag{4}$$

Instructions #5 and # 8 are the two matrix-matrix multiplications required to implement minimal norm Least-Squares with the regularization parameter. Operation #5 computes the matrix multiplication between H and its transpose:

$$H.prod[L \times L] = H[L \times N]t(H)[N \times L] \tag{5}$$

while operation # 5 multiplies the inverted matrix obtained after adding the regularization term and H:

$$mult[L \times N] = inverse[L \times L]H[L \times N] \tag{6}$$

Looking at the dimensions of these multiplications, number of features d only influences operations # 1 and # 12. According to this, results of Table 1 show that execution time in operation # 1 increased 115 times, from 0.44 to 50.82 s, when the database of 1,000 features was used. Other operations barely remained constant when the number of features was varied.

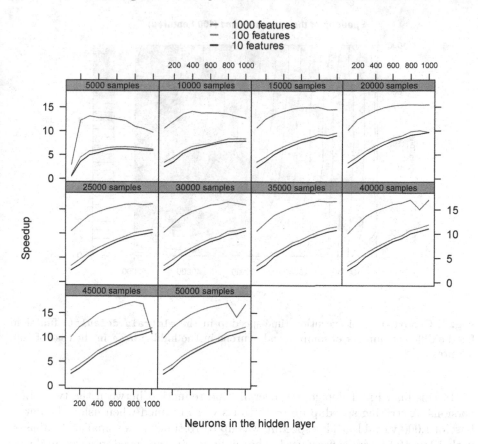

Fig. 1. Execution time speedup (vertical axis) in the `elmtrain.default()` function for the different combinations of samples, features and neurons in the hidden layer

Modifying the number of samples N and the number of neurons in the hidden layer d had a similar impact on the execution time. The execution time of multiplications # 1, # 5, # 8 and # 12 considerably grew. On the contrary, the execution time of some of the remaining operations such as the activation function (# 4), the calculation of the regularization term (# 6), matrix-vector multiplications (# 10 and # 16) or computing the inverse (# 8) experimented a virtually negligible increase. This was the reason why only matrix-matrix multiplications were implemented in the GPU.

Table 2 shows execution times in seconds using the same databases but with the GPU-accelerated ELM. Remarkable time reductions were obtained in most demanding computations. For instance, with the 50,000 sampled database, time required by all matrix-matrix multiplications was around 2 s, which is now in the same range of other computations such as the arithmetic operations implemented by the sigmoid activation function (# 4). What is more, using 1,000 neurons in the hidden layer, time required by matrix multiplications was eventually half of the time spent to obtain the inverse (# 7).

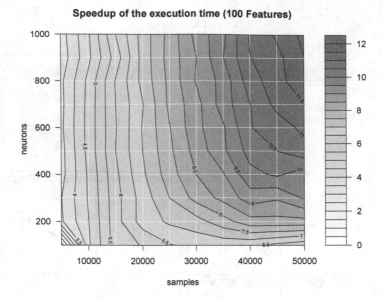

Fig. 2. Contour plot of execution time speedup in the `elmtrain.default()` function for the different number of samples and neurons in the hidden layer in the case of 100 features

In this line, Fig. 1 depicts the overall time reduction between the two ELM versions. A striking speedup up to 15 times was obtained when using the database of 1,000 variables. This speedup was up to 10 times when smaller databases with 10 or 100 features were used. The slight fall in the speedup curve in databases with 1,000 features and 40,000, 45,000 or 50,000 samples was caused by RAM limitations in the workstation.

The case of 100 features was further analyzed in detail in Fig. 2 with a contour plot, where samples and neurons were selected as x and y axis respectively while speedup was the third dimension. It can be appreciated that the higher speedups were obtained when both the number of samples and neurons increased proportionally. On the contrary, the speedup slightly increased and even decreased when only neurons or samples were raised alone. This explained why in Fig. 1, when low number of samples were used, the speedup curve stagnated of even started to decreased when the number of neurons was raised. Similar patterns were observed with 10 and 1,000 features (data not shown).

Finally, the applicability of the GPU-accelerated ELM was evaluated with a real case of study of model selection using GA, where 12,800 ELMs were computed. Although the GA procedure introduces some sources of uncertainty in different steps of the procedure, such as the creation of initial generation or mutations, preliminary results have proved the robustness of this methodology by repeating GA several times. This robustness was again verified in this case of study, as the evolution followed in GA by both ELM versions presented a similar trend (data not shown). Besides, the final solution reached (best individual of

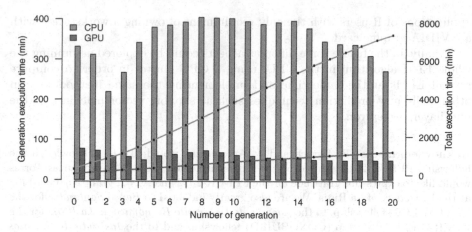

Fig. 3. Total execution time (lines) and execution time per generation (bars) in minutes spent by CPU and GPU versions of ELM through the GA optimization process

last generation) of both ELMs was roughly equivalent. With the CPU version, an ELM with 8 selected features, 472 neurons in the hidden layer and a cost of 2^9 was obtained with a normalized testing MAE of 0.059, while in the GPU version, an ELM with the same 8 selected features, 524 neurons in the hidden layer and a cost of 2^{11} was obtained with a normalized testing MAE of 0.060.

As a result, the computational cost through each generation were comparable in terms of complexity. However, when looking at execution times, Fig. 3 shows how the GPU-accelerated ELM significantly outperforms the CPU version achieving a total overall speedup of roughly 6 times. The CPU version took around 123 hours to run all generations whilst the proposed GPU-accelerated ELM spent only 20 hours.

5   Conclusions and Future Work

General purpose computing of graphics processing units (GPGPU) is emerging as one of the most appealing technologies to deal with nowadays computational challenges in data analysis. In the previous study, a GPU-accelerated version of ELM has been proposed by modifying the R package elmNN. Preliminary trials showed how by only running matrix-matrix multiplications in the GPU, speedups up to 15 times were obtained in the most demanding situations with high number of features, samples and neurons on the hidden layer. The methodology was also proved useful in a real case where a relatively-small database was used but a vast amount of models had to be computed in the context of model selection meta-heuristics. In this case, an overall reduction around 6 times was obtained using GA to perform a fine-tuning of an ELM.

The GPU-accelerated version of package elmNN has been freely released at https://github.com/maaliam/EDMANS-elmNN-GPU.git for future applications of R users with the only requirement of owning a workstation with a NVIDIA graphic card.

Finally, in the future some different aspects could be explored as running the whole ELM algorithm in the GPU, using a GPU cluster in order to compute several ELMs at the same time and implementing the same methodology in other well-know prediction techniques such as support vector machines or the multilayer perceptron.

Acknowledgments. R. Urraca and J. Antonanzas would like to acknowledge the fellowship FPI-UR-2014 granted by the University of La Rioja. F. Antonanzas-Torres would like to express his gratitude for the FPI-UR-2012 and ATUR grant No. 03061402 at the University of La Rioja. We are also greatly indebted to *Banco Santander* for the PROFAI-13/06 fellowship, to the *Agencia de Desarrollo Económico de La Rioja* for the ADER-2012-I-IDD-00126 (CONOBUILD) fellowship and to the *Instituto de Estudios Riojanos* (IER) for funding parts of this research.

References

1. Hashem, I.A.T., Yaqoob, I., Anuar, N.B., Mokhtar, S., Gani, A., Ullah Khan, S.: The rise of "big data" on cloud computing: review and open research issues. Inf. Syst. **47**, 98–115 (2015)
2. Chyzhyk, D., Savio, A., Graña, M.: Evolutionary ELM wrapper feature selection for alzheimer's disease CAD on anatomical brain MRI. Neurocomputing **128**, 73–80 (2014)
3. Peddie, J.: The new visualization engine - the heterogeneous processor unit. In: Dill, J., Earnshaw, R., Kasik, D., Vince, J., Wong, P.C. (eds.) Expanding The Frontiers Of Visual Analytics And Visualization, pp. 377–396. Springer International Publishing, London (2012)
4. Urraca, R., Antonanzas, J., Martinez-de Pison, F.J., Antonanzas-Torres, F.: Estimation of solar global irradiation in remote areas. J. Renew. Sustain. Energy (In Press)
5. van Heeswijk, M., Miche, Y., Oja, E., Lendasse, A.: GPU-accelerated and parallelized ELM ensembles for large-scale regression. Neurocomputing **74**(16), 2430–2437 (2011)
6. Team, R.C.: R: A language and environment for statistical computing. R Foundation for Statistical Computing, Vienna, Austria (2014)
7. Buckner, J., Wilson, J., Seligman, M., Athey, B., Watson, S., Meng, F.: The gputools package enables GPU computing in R. Bioinformatics **26**(1), 134–135 (2010)
8. Huang, G.B., Zhu, Q.Y., Siew, C.K.: Extreme learning machine: theory and applications. Neurocomputing **70**, 489–501 (2006)
9. Salcedo-Sanz, S., Casanova-Mateo, C., Pastor-Sanchez, A., Giron, M.S.: Daily global solar radiation prediction based on a hybrid coral reefs optimization - extreme learning machine approach. Sol. Energy **105**, 91–98 (2014)
10. Huang, G.B.: Extreme learning machine for regression and multiclass classification. IEEE Trans. Syst. Man Cybern.-Part B: Cybern. **42**(2), 513–529 (2012)
11. Gosso, A.: elmNN: Implementation of ELM (Extreme Learning Machine) algorithm for SLFN (Single Hidden Layer Feedforward Neural Networks). R package version 1.3 (2012)

12. Urraca-Valle, R., Sodupe-Ortega, E., Antoñanzas Torres, J., Antoñanzas-Torres, F., Martínez-de-Pisón, F.J.: An overall performance comparative of GA-PARSIMONY methodology with regression algorithms. In: de la Puerta, J.G., Ferreira, I.G., Bringas, P.G., Klett, F., Abraham, A., de Carvalho, A.C.P.L.F., Herrero, A., Baruque, B., Quintián, H., Corchado, E. (eds.) International Joint Conference SOCO'14-CISIS'14-ICEUTE'14. AISC, vol. 299, pp. 53–62. Springer, Heidelberg (2014)
13. Ye, J.: On measuring and correcting the effects of data mining and model selection. J. Am. Stat. Assoc. **93**(441), 120–131 (1998)
14. Seni, G., Elder, J.: Ensembe Methods In Data Mining. Improving Accuracy Through Combining Predictions. Morgan & Claypool, Chicago (2010)

Real Implantation of an Expert System for Elderly Home Care

Aitor Moreno-Fernandez-de-Leceta[1], Unai Arenal Gómez[1],
Jose Manuel Lopez-Guede[2,4(✉)], and Manuel Graña[3,4]

[1] Instituto Ibermática de Innovación,
Sistemas Inteligentes de Control y Gestión, San Sebastián, Spain
[2] Department of Systems Engineering and Automatic Control,
University College of Engineering of Vitoria,
Basque Country University (UPV/EHU), Vitoria, Spain
[3] ENGINE centre,Wroclaw University of Technology, Wroclaw, Poland
[4] Computational Intelligence Group of the Basque Country University (UPV/EHU),
Vitoria, Spain
jm.lopez@ehu.eus

Abstract. This paper presents an intelligent system for elderly people care at home that has been implemented and tested in real life environments. The expert system is based on the principle of no intrusion. It uses plug-and-play sensors and machine learning algorithms to learn the elderly's usual activity. If the system detects that something unusual happens (in a wide sense), it sends at real-time alarm to the family, care center or medical agents, without human intervention. The system is actually running in dozens of homes with an accuracy larger that 81 %.

1 Introduction

European population is aging rapidly, threatening to overwhelm the society's capacity for taking care of its elderly members. The projected estimated percentage of persons over 65 years old in the European Union will rise from 17.4 % in 2010 to 28.8 % in 2050 [1]. As a consequence, there will be less than two persons of working age (20–64) for every person aged over 65 years. Such projections drive the urgent development of ambient assisted living solutions to help the elderly live longer independently with minimal support from the working-age population. The increase in demand for home care and telecare is driven by the following circumstances:

- Increased demand for home security and social assistance, prompted by conclusive clinical and social studies on the benefits of telecare for citizens and professionals.
- Public policies in home care, related to reducing costs and improving the service quality.
- The motivation and cost of training of professionals and institutions responsible for the attention of elder citizens.

© Springer International Publishing Switzerland 2015
E. Onieva et al. (Eds.): HAIS 2015, LNAI 9121, pp. 668–678, 2015.
DOI: 10.1007/978-3-319-19644-2_55

Despite of this increasing demand, the success of these systems is hindered by high cost of tele-assistance devices, applications and services, difficulty for the elderly in using the tele-assistance equipment and services, resistance of large organizations responsible for establishing working practices to incorporate new routines and management models. The main objective of the work described in this paper is to create a collection of intelligent services that make up a monitorization system of the parameters characterizing the habits of elderly people who are still self-sufficient but require a little help.

Prior knowledge about the elderly's activity is a good starting point to detect behavioral patterns and help to assess his/her status. Moreover, it therefore provides valuable input for intention detection. Various experiments, particularly for ambient assisted living environments have demonstrated the possibilities and the complexities of intention detection [2]. User actions measurement and monitorization of user experience in real-time are enablers for a new range of innovative systems and a key enhancement to existing products.

The main objectives of the system, which in fact have been achieved (the system is already running in dozens of homes), are the following:

- Create a set of services that enables intelligent monitorization of a particular elderly so that the system adapts to him, creating automatically rules that determine the usual values for each individual and evolve with the elderly, so that they are always up to date. These rules allow launching fully customized alerts without human intervention.
- Create a telecare third-party system based on an expert system and an inference engine that can automatically detect dangerous situations decreasing false positives, firing events only at abnormal circumstances.

The remainder of the paper is organized as follows. Section 2 introduces the system architecture. In Sect. 3 details about the machine learning processes of the system are given, while Sect. 4 explains the implantation of the system and discuss the results. Finally, Sect. 5 presents our conclusions and future work.

2 System Architecture

The system is designed to fulfill two main requirements. On one hand, the extraction, transformation, and load of sensor information is carried out in a simply way: the sensor is plugged on the network, and its raw data automatically are integrated in the platform. On the other hand, the platform is able to measure the elderly's habits in order to track their behavior to find deviations from their daily tasks (e.g. wake up times, sleep habits, diary strolls, etc.), and provide a detailed summary to the caregivers and the family about their evolution. All services provided by the system are addressed to be a robust, easily-deployable solution and a cost-contained model. The benefits will directly affect the elderly, the family and the caregivers.

As can be seen in Fig. 1, the platform is organized in three main modules to tackle and process the input sensors data:

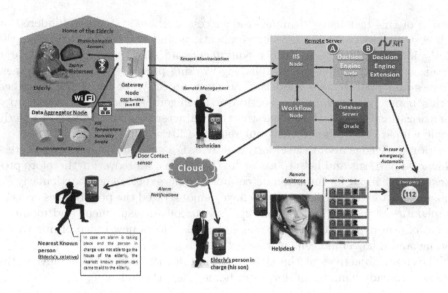

Fig. 1. Platform over real housing with care systems

- Data capture from a set of sensors of different types
- Remote processing of the data received
- Machine Learning and Inference Machine system

One important achievement is that the system has been successfully accepted in the UNIVERsal open platform and reference Specification for Ambient Assisted Living (UniversAAL) [3] reference architecture, which is expected to be the Ambient Assisted Living (AAL) reference architecture for future developments with a wide-spread acceptance. UniversAAL aims to produce an open platform that provides a standardized approach making it technically feasible and economically viable to develop AAL solutions.

The main component of this platform at the gateway level is the so-called Home Box Services (HSB), which consists of a structured software system, flexible and portable that can run on different hardware platforms, and is the processing kernel of the system on the remote data received.

The HSB includes a software architecture based on a layered structure with an operating system (Linux, Android or Windows), a layer of Java language, an OSGi service layer, and a set of software applications. The OSGi layer is a module system and service platform for the Java programming language that implements a complete and dynamic component model.

Regarding the technologies involved, UPnP [4] is a highlighted protocol which does not only cover internet protocols such as TCP/IP, HTTP, SOAP, UDP or XML, but also integrates Zigbee, USB, IEEE802.11, BT, BLE Wi-Fi, and security considerations using security techniques like X.509 certificates. Moreover, this protocol is open and it can be extended (e.g. to define a specific type of message adding extra attributes). This project contains the three types of sensors: environmental, physiological, embedded service and audiovisual sensors, connected to one or more hubs.

So, with the described architecture, the alarm services are able to capture the data from a set of sensors deployed in the house, process the data captured locally and send the information to a remote server to process it.

3   Machine Learning and Inference Machine

The main objective is to create a health care system that is able to detect dangerous situations in real-time, such as dropping or loss of consciousness, which are two of the most common problems in elderly care. The idea is to monitorize the elderly's behavior over long periods of time and to detect changes that indicate a decrease in attention, agility and performance, and could denote an increase of certain disorders without evidence, so they could be taken as signs in order to a deeper study of the elderly.

Several systems were introduced in recent years to address some of the issues related to elderly care, principally, in fall detection systems. However, most of the systems developed in this context are either too expensive for mass use or of low quality. Most commercial solutions are capable only of fall detection, meaning that they recognize only a small set of hazardous situations [5].

Human behavior and habits are characterized by three attributes of daily activities, namely time, duration and frequency [6]. The drifts in behavior can be identified looking at the changes in those attributes. For example, sleeping and napping behaviors of persons during a day. Any subtle change in sleeping or napping durations can be a sign of a serious disease, especially for the elderly, or an indicator in the progress of a mental disease (like Alzheimer's disease) in the long term [7]. One of the easier way to detect changes and behavior anomalies is to compare the real situation or state of the elderly with one prediction of his state. However, to make accurate predictions, we have not only to consider the elderly's data and the nearest environmental sensors, but also need to add external information such as the outdoor weather. For example, if it is raining, even though it is summer, the elderly probably does not go outdoor unless he likes to walk in the rain. These subjective observations should be processed and the system must be able to learn these characteristics. Defining personalized and adaptive elderly's behavior models is a key challenge when considering the issue of predicting elderly's intentions.

Machine learning deals with the development of algorithms that enable computer programs to learn and automatically improve with experience [8]. The first problem concerning the experience is that, in a first moment, one does not have custom data about elerly's behavior. Therefore, given that the system is configured as a plug-and-play platform, that, once placed sensors (any type of sensor), it begins to send information directly to the inference engine to analyze from the outset, if the user behavior is normal. However, without experience it is impossible to generate automatic control systems. So, there is provided an expert system composed of experts' rules written by telecare agents who collaborate intensively with us in the installation and configuration of the platform in actual homes and care services. On the other hand, the incorporation of expert knowledge overcomes the problem of classifier over-fitting observed with classifiers induced with machine learning [9].

So, the system has a hybrid inference engine that joins heuristic rules (first conditions to check without user data) with a supervised system in order to discover new rules, adapting the heuristic rules to the personal behavior changing and with an unsupervised system, with two objectives:

- Detect unknown alerts (not registered in heuristics or supervised system)
- Join similar elderly's behaviors in homogeneous groups (segment usual activity, customizing automatically the user usual activity), in order to send new knowledge to the medical and care agents about the general behaviors of theirs patients.

In general, after the home installation, the inference machine run the following tasks:

- Identification of the observable behavior of the elderly
- Matching the heuristic rules to detect abnormal facts
- Start the learning process during the learning period
- Put the learned behavior model into practice, modifying the heuristic rules by personal rules

The intention aware elderly care application can predict the activities of the user based on historic usual activity, customizing automatically the user usual activity information. An advantage of the system is the detection of the elderly through very cheap hardware sensors, but with the support of a context inference engine, which minimizes false positives. The key is the automatic adaptation to the users behaviors automatically. In fact, the inference engine is an activity tracker system, and it is intended to track daily activities of the elderly via automatic/manual input. The activity tracker system provides three services for the intention aware elderly activities API:

- Current activity (performed by the elderly at the present time)
- Last 14 hour activities (split into 5 min slots time)
- Prediction next 5 min activity: service to infer the next activity that will perform the elderly based on the historic data of the elderly's intention. This service will provide the likelihood of happening the tracked activities, and takes the activity whose probability is higher than the remaining.

3.1   Rule Based Expert Subsystem

The knowledge of an expert can be easily integrated into an automatic system. Improvements in information gathering, processing and integration can help medical agents to work more effectively to prevent injury and loss of life, as well as minimize property damage. The system exploits advantages of join different sensors raw data to create a formal representation of context information, which in our domain includes environment entities, user profiling and health aspects.

This information constitutes the knowledge base of the system. Three types of reasoning are applied upon this knowledge: a first rule-based reasoning level for inferring additional information about the context, a case based reasoning level for recognizing the current activity and a final reasoning level that offers personalized assistance in the form of rules expressed in a high-level rule language. The rules about the assistance conclude to actions related with the recognized activity, aspects of the person's health or emergency situations. Compared to the information services in traditional office environments, context-awareness is an important concept for the usability of pervasive systems because it reduces the need for explicit inputting and it takes advantage of changes in information relating to users, devices and environments.

To this end, bearing in mind that in the first moment the system does not have enough information to model custom behaviors of patients at home, it is necessary to turn to experts in the field of telecare who have help us to define a set of general rules of behaviors that indicate risk alerts or states, with the intention that the system is fully operational since the beginning. These rules have been inserted into the inference system using the manual mode (see Fig. 2). This allows modify easily them based on new medical knowledge or changes in patterns without any programming. Later the rules are directly applied by the Decision Engine (see Fig. 3) against each transaction or set of raw data that are received by the system in real-time.

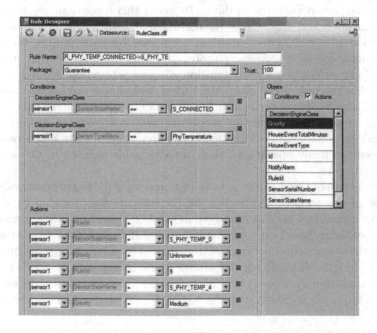

Fig. 2. Rule designer

Decision Engine Monitor

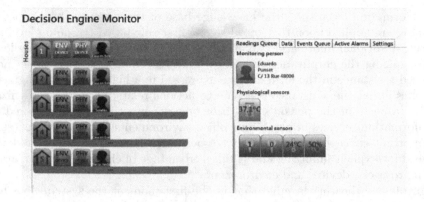

Fig. 3. Decision engine monitor

3.2   Rule Discover Subsystem

It is important that general rules generated by an expert will be adapted automatically to each elderly by the platform with implicit knowledge, so the system will personalize the information to each patient, their current parameters, and their last actions allowing to eliminate the false positives.

Usually, interest-driven analysis (driven by supervised analysis) tends to overlook unexpected patterns in data. To avoid this inconvenience the system contains unsupervised algorithms (clustering and association models). Anomaly detection is a well known problem addressed by data mining techniques. Anomaly detection is an extremely useful tool that running together with clustering techniques enables the recognition of data sets whose behavior is very different from the rest of the data [10]. Often these items are known as outliers [11]. The anomaly detection is also known as detection of deviations, because anomalous objects have values of attributes with a significant deviation from the typical expected values. Although these abnormalities are often treated as noise or error in many operations, they are a valuable element in the search for atypical behaviors.

The objective of this module is to obtain new knowledge automatically (very important in this scenario), collecting all the information provided by different sensors in a centralized service. The system must be able to update automatically its own knowledge based on each patient, using data collected by the sensors, analyzing them and subsequently identifying the user's behavior patterns. Based on these techniques of intelligent information processing, we give special emphasis to the detection and prediction of anomalies (trend analysis, deviations of the data, etc.), such as lifestyle changes, poorly executed exercises, etc.

3.3   Multivariate Analysis over Time

Statistical models, when are referred to clinic records, loose knowledge if they do not take into account their evolution along time. The time factor has been barely studied in large repetitive series of data in the medical domain. The results presented in the literature have not tackled the issue of analyzing medical procedures through the time line, something of great importance under this specific domain. In this work algorithms containing inference rules taking into account the influence of time have been developed. The analysis of rules within the time series of medical data is still an open field, although typical methods used in data mining as FP-Growth and A-priory, allow to obtain rules (i.e., "If the event X occurs, then the event Y will occur between times T_1 and T_2). This will allow to introduce a new approach to find out association rules among the quantitative values in relational databases. Some of the most popular approaches for obtaining rules are the use of linear probability models employing the auto-regressive model (AR), the moving average (MA) and the autoregresive integrated moving average (ARIMA) methods, or a combination of them [12].

In order to introduce the time component in a multivariate system, the association rules acquisition and relationships between antecedent and consequent along the time, a classification method based on rule extraction from sliding windows in function of time is used by the system. This method applied to previous state and next state is based on the data expansion along time taking into consideration the previous states and their multiple variables in such situations.

Compared to the current technology for evaluating context-aware systems, we focus in particular on the quantitative evaluation of the properties of our rule-based system. The challenge of this approach is to evaluate, on the basis of different validation methods, the accuracy and priority of the rules to send to the context decision module the most relevant in real-time to be executed. So, evaluations of rules in terms of precision and sensitivity are carried out by the real-time decision system. To develop this approach, the system must be able to resolve rule conflicts in two senses: a particular/general conflict situations and the answer time needed to suggest a critical decision.

4   Implantation and Results

At the beginning of 2015, 60 homes are equipped with the described system, checking online the elderly's everyday life, over three different patient segments: dependent elderly people, elderly whose habits are worsening due to the aging and elderly people who are suffering the first symptoms of dementia. As said before, the expert rules are running from the first moment, besides the system starts to obtain the elderly's behavior from raw data collected during the first month and later. The tasks performed by the systems are the following:

- The raw data of environmental sensors are processed by the expert system to determine which is the elderly's context at any time, transforming the data into a structured table with the information about person, date, hour, and the state of the elderly in that moment (deduced from the expert rules with a period of 5 min): Sleeping (S), Cooking (C), Eating (E), Doing Housework (D), Outdoor (O), Outdoor sport (U), Using tablet (T), Using mobile (M) or Spare time (X).

- The system checks continuously the physiological status of the users (i.e., temperature, heart pulse, blood pressure, etc.). Data will be managed in more compact fashion and only the relevant information to analyze the conditions of the alerts (like "The elderly has a fever unusual at 08:02 more than 15 min") is taken into account. Initially the thresholds are defined manually by the doctors, for example a temperature of 36,5C, leaving the statistical detection of thresholds for later, where the average temperature threshold is modified by historical data, statistical processes and unsupervised algorithms.
- The system checks continuously the environmental sensors such as smoke, temperature and humidity sensors, throwing alerts when activated.
- Finally, the system takes external data to integrate into elderly's data, at every moment, with these values: Haze (C), fog (N), low fog (N), fog (I), precipitation (P), drizzle (L), rain (U), torn rain (V), tornado sight (R), rain shower (H), rain (E), snow (E), shower hail (T), freezing rain (T).

In order to design a model to predict the current state of the elderly (i.e., its behavior), several variables as the hour, the outdoor weather conditions and the day of the week were taken into account initially, based on intuitive criterion. In this way, the inference system generates several rules in order to predict the next action taking into account these variables; however, using only that information the accuracy reached by the models was quite poor (only 67,95 %), as can be seen in the confusion matrix of Fig. 4.

To overcome that problem a correlation analysis was performed, whose results are in Fig. 5. There can be seen that the variable that has the highest correlation is the last action, the second is the hour of the day and the third is the outdoor weather conditions. In this way the accuracy of the system increases significantly (see Fig. 6), reaching the 81,80 %. Thus, if the predicted state does not match with the actual state, and this situation has a high significance rate, the system send an alert to remote care services to immediately launch emergency protocols. The system is a new development and a reformulation of the current model of care taking into account the characteristics and preferences of each person, obtaining a personal behavior model for each elderly (see Fig. 7).

accuracy: 68.12% +/- 0.16%									class
	true S	true P	true E	true T	true O	true C	true D	true U	true X precision
pred. S	14450	1065	13	0	68	50	1	0	1 92.34%
pred. P	940	3800	695	405	326	1016	52	29	10 52.25%
pred. E	10	320	592	105	41	358	185	0	0 36.75%
pred. T	0	123	177	1566	293	91	201	39	0 62.89%
pred. O	102	296	70	298	1203	242	9	342	28 46.45%
pred. C	44	703	888	40	224	1854	484	85	0 42.90%
pred. D	0	31	175	38	0	138	183	0	0 32.39%
pred. U	0	13	0	73	215	2	0	218	14 40.75%
pred. X	0	0	0	0	1	0	0	2	3 50.00%
class recall	92.95%	59.83%	22.68%	62.02%	50.74%	49.43%	16.41%	30.49%	5.36%

Fig. 4. Confusion matrix (hour, outdoor weather conditions, day of the week)

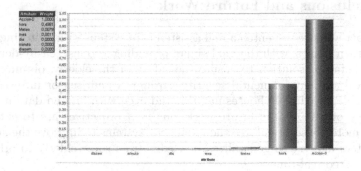

Fig. 5. Correlation analysis

	true S	true P	true E	true T	true O	true C	true D	true U	true X	class precision
pred. S	7404	270	9	2	74	23	0	0	3	95.11%
pred. P	313	2318	136	51	66	207	23	2	0	74.39%
pred. E	16	175	851	84	6	68	124	0	0	64.27%
pred. T	0	73	17	994	126	27	6	38	1	77.54%
pred. O	0	87	44	6	843	119	1	72	14	71.08%
pred. C	36	197	244	42	3	1321	56	0	0	69.56%
pred. D	2	25	0	83	8	75	345	0	0	64.13%
pred. U	0	28	2	0	59	33	2	242	5	65.23%
pred. X	0	0	0	0	1	0	0	0	2	33.33%
class recall	95.28%	73.05%	65.31%	78.76%	71.08%	70.53%	61.94%	67.79%	8.00%	

accuracy: 81.80%

Fig. 6. Confusion matrix (adding the previous state)

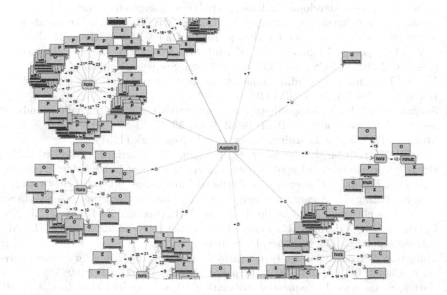

Fig. 7. Personal behavior model obtained by the system (one per elderly)

5   Conclusions and Future Work

In this paper we have presented a real assisted care system for monitoring elderly people at their homes, with the final aim of providing a robust, easily-deployable and cost-contained solution to ensure the safety of the elderly, obtaining both physiological and environmental security through a multisensor infrastructure. It has been deployed in 60 houses in 2015, and even with limited data it reaches an accuracy of 81,80 %. As future work, our next objectives are to extent the system to more houses, reinforce the intelligent systems to improve the accuracy of the system and try to generalize knowledge from some elderly to others, all in an unassisted real-time way.

Acknowledgements. The research was supported by Grant UFI11-07 of the Research Vicerectorship, Basque Country University (UPV/EHU). The Computational Intelligence Group is funded by the Basque Government with grant IT874-13. ENGINE project is funded by the European Commission grant 316097.

References

1. Eurostat, Demography report 2010, European Union, Technical report (2011)
2. Giroux, S., Bauchet, J., Pigot, H., Lussier-Desrochers, D., Lachappelle, Y.: Pervasive behavior tracking for cognitive assistance. In: The 3rd International Conference on Pervasive Technologies Related to Assistive Environments, Petra 2008, Greece, 15–19 July 2008 (2008)
3. UniversAAL. http://universaal.org/
4. UPnP. Upnp open development tools. http://pupnp.sourceforge.net/
5. Kaluža, B., Mirchevska, V., Dovgan, E., Luštrek, M., Gams, M.: An agent-based approach to care in independent living. In: de Ruyter, B., Wichert, R., Keyson, D.V., Markopoulos, P., Streitz, N., Divitini, M., Georgantas, N., Mana Gomez, A. (eds.) AmI 2010. LNCS, vol. 6439, pp. 177–186. Springer, Heidelberg (2010)
6. Noyes, J.: Human reliability analysis: context and control by Hollnagel, E. Ergonomics **38**(12), 2614–2615 (1995)
7. Suryadevara, N.K., Mukhopadhyay, S.C.: Determining wellness through an ambient assisted living environment. IEEE Intell. Syst. **29**(3), 30–37 (2014)
8. Mitchell, T.: Machine Learning. McGraw Hill, New York (1997)
9. Luštrek, M., Kaluža, B., Cvetković, B., Dovgan, E., Gjoreski, H., Mirchevska, V., Gams, M.: Confidence: ubiquitous care system to support independent living. In: DEMO at European Conference on Artificial Intelligence, pp. 1013–1014 (2012)
10. Niu, K., Huang, C., Zhang, S., Chen, J.: ODDC: outlier detection using distance distribution clustering. In: Washio, T., Zhou, Z.-H., Huang, J.Z., Hu, X., Li, J., Xie, C., He, J., Zou, D., Li, K.-C., Freire, M.M. (eds.) PAKDD 2007. LNCS (LNAI), vol. 4819, pp. 332–343. Springer, Heidelberg (2007)
11. Milligan, G.: A validation study of a variable weighting algorithm for cluster analysis. J. Classif. **6**(1), 53–71 (1989). http://dx.doi.org/10.1007/BF01908588
12. Harms, S., Deogun, J.: Sequential association rule mining with time lags. J. Intell. Inf. Syst. **22**(1), 7–22 (2004)

A Novel Hybrid Algorithm for Solving the Clustered Vehicle Routing Problem

Andrei Horvat Marc[1], Levente Fuksz[2], Petrică C. Pop[1(✉)],
and Daniela Dănciulescu[3]

[1] Department of Mathematics and Computer Science,
Technical University of Cluj-Napoca, North University Center of Baia Mare,
Cluj-Napoca, Romania
petrica.pop@cunbm.utcluj.ro
[2] Indeco Soft, Baia Mare, Romania
[3] Faculty of Exact Sciences, Department of Informatics, University of Craiova,
Craiova, Romania

Abstract. This paper presents a new hybrid optimization approach based on genetic algorithm and simulated annealing for solving the clustered vehicle routing problem (CluVRP). The problem investigated in this paper is a NP-hard combinatorial optimization problem that generalizes the classical vehicle routing problem (VRP) and it is closely related to the generalized vehicle routing problem (GVRP). Preliminary computational results on two sets of benchmark instances are reported and discussed.

1 Introduction

The clustered vehicle routing problem (CluVRP) is a generalization of the classical vehicle routing problem and belongs to the class of generalized combinatorial optimization problems. This class of problems generalizes in a natural way the classical combinatorial optimization problems and it is characterized by the fact that the nodes are partitioned into clusters and the original problem's feasibility constraints are expressed in terms of the clusters instead of individual nodes. For more information on the class of generalized combinatorial optimization problems and different problems belonging to this class we refer to [8].

Given a depot and a set of customers which are grouped into a number of predefined clusters, the CluVRP consists on finding optimally delivery or collection routes from the depot to the customers subject to capacity constraints and with the additional constraint that all the customers belonging to a cluster must be visited consecutively. CluVRP was introduced by Sevaux and Sörensen [13] and is closely related to the following two problems:

- the generalized vehicle routing problem (GVRP) which consists on designing optimally delivery or collection routes from the depot to the customers subject to capacity constraints but with the additional constraint that from each cluster must be visited exactly one node. GVRP was first introduced by Ghiani and Improta [6] and was lately intensively studied. For more information on this problem we refer to [9–11].

© Springer International Publishing Switzerland 2015
E. Onieva et al. (Eds.): HAIS 2015, LNAI 9121, pp. 679–689, 2015.
DOI: 10.1007/978-3-319-19644-2_56

– the problem of finding optimally delivery or collection routes from a given depot to the customers subject to capacity constraints but with the additional constraint that from each cluster must be visited at least one node consecutively. This problem was considered by Baldacci and Laporte [1].

The existing literature concerning CluVRP is rather scarce: as we have already mentioned the problem was introduced by Sevaux and Sörensen [13] motivated by a practical application, namely parcel delivery. In this application, we have a depot and many of known customers which are grouped in zones (clusters) and the aim is to find an optimal collection of routes with the constraints: once a customer from a cluster is visited then all the other customers belonging to the same cluster have to be visited consecutively before visiting other customers from different clusters or returning to the depot. It is assumed that one cluster is always visited by a single truck and one truck may visit more than one cluster if the capacity constraints are fulfilled. Pop et al. [10] described two integer programming based models for CluVRP adapted from the corresponding formulations in the case of the GVRP. Battarra et al. [2] described two exact algorithms for CluVRP, namely a Branch&Cut algorithm and a Branch&Cut&Price algorithm. A hybrid approach based on genetic algorithms for solving the CluVRP was presented by Pop and Chira [12].

   The aim of this paper is to describe a novel hybrid approach for solving the CluVRP. Our hybrid algorithm is obtained by combining a genetic algorithm applied to the clustered graph (see details in Sect. 3) with a Simulated Annealing algorithm used to calculate the shortest Hamiltonian path between the nodes belonging to a given cluster. The results of preliminary computational experiments on two benchmark instances from the literature are presented and analyzed.

   The rest of the paper is structured as follows: the definition of the CluVRP is presented in Sect. 2, the hybrid algorithm is described in Sect. 3, computational experiments and results are presented and discussed in Sect. 4 and finally, the conclusions are depicted in Sect. 5.

2   Definition of the Clustered Vehicle Routing Problem

In this section we give a formal definition of the Clustered Vehicle Routing Problem as a graph theoretic model.

   Let $G = (V, E)$ be an undirected graph with $V = \{0, 1, 2, ..., n\}$ as the set of vertices and the set of edges

$$E = \{e = (i, j) \mid i, j \in V, i \neq j\}.$$

Vertices $i \in \{1, ..., n\}$ correspond to the customers and the vertex 0 corresponds to the depot. The entire set of vertices $\{0, 1, ..., n\}$ is partitioned into $k + 1$ mutually exclusive nonempty subsets, called clusters, $V_0, V_1, ..., V_k$, i.e. the following conditions hold:

1. $V = V_0 \cup V_1 \cup ... \cup V_k$
2. $V_l \cap V_p = \emptyset$ for all $l, p \in \{0, 1, ..., k\}$ and $l \neq p$.

The cluster V_0 has only one vertex 0, which represents the depot, and remaining n vertices are belonging to the remaining k clusters.

We have defined two kinds of edges: edges between vertices belonging to the same cluster, called intra-cluster edges and edges between vertices belonging to different clusters, called inter-cluster edges. The graph G is assumed to be strongly connected and in general it is even assumed to be complete.

A nonnegative cost c_{ij} is associated with each edge $e = (i,j) \in E$ and represents the travel cost spent to go from vertex i to vertex j. The cost of a route is equal to the sum of the costs of all the edges belonging to the route. Each customer i ($i \in \{1, ..., n\}$) has a known nonnegative demand d_i to be delivered and the depot has a fictitious demand $d_0 = 0$. There exist m identical vehicles, each with a capacity Q and to ensure feasibility we assume that $d_i \leq Q$ for each $i \in \{1, ..., n\}$. It is assumed that each of the vehicles may perform at most one route, one cluster is always visited by a single vehicle and one vehicle may visit more than one cluster if the capacity constraints are fulfilled.

The *clustered vehicle routing problem* (CluVRP) consists in finding a collection of routes visiting all the clusters and all the vertices with minimum cost, such that the following constraints hold: each route starts and ends at the depot vertex, all the vertices of each cluster must be visited consecutively and the sum of the demands of the visited vertices by a route does not exceed the capacity of the vehicle, Q.

An illustrative scheme of the CluVRP and a feasible tour is shown in the next figure (Fig. 1).

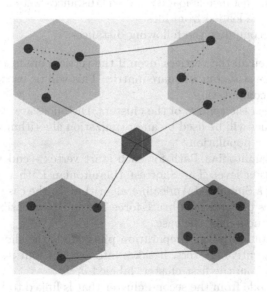

Fig. 1. A feasible solution of the CluVRP

The CluVRP is NP-hard because it includes the classical Vehicle Routing Problem as a special case when all the clusters are singletons.

3   The Hybrid Algorithm for Solving the CluVRP

In this section we present our hybrid algorithm for solving the CluVRP obtained by combining a genetic algorithm applied to the global graph with a Simulated Annealing algorithm used for computing all the Shortest Hamiltonian Paths for each start vertex - end vertex combination at each cluster level.

We denote by G' the graph obtained from G after replacing all the nodes of a cluster V_i with a supernode representing V_i, $\forall i \in \{1, ..., k\}$, the cluster V_0 (depot) consists already of one vertex. We will call the graph G' the *global graph*. For convenience, we identify V_i with the supernode representing it. Edges of the graph G' are defined between each pair of the graph vertices $V_0, V_1, \ldots, V_k$ and the corresponding costs are the euclidean distances between the mass centers of the clusters.

By applying the genetic algorithm to the global graph we reduce considerably the solution space of the problem. The GA provides a collection routes visiting the clusters in a given order. We will call such a route a clustered route.

3.1   Preparation Phase

In this phase a number of distances between elements are computed and stored in files so subsequent algorithm runs do not need to compute these values again. The pre-computed distances are used when a solution is evaluated in terms of quality. This preparation phase is triggered when a new instance is loaded for the first time. When an instance is loaded and the distances were already computed before, the values are loaded from files.

The algorithm computes the following distances:

- Distances between all the vertices, even if the vertices are in separate clusters. The distances are stored in a square matrix. This will be used in almost every future distance computation.
- Distances between the centers of the clusters. Distances are stored in a square matrix. The values will be used by an optimization algorithm when generating the initial genetic population.
- The Shortest Hamiltonian Path for each start vertex - end vertex combination at each cluster level. The Shortest Hamiltonian Path within a cluster is computed using a Simulated Annealing algorithm. In the case of the instances with few vertices per cluster a brute-force method was feasible but on larger instances this is no longer the case.
- The last computation in the preparation phase finds the shortest way to traverse three consecutive clusters. It takes into account four nodes:
  - the exit node from the first cluster, labeled v_1^{out};
  - the entering node from the second cluster that is linked to v_1^{out}, labeled v_2^{in};
  - the exit node from the second cluster, labeled v_2^{out};
  - the entering node from the third cluster that is linked to v_2^{out}, labeled v_3^{in};

  In our approach, we are using the Shortest Hamiltonian Path computed before to link nodes v_2^{in} and v_2^{out}.

3.2   The Genetic Algorithm

Representation. It is known that a good representation scheme is important for the performance of the GA and it should define noteworthy crossover, mutation and other specific genetic operators to the problem in order to minimize the computational effort within these procedures.

In order to meet this requirement we use an efficient representation in which the chromosome for each candidate solution is represented as an array of clusters for each route ordered in conformity with the order in which the clusters are visited. The deposit is also marked in the chromosome by a special virtual cluster that only contains the deposit. For example, if a solution is composed by two routes that visit clusters V_1, V_2, V_3 and V_4, V_5, V_6, the chromosome for this solution is represented by an array like $V_1, V_2, V_3, V_0, V_4, V_5, V_6$. As you can see the actual nodes that form a cluster are not represented inside the chromosome. Each chromosome representing the order in which clusters are visited can be expanded to the corresponding vertices that are visited by using the pre-computed optimal route including vertices between three consecutive clusters obtained in the preparation phase.

The fitness function for each proposed solution returns the total length of the routes. This distance also takes into account the order in which the nodes inside a cluster are visited. Our goal is to minimize this total distance.

Initial Population. The construction of the initial population is of great importance to the performance of GA, since it contains most of the material the final best solution is made of.

In our case, the initial population was generated using a genetic algorithm that solves the generalized number partitioning problem at cluster demand level [5]. The input for this algorithm is the list of demands per cluster, the output is the demands split up in a number of partitions that match the number of routes needed by the specific instance. Basically, this algorithm splits up the demands evenly for the number of routes.

After solving the number partitioning part for the demands, solutions are constructed by replacing the demand values with the clusters that request that demand. If there are multiple clusters with the same demand, multiple variations are getting constructed.

Also, to increase the number of the solutions in the initial population a limited balancing operation is executed. This operation tries to switch clusters between the routes determined by the number partitioning algorithm while keeping the total demand per route inside the vehicle capacity. After obtaining the initial population, which consists of randomly arranged clusters that just satisfy the capacity of the vehicle an optimization takes place. This optimization uses the Clarke-Wright algorithm to rearrange the clusters per route in each initial solution so that the arrangement is optimal relative to the distances between the centers of the clusters.

Selection. For solving the CluVRP we used a rank based selection. The first step for the selection is to order the population in terms of the fitness value of the individuals (candidate solutions). The newly obtained list will have the worst candidate solution in the first position and the best candidate solution in the last position. After ordering the list, a rank is computed based on the position of the candidate solution and a selection pressure. Random numbers are generated and solutions are selected from the initial population based on their rank relative to the obtained random number. This operation is continued until a new population is obtained. We decided that only distinct candidate solutions are to be used as input to the selection function.

Crossover. Our algorithm uses a custom version of the one point crossover. The crossover function takes two parent candidate solutions as input and outputs four solutions that are derived from the parents. The crossover is applied to the population resulted from the selection algorithm by taking two parents in an iterative manner. The first iteration goes from $i = 1$ to N, where N is the total number of candidate solutions in the selected population while the second goes from $j = i + 1$ to N.

As we mentioned before, the crossover for the i-th and j-th elements is using a custom one point crossover. This operation generates a random number between 1 and N, where N is the length of the chromosome and splits the chromosome of each parent into two parts. There are four ways in which the resulting parts can be recombined. For example, if the first parent is split up into two part labeled A and B, and the second into X and Y, four descendants can result using the following combinations AY, XB, YA and BX.

Mutation. After obtaining the children solutions from the crossover algorithm a mutation operator is applied. The mutation operation has a probability to be applied, probability that is set before solving the problem.

In our case the mutation does two things: first of all it picks two random genes from the chromosome and swaps them, without taking any rule into consideration and the second operation takes two random genes from the chromosome but from different routes and swaps them.

Genetic and Simulated Annealing Parameters. The parameters involved in our algorithm are very important for the success of our hybrid approach. Based on preliminary computational experiments, we set the following parameters:

- the genetic parameters: the population size μ has been set to 70, the mutation probability was set at 20 % and the maximum number of generations (epochs) in our algorithm was set to 200.
- the SA parameters: the initial temperature was set to 1000 and the cooling rate $r = 0.99$ was used to reduce the temperature in each step.

4   Computational Results

In this section we present preliminary computational results in order to assess the effectiveness of our proposed hybrid algorithm for solving the CluVRP.

We conducted our computational experiments for solving the CluVRP on two sets of instances:

- The first set of instances were generated through an adaptation of the existing instances in the Capacitated Vehicle Routing Problem (CVRP)-library available at http://branchandcut.org/VRP/data/. The naming of the generated instances follows the general convention of the CVRP instances available online, and follows the general format $X - nY - kZ - C\Omega - V\Phi$, where X corresponds to the type of the instance, Y refers to the number of vertices, Z corresponds to the number of vehicles in the original CVRP instance, Ω is the number of clusters and Φ is the number of vehicles in the instance. These instances were used by Bektas et al. [3] and Pop et al. [11] in their computational experiments in the case of the GVRP.
- The second set of instances have been adapted from the 11 large-size CVRP instances described by Golden et al. [7] and available at http://www.rhsmith. umd.edu/faculty/bgolden/vrp_data.htm.

Originally the set of nodes in these problems were not divided into clusters. Fischetti et al. [4] proposed in the case of the generalized traveling salesman problem a procedure to partition the nodes of the graph into clusters, called CLUSTERING. This procedure sets the number of clusters $s = \lceil \frac{n}{\theta} \rceil$, identifies the s farthest nodes from each other and assigns each remaining node to its nearest center.

The proposed hybrid algorithm for solving the CluVRP has been implemented and in our experiments we performed 30 independent runs for each instance as in [12].

The testing machine was an Intel(R) Core(TM)i7-3612QM CPU @ 2.10 GHz. The algorithm was developed in Microsoft.NET. Framework using C#.

In the next table we present the computational results achieved in the case of the small and medium instances described by Bektas et al. [3] (Table 1).

Table 1. Experimental results in the case of the small and medium size instances described by Bektas et al. [3]

Instance	HGA-1.5			HGA-1.7			HGA-1.9		
	Gen	Best solution	Average solution	Gen	Best solution	Average solution	Gen	Best solution	Average solution
A-n32-k5-C16-V2	7	523.518	523.518	8	523.518	523.518	14	523.518	523.518
A-n33-k5-C11-V2	6	472.905	472.905	9	472.905	472.905	6	472.905	472.905
A-n33-k6-C11-V2	13	563.534	563.534	31	563.534	563.534	36	563.534	563.534
A-n34-k5-C12-V2	19	548.085	548.085	4	548.085	548.085	2	548.085	548.085
A-n36-k5-C12-V2	14	590.464	590.464	17	590.464	590.464	19	590.464	590.464
A-n37-k5-C13-V2	10	572.745	573.415	76	574.085	574.085	10	574.085	574.085
A-n37-k6-C13-V2	56	618.744	621.132	142	625.908	628.712	43	625.161	628.270
A-n38-k5-C13-V2	54	510.310	510.310	8	510.310	510.310	31	510.310	510.310
A-n39-k5-C13-V2	16	620.301	620.301	23	620.301	620.301	15	620.301	620.301
A-n39-k6-C13-V2	37	614.732	617.759	46	614.732	614.732	18	614.732	620.785
A-n44-k6-C15-V2	24	719.958	743.757	76	717.763	731.176	7	737.226	742.607
A-n45-k6-C15-V3	14	715.515	718.575	68	715.515	715.515	98	715.515	715.515
A-n45-k7-C15-V3	36	672.410	681.846	42	672.410	681.846	26	672.410	672.410
A-n48-k7-C16-V3	71	688.038	704.231	75	688.038	696.164	34	688.038	701.680

The first column in the table gives the name of the instances, the next columns contain the generation in which was reached the best solution and the values of the best solutions respectively the average solutions achieved by our proposed hybrid genetic based algorithm (HGA) using a rank-based selection with selective pressure set as 1.5, 1.7 and 1.9.

In the next table we present the computational results achieved in the case of the large size instances described by Golden et al. [7] (Table 2).

The first column in the table gives the name of the instances, the second column provides the number of the clusters and the third column contains the total number of nodes. The next two columns contain the values of the best solutions respectively the average solutions obtained using the hybrid genetic algorithm [12] and the last two columns contain the values of the best solutions respectively the average solutions obtained using our novel hybrid algorithm.

Analyzing the computational results, we observe that the proposed hybrid algorithm provides better best and average solutions in comparison to the previous hybrid based genetic algorithm for solving the CluVRP. Another observation is that the best solutions were reached in the early phases of the generations, therefore in the future we plan to maintain the diversity in order to avoid premature convergence by choosing other mutation operators and by changing the selection pressure.

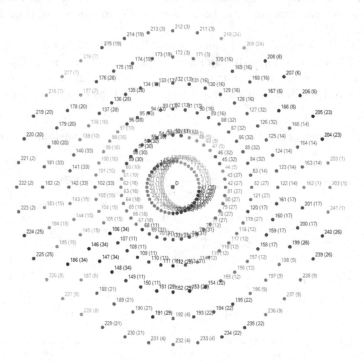

Fig. 2. A partition of the vertices into clusters. The vertices belonging to a specific cluster have the same color (Color figure online).

Table 2. Experimental results in the case of the large size instances described by Golden et al. [7]

Instance name	Number of clusters	Number of nodes	Previous results [12]		New results	
			Best solution	Average solution	Best solution	Average solution
Golden1_C17_N241	17	241	5403.37	5425.32	4938.672	4963.389
Golden1_C18_N241	18	241	5373.88	5409.30	4961.67	4992.616
Golden1_C19_N241	19	241	5426.37	5461.08	4972.778	4987.803
Golden1_C21_N241	21	241	5355.10	5396.02	5081.547	5123.834
Golden1_C22_N241	22	241	5470.34	5506.15	4998.291	5060.427
Golden1_C25_N241	25	241	5525.57	5585.07	5058.552	5193.067
Golden1_C27_N241	27	241	5588.96	5631.01	5140.656	5225.360
Golden1_C31_N241	31	241	5903.34	5971.26	5325.361	5408.976
Golden1_C35_N241	35	241	6113.88	6199.17	5328.243	5565.115
Golden1_C41_N241	41	241	6042.80	6163.40	5794.605	5928.835
Golden1_C49_N241	49	241	5946.17	6066.17	5904.874	6081.703

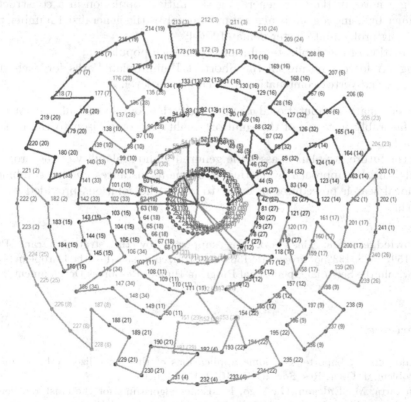

Fig. 3. The best solution of the CluVRP corresponding to the instance *Golden1_C35_N*241 (Color figure online)

Next we present an example derived from a large-size CVRP instance, namely test problem *Golden*1_*C*35_*N*241, introduced by Golden et al. [7], which has 241 vertices partitioned into 35 clusters (Figs. 2 and 3).

5   Conclusions

In this paper, we considered the clustered vehicle routing problem, where given a depot and a set of customers which are grouped into a number of predefined clusters, we are interested in finding optimally delivery or collection routes from the depot to the customers subject to capacity constraints and with the additional constraint that all the customers belonging to a cluster must be visited consecutively before visiting customers from other clusters.

We developed an efficient hybrid approach to the problem that combines the use of genetic algorithms (GA) and Simulated Annealing (SA). Some important features of our hybrid algorithm are:

- using a novel method for generating the initial population in a constructive manner by using a genetic algorithm that solves the generalized number partitioning problem at cluster demand level;
- elimination of the duplicate solutions from each population;
- using SA for computing all the Shortest Hamiltonian Paths for each start vertex - end vertex combination at each cluster level.

The preliminary computational results show that our hybrid algorithm compares favorably in terms of the solution quality in comparison to the existing approaches.

In the future, we plan to asses the generality and scalability of the proposed hybrid heuristic approach by testing it on more instances and to combine it with local search procedures in order to refine the solutions provided by our algorithm.

Acknowledgements. This work was supported by the strategic grant POS-DRU/159/1.5/S/133255, Project ID 133255 (2014), co-financed by the European Social Fund within the Sectorial Operational Program Human Resources Development 2007-2013.

References

1. Baldacci, R., Laporte, G.: Some applications of the generalized vehicle routing problem. J. Oper. Res. Soc. **61**(7), 1072–1077 (2010)
2. Battarra, M., Erdogan, G., Vigo, D.: Exact algorithms for the clustered vehicle routing problem. Oper. Res. **62**(1), 58–71 (2014)
3. Bektas, T., Erdogan, G., Ropke, S.: Formulations and branch-and-cut algorithms for the generalized vehicle routing problem. Transp. Sci. **45**(3), 299–316 (2011)
4. Fischetti, M., Salazar, J.J., Toth, P.: A branch-and-cut algorithm for the symmetric generalized traveling salesman problem. Oper. Res. **45**(3), 378–394 (1997)

5. Fuksz, L., Pop, P.C.: A hybrid genetic algorithm with variable neighborhood search approach to the number partitioning problem. In: Pan, J.-S., Polycarpou, M.M., Woźniak, M., de Carvalho, A.C.P.L.F., Quintián, H., Corchado, E. (eds.) HAIS 2013. LNCS, vol. 8073, pp. 649–658. Springer, Heidelberg (2013)
6. Ghiani, G., Improta, G.: An efficient transformation of the generalized vehicle routing problem. Eur. J. Oper. Res. **122**(1), 11–17 (2000)
7. Golden, B.L., Wasil, E.A., Kelly, J.P., Chao, I.-M.: Metaheuristic in vehicle routing. In: Crainic, T.G., Laporte, G. (eds.) Fleet Management and Logistics, pp. 33–56. Kluwer, Boston (1998)
8. Pop, P.C.: Generalized Network Design Problems, Modelling and Optimization. De Gruyter, Germany (2012)
9. Pop, P.C., Matei, O., Sitar, C.P., Chira, C.: A genetic algorithm for solving the generalized vehicle routing problem. In: Corchado, E., Graña Romay, M., Manhaes Savio, A. (eds.) HAIS 2010, Part II. LNCS(LNAI), vol. 6077, pp. 119–126. Springer, Heidelberg (2010)
10. Pop, P.C., Kara, I., Horvat Marc, A.: New mathematical models of the generalized vehicle routing problem and extensions. Appl. Math. Model. **36**(1), 97–107 (2012)
11. Pop, P.C., Matei, O., Pop Sitar, C.: An improved hybrid algorithm for solving the generalized vehicle routing problem. Neurocomputing **109**, 76–83 (2013)
12. Pop, P.C., Chira, C.: A hybrid approach based on genetic algorithms for solving the clustered vehicle routing problem. In: Proceedings of IEEE Congress on Evolutionary Computation (CEC-2014), Beijing, China, pp. 1421–1426 (2014)
13. Sevaux, M., Sörensen, K.: Hamitonian paths in large clustered routing problems. In: Proceedings of EU/MEeting Workshop on Metaheuristics for Logistics and Vehicle Routing, Troyes, France (2008)

Trading-off Accuracy vs Energy in Multicore Processors via Evolutionary Algorithms Combining Loop Perforation and Static Analysis-Based Scheduling

Zorana Banković[1], Umer Liqat[1], and Pedro López-García[1,2]([✉])

[1] IMDEA Software Institute, Madrid, Spain
{zorana.bankovic,umer.liqat,pedro.lopez}@imdea.org
[2] Spanish Council for Scientific Research (CSIC), Madrid, Spain

Abstract. This work addresses the problem of energy efficient scheduling and allocation of tasks in multicore environments, where the tasks can permit certain loss in accuracy of either final or intermediate results, while still providing proper functionality. Loss in accuracy is usually obtained with techniques that decrease computational load, which can result in significant energy savings. To this end, in this work we use the loop perforation technique that transforms loops to execute a subset of their iterations, and integrate it in our existing optimisation tool for energy efficient scheduling in multicore environments based on evolutionary algorithms and static analysis for estimating energy consumption of different schedules. The approach is designed for multicore XMOS chips, but it can be adapted to any multicore environment with slight changes. The experiments conducted on a case study in different scenarios show that our new scheduler enhanced with loop perforation improves the previous one, achieving significant energy savings (31 % on average) for acceptable levels of accuracy loss.

1 Introduction

Task scheduling and allocation for energy efficiency in multicore environments is a well-known NP-hard problem which can be efficiently solved with heuristic algorithms, such as evolutionary algorithms. One example is our approach for scheduling and allocation, which is based on evolutionary algorithms (EAs) [1]. The algorithm was shaped for its application to XMOS multicore chips, which give support for dynamic voltage and frequency scaling (DVFS) at chip level, i.e., all cores have the same voltage and frequency. However, the approach can be adapted to any multicore environment with slight modifications. In this work we want to deal with optimally scheduling tasks which can permit certain accuracy loss.

As a matter of fact, the great majority of today's processors are designed in a way that can provide a high level of accuracy. However, there are numerous applications that allow certain accuracy loss, which still permits them to function

© Springer International Publishing Switzerland 2015
E. Onieva et al. (Eds.): HAIS 2015, LNAI 9121, pp. 690–701, 2015.
DOI: 10.1007/978-3-319-19644-2_57

properly, such as video streaming, machine learning, etc. Since decreasing the accuracy is usually achieved by reducing the computational load, this can lead to both increase in performance and decrease in energy consumption, so here we deal with a trade-off between accuracy on one side and performance and/or energy on the other. One technique that achieves this is loop perforation [7], which in essence consists in skipping every n-th loop iteration, for a given n. Broadly speaking, accuracy can be considered as one aspect of quality of service (QoS), so we can say that in this work we deal with the QoS/energy trade-off.

Thus, in this work we solve the following scheduling problem: given a set of tasks with known release time and number of cycles to compute them, find proper allocation and scheduling of the tasks, as well as a (V, f) assignment (i.e., voltage and frequency pair) to the cores in a way the total energy is minimised, while accuracy is maximised, meeting a minimal acceptable level of accuracy. Different levels of accuracy are achieved by applying the loop perforation technique with different n, where every n-th loop iteration is skipped.

Hence, we deal with two objectives: accuracy and energy. Accuracy is defined in terms of deviations of the output signal after applying the loop perforation, while in order to estimate energy consumption, we use an existing static analysis which, at compile time, with no need of executing the programs, and in a matter of seconds, gives a safe estimation of the energy consumed by programs. The energy consumption often depends on (the size of) input data, which is not known at compile time. For this reason, the static analysis provides the energy as a function of the input parameters, which is evaluated when input values are known at runtime. The energy consumption estimated by using the static analysis for a given scheduling is calculated as the sum of energies of the tasks running on different cores. This gives a safe upper bound on the total energy consumption, which is good enough for deciding which schedule consumes less energy, and can provide acceptable estimations of energy savings.

The rest of the paper is organised as follows. Section 2 gives more details of our proposed approach. Section 3 presents an experimental evaluation of it. Some related work is discussed in Sect. 4 and finally, some conclusions are drawn in Sect. 5.

2   Proposed Approach

2.1   Loop Perforation

The loop perforation technique consists in skipping some loop iterations, for example skipping every n-th iteration [7], where n can be varied in order to trade accuracy with energy, i.e., for higher n, less instructions are skipped, so the accuracy is higher, while more energy is saved for lower values of n. This trade-off between accuracy and energy consumption justifies the usage of a multiobjective algorithm. As we will see in the following, in this work the loop perforation technique is implemented as one possibility for the mutation operator.

2.2   Evolutionary Algorithm (EA)

The work presented in this paper is an extension of our previous work where we developed a custom algorithm based on an NSGA-II multiobjective evolutionary algorithm [1]. The conflicting objectives are accuracy and energy consumption, since we want to decrease the energy consumption, while maintaining the accuracy level as high as possible (always above a given threshold).

The non-dominated solutions are generated using the well-known NSGA-II algorithm [2], while the EA follows the standard steps of evolutionary algorithms: initialisation, evolution, where the selection process is implemented as standard tournament selection, and our custom-made crossover and mutation operators are applied. In the following we give more detail on the particular improvements carried out in this work.

Individual. A solution to the problem we are solving has to contain information about scheduling and allocation of each task, how many cycles of each task are executed in the current run (since we support task migration), and voltage and frequency levels of the core at each moment. In this work we add a new dimension to the problem, which is the possibility to decrease accuracy through loop perforation and thus it also has to be encoded in the individual. For this reason, we add one more field after each task, which encodes n, i.e., the iterations which can be skipped in one or more loops previously identified in each task. An example of a part of an individual is given in Fig. 1, and can be read in the following way: on core 1 in state 2 we execute in this order,

- 48 cycles of task 1, without performing loop perforation on it, and
- 77 cycles of task 5, where we skip every 4th iteration in the loop previously defined.

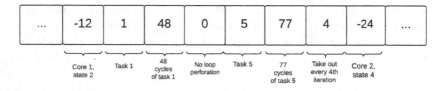

Fig. 1. Representation of an individual

Population Initialisation. Individuals in the initial population are created by randomly assigning tasks to random cores in random (V, f) settings with equal probability. However, in order to provide a load balanced solution (as much as possible), the probability of choosing a core decreases as its load increases. The number of cycles of a task executed in each run, as well as the loop iterations to be skipped are also randomly chosen.

The Crossover Operator. Our custom crossover operator is designed in the following way:

- Each child preserves the order of appearance of the tasks, as well as their allocation from one of the parents,
- But, can take the distribution of the number of cycles, as well as the number of loop iterations to be skipped of one of them with equal probability.

The Mutation Operator. The mutation operator can perform different operations involving one or two tasks (designated as i and t in the following text). In each generation we perform one of the following operations with the same probability:

- *Swapping:* i and t, together with their corresponding number of cycles and loop iterations to be skipped, change their positions in the solution. However, in order to avoid creating solutions which are not viable, i and t have to belong to the cores which are executed in parallel.
- *Moving:* move i to a random position j. For the same reason as before, the position j has to belong to a core being executed in the same state as i's original state.
- *Changing the Cycle Distribution:* Randomly change distribution of the cycles of task i between its appearances on different cores.
- *Loop Perforation:* For a random task i, assign randomly the number of loop iterations to be skipped, update the total number of cycles, i.e., decrease the total number of cycles for the amount corresponding to the cycles of the skipped loops, and share them randomly between the existing appearances of the task i in the solution.

These operators are depicted in Fig. 2:

- *Swapping:* Tasks 1 and 2 are swapped between cores 1 and 2 while both in state 1.
- *Moving:* First part of task 1 (40 cycles) are moved to core 2 before task 2.
- *Changing the Number of Cycles:* Task 1 now executes 25 cycles on core 1 in state 1 and 45 cycles on core 2 and state 2.
- *Loop Perforation:* Task 1, where loop perforation has not been performed, now skips every 20th task in the defined loop, which results in decreased number of cycles, i.e., it has 60 cycles, where the first 35 cycles are executed in the first appearance of the task 1, while the remaining 25 cycles are executed in its second appearance.

Objective Functions: Energy Consumption. This objective represents the total energy consumption of the given schedule, and it should be minimised. It is given with the following formula:

$$E = \sum_{1 \leq i \leq n} \left(P_{st,i} \cdot T + \sum_{1 \leq j \leq k} (x_{i,j} \cdot p_{i,j} \cdot \tau_{i,j}) \right) \tag{1}$$

where $P_{st,i}$ is the static power of the core i, T is the total execution time of the schedule, i.e., the moment when the last task finishes its execution, $\tau_{i,j}$ is

Original:

-11	1	40	0	-21	2	30	10	-12	2	50	10	-22	1	30	0

Swapping:

-11	2	30	10	-21	1	40	0	-12	2	50	10	-22	1	30	0

Moving:

-11	-21	1	40	0	2	30	10	-12	2	50	10	-22	1	30	0

Changing the number of cycles:

-11	1	25	0	-21	2	30	10	-12	2	50	10	-22	1	45	0

Loop perforation:

-11	1	35	20	-21	2	30	10	-12	2	50	10	-22	1	25	20

Fig. 2. Different possibilities for mutation

the execution time of task j on core i, $x_{i,j}$ is a binary value, $x_{i,j} \in \{0,1\}$, that represents whether the task j is executed on the core i ($x_{i,j} = 1$) or not ($x_{i,j} = 0$), and $p_{i,j}$ is the power of task j when executed on core i.

Objective Functions: Accuracy. In this work accuracy is defined as an average error of the output after applying loop perforation, and it should be minimised. If a task performs some sort of signal processing, where the output is a digital signal consisting of a number of samples, the error is calculated as the Euclidean distance between the outputs obtained with and without loop perforation.

2.3   Energy Static Analysis as Input

In order to statically estimate the energy consumed by programs we use an existing static analysis. It is a specialization of the generic resource analysis presented in [8] for programs written in a high-level C-based programming language, XC [9], running on the XMOS XS1-L architecture, that uses the instruction-level energy cost models described in [3]. The analysis is general enough to be applied to other programming languages and architectures (see [4,5] for details). It enables a programmer to symbolically bound the energy consumption of a program P on input data $\bar{x}$ without actually running $P(\bar{x})$. It is based on setting up a system of recursive cost equations over a program P that capture its cost (energy consumption) as a function of the sizes of its input arguments $\bar{x}$. Consider for example the following program written in XC:

```
int fact(int N) {
   if (N <= 0) return 1;
   return N * fact(N - 1);
}
```

The transformation based analysis framework of [4,5] would transform the assembly (or LLVM IR) representation of the program into an intermediate semantic program representation (HC IR), that the analysis operates on, which is a series of connected code blocks, represented as Horn Clauses. The analyzer deals with this HC IR always in the same way, independent of where it originates from, setting up cost equations for all code blocks (predicates).

$$fact_e(N) = fact\_if_e(0 \leq N, N) + c_{entsp} + c_{stw} + c_{ldw} + c_{ldc} + c_{lss} + c_{bf}$$

$$fact\_if_e(B, N) = \begin{cases} fact_e(N-1) + c_{bu} + 2\ c_{ldw} + c_{sub} + \\ \qquad\qquad + c_{bl} + c_{mul} + c_{retsp} & \text{if } B \text{ is true} \\ c_{mkmsk} + c_{retsp} & \text{if } B \text{ is false} \end{cases}$$

The cost of the function $fact$ is captured by the equation $fact_e$ which in turn depends on the equation $fact\_if_e$, that captures the cost of the two clauses representing the two branches of the if statement, and a sequence of low-level instructions. The cost of low-level instructions, which constitute an energy cost model, is represented by c_i where $i \in \{entsp, stw, ldw, ...\}$ is an assembly instruction. Such costs are supplied by means of assertions that associate basic cost functions with elementary operations.

If we assume (for simplicity of exposition) that each instruction has unitary cost in terms of energy consumption, i.e., $c_i = 1$ for all i, we obtain the energy consumed by fact as a function of its input data size (N): $fact_e(N) = 13\ N + 8$.

3   Experimental Evaluation

3.1   Testing Environment

XMOS Chips. In this work we target the XS1-L architecture of the XMOS chips as a proof of concept. Although these chips are multicore and multi-threaded, in this work we assume a single core architecture with 8 threads, which is the architecture for which we have an available energy model. All threads have their own register set and up to 4 instructions per thread can be buffered, which are scheduled in a way to minimize simultaneous memory accesses by consecutive threads. The threads enter a 4-stage pipeline, meaning that only one instruction from a different thread is executed at each pipeline stage. If the pipeline is not full, the empty stages are filled with $NOPs$ (no operation). Effectively, this means that we can assume that the threads are running in parallel, with frequency F/N, where F is the frequency of the chip, and $N = max(4, numberOfThreads)$.

DVFS is implemented at the chip level, which means that all the threads have the same voltage and frequency at the same time. All XMOS chips support frequency scaling. However, only the XS1-SU01A-FB96 [6] chip provides the possibility of voltage scaling enabled by two DC-DC converters whose output voltage belongs to the range (0.6V, 1.3V). In order to apply DVFS, we need list of Voltage-Frequency (V,f) pairs or ranges that provide a correct chip functioning.

Table 1. Viable (V, f) pairs for XMOS chips.

$Voltage(V)$	0.95	0.87	0.8	0.8	0.75	0.7
$frequency(MHz)$	500	400	300	150	100	50

We have experimentally concluded that the XMOS chips can function properly with the voltage and frequency levels given in Table 1.

Task Set. We use two real world programs for testing:

- fir(N): Finite Impulse Response (FIR) filter. In essence, it computes the inner-product of two vectors: a vector of input samples, and a vector of coefficients.
- biquad(N): Part of an equaliser implementation, which uses a cascade of Biquad filters. The energy consumed depends on the number of filters in the cascade, also known as banks N.

These filters are often used in signal processing, where some certain level of accuracy loss can be permitted. This makes them good candidates for experimenting with the accuracy/energy trade-off. We have used four different FIR implementations, with different number of coefficients: 85, 97, 109 and 121. Furthermore, we have used four implementations of the biquad program, with different number of banks: 5, 7, 10 and 14. We have tested our approach in scenarios with 32 tasks, each one corresponding to one of the above mentioned implementations. The tasks corresponding to the same implementation have different release times.

The energy consumed by the programs is inferred at compile time by the static analysis described in Sect. 2.3. This energy is expressed as a function of an input parameter N, which is known at run time only. In the case of FIR, N is the number of coefficients, while in the case of the Biquad cascade, N is the number of banks. These functions are given in Table 2. The analysis assumes that a single program is running on one thread on the XMOS chip, while all other threads are inactive. This means that only the first stage of the pipeline is occupied with an instruction, while the rest are empty, i.e., occupied with NOPs. In this implementation, the EA algorithm approximates the total energy of a schedule taking the sum of the energies of all the tasks running on different cores, i.e., threads, as we have seen in Sect. 2.2. However, in reality if all the threads are active and execute a program, each pipeline stage will contain an instruction from a different thread. For this reason, we can say that the estimation produced by the static analysis of the energy consumed by a set of tasks is an upper bound on the actual energy consumption. However, this estimation provides precise enough information for the EA to decide which schedule is better.

3.2   Testing Scenario

We have tested our approach on a scenario of 32 tasks, where each task implements either an FIR or a Biquad cascade previously described. For the case of

Table 2. Energy functions for 3 different pairs of voltage (V) / frequency (F, in MHz)

	V = 0.70 F = 50	V = 0.75 F = 100	V = 0.80 F = 150
$fir(N)$	$74.93\ N + 124.5$	$43.36\ N + 71.9$	$33.41\ N + 55.2$
$biquad(N)$	$386\ N + 128$	$223.6\ N + 74.2$	$172.5\ N + 57.2$
	V = 0.80 F = 300	V =0.87 F = 400	V = 0.95 F = 500
$fir(N)$	$20.14\ N + 33.2$	$18.95\ N + 31.09$	$19.15\ N + 31.3$
$biquad(N)$	$104.3\ N + 34.4$	$98.31\ N + 32.4$	$99.48\ N + 32.7$

FIR, loop perforation takes out a few coefficients, while in the case of Biquad cascade, it takes out a few banks. All tasks have different release time. Task deadlines do not exist. However, we should bear in mind that in the case of DVFS it is not beneficial to scale down voltage and frequency indefinitely, since at some point static power consumption becomes more significant than dynamic power consumption. Thus, if we keep decreasing the dynamic power, the static power is increased at the same time, and as a result, the total energy consumption increases. The input signal to all tasks is a standardised set of input samples for testing in signal processing.

3.3   Obtained Results and Discussion

The EA has been trained with the following parameters: population of 200 individuals, evolved for 150 generations, crossover rate: 0.9, and mutation rate: 0.9 - since mutation introduces loop perforation, a high rate is needed.

   In order to illustrate the energy savings provided by loop perforation (referred to as *Case 1* in the following text), we have trained another EA, where the objectives are to minimize energy and execution time, without the possibility of loop perforation (referred to as *Case 2* in the following). This algorithm has been trained with the same parameters given above. Since both algorithms are multiobjective, the result of the training of both is a Pareto front of possible solutions with different trade-off between the objectives. Examples of Pareto fronts obtained in *Case 1* and *Case 2* are given in Figs. 3 and 4 respectively. In *Case 1* we have picked a solution with the smallest energy objective value, whose maximal deviation from the final result (accuracy) is below (above) a given threshold, while in *Case 2* we have chosen a solution with the smallest energy objective. The results are presented in Table 3, with the following columns:

- *Column 1:* Maximal acceptable average error (or equivalently, minimal acceptable level of accuracy) of the final result.
- *Column 2:* Average energy of the final schedule obtained in a set of experiments of *Case 1* estimated by static analysis given in mJ (mili Joules).

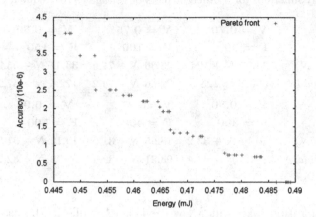

Fig. 3. Pareto front for Energy/Accuracy trade-off EA (Case 1)

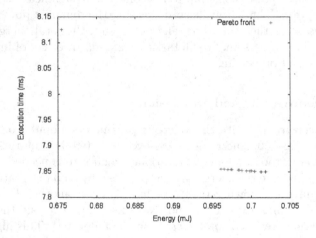

Fig. 4. Pareto front for Energy/Time trade-off EA (Case 2)

Table 3. Obtained savings with different levels of minimal acceptable accuracy.

| Max. | Case 1: | Case 2: | Savings(%) | |
Avg. Error	Avg. En.(mJ)	Avg. En.(mJ)	Avg.	CI0.05
10^{-6}	0.487	0.721	16.18	0.93–31.42
$2 \cdot 10^{-6}$	0.461	0.597	18.21	3.54–32.87
$3 \cdot 10^{-6}$	0.434	0.666	31.04	13.72–48.37

– *Column 3:* Average energy of the final schedule obtained in a set of experiments of *Case 2* estimated by static analysis given in mJ (mili Joules).
– *Column 4:* Obtained savings expressed as % and calculated as $\frac{Column3 - Column2}{Column3} \cdot 100$.
– *Column 5*: Statistics of the experiments expressed as 0.05 confidence interval, i.e., we can claim with 95 % certainty that the final result will belong to this interval.

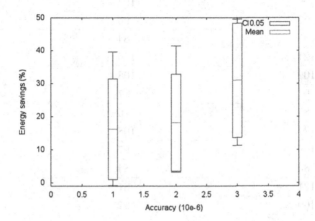

Fig. 5. Energy savings for different accuracy levels

As we can observe, energy savings that can be obtained with loop perforation are significant and range from 3 % to 40 % in different experiments, even with small permitted level of error. As we increase the accepted level of average error, the savings increase, as expected, which is clearly depicted in Fig. 5. However, the relationship between the accuracy and the energy savings depends on the application: some applications can preserve acceptable accuracy by skipping more loop iterations (and hence achieve bigger energy savings) than others that lose acceptable accuracy by skipping less loop iterations (and hence achieve smaller energy savings).

Fluctuations in the final result in different experiments appear due to the imprecision of the static analysis, since currently it gives an upper bound, rather than a realistic estimation of energy consumption. This can explain the big confidence intervals. Since the acceptable level of error is small, we could observe that in the final result only tasks that perform FIR could skip a few iterations, while some of the tasks that perform biquad could skip one iteration at most, since the number of iterations is bigger in FIR than in the case of the biquad cascade. In Table 4 we present an example of a part of an output containing tasks where loop perforation was applied, where the maximal acceptable error is 10^{-6}. In the table, for each task, we show the original number of loop iterations, the number of loop iterations after applying loop perforation, and N, where every N-th loop is skipped. The actual error of this example is $7.8 \cdot 10^{-7}$, but we still achieve significant energy savings.

Table 4. Result of an experiment: tasks whose final number of loop iterations has been changed.

Task	Original num. of loop iterations	Final num. of loop iterations	N
FIR97-1	97	87	9
FIR85-1	85	76	9
FIR121-1	121	108	9
FIR109-1	109	104	21
FIR97-2	97	96	96
FIR85-2	85	84	84
FIR121-2	121	120	120
FIR109-2	109	108	108
FIR97-3	97	87	9
FIR85-3	85	76	9
FIR121-3	121	108	9
FIR109-3	109	97	9
FIR85-4	85	84	1
FIR121-3	121	81	3
FIR109-3	109	97	9

4   Related Work

In the existing literature techniques that include QoS as an objective in scheduling are mainly designed for Grid or Cloud Computing environments, where QoS is measured as either execution time, cost, etc., which has to be provided according to the signed Service Level Agreement (SLA) between the provider and the customer [10–12]. Multiobjective genetic algorithms were used in [12] to minimize cost and execution time, since they can be in conflict. A similar approach is presented in [11]. However, in the recent past, energy consumption has become a bottleneck, so it has become very important to reduce it. One such work is given in [10], where the authors try to minimize energy and maximize QoS at the same time in a Cloud Computing environment. The multiobjective optimisation problem is solved using particle swarm optimisation.

However, as far as we know, none of the approaches in the literature propose to trade-off QoS (accuracy in our case) with energy or performance in a scheduling problem by transforming the code, in our case by using loop perforation.

5   Conclusions

In this work we have presented an approach for energy efficient scheduling in multicore environments, adapted to multicore XMOS processors, where significant additional energy can be saved if a certain level of accuracy reduction in final result is allowed. Accuracy reduction is performed by using the loop perforation technique. Our experimental results show that, even with small acceptable levels of error in the result, significant energy savings can be obtained.

However, the energy estimation of different schedules is based on a static analysis that can only provide an upper bound. Although it is still capable of providing energy savings, better results could be achieved with more precise energy estimations. For this reason, we are developing an energy analysis of concurrent program, which is expected to provide additional savings.

Acknowledgements. The research leading to these results has received funding from the European Union 7th Framework Programme under grant agreement 318337, ENTRA - Whole-Systems Energy Transparency, Spanish MINECO TIN'12-39391 *StrongSoft* and TIN'08-05624 *DOVES* projects, and Madrid TIC-1465 *PROMETIDOS-CM* project.

References

1. Banković, Z., Lopez-Garcia, P.: Stochastic vs. deterministic evolutionary algorithm-based allocation and scheduling for XMOS chips. Neurocomputing **150**, 82–89 (2014)
2. Deb, K., Pratap, A., Agarwal, S., Meyarivan, T.: A fast elitist multi-objective genetic algorithm: NSGA-II. IEEE Trans. Evol. Comput. **6**, 182–197 (2000)
3. Kerrison, S., Eder, K.: Energy modelling of software for a hardware multi-threaded embedded microprocessor. ACM Trans. Embed. Comput. Syst. (TECS) (2015, to appear)
4. Liqat, U., Kerrison, S., Serrano, A., Georgiou, K., Lopez-Garcia, P., Grech, N., Hermenegildo, M.V., Eder, K.: Energy consumption analysis of programs based on XMOS ISA-level models. In: Gupta, G., Peña, R. (eds.) LOPSTR 2013, LNCS 8901. LNCS, vol. 8901, pp. 72–90. Springer, Heidelberg (2014)
5. López-García, P. (ed.) Initial Energy Consumption Analysis. ENTRA Project: Whole-Systems Energy Transparency (FET project 318337), April 2014. Deliverable 3.2, http://entraproject.eu
6. XMos Ltd., Xs1-su01a-fb96 datasheet, November 2012
7. Hoffmann, H., Misailovic, S., Sidiroglou, S., Rinard, M.: Managing performance vs. accuracy trade-offs with loop perforation. In: Proceedings of FSE 2011. ACM Press (2011)
8. Serrano, A., Lopez-Garcia, P., Hermenegildo, M.: Resource usage analysis of logic programs via abstract interpretation using sized types. In: Theory and Practice of Logic Programming, 30th Int'l. Conference on Logic Programming (ICLP 2014) Special Issue, 14(4–5):739–754, (2014)
9. Watt, D.: Programming XC on XMOS Devices. XMOS Limited (2009)
10. Yassa, S., Chelouah, R., Chelouah, R., Granado, B.: Multi-objective approach for energy-aware workflow scheduling in cloud computing environments. Sci. World J. 2013, Article ID: 350934, 1–13 (2013)
11. Ye, G., Rao, R., Li, M.: A multiobjective resources scheduling approach based on genetic algorithms in grid environment. In: Fifth International Conference on Grid and Cooperative Computing Workshops, GCCW 2006, pp. 504–509, October 2006
12. Yu, J., Kirley, M., Buyya, R.: Multi-objective planning for workflow execution on grids. In: Proceedings of the 8th IEEE/ACM International Conference on Grid Computing, GRID 2007, pp. 10–17. IEEE Computer Society, Washington, DC (2007)

Distributed Tabu Searches in Multi-agent System for Permutation Flow Shop Scheduling Problem

Olfa Belkahla Driss[1,2] and Chaouki Tarchi[1,2(✉)]

[1] Stratégies d'Optimisation et Informatique intelligentE (SOIE),
High Institute of Management, University of Tunis,
41, Street of Liberty Bouchoucha-City, 2000 Bardo, Tunis, Tunisia
[2] Higher Business School of Tunis, University of Manouba, Manouba, Tunisia
olfa.belkahla@isg.rnu.tn,
chaouki.tarchi@gmail.com

Abstract. In this paper, we propose a distributed multi-agent approach to solve the permutation flow shop scheduling problem for the objective of minimizing the makespan. This approach consists of two types of agents that cooperate to find a solution for this problem. A mediator agent who is responsible for generating the initial solution with NEHT heuristic, and scheduler agents, each applying a tabu search to refine a specific sequence of jobs which differs from those of other agents. Computational experiments confirm that our approach provides good results equal to or better than the ones given by other approaches with which we have made comparisons.

Keywords: Permutation flow shop scheduling · Makespan · Tabu search · Multi-agent system

1 Introduction

The Flow Shop Problem (FSP) is a complex combinatorial optimization problem with many variations. In the permutation FSP (PFSP), a set $N = \{1...n\}$ of n independent jobs has to be processed in the same order on a set $M = \{1...m\}$ of m machines and the goal is to find a job permutation that minimizes a specific performance criterion. The criterion that is most commonly studied in the literature is the minimization of the total completion time, also called makespan or Cmax. The makespan minimization PFSP is denoted as Fm|prmu|Cmax following the notation introduced by [11], where m is the number of machines, prmu denotes that only permutation schedules are allowed, and Cmax denotes the makespan minimization as the optimization criterion. In the PFSP, job passing in the sequence is not allowed; that is, the processing sequence on the first machine is maintained throughout the remaining machines.

Since the pioneering work of Johnson [14] on the two machine problem, many methods have been introduced for solving PFSP with the objective of minimizing the makespan criterion. However, due to huge computation time, exact algorithms such as branch and bound method [15] and the empirical analysis of integer programming method [25] cannot be applied to the middle and large-scale problems with acceptable time.

© Springer International Publishing Switzerland 2015
E. Onieva et al. (Eds.): HAIS 2015, LNAI 9121, pp. 702–713, 2015.
DOI: 10.1007/978-3-319-19644-2_58

Heuristic algorithms based on the constructive operation were then proposed to solve the large-sized scheduling problems, such as the CDS heuristic [3] which is an extension of the Johnson [14] algorithm for $m > 2$ and the NEH heuristic [20] which is considered as the best method among simple constructive heuristics for flow shop scheduling. Also, the improvement heuristics that start from the previous generated solutions and subsequently achieve the optimal solution by improving the solutions with domain dependent knowledge like [4] which is a variant of NEH heuristic. The meta-heuristics mainly include Simulated Annealing algorithm (SA) [22], Genetic Algorithm (GA) [19], Particle Swarm Optimization algorithm (PSO) [14], Bee Colony algorithm (BCO) [16], tabu search algorithm [10].

Few SMA-based works has actually been proposed in the literature for solving the FSP such as [5] and in particular for PFSP by the new multi-agent model based on tabu search [2]. The encouraging results from the latest model lead us to use the tabu search meta-heuristic, but in a distributed way on multiple agents.

The remainder of this paper is organized as follows. In Sect. 2, the formulation of the PFSP with total completion time criterion is presented. In Sect. 3, the principle of the Tabu search meta-heuristic is discussed in detail. Section 4 describes the proposed Multi-Agent approach. In Sect. 5, an adaptation of Tabu search in the proposed approach is presented. The computational results are illustrated and analyzed in Sect. 6, and the paper is concluded in Sect. 7.

2 PFSP Formulation

The PFSP minimizing makespan can be formally defined as follows. A set of jobs $N = \{1...n\}$ available at time zero must be processed on m machines, where $n >= 1$ and $m >= 1$, p is the processing time and Cmax is the makespan. A job permutation is denoted by $\pi = \{\pi_1, \pi_2,..., \pi_n\}$ and $C(\pi_j, m)$ denote the completion time of job π_j on machine m. The completion time of the permutation flow shop scheduling problem according to the processing sequence $\pi = \{\pi_1, \pi_2,..., \pi_n\}$ is shown as follows:

$C(\pi_1, j) = p\pi_1, 1.$
$C(\pi_1, j) = C(\pi_{i-1}, i) + p\pi_i, 1, i = 2,...,n.$
$C(\pi_1, j) = C(\pi_1, j - 1) + p\pi_1, j, j = 2,...,m.$
$C(\pi_1, j) = \max(C(\pi_{i-1}, j), C(\pi_i, j - 1)) + p\pi_i, j, i = 2,...,n, j = 2,...,m.$

Then makespan can be defined as: $Cmax(\pi) = C(\pi_n, m)$.

The goal of the permutation flow shop problem is to find the most suitable arrangement of π^* such as: $Cmax(\pi^*) \le C(\pi_n, m) \ \forall \pi \in \prod$.

3 The Tabu Search Meta-heuristic

Tabu Search is a local search based optimization method proposed by Glover [9]. This method has been successfully used to solve many hard combinatorial optimization problems such as timetabling, routing, and particularly in the scheduling area.

Briefly speaking, the basic idea of this method consists in starting from an initial permutation of n jobs and searching through its neighborhood, a set of permutations in order to find one that gives the lowest makespan. Then the search is repeated starting from the best permutation, as a new current permutation, and the process is continued. The neighborhood of the permutations is generated by the moves. A move changes the location of some jobs in the current permutation. In order to avoid being trapped in local optimum, the Tabu Search uses a memory structure called tabu list. The elements of the tabu list define moves that cannot be applied for certain number of iterations equals to the tabu list size. The list content is refreshed when a new current permutation is found; the oldest element is removed and the new move is added. The search stops when a given number of iterations has been reached without improving the currently best makespan, or when the algorithm has performed a maximum number of iterations. A simple tabu search requires the following elements: Initial solution, Mechanism for generating neighborhood, Move strategy, Tabu list, Diversification scheme and Stopping criteria.

The next section illustrates in details the proposed Multi-Agent approach.

4   The Proposed Multi-agent Approach

The need for the use of Multi-Agent System (MAS) was born following the increasing complexity and the wide distribution of applications and data. In fact, an information request can be satisfied from multiple distributed systems requiring the recovery of the response by a manager entity. So the exchange of data and the distribution of tasks of a distributed application require interaction between different entities (agents) through the network. Each agent in this network must perform an important role; it can communicate, collaborate, coordinate and negotiate with other agents in order to accomplish the objective that is assigned.

Our proposed Multi-Agent approach illustrated in Fig. 1 is called "Distributed Tabu Searches in Multi-Agent system for FSP" (DTS-MAFSP). It is based on two types of agents; One Mediator agent and "n" Scheduler agents with "n" refers to the number of jobs. Each agent is assigned from the beginning to a specific position in the sequence of scheduling. This position is determined by an exact match to the rank of this agent, e.g. the first scheduler agent is assigned to the first position. To solve the PFSP with minimizing makespan, tabu searches are distributed on all scheduler agents. The global optimization process of our approach and the role of each type of agents are explained in detail below.

4.1   The Mediator Agent

It is the agent, who launches the program, it is initially responsible for creating n scheduler agents, and sends for them the data needed for their operation corresponding to the number of jobs and machines and execution times of each job on each machine. Then, it generates the initial solution which is the origin of the desired optimal solution. It is generated by the NEHT heuristic [24]. It selects thereafter the least well inserted

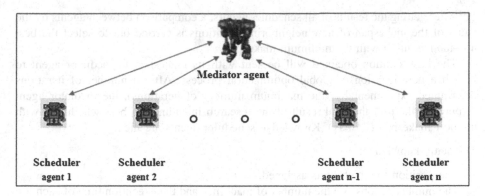

Fig. 1. DTS-MAFSP architecture

job in the initial solution with the extension of the Taillard's implementation in the case of a job remove [20], and it sends to the "n" scheduler agents the initial solution to refine and the least well inserted job to move. Towards the end of the optimization process based on tabu searches implemented in scheduler agents, it returns to the user the search results that contain the best makespan (C*max) and the best scheduling of all jobs on different machines. The knowledge of this agent may be static or dynamic. Static knowledge consists of:

– The number of jobs and the number of machines and the execution time of each job on each machine.
– The initial solution and the value of its makespan.

Dynamic knowledge consists of:

– The job to remove (the least well inserted).
– The current solution and the value of its makespan.
– The optimal solution and the value of its makespan at the end of the research process.

4.2   Scheduler Agents

These are exactly equal to the number of jobs, that is to say n agents. Each scheduler agent has an important role in our approach. It allows refining the solution received from the mediator agent. This improvement is achieved through tabu search meta-heuristic, which will be implemented in each scheduler agent, which allows us to have a global optimization process based on Distributed Tabu Searches across all scheduler agents.

In fact, after receiving the initial solution and the job to move from the mediator agent, each agent scheduler is responsible for placing the job in the position to which it is assigned. Subsequently, it launches the process of tabu search to calculate the value of the makespan of the new constructed sequence.

After getting the results of all scheduler agents, a comparison between agents by the value of the makespan of new neighboring solutions is carried out to select the best non-tabu solution with the minimum makespan.

The best solution obtained will be sent with its makespan to mediator agent to launch a new iteration of global optimization process. After a number of iterations determined experimentally (the maximum number of iterations), the mediator agent displays to the user the final result of the research including the best scheduling with the best makespan (C*max). Knowledge scheduler agents are then:

The static knowledge:

- The position to which he is assigned.
- The number of jobs and the number of machines and the execution time of each job on each machine.
- The stopping criterion «nbr_itr_max»: the maximum number of iterations of the tabu search.
- The size of the tabu list.
- The criterion of diversification "seuil_diver": the number of iterations between two successive improvements.

The dynamic knowledge:

- The job to move.
- The current solution and its makespan.
- The best solution found until the current iteration and its makespan.
- Elements of the tabu list.
- The number of iterations performed.
- The number of iterations "nbr_itr_diver" after the last improvement.

5 Adaptation of Tabu Search Meta-Heuristic in "DTS-MAFSP"

In this section, we introduce an adaptation of the tabu search in our approach "DTS-MAS" to solve the PFSP minimizing makespan.

5.1 Initial Solution

The initial solution is the first step in the tabu search. This solution can be chosen randomly or on the basis of a heuristic. In fact, the choice of the method of generating the initial solution is very useful because it influences the efficiency of research and speed of convergence to the global optimum.

It has been shown that the effectiveness of the approach based on the principle of local search depends heavily on the quality of the initial solution [13].

In "DTS-MAFSP", we choose to generate the initial solution at the mediator agent by applying NEH heuristic [20] improved by the Taillard's implementation [24]. This improvement allows accelerating the insertion phase, which reduces the complexity of NEH from $O(n^3m)$ to $O(n^2m)$.

5.2   Neighborhood Function

The neighborhood N(s(i)) of the current solution is a set of neighboring solutions generated by an elementary transformation from a solution s(i) to another solution s(j) making a slight modification of the structure s(i). This operation is called move that cannot be necessarily better than s(i). The effectiveness of this transformation is based on the type of movement adopted to generate the entire neighborhood.

We quote at this level the main movements in the literature:

- **Exchange Moves:** this type of neighborhood is to swap the positions p_i and p_j of any two jobs. This movement generates a neighborhood of size n $(n-1)/2$, and exploring the neighborhood reaches $O(n^3m)$ which can cause a considerable computation time for large size instances.
- **Swap Moves:** this type of neighborhood is to reverse two successive elements in the current solution. This movement generates a neighborhood of size $(n-1)$, which can be explored in $O(n^2m)$. Local search algorithms based on this type of movement does not provide solutions of good quality [6].
- **Insertion Moves:** this type of neighborhood is to move a job from its original position pi to a new position pj. This movement generates a neighborhood of size $(n-1)^2$, but it can be evaluated in $O(n^2m)$. This type of neighborhood is considered the most effective, and it is the most used in several approaches in literature. Then, we choose to use this type of neighborhood because of its efficiency in terms of the quality of solution and running time.

In our approach "DTS-MAFSP", the neighborhood generation is performed by cooperation between the mediator agent and scheduler agents. Indeed, at each iteration the mediator agent chooses the least well inserted job into the current solution by applying the extension of the Taillard's implementation to remove a job [7]. It sends this job to scheduler agents. Each agent puts this job in the position assigned to it, and launches the tabu search by applying the Taillard's implementation [24] to calculate the new solution and its makespan. Subsequently, comparison between agents by the value of the makespan of new neighborhood solutions is performed to select the best solution not tabu to be sent to the mediator agent to start the next iteration, see Fig. 2.

5.3   Move Strategy

After choosing the best non-tabu solution, a step of evaluation of this solution is performed. In fact, each scheduler agent replaces the current solution by the best non-tabu neighborhood solution. If the makespan of the new current solution is less than the makespan of the best solution, the value of the best makespan is replaced by the makespan of the new current solution and the best scheduling is replaced by the new current scheduling.

When a new best solution cannot be found after a diversification threshold, the diversification phase is triggered to generate new solutions.

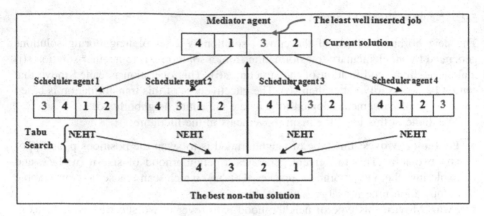

Fig. 2. The proposed neighborhood structure

5.4 Tabu List

Tabu list is a short-term memory, which saves the last visited solutions called tabu solutions to avoid cycles and local optima. The items in this list are of great importance during the optimization process, which can be makespan of visited solutions, displaced jobs and their positions... and the size of the tabu list can be static or dynamic. The size of the tabu list is a very important parameter. Several studies were carried out to optimize the length of the static [18] or dynamic [1] tabu list.

In our approach "DTS-MAFSP", we propose to use a tabu list with static size experimentally determined which stores the makespan of solutions already visited. When the list becomes full, its content is updated in the FIFO order (First In First Out); i.e. the oldest element is removed and the new move is added.

5.5 Diversification Scheme

Tabu search is a very effective method in the exploitation of an area of the search space. However, it is less effective when it comes to exploring the search space [1]. Diversification phase is started in the case where after a number of iterations, set in advance, a new best solution cannot be found. In "DTS-MAFSP", the solution of diversification phase is randomly generated based on the best solution from the scheduler agents. When the number of iterations increases without noticing that the current solution is improved; that is to say, when it reaches the threshold value of diversification "seuil_diver" that we experimentally fix and no better solution is found, we launch the diversification phase. After the random generation of the new sequence, we apply Taillard's implementation [24] to refine this solution and calculate the value of its makespan. This solution will be the new current solution, the "nbr_itr_diver" is reset and the global optimization process carries on reaching the maximum number of iterations "nbr_itr_max" which corresponds to the stop condition.

5.6 Stopping Criterion

In "DTS-MAFSP", the stopping criterion is set as the maximum number of iterations "nbr_itr_max" experimentally determined at the launch of tabu search.

6 Experimental Evaluations

The implementation of the proposed approach was made with the JADE platform on a PC Intel Pentium 2.1 GHz with 4 GB of RAM. To test the parameters of our system " DTS-MAFSP ", we use a set of instances of two benchmarks of literature; Taillard's benchmarks [23] and those of Reeves and Yamada [21]. To measure the performance of our approach, we made comparisons with the NEHT heuristic [11], the NEGA approach [26] and the MAFSP approach [2] with Taillard's benchmarks, and HDABC approach [17] and MAFSP approach [2] with Reeves and Yamada benchmarks. The brand "*" means that the result obtained by our approach is optimal.

Table 1. Experimental results for Taillard's instances of 20 jobs

Instances	J*M	C*max	NEHT	NEGA	MA FSP	DTS-MAF SP	Deviation pourcentage			
							NEHT	NEGA	MAF SP	DTS-MAFS P
TA001	20*5	1278	1286	1278	1278	1278*	0.626	0.00	0.00	0.00
TA002		1359	1365	1359	1359	1359*	0.441	0.00	0.00	0.00
TA003		1081	1159	1081	1081	1081*	0.215	0.00	0.00	0.00
TA004		1293	1325	1293	1293	1293*	2.475	0.00	0.00	0.00
TA005		1235	1305	1235	1235	1235*	5.668	0.00	0.00	0.00
TA006		1195	1228	1195	-	1195*	2.761	0.00	-	0.00
TA007		1239	1278	1239	-	1239*	3.148	0.00	-	0.00
TA008		1206	1223	1206	-	1206*	1.410	0.00	-	0.00
TA009		1230	1291	1230	-	1230*	4.960	0.00	-	0.00
TA010		1108	1151	1108	-	1108*	3.880	0.00	-	0.00
Average							2.559	0.00	-	0.00
TA011	20*10	1582	1680	1582	1582	1582*	6.195	0.00	0.00	0.00
TA012		1659	1729	1659	1659	1671	4.219	0.00	0.00	0.723
TA013		1496	1557	1496	1496	1508	4.077	0.00	0.00	0.802
TA014		1377	1439	1377	1377	1381	4.502	0.00	0.00	0.290
TA015		1419	1502	1419	1419	1425	5.849	0.00	0.00	0.422
TA016		1397	1453	1397	-	1414	4.009	0.00	-	1.217
TA017		1484	1562	1484	-	1484*	5.257	0.00	-	0.00
TA018		1538	1609	1538	-	1550	4.617	0.00	-	0.780
TA019		1593	1647	1593	-	1603	3.390	0.00	-	0.628
TA020		1591	1653	1591	-	1604	3.897	0.00	-	0.818
Average							4.601	0.00	-	0.568
TA021	20*20	2297	2410	2297	2297	2306	4.919	0.00	0.00	0.391
TA022		2099	2150	2099	2099	2101	2.430	0.00	0.00	0.096
TA023		2326	2411	2326	2326	2350	3.654	0.00	0.00	1.031
TA024		2223	2262	2223	2223	2230	1.754	0.00	0.00	0.315
TA025		2291	2397	2291	2291	2308	4.627	0.00	0.00	0.742
TA026		2226	2349	2226	-	2246	5.526	0.00	-	0.899
TA027		2273	2362	2273	-	2293	3.916	0.00	-	0.880
TA028		2200	2249	2200	-	2212	2.223	0.00	-	0.546
TA029		2237	2320	2237	-	2246	3.710	0.00	-	0.402
TA030		2178	2277	2178	-	2181	4.546	0.00	-	0.138
Average							3.730	0.00	-	1.088

Bold values indicate that the results obtained by our approach are better or equal to the results of the approaches by which we performed comparisons, and when the deviation percentage is equal to zero it means that our approach gave an optimal solution. With:

$$\text{Deviation percentage} = \frac{Cmax - Cmax*}{Cmax*} * 100$$

We give first, in Tables 1, 2 and 3 the results of comparison between NEHT, NEGA, MAFSP and DTS-MAFSP on Taillard's benchmarks [23].

Table 2. Experimental results for Taillard's instances of 50 jobs

Instances	J*M	C*max	NEHT	NEGA	M.A. FSP	DTS-MAFSP	Deviation pourcentage			
							NEHT	NEGA	MAFSP	DTS-MAFSP
TA031	50*5	2724	2733	2724	2724	**2724***	0.330	0.00	0.00	**0.00**
TA032		2834	2843	2834	-	2838	0.318	0.00	-	0.141
TA033		2621	2640	2621	-	**2621***	0.725	0.00	-	**0.00**
TA034		2751	2782	2751	-	2753	1.127	0.00	-	0.072
TA035		2863	2868	2863	-	**2863***	0.175	0.00	-	**0.00**
TA036		2829	2850	2829	-	**2829***	0.742	0.00	-	**0.00**
TA037		2725	2758	2725	-	2728	1.211	0.00	-	0.110
TA038		2683	2721	2683	-	**2683***	1.417	0.00	-	**0.00**
TA039		2552	2576	2552	-	2558	0.940	0.00	-	0.236
TA040		2782	2790	2782	-	**2782***	0.288	0.00	-	**0.00**
Average							0.728	0.00	-	0.056
TA041	50*10	2991	3135	3021	3025	3086	4.814	1.00	1.137	3.177
TA042		2867	3032	2902	-	2971	5.756	1.22	-	3.628
TA043		2839	2986	2871	-	2934	5.178	1.13	-	3.347
TA044		3063	3198	3070	-	3106	4.408	0.23	-	1.403
TA045		2976	3160	2998	-	3062	6.182	0.74	-	2.890
TA046		3006	3178	3024	-	3076	5.721	0.60	-	2.329
TA047		3093	3277	3122	-	3162	5.949	0.94	-	2.230
TA048		3037	3123	3063	-	3080	2.831	0.86	-	1.416
TA049		2897	3002	2914	-	2981	3.625	0.59	-	2.900
TA050		3065	3257	3076	-	3160	6.265	0.36	-	3.100
Average							5.072	0.767	-	2.642
TA051	50*20	3850	4082	3874	3895	3984	6.026	0.62	1.169	3.480
TA052		3704	3921	3734	-	3843	5.859	0.81	-	3.752
TA053		3640	3927	3688	-	3798	7.885	1.32	-	4.340
TA054		3720	3969	3759	-	3858	6.693	1.05	-	3.710
TA055		3610	3835	3644	-	3764	6.232	0.94	-	4.266
TA056		3681	3914	3717	-	3823	6.330	0.98	-	3.858
TA057		3704	3952	3728	-	3844	6.696	0.65	-	3.780
TA058		3691	3938	3730	-	3816	6.691	1.06	-	3.387
TA059		3743	3952	3779	-	3875	5.583	0.96	-	3.527
TA060		3756	4079	3801	-	3885	8.600	1.20	-	3.435
Average							6.660	0.959	-	3.753

Table 1 shows that the approach "DTS-MAFSP" achieves the optimum solution for 100 % of instances of 20*5 size. It achieves the optimal solution for 2 instances of 20*10 size. The average deviation percentage compared to the optimal solution for 20*10 size instances is 0.568, and for 20*20 size instances is 1.088.

Table 2 shows that the approach "DTS-MAFSP" gives 60 % of optimal solutions for 50*5 size instances.

The average deviation percentage compared to the optimal solution for 50*10 size instances is 2.642, and for 50*20 size instances is 3.753.

Table 3 shows that the approach "DTS-MAFSP" achieves the optimum solution for 70 % of instances of 100*5 size. The average deviation percentage compared to the optimal solution for 100*10 size instances is 1.010, and for 100*20 size instances is 3.90.

We then compare our approach with HDABC on Reeves and Yamada Benchmarks [21]. Table 4 shows that "DTS-MAFSP" achieves the optimal solution for 2/3 of the 20*5 size instances and the 20*10 size instances, and for 1/3 of the 20*15 size instances.

We also note that our approach gave a better solution than HDABC approach in Rec15 instances and the same results for both instances Rec13 and Rec21.

Table 3. Experimental results for Taillard's instances of 100 jobs

Instances	J*M	C*max	NEHT	NEGA	MA FSP	DTS- MAF SP	Deviation pourcentage			
							NEHT	NEGA	MAF SP	DTS- MAFSP
TA061	100*5	5493	5519	5493	5493	5493*	0.473	0.00	0.00	0.00
TA062		5268	5348	5268	-	5268*	1.519	0.00	-	0.00
TA063		5175	5219	5175	-	5175*	0.850	0.00	-	0.00
TA064		5014	5023	5014	-	5018	0.180	0.00	-	0.08
TA065		5250	5266	5250	-	5250*	0.305	0.00	-	0.00
TA066		5135	5139	5135	-	5135*	0.078	0.00	-	0.00
TA067		5246	5259	5246	-	5246*	0.248	0.00	-	0.00
TA068		5094	5120	5094	-	5099	0.510	0.00	-	0.099
TA069		5448	5489	5448	-	5448*	0.752	0.00	-	0.00
TA070		5322	5341	5322	-	5327	0.358	0.00	-	0.093
Average							0.527	0.00	-	0.027
TA071	100*10	5770	5846	5770	5770	5805	1.317	0.00	0.00	0.607
TA072		5349	5453	5358	-	5404	1.945	0.17	-	1.028
TA073		5676	5824	5676	-	5691	2.608	0.00	-	0.265
TA074		5781	5929	5792	-	5901	2.560	0.19	-	2.076
TA075		5467	5679	5467	-	5556	3.878	0.00	-	1.628
TA076		5303	5375	5311	-	5334	1.358	0.15	-	0.585
TA077		5595	5704	5605	-	5624	1.949	0.18	-	0.519
TA078		5617	5760	5617	-	5700	2.546	0.00	-	1.478
TA079		5871	6032	5877	-	5947	2.142	0.10	-	1.295
TA080		5845	5918	5845	-	5881	1.249	0.00	-	0.616
Average							2.155	0.079	-	1.010
TA081	100*20	6202	6541	6303	6283	6482	5.466	1.63	1.306	4.517
TA082		6183	6523	6266	-	6419	5.499	1.34	-	3.817
TA083		6271	6639	6351	-	6497	5.869	1.28	-	3.603
TA084		6269	6557	6360	-	6488	4.595	1.45	-	3.493
TA085		6314	6695	6408	-	6556	6.035	1.49	-	3.832
TA086		6364	6664	6453	-	6609	4.715	1.40	-	3.850
TA087		6268	6632	6332	-	6523	5.808	1.02	-	4.069
TA088		6401	6739	6482	-	6694	5.280	1.27	-	4.578
TA089		6275	6677	6343	-	6545	6.407	1.08	-	4.302
TA090		6434	6677	6506	-	6623	3.777	1.12	-	2.938
Average							5.346	1.308	-	3.90

Table 4. Experimental results of HDABC, MAFSP and DTS-MAFSP

Instances	J*M	C*max	HDABC	MA FSP	DTS- MAF SP	Deviation pourcentage		
						HDABC	MAF SP	DTS- MAFSP
Rec01	20*5	1247	1247	1247	1249	0.00	0.00	0.160
Rec03		1109	1109	1109	1109*	0.00	0.00	0.00
Rec05		1242	1242	1242	1242*	0.00	0.00	0.00
Rec07	20*10	1566	1566	1566	1572	0.00	0.00	0.383
Rec09		1537	1537	1537	1537*	0.00	0.00	0.00
Rec11		1431	1431	1431	1431*	0.00	0.00	0.00
Rec13	20*15	1930	1932	1930	1932	0.103	0.00	0.103
Rec15		1950	1963	1950	1950*	0.667	0.00	0.00
Rec17		1902	1917	1902	1926	0.789	0.00	1.261
Rec19	30*10	2093	2101	2099	2120	0.382	0.287	1.290
Rec21		2017	2046	2019	2046	1.438	0.099	1.438
Rec23		2011	2020	2018	2037	0.448	0.348	1.292
Rec25	30*15	2513	2542	2522	2571	1.153	0.358	2.308
Rec27		2373	2392	2379	2418	0.800	0.253	1.897
Rec29		2287	2310	2289	2418	1.00	0.087	5.729

7   Conclusions and Future Works

This paper presents our approach "Distributed Tabu Searches in Multi-Agent system for FSP" (DTS-MAFSP) to minimize makespan criterion. It is composed of two types of agents; One Mediator agent and "n" Scheduler agents looking to find the best solution to the PFSP.

Experiments show that the results of our approach are encouraging that motivate us to pursue the following lines of research:

- Explore other optimization criteria for PFSP such as total flow time, the sum of delays...
- The adaptation of our approach for hybrid flow shop where each machine can have multiple copies running in parallel.
- Explore other types of scheduling problems such as the Job shop problem or the Open shop problem.

References

1. Battiti, R., Protasi, M.: Reactive search, a history-sensitive heuristic for max-sat. J. Exp. Algorithmics JEA **2**(2) (1997)
2. Bargaoui, H., Driss, O.B.: Multi-Agent Model based on Tabu Search for the Permutation Flow Shop Scheduling Problem. Advances in Distributed Computing and Artificial Intelligence. Springer International Publishing, Switzerland (2001)
3. Campbell, H.G., Dudek, R.A., Smith, M.L.: A heuristic algorithm for the n job, m machine sequencing problem. Manage. Sci. **16**(10), B630–B637 (1970)
4. Dong, X., Huang, H., Chen, P.: An improved NEH-based heuristic for the permutation flow shop problem. Comput. Oper. Res. **35**(12), 3962–3968 (2008)

5. Daouas, T., Ghedira, K., Muller, J.P.: How to schedule a flow shop plant by agents. In: Applications of Artificial Intelligence in Engineering, Computational Mechanics, pp. 73–80 (1995)
6. Deroussi, et al.: New effective neighborhoods for the permutation flow shop problem. Research report LIMOS/RR-06-09 (2006)
7. Deroussi, L., Gourgand, M., Norre, S.: Une adaptation efficace des mouvements de Lin et Kernighan pour le flow-shop de permutation. In: 8eme Conférence Internationale de MOdélisation et SIMulation: MOSIM, Tunisie (2010)
8. Duvivier, D.: Etude de l'hybridation des métaheuristiques, application à un problème d'ordonnancement de type job shop, Université du Littorial côté d'opale (2000)
9. Glover, F.: Future paths for integer programming and links to artificial intelligence. Comput. Oper. Res. 13, 533–549 (1986)
10. Grabowski, J., Wodecki, M.: A very fast tabu search algorithm for the permutation flowshop problem with makespan criterion. Comput. Oper. Res. 31, 1891–1909 (2004)
11. Graham, R.L., Lawler, E.L., Lenstra, J.K., Kan, A.R.: Optimization and approximation in deterministic sequencing and scheduling: a survey. Ann. Discrete Math. 5, 236–287 (1979)
12. Hajinejada, D., Salmasib, N., Mokhtari, R.: A fast hybrid particle swarm optimization algorithm for flow shop sequence dependent group scheduling problem. Scientia Iranica 18(3), 759–764 (2011)
13. Jain, A., Rangaswamy, B., Meeran, S.: Job shop neighborhoods and move evaluation strategies, Department of Applied Physics, Electronic and Mechanical Engineering, University of Dundee, Dundee, Scotland (2000)
14. Johnson, S.M.: Optimal two- and three-stage production schedules with setup times included. Naval Res. Logistics Q. 1, 61–68 (1954)
15. Ladhari, T., Haouari, M.: A computational study of the permutation flow shop problem based on a tight lower bound. Comput. Oper. Res. 32, 1831–1847 (2005)
16. Li, X., Yin, M.: A discrete artificial bee colony algorithm with composite mutation strategies for permutation flow shop scheduling problem. Scientia Iranica 19(6), 1921–1935 (2012)
17. Liu, Y.F., Liu, S.Y.: A hybrid discrete artificial bee colony algorithm for permutation flowshop scheduling problem. Appl. Soft Comput. 13(3), 1459–1463 (2013)
18. Mazure, B., Saïs, L., Grégoire, E.: Boosting complete techniques thanks to local search methods. Ann. Math. Artif. Intell. 22(3–4), 319–331 (1998)
19. Nagano, M.S., Ruiz, R., Lorena, L.A.N.: A constructive genetic algorithm for permutation flowshop scheduling. Comput. Ind. Eng. 55, 195–207 (2008)
20. Nawaz, M., Enscore, E.E., Ham, I.: A heuristic algorithm for the m-machine, n-job flow-shop sequencing problem. OMEGA Int. J. Manage. Sci. 11(1), 91–95 (1983)
21. Reeves, C., Yamada, T.: Genetic algorithms, path relinking and the flowshop sequencing problem. Evol. Comput. 6(1), 45–60 (1998)
22. Yellanki, S.: Simulated Annealing Approach to Flow Shop Scheduling (2013)
23. Taillard, E.: Benchmarks for basic scheduling problems. Eur. J. Oper. Res. 64(2), 278–285 (1993)
24. Taillard, E.: Some efficient heuristic methods for the flowshop sequencing problem. Eur. J. Oper. Res. 47, 65–74 (1990)
25. Tseng, F.T., Stafford Jr., E.F., Gupta, J.N.D.: An empirical analysis of integer programming formulations for the permutation flowshop. OMEGA Int. J. Manage. Sci. 32(4), 285–293 (2004)
26. Zobolas, G.I., Tarantilis, C.D., Ioannou, G.: Minimizing makespan in permutation flow shop scheduling problems using a hybrid metaheuristic algorithm. University of Economics and Business (2008)

Content Based Image Retrieval for Large Medical Image Corpus

Gjorgji Strezoski[✉], Dario Stojanovski, Ivica Dimitrovski,
and Gjorgji Madjarov

Faculty of Computer Science and Engineering, Skopje 1000, Macedonia
{strezoski.g,stojanovski.dario}@gmail.com,
{ivica.dimitrovski,gjorgji.madjarov}@finki.ukim.mk
http://www.finki.ukim.mk

Abstract. In this paper we address the scalability issue when it comes to Content based image retrieval in large image archives in the medical domain. Throughout the text we focus on explaining how small changes in image representation, using existing technologies leads to impressive improvements when it comes to image indexing, search and retrieval duration. We used a combination of OpponentSIFT descriptors, Gaussian Mixture Models, Fisher kernel and Product quantization that is neatly packaged and ready for web integration. The CBIR feature of the system is demonstrated through a Python based web client with features like region of interest selection and local image upload.

Keywords: Image processing · Opponent SIFT · Medical image retrieval · Fisher vectors · PCA · Product quantization

1 Introduction

As we explore new boundaries and create new technologies we thrive towards bettering our lives in a variety ways. These technological advances are highly dependent on the data that is constantly being collected from any field imaginable. From simple movie databases, to complex medical imaging, vast quantities of data is being stored and processed on daily basis. Throughout time very large collections of data have been generated which are hard to manage and extract information from, therefore an efficient technique of information retrieval is crucial.

In the medical domain, imaging plays a fundamental role in research, education, diagnostics and even treatment. Almost every type of medical condition can be in a way expressed through an image, so there is a lot of information in the image itself. The sole tangible nature of an image is probably the most important factor in choosing images over other types of data. Until recent years medical image retrieval systems have been text based, which is not that convenient especially because for the text based image retrieval system to work, all of the images that would be used need to be annotated. Having in mind that there

© Springer International Publishing Switzerland 2015
E. Onieva et al. (Eds.): HAIS 2015, LNAI 9121, pp. 714–725, 2015.
DOI: 10.1007/978-3-319-19644-2_59

are over 12400 different categories of medical conditions [1] for which images can be collected, an efficient way of searching through this massive collection of data is also required. This presents a major problem for the medical community which grows over time and needs to be addressed.

Hospitals, clinics and other medical institutions have adopted technologies like Picture Archiving and Communication Systems (PACS) [2], Radiological Information Systems (RIS) [2] and Hospital Information Systems (HIS) [2]. The purpose of these systems is entering, storing and managing the patient data, but the sheer volume of data overwhelms the current information indexing and retrieval algorithms. As mentioned before, the text based nature of these systems limits their users to some kind of keyword based searches (image header keywords, patient ids, diagnosis ids...), which does not necessary capture the scope of the required query, some valuable visual characteristics that are proprietary to the image may be missing.

The CBIR systems create the possibility for searching these vast image collections, with visual queries that consist of sketches, textures, color characteristics, textures or cropped patches from existing images. Therefore the query gains contextual significance and captures those evading features that escaped the text based query approach.

In this paper we present a complete system for medical image retrieval that uses state-of-the-art techniques for feature representation, indexing and querying a large image archives. The remainder of this paper is organized as follows. Section 2 presents related systems and solutions in the CBIR field. Section 3 elaborates our system's architecture and implementation in detail, while Sect. 4 describes the dataset, results and the experimental setup. Finally in Sect. 5 we expressed our future intentions regarding this system and we gave our concluding thoughts.

2   Related Work

The earliest text-based image retrieval systems can be traced back to the 1970s [3] so we can safely say that image retrieval systems have always been a very popular research topic. So far text based search has proven satisfactory results and is widely used today. There are a lot of systems that operate in the Medical field that use text based retrieval.

One of those systems is Goldminer[1] which retrieves images by looking at figure captions of journal articles from the Radiological Society of North America (RSNA). The idea of this system is that the keywords of the captions can be extracted and then mapped to UMLS concepts.

Yale have created the Yale Image Finder[2] (YIF) which through optical character recognition recognizes text in the image. The recognized text is then combined with features from captions, titles and abstracts from medical journal articles.

---

[1] http://goldminer.arrs.org/home.php.
[2] http://krauthammerlab.med.yale.edu/imagefinder/.

Stathopoulos et al. make a field-based representation of the images and index it using Lucene[3]. In the retrieval phase they add different weights to the fields of representation based on the part of the article they were extracted from.

All of the above systems rely on text based features to retrieve a list of relevant images to each query. But in medical imaging a more precise type of retrieval is required, especially because not all annotations can be interpreted in a same way. We need to retrieve images with relevant visual features to those of the query image. These visual features at specific points in each image can be described with image descriptors. Initially content based retrieval systems implemented a more global approach on image description using global descriptors like color histograms and texture values. Thus, results have shown that global descriptors do not apply well in medical image retrieval. This is because the key feature of the image, the segment of the image with the most clinically relevant information is usually located in a very small area and global descriptors fail to grasp this detail. Eakins [2] has divided image features into three levels:

Level 1 - This level deals with primitive features like color, texture, shape or some spatial information about the objects in the picture. This way we can filter images on a more global scale based on form or color. This can be used for finding images that are visually similar to the query image.

Level 2 - This level introduces the logical features or derived attributes which involve some degree of inference about the identity of the objects depicted in the image. So a typical query in a medical scope would be "Find images of a kidney".

Level 3 - Most complex of all levels, as it requires complex reasoning about the significance of the objects depicted. In this case the query would look like "Find image of an infected kidne".

Most of the developed systems offer us level 1 retrieval. There are some systems in an experimental faze that allow level 2 retrieval but there are none level 3 systems so far. Recent systems for content based image retrieval in the medical domain are ASSERT system for high resolution computed tomography (CT) images of lungs, the Flexible Image Retrieval Engine (FIRE) which is used for a wide variety of medical images and the Image Retrieval for Medical Applications (IRMA) system that classifies images in viewpoints, modalities and anatomical areas.

The ASSERT system lets users extract valuable pathological data from lung images in specific pathology-bearing regions. The images are described by their texture, gray-scale and shape attributes.

All of the above mentioned systems have the common fault of low scalability. Searching a large image database is in it self a slow process, combined with the fact that biomedical image archives grow all the time, scalability is becoming a great concern. In our system the major improvement is in fact the scalability factor. We implement a very efficient image querying method that is almost invariant to the size of the data-set.

---

[3] http://lucene.apache.org/

3 Content Based Image Retrieval System for Large Biomedical Archives

Our system can be logically separated into two phases: an online phase and an offline phase. The offline phase is consisted of various methods of feature extraction, dimension reduction and quantization that increase system efficiency, while the online phase is basically a image search engine. Also because our system effectively powers a web client, the online phase can also be divided into two functional segments: a front end and a back end. The back end is basically a real time, slightly modified, on-call offline phase, while the front end delivers a user friendly interface. Once an image query is uploaded to the system, it immediately passes through the whole pipeline and a suitable representation is generated. Then the search is performed using a pre-indexed structure from the image archive in question. The results for the uploaded query image are then ordered by similarity and returned to the web client as a list from which image paths and relevant medical articles are constructed. Every query gets up to a 1000 result images. The similarity coefficient is also included in the result display.

3.1 Offline Phase

As mentioned above, the offline phase carries the whole system logic. It contains the image transformation, feature extraction, dimension reduction, distribution analysis, representation altering, product quantization and search functions. Each of these steps is vital to the end result and will be thoroughly described in the sections bellow. First the images from the training set are fed to the system because they are a fair representation of the whole image archive and a viable feature distributions can be extracted from them. With the help of the feature distributions we apply the Fisher vector encoding over the generated descriptors, resulting in one vector per picture representation of the image descriptors. Fisher vectors help us to significantly reduce the size of the information kept for each image and thus speed up search and indexing in the latter part of the process. Once the data analysis is complete, and all required coefficients for Fisher vector generation are retrieved we generated Fisher vectors on the whole 305 638 image set. We then fed the whole 305 638 image set once to the Product Quantization (PQ) pipeline extracted the structures needed for quick retrieval. Once we extracted the PQ structures the system was ready for integration with the online client for CBIR.

Image Transformation. In order to improve the scalability of the system, the images are preprocessed before feature extraction and indexing is performed. As illustrated on Fig. 1, the first step in the image processing pipeline is a physical transformation of the image itself. The transformation consists of reducing the dimensions of the image to the x768 dimension while keeping the aspect ratio. The aspect ratio is important so that the image does not appear warped and distorted upon processing. Also sometimes valuable information can be lost if

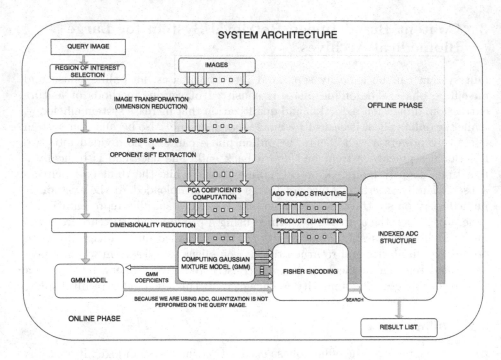

Fig. 1. Full system architecture

the aspect ratio is not kept intact. This transformation of the images is done via the djpeg package from the Ubuntu software repositories. After the scaling is complete, the image continues to be processed in Portable Pixel Map (PPM) or jpeg format.

Both images from the training set, indexing set and the user uploads undergo this process so that the consistency of the data is preserved.

OpponentSIFT. Van de Sande et al. (2010) [4] performed a study of the invariance properties of different color representations under different types of illumination transformations, encompassing light intensity changes, light intensity shifts, light color changes and light color shifts. We chose this descriptor over the regular grey-scale SIFT descriptor because even though SIFT is invariant to rotation, translation or scaling it does not capture the color features of the image. OpponentSIFT combines the best of both worlds in this case, it keeps the spatial invariance and adds color information. In medical imaging often times color can be the key semantic difference between two images (Example: infected vs healthy) so it was very important to capture this information.

The OpponentSIFT descriptor is 384 dimensional. This means that 384 values describe each point of interest or key point detected on the image. There are 128 values describing each of the opponent color channels - red vs green, blue vs yellow and black vs white. We used this descriptor in combination with dense sampling in order to extract as much information from the images as possible. All images were sampled with a window of 6×6 pixels on one scale and we saved the descriptors in a binary format proprietary for the ColorDescriptor tool we used for extraction.

Dimension Reduction. Once the opponent SIFT features are extracted, we have a matrix in which every key-point in the image is described by a 384 dimensional vector. Because of the dense extraction, the number of key-points is directly related to the size of the image and the step of key-point extraction. In our case the dimension of the image descriptors (384) is not optimal for working with a large number of images. The resource consumption would be too high and the performance will suffer. That is why we reduce the dimension of the descriptors by half using Principal Component Analysis (PCA). Principal component analysis (PCA) is a standard tool [5] for dimensionality reduction: the eigen vectors associated with the most energetic eigenvalues of the empirical vector covariance matrix are used to define a matrix M mapping a vector $x \epsilon R128$ to a vector $x = M_x$ in a lower-dimensional space [6].

Dimension reduction using PCA is a two step process. First random key-points from each image descriptor file are extracted and concatenated in a matrix. It is computationally inefficient to use all key-points from every image, because we are interested in a general distribution of features and that can be accomplished with as low as 800 key-points per image (depending on the image size). This gives us an object on which a suitable distribution analysis can be performed. The analysis starts with mean extraction from each of the 384 descriptor vectors for each randomly selected key-point. Every mean vector is then added to a matrix that will further be used in the dimension reduction process. After the mean extraction is complete, a principal component for each descriptor vector is also computed. The principal components actually represent the coefficients by which we multiply the original 384 dimensional descriptor in order reduce its size. The multiplication of these matrices is the actual dimension reduction part. There are 384 principal components generated for each of the 384 descriptor vectors. We can choose dimension of the resulting descriptor by limiting the number of principal component used in the multiplication.

In our case we reduce the descriptors dimension in half, so we multiply by a 192×384 dimensional PCA matrix. This kind of dimension reduction can be performed on the resulting fisher vector representation of the images, but the trade off between vector dimension and accuracy does not favor accuracy.

Fisher Vector Representation. The Fisher kernel combines all the benefits of generative and discriminative approaches when it comes to transforming an incoming variable size set of independent samples into a fixed sized vector representation [7,8]. The only assumption that has to be made during this process is that the samples in question follow some kind of parametric generative model estimated on a training set. In the world of image classification and retrieval the Fisher kernel extends the popular Bag of Visual Words (BOV) and has shown to improve state-of-the-art results. Because of the convenient size of the end representation the Fisher kernel is also quite suited for large scale image classification and retrieval. Having this in mind we chose the Fisher kernel as a suitable representation for our data.

Another advantage of the Fisher kernel is that it naturally gives a similarity measure that takes into account the underlying probability distribution. For example in our case we use each image of the indexed set to generate a Gaussian Mixture Model (GMM). This way we extract weights of the mixture elements, number of centroids and the diagonal of the covariance matrix. After this it is easy to calculate how much a new data entry would stretch the parameters of the trained model. It also gives the direction in parameter space into which the learned distribution should be modified to better fit the observed data. This representation in comparison with the BOF representation shows that fewer visual words are required by this more sophisticated representation.

Product Quantization. This section addresses the problem of coding an image vector. Given a D-dimensional input vector, we want to produce a code of B bits encoding the image representation, such that the nearest neighbors of a (non-encoded) query vector can be efficiently searched in a set of n encoded database vectors. With our vectors we have 12288 (192 × 64) dimensions and we encode them into 8 bit codes.

The whole procedure takes place in two steps, first a suitable projection that reduces dimensionality of the vector is generated and second, quantization is used to index the resulting vectors. The best choice of action for this problem with large image corpora are approximate nearest neighbor search methods. Most of the popular approximate nearest neighbor search techniques require several hash tables to be present in memory all the time. With a body of images this size, that is not efficient. So we chose the Spectral Hashing [9,10] method which embeds the vector into binary space and better adapts to memory requirements. Spectral hashing, similarly to Semantic Hashing, has each image in the data-set represented by a compact binary code. Similar images in the data-set have similar codewords, and similarity is measured by Hamming distance.

This method has several approaches, from which we chose the asymmetric distance computation (ADC) approach. Jegou et al. [11] have provided a compact coding scheme which is combined with an inverted file system and the ADC approach significantly improves results in terms of the trade-off between search quality and memory usage. Proprietary for this method is the fact that it encodes all the vectors in the database but it does not encode the query vector. So let $x \epsilon \Re^d$ be the query vector for which we need to find the nearest neighbors $NN(x)$ in the data-set $Y = \{y_1, ..., y_n\}$. The ADC approach consists in encoding each vector y_i by a quantized version $c_i = q(y_i)$. For the quantization we use a quantizer $q(.)$ of k centroids [12]. This means that the vector will be encoded by $\log_2(k)$ bits, where k is a power of 2. After the quantization is complete, finding the a nearest neighbors of x is just a matter of computing this simple equation:

$$NN_a = a - \arg\min \|x - q(y_i)\|^2$$

From this equation we also notice that because there is no quantization of the query vector, there exists no approximation error on the query side. The ADC search function is called every time a query is made. So it is very important that the function duration is as short as possible.

3.2   Online Phase

The online phase of this pipeline creates a user friendly environment for querying the CBIR system. The pipeline changes track after the indexing of the large data-set so the new query images are processed much faster. This is due to the pre indexed structures and distributions that do not need to be recomputed for each query. The Gaussian mixture model is constructed on the indexed data set, the PCA coefficients required for dimensionality reduction are also precomputed with the indexed set images.

When it comes to the Product Quantization we also have a significant speed up. Because we use the Asymmetric distance computation method we have no quantization on the query vector, so no additional time is spent. The only time consuming procedure that is left in the whole query process is the generation of descriptors for the query image. In an effort to reduce descriptor size we added a region of interest tool in the web endpoint. This way users can select only the part of the image that they want to search thus effectively reducing image size.

3.3   Implementation

Back End. The back end of the online phase of the system is powered by Python[4] and MATLAB. We use the Flask[5] micro-framework for Python in order to speed up development. Also, with speed in mind, all of the MATLAB functions required for query image processing are precompiled and permanently added to the MATLAB work-path.

Front End. The front end is constructed with the Bootstrap[6] 3 framework. It features content based, text based and mixed retrieval. On this endpoint a user can upload the query image via drag and drop or regular upload from a file browser. Additionally a region of interest tool is added in order to effectively reduce input size and increase effectiveness. Research has shown that other than improving efficiency, cropping the query image to only the region of interest generates better retrieval results [13].

Figure 2 illustrates the front end of our CBIR. In the upper left corner there is a region for uploading a query image. Bellow the query segment there is a vertical list with resulting images accompanied by relevant medical articles altogether.

---

[4] https://www.python.org/.
[5] http://flask.pocoo.org/.
[6] http://getbootstrap.com/.

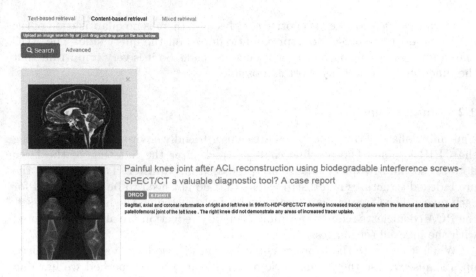

Fig. 2. Web client interface

4   Experiments and Results

4.1   Dataset

Our system performs retrieval over the ImageCLEFmed 2013 data-set. This data-set comprises a large subset (over 300 000 images from over 45 000 different biomedical research articles) of the PubMed Central (R) repository hosted by the U.S. National library of Medicine. From this subset over 5000 images are extracted and manually annotated with applicable categories. This dataset has been used in various tasks for modality classification and image retrieval as a part of the ImageCLEF[7] challenge.

4.2   Experimental Setup

For our experiments we used a HP Z800 Workstation with a 4 Core Intel Xeon processor E5620 that runs on 2.40 GHz with 12 MB cache. Our workstation is also equipped with 24 GB 1066 MHz RAM memory and a hard disk drive of 1 TB. All of the experiments were run on a 64 bit Debian 3.16.3-2 operating system, codename Jessie, running MATLAB[8] 2014 R8. The computationally demanding functions were optimized on the lowest possible level by using Inria's YAEL[9] library for MATLAB. As mentioned above in the text, feature extraction was performed using Van de Sande's ColorDescriptor software (Fig. 3).

---

[7] http://www.imageclef.org/.
[8] http://www.mathworks.com/products/matlab/.
[9] https://gforge.inria.fr/projects/yael/.

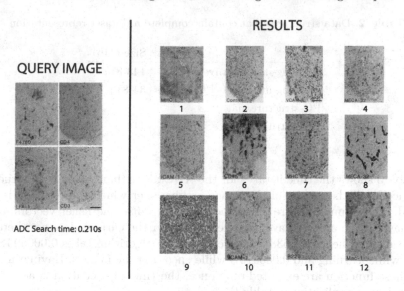

Fig. 3. Query results

4.3   Results and Discussion

In terms of memory consumption, results show that a structure which sizes up in Gigabytes can be effectively represented in a structure of just few tens of Megabytes. Table 2 shows a comparison between the combined set size before and after the product quantization. The first entry illustrates the size of the descriptors in the training set with PCA dimension reduction performed while the latter two entries show the suitable representations for the entire data-set after product quantization. This extreme shrinkage is due to substituting the vector representation of the images with a suitable code. Table 1 shows an example image descriptor file before and after the PCA dimension reduction has been performed. The PCA function is implemented in the Yael library for MATLAB. This part of the process is crucial because it speeds up the learning and search operations and reduces memory consumption from descriptor storage thus improving system scalability multiple times.

Table 1. Descriptor file dimensions and size

File name	Dimensions	Dimension (after PCA)	Size	Size (after PCA)
image1.siftgeo	16250 × 384	16250 × 192	5500 Kb	1370 Kb
image2.siftgeo	9250 × 384	9250 × 192	3700 Kb	820 Kb

The first two entries in Table 2 relates to the size of the image training set before and after PCA dimension reduction accordingly. There is a four fold dimension difference between the PCA reduced and the former, original size dataset.

Table 2. Data structures that contain complete a dataset representation

File	Size (Mb)
Training-image-set.fvecs	143 812
Training-image-set-[PCA].fvecs	34 816
PQ-structure.mat	70
ADC-structure.fvecs	11

Table 3 shows the time it takes for the ADC algorithm to learn the structure and encode all the entries of the image archive over which the retrieval is performed. These functions are only executed once, after the fisher vectors for all the image in the archive have been generated. In the current data set there are 306538 images, hence 306538 fisher vectors. The algorithm takes 0.000393 S per image while learning and 0.000513 S while encoding the images. Having in mind that these function are executed only once, the time of execution is acceptable in even larger applications (Table 4).

Table 3. ADC structure generation duration

Function	Execution time
ADC learn	120.600 s
ADC encode	157.300 s

Table 4. ADC search for 1 vector in a database of 306538

Function	Execution time
ADC Search	0.320 s

5 Conclusion and Future Work

In this paper we explained a content based image retrieval system which applies dimensionality reduction and product quantization methods in order to get a better trade-off ratio between search time and memory consumption. This better trade-off means greater scalability for the system. According to our results we can conclude that Product Quantization of Fisher vectors in content based image retrieval significantly improves the scalability and timing factors. The current state our system does not support multi-image queries. This is an important feature because sometimes medical conditions can not be expressed through a single image. The implementation of this feature is a near future goal and in the meantime we will continue to work on improving the system and report even faster search times.

Acknowledgments. We would like to acknowledge the support of the European Commission through the project MAESTRA - Learning from Massive, Incompletely annotated, and Structured Data (Grant number ICT-2013-612944)

References

1. Dye, C., Reeder, J.C., Terry, R.F.: Research for universal health coverage. World Health Organization (2013)
2. Hwang, K.H., Lee, H., Choi, D.: Medical image retrieval: past and present. Healthc. Inf. Res. **18**(1), 3–9 (2012)
3. Long, F., Zhang, H., Feng, D.D.: Fundamentals of content-based image retrieval. In: Feng, D.D., Siu, W.-C., Zhang, H.-J. (eds.) Multimedia Information Retrieval and Management. Signals and Communication Technology, pp. 1–26. Springer, Heidelberg (2003)
4. van de Sande, K.E.A., Gevers, T., Snoek, C.G.M.: Evaluating color descriptors for object and scene recognition. IEEE Trans. Pattern Anal. Mach. Intell. **32**(9), 1582–1596 (2010)
5. Bishop, C.M.: Pattern Recognition and Machine Learning. ISS, 1st edn. Springer, New York (2006)
6. Jegou, H., Perronnin, F., Douze, M., Sanchez, J., Perez, P., Schmid, C.: Aggregating local image descriptors into compact codes. IEEE Trans. Pattern Anal. Mach. Intell. **34**(9), 1704–1716 (2012)
7. Douze, M., Ramisa, A., Schmid, C.: Combining attributes and Fisher vectors for efficient image retrieval. In: CVPR 2011 IEEE Conference on Computer Vision and Pattern Recognition, Colorado Springs, United States, pp. 745–752. IEEE, June 2011
8. Sewell, M.: The fisher kernel: A brief review (2011)
9. Weiss, Y., Torralba, A.,Fergus, R.: Spectral hashing. In: Weiss, Y., Schölkopf, B., Platt, J., (eds.) NIPS (2008)
10. Weiss, Y., Torralba, A., Fergus, R.: Spectral hashing. In: Advances in Neural Information Processing Systems, pp. 1753–1760 (2009)
11. Jegou, H., Douze, M., Schmid, C.: Product quantization for nearest neighbor search. IEEE Trans. Pattern Anal. Mach. Intell. **33**(1), 117–128 (2011)
12. Jégou, H., Douze, M., Schmid, C., Pérez, P.: Aggregating local descriptors into a compact image representation. (June 2010)
13. Russakovsky, O., Deng, J., Su, H., Krause, J., Satheesh, S., Ma, S., Huang, Z., Karpathy, A., Khosla, A., Bernstein, M., Berg, A.C., Fei-Fei, L.: Imagenet large scale visual recognition challenge (2014)

Twitter Sentiment Analysis Using Deep Convolutional Neural Network

Dario Stojanovski[✉], Gjorgji Strezoski, Gjorgji Madjarov,
and Ivica Dimitrovski

Faculty of Computer Science and Engineering,
Saints Cyril and Methodius University,
Rugjer Boshkovikj 16, 1000 Skopje, Macedonia
{stojanovski.dario,strezoski.g}@gmail.com,
{gjorgji.madjarov,ivica.dimitrovski}@finki.ukim.mk

Abstract. In the work presented in this paper, we conduct experiments on sentiment analysis in Twitter messages by using a deep convolutional neural network. The network is trained on top of pre-trained word embeddings obtained by unsupervised learning on large text corpora. We use CNN with multiple filters with varying window sizes on top of which we add 2 fully connected layers with dropout and a softmax layer. Our research shows the effectiveness of using pre-trained word vectors and the advantage of leveraging Twitter corpora for the unsupervised learning phase. The experimental evaluation is made on benchmark datasets provided on the SemEval 2015 competition for the Sentiment analysis in Twitter task. Despite the fact that the presented approach does not depend on hand-crafted features, we achieve comparable performance to state-of-the-art methods on the Twitter2015 set, measuring F1 score of 64.85 %.

Keywords: Twitter · Sentiment analysis · Convolutional neural networks · Word embeddings · Deep learning

1 Introduction

Sentiment analysis is an area of Natural Language Processing (NLP) that focuses on understanding human emotion in text. With the spread of social media and microblogging websites, sentiment analysis in social networks has gained increasing popularity amongst scientific researchers. Users on these services share their ideas and opinions on various topics, events and products. As of 2014 Twitter has over 284 million monthly active users and about 500 million messages are sent on a daily basis[1], which positions Twitter as the focal point for research in sentiment analysis. This motivates companies to poll data from social networks to get a better understanding of the reactions their products and services get.

---

[1] https://about.twitter.com/company.

© Springer International Publishing Switzerland 2015
E. Onieva et al. (Eds.): HAIS 2015, LNAI 9121, pp. 726–737, 2015.
DOI: 10.1007/978-3-319-19644-2_60

Sentiment analysis in social networks and microblogs is more challenging due to the informal nature of the language. Unlike text from movie or product reviews, tweets have limitation of 140 characters and users tend to use a lot of abbreviations, slang and URLs along with Twitter specific terms such as user mentions and hashtags.

Deep learning techniques have recently shown great improvements over existing approaches in computer vision and speech recognition. In the field of NLP, deep learning methods are primarily used for learning word vector representations [1, 2], part-of-speech tagging, semantic role labeling, named entity recognition [3] etc. Traditional NLP methods are based on hand-crafted features which is both time-consuming and leads to over-specified and incomplete features. Feature generation is inherently built into deep neural networks and they enable the model to learn increasing levels of complexity. Recently there have been attempts of using deep learning for sentiment analysis, primarily through utilizing deep convolutional neural networks. Deep CNNs have one key advantage over existing approaches for sentiment analysis that rely on extensive feature engineering. CNNs automate the feature generation phase and learn more general representations, thereby making this approach robust and flexible when applied to various domains.

In this paper, we tackle the problem of sentiment analysis on Twitter messages by using a deep CNN architecture. The architecture is based on the model proposed in [4] which reported state-of-the-art performance on 4 out of 7 sentence classification tasks. Unlike the aforementioned network that has only one fully connected layer, we employ a more deep architecture. We have two fully connected non-linear layers with dropout and a softmax layer. Our model resembles the architecture of the network proposed in [3] and [5], the difference being that we use multiple filters in the convolutional layer. Additionally, our model has multiple layers of non-linearity which enables for learning more complex representations.

Though some of the work so far have relied on emoticons for labels in order to obtain a larger training set, we only utilize manually labeled tweets. Training and test sets were provided by the organizers of the SemEval competition, but we additionally extend our train set with other available manually annotated Twitter data. Evaluation metrics that are used are accuracy and average macro-F1 score on positive and negative labels.

The main contributions of this paper are three fold:

- We evaluate several pre-trained word vectors and the usefulness of leveraging Twitter corpora as training data when applied to the task of Twitter sentiment analysis.
- We present an architecture for deep convolutional neural network that, to our knowledge, has not been used for sentiment analysis on Twitter data.
- We report our results on the benchmark test sets on the Twitter Sentiment Analysis Track in SemEval 2015.

The rest of the paper is organized as follows. Section 2 outlines current approaches on sentiment analysis, with emphasis on Twitter sentiment analysis and deep learning methods. Section 3 presents the details of the model proposed in this paper, the pre-processing phase and an overview of the pre-trained word vectors used in our work. In Sect. 4, the experimental setup is explained in detail along with the datasets being used. We present and elaborate on the performance achieved using our approach and provide insight on the findings of our research in Sect. 5. Finally, we conclude our work and discuss future directions in Sect. 6.

2   Related Work

There has been a lot of work done in the field of sentiment analysis in natural language and social network posts. The research ranges from document level classification [6], contextual polarity disambiguation to topic based sentiment classification. Twitter messages have 140 character limitation which makes the task of Twitter sentiment analysis closest to sentence level sentiment detection.

Most of the work done so far in Twitter sentiment analysis have revolved around extensive feature engineering which is both labor intensive and is likely to be too domain specific. In 2013, the best performance on classifying tweets polarity was reported by Mohammad et al. [7]. The features used in their method are word and character ngrams, the number of words with all characters in upper case, the number of hashtags, the number of contiguous sequences of exclamation marks, the presence of elongated words, the number of negated contexts etc. The system also depends on the use of several lexicons to determine the sentiment score for each token in the tweet, part-of-speech tag and hashtag.

The authors of [8] developed around 100 features and compared the effectiveness against unigram features. Their approach separates the features in multiple categories based on whether they are generated using POS tagging, carry polarity information and their type(integers, booleans or real values).

Classifiers that are mostly used by the aforementioned methods are Naive Bayes, Maximum Entropy and Support Vector Machines (SVM). In the work of [9], these commonly used classifiers were evaluated on unigram and bigram features and showed that all classifiers perform similarly. While most of the methods use hand-crafted features, some approaches rely on lexicons with words and their polarity score. These approaches map the words polarity score and compute the sentiment of the tweet.

On the other hand, deep convolutional neural networks do not depend on extensive manual feature engineering and extract the features automatically. They have the advantage of inherently taking into account the ordering of the words and by using word vectors they encompass syntactic and semantic meaning of words. Socher et al. [10] introduced a Recursive Neural Tensor Network that maps phrases through word embeddings and a parse tree. Afterwards, vectors for higher nodes in the tree are computed and tensor-based composition function for all nodes is used. The method pushed state-of-the-art results on fine-grained and positive/negative sentiment classification of movie reviews. However, RNTN depends on the syntactic structure of the text as input.

CNNs have already started to give better results on several tasks in NLP. Kalchbrenner et al. [11] showed that their Dynamic Convolutional Neural Network outperforms other unigram and bigram based methods on classification of movie reviews and tweets. However, we can't directly compare with the aforementioned method as they only report the accuracy their model achieves and not the F1 score. The authors of [12] proposed a neural network architecture that exploits character-level, word-level and sentence-level representations. Character-level features proved to be useful for sentiment analysis on tweets, because they capture morphological and shape information.

Using pre-trained word representations for sentiment analysis has one obvious disadvantage. Since the training is done in an unsupervised manner, there is no sentiment information encoded in the word vectors. Tang et al. [13] attempt to resolve this issue by learning sentiment specific word embeddings (SSWE) from massive distant-supervised tweets. The proposed method uses noisy-labeled tweets where labeling is based on the presence of positive and negative emoticons. Besides these word embedding features, the system they proposed at SemEval 2014 Task 9 [14] also consists of hand-crafted features which are based on the SemEval 2013 winning system [7].

3   System Architecture

3.1   Deep Convolutional Neural Network

In this work, we propose a deep convolutional neural network for classification of tweets into positive, negative and neutral classes. Our approach is based on the approaches proposed by Kim [4] and Collobert et al. [3], incorporating elements from both architectures. Kim [4] propose an architecture that uses multiple filters with varying window sizes that are applied on each given sentence. We modify the aforementioned model by adding two fully connected layers with dropout and a softmax layer to the architecture. The first layer consists of sigmoid activated units since using a linear layer showed worse performance. The second layer is a hyperbolic tangent layer to which a standard softmax layer is appended.

CNNs with pooling operation deal naturally with variable length sentences and they also take into account the ordering of the words and the context each word appears in. This solves the problem of negations which may appear in different places in a sentence. For simplicity, we consider that each tweet represents one sentence. The architecture of the model is depicted in Fig. 1 and is somewhat similar to the one presented in [3].

Let's consider a tweet t with length of n tokens with the appropriate padding at the beginning and at the end of the tweet. Padding length is defined as $h/2$ where h is the window size of the filter. The first step is mapping tokens to the corresponding word vectors from a lookup table $L \in R^{k \times |V|}$, where k is the dimension of the word vectors and V is a vocabulary of the words in the lookup table (more details on the lookup table are provided in Sect. 3.2). Each word or token is projected to a vector $w_i \in R^k$. After the mapping, a tweet is represented as a concatenation of the word embeddings

$$x = \{w_1, w_2, \ldots w_n\}. \tag{1}$$

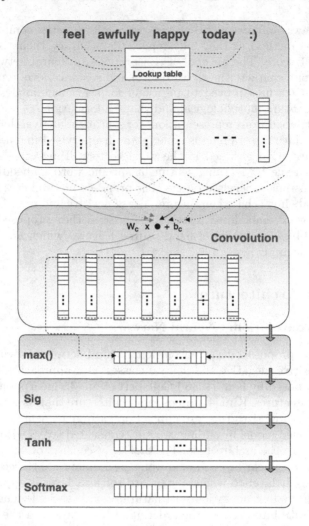

Fig. 1. Deep convolutional neural network architecture.

The next step is the convolution operation in which we apply multiple filters with varying window sizes h. Filters are applied to every possible window of words in the tweet and a feature map is produced as a result. For each of the filters, a weight matrix $W_c \in R^{h_u \times hk}$ and a bias term b_c are learned, where h_u is the number of hidden units in the convolutional layer. The weight matrix is used to extract local features around each word window. The convolution operation can be formally expressed as

$$x'_i = h(W_c \cdot x_{i:i+h-1} + b_c), \tag{2}$$

where $h(\cdot)$ is the hyperbolic tangent function and $x_{i:i+h-1}$ is the concatenation of word vectors from position i to position $i + h - 1$.

We then apply a max-over-time pooling operation on the feature map x' computed from the convolution operation (3).

$$x' = max\{x'_1, x'_2 \ldots x'_{n-h+1}\}. \tag{3}$$

As a result, we get a fixed size vector for the tweet and extract the most important features for each feature map. The size of the vector is a hyper-parameter to be determined by the user and corresponds to the number of hidden units in the convolutional layer. This is the process for generating one feature for one filter. In order to utilize more filters, the fixed size vectors generated by the max-over-time pooling operation are concatenated and fed to the first layer of the network architecture.

The rest of the architecture is a classical feed forward neural network consisting of three separate layers. The first layer contains units with sigmoid activation function. We have experimented with a linear layer as was done in [3], but using sigmoid function yielded better results.

$$x^1 = f(W^1 \cdot x' + b^1), \tag{4}$$

where f is the sigmoid activation function. The sigmoid layer is followed by another non-linear layer for which we chose a hyperbolic tangent function. The final layer of the architecture is a softmax layer that gives a probability distribution over the labels. The network is trained using stochastic gradient descent over shuffled mini-batches with the Adadelta update rule [15].

Deep neural networks suffer from overfitting due to the high number of parameters that need to be learned. To counteract the problem of large number of hidden units and connections between them we utilize dropout regularization. The idea behind this technique is that during the training process random units along with their connections are dropped (set to zero). The proportion of units to be dropped is a hyper-parameter to be determined by the user. Dropout regularization is applied to the fully connected layers.

3.2   Pre-training

Pre-processing. Preprocessing is a common stage in any task involving Twitter data because of the language irregularities that are present in tweets. We do several pre-processing actions in order to clean the input data from noise. As URLs carry no information for the sentiment of a tweet we remove all instances of URLs. We clean tweets from all HTML entities, user mentions and punctuation with the exception of exclamation and question marks. We keep hashtags and emoticons as emoticons are probably the strongest indicator for the sentiment a tweet caries.

Users on social media tend to elongate words in order to emphasize the emotion they are trying to convey. The length of one word (the number of character repetitions) may differ in different tweets, but they essentially carry the same information. One simple example is that a tweet can contain the token "haaaapy" and another the token "haaaaapy". In order not to differentiate between these variations, we shorten the repeated characters to maximum 3 repetitions.

We tried replacing abbreviations with their actual meaning, but in our experiments this approach didn't bring the expected performance improvements. We contribute this to the fact that the network is well suited to learn an appropriate word vector for these abbreviations even if they are not present in the lookup table. Consequently, we decided to leave out this pre-processing step.

Pre-trained Word Vectors. Learning word representations from massive unannotated text corpora have recently been used in many NLP tasks. Leveraging large corpora for unsupervised learning of word representations enables capturing of syntactic and semantic characteristics of words.

One possibility is to randomly initialize the word vectors and let the model learn appropriate representation for each word. Kim [4] and Santos et al. [12] reported better results by initializing word vectors with ones obtained from an unsupervised neural language model. Therefore, we decided not to explore the effect of random initialization since this has already been studied and proven considerably less effective than using pre-trained vectors.

In our research we evaluate three different methods for generating word vectors and their applicability to sentiment analysis. Apart from the widely popular *word2vec*[2] [1], we also use global vectors for word representation [2], referred throughout the paper as GloVe word embeddings[3] and the semantic specific word embeddings (SSWE) from [13]. Details of the word embeddings are presented in Table 1. Note that corpora size is expressed in token count with the exception of SSWE where the authors only report the number of tweets on which vectors were learned. GloVe Crawl embeddings were trained on web data, while for *word2vec* vectors, data from Google News was used.

Table 1. Details about the word embeddings used for the lookup table. Corpora size is expressed in token count with the exception of SSWE where only the number of tweets is provided.

	Dimension	Corpora	Vocabulary
SSWE	50	10 M	137 K
word2vec	300	100 B	3 M
GloVe Crawl	300	840 B	2.2 M
GloVe Twitter	200	20 B	1.2 M

Unsupervised learning of word embeddings has the drawback of not having sentiment information encoded in their representation. A simple example is that

---

[2] https://code.google.com/p/word2vec/.
[3] http://nlp.stanford.edu/projects/glove/.

"good" and "bad" are neighboring words based on cosine similarity. This stems from the fact that these words appear in similar context in the large text corpora that is used for the training process.

Our model tackles this issue differently than [13]. Instead of doing the pre-training phase ourselves, we use available word vectors and by backpropagation, during the training of the network, update them in order to adapt to the specific task at hand. Kim [4] showed that by using non-static word vectors, their approach was able to capture sentiment regularities in words. They showcase this by comparing top-4 neighboring words of "good" before and after training. Non-static word vectors managed to learn that "bad" is not similar to "good". One could see the benefit from this method if sentiment detection system is put into production use. In time, the model will adapt to changes in language that may arise and which in fact occur frequently in microblogging environments.

For words that are not present in the vocabulary of word vectors, we use random initialization. Kim [4] suggest to use a range of $[-a, a]$ where a is set so that random initialized words have the same variance as the pre-trained ones. In our case, we set a to 0.25.

4 Experimental Design

4.1 Datasets

We train and test our model on the benchmark sets from the SemEval Task 10 challenge. The sets were manually annotated by the organizers of the challenge with three labels, positive, negative and neutral. Unfortunately, we were not able to retrieve all of the tweets because some of them were most likely removed or had altered privacy status. The overall number of tweets was somewhat smaller than what some teams reported in this year's challenge. This year the organizers of SemEval Task 10, decided not to constrain competitors by allowing them to use data outside of the one provided by them. Therefore, we extended our training set with another manually labeled set of tweets[4], which were collected with respect to 4 topics. The results presented in this paper are on the latest Twitter2015 test set along with the test sets from Subtask B from previous years. Classes distribution are depicted in Table 2.

Table 2. Distribution of labels on the training and test sets

	Positive	Negative	Neutral
Train	4000	2101	6653
TW13	1572	601	1640
TW14	982	202	669
TW15	1038	365	987

---

[4] http://www.sananalytics.com/lab/twitter-sentiment/.

4.2   Experimental Setup

In our experiments, we reused some of the hyper-parameters reported in [4] such as a mini-batch size of 50, l_2 constraint of 3 and filter windows of 3, 4 and 5. We experimented with other combinations of filter windows, but this proved to be a suitable combination because of the limitation of Twitter messages. In our case, we observe that using hyperbolic tangent activated units performs better than rectified linear units for the convolutional layer. We set the learning rate to 0.02 and apply a regularization with a dropout rate (0.7, 0.5) on the fully connected layers in the network respectively.

We started with 100 hidden units in each layer and 100 feature maps for the different filter windows. However, results were slightly improved by using 500 hidden units in the first layer and 300 in the second, while increasing feature maps size to 300.

5   Results and Discussion

In this paper we present performance achieved on the test set of this year's SemEval Task 10. Results are presented in Tables 3 and 4. We use two evaluation metrics, accuracy and average macro-F1 score on positive and negative labels.

We observe that using GloVe word embeddings gives better performance than other approaches. It is interesting to see that GloVe Twitter and GloVe Crawl

Table 3. Performance using different word vectors on Twitter2015

	SSWE	word2vec	GloVe Crawl	GloVe Twitter
Accuracy	61.59	66.44	68.77	66.99
Macro-F1	58.76	60.26	64.72	64.85

Table 4. Macro-F1 score on positive, negative and neutral classes. TW13, TW14 and TW15 are Twitter2013, Twitter2014 and Twitter2015 respectively. Table 4 is structured into three main sections. The first section contains top performing approaches using hand-crafted features and SVM, followed by methods using a combination of deep learning and manual feature engineering. The last section contains pure deep learning approaches.

Team	TW13	TW14	TW15
Webis	68.49	70.68	64.84
Isislif	71.34	71.54	64.27
CIS-positiv	64.82	66.05	59.57
Splusplus	**72.8**	**74.42**	63.73
unitn	72.79	73.6	64.59
Finki	69.07	72.75	**64.85**

perform similarly, even though GloVe Twitter embeddings have a dimension of 200 in comparison to the 300-dimensional GloVe Crawl and *word2vec* word vectors. Using SSWE vectors did not produced comparable results, and it would take further research to determine whether this is due to the lower dimensionality and smaller corpora size. On the other side, *word2vec* word vectors were not as effective as GloVe embeddings. Whether the reason for the difference in performance is the type of corporas used or the methods themselves requires further examination.

We compare our approach with the submissions from the latest SemEval challenge. Results for the Twitter2015 test set were considerably worse than for the Twitter2013 and Twitter2014 sets, with almost 10 % margin between the top results. Our system, Finki, performs well on Twitter2013 and is in top-3 on Twitter2014, while outperforming other approaches on the Twitter2015 test set. It is obvious from Table 4, that deep learning techniques provide more consistent results across datasets.

As was mentioned before, the training set was extended with an additional manually labeled set. Although the added training set that we use has limited domain, combining the sets improved performance. This only confirms the intuition that deep learning techniques are more flexible than approaches with hand-crafted features and can greatly benefit from a larger training set. From the presented results, we can also observe the significance word embeddings have on performance in Twitter sentiment analysis, especially ones that are trained on corpora originating from Twitter.

6   Conclusion and Future Work

In this paper, we present a deep convolutional neural network for sentiment analysis on Twitter posts. To our knowledge this specific architecture, with multiple filters and non-linear layers on top of the convolutional layer has never been used for classifying Twitter messages. We experimented with different word embeddings, trained on both Twitter and non-Twitter data.

Unsupervised pre-training of word embeddings on Twitter based corpora offers improvements over non-Twitter based corpora, as was made evident from our experimentations and we would like to further explore the effect of using Twitter corpora as training data. Utilizing the GloVe Twitter word vectors already provided slightly better results than Glove Crawl, despite having 200 dimensions and being trained on a considerably smaller corpora. We would like to see the performance of *word2vec* when trained on Twitter data and the effectiveness of SSWE vectors if they would be trained on larger corpora and have a bigger dimensionality. We would also like to further investigate on why using first linear layer did not provided similar results to our current model.

We report our results on test sets from the SemEval 2015 Task 10, for 3-way sentiment classification of tweets. Our method performs comparable to state-of-the-art approaches in this challenge, despite the fact it does not depend on any hand-crafted features or polarity lexicons. The network achieved 64.85 % F1 score on the Twitter2015 set. We can finally conclude that CNN that leverage pre-trained word vectors perform well on the task of Twitter sentiment analysis.

Acknowledgments. We would like to acknowledge the support of the European Commission through the project MAESTRA Learning from Massive, Incompletely annotated, and Structured Data (Grant number ICT-2013-612944).

References

1. Mikolov, T., Sutskever, I., Chen, K., Corrado, G.S., Dean, J.: Distributed representations of words and phrases and their compositionality. In: Burges, C., Bottou, L., Welling, M., Ghahramani, Z., Weinberger, K. (eds.) Advances in Neural Information Processing Systems 26, pp. 3111–3119. Curran Associates, Inc. (2013)
2. Pennington, J., Socher, R., Manning, C.: Glove: global vectors for word representation. In: Proceedings of the 2014 Conference on Empirical Methods in Natural Language Processing (EMNLP), pp.1532–1543. Association for Computational Linguistics, Doha, October 2014
3. Collobert, R., Weston, J., Bottou, L., Karlen, M., Kavukcuoglu, K., Kuksa, P.: Natural language processing (almost) from scratch. J. Mach. Learn. Res. **12**, 2493–2537 (2011)
4. Kim, Y.: Convolutional neural networks for sentence classification. In: Proceedings of the 2014 Conference on Empirical Methods in Natural Language Processing (EMNLP), pp. 1746–1751. Association for Computational Linguistics, Doha, October 2014
5. Chintala, S.: Sentiment Analysis Using Neural Architectures. New York University, New York (2012)
6. Pang, B., Lee, L.: Opinion mining and sentiment analysis. Found. Trends Inf. Retrieval **2**(1–2), 1–135 (2008)
7. Mohammad, S., Kiritchenko, S., Zhu, X.: Nrc-canada: building the state-of-the-art in sentiment analysis of tweets. In: Proceedings of the Seventh International Workshop on Semantic Evaluation Exercises (SemEval-2013), Georgia, June 2013
8. Agarwal, A., Xie, B., Vovsha, I., Rambow, O., Passonneau, R.: Sentiment analysis of twitter data. In: Proceedings of the Workshop on Languages in Social Media. LSM 2011, pp. 30–38. Association for Computational Linguistics, Stroudsburg, (2011)
9. Go, A., Bhayani, R., Huang, L.: Twitter sentiment classification using distant supervision. CS224N Project Report, Stanford, pp. 1–12 (2009)
10. Socher, R., Perelygin, A., Wu, J.Y., Chuang, J., Manning, C.D., Ng, A.Y., Potts, C.: Recursive deep models for semantic compositionality over a sentiment treebank. In: Proceedings of the Conference on Empirical Methods in Natural Language Processing (EMNLP), pp.1631–1642. Citeseer (2013)
11. Kalchbrenner, N., Grefenstette, E., Blunsom, P.: A convolutional neural network for modelling sentences, arXiv preprint (2014). arXiv:1404.2188
12. dos Santos, C., Gatti, M.: Deep convolutional neural networks for sentiment analysis of short texts. In: Proceedings of COLING 2014, the 25th International Conference on Computational Linguistics: Technical Papers, pp. 69–78. Dublin City University and Association for Computational Linguistics (2014)

13. Tang, D., Wei, F., Yang, N., Zhou, M., Liu, T., Qin, B.: Learning sentiment-specific word embedding for twitter sentiment classification. In: Proceedings of the 52nd Annual Meeting of the Association for Computational Linguistics, vol. 1, Long Papers, pp. 1555–1565. Association for Computational Linguistics (2014)
14. Tang, D., Wei, F., Qin, B., Liu, T., Zhou, M.: Coooolll: A deep learning system for twitter sentiment classification. In: Proceedings of the 8th International Workshop on Semantic Evaluation (SemEval 2014), pp. 208–212. Association for Computational Linguistics and Dublin City University, Dublin, August 2014
15. Zeiler, M.D.: Adadelta: An adaptive learning rate method, arXiv preprint (2012). arXiv:1212.5701

Author Index

Printed in the United States
By Bookmasters